Intelligence, Espionage and Related Topics

Intelligence, Espionage and Related Topics

An Annotated Bibliography of Serial Journal and Magazine Scholarship, 1844–1998

Compiled by
James D. Calder

Bibliographies and Indexes in Military Studies, Number 11

GREENWOOD PRESS
Westport, Connecticut • London

Library of Congress Cataloging-in-Publication Data

Intelligence, espionage and related topics : an annotated
    bibliography of serial journal and magazine scholarship, 1844–1998
    / compiled by James D. Calder.
        p.   cm.—(Bibliographies and indexes in military studies,
    ISSN 1040–7995 ; no. 11)
      Includes bibliographical references and indexes.
      ISBN 0–313–29290–6 (alk. paper)
      1. Intelligence service—Periodicals Indexes.   2. Espionage—
    Periodicals Indexes.   I. Calder, James D.   II. Series.
    UB250.I565   1999
    327.12—dc21   99–39950

British Library Cataloguing in Publication Data is available.

Library of Congress Catalog Card Number: 99–39950
ISBN: 0–313–29290–6
ISSN: 1040–7995

First published in 1999

Greenwood Press, 88 Post Road West, Westport, CT 06881
An imprint of Greenwood Publishing Group, Inc.
www.greenwood.com

Printed in the United States of America

The paper used in this book complies with the
Permanent Paper Standard issued by the National
Information Standards Organization (Z39.48–1984).

10 9 8 7 6 5 4 3 2 1

To the memory of my father, William Douglas Calder,

cartographer and intelligence consumer,

to my mother, Margaret O. Calder, for her appreciation of history,

and to my wife, Monika Calder, for her patience and support

Contents

Preface

Studies of intelligence and espionage (arguably two sides of the same coin) have attracted profoundly more serious intellectual attention than is suggested by commonplace images of spies and spy operations featured in popular media. Books and articles of all types on these subjects now fill library shelves. The body of knowledge, unorganized and far less mature just thirty years ago, has been crafted and multiplied mainly by a new cadre of serious researchers and writers. This bibliography of only one dimension of that literature contains significant evidence of an evolving and distinctive collection worthy of special accounting.

Known loosely as "intelligencers," scholars of intelligence, espionage, and related subjects have contributed volumes of serious inquiry about activities of spies and spy organizations, and about multifarious topics linked to collection, analysis, and distribution of open and secret information. Some of their most concise and documented work has appeared worldwide in hundreds of serial journals or professional magazines. The majority of the work has been rigorously vetted, a process by which articles are subjected to critical evaluation by anonymous peer reviewers. Assumptions, content, focus, methodology, and conclusions are all challenged, and article length is restricted. Serial journals are usually, but not exclusively, linked to academic disciplines, such as international affairs, history, law, or political science, while professional magazines generally publish discussions of new modes of organizational thought, case analyses, professional trends, or reflections upon issues. Journals and magazines appear in many different forms and publication policies vary from discipline to discipline, from nation to nation, and subject to subject.

This collection has grown from a small pile of three-by-five cards, banded and tossed carelessly in my briefcase, to what you find here. Originally, the approach was limited to gathering citations to add to my list of required or recommended readings for students in my course on intelligence and national security. After bursting the glue and tape on several card boxes, it was time for a primitive computer list, and ultimately the rudiments of a manuscript. Motivation to carry through the hours of tedium in this project appears to have three sources: first, a frustration that the explosive volume of non-book literature had not been sharply distinguished from popular press journalism; second, an obsession for representing the corpus of scholarship back to its origins in at least the American journals and magazines; and third, a desire to bring together a range of topics that already had been linked to traditional discussions of intelligence and espionage, or which could find direct application in further studies. Of course, the collection effort will continue, and it may be appropriate in future years to publish an addendum to this work.

PURPOSES AND SCOPE OF THIS BIBLIOGRAPHY

I began this collection intending only a list of the most frequently cited articles on intelligence and world affairs. In the early stages, I estimated the corpus of this literature at less than a thousand items. Hours of research in paper indexes, some dating to the mid-nineteenth century, eventually gave way to equally irksome but productive computer searches. The collection soon expanded to several thousand articles, but even the marvels of computer searches delivered many off-point items and items that ranged outside the scope of interest. More obscure citations, including gems from shortly after the Civil War, required discovery by methods more akin to finding a needle in the proverbial haystack. The completed collection, however, reflects a reasonably dogged hunt for the oldest and most current articles. It is limited mainly to articles in English, although many citations are to journals in Chinese, French, German, Italian, Japanese, Polish, Romanian, Spanish, Russian, and other languages. I do not claim that the total collection represents a universe of journal articles, but undoubtedly it represents a large portion of the journal and magazine scholarship. The cutoff date for acquisition of citations was December 1, 1998.

A bibliography of scholarship is a risky enterprise. The product is likely to imply that its author holds an unequivocal standard of what should or should not be included. Admittedly, this collection emanates from a discriminating view that reasoned and vetted analysis can be distinguished from straight fact reporting and brief and unsourced anecdotal interpretations found in newspapers and popular magazines. When I began this project my assumptions about this distinction were clear and unbending, but they grew more elusive (like the topics they chased) with every extension of the project's scope and with every passing year of investigation. Originally, I imagined a universal, or at least a widely accepted, understanding of the kind and quality of writing that should properly represent the cutting edge of academic and professional analysis. I was not able to find universally acceptable criteria upon which to accurately and fairly separate all the items I found in print. Without question, however, I could apply elements of a common standard to most of the cited material, and many articles measured up to the most restrictive tests for inclusion.

Because my objective was to build an interesting and useful research tool, I shifted the focus of judgment toward works that expand and diversify critical analysis, and that appear to encourage further inquiry and publication in the topical areas of espionage and intelligence. I was obligated to challenge the merits of every piece, but it seemed less and less reasonable to arbitrarily exclude articles in view of the fact that neither colleagues nor the academic literature could supply clear, untarnished selection criteria. For example, I discovered no uniformity in journal vetting practices on the issue of methodological approach or rigor of analysis. Journal reputations, author credentials, and legacies of editorial board membership also proved impossible to measure and apply. Moreover, I was not convinced that principles and values underlying journal or magazine article acceptance practices related in any way to traditional measures of journal standing, e.g., "leading," "secondary" or "lower-end." I concluded, also, that if academic credentials are ignored, "insider" reflections on the murky realities of espionage may shed more informed light on the need for further investigation in ways that no "outsider" could credibly allege. Equally, however, those on the outside, despite tendencies toward detached analyses and wanderings in the thicket of concepts, theory, and publicly available data, can aggressively challenge insider assumptions and biases. Thus, the collection in this book reflects my sincere intention to include where exclusion is arguably indefensible.

This annotated bibliography has two major purposes. First, it attempts to distinguish scholarship from popular literature in the areas of intelligence, espionage, and related topics. I intended an accessible and informative resource. Principally, it will be used by academics, students, and intelligencers who are concerned with advancing theory, conducting systematic investigations, and debating implications of activities of individuals and organizations engaged in spying. It presumes that the content of journals or professional magazines results from a process of review that permits scholars an opportunity to carefully critique articles with respect to author assumptions, data sources, methodology, and conclusions. Article vetting practices, however, vary greatly within and across disciplines, and they are subject to significant imperfections. There are no guarantees, in fact, that journal articles reflect the most current or respected analyses. Readers of this resource can be expected to make judgments about whether or not particular citations should have been included, but they will have the critical mass of serial journal and magazine scholarship from which to discriminate.

Secondly, this work furnishes a practical finding aid for scholars and students who have general or special interests in particular topics. The extensive index, for example, provides important suggestions about which subjects have attracted journal publication. In this connection, citations are purposely eclectic in the reporting, keeping the main priority in mind concerning topics generally regarded as the bread and butter of intelligence and espionage studies. The expectation is that a source that is friendly to use and thorough, but one that mainly excludes popular literature, will shorten research time, thus encouraging students and scholars to expand the body of quality literature. Unquestionably, this expansion will require investigators to cross boundaries of thought in their respective fields, thus calling for sources that invite analysis not previously contemplated. In recent years, for example, the disciplines of history and political science have been overheard to admit that too little attention has been paid to the significance of intelligence in major world events and policy decisions. My own discipline of criminology is woefully behind, but catching up quickly, in accepting the role of systematic collection and interpretation of street-level intelligence in planning crime prevention strategies. Partial blame can be placed on government sequestration of essential records. A generalized unwillingness to credit intelligence operations with significant contributions to particular historical outcomes is also to blame. In any event, one tangible objective is to encourage broader use of the scholarly journal sources in the cross-fertilization of research interests.

The scope of article selection included has followed some formal rules. An effort was made to remain loyal to my rules, but admittedly violations occurred where, say, a popular magazine article revealed the personal experiences of an intelligence careerist, or where an article attracted acclaim or controversy. Consistent with my intended objectives, selection rules were:

1. Articles on intelligence, espionage and reasonably related topics appearing in serial periodicals with known traditions of article vetting, regardless of debates about journal stature. In most cases, this criterion identified articles in major or universally recognized journals across the social and behavioral sciences.

2. Articles appearing in serial publications with commonly accepted traditions of publication of new theory, research, or discourse relevant to a particular field of study. Fields included in searches for citations were history, political science, sociology, psychology, criminology and criminal justice, foreign affairs, international relations, business, communications, humanities, popular culture, law, mathematics, and physics.

3. Articles appearing in journals or magazines which appear no more frequently than monthly, sometimes available at newsstands, but which have high intellectual acclaim as authoritative in U. S. or European domestic or international affairs.

4. Articles appearing in specialized professional or discipline-specific journals and magazines which appear to guard publication standards. This includes a small sample of popular press articles written about or written by persons with special credibility in the realm of intelligence, or articles about subjects for which there was little coverage in academic journals.

5. Book review essays, generally considered more lengthy and analytical than standard book reviews.

Excluded were weekly magazines and daily newspapers, most magazines or journals aimed at general readership (what I call popular press publications), most professional bulletins, mimeographed materials, conference papers and informal proceedings, books and monographs, book reviews (unless in essay form), and government reports.   To the researcher engaged in current investigation, perhaps on topics about which there is little developed intelligence, these sources are critical repositories of information. To the intelligence analyst, however, they may be regarded as raw data. News is news. But reflective and vetted intellectual analyses on complex issues related to espionage and intelligence have entirely different audiences. The decision to leave out many excellent citations from respected daily and weekly publications was sometimes painful, but overall consistency was regarded as an issue of fairness to the self-perceptions of the scholars mentioned herein who expended the labor to publish for the purpose of recognition from respected peers. As deeply analytical as the <u>New York Times</u>, the <u>Washington Post</u>, selected other daily papers, or <u>Time</u> magazine may be, the authors of articles appearing in the <u>American Political Science Review</u>, in <u>International Affairs</u> (Great Britain), in the <u>Stanford Law Review</u>, in <u>Intelligence and National Security</u>, or in the <u>International Journal of Intelligence and Counterintelligence</u> are likely to have different views of their contributions to new knowledge than the authors of popular press articles. To be clear, therefore, the reputations of the authors reflected in this volume, regardless of apparent political persuasion or relative statuses in their disciplines, deserve recognition among relatively equal measures of contribution. The principal measure I have used to judge contributions to understanding of subjects associated with espionage and intelligence, therefore, is publication in journals and magazines regarded by various disciplines to contain intellectual analysis, not news.

ORGANIZATION AND TIPS FOR USING THIS BIBLIOGRAPHY

Citations are arranged in alphabetical order, mainly to give center stage to the contributors, living and deceased. An author-driven bibliography also focusses attention on the corpus of a writer's journal work, recognizing, of course, that many contributors have published outside the scope of this collection. The need for duplicate listings is eliminated. Users who have some familiarity with the major authors in the subject areas will find this resource convenient for confirming citation details or learning about sources in obscure journal locations. For these users, this work may offer substantial browsing value. An appendix supplies a list of journals cited, useful to authors who may need a quick reference to the types of publications that will accept manuscripts relevant to topical areas associated with espionage and intelligence. A key word or term index is provided to encourage topical investigation. The co-author index can be used to find the second authors of articles where applicable.

Selections included in this work were made without regard to judgments about the quality of presentation, intellectual impact, and/or ideological perspective. In some cases, I have observed the value of a particular piece in connection with particular types of research which may be conducted by new or seasoned scholars. I have purposely included pieces that reflect conflicting political views on the intelligence organizations, their activities, operations, and products. I believe that further study and writing, especially responsible scholarship, can proceed only through research tools that provide ready access to diverse and sometimes disagreeable perspectives. Perhaps the range of citations represented here will encourage research on the sources that the contributors have used to support their findings or to lend credibility to their arguments.

Following the 'Z' collection, citations also appear in the "author unknown" collection. Anonymous authorship reflects the personal preference of the author, the affiliation or prior associations of the author, agency or organization policy, or the publisher's policy. In a few cases, pseudonyms are used. Given the occasional insistence upon secrecy in the intelligence field, there should be no surprise in a lack of attribution to some authors who wished to remain anonymous. I can only presume that the material in these pieces is credible. Anonymity can also result from a publication policy held by some law journals prohibiting attribution of law notes or comments to authors who are often third-year law students writing under faculty supervision. Each item in the "author unknown" collection, therefore, is listed according to the first major word in the title. In some cases, citations reflect declassified documents which appeared in serial journals; other cases suggest authorship by editors or editorial staff. Where an author's name could be found, however, it was arranged in the main alphabetical listing or in the "late entries" collection.

A "late entries" collection appears after the "author unknown" collection. This list was added after a cutoff date in 1997; accession numbers were assigned after December 1, 1998. Readers will note that this collection contains mainly sources with an author, but some unauthored pieces are included in alphabetical order of the first key word in the title. An index of co-authors is supplied to give credit to authors who contributed equally to an article by assisting in the research or writing, or authors who fell victim to journal policy of alphabetical arrangement of names.

The key word or term index was constructed mainly from the content of article titles and annotations. Most titles include sufficient topical details to allow for primary discovery or cross-referencing. Redundancies have been provided in the index of key words or terms by using at least two title or annotation elements, and by listing many citation numbers on more than one occasion. For example, if the title was "The Espionage Career of Paul Jones Against the Japanese in World War II, 1942-1944," index listings would most likely appear under "career," "Jones, Paul," "Japan[ese]," "World War II," and "1942." Please note that citations containing a year parameter, such as "1942," will be listed at the beginning of the "N" (for nineteen) collection; "E" (for eighteen); etc. I hope that researchers will find the index friendly to their needs, and that future writing will be encouraged by drawing on the diversity of sources relevant to particular subjects.

My sincere hope is that the collection magnifies the role of academic journals and professional magazines in the study of intelligence, espionage, and related topics. Since 1947 and congressional passage of the National Security Act, scholars have been virtually guaranteed a place at the national security table. Their opportunity, and perhaps even their duty, is to keep open the lines of investigation into the fundamental processes of information gathering and to the complex circumstances in which information may be manipulated, distorted, and occasionally incorporated in the decision making processes of national and corporate leaders. Scholars of these topics have relied heavily on the journal or professional magazine as important, yet somewhat elusive, media for sustaining their participation in the continuing discourse about spies, spy work, and spy organizations in old and new worlds. Perhaps publication of this collection will encourage more journal publication in the twenty-first century, most likely in some similar forms but predictably in many different forms.

I take full responsibility for any failure to include an author's journal or magazine scholarship. In view of the need to continue this project, I hope that authors will communicate directly with me by e-mail at JCalder@utsa.edu or by regular mail addressed to The University of Texas at San Antonio, Division of Social and Policy Sciences, San Antonio, Texas 78249-0655.

Acknowledgments

The authors cited in this bibliography are owed a full measure of recognition for advancing critical thought and open discussion about intelligence, espionage, and related topics. Each has enriched our understanding of the complex and elusive actions of spies, spy organizations, and the masters they serve. Their works have peaked our interest in secret activities of government and private organizations, and they have cast significant light on schemes and undercurrents floating below the surface of glitter and pretentiousness in international relations. Clearly, their contributions tell important stories about the circumstances under which nations employ intelligence services to inform policy, to adjust to foreign or domestic circumstances, or even to do evil or good in the name of economic or national interests. This collection, then, is dedicated mainly to past and present scholars who have shared experiences, insights, and reflections on subjects which have intruded into the foreground and background of recorded history. The new millennium will be supplied with citations to nearly ten-thousand four-hundred formal articles in the broad and expanding body of knowledge concerned with intelligence and espionage studies.

Special acknowledgments are owed to Mr. Charles Thurston, senior reference librarian at The University of Texas at San Antonio, who on many occasions offered valuable advice and assistance in conducting topical searches. Like Charles, there are many librarians across the nation who contributed directly or indirectly to this project, and to each of them I say thank you for your kindness and support. Special thanks are due to my sister, Katherine E. Riskam, for sharing her knowledge of search strategies for extracting valuable information from the vast computer resources now available to bibliographers. I profited from many excellent bibliographic sources that pioneered the collection and organization of journal and magazine writings, especially the works of Jonathan M. House, Neal H. Petersen, Myron J. Smith, Jr., Raymond G. Rocca, and John J. Dziak. Several encyclopedias ensured that the fine points of historical events and personalities were properly interpreted, in particular the works of Norman Polmar and Thomas B. Allen, Jeffrey T. Richelson, Richard Deacon, and Ernest Volkman. H. Bradford Westerfield's study of declassified articles in the Central Intelligence Agency's internal journal was exceptionally helpful in cleaning up many citation errors I found in secondary sources.

Throughout the years of collecting and annotating sources, I learned the value of readily available index resources and a good collection of serial journals and magazines. In fact, I owe a huge debt of gratitude to the reference and journals acquisition librarians at Trinity University library, St. Mary's University regular and Law Center libraries, the Honnold Library of the Claremont Colleges, The University of Texas at Austin Perry Casteneda and law libraries, the University of Maryland McKeldin graduate library, the library of the U. S. Army War College, Georgetown University Edward Bennett Williams law library, and the John Peace Library of The University of Texas at San Antonio.

So many students have also rendered exceptional contributions through the sixteen years of this project, and to you I offer my sincere gratitude. Valuable technical advice was supplied by UTSA staff member Kevin Bryan, and by Robert Behrens, J.D. Susan Baker and Jane Lerner of the production staff at Greenwood have provided many helpful tips to ease the pain of the drafts of this book and my earlier history of the Hoover administration's crime control policies. My good friend and bowling partner, Mr. Henry Alvarado (deceased), and his UTSA staff, offered dedicated assistance in putting citations in computer form in the early years. Wherever you are, Henry, please know that you are in our thoughts, and your spirit, your smile, and your thoughtfulness are missed.

Frankly, I could not have acquired the peace of mind necessary to complete this project without the love and devotion of my wife, Moni Calder. I admire and respect her patience, especially for withstanding thousands of hours of dialogues, editing, German translations, library assistance, and tons of moral support in the many steps to final production.

To my loyal adviser and friend, Mr. John Harney, Book Consultants of Boston, I offer a large debt of gratitude. The final product has depended on his continued inspiration and gentle prodding. To Dr. James Sabin, thanks for your faith in this project throughout its many delays. Intelligencers will thank both of you.

Introductory Essay

"And what are you?, said he. "It will not satisfy me to point to this fantastic show of an Intelligence Office and this mockery of business. Tell me what is beneath it, and what your real agency in life, and your influence upon mankind."

Nathaniel Hawthorne, "The Intelligence Office," <u>Democratic Review</u>, 1844

In the 1930s Thurman Arnold issued a stern warning to a budding social science community. "[T]he social sciences are stationary,"[1] he charged. His criticism slashed at the aloofness of much social inquiry in a time of worldwide ideological turmoil and gripping economic depression. Intellectuals, he believed, had a larger calling to be more deeply focussed on improving the human condition. Indeed, Arnold was impatient with some of his colleagues and with the pace of social reform. He had concluded that these were outcomes of rigid departmentalization of the social sciences and shortages of transdisciplinary scholarship.[2] The words stung deeply, but their objective was to hasten diversification and expansion of the social sciences.

Oddly, Arnold's charge offers a lesson for modern and future studies in the social sciences, and in particular, the scholarly study of intelligence, espionage and related topics. The world will become an even smaller place in the new millennium. Accordingly, social science inquiry will be obligated to become less stationary and vastly more transdisciplinary in acquisition and analysis of critical data. In particular, the success of scientific investigations and policy results concerning, for example, prevention of nuclear war, disaster response, famine relief, and terrorism containment will require new assignments for secret services, and new definitions of information control and secrecy in international relations. No doubt the social sciences will more forthrightly consider the place and responsibilities of secret information collectors and information analysts in positions of influence in democratic and non-democratic political systems. And they will most likely be unable to avoid the implications of information compromise in the smaller and more tightly wound setting of international conflict and cooperation. Indeed, the expectation is that the social sciences will contribute more to the cause of world peace and to the integrity of nation-state sovereignty as they reveal in their publications a broadened understanding of how intelligence-gathering and espionage influence national and organizational decision-making. Arnold's warning, therefore, is likely to have new life in the future since any residual aloofness of the social sciences about the gathering and control of vital information, either by open or clandestine means, serves no useful purpose.

The corpus of citations in this bibliography presents a circumstantial case for recognizing the correctness of Arnold's critique. Many new disciplines and subdisciplines have grown up under the broad umbrella of traditional social and behavioral sciences. Diversity of research and publication within these disciplines, some of which has experienced only grudging toleration, have changed permanently the boundaries of social science writing. New disciplines, such as foreign affairs, international relations, public administration, criminal justice, urban geography, legal studies, military studies, various forms of cultural and ethnic studies, and most recently intelligence studies,[3] now share office space and transdisciplinary interests with traditional fields. Dismaying some and delighting others, newer disciplines within colleges of social science are less confined by philosophical, topical, or methodological agendas of the traditional disciplines. Concepts and terminologies are borrowed across academe's internal grids, and information systems enhance the ability of scholars to overlay methodologies and to expand research interests. Faculties in the new mix of disciplines are often, but not always, expected to cross the well-guarded walls of inquiry and to share concepts and research methods aimed at bridging theory and practice. The new discipline of intelligence studies owes its existence to the willingness of many traditionally trained scholars to take up Thurman Arnold's challenge.

In some ways the new disciplines spring from Arnold's more reasonable instruction that academic pursuits should invest as much in understanding modern realities as in developing assumptions about conditions that may not exist or moral expectations that may be impossible to fulfill. "The road to discovery," Arnold reasoned, "is...closed to all who refuse to accept the world as it is."[4] The formal study of intelligence and espionage, like other studies under the modern mantle of social science, begins with assumptions about ancient and modern realities associated with social and international relations. The mounting collection of scholarly articles and books on these subjects makes clear that modern social sciences not only reflect advancements since Arnold's "stationary" thesis, but it speaks to a new manner of thought about the realities of human relations in the United States and around the world. If he were around today, I believe Arnold would approve of the interest taken by scholars from many disciplines in the place of secrecy systems and organizations in a world where information is a vital exchange commodity, bargaining chip, and protective coating.

A detailed explanation of social science investment in topics like intelligence and espionage belongs elsewhere. Suffice to suggest that new disciplines and subfields often evolve from the particularly profound insights of established scholars or from pioneering work at the intellectual borders of traditional disciplines. Sociology, for example, developed an interest in organizational secrecy, drawing credibility from the work of Georg Simmel,[5] and more recently from the work of Edward Shils on the McCarthy era and the "torment of secrecy."[6] American historians expanded their interest in espionage from the scholarship of Carl Van Doren[7] and James Thomas Flexner,[8] each an analyst of the role of espionage and intelligence operations in the American Revolution. Political science has many intellectual icons who have taken special interest in the political implications of secrecy and management of spy systems, including Charles Merriam's work on the underside of Chicago politics and the tools of government for controlling gangster organizations;[9] Harry Howe Ransom's studies of the Central Intelligence Agency;[10] Frank Trager's legacy in national security studies;[11] and more recently the blending of history, political science, and international relations in the work of Walter Laqueur.[12] Economics draws on uncounted contributions to modern scholarship on the role of information in domestic and international market change, especially where information is critical to investments in major scientific or technological advancements.[13] Economic intelligence (or espionage), after all, is a natural by-product of economic forces. Perhaps a significant impetus for the expansion of social science interest in intelligence and espionage lies in the economic, social, and political quest to understand and control channels and sources of information.[14] Indeed, at the heart of all the social sciences resides an enduring interest in the circumstances of information control and how the distribution of information resources may likely raise or lower the quality of life among peoples of the world.

Several indicators suggest that traditional subtext concerns for espionage and intelligence are now given more central consideration in social science writing about international and domestic issues. An important indication of this development is gleaned from the writings of scholars with crystal-clear academic standing in traditional areas of history, politics, and biography. Vitae contain citations to research into espionage cases and implications involving the actions of spies, techniques and objectives of spying, and operational activities of intelligence services. Stephen Ambrose, for example, a recognized biographer of Dwight Eisenhower, Crazy Horse and Custer, Henry Halleck, and others, inquired into the rise of U. S. intelligence services during the 1950s, as reflected in his book, Ike's Spies: Eisenhower and the Espionage Establishment (1981). Biographer Clare Brandt expanded her interest in the Livingston family, early American aristocrats, with her study of a Revolution-era traitor: The Man in the

Mirror: A Life of Benedict Arnold (1994). Historian of the Nuremberg trials, Bradley F. Smith, produced an acclaimed history of the predecessor to the Central Intelligence Agency in The Shadow Warriors: O.S.S. and the Origins of the C.I.A. (1983); and more recently, Sharing Secrets with Stalin: How the Allies Traded Intelligence, 1941-1945 (1996). Even British historian Rhodri Jeffreys-Jones, consummate observer of American foreign and domestic affairs, has contributed articles on private intelligence operations against labor organizers in the United States and a book on U. S. intelligence practices: The CIA & American Democracy (1989). And Peter Grose, foreign and diplomatic correspondent specializing in Middle East affairs, and later executive director of Foreign Affairs, has recently published a rich biography of Allen Dulles: Gentleman Spy: The Life of Allen Dulles (1994). Who could overlook the memory of Carl Van Doren's work in Secret History of the American Revolution (1941), particularly in view of the fact that the author is acclaimed for biographies of Benjamin Franklin, Jonathan Swift, Thomas Love Peacock, James Branch Cabell, and Sinclair Lewis? Numerous other full treatments by scholars who are generally recognized for work in more mainstream areas lend credence to the notion that espionage and intelligence more properly inhabit the center rather than the periphery of historical, political, and social dialogue. A work of special significance to me is Robin W. Winks's book, Cloak and Gown: Scholars in the Secret War, 1939-1961, which demonstrates clearly the previous closeness of the relationship between scholars and intelligence work.

Another indicator is revealed by the many bibliographies and encyclopedias on intelligence and espionage which are now in print or accessible in first-rate academic libraries. Following the focussed work of Harry Howe Ransom on the Central Intelligence Agency, interest widened to study other intelligence organizations and to compare U. S. organizations with spy groups around the world. Several compilations published from the late 1970s to the 1990s cite thousands of books, reports, and articles. Convenience of access to these types of sources stimulated introduction of university courses and seminars. Noteworthy in this era are Myron J. Smith, Jr.'s three-volume work, The Secret Wars: A Guide to Sources in English (1980), Raymond G. Rocca and John J. Dziak's Bibliography on Soviet Intelligence and Security Services (1985), Neal H. Petersen's American Intelligence, 1775-1990: A Bibliographical Guide (1992), and John M. House's Military Intelligence, 1870-1991: A Research Guide (1993). Beginning in 1979, the Consortium for the Study of Intelligence published several reference works, including listings of monographs and congressional hearings and reports, all aimed at expanding academic interest and research. Professor of international studies and political science at Yale, H. Bradford Westerfield has recently offered a detailed analysis of declassified articles from the Central Intelligence Agency's internal journal, Studies in Intelligence, in his book, Inside CIA's Private World (1995). Most recently, Norman Polmar and Thomas B. Allen have published an encyclopedia, Spy Book: The Encyclopedia of Espionage, a useful addition to similar works by Jeffrey T. Richelson, A Century of Spies: Intelligence in the Twentieth Century (1995) and Ernest Volkman, Spies: The Secret Agents Who Changed the Course of History (1994). The prestigious Encyclopedia of Foreign Relations (1997 edition) contains numerous new entries relevant to intelligence operations and persons associated with events linking intelligence with broader foreign relations issues.

Extensive bibliographies and document collections found in books on particular subjects loosely categorized as relevant to intelligence or espionage include references to hundreds of formal studies on issues and personalities. Naturally, this is not a convenient place to itemize these resources, but a short list of recommendations, highly selective at best, may include Robert M. Hatch, Major John Andre: A Gallant in Spy's Clothing (1986); William A. Tidwell, James O. Hall and David W. Gaddy, Come Retribution: The Confederate Secret Service and the Assassination of Lincoln (1988); William A. Tidwell, April '65: Confederate Covert Action in the American Civil War (1995); Edwin C. Fishel, The Secret War for the Union: The Untold Story of Military Intelligence in the Civil War (1996); William R. Corson, The Armies of Ignorance: The Rise of the American Intelligence Empire (1977); Michael L. Lanning, Senseless Secrets: The Failures of U.S. Military Intelligence from George Washington to the Present (1996); John Ranelagh, The Agency: The Rise and Decline of the CIA from Wild Bill Donovan to William Casey (1986); Loch K. Johnson, America's Secret Power: The CIA in a Democratic Society (1989) and A Season of Inquiry: Congress and Intelligence (1988); Stephen F. Knott, Secret and Sanctioned: Covert Operations and the American Presidency (1996); Frank J. Donner, The Age of Surveillance: The Aims and Methods of America's Political Intelligence System (1980); Athan G. Theoharis, Spying on Americans: Political Surveillance from Hoover to Huston (1978); Richard G. Powers, Secrecy and Power: The Life of J. Edgar Hoover (1987); Curt Gentry, J. Edgar Hoover: The Man and the Secrets (1991); Ronald Kessler, The FBI (1993); and Mark Riebling, Wedge: The Secret War Between the FBI and CIA (1994). A long list of excellent resources refers readers to intelligence and espionage concerns beyond American borders, such as John O. Koehler, STASI: The Untold Story of the East German Secret Police (1999); Gordon Thomas, Gideon's Spies: The Secret History of the Mossad (1999); R. Lamont-Brown, Kempeitai: Japan's Dreaded Military Police (1998); Maria Emilia Paz, Strategy, Security, and Spies: Mexico and the U. S. as Allies in World War II (1997); Douglas Porch, The French Secret Services: From the Dreyfus Affair to the Gulf War (1995); Nicholas Eftimiades, Chinese Intelligence Operations (1994); Ian Black and Benny Morris, Israel's Secret Wars: A History of Israel's Intelligence Services (1991); Jeffrey T. Richelson, Foreign Intelligence Organizations (1988); Jeffrey T. Richelson and Desmond Ball, The Ties That Bind: Intelligence Cooperation between the UKUSA Countries--the United Kingdom, the United States of America, Canada, Australia and New Zealand (1985, 1990); or Walter Laqueur, A World of Secrets: The Uses and Limits of Intelligence (1985). Even popular culture is represented in bibliographies of spy novels: LeRoy L. Panek, The Special Branch: The British

Spy Novel, 1890-1980 (1981); and Myron J. Smith, Jr., Cloak and Dagger Fiction: An Annotated Guide to Spy Thrillers (1982).

A third indicator brings us to the rationale for this bibliography: the remarkable growth and sophistication of research on espionage and intelligence appearing in both traditional and new journals of scholarship. In fact, the frequency of article publication in the last two decades may serve as the strongest indicator of an emergent discipline. Before Harry Ransom's work nearly four decades ago, the journal literature on intelligence and intelligence services was thin and virtually unrecognized in the flood of mainstream social science publication. Some formal writing appeared within the tight circle of academic colleagues with special interests in social science study of intelligence, former intelligence officers of the World War II era, or people who were employed in secret services, such as OSS, CIA, military intelligence or signals operations, or National Security Agency. The literature generated by "insiders," i.e., current or former intelligence personnel, was published mainly in book form, but it was rarely vetted in a manner that social scientists would accept or in a manner normally applied to articles appearing in academic journals.[15] Outsiders settled for tidbits of insider data, frequently acquiring it from private interviews, autobiographical accounts, popular magazines, or occasional documentary sources.

The modern experience is substantially different. Publishing houses sponsor whole journals devoted to intelligence and espionage topics, such as Frank Cass Publishers in London who control Intelligence and National Security (now in volume 14); specially organized publishers, such as the Joint Military Intelligence College Foundation in Washington, D.C., who control Defense Intelligence Journal (now in volume 8); and Taylor and Francis, Inc., who publish International Journal of Intelligence and Counterintelligence (now in volume 12). Articles in these publications demonstrate extensive research into primary records and validation of some of the insider-supplied information from previous years. Journal publishers in history, political science, and international affairs also have compiled a substantial record of article publication exclusively or partly aimed at intelligence and espionage topics, e.g., Foreign Affairs; Foreign Policy; Orbis; American Historical Review; and American Political Science Review. Each of these leading academic journals, and dozens of other highly respected journals of all rankings, have vetted and published articles on intelligence and espionage in complete issues or within a mix of other articles.

Ironic, perhaps, is the fact that concepts and issues relevant to intelligence and espionage have been accommodated by the social sciences at a time when the methods for transmitting knowledge, such as serial journals, are changing form and possibly declining in value. The traditional academic journal in paper form, the main source for sharing advances in theory and research, may shortly become a dinosaur, yielding to faster means of transmission through Internet capabilities. In the near future access to primary information sources could become so widely disseminated that the slow and specialized nature of analysis associated with traditional paper journals will be surpassed by a broad field of equally competent analysts armed with more data and unlimited space. Without question, the vetting process will become increasingly critical to scientific and analytical advancements in all fields as technologies influence the process and form of journals.[16]

As researchers who have primary or secondary interests in intelligence and espionage await these emerging developments, perhaps the main contribution of this bibliography is to present a compilation of serial journal scholarship in one source. Spanning 150 years of writing, this collection cites nearly 10,400 articles. It brings special focus to this new and unique area of scholarship. On a practical level, also, it provides a convenient research finding aid that recognizes the individual and collective efforts of the authors. I hope that it will be used as a preliminary source for authors who have aimed research questions at the role of intelligence and espionage in the decision-making processes of public and private organizations.

JOURNALS AND THE STUDY OF INTELLIGENCE AND ESPIONAGE

The serial journal offers a unique contribution to information transfer. Like books and other publication forms, article publishing follows certain practices and traditions that have become standardized over time and across academic disciplines. While scholars are all too familiar with these practices, general users of this bibliography may wish to consider some of the dynamics of vetted article publications. Articles about intelligence, espionage, and related topics reach print in the same way other social and behavioral science writings are published. Some characteristics of these topics, however, present challenges to traditional article vetting practices

Serial journal articles are not intended to be comprehensive treatises. Their length ranges, on average, between fifteen and thirty-five pages, and subscription costs are generally high by comparison with costs of sophisticated popular magazines found at newsstands. Thus, they are not readily consumed by general readership audiences. Contrasted with books or monographs they contain articles generally regarded as narrowly focused, specialized contributions at the leading edge of scholarly inquiry. New journals frequently reflect sophistication of an advancing new field or subspecialization. Journals devoted exclusively to topics of intelligence and espionage have grown up around the attention visited upon the world and actions of spies since the 1970s. So far, their subject matter has had limited range, largely resulting from limited access to critical agency records. Another important factor included the broadening of topical diversity of editorial policies in the mainstream social science journals, resulting in part from new coalitions among scholars across disciplines and new specializations within traditional areas of research and publication.

The principal market for serial journals is college and university libraries where serious publications serve as vital information resources for undergraduate and graduate students, and faculty and consultants who conduct research in connection with teaching or specialized institutes and schools (e.g., foreign affairs institutes, medical schools, or law schools). Academics who are expected to publish have the largest stake in journal publication. Some appeal is sustained by professionals who identify with, benefit from, use, or contribute to research products. Demand for journal information is correlated with graduate studies or professional advancement programs since the faculty must read beyond the level of the students they instruct. Unquestionably, the economics of publication make journals risky propositions, since they service highly specialized audiences, and since they are inherently concerned with changing conditions and information.

Journal information is consumed differently from information found in newspapers or popular magazines. Customarily, for example, general readers do not visit medical school libraries to read the latest cancer research found in the Journal of the American Medical Association. Typically, they will not visit a law library to learn how to write a contract. It is also uncommon for law students, general practitioner lawyers or doctors, or technicians to consistently review articles appearing in serial journals. All may read the local newspaper, Time, or Newsweek, but usually people who hold advanced degrees represent the predominant subscribers to serial journals. Like others, scholars of intelligence-related topics visit research libraries where they read what others have investigated concerning, for example, historical case studies on strategic or tactical surprise, how spies may have changed the course of history, or problems associated with the CIA's changing organizational culture. Journal readership, therefore, is substantially dissimilar from book or popular magazine readership. Articles tend to avoid lengthy background details since the reader is presumed to be reasonably well informed. Tight writing and collections of endnotes confirm that articles are aimed mainly at extending or adjusting what the reader already knows. In essence, then, serial journal articles contain information produced by scholars specifically for scholars or people who have highly specialized interests in new knowledge discovery.

A finished article is the product of a generally limited treatment of issues, research findings, or theoretical approaches. Generally, two or three members of a journal's editorial board read and comment on whether or not an article comports with journal focus, tradition, and policy. They also screen articles on matters of methodology, data, conclusions, and overall coherence of writing style. Editorial boards, usually comprised of leading scholars in a field or subfield, challenge submissions on efficiency of presentation, evidentiary support for the argument presented, methodological and analytical rigor, research implications, and conclusions tied to the data. The process disallows straying too far from mainstream issues and approaches, thus in theory advancing and reinforcing the body of knowledge. For years, the argument has been offered that leading journals of scholarship invest more energy in guarding the gates of topical inquiry than in encouraging different modes of research and knowledge development. The debate about this problem will continue to occupy the time of traditional academic tribes. By implication, the dialogue will also affect studies of intelligence functions, particularly in view of strong forces of consensus in the world of spy organizations where dissent is held in check by the pull of secrecy imperatives and systematic methods for extracting, organizing, and reporting data.[17]   In many ways, the value system of journal publication is fully consistent with mainstream requirements for success in intelligence work.

Articles that survive review tests, sometimes after significant refinement, are accepted as additions to the body of advancing scholarship. The published product is likely to reflect intensive study of small pieces of a much larger pie. After publication, an article's life is served on a library shelf, probably amounting to little more than a microdot in history, perhaps an endnote in someone else's article, or with any luck the basis of a new way of thinking. Other academics will judge the long-term value of the piece, a kind of impact assessment which is partly dependent on the frequency of a microdot's appearance in the work of others. Scholarship, it is argued, depends on an expanding collection of narrowly focussed journal articles, most of which represent attempts to extend or modify other research. The critical mass of specialized literature builds and sustains the art and science.

All disciplines of scholarship confront a difficult dilemma as they advance and subdivide: how to evaluate journal articles written by scholars who conduct research at the margins of mainstream intellectual interests, articles on subjects only marginally outside the borders of editorial policy, or articles by authors who express perspectives that contrast sharply with editors' views. This dilemma is not easily or comfortably resolved, since the mission of an academic journal is mainly to restrict publication to authors who write within the commonly accepted lines of editorial policy. Theoretically, editorial policy maintains journal objectives so that a reputation which has been sanctioned by a community of like-minded scholars can be maintained. The problem comes when the guardians of editorial policy overlook or misunderstand the significance of new realities or trends. Deviation from a journal's publishing history threatens continuity and orderly progress.

Widely recognized in most fields is the fact that journals reject more articles than they accept, thus leading to an equally widely accepted view among scholars that only "good" articles reach publication. Setting aside rejections that should result from plainly bad research, bad analysis, or bad writing, journal literature, already limited in audience appeal, is vulnerable to progressive sclerosis. Articles can be rejected because they do not fit a predetermined publication formula. This outcome may be tied in part to afflictions of editorial policy, such as creeping journal politics or hidden preferences of editors. Articles on subjects pertaining to intelligence and espionage can easily fall outside the publication traditions of most social science journals. These are subjects about which social scientists can experience intellectual discomfort, the sources of which are complex and often unreachable.

General practices of journal publication have been adopted and reinforced in the social sciences for about a hundred years. All of them have implications for scholars engaged in research associated with intelligence or espionage. Only in the last two decades has it been possible to publish articles explicitly on topics of intelligence or espionage in the so-called leading journals in the social sciences. Fair judgment would insist, however, that the explosive pace of intelligence and espionage scholarship, beginning in the early 1980s, could not have been accommodated by traditional social science journals. An inadequate number of journals was available until recent times, and even if pages had been more open for the arguably best pieces, total page allocations were limited by the economics of issue length. In contrast, however, it is equally reasonable to say that some meritorious writings on intelligence and espionage may have been rejected on grounds that they represented a dark side of democratic life and politics.[18] This bibliography may encourage further consideration of how scholarship on intelligence and espionage finds its way into traditional social science journals.

Journals aimed specifically at publication of articles on intelligence and espionage emerged in the 1980s, partly in response to editorial practices of mainstream social science journals. British scholars of intelligence history, for example, introduced Intelligence and National Security in 1986. The editorial board included recognized academics in several subspecializations of history, political science, and international relations, among them Richard K. Betts and Robert Jervis of Columbia University, Harry Howe Ransom at Vanderbilt University, John Ferris of the University of Calgary, Alexander L. George of Stanford University, Roy Godson of Georgetown University, Samuel P. Huntington, Anthony G. Oettinger, Ernest May and Thomas C. Schelling of Harvard University, Klaus-Jurgen Muller of the University of Hamburg, David Stafford of the Canadian Institute of International Affairs, D. Cameron Watt of the London School of Economics, and Aharon Yariv of the University of Tel Aviv. Currently, this journal's editors include Wesley Wark of the University of Toronto and Richard J. Aldrich of the University of Nottingham and a distinguished editorial board comprised of scholars from the U. K., the U. S., Australia, Belgium, France, Germany, and Israel. Responding to American demands for a quality journal, former business executive F. Reese Brown introduced, also in 1986, the International Journal of Intelligence and Counterintelligence, "devoted to exploring the methods and techniques used in the various facets of intelligence work as well as investigating the processes used in developing national estimates and other forms of finished intelligence."[19] Board membership for this journal has tended to include more representation from intelligence field specializations, but recognized academic members currently include David M. Barrett of Villanova University, Gideon Doron of Tel Aviv University, Frederick P. Hitz of Princeton University, Robert Jervis of Columbia University, Loch K. Johnson of the University of Georgia, Sheila Kerr of the University of Salford, Amy Knight of George Washington University, Richard Pipes of Harvard University, John D. Stempl of the University of Kentucky, Michael A. Turner of U. S. International University, Peter C. Unsinger of San Jose State University, Richard R. Valcourt of the American Military University, H. Bradford Westerfield of Yale University, and James J. Wirtz of the Naval

Postgraduate School.   Less widely distributed in academic circles and more narrow in scope, but no less important to diversity of article publication, are such documents as Defense Intelligence Journal (Joint Military Intelligence College Foundation), Military Intelligence (an Army publication), Naval Intelligence Professionals Quarterly (an outlet of the Naval Intelligence Professionals Association), and American Intelligence Journal (Association of Former Intelligence Officers).

No specialized journal currently published is older than the CIA's internal classified journal, Studies in Intelligence, a refereed outlet since 1955 for CIA analysts and operations personnel.   In recent years, CIA has been pressured by scholars in various disciplines to declassify articles to promote more public and scholarly investigation of intelligence community organizations.[20]   In each case, these journals give intensive consideration to a broad range of subjects, from ancient Roman intelligence history, to European and other contexts of intelligence operations, to recent policy issues on restructuring American and foreign intelligence services.   To date, there are few evaluations of articles published in these journals.   This bibliography may assist in the advancement of article evaluation research, a necessary step in strengthening the quality and respect for the journal literature.

AN EXPLOSION OF ARTICLES, A FUSION OF CONDITIONS

In the 1970s, several conditions combined to crack open opportunities for research and publication on intelligence and related subjects.   The principal contributing factor for the explosion of article and book publications was a movement in several Western nations to unseal vast stockpiles of records held secret for decades by government agencies.   Beginning in the 1960s, interest groups in the United States, Canada, Great Britain, and France lobbied legislative bodies to change laws to allow greater access to documents containing information about foreign and domestic conflicts, environmental hazards, nuclear weapons, national security, and the activities of secret intelligence services.   The movement attracted vigorous opposition and was undermined for a period of time by federal investigative agencies at least in the United States.   Legislation, such as the Freedom of Information Act installed by the U. S. Congress in 1966 (revised in 1974), opened millions of files to researchers and citizens.   Once scholars and others mastered the cumbersome bureaucratic process for accessing files, paths were beaten to offices and archives in Washington, D.C.   Documents stored in federal agencies and at the National Archives and Records Administration in Washington (the historian's research laboratories for investigating controversies) were pored over and copied by the reams of paper.   Most scholars searched for evidence to challenge earlier explanations given by public officials, or never-explored explanations for the decisions taken by presidents, members of Congress, key inside advisers, directors of agency intelligence functions, and various players in all areas of civil and military intelligence work, domestic and foreign.   The most intensive and thorough research required several years to accomplish, thus delaying the full impact of the results until the late 1970s. Historians, such as Athan Theoharis, Anthony Cave Brown, Joseph Persico, Ladislas Farago, and others with traditional historical credentials, mined and digested tall stacks of formerly secret documents for new perspectives on FBI, CIA, NSA, and other intelligence agency operations. A large number of articles and dozens of books resulted from this work. The net product increased public oversight of governmental records, expanded participation in decision-making processes, and brought about new forms of accountability for administrative actions. Perhaps a negative result was heightened and generalized distrust of government. But the overall effort has clearly matured the kind and quality of scholarly reflection on intelligence activities, and it has most likely checked intelligence agency fears that limited revelations would somehow injure essential intelligence functions.

A second major cause was a gradual recognition by the superpowers, in particular the United States and the former Soviet Union, that narrow cold war hostilities had become considerably less appealing to respective internal audiences. Secrecy no longer carried the aura of previous decades, and unquestionably the stakes for failure or misunderstanding were much higher. Mistakes in judgment (e.g., the 1961 Bay of Pigs invasion), dangerous nuclear brinkmanship (e.g., the 1962 missile crisis), monstrous overzealousness and constitutional invasions of private rights (e.g., anti-Vietnam war dissent, Watergate, and Iran-Contra), allegations of miscalculations of world conditions by the intelligence community (e.g., the Hungarian and Czechoslovakian invasions, the fall of the Shah, and the fall of the Soviet Union), and counterintelligence organization abuses or failures (e.g., military and CIA surveillance of American citizens in the United States; the Boyce-Lee, Walker, and Ames espionage cases) all raised significant questions about government credibility. Even in domestic matters, such as presidential assassinations, links between government officials and organized crime, civil rights enforcement, riot control, or the handling of disasters, excessive and unreasonable government secrecy weakened credibility of government action. Diverse channels of information access challenged traditional methods by which people learned about government practices and cover-ups of mistakes.

More publication evolved from calls to expand oversight of intelligence agencies from the early 1970s to the late 1980s. Public hearings and investigations of alleged wrongdoings in the intelligence community, and in the supervising national security structure, stirred controversies worthy of formal academic analyses. A cadre of university scholars, some of whom had already been bitterly alienated by domestic and foreign intrigues of earlier decades, opened the dialogue, but the fact that most argued from an outside position guaranteed they would speak only to themselves. A substantial amount of the journal literature from this period expresses deep frustration with the manner in which government decisions were made, particularly the willfulness by which democratic processes were set aside while ego-inflated personalities and raw exercises of power appeared to control policy outcomes. Despite incomplete evidence to prove their cases beyond a reasonable doubt, authors of many articles of dissent produced a strong circumstantial case for government malfeasance, misfeasance, and even non-feasance. The collection of published articles achieved significant public recognition. Clearly, the aggregate collection of publications from this era contributed to increased functional oversight of the intelligence community, presumably informing other scholars and the public about values, thought processes, corrupting influences, and actions of national security leaders.

In the early 1980s, a new group of scholars emerged with closer affiliations to agency personnel. A moderate display of enlightenment had entered operational intelligence functions in the late 1970s, and some insiders wanted to communicate with academic critics, partly out of a desire to educate uninformed critics, partly to reinstate credibility of intelligence organizations, and partly to provide a limited amount of case material to encourage more objective evaluation. New associations, lecture series, and open access to insiders encouraged dozens of scholars to add intelligence subjects to their list of publications. Several thousand papers, monographs, articles, and books have been published from this period, which seemed to suffer a small measure of burn-out by the mid-1990s.

Several other conditions also contributed to the explosion of articles over the last few decades. Some university history departments developed strong military history specializations that encouraged research on dynamics of surprise and deception in warfare and strategic planning. Historians mined documents for facts and insights relevant to classic cases of tactical or strategic surprise, searching for factors ignored or overlooked in earlier studies of battles, force movements, or wars. Studies were extended to other areas of interest: leaders and the acceptance of intelligence information, deceptions, and diplomacy; strategy and technological achievements; dynamics of intelligence failures; competing analytical methodologies for calculating the size, capabilities, and equipment of enemy forces; and the impact of "group think" psychology on intelligence.

The humanities contributed analyses of spy novels and films. Analysts took interest, once again, in the spy's role in competition between committed and deadly serious superpowers. John LeCarre's 1963 novel, The Spy Who Came in from the Cold, amplified in Richard Burton's coldly humorless role in the 1965 film by the same title, characterized the human functionaries serving at the razor's edge of big power decisions in the cold war. As the list of spy novels and novelists lengthened, the genre of espionage literature explored scenarios and characteristics of players and pawns in the international spy game. Formal analyses and numerous articles emerged in cultural studies, literature, and humanities journals. The significance of this body of literature lies mainly in the fact that novelists in Britain and the United States placed the spy center stage in the competitive and deadly game of nations for nearly a hundred years. Modern literary analysts have returned to the earliest works to find overlooked gems of wisdom offered by Erskine Childers, The Riddle of the Sands: A Record of Secret Service (1903); Joseph Conrad, Secret Agent (1907) and Under Western Eyes (1911); semi-fictional domestic spy tales by Allen Pinkerton (e.g., The Spy of the Rebellion, 1883), and many pre- and post-World War I novels of John Buchan (e.g., The Thirty Nine Steps, 1915; Greenmantle, 1915; Mr. Standfast, 1919; and Courts of the Morning, 1929), Somerset Maugham (e.g., Ashenden: or, The British Agent (1928), William LeQueux (e.g., The Great War in England in 1897, 1894; The Luck of the Secret Service, 1921; and Crinkled Crown, 1930), and E. Phillips Oppenheim (e.g., The Mysterious Mr. Sabin, 1905; The Great Secret, 1907; and The Great Impersonation, 1920). A special issue of Intelligence and National Security (October 1990) was devoted to "Spy Fiction, Spy Films and Real Intelligence"; and Michael Cox has recently edited an anthology titled The Oxford Book of Spy Stories (Oxford University, 1996).

A substantial number of citations in this book result from the legal community's huge involvement in modern national security issues. Legal scholars and students contributed to the literature in lengthy analyses of legislation regarding oversight of intelligence organizations, law enforcement strategies for investigating espionage and government information leaks, and clarification of legal procedures which guide criminal matters involving national security. Several hundred law review articles examined legal principles and policy issues at the foundation of covert action decisions, use of informants, electronic surveillance in domestic policing and foreign espionage cases, constitutional limits on search and seizure in national security matters, challenges to agency and judicial restrictions on classified information releases, international arms transfers, industrial espionage and trade secrets theft, and publication of agency secrets by former intelligence community insiders. Articles appeared in law school journals from the most prestigious schools like Harvard, Yale, Columbia, UCLA and UC-Berkeley to small public and private schools with little national recognition. Foreign law journals, mainly from Britain, Canada, and Australia, published pieces concerning controls on intelligence services and challenges to information held secret under more rigid laws like the British Officials Secrets Act. Many law journal citations came from third-year students, a result usually of a law school professor's interest in a subject or willingness to mentor a student who desired to investigate a current legal question. Numerous appellate court decisions have encouraged substantial publication from the discipline of law.

Finally, some journals devoted exclusively to intelligence subjects signed on to a significant dispute, mainly in English-speaking countries, over changes in intelligence agency operating practices or reductions or outright eliminations of traditional spy agency functions. In general, most of the material in this collection presumes an inherent value in intelligence services in the foreign policy apparat, finding grounds on which to permit services to continue their missions under more watchful eyes. The demise of the Soviet Union has fired up challenges from liberal, conservative, and administrative-reform perspectives. The Left has argued for more rigorous oversight of agencies, such as CIA and FBI, often heard to dredge up the ghosts of Watergate and unlawful or unethical actions from Iran-Contra back to the earliest foreign or domestic covert actions. The Right argues for expansion of covert actions and strengthening of domestic and foreign counterintelligence resources. Administrative reformers argue for separating intelligence collection specialties from the analytical function. In theory this design would allow the inevitable embarrassments resulting from clandestine collection or covert operations to be aired without injury to analytical and political advisement functions. Some journal articles aimed at these issues appear to be less intellectually durable, but the total complement serves to emphasize the fact that all policy is linked to actions by real organizations employing real people who work in real and sometimes unruly bureaucratic structures. Other pieces are reasoned and data-supported contributions that have achieved recognition for insights and proposals for change among national security policy leaders. ·

Future journal articles will, no doubt, continue the dialogue on these matters. Pressures to reshape the intelligence community will probably attract the active attention of scholars for another century because spy work is difficult to measure in terms of economic value; because structural reorganization is inherent in bureaucratic organizations; and because restrictions on chartered activities of democratic spy agencies must be consistently and closely guarded. Substantially more investigation of old and new controversies must be undertaken. Spying will remain contentious and intellectually distasteful for the next 2000 years, but the social and behavioral sciences will likely have the largest burden to understand it, to contribute to disciplinary maturity about its constructive role and its cancerous qualities, and to follow the evidence to challenge assumptions of intelligence community analysts, political leaders, and even other scholars. The informational resource of the serial journal can be expected to contribute in new ways to the education of scholars and decision makers alike concerning the actions of spies and their organizations.

NOTES

1. Thurman Arnold. The Symbols of Government. New Haven: Yale University, 1935.

2. Edward N. Kearny. Thurman Arnold, Social Critic: The Satirical Challenge to Orthodoxy. Albuquerque: University of New Mexico, 1970.

3. Formal study of intelligence concepts and issues was greatly expanded in the past twenty years through tireless efforts of Georgetown University Professor Roy Godson and colleagues associated with the Consortium for the Study of Intelligence. Several topical monographs under a main title of Intelligence Requirements for the 1980s (and updated for the 1990s) provided a framework for academic courses and seminars. One particular article set forth an exceptionally detailed outline of the uses and misuses of intelligence products in the policy process: Richard K. Betts, "Analysis, War, and Decision: Why Intelligence Failures Are Inevitable," World Politics 31 (October 1978): 61-89. Reflections on the expansion and gaps in current intelligence studies are found in Stafford T.

Thomas, "Assessing Current Intelligence Studies," International Journal of Intelligence and Counterintelligence 2/2 (Spring 1988): 217-244; and D. Cameron Watt, "Intelligence Studies: The Emergence of the British School," Intelligence and National Security 3/2 (April 1988): 338-341. A few of the many examples of textbooks now used in undergraduate and graduate courses on intelligence include: Bruce D. Berkowitz and Allan E. Goodman, Strategic Intelligence for American National Security (Princeton, 1989); Adda B. Bozeman, Strategic Intelligence & Statecraft (Brassey's, 1992); Abram N. Shulsky, Silent Warfare: Understanding the World of Intelligence (Brassey's, 1991); Walter Laqueur, A World of Secrets: The Uses and Limits of Intelligence (Basic Books, 1985); and Roy Godson, Dirty Tricks or Trump Cards: U.S. Covert Action and Counterintelligence (Brassey's, 1995).

4. Kearny, op. cit., p. 6.

5. Georg Simmel. "The Sociology of Conflict," American Journal of Sociology 9 (1904): 490-525.

6. Edward Shils. The Torment of Secrecy: The Background and Consequences of American Security Practices. New York: Free Press, 1956.

7. Carl Van Doren, Secret History of the American Revolution. New York: Viking, 1941.

8. James Thomas Flexner. The Traitor and the Spy: Benedict Arnold and John Andre. Syracuse: Syracuse University Press, 1991, 1975, 1953.

9. B. D. Karl. Charles E. Merriam and the Study of Politics. Chicago: University of Chicago Press, 1974. On the evolution of political science as a discipline, see also E. J. Harpham. Disenchanted Realist: Political Science and the American Crisis, 1884-1984. Albany: State University of New York Press, 1985.

10. Harry Howe Ransom. Central Intelligence and National Security. Cambridge: Harvard University Press, 1958. This was followed by several articles and books on American intelligence organizations, then The Intelligence Establishment. Cambridge: Harvard University Press, 1970.

11. See for example Frank N. Trager. "The National Security Act of 1947: Its Thirtieth Anniversary," Air University Review 29/1 (November-December 1977): 2-15.

12. Walter Laqueur. A World of Secrets: The Uses and Limits of Intelligence. New York: Basic Books, 1988.

13. Jeffrey T. Richelson. A Century of Spies: Intelligence in the Twentieth Century. New York: Oxford University Press, 1995, pp. 426-428. See also Peter Schweizer. Friendly Spies: How America's Allies Are Using Economic Espionage to Steal Our Secrets. New York: Atlantic Monthly Press, 1993.

14. See for example Adda B. Bozeman. Strategic Intelligence & Statecraft: Selected Essays. Washington, D.C.: Brassey's, 1992, pp. 180-212.

15. It is widely understood that intelligence professionals who have signed a secrecy agreement with the United States government are legally obligated to submit any manuscripts to the respective agency of employment for purposes of editorial review. Following is a small sample of the books published by former CIA insiders in the last two decades: Duane R. Clarridge, A Spy for All Seasons: My Life in the CIA (1997); William Colby with James McCargar, Lost Victory: A Firsthand Account of America's Sixteen-Year Involvement in Vietnam. Chicago: Contemporary Books, 1989; Stansfield Turner, Secrecy and Democracy: The CIA in Transition. Boston: Houghton Mifflin, 1985; Cord Meyer, Facing Reality: From World Federalism to the CIA. Washington, D.C.: University Press of America, 1980; William Colby, Honorable Men: My Life in the CIA. New York: Simon & Schuster, 1978; and David Phillips, The Night Watch (1977).

16. The future of journals is cogently summarized by Lauren H. Seiler in "The Future of the Scholarly Journal," Academic Computing (September 1989), pp. 14-16, 66-69. Seiler has concluded, "Print is moving toward extinction. The digital electronic medium is rapidly supplanting it while at the same time combining and integrating with it the myriad other forms of information" (p. 69).

17. Many intelligence insiders and outsiders have commented on this problem, but a book worthy of reader attention is the late Sam Adams's War of Numbers: An Intelligence Memoir. South Royalton, Vermont: Steerforth Press, 1994. Numerous journal articles have addressed this point, particularly with respect to the negative implications for analysis of critical national security threats.

18. Edward Sayle's article, for example, "The Historical Underpinnings of the U.S. Intelligence Community," which appeared in the Spring 1986 issue of The International Journal of Intelligence and Counterintelligence, was at least equivalent to any number of articles appearing in Journal of American History, other history journals, and any of several political science journals with policy orientations. Sayle, however, was not a mainstream academic historian situated in a university department of history, and his position at the time of historical curator at the Central Intelligence Agency could easily have raised flags among journal editors.

19. F. Reese Brown, "From the Editor...," International Journal of Intelligence and Counterintelligence 1/1 (Spring 1986), p. i.

20. Recently, Yale professor H. Bradford Westerfield published Inside CIA's Private World (Yale University Press, 1995), a collection of articles from CIA's in-house classified journal, Studies in Intelligence. CIA declassified several articles published between 1955 and 1992 from which Westerfield selected and edited the pieces he believed would have further value to academics engaged in research on intelligence processes of collection, analysis, dissemination, and of applications of intelligence in policy formation.

Journal Articles, by Author's Last Name

A

"A Number to Live With"
(<u>War of Numbers</u> by Sam Adams, p. 212)

1. Aalders, G. and C. Wiebes. "Stockholm's Enskilda Bank, German Bosch and IG Farben: A Short History of Cloaking," <u>Scandinavian Economic History Review</u> 33/1 (1985): 25-50.

2. Abeles, Francis and Stanley H. Lipson. "Some Victorian Periodic Polyalphabetic Ciphers," <u>Cryptologia</u> 14/2 (April 1990): 128-134.
This journal publishes numerous articles on the history and techniques of cryptology.

3. Abell, Richard B. "Effective Systems for Regional Intelligence Sharing," <u>Police Chief</u> 55 (November 1988): 58-59.
Discusses a proposal to create a seven-state project to advance the cooperation between states on criminal intelligence. Useful in studies of domestic or police intelligence practices.

4. Abbott, James P. "The Intelligence Puzzle Has Seven Pieces: The Essential Elements of Information," <u>Army</u> 7 (August 1956): 48-49.
This article appears in a US Army professional magazine, a rare discussion of intelligence matters in the decade of the 1950s.

5. Abbott, Roger S. "The Federal Loyalty Program: Background and Problems," American Political Science Review 42 (1948): 486-499.

Analysis of employee loyalty law, beginning with Executive Orders of 1947, having their origins in a growing fear of communism in government.

6. Abbott, Steve. "The Wizards of War," Soldier 36 (May 1981): 28-31.

A profile of the 11th Military Intelligence Battalion, an Army organization aimed at analysis of weapons and equipment of enemy nations.

7. Abbott, W. C. "English Conspiracy and Dissent, 1669-74," American Historical Review 14 (1908-1909): 502-528.

8. Aberbach, Joel D. "Changes in Congressional Oversight," American Behavioral Scientist 22 (May-June 1979): 493-515.

Discusses congressional oversight of executive branch functions; factors that promote oversight and factors that increase the quality of oversight; congressional behavior and oversight actions; and research on oversight.

9. Aberbach, Joel D. "The Congressional Committee Intelligence System: Information, Oversight and Change," Congress & the Presidency 14 (Spring 1987): 51-76.

Discusses congressional oversight intelligence agency activities and program performance. Major sections include discussions of goals of intelligence oversight; data gathering methods; division of information in networks; and internal congressional communications.

10. Abernathy, Thomas P. "The Commercial Activities of Silas Deane in France," American Historical Review 39 (April 1934): 477-485.

Discusses the role of Silas Deane, an American agent charged with gathering economic information from Great Britain, in serving the economic interests of the colonies as well as his own interests. Accounts for British information gathering in Deane's affairs and the extent of Deane's profiteering.

11. Ablett, Charles B. "Shoot What? Shoot Where?," Military Review 44/2 (1964): 48-57.

12. Ablett, Charles B. "Electronic Warfare: A Modern Weapons System," Military Review 46/11 (November 1966): 3-11.

A summary of the use of electronic warfare in World War II, including Magic codes, navigation applications, and radar. Emphasizes that the secret of US military superiority could not be revealed during the war for obvious reasons.

13. Abosch, Heinz. "In the Shadow of Big Brother," Frankfurter Hefte 22/5 (1967): 302-304.

14. Abramov, S. Z. "The Agranat Report and Its Aftermath," <u>Midstream</u> 20/6 (June-July 1974): 16-28.

The author, a member of the Israeli Liberal Party and Speaker of the Knesset, summarizes the contents and implications of a commission report concerning the failures of Israeli intelligence and military operations prior to the Yom Kippur war.

15. Abrams, Floyd; Henry M. Holzer; Don Oberdorfer; and Richard K. Willard. "The First Amendment and National Security," <u>University of Miami Law Review</u> 43/1 (September 1988): 61-90.

Article contains statements made at a symposium by two law professors, a reporter and a former US Assistant Attorney General. Political discourse on proper manner by which to treat individuals in media and government employees who leak sensitive information. Holzer and Willard advocate punishment and prior restraint while Abrams and Oberdorfer oppose.

16. Abrams, Stuart E. "Threats to the President and the Constitutionality of Constructive Treason," <u>Columbia Journal of Law and Social Problems</u> 12/3 (Summer 1976): 351-392.

Analyses the history of Title 18, U.S. Code Section 871, relating to verbal and written threats upon the President and certain federal officials. Suggests legislative changes in order to protect the President while remaining constitutionally acceptable.

17. Abshire, David and Brian Dickson. "War by Miscalculation: The Forgotten Dimension," <u>Washington Quarterly</u> 6/4 (1983): 114-124.

Discusses origins of four wars (World Wars I and II, Korea and Falklands/Malvenas), emphasizes the significance of miscalculations about military strengths and weaknesses.

18. Abu-Jaber, Faiz. "American Leadership in the Cold War," <u>Indian Political Science Review</u> 12/1 (1978): 107-116.

19. Achard, James. "The Intelligence Service in the Future," <u>Military Review</u> 28 (November 1948): 90-94.

20. Achard, James. "Intelligence in Atomic Warfare," <u>Military Review</u> 36 (June 1956): 102-106.

21. Acheson, Dean. "Dean Acheson's View of Robert Kennedy's View of the Cuban Missile Crisis," <u>Esquire</u> (February 1969): 44-45; 76-78.

The author's observations of the missile crisis, arguing that President Kennedy had received an incomplete analysis of the situation from Robert Kennedy, thereby making a favorable outcome essentially a matter of risk.

22. Ackerman, Jennifer G. "Intelligence and Its Literature: A Collector's Trove in the Watergate," Yale Alumni Magazine and Journal 47/3 (December 1983): 24-27.

23. Ackerman, Robert K. "The Art of Deception," Signal 43/1 (September 1988): 47-51.
　　　Use of battlefield decoys on the ground, in aircraft positioning and naval areas.

24. Adam, John A. "Counting the Weapons," IEEE Spectrum 23/7 (July 1986): 46-56.
　　　Summation of the context and roles of satellite technologies used to monitor weapons agreements, crop yields, disasters and other earth phenomena. Discusses nuclear weapons concealment and the need for "tagging" concealable weapons.

25. Adam, John A. "Cryptography = Privacy?," IEEE Spectrum 29/8 (August 1992): 29-35.

26. Adams, Bruce. "The Extraordinary Career of Vasili Shul'gin," Revolutionary Russia 5/2 (1992): 193-208.

27. Adams, Ephraim D. "British Correspondence Concerning Texas," Southwestern Historical Quarterly 20 (1917): 50-99.

28. Adams, George E. "With the OSS in China," Studies in Intelligence 34/4 (Winter 1990).

29. Adams, Ian. "You and Me and the RCMP," Canadian Dimension 13/3 (1978): 3-8.

30. Adams, Jefferson. "Crisis and Resurgence: East German State Security," International Journal of Intelligence and Counterintelligence 2/4 (Winter 1988): 487-512.
　　　An analysis of the history and development of the East German state security system, including sections on Ernst Wollweber's influence, restructuring of intelligence agencies in the early 1950s, the intelligence service and the Communist Party, the appointment of Enrich Mielke to succeed Wollweber, the tightening of Party control, and strengthening of ties with the Soviet Union.

31. Adams, Milton B. "Where Is He?," Air University Review 20/2 (January-February 1969): 113-115.

32. Adams, Paul. "New Zealand 'Spy Base' Targeted by Faltering Protest Movement," <u>Armed Forces Journal International</u> (July 1988): 30.

33. Adams, Robert H. "Developments in Air Targeting: The Air Battle Model," <u>Studies in Intelligence</u> 2/1 (Spring 1958).

34. Adams, Samuel A. "Vietnam Cover-Up: Playing War with Numbers"; "Statistics on Viet Cong Strength Ignored by the CIA," <u>Harper's</u> 250 & 251 (May and July 1975): 41-44, 62-73; 14-16.

 A frequently cited two-part article describing the author's evidence of a major intelligence assessment coverup regarding enemy strengths and weaknesses in Vietnam. Implicates several key operational and policy figures in the cover-up.

35. Adelman, Kenneth L. "Zaire's Year of Crisis," <u>African Affairs</u> 77 (January 1978): 36-44.

 Discusses economics, internal and external security, politics, and future prospects for Zaire. Mentions the CIA.

36. Adelman, Kenneth L. "A Clandestine Clan: A Review Essay," <u>International Security</u> 5/1 (Summer 1980): 152-171.

 A book review essay concerning <u>The Man Who Kept the Secrets: Richard Helms and the CIA</u> by Thomas Powers, and <u>Countercoup: The Struggle for the Control of Iran</u> by Kermit Roosevelt.

37. Adelman, Kenneth L. "Why Verification Is More Difficult and Less Important," <u>International Security</u> 14/4 (Spring 1990): 141-146.

 Discusses the ineffectiveness of satellite verification in the absence of enforcement. Focusses also on weaknesses of the "START" agreement with the Soviet Union.

38. Adelman, Kenneth L. and Robert Ellsworth. "Foolish Intelligence," <u>Foreign Policy</u> 36 (Fall 1979): 147-159.

 Main emphasis is on CIA failures in Iran and in estimating Soviet MIRV technology. Major sections include discussion of a legacy of CIA estimation failures; the firestorm of criticism; poor preconception; and answering the unanswerable.

39. Adelson, Richard H. "Politics and Intrigue: John Henry and the Making of a Political Tempest," <u>Vermont History</u> 52/2 (1984): 89-102.

 Examines the failed efforts of federalist John Henry and Canadian Governor James Craig to induce the northeastern states to secede from the Union.

40. Adiseshiah, W. T. "The Role of Intelligence in War Strategy," <u>Military Review</u> 34/12 (December 1954): 83-87.

41. Adler, Emanuel. "Executive Command and Control in Foreign Policy: The CIA's Covert Activities," Orbis 23/3 (Fall 1979): 671-696.

Deals with the command and control processes involved in covert actions, institutional and procedural deficiencies, theoretical considerations, and policy conclusions and recommendations.

42. Adler, Mark S. "National Security Information Under the Amended Freedom of Information Act: Historical Perspectives and Analysis," Hofstra Law Review 4/3 (Spring 1976): 759-804.

Reviews basis of governmental withholding of information before the FOIA; examines the 1966 act on executive privilege in this area, and discusses the 1974 amendments.

43. Adomeit, Hannes. "Soviet Crisis Prevention and Management: Why and When Do the Soviet Leaders Take Risks?," Orbis 30/1 (Spring 1986): 42-64.

Soviet leaders are keenly aware of the "objective" and "subjective" factors involved in planning and executing risks of international crises. Contains discussion of the role of secrecy and deception in surprise and risk taking.

44. Aftergood, Steven. "The Perils of Government Secrecy," Issues in Science and Technology 8 (Summer 1992): 81-88.

45. Agee, Jerry. "Naval Security and Investigative Command, Naval Intelligence Professionals Quarterly 3/1 (Winter 1987): 2-3.

46. Agee, Philip. "How to Neutralize the CIA," Skeptic 7 (May-June 1975): 50-51.

Former CIA agent and self-proclaimed critic characterizes the Agency's work as illegal and immoral, therefrom suggesting that such work should be neutralized by exposes of intelligence operations.

47. Agee, Philip. "Why I Split the CIA and Spilled the Beans," Esquire 83 (June 1975): 128-130.

Former case officer Agee discusses his reasons for leaving his chosen career as a spy, including his charges against the Central Intelligence Agency for covert operations, problems encountered in publishing his book (Inside the Company: CIA Diary), and his future plans.

48. Agee, Philip. "The American Security Services: Where Do We Go From Here?," Journal of Contemporary Asia 7 (Spring 1977): 251-259.

49. Agee, Philip. "How the Director of Central Intelligence Projected U.S. Intelligence Activities for 1976-1981," Covert Action Information Bulletin 6 (1979): 13-24.

50. Aglan, Alva. "A French Network of the Intelligence Service: 'Jade-Fitzroy,'" <u>Revue d'Histoire Moderne et Contemporaine</u> 40/2 (1993): 289-302.

51. Agnor, Francis. "The Interpreter as an Agent," <u>Studies in Intelligence</u> 4/4 (Winter 1960): 21-27.
　　　Discusses the role of the language interpreter in the overseas environment and his possible use as an intelligence collector. Outlines the preparation for such role.

52. Agranat Commission. "The Agranat Report," <u>Jerusalem Journal of International Relations</u> 4/1 & 2 (1979): 69-90, 95-128.
　　　A partially reprinted report of the Commission of Inquiry set up by Israel to learn about weaknesses in her own defense system following the 1967 war with Egypt.

53. Agrell, Wilhelm. "Strategy on False Assumptions--A Study of the Egyptian Headquarters 1967," <u>Journal of the Academy of War-Science</u> 5 (1973).

54. Agursky, Mikhail. "Soviet Disinformation and Forgeries," <u>International Journal of World Peace</u> 6/1 (January-March 1989): 13-30.
　　　The use of forgeries by Soviet intelligence services to set up counterintelligence against conspiracies and to penetrate various types of groups. Offers case studies of forgeries in the 1920s.

55. Agursky, Mikhail and Hannes Adomeit. "The Soviet Military-Industrial Complex," <u>Survey</u> 24/544 (Spring 1979): 106-124.

56. Ahlstrom, John D. "Leyte Gulf Remembered," <u>U.S. Naval Institute Proceedings</u> 110/8978 (August 1984): 45-54.
　　　An air intelligence officer describes the battle of Leyte Gulf in World War II.

57. Ahluwai, Mr. "The Question of the U-2 Incident and International Law," <u>Indian Journal of International Law</u> 1 (1961): 301-307.
　　　Author provides editorial comment on two main issues: first, whether the U-2 flight violated Soviet "territorial sovereignty"; and second, whether Soviets were justified in bringing down the U-2 under international law. Provides answers through analysis of then existing international law and conventions, and Soviet responses to similar incidents in the past.

58. Ailes, Catherine P.; James E. Cole; and Charles H. Movit. "Soviet Economic Problems and Technological Opportunities," <u>Comparative Strategy</u> 1/4 (1979): 267-295.

59. Ainsztein, Reuben. "Stalin and June 22, 1941: Some New Soviet Views," International Affairs (Great Britain) 42/4 (October 1966): 662-672.

A book review essay of the 6 volumes, Istoriya Velikoi; Otechestvennoi; Voiny Soveskogo Soyuza; Na Rubezhe Mira; Voiny; and Pared Voini. Suggests that the Soviet people allowed Stalin to aggrandize power at the expense of potential German or other surprise attack (BARBAROSSA).

60. Aitchison, Danae J. "Reining In the Glomar Response: Reducing CIA Abuse of the Freedom of Information Act," U. C. Davis Law Review 27 (Fall 1993): 219-254.

Major topics are the roots of the Freedom of Information Act; the origin and evolution of the Glomar response; the CIA's abuse of the Glomar response; elimination of CIA's abuse of the Glomar response; and conclusions.

61. Akinsanya, Adeoye. "The 'Pueblo' Affair and International Law," Indian Journal of International Law 15/4 (October-December 1975): 485-500.

Applies the controversial international law principles relating to the breadth of the international sea to the seizure of the U.S.S. Pueblo in February 1968. Outlines various international conference rules, rights of coastal states over the territorial sea, background of the Pueblo incident, the Pueblo affair in international law, and implications.

62. Akritas, Alkiviadis G. "Applications of Vincent's Theorem to Cryptography," Cryptologia 6/4 (October 1982): 312-318.

63. Albergotti, Robert D. "Search and Seizure: Warrantless Foreign National Security Wiretaps," Tulane Law Review 49/4 (May 1975): 1153-1160.

Brief note discussing the issues surrounding U. S. v. Butenko 494 F.2d 593 (3rd Cir.). Concludes that warrants for security surveillance by wiretap are a small price to pay to uphold the Fourth Amendment.

64. Albert, Douglas J. "Combatting Software Piracy by Encryption and Key Management," Computer 17 (April 1984): 68-73.

Discusses the application of new encryption programs to reduce computer piracy. Major sections discuss the rationale for key management; processor and key management schemes; security of key management; implementation; and resulting profits.

65. Aldrich, George H. "New Life for the Laws of War," American Journal of International Law 75/4 (October 1981): 764-783.

Analyses the protocols in force in December 1978 and October 1980 with regard to the "protecting power system," the guerilla problem, combatants and POW status, spies, mercenaries, and conduct of hostilities.

66. Aldrich, George H. "Questions of International Law Raised by the Seizure of the U.S.S. Pueblo," Proceedings of the American Society of International Law 63/2 April (1969): 2-6.

Argued at the ASIL meeting in April 1969 that the legal position of the US in the Pueblo affair was a strong one. Says that the North Koreans violated the international law of the sea and the international law of self-defense. Reports upon status of crew in detention and the espionage charges leveled against crew.

67. Aldrich, Richard J. "Imperial Rivalry: British and American Intelligence in Asia, 1942-46," Intelligence and National Security 3/1 (January 1988): 5-55.

Discusses political context of intelligence in Asia; intelligence collection; operational conflict; the question of rivalry or rivalries; the post-war period; conclusions. Concludes that the British and American rivalries dwindled as the political questions which spawned them became increasingly irrelevant.

68. Aldrich, Richard J. "Soviet Intelligence, British Security and the End of the Red Orchestra: The Fate of Alexander Rado," Intelligence and National Security 6/1 (January 1991): 196-217.

Discusses Rado's defection in Cairo and his forcible repatriation during World War II. Author examines the operations of the GRU (Soviet military intelligence) against the German military in World War II.

69. Aldrich, Richard J. "Conspiracy or Confusion?: Churchill, Roosevelt and Pearl Harbor," Intelligence and National Security 7/3 (July 1992): 335-346.

A detailed book review essay regarding Betrayal at Pearl Harbour: How Churchill Lured Roosevelt Into War by J. Rusbridger and E. Nave. The book addresses the British and American cryptanalytical work against Japan in the 1930s.

70. Aldrich, Richard J. "Intelligence, Anglo-American Relations and the Suez Crisis, 1956," Intelligence and National Security 9/3 (July 1994): 544-554.

A book review essay of five books: David Calhoun, Hungary and Suez, 1956: An Exploration of Who Makes History; Peter Hahn, The United States, Great Britain and Egypt, 1945-1956; Diane Kunz, The Economic Diplomacy of the Suez Crisis; Keith Kyle, Suez; W. Scott Lucas, Divided We Stand: Britain, the US and the Suez Crisis.

71. Aldrich, Richard J. "The Waldegrave Initiative and Secret Service Archives: New Materials and New Policies," Intelligence and National Security 10/1 (January 1995): 192-197.

Reviews a collection of documents released under the British Public Record Office Act: Louise Atherton, Top Secret: An Interim Guide to Recent Releases of Intelligence Records at the Public Record Office; Louise Atherton, SOE Operations in the Far East: An Introductory Guide to the Newly Released

Records of the Special Operations Executive in the Public Record Office; Louise Atherton, SOE Operations in Scandinavia; FCO Historical Branch, Changes in British and Russian Records Policy: Occasional Papers No. 7; and FCO Historical Branch, FCO Records: Policy Practice and Posterity, 1782-1993.

72. Aldrich, Richard J. "British and American Policy on Intelligence Archives: Never-Never Land and Wonderland," Studies in Intelligence 38/5 (1995): 17-26.

A version of this article containing end notes and a slightly different title appeared in the British journal Contemporary Record 8/1 (Summer 1994): 133-152. Major sections discuss the JIC and Pearl Harbor; British and American archives compared; British documents in the US archives; the government-historian interface; and published documents and classified histories.

73. Aldrich, Richard J. and Michael Coleman. "The Cold War, the JIC and British Intelligence, 1948," Intelligence and National Security 4/3 (July 1989): 535-549.

Analysis of the British signal intelligence priorities as defined by the Joint Intelligence Committee in the late spring of 1948. Explores evidence of British targeting of high priority signals and argues that such efforts were not very successful.

74. Alem, Jean-Pierre. "Culper's Network," Magazin Istoric 14/10 (1980): 47-50.

This article appears in a journal published in Romania. This is an approximate translation of the title.

75. Alem, Jean-Pierre. "Pinkerton the Detective," Magazin Istoric 14/11 (1980): 56-58.

A Romanian journal article and approximate translation.

76. Alem, Jeanne-Pierre. "The Arsenal of Secret War," Magazin Istoric 14/12 (1980): 33-35.

A Romanian journal article and approximate translation.

77. Alexander, A. John. "An Intelligence Role for the Footnote," Studies in Intelligence 8/2 (Summer 1964).

78. Alexander, Christine. "Preserving High Technology Secrets: National Security Controls on Research and Teaching," Law and Policy in International Business 15/1 (1983): 173-240.

Author argues that the extension of controls upon technology transfers to university exchanges, teaching and research merely inhibits US technological progress while only retarding other nations' technological gains. She argues for a balance between national security interests an academic freedom.

79. Alexander, Manfred. "The Trial of Vojteck Tuka Based on Reports of the German Consulate in Bratislava: Documentary Supplements," Historicky Casopis 40/6 (1992): 714-730.

80. Alexander, Martin S. "Did the Deuxieme Bureau Work?: The Role of Intelligence in French Defence Policy and Strategy, 1919-39," Intelligence and National Security 6/2 (April 1991): 293-333.

Sections discuss French intelligence historiography as to whether it amounts to myth or demystification; French intelligence institutions and policies; intelligence staffs and the decision makers; and intelligence and defense choices in terms of three case studies.

81. Alexander, Martin S. "In Lieu of Alliance: The French General Staff's Secret Co-operation with Neutral Belgium, 1936-1940," Journal of Strategic Studies 14/4 (December 1991): 413-427.

Includes substantial discussion of espionage activities carried out by the French in Belgium after Belgium returned to neutrality. Some of the espionage was carried out by civilian personnel in contact with French military intelligence.

82. Alexander, Milnor. "Political Repression in the USA," Canadian Dimension 11/6 (1976): 16-22.

Discusses repression of political dissidents, the plight of citizens and radicals alike in the fall of the HUAC, the McCarran Act and loyalty oaths.

83. Al-Kadi, Ibrahim A. "Origins of Cryptology: The Arab Contribution," Cryptologia 16/2 (April 1992): 97-126.

84. Alkhimenko, A. "Strategic Equipment in Naval War Theaters," Morskoi Sbornik 1 (1980): 15-20.

85. Alkhimenko, A. "The NATO Base Network in the Atlantic," Morskoi Skornik 3 (1984): 30-37.

This is an approximate translation of the original Russian title.

86. Allard, C. Kenneth. "Intelligence and Arms Control: Process and Priorities," Fletcher Forum of World Affairs 5/1 (Winter 1981): 1-26.

Discusses the significance of intelligence monitoring and verification arising from the SALT II Treaty and future strategic arms talks. Evaluates the intelligence process, identifies technological applications to verification and summarizes issues of intelligence and arms control policy.

87. Allen, Deane J. "Interview with Deane Allen, DIA," Federalist 6/1 (March 1985): 1, 6-8.

88. Allen, Deane J. "DIA: The First Twenty-five Years," American Intelligence Journal 8/1 (January 1987).

89. Allen, Deane J. "Reviewing the Literature: Harbingers, Gadflies, and Mentors...On Change," Defense Intelligence Journal 2/1 (Spring 1993): 105-114.
       A book review essay of John A. Gentry's Lost Promise: How CIA Analysis Misserves the Nation (1992).

90. Allen, Edward L. "Industrial Planning in the US and the USSR," Studies in Intelligence 2/3 (Fall 1957).

91. Allen, Francis A. "The Wolf Case: Search and Seizure, Federalism, and the Civil Liberties," Illinois Law Review 45 (March-April 1950): 1-30.
       An extensive discussion of judicial decisions relating to a federal "right" of privacy following the Wolf case.

92. Allen, Gary W. and Anthony J. Ramienski. "A Survey of Intelligence Literature," Military Intelligence 12/2 (1986): 54-56.

93. Allen, George. "The Professionalization of Intelligence," Studies in Intelligence 26/1 (Spring 1982).

94. Allen, George W. "Intelligence in Small Wars," Studies in Intelligence 35/4 (Winter 1991).
       A discussion of the lessons learned in the Vietnam war.

95. Allen, Leola. "Anti-German Sentiment in Iowa During World War I," Annals of Iowa 42/6 (1974): 418-429.

96. Allen, Louis. "Japanese Intelligence Systems," Journal of Contemporary History 22/4 (October 1987): 547-562.
       A view of Japan's intelligence capabilities, including the OPSEC deficiencies at Pearl Harbor. Japan's SIGINT from China and the evolution of cryptology up to the surrender.

97. Allen, Louis. "Burmese Puzzles: Two Deaths that Never Were," Intelligence and National Security 5/1 (January 1990): 193-198.
       A brief analysis of British and Burmese guerilla actions in Burma in the last days of World War II, including the question of whether or not two Japanese generals had ever been killed in Burma.

98. Allen, Louis. "The Campaigns in Asia and the Pacific," Journal of Strategic Studies 13/1 (1990): 162-192.

99. Allen, Thomas B. "Year of the Questions--Spies, Software, Moles, and Subversive Agents," Sea Power 29 (June 1986): 32-33+.

100. Aller, James C. "Electronic Warfare Concept," Naval War College Review 22 (May 1970): 75-79.

101. Alletto, William C. "The Arson Squad and Intelligence Operations," Police 16/4 (December 1971): 38-41.

102. Allison, Graham. "Conceptual Models and the Cuban Missile Crisis," American Political Science Review 63/3 (September 1969): 689-718.
    An analysis of the assumptions and categories employed by analysts in thinking about foreign and military affairs engaged in by governmental officials. Three propositions are offered that relate to implicit thinking, rational policy model, organizational process model and bureaucratic politics model. Contains section on organizational intelligence.

103. Allport, F. H. "Broadcasting to an Enemy Country: What Appeals Are Effective and Why," Journal of Social Psychology 23 (May 1946): 217-224.
    An analysis of the strategies and language of psychological warfare by radio broadcasting during World War II. Considers the effectiveness of German and Italian propaganda and establishes five categories of propaganda: defeatism; division; derogation of our aims and methods; destiny; and axis ennoblement.

104. Allyn, Bruce J.; James G. Blight; and David A. Welch. "Essence of Revision: Moscow, Havana and the Cuban Missile Crisis," International Security 14/3 (Winter 1989-1990): 136-172.
    A discussion of the modification of agreements between the Soviet Union and the Cuban government concerning the supply of nuclear weapons to Cuba. Cubans sought only to allow the Soviets to supply weapons on a basis of mutual military assistance rather than on a basis of assisting the revolution.

105. Alotta, Robert I. "Codenamed Operations in World War II: An Interpretation," Names 30/1 (1982): 5-14.

106. Alpatov, V. "Look for Him on the Shooting List," Aziia i Afrika Segodnia 12 (1991): 37-38.

107. Al'perovich, M. S. "Concerning the Activities of American Diplomacy in France 1870-1871," Voprosy Istorii 7 (1956): 110-115.

108. Alpert, Eugene J. "Capabilities, Perception, and Risks: A Bayesian Model of International Behaviors," International Studies Quarterly 20/3 (September 1976): 415-440.

Applies a formal decision making model to conceptualize the role of uncertainty in war. Applies the model to the intelligence analysis task.

109. Alsop, Joseph and Stewart Alsop. "We Accuse," Harper's 209 (October 1954): 25-45.

A lengthy analysis of J. Robert Oppenheimer's role in opposing the construction and deployment of the H-bomb on both moral, technical and strategic grounds. Includes discussion of the internal security initiatives to investigate Oppenheimer in order to destroy his credibility.

110. Alter, Jonathan. "Slaying the Message: How the Frank Snepp Case Hurts Us All," Washington Monthly 13/6 (June 1981): 43-50.

Discusses the negative implications of the CIA ex-employee's Supreme Court decision concerning a book he wrote titled Decent Interval. The Court held that the proceeds from the book could not be turned over to Snepp. The Court said the book violated Snepp's secrecy oath with CIA.

111. Alter, Scott M. "Selecting Protection for Computer Programs," Federal Bar News & Journal 39 (May 1992): 264-268.

112. Alton, T. W. "S-2 at Work," Infantry Journal 56 (May 1945): 38-39.

113. Alvarez, David. "Vatican Intelligence Capabilities in the Second World War," Intelligence and National Security 6/3 (July 1991): 593-607.

A discussion of the Papal diplomatic service; the foreign diplomatic corps; the bishops, priests, religious and lay people in the service; the Vatican police; communications; intelligence with respect to Operation BARBAROSSA and the Final Solution, 1941-42. Discusses the methods of Vatican collection of intelligence.

114. Alvarez, David. "A Papal Diplomatic Code," Cryptologia 16/2 (April 1992): 174-176.

115. Alvarez, David. "Vatican Communications Security, 1914-18," Intelligence and National Security 7/4 (October 1992): 443-453.

Discusses the reasons for the Vatican's need to secure communications, security problems with personnel, and steps taken to proceed with secure communications.

116. Alvarez, David. "The Papal Cipher Section in the Early Nineteenth Century," Cryptologia 17/2 (April 1993): 219-224.

117. Alvarez, David. "A Dutch Enciphered Code," Cryptologia 19/3 (July 1995): 261-264.

118. Alvarez, David. "Italian Diplomatic Cryptanalysis in World War II," Cryptologia 20/1 (January 1996): 1-10.

119. Alvarez, David. "A German Agent at the Vatican," Intelligence and National Security 11/2 (April 1996): 345-356.
　　　A detailed accounting of the history of Vatican espionage in World War I. The Vatican, it seems, was a major target location for European spy schemes. The distrust between the Vatican and the Italian state made matters worse.

120. Alvarez, David. "Diplomatic Solutions:　German Foreign Office Cryptanalysis, 1919-1945," International Journal of Intelligence and Counter-intelligence 9/2 (Summer 1996): 169-185.
　　　Author argues that Germany's weak position after World War I caused reconsideration of the role of diplomatic cryptanalysis. He concludes that new plans for cryptanalysis could not have influenced Nazi leadership or　foreign policy by 1939.

121. Amalrik, Andrei A. "Arrest on Suspicion of Courage:　Detention by the KGB," Harper's 253 (August 1976): 37-44+.
　　　A tale of Amalrik's oppression inside the Soviet Union, caused fundamentally by the regime's perceptions of its own weaknesses.　Author suggests that the regime could not determine a path to national economic improvement while staying in power.

122. Ambrose, Stephen E. "Eisenhower, the Intelligence Community in World War II," Journal of Contemporary History 16/1 (January 1981):　153-166.
　　　A brief discussion of the evolution of Dwight Eisenhower from good military leader to superior intelligence information user throughout the Second World War.

123. Ambrose, Stephen E. "Eisenhower, the Intelligence Community, and the D-Day Invasion," Wisconsin Magazine of History 64/4 (Summer 1981):　261-277.
　　　A well-documented summation of the use of intelligence by General Eisenhower in his planning and execution of D-Day.　A more extensive analysis was published in a later book by the author.

124. Ambrose, Stephen E. "Operation Overlord: A Secret Chapter," Magazin Istoric 18/3; 5 (1984):　49-54; 47-52; 41-46, 62.
　　　This multi-part article looks at the Allied invasion of France and the role of military intelligence in the outcome.

125. Ambrose, Stephen E.　"The Bulge," MHQ:　The Quarterly Journal of Military History 1/3 (Spring 1989):　22-33.

An overview of the circumstances of the infamous Battle of the Bulge in the winter of 1944, sometimes referred to as an intelligence failure during Hitler's efforts to break out to the west in a desperation counteroffensive.

126. Ambrose, Stephen E. "Eisenhower's Legacy," Military Review 70/10 (October 1990): 4-14.
Discusses the two major legacies of the Eisenhower presidency: pursuit of freedom in the fight against Senator Joseph McCarthy's anticommunist attacks, and abhorrence of war by using covert actions as a means of unseating communist governments or insurgencies. Discusses the roles of the CIA and the FBI in the Eisenhower years. An article with the same title appeared in Prologue: Quarterly Journal of the National Archives 22/3 (1990), then reprinted in Prologue 26/special issue (1994): 160-167.

127. Amery, Julian. "Of Resistance," Nineteenth Century (March 1949): 138-149.

128. Amiantov, I. N. and Z. N. Tikhonova. "Materials of the Commission of Inquiry of the Central Committee of the Russian Social Democratic Workers' Party in the Matter of Roman V. Malinowski, May-November 1914," Voprosy Istorii 10 (1993): 91-108.

129. Amon, Moshe. "Cultural Clues: The Nature of Intelligence After Rabin's Assassination," International Journal of Intelligence and Counterintelligence 9/1 (Spring 1996): 1-15.
Major sections discuss the search for clues; the American connection; misinterpretation of many events; haughtiness on high horses; the here and now; land and religion; ignoring the signs; poets and philosophers; and the unread script. An insightful piece for analysts of terrorism or assassinations.

130. Amory, Robert, Jr. "John Andre, Case Officer for Benedict Arnold," Studies in Intelligence 5/2 (Summer 1961).

131. Anastaplo, George. "Clausewitz and Intelligence: Some Preliminary Observations," Teaching Political Science 16/2 (Winter 1989): 77-84.

132. Anawalt, Howard C. "A Critical Appraisal of Snepp v. United States: Are There Alternatives to Government Censorship?," Santa Clara Law Review 21/3 (Summer 1981): 697-726.
Profits from the sale of Decent Interval by Frank Snepp were denied to the author in Snepp v. U. S. Article argues that Snepp is a highly knowledgeable former government employee of CIA whose ideas and comments should be free from government controls, and that the government should be obligated to prove national security necessity if it wishes to control information.

133. Anders, Roger M. "The Rosenberg Case Revisited: The Greenglass Testimony and the Protection of Atomic Secrets," American Historical Review 83/2 (April 1978): 388-400.

Argues that Greenglass told the truth about the scientific features of the atomic bomb. Discusses Atomic Energy Commission security measures to protect secrets while it allowed Greenglass to explain his story.

134. Anderson, David A. "The Origins of the Press Clause," UCLA Law Review 30 (February 1983): 455-541.

Author recaps the legislative history and process of creating and ratifying press clause in the First Amendment. Offers interpretation of history and contrasts and compares the history with the "Levy interpretation". Further, discusses the concept of freedom of the press as perceived in 1789 and as it related to sedition pre-and post-Sedition Act of 1798. Includes other, broader views held by then current thinkers on the subject.

135. Anderson, David A. "Spying in Violation of Article 106, UCMJ: The Offense and the Constitutionality of Its Mandatory Death Penalty," Military Law Review 127 (Winter 1990): 1-61.

Offers historical background on crime of espionage and punishment, case precedents of the US Supreme Court and Court of Military Appeals relating to mandatory penalties and death penalty, treatment of espionage under then current international law and opinion.

136. Anderson, David L. "J. Lawton Collins, John Foster Dulles, and the Eisenhower Administration's Point of No Return in Vietnam," Diplomatic History 12/2 (Spring 1988): 127-147.

Considers various negotiations between the US, France and Vietnam in the 1950s to resolve internal warfare in Vietnam. Discusses the role of various factions in the process of negotiating a resolution to conflict.

137. Anderson, Dillon. "The President and National Security," Atlantic Monthly (January 1966): 42-48.

138. Anderson, Godfrey T. and Dennis K. Anderson. "Edward Bancroft, M.D., F.R.S., Aberrant "Practitioner of Physick," Medical Historian 17/4 (1973): 356-367.

An account of Bancroft's activities as a double agent during the American Revolution and his possible involvement in the death of Silas Deane.

139. Anderson, Judith B. "The Constitutionality of the Foreign Intelligence Surveillance Act of 1978," Vanderbilt Journal of Transnational Law 16/1 (Winter 1983): 231-259.

Discusses the legal background of the Act; U. S. v. Falvey; U. S. v. Belfield; analysis of the national security exception, and applications of the First, Fourth, Fifth and Sixth Amendments. Author concludes that the Falvey and Belfield cases give deferential but incomplete support for the FISA exception to Fourth Amendment warrant requirements.

140. Anderson, Paul A. "Decision Making by Objection and the Cuban Missile Crisis," Administrative Science Quarterly 28/2 (June 1983): 201-222.

Acknowledges the two main attacks on rational decision making theory, but suggests that the attacks have not been empirically based. Decision making during the missile crisis involved sequential choice over a collection of noncompeting possibilities; the act of making decisions led to goals; and decision makers were less interested in success than in avoiding failure. Offers an alternative theory of decision making.

141. Anderson, Paul A. and Stuart J. Thorson. "Artificial Intelligence Based Simulations of Foreign Policy Decision Making," Behavioral Science 27/2 (April 1982): 176-193.

Offers techniques for using artificial intelligence in the development of theories of foreign relations with other countries. Argues that causal and teleological explanations should be combined in order to improve explanations of foreign policy behavior. Offers computer simulations for accomplishing the combination.

142. Anderson, Ralph V. "If I Remember," Cryptologia 6/1 (January 1982): 40-44.

Personal recollections of the author from his service in the Navy Department's Code Room in World War II.

143. Anderson, Robert C. "C³CM--Lessons from the Past," Islamic Defense Review 6/2 (1981): 33-39.

144. Anderson, Roland. "Improving the Machine Recognition of Vowels in Simple Substitution Ciphers," Cryptologia 10/1 (January 1986): 10-22.

145. Anderson, Roland. "Cryptanalytic Properties of Short Substitution Ciphers," Cryptologia 13/1 (January 1989): 50-60.

146. Anderson, Roland. "Recognizing Complete and Partial Plaintext," Cryptologia 13/2 (April 1989): 161-166.

147. Anderson, Roland. "Extending the Concept of Interval," Cryptologia 15/4 (October 1991): 314-324.

148. Anderson, Ross J. "Solving a Class of Stream Ciphers," Cryptologia 14/3 (July 1990): 285-287.

149. Anderson, Ross J. "Tree Functions and Cipher Systems," Cryptologia 15/3 (July 1991): 194-202.

150. Anderson, Ruth. "Witness to an Evolutionary Revolution," American Intelligence Journal 13/3 (Summer 1992): 63-70.
        A personal account of the author's experiences in Hungary in July 1988 during the gradual breakup of the Soviet Union. Subjects include earning accreditation as an air attache; the Soviet connection; freedom won out in 1989; the military in transition; lessons from the dismal science; flexibility is the key to airpower; unfinished business; and attache management.

151. Anderson, Scott. "'With Friends Like These...': The OSS and the British in Yugoslavia," Intelligence and National Security 8/2 (April 1993): 140-171.
        An account of the strained relations between the US OSS and British intelligence services in the dealings over Yugoslavia during and after World War II. The respective services, concludes the author could not agree on a policy of intervention in Yugoslavia.

152. Anderson, Scott. "The Evolution of the Canadian Intelligence Establishment, 1945-1950," Intelligence and National Security 9/3 (July 1994): 448-471.
        Argues that Canadian intelligence agencies evolved in response to the Cold War, while directions taken were determined by historical experience.

153. Anderson, Thomas D. "Progress in the Democratic Revolution in Latin America: Country Assessment--1987," Journal of Inter-American Studies and Worlds Affairs 29/1 (Spring 1987): 57-71.
        Drawing on CIA and other official sources, the author ranks thirty-three Latin American countries in terms of movement toward democratization. Concludes that the majority of the countries have institutionalized the democratic process.

154. Anderson, William H. "Probability Analysis for the Case of Yellow Rain," International Journal of Intelligence and Counterintelligence 3/1 (Spring 1989): 77-82.
        Application of probability analysis to estimate the likelihood of the use of mycotoxins in Southeast Asia following the discovery of some evidence that such toxins were used against indigenous people. Major sections discuss the Bayesian analysis and conclusions; and definition of terms.

155. Andrew, Christopher M. "Dechiffrement et Diplomatie: Le Cabinet Noir du Quai d'Orsay sous la Troisieme Republique," Relations Internationales 3/5 (1976): 37-64.

156. Andrew, Christopher M. "The British Secret Service and Anglo-Soviet Relations in the 1920s, Part I: From the Trade Negotiations to the Zinoviev Letter," Historical Journal 20/3 (1977): 673-706.

A detailed inquiry into the various internal and external bits of evidence to sustain or reject the theory that the Zinoviev letter was a hoax. Covers the evidence suggesting an intelligence service participation in the alleged plot.

157. Andrew, Christopher M. "Whitehall, Washington and the Intelligence Services," International Affairs (Great Britain) 53/3 (July 1977): 390-404.

Argues for more openness with respect to the affairs and activities of the intelligence services. Discusses two problems created by the success of American intelligence collection: the cost of technologies of collection; and the information explosion. Also discusses the preservation of political power through the cult of secrecy.

158. Andrew, Christopher M. "Governments and Secret Services: A Historical Perspective," International Journal 34/2 (Spring 1979): 167-186.

The author argues that the complexities of modern intelligence operations are not necessarily new. Suggests that democracy is enriched by a publicly visible system of accountability for the intelligence services. Western governments have failed to consider public confidence in the operations of intelligence services.

159. Andrew, Christopher M. "British Intelligence and the Breach with Russia in 1927," Historical Journal 25/4 (December 1982): 957-964.

Argues that British intelligence services participated in the efforts aimed at breaching the Anglo-Soviet diplomatic relations in 1927. The author says that this article follows on his earlier piece in Historical Journal in 1977. Implicates the intelligence services in deception and failure to provide all information to government officials.

160. Andrew, Christopher M. "Christopher Andrew Questions Official Policy Toward the History of British Intelligence," History Today 33 (January 1983): 3-4.

The author critiques official British policy with respect to the restrictions on official documents pertaining to British intelligence services. Argues that there has been pointless censorship and secrecy.

161. Andrew, Christopher M. "Happy New Year from M.I.5," History Today 33 (January 1983): 5-7.

Argues for more openness in the discussion and study of intelligence services in the US and Britain; the information explosion; and reasons for the cult of secrecy.   Suggests that Britain's Parliament needs to move closer to the American model of openness.

162.   Andrew, Christopher M.   "Codebreaking and Signals Intelligence," Intelligence and National Security 1/1 (January 1986): 1-5.

163.   Andrew, Christopher M.   "Churchill and Intelligence," Studies in Intelligence 30/3 (Fall 1986).

164.   Andrew, Christopher M.   "Churchill and Intelligence," Intelligence and National Security 3/3 (July 1988): 181-193.
Part of a special issue devoted to leaders and intelligence, this article concludes that Churchill's interest in intelligence organizations and their contributions to the war effort hastened coordination and advancement.

165. Andrew, Christopher M. "The Evolution of Australian Intelligence," Studies in Intelligence 32/3 (Fall 1988).

166.   Andrew, Christopher M.   "The Growth of the Australian Intelligence Community and the Anglo-American Connection," Intelligence and National Security 4/2 (April 1989): 213-256.
Major sections discuss the British connection; between the wars; the Second War; the American connection; post-war reorganization; the Australian Security Intelligence Organization; the Australian Secret Intelligence Service; scientific intelligence; the Anglo-American connection in the 1960s; the Joint Intelligence Organization; the Whitlam era; the Hope reports; reassessing the Anglo-American connection; the Australian Security and Intelligence Community.

167.   Andrew, Christopher M.   "From the Okhrana to the KGB," Studies in Intelligence 33/3 (Fall 1989).

168. Andrew, Christopher M. "KGB Foreign Intelligence from Brezhnev to the Coup," Intelligence and National Security 8/3 (July 1993): 52-67.
Part of a special issue on espionage: past, present and future, this article discusses the power politics at the top level of Soviet politics and government as they relate to the KGB's foreign intelligence projects from the late 1960s to 1991.

169.   Andrew, Christopher M.   "American Presidents and Their Intelligence Communities," Intelligence and National Security 10/4 (October 1995): 95-112.
Summarizes the relationship between intelligence agencies and presidents from Franklin Roosevelt to Bill Clinton. Considers the three ages of development

of the relationship: age of innocence; age of transformation; and age of uncertainty.

170. Andrew, Christopher M. and Keith Neilson. "Tsarist Codebreakers and British Codes," Intelligence and National Security 1/1 (January 1986): 6-12.

171. Andrews, Clarence A. "Floyd Dell in the Western Illinois Region," Western Illinois Regional Studies 8/2 (1985): 17-33.

172. Andrews, R. E. "Confessions of a Battalion S-2," Marine Corps Gazette 48 (September 1964): 41-43.

173. Andrews, Robert H. "Benedict Arnold: Dark Eagle of the American Revolution," Mankind 3/2 (1971): 10-17, 57-60.

174. Andrews, Robert H. "How the CIA Was Born," Mankind 5/4 (April 1975): 14-15, 68.
This article suggests the CIA's origins can be found in Thomas Jefferson's attitude toward intelligence collection in the American Revolution.

175. Andrianov, V. N. "Partisan Reconnaissance During the Years of the Great Patriotic War," Voenno-Istoricheskii Zhurnal 8 (August 1986): 36-46.
Article is in Russian: translated by Joint Publications Research Service, January 15, 1987, pp. 36-46. Author is a Soviet General.

176. Andriesen, S. K. "The Gibson Affair," Spiegel Historiael 15/1 (1980): 44-48.
This article appears in a Dutch journal and this is an approximate translation.

177. Andriole, Stephen J. "Indications, Warnings and Bureaucracies," Military Intelligence 10/3 (1984): 18-24.

178. Andriole, Stephen J. "Indications and Warnings Research Development: Problems and Prospects," (Pt. 1) American Intelligence Journal 6/4 (February 1985): 6-13.

179. Andriole, Stephen J. "Indications and Warnings Research Development: Problems and Prospects," (Pt. 2) American Intelligence Journal 7/1 (June 1985): 10-17.

180. Androvelle, Edward. "Somebody Forgot to Tell," Infantry Journal 62 (July 1948): 51-52.

A personal recollection of a World War II intelligence experience by the author.

181. Angevine, Robert G. "Gentlemen Do Read Each Other's Mail: American Intelligence in the Interwar Era," Intelligence and National Security 7/2 (April 1992): 1-29.

Argues that the reduction of US intelligence activities in the interwar years was a logical result of US national security policy. Major sections discuss the post World War I situation; the decline of US intelligence; the end of the Black Chamber; the rebirth of COMINT; and the political context of demobilization.

182. Ano, Masaharu. "Loyal Linguists: Nisei of World War II Learned Japanese in Minnesota," Minnesota History 45/7 (1977): 273-287.

183. Ansbacher, Richard. "Passport Revocation: Balancing Constitutional Freedoms with National Security Concerns," University of Florida Law Review 33/5 (Fall 1981): 763-776.

Argues that the revocation of Philip Agee's passport (Agee, a former CIA agent) set a dangerous precedent by giving the Secretary of State the power to control passports for any reason. Accordingly, executive power is extended too far.

184. Antonov, A. "CIA: Ideological Subversion," International Affairs (USSR) 1 (January 1979): 87-92.

A Soviet view of international operations of the US Central Intelligence Agency.

185. Aplington, Henry, II. "Remembrance of Duty in ONI," Naval Intelligence Professionals Quarterly 5/2 (Summer 1989): 10-11.

186. Appich, Thomas. "Tilting at the Tower of Babel," Studies in Intelligence 35/3 (Fall 1991).

187. Arbatov, Georgi. "A New Cold War," Foreign Policy 95 (Summer 1994): 90-104.

188. Arbenny, John. "ITAC: The Unique Organization," INSCOM Journal (February 1982): 3-4.

189. Archdeacon, Maurice. "The Heritage Front Affair," Intelligence and National Security 11/2 (April 1996): 306-312.

Discusses the Canadian Security Intelligence Review Committee report on the Heritage Front affair. Main sections consider the composition of the

Committee; ministerial direction; the Sub-committee on National Security; evidence; trust; the Reform Party; election contributions; the title; and the media.

190. Archibald, Sam. "The Early Years of the Freedom of Information Act-- 1955 to 1974," PS: Political Science & Politics 26/4 (December 1993): 726-731.

191. Ardman, Harvey. "U.S. Code-breakers v. Japanese Code-breakers in World War II," American Legion Magazine 94 (May 1972): 18-23; 38-42.

192. Arens, Ilmar. "Otsa Jurgen's Honorary Vassalage for His Espionage Services to the Swedish Army in Tartu, 1656-57," Eesti Teaduslihu Seltsi Noatsis Aastar Aamat 9 (1980-1984): 85-97.

193. Arguelles, Lourdes. "The US National Security State: The CIA and Cuban Emigre Terrorism," Race and Class 23/4 (Spring 1982): 287-304.
    A preliminary study of the political economy of the national security state from a leftist perspective. Discusses the CIA and the Cuban revolution, CIA operatives, and Cuban emigre terrorism in the Reagan era.

194. Arkin, William M. "Long on Data, Short on Intelligence," Bulletin of the Atomic Scientists 43/5 (June 1987): 5-6.
    Criticizes poor analysis of US intelligence concerning Soviet radar in Siberia. Focus is on use of SPOT satellite commercial imagery by government, plus leaks to press to make a point.

195. Arkin, William M. "Spying in the Black Sea," Bulletin of the Atomic Scientists 44 (May 1988): 5-6.
    An brief account of the collision at sea of the USS Yorktown and the USS Carron with Soviet frigates in 1988. The Carron was a signals intelligence vessel. Author argues that the Carron's mission escalated tensions between the US and the USSR by performing collection missions in the Black Sea.

196. Arkin, William M. and Richard W. Fieldhouse. "Focus on the Nuclear Infrastructure," Bulletin of the Atomic Scientists 41/6 (1985): 11-15.

197. Armacost, R. L.; J. C. Hosseini; S. A. Morris; and K. A. Rehbein. "An Empirical Comparison of Direct Questioning, Scenario, and Randomize Response Methods for Obtaining Sensitive Business Information," Decision Sciences 22 (December 1990): 1070-1090.

198. Armbrister, William A. "The Pueblo Crisis and Public Opinion," Naval War College Review 24 (1971): 84-110.

Lengthy discussion of the case facts, including the background, imprisonment of the Pueblo crew, and the final decision of the Secretary of the Navy. Navy intelligence was implicated in the failure of the mission.

199. Armengaud, Jean-Louis. "La Reconnaissance de l'Ennemi par l'Armee de l'Air et la Manoeuvre Strategique des Armees de Terre," <u>Revue Militaire Francaise</u> 154 (April-June 1934): 43-81.

200. Armer, Paul. "Computer Technology and Surveillance," <u>Computers and People</u> 24 (September 1975): 8-11.

201. Armes, Keith. "Chekhists in Cassocks: The Orthodox Church and the KGB," <u>Demokratizatsiya: Journal of Post-Soviet Democratization</u> 1/4 (Fall 1993-1994): 72-83.

202. Armor, Marshal H., Jr. "Where Will It Hurt the Most?," <u>Military Review</u> 35/7 (October 1955): 37-44.
        Discusses tactical military intelligence estimates and ways to revise their format.

203. Armour, Ian D. "Colonel Redl: Fact and Fantasy," <u>Intelligence and National Security</u> 2/1 (January 1987): 170-183.
        Brief history of the role of Colonel Alfred Redl in the Austro-Hungarian Army, and allegations and facts pertaining to Redl's espionage work for the Russians.

204. Armstrong, A. G. "The Art of Surprise," <u>Journal of the Royal United Services Institution</u> (November 1940): 650-654.

205. Armstrong, Anne. "Bridging the Gap: Intelligence and Policy," <u>Washington Quarterly</u> 12/1 (Winter 1989): 23-34.
        A general discussion of the linkages between intelligence analysis and policy processes. Rapid changes in world conditions, particularly with respect to the Soviet Union, demand a closer link between the two functions. Limitations on intelligence resources call for priorities of focus.

206. Armstrong, Peter F. "Capabilities and Intentions," <u>Marine Corps Gazette</u> 70/9 (September 1986): 38-47.
        Concerns Armstrong's description of how his military unit gathered intelligence on attacks by and against the North Vietnamese in 1972.

207. Armstrong, Richard. "Countering the Third Dimension," <u>Military Intelligence</u> 10/1 (1984): 16-21.

208. Armstrong, Scott. "Preserving the Institutional Memory: An Interview with Scott Armstrong, Executive Director of the National Security Archive," Government Publications Review 16 (July-August 1989): 331-344.

Mr. Armstrong was interviewed by Bruce Morton and Steven Zink, both of the Review. Discussion focused on the role of the National Security Archives, trends in the classification and declassification of government information, FOIA requests, federal information policy, and related issues.

209. Armstrong, Scott. "Iran-Contra: Was the Press Any Match for All the President's Men," Columbia Journalism Review 28 (1990): 27-35.

210. Armstrong, W. P. "Trial of the Nazi Saboteurs: Excerpts from Address to American Bar Association," Journal of Criminal Law and Criminology 33/4 (November 1942): 326-327.

ABA President Walter P. Armstrong's speech to the ABA meeting in Detroit in 1942. He praised the diligence and demeanor of the attorneys in the case against the German saboteurs.

211. Armstrong, Willis C.; William Leonhart; William J. McCaffrey; and Herbert C. Rothenberg. "The Hazards of Single-Outcome Forecasting," Studies in Intelligence 28/3 (Fall 1984): 57-70.

Attempts to determine the causes of intelligence community failure to anticipate significant events of world change, and attempts to identify measures for improving future forecasting of events. Draws on 12 cases from 1945 to 1978.

212. Army Security Agency. "Examples of Intelligence Obtained from Cryptanalysis (August 1946)," Cryptologia 7/4 (October 1983): 315-326.

213. Arndt, Karl J. "The Louisiana Passport of Pennsylvania's Charles Sealsfield," Pennsylvania Folklife 33/3 (1984): 134-137.

214. Arndt, Richard T. "Agents from Academe," Virginia Quarterly Review 64/4 (1988): 736-739.

215. Arnold, Isaac N. "Something New of Benedict Arnold and his Descendants in England," Magazine of American History 10 (July-December 1883): 307-319.

216. Arnold, Jonathan P. "Herbert O. Yardley, Gangbuster," Cryptologia 12/1 (January 1988): 62-64.

217. Arnold, Joseph C. "Omens and Oracles," U.S. Naval Institute Proceedings 106/8 (August 1980): 47-53.

A discussion of intelligence factors by US since World War II, and suggests that capabilities estimates are far more useful than estimates of intentions.

218. Arnold, Philip M. "A Forgotten Book on Ciphers," Cryptologia 2/2 (July 1978): 232-235.

219. Arnold, Philip M. "Ciphers for the Educated Man," Cryptologia 3/4 (October 1979): 215-216.

220. Arnold, Philip M. "A German Code Book," Cryptologia 3/4 (October 1979): 243-245.

221. Arnold, Philip M. "Palatino and Bibliander on Ciphers," Cryptologia 5/3 (July 1981): 149-154.

222. Arokay, Lajos. "The Workings of the Disguised Military Attache Service, 1923-28," Hadtrtnelmi Kzlemnyek 30/4 (1983): 574- 592.
    A review of the controversy within the Hungarian government regarding covert military operations.

223. Aronsen, Lawrence R. "Some Aspects of Surveillance: 'Peace, Order and Good Government' During the Cold War - The Origins and Organization of Canada's Internal Security Program," Intelligence and National Security 1/3 (September 1986): 357-380.

224. Artemiev, Vyacheslav P. "OKR: State Security in the Soviet Armed Forces," Military Review 43/9 (September 1963): 21-31.
    Discusses the level of security produced by intelligence and state security forces inside the ranks of the Soviet military. An excellent case study of the benefits and costs of diligent internal security.

225. Arthur, Richard O. "The Subversive in the Police Department," Law and Order 12/7 (July 1964): 64-65.
    Description of subversive infiltration of police agencies and counter intelligence activities.

226. Ashcroft, Bruce. "Air Force Foreign Materiel Exploitation," American Intelligence Journal 15/2 (Autumn-Winter 1994): 79-82.
    A brief history and discussion of the role of the National Air Intelligence Center.

227. Ashkenas, Bruce F. "A Legacy of Hatred: The Records of A Nazi Organization in America," Prologue: Quarterly Journal of the National Archives 17 (Summer 1985): 93-106.

Recounts the history of a Nazi Bund in the US and the Bund's activities before World War II.   Also discusses the reactions of American citizens, investigative agencies and legal community brought to suppress activities.

228. Ashley, Robert P. "The St. Albans Raid," Civil War Times Illustrated 6/7 (1976): 18-27.

229. Ashman, Allan. "Military Justice ... Violation of Plea Agreement," American Bar Association Journal 68 (July 1982): 855-856.
Reports on the writ of mandamus by the US Court of Military Appeals directing the dismissal of charges for espionage against 2d lieutenant Christopher M. Cooke.

230. Ashman, Allan. "C.I.A. Sat on Jonestown Death Data in Bad Faith," American Bar Association Journal 69 (April 1983): 512.
Brief account of the FOIA suit by F. M. McGehee against the CIA for records pertaining to the knowledge of the CIA in the Jonestown suicides and forced deaths of 1978.

231. Ashman, Allan. "Lawyers Denied Surveillance Material from Law Office Bug. Application of United States (Carreras), In re-723 F.2d 1022 (1st Cir. 1983)," American Bar Association Journal 70 (May 1984): 137-138.
News summary of US Court of Appeals holding. First Circuit held that persons named in order for application for wiretap and attorneys/clients whose conversations were recorded by same as part of grand jury investigation were not entitled to inspect materials obtained.

232. Ashmore, Harry. "The Policy of Illusion, The Illusion of Policy," Center Magazine (May 1970): 2-10.
A discussion of the Nixon doctrine and a comparison of the Nixon and Johnson administrations with respect to the Vietnam war. Argues that the Nixon and Johnson policies toward ending the war have produced and illusion of commitment about termination, based in part on intelligence reports.

233. Askin, Frank. "Police Dossiers and Emerging Principles of First Amendment Adjudication," Stanford Law Review 22/2 (January 1970): 196-220.
Offers arguments to constrain the practice of police for maintaining dossiers on political dissidents. Suggests that the New Jersey plan should be a model for other states as a means of protecting First Amendment rights of free speech.

234. Askin, Frank. "Surveillance: The Social Science Perspective," Columbia Human Rights Law Review 4/1 (Winter 1972): 59-88.

Discussion of the social consequences of excessive internal security as applied to dissidents and others who exercise their First Amendment rights.

235. Askin, Frank. "Secret Justice: When National Security Trumps Citizen Rights," American Prospect (Spring 1994): 62-67.

236. Aslop, J. D. "Thomas Nairne and the 'Boston Gazette No. 216' of 1707," Southern Studies 22/2 (1983): 209-211.
Article discusses the imprisonment of Nairne and his plea of innocence against reason charges. Research suggests he was guilty.

237. Aspaturian, Vernon V. "The Soviet Union as a Global Power: Soviet Perceptions of the Changing Correlation of Forces," Problems of Communism (April-May 1980).

238. Aspin, Les. "The Verification of the SALT II Agreement," Scientific American 140/2 (February 1979): 38-45.
Former US Representative argues that intelligence analysts do not carefully study Soviet intentions and priorities. Suggests three major improvements in forecasting, negotiating strategies, and assessments of strategic forces.

239. Aspin, Les. "Debate Over U.S. Strategic Forecasts: A Mixed Record," Strategic Review 8/3 (Summer 1980): 29-43, 57-59.

240. Aspin, Les. "Misreading Intelligence," Foreign Policy 43 (Summer 1981): 166-172.
Discussion of the greatest difficulties confronting intelligence analysts in interpreting the intentions of political leaders in the Soviet Union. Improvements could be made is such areas as forecasting Soviet strategic plans; devising new bases for negotiations; and intelligence for US strategic forces.

241. Asselin, Fred. "Technology Diversion," Washington Quarterly 7/3 (Summer 1984): 99-112.
An examination of the USSR's ability to compromise Western military technology and the apparent inability of US counterintelligence agents to stop the leaks.

242. Association of the Bar of the City of New York. "Military Surveillance of Civilian Political Activities: Report and Recommendations for Congressional Action," Record of the Association of the Bar of the City of New York 28 (October 1973): 651-676.

Committee report calling for congressional action to control military surveillance of civilians. Contains nature and extent of the problem, the state of the law, and conclusions. See also items 1576, 1577, and 1578.

243. Association of the Bar of the City of New York. "Judicial Procedures For National Security Electronic Surveillance," Record of the Association of the Bar of the City of New York 29 (December 1974): 751-774.

Committee report in support of Senator Gaylord Nelson's bill, "Surveillance Practices and Procedures Act." Bill was designed to establish judicially administered procedures for electronic surveillance. Contains historical background, the bill's sections, constitutional issues and policy considerations. See also items 1576, 1577, and 1578.

244. Association of the Bar of the City of New York. Special Committee on Communications Law. "The Espionage and Secrecy Provisions of the Proposed New Federal Criminal Code," Record of the Association of the Bar of the City of New York 31 (November 1976): 572-592.

Committee argues proposed provisions would effectively trade ambiguities under the old law for incompatibility with free speech. New provisions threatened to both diminish importance of public awareness on national security issues and enhance likelihood of prosecution. Discusses existing legislation and new provisions, including meaning of "espionage," "mishandling national security information," "clandestine," and suggestion for new legislation. See also items 1576, 1577, and 1578.

245. Assoulini, Pierre. "The Puzzle of Georges Paques: A Soviet 'Mole' in Paris," Histoire 81 (1985): 10-25.

246. Astor, David. "Why the Revolt Against Hitler Was Ignored," Encounter 32/6 (June 1969): 3-13.

Discusses the loyalty of Hitler's intelligence services, a key factor in determining Hitler's power and in overcoming the revolt in 1944.

247. Aswell, Edward C. "The Case of the Ten Nazi Spies: How They Worked - How the FBI Caught Them," 185 Harper's (June 1942): 1-21.

A summary of the capture and prosecution of Nazi spies at the beginning of World War II, including discussion of the German intelligence efforts to penetrate the US borders and war facilities.

248. Atha, Robert I. "BOMBE! 'I Could Hardly Believe It'!," Cryptologia 9/4 (October 1985): 332-336.

249. Athanasiou, T. "Encryption Technology, Privacy, and National Security," Technology Review 89 (August-September 1986): 56-64+.

A discussion of applications of encryption technologies in both positive and negative terms. Also discusses the role of the National Security Agency in developing cipher devices. Sections discuss secret cryptography, NSA's peculiar history, the public uses of cryptography, and implications of a dossier society.

250. Atkeson, Edward B. "When Turfs Overlap: A Study of Organizations in Collision," Army 30 (November 1980): 38-43.

251. Atkey, Ronald G. "Freedom of Information: The Problem of Confidentiality in the Administrative Process," University of Western Ontario Law Review 18/1 (Winter 1980): 153-184.
        Discusses Canadian legislation introduced in 1977 and its potential impact on administration of government. Topics include ministerial responsibility; section 41(2) of the Canadian Federal Court Act; coverage of proposed legislation; exemptions founded on considerations of business competition, exemption for protecting privacy; whether special interests of requesting parties need to be considered; and some special problems for tribunals such as "internal law" of agencies, staff reports, and discovery procedures.

252. Atkey, Ronald G. "Reconciling Freedom of Expression and National Security," University of Toronto Law Journal 41 (Winter 1991): 38-59.

253. Atkinson, Leonard. "The Origins of Wiretapping in Connecticut," University of Bridgeport Law Review 12/1 (Winter 1991): 247-292.
        Details history of eavesdropping and wiretapping, including common law, case law, and the Omnibus Crime Control and Safe Streets Act of 1968 containing Title III (wiretap statute). Contends the Connecticut statute is more restrictive than Title II and provides an analysis under Fourth Amendment principles.

254. Atkinson, Russell. "Ciphers in Oriental Languages," Cryptologia 9/4 (October 1985): 373-380.

255. Attanasio, Dominick B. "The Multiple Benefits of Competitor Intelligence," Journal of Business Strategy 9/3 (May-June 1988): 16-19.

256. Atwal, Kay. "No Risk Snooping: Unmanned Aerial Vehicles," Defence 24 (June 1993): 25-30.

257. Atyeo, Henry C. "Political Developments in Iran, 1951-1954," Middle East Affairs 5 (August-September 1954): 249-259.

258. Aubin, Stephen. "Covert Action--Renegade Operations Out of Control?," International Combat Arms: The Journal of Defense Technology 7 (May 1989): 20-25.

259. Aubry, Arthur S., Jr. "The Internal Revenue Service Intelligence Division," Police (March-April 1969): 35-41.

Discussion of the organization, direction, division responsibilities, history, special agent duties, special agent requirements, training and investigative and enforcement functions.

260. Audet, William M. "Electronic Detection Devices: A Search By Any Other Name . . . (9th Circuit Survey: August 1, 1981 - July 31, 1982)," Golden Gate University Law Review 13 (Spring 1983): 177-192.

Author discusses 9th Circuit decision in U. S. v. Brock, where DEA agents placed a beeper in drum of chemicals used for manufacture of amphetamines. Compares result with previous 9th Circuit decisions and those of other circuits. Also focusses on justices' majority and concurring opinions. Critique finds fault in majority holding that there was no search.

261. Auerbach, Carl A. "The Communist Control Act of 1954: A Proposed Legal-Political Theory of Free Speech," University of Chicago Law Review 23/2 (Winter 1956): 173-220.

Analyzes the history and provisions of the Act, constitutionality and the wisdom of the Act. Concludes that the Smith and Communist Control Acts are unwise because the negative impact on democracy outweighs any positive value in controlling the spread of communism.

262. August, David. "Information Theoretic Approach to Secure LSFR Ciphers," Cryptologia 9/4 (October 1985): 351-359.

263. August, David. "Cryptography and Exploitation of Chinese Cryptosystems, Part I: The Encoding Problem," Cryptologia 13/4 (October 1989): 289-302.

264. August, David. "Cryptography and Exploitation of Chinese Manual Cryptosystems, Part II: The Encryption Problem," Cryptologia 14/1 (January 1990): 61-78.

265. Augustini, Jeff. "From Goldfinger to Butterfinger: The Legal and Policy Issues Surrounding Proposals to Use the CIA for Economic Espionage," Law and Policy in International Business 26 (Winter 1995): 459-495.

266. Aulard, F. A. "Organisation du Service des Agents Secrets dans la Premiere Republique," La Revolution Francaise 12 (1887): 1117-1128.

267. Aulard, F. A. "Instructions Generales aux Agents Diplomatiques de la Republique Francaise," La Revolution Francaise 13 (1887): 66-73.

268. Ausems, Andre. "The Bureau Inlichtingen (Intelligence Service) of the Netherlands Government in London, November 1942-May 1945: An Overview of its Mission, Agents and Undercover Radio Traffic," Military Affairs 45/3 (October 1981): 127-132.

A detailed discussion of the highly successful service operated out of London on the heels of other intelligence disasters in sending agents into the Netherlands.

269. Ausems, Andre. "The Netherlands Military Intelligence Summaries 1939-1940 and the Defeat in the Blitzkrieg of May 1940," Military Affairs 50/4 (October 1986): 190-199.

Accounts for the weaknesses in Dutch preparation for war with Germany in the years 1939 to 1940.

270. Austin, C. Grey. "Credibility Gap," Journal of Higher Education 38 (May 1967): 278-280.

An editorial on the misapplication of wiretapping, especially with respect to educational, labor and religious organizations. Refers specifically to CIA recruitment of National Student Association personnel and FBI wiretaps of embassies in Washington, D.C.

271. Austin, Roger. "Propaganda and Public Opinion in Vichy, France: The Department of Herault, 1940-44," European Studies Review 13/4 (October 1983): 455-477.

A discussion of the employment and failure of propaganda in France in World War II. Suggests that small gains in the use of propaganda were eventually lost when the Nazi's brought occupation to France after 1940.

272. Austin, Roger. "Surveillance and Intelligence Under the Vichy Regime: The Service du Controle Technique, 1939-45," Intelligence and National Security 1/1 (January 1986): 123-137.

273. Austra, Kevin R. "The Battle of the Bulge: The Secret Offensive," Military Intelligence 17/1 (January-March 1991): 26-33.

274. Auvergne, Caroline. "Early American Destinations: Blenner Hassett," Early American Life 16/4 (1985): 49-51, 75-76.

An account of the lives of Harman and Margaret Blenner Hassett and charges of treason rendered against them.

275. Auxier, George W. "The Propaganda Activities of the Cuban 'Junta' in Precipitating the Spanish-American War, 1895-1898," Hispanic American Historical Review 19 (1939): 286-305.

Argues that the Cuban Junta was an essential ingredient in stirring American support for the Cuban cause in the Spanish-American conflict between 1895 and 1898. Based on interpretation of forty Midwest American newspaper articles and editorials. The Junta was composed mainly of naturalized Cubans living in cities along the Atlantic seaboard.

276. Avery, Donald. "Secrets Between Different Kinds of Friends: Canada's Wartime Exchange of Scientific Military Information with the United States and the USSR, 1940-1945," Historical Papers (1986): 225-253.

Article deals with Canada's efforts to maintain good relations with the US and USSR during World War II in spite of espionage and spying ventures between the three nations.

277. Avery, Donald. "Allied Scientific Co-operation and Soviet Espionage in Canada, 1941-45," Intelligence and National Security 8/3 (July 1993): 100-128.

Offers answers to questions pertaining to Canada's involvement with alliance military technology in World War II. Includes questions about reasons for Canada's access to top secret information; extent of Canadian scientific involvement in atomic weapons research; Soviet targeting of Canadian scientists; and willingness of some scientists to compromise secret research for the Soviets.

278. Avtorkhanov, Abdurakhman. "The Soviet Triangular Dictatorship: Party, Police and Army: Formation and Situation," Ukrainian Quarterly 34/2 (Summer 1978): 135-153.

279. Avtorkhanov, Abdurakhman. "What is the Significance of the Change in the Name of the KGB?," Posev 9 (September 1978): 3-5.

280. Axelrod, Robert. "Schema Theory: An Information Processing Model of Perception and Cognition," American Political Science Review 67/4 (December 1973): 1248-1266.

Outlines purposes and values of schema theory on methods by which information is taken in, interpreted and reformulated. Contains elements of a model, model dynamics, evidence relating to parts of the model, comparison with other theoretical approaches and applications to such areas as intelligence.

281. Axelrod, Robert. "The Rational Timing of Surprise," World Politics 31/2 (January 1979): 228-246.

Offers a theory of surprise based on behavioral patterns of opponents and commitment to action. A key source in the study of deception and surprise theory. Major sections discuss the resources for surprise; a math model of surprise; and policy implications. Discusses the question of when a resource for surprise should be exploited. Cites examples from World War II and Middle East conflicts.

B

"This is a research ship that has nothing to do with the CIA..."
(Bucher: My Story by Lloyd M. Bucher, p. 218)

282. Babcock, Fenton. "Assessing DDO Human Source Reporting," Studies in Intelligence 22/3 (Fall 1978): 51-57.
A discussion of the Directorate of Operations at CIA, this article's major sections include: value assessment in the field; value assessment in the headquarters divisions; value assessment at the directorate level; a careful approach to quantification of value; and relevance at the intelligence community level.

283. Babcock, James H. "Intelligence and National Security," Signal 33 (March 1978): 16-18, 20.

284. Babcock, James H. and Peter C. Oleson. "Intelligence Concerns for the 1990s," Signal 43/10 (June 1989): 147-156.
Discusses trends approaching the 1990s, redefining national security, funding outlook, Perestroika, surprise and warning, technology, and concerns and alternatives.

285. Baber, James G. "Constitutional Torts--The Creation of a Uniform Standard for Determining When a Special Relationship Exists: FBI Informant's Duty to Prevent a Murder," Southern Illinois University Law Journal 1985/1 (Winter 1985): 97-111.
Author discusses Beard v. O'Neal, 728 F.2d 894 (7th Cir.), cert. denied,

105 S.Ct. 104 (1984), wherein the Court held FBI informant had no duty to prevent a murder in his presence, and in turn, FBI was not liable either. Court found no special relationship between informant and victim. Author criticizes this result.

286. Bachelder, Ed. "The Saga of the Intelligent Beach Master," Naval Intelligence Professionals Quarterly 4/1 (Winter 1988): 17-18.

287. Backscheider, Paula R. "Daniel Defoe and Early Modern Intelligence," Intelligence and National Security 11/1 (January 1996): 1-21.
Argues that Defoe's work offers great insights into the integration of intelligence work into the political history of democratic society.

288. Bacon, John. "The French Connection Revisited," International Journal of Intelligence and Counterintelligence 4/4 (Winter 1990): 507-524.
Extensive inquiry into the background and circumstances of the US Treasury Department's intelligence and law enforcement efforts against major Italian narcotic distributors. Includes sections on the origins of police intelligence; the wrong goals of the Federal Bureau of Narcotics; intelligence and drug control; the systems concept; the French Connection organization; Bureau of Narcotic and Dangerous Drugs intelligence office and its files; the links between BNDD and CIA; Project Pilot and the discovery of mafia connections for drug smuggling to the US; Pilot's legacy and impact; and recent efforts. Article is critical of shortsightedness of the Drug Enforcement Agency's intelligence.

289. Baden-Powell, R. "Adventures As a Spy," Everybody's 32 (February 1915): 184-192.

290. Baggett, Candace S. "Fourth Amendment--Absent Exigent Circumstances, Prior Judicial Authorization of Electronic Surveillance of United States Citizens Abroad Is Constitutionally Required: Berlin Democratic Club v. Rumsfeld, 410 F. Supp. 144 (D.D.C. 1976)," Texas International Law Journal 12/2-3 (Spring-Summer 1977): 362-369.
Relates the facts of the case, threshold issues concerning wiretapping, Fourth Amendment issues and first and Sixth Amendment damages.

291. Baggett, Lee, Jr. "C³I Requirements within the Atlantic Command," Signal 42 (June 1988): 31-32.

292. Bagley, Tennant H. "Treason in the KGB: New Facts from Inside," International Journal of Intelligence and Counterintelligence 5/1 (Spring 1991): 63-76.
An account of the work of Major General Oleg Kalugin to move toward democratization in the Soviet Union and Kalugin's call for a cutback in KGB

work against Western intelligence. Contains the phases and events in the Kalugin treason and reactions by his superiors; the Yurchenko affair; and the need for answers to many additional questions pertaining to internal KGB treason. Extensive and useful notes.

293. Bagley, Tennant H. "Bane of Counterintelligence: Our Penchant for Self-Deception," International Journal of Intelligence and Counterintelligence 6/1 (Spring 1993): 1-20.
    An extensive analysis of deception and self-deception as they apply in the realm of counterintelligence. Discusses self-deception examples; Lenin and internal intrigues; Trotsky; the origins of the "Trust," a Soviet deception operation in the 1920s; the creation of British double agents; ULTRA; the Philby conspiracy; the Hiss case; the Nalivaiko case; the question of why we deceive ourselves; the perils of bureaucracy; and a questionable antidote.

294. Bagnall, J. J. "The Exploitation of Russian Scientific Literature for Intelligence Purposes," Studies in Intelligence 2/2 (Summer 1958): 45-49.

295. Bahro, Rudolf. "He Who Does Not Howl with the Wolves Is Out," Samtiden 90/1 (1981): 61-67.
    This article concerns the experiences of the author, who was imprisoned for espionage and betrayal of state secrets.

296. Bailey, Bill. "Summer of '57," Naval Intelligence Professionals Quarterly 3/2 (1987): 3-5.

297. Bailey, Norman and Stephan A. Halper. "National Security for Whom?," Washington Quarterly 9/1 (Winter 1986): 187-192.

298. Bailey, S. D. "Police Socialism in Tsarist Russia," Review of Politics 19 (October 1957): 462-471.
    Argues that police socialism was the most significant element in the decline of Tsarist Russia. Accounts for four individuals who played important roles in the Tsarist police: Asev; Gapon; Bogrov; and Malinovsky.

299. Bain, Chester A. "Viet Cong Propaganda Abroad," Foreign Service Journal 45/10 (October 1968): 18-21, 47.
    Discusses the World Federation of Democratic Youth as a Moscow-created propaganda organization to disrupt support for American war policy in Vietnam.

300. Bair, Arthur H., et al. "Unconventional Warfare: A Legitimate Tool of Foreign Policy," Conflict: An International Journal 4/1 (1983).

301. Baird, Jay W. "The Political Testament of Julius Streicker: A Document from the Papers of Captain Dolibois," Vierteljahrshefte fuer Zeitgeschichte 26/4 (1978): 660-693.

302. Bakeless, John E. "General Washington's Spy System," Manuscripts 12/2 (1960): 28-37.

303. Bakeless, John E. "Catching Harry Gilmor," Civil War Times Illustrated 10/1 (1971): 34-40.

304. Bakeless, John E. "Incident at Fort Granger," Civil War Times Illustrated 8/1 (1969): 10-16.

305. Bakeless, John E. "James Harrison: Rebel Enigma," Civil War Times Illustrated 9/1 (1970): 12-20.

306. Bakeless, John E. "The Mystery of Appomattox," Civil War Times Illustrated 9/3 (1970): 18-32.

307. Bakeless, John E. "Spies in the Revolution," American History Illustrated 6/3 (March 1971): 36-45.
    A summary of the strengths and weaknesses of colonial and British intelligence operations in the American Revolution. Suggests that British and colonial spies applied different tradecraft to acquire information and to mislead the opposition.

308. Bakeless, John E. "Lincoln's Private Eye," Civil War Times Illustrated 14/6 (October 1975): 22-30.
    Discusses the career of William Lloyd, a personal spy for Lincoln in Richmond during the Civil War.

309. Baker, Brent. "Leakology: The War of Words," U.S. Naval Institute Proceedings 103/7 (July 1977): 43-49.
    Discusses the problem of leaks and their impact on intelligence operations.

310. Baker, Bruce R. "Policy and Procedures for the Portland Police Intelligence Division," Police Chief 43/3 (March 1976): 58-61.
    Describes Portland's intelligence gathering policies and how information on criminals is acquire, stored and retrieved.

311. Baker, E. Jo and C. Michael York. "Communication or Confrontation," Law and Order 20/10 (October 1972): 86-89.
    Activities of civil disorder technical assistance unit within Georgia

Department of Public Safety.

312. Baker, Henry M. "Why Did Benjamin Thompson, Now Known as Count Rumford, Become a Tory?," Magazine of American History 8 (September-October 1908): 136-142, 196-204.
  An excellent old resource to begin study of Thompson's work as a spy.

313. Baker, Stewart A. "Should Spies Be Cops?," Foreign Policy 97 (December 1994): 36-52.
  Considers the question of CIA's involvement in law enforcement activities; the risks to civil liberties; and problems associated with dissemination of information.

314. Baker, William M. "Secrecy and the Media," Studies in Intelligence 34/1 (Spring 1990).

315. Balcer, Jack M. "The Athenian Episkopos and the Achaemenid King's Eye," American Journal of Philology 98/3 (1977): 252-263.
  Among other roles of Athenian Episophes was the Office of the King's Ear, an organization responsible for eavesdropping on citizens. Discusses the earliest references to the Episkopos, jurisdiction of Episkopos, the King's Ear, Satraps, Imperials, and the King's Eye.

316. Baldino, Nancy C. "The C^3I Budget: Continued Priority," Signal (March 1985): 35-36.

317. Baldwin, David A. "Foreign Aid, Intervention, and Influence," World Politics 21/3 (April 1969): 425-447.
  Discusses the concept of intervention, types of foreign aid, and recommended policy toward trade rather than aid. A useful background piece for discussions of forms of national security intervention.

318. Baldwin, David A. "Thinking About Threats," Journal of Conflict Resolution 16 (March 1971): 71-78.
  A discussion of the interpretation of threats, the differences between threats and promises, variations in coerciveness, the interplay between threats and costs, and the relationship between threats and policy responses.

319. Baldwin, Gordon B. "Congressional Power to Demand Disclosure of Foreign Intelligence Agreements," Brooklyn Journal of International Law 3/1 (Fall 1976): 1-30.
  Examines the historical, legislative and judicial bases of the President's power to withhold information relating to international agreements from the Congress. Includes the nature of intelligence agreements (liaison activities),

legislative history of the Case Act, interpretation of the Case Act, other statutes, Presidential power to effect agreements, balance of powers between Congress and the President and conclusions. One of very few discussions of secretive liaison activities.

320. Baldwin, Gordon B. "The Foreign Affairs Advice Privilege," Wisconsin Law Review 1976 (1976): 16-46.

Author focusses on issue of foreign affairs privilege of Secretary of State in context of congressional attempts to investigate executive action and force disclosure of dialogue between executive officials. Writer argues that there is a qualified advice privilege based in the Constitution which is sustained by US Supreme Court opinions.

321. Baldwin, Hanson W. "Battlefield Intelligence: The Battle of the Bulge as a Case History," Combat Forces Journal 3 (February 1953): 30-41.

322. Baldwin, Hanson W. "Slow-down the Pentagon," Foreign Affairs 43/1 (January 1965): 262-279.

Discusses the creeping politicization of the Pentagon and the influences of various agencies, such as NASA, CIA, Bureau of the Budget and the Joint Chiefs of Staff, on weapons development.

323. Baldwin, Hanson W. "The Future of Intelligence," Strategic Review 4/3 (Summer 1976): 6-24.

Offers several suggestions for improving the organization and limitations on the intelligence community in light of President Gerald Ford's executive order.

324. Baldwin, Hanson W. "America at War: Three Bad Months," Foreign Affairs 70/5 (Winter 1991-1992): 162-165.

This is a reprint of the original article published in the same journal, April 1942. It is a classic piece of close-in reflection upon the Pearl Harbor attack and the succeeding months of difficult warfare.

325. Baldwin, Peter M. "Clausewitz in Nazi Germany," Journal of Contemporary History 16/1 (January 1981): 5-26.

A study of the influence of Clausewitz on war policy and strategy in Hitler's Germany. Discusses the perversion of Clausewitz's writings by the Nazi regime and the heavy emphasis on Clausewitz's philosophy in German propaganda.

326. Baldwin, Roger and Alan F. Westin. "The ACLU and the FBI: A Conversation Between Roger Baldwin and Alan F. Westin," Civil Liberties Review 4/4 (November-December 1977): 17-25.

A discussion of the role of the ACLU in the pre-World War I period through the 1920s. Role of the FBI in these years is also discussed.

327. Baldwin, Simeon E. "The Law of the Air-Ship," American Journal of International Law 4/1 (January 1910): 94-108.
Opens with an observation of the then new law of air navigation, referring to the negative aspects: "It will be seized as an aid in evil-doing by smugglers, spies, burglars. . ." Asks if there is a right to navigate the air. Discusses international regulation and ends with a poem from Locksley Hall. Useful in historical studies of airpower and intelligence collection. A classic article useful in historical studies of airpower and intelligence gathering.

328. Balet, Sebastian. "Marlowe: Playwright, Nonbeliever and Spy," Historia y Vida 18/203 (1985): 104-113.

329. Ball, Desmond J. "Allied Intelligence Cooperation Involving Australia During World War II," Australian Outlook: Journal of the Australian Institute of International Affairs 32/4 (December 1978): 299-309.

330. Ball, Desmond J. "U.S. Strategic Forces: How Would They Be Used?," International Security 7/3 (Winter 1982-1983): 31-60.
A detailed review of the strategic forces of the US and the USSR and the need for controlling the processes of escalating nuclear capabilities. Useful background piece for conditions in the early 1980s.

331. Ball, Desmond J. "Soviet Signals Intelligence: Vehicular Systems and Operations," Intelligence and National Security 4/1 (January 1989): 5-27.
A detailed study of contemporary Soviet signals operations, including counter-espionage and counter-intelligence; European operations; American operations; and conclusions.

332. Ball, Desmond J. "Sharing Nurrungar," Asia-Pacific Defence Reporter (November 1991): 6-10.

333. Ball, Desmond J. "Signals Intelligence in India," Intelligence and National Security 10/3 (July 1995): 377-407.
Major sections discuss wartime operations in North-West India; SIGINT operations in Ceylon; Post-independence activities; US-Indian cooperation; the 1970 ITU report; Soviet SIGINT in India; the Indian SIGINT establishment; SIGINT operations at the tactical level; coordination machinery; and politicization of the Indian SIGINT establishment.

334. Ball, Desmond J. "Signals Intelligence in India," Jane's Intelligence Review 6 (1995): 365-370.

335. Ball, Desmond J. "Signals Intelligence in Taiwan," Jane's Intelligence Review 11 (1995): 506-510.

336. Ball, Desmond and Robert Windrem. "Soviet Signals Intelligence (Sigint): Organization and Management," Intelligence and National Security 4/4 (October 1989): 621-659.

Outlines Soviet intelligence organizations and systems. Major sections cover the KGB; the Chief Directorate of Strategic Deception in the Soviet general staff; Sigint activities of the Soviet ground forces; higher level management; tasking and lines of reporting in the Soviet Sigint establishment.

337. Ball, Donald W. "Covert Political Rebellion As Ressentiment," Social Forces 43/1 (October 1964): 93-101.

Concerns the potential for youthful passive rebellion against parental direction on issues of politics. Suggests that passive rebellion in youths derives from two stages, first alienation, and second, low sense of perceived control over environmental conditions. Stages result in ressentiment, an inversion of particular values held by the object of hostility. Indirectly relevant to intelligence in terms of the potential for recruiting those alienated by parental domination of political views and perceived lack of environmental control.

338. Ball, Eve. "The Apache Scouts: A Chiricahua Appraisal," Arizona and the West 7/4 (1965): 315-328.

339. Ball, George W. "Top Secret: The Prophesy the President Rejected," Atlantic Monthly 230/7 (July 1972): 35-49.

Originally, this piece was titled "How Valid Are the Assumptions Underlying Our Viet-Nam Policies?", appearing in the October 5, 1964 issue of Atlantic Monthly. Presents the author's options for the US to approach a resolution to the Vietnam war. Argues that military plans to attack North Vietnam should be set aside. Good background piece for the role of intelligence analysis in the decision making process.

340. Ball, George, et al. "Should the U.S. Fight Secret Wars? Overt Talk on Covert Action," Harper's 269/1612 (September 1984): 33-39, 42-47.

A debate forum on the merits and demerits of covert actions to assist foreign governments. Cites several examples of covert action schemes, many of which reflect failures.

341. Ballantine, Joseph W. "Mukden to Pearl Harbor: The Foreign Policies of Japan," Foreign Affairs 27/4 (July 1949): 651-664.

Discusses three main stages of Japan's evolving actions to go to war against Western powers: expansionist moves of the Army without the approval of higher levels of authority; adoption of a policy of expansion; and the decision to proceed with expansionism despite the implications for war.   Excellent background piece on the failures of the decision making process.

342. Ballard, Michael B. "Lightning Ellsworth's Electronic Warfare: Deceit by Telegraph," Civil War Times Illustrated 22/6 (1983): 22-27.

343. Ballendorf, Dirk A. "Earl Hancock Ellis: The Man and His Mission," U.S. Naval Institute Proceedings 109/11 (November 1983): 53-60.
    A tribute to Ellis' contributions to Naval intelligence history during the 1920s, and a commentary on his personality disorders.

344. Ballendorf, Dirk A. "Secrets Without Substance: U.S. Intelligence in the Japanese Mandates, 1915-1935," Journal of Pacific History 19/1-2 (1984): 83-99.
    Argues that US naval intelligence had extensive intelligence on pre-war Japan's activities and interests in the South Pacific.

345. Ballou, Eric E. and Kyle E. McSlarrow. "Plugging the Leak: The Case for a Legislative Resolution of the Conflict Between the Demands of Secrecy and the Need for an Open Government," Virginia Law Review 71/5 (June 1985): 801-868.
    Addresses the problem created by disclosure of government secrets and discusses statutory solutions for criminalizing leaks of such secrets and any resulting publication. Discusses government controls on secrets, the tension between national security and the First Amendment, problems of legislative solutions to controls, and criminal sanctions.

346. Balticus. "The Two 'G's': Gestapo and GPU, Phenomena of Modern Revolution," Foreign Affairs 17/3 (April 1939): 489-507.
    Presents a theory of the role of secret police in the stability of the progress of revolutions. The expansion of the role of the secret police in revolutions comes with every "mission into the living organism of the nation...socially, economically or politically..."

347. Bamford, James. "NSA--Projects and Prospects," Intelligence Quarterly 1/2 (July 1985): 5-6.
    The author published a full-length study of the National Security Agency.

348. Bamford, James. "The Walker Espionage Case," U.S. Naval Institute Proceedings 112/5 (May 1986): 110-119.
    This is an excellent summation of this espionage case, including a listing of all the Navy-Marine Corps espionage cases from 1981-1986.

349. Bandmann, Yona and Yishai Cordova. "The Soviet Nuclear Threat Towards the Close of the Yom Kippur War," Jerusalem Journal of International Relations

5/1 (1980): 94-110.

Outlines the main events of the military front and on the political scene which preceded the threat. Presents accounts of news reports and their interpretations. Concludes that the evidence is thin on whether the US Central Intelligence Agency purposely leaked information regarding Soviet nuclear deliveries to Egypt.

350. Banfill, Charles Y. "Military Intelligence and Command," Infantry Journal 62 (February 1948): 28-30.

Discusses standards for the intelligence staff, intelligence as everybody's business, and military intelligence as an end product.

351. Banford, Harry C. "Intelligence Communication in a Changing World," American Intelligence Journal 11/3 (Summer-Fall 1990): 19-22.

Discusses intelligence communications architecture in current and future terms. Includes a schematic of the ITDN generic architecture.

352. Banford, Harry C. and Paul L. High, Jr. "Intelligence Communications in the Age of Information Warfare," American Intelligence Journal 15/2 (Autumn-Winter 1994): 52-57.

Explores the intelligence process; the flow of information; the driving force of technology; architectures and implementation tools; the rapid pace of technology; INTELINK; and interoperability.

353. Bank, Harold W. "Espionage: The American Judicial Response: An In Depth Analysis of the Espionage Laws and Related Statutes," American University Law Review 21 (1972): 329-373.

Major sections include espionage and censorship laws, conspiracy, constitutionality of the espionage laws, statutory provisions prohibiting activities related to espionage, penalties, immunity, and exchanges of spies. Concludes that espionage laws have not hindered espionage activities, but they are adequate for reaching convictions.

354. Banks, Thomas C. "Use of Surveillance Evidence Under Title III: Bridging the Legislative Gap Between the Language and Purpose of the Sealing Requirement," Vanderbilt Law Review 36/2 (March 1983): 325-360.

Discusses Title III scheme of sealing requirement of information obtained by wiretap. Sections discuss Supreme Court abandonment of trespass doctrine; Berger v. Katz cases; statutory remedy of suppression; interpretations of the various Circuit courts; and analyzes effectiveness of decision in furthering safeguards and purpose of sealing requirements.

355. Banks, William C. "While Congress Slept: The Iran-Contra Affair and Institutional Responsibility for Covert Operations," Syracuse Journal of

International Law and Commerce 14/3 (Spring 1988): 291-361.

Details the development of the Iran-Contra affair, congressional committee investigation results (based on committee reports), and recommendations. Criticizes procedural shortcomings of investigation and congressional short-sightedness in failing to further pursue issues of US role in various operations. Suggests need for clarification of constitutional issue of war power control and offers suggestions for improvement. An extensive discussion of this much-ignored controversy.

356. Baram, Michael S. "Trade Secrets: What Price Loyalty?," Harvard Business Review 46/6 (November-December 1968): 66-74.

Discusses the corporate response to employee movement to other companies, sometimes taking with them the valuable secrets of intellectual property. Proposes alternatives to litigation in order to introduce preventive measures.

357. Barathy, Frederick D. "Cover: Property Restitution," Studies in Intelligence 5/2 (Spring 1961).

358. Baratz, Morton S.; Derek C. Bok; and Stansfield Turner. "Universities and the Intelligence Community," Academe 65/1 (February 1979): 15-26.

Former CIA Director Turner comments on the remarks before Congress of Morton Baratz and Derek Bok concerning the role of the CIA in university research missions. Baratz and Bok had testified in 1978 that university professors had been used by the CIA to travel abroad, to engage in recruiting activities, and to sponsor in a clandestine fashion university organizations.

359. Barber, Charles H. "Some Problems of Air Intelligence," Military Review 26/5 (August 1946): 76-78.

Discusses evolution of air intelligence procedures during World War II. Suggests formalization of procedures within every level of the Air Force.

360. Barber, Laurie and Garry Clayton. "The Spider and the Web: Intelligence Networks of the 2nd New Zealand War," Army Quarterly and Defence Journal 119/4 (October 1989): 453-457.

A short article which discusses the role of intelligence in the British wars in New Zealand, 1860-1872.

361. Barbosa, Roberto; P. Brogan; and C. Burns. "The CIA and the Press: Foreign Reaction to Disclosures of Media Manipulation," Atlas 25 (March 1978): 22-25.

362. Barde, Robert E. "Midway: Tarnished Victory," Military Affairs 47/4 (1983): 188-192.

Interprets the meaning of the capture, interrogation and execution of American pilots captured in the Midway sea battle of 1942. Japanese intelligence harvested information regarding US naval capabilities through brutal treatment of pilots, and the incident resulted in the creation of the military code of conduct under capture.

363. Barendt, Eric. "Spycatcher and Freedom of Speech," Public Law (Summer 1989): 204-212.

Discusses the implications of the British House of Lords decision to lift all injunctions against Guardian Newspapers for publishing excerpts of Peter Wright's Spycatcher. Mentions US decisions in cases involving CIA personnel who have published memoirs.

364. Barghoorn, Frederick C. "Cultural Exchanges Between Communist Countries and the United States," Annals of the American Academy of Political and Social Science 372 (1967): 113-123.

Attempts to extend the limited scholarly discussion of cultural exchanges. Argues that there are propaganda and information/intelligence problems in such exchanges. Mentions the CIA and the KGB.

365. Bar-Joseph Uri. "Methodological Magic," Intelligence and National Security 3/4 (October 1988): 134-155.

A lengthy and detailed book review essay concerning Ariel Levite's book, Intelligence and Strategic Surprise, 1987. The author considers Levite's elements of the study; two fundamental methodological mistakes; and suggestions for future studies of strategic surprise.

366. Bar-Joseph, Uri. "Israel's Intelligence Failure: New Evidence, a New Interpretation, and Theoretical Implications," Security Studies 4/3 (Spring 1995): 584-609.

367. Bar-Joseph, Uri. "Israel Caught Unaware: Egypt's Sinai Surprise of 1960," International Journal of Intelligence and Counterintelligence 8/2 (Summer 1995): 203-219.

An account of the Egyptian operation Rotem, a surprise aggressive act aimed at shocking the Israeli defense system. Major sections discuss the setting; a strategic surprise against Israel; analysis of the events; and lessons learned.

368. Bar-Joseph, Uri. "The Wealth of Information and the Poverty of Comprehension: Israel's Intelligence Failure of 1973 Revisited," Intelligence and National Security 10/4 (October 1995): 229-240.

A book review essay covering four titles: Yoel Ben-Porat, Neila: Locked-On; Arie Braun, Moshe Dayan and the Yom Kippur War; Eli Zeira, The October 73 War: Myth Against Reality; and The Investigation Committee-The

Yom Kippur War, <u>An Additional Partial Report: Reasoning and Completion to the Partial Report of April 1, 1974</u> (7 volumes).

369. Barker, Bernard and Eugenio R. Martinez. "Mission Impossible: The Watergate Bunglers," <u>Harper's</u> 249 (October 1974): 50-58.
This article contains portions of interviews with the authors, two men involved in the Watergate breakin scandal during the Nixon administration. Other related articles in this issue address the Watergate affair.

370. Barker, Edward L. "Air Combat Intelligence," <u>Naval Intelligence Professionals Quarterly</u> 5/1 (Winter 1989): 11-15.

371. Barker, Elisabeth. "The Berlin Crisis 1958-1962," <u>International Affairs</u> (Great Britain) 39/1 (January 1963): 59-73.
Analyzes and reports upon the four major crisis periods of the Berlin issue, originating, says the author, with Soviet confidence following Sputnik. Could be used in connection with other intelligence events in this period, e.g., V-2 shoot-down, Bay of Pigs, Missile crisis.

372. Barker, Eugene. "President Jackson and the Texas Revolution," <u>American Historical Review</u> 12/4 (July 1907).
A useful background piece for studies of conflicts with Mexico.

373. Barker, Nancy N. "In Quest of the Golden Fleece: Dubois De Saligny and French Intervention in the New World," <u>Western Historical Quarterly</u> 3/3 (1972): 153-168.
Discusses French interventionist policies, particularly Frances Alphonse Dubois de Saligny's covert actions in the newly formed Republic of Texas during the 1800s.

374. Barker, Wayne G. "Solving a Hagelin, Type CD-57 Cipher," <u>Cryptologia</u> 2/1 (January 1978): 1-8.

375. Barker, Wayne G. "The Unsolved D'Agapeyff Cipher," <u>Cryptologia</u> 2/2 (April 1978): 144-147.

376. Barker, Wayne G. "Opportunities for the Amateur Cryptanalyst Can Be Anywhere," <u>Cryptologia</u> 4/3 (July 1980): 169-172.

377. Barkin, Edward S. and L. Michael Meyer. "COMINT and Pearl Harbor: FDR's Mistake," <u>International Journal of Intelligence and Counterintelligence</u> 2/4 (Winter 1988): 513-532.
Introduces the two main views on the attack at Pearl Harbor: The mainstream school which argues that bureaucratic failures caused the attack, and

the revisionist school which argues that Franklin Roosevelt plotted to drag the US into war with Japan. Major sections discuss the views of the neo-revisionists; the question of Japanese radio silence; Roosevelt's decisionmaking; and crisis analysis.

378. Barksdale, William S. "Aerial Combat Photography," Air University Review 17/5 (July-August 1966): 60-69.

379. Barland, Gordon H. and David C. Raskin. "An Evaluation of Field Techniques in Detection of Deception," Psychophysiology (1976): 321-330.
    Addresses factors involved in deceiving devices for detecting deception, such as the polygraph.

380. Barlow, John P. "Dycrypting the Puzzle Palace," Communications of the ACM 35 (July 1992): 25-31.

381. Barlow, Mike. "A Machine Solution of the AMSCO Cipher," Cryptologia 10/1 (January 1986): 23-33.

382. Barlow, Mike. "The Voynich Manuscript - By Voynich?," Cryptologia 10/4 (October 1986): 210-216.

383. Barlow, Mike. "A Mathematical Word Block Cipher," Cryptologia 12/4 (October 1988): 256-264.

384. Barnds, William J. "Intelligence and Foreign Policy: Dilemmas of a Democracy," Foreign Affairs 47/2 (January 1969): 281-295.
    Discussion of the dilemmas facing intelligence services in the US following the loss of consensus as to their value in the 1960s. Considers the evolution of CIA, use of intelligence agencies, and relationship between intelligence and foreign policy.

385. Barnes, Joseph. "Fighting with Information: OWI Overseas," Public Opinion Quarterly 7/1 (Spring 1943): 34-45.
    Sets forth the overseas information activities of the Office of War Information. Major sections include discussion of the intelligent use of truth; Voice of America; the need for alignment with foreign policy initiatives; the director of overseas operations; regional divisions; Atlantic operations; overseas radio bureau; motion picture bureau; publications bureau; overseas news and feature bureau; Pacific operations; outpost service bureau; overseas bureau of research and analysis; and communications facilities bureau.

386. Barnes, S. "The Navaho's Secret Weapon," American Legion Magazine 104/2 (February 1978): 14-18.
    Examines the effective use of the uncommon Navajo language in safe and

effective communications during the island combat missions in World War II against Japan.

387. Barnes, Trevor. "Special Branch and the First Labour Government," Historical Journal 22/4 (December 1979): 941-952.

A study of British domestic intelligence services in the early 1920s. The news Labour government of 1924 viewed the Special Branch as a necessary contributor to the defensive posture taken by the British to the fear of a communist sweep of Western governments.

388. Barnes, Trevor. "The Secret Cold War: The C.I.A. and American Foreign Policy in Europe, 1946-1956, Part I," Historical Journal   24/2 (June 1981): 399-415.

First part of a lengthy discussion of US covert actions origins. This piece addresses the three formative years of CIA from 1945 to 1948.

389. Barnes, Trevor. "The Secret Cold War: The C.I.A. and American Foreign Policy in Europe 1946-1956. Part II," Historical Journal 25/3 (September 1982): 649-670.

Second part of a lengthy discussion of the US involvement in covert actions in Europe, emerging out of the Marshall Plan and the fear of expansion of communist parties.

390. Barnet, Richard J. "Dirty Tricks and the Intelligence Underworld," Society 12/3 (March-April 1975): 52-57.

This article asserts that there is a double standard of public opinion which distinguishes intelligence service operations at home and abroad. Captures many of the popular rancor about the intelligence community in the1970s.

391. Barnet, Richard J. "The Ideology of the National Security State," Massachusetts Review 26/4 (Winter 1985): 483-500.

Addresses the arms build-up between the US and USSR from World War II to the present.

392. Barnett, James D. "Passport Administration and the Courts," Oregon Law Review 32 (April 1953): 193-209.

Brief history of passport administration; review of Bauer v. Acheson overturning State Department revocation of passport, and new regulations imposed to administer passport issuance.

393. Barnett, Stephen R. "The Puzzle of Prior Restraint," Stanford Law Review 29/3 (February 1977): 539-560.

Discussion of Nebraska Press Assn. v. Stuart, 96 S.Ct. 2791 (1976), where Supreme Court refused to accept a blanket rule against gag orders. Argues balancing test in prior restraint cases weakens First Amendment protection and is more restrictive than the test in the earliest prior restraint cases. Provides history, development and application of prior restraint doctrine.

394. Barnett, Harvey. "Legislation-based National Security Services: Australia," Intelligence and National Security 9/2 (April 1994): 287-300.

Details the birth, recruitment, and operations of the Australian Security and Intelligence Organization (ASIO). Argues that the arrangement between the Australian government and the ASIO is satisfactory at present, and that the overseer of the intelligence functions should, themselves, be overseen.

395. Barnett, Roger W. "Fathoming Soviet Intentions," U.S. Naval Institute Proceedings 111/7 (July 1985): 30-36.

A piece offering some conclusions on the subject of Soviet intentions in warfare.

396. Barques, Mark J. "Soviet Naval Spetsnaz Forces," Naval War College Review 41/2 (Spring 1988): 5-21.

397. Barrett, Michael J. "Espionage and the Legal Norm: The Legal and Moral Status of the Intelligence Profession in a Free Society" (Pt. I), Defense and Diplomacy 2/2 (February 1984): 12-25+.

398. Barrett, Michael J. "Honorable Espionage" (Parts I, II, III), Defense & Diplomacy 2/2 (1984): 13-21, 25, 63; 2/3 (1984): 12-17, 62; 2/4 (1984): 17-21.

399. Barrett, Michael J. "Patterns of Terror," Defense & Diplomacy 4/3 (1986): 40-44.

400. Barrett, Raymond J. "Psyop: What Is It? and What Should We Do About It?," Military Review 52/3 (March 1972): 57-72.

A discussion of psychological operations and their roles in national security policy making. Offers a framework for administrative controls on such operations.

401. Barrett, Raymond J. "Graduated Response and the Lessons of Vietnam," Military Review 52/5 (May 1972): 80-91.

A discussion of graduated response methodology, reflecting upon an increase and reallocation of bombing missions in Vietnam. Argues that enemy intelligence picked up on the timing of graduated response, thereby defeating the method. Offers alternatives.

402. Barron, John. "Espionage As An Instrument of Communist Policy," Survey 136 (July 1960): 1-24.

403. Barros, Andrew. "A Window on the 'Trust': The Case of Ado Birk," Intelligence and National Security 10/2 (April 1995): 273-293.

Sheds additional light on the early days of the Soviet security services through the case of Ado Birk, former Estonian Minister in Moscow. Concludes that "The Trust," a front organization that operated by direction of Feliks Dzerzhinskii, grew from defensive to offensive protection of the Bolshevik revolution.

404. Barros, James. "Alger Hiss and Harry Dexter White: The Canadian Connection," Orbis 21/3 (Fall 1977): 593-606.

Reveals the views of Canadian Prime Minister King regarding the allegations of espionage against Hiss and White. King's recollections were contained in notes taken from conversations with Igor Gouzenko. One of very few pieces associating these two characters in post-war Canadian espionage.

405. Barry, James A. "Managing Covert Political Action: Guideposts from Just War Theory," Studies in Intelligence 36/3 (Fall 1992): 19-31.

Major topics under discussion in this piece, published in CIA's internal journal, include: covert action and the new world order; Just War theory; the theory of covert action; the Chile case; the 1964 election operation; the 1970 elections and "Track II"; evaluating the two operations; reforms since the 1970s; and approach for the 1990s; and the casuistry of covert action. Reprinted: see next citation.

406. Barry, James A. "Covert Action Can Be Just," Orbis 37/3 (Summer 1993): 375-390.

Major sections include discussion of covert action and the new world order; just war theory; just war and covert action; just war and Chile, 1964; covert action in the 1970 election in Chile; evaluation of the 1964 and 1970 operations; an approach for the 1990s; and policy implications.

407. Bar-Siman-Tov, Yaacov. "Constraints and Limitations in Limited Local War: The Case of the Yom Kippur War," Jerusalem Journal of International Relations 5/2 (1981): 46-61.

408. Bar-Siman-Tov, Yaacov. "Crisis Management by Military Cooperation with a Small Ally: American-Israeli Cooperation in the Syrian-Jordanian Crisis, September, 1970," Cooperation and Conflict 17/3 (1982): 151-162.

Identifies factors limiting local war involvement between small actors and examines these factors in the case of the 1967 Yom Kippur war. Distinction is made between constraints and limitations.

409. Bartels, John R. Jr. "Drug Enforcement Administration's Unique Concept: Unified Intelligence," Police Chief 42/7 (July 1975): 38-39.

Addresses the problem of conflicting interests between local, state and federal law enforcement agencies, and of effective solution of an operational task force used in the 1970s New York drug wars.

410.   Barthel, Robert.   "The Interpreter Officers of the Marine Intelligence Service," Revue Historique des Armes 1 (1989): 77-96.

411. Bartlett, C. J. "The US Army and Global Politics, 1917 to 1927," Journal of American Studies 14/2 (1980): 249-252.
A review essay of Richard Challener's book, United States Military Intelligence, 1917-27 (1979, 30 volumes).   Argues the learned benefits of intelligence in World War I for later application.

412.   Bartley, Robert L. and William P. Kucewicz.   "'Yellow Rain' and the Future of Arms Agreements," Foreign Affairs 61/4 (Spring 1983): 805-825.
Presents evidence of previous Soviet-backed chemical attacks upon the H'Mong tribe by the North Vietnamese and Laotian People's Liberation Army. Outlines the evidence and argues that the American news media refused to accept the story of Laotian defector. CIA reported efforts to determine the type chemical agent in use, resolving that a mycotoxin had been used. The CIA finding was rejected by leaders in the press as a hoax.

413. Bartos, Milan. "International Terrorism," Review of International Affairs 23 (April 1972): 25-26.

Briefly mentions the importance of information control in the defense against terrrorism.

414. Barzun, Jacques. "Meditations on the Literature of Spying," American Scholar 34/2 (Spring 1965): 167-178.
Critiques topical spy literature of his time, including LeCarre's The Spy Who Came in from the Cold, Candy by Terry Southern and Mason Hoffenberg, and The Spy by James Fennimore Cooper.

415. Bashkin, V. "The Israeli Special Services: Instruments of Aggression and Terror," Mirovaia Ekonomika i Mezhdunarodyne Otnasheniia 1 (1985): 142-145.

416. Bashkirov, I. "A Master Razvedka," Voenno Istoricheskiy Zhurnal 1 (January 1983): 39-42.

417.   Basik, Theodore S.   "Constitutional Law - Criminal Procedure - Eavesdropping - Title III of the Omnibus Crime Control and Safe Streets Act of 1968: A Search Without a Warrant? Dalia v. United States, 441 U.S. 238 (1979)," University of Baltimore Law Review 9 (Winter 1980): 308-341.

This four-part article accounts for the evolution of case history concerning eavesdropping, Title III of the Omnibus Crime Control and Safe Streets Act of 1968, and Basik's own disagreement with the Supreme Court's ruling in Dalia v. U. S..

418. Basile, James F. "Congressional Assertiveness, Executive Authority and the Intelligence Oversight Act: A New Threat to the Separation of Powers," Notre Dame Law Review 64/4 (1989): 571-598.

Examines the constitutionality of the Intelligence Oversight Act. Major sections discuss the Act; the Act and the president's foreign affairs program; the Act and executive privilege; and alternatives to legislative usurpation of executive privilege.

419. Baskir, Lawrence M. "Reflections on the Senate Investigation of Army Surveillance," Indiana Law Journal 49 (Summer 1974): 618-653.

An extensive review of the Senate investigation: Early stage of the investigation, the approach to public hearings, witnesses, difficulties with the Department of Defense, litigating military surveillance, drafting legislation, and conclusions.

420. Basoco, Richard M. "A British View of the Union Navy, 1864," American Neptune 27/1 (1967): 30-45.

The British view is rarely presented.

421. Bass, Robert H. "Communist Fronts: Their History and Function," Problems of Communism 9 (September-October 1960): 8-16.

Discusses the theoretical formulations of front organizations; extension from theory to practice; the role of the Red International of Labor Unions and the Young Communist International; the short-lived success of prewar fronts; the postwar hiatus; the costs of loyalty of front organizations; new policies and new functions; and overall successes and failures.

422. Bass, Streeter. "Nathan Hale's Mission," Studies in Intelligence 17/4 (Winter 1973): 67-74.

423. Bassiouni, M. Cherif. "Protection of Diplomats Under Islamic Law," American Journal of International Law 74/3 (July 1980): 609-633.

Included in the broader discussion of Islamic law pertaining to diplomatic immunities, the author discusses the relevant portions of law dealing with espionage.

424. Bassiouni, M. Cherif. "Media Coverage of Terrorism: The Law and the Public," Journal of Communication 32/2 (Spring 1982): 128-143.

Publication of information concerning terrorist actions presents difficulties for law enforcement, but media also serve to pass on tactical intelligence. Recommendations for media self-regulation are offered.

425. Bastide, C. "Ethics of Espionage," Fortnightly 83 (January 1905): 39-44.
Discusses internal espionage in the French government and society during the early 1900s, in particular the motivations of the spies of that era.

426. Batatu, Hanna. "Iraq's Underground Shi'a Movements: Characteristics, Causes and Prospects," Middle East Journal 35/4 (Autumn 1981): 578-594.
Identifies and discusses each of the major underground movements; then asks how the regime reacted to militant Shi'a activities and what are the prospects for the Shi'a underground.

427. Bateman, Gary M. "The Enigma Cipher Machine," American Intelligence Journal 5/2 (July 1983): 6-11.

428. Bates, E. Asa. "National Technical Means of Verification," RUSI Defence Studies Journal 123 (June 1978): 64-73.
The earlier title of this journal was Royal United Services Institute Journal (hereafter referenced under either title). National technical means of intelligence gathering are considered, including friendly platforms, Soviet capabilities and satellite vulnerabilities.

429. Bates, David H. "A Rebel Cipher Despatch: One Which Did Not Reach Judah P. Benjamin," Harper's 97 (June 1898): 105-109.
Discusses a form of cryptology used during the Civil War. A code was recovered from the body of John Wilkes Booth after Lincoln's assassination.

430. Bates, Dick. "Writing About Naval Intelligence," Naval Intelligence Professionals Quarterly (several volumes and issues (1986-1995).
There are numerous contributions of this author on this subject in the NIP Quarterly. In the Fall 1995 issue, the author includes a history of the Naval Intelligence Professionals organization

431. Bates, J. Leonard. "Watergate and Teapot Dome," South Atlantic Quarterly 73/2 (1974): 145-159.

432. Bates, Richard W. "Intelligence and Academe: Estranged Communities," American Intelligence Journal 4/1 (Summer 1981): 10-13.

433. Bates, Richard W. "The Intelligence Profession," American Intelligence Journal 4/3 (May 1982): 19-23.

434. Bates, Richard W. "Writing About Naval Intelligence," Naval Intelligence

Professionals Quarterly (Winter 1995): 14-15.

435. Bath, Alan. "Double-Cross and Deception Revisited," Naval Intelligence Professionals Quarterly 7/3 (Summer 1991): 16-17.

436. Bathurst, Robert B. "Crisis Mentality: A Problem of Cultural Reality," Naval War College Review 26/4 (1974): 55-62.
The author argues that US crisis analysts fail to analyze the enemy properly and in the future this ignorance could be disastrous. The invasion of Czechoslovakia in 1968 and the Arab-Israeli War of 1967 are both addressed. Few articles address the intelligence failures regarding the Czech invasion.

437. Batten, J. "Joe Sedgwick and Gouzenko's Spy," Canadian Lawyer 6/5 (1982): 10-16, 40.
Discusses history of espionage case against Eric Adams, accused of spying for the Soviets from 1942 to 1945.

438. Batyushin, N. "Cryptography During World War I: A Tsarist Russian's View," Studies in Intelligence 21/2 (Summer 1977).

439. Baudouin, Roger. "Chiffre et Cryptographie: Le Chiffre et son Emploi Militaire, par le Capitaine Baudouin," Revue de l'Armee de l'Air 114 (January-February 1939): 5-22.

440. Baudouin, Roger. "Chiffre et Cryptographie: Solution des Problemes Poses dand Notre Dernier Numero, par le Capitaine Baudouin," Revue de l'Armee de l'Air 115 (March-April 1939): 192-194.

441. Bauer, Friedrich L. "Cryptological Devices and Machines in the Deutsches Museum, Munich," Cryptologia 20/1 (January 1996): 11-13.

442. Bauer, Raymond. "Problems of Perception and the Relations Between the U.S. and the Soviet Union," Journal of Conflict Resolution 5/3 (September 1961): 223-229.
Argues that positive relations between nations are enhanced by mutual understanding of social and political institutions. Perceptions of each nation are critical to better understanding between the US and the Soviet Union, and overreaction by either country can lead to miscalculations. Cautions intelligence analysts to avoid admission of personal perceptions to the analytical process.

443. Baumard, Phillipe. "From Noticing to Making Sense: Using Intelligence to Develop Strategy," International Journal of Intelligence and Counterintelligence 7/1 (Spring 1994): 29-73.
An extensive and detailed discussion of methods of corporate intelligence

analysis. Major sections discuss the background of company information efforts; reasoning and methods of corporate research; how and why do corporations notice?; how and why do corporations filter their perceptions?; how and why corporations give sense and produce intelligence?; case study research, method and results; learning from past intelligence failures; intelligence sharing; intelligence roots and early seekers; evolution of intelligence language; intelligence and corporate change; and enhancing intimacy through experience sharing.

444. Bax, Francis R. "The Legislative-Executive Relationship in Foreign Policy: New Partnership or New Competition?," Orbis 20/4 (Winter 1977): 881-904.

Discusses the changing role of Congress in foreign policy oversight, structural differences in Congress, the historical background, and analysis of the current relationship.

445. Baxter, Richard R. "So-Called 'Underprivileged Belligerency' Spies, Guerillas, and Saboteurs," British Yearbook of International Law 28 (1951): 323-345.

Detailed examination of international law applied to war; hostile conduct of spies, guerillas and saboteurs. Offers conclusions that international law is entirely unclear on the protection of these forms of belligerency.

446. Baxter, Ronald W. "Her Majesty's Very Secret Service," World and I 1/11 (November 1986): 64-67.

447. Baxter, William P. "What Ivan Knows About Us," Army 30 (May 1980): 33-35.

448. Bayley, Harold. "The Dignity of Cypher Writing," Baconiana 10 (1902): 123-126.

449. Baylis, John. "British Wartime Thinking About a Post War European Security Group," Review of International Studies 9/4 (1983): 273-277.

450. Baynham, Simon. "Quis Custodiet Ipsos Custodes?: The Case of Nkrumah's National Security Service," Journal of Modern African Studies 23/1 (March 1985): 87-103.

Reviews to conflict of civilian control of the military in the period 1960-1966.

451. Baynham, Simon. "Security Strategies for a Future South Africa," Journal of Modern African Studies 28/3 (September 1990): 401-430.

Discusses current security policy in South Africa; three possible scenarios; and alternative security options. Mentions the security services.

452. Bazan, Elizabeth B. "Espionage and the Death Penalty," <u>Federal Bar News & Journal</u> 41 (October 1994): 615-619.
　　　A brief discussion of the law and implications of capital punishment in espionage cases.

453. Bazant, Jan. "Sequestration for Treason," <u>Historical Mexicana</u> 32/4 (1983): 554-576.
　　　Deals with the taking of private property by the Juarez government as a means of control over the population.

454.   Bazotosnyi, V. M.   "Napolean's Intelligence in Russia Before 1912," <u>Voprosy Istorii</u> 10 (1992): 86-94.

455. Beach, Edward L. "Who's To Blame?," <u>U.S. Naval Institute Proceedings</u> 117/12 (1991): 32-40.

456. Beach, Moses S. "Origins of the Treaty of Guadalupe-Hidalgo," <u>Scribner's Magazine</u> 17 (November 1878): 299-300.
　　　A rare article and one of the oldest pieces in this collection.

457. Beach, Moses S. "A Secret Mission to Mexico," <u>Scribner's Magazine</u> 18 (May 1879): 136-140.

458. Beachley, David R. "Soviet Radio-Electronic Combat in World War II," <u>Military Review</u> 61/3 (March 1981): 66-72.
　　　A general outline of Soviet use of ground signals intelligence and deception in World War II.

459.   Beam, John C.   "The Intelligence Background of Operation Torch," <u>Parameters: Journal of the U.S. Army War College</u> 13/4 (December 1983): 60-68.
　　　A discussion of the intelligence collection work of Robert Murphy, President Roosevelt's charge d'affaires to Vacua, France during the Second World War. This article was reprinted in <u>Studies in Intelligence</u> 28/1 (Spring 1984).

460.   Beames, M. R.   "Rural Conflict in Pre-Famine Ireland: Peasant Assassinations in Tipperary, 1837-1847," <u>Past and Present</u> 81 (November 1978): 75-91.

461. Beane, Joy. "Passport Revocation: A Critical Analysis of Haig v. Agee and the Policy Test," <u>Fordham International Law Review</u> 5/1 (1981): 185-211.
　　　Discusses passports and their regulation to <u>Kent v. Dulles</u>; the Kent case as a test for determining the Secretary of State's power to revoke passports; <u>Haig v. Agee</u> and the policy test and the Fourth Amendment; and conclusions.

462. Beans, James D. "Marine Corps Counterintelligence: 1990-2000," American Intelligence Journal 10/2 (Summer-Fall 1989): 47-50.
    Discusses the historical development of Marine Corps CI in the 1950s, 1960s, 1970s, 1980s, and 1990s.

463. Beans, James D. "Marine Corps Intelligence in Low Intensity Conflicts," Signal 43/7 (March 1989): 27-32.
    Marine Corps history in LIC, current and new Marine Corps intelligence operations, and future challenges.

464. Beard, William W. "YIYKAEJBGZQSYWX," U.S. Naval Institute Proceedings 44/8 (1918).

465. Beardsley, E. H. "Secrets Between Friends: Applied Science Exchange Between Western Allies and the Soviet Union During World War II," Social Studies of Science 7/4 (1977): 447-474.
    Characterizes the conflicts between these nations over the content and possible outcomes of providing or trading information with the Soviets.

466. Beasley, Norman. "The Capture of the German Rocket Secrets," American Legion Magazine (October 1963).

467. Beaumarchais, Pierre-Augustin Caron de. "Covert Action, State Policy, and Public Morality," Studies in Intelligence 23/3 (Fall 1979).

468. Beaumont, Frederick F. "On Balloon Reconnaissance as Practiced by the American Army," Papers of the Royal Engineer Corps 12 (1863): 71-86.

469. Beaumont, Roger A. "The Flawed Soothsayer: Willoughby--General MacArthur's G-2," Espionage 1/4 (July 1985): 20-37.

470. Beaver, W. C. "The Intelligence Division Library 1854-1902," Journal of Library History 11/3 (July 1976).

471. Bebier, Dusan. "Allied Military Missions on the Slovene Coast 1943-1945," Voynaistoryski Glasnik 34/3 (1983): 131-144.

472. Bebier, Dusan. "The Arrival of The British Military Mission 'Typical' at the Supreme Headquarters of the Yugoslav National Liberation Army and Partisan Detachments," Voynaistoryski Glasnik 35/1 (1984): 399-403.

473. Bechtel, M. "A Fresh Look at Afghanistan," New World Review 51/5 (September 1983): 22-25.

474. Beck, Kent M. "Necessary Lies, Hidden Truths: Cuba in the 1960 Campaign," Diplomatic History 8/1 (Winter 1984): 37-59.

Explores in detail the circumstances of the presidential campaign discussions of US-Cuban relations and the secret plan to invade Cuba, held secret by the candidates in the 1960 campaign.

475. Becker, Abraham C. "Intelligence Fiasco or Reasoned Accounting--CIA Estimates of Soviet GNP," Post-Soviet Affairs 10/4 (October-December 1994): 291-329.

Major sections discuss the growth of Soviet GNP (including CIA estimates); comparative size of the Soviet economy and criticisms of the CIA estimates; and reflections on the debate.

476. Becker, Howard. "The Nature and Consequences of Black Propaganda," American Sociological Review 14 (April 1949): 221-235.

Defines propaganda and types of propaganda, including "black propaganda" and "psychological warfare." Discusses uses of propaganda as an intelligence weapon.

477. Becker, Jerrold L. "The Supreme Court's Recent 'National Security' Decisions: Which Interests Are Being Protected?," Tennessee Law Review 40/1 (1972): 1-27.

Author discusses interaction between individual freedoms under 1st and 4th Amendments to the Constitution and government security interests. Seeks to show that standards for resolving such conflicts have been developed, and that continual change in the standards is related more to change in who sits on the Court than to lack of case precedent. Focusses on Chief Justice Warren Burger's Court decisions as compared to the Chief Justice Earl Warren Court. Extensive notes.

478. Becker, Richard T. "Interpretation of the Smith Act," Marquette Law Review 42/1 (Summer 1958): 125-131.

A brief case note concerning Supreme Court interpretations in several cases hinging on terminology in the 1940 Smith Act.

479. Beckerly, J. G. "The Impact of Government Information and Security Controls on Competitive Industry," Bulletin of the Atomic Scientists 11 (1955): 123-127.

Discusses the basic information security controls, government personnel security clearances, the need-to-know requirement, negative features of excessive security controls, and the role of information controls on trade secrets and patent administration.

480. Beckett, Ian F. W. "A Note on Government Surveillance and Intelligence

During the Curragh Incident, March 1914," Intelligence and National Security 1/3 (September 1986): 435-440.

481. Beebe, Lewis. "Journal of a Physician on the Expedition Against Canada, 1776," Pennsylvania Magazine of History and Biography 59 (1935): 321-361.

482. Beecher, William. "Spy Satellites Will Monitor the Pacts: Small Silent Sentinels in Outer Space and Beyond," Sea Power 15/7 (July-August 1972): 20-24.

483. Beeley, Harold. "The Changing Role of British International Propaganda," Annals of the American Academy of Political and Social Sciences 398 (November 1971): 124-129.

484. Beer, Siegfried. "Der Agent 'Ernest Cole'," Steirische Berichte 3 (1985): 16-20.

485. Beer, Siegfried. "Karten im Fruhsommer 1945: Drei Berichte und Analysen des Amerikanischen Geheim-und Nachrichtendienstes OSS zu Politik, Wirtschaft und Gesellschaft in einem Britisch-Besetzten Bundesland," Carinthia 177 (1987): 415-452.

486. Beesly, Patrick. "Naval Intelligence in the Nuclear Age: From Two World Wars - Six Still Valid Lessons," Navy International (April 1977).

487. Beesly, Patrick. "Who Was the Third Man at Pyry?," Cryptologia 11/2 (April 1987): 78-80.

488. Beesly, Patrick. "Convoy PQ17: A Study of Intelligence and Decision-Making," Intelligence and National Security 5/2 (April 1990): 292-322.
        Discusses the case of Sir Dudley Pound's dispatch of Convoy PQ17 to the Soviet Union as a decoy for German aircraft. His decision to dispatch was based on a misunderstanding of intelligence information.

489. Beesly, Patrick; David Stafford; and Erven Montagu. "What You Don't Know by What You Do," International History Review 5/2 (May 1983): 279-290.

490. Behm, A. J. "Terrorism, Violence Against the Public, and the Media: The Australian Approach," Political Communication and Persuasion 8/4 (October-December 1991): 233-246.

491. Beichman, Arnold. "How Weak Is the CIA?," Freedom At Issue 52 (September-October 1979): 12-16.
        The author's summary of papers delivered at the 1979 colloquium in

Washington, "Intelligence Requirements for the 1980s."

492. Beichman, Arnold. "Can Counterintelligence Come In From the Cold?," Policy Review 15 (Winter 1981): 93-101.

The author charges that the Congress has overlooked funding for the counterintelligence program of the FBI. Discusses the function of counterintelligence and the obstacles to rebuilding its capabilities.

493. Beier, Norman S. and Leonard B. Sand. "The Rosenberg Case: History and Hysteria," American Bar Association Journal 40 (December 1954): 1046-1050.

Discusses the Rosenberg espionage case from the perspective of the organized effort in Europe and the United States to defend the innocense of the executed spies. Covers other testimony establishing guilt; observes the absence of public clamor over other executions.

494. Beitz, Charles R. "Covert Intervention as a Moral Problem," Ethics and International Affairs 3 (1989): 45-60.

A rare discussion of the ethical framework of covert action.

495. Belair, Robert R. "Less Government Secrecy and More Personal Privacy?," Civil Liberties Review 4/1 (1977): 10-18.

Discusses the need for reforming the Freedom of Information Act of 1974 and the Privacy Act of 1975.

496. Belair, Robert R. and Charles D. Bock. "Police Use of Remote Camera Systems for Surveillance of Public Streets," Columbia Human Rights Law Review 4/1 (Winter 1972): 143-202.

Arising from the case of Mt. Vernon, New York, [police experimentation with camera surveillance] the author discusses First Amendment implications of the mere observation as a search, and public policy considerations.

497. Belchem, John. "Chartist Informers in Australia: The Nemesis of Thomas Powell," Labour History 43 (1982): 83-89.

498. Belden, Thomas G. "Indications, Warning, and Crisis Operations," International Studies Quarterly 21/1 (March 1977): 181-198.

Argues that the national intelligence system has not been adequately organized to do systematic analysis of warnings and indications. We have not adequately studied the warning process. Suggests remedial steps to improve weak communications links.

499. Belenko, Victor. "Defense Electronics Talks with Victor Belenko - An Exclusive Interview: The Escaped Fighter Pilot Pulls No Punches in Discussing

Soviet Technology, Politics, and Policies," Defense Electronics (June 1988): 95-110.

500. Belk, G. M. "Task of Intelligence," Enforcement Journal 15/1 (January-March 1976): 10-13.

Describes drug enforcement intelligence activities and the creation of the National Narcotics Intelligence System.

501. Belknap, Michael R. "The Mechanics of Repression: J. Edgar Hoover, The Bureau of Investigation and the Radicals, 1917-1925," Crime and Social Justice 7 (Spring-Summer 1977): 49-58.

Argues that J. Edgar Hoover's domestic intelligence policies relied upon bureaucratic considerations and personal ambition to influence the scope and intensity of governmental attacks on dissent.

502. Belknap, Michael R. "The Supreme Court Goes to War: The Meaning and Implications of the Nazi Saboteur Case," Military Law Review 89 (1980): 59-95.

A discussion of the Supreme Court case, Ex Parte Quirin (1942) and the role of wartime military commissions with jurisdiction over cases involving spying and trading with the enemy.

503. Belknap, Michael R. "Uncooperative Federalism:. The Failure of the Bureau of the Investigation Intergovernmental Attack on Radicalism," Publius 12/2 (Spring 1982): 25-47.

An interesting case of failure of intergovernmental work expectations. The Bureau believed that the State of Michigan was equally committed to the prosecution of persons suspected of communist affiliations. This is a case of the failure of cooperative federalism in law enforcement.

504. Belknap, Michael R. "Frankfurter and the Nazi Saboteurs. (Supreme Court Justice Felix Frankfurter)," Supreme Court Historical Society Yearbook (1982): 66-71.

An analysis and discussion of Frankfurters opposition to the Supreme Court's rejection of and appeal by 8 Nazi saboteurs during the Second World War.

505. Belknap, Michael R. "The Vindication of Burke Marshall: The Southern Legal System and the Anti-Civil Rights Violence of the 1960's," Emory Law Journal 33/1 (Winter 1984): 93-133.

Discusses mainly the policy position of the Justice Department regarding violence and the civil rights movement in the South in the 1960s. FBI opposition to direct involvement in law enforcement is also discussed. May be useful for those wishing to study the contradiction between FBI's opposition here and its activist role in spying on civil rights leaders.

506. Belknap, Michael R. "Above the Law and Beyond Its Reach: O'Reilly and Theoharis on FBI Intelligence Operations," American Bar Foundation Research Journal 1985 (Winter 1985): 201-215.

A book review essay on O'Reilly's, Hoover and the Un-Americans: The FBI, HUAC and the Red Menace (Philadelphia: Temple University, 1983) and Theoharis', Beyond the Hiss Case: The FBI, Congress and the Cold War (Philadelphia: Temple University, 1982).

507. Belkora, Jeff. "Belkoranic Hill Ciphering," Cryptologia 13/1 (January 1989): 43-49.

508. Bell, George. "The Background of the Hitler Plot," Contemporary Review 168 (1945): 203-208.

509. Bell, Griffen B. "Electronic Surveillance and the Free Society," St. Louis University Law Journal 23/1 (1979): 1-10.

Topic of the article is Electronic Surveillance Act of 1978 and whether safeguards are sufficient to prevent abuses by government, and whether Act limits or takes away inherent power of president, if any, to order surveillance. Addresses dilemma confronted by Attorney General in performing conflicting duties of law enforcement, apprehension of spies and protection of liberties. Discusses Senate Select Committee on Intelligence report in 1976 which concluded intelligence gathering was too broad in including persons who were not enemies.

510. Bell, Coral. "The October Middle East War: A Case Study in Crisis Management During Detente," International Affairs (Great Britain) 50/4 (October 1974): 531-543.

Explores the relationships between US and Soviet Union in the era of detente, and the impact these had on crises between the clients of these nations in the Middle East. Discusses Soviet bids for 'condominium'; early signals and Soviet views of detente are also discussed.

511. Bell, Daniel. "Ten Theories in Search of Reality: The Prediction of Soviet Behavior in the Social Sciences," World Politics 10/3 (April 1958): 327-365.

The author, an internationally recognized social theorist, examines ten discrete social theories of Soviet behavior: Anthropological; psychoanalytic; social system; ideal types; Marxist; neo-Marxist; totalitarian; Kremlinological; Slavic institutions; and geo-political. The author was a well-recognized urban sociologist in the 1950s.

512. Bell, J. Bowyer. "National Character and Military Strategy: The Egyptian Experience, October 1973," Parameters: Journal of the U.S. Army War College 5/1 (1975): 6-17.

Suggests that some generalizations about Egyptian national character have merit. Says Egyptians, prior to the 1973 war, were not oriented to accepting the realities of conflict with the Israelis, tending to elevate honor and national pride above capabilities.

513. Bell, J. Bowyer. "Aspects of the Dragonworld: Covert Communications and the Rebel Ecosystem," International Journal of Intelligence and Counter-intelligence 3/1 (Spring 1989): 15-44.
Rich analysis of the world and ecosystems of revolutionary and terrorist groups. Major sections discuss tradecraft in the dragonworld; consequences and sacrifices; the rebels arena; costs of covert communication; the core of covert communications; and conclusions about rebel organizations.

514. Bell, J. Bowyer. "Revolutionary Dynamics: The Inherent Inefficiency of the Underground," Terrorism and Political Violence 2/2 (Summer 1990): 193-211.

515. Bell, J. Bowyer. "Dragonworld (II): Deception, Tradecraft, and the Provisional IRA," International Journal of Intelligence and Counterintelligence 8/1 (Spring 1995): 21-50.
Continuation of the author's study of earlier eras of revolutionary organizations. Argues that effectiveness of these groups is balanced by an ecosystem that raises costs for persistence and efficiency in the long run. Major sections discuss the rebel ecosystem; shared characteristics; deception; rebels as covert actors; orthodox tradecraft; underground structure of deceptions; the Irish Republican Movement; the problem of the normal; tradecraft and transmission; and deception and counterdeception.

516. Bell, J. Bowyer. "The Armed Struggle and Underground Intelligence: An Overview," Studies in Conflict and Terrorism 17/2 (April-June 1994): 115-150.
Develops a conceptual interpretation of the role of intelligence in underground movements to bring about internal rebellion. Argues that the main focus of intelligence in rebel organizations is state organs and their security forces.

517. Bellemare, Daniel A. "L'Indemnisation des Victimes d'Interception ou de Divulgation," Revue Barreau Quebec 41 (May-June 1981): 355-358.

518. Bellemare, Daniel A. "La Partie IV.1 du Code Criminel et la Protection des Communications Privilegies de l'Avocat," Revue Barreau Quebec 44 (March-April 1984): 382-392.

519. Belleranti, Shirley W. "Code Talkers," Westways 75/5 (1983): 40-42, 76.
A discussion of the work of Navajo Code Talkers who developed secret communication codes for use in World War II, Korean and Vietnam wars.

520. Belote, James H. "The Lohmann Affair," Studies in Intelligence 4/1 (Spring 1960).

521. Bemis, Samuel F. "British Secret Service and the French-American Alliance," American Historical Review 29/3 (April 1924): 474-495.
A careful and classic treatment of the British attempts to use secret service operations to destroy the relationship between America and France during the American revolution.

522. Bemis, Samuel F. "Secret Intelligence, 1777: Two Documents," Huntington Library Quarterly 24/3 (1961): 233-249.
In the difficult days of the American revolution in 1777, the main British objective was to determine the amount and nature of French supplies leaving France for the colonies. The author provides a brief narration of the background, then presents two intelligence documents written by British spies to the Crown.

523. Benadom, Gregory A. and Robert U. Goehlert. "The CIA: Its History, Organization, Functions, and Publications," Government Publications Review 6/3 (1979): 195-212.
The title captures the content of this article. The main objective is to outline the publications of the CIA, including those most easily accessible and those which are difficult to acquire. Includes an extensive bibliography of CIA publications.

524. Bender, Edward J., Jr. "Maritime Terrorism: Are We Prepared?," American Intelligence Journal 5/2 (July 1983): 25-34.

525. Bender, Gerald J. "Angola, the Cubans, and American Anxieties," Foreign Policy 31 (Summer 1978): 3-30.
Discusses the Soviet and Cuban involvement in Angola and the impact of that combination of interests on US foreign policy before and during the Carter presidency. Useful for its insight into the deeper interpretations of proxy presence in contested interest areas.

526. Bender, Gerald J. "Angola: Left, Right and Wrong," Foreign Policy 43 (Summer 1981): 53-69.
Discusses the need for careful assessment of the facts about internal and external dynamics of Angola before setting course toward methods designed to yield even more confusion about US policy. Mentions the Reagan administration's proposal to change the Clark Amendment to permit covert actions to return to Angola.

527. Bendikson, L. "The Restoration of Obliterated Passages and of Secret Writing in Diplomatic Missives," Franco-American Review 1 (1937): 243-256.

Gives a scenario of the methods used by diplomats to communicate with colleagues via secret writing. Information on ways to decipher passages using light reflection and microscopy. Refers to John Jay's use of obliterated passages.

528. Bendiner, Robert. "Explaining What You Are After Is the Secret of Diplomacy," American Heritage 34/5 (May 1983): 48-55.
This is the author's article based on an interview with Henry A. Kissinger. Gives Kissinger's answers to questions about the foreign service, the role of the CIA in national security, rights of journalists, and the search for a coherent foreign policy. Discusses, also, the nature of secrecy in a democracy.

529. Ben-Israel, Isaac. "Philosophy and Methodology of Intelligence: The Logic of Estimate Process," Intelligence and National Security 4/4 (October 1989): 660-718.
Major sections discuss an apparent analogy between science and intelligence; a criteria of applicability; intelligence and the policy makers; truism and corruption of language: Are there no laws in social science? Considers several aspects of the role of social science in the intelligence process.

530. Bennett, Barbara. "The Melvin Adams Hall Papers," Princeton University Library Chronicle 53/2 (1992): 217-225.

531. Bennett, Burney B. "The Greater Barrier," Studies in Intelligence 2/3 (Fall 1958).

532. Bennett, Charles F. "The Mayaguez Re-Examined: Misperceptions in an Information Shortage," Fletcher Forum of World Affairs 1/1 (Fall 1976): 15-31.
An analysis of the Ford administration's failed attempts to rescue and retrieve the container ship Mayaguez. Particular emphasis place on the lack of information in the hands of the president.

533. Bennett, Colin. "From the Dark to the Light: The Open Government Debate in Britain," Journal of Public Policy 5 (May 1985): 187-213.
Efforts of the British government to loosen the secrecy restraints on government information. Discusses the basic values underlying the British secrecy system and the hindrances of secrecy in decision making.

534. Bennett, Donald G. "Spot Report: Intelligence, Vietnam," Military Review 46/8 (August 1966): 72-77.
Emphasizes the use of document sources in the tactical intelligence mission in South Vietnam. Other sources are discussed also.

535. Bennett, Donald H. "An Unsolved Puzzle Solved," Cryptologia 7/3 (July 1983): 218-234.

536. Bennett, Douglas J., Jr. "Congress in Foreign Policy: Who Needs It?," Foreign Affairs 57/1 (Fall 1978): 40-50.

The evolution of congressional involvement in foreign policy decision making is discussed, particularly dating from the Gulf of Tonkin resolution. Argues that the congressional role in foreign policy should continue. This is good background piece for historical discussions of the political atmosphere surrounding intelligence operations and policy in the l960s and 1970s.

537. Bennett, J. Bradley; George W. Bilicic Jr.; and James W. Black. "Electronic Surveillance. (Sixteenth Annual Review of Criminal Procedure: United States Supreme Court and Courts of Appeals 1985-1986)," Georgetown Law Journal 75 (February 1987): 790-817.

Discusses use of electronic surveillance in context of police practices and under requirements of Title III of the Omnibus Crime Control and Safe Streets Act of 1968. Reviews constraints of Title III and procedures for obtaining orders to permit such surveillance, including duties imposed after order is obtained and protective measures and remedies administered. Also includes exemptions of certain types of surveillance.

538. Bennett, James R. "Soviet Scholars Look at U.S. Media," Journal of Communication 36/1 (1986): 126-132.

Considers Central Intelligence Agency secrecy and control of the media within the framework of a larger emporium of the United States and Soviet Union media systems.

539. Bennett, James R. "The Agencies of Secrecy: A Bibliographic Guide to the U.S. Intelligence Apparatus," National Reporter 9/3-4 (1986): 41-47.

540. Bennett, John. "Analysis of Encryption Algorithm Used in Word Perfect Word Processing Program," Cryptologia 11/4 (October 1987): 206-210.

541. Bennett, Ralph. "Ultra and Some Command Divisions," Journal of Contemporary History 16/1 (January 1981): 131-151.

The role of the ULTRA breakthrough in benefitting the Allies in World War II, especially in breaking German codes pertaining to decisions at a level just below grand strategy. Accounts also for the two major failings in the full use of ULTRA: inexperience and inability to comprehend ULTRA. Draws on excellent sources.

542. Bennett, Ralph. "Knight's Move at Drvar: Ultra and the Attempt on Tito's Life, 25 May 1944," Journal of Contemporary History 22/2 (April 1987): 195-208.

An account of the German surprise attack on Drvar. Yugoslavia's Marshal Josip Tito held out for victory as discussed along with the future of Ultra.

543. Bennett, Ralph. "World War II Intelligence: The Last 10 Years' Work Reviewed," Defense Analysis 3/2 (June 1987): 103-117.

An overview of the major British literature on intelligence topics since World War II. Notes the trends to focus on the institutions of intelligence gathering, and the isolation of intelligence in the accounts of the major civilian and military leaders in crises situations.

544. Bennett, Ralph. "The 'Vienna Alternative', 1944: Reality or Illusion?," Intelligence and National Security 3/2 (April 1988): 251-271.

A case study of the situation in which intelligence and policy moved in opposite directions, in particular reference to Field Marshal Earl Alexander's proposal in 1944 to strike from the head of the Adriatic towards Vienna. The record of intelligence involvement in the outcome of proposal is thin. The author argues that the rejection of the plan resulted from the dominance of one view over another in the persistent Allied strategy debate.

545. Bennett, Ralph. "Fortitude, Ultra and the 'Need to Know,'" Intelligence and National Security 4/3 (July 1989): 482-502.

Examines the intelligence art of deception and misdirection by means of offensive and counter-offensive actions. Uses the intelligence offensive 'Fortitude' to outline main points. Fortitude refers to American and Soviet counterintelligence against Nazi Germany in World War II.

546. Bennett, Ralph. "Intelligence and Strategy: Some Obversations on the War in the Mediterranean," Intelligence and National Security 5/2 (April 1990): 444-464.

The author summarizes his conclusions drawn in a book titled Ultra and Mediterranean Strategy, observing in particular the need for thorough preparation of intelligence officers.

547. Bennett, Ralph. "A Footnote to Fortitude," Intelligence and National Security 6/1 (January 1991): 240-241.

A translation of what the author considers to be even more evidence that the Germans expected a US/Allied invasion through Denmark in January 1945. A small piece of literature on deception.

548. Bennett, Ralph; William Deakin; David Hunt; and Peter Wilkinson. "Mihailovic and Tito," Intelligence and National Security 10/3 (July 1995): 527-529.

Brief discussion by the authors, all of whom were intelligence officers in World War II, with special knowledge of the relationship between the subjects.

549. Bennett, Sherrie L. "The Broadening of the Pentagon Papers Standard: An Impermissible Misapplication of the National Security Exception to the Prior

Restraint Doctrine," <u>University of Puget Sound Law Review</u> 4 (Fall 1980): 123-142.

      Discusses the evolution of the Pentagon Papers standard, the Marchetti case, the Progressive case, and the author's application of the 'Papers' standard. some good notes to begin research on these cases.

550. Bennett, William R. "Secret Telephony as a Historical Example of Spread-Spectrum Communication," <u>IEEE Transactions on Communications</u> 31 (January 1983): 98-104.

551. Benson, Raymond. "On the Trail of Ian Fleming," <u>Dossier: The Official Journal of the International Spy Society</u> 6 (November 1983): 22-23.

552. Benson, Robert L. "Early Efforts (and Failures) in Joint Intelligence: A Shaky Beginning," <u>Joint Perspectives</u> (Fall 1980).

553. Benson, Sumner. "The Historian as Foreign Policy Analyst: The Challenge of the CIA," <u>Public Historian</u> 3/1 (Winter 1981): 15-25.

554. Benson, Sumner. "The Impact of Technology Transfer on the Military Balance," <u>Air University Review</u> 36/1 (November-December 1984): 4-15.

555. Bentley, Hannah. "Keeping Secrets: The Church Committee, Covert Action, and Nicaragua," <u>Columbia Journal of Transnational Law</u> 25 (Summer 1987): 601-645.

      Using Iran-Contra as a backdrop case, author discusses constitutional bases of covert action prior to 1974, including presidential authority, the National Security Act of 1947, and acquiescence by Congress. Then discusses Hughes-Ryan Amendment of 1974. Continues with topics including congressional oversight, executive control, War Powers Resolution, and changes initiated by Intelligence Oversight Act of 1980. Concludes with review of developments leading to Iran-Contra affair.

556. Benyon, John. "Policing the European Union: The Changing Basis of Cooperation on Law Enforcement," <u>International Affairs</u> (Great Britain) 70/3 (1994): 497-517.

      Discusses cross-border crime in Europe; immigration and the "ring of steel" at the external frontiers; levels of police cooperation, including intelligence; arrangements for police cooperation; other structures for police cooperation; and obstacles for further development here.

557. Ben-Zvi, Abraham. "American Preconceptions and Policies Toward Japan, 1940-1941: A Case Study in Misperception," <u>International Studies Quarterly</u> 19/2 (June 1975): 228-248.

Offers three categories of American policymakers in the period of 1940-41: the globalist-realist; the globalist-idealist; and the nationalist-pragmatist.

558. Ben-Zvi, Abraham. "Hindsight and Foresight: A Conceptual Framework for Analysis of Surprise Attacks," World Politics 28/3 (April 1976): 381-395.

Acknowledges the contribution of Wohlstetter's Pearl Harbor: Warning and Decision, and sets out to theorize about expectations and surprise. Contains a theoretical framework and a series of variables important for analyzing surprise in warfare.

559. Ben-Zvi, Abraham. "Misperceiving the Role of Perception: A Critique," Jerusalem Journal of International Relations 2/2 (Winter 1976-1977): 74-93.

Examines series of studies designed to explain perceptual predispositions and their relationships to the inability of nations to predict impending attack.

560. Ben-Zvi, Abraham. "The Outbreak and Termination of the Pacific War: A Juxtaposition of American Preconceptions," Journal of Peace Research 15/1 (1978): 33-49.

Argues that US policymakers chose opted to give greater credibility to their strategic assumptions and interests than to tactical field information in the months and years preceding the war. This study compares preconceptions regarding Japanese capabilities with outcomes of the war on the Japanese side. An excellent piece of research for those studying perceptions and misperceptions.

561. Ben-Zvi, Abraham. "The Study of Surprise Attacks," British Journal of International Studies 5/2 (1979): 129-149.

A study of the surprise attacks at Pearl Harbor, in the Korean War and in the Arab-Israeli war of 1967. Concludes that particular schools of thought about surprise have not adequately accommodated all the elements of surprise found in these cases.

562. Ben-Zvi, Abraham. "Perception, Action and Reaction: A Comparative Analysis of Decision-Making Processes in Bilateral Conflicts," Journal of Political Science 7/2 (1980): 95-111.

Argues that decisionmakers respond to crises on the basis of their preconceptions rather than upon reality. Uses the Arab-Israeli wars of 1967 and 1973 and the war between the US and Japan as laboratories for testing the theory.

563. Ben-Zvi, Abraham. "Between Warning and Response: The Case of the Yom Kippur War," International Journal of Intelligence and Counterintelligence 4/2 (Summer 1990): 227-242.

Reviews the theory of surprise attacks and their warnings. Major sections discuss misperception and surprise; the distinctive nature of surprise; the Yom Kippur surprise; political versus military response; and conclusions regarding the nature of misperceptions prior to the Yom Kippur war.

564. Bequai, August. "Management Can Prevent Industrial Espionage," Advanced Management Journal 50/1 (Winter 1995): 17-19.

565. Berardino, Dick. The G-2 GS 1942-1944," American Intelligence Journal 4/4 (September 1982): 24-26.

566. Berch, Michael A. "Money Damages for Fourth Amendment Violations by Federal Official: An Explanation of Bivens v. Six Unknown Named Agents of Federal Bureau of Narcotics," Law and Social Order 1971/1 (1971): 43-63.
    Discusses claim of money damages based on unreasonable search and seizure by federal officers. In Bivens, Court held action was an implied right under the Fourth Amendment. Case did not decide issues on immunity of limits of action.

567. Berens, John F. "The FBI and Civil Liberties from Franklin Roosevelt to Jimmy Carter: An Historical Review," Michigan Academician 13/2 (1980): 131-144.
    Simply a history of the subject, focussing on Roosevelt's charge to the FBI to enter the domestic intelligence field.

568. Beres, Louis R. "On Assassination as Anticipatory Self-Defense: The Case of Israel," Hofstra Law Review 20/2 (Winter 1991): 321-340.
    Aside from this article, this author is a distinguished scholar of the self-defense issue as it is considered in the Middle East and Israeli contexts. See any social science or law index system for a complete collection of journal references. The below listed citation contains a substantial number of his citations. This self-defense issue is addressed in several articles by this author.

569. Beres, Louis R. "The Iranian Threat to Israel: Capabilities and Intentions," International Journal of Intelligence and Counterintelligence 9/1 (Spring 1996): 51-61.
    Major sections the author's theory of the situation; political bluster and synergy; Palestinian separatism; the first move; responding to initiatives; and a dialectic of thoughts.

570. Beres, Louis R. "Intelligence and Nuclear Terrorism: Preventing 'Pain into Power,'" International Journal of Intelligence and Counterintelligence 9/2 (Summer 1996): 159-167.
    Author introduces a series of questions that need to be asked by intelligence and other personnel in the development of a strategy of counternuclear terrorism. Other major sections consider turning pain in power; and the "healing medicine."

571. Beresford, Spencer M. "Surveillance Aircraft and Satellites: A Problem of International Law," Journal of Air Law and Commerce 27/2 (Spring 1960): 107-118.

Author addresses need for agreements similar to international flight agreements to govern air sovereignty over "outer space," and need for determination of boundary between "airspace" and "outer space."

572. Beresford, C. F. "Tactics as Affected by Field Telegraphy," Journal of the Royal United Service Institute 31 (1887).

573. Berezhkov, Valentin. "Stalin's Error of Judgement," International Affairs (USSR) (August 1989): 13-26.

574. Bergbauer, F. "Recruiting and Administering Police Undercover Agents, Legal Problems--West Germany," Kriminalist 8/10-11 (October and November 1976): 607-608; 610-613.

This is a two-part article on instructions for managing undercover operations of the German Police. Methods of the operations are also discussed and recommendations are offered.

575. Berger, Raoul. "War, Foreign Affairs, and Executive Secrecy," Northwestern University Law Review 72/3 (July-August 1977): 309-345.

Compares constitutional practices related to secrecy in the US and Britain. Evaluates executive and legislative powers regarding secrecy. Observes the negative aspects of power fragmentation in foreign policy. Calls for constitutional revisions to address tensions between President and Congress over secrecy.

576. Bergeron, Arthur, Jr. "Robert C. Kennedy: Louisiana Confederate Secret Agent," Revista de Louisiane 6/2 (1977): 135-145.

577. Bergonzi, Bernard. "The Case of Mr. Fleming," Twentieth Century (March 1958): 288-289.

578. Bergstrom, Robert L. "The Applicability of the "New" Fourth Amendment to Investigations by Secret Agents: A Proposed Deliberation of the Emerging Fourth Amendment Rights to Privacy," Washington Law Review 45/4 (June 1970): 785-815.

Discusses the Constitution and secret agents, the application of the Fourth Amendment, the development of a privacy model, secret agents in the Supreme Court, and secret agents and the privacy model.

579. Berkeley, Bill. "Warlords of Natal," Atlantic Monthly 273/3 (March 1994): 85-100.

580. Berkner, Lloyd V. "Earth Satellites and Foreign Policy," Foreign Affairs 36/2 (January 1958): 221-231.

An early analysis of the symbol of military progress and intellectual growth in the development of earth satellites. Compares American and Soviet scientific styles in approaching the intellectual race to space.

581. Berkovits, Shimshon. "Factoring Via Superencryption," Cryptologia 6/3 (July 1982): 229-237.

582. Berkowitz, Bruce D. "A New Role for Intelligence in Arms Control," Studies in Intelligence 29/1 (Spring 1985).

583. Berkowitz, Bruce D. "Intelligence in the Organizational Context: Coordination and Error in National Estimates," Orbis 29/3 (Fall 1985): 571-596.

Addresses the problem of predicting the number of Soviet ICBM's that could be deployed in near-future years. Focuses on coordination of estimates within the intelligence community. Demonstrates that the coordination process produces error, and that some organizational problems which have produced error may be predictable.

584. Berkowitz, Bruce D. "Congressional Oversight of Intelligence," Studies in Intelligence 30/2 (Summer 1986).

585. Berkowitz, Bruce D. and Allen E. Goodman. "Why Spy--and How--in the 1990s," Orbis 36/2 (Spring 1992): 269-280.

Discusses the continuing need for intelligence collection, analysis and dissemination to policy makers in a new world replete with ethnic, military and resource conflicts. Discusses some recommendations for establishing the structural ingredients for new effectiveness in intelligence work.

586. Berkowitz, Bruce D. and Jeffrey T. Richelson. "The CIA Vindicated: The Soviet Collapse Was Predicted," National Interest 419 (Fall 1995): 36-47.

Challenges the notion that the CIA had failed to predict the downfall of the Soviet Union.

587. Berkowitz, Marc J. "Soviet Naval Spetsnaz Forces," Naval War College Review 41 (Spring 1988): 5-21.

One of few articles on this subject.

588. Berle, A. A., Jr. "The Protection of Privacy," Political Science Quarterly 79 (1964): 162-168.

589. Berlet, Chip. "Frank Donner: An Appreciation," Covert Action Quarterly 53 (Summer 1995): 17-19.

This is a remembrance of the principles and chief writings of Professor Frank Donner and his work to highlight the domestic excesses of the investigative, intelligence and police agencies of the US.

590. Berlin, Don L. "Why Intelligence Estimates Won't Mislead Us Anymore," Defense Intelligence Journal 3/2 (Fall 1994): 21-36.

Discusses forecasting in defense intelligence; differences between past and current defense intelligence forecasting needs; previous experience with misleading estimates; the alternative futures approach; and other important considerations.

591. Berman, Jerry J. "FBI Charter Legislation: The Case for Prohibiting Domestic Intelligence Investigations," University of Detroit Journal of Urban Law 55/4 (Summer 1978): 1041-1077.

Charter legislation to regulate FBI intelligence operations is defended as a means of protecting civil rights of political dissenters. Case law examples are offered as evidence of abuse of intelligence role of FBI.

592. Berman, Jerry J. and Morton H. Halperin. "Protecting Our Freedoms," Society 19/3 (March-April 1982): 71-75.

Discusses fears of Senate bill 391, the National Security Act Amendment, making it unlawful for any present or past government employee to reveal the identity of intelligence agents and intelligence relationships overseas. Authors argue that the bill would introduce serious First Amendment concerns.

593. Berman, Sylvan M. "The 1976 Israeli Attack on the American Electronic Spy Ship Revisited: An Historical Note," International Problems 18/3 & 4 (1979): 59-63.

The author offers a retort to criticisms of the Israeli attack offered by Richard K. Smith and Smith Hempstone.

594. Bermingham, John. "Ruse de Guerre," U.S. Naval Institute Proceedings (August 1938): 1156-1161.

595. Bermudez, Joseph S., Jr. "North Korea's Intelligence Agencies and Infiltration Services," Jane's Intelligence Review 3/6 (June 1991): 269-277.

Discusses in some detail the operations of the North Korean intelligence services, and the equipment, organization and training of these functions targeted mainly at Japan and South Korea.

596. Bernard, Paul P. "Kaunitz and Austria's Secret Fund," East European Quarterly 16/2 (Summer 1982): 129-136.

597. Berner, Richard O. "The Effects of the 1976 Amendment to Exemption

Three of the Freedom of Information Act," Columbia Law Review 1976/6 (1976): 1029-1047.

Provides a framework for determining whether a nondisclosure statute qualifies as an exempting statute under exemption 3.   Contains judicial interpretations of exemption 3 of the FOIA, analyzes the Robertson case applications, legislative history of exemption 3, and approaches to problems of interpretation.

598. Bernstein, Barton J. "Roosevelt, Truman, and the Atomic Bomb, 1941-1945: A Reinterpretation," Political Science Quarterly 90/1 (Spring 1975): 23-69.

A detailed examination of the background conditions and circumstances under which the two presidents decided to build and deploy the atomic bomb. Major sections discuss Roosevelt and the bomb; Truman and the bomb; leaving open the options for atomic diplomacy; the bomb and dealing with the Soviets; alternatives to the use of the bomb; why the bomb was used; atomic diplomacy after Hiroshima; and the bomb and the Cold War.

599. Bernstein, Barton J. "The Week We Almost Went to War," Bulletin of the Atomic Scientists 32 (February 1976): 13-21.

Argues that the Cuban missile crisis may have been an unnecessary risk for the United States. Sections discuss President John Kennedy's decision; the blockade of Soviet Union's ships; the ExComm's analysis; personalities and politics surrounding the leadership in each country; missiles in Turkey; perils of invasion and war; and costs of victory.

600. Bernstein, Barton J. "The Road to Watergate and Beyond: The Growth and Abuse of Executive Authority Since 1940," Law and Contemporary Problems 40/2 (Spring 1976): 58-86.

Article asserts that Watergate was the culmination of the growth of presidential power. Includes discussion of the lack of expectation that Watergate would unravel this power, erosion of civil liberties, growth of abuse of executive power in foreign affairs.   Asks whether the system has been transformed. Discusses FBI and CIA.

601. Bernstein, Barton J. "The Week We Almost Went to War: American Intervention in the Korean Civil War," (Part I and II) Foreign Service Journal 54/1 & 54/2 (1977): 6-9, 33-35; 8-11, 33-34.

This two-part feature article follows on similar work by the author concerning the Cuban missile crisis. Includes discussion of the United Nations coalition, background political concerns, Soviet intentions, and the US policy process. Intelligence is mentioned in connection with the policy process. The author says that the US would have been wise to have stayed out of the contest to save South Korea.

602. Bernstein, Barton J. "The Cuban Missile Crisis: Trading the Jupiters in Turkey?," Political Science Quarterly 95/1 (Spring 1980): 97-126.

Based on then recently released documents, article concludes that President Kennedy was partly responsible for installing missiles in Turkey and that Kennedy and some of his advisers were more flexible on negotiating about those missiles than was earlier credited.

603. Bernstein, Barton J. "Truman at Potsdam: His Secret Diary," Foreign Service Journal 57/7 (July-August 1980): 29-36.

Observes conditions and issues surrounding President Truman's diary notes regarding his seven-day visit with Stalin, the plan to use the atomic bomb against Japan, and the rationale for using the bomb. Diary covers the period of July 16-30, 1945.

604. Bernstein, Barton J. "Truman's Secret Thoughts on Ending the Korean War," Foreign Service Journal 57/10 (November 1980): 31-33, 44.

Discusses the contents of three documents from the Truman presidency which tend to demonstrate Truman's frustration with the Korean war, including the potential for expanding the war to China and implementing a sea blockade of the North. Good background piece for intelligence histories of the Truman era.

605. Bernstein, Barton J. "Nuclear Deception: The U.S. Record," Bulletin of the Atomic Scientists 43/7 (1986): 40-43.

Discusses US cover-up of its nuclear program, including intentional and unintentional release of radiation into the air and water.

606. Bernstein, Barton J. "Churchill's Secret Biological Weapons," Bulletin of the Atomic Scientists 43/1 (January-February 1987): 46-50.

Argues that the fear of German retaliation was uppermost in containing Britain's plans to use biological weapons in World War II. Refers to intelligence services work on this subject.

607. Bernstein, Barton J. "Commentary: Reconsidering Krushchev's Gambit--Defending the Soviet Union and Cuba," Diplomatic History 14/2 (Spring 1990): 231-239.

Argues that more attention has been given to President Kennedy's decisions in the Cuban missile crisis than has been given to Soviet intentions, politics and problems. Neither the US nor the USSR realized the danger in the emerging crisis.

608. Bernstein, Cyrus. "The Saboteur Trial: A Case History," George Washington Law Review 11/2 (February 1943): 131-190.

Reviews the history of the case of eight German soldiers who entered the US by submarine in 1942 on a mission of wartime sabotage. Major sections discuss the federal investigation of the mission; the petitioners' contentions; the respondent's contentions; argument before the Supreme Court; Supreme Court opinion; and denouement.

609. Bernstein, Daniel. "The Defrocking of Tom Dooley: A Biographical Sketch," Gateway Heritage 9/3 (1988-1989): 28-37.

610. Bernthal, Craig A. "Treason in the Family: The Trial of Thumpe v. Horner," Shakespeare Quarterly 42 (Spring 1991): 44-54.

611. Berresford, John W.. "Whittaker Chambers and Alger Hiss: The Courts Decide; A Look at the Court's Decisions within the Larger Story," Federal Bar News & Journal 40 (February 1993): 96-108.
    Examines court decisions including roles of evidence, strategy, political issues, and psychology. Topics covered include background, Chambers' deposition, testimony (both of Hede Massing and concerning the mental condition of Chambers), Hiss's petition to reopen the case, and a conclusion that still sees Hiss as guilty.

612. Berridge, G. R. "The Ethnic 'Agent in Place': English-Speaking Civil Servants and Nationalist South Africa 1948-57," Intelligence and National Security 4/2 (April 1989): 257-267.
    Discusses the sensitive position and use of intelligence agents in place in foreign countries, as suggested by the espionage case of Jonathan Pollard. Includes several case examples to argue the vulnerability of such agents. Will become a useful reference article in the current debate about Pollard.

613. Berry, A. G. "The Beginning of the Office of Naval Intelligence," U.S. Naval Institute Proceedings 63 (January 1937): 102-103.

614. Berry, F. Clifton, Jr. and Deborah Kyle. "The 'Other Cabinet': The National Security Council Staff," Armed Forces Journal International 114 (July 1977): 12-20.

615. Berry, Neil. "Encounter," Antioch Review 51/2 (Spring 1993): 194-211.
    A rich analysis of the periodical, Encounter, once clandestinely sponsored by the CIA, says the author. The periodical ceased publication in 1991.

616. Berry, Peter T. and Donna B. Miles. "Operation Desert Shield/Desert Storm: The CID's Law Enforcement Role," Police Chief 58/10 (October 1991): 86, 88.

617. Berry, Steven J. "Criminal Law - Search and Seizure - Monitoring of Beeper Signal Emanating from Private Residence Violates Fourth Amendment

Rights of Those Who Have An Expectation of Privacy in the Home," St. Mary's Law Journal 16/3 (Summer 1985): 709-729.

Discusses U. S. v. Karo, where Supreme Court held no warrant was needed where beeper was installed with original owner's consent, even as to subsequent owners, but that warrantless monitoring of beeper in a home is a violation of Fourth Amendment privacy rights.

618. Bertelsman, William O. "The Challenge of Our Constitution" (Bicentennial Issue: Celebrating 200 Years of Democracy), Kentucky Bench and Bar 51 (Fall 1987): 44-46.

A brief discussion of the early American history of treason and the US Constitution.

619. Bessette, Carol S. "An Intelligence Tour of World War II England," American Intelligence Journal 9/3 (Fall 1988).

620. Bethe, Hans A.; Kurt Gottfried; and Roald Sagdeev. "Did Bohr Share Nuclear Secrets?," Scientific American 272 (May 1995): 84-90.

621. Bethel, Elizabeth. "The Military Information Division: Origin of the Intelligence Division," Military Affairs 11/1 (Spring 1947): 17-24.

A brief history of the origins of the M. I. D. in 1885.

622. Bethell, Nicholas. "After 'The Last Secret,'" Encounter 45 (November 1975): 82-88.

Discusses the escape of Russian Cossacks, who subsequently aided the German cause in World War II, but also who were sacrificed to save American POW's. Evaluates the moral versus political issues involved.

623. Bethell, Nicholas, "The Klagenfurt Conspiracy: War Crimes and Diplomatic Secrets," Encounter 60 (May 1983): 24-37.

Discusses Prime Minister Macmillan's policy to return Croat and Serbian escapee emigres from Tito's Yugoslavia, most of whom were subsequently executed. Sections discuss the prison camps, the massacre at Korevje; Tito's pressure on the British; and the Macmillan policy failure.

624. Bethell, Thomas N. "The Mailer-CIA Connection," Washington Monthly 8 (October 1976): 54-59.

A summary of author Norman Mailer's criticisms of CIA and FBI involvement in the Watergate affair.

625. Bethell, Thomas N. "The Spy Who Went Out in the Cold: The Problem of Choosing Wars Wisely," Washington Monthly 12/3 (March 1980): 28-41.

A book review essay developed around Thomas Powers' award-winning book, The Man Who Kept the Secrets: Richard Helms and the CIA.

626. Bethell, Thomas N. and Charles Peters. "The Imperial Press," Washington Monthly 8/9 (1976): 28-34.

  An analysis of the House Ethics Committee investigation of reporter Daniel Schorr's leak of information asserted to be vital to national security.

627. Betts, Richard K. "Analysis, War and Decision: Why Intelligence Allures Are Inevitable," World Politics 31 (Spring 1978): 61-89.

  Clearly, one of the most scholarly treatments ever in journal form of the intelligence analysis process. Argues that intelligence can be improved marginally, but not radically, by changing the analytical process. This article was reprinted in CIA's Studies in Intelligence 23/3 (Fall 1979).

628. Betts, Richard K. "Intelligence for Policymaking," Washington Quarterly 3/3 (Summer 1980): 118-129.

  Argues that intelligence plays an important role in the policy making process, mainly in the realm of minimizing error. Improved organization and coordination of the intelligence community can result in improved foreign policy decisions.

629. Betts, Richard K. "Strategic Intelligence Estimates: Let's Make Them Useful," Parameters: Journal of the U.S. Army War College 10/4 (December 1980): 20-26.

  Describes the author's objections to the manner in which the intelligence community, especially the Central Intelligence Agency, compiles National Intelligence Estimates (NIE's). He suggests that the organizational structure of the community limits the degree to which creativity and speculation can be imparted in the estimates. Creativity and speculation are necessary adjuncts to improved estimates. This piece was reprinted in CIA's Studies in Intelligence 25/1 (Spring 1981).

630. Betts, Richard K. "Surprise Despite Warning: Why Sudden Attacks Succeed," Political Science Quarterly 95/4 (Winter 1980-1981): 551-572.

  Discusses intelligence and warning; obstacles to warning; limits to predictability; indecision, false alerts and fluctuation; deferring decisions; deception; circumvention; technical surprise; doctrinal surprise.

631. Betts, Richard K. "Nuclear Surprise Attack: Deterrence, Defense and Conceptual Contradictions in American Policy," Jerusalem Journal of International Relations 5/3 (1981): 73-99.

  Discusses background and catalysts of a nuclear threat, surprise, soviet views, Soviet incentives for surprise, escalation, doctrines, self-surprise, theater dilemmas, chemical warfare, and current conditions.

632. Betts, Richard K. "Surprise Attack: NATO's Political Vulnerability," International Security 5/4 (Spring 1981): 117-149.

Discusses the position of NATO in the case of a Soviet attack on Western forces in terms of the prelude to surprise, compound crises, Soviet defensive surprise, preemptive attack, and preventive war.

633. Betts, Richard K. "Hedging Against Surprise Attacks," Survival 23/4 (July-August 1981): 146-156.

Argues that NATO responses to warnings of attack ought to be structured, and that more could be done to structure forces and encourage arms control negotiations to lessen the probability of surprise attack.

634. Betts, Richard K. "Warning Dilemmas: Normal Theory vs. Exceptional Theory," Orbis 26/4 (Winter 1983): 828-833.

Discusses the significant differences between normal analyses in regard to future objectives of an enemy from the exceptional conditions that may reasonably call for a warning of impending attack. Includes evaluation of normal theory, exceptional theory, and the 'cry wolf' condition.

635. Betts, Richard K. "Conventional Deterrence: Predictive Uncertainty and Policy Confidence," World Politics 37/2 (January 1985): 153-178.

Discusses the role and performance of NATO forces in the overall deterrence equation.

636. Betts, Richard K. "Policy-makers and Intelligence Analysts: Love, Hate or Indifference?," Intelligence and National Security 3/1 (January 1988): 184-189.

Considers the subject in terms of accuracy versus influence; combination of functions; managing politicization; and marketing.

637. Betts, Richard K. "Surprise, Scholasticism and Strategy: A Review of Ariel Levite's Intelligence and Strategic Surprise," International Studies Quarterly 33/3 (September 1989): 329-343.

Levite's book was published by Columbia University in 1987. Betts says it is the first serious revisionist examination of the dominant theories of strategic surprise. Betts suggests that is fails, however, because the methodology artificially narrows the issue, "excludes essential political variables, relies on faulty definitions and standards of comparison, and does not support the assumption that the analysis of success in wartime intelligence would apply to decisions in pre-war crises."

638. Betts, T. J. "Operation Columba," Studies in Intelligence 5/2 (Spring 1961).

639. Bevan, Vaughan. "Is Anybody There? Malone v. Commissioner of Police (1979)," Public Law (Winter 1980): 431-453.

Discussion of English law of "telephone tapping," including extent and need. Author argues that neither theory nor practice has proved its necessity and it ought to be disallowed.   Discusses major British case of Malone v. Commissioner of the Police for the Metropolis, which permitted tapping. Author contends there are several grounds for prohibiting tapping, including the European Convention on Human Rights. Then discusses controls necessary if tapping is to be permitted, whether controls should apply in case involving national security, exclusionary rule of England, and response by government. An exceptionally good insight into British approaches to the telephone tap issue.

640. Bevilacqua, Allan C. "Beating the Drum for Intelligence," Marine Corps Gazette 55 (September 1971): 33-36.
    Discusses the role of intelligence in the Marine Corps.

641. Bevilacqua, Allan C. "Intelligence and Insurgency," Marine Corps Gazette 44 (January 1960): 40-46.

642. Bevilacqua, Allan C. "Intelligence Made Easy," Marine Corps Gazette 64 (October 1980): 54-59.

643. Bevilacqua, Allan C. "Combat Intelligence in a Maneuver Environment," Marine Corps Gazette 69 (July 1985): 60-65.

644. Beyea, Richard S., Jr. "Security Countermeasures: The 'Prodigal Son' of Counterintelligence," American Intelligence Journal 10/2 (1989): 25-27.

645. Beymer, William G. "Timothy Webster, Spy," Harper's 121 (October 1910): 761-772.
    An account of Webster's work for Allan Pinkerton, in particular, his role as a double agent for the North during the Civil War.

646. Beymer, William G. "Miss Van Lew," Harper's 122 (June 1911): 86-99.
    An account of the life and Civil War espionage work for the Union of Miss Van Lew. Includes discussion of her tradecraft and her contributions to the Northern cause.

647. Beymer, William G. "Phillipses: Father and Son," Harper's 123 (October 1911): 743-753.
    An account of the Phillips family espionage methods for the Union during the Civil War. Neither father nor son were captured before the surrender at Appomattox.

648. Beymer, William G. "Mrs. Greenhow, Confederate Spy," Harper's 124 (March 1912): 563-576.

Activities of the Confederate spy, Mrs. Greenhow. She had access to social circles in Washington, maintained communications even after her capture by Allan Pinkerton, and may have continued to spying after her release from prison.

649. Bialer, Uri. "Telling the Truth to People: Britain's Decision to Publish the Diplomatic Papers of the Inter-War Period," Historical Journal 26/2 (June 1983): 349-367.

A discussion of the British publication of documents concerning war appeasement efforts in the interwar years, 1919-1939, and the controversies surrounding the opening of these records.

650. Bialer, Uri. "The Iranian Connection in Israel's Foreign Policy, 1948-1951," Middle East Journal 39/2 (Spring 1985): 292-315.

651. Biard, Forrester R. "The Pacific War Through the Eyes of Forrester R. 'Tex' Biard," Cryptolog 10/2 (1989): entire issue.

652. Biddiscombe, Perry. "Operation Selection Board: The Growth and Suppression of the Neo-Nazi 'Deutsche Revolution,'" Intelligence and National Security 11/1 (January 1996): 59-77.

Contributes to our understanding of the survival of some Nazi revolutionary movements in Germany after the end of World War II in defiance of occupation forces. This article reports on the third tier groups, or groups characterized by a relatively advanced political program.

653. Biddle, Francis. "Sickness of Fear: The Larger Meaning of Loyalty Investigations and Their Impact on Traditional Free Thought," Bulletin of the Atomic Scientists 7 (November 1951): 323-326, 336.

A brief overview of the federal loyalty security program and the implications of the program for scientists. Major sections discuss the disloyal scientist; loyalty programs; registration; loyalty and conformity; and thought control.

654. Biddle, W. Craig. "Court-Supervised Electronic Searches: A Proposed Statute for California," Pacific Law Journal 1 (1970): 97-132.

Discusses requirements of Title III if the Safe Streets Act of 1968, relating to electronic surveillance. Includes reviews of case law prior to enactment of Title III. Continues with proposal for California statute, analyzing compliance with strictures of Title III and concluding proposed law exceeds minimum standards of compliance. Includes appendix with text of proposed statute.

655. Bigel, Alan I. "The First Amendment and National Security: The Court

Responds to Governmental Harassment of Alleged Communist Sympathizers," Ohio Northern University Law Review 19/4 (1993): 885-926.

Explores congressional and state investigations of alleged Communist Party members and activities; federal loyalty program and loyalty oaths as a condition of employment; the right of alleged party members to remain in the US and to travel abroad; and conclusions.

656. Bigelow, Michael E. "The Apache Campaigns Under General Crook: A Historical Perspective on Low-Intensity Conflict," Military Intelligence 16/3 (July-September 1990): 38-40.

A brief discussion of General Crook's applications of fighting strategies suited for countering the Apaches. Considers the role of intelligence in terrain analysis.   Relevent to modern studies of low intensity conflicts.   A rare consideration of intelligence aspects of the wars against Native Americans.

657. Bigelow, Michael E. "Van Deman," Military Intelligence 16/4 (1990): 38-40.

Discusses the life of Ralph Van Deman, in particular, his leadership and commitment to encouraging the development of Army intelligence prior to World War I.

658. Bigelow, Michael E. "Disaster Along the Ch'ongch'on: Intelligence Breakdown in Korea," Military Intelligence 18/3 (July-September 1992): 11-16.

The failures of American intelligence during the Korean war are summarized: lack of human intelligence and heavy dependence on a limited supply of prisoner interrogation and air surveillance.

659. Bill, James A. "Iran and the Crisis of '78," Foreign Affairs 57/2 (Winter 1978-1979): 323-342.

Evaluates the stability of the Shah's regime, growing internal tensions, the Shah's policies, opposition forces, American contribution to instability, and possible solutions and outcomes.

660. Billik, B. H. and H. L. Roth. "On the Logical Establishment of Global Surveillance and Communication Nets," Journal of Astronautical Sciences 12 (Fall 1965): 88-99.

661. Bimmerle, George. "'Truth' Drugs in Interrogation," Studies in Intelligence 5/2 (Spring 1961): 1-19.

662. Bindler, Susan. "Peek and Spy: A Proposal for Federal Regulations of Electronic Monitoring in the Work Place," Washington University Law Quarterly 70 (Fall 1992): 853-885.

Discusses "business-extension" and "consent" exemptions under Title III of the Safe Streets Act of 1968 which permit employers to monitor conversations of employees. Contends that courts have been troubled in interpreting exemptions and that such interpretations could result in civil or criminal liability for employers. Further discusses then-proposed "Privacy for Consumers and Workers Act." Critiques both the Title III exemptions and the proposed act, proposing instead, federal regulation of such monitoring. Argues that legislation should focus on granting specific rights to employees, rather than on methods and equipment.

663. Bing, Jon. "Reflections on Data Protection Policy," Yearbook of Law, Computers & Technology," 5 (1991): 164-179.

664. Bingham, Woodbridge. "Historical Training and Military Intelligence: Value of Trained Historians in the World War," Pacific Historical Review 15 (June 1946): 201-206.
    Describes the role of scholarly training that proved valuable during World War II to advance the successes of military intelligence.

665. Bird, Kai. "The Decline of Dissent," Foreign Service Journal 62/2 (February 1985): 26-31.
    Addresses the system established in 1971 by which Foreign Service Officers in analytical positions could offer dissent to policy decisions. Suggests that despite the intentions for a more open system of analysis, several FSO careers were negatively impacted by through use of the system. Offers lessons for those involved in the dissent process in the intelligence community.

666. Birkenstock, Gregory E. "The Foreign Intelligence Surveillance Act and Standards of Probable Cause: An Alternative Analysis," Georgetown Law Journal 80 (February 1992): 843-871.
    Discusses FISA as compromise between protecting US citizens' rights while permitting executive discretion in using surveillance to gather foreign intelligence. States that courts continue to use foreign intelligence exception to probable cause language of Fourth Amendment. Argues that courts should analogize to other lines of decisions involving Fourth Amendment rather than constitutionalizing another exception to it. Topics include FISA's requirements; mechanics; probable cause standard; court decisions involving foreign intelligence searches; and potential use of administrative search doctrine.

667. Birks, Peter. "A Lifelong Obligation of Confidence," Law Quarterly Review 105 (October 1989): 501-508.
    Reviews the British House of Lords decision to set aside injunctions against Guardian Newspapers in the case of Spycatcher, a memoir of Peter Wright's work in British intelligence. Considers contractual and constitutional perspectives.

668. Bishara, Ghassan. "The Israeli Raid on the Iraqi Reactor," Journal of Palestine Studies 2/3 (Spring 1982): 58-76.

669. Bisher, Jamie. "A Travelling Salesman Fills a Crucial Gap," Military Intelligence 15 (January-March 1989): 36-37.
        A brief discussion of the Military Intelligence Division activities in Latin America.

670. Bisher, Jamie. "German and Chilean Agents in Peru: Entwined by a Yen for Espionage," International Journal of Intelligence and Counterintelligence 6/2 (Summer 1993): 205-212.
        An historical account of the work of Chile's spymaster, Colonel Carlos Hurtado Wilson, against Chile's prime target, Peru, from 1918 to 1920.

671. Bishop, Joseph W., Jr. "The Executive's Right of Privacy: An Unresolved Constitutional Question," Yale Law Journal 66 (1957): 477-491.
        Concludes that neither the executive branch nor the legislative branch comprehends the limits of information held by the executive. Discusses the withholding of classified information and intelligence reports. Offers several propositions regarding the confirmation of this constitutional dilemma. An excellent beginning article on this subject.

672. Bishop, Wayne H. "LEIU (Law Enforcement Intelligence Unit): An Early Warning System," Police Chief 38/9 (September 1971): 30-32.
        A description of the Law Enforcement Intelligence Unit and its role in exchanging information on criminals and criminal organizations. LEIU was an informal, volunteer confederation of police agencies for intelligence purposes.

673. Bissell, Richard M., Jr. "Response to Lucien S. Vandenbroucke, The "Confessions" of Allen Dulles: New Evidence on the Bay of Pigs,'" Diplomatic History 8/4 (Fall 1984): 377-380.

674. Bissell, Richard M., Jr. "Reflections on the Bay of Pigs: Operation ZAPATA," Strategic Review 8 (Fall 1984): 66-70.

675. Bissell, Richard M., Jr. "Origins of the U-2: Interview with Richard M. Bissell, Jr.," Air Power History 36/4 (1989): 15-23.

676. Bissell, Schuyler and Daniel G. Kniola. "Intelligence for War Fighting," Signal 41 (September 1986): 48-49.

677. Bissy, J. de Lannoy de. "Les Photographies Aeriennes et l'Etude au Point de Vue Militaire," Revue Militaire Francaise 12 (April-June 1924): 257-277.

678. Bittman, Ladislav. "The Use of Disinformation by Democracies," International Journal of Intelligence and Counterintelligence 4/2 (Summer 1990): 243-262.

Discusses the role of disinformation in the general covert action realm of democratic regimes, in particular, the United States. Major sections discuss the background of the demise of Czechoslovakian democracy; the disinformation controversy; Soviet active measures; advantages and drawbacks of disinformation; mind games; defining disinformation; disinformation in US policy; risks and dangers; the Reagan years; and disinformation and democracy.

679. Bivins, Robert W. "Silencing the Name Droppers: The Intelligence Identities Protection Act of 1982," University of Florida Law Review 36/4 (Fall 1984): 841-869.

Discusses the background of the Act, First Amendment considerations and conclusions. Central issues are the compelling interest test, clear and present danger test and other tests.

680. Bizzarro, Salvatore. "Rigidity and Restraint in Chile," Current History 74/434 (February 1978): 66-69, 83.

Discussion of economic and political conditions in Chile, including areas of progress and failure. Mentions the elimination of the hated DINA secret police and the movement toward civilian control of the government.

681. Bjelajac, Stavko N. "Psywar: The Lessons from Algeria," Military Review 42/12 (December 1962): 2-7.

682. Bjelajac, Stavko N. "A Design for Psychological Operations in Vietnam," Orbis 10 (Spring 1966): 126-137.

Argues the need for psychological operations in Vietnam as the key to win support of the indigenous people. Sections include discussion of the Viet Cong penetration of the masses; concept for a government program; rooting out the underground; targeting and reaching the people; sampling word of mouth propaganda; the distribution of printed materials; and broadcasts.

683. Black, Cyril E. "The Start of the Cold War in Bulgaria: A Personal View," Review of Politics 41/2 (April 1979): 163-202.

A general discussion of conditions under which the US and the USSR conducted Cold War activities in the late 1940s, mainly over the issue of Soviet domination of economic, political and social freedoms. Mentions Soviet control of the Bulgarian police.

684. Black, Edwin F. "Laos: A Case Study," Military Review 44/12 (December 1964): 49-59.

A discussion of the country of Laos and the strategy the communists used to bring it under control.

685. Black, Forrest R. "An Ill-Starred Prohibition Case," <u>Georgetown Law Journal</u> 23/2 (January 1930): 120-129.
  A discussion of the first federal case on wiretapping: <u>Olmstead</u>. A good beginning piece for a seminar on wiretapping policy development in the US.

686. Black, Forrest R. "<u>Debs v. The United States</u>--A Judicial Milepost on the Road to Absolutism," <u>University of Pennsylvania Law Review</u> 81/2 (December 1932): 160-175.
  Discusses <u>Debs</u> in context of <u>Schenck</u> "clear and present danger" case decided only three weeks before <u>Debs</u>. Claims departure was made in order that government could "get its man." Then discusses historical developments of free speech theories, including "use-abuse" theory, Blackstonian "bad tendency" theory, Freudian "damning doctrine of inferential intent," concluding with four important elements of <u>Schenck</u>.

687. Black, Gregory D. and Clayton R. Koppes. "OWI Goes to the Movies: The Bureau of Intelligence's Criticism of Hollywood, 1942-43," <u>Prologue: Quarterly Journal of the National Archives</u> 6/1 (1974): 44-59.
  An account of the criticisms of the Office of War Information made by the Bureau of Intelligence following President Roosevelt's appointment of Elmer Davis to head the organization.

688. Black, Ian. "The Origins of Israeli Intelligence," <u>Intelligence and National Security</u> 2/4 (October 1987): 151-156.
  A review article of stressing the importance of intelligence in the new state of Israel, beginning in the late 1940s.

689. Black, Jeremy. "Sir Robert Ainslie: His Majesty's Agent-Provocateur? British Foreign Policy and the International Crisis of 1787," <u>European History Quarterly</u> 14/3 (July 1984): 253-283.
  Examines the history of British spies in 1787, in particular the role of Sir Robert Ainslie in the war of the Russians and the Ottoman Turks. Ainslie served as ambassador to Constantinople as he purportedly stirred up trouble between the Turks and the Russians without significant oversight from London.

690. Black, Jeremy. "The Need for a Consular Service in France: An Eighteenth-Century British Memorandum," <u>Bulletin of the Institute of Historical Research</u> 59/140 (1986): 229-231.
  Discusses secret British writings that called for the organization of a consular service in France for the purpose of providing commercial assistance and naval espionage.

691. Black, Jeremy. "British Intelligence and the Mid-Eighteenth-Century Crisis," <u>Intelligence and National Security</u> 2/2 (April 1987): 209-229.

Brief history of intelligence during the era of British monarch George II beginning in 1727. Suggests that British successes in information gathering picked up in the sedcond half of the eighteenth century in the era of Sir Robert Walpole in surveillance of Jacobite activities.

692. Blackburn, Clifton A., Jr. "Terrain Intelligence," <u>Military Engineer</u> (July-August 1958): 280-283.

693. Blackburn, Clifton. "Terrain Intelligence for the Pentomic Army," <u>Military Engineer</u> (November-December 1959): 482-485.

This piece was reprinted in CIA's <u>Studies in Intelligence</u> 3/3 (Fall 1959).

694. Blackburn, N. Glenn. "Computers: A Counterintelligence Concern," <u>Military Intelligence</u> 11/2 (April-June 1985): 38-42.

A brief discussion of computer security in the Defense Department. concludes the importance of training, background investigations, limitations on access; risk analysis for potential threats, and research on service-peculiar problems.

695. Blackley, Allan B. "Airborne Surveillance in a Post-CFE Environment: A Central Region Perspective," <u>Military Technology</u> 15/2 (February 1991): 62-64.

Briefly explores air surveillance in support of forces in contemporary Europe.

696. Blackman, Deanne R. "The Gromark Cipher, and Some Relatives," <u>Cryptologia</u> 13/3 (July 1989): 273-282.

697. Blackstock, Paul W. "The CIA and the Penkovskiy Affair," <u>Worldview</u> 9 (February 1966): 11-15.

698. Blackstock, Paul W. "CIA: A Non-inside Report," <u>Worldview</u> 9/5 (May 1966): 10-13.

699. Blackstock, Paul W. "'Books for Idiots': False Soviet 'Memoirs'," <u>Russian Review</u> 25/3 (July 1966): 285-296.

Considers the work of the special operations of the KGB responsible for drafting and publishing false memoirs and biographies to serve as disinformation vehicles. The author cites Gregori Bessedovky's job in the Soviet disinformation bureau as aimed at "writing books for idiots." Includes a detailed background on Bessedovsky.

700. Blackstock, Paul W. "Political Surveillance and the Constitutional Order,"

<u>Worldview</u> 14 (May 1971): 11-14.

701. Blackstock, Paul W. "A Look at the Intelligence Establishment," <u>Worldview</u> 14 (September 1971): 17-19.
This author developed one of the first bibliographies on intelligence.

702. Blackstock, Paul W. "The Intelligence Community Under the Nixon Administration," <u>Armed Forces and Society</u> 1/2 (February 1975): 231-250.
Explains the intelligence community reforms in the Nixon presidential years before Watergate. Includes discussion of the James R. Schlesinger mandate; the clash of budgetary interests; personnel purge and structural changes; and the intelligence community under William Colby.

703. Blain, William T. "Challenge to the Lawless: The Mississippi Secret Service, 1870-1871," <u>Mississippi Quarterly</u> 31/2 (1978): 229-240.
Discusses Governor James Alcorn's use of secret police to fight white marauders and the KKK in the years following Mississippi's readmission to the Union.

704. Blain, William T. "Challenge to the Lawless: The Mississippi Secret Service, 1870-1871," <u>Journal of Mississippi History</u> 40/2 (1978): 119-131.
See previous citation.

705. Blair, Arthur H., Jr., et al. "Unconventional Warfare: A Legitimate Tool of Foreign Policy," <u>Conflict: An International Journal</u> 4/1 (1983): 59-81.

706. Blair, Dennis C. "The Future of Intelligence Support to the Armed Forces," <u>Defense Intelligence Journal</u> 4/2 (Fall 1995): 7-16.
Explores the phases of military operations; preparation and planning; deployment and employment; conflict termination; and concerns for where we go from here.

707. Blair, Leon B. "Amateurs in Diplomacy: The American Vice Consuls in North Africa 1941-1943," <u>Historian</u> 35/4 (1973): 607-620.
Discussion of American consulate activities in Morocco. failures of reporting political intelligence, and successes in passing military information. Concludes that consul activities were ineffective with respect to the policy on Morocco.

708. Blair, William R. "Army Radio in Peace and War," <u>Annals of the American Academy of Political and Social Science</u> 142 (March 1929) 86-89.

709. Blais, J. J. "The Political Accountability of Intelligence Agencies - Canada," <u>Intelligence and National Security</u> 4/1 (January 1989): 108-118.

An account and analysis of the Canadian Security Intelligence Act of 1984. Considers elements of the Act; the review process for proposed intelligence operations; the complaints process; the Parliament's committee processes; access to information; disclosure and publication; and disclosure and the complaints process.

710.   Blake, George.   "There Is No Other Way," Mirovaia Ekonomika i Mezhdunarodnye Otnosheniia 7,8,10,11,12 (1991): 136-142; 136-145; 131-140; 122-135; 108-125.

711.   Blakely, Bob and G. R. Blakely.   "Security of Number Theoretic Public Key Cryptosystems Against Random Attack," (Parts I, II & III) Cryptologia 2/4 (October 1978); 3/1 (January 1979); (April 1979): 305-321; 29-42; 105-118.

712.   Blakey, G. Robert and James A. Hancock.   "A Proposed Electronic Surveillance Control Act," Notre Dame Lawyer 43/5 (June 1968): 657-683.
Authors acknowledge debate on electronic surveillance. They note that the presidential commission concluded there was a need for legislation, especially considering U. S. Supreme Court decisions in Berger v. New York and Katz v. U. S., which permitted such surveillance, and public opinion favoring enactment of controls. Recognizing that legislation was then pending in some states and Congress, the authors submit their proposed statute as the bulk of the article.

713.   Blanchard, Robert O.   "Present at the Creation: The Media and the Moon Committee," Journalism Quarterly 49/2 (1972): 271-279.
Discusses role of the media with respect to House Special Subcommittee on Government Information.

714.   Blanchard, William H.   "National Myth, National Character and National Policy: A Psychological Study of the U-2 Incident," Journal of Conflict Resolution 6/2 (Spring 1962): 143-148.
Argues that the important consideration in foreign policy development is comprehension of national attitudes and characteristics of people in foreign lands. Crises usually force definition of the public persona, and previously subdued cultural attitudes rise to the surface. The U-2 incident of 1960 shocked the French in terms of the willingness of the US to admit guilt for its espionage activities.

715.   Blankenhorn, Heber.   "The Battle of Radio Armaments," Harper's 12 (December 1931): 83-91.
A review of the uses of radio in the international context in the 1920s. Discussion of technical problems with radio installations, international broadcasting, and a case of abuse of power by the Brazilian president in crushing radio installations.

716. Blanton, Eugene T. "Air Operations in Vietnam: COIN Weather Support," Air University Review 15/4 (May-June 1964): 66-72.

Discusses an air support squadron in the early stages of the Vietnam war. A useful glimpse at the early days of the Vietnam war.

717. Blanton, Margaret G. "Moment of Truth For a Spy," Civil War Times Illustrated 6/6 (1967): 20-23.

718. Blash, Edmund C., II. "Strategic Intelligence Analysis and National Decisionmaking: A Systems Management Approach," International Journal of Intelligence and Counterintelligence 6/1 (Spring 1993): 55-68.

Discussion of strategic intelligence analysis from a systems management perspective. Major sections discuss the history and background of strategic analysis aimed at the Soviets; matrix analysis; the relativity of scores; the environment today; potential applications for evaluating military power; and limitations of the analytical models.

719. Blasi, Vincent. "Toward a Theory of Prior Restraint: The Central Linkage," Minnesota Law Review 66/1 (November 1981): 11-93.

Analyses prior restraint theory and analogies to injunction and administrative licensing systems. Discusses whether similar features of both are significant enough to be treated differently under First Amendment than after-the-fact criminal and/or civil liabilities. Also reviews "self-censorship," adjudication in the abstract, overuse of injunction and licensing, impact of system on audience, and unacceptable premises.

720. Blechman, Barry M. and William J. Durch. "Bay of Pigs + 20," Washington Quarterly 4/4 (Autumn 1981): 86-100.

721. Blechman, Barry M. and Robert Powell. "What in the Name of God Is Strategic Superiority?," Political Science Quarterly 97/4 (1982-1983): 589-602.

Analysis of the variations in the definition of strategic superiority from the 1960s to the 1980s. Considers Eisenhower and the Korean war; substance of US nuclear warnings in 1953; risks inherent in nuclear threats; and Soviet attitudes. Background piece for studies of surprise and threat management.

722. Blecker, Robert I. "Beyond 1984: Undercover in America - Serpico to Abscam," New York Law School Law Review 28/4 (1984): 823-1024.

Discusses wiretapping and taping as investigative techniques, police corruption, entrapment as a defense, probable cause, distinction between private and public parties, and jurisdiction. Includes review of several important cases on point.

723. Bledsoe, Caroline H. and Kenneth M. Robey. "Arabic Literacy and Secrecy

Among the Mende of Sierra Leone," Man 21 (June 1986): 202-226.
        Discusses psychology and sociolinguistics of this African Arabic language tribe.

724. Bleiler, E. F. "Jules Verne and Cryptography," Extrapolation 27 (Spring 1986): 5-18.
        Examines Verne's use of cryptograms in three novels: Journey to the Center of the Earth (1864); The Grant Raft (1887); Mathias Sandorf (1889).

725. Blevins, Don. "The Forgotten Peacemaker, Nicholas Trist," American History Illustrated 14 (June 1979): 4-8, 42-47.
        Evaluates Trist's role in negotiating the Treaty of Guadalupe Hidalgo in the nineteenth century controversy over the determination of the Texas-Mexico border.

726. Blickle, Peter and Mark Edwards. "The Criminalization of Peasant Resistance in the Holy Empire: Toward a History of the Emergence of High Treason in Germany," Journal of Modern History 58/4 (December 1986): 588-597.
        An account of the peasant revolt against a penal ordinance issued by Charles V which lasted from 1500-1532.

727. Blight, James G., Joseph S. Nye, Jr. and David A. Welch. "The Cuban Missile Crisis Revisited," Foreign Affairs 60 (Fall 1987): 170-188.
        A discussion of several lessons learned from the missile crisis of 1962: plan; variety of options; dependence on those with knowledge of the Soviet Union; retain civilian control; attention to world opinion; avoid humiliation of opponent; awareness of potential for inadvertence.

728. Blitzer, Wolf. "The Journalist and the Spy," WJR 11 (May 1989): 29-30+.

729. Bloch, Gilbert. "La Contribution Francaise a la Reconstitution au Decryptement de l'Enigma Militaire Allemande en 1931-32," Revue Historique des Armes 4 (1985): 17-25.

730. Bloch, Gilbert. "ENIGMA Before ULTRA: Polish Work and the French Connection," Cryptologia 12/3 (July 1988): 178-184.

731. Bloch, Gilbert and Ralph Erskine. "ENIGMA: The Dropping of the Double Encipherment," Cryptologia 10/3 (July 1986): 134-141.

732. Bloch, Gilbert and Ralph Erskine. "ENIGMA Before ULTRA: Polish Work and the French Connection," Cryptologia 11/3 (July 1987): 142-155.

733. Bloch, Gilbert and Ralph Erskine. "Enigma Before Ultra: The Polish Success and Check," Cryptologia 11/4 (October 1987): 227-234.

734. Block, Alan R. "Violence, Corruption and Clientelism: The Assassination of Jesus De Galindez, 1956," Social Justice 16/2 (1989): 64-88.
       Review of the KGB's use of assassination. Reviews clientelism in US policy toward the Dominican Republic, the era of the Trujillo government, and the murder of opposition leader Jesus Galindez. Cites CIA knowledge of actions leading up to the assassination.

735. Block, Alan R. "IRS Intelligence Operations under the Alexander Regime: A Commentary on Undercover Operations," Crime, Law and Social Change 18/1-2 (September 1992): 61-90.
       A careful and detailed analysis of the Nixon administration, the Internal Revenue Service, and the rise of Donald C. Alexander; the concerns of author David Wise in The American Police State; IRS covert operations in The Bahamas; the political use of Operation Leprechaun; targets of Leprechaun; and Leprechaun's bogus reputation.

736. Block, Alan R. "Issues and Theories on Covert Policing," Crime, Law, and Social Change 18/1-2 (1992): 1-2.
       The editor of this volume opens with an introduction on the subject to which the entire issue is devoted. Contains a brief overview of other articles in the issue.

737. Block, Alan R. and John C. McWilliams. "On the Origins of American Counterintelligence: Building a Clandestine Network," Journal of Policy History 1/4 (1989): 353-372.

738. Block, Lawrence J. and David B. Rivkin, Jr. "The Battle to Control the Conduct of Foreign Intelligence and Covert Operations: The Ultra-Whig Counterrevolution Revisited," Harvard Journal of Law & Public Policy 12/2 (Spring 1989): 303-355.
       Argues that Vietnam War and Watergate prompted legislative takeover of executive power. Focusses on conflict between president and congress concerning control of intelligence policy and activity. Topics include constitutional origins of executive authority over foreign intelligence, constitutional "myths" and associated concerns, history of intelligence activities, current developments, and conclusions.

739. Blockeley, Roger. "Internal Self-Policing in the Late Roman Administration: Some Evidence from Ammianus Marcellinus," Classica et Medievalia 30 (1969): 403-419.

740. Blockeley, Roger.   "The Coded Message in Ammianus Marcellinus 18.6.17-19," Classical Views 30/5 (1986): 63-65.

741. Blodgett, Nancy.   "Is It Espionage?   Photo Leak to Media at Issue," American Bar Association Journal 71 (May 1985): 18.
        Brief report of the application of 18 U.S.C. 793(d) to the case of U. S. v. Morison.

742. Bloom, Murray T.   "Uncle Sam: Bashful Counterfeiter," International Journal of Intelligence and Counterintelligence 2/3 (Fall 1988): 345-358.
        An account of US plans to distribute phony money in Germany and Italy during World War II.   Briefly follows the idea of counterfeiting the enemy's currency after the war.

743. Bloom, Murray T.   "The Bank Note World's Security Obsession," International Journal of Intelligence and Counterintelligence 2/4 (Winter 1988): 533-546.
        General discussion of the significance of bank note makers of the major currency nations of the world, including the US Bureau of Engraving and Printing; the Bank of England Printing Works; the Bank of France; and GOSNAK of the USSR.   Considers bank note security problems and their role in international financial crises.

744. Bloomfield, Lincoln P., Jr. "The Legitimacy of Covert Action: Sorting Out the Moral Responsibilities," International Journal of Intelligence and Counterintelligence 4/4 (Winter 1990): 525-538.
        Assuming the need for a US covert action capability, asks how the US can ensure that the Executive Branch can execute covert actions in a manner consistent with the Constitution.   Major sections discuss issues raised by Iran-Contra; the limits of covert action; the quest for perfection--the enemy of good government; accountabilty--when overseers overreach; and problems with ends/means considerations.

745. Bloomfield, Lincoln P., Jr. and Barton Whaley.   "The Political-Military Exercise: A Progress Report," Orbis 8/4 (1965): 854-870.
        Sections consider the policy-type political-military exercise; implications for policy; educative uses of the policy-type exercise; and problems for future research on gaming.

746. Blow, Tom.   "Soviet Space Weapons: The Greatest Challenge to Intelligence Art," Jane's Soviet Intelligence Review 1/5 & 1/6 7 1/7 (May, June & July 1989): 197-199; 252-253; 328-329.

747. Blue, William. "Ronald Reagan's Legacy: Eight Years of CIA Covert Action," Covert Action Information Bulletin 33 (Winter 1990): 8-11.

748. Blum, Joseph; Robert L. Kirby; and Jack Minker. "Eloge: Walter W. Jacobs, 1914-1982," Annals of the History of Computing 6/2 (1984): 100-105.

749. Blum, Robert M. "Surprised by Tito: Anatomy of an Intelligence Failure," Studies in Intelligence 29/2 (Summer 1985).
    Discussion of the intelligence failure in evaluating Soviet-Yugoslav relations after World War II. Understaffing and misinterpretations were two problems leading to failures in collection and analysis. This article was published later in Diplomatic History 12 (Winter 1988): 39-57.

750. Blumberg, Arnold. "The Strange Career of Joseph Binda," South Carolina History Magazine 67/3 (1966): 155-166.

751. Blumenson, Martin. "The Early French Resistance in Paris," Naval War College Review (Summer 1977): 64-72.
    A summary of the sophisticated espionage system set up by the French resistance forces in support of the allies in World War II. The author recognizes the value of the French missions and the sacrifices made.

752. Blumenson, Martin. "Intelligence in World War II: Will 'Ultra' Rewrite History?," Army 28/8 (August 1978): 42-48.
    Suggests that F. W. Winterbotham's publication of the facts of the Ultra secret will not have significant impact on the history of the Western nations' victories in decoding the Japanese and German cryptographic systems in the 1930s.

753. Blumenthal, Sidney. "The CIA's Hypnotically Trained Assassins," Saga 55/5 (1978): 14-17+.

754. Blumrosen, Alfred W. "Repeated Federal Employee Security Adjudications," Wayne Law Review 1/2 (Spring 1955): 77-104.
    Considers the history of administrative tribunals; federal employment security program; possible remedies for federal employees; and conclusions. Contains excellent references for studies of government personnel security history.

755. Boatner, Helene L. "The Evaluation of Intelligence," Studies in Intelligence 28/2 (Summer 1984).

756. Bobb, Merrick J. "Preventive Intelligence Systems and the Courts," California Law Review 58/4 (June 1970): 914-939.
    Discusses the rapid growth of preventative intelligence systems, i.e.,

sophisticated computer banks containing the dossiers and political activities of individuals and groups. It asks what role the courts should play in challenging the right of police agencies to compile such records.

757. Bock, Joseph G. and Duncan L. Clarke. "The National Security Assistant and the White House Staff: National Security Policy Decisionmaking and Domestic Political Considerations, 1947-1984," Presidential Studies Quarterly 16/2 (Spring 1986): 258-279.
     Explores the emergence and expansion of roles of the national security affairs advisor to presidents from Truman to Reagan. Offers two main conclusions: the subject requires more scholarly attention; there are few clear conclusion.

758. Bock, P. G. "Transnational Corporation and Private Foreign Policy: ITT in Chile," Society 11 (January 1974): 44-49.
     Discusses the growth of the ITT Corporation in Chile and the links between ITT's company postures and US foreign policy and CIA personnel. Background information for understanding US covert action in Chile in the early 1970s.

759. Bocklett, Richard. "HUMINT Is Still the Best Intelligence," National Guard 43 (April 1989): 26-28.

760. Bode, William R. "The Reagan Doctrine," Strategic Review 14 (Winter 1986): 21-29.

761. Bodger, Walter C. "The Hidden World of Kurdistan," Naval Intelligence Professionals Quarterly 11/2 (Spring 1995): 8-10.

762. Bodle, Walter S. "The Black Soldier in World War I," Social Education 49/2 (1985): 129-132.
     A brief summation of the role of black soldiers in World War I, and the difficulties that many sodiers had when they returned to a society that had not changed its outlook on race. May have some relevence to studies of black soldiers in the intelligence missions of the war.

763. Boehm, Eric H. "The 'Free German' in Soviet Psychological Warfare," Public Opinion Quarterly 14 (Summer 1950): 285-295.
     Reviews the activities of the Free Germany Committee formed by the Soviets in 1943. Discusses the psychological warfare tactics of this group. Concludes that measures of effectiveness of this group's work are difficult to construct. Useful in evaluating cases of encouraging internal dissent.

764. Boehmer, Robert G. "Artificial Monitoring and Surveillance of Employees:

The Fine Line Dividing the Prudently Managed Enterprise from the Modern Sweatshop," <u>DePaul Law Review</u> 41/3 (Spring 1992): 739-819.

Argues law provides little guidance for employers on subject of monitoring employees. Provides overview of the current state of monitoring practices by employers and the massive but inadequate regulations on the practice. Gives exhaustive analysis of federal and state law and discusses interaction of increasing sophistication of monitoring with changing workplace conditions. Analyzes whether the combined circumstances warrant passing of the proposed "Privacy for Consumers and Workers Act," and concludes the law is necessary. Adds recommendations.

765. Boesche, Roger. "Why Could Tocqueville Predict So Well?," <u>Political Theory</u> 11/1 (February 1983): 79-103.

Discusses analytical approaches to comprehending Tocqueville's successes in foretelling various domestic and international events in American history. Sections discuss Tocqueville's conception of society; the social pattern of meaning; and historical and political prediction. Particularly useful in analyses of the role of cultural immersion and the potential for crises prediction.

766. Bofrone, Kenneth E. "Intelligence Photography," <u>Studies in Intelligence</u> 5/2 (Spring 1961): 9-16.

Strategies for capturing vital information on still film through the use of off-the-shelf photo equipment.

767. Bogue, Joy R. "Intelligence Training," <u>Military Review</u> 27/4 (April 1947): 55-60.

Discusses the purpose of intelligence training in the removal of a commander's analytical blindfolds. Identifies specific contributions of soldier training in intelligence.

768. Bok, Sissela. "Secrets and Deception: Implications for the Military," <u>Naval War College Review</u> 38/2 (March-April 1985): 73-80.

Extensive discussion of the meaning and implications of distrust, in particular reference to political relations between East and West. Secrecy and deception, the author suggests, raise the tension between nations and each can lead to abuses and self-defeating actions. Makes reference to President Carter's handling of the Iran hostage rescue case, and the frequent US use of covert action. Argues for more openness in international relations.

769. Bok, Sissela. "Distrust, Secrecy, and the Arms Race," <u>Ethics</u> 95 (April 1985): 712-727.

This is a transcript of the Aspen Conference on the Ethics of Nuclear Deterrence and Disarmament, Aspen Colorado, September 1-4, 1984.

770. Bold, Christine. "Secret Negotiations: The Spy Figure in Nineteenth-Century American Popular Fiction," <u>Intelligence and National Security</u> 5/4 (October 1990): 17-29.

Considers the emergence of James Fennimore Cooper's <u>The Spy</u> in 1821 and the slow, reluctant acceptance of the spy novel by the late 19th century. Explores the dime novels and story papers of the 1860s and 1870s.

771. Bold, Christine. "'Under the Very Skirts of Britannia': Re-reading Women in the James Bond Novels," <u>Queen's Quarterly</u> 100/2 (Summer 1993): 311-328.

Argues that a re-reading of the Ian Fleming novels suggests that the creator of the character James Bond may have sought to protect a particular order of political, sexual, and racial propriety of his times. This contrasts with a traditional view that the Bond books and films represented mere escapism.

772. Bolger, Daniel P. "Operation Urgent Fury and Its Critics," <u>Military Review</u> 66/7 (1986): 57-69.

773. Bolmer, John E., II. "The Public Forum Doctrine and Haig v. Agee," <u>Hastings Constitutional Law Quarterly</u> 10 (Fall 1982): 187-212.

Discusses domestic forum denials, comparison of foreign and domestic forums, early passport cases, Haig v. Agee, applicability of the domestic doctrine abroad, alternative holdings, implications of Haig v. Agee, and conclusions.

774. Bol'shakov, V. V. "In the Service of Imperialism," <u>Novaia i Noveishaia Istoriia</u> 4 (1972): 120-135.

Explores Zionism since World War II. Links Israeli intelligence services with those of Western countries and cites examples. Claims motivations of Zionism is national prejudice and religious dominance.

775. Boltax, Phyllis E. "The Right to Travel and Passport Revocation: (<u>Haig v. Agee</u>)," <u>Brooklyn Journal of International Law</u> 8/2 (Summer 1982): 391-428.

Contains a summary of Agee's attempt to secure a US passport, origins of the common law right to travel, later developments re: passports, modern case law re: travel passports in international law, and applications to the Agee case.

776. Bolten, Joshua B. "Enforcing the CIA's Secrecy Agreement Through Postpublication Civil Action: <u>United States v. Snepp</u>," <u>Stanford Law Review</u> 32/2 (January 1980): 409-431.

Discusses the validity and importance of the prior restraint agreement, the design of an adequate post-publication remedy and conclusions.

777. Bonen, Z. "The Role of Target Acquisition in Combat Intelligence Past and Future," <u>Intelligence and National Security</u> 4/1 (January 1989): 119-126.

Discusses target acquisition for extended current battle; decision loop and the execution/fire control loop; sensors for target acquisition; elevated observation equipment; classification and allocation of separate target acquisition platforms; technical and operational problems; and the wider context of combat intelligence.

778. Bonham, Francis G. "Deception in War," Infantry Journal (July-August 1934): 272-278.

779. Bonham, G. Matthew; Michael J. Shapiro; and Thomas L. Trumble. "The October War: Changes in Cognitive Orientation Toward the Middle East Conflict," International Studies Quarterly 23/1 (March 1975): 3-44.
    Examines adjustments that foreign policy officials make in their thinking to accommodate new information. Contains results of sample survey of some policy makers during the 71-72 and 74-75 periods. Considers covert actions, disorder of the secret bureaucracy and conclusions.

780. Bonney, Richard. "The Secret Expenses of Richelieu and Mazarin, 1624-1661," English Historical Quarterly 91 (October 1976): 825-836.

781. Bontecou, Eleanor. "The English Policy As to Communists and Fascists in the Civil Service," Columbia Law Review 51/5 (May 1951): 564-586.
    Explores the genesis of the policy, official intentions, policy operation, safeguards, and appraisal and comment. Includes text of official documents.

782. Bonthous, Jean-Marie. "Understanding Intelligence Across Cultures," International Journal of Intelligence and Counterintelligence 7/3 (Fall 1994): 275-313.
    Major sections discuss cultural influences on intelligence; the German approach to intelligence; the French approach to intelligence; the Swedish approach to intelligence; the Japanese approach to intelligence; the US approach to intelligence; and transcending perceptual biases and developing an intelligent nation/organization. Emphasizes economic and business intelligence.

783. Boog, Horst. "German Air Intelligence in World War II," Aerospace Historian 33/2 (Summer 1986): 121-129.
    Presents a highly negative view of the capabilities, biases and ultimate effectiveness of the Lufewaffe intelligence branch. German intelligence officers had no particular calling in the upper echelons of decision making, and they were not prepared for the rigors of intelligence analysis on a wide scale.

784. Boog, Horst. "Josephine and the Northern Flank," Intelligence and National Security 4/1 (January 1989): 137-160.
    A detailed account of effective British deception efforts through Scotland in 1944.

785. Boog, Horst. "German Air Intelligence in the Second World War," Intelligence and National Security 5/2 (April 1990): 350-424.
    This article compares with the author's earlier piece on the same subject, but it is more extensively noted and detailed in its characterization of the ineffectiveness of the Luftwaffe intelligence service.

786. Booth, Alan R. "Economic Advice at the Centre of British Government, 1939-1941," Historical Journal 29/3 (1986): 655-675.

787. Booth, Alan R. "The Development of the Espionage Film," Intelligence and National Security 5/4 (October 1990): 136-160.
    Major sections discuss spies and their invasion of the silent screen; the spy as amateur gentleman hero before World War I; espionage in World War II films; labyrinths of betrayal in Cold War films; ambiguities of loyalty in the twilight of the Cold War; and the role of murder in Cold War films.

788. Booth, Marilyn. "The Jennifer Triangle: Hughes, Glomar, and the CIA," Harvard Political Review 4 (Spring 1976): 17-25.

789. Booth, Waller R., Jr. "Operation Swamprat," Combat Forces Journal 1/3 (October 1950): 23-26.

790. Booth, Waller R., Jr. "How S-2 Caught the Crooks," Combat Forces Journal 5 (February 1955): 38-39.

791. Booth, Waller R., Jr. "Allies or Hirelings," Army 22 (May 1972): 43-47.

792. Booth, Waller R., Jr. "War by 'Other Means,'" Army 25/1 (1975): 21-24.
    A brief discussion of operations in Spain by the Coordinator of Information, and later the Office of Strategic Services.

793. Borcke, Astrid von. "The Role of the Secret Service in Soviet Policy: The Invisible 'Fourth Dimension,'" Polilische Studien 283 (September-October 1985): 520-529.

794. Borcke, Astrid von. "From KGB to MBRF: The End of the Soviet Committee for State Security and the New Russian Secret Service," Aus Politik und Zeitgeschichte 21 (May 1992): 33-38.

795. Borel, Paul A. "Automation for Information Control," Studies in Intelligence 11/4 (Winter 1967).

796. Boren, David L. "Counterintelligence in the 1990's," American Intelligence Journal 10/2 (1989): 9-14.

797. Boren, David L. "Comments on Intelligence Reorganization," <u>American Intelligence Journal</u> 13/1&2 (Winter-Spring 1992): 6-7.

798. Boren, David L. "The Winds of Change at the CIA," <u>Yale Law Journal</u> 101/4 (January 1992): 853-865.
Argues need for change in philosophy toward economic strength and ability to provide social and political models as a means to maintain international influence. Topics include discussion of challenges, congressional initiatives to improve oversight, recommendations for changing structure of intelligence community (integration of Department of State, Department of Defense, and CIA); human intelligence; economic intelligence; analysis; role of CIA directors; other threats; conclusions.

799. Boren, David L. "Rethinking US Intelligence," <u>Defense Intelligence Journal</u> 1/1 (Spring 1992): 17-30.
Considers Senate bill 2198, Intelligence Reorganization Act of 1992 and each major component of proposed changes; the case for change; deficiencies in the existing management structure; the management structure for defense intelligence; functional management; and the outlook for legislation. The author, a former US Senator, chaired the Senate Intelligence Committee.

800. Boren, David L. "The Intelligence Community: How Crucial?," <u>Foreign Affairs</u> 71/3 (Summer 1992): 50-62.
A former US senator argues that the analytical function at CIA should be separated from the Agency and placed in the hands of a National Intelligence Council. Defends the oversight functions of the Congress in monitoring civilian and defense intelligence operations.

801. Borosage, Robert L. "Para-Legal Authority and Its Perils," <u>Law and Contemporary Problems</u> 10/3 (Summer 1976): 166-188.
Presidential justification of covert action by the CIA is based on three doctrines, inherent powers, congressional delegation, and post hoc ratification. Discusses CIA's covert actions, disorder of the secret bureaucracy and conclusions.

802. Borosage, Robert L. "Secrecy vs. the Constitution," <u>Society</u> 12/3 (March-April 1975): 71-75.
Discussion of the Constitution's principle of separation of powers and presidential license during the Depression and World War II. Sections discuss law and para-law; covert actions and executive war-making; the end of distinction between war and peace; and the case of Victor Marchetti's battle with the CIA over the secrecy agreement.

803. Borosage, Robert L. "What To Do With the Intelligence Agencies,"

Working Papers for a New Society 4/4 (Winter 1977): 38-45.
    Involves a discussion of the need for legislative reforms to limit CIA and other intelligence agency activities in the 1970s.

804. Borowy, Stefan. "Military Intelligence Behind Enemy Lines," Studies in Intelligence 2/2 (Summer 1958).

805. Borrelli, George A. "Revolution, Portuguese Style," Naval Intelligence Professionals Quarterly 10/2 (Spring 1994): 11-12.

806. Bortnik, M. "1901-1904 in the Petersburg Pipe Factory: From the History of the Revolutionary Movement in the Factory," Krasnaia Letopis' 1/28 (1929): 182-219.
    In Russian, this article discusses the political actions of the Social Democratic Party in the years 1901-1904, and the intelligence data collected by the Okhrana.

807. Borza, Eugene N. "Alexander's Communications," Ancient Macedonia 2 (1977): 295-303.

808. Bosch, Brian J. "Intelligence in the Army of the Andes," Military Review 47/2 (February 1967): 9-14.
    Discusses the intelligence network diversity of Jose de San Martin during the nineteenth century conflict between Chile and Argentina. Sections discuss the invasion plans; axes of advance; tactical plans; espionage mission; and use of double agents. An effective military intelligence system was the key to de San Martin's successes.

809. Bose, Nikhilesh. "Strategic Intelligence and National Security," United Service Institution of India Journal 96 (January-March 1966): 1-14+.

810. Boshier, Roger. "Footsteps Up Your Jumper: The Activities of the New Zealand Security Service," Perspective 6 (1969): 17-18.

811. Boss, Robert. "Communist Fronts: Their History and Function," Problems of Communism (September-October 1960).

812. Bossy, John. "Surprise, Surprise: An Elizabethan Mystery," History Today 41 (September 1991): 14-19.
    A brief historical note on French intelligence operations against the British in the 15th and 16th centuries.

813. Bostwick, Gary L. "A Taxonomy of Privacy: Repose, Sanctuary, and Intimate Decision," California Law Review 64 (1976): 1447-1483.

Suggests that the right of privacy in fact encompasses three separate rights. Major topics consider spacing mechanisms and zones of privacy; the privacy of repose; the privacy of sanctuary; the privacy of intimate decision; and a compendium of privacy protection.

814. Bosworth, C. E. "The Section on Codes and their Decipherment in Qalqashandi's Subh al-a'sha," Journal of Semitic Studies 8 (Spring 1963): 17-33.

A discussion of the ancient history of cryptology, the development of codes, and the decipherment of ancient Arabic text of Subh al-a'sha. Ancient code security protections are discussed in the context of the Greeks, Romans, Egyptians, Jews and Arabs.

815. Bottom, Norman R., Jr. "Overview of Espionage," Journal of Security Administration 6/2 (January 1984): 9-15.

A brief narration of articles in the issue written by academics interested in pushing out new limits of research on the topic.

816. Bottom, Norman R., Jr. "Security Intelligence," Security Management 20 (July 1976): 36-39.

817. Bottom, Norman R., Jr. "Security Intelligence: A Definite Process Is Necessary to Collect Intelligence," Journal of Security Administration 5/1 (June 1982): 33-40.

A description of the fundamental processes of intelligence collection and analysis.

818. Bottom, Norman R., Jr. "Something New for Police Intelligence," Police Journal 52/4 (October 1979): 390-393.

A descriptive application of fundamentals of national intelligence to police intelligence.

819. Boudin, Leonard B. "The Constitutional Right to Travel," Columbia Law Review 56/1 (January 1956): 47-75.

An early legal examination of what later became an important issue in Agee v. U. S. Author examines the constitutional basis, the necessity for travel, judicial protection, history of passports and conclusions. A useful reference for studies of the power of the Secretary of State to control passport issuance.

820. Boulding, Kenneth E. "National Images and International Systems," Journal of Conflict Resolution 3/2 (June 1959): 120-131.

Addresses the importance of image and perceptions in world relations. Two group images exist in most societies: the existence of a small and powerful elite that controls the switches of decision making; and the extent to which hostile and friendly relations can change on short notice. Includes case studies and statistical analyses to explain the dynamics of international systems and the balance of power.

821. Boulton, Charles K. "A Fragment of the Diary of Enos Stevens, Tory, 1777-1778," New England Quarterly 11 (June 1938): 374-388.

Presents a small amount of the total diary of Enos Stevens, a Tory and counterrevolutionary. The remainder of the diary was lost in a fire.

822. Bouman, J. L. "Abdul Njdi: Ally and Enemy of the Portugese in Guined Bissair," Journal of Algerian History 27/3 (1986): 463-479.

Njdi helped the Colonial subjugation and occupation of the Portuguese of Guinea-Bissau. As reward for his services, the Portuguese granted NJAI the Oio province. Using force to maintain power in Oio, Njdi was later captured and deported in 1919 when the colonial administration perceived him a threat to their exploiting the territory.

823. Bourne, Kenneth. "Mr. Smith: An Early Honorary Member," New York Historical Society Quarterly 52/2 (1968): 184-191.

824. Bouza, Anthony. "Anderson v. Sills: The Constitutionality of Police Intelligence Gathering," Northwestern University Law Review 65/3 (1970): 461-485.

Discusses creation of law enforcement intelligence units in response to civil disorders. Anderson v. Sills addressed the question of "standing" in whether or not citizens could challenge the Attorney General's memo on intelligence reports. Also discusses deterrent effects of intelligence on free speech and potential for conducting domestic intelligence operations under the Court's guidelines in Anderson.

825. Bovey, John. "The Ashes of the Marshal," Blackwood's Magazine 322/1941 (July 1977): 32-41.

The author, a former member of the American foreign service, recalls events and conditions surrounding the service of CIA's Norwegian chief of station Charles Cappadose in the 1960s.

826. Bovey, Robert. "The Quality of Intelligence Analysis," American Intelligence Journal (Winter 1980-1981): 6-11.

827. Bovey, Robert. "The Quality of Intelligence Analysis," Analytical Methods Review (February 1980): 1-16.

828. Bovey, Wilfrid. "Confederate Agents in Canada During the American Civil War," Canadian Historical Review 2 (March 1921): 46-57.

829. Bowen, D. G. and Benjamin V. Cox. "Tactical Communication to Support Intelligence," Signal 42/6 (June 1988): 185-188+.

830. Bowen, Gordon L. "U.S. Foreign Policy Toward Radical Change: Covert Operations in Guatemala, 1950-1954," Latin American Perspectives 10/1 (Winter 1983): 88-102.
　　　　Discusses the overthrow of the Jacobo Arbenz government in Guatemala and the role of the CIA in the effort. Uses some declassified documents to suggest private corporate motivations for the overthrow. A useful perspective on this much-studied event.

831.   Bowen, James S.   "'Who's Watching the Watcher'?   The Law of Conspiracy in the Context of the FBI's Record of Surveillance of Black Folk in America," Western State University Law Review 21/1 (Fall 1993): 219-240.
　　　　Major topics consider the critical view towards conspiracy; FBI guidelines on "subversive groups"; conspiracy applications; surveillance and containment; and conclusions.

832. Bowen, N. St. John and E. J. Hughes. "Guatemala, 1954: Intervention and Jurisdiction," International Relations 4 (May 1972): 78-93.

833.   Bowen, Roger.   "Death of an Ambassador," Canadian Dimension 15/6 (1981): 31-34.
　　　　This piece contemplates the accusation that Canadian diplomat Herbert Norman conducted spy activities against the US Senate Committee on Internal Security. It is alleged that Norman's death was attributable to the false accusations.

834. Bowen, Russell J. "Soviet Research and Development: Some Implications for Arms Control Inspection," Journal of Conflict Resolution 7/3 (September 1973): 426-448.
　　　　A summary of open source information on Soviet trends in weapons research up to 1963, including brief discussion of the role of the intelligence community in developing additional information to aid the weapons negotiation processes.

835. Bowen, Russell J. "An Engineering Approach to Literature Appreciation," Studies in Intelligence 24/1 (Spring 1980).

836. Bowen, Russell J. "The Quality of Intelligence Literature," Studies in Intelligence 34/4 (Winter 1990).

837. Bowers, Ray L. "The American Revolution: A Study in Insurgency," Military Review 46/7 (July 1966): 64-72.

Discusses various methods used by the American patriots to break up support for the loyalist forces, including intrusion into loyalist meetings and use of propaganda. Major sections discuss the nature of internal civil war; patriot dominance; organized militia forces; the propaganda weapon; political and cultural aspects; counterinsurgency psychology; partisan warfare techniques; improvised weapons; and Black loyalist support.

838. Bowers, Stephen R. "The Political Evolution of Intelligence," Army Quarterly and Defence Journal 114/2 (April 1984): 168-177.
      A brief history of intelligence, including section addressing sophistication, demands, political adaptations, service of the state, intelligence in the world wars, and the Soviet example.

839. Bowie, Robert R. "Formulation of American Foreign Policy," Annals of the American Academy of Political and Social Sciences 330 (1960): 1-10.
      Argues for the improvement of the methods and machinery for foreign policy making. Asserts that machinery is no substitute for able individuals and leadership, and the best policy will not yield and orderly world. Includes a brief discussion of the NSC, the DoD, State Department and CIA.

840. Bowman, James E. "Ethics in the Federal Service: A Post-Watergate View," Midwest Review of Public Administration 11/1 (March 1977): 3-20.
      Discusses findings of a survey of government executives regarding ethics in government, including ethical practices of the Federal Bureau of Investigation and the Central Intelligence Agency.

841. Bowman, M. E. "Prosecuting Spies: An Uneasy Alliance of Security, Ethics and Law," American Intelligence Journal 11/2 (1990): 29-39.

842. Bowman, M. E. "Prosecuting Spies: An Uneasy Alliance of Security, Ethics and Law," Defense Intelligence Journal 4/1 (Spring 1995): 57-81.
      A reprint of the citation above. Considers the phases in espionage cases, such as the charges, discovery, and evidence; using classified information and the impact of the Classified Information Procedures Act; defenses; and sentencing.

843. Bowman, M. E. "Intelligence and International Law," International Journal of Intelligence and Counterintelligence 8/3 (Fall 1995): 321-335.
      An assessment of the dialectic of customary international law; international expectations; norms; the need for rules; the US experience; and the international norm of intelligence.

844. Boyce, Peter J. "The Influence of the United States on the Domestic Debate in Australia," Australian Outlook 38/3 (1984): 159-162.
      Identifies reasons why US military and intelligence presence in Australia

continues to attract support from Australian cities.

845. Boyce, Robert J. "The 19-Year Ordeal of Dhoruba bin-Wahad," <u>Covert Action Information Bulletin</u> 36 (Spring 1991): 12-16.

846. Boyd, Carl. "The Significance of MAGIC and the Japanese Ambassador to Berlin: (I) The Formative Months Before Pearl Harbor," <u>Intelligence and National Security</u> 2/1 (January 1987): 150-169.

      This is a 5-part article (see below) which discusses the extensive role of the MAGIC descriptions to the advantage of the US and allies. As indicated by the number of articles, the author is an expert on MAGIC documents.

847. Boyd, Carl. "The Significance of MAGIC and the Japanese Ambassador to Berlin: (II) The Crucial Months After Pearl Harbor," <u>Intelligence and National Security</u> 2/2 (April 1987): 302-319.

      Continuation of this 5-part study, covering the reports of Oshima during 1942.

848. Boyd, Carl. "Significance of MAGIC and the Japanese Ambassador to Berlin: (III) The Months of Growing Certainty," <u>Intelligence and National Security</u> 3/4 (October 1988): 83-102.

      Continues the investigation into the role of the Japanese ambassador to Berlin, Oshima Hiroshi, in American intelligence assessments of Hitler's plans in Europe. Explores details of the US intelligence successes in intercepting the ambassador's messages to Tokyo, a vital asset to US intelligence about Hitler's plans.

849. Boyd, Carl. "Significance of MAGIC and the Japanese Ambassador to Berlin (IV): Confirming the Turn of the Tide on the German-Soviet Front," <u>Intelligence and National Security</u> 4/1 (January 1989): 86-107.

      Argues that Oshima had significant difficulty in advising his superiors in Japan that the battles on the German-Soviet front in 1942 were not proceeding according to Germany's planned swift victories. Explores Japanese opportunities to conduct espionage against the Soviet Union.

850. Boyd, Carl. "Significance of MAGIC and the Japanese Ambassador to Berlin: (V): News of Hitler's Defense Preparations for Allied Invasion of Western Europe," <u>Intelligence and National Security</u> 4/3 (July 1989) 461-481.

      Discusses American decryptographers and their interceptions of Japanese communications from Berlin to Tokyo via the Japanese ambassador. Examines the economic, political, and military intelligence intercepted by MAGIC signal intelligence.

851. Boyd, Carl. "Anguish Under Siege: High-Grade Japanese Signal

Intelligence and the Fall of Berlin," Cryptologia 13/3 (July 1989): 193-209.

852. Boyd, Carl. "American Naval Intelligence of Japanese Submarine Operations Early in the Pacific War," Journal of Military History 53/2 (April 1989): 169-189.

Discusses US Navy operations in the Pacific war against Japan in early 1942, including the successes in acquiring intelligence on the Japanese fleet and submarine deployments. Mentions the successes in breaking the JN-25 code system.

853. Boyd, Julian P. "Silas Deane: Death By a Kindly Teacher of Treason?," William and Mary Quarterly 16/2 (April 1959): 165-187; 16/3 (July 1959): 319-342; 16/4 (October 1959): 515-550.

An account of espionage and counterespionage during the American Revolution involving Silas Deane, spy and first emissary to a foreign nation, Edward Bancroft, double-agent, and Thomas Jefferson, minister to France. Boyd argues that Bancroft murdered Deane in order to protect Jefferson.

854. Boydston, H. E. "The Santa Claus Valley Intelligence Unit," Texas Police Journal 22/1 (1974): 16-19; 22/2 (1974): 12-15.

855. Boyer, Jacques. "German Spies and Invisible Writing," Conquest (December 1921): 56-58.

856. Boyes, Jon L. "C³I and D-Day," Signal 38 (June 1984): 13-14.

857. Boyes, Jon L. "C³I Technologies: A Deterrent to Terrorism," Terrorism: An International Journal 10/3 (1987): 271-273.

858. Boyle, Andrew J. "Scientific and Technical Exploitation," Military Review 31/12 (December 1951): 7-13.

859. Boyle, Robert J. "Grand Jury Testimony Derived from Electronic Surveillance," Search and Seizure Law Reporter 11 (June 1984): 37-43.

860. Bozeman, Adda B. "Iran: U. S. Foreign Policy and the Tradition of Persian Statecraft," Orbis 23/2 (Summer 1979): 387-402.

Argues that American foreign policy in the Carter administration regarding Iran was defective. Policy reflected ignorance and misperceptions about the culture and its religious elements relevant to the defects of the analytical and policy advice processes.

861. Bozeman, Adda B. "Human Rights and National Security," Yale Journal of World Public Order 9/1 (Fall 1982): 40-78.

Topics discussed include: The "international community" and human rights; the individual and the state; global realities and the American perception of human rights; culture, human rights and American foreign policymaking; and human rights in East Asia.

862. Bozeman, Adda B. "Statecraft and Intelligence in the Non-Western World," Conflict 6/1 (1985): 1-35.

Discusses the extent to which foreign policy and intelligence failures of the United States are attributable to our failure to understand other cultures.

863. Bozeman, Adda B. "Non-Western Orientations to Strategic Intelligence and Their Relevance for American National Interests," Comparative Strategy 10/1 (January-March 1991): 53-72.

864. Brace, Kimbal, Doug Chapin and Wayne Arden.   "Whose Data Is It Anyway?: Conflicts Between Freedom of Information and Trade Secret Protection in Legislative Redistricting," Stetson Law Review 21 (Summer 1992): 724-742.

Privatization of some state and local government work on redistricting raises the issue of access to private vendor information through FOIA type laws. Discusses various aspects of this situation in relation to vendor trade secrets.

865. Bracion, Henri de. "Dien Bien Phu, or the Clash of Opposing Artillery Forces," Revue Historique des Armes 4 (1992): 104-119.

866. Brackenbury, C. B. "The Intelligence Duties of the Staff Abroad and at Home," Journal of the Royal United Services Institution 19 (1875): 242-267.

867. Bradbury, Malcolm. "Ezra Pound and Treason: The National Skeleton," Encounter 63 (December 1984): 47-48+.

868. Braden, Spruille. "The Germans in Argentina," Atlantic Monthly 177 (April 1946): 37-43.

Discusses German scientists and others in Argentina during and following World War II. Useful for studies of the post-war acquisition of German scientific and technical skills.

869. Braden, Tom. "The Birth of the CIA," American Heritage 28/2 (February 1977): 4-13.

Discusses the development of the Central Intelligence Agency as it emerged from the National Security Act of 1947. A classic overview of the CIA and its historical roots

870. Braden, Tom. "The Spies Who Came in From the Cold: The World

Changed. Can the CIA?," Washington Monthly 24 (March 1992): 18-23.

Discusses the role of the Central Intelligence Agency in the post cold war era, and the suggestion that the CIA be abolished. Contains insights into these matters by Clark Clifford, Richard Helms, William Colby, and Ray Cline.

871. Bradford, Donald R. "Consent to Electronic Surveillance by a Party to a Conversation: A Different Approach," Tulsa Law Journal 10 (1975): 386-397.

This is a case note article which discusses 3 arguments: (1) that intercepted and taped conversations capture substance beyond criminal information; (2) democratic society mandates a right of privacy; and (3) reasonable expectation of privacy is the test of Fourth and Fifth Amendment protections.

872. Bradley, A. Day. "New York Friends and the Loyalty Oath of 1778," Quaker History 57 (1968): 112-114.

873. Bradley, J. F. N. "The Russian Secret Service in the First World War," Soviet Studies 20/2 (October 1968): 242-248.

Evaluates conditions in the Russian intelligence networks during the period of 1908-1917. Focusses on German and Austrian efforts to control Russian espionage. Espionage sources for the relatively ineffective Russian service came primarily from captured spies and double agents.

874. Bradley, Edwin J. and James E. Hogan. "Wiretapping: From Nardone to Benanti and Rathbun," Georgetown Law Journal 46/3 (Spring 1958): 418-442.

Explores discovery of the federal wiretap statute; the rule of exclusion; definition of an interception; and conclusions. Interprets the progression of Supreme Court decisions in wiretapping matters.

875. Bradley, Margaret. "Engineers as Military Spies? French Engineers Come to Britain, 1780-1790," Annals of Science 49/2 (1992): 137-161.

876. Bradner, Stephen. "Our Korean Connection," American Intelligence Journal 2/3 (Fall 1979).

877. Bradshaw, J. "Trouble in the South Tyrol," Blackwood's Magazine 263 (April 1948): 264-270.

878. Bradsher, James G. "Researchers, Archivists, and the Access Challenge of the FBI Records in the National Archives," Midwestern Archivist 11/2 (1986): 95-110.

Addresses the problem of public access to FBI records stored at the National Archives in Washington, D.C.

879. Brady, Charles A. "John LeCarre's Smiley Saga," Thought 60/238 (September 1985): 274-296.

Evaluates detective and spy novels, including Joseph Conrad's Kim, James Fennimore Cooper's Deer Slayer, and the works of John LeCarre. Includes discussion of authors and characters.

880. Brady, Christopher. "Intelligence Failures: Plus Ca Change...," Intelligence and National Security 8/4 (October 1993): 86-96.

Argues the point that, despite many views to the contrary, not every surprise can be interpreted in advance, and that successes in the applications of intelligence knowledge to conditions of surprise are less likely than failures.

881. Brait, Richard A. "The Unauthorized Use of Confidential Information," Canadian Business Law Journal 18 (November 1991): 323-381.

Discusses topic of confidential information in the context of trade secrets. Topics include confidential information received without written obligation (unsolicited and pre-contract disclosures), written agreements (marking requirements, use restrictions, requirement to exercise due care, and publicly available info), third parties receiving info with and without knowledge, remedies (contract, equity, injunction, constructive trust, fiduciary duty, etc.), and statute reform (Uniform Trade Secrets Act and proposed Canadian legislation).

882. Braithwaite, John; Brent Fisse; and Gilbert Geis. "Covert Facilitation and Crime: Restoring Balance to the Entrapment Debate," Journal of Social Issues 43/3 (1987): 5-42.

A detailed exploration of the issue of covert facilitation of criminal actions by police. Major sections discuss covert facilitation and erosion of privacy; controlling the manufacture of criminal liability; invisible offenses; illustrative cases; responsibility to engage in facilitation; privacy; corporations and probable cause; and civil sanctions.

883. Brams, Steven J. "Deception in 2 x 2 Games," Journal of Peace Science 2 (Spring 1977): 171-203.

884. Branch, Taylor. "The Censors of Bumbledom," Harper's 250 (January 1974): 56-63.

Discusses the case of former CIA employee Victor Marchetti who wrote an account of the defects of the collection and analytical phases of intelligence. Relates the CIA's efforts to suppress publication of Marchetti's book.

885. Branch, Taylor. "The Scandal-Makers," More (March 1975).

A brief discussion of competition between newspapers and reporters for leaks concerning the CIA.

886. Branch, Taylor. "Raising a Glass to Beau Geste," Esquire 86 (August 1976): 30-33.

An account of the French Foreign Legion members who served in Vietnam, in particular, Lucien Conein's experiences in training then fighting Ho Chi Minh.

887. Branch, Taylor. "Playing Both Sides Against the Middle: M. Rogovin Representing the CIA and Public Interest Clients," Esquire 86 (September 1976): 17-18.

Discussion of the government agent work of Mitchell Rogovin, former IRS liaison officer to the CIA. Rogovin's legal experience included cases brought against and on behalf of CIA and FBI.

888. Branch, Taylor. "Sam Jaffe and the New Blacklist," Esquire 87 (March 1977): 36, 40, 42.

An account of Sam Jaffe's search for the records reflecting an accusation that Jaffe was a spy. Useful piece in reflecting upon the relationship between the CIA and the press.

889. Branch, Taylor. "Man Who Called Walter Cronkite a Spy, S. Jaffe," Esquire 87 (April 1977): 34-46.

An account of Sam Jaffe's accusations that other journalists and reporters at CBS were informers for the CIA. Jaffe had been accused of spying for the CIA while serving in his correspondent position in Moscow.

890. Branch, Taylor and George Crile, III. "The Kennedy Vendetta: How the CIA Waged a Silent War Against Cuba," Harper's 251 (August 1975): 49-63.

Authors discuss the Kennedy administration's efforts to overthrow the Castro government in Cuba. Sections discuss the secret command; strategy of sabotage; the Cuban recruits; the cowboy plan; and secret war surfaces. Considering volatility of concerns at this time, this is a useful research citation.

891. Branch, Taylor and John Rothchild. "The Incident: Investigating the Cuban Connection to the Orlando Letelier Murder in Venezuela," Esquire 87 (March 1977): 55-58, 139, 149.

Authors discuss their travels from Miami to Caracus, Venezuela to find leads to the murder of Orlando Letelier. Argues that the CIA, FBI and Miami police thwarted their search for information.

892. Brands, H. W., Jr. "The Cairo-Tehran Connection in Anglo-American Rivalry in the Middle East, 1951-1953," International History Review 11/3 (1989): 434-456.

A discussion of President Dwight Eisenhower's decision to apply CIA resources to the overthrow of Iran's political leader Mossadegh in 1953. Outlines

Project AJAX, the CIA plan to carry out the assistance to internal forces to unseat the leader, to gain a stronghold in the Middle East.

893. Brands, H. W., Jr. "The Limits of Manipulation: How the United States Didn't Topple Sukarno," Journal of American History 76/3 (December 1989): 785-808.

Discusses the US role in a covert action to overthrow the Sukarno government in 1960s Indonesia. Sections discuss a US treaty with Indonesia; Lyndon Johnson's position on Indonesia; Sukarno's appeal to the Soviets and China; Sukarno's threats of war in Malaysia; and the plot to overthrow the Sukarno regime.

894. Brandstrom, Hugo. "A Public-Key Cryptosystem Based Upon Equations Over a Finite Field," Cryptologia 7/4 (October 1983): 347-358.

895. Brandwein, David S. "Maxims for Analysis," Studies in Intelligence 22/4 (Winter 1978).

896. Branfman, Fred and Steve Cohn. "The CIA: A Visible Government in Indochina," Computers and Automation 21 (February 1972): 41-42.

Discusses the role of the Central Intelligence Agency in Indochina, myths concerning the CIA, and the four main directorates of CIA (Intelligence; Operations; Administration; and Science and Technology).

897. Bratzel, John F. and Leslie B. Rout, Jr. "Pearl Harbor, Microdots, and J. Edgar Hoover," American Historical Review 87/5 (December 1982): 1342-1351.

Argues that J. Edgar Hoover withheld from President Roosevelt a major report concerning a German intelligence request for information about military facilities on Oahu island.

898. Bratzel, John F. and Leslie B. Rout, Jr. "Abwehr Ciphers in Latin America," Cryptologia 7/2 (April 1983): 132-144.

899. Bratzel, John F. and Leslie B. Rout, Jr. "Heinrich Jurges and the Cult of Disinformation," International History Review 6/4 (November 1984): 611-623.

900. Bratzel, John F. and Leslie B. Rout, Jr. "FDR and the 'Secret Map,'" Wilson Quarterly 9/1 (January 1985): 167-173.

Accounts for Franklin Delano Roosevelt's efforts in late 1941 to influence the isolationists by presenting them with a secret map showing Japanese and German plans to reorganize South America. Discusses the map as a forgery and reveals the intelligence processes by which the map was acquired.

901. Braun, A. Z. and Dov Levin. "Factors and Motivations in Jewish

Resistance," Yad Vashem Bulletin 2 (December 1957): 4-6+.

902. Braunstein, Michael. "Constitutional Law--Jurisdiction of Federal Courts--First Amendment Chill Resulting from Army Surveillance Non-justiciable," Tulane Law Review 47/2 (February 1973): 426-436.

Discusses Laird v. Tatum, focussing on issue of justiciability. US Supreme Court held mere fact that Army was conducting surveillance activity and claim that same chilled First Amendment rights did not invoke jurisdiction of federal courts.

903. Brausch, Gerd. "Sudan 1940: Deuxieme Bureau and Strategic Surprise," Militargeschichtliche Mitteilungen 2 (1967): 15-92.

In German, this is a lengthy analysis of the French intelligence service before the Sudan surprise attack in May 1940.

904. Bravo Nuche, Raman. "Servicios De Inteligencia," Revista General de Marina 193/8-9 (1977): 185-197.

Discusses the winding path of decentralized US intelligence services to the creation of the CIA, an agency which eventually became too centralized. The author argues for a balance between centralization and decentralization.

905. Brawley, J. V. and Jack Levine. "Equivalences of Vigenere Systems," Cryptologia 1/4 (October 1977): 338-361.

906. Bray, H. "Journalists As Spooks: CIA Use of Newsmen for Intelligence Operations," Progressive 41 (February 1977): 9-10.

Inquires into the relationship between the CIA and the major news organizations in newsprint, TV and foreign broadcast forms. Suggests that media were manipulated by purposeful Agency propaganda. Includes reactions by House and Senate intelligence committees.

907. Breaks, Katherine. "Ladies of the OSS: The Apron Strings of Intelligence in World War II," American Intelligence Journal 13/3 (Summer 1992): 91-96.

908. Brecher, Michael. "Toward a Theory of International Crisis Behavior," International Studies Quarterly 21 (March 1977): 39-74.

909. Brecher, Michael. "A Theoretical Approach to International Crisis Behavior," Jerusalem Journal of International Relations 3/2-3 (Winter-Spring 1978): 5-24.

Focusses on crisis definition and construction in the military-security issue area. Defines intra-war crisis, dimensions of crisis, actor attributes, characteristics of the decisional units. Offers a crisis model.

910. Brecher, Michael and Benjamin Geist. "Crisis Behavior: Israel, 1973," Jerusalem Journal of International Relations 3/2-3 (1978): 197-228.

Discusses Israel's political behavior during the Yom Kippur war of 1973 in terms of the psychological climate for decisions, the composition of consultative and decisional units; participants in the decisional process; decisional structures; stress and the pattern of information, and effect of stress on the search for alternatives.

911. Brecher, Michael and Mordechai Rtz. "Images and Behavior: Israel's Yom Kippur Crisis 1973," International Journal 32/3 (1977): 475-500.

Brecher's book on the subject is Decisions in Crisis, 1980.

912. Breckinridge, Scott D. "Clandestine Intelligence: International Law," International Studies Notes 9/2 (Summer 1982): 8-12.

913. Breckinridge, Scott D. "CIA's Inspector General -- The DCI's Independent Eye: Another View," International Journal of Intelligence and Counterintelligence 3/3 (Fall 1989): 419-424.

Brief remarks reflecting the author's professional experiences in the CIA, reflecting upon an article by Frederick M. Kaiser, "The Watcher's Watchdog: The CIA Inspector General." Opposes the view taken that the IG should become an instrument of the Congress.

914. Breckinridge, Scott D. "The Shape of Post-Cold War Intelligence," International Journal of Intelligence and Counterintelligence 8/1 (Spring 1995): 1-10.

Considers proposals for changing the structure and foci of the US intelligence community. Sections discuss the continuing crises in the post-Cold War world; concerns for the Peoples Republic of China and North Korea; smolderings in Cuba and states in the Middle East; the trade dimension, including NAFTA, GATT and WTO; and the nature of intelligence amid new crises.

915. Breemer, Jan S. "The Submarine Gap: Intelligence Estimates, 1945-1955," Navy International 91/2 (February 1986): 100-105.

916. Breemer, Jan S. "Soviet Naval Capabilities," International Journal of Intelligence and Counterintelligence 1/4 (Winter 1986-1987): 119-130.

Argues that intelligence analysts must take care to distinguish between capabilities and intentions of an enemy. Overemphasis on consideration of capabilities leads to the rejection of new data. Refers to examples of overemphasis on Soviet naval capabilities during the cold war. Observes the interaction between analyses of capabilities and intentions.

917. Breguet, Claude. "La Reconnaissance Aerienne et la Bataille de la Marne,"

Revue Militaire Francaise 166 (March 1987): 92-100.

918. Breight, Curtis C. "Duelling Ceremonies: The Strange Case of William Hacket, Elizabethan Messiah," Journal of Medieval & Renaissance Studies 19 (Spring 1989): 35-67.
        Includes some discussion of treason in connection with this fifteenth century account in Tudor history.

919. Breindel, Eric M. "Do Spies Matter?," Commentary 85/3 (March 1988): 53-58.
        A book review essay on the question, referring to several books, such as, Peter Wright's Spycatcher; Barrie Penrose and Simon Freeman's Conspiracy of Silence: The Secret Life of Anthony Blunt; Norman Moss' Klaus Fuchs: The Man Who Stole the Atom Bomb; Robert C. Williams' Klaus Fuchs: Atom Spy; and Chapman Pincher's Traitors: The Anatomy of Treason.

920. Breindel, Eric M. "Alger Hiss: A Glimpse Behind the Mask," Commentary 86/5 (November 1988): 55-58.
        A discussion of the allegations and evidence against State Department employee Alger Hiss in the early 1950s. A book review essay of Hiss' autobiography, Recollections of a Life.

921. Breitman, Richard. "The Allied War Effort and the Jews, 1942-1943," Journal of Contemporary History 20/1 (1985): 135-156.

922. Bremner, R. M. "My Visit to the Australian Intelligence Corps," Rose and the Laurel 8/34 (December 1972): 57-58.
        Describes the facilities and organizations of Australian intelligence services positioned for ocean surveillance. Also indicates measure of US involvement in Australian communications intelligence.

923. Breneman, Gary M. "Lawrence R. Houston: A Biography," Studies in Intelligence 30/1 (Spring 1986).

924. Brennan, Bonnie C. and Katherine Gilbert. "Investigating the Puzzle Palace: An Interview With James Bamford" and "The National Security Agency: The High Technology of Global Surveillance," Fletcher Forum of World Affairs 7/1 (Winter 1983): 199-215.
        A book review of James Bamford's The Puzzle Palace. This is a similar piece to a review by the same authors cited in this bibliography, but it includes the authors' interview with Bamford.

925. Brennan, Bonnie C. and Katherine Gilbert. "The Puzzle Palace: A Report on America's Most Secret Agency," Boston College International and Comparative

Law Review 6 (Spring 1983): 625-635.

A book review essay of James Bamford's The Puzzle Palace. Contains sections tiled "History of the NSA," "NSA Monitoring Stations Revealed," "Big Brother?," "NSA's Legal Status," "NSA Efficiency," and "Searching Out the Margin."

926. Brennan, John C. "General Bradley T. Johnson's Plan to Abduct President Lincoln," Chronicles of St. Mary's 22 (November-December 1974): 413-424.

927. Brennan, Sheila M. "Popular Images of American Women in the 1950's and Their Impact on Ethel Rosenberg's Trial and Conviction," Women's Rights Law Reporter 14 (Winter 1992): 43-63.

928. Breslauer, Irving H. "Fourth Allied Tactical Air Force," Canadian Forces Sentinel 3/2 (1967): 18-21.

929. Bresler, Robert J. "Hoover and Donovan: The Politics of Bureaucratic Empire Building," International Journal of Public Administration 16/1 (1993): 67-105.

Argues that FBI's J. Edgar Hoover and OSS director William J. Donovan were locked in a struggle for supremacy in controlling US intelligence operations during World War II.

930. Brethauer, Todd. "Adam Smith Examines the Intelligence Economy," Studies in Intelligence 39/5 (1996): 71-73.

Major sections discuss the business of intelligence; the cold war, risk avoidance, and central planning; new world disorder, risk management, and market forces; the intelligence marketplace; and imposing budgetary restraint.

931. Brewer, Gary D. and Paul Bracken. "Some Missing Pieces of the C^3I Puzzle," Conflict Resolution 28/3 (September 1984): 451-469.

Defines command, control and communications and their role in national defense of the US. Argues the importance of maintaining strength in C^3I capabilities in order to hedge against surprise attacks. Suggests changes in C^3I systems to be more responsive to national policy objectives.

932. Brewer, Robert T. "Albania: New Aspects, Old Documents," East European Quarterly 26/1 (Spring 1992): 31-54.

Discusses recently declassified documents concerning British work with the American OSS during World War II in Albania. OSS recruited many Albanians for intelligence missions and for guerilla and sabotage missions. Focusses also on operation Birdset aimed at infiltrating intelligence agents into Albania.

933. Brickell, Ernest F. and Andrew M. Odlyzko. "Cryptanalysis: A Survey of Recent Results," Proceedings of the IEEE 76 (May 1988): 578-593.

934. Bricker, Bill. "The S2 in Counterguerilla Operations," Infantry 56 (July-August 1966): 12-15.

935. Brickhill, Joan. "Trouble in Jamaica: Is the CIA Harassing the Island's Socialist Regime?," Atlas 24 (March 1977): 112+.

936. Bridge, T. D. "Admiral John Godfrey RN: Genius Without Recognition," Army Quarterly and Defence Journal 3/3 (July 1981): 323-326.

937. Bridges, Brian. "Britain and Japanese Espionage in Pre-War Malaya: The Shinozaki Case," Journal of Contemporary History 21 (January 1986): 23-25.
    Shinozaki was press attache in Singapore. This is the story of his arrest, detention and subsequent release on a charge of espionage. Later, he contributed to the new Singapore administration.

938. Bridges, Hal. "A Lee Letter on the 'Lost Dispatch' and the Maryland Campaign of 1862," Virginia Magazine of History and Biography 66/2 (1958): 161-168.

939. Bridges, Horace J. "A Suggestion Toward a New Definition of Treason," Journal of the American Institute of Criminal Law and Criminology 30/4 (November-December 1939): 470-484.
    Remarks on long moral decline in international relations. Argues that certain speech be included in established definition of treason as "acts by which war is brought into existence."

940. Brietzke, Paul H. "Public Policy: Contract, Abortion, and the CIA," Valparaiso University Law Review 18 (Summer 1984): 741-940.
    An extensive scholarly examination of the policy making process, especially that portion of which concerns the formulation of policy alternatives, often done in a simplistic fashion. A major section addresses the CIA: "Funding the Horns of the False Dichotomy." Required reading for all analysts and scholars of intelligence topics.

941. Brigden, Susan. "Henry Howard, Earl of Surrey, and the 'Conjured League,'" Historical Journal 37 (September 1994): 507-537.
    Discussion of treason in sixteenth century British literature.

942. Briggs, Michael W. "Constitutional Law -- A Police Officer's Naked-eye Observations of the Interior of a Partially-covered Greenhouse from the Vantage Point of a Helicopter Circling at an Altitude of 400 Feet Is Not a Search for

Which a Warrant Is Required Under the Fourth Amendment," <u>Drake Law Review</u> 40/3 (Spring 1991): 615-627.

      Discusses result of <u>Florida v. Riley</u>. Provides Florida Supreme Court analysis and US Supreme Court analysis. Discusses standard of <u>Katz v. U. S.</u> and Supreme Court's failure to apply the <u>Katz</u> standard in <u>Riley</u>.

943. Briggs, Ralph T. "The Day VADM Yamagata Joined His Honorable Ancestors," <u>Cryptolog</u> 10/5 (1989): 1-14.
      Also appears in <u>Naval History</u> 3/2 (1989): 29-35.

944. Briggs, Ralph T. "Intelligence Analects and News Bytes," <u>NICA Shield</u> 3/2 (March-April 1994): 4-14.

945. Brigham, C. S. "Edgar Allan Poe's Contributions to Alexander's Weekly Messenger," <u>American Antiquarian Society Proceedings</u> 52 (April 1942): 45-125.

946. Bright, C. "Telegraphs in War-Time," <u>Nineteenth Century</u> (April 1915): 874-875.

947. Bright, Herbert S. "Cryptanalytic Attack and Defense: Ciphertext-only, Known Plaintext, Chosen=Plaintext," <u>Cryptologia</u> 1/4 (October 1977): 366-370.

948. Bright, Herbert S. "High Speed Indirect Encryption," <u>Cryptologia</u> 4/3 (July 1980): 133-139.

949. Brill, Steven. "The Two Persuaders," <u>American Lawyer</u> 2 (May 1980): 5-6.
      Discusses briefly the Department of Justice victory against former CIA case officer Frank Snepp, where United States Supreme Court held that Snepp was enjoined from publishing his book (<u>Decent Interval</u>) due to his failure to obtain Central Intelligence Agency approval. Snepp was ordered to give the government all his earnings from the book.

950. Brinton, Crane. "Letter from Liberated France," <u>French Historical Studies</u> 2/1 & 2/3 (Spring and Fall 1961): 1-27; 133-156.

951. Briscoe, N. B. "Combat Intelligence," <u>Cavalry Journal</u> (September-October 1940).

952. Brisse, Gerard. "Cambodia: A People Murdered," <u>Annee Politique et Economie</u> 46 /235-236 (1973): 295-335.
      A detailed discussion in French of the role of the CIA in Cambodia in association with the Sihanouk government.

953. Brissenden, R. F. "A Perfect Spy: 'Like Huckleberry Finn,'" Quadrant 30 (December 1986): 45-49.

954. Bristoll, William M. "Escape From Charleston," American Heritage 26/3 (March 1975): 24-27, 82-88.
 A tale of Civil War espionage and intelligence. A Charleston shopkeeper is the first to be tried under the Confederate Sequestration Act, then escapes to the North after capture and interrogation.

955. Broadwell, Wendell S. "Commercial Espionage: The Phenomenon of Information Theft," Journal of Security Administration 6/2 (January 1984): 41-51.
 Applies an expectancy model of behavior to explain the alleged increase in commercial espionage. Proposes that the advantage gained from the behavior and the availability of resources and talent to engage the activity determine the frequency of occurrence. Major sections discuss business, technology and secrecy; intelligence and business competition; and answer to the question of who commits commercial espionage; advantages of engagement; and resources and talent needed.

956. Brock, Darla. "'Our Hands Are At Your Service': The Story of Confederate Women in Memphis," West Tennessee Historical Society Papers 45 (1991): 19-34.

957. Brockel, Harry C. "World War II Secrets of Lake Michigan," Inland Seas 34/2 (1978): 103-112.
 Discusses a wide variety of wartime activities on Lake Michigan in connection with training and logistics.

958. Brodeur, Jean-Paul. "High Policing and Law Policing: Remarks About the Policing of Political Activities," Social Problems 30/5 (June 1983): 507-520.
 A theoretical discussion of two types of policing strategies employed to maintain social control. Author suggests that low policing is potentially dangerous, as it involves the invasion of privacy and violation of civil rights. Useful piece for analyses of domestic intelligence activities.

959. Brodeur, Jean-Paul. "Undercover Policing in Canada: Wanting What Is Wrong," Crime, Law and Social Change 18/1-2 (September 1992): 105-136.
 Considers undercover operations in Canada; the Canadian police apparatus; the concept of intention in undercover work; the consequences of undercover policing; and conclusions.

960. Brodie, Bernard. "Military Demonstration and Disclosure of New Weapons," World Politics 5/3 (April 1953): 281-301.
 Author contrasts the objective results of demonstration of weapons to the

enemy (one's military intentions) and disclosure of new weapons (one's military capabilities). Discusses in detail weapons development in the United States and the role of secrecy in scientific advancements of military strengths. A useful resource for studies of the value and limitations of secrecy management.

961. Brodie, Bernard. "Why Were We So (Strategically) Wrong?," Foreign Policy 5 (Winter 1971-1972): 151-161.

Argues that high level decision making that led to the entanglements in Vietnam was tainted by misperceptions of the determination of the North Vietnamese to fight and by decisions based in earlier wars. Author finds great fault with the analytical biases that inched their way into the decision making processes.

962. Brodin, Katarina. "Surprise Attack: The Case of Sweden," Journal of Strategic Studies 1/1 (May 1978): 98-110.

Analysis of the Swedish defense capabilities and the philosophy of perpetual mobilization against potential attack.

963. Brody, Peter M. "The First Amendment, Governmental Censorship, and Sponsored Research," Journal of College and University Law 19/3 (Winter 1993): 199-215.

Discusses the doctrine of academic freedom; unconstitutional conditions; the "non-subsidy" doctrine; the Stanford case; and conclusions.

964. Brody, Richard. "The Limits of Warning," Washington Quarterly 6/3 (Summer 1983): 40-48.

965. Broeder, Dale W. "Wong Sun v. United States: A Study in Faith and Hope," Nebraska Law Review 42/3 (April 1963): 483-621.

Discusses the many issues in the Wong Sun decision, such as unlawful arrest (including searches incident to arrest, reliability, flight evidence, etc.), "fruits" doctrine, corpus delicti, application to the states, McNabb-Mallory rule, due process, right to counsel, wiretapping, and Fifth Amendment and dual sovereignty.

966. Brogan, Mark. "The Royal Commission on Australia's Security and Intelligence Agencies," Archives and Manuscripts 12/2 (1984): 105-115.

An examination of the status of security and intelligence agency records in Australia.

967. Brommel, Bernard J. "Kate Richards O'Hare: A Midwestern Pacifist's Fight for Free Speech," North Dakota Quarterly 44/1 (1976): 5-19.

968. Bronson, Judith G. "Unfriendly Eyes," IEEE Transactions on Professional

Communication 30/3 (September 1987): 173-178.

As part of the professional communication volumes of this series, this article considers issues related to industrial espionage and trade secrets compromises, including countermeasures.

969. Brooker, Gregory G. "FOIA Exemption 3 and the CIA: An Approach to End the Confusion and Controversy," Minnesota Law Review 68/6 (June 1984): 1231-1263.

Analyses the differing standards by which courts have applied exemption 3 to CIA documents. Examines the legislative history of exemption 3 where CIA admits existence of documents. Considers exemption 3 in light of CIA refusals to confirm or deny.

970. Brooks, Harvey. "Notes on Some Issues on Technology and National Defense," Daedalus 110/1 (Winter 1981): 129-136.

Raises questions and offers a typology concerning the impact of technology on military operations. Discusses briefly the United States response to the Sputnik surprise of 1957.

971. Brooks, Robert O. "Surprise in the Missile Era," Air University Review 11/1 (Spring 1959): 76-83.

972. Brooks, Sydney. "The German Spy System," Atlantic Monthly 115 (February 1915): 253-261.

An early account of espionage system of a man named Wilhelm Stieber, later described as the genius behind Bismarck's imperialist foreign policy. A classic historical article.

973. Brooks, Thomas A. "The Ultimate Intelligence System," American Intelligence Journal 4/3 (May 1982): 24-25.

974. Brooks, Thomas A. "Soviet Navy: An Update; Intelligence Collection," U.S. Naval Institute Proceedings 111 (December 1985): 47-49.

975. Brooks, Thomas A. "Naval Intelligence in the Nineties," American Intelligence Journal 11/3 (1990): 9-10.

976. Brophy, W. J. and T. G. Paterson. "October Missiles and November Elections: The Cuban Missile Crisis and American Politics, 1962," Journal of American History 73 (June 1986): 87-119.

A lengthy review of the Cuban missile crisis in terms of its significance to the fall elections of 1962. Breaks down the time periods prior to the elections and evaluates positions of President Kennedy at each phase.

977. Brower, Brock. "Why People Like You Joined the CIA," <u>Washington Monthly</u> 8/9 (November 1976): 50-60.
A light commentary on the early days at CIA and the experiences of one member who was known to the author.

978. Brower, K. S. "The Yom Kippur War," <u>Military Review</u> 64/3 (March 1984): 18-23.

979. Brown, Canter, Jr. "Tampa's James McKay and the Frustration of Confederate Cattle-Supply Operations in South Florida," <u>Florida Historical Quarterly</u> 70/4 (1992): 409-433.

980. Brown, Dallas C. "Combat Intelligence Today," <u>Armor</u> 73 (October 1964): 20-23.

981. Brown, Drusilla. "Psychological Operations (PSYOP): United States-- Soviet Union," <u>Military Intelligence</u> 8/4 (1982): 46-48.

982. Brown, F. C. "The Phoenix Program," <u>Military Journal</u> 2 (Spring 1979): 19-21, 49.

983. Brown, George E., Jr. "Politics and Secrecy: Easing the Tension," <u>American Intelligence Journal</u> 9/1 (Summer 1988): 30-31.
Brief remarks concerning the impact of overclassification of technology and the hindrance such overclassification has on the development of satellite technologies.

984. Brown, Harold. "The Military Planner's Challenge: Reconciling Technology with Policy," <u>Foreign Affairs</u> 45/2 (1967): 277-290.
Discusses the uncertainty with which the Department of Defense addressed planning for future United States military force applications. Argues that intelligence should be raised from a secondary input among various decision processes to a more central place in the development of military systems.

985. Brown, Julia C. "I Was a Spy for the FBI," <u>Ebony</u> 16/5 (March 1961): 94-103.
This publication is normally not included among scholarly journals, but the subject matter and circumstances of the case are unique and rarely explored in journal literature, thus making the article worthy of citation here. More research on African-American connections with the FBI and the CIA is needed.

986. Brown, Kathryn. "Intelligence and the Decision to Collect It: Churchill's Wartime Diplomatic Signals Intelligence," <u>Intelligence and National Security</u> 10/3 (July 1995): 449-467.

Based on newly released Public Information Office records, the author addresses the matter of Churchill's access to American diplomatic traffic by way of signals intercepts prior to US involvement in the war.

987. Brown, MacAlister. "Third Reich's Mobilization of the German Fifth Column in Eastern Europe," Journal of Central European Affairs 19 (July 1959): 128-148.

Advances the view that ethnic Germans aided Hitler's SS by conducting espionage in Eastern European countries. Argues that Hitler played an important part in the management of ethnic minority affairs, and he used the argument of the abuse of German ethnic minorities as a reason for his invasions into Eastern Europe.

988. Brown, Neville. "Reconnaissance from Space," World Today 27/2 (February 1971): 68-76.

Mainly an historical review of US satellite reconnaissance programs and military assets in space. Concludes with a discussion of the possible abuses of satellite use by the US and other nations.

989. Brown, Neville. "Jordanian Civil War," Military Review 51 (September 1971): 38-48.

Discusses terrorism in Jordan, and brief mention of the role of intelligence.

990. Brown, Peter M. "The Great Wiretapping Debate and the Crisis in Law Enforcement," New York Law Forum 6 (1960): 265-282.

Discusses concerns about wiretapping in years prior to enactment of Omnibus Crime Control and Safe Streets Act of 1968 and its Title III wiretap provision. Covers state debates, background, important points in history of the problem.

991. Brown, Peter M. and Richard S. Peer. "The Wiretapping Entanglement: How to Strengthen and Preserve Privacy," Cornell Law Quarterly 44/2 (Winter 1959): 175-185.

Discusses the confusion in the law regarding wiretapping procedures. Calls for congressional action to change the law and to codify the principles.

992. Brown, Ralph S., Jr. "The Operation of Personnel Security Programs," Annals of the American Academy of Political and Social Science 300 (1955).

993. Brown, Ralph S., Jr. and John D. Fassett. "Security Tests for Maritime Workers: Due Process Under the Port Security Program," Yale Law Journal 62/8 (July 1953): 1163-1208.

Concerns federal loyalty-security programs, particularly the Port Security

Program administered by the US Coast Guard.   Topics covered include communism and the shipping industries, the role of the Coast Guard in the voluntary security program, criteria for denying clearances, review process, operation of responses to and authority for the program delegation, due process and the Administrative Procedures Act, the Fifth Amendment, proposals for procedures.

994. Brown, Raymond J. "Break My Day, or the Intelligence Officer's Lament," Naval Intelligence Professionals Quarterly 10/1 (Winter 1994): 7-8.

995. Brown, Raymond J. "Weather Intelligence: A Personal Encounter," Naval Intelligence Professionals Quarterly 12/1 (Winter 1996): 5-6.
   More research and publication should be engaged on this subject.

996. Brown, Richard C. "General Emory Upton--the Army's Mahan," Military Affairs 17 (1953): 125-131.
   A brief history of the life of General Emory Upton that compares his studies of the world's armies to Admiral Mahan's studies of the world's navies. Upton's grand contributions to the Army were cut short by his suicide in 1881.

997. Brown, Richard C. "Three Forgotten Heroes: John Andre Encounters Yankee Doodle," American Heritage 26/5 (May 1975): 25-29.
   A recognition account of the three men (John Paulding; Isaac Van Wert; David Williams) who captured British spy Major John Andre in September 1780.

998. Brown, Robert K. "The Phantom Navy of the CIA," Sea Classics 8 (May 1975): 50-62.

999. Brown, Sanborn C. and Kenneth Scott. "Count Rumford: International Informer," New England Quarterly 21 (March 1948): 34-49.
   An account of Benjamin Thompson, a charismatic school teacher, who moved into elite circles before and during the American revolution to become a military and political informer. It is argues that his espionage work helped him politically and financially.

1000. Brown, Sanborn C. and E. Stein. "Benjamin Thompson and the First Secret Ink Letter of the American Revolution," American Journal of Police Science 40 (1950): 627-628.

1001. Brown, William F. and Americo R. Cinquegrana. "Warrantless Physical Searches for Foreign Intelligence Purposes: Executive Order 12,333 and the Fourth Amendment," Catholic University Law Review 35/1 (Fall 1985): 97-179.
   Discusses utility of warrantless searches, constitutional grounds in Fourth Amendment and creation of foreign intelligence exception for foreign intelligence

collection as well as standards for permitting exceptions to the warrant clause of the Fourth Amendment. Reviews scope of exception, its requirements and test used by courts, congressional initiatives, such as Foreign Intelligence Security Act, and the "zone of twilight" in the conflict between executive power and congressional authority.

1002. Brown, William H. "J58/SR71 Propulsion Integration," Studies in Intelligence 26/2 (Summer 1982).

1003. Browne, Donald R. "R.I.A.S. Berlin: A Case Study of a Cold War Broadcast Operation," Journal of Broadcasting 10 (Spring 1966): 119-135.
    Account of the post-war operations of Radio in the American Sector of Berlin (R.I.A.S.), an autonomous branch of Voice of America. Discusses the establishment of the radio operations, basic policy, operating principles, measuring the impact of RIAS, and the competition of television.

1004. Browne, Donald R. "Broadcasting in Industrially-Developed Nations: An Annotated Bibliography," Journal of Broadcasting 19/3 (Summer 1975): 341-354.
    A bibliography of books only reflecting resources in various nations of the world. Categorized by country of publication.

1005. Browne, Malcolm. "A Reporter Looks Back: The CIA and the Fall of Vietnam," Washington Journalism Review (January-February 1978): 18-19.

1006. Brownell, Herbert, Jr. "The Public Security and Wiretapping," Cornell Law Quarterly 39/2 (Winter 1954): 195-213.
    Discusses history of wiretapping and treatment by US courts and how existing law hindered prosecution for espionage. Considers then-pending legislation in Congress and its potential to remedy problems of existing law.

1007. Brownlee, Robert W. "Key Man on the Combat Intelligence Team," Army Digest 23 (January 1968): 12-16.

1008. Brownstein, Ronald. "Inside the Puzzle Palace," Student Lawyer 11/5 (January 1983): 10-14, 38-39.
    Describes James Bamford's research under the FOIA to acquire NSA documents. Material was used in his book, The Puzzle Palace.

1009. Brown University Students CIA Action Group. "Citizens' Arrest of CIA Recruiters: The Buck Stops Here," National Lawyers Guild Practitioner 42/2 (Spring 1985): 61-64.
    Details charges made against CIA and its recruiters in the 1984 citizens arrest of CIA recruiters at Brown. Most charges focussed on CIA involvement in Nicaragua as violations of several laws, treaties, orders, and international

organization provisions.

1010. Broyles, David. "Fundamentals of Intelligence: Prudential Reason and the Founders' Executive," Teaching Political Science 16/3 (Spring 1989): 99-106.

1011. Bruce, David K. E. "The National Intelligence Authority," Virginia Quarterly Review 22 (Summer 1946): 355-369.

1012. Bruce, David K. E. "Have We an Intelligence Service?," Atlantic Monthly 181 (April 1948): 66-70.
    Argues that US intelligence services were in a state of decline following World War II, suggesting the need for stronger congressional support for the role of intelligence in national security.

1013. Bruce-Briggs, B. "Another Ride on Tricycle," Intelligence and National Security 7/2 (April 1992): 77-100.
    A new look at the Tricycle affair in connection with background political and military conditions following review of FBI archives. Major sections discuss a British assault on J. Edgar Hoover; an American assault on J. Edgar Hoover; the question of Hoover's exoneration; the redemption question concerning Popov; the Gronau forecast; the reconsideration of the Tricycle questionnaire; and the question of an assault on American intelligence.

1014. Bruemmer, Russell J. "Intelligence Community Reorganization: Declining the Invitation to Struggle," Yale Law Journal 101/4 (January 1992): 867-891.
    Considers how to restructure intelligence community in context of current developments in international arena. Argues need for more emphasis on economic and social issues and less on military, especially regarding former Soviet Republic countries and Eastern Europe, as well as Middle East and Africa. Discusses authority and responsibility in the intelligence community, and proposals for reorganization.

1015. Bruemmer, Russell J. and Marshall H. Silverberg. "The Impact of the Iran-Contra Matter on the Congressional Oversight of the CIA," Houston Journal of International Law 11/1 (Fall 1988): 219-243.
    Focusses on the role of the CIA in the Iran-Contra affair. Contains background of congressional oversight of CIA and covert action; summarizes CIA's role in Iran-Contra; describes CIA internal measures to preclude future controversies of a similar nature; and includes two additional congressional oversight proposals.

1016. Brugioni, Dino A. "Spotting Photo Fakery," Studies in Intelligence 13/4 (Winter 1969): 57-67.
    See author's book on the Cuban Missile Crisis: Eyeball to Eyeball, 1990.

1017. Brugioni, Dino A.   "The Unidentifieds," Studies in Intelligence 13/2 (Summer 1969): 1-20.

Discusses the problems and methodology involved in photographic interpretation, in particular, cases calling for other sources of confirmation of what appeared at first conclusion to have been military installations. Several photos included.

1018. Brugioni, Dino A.   "The Serendipity Effect," Studies in Intelligence 14/1 (Spring 1970).

1019. Brugioni, Dino A.   "The Cuban Missile Crisis: Phase I," Studies in Intelligence 16/3 (Fall 1972).

1020. Brugioni, Dino A.   "The Case of the Missing Diamond," Studies in Intelligence 23/1 (Spring 1979).

1021. Brugioni, Dino A.   "President Truman and the Congolese SAM," Studies in Intelligence 23/3 (Fall 1979).

1022. Brugioni, Dino A.   "Auschwitz-Birkenau: Why the World War II Photo Interpreters Failed to Identify the Extermination Complex," Military Intelligence 9/1 (January-March 1983): 50-55.

An explanation of the subject by an author with first hand knowledge of the oversight.

1023. Brugioni, Dino A.   "Hiding the Aircraft Factories," Air Force Magazine 66/3 (1983): 112-115.

Camouflage actions on the West Coast to protect US war plants from expected bombing by the Japanese, mainly in 1942 and 1943.

1024. Brugioni, Dino A.   "Aerial Photos--An Overlooked Resource," American Intelligence Journal 6/1 (March 1984): 19-24.

1025. Brugioni, Dino A.   "Aerial Photography: Reading the Past, Revealing the Future," Smithsonian 14/12 (1984): 150-161.

1026. Brugioni, Dino A.   "Photo Interpretation and Photogrammetry in World War II," Photogrammetric Engineering and Remote Sensing 50/9 (1984): 1313-1318.

1027. Brugioni, Dino A.   "Naval Photo Intell in WW II," U.S. Naval Institute Proceedings 113/6 (June 1987): 46-51.

A discussion of the development of naval photographic intelligence during war: terrain modeling, US Naval Underwater Demolition teams, flak charts, use of Naval information, aerial cameras, Operation Overlord.

1028. Brugioni, Dino A. "The Serendipity Effect of Aerial Reconnaissance," Interdisciplinary Science Reviews 124/1 (1989).
    Contains the author's findings from a review of aerial reconnaissance of the Nazi camp at Auschwitz.

1029. Brugioni, Dino A. "Genetrix--The Intelligence Balloon," Military Intelligence (January-March 1989): 26-28.
    Discusses the developments in reconnaissance balloons during the Eisenhower presidency. Sections discuss advances in chemistry, Project Skyhook, the Genetrix balloon, technical problems, the Soviet and US testing of nuclear weapons, balloon test programs, Eisenhower's balloon policy, and balloon propaganda.

1030. Brugioni, Dino A. "The Impact and Social Implications of Commercial Remote-Sensing Satellites," Technology in Science 11 (1989): 1-10.

1031. Brugioni, Dino A. "Antoine De Saint Exupery, Reconnaissance Pilot Par Excellence," American Intelligence Journal 13/1&2 (Winter-Spring 1992): 75-79.

1032. Brugioni, Dino A. "A Legacy of Excellence: Remembering Art Lundahl," Studies in Intelligence 36/4 (Winter 1992).
    A dedication to the Arthur C. Lundahl, the photo interpretation specialist in the early years of the CIA who was charged with organizing the National Photographic Interpretation Center.

1033. Brugioni, Dino A. and Robert F. McCort. "Personality: Arthur C. Lundahl," The Art of Photography: Photogrammetry and Remote Sensing 54/2 (February 1988): 270-272.

1034. Brugioni, Dino A. and Robert G. Piorier. "The Holocaust Revisited, A Retrospective Analysis of the Auschwitz-Birkenau Extermination Complex," American Intelligence Journal 2/1 (Spring 1979): 14-23.
    This piece appeared originally in CIA's Studies in Intelligence 22/4 (Winter 1978): 11-29, under the same title. This is a study of the remaining declassified photos of these two holocaust death camps.

1035. Brunn, Bruce E. "Intelligence Support of the Forward Deployed MAGTF," Marine Corps Gazette 69 (March 1985): 65-70.

1036. Bryan, G. S. "Famous Spies in American History," Mentor 9 (September 1921): 1-12.

1037. Bryan, John R. "Balloons Used for Scout Duty: Terrible Experiences of a Confederate Officer Who Saw the Enemy from Dizzy Heights," Southern Historical Society Papers 33 (1905): 32-42.

1038. Bryan, Kenneth D. "Cryptography for Secure Networks," Journal of Electronic Defense 10 (June 1987): 43-44+.

1039. Bryant, F. C. "The Capture of Togoland," Cavalry Journal 26/60 (April 1926): 145-146.

1040. Bryant, Pat. "Justice vs. the Movement," Radical American 14/6 (1980): 7-22.
     Discusses the intelligence activities of the Justice Department's Community Relations Service in relation to certain demonstrations and incidents involving civil rights groups.

1041. Brzezinski, Zibignew. "The NSC's Midlife Crisis," Foreign Policy 69 (Winter 1987-88): 80-87.
     A detailed analysis of the National Security Council's evolution: institutionalization over-personalization and degradation. The author identifies factors needed to restore NSC to its original institutionalized role.

1042. Brzoska, Michaels. "Arms Transfer Data Sources," Journal of Conflict Resolution 26/1 (March 1982): 77-108.
     Within this extensive discussion of the sources of arms control data from private and intelligence sources, the author suggests that American intelligence figures contain errors.

1043. Bucans, Lawrence M. "Publicizing Soviet Scientific Research," Studies in Intelligence 4/4 (Winter 1960).

1044. Buchen, Philip W. "Secrets of History and the Law of Secrets," American Archivist 40/1 (1977): 51-55.
     Discusses the conflicts between the efforts to open government via the Freedom of Information Act and the effects of openness upon government decisionmakers.

1045. Bucher, Erwin. "On the Masson-Schellenberg Line," Schweizerische Zeitscrift fuer Geschichte 38/3 (1988): 276-302.

1046. Bucher, Lloyd M. "The Pueblo Incident: Commander Bucher Replies," Naval History (Winter 1989): 44-50.
     The commander of this intelligence collection vessel responded to the Journal editor's critique of his actions.

1047. Buchwald, Don D. "Eavesdropping, Informers, and the Right of Privacy: A Judicial Tightrope," Cornell Law Quarterly 52/6 (Summer 1967): 975-1001.

Discusses history of law relating to intercepted conversation, distinction between wiretap and eavesdrop, tangibility requirement of Fourth Amendment as stated in Olmstead v. U. S. and its subsequent removal in Irvine v. California, the trespass theory and its development, relevances for voluntariness, requisite of corroboration, application of Fourth Amendment warrant clause, and trends in the law. Also considers informers and potential conflicts with rights to counsel and against self-incrimination, as well as issues of solicitation, credibility, and entrapment.

1048. Buck, James H. "Japan's Defense Policy," Armed Forces and Society 8/1 (Fall 1981): 79-98.

Extensive characterization of the many factors involved in the maintenance of Japan's defense posture, including the internal problem of no laws against espionage.

1049. Buck, Kathleen A. "The First Amendment - An Absolute Right?," William and Mary Law Review 26/5 (Special Issue 1985): 851-862.

Discusses limitations on First Amendment, including national security, lack of right to special access to government information, free speech restraints on government employees.

1050. Buckley, Peter. "Labor of Love," Horizon 26/6 (1983): 45-49.

1051. Buckman, John. "Brainwashing, LSD, and the CIA: Historical and Ethical Perspectives," International Journal of Social Psychology 23 (Spring 1977): 8-19.

A useful interpretation of this controversy.

1052. Buckner, H. T. "A Theory of Rumor Transmission," Public Opinion Quarterly 29 (1965): 54-70.

1053. Buel, Larry V. "Intelligence Preparation of the Battlefield," Military Review 67/10 (October 1987): 24-33.

Explains intelligence planning at the operational level in terms of collection of information on military posturing, and analysis of economic, industrial, political, psychological, and sociological data as part of an overall plan.

1054. Buffotot, Patrice. "La Perception du Rearmement Allemand par les Organismes de Renseignement Francais do 1936 a 1939," Revue Historique des Armees 3 (1979): 173-184.

1055. Bukovsky, Vladimir. "The Peace Movement and the Soviet Union," Commentary 73/5 (1982): 1-36.

Major sections include discussion of Cold War propaganda, the peace movement and detente, the Afghanistan invasion, nuclear disarmament, the Bulgarian peace movement, Soviet expansionism, and aggressive encirclement.

1056. Bull, George C. "The Elicitation Interview," Studies in Intelligence 14/3 (Fall 1970): 115-122.

The author lays out a methodology for acquiring information in the scientific sphere without appearing to conduct an interrogation. Sections discuss the reason for an interview; finding the potential source; identifying the prospect; and maintaining cover while keeping the source on the subject.

1057. Bull, Martin. "Villains of the Peace: Terrorism and the Secret Services in Italy," Intelligence and National Security 7/4 (October 1992): 473-478.

A review article evaluating the 1991 books by R. Catanzaro, The Red Brigades and Left-Wing Terrorism in Italy and P. Willan, Puppet Masters: The Political Use of Terrorism in Italy.

1058. Bullard, F. Lauriston. "Abraham Lincoln and George Ashmun," New England Quarterly 19/1 (March 1946).

1059. Bulloch, Chris. "View from the Top--Intelligence Gathering from Aircraft and Spacecraft," Interavia 39 (January 1984): 543-548.

1060. Bullock, Joan G. "Intelligence Support of Military Operations: A Perspective," International Journal of Intelligence and Counterintelligence 4/2 (Summer 1990): 181-198.

Considers in detail the question of how joint intelligence support is provided to Naval Air Forces tasked to support Army-Air Force land campaigns. Major sections discuss employment of Naval Air Forces to support land operations; intelligence requirements; competing structures; historical perspectives; intelligence capabilities; new systems; and recommendations.

1061. Bullock, Joan R. M. "National Security Interests vs. the First Amendment," University of Toledo Law Review 13/4 (Summer 1982): 1437-1467.

Examines the Haig v. Agee case as a standard for conflicts between national security and the First Amendment. Discusses the clear and present danger test, the balancing test, the prior restraint doctrine, secrecy agreements, and conclusions.

1062. Bundy, McGeorge and James G. Blight. "October 27, 1962: Transcripts of the Meetings of the ExComm," International Security 12/3 (Winter 1987-1988): 30-94.

Discusses the transcripts of meetings concerning the Cuban missile crisis.

Major sections discuss the second Khrushchev letter to President Kennedy; the standstill agreement and the problem of two different audiences; the prospect of war and the elements of a way out; the approval of the Trollope ploy; the shootdown of the U-2; the refocus on Cuba; and turning up the temperature in Cuba.

1063. Bundy, William P. "The Guiding of Intelligence Collection," Studies in Intelligence 3/4 (Winter 1959): 37-53.

1064. Bundy, William P. "From the Depths to the Heights," Cryptologia 6/1 (1982): 65-74.
      A book review essay of several books pertaining to the deployment of the Ultra weapon by American intelligence at the British Bletchley Park.

1065. Bundy, William P. "The National Security Process: Plus Ca Change...?," International Security 7/3 (Winter 1982-1983): 94-109.
      Discusses in detail the foreign policy organization and plans of the Truman, Eisenhower, Kennedy and Johnson administrations. Begins with Truman's initiative to secure passage of the National Security Act of 1947, then discusses each president's use of the National Security Council.

1066. Bundy, William P. "Some of My Wartime Experiences," Cryptologia 11/1 (April 1987): 65-76.

1067. Bunker, Ellsworth. "Vietnam in Perspective," Studies in Intelligence 18/1 (Spring 1974).

1068. Bunn, George. "Satellites for the Navy: Shielded for Arms Control," Naval War College Review 38/5 (July-August 1985): 55- 69.
      Discusses Navy's dependence on surveillance satellites, existing international law on satellites and ASAT's, the ban on ASAT testing or deployment in space, ASAT verification, and ASAT's and national security threats.

1069. Bunting, Jerry E. "Corps Coastal Survey Teams," Marine Corps Gazette 55 (June 1971): 50-51.

1070. Burdick, Charles B. "A House on Navidad Street: The Celebrated Zimmermann Note on the Texas Border?," Arizona and the West 8/1 (1966): 19-34.
      A detailed historical account of a World War I espionage case that was centered in San Antonio, Texas--on Navidad Street. German spies and illegal immigrants were at the center of an espionage ring.

1071. Burdick, Charles B. "The American Military Attaches in the Spanish Civil War, 1936-1939," Militaergeschichtliche Mitteilungen 2 (1989): 61-77.

1072. Burford, Russell E., Jr. "Getting the Bugs Out of Socialist Legality: The Case of Joseph Brodsky and the Decade of Soviet Anti-Parasite Legislation," American Journal of Comparative Law 22 (Summer 1974): 465-508.
    Explores the atmosphere and workings of a Soviet court through an unofficial trial transcript, a link between the transcript and Brodsky who lives in the United States, and analyzes the efficacy of anti-parasite laws. Issue is the writer as enemy of the state.

1073. Burger, Ethan. "The East European Response to the Soviet Invasion of Afghanistan," American Intelligence Journal 5/1 (February 1983): 14-25.

1074. Burger, Robert H. "Privacy, Secrecy, and National Information Policy," Library Trends 35 (Summer 1986): 3-182.

1075. Burgess, Don. "Tarahumara Folklore: A Study in Cultural Secrecy," Southwest Folklore 5/1 (Winter 1981): 11-22.
    Role of secrecy among the Tarahumara indians of the Sierra Madre and Chihuahua, Mexico. The secrecy system has been used effectively against outsiders for centuries.

1076. Burgess, William H., III. "Strategic Targeting for Special Operations Forces," Armed Forces Journal International 122 (March 1985): 66-75.
    Discusses "new markets" for SOF's, funding, organizational locations of SOF's, initiatives, and suggested intelligence coordination lines.

1077. Burgess, William H., Jr. "Iranian Special Operations in the Iran-Iraq War: Implications for the United States," Conflict: An International Journal 8/1 (1988): 23-40.

1078. Burhans, William. "Radiodezinformatsiya," Journal of Electronic Defense (May 1986): 22-23.

1079. Burk, Dan L. "Protection of Trade Secrets in Outer Space Activity: A Study in Federal Preemption," Seton Hall Law Review 23/2 (Spring 1993): 560-640.
    Discusses commercial activity in outer space including issues of commercialization and privatization of various research activities; legal considerations under treaties; the Intergovernmental Agreement, patent law and trade secrets law; federal preemption in context of patents and trade secrets and application of doctrine of intellectual property interests in outer space. Examines similar problems as a means of answering problems of protecting outer space trade

secrets and offers potential solutions.

1080. Burke, Christine A.   "Foreign Intelligence Surveillance: Intelligence Gathering or Prosecution?," Fordham International Law Review 6/3 (1982-1983): 501-529.
Considers the implications of United States v. Falvey and the constitutionality of the Foreign Intelligence Surveillance Act.   Considers the permissible use of FISA in light of the Fourth Amendment to the United States Constitution.

1081. Burke, Colin.   "An Introduction to an Historic Computer Document: The 1946 Pendergass Report on Cryptanalysis and the Digital Computer," Cryptologia 17/2 (April 1993):   113-123.

1082. Burke, James F.   "Recently Released Material on Soviet Intelligence Operations," Intelligence and National Security 8/2 (April 1993):   238-249.
Brief description of sources of recently released documents from Soviet files on intelligence operations.   List of types of documents concerning Soviet intelligence activities in the former USSR, and materials concerning foreign intelligence operations.

1083. Burke, James F.   "Romanian and Soviet Intelligence in the December Revolution," Intelligence and National Security 8/4 (October 1993):   26-58.
Traces the history and development of the Romanian intelligence service, Sucuritate.   Sections discuss Romanian security and intelligence organizations; Soviet ties; pressures on the Ceausesceau regime in the 1980s; the December revolt and coup; the origins of the National Salvation Front; and the aftermath.

1084. Burke, James F.   "The Role of Capital Markets Intelligence in Corporate Management," International Journal of Intelligence and Counterintelligence 7/4 (Winter 1994):   429-433.
Brief outline of the definition and roles of capital market intelligence in terms of organization, missions and analytical products.

1085. Burke, Karen C.   "Secret Surveillance and the European Convention on Human Rights," Stanford Law Review 33/6 (July 1981):   1113- 1140.
Discusses wiretapping practices of the European Convention in terms of privacy rights and judicial discretion.   Argues for a more principled approach to judicial discretion if it is to be effectively applied.

1086. Burkhalter, Edward A., Jr.   "Soviet Industrial Espionage," Signal 37/7 (March 1983):   15-20.
Major sections discuss announced Soviet objectives; Soviet industry; highest priorities; the Bell-Zacharsky spy case; software purchase; sophisticated

schemes; and countermeasures.

1087. Burkhalter, Edward A., Jr. "The Role of the Intelligence Community Staff," Signal 39 (September 1984): 33-35.

1088. Burkhalter, Edward A., Jr. "The Soviet Union's Subversive War Against America," American Intelligence Journal 7/2 (September 1985): 1-5.

1089. Burkhalter, Edward A., Jr. "Leaks and Our National Security," Signal 40 (September 1985): 17-18.

1090. Burkhardt, Ernst. "'Aerial Warfare: Secret German Plans': Revelations or Forgeries?," Nineteenth Century and After 116/9 (1934): 331-336.

1091. Burlingame, Bo. "Paranoia in Power," Harper's 249 (October 1974): 26, 28-32, 36-37.

1092. Burnet, David and Richard Thomas. "Spycatcher--The Commodification of Truth," Journal of Law and Society 16/2 (Spring 1989): 210-224.
    Considers the Peter Wright litigation to achieve publication of a book, Spycatcher, in Britain. Takes in British and Australian government positions on the issue and concludes that there are basic reasons for the secrecy obsession in British political culture.

1093. Burnett, Edmund C. "Ciphers of the Revolutionary Period," American Historical Review 22/2 (January 1917): 329-334.
    Discusses rather extensively the use of cipher systems and practices in the American revolution.

1094. Burns, Arthur L. "The International Consequences of Expecting Technological Surprise," World Politics 10/4 (July 1958): 512-536.
    Reviews the escalation of weapons systems in relation to strategic surprise. Concludes that there is a continuing need to prevent nuclear warfare by constructing superior defensive systems. Excellent observations of the situation at the end to the 1950s, prior to the Cuban missile crisis.

1095. Burns, R. C. "Intelligence Across the Andes: How San Martin Used It," Military Review 57/7 (July 1977): 68-75.
    Recounts the activities of Jose Francisco de Martin in establishing an espionage network in Chile and psychological warfare strategies in pursuit of the independence of Chile.

1096. Burns, R. C. "How the RAF Led the Way," Aerospace Historian 26/1 (1979): 12-16.

1097. Burns, Richard D.   "Inspection of the Mandates, 1919-1941," Pacific Historical Review 37/4 (November 1968): 445-462.

Difficulties in the inspection of Japanese islands of the Marianas, the Carolines and the Marshalls during the interwar years. American intelligence did not have sufficient proof to argue that Japan was fortifying these islands for military purposes. Information came mainly from an American doctor living in Japan.

1098. Burns, Richard D. "International Arms Inspection Policies Between World Wars, 1919-1934," Historian 31 (August 1969): 583-603.

1099. Burpo, John H. "Electronic Surveillance by Leave of the Magistrate: The Case for the Prosecution," Tennessee Law Review 38/1 (1970): 14-32.

Discusses several issues pertaining to the constitutionality of electronic surveillance. Discusses Title III of the Omnibus Crime Control and Safe Streets Act regarding electronic surveillance.

1100. Burris, William C.   "The Uses of History of Intelligence Analysis," International Journal of Intelligence and Counterintelligence 6/3 (Fall 1993): 297-302.

An essay on the dangers of employing history in the justification of a particular theory applied in the intelligence field. Includes brief discussion of the James Angleton affair. Warns against the over-application of social science methods in the realm of intelligence.

1101. Bursell, William R. "American Sound Ranging in Four Wars," Field Artillery Journal 49/6 (November-December 1989): 53-55.

1102. Burt, Struthers. "Secret Agent on Skis," Harper's 204 (February 1952): 84-92.

An account of the German use of secret agents during World War II, including two particular agents who operated in mountainous regions in the United States.

1103. Burtness, Paul S. and Warren U. Ober. "Research Methodology: Problem of Pearl Harbor Intelligence Reports," Military Affairs 25/3 (Fall 1961): 132-146.

Authors critique a report by Takeo Ysohikawa, as interpreted by Lt. Col. Norman Stanford concerning espionage in Honolulu, Hawaii before the attack on Pearl Harbor. Suggests that the US was reading Yoshikawa's dispatches but it failed to appreciate their significance, thus introducing a failure of analysis, not a failure of information receiving. A detailed consideration of the information regarding Japanese agent reports of conditions of the US naval fleet prior to December 7, 1941. Suggests that a large number of agents would have been required to have dispatched as much information as some accounts suggest was in the hands of the Japanese. Observes the need for painstaking attention to details as a key element in successful intelligence gathering and reporting.

1104. Burton, Donald F. "Estimating Soviet Defense Spending," Problems of Communism 32/2 (1983): 85-93.

A reasonably detailed defense of the manner in which the Central Intelligence Agency gathers and evaluates Soviet defense expenditures.

1105. Burton, Ralph W. "Military Intelligence Support to Corps and the Air/Land Battle," Military Intelligence 7/3 (July-September 1981): 6-8.

Discussion of the use of various intelligence technologies capable of identifying, jamming, and targeting the enemy.

1106. Burton, Shirley and Kellee Green. "Defining Disloyalty: Treason, Espionage, and Sedition Prosecutions, 1861-1946," Prologue: Quarterly Journal of the National Archives 21/3 (1989): 215-221.

Discusses the historical difficulties in defining treason against the US government, some historical examples of alleged treason, and various laws passed since 1798 to deal with treason.

1107. Burtzev, Vladimir. "Police Provocation in Russia: Azef, the Tsarist Spy," Slavonic and East European Review 6 (December 1927): 246-260.

Original spelling of the author's name was Bourtzeff. Reflections from the author's interviews with the Russian terrorist and spy Yevno Azef.

1108. Bush, George. "The Central Intelligence Agency and the Intellectual Community: A Banquet Address, June 9, 1976," Signal 30 (August 1976): 36-37+.

1109. Bush, George. "The Objective Is to Keep the Peace," Studies in Intelligence 27/3 (Fall 1983).

1110. Bush, Larry. "JSIPS: Deployable Imagery Intelligence Goes Softcopy," American Intelligence Journal 13/1&2 (Winter-Spring 1992): 57-60.

1111. Bushinsky, J. "From Tel Aviv: Spies and Spooks," Present Tense 4/3 (1977): 21-24.

1112. Bussey, Donald S. "Ultra and the American 7th Army," Revue d'Histoire de la Deuxieme Guerre Mondiale et des Conflits Contemporains 34/133 (1984): 59-64.

Addresses a report of the 7th Army intelligence officers completed in 1945. Concerns the experiences of an intelligence-gathering group known as the Ultra team. Article is in French.

1113. Butler, Alfred J. "Some Elizabethan Cipher Books," <u>Transactions of the Bibliographical Society</u> 6/1 (December 1901): 127-135.

1114. Butler, Charles W. and Norman O. Schultz. "Divising An Intelligence Collection Plan," <u>Security Management</u> 37/3 (March 1993): 66, 68.
Application of basic intelligence collection methods in the corporate setting.

1115. Butler, William E. "The Pueblo Crisis: Some Critical Reflections," <u>Proceedings of the American Society of International Law</u> 63/1 (April 1969): 7-13.
Argued at the ASIL meeting, April 24, 1969, that the Pueblo matter raised legal issues of great scope and diversity. Especially important is the inappropriateness of international law re: coastlines and boundaries in the face of electronic intelligence gathering.

1116. Butterfield, Lyman H. "Psychological Warfare in 1776: The Jefferson-Franklin Plan to Cause Hessian Desertions," <u>Proceedings of the American Philosophical Society</u> 94/3 (June 1950): 233-241.
Discusses plans and operations of King George III to deploy Hessian mercenaries to fight for the British after 1775 in the American revolution. The Jefferson-Franklin plan to counter this move was an example of successful psychological warfare.

1117. Button, Robert E. "Ultra in the European Theatre of Operations," <u>Revue d'Histoire de la Deuxieme Guerre Mondiale et des Conflits Contemporains</u> 34/133 (1984): 43-52.
In French, this article discusses the cooperative efforts between British and American intelligence gathering teams during World War II.

1118. Butts, John L. "U.S. Navy Intelligence," <u>Military Intelligence</u> 9/3 (July-September 1983): 16-18.
Supplies a complete outline of US Navy intelligence organizations and respective missions.

1119. Butz, J. S. "New Vistas in Reconnaissance from Space," <u>Air Force and Space Digest</u> 51 (March 1968): 46-56.

1120. Buultjens, Ralph. "Words and Deed: Indian Intervention in South Asia," <u>Ethics & International Affairs</u> 3 (1989).

1121. Buzek, Antonin. "Diplomacy and Espionage," <u>Military Review</u> 43/1 (January 1963): 85-88.

1122. Buzek, Antonin. "Diplomacy and Espionage," East Europe 11/8 (August 1982): 10-11.
A brief discussion of the activities of Czech intelligence services.

1123. Byrd, Harry F. "Hitler's Experts Work for Us," American Magazine 3 (1945): 24-25, 136-138.

1124. Byrne, John; Cipher A. Deavours; and Louis Kruh. "Chaocipher Enters the Computer Age When Its Method Is Disclosed to Cryptologia Editors," Cryptologia 14/3 (July 1990): 193-198.

1125. Byrne, Leonard. "Nathan Hale: A Testament of Courage," New England Galaxy 16/4 (1975): 13-22.
Traces Hale's career to his execution as a spy against the British during the American Revolution.

1126. Byrne, Robert. "Combat Intelligence: Key to Victory at Gettysburg," Military Intelligence 2 (Fall 1976): 5-9.

1127. Byrnes, James F. "Why We Must Give the President a Clear Road," American Magazine (August 1945).
An argument for a centralized coordination of intelligence and the elimination of duplications between the various elements of the evolving concept of an intelligence community.

1128. Byrnes, Robert F. "Harvard, Columbia, and the CIA: My Training in Russian Studies," Russian History 15/1 (1988): 93-113.
A personal history of the author's experiences in Russian studies at Harvard, Columbia and the Central Intelligence Agency. Argues that experts in Russian studies should be removed from positions of authority and decision making at CIA in order to allow a better relationship with current research and analysis. Opposes covert government support for Russian studies in universities.

C

"...I was jumping from frying pans to fires...But I was
exhilarated doing it."
(Honorable Men by William E. Colby, p. 424)

1129. Cabaniss, H., Jr. "Espionage and Sabotage Legislation," California State
Bar Journal 17 (May-June 1942): 116-120.

1130. Cable, James. "The Falklands Conflict," U.S. Naval Institute Proceedings
108 (September 1982): 14-23.

1131. Cable, Larry. "Piercing the Mists: Limited and Ambiguous Conflicts,"
International Journal of Intelligence and Counterintelligence 4/1 (Spring 1990):
59-76.
    An analysis of the relationship between policy formulation and execution
in situations involving actual or imminent insurgency, partisan guerilla conflict,
terrorism, and strategic special operations. Contains major sections on intelligence
products; difficult relations regarding several insurgency cases in the 1960s;
assessment of performance; evaluating CIA estimates; and recommended changes.

1132. Caccamo, Joseph A. "A Comparison and Analysis of Immunities Defenses
Raised by Soviet Nationals Indicted Under United States Espionage Laws,"
Brooklyn Journal of International Law 6/2 (Summer 1980): 259-288.
    Discusses the issue of diplomatic immunity as it impacts cases in which
Soviet nationals are indicted under US espionage statutes. Where diplomatic
immunity is clearly established via diplomatic status, US courts have no

jurisdiction. Functional immunity, however, is not a defense against charges of espionage.

1133. Cachinero, Jorge and Julio Trujillo. "The Silent War: The Future of Intelligence Services," Politica Exterior 34 (Summer 1993): 115-125.
Considers the role and suggested reorganization of intelligence services in the 1990s and beyond, including the Spanish intelligence service.

1134. Cadwalader, John. "Operation Coldfeet: An Investigation of the Abandoned Soviet Arctic Drift Station Np 8," ONI Review 17 (August 1962): 344-355.

1135. Cagle, Malcolm W. "Errors of the Korean War," U.S. Naval Institute Proceedings 84 (March 1958): 31-35.

1136. Cahill, John. "Intelligence Unit Is a Key Division of a Police Agency," FBI Law Enforcement Bulletin 31/9 (September 1962): 4-7.

1137. Cain, Frank. "Missiles and Mistrust: U.S. Intelligence Responses to British and Australian Missile Research," Intelligence and National Security 3/4 (October 1988): 5-22.
Outlines the role of intelligence in the progress of atomic energy research and missiles in the post World War II era. Explores the points of interaction between Australian, British, and US efforts to protect sensitive information.

1138. Cain, Frank. "An Aspect of Post-War Relations with the United Kingdom and the United States: Missiles, Spies and Disharmony," Australian Historical Studies 23/92 (1989): 186-202.

1139. Cain, Frank. "ASIO and the Australian Labour Movement - An Historical Perspective," Labour History 58 (May 1990): 1-16.

1140. Cain, Frank. "Intelligence Writings in Australia," Intelligence and National Security 6/1 (January 1991): 242-253.
Briefly summarizes several books concerning the Australian intelligence services: The Secret Army and the Premier; Defending the National Tuck Shop; The Petrov Affair, Politics and Espionage; Sanctuary: Nazi Fugitives in Australia; Pine Gap, Australia and the U.S. Geostationary Signals; and A Base for Debate.

1141. Cain, Frank. "The Right to Know: ASIO, Historians and the Australian Parliament," Intelligence and National Security 8/1 (January 1993): 87-101.
Discusses the background and development of the Australian Security Intelligence Organization, including current events and the role of the historian researcher. Sections discuss the political history of ASIO; Parliamentary

oversight; ASIO arguments; and the historian's case.

1142. Cairns, Donald W. "UAV--Where We Have Been," Military Intelligence 13 (March 1987): 18-20.
　　　　Discusses the history of US unmanned aerial reconnaissance from 1915 to 1972.

1143. Calder, James D. "Industrial Espionage--Some Textbook Assumptions: Toward a New Multidisciplinary Research Agenda," Journal of Security Administration 6/2 (January 1984): 53-69.
　　　　Examines the underlying assumptions concerning the traditional and generally narrow discussions of industrial espionage found in the leading security management books. Argues for a substantially larger conception of the behavior involved in industrial espionage.

1144. Calder, James D. "Al Capone and the Internal Revenue Service: State-sanctioned Organized Crime," Crime, Law and Social Change 17/1 (April 1992): 1-23.
　　　　Discussion of the Internal Revenue Service's Intelligence Division investigation of gangster Al Capone, and the author's federal court litigation to gain access to the Intelligence Division records. Argues that the continued secrecy controls on the Capone records restricts study of organized crime to state-approved theories.

1145. Caldwell, Dan. "Department of Defense Operations During the Cuban Crisis: A Report by Adam Yarmolinsky," Naval War College Review 32/4 (July-August 1979): 83-99.
　　　　A detailed report, declassified in 1979, of US responses to Soviet submarine activity during the 1962 Cuban missile crisis. Shows the direct control and use of intelligence during the most tense period of the cold war.

1146. Caldwell, Dan. "A Research Note on the Quarantine of Cuba: October 1962," International Studies Quarterly 22/4 (December 1978): 625-633.

1147. Caldwell, Dan. "Cuban Missile Affair and the American Style of Crisis Management," Parameters: Journal of the U.S. Army War College 19/1 (March 1989): 49-60.
　　　　Major sections discuss the American style of crisis management; criticism of the American style of crisis management; conclusions regarding the Cuban missile crisis; and predictability of such events.

1148. Caldwell, Edward C. "Censorship of Radio Programs," Journal of Radio Law 1/3 (October 1931): 441-476.
　　　　Discusses the then-emerging concern for constitutional protections for

information transmitted by radio broadcasts, especially when broadcasts deal with matters of politics, society and economics.

1149. Caldwell, George. "The Mob in the Streets," Studies in Intelligence 29/4 (Winter 1985).

1150. Calendrillo, Linda T. "Role Playing and 'Atmosphere' in Four Modern British Spy Novels," Clues 3/1 (Spring-Summer 1982): 111-119.
    Discusses comparisons of roles found in Graham Green's The Confidential Agent, LeCarre's The Spy Who Came in from the Cold, and Joseph Conrad's The Secret Agent.

1151. Caldwell, Stephen L. "Defense Intelligence Training: Changing to Better Support the Warfighter," Defense Intelligence Journal 4/2 (Fall 1995): 83-100.
    Explores shifts in regional focus; joint topics; combined operations; and more flexibility through variety of topics.

1152. Calkin, Homer L. "James Leander Cathcart and the United States Navy," Irish Sword 3/12 (1958): 145-152.

1153. Callahan, David. "Robert Gates: Bush's Man at Langley," Foreign Service Journal 68/12 (December 1991): 14-21.
    Summation of CIA director Gates' career and controversies surrounding his last year at CIA.

1154. Callen, Earl. "A Freedom of Information Fable...What's in a Name File?," Civil Liberties Review 3/2 (June-July 1976): 58-67.
    The author, a physicist and university professor, describes his search for, and acquisition of, information about himself obtained through the Freedom of Information Act.

1155. Callimahos, Lambros D. "The Legendary William F. Friedman," Cryptologia 15/3 (July 1991): 219-236.

1156. Calloway, Colin G. "Rhode Island Renegade: The Enigma of Joshua Tefft," Rhode Island History 43/4 (1984): 137-145.

1157. Callwell, C. E. "War Office Reminiscences," Blackwood's Magazine 140 (1911).

1158. Calvert, Michael. "Some Aspects of Guerrilla Warfare: Socio-Economic Poliwar and Psywar," RUSI Defence Studies Journal 117 (September 1972): 20-24.

1159. Calvocoressi, Peter J. "The Secrets of Enigma," Listener 97 (January-February 1977): 70-71, 112-114, 135-137.

1160. Cameron, Iain. "Telephone Tapping and the Interception of Communications Act 1985," Northern Ireland Legal Quarterly 37/2 (Summer 1986): 126-150.
  Discusses background leading to passage of Act, which allows executive to intercept communications while making an offense for others to do the same intercepts. Details the specific requirements under the Act.

1161. Cameron, Iain. "Commission of Inquiry Concerning Certain Activities of the Royal Canadian Mounted Police. Second Report: "Freedom and Security Under the Law," Modern Law Review 48 (March 1985): 201-211.
  One in a series of reports on unauthorized/illegal activities of the Royal Canadian Mounted Police and a precursor to Canadian legislation governing intelligence operations. Includes description of wrongful activities and suggested approach for authorization of intelligence operations.

1162. Cameron, Roy L. "Passport Control in the National Interest and Freedom to Travel," Temple Law Quarterly 33/3 (Spring 1960): 332-345.
  Considers whether right to travel outside US may be restricted and if so, what due process is required. Discusses passport procedures in other countries and reviews history of passports in the US, court decisions, area restrictions, criticism of data used by Supreme Court, and recommendations.

1163. Camp, Alida. "Enforcement of CIA Secrecy Agreements: A Constitutional Analysis," Columbia Journal of Law and Social Problems 15/4 (Summer 1980): 455-505.
  An analysis of the Snepp case in terms of the First Amendment. Considers the legislative and executive authority for secrecy agreements, the standard of prior restraint, and employer-employee relationships as a CIA agent.

1164. Camp, Richard D., Jr. "The Listening Post: Tool for Detection," Marine Corps Gazette 53 (August 1969): 50-51.

1165. Campbell, A. I. L. "Ponting and Privilege," Public Law (1985): 212-214.
  Brief observations of the relationship between the British Official Secrets Act of 1911 and parliamentary privilege following the acquittal of Clive Ponting for alleged violation of the Act.

1166. Campbell, Douglas A. and Robert W. McKinney. "Predictive Intelligence: An Old Lesson Unlearned," Military Review 70/8 (August 1990): 50-58.
  A lengthy argument about the need for revising Army intelligence doctrine to return to a system of evaluating enemy capabilities.

1167. Campbell, Duncan. "Global Boom in Eavesdropping: Signals Intelligence," Atlas 26 (1979): 26-28.

1168. Campbell, John P. "Air Operations and the Dieppe Raid," Aerospace Historian 23 (1976): 10-20.

1169. Campbell, John P. "The Ultra Revelations: The Dieppe Raid...," Canadian Defence Quarterly 6 (Summer 1976): 36-42.

1170. Campbell, John P. "D-Day 1943: The Limits of Strategic Deception," Canadian Journal of History 12 (December 1977): 207-237.
    Argues that the Germans were at a technological disadvantage. The British used aerial photographs and visual reports. Tactical intelligence provided useful clues for prisoner-of-war interrogations. Intelligence was the weakest link in the German General Staff.

1171. Campbell, John P. "'Give a Dog a Bad Name': The Curious Case of F. E. Smith and the 'Black Diaries' of Sir Roger Casement," History Today 34/9 (September 1984): 14-19.
    A brief history of the 1916 trial, conviction, and execution for treason of British political activist F. E. Smith. Smith was tried for treason for his role in actions in POW camps in Germany in World War I.

1172. Campbell, John P. "Garbo," Intelligence and National Security 2/2 (April 1987): 374-375.
    A brief book review essay of a book by the same title by Juan Pujol and Nigel West.

1173. Campbell, John P. "Operation Starkey 1943: 'A Piece of Harmless Playacting,'" Intelligence and National Security 2/3 (July 1987): 92-113.
    Discusses British deception operations in 1943 to dissuade the Germans of any weaknesses in the British military strength. Includes relationships between the allies in carrying off various deception plans.

1174. Campbell, John P. "An Update on the Interpretation on the Ultra Documentation," Archivaria 26 (1988): 184-188.

1175. Campbell, John P. "Some Pieces of the Ostro Puzzle," Intelligence and National Security 11/2 (April 1996): 245-263.
    A discussion of the espionage work of Paul Fidrmuc ("Ostro"), a Czech businessman and spy in residence in Lisbon, Spain in World War II.

1176. Campbell, Kenneth H. "Bedell Smith's Imprint on the CIA," International Journal of Intelligence and Counterintelligence 1/2 (Summer 1986): 44-62.

A bibliographic account of Walter Bedell Smith, including references to his career as four star general, Ambassador to the Soviet Union, Director of CIA, and Undersecretary of State.

1177. Campbell, Kenneth J.   "Ethan Allen Hitchcock: Intelligence Leader-Mystic," Intelligence Quarterly 2/3 (1986):   13-14.

1178. Campbell, Kenneth J.   "A Profile of Philip Agee," Intelligence Quarterly 3/2 (1987):   6-9.

1179. Campbell, Kenneth J.   "Major General Ralph Van Deman, Father of Modern American Military Intelligence," American Intelligence Journal 8 (Summer 1987):   13-19.

1180. Campbell, Kenneth J.   "John A. McCone: An Outsider Becomes DCI," Studies in Intelligence 32/2 (Summer 1988):   49-60.

1181. Campbell, Kenneth J.   "William J. Donovan: Leader and Strategist," American Intelligence Journal 11/1 (Winter 1989-1990):   31-36.
        A brief history of the OSS chief's life beginning with the central theme of Donovan's life; the interwar years; achievements in intelligence; Donovan as leader and administrator; and Donovan as he is remembered.

1182. Campbell, Kenneth J.   "Robert L. Johnson: The Army's Johnnie Walker," American Intelligence Journal 11/2 (Spring 1990):   5-10.
        Extensive evaluation of the espionage case of an Army spy, Robert L. Johnson, which took place from 1953 to 1963.   Argues that Johnson was a pathological traitor.   Sections discuss Johnson's early life and Army career; Johnson as others saw him; and lessons learned from the case.

1183. Campbell, Kenneth J.   "Allen Dulles: An Appraisal," Studies in Intelligence 34/1 (Spring 1990).

1184. Campbell, Kenneth J.   "Profiles in Treason: Jonathan Jay Pollard, A Corrupted Ideologue," American Intelligence Journal 14/1 (Autumn-Winter 1993): 55-59.

1185. Campbell, M. R. Ian.   "The Russian Convoys, 1941-1945," Journal of the Royal United Service Institution 102 (May 1946):   227-240.

1186. Campbell, Ruth.   "Sentence of Death by Burning for Women," Journal of Legal History 5 (May 1984):   44-59.
        Of value in this article is the discussion of women put to death for petty treason, a charge levied only against women for the killing of their husbands.

1187. Canan, Howard V. "Influence of Military Intelligence (Battle of Second Manassas)," Armor 64 (September-October 1955): 34-41.

A brief history of the second battle of Manassas during the American Civil War.

1188. Canan, Howard V. "Balloons in the Civil War," Signal 12/1 (September 1957): 26-29.

Discusses the work of the first balloonist, James Allen, and the efforts to incorporate balloons into intelligence gathering.

1189. Canan, Howard V. "Phil Sheridan, A Superb Combat Intelligence Officer," Armor 71 (November-December 1962): 56-61.

1190. Canan, Howard V. "Confederate Military Intelligence," Maryland Historical Magazine 59/1 (March 1964): 34-51.

1191. Canan, James W. "Steady Steps in Strategic C³I," Air Force Magazine 70 (June 1987): 44-51.

1192. Canan, James W. "Recovery in Space," Air Force Magazine 71/8 (1988): 68-73.

1193. Canby, Thomas Y. "Satellites that Serve Us," National Geographic 164/3 (July 1983): 280-335.

1194. Canby, Thomas Y. "Are the Soviets Ahead in Space?," National Geographic 170/4 (October 1986): 420-458.

The author's major objective is to document the history, successes and failures of the Soviet space program, including Soviet strengths such as the building block approach, commitment, imaginative goals, manned programs, and a busy launch schedule. Useful in historical studies of space intelligence platforms.

1195. Candeloro, Dominic. "Louis F. Post and the Red Scare of 1920," Prologue: Quarterly Journal of the National Archives 11/1 (Spring 1979): 41-55.

An account of Post's activist and unceasing attempts to oppose enforcement of the Alien Anarchist Act of 1918. Post argued for due process for foreign born radicals.

1196. Canfield, Jeffrey L. "Gerbil Redux: What Course Ahead for Naval Intelligence?," International Journal of Intelligence and Counterintelligence 6/3 (Fall 1993): 271-296.

Extensive consideration of Naval intelligence within the broader consider of intelligence and the new world order; plotting a course ahead for naval intelligence; the first pillar, a naval intelligence doctrine to bridge service and joint missions; the second pillar, articulation and implementation of a new operational paradigm for naval intelligence; the third pillar, heightened emphasis on professionalization; and the fourth pillar, a leadership role for naval intelligence.

1197. Canham-Clyne, John. "Business As Usual: Iran-Contra and the National Security State," World Policy Journal 9/4 (1992): 617-638.

Author argues that the Iran-Contra affair was not an aberration in the annals of US government foreign policy matters, rather it was business as usual. Discusses the role of CIA. Major sections discuss the quid pro quo as policy; the National Security Council goes operational; private citizens and the 'Company'; mixed messages in the Middle East; institutional secrecy and congressional complicity; and efforts to uncover the actions of key players.

1198. Canon, David. "Intelligence and Ethics: The CIA's Covert Operations," Journal of Libertarian Studies 4/2 (Spring 1980): 197-214.

1199. Canton, John S. "MAGIS (Marine Air Ground Intelligence System)," Marine Corps Gazette 53 (February 1969): 18-24.

1200. Cantril, H. "Evaluating the Probable Reactions to the Landing in North Africa in 1942: A Case Study," Public Opinion Quarterly 29 (Fall 1965): 400-410.

An account of a military intelligence study in early 1942 to determine the popular appeal of an invasion of the United States. Purpose of the study was to draw out information on psychological warfare dynamics.

1201. Cantwell, John. "The Public Record Office: The Legal and Departmental Records," Journal of Legal History 2/3 (December 1981): 227-237.

A brief history of the Office, beginning with the Public Records Act of 1838.

1202. Cantwell, John. "The Right to Know: The Unfolding of the Public Records," Government and Opposition 17/2 (Spring 1982): 157-163.

1203. Capassakis, Evelyn. "Passport Revocations or Denials on the Ground of National Security and Foreign Policy," Fordham Law Review 49/6 (May 1981): 1178-1196.

Asks whether Congress has delegated to the Secretary of State the authority to revoke or deny passports on the grounds of national security and foreign policy. Author concludes in the affirmative. She discusses implied authorization and constitutional considerations.

1204. Capen, E. C. "The Difficulty of Assessing Uncertainty," Journal of Petroleum Technology (August 1976): 843-850.

1205. Caplan, Jonathan. "The Criminal Liability of the Media Under Section 2 of the Official Secrets Act (Great Britain)," Journal of Criminal Law 52 (February 1988): 67-74.
   Discusses "catch-all" effect of section 2 and failed efforts to amend it. Topics include background on offense of "wrongful communication," the "new" section 2 (of the 1911 Act), defenses, and discretion of prosecution.

1206. Capps, Freddie L., Jr. "Espionage Awareness Programs," FBI Law Enforcement Bulletin 60/9 (September 1991): 17-19.

1207. Caraley, Demetrios, et al. "American Political Institutions After Watergate--A Discussion," Political Science Quarterly 89/4 (Winter 1974-1975): 713-749.
   A seminar of the editors of PSQ discusses the long term implications for American political institutions of the Watergate affair. An excellent piece of background material for intelligence and national security agency implications.

1208. Caravelli, John M. "The Role of Surprise and Preemption in Soviet Military Strategy," International Security Review 6/2 (Summer 1981): 209-236.

1209. Carchio, Francis A. "Constitutional Law -- Pennsylvania Upholds First Amendment Protection for Publication of Private Truthful Information," Temple Law Review 65/2 (Summer 1992): 663-677.
   Discusses Pennsylvania case in which state supreme court held that newspaper was not liable for publication of material lawfully intercepted under state wiretap statute. Criticizes court's reasoning that the particular conversations were not meant to be protected by the statute, arguing that media should not be held liable for publishing truthful information if state does not use less restrictive means. Discusses US Supreme Court precedent and its application to Pennsylvania case.

1210. Carey, Warren and Myles Maxfield. "Intelligence Implications of Disease," Studies in Intelligence 16/1 (Spring 1972): 71-78.
   An inquiry into the communicable diseases in various restricted parts of the world.

1211. Carey, William D. "The Secrecy Syndrome," Bulletin of the Atomic Scientists 39/7 (August-September 1983): 2.
   A brief commentary on the implications of administration-congressional arguing over the Export Administration Act, as to controls on unclassified scientific information.

1212. Carey, William D. "Force, Foresight and Science," Society 22/2 (1985): 5-7.

The US limitations on, and enforcement of restrictions on research information that can compromise national security.

1213. Carlisle, Jeffrey J. "Extradition of Government Agents as a Municipal Law Remedy for State-Sponsored Kidnapping," California Law Review 81/6 (December 1993): 1541-1586.

Author notes cross-border abductions by agents of the US government violate international law and the foreign states municipal law. Mentions foreign security and intelligence services.

1214. Carlon, Joseph R. and John Vezeris. "The Secret Service Master Central Index," Police Chief 52 (November 1985): 18-21.

Observations of the implications of technology in the Secret Service and the operational role of a new information system.

1215. Carlson, Elliott. "Chief of Spies: The Feisty, Dramatic and Controversial Stansfield Turner," Modern Maturity 28/6 (December 1985-January 1986): 71-75.

May have value in research of popular press interviews by the CIA chief.

1216. Carlton, Stephen A. "Industrial Espionage: Reality of the Information Age," Research-Technology Management 35/6 (November-December 1992): 18-24.

A brief summary of the problem of industrial espionage and the economic and security threats posed by this problem.

1217. Carlucci, Frank C. and Floyd Abrams. "Jail for Naming CIA Agents?," American Lawyer 2 (December 1980): 37-38.

Debate between authors on proposed legislation which would make disclosing the name of intelligence agents a criminal offense. Carlucci favors the penalties on the grounds that the statute only covers those private citizens engaged in a pattern of activity intended to expose agents with reason to know it will impair intelligence. Abrams opposes the position so far as private citizens are covered by the proposed statute, arguing the statute violates the First Amendment.

1218. Carmichael, Joel. "The Kingdom of God and the KGB," Midstream 31/5 (May 1985): 3-9.

Discusses the infiltration of Marxist theology into the Catholic faith in several Latin American countries, thus allowing for greater confusion in "Kingdom of God." Sections discuss liberation theology; Marxism; Latin American churchmen and the incursion of the KGB; Soviet extension; the Pope and "The Letter on Economy."

1219.   Carnahan, Burrus M.   "United States v. Whiting: International Agreements, Human Rights, and Military Law," Air Force Law Review 23 (Spring 1982-1983): 271-281.

Discusses the trial of Sergeant Whiting for unauthorized possession of classified documents. Sgt. Whiting argued that the "status of forces agreements" between the US and Germany conferred upon individuals certain rights pertaining to search and seizure, such as the search of an off base apartment.

1220. Carne, Greg. "Official Secrets and the Gibbs Report: A Charter for Reform or a Tug of the Legal Forelock?," University of Tasmania Law Review 12 (1993): 11-25.

1221. Carnegie Endowment for International Peace and Institute for International Economics. "Special Report: Policymaking for a New Era," Foreign Affairs 71/5 (Winter 1992-1993): 175-189.

Calls for substantial changes in national security, economic and domestic affairs policy making.   Refers to the National Security Council, Central Intelligence Agency, and the role of the intelligence community in a post-Cold War world.

1222. Carnes, Calland F. "Soviet Military Intelligence: How Significant?," Military Intelligence (January-March 1981): 6-10.

1223.   Carnes, Calland F.   "Soviet Intelligence Support to International Terrorism," American Intelligence Journal 7/3 (January 1986).

1224. Carnes, Calland F. "Inside Soviet Naval Intelligence," Naval Intelligence Professionals Quarterly 6/2 (Summer 1990): 5-8.

1225. Carney, Donald J. and Thomas C. Indelicarto. "Indications and Warning and the Drug War," Defense Intelligence Journal 3/1 (Spring 1994): 89-106.

Discusses the drug war and warning; factors affecting strategic and tactical warning; reinvigorating intelligence theories and techniques; and development of an analysis matrix for drug intelligence.

1226. Carney, John J. "Managing the Intelligence Function," Criminal Justice Journal 1/10 (October 1982): 1-5.

Discussion of Pennsylvania's Commission on Crime and Delinquency and the creation of an intelligence unit. Argues that the introduction of an intelligence unit in police organizations poses management problems in terms of their potential for becoming elite investigative activities. Discusses how this outcome can be avoided through management monitoring of criteria and productivity. Useful in studies of domestic intelligence conducted by police agencies.

1227. Caron, Yves. "Rado: History of a Great Soviet Espionage Network," Est et Quest 662 (April 1982): 446-452.

In French, a review of the espionage activities involving Alexander Rado, including an account of his death.

1228. Carpeaux, Otto M. "Camelots," Atlas 10/4 (October 1965): 231.

A translation into English of the author's assertions about Project Camelot, a Defense Department program in the 1960s, disbanded by 1965, to enlist academics to study the potential for internal wars in Latin America.

1229. Carpenter, Clifton C. "Modern Technology and Political Geography," Military Review 53/1 (1973): 69-76.

Advances in intelligence gathering techniques have made it more difficult for governments to sustain themselves merely by power based on geographic location.

1230. Carpenter, Humphrey. "'This Is Ole Ezra Speaking'! Ezra Pound's Wartime Broadcasts," Encounter 71 (June 1988) 3-15.

1231. Carpenter, Richard C. "007 and the Myth of the Hero," Journal of Popular Culture 1/2 (1967): 79-87.

1232. Carpenter, Richard C. "I Spy and Mission Impossible: Gimmicks and a Fairytale," Journal of Popular Culture 1/3 (1967): 286-290.

Argues that television programs like "I Spy" and "Mission Impossible" are not intended to demonstrate true tradecraft of espionage work.

1233. Carr, Caleb. "Aldrich Ames and the CIA's Dark History," Harper's 289/1734 (November 1994): 24-28.

This is an extract of a longer article: "Aldrich Ames and the Conduct of American Intelligence," World Policy Journal 11/3 (Fall 1994): 19-28. Observations of the impact of the Aldrich Ames espionage case on the CIA and the intelligence functions. Major sections of the longer article in World Policy Journal discuss the background of the CIA; the obstacles in the 1950s; the patterns of failure in the 1960s; the true dangers of espionage; and the limits of intelligence.

1234. Carr, E. H. "The Origin and Status of the Cheka," Soviet Studies 10/1 (July 1958): 1-11

Discusses the origins of the Soviet secret police, the Cheka, and the emergence of the modern Soviet intelligence service, the KGB. Efforts by Bolshevik leaders to use and control the Cheka are discussed, including the issue of legislative reforms.

1235. Carr, James G. "Wiretapping in West Germany," <u>American Journal of Comparative Law</u> 29/4 (Fall 1981): 607-645.

     Provides a comparative analysis of West German and American wiretap laws enacted in 1968. Topics include constitutional contexts, review and notice, issuance and orders (when, where, who), procedural requisites, execution, and restrictions on admissibility of intercepted communications.

1236. Carroll, John M. and Lynda E. Robbins. "The Automated Cryptanalysis of Polyalphabetic Ciphers," <u>Cryptologia</u> 11/4 (October 1987): 193-205.

1237. Carroll, John M. and Lynda E. Robbins. "Using Binary Derivatives to Test an Enhancement of DES," <u>Cryptologia</u> 12/4 (October 1988): 193-208.

1238. Carroll, John M. and Lynda E. Robbins. "Computer Cryptanalysis of Product Ciphers," <u>Crytologia</u> 13/4 (October 1989): 303-326.

1239. Carroll, John M. and Steve Martin. "The Automated Cryptanalysis of Substitution Ciphers," <u>Cryptologia</u> 10/4 (October 1986): 193-209.

1240. Carroll, John M.; Jeff Verhagen; and Perry T. Wong. "Chaos in Cryptography: The Escape from the Strange Attractor," <u>Cryptologia</u> 16/1 (January 1992): 52-72.

1241. Carroll, John M. and Sri Nurdiati. "Weak Keys and Weak Data: Foiling the Two Nemeses," <u>Cryptologia</u> 18/3 (July 1994): 253-280.

1242. Carroll, Robert C. "Six Men Alone," <u>Infantry</u> 65 (January-February 1975): 41-43.

1243. Carroll, Thomas F. "Freedom of Speech and the Press in War Time: The Espionage Act," <u>Michigan Law Review</u> 17/8 (June 1919): 621-665.

     Extensive review of provisions of the Espionage Act, including some background to its enactment. Covers censorship, exclusion from the mail and interstate commerce, disloyal statements, conspiracy, treason, and analysis of constitutional implications.

1244. Carroll, Thomas F. "Freedom of Speech and of the Pen in the Federalist Period: The Sedition Act," <u>Michigan Law Review</u> 18/7 (May 1920): 615-651.

     Historical background and analysis of passage of Sedition Act and its impact on First Amendment freedom of speech, as determined by court decisions, including constitutional implications.

1245. Carrow, Milton M. "Governmental Nondisclosure in Judicial Proceedings," <u>University of Pennsylvania Law Review</u> 107/2 (December 1958): 166-198.

Includes discussion of the legal basis for nondisclosure; the nature of the interest affected; types of information that may be privileged; the function of the court in determining applicability of "the privilege"; and conclusions. Refers to national security information and problems arising from the Army-McCarthy hearings of 1954.

1246. Carson, John. "Army Alpha, Army Brass, and the Search for Army Intelligence," Isis 84/2 (1993): 278-309.

1247. Carter, Barry E. "The Strategic Debate in the United States," Proceedings of the Academy of Political Science 33/1 (1978): 15-29.
Discusses in part the role of the Central Intelligence Agency in the assessment of strategic forces of various countries including the Soviet Union.

1248. Carter, Carolle J. "Ireland: America's Neutral Ally, 1939-1941," Eire-Ireland 12/2 (1977): 5-14.

1249. Carter, Dan. "Marine Corps Counterintelligence in Somalia and Beyond," Defense Intelligence Journal 4/1 (Spring 1995): 83-89.
Summarizes Marine Corps CI actions in the Somalia mission, in particular, the human intelligence aspects. Major sections discuss the Marine CI mission; the mission as applied to Somalia, and adaptations for future missions.

1250. Carter, Marshall N. "To Kill or Capture," Marine Corps Gazette 57/6 (June 1973): 31-35.
Discussion of a specific incident from the Vietnam war in which good intelligence gained significant advantage for the Marines over the enemy.

1251. Cartier, Francois. "Le Service d'Ecoute Pendant la Guerre," Radio-Electricite 4 (1923): 453-460; 491-498.

1252. Carver, George A., Jr. "The Real Revolution in South Viet Nam," Foreign Affairs 43/3 (April 1965): 387-408.
Addresses the social revolution in South Vietnam among the Buddhists and the Catholics, and the author suggests that the intelligence community chose to focus more on the military dimensions of war than on social dimensions, thus implying the need for care on this point by intelligence community analysts.

1253. Carver, George A., Jr. "The Faceless Viet Cong," Foreign Affairs 44/3 (April 1966): 347-372.
Review of the history of the Viet Cong from the formation of the National Front and the Peoples' Revolutionary Party. Describes the Viet Cong uses of subversive insurgency to develop political power. Useful in analyses of intelligence misjudgments about the political appeal of insurgencies.

1254. Carver, George A., Jr. "Covert Action an Essential Form of Diplomacy," Human Events 12 (December 1987).

1255. Carver, George A., Jr. "Washington: The Fifth Man," Atlantic Monthly 262/3 (September 1988): 26-29.
        With the death of spy Kim Philby, the question remains whether there was a fifth man in the spy ring of Burgess, Maclean, Blunt and Philby.

1256. Carver, George A., Jr. "Intelligence in the Age of Glasnost," Foreign Affairs 69/3 (Summer 1990): 147-166.
        Considers alterations to the intelligence community responses to conditions in the Soviet Union in the last years of the 1980s. Argues for the maintenance of a strong counterintelligence community to observe the changes in Eastern Europe.

1257. Carver, George A., Jr. and Morton Halperin. (Critiques of the Szanton and Allison article, same issue) Foreign Policy 22 (Spring 1976): 206-214.
        Critiques are generally supportive of the Szanton and Allison piece, yet offer additional remarks and suggestions.

1258. Cary, Lorin L. "The Bureau of Investigation and Radicalism in Toledo, Ohio: 1918-1920," Labor History 21/3 (1980): 430-440.
        Discusses the relevance of Bureau of investigation records in the early domestic intelligence cases on the International Workers of the World.

1259. Case, Blair. "Project Window: The First Air Defense Countermeasure," Air Defense Artillery (Summer 1983): 20-23.

1260. Casey, Francis M. "Threat Perception: Key to Strategy," Marine Corps Gazette 70 (June 1986): 48-54.

1261. Casey, William J. "The Clandestine War in Europe (1942-1945)," Studies in Intelligence 25/1 (Spring 1981): 1-7.

1262. Casey, William J. "The American Intelligence Community," Presidential Studies Quarterly 12/2 (Spring 1982): 150-153.
        A basic outline of the history of the US intelligence community with and argument to limit information flows by way of the Freedom of Information Act.

1263. Casey, William J. "Economic Intelligence for the Future," Studies in Intelligence 26/2 (Summer 1982).

1264. Casey, William J. "The Threat and the Need for Intelligence," Signal 38 (October 1983): 11.

1265. Casey, William J. "War Behind the Lines," Studies in Intelligence 26/4 (Winter 1982).

1266. Casey, William J. "CIA: Confronting 'Undeclared War,'" American Legion Magazine 116/6 (June 1984): 12-14, 37.

1267. Casey, William J. "Scouting the Future," Presidential Studies Quarterly 16/3 (Summer 1986): 421-427.
Former CIA director Casey talks about economic and geo-political aspects of world stability. Discusses new initiatives regarding US intelligence.

1268. Casey, William J. "OSS: Lessons for Today," Studies in Intelligence 30/4 (Winter 1986).

1269. Casey, William J. "Focus on the Third World: Challenges and Opportunities," Presidential Studies Quarterly 17/1 (Winter 1987): 19-26.
The former director of the Central Intelligence Agency observes that new competition in technological advancements among the world's nations. Argues for US policy to become increasingly the guarantors of private investment in Third World nations.

1270. Cash, Robert B. "Presidential Power: Use and Enforcement of Executive Orders," Notre Dame Lawyer 39/1 (December 1963): 44-55.
Discusses history of use and organization of executive orders, scope of orders (extent and limitations of executive authority), and administrative and judicial enforcement, and conclusions.

1271. Cashin, Edward J. "The Trembling Land: Covert Activity in the Georgia Backcountry During the American Revolution," Proceedings and Papers of the Georgia Association of History (1982): 31-39.
The article chronicles the behind the scenes activities and scandals of many post war heroes during the American Revolution in rural Georgia.

1272. Casper, Gerhard. "Comment: Government Secrecy and the Constitution," California Law Review 74 (May 1986): 923-926.
The author argues that the First Amendment is too broad for application to matters involving government control of information. Discusses the relevance of secrecy principles to employee rights.

1273. Casper, Jonathan D. "Lawyers and Loyalty-Security Litigation," Law and Society Review 3/4 (May 1969): 575-585.
Author reports findings of a study concerning attorneys who defended loyalty-security cases resulting in Supreme Court decisions in the years from 1957 to 1966.

1274. Casper, Stewart M. "Looking Fraudulent Surveillance in the Eye: How to Refute Distorted Evidence," Trial 29/1 (January 1993): 136-142.
Discusses secret surveillance of plaintiffs by defense lawyers in order to negate personal injury claims. Author argues some valid claims may be adversely affected when improper techniques are employed and evidence is abused. Suggests methods to expose abuses.

1275. Cassady, Ralph. "The Intelligence Function and Business Competition," California Management Review (Spring 1964): 14-23.

1276. Cassandra, I. "C³I as a Force Multiplier--Rhetoric of Reality?," Armed Forces Journal International 115/5 (January 1978): 16-18.

1277. Castel, Albert. "The Guerilla War, 1861-1865," Civil War Times Illustrated 12 (1974): 14-19.

1278. Castel, Albert. "Samuel Ruth: Union Spy," Civil War Times Illustrated 14/10 (1976): 36-44.
Considers Ruth's spy work in Virginia and Robert E. Lee's ultimate suspicion of his role in building pro-Union sympathies.

1279. Castillo Armas, Carlos. "How Guatemala Got Rid of the Communists," American Mercury 80 (January 1955): 140-141.
The source publication is considered journalistic and affiliated with popular press magazines, but due to the author's prominence as a fugitive Guatemalan colonel and leader of the opposition to the Arbenz government in the coup of 1954, the article may have value to researchers of the US intelligence community's role in the overthrow. Unplanned and somewhat ironic is the order of this piece in relation to the next piece by Fidel Castro.

1280. Castro, Fidel. "Fidel Castro Denounces Aggressions Against Cuba," Black Scholar 8/3 (December 1976): 10-17.
This is a speech by the Cuban dictator on October 15, 1976, to present alleged evidence that the CIA was responsible for attacks on Cuban airlines and diplomatic outposts.

1281. Cate, Charles V. "Counterintelligence for National Security," Studies in Intelligence 2/3 (Fall 1958).

1282. Catton, Bruce. "The Inspired Leak," American Heritage 28/2 (February 1977): 44-49.
Discusses the origin of the leak of secret information in American history.

1283. Catudal, Honore M., Jr. "Kennedy and the Berlin Crisis," Schweizeriche Zeitschrift Geschichte 29/2 (1979): 418-437.

1284. Cavallini, Enrique H. J. "The Malvinas/Falkland Affair: A New Look," International Journal of Intelligence and Counterintelligence 2/2 (Summer 1988): 203-216.
      Argues that there were several foreign policy blunders made in the Argentinean decision to engage war with Great Britain over the Malvinas/Falkland Islands. Includes discussion of the domestic situation in Argentina, Argentinean intelligence services, and the Argentine-US relationship.

1285. Cavanaugh, Catherine F. "Stories of Our Government Bureaus: George Washington and the Secret Service," Bookman 33 (1911): 384-387.

1286. Cecil, Robert. "Legends Spies Tell," Encounter 50/4 (April 1978): 9-17.
      Lengthy discussion of the Burgess-Maclean-Philby espionage ring. Attempts to dispel the view that the ring brought significant damage to the British intelligence system.

1287. Cecil, Robert. "Of Secrecy and Intelligence: British Dilemmas," Encounter 64/5 (May 1985): 28-32.
      Discussion and contrast between US and Britain in area of legislative oversight of intelligence. Cites recent British TV expose of MI-5 and recent spy cases in Britain. (Editorials) Interesting Side Stories from the London Times "Mole Hunt" by Chapman Pincher, "Tapping Wires" by Bernard Levin and "A Polish Murder Trial" by Leopold Lobedz (about murder of a Pro-Solidarity Priest).

1288. Cecil, Robert. "C's War," Intelligence and National Security 1/2 (May 1986): 170-188.
      A fairly detailed narration and analysis of the career of H. A. R. Kim Philby, the British spy for the Soviet Union.

1289. Cecil, Robert. "Five of Six at War: Section V of MI6," Intelligence and National Security 9/2 (April 1994): 345-353.
      Discusses the credibility and effectiveness problems of the counterintelligence section of MI6, accounting for some of the sources of the problems. Suggests that British counterintelligence function was guided by certain individuals who may not have deserved the praise they received.

1290. Cecil, Robert. "Philby's Spurious War," Intelligence and National Security 9/4 (October 1994): 764-768.
      A book review essay that reflects upon the espionage career of Soviet spy Kim Philby, and mainly a reflection upon Philby's autobiography, My Silent War.

Discusses Philby's early career; career in SOE; career in SIS; and his days in Washington and after.

1291. Cedergren, Ernest W. "I Flew at Dien Bien Phu," Flying 56 (February 1955): 26-27, 66-67.

1292. Celine, Louis F. "Reply to Charges of Treason Made by the French Department of Justice," South Atlantic Quarterly 93 (Spring 1994): 531-539.
    A document in the record of alleged wartime French collaborationist Louis F. Celine, as translated by Julien Cornell.

1293. Cerveny, Randy and Melvin G. Marcus. "Elements of Espionage," Weatherwise 47 (October-November 1994): 14-18.

1294. Chace, William M. "Ezra Pound: "Insanity," "Treason," and Care," Critical Inquiry 14 (Autumn 1987): 134-141.

1295. Chadbourne, R. D. "Industrial Espionage: The Silent Road to Bankruptcy," Supervision 49/4 (April 1987): 14-17.

1296. Chafe, William. "The Greensboro Sit-Ins," Southern Exposure 6/3 (Fall 1978): 78-87.
    A detailed analysis of the circumstances leading to, and involving, the 1960 sit-ins by four black college students in a Greensboro, North Carolina Woolworth's store. Although not directly an article about intelligence matters, this piece may be useful in research and writing about FBI intelligence on the sit-in demonstrations in the South.

1297. Chafee, Zechariah, Jr. "A Contemporary State Trial--The United States Versus Jacob Abrams, et al.," Harvard Law Review 33 (April 1920): 747-774; 35 (1921): 9-28.
    A classic article in two parts that addresses the application of the Espionage Act to the arrest and conviction of persons who opposed dispatching US troops to Russia.

1298. Chafee, Zechariah, Jr. "The Registration of 'Communist-Front' Organizations in the Mundt-Nixon Bill," Harvard Law Review 63 (1950): 1382-1390.
    A brief but thorough review of proposed legislation aimed at imposing compulsory registration of every Communist political or front organization.

1299. Chaffee, Wilbur. "Two Hypotheses of Asia-Soviet Relations as Concerns the Instigation of the Korean War," Journal of Korean Affairs 6/3-4 (October 1976-January 1977): 1-13.

1300. Chaigneau, Pascal. "The KGB and Africa," Politique Internationale 20 (1983-84).

1301. Chaliand, Gerard. "Ideology and Society: The Pentagon Papers and North Vietnam," Esprit 40/6 (1972): 931-942.

1302. Chaliand, Gerard. "Ethnic Minorities: An Overview," Defense Intelligence Journal 1/2 (Fall 1992): 129-136.
     Discusses historical background of ethnic minorities in Europe; minorities and the fall of the communism; contempory international approaches; and minorities and US national security.

1303. Chalk, Rosemary. "Secrecy and Science," Bulletin of the Atomic Scientists 38/5 (May 1982): 9-10.
     Discusses the role of the Freedom of Information Act in opening scientific information flows.

1304. Chalk, Rosemary. "Security and Scientific Communication," Bulletin of the Atomic Scientists 39/7 (August-September 1983): 19-23.
     Argues that the Reagan administration's clamps on scientific information may undermine US vitality and progress.

1305. Chalk, Rosemary. "Continuing Debate Over Science and Secrecy," Bulletin of the Atomic Scientists 42 (March 1986): 14-16.
     Discusses National Security Directive 189 which exempted certain types of fundamental defense research from national security controls. Various implications of the policy are discussed in terms of the academic community, the government, the Defense Department, and the intelligence agencies.

1306. Chamberlain, Eugene K. "Nicholas Trist and Baja California," Pacific Historical Review 32/1 (1963): 49-63.
     An account of Trist's role in the Treaty of Guadalupe Hidalgo at the end of the war with Mexico in 1848. Partially a case example of the role of accurate and timely information.

1307. Chambliss, Lauren and William J. "Crimes of State: Drug Dealing, Iran and the Contras," Canadian Dimension 21/5 (September 1987): 35-38.

1308. Chambliss, William J. "State-Organized Crime," Criminology 2/2 (May 1989): 183-208.
     A noted criminologist observes a relationship between criminality, social structure and political economy. Discusses the methods and justifications of government officials who conducted smuggling of narcotics during the Vietnam war and arms smuggling in later years. Other forms of state organized crime

include, he argues, the FBI's counterintelligence operations, COINTELPRO.

1309. Chamorro, Edgar. "Packaging the Contras: A Case of CIA Disinformation," Radical American 21/2-3 (1987): 72-79.

1310. Chan, Steve. "The Intelligence of Stupidity: Understanding Failures in Strategic Warning," American Political Science Review 73/1 (March 1979): 171-180.
       Discusses the implications of cognitive and organizational factors for the evolution and avoidance of failures in strategic warning. Three diverse arguments are raised concerning warning systems.

1311. Chandler, Stedman. "Find'em! Fix'em! Fight'em!," Infantry Journal 54/9 (September 1949): 15-17.
       Discusses examples of Civil War intelligence and information transmissions.

1312. Chandler, Stedman and R. W. Robb. "Front-line Intelligence," Infantry Journal 51 (1946).

1313. Chang, Gordon H. "JFK, China, and the Bomb," Journal of American History 74/4 (1988): 1287-1310.
       Discusses a US national security plan to attack and destroy China's emerging nuclear capability in the early 1960s. Accounts for the CIA analysis of Sino-Soviet relations, in particular the view that the USSR and China would continue their competition.

1314. Chang, Y. Kurt. "Special 301 and Taiwan: A Case Study of Protecting United States Intellectual Property in Foreign Countries," Northwestern Journal of International Law & Business 15 (Fall 1994): 206-230.
       Includes discussion of industrial espionage in the context of the Omnibus Trade and Competitiveness Act of 1988, and in particular consideration of relations with Asian nations.

1315. Channon, James B. "Graphic Intelligence," Infantry 60 (January-February 1960): 54-56.

1316. Channon, James B. "Intelligence Instinct Can Be Developed," Infantry 62 (May-June 1962): 28-31.

1317. Chapin, B. "Colonial and Revolutionary Origins of the American Law of Treason," William and Mary Quarterly 17 (January 1960): 3-21.
       Traces the roots of US treason law back to English origins and contrasts its history in terms of the differences between monarchical versus representative

governments. Discusses the definitions of treason and espionage.

1318. Chaplin, Duncan D. "Integrated Combat Intelligence," <u>Marine Corps Gazette</u> 50 (July 1966): 50-51.

1319. Chapman, John J. M. "Pearl Harbor: The Anglo-Australian Dimension," <u>Intelligence and National Security</u> 4/3 (July 1989): 451-460.
  An evaluation of Australian intelligence collection on Japanese capabilities and intentions prior to the Pearl Harbor attack.

1320. Chapman, John W. M. "No Final Solution: A Survey of the Cryptanalytical Capabilities of German Military Agencies, 1926-35," <u>Intelligence and National Security</u> 1/1 (January 1986): 13-47.

1321. Chapman, John W. M. "A Dance on Eggs: Intelligence and the 'Anti-Comintern,'" <u>Journal of Contemporary History</u> 22/2 (April 1987): 333-372.
  Article demonstrates that longstanding covert links among arms industries, military naval hierarchies, and intelligence agencies between Germany and Japan from 1919-1938. New evidence reveals German secret police manipulation of German foreign policy.

1322. Chapman, John W. M. "Signals Intelligence Collaboration Among the Tripartite States on the Eve of Pearl Harbor," <u>Japan Forum</u> 3/2 (1991): 231-256.

1323. Chapman, John W. M. "Tricycle Recycled: Collaboration Among the Secret Intelligence Services of the Axis States, 1940-41," <u>Intelligence and National Security</u> 7/3 (July 1992): 268-299.
  Dusko Popov ('Tricycle') was a World War II spy. He said that he warned the US of imminent attack at Pearl Harbor. Author disputes the value of the information received, suggesting Japanese success turned on other factors.

1324. Charkes, Susan D. "The Constitutionality of the Intelligence Identities Protection Act of 1982," <u>Columbia Law Review</u> 83/3 (April 1983): 727-754.
  Examines the Act in light of First Amendment principles. Analyses Supreme Court decisions in the area of disclosure by government of national security information. See similar article in <u>Conflict Quarterly</u> (Winter 1982).

1325. Charlevois, J. J. "Nothing to Hide," <u>Studies in Intelligence</u> 9/1 (Spring 1965).
  Deals with Ben Franklin's philosophy on intelligence.

1326. Charlot, Claire. "Senior Civil Servants and Leaks in Great Britain: The 'Ponting Affair,'" <u>Revue Francaise de Sciencepolitique</u> 35/6 (December 1985): 1064-1079.

1327. Charlson, Michael L. "The Constitutionality of Expanding Prepublication Review of Government Employees' Speech," California Law Review 72 (September 1984): 962-1018.

Examines beginnings of prepublication review during the Reagan administration, including discussion of leaks, and an interdepartmental report ordered by Reagan which found that four basic harms are caused by leaks and that criminal prosecution is inadequate when based on pragmatic considerations. Considers National Security Decision Directive 84, as well as the Sensitive Compartmented Information Nondisclosure Agreement and its requisites, remedies, and review procedures. Analyzes SCI under First Amendment prior restraint, overbreadth and vagueness, and unconstitutional conditions doctrines. Suggests alternatives.

1328. Charns, Alex. "FBI's Cointelpro Revisited," Southern Exposure 13/1 (January-February 1985): 53-57.

Documentation of FBI activities, involving the suppression of demonstrators and marchers, during the 60s and 70s.

1329. Charteris, M. M. C. "A Year As an Intelligence Officer in Palestine," Middle East Society Journal 1 (October 1946): 15-23.

1330. Charters, David A. "Intelligence and Psychological Warfare Operations in Northern Ireland," RUSI Defence Studies Journal 122/3 (September 1977): 22-27.

1331. Charters, David A. "Special Operations in Counter-Insurgency: The Farren Case, Palestine 1947," RUSI Defence Studies Journal 124/2 (June 1979): 51-61.

1332. Charters, David A. "Security Services in an Open Society," Conflict Quarterly 1/2 (Summer 1980): 8-14.

1333. Charters, David A. "Sir Maurice Oldfield and British Intelligence: Some Lessons for Canada?," Conflict Quarterly 2/3 (Winter 1982): 40-51.

A biography of Oldfield, the first chief of the British Secret Intelligence Service. Argues that Canada's security service will be successful if it can attract the same class and effectiveness of people like Oldfield.

1334. Charters, David A. "British Intelligence in the Palestine Campaign, 1945-47," Intelligence and National Security 6/1 (January 1991): 115-140.

Sections discuss insurgency and the British response; intelligence producers and intelligence production; and assessment of the intelligence product. Discusses British intelligence in Palestine, 1945-47 and assesses its contribution to the counterinsurgency campaign. Discusses reasons for intelligence failures.

1335. Charters, David A. "Terrorism and Democracy," Intelligence and National Security 9/3 (July 1994): 567-569.
　　　A book review essay of former CIA director Stanfield Turner's book by the same title.

1336. Chartrand, Rene. "The United States Forces of 1812-1816 as Drawn by Charles Hamilton Smith, Officer and Spy," Military Collector and Historian 35/4 (Winter 1983): 142-150.

1337. Chase, Harold W. and Robert W. Chandler. "Review of War Ideas: The U.S. Propaganda Campaign in Vietnam," Marine Corps Gazette 66 (January 1982): 68-69.

1338. Chase, Michael T. "All-Source Intelligence: A New Name for an Old Thoroughbred," Military Review 56/7 (July 1976): 43-49.
　　　Explains intelligence community adoption of term "all-source intelligence", but recognizes that the concept has existed for 50 years. Discusses the meaning of the concept in 1976 and some problems associated with collection and utilization of data, and relevance of all-source to field commanders. Examples from the Vietnam war.

1339. Chase, Pliny E. "Mathematical Holocryptic Cyphers," Mathematical Monthly 1 (March 1859): 194-196.
　　　One of the earliest published discussions in America of the role and methods of cypher construction for secret correspondence. Use of holographic cypher systems can make translations difficult, says the author.

1340. Chastain, James G. "Bakunin As a French Secret Agent in 1848," History Today 31 (August 1981): 5-9.
　　　Bakunin's role as propagandist and militant for the Provisional Government of revolutionary France is discussed, especially in terms of the overthrow of the Tsar.

1341. Chatterjee, Pratap. "Spying for Uncle Sam," Covert Action Quarterly (Winter 1995-1996): 41-45+.

1342. Chayes, Antonia H. and Abraham Chayes. "From Law Enforcement to Dispute Settlement: A New Approach to Arms Control Verification and Compliance," International Security 14/4 (Spring 1990): 147-164.
　　　Discusses the proposition that arms control advances with the Soviets can proceed if both the United States and the Soviet Union can accept the need to live under a complex treaty regime involving management of a stream of disputes and interpretations. Role of intelligence is mentioned in the scheme.

1343. Cheatham, Tom. "Message Decryption and Spelling Checkers," Cryptologia 11/2 (April 1987): 115-118.

1344. Cheema, Pervaiz I. "The Afghanistan Crisis and Pakistan's Security Dilemma," Asian Survey 23/3 (March 1983): 227-243.

Explores the complexities of the Soviet invasion of Afghanistan, including brief discussion of the role of Soviet espionage in refugee camps.

1345. Cheh, Mary M. "The Progressive Case and the Atomic Energy Act: Waking to the Dangers of Government Information Controls," George Washington Law Review 48/1 (November 1979): 163-210.

Discusses potential liability under Atomic Energy Act for those who publish privately developed information that would be "restricted data" under the Act, including history and legislative developments of Act. Reviews how controls have been used and whether the controls are justifiable. Focusses on legislative intent regarding whether privately generated information was meant to be regulated under the Act.

1346. Cheh, Mary M. "Government Control of Private Ideas--Sticking a Balance Between Scientific Freedom and National Security," Jurimetrics Journal 23/1 (Fall 1982): 1-32.

Discusses nature and scope government information controls developed by private individuals, including information on atomic energy, technical data, and cryptology. Laws on information controls are discussed. Examines countervailing arguments of national security versus First Amendment challenges.

1347. Cheh, Mary M. "Secrecy: Why Is It Still With Us?," Bulletin of the Atomic Scientists 38/10 (December 1982): 66-70.

Discusses atomic energy secrecy and its relationships to all other secrets of government.

1348. Cheh, Mary M. "Judicial Supervision of Executive Secrecy: Rethinking Freedom of Expression for Government Employees and the Public Right of Access to Government Information," Cornell Law Review 69 (April 1984): 690-734.

Argues that courts can and should supervise executive decisions regulating how secrets are kept by requiring the President to protect government employee free speech rights. There is, however, a more limited role for courts in telling President what information should be kept.

1349. Cheney, Richard B. "Clarifying Legislative and Executive Roles in Covert Operations," George Mason University Law Review 11/1 (Fall 1988): 203-219.

Discusses oversight of covert operations; the proposed 48-hour rule; substitution for public debate, the real issue; and an alternative approach.

1350. Cheney, Richard B.   "The Geostrategic Threat," <u>Signal</u> 44 (December 1989): 25.

1351. Chernavin, Victor. "What the Allies Knew of the German Military Plan Before the Outbreak of the Great War," <u>Army Quarterly</u> 19 (1935): 287-296.
    The author, a former general in Imperial Russia, argues that French intelligence was provided the German military plans for war but never used them to plan a defensive posture.

1352. Cherne, Leo. "Intelligence Cannot Help a Nation Find Its Soul. It Is Indispensable, However, to Help Preserve That Nation's Safety While It Continues the Search," <u>Freedom At Issue</u> 35 (1976): 6-11.
    Intelligence operations, it is pointed out, are essential to the fight against terrorism as well as in guiding the economics of foreign policy.

1353. Cherne, Leo. "Need to Know," <u>Journal of Defense & Diplomacy</u> 4 (May 1986): 38-41.

1354. Chertok, Mark A. and Stanley Marcus. "Chilling Political Expression by Use of Police Intelligence Files: Anderson v. Sills," <u>Harvard Civil Rights and Civil Liberties Law Review</u> 5/1 (January 1970): 71-88.
    Examines New Jersey court decision which found that police collection of information on "potential civil disorder problems" violated First Amendment. Argues such collection chills First Amendment rights and that collection should only occur where systematic violent behavior is present.

1355. Chevigny, Paul G. "Philosophy of Language and Free Expression," <u>New York University Law Review</u> 55/2 (May 1980): 157-194.
    Offers reason for free speech without reference to political philosophies based on individualism. Argues for inclusion of right to reach audiences to have them listen and respond is the core concept of free speech. Otherwise essence of free speech is ignored since words without discourse are meaningless.

1356. Chevigny, Paul G. "Politics and Law in the Control of Local Surveillance," <u>Cornell Law Review</u> 69/4 (April 1984): 735-784.
    Discusses law of police surveillance in the 1970s; federal litigation in New York, Chicago and Memphis; state courts and city councils in Los Angeles, Detroit and Seattle; and the flight into private investigation.

1357. Child, Clifton J. "In Defence of 'Tom' Delmer and Dr. Otto John: Notes for the Record," <u>Intelligence and National Security</u> 4/1 (January 1989): 127-136.
    The author writes a defense of the actions of Delmer and John based on his experiences during World War II with both intelligence officers. Argues that Delmer and John were both bitterly anti-Hitler and anti-Stalin.

1358. Childs, Harwood L. "American Government in War-Time: Public Information and Opinion," American Political Science Review 37/1 (February 1943): 56-68.

Contains a historical account of the years immediately preceding World War II in which war information policies were established; organization chart and discussion of the Office of War Information, including intelligence operations.

1359. Childs, Harwood L. "The Office of War Information," Public Opinion Quarterly 7/1 (1943): 3-4.

Introduces several articles in this issue on the OWI. Points out that many people are critical of the Office's functions, but he counters with a recognition that information control is critical to controlling the direction of war.

1360. Childs, J. Rives. "My Recollections of G.2 A.6," Cryptologia 2/3 (July 1978): 201-214.

1361. Childs, J. Rives. "Breaking Codes Was This Couple's Lifetime Career," Smithsonian 18/3 (September 1987): 128-130+.

A discussion of the codebreaking work of William and Elizabeth Friedman.

1362. Chilton, C. W. "Roman Law of Treason Under the Early Principate," Journal of Roman Studies 45 (1955): 73-81.

A detailed consideration of two questions: "Under what law or laws were charges brought in cases of treason during the first years of the Principate?; What were the penalties prescribed by that law or those laws?"

1363. Chimes, Lewis. "National Security and the First Amendment: The Proposed Use of Government Secrecy Agreements Under National Security Directive 84," Columbia Journal of Law and Social Problems 19/3 (Fall 1985): 209-251.

Examines extent of operation of prepublication review of writings on national security by current or ex-government employees. Discusses case law and reviews Snepp v. U. S. analysis used in determining validity of such programs. Also contains analysis of NSD 84. Concludes that NSD 84 does not satisfy any of the requirements in the Snepp case.

1364. Chin-Chen, Chang and Ren-Junn Hwang. "Master Keys for M3 Cryptoscheme," Cryptologia 17/2 (April 1993): 175-186.

1365. Chin, Yuan-Chung; PeCheng Wang; and Jing-Jang Hwang. "Cryptanalysis on Schwartz Graphical Encryption Method," Cryptologia 17/3 (July 1993): 301-304.

1366. Chirico, Guy W. "The Right to Travel and Presidential Emergency Authority: The Supreme Court Lowers the Standard of Review in <u>Regan v. Wald</u>," <u>Albany Law Review</u> 49/4 (Summer 1985): 1001-1031.

In <u>Regan v. Wald</u> respondents were denied travel authority to Cuba for educational, political and religious study under Regulation 560. Article includes application of the case, <u>Haig v. Agee</u>, to this case. Agee had been denied a passport and readmission to the US.

1367. Chistaikov, N. F. "Sotsialisticheskaia Zakonnost' i Sviaz's Sovetskoi Obshchestvennost' is - Osnovnuy Printsipy Deiatel'nosti Sledstevennogo Apparate Organov Gosudar Stvenoi Bezopasnosti," <u>Sovetskoe Gosudarstvo i Pravo</u> 11 (1960): 34-41.

1368. Chittick, William O. "American Foreign Policy Elites: Attitudes Toward Secrecy and Publicity," <u>Journalism Quarterly</u> 47 (Winter 1970): 689-696.

1369. Chomeau, John B. "Covert Action's Proper Role in U.S. Policy," <u>International Journal of Intelligence and Counterintelligence</u> 2/3 (Fall 1988): 407-414.

Discussion of the proper role of covert action in a spectrum of conflict ranging from diplomacy on the low side to conventional war on the high side. Major sections discuss a defense of the initiative; warning signs; CIA's role; the right way to conduct covert action; forms of covert action; and covert action's future.

1370. Chong-Sik Lee. "South Korea 1979: Confrontation, Assassination, and Transition," <u>Asian Survey</u> 20/1 (January 1980): 63-76.

Discusses the political developments in South Korea following the assassination of President Park by the head of the Korean Central Intelligence Agency. Suggests that the future holds political instability.

1371. Choucri, Nazli. "Applications of Econometric Analysis to Forecasting in International Relations," <u>Peace Research Society International Papers</u> 21 (1973): 15-39.

1372. Christianson, Paul. "The 'Obligated' Portions of the House of Lords Journals Dealing with the Attainder of Strafford, 1641," <u>English Historical Journal</u> 95/375 (April 1980): 339-353.

A brief discussion of the journal records pertaining to the impeachment, trial, attainder, and execution of the first Earl of Strafford in 1662.

1373. Christie, George C. "Government Surveillance and Individual Freedom: A Proposed Statutory Response to <u>Laird v. Tatum</u> and the Broader Problem of Government Surveillance of the Individual," <u>New York University Law Review</u>

47/5 (November 1972): 871-902.

Discusses the symbolic significance of surveillance in both of its extreme meanings in the political arena. Suggests a federal statute to delineate the circumstances of surveillance among government and private agencies.

1374. Christol, Carl Q. and Charles R. Davis. "Maritime Quarantine: The Naval Interdiction of Offensive Weapons and Associated Material to Cuba, 1962," American Journal of International Law 57/3 (July 1963): 525-545.

Discusses international law pertaining to the maritime quarantine rule, self-defense, maintenance of international peace and security, applicability of the convention on the high seas, proportionality, and clearance certifications.

1375. Chroust, A. H. "Treason and Patriotism in Ancient Greece," Journal of the History of Ideas 15 (April 1954): 280-288.

Describes political 'clubs' in seventh century Greece and defines their goals. Traces the origins of democracy and the earliest definitions of treason and patriotism. Patriotism was an act that benefitted onesself or one's club since the country was divided.

1376. Chrzanowski, Bogdan. "The Organization of an Evacuation Network from Poland to Sweden by Sea During the Nazi Occupation: 1939-45," Stutthof Zaazyt y Muzaum 5 (1984): 13-46.

1377. Chrzanowski, Bogdan. "Intelligence Activities of the Organization for Armed Struggle: Home Army in Pomerania," Stutthof Zaazyt y Muzaum 6 (1985): 5-38.

A Polish article, continuation is found in 7 (1987): 5-31.

1378. Chubatyi, Nicholas D. "The Ukrainian Underground," Ukrainian Quarterly 2 (Winter 1946): 154-166.

1379. Chukseyev, V. "CIA -- Another Scandal," International Affairs (USSR) 5 (May 1975): 142-149.

1380. Chumbley, Douglas J. "Criminal Procedure: The Foreign Intelligence Exception to the Warrant Requirement," Washington and Lee Law Review 38/2 (Spring 1981): 551-563.

Discusses U. S. v. Truong Dinh Hung in which the Fourth Circuit Court applied an exception to the Fourth Amendment warrant requirement for government investigations of foreign intelligence activities.

1381. Chung, Daniel C. "Internal Security: Establishment of a Canadian Security Intelligence Service--Canadian Security Intelligence Service Act, ch. 21, 1984, Can. Stat.," Harvard International Law Journal 26/1 (Winter 1985):

234-249.

Legislative history of the transfer of national security responsibilities from the RCMP to the autonomous civilian agency, the CSIS. Discusses each part of the legislation.

1382. Church, Frank. "Pacem in Terris IV: The CIA and Covert Operations," Center Magazine 9/2 (March-April 1976): 21-38.

A review of CIA activities known as covert actions from 1947 to the 1970s.

1383. Church, Frank. "Covert Action: The Swampland of American Foreign Policy," Bulletin of Atomic Scientists 32/2 (February 1976): 7-11.

A review of CIA activities in covert actions by the CIA in the post World War II era.

1384. Church, Katrina J. "The Briar Patch of Reality: A Legal Analysis of the Mining of Nicaragua's Harbors," New York University Journal of International Law and Politics 18 (Fall 1985): 169-227.

Examines the decision to mine the harbors and CIA involvement; the law underlying the policy; the history of similar interventions; and the lessons of history. Argues for more congressional controls on executive sidestepping of international law.

1385. Church, Larry D. "Intelligence Requirements of the Tactical Commander," American Intelligence Journal 8/3 (Summer 1987).

1386. Churchill, Marlborough. "The Military Intelligence Division, General Staff," Journal of the United States Artillery 52/4 (April 1920): 293-315.

Based essentially on the author's lecture on the topic of September 4, 1919 at the War Department's General Staff College. It is a fundamental outline of the MID's organization during World War I. An excellent source document for the period.

1387. Churchill, Ward. "U.S. Mercenaries in Africa: The Recruitment Network and U.S. Policy," Africa Today 27/2 (1980): 21-46.

1388. CIA History Staff. "Fifteen DCI's First Hundred Days," Studies in Intelligence 39/5 (1995): 53-63.

Briefly summarizes the contributions of fifteen CIA directors: Sidney Souers; Hoyt Vandenburg; Roscoe Hillenkoetter; Walter Smith; Allen Dulles; John McCone; William Raborn; Richard Helms; James Schlesinger; William Colby; George Bush; Stansfield Turner; William Casey; William Webster; and Robert Gates.

1389. Cimbala, Stephen J. "Counterintelligence: The Necessary Skepticism," National Defense 49 (November 1984): 61-62, 65.

A general description of the role of counterintelligence and the responsible authorities for its execution in the intelligence community.

1390. Cimbala, Stephen J. "Is a Soviet 'Bolt from the Blue' Impossible?," Air University Review (May-June 1985): 23-31.

1391. Cimbala, Stephen J. "Amorphous Wars," International Journal of Intelligence and Counterintelligence 2/1 (Spring 1988): 73-90.

Discusses the relationship between intelligence and amorphous wars, e.g., terrorism, low intensity conflict, insurgency, and guerilla warfare. Sections include discussion of the ambiguity of the threats from such wars, the impact of terrorism, and the overall role of intelligence in fighting terrorism.

1392. Cimbala, Stephen J. "The SIOP: What Kind of War Plan?," Air Power Journal 2 (Summer 1988): 4-10.

1393. Cimbala, Stephen J. "Mainstreaming Military Deception," International Journal of Intelligence and Counterintelligence 3/4 (Winter 1989): 509-536.

Discusses war and uncertainty; intelligence and deception; capabilities and intentions; perception and estimate; intelligence, deception, and operational art; global objectives of intelligence estimates; resources and staying power; and unexpected attacks.

1394. Cinquegrana, Americo R. "Dancing in the Dark: Accepting the Invitation to Struggle in the Context of 'Covert Action' the Iran-Contra Affair and the Intelligence Oversight Process," Houston Journal of International Law 11/1 (Fall 1988): 177-209.

Explores sources and extent of guidance concerning "covert action" and "special activities" of the intelligence community. Major sections discuss the Hughes-Ryan Amendment; the Church Committee; the Pike Committee; executive orders of Presidents Ford, Carter and Reagan; the Intelligence Oversight Act of 1980; the congressional response to covert action; and Iran-Contra and the Congress.

1395. Cinquegrana, Americo R. "The Walls (and Wires) Have Ears: The Background and First Ten Years of the Foreign Intelligence Surveillance Act of 1978," University of Pennsylvania Law Review 137/3 (January 1989): 793-828.

Legal and political bases of the FISA, contents, and ramifications of enactment. Covers Court review and amendments recommended by the President.

1396. Cipolla, Richard J., Jr. "A Practitioner's Guide to Oklahoma Trade Secrets Law, Past, Present, and Future," Tulsa Law Journal 27 (Winter 1991): 137-179.

Discusses adoption by Oklahoma legislature of Uniform Trade Secrets Act, elements of trade secret cause of action, and application of legal precedents, defenses, damages, etc. Includes and definition of trade secrets.

1397. Cirillo, Vincent A. "Liberty v. Tyranny: The Pennsylvania Supreme Court Encounters Old Combatants on a New Battlefield," Temple Law Review 65 (Summer 1992): 615-621.

Lower court judge reflects on cases of previous year in Pennsylvania Supreme Court. Discusses cases involving trial using closed circuit testimony, wiretaps, and computer files, etc.

1398. Civiletti, Benjamin R. "Intelligence Gathering and the Law: Conflict or Compatibility?," Fordham Law Review 48/6 (May 1980): 883-906.

Discusses the relationship between the rule of law and intelligence gathering activities of the US government: Nature and role of intelligence gathering; developments of intelligence law; constitutional problems; the future of intelligence law.

1399. Civiletti, Benjamin R. "Post-Watergate Legislation in Retrospect," Southwestern Law Journal 34/5 (February 1981): 1043-1062.

A lecture regarding reform legislation, including the FOIA, the Privacy Act, the Ethics in Government Act, the War Powers Resolution, the Hughes-Ryan Amendment, and charters for the CIA and FBI.

1400. Civiletti, Benjamin R. "Intelligence Gathering and the Law," Studies in Intelligence 27/2 (Summer 1983).

1401. Claburn, Jeffrey. "Public Constraints on Assassination as an Instrument of U.S. Foreign Policy," International Journal of Intelligence and Counterintelligence 7/1 (Spring 1994): 97-109.

Raises and considers several questions relating to the role and retreat from political assassination in US foreign relations. Considers morality versus realpolitik; the nature of leadership; public squeamishness; the pros and cons of assassination; circumventing the ban on assassinations; and the making of hard choices.

1402. Clancy, Paul. "The Bureau of the Bureaus," Quill (February 1986): 12-18.

The role and operations of the FBI against activist groups is discussed, including allegations of FBI-authored stories for media consumption. Continued in the March 1976 issue, pp. 12-15.

1403. Clapper, James R., Jr. "Air Force Intelligence: Working Smarter in the 90's," American Intelligence Journal 11/3 (Summer-Fall 1990): 11-12.

A brief discussion of the impact of budget cuts and realignments in defense policy will have on Air Force intelligence.

1404. Clapper, James R., Jr. "Imagery -- Gulf War Lessons Learned and Future Challenges," American Intelligence Journal 13/1&2 (Winter-Spring 1992): 13-17.
Discusses the imagery situation in the 1990 Gulf War, in particular, operation Desert Shield and Desert Storm; lessons learned; and future challenges.

1405. Clapper, James R., Jr. "Defense Intelligence Reorganization and Challenges," Defense Intelligence Journal 1/1 (Spring 1992): 3-16.
Discusses the new world order; new challenges for the Defense Intelligence Agency and the overall intelligence community; operations Desert Shield/Desert Storm; increased responsibility for DIA; the role of Congress; and meeting the challenges.

1406. Clapper, James R., Jr. "Reorganization of DIA and Defense Intelligence Activities," American Intelligence Journal 14/3 (Autumn-Winter 1993-1994): 9-16.
Discusses the era of change and reorganization at the Defense Intelligence Agency. Major sections cover the post-Cold War security environment; the role of intelligence; restructuring the community; the DIA reorganization plans; and integration through the Military Intelligence Board.

1407. Clapper, James R., Jr. "Challenging Joint Military Intelligence," Joint Forces Quarterly (Spring 1994): 93-94.

1408. Clark, Clairborne. "Congress's Turbulent Relationship and Intelligence," World and I 1/11 (November 1986): 30-37.

1409. Clark, Andrew; Ed Dawson; and Helen Bergen. "Combinational Optimization and the Knapsack Cipher," Cryptologia 20/1 (January 1996): 85-93.

1410. Clark, Herbert H. and Edward F. Schaefer. "Concealing One's Meaning from Overhearers," Journal of Memory and Language 26 (April 1987): 209-225.

1411. Clark, J. "Bovine Balloons and the Odiferous Option," Washington Monthly 16 (November 1984): 24-25.
Discusses briefly the history of OSS's development of weapons.

1412. Clark, James C. "Robert Henry Best: The Path to Treason, 1921-1945," Journalism Quarterly 67 (Winter 1990): 1051-1061.

1413. Clark, Jane. "Metcalf Bowler as a British Spy," Rhode Island Historical Society Collections 23/4 (1930): 101-117.

1414. Clark, M. Wesley. "Electronic Surveillance and Related Investigative Techniques," Military Law Review 128 (Spring 1990): 155-224.

Discusses military law as applied to electronic surveillance. Major sections discuss definitions; consensual interceptions; steps and processes of consensual intercepting requests; Army and other regulations; related considerations; nonconsensual intercepts; and pen registers.

1415. Clark, Phillip S. "The Soviet Photo-Reconnaissance Satellite Programme," Jane's Soviet Intelligence Review 2/2 (February 1990): 84-90.

Several generations of Soviet satellites are discussed in terms of their characteristics.

1416. Clark, Phillip S. "Soviet Worldwide ELINT Satellites," Jane's Soviet Intelligence Review 2/7 (July 1990): 330-333.

A summary of schedules and orbits of such satellites, beginning in 1970.

1417. Clark, Phillip S. "Soviet ELINT Satellites for Monitoring Naval Transmissions," Jane's Soviet Intelligence Review 2/8 (August 1990): 378-381.

Refers to ELINT capabilities since 1974, including coverage during the Falklands War.

1418. Clark, Phillip S. "Soviet Nuclear Satellites for Observing Western Navies," Jane's Soviet Intelligence Review 2/9 (September 1990): 423-429.

A detailed explanation of Soviet capabilities from the late 1960s.

1419. Clark, Robert M. "Scientific and Technical Intelligence Analysis," Studies in Intelligence 19/1 (Spring 1975): 39-48.

Major sections consider the purpose of S & T intelligence; cases of S & T intelligence; sources of S & T intelligence; the cardinal principle of scientific intelligence; S & T intelligence maxims; and a postscript.

1420. Clark, Tom. "Wiretapping the Constitution," California Western Law Review 5/1 (Fall 1968): 1-6.

Short discussion of wiretapping/eavesdropping case law history followed by slightly longer coverage of Title III of the Safe Streets Act of 1968. The author is former associate justice of the US Supreme Court.

1421. Clark, William B. "John the Painter," Pennsylvania Magazine of History and Biography 63/1 (January 1939): 1-23.

An account of the life and criminal activities of one James Aitken, known also as John the Painter. His more common crimes were thievery and arson. He was known to Silas Deane, American commissioner in France, and to Edward Bancroft, a double agent who spied on Benjamin Franklin in Paris. He was hanged in 1777.

1422.   Clark, William B.   "In Defense of Thomas Digges," Pennsylvania Magazine of History and Biography 77 (1953): 381-438.
         An account of the life in crime, including espionage for the British, of a Maryland gentleman who had come to America during the American Revolution.

1423.   Clarke, Bruce C.   "G-2: Member of the Operations Team," Military Review 47/9 (September 1967): 73-76.

1424.   Clarke, Carter W.   "From the Archives: Account of Gen. George C. Marshall's Request of Gov. Thomas E. Dewey," Cryptologia 7/2 (April 1983): 119-128.

1425.   Clarke, David.   "Open Government: The French Experience," Political Quarterly 57/3 (July-September 1986): 278-294.
         Discusses the trends in French government away from secrecy and toward openness, in particular the passage of a freedom of information act in 1969 and a data processing act of 1978. Also discusses the lessons learned along the way toward operating a more open form of government and the administration of citizen requests for information.

1426.   Clarke, Duncan L. and Edward L. Neveleff.   "Secrecy, Foreign Intelligence, and Civil Liberties: Has the Pendulum Swung Too Far?," Political Science Quarterly 99/3 (Fall 1984): 493-513.
         Discusses E.O. 12333 of 1981, physical foreign intelligence searches, Intelligence Identities Protection Act of 1982, public access to information, classification provisions, and Reagan directive on unauthorized disclosure.

1427.   Clarke, George W.   "Disclosure Problems in Espionage Prosecutions," Studies in Intelligence 28/1 (Spring 1984).

1428.   Clarke, I. F.   "World-War-II, or, What Did the Future Hold," Futures 26/3 (April 1994): 335-344.

1429.   Clarke, William F.   "Government Code and Cypher School: Its Foundation and Development with Special Reference to Its Naval Side," Cryptologia 11/4 (October 1987): 219-226.

1430.   Clarke, William F.   "The Years Between," Cryptologia 12/1 (January 1988): 52-58.

1431.   Clarke, William F.   "Bletchley Park 1941-1945," Cryptologia 12/2 (April 1988): 90-97.
         This is a reprint of a report by the author.

1432. Clarke, William F.   "Post War Organization," Cryptologia 12/3 (July 1988): 174-177.
This is a reprint of a post World War II report by the author.

1433. Clarke, William F.   "Post War Organization," Cryptologia 13/2 (April 1989): 118-122.

1434. Clarkson, Edward J.   "An Unknown Warrior," Marine Corps Gazette 54 (August 1970): 38-43.

1435. Clasby, Francis X. and Robert A. Koch.   "Wartime Naval Photography of the Electronic Image," Society of Motion Picture Engineers 50 (March 1948): 189-198.

1436. Claveloux, Ronald L.   "The Conflict Between Executive Privilege and Congressional Oversight: The Gorsuch Controversy," Duke Law Journal 1983/6 (December 1983) 1333-1358.
Presents background of disputes and eventual resolution of conflict between president and congress.   Discusses executive privilege and right of oversight as interpreted by courts in case law.   Argues that compromise is preferred as means to resolve such issues, but also suggests grounds for judicial analysis.

1437. Clawson, Patrick.   "Coping with Terrorism in the United States," Orbis 33/3 (Summer 1989): 341-356.
Poses a question: How should US law enforcement handle US-based supporters of terrorist groups, both foreign and domestic?   Analyzes the CISPES case, offer four models of counter-terrorism, and conclusions.

1438. Clemens, Martin.   "Coastwatchers Diary: Guadalcanal," American Heritage 17/2 (February 1966): 104-110.
An account of the British and Australian coastwatchers who collected military intelligence about Japanese naval activities in early 1942.   Information taken from the diaries of the author between February and August 1942.

1439. Clement, David.   "Le My, Study in Insurgency," Marine Corps Gazette 51 (July 1967): 18-24.

1440. Clendenen, Clarence C.   "A Confederate Spy in California: A Curious Incident of the Civil War," Southern California Historical Society Quarterly 45/3 (1963): 219-233.
The story of one Captain H. Kennedy, sent to California as a Confederate soldier to strengthen the secret conspiracy to organize forces in the West. Sections discuss the evolution of the California conspiracy; the willingness of

volunteers to join and remain committed to the Confederate Army; the roles of Albert Sidney and Lansford W. Hastings; Kennedy's arrival and eventual escape to Texas.

1441. Cleveland, Harlan and Stuart G. Brown. "The Limits of Obsession: Fencing in the 'National Security' Claim," Administrative Law Review 28 (1976): 327-346.

Discusses development of executive discretion; development of national security; the "need to know" doctrine; the trouble with secrecy; the "national security" claim; fencing in the executive; and public face and private face.

1442. Clifford, J. Garry. "A Connecticut Colonel's Candid Conversation with the Wrong Commander-in-Chief," Connecticut History 28 (1987): 24-38.

1443. Clifford, Ray T. and Donald C. Fischer, Jr. "Foreign Language Needs in the U.S. Government," Annals of the American Academy of Political and Social Science 511 (September 1990): 109-121.

Discusses the language needs of several US government agencies, including the Central Intelligence Agency, Federal Bureau of Investigation, National Security Agency, and the Drug Enforcement Administration.

1444. Clift, A. Dennis. "The Five-Legged Calf: Bringing Intelligence to the National Security Debate," American Intelligence Journal 11/1 (Winter 1989): 24-30.

1445. Clift, A. Dennis. "National Security and National Competitiveness: Open Source Solutions," American Intelligence Journal 14/2&3 (Spring-Summer 1993): 25-28.

Major sections of this piece discuss scientific and technical intelligence in terms of open source solutions; other open source intelligence interaction; general defense intelligence program strategy; and GDIP priorities.

1446. Clinard, Outten J. "Developments in Air Targeting: Data-Handling Techniques," Studies in Intelligence 3/1 (Spring 1959).

1447. Cline, Mary A. "The Growing Importance of the Intelligence Community in Information Warfare," Defense Intelligence Journal 5/1 (Spring 1996): 83-86.

A brief commentary on the increasing dependence of decision makers on the intelligence officer. Argues that the future intelligence officer with the most complete and accurate information which is protected from compromise will have the advantage.

1448. Cline, Ray S. "Is Intelligence Over-Coordinated?," Studies in Intelligence 2 (Fall 1957).

1449. Cline, Ray S. "Policy Without Intelligence," Foreign Policy 17 (Winter 1974-1975): 121-135.

Argues for a reconsideration of the interagency staff system supporting the National Security Council.

1450. Cline, Ray S. "US Foreign Intelligence, 1939-41," Foreign Service Journal 53/11 (1976): 17-20.

A brief history of the origins of the highly experimental early intelligence branches, especially those most useful to the foreign service officers. See this author's book, The CIA Under Reagan, Bush & Casey. He had a long and distiguished career at CIA, and also inspired many academic research projects.

1451. Cline, Ray S. "Terrorism: Seabed for Soviet Influence," Midstream 26 (May 1980): 5-8.

1452. Cline, Ray S. "A CIA Reminiscence," Washington Quarterly 5/4 (Autumn 1982): 88-92.

A brief summary of the author's lengthy career in the CIA, in particular his role in the Cuban missile crisis of 1962.

1453. Cline, Ray S. "Technology and Intelligence," Terrorism: An International Journal 10/3 (1987): 253-255.

A brief article concerning the role of intelligence analysts and advanced technology. Argues that the role of human judgment must continue to be regarded in the overall analytical effort.

1454. Cline, Ray S. "Covert Action as Presidential Prerogative," Harvard Journal of Law & Public Policy 12/2 (Spring 1989): 357-369.

A general discussion of the history and development of presidential actions in the conduct of covert action. Argues for reduction of congressional oversight due to its alleged exposures of classified information, micro-management of covert operations, and obstruction of presidential foreign policy efforts.

1455. Cline, Ray S. "Commentary: The Cuban Missile Crisis," Foreign Affairs 68/4 (Fall 1989): 190-196.

Argues that no American policy to invade Cuba was responsible for Soviet actions to install offensive weapons in Cuba in 1962.

1456. Cline, Ray S. "Old Spies, New Day," Naval Intelligence Professionals Quarterly 6/2 (Spring 1990): 6.

1457. Cline, Ray S. "Streamlining Congressional Oversight of the CIA," World & I (June 1991): 114-117.

1458. Clinton, Henry. "Original Documents: Sir Henry Clinton's Original Secret Record of Private Daily Intelligence," Magazine of American History 10 (1883): 327+; 11 (1884): 53+.

1459. Clinton, Henry. "The Treason of Benedict Arnold, as Presented in Letters of Sir Henry Clinton to Lord George Germain," Pennsylvania Magazine of History and Biography 22 (January 1899): 410-422.

1460. Clive, Nigel. "The Management of Intelligence," Government and Opposition 22 (Winter 1987): 93-100.
    A book review essay of The Ties That Bind by Jeffrey Richelson and Desmond Ball, and Secrecy and Democracy by Stansfield Turner.

1461. Clive, Nigel. "From War to Peace in SIS," Intelligence and National Security 10/3 (July 1995): 512-513.
    A brief account of the work of the author in the Secret Intelligence Services (SIS).

1462. Clotworthy, Orrin. "Some Far-Out Thoughts on Computers," Studies in Intelligence 6/3 (Fall 1962).
    Consider the age and subject matter of this article in modern terms.

1463. Clubb, O. Edmund. "Security Risks: National Security and the State Department," Worldview 16/8 (August 1973): 43-45.
    An historical assessment of US foreign policy as developed by the State Department in the post World War II era. The issue of security risks among foreign service officers is also raised.

1464. Cluseau, D. "L'Arrestation par les Allemands du Personnel du 2eme Bureau Francais," Revue d'Histoire de la Deuxieme Guerre Mondiale 29 (1958): 32-48.

1465. Clutterbuck, Richard L. "The SEP Guerilla Intelligence Source," Military Review 42/10 (October 1962): 13-21.
    Discussion of the "surrendered enemy personnel" system.

1466. Clutterbuck, Richard L. "Communist Defeat in Malaya: A Case Study," Military Review 43/9 (September 1963): 63-78.
    A detailed analysis of the role of information security concerning insurgent activities in Malaya.

1467. Coady, W. F. "Automated Link Analysis: Artificial Intelligence-Based Tool for Investigators," Police Chief 52/9 (September 1985): 22-23.

1468. Coates, G. P. "Reconnaissance Satellites," Spaceflight 3 (May 1961): 100-104.

1469. Cobb, Dawna M. "Prohibiting Indirect Assistance to International Terrorists: Closing the Gap in United States Law," Fordham International Law Journal 6/3 (1982-1983): 530-555.

Considers the applicable statutes; a proposal for the legislation; countervailing arguments; and conclusions. Argues that rendering assistance to terrorists should not go unpunished.

1470. Cobb, Elizabeth H. "Covert Entry, Electronic Surveillance, and the Fourth Amendment," Louisiana Law Review 40 (Summer 1980): 951-962.

A case note discussion of Dalia v. United States, 441 U.S. 238 (1979).

1471. Cobb, Tyrus W. "The Future of the Soviet Defense Burden: The Political Economy of Contemporary Soviet Security Policy," Naval War College Review 33 (July-August 1981): 30-52.

1472. Cobban, Alfred. "British Secret Service in France, 1784-1792," English Historical Review 69 (April 1954): 226-261.

Argues that the British government allocated small expenditures for secret service agents. The quality of persons working for the British was, therefore, diminished with few exceptions. Discusses the Brest plot, the Civil List Act, and British agents in France.

1473. Cobban, Alfred. "Beginning of the Channel Isles Correspondence, 1789-1794," English Historical Review 77 (January 1962): 38-52.

Discusses the Channel of Isles intelligence network established to provide the British with information on French naval operations. The network continued after the war with France. Sections discuss the collection of information about French preparations for war; military operations and the determination of British supporting factions; and agent traffic following the war.

1474. Cobban, Alfred. "The Great Mystification of Mehee de la Touche," Bulletin of the London University Institute of Historical Research 41 (May 1968): 100-106.

1475. Cochran, Alexander S., Jr. "'Magic,' 'Ultra,' and the Second World War: Literature, Sources, and Outlook," Military Affairs 46/2 (April 1982): 88-92.

A critical review of how historians of the codebreaking efforts of American and British agencies have reported the Magic and Ultra projects.

1476. Cochran, Alexander S., Jr. "MacArthur, Ultra, and the War in the Pacific," Revue d'Histoire de la Deuxieme Guerre Mondiale et des Conflits Contemporains

34/133 (1984): 17-27.

This article chronicles General Douglas MacArthur's fight against the installation of secret data gathering programs, over which he had no control or access.

1477. Cochran, Alexander S., Jr. "Protecting the Ultimate Advantage," Military History 1 (June 1985): 42-49.

1478. Cockburn, A. "Tinker with Gadgets, Tailor the Facts," Harper's 270 (April 1985): 65-70.

A book review essay concerning eight books on intelligence topics.

1479. Cockburn, Leslie, et al. "Forum: Hearing Nothing, Saying Nothing: The Iran-Contra Investigation," Harper's 276 (February 1988): 45-56.

Six authors and news analysts evaluate the 690-page text of the Iran-Contra matter, and how intelligence is controlled or not controlled at the highest levels of government. Concludes that the report was entirely incomplete and more was occurring in the affair that investigators wished to uncover.

1480. Cockle, Paul. "Analyzing Soviet Defence Spending: The Debate in Perspective," Survival 20/5 (September-October 1978): 209-219.

1481. Coddon, Karin S. "'Unreal Mockery': Unreason and the Problem of Spectacle in Macbeth," ELH 56 (Fall 1989): 485-501.

1482. Codevilla, Angelo. "The CIA: What Have Three Decades Wrought?," Strategic Review 8/1 (Winter 1980): 68-71.

1483. Codevilla, Angelo. "The Substance and the Rules," Washington Quarterly 6/3 (Summer 1983): 32-39.

Debates the 1970s rules and restrictions on US intelligence services and argues that new decisions about these services must be crafted in order to provide clear signals for necessary operations.

1484. Codevilla, Angelo. "The Challenge of Special Operations," Defense & Diplomacy 3/6 (June 1985): 18-22.

Military intelligence technology and modern devices affect the form but not the substance of special operations. Successful operations depend upon good intelligence planning and command.

1485. Codevilla, Angelo. "Ignorance vs. Intelligence," Commentary 83/5 (May 1987): 77-80.

A book review essay of William Burrough's Deep Black. The author presents several concerns for the accuracy of the book, mainly concerns for the book's sources. The author offers an alternative perspective on technologies of spying and how technologies affect intelligence operations in other countries.

1486. Codevilla, Angelo. "Arms and Intelligence," Global Affairs 2/1 (Winter 1987): 34-46.

1487. Codevilla, Angelo. "Is There Still a Soviet Threat?," Commentary 87 (November 1988): 23-24.

1488. Codevilla, Angelo. "The CIA's Identity Crisis," American Enterprise (January-February 1992): 29-37.

1489. Coe, Roger N. "Keeping Trade Secrets Secret," Journal of the Patent and Trademark Office Society 76 (November 1994): 833-839.

1490. Coffman, Edward M. "Captain Hines' Adventures in the Northwest Conspiracy," Register of the Kentucky Historical Society 63/1 (1965): 30-38.

1491. Cogan, Charles G. "The Response of the Strong to the Weak: The American Raid on Libya, 1986," Intelligence and National Security 6/3 (July 1991): 608-620.
    Major sections discuss the smoking discotheque, intimidation and terror, 1981-86; planning for attack; the balance sheet and the aftermath; and implications for the future. The case illustrates the secrecy environment of major military operations.

1492. Cogan, Charles G. "The In-Culture of the DO," Studies in Intelligence 35/2 (Summer 1991).
    The article was published under the same title in Intelligence and National Security 8/1 (January 1993): 78-86. A personal reflection by the author on the development of two distinct cultures at CIA: the analytical and the operational. Recognizes the major differences in problem definition and approach of each of the cultures.

1493. Cogan, Charles G. "Partners in Time: The CIA and Afghanistan Since 1979," World Policy Journal 10/2 (Summer 1993): 73-82.
    Discusses the segmented society of Afghanistan, the 1979 coup; President Carter's rapid reaction and covert action order; and American responsibility in succeeding years.

1494. Cogan, Charles G. "Intelligence and Crisis Management: The Importance of the Pre-Crisis," Intelligence and National Security 9/4 (October 1994): 633-650.
    Analyzes the phases of crisis development and pays particular attention

to the tension between policy makers and intelligence analysts in the pre-crisis period. Majors sections discuss types of crises; divergence of planning; errors of appreciation; improving the intelligence approach to crises; and improving the policy approach to crises. An article with a similar title and subject matter appeared in French in a French journal, Revue d'Histoire Diplomatique 108/3 (1994): 257-276.

1495. Cogan, Charles G. "Covert Action and Congressional Oversight: A Deontology," Studies in Conflict and Terrorism 16 (April-June 1993): 87-97.
Cold war intelligence operations controls are discussed. Special emphasis is placed on clandestine and covert operations.

1496. Cogan, Charles G. "Restructuring the CIA," Foreign Service Journal 73/2 (February 1996): 32-39.
Itemizes the areas of critical reform efforts needed with respect to the organization and missions of the Central Intelligence Agency. Argues that CIA reforms are needed in order to preclude isolation and marginalization of the agency in the policy process.

1497. Cogan, Charles G. "Historical Fluke: US Intelligence at the Crossroads," Intelligence and National Security 11/2 (April 1996): 374-378.
A book review essay pertaining to two books: Roy Godson, Ernest May and Gary Schmitt, US Intelligence at the Crossroads: Agendas for Reform; and Roy Godson, Dirty Tricks or Trump Cards: US Covert Action and Counterintelligence.

1498. Coghlan, David. "Industrial Espionage--Measures and Countermeasures," International Security Review 20 (November-December 1982): 52-57.

1499. Cohan, Jerome A. "Comments" [RE: discussion of Pueblo incident offered by George A. Aldrich and William E. Butler, in this bibliography], Proceedings of the American Society of International Law 63 (April 1969): 19-30.
Questions facts pertaining to the Pueblo incident, the problem of intelligence gathering and international law, and whether a state can detain military persons on a charge of espionage involving a ship. American naval personnel were held by North Korea for over one year.

1500. Cohan, Leon, Jr. "Intelligence and Vietnam," Marine Corps Gazette 50/2 (February 1966): 47-49.

1501. Cohen, Barry. "U.S. Agencies and Chile's Coup," Labour Monthly 56 (June 1974): 280-284.

1502. Cohen, Eliot A. "Why We Should Stop Studying the Cuban Missile Crisis," National Interest (Winter 1986): 3-13.

1503. Cohen, Eliot A. "Toward Better Net Assessment: Rethinking the Conventional Balance in Europe," International Security 13/1 (Summer 1988): 50-89.
        Discusses six flaws in the optimistic view of the conventional balance of forces in Europe, including the view of "perfect intelligence"; the Soviet calculus; and how the US should think about the balance.

1504. Cohen, Eliot A. "The Chinese Intervention in Korea, 1950," Studies in Intelligence 32/3 (Fall 1988).

1505. Cohen, Eliot A. "'Only Half the Battle': American Intelligence and the Chinese Intervention in Korea, 1950," Intelligence and National Security 5/1 (January 1990): 129-149.
        Discusses intelligence in the Korean War from Inchon to the Yalu; intelligence structure and sources; the real story; American estimates up to the 38th parallel and from the 38th parallel to the first phase offensive; the resumption of the offensive; and conclusions regarding Korea as an intelligence failure.

1506. Cohen, Jacob. "Conspiracy Fever," Commentary 60/4 (October 1975): 33-42.
        A lengthy analysis of the various conspiracy theories of the 1970s, particularly the theories about John Kennedy's assassination. CIA is discussed.

1507. Cohen, Maxwell. "Espionage and Immunity: Some Recent Problems and Developments," British Yearbook of International Law 25 (1948): 404-414.
        An excellent analysis of the accommodation of spies in international law during peace time rather than during war time. Uses the Igor Gouzenko case for analytical purposes.

1508. Cohen, Michael J. "Secret Diplomacy and Rebellion in Palestine, 1936-1939," International Journal of Middle East Studies 8/3 (July 1977): 379-404.
        Discusses at length the Arab rebellion in Palestine and the outbreak of terrorism in 1936. Useful in research and writing on Middle East deception activities of Zionist and Arab leaders.

1509. Cohen, Paul. "The Police, the Home Office and the Surveillance of the British Union of Fascists," Intelligence and National Security 1/3 (September 1986): 416-434.

1510. Cohen, Raymond. "Threat Perception in International Crisis," <u>Political Science Quarterly</u> 93/1 (Spring 1978): 93-107.

Examines empirically, on the basis of historical and comparative analysis, the conditions under which threat is perceived. Uses 6 historical examples: the 'war in sight' crisis of 1875; the Italian invasion scare of 1889; the Liman Von Sanders crisis of 1913; the Britain and Prague crisis of 1939; the Poland crisis of 1939 and the Straits Question of 1946.

1511. Cohen, Raymond. "Israeli Military Intelligence Before the 1956 Sinai Campaign," <u>Intelligence and National Security</u> 3/1 (January 1988): 100-140.

Argues that the <u>Aman</u> military intelligence was highly effective in its role in the Israeli defeat of the Egyptian forces.

1512. Cohen, Raymond. "Early Warning Systems," <u>Studies in Intelligence</u> 33/3 (Fall 1989).

1513. Cohen, Raymond. "Threat Assessment in Military Intelligence: The Case of Israel and Syria 1985-86," <u>Intelligence and National Security</u> 4/4 (October 1989): 735-764.

Major sections discuss Israeli approaches to threat assessment and Israeli assessments of the Syrian threat in 1985-86. Highlights the Israeli problems in structuring and organizing early intelligence. Author notes the effects of having limited confidence in one's own intelligence.

1514. Cohen, Robert A. "United States Exclusion and Deportation of Nazi War Criminals: The Act of October 30, 1978," <u>New York University Journal of International Law and Politics</u> 13/1 (Spring 1980): 101-133.

The amendment to the Immigration and Nationality Act of 1952, signed by President Carter, was designed to exclude from the United States any alien of Nazi Germany who had persecuted any person because of race, religion, national origin or political opinion. Discusses deportation, the new Act, international agreements, bills of attainder and ex post facto problems, and denaturalization.

1515. Cohen, Samuel T. and Joseph D. Douglass, Jr. "Selective Targeting and Soviet Deception," <u>Armed Forces Journal</u> (September 1983): 95-101.

1516. Cohen, Samuel T. and Joseph D. Douglass, Jr. "Arms Control, Verification, and Deception," <u>Journal of Defense & Diplomacy</u> 4 (June 1986): 7-10.

1517. Cohen, Shaye J. D. "Josephus, Jeremiah, and Polybius," <u>History and Theory</u> 21/3 (October 1982): 366-381.

An analysis of the Roman emperor Josephus's book, <u>Jewish War</u>, in particular the book's details concerning the use of propaganda in convincing the

Jews to surrender to Roman authority during a revolution. The setting of the book is 66-88 A.D. Josephus is considered to be like Jeremiah and Polybius. He is regarded as a prophet, a leader, and a controlling dictator whose propaganda may have prevented a revolution that might easily have crushed the Jewish state.

1518. Cohen, Sheldon S. "Hannah Levy and the General: An Historical Enigma," Mid-America 68/1 (1986): 5-13.
A insightful look at the relationship between Hannah Levy and Benedict Arnold and her possible influence on him.

1519. Cohen, Stanley A. "Invasion of Privacy: Police and Electronic Surveillance in Canada," McGill Law Journal 27/4 (November 1982): 619-675.
Discusses "police function" and crime prevention (including history), the rule of law as related to crime prevention, democratic principles governing police role, proactive and reactive policing, organized crime, powers of surveillance, discretion, and privacy (definition, rights) and its relationship to intelligence gathering and law enforcement.

1520. Cohen, Stephen P. "U.S. Weapons and South Asia: A Policy Analysis," Pacific Affairs 49/1 (Spring 1976): 49-69.
Discusses the author's observations of US involvement in South Asia from 1945 to the early 1970s, in particular the US roles in supplying arms to India and Pakistan, and the US role in stabilizing the region. Useful in historical analyses of the region.

1521. Cohen, Sylvester, Jr. "In Search of Enemies: A Review," African Studies Review 22/2 (September 1979): 139-140.
A book review essay concerning John Stockwell's controversial analysis of CIA operations in Angola.

1522. Cohen, William. "Riots, Racism, and Hysteria: The Response of Federal Investigative Officials to the Race Riots of 1919," Massachusetts Review 13/3 (Summer 1972): 373-400.
A brief commentary on thirteen documents in the files of the Army's Military Intelligence Division pertaining to "Negro subversion" during World War I. The text of the documents is included.

1523. Cohen, William. "Justice Douglas and the Rosenberg Case: Setting the Record Straight," Cornell Law Review 70/2 (January 1985): 211-252.
Evaluates the role of the Supreme Court in the case, especially in terms of certain questions: Should the Court have reviewed it without reference to the substantiality of the issues?; Did the Rosenbergs' attorneys raise substantial issues for a Court review? Contains a chronology of the case.

1524. Cohen, William and Helena Czepiec. "The Role of Ethics in Gathering Corporate Intelligence," Journal of Business Ethics 7/3 (March 1988): 199-203.

An academic analysis of attitudes toward corporate intelligence gathering techniques, finding that social occasions are places of major information exchange, and most intelligence gathering is condoned by companies.

1525. Cohen, William S. "Congressional Oversight of Covert Actions," International Journal of Intelligence and Counterintelligence 2/2 (Summer 1988): 155-162.

Author, a US Senator with intelligence committee service, argues that the Intelligence Oversight Act of 1980 will not have deleterious effects upon presidential decision making in foreign policy. Major sections discuss the question of oversight in relation to threatening presidential power, the author's perspectives on oversight, and the relationship between oversight and national security arrangements.

1526. Cohen, William S. "Congressional Oversight of Covert Actions: The Public's Stake in the Forty-Eight Hour Rule," Harvard Journal of Law & Public Policy 12/2 (Spring 1989): 285-301.

Discussion of the author's bill to require the President to notify both congressional intelligence oversight committees or the congressional leadership within 48 hours of approving a covert action. Discusses background of the legislation; the rule as a public policy issue; conclusions.

1527. Cohn, Art. "An Incident Not Known to History: Squire Ferris and Benedict Arnold at Ferris Bay, October 13, 1776," Vermont History 55/2 (Spring 1987): 96-112.

1528. Coker, William S. "How General Jackson Learned of the British Plans Before the Battle of New Orleans," Gulf Coast Historical Review 3/1 (1987): 84-95.

1529. Colangelo, Philip. "The Secret FISA Court: Rubber Stamp on Rights," Covert Action Quarterly 53 (Summer 1995): 43-49.

A review of the activities of the secret court established under the Foreign Intelligence Surveillance Act to evaluate government justifications for electronic intercepts

1530. Colburn, Forrest. "Revolutionary Comics: Political Humor from Nicaragua," Caribbean Review 15/1 (Winter 1986): 16-17.

A brief account of the political cartoons of Roger S. Flores, including six cartoons, among them a lampoon of the Central Intelligence Agency's support for the Contras.

1531. Colby, Elbridge. "Training an Intelligence Section," Infantry Journal 15/3 (September 1918): 221-227.

Discusses the author's training courses for intelligence personnel, including report writing, sketching and use of sources. Includes mention of a book titled Military Map Reading and Intelligence Training by Captain Barber, C.E.F., published by E. C. McKay of Cleveland, Ohio. Pages 3-15 discuss intelligence and the training of scouts, observers and snipers.

1532. Colby, Jonathan E. "The Developing International Law on Gathering and Sharing Security Intelligence," Yale Journal on World Public Order 1 (1974): 49-92.

This citation lists the more recent title of this journal.

1533. Colby, William E. "Intelligence in the 1980's," Information Society 1/1 (Spring 1981): 53-69

Discusses evolution of CIA in terms of its historical development of a worldwide intelligence service, the emergence of technologies to the collection effort, and the institutionalization of intelligence within the American constitutional framework. Suggests that future developments should include the improvement of intelligence estimates and warnings to match quantitative improvements in information collection and management. Argues that intelligence growth is too important to remain totally within government control and direction. This article also appeared in Studies in Intelligence 25/2 (Summer 1981).

1534. Colby, William E. "The CIA's Covert Actions," Center Magazine 8/2 (March-April 1975): 71-80.

Former CIA director's remarks and responses to questions at a conference held at the Center for National Security Studies, mainly concerned with the history of US covert actions.

1535. Colby, William E. "Can We Do Without Secret Intelligence Operations?," Skeptic 7 (May-June 1975): 36-39.

1536. Colby, William E. "Secrecy in an Open Society," Center Magazine 9/2 (1976): 26-38.

The author argues that covert action by the Central Intelligence Agency are vital to foreign policy advancements. Included in this piece are the critiques of covert actions.

1537. Colby, William E. "Intelligence, Secrecy and Security in a Free Society," International Security 1/2 (Fall 1976): 3-14.

A general discussion of the author's perspectives on access to information pertaining to intelligence operations.

1538. Colby, William E. "Why I Was Fired from the CIA," Esquire 89 (May 1978): 59-62+.

1539. Colby, William E. "Verifying SALT," Worldview 22 (April 1979): 4-7.

1540. Colby, William E. "A New Charter for the CIA," America 142 (March 1980): 243-244.
      Provides an overview of the National Intelligence Act of 1980, its goals and weaknesses. Regards the Act as a new leash on the CIA and a clear response to previous CIA abuses. Considers such issues as range of intelligence activities, latitude of agents, priorities of control, and means for controlling information.

1541. Colby, William E. "Intelligence Looks Ahead: The World of the 80's," New York State Bar Journal 53/2 (February 1981): 96-99, 125-128.
      Former head of the CIA addresses the New York State Bar Association with ideas about the historical development and future of intelligence in free societies. He encourages more study of the sociological, political, psychological and economic forces in world relations and intelligence.

1542. Colby, William E. "Public Policy, Secret Action," Ethics and International Affairs 3 (1989): 61-72.
      Argues for a theory of covert action based on "...a standard for selection of covert actions that are just and can be developed by analogy with the longstanding efforts to differentiate just from unjust wars."

1543. Colby, William E. "Intelligence in a New World," Mediterranean Quarterly 1/4 (Fall 1990): 46-59.
      A firm and detailed position statement in favor of continued work on the part of American intelligence services in a new world of new tensions and threats of violence. Suggests need for intelligence community alterations to accommodate new information gathering and analytical demands.

1544. Colby, William E. "Retooling the Intelligence Industry: After the Cold War, What Do We Do With Our Spies?," Foreign Service Journal 69/1 (January 1992): 21-25.
      The former director of the CIA considers the reforms that will be needed to keep a viable, respected intelligence community. Considers the analytical function; countering technology spies; and new areas for intelligence.

1545. Colby, William E. "Tactical Intelligence: The Need for Improvement," Defense Intelligence Journal 1/1 (Spring 1992): 75-80.
      Discussion of the need for, and possibilities associated with, blending strategic and tactical intelligence. Acknowledges the validity of some military complaints about inadequacy of CIA and DIA intelligence during the Gulf War.

1546. Colby, William E. "Interview" (with William Colby), <u>Omni</u> (February-March 1993): 75-76, 78, 89-92.

1547. Colby, William E. "Interview" (with William Colby), <u>Special Warfare</u> (April 1994): 40-43.
   The former director of CIA offers his views on the intelligence community and world events.

1548. Colby, William E.; Walter F. Mondale; Porter Szanton; and Graham Allison. "Reorganizing the CIA: Who and How," <u>Foreign Policy</u> 23 (Summer 1976): 53-63.
   Brief discussion about suggestions for restructuring the American intelligence community and the need for governmental secrecy concerning operations.

1549. Cole, C. Robert. "The Conflict Within: Sir Stephen Tallents and Planning Propaganda Overseas Before the Second World War," <u>Albion</u> 14/1 (Spring 1982): 50-71.
   Details the role of foreign propaganda prior to World War II in Great Britain, describing also the properties and uses of propaganda. During the appeasement period, propaganda was used to minimize dissent in Britain's colonies and among the allies. During the war it was used against enemy nations.

1550. Cole, David. "Challenging Covert War: The Politics of the Political Question Doctrine," <u>Harvard International Law Journal</u> 26/1 (Winter 1985): 155-188.
   Argues that US courts should apply principles of international law as rigorously to US officials as to foreign officials.

1551. Cole, Leonard A. "Yellow Rain or Yellow Journalism," <u>Bulletin of the Atomic Scientists</u> 40/7 (August-September 1984): 36-38.
   Argues that the press, specifically the <u>Wall Street Journal</u>, may have fallen victim to the use of CIA-supplied information about alleged Soviet use of biological weapons in Laos. Emphasizes difficulties facing CIA if it attempts to use the press to advocate positions not based in facts. Uses the Vietnam war as a background example of eventual press skepticism of the intelligence community.

1552. Cole, Patrick. "The Relevance of Human Rights Provisions to American Intelligence Activities," <u>Loyola of Los Angeles International and Comparative Law Journal</u> 6 (Winter 1983): 37-63.
   Discusses the status of human rights in US foreign policy; violations of human rights principles by the CIA; executive orders on intelligence and whether human rights provisions were meant to apply in the intelligence arena; and the case for using international law to control intelligence activities.

1553. Cole, Patrick E. "The Freedom of Information Act and the Central Intelligence Agency's Paper Chase: A Need for Congressional Action to Maintain Essential Secrecy for Intelligence Files While Preserving the Public's Right to Know," Notre Dame Law Review 58/2 (December 1982): 350-381.

Contains discussion of the origins of the FOIA, exemptions covering most sensitive information, a search for a compromise between secrecy and openness, and a proposal for a limited exemption for information provided by a foreign contact.

1554. Cole, Wayne S. "American Entry into World War II: A Historiographical Appraisal," Mississippi Valley Historical Review 43 (1957): 595-617.

A bibliographical essay on the topic.

1555. Colebrook, Joan. Israel--With Terrorists," Commentary 58/1 (July 1974): 30-39.

Recounts the author's experiences in discussing terrorism with Israelis, including mention of terrorist groups and the Soviet KGB.

1556. Colella, Frank G. "Beyond Institutional Competence: Congressional Efforts to Legislate United States Foreign Policy Toward Nicaragua--The Boland Amendments," Brooklyn Law Review 54 (1988): 131-155.

Concludes that legislation such as the Boland amendments will ultimately prevent the US from speaking with one voice in foreign affairs. Examines tensions over foreign affairs; the Boland prohibitions; analysis of the amendments; and conclusions

1557. Coleman, C. A. and A. K. Bottomley. "Police Conceptions of Crime and 'No Crime'," Criminal Law Review (June 1976): 344-360.

Within a larger concern for how police decide upon a label for crimes is brief mention of the police classification system which draws on intelligence information.

1558. Coleman, Charles H. "The Use of the Term 'Copperhead' During the Civil War," Mississippi Valley Historical Review 25 (September 1938): 263-264.

1559. Coleman, Michael and Richard Aldrich. "The Cold War, the JIC and British Signals Intelligence, 1948," Intelligence and National Security 4/3 (July 1989): 535-549.

Examines the British intelligence gathering operations at the outset of the Cold War (1948), and attempts to analyze a few documents available on signal intelligence priorities defined by the Joint Intelligence Committee (JIC).

1560. Coletta, Paolo E. "French Ensor Chadwick: The First American Naval Attache, 1882-1889," American Neptune 39 (April 1979): 126-141.

1561. Colhoun, Jack. "BCCI: The Bank of the CIA," Covert Action Quarterly 44 (Spring 1993): 40-45.
      Offers some evidence that BCCI funded some CIA clandestine activities.

1562. Coliver, Sandra. "Electronic Surveillance: How Much Is Too Much?," Trial 18 (September 1982): 61-64.
      Argues that increase in federal agency electronic surveillance threatened the rights of accused persons. The amount of time and money required to sift and interpret surveillance tapes delays the defendant's right to speedy trial.

1563. Coll, Alberto R. "Normative Prudence as a Tradition of Statecraft," Ethics and International Affairs 5 (1991): 36-46.

1564. Collier, Peter and David Horowitz. "Another "Low Dishonest Decade" on the Left," Commentary 83/1 (January 1987): 17-24.
      Experiences of the authors in their associations with the New Left. Mentions the US National Security Agency, the KGB, and CISPES.

1565. Collins, F. W. "In Defence of the C.I.A. Too Much Pious Hypocrisy," Round Table 225 (January 1967): 115-121.
      This article, unique for its subject, appears in a British journal.

1566. Collins, R. "Army Counter-Intelligence Operations," Army Information Digest 19/9 (September 1964).

1567. Collins, George W. "The War in Afghanistan," Air University Review 37/3 (March-April 1986): 42-49.
      Major sections discuss Soviet intervention; military development; use of artillery; Soviet military problems; Afghan Freedom Fighters; and various problems in the war. Mentions US intelligence support for the Freedom Fighters; argues that the likelihood of a Soviet withdrawal as a function of the successes of the Fighters' activities was good.

1568. Collums, Haley D. "The Letelier Case: Foreign Sovereign Liability for Acts of Political Assassination," Virginia Journal of International Law 21/2 (Winter 1981): 251-268.
      Letelier v. Republic of Chile was a civil action by the survivors of the Letelier-Moffitt car bomb murders in 1976. Plaintiffs alleged the bomb was placed by members of Chilean intelligence. Examines background of immunity law, the Letelier decision, implications of the case and conclusions.

1569. Colton, David E. "Speaking Truth to Power: Intelligence Oversight in an Imperfect World," University of Pennsylvania Law Review 137/2 (1988): 571-613.

Discusses at length the history of intelligence oversight by Congress, oversight and the US Constitution, and the policy compromises that are necessary for effective and balanced oversight. Concludes that statutory oversight should be reduced in favor of oversight by competing political forces.

1570. Columb, J. C. R. "Naval Intelligence and Protection of Commerce in War," Journal of the Royal United Services Institution 25 (1881): 553-590.

1571. Colvin, John. "Horror in My Time," Washington Quarterly 4/2 (Spring 1981): 138-154.

1572. Colwell, Robert N. "Intelligence and the Okinawa Battle," Naval War College Review 38/2 (March-April 1985): 81-95.
        An examination of the role of photographic intelligence in the location and placement of underwater weapons and apparatus during the Okinawa invasion.

1573. Colwell, Robert N. "One Naval Intelligence Officer's OJT Experiences at Guadalcanal," Naval Intelligence Professionals Quarterly 7/2 (Spring 1991): 7-10.

1574. Comer, Robert; John W. Powell; and Bert V. A. Rolling. "Japan's Biological Weapons: 1930-1945," Bulletin of the Atomic Scientists (October 1981): 43-54.

1575. Cometti, Elizabeth. "Women in the American Revolution," New England Quarterly 20 (September 1947): 329-346.

1576. Committee on Civil Rights and International Human Rights, New York City Bar Association. "The Central Intelligence Agency: Oversight and Accountability," Record of the New York City Bar Association 30 (1975): 255-301.
        Summarizes the creation and legal development of the CIA; discusses CIA's domestic activities and their relations to the laws governing CIA and to the Constitution; discusses foreign activities of CIA and the legal bases for such activities; describes present funding of CIA; and discusses remedies and offers recommendations for regulation. See also items 242, 243, and 244.

1577. Committee on Criminal Law, New York City Bar Association. "The Felt-Miller Presidential Pardon," Record of the New York City Bar Association 36/6 (October 1981): 411-419.
        Argues that President Reagan's pardon of FBI agents Felt and Miller poses a danger to the federal criminal justice system. Both had been convicted for alleged illegal activities against the Weather Underground Organization in the early 1970s. Both were members of FBI's Domestic Intelligence Division. See also items 242, 243, and 244.

1578. Committee on Federal Legislation, New York City Bar Association. "The Response to Snepp v. United States: A Proposal for the 97th Congress," Record of the New York City Bar Association 36/5 (May- June 1981): 299-327.

Reviews the Snepp decision and other judicial authorities concerning disclosures by former CIA or other agents; offers analysis of the problems presented by Supreme Court sanctions; and concludes with a proposal to balance government secrecy needs with the First Amendment. See also items 242, 243, and 244.

1579. Conable, Gordon M. "The FBI and You," American Libraries 21 (March 1990): 245-246+.

1580. Conant, Hollyn. "Genghis Khan's Communication Network," Military Review 94/8 (August 1994): 65-77.

Argues that Genghis Khan was an exacting strategist whose intelligence network and communications capabilities rivaled those of his 13th century European counterparts.

1581. Conde, David. "The Communist Spy Plot," Eastern Horizon 7 (January 1968): 49-54.

Considers issues related to Korean intelligence services.

1582. Condon, John P. "Bringing Down Yamamoto," U.S. Naval Academy Proceedings 116/11 (1990): 86-90.

1583. Conley, Michael C. "The Strategy of Communist-Directed Insurgency and the Conduct of Counterinsurgency," Naval War College Review (May 1969): 73-93.

Defines and describes communist insurgency and the role of counterinsurgency. Concludes that established groups should be moved closer to the center and they should be induced to support the government. Unorganized groups should be moved to places where they can serve as social groups. This is the text of the author's October 1968 address at the Naval War College.

1584. Conlon, Thomas F. "Portuguese Timor: An Estimative Failure," Studies in Intelligence 4/4 (Winter 1960).

Discusses this important intelligence failure which the author concludes was a contributing factor to an Allied occupation.

1585. Connell, Charles. "An Analysis of NEWDES: A Modified Version of DES," Cryptologia 14/3 (July 1990): 217-224.

1586. Conner, William E. "Reforming Oversight of Covert Actions After the Iran-Contra Affair: A Legislative History of the Intelligence Authorization Act of FY 1991," Virginia Journal of International Law 32/4 (Summer 1992): 871-928.

Reviews provisions of the Act. Major sections discuss congressional oversight of intelligence; covert action oversight and the impetus for reform; oversight following the Iran-Contra affair; executive concerns and analysis; and conclusions.

1587. Conner, William E. "Congressional Reform of Covert Action Oversight Following the Iran-Contra Affair," Defense Intelligence Journal 2/1 (Spring 1993): 35-64.

Discusses the nature of intelligence and covert action; outline of the intelligence community; congressional oversight of intelligence activities; the impact of the Iran-Contra affair; and three pieces of legislation regarding oversight proposals.

1588. Conners, Kerry B. "Warrants for Videotape Surveillance Issuable Despite Lack of Statutory Authority," St. John's Law Review 54 (Summer 1980): 790-796.

A survey of New York practice, especially following People v. Teicher, 395 N.Y.S. 2d 587 (Sup. Ct. N.Y. Co. 1977).

1589. Conrad, Sherri J. "Executive Order 12,333: 'Unleashing' the CIA Violates the Leash Law," Cornell Law Review 70/5 (June 1985): 968-990.

Argues that the Order is a statutorily impermissible license for renewed government intrusion and it should be revoked. Contains history of CIA, CIA authority, the Order, and conclusions.

1590. Constantinides, George C. "Tradecraft: Follies and Foibles," International Journal of Intelligence and Counterintelligence 1/4 (Winter 1986-1987): 97-110.

Discusses the significance of intelligence tradecraft for avoiding mistakes of control in collection missions. Cites several mistakes of intelligence officers from the history of intelligence.

1591. Constantinides, George C. "A Brief Review of OSS Literature," Studies in Intelligence 35/4 (Winter 1991).

1592. Constantine, Edward L. "Low Intensity Conflict: Are We Prepared?," Military Intelligence 13/2 (June 1987): 39-41.

Argues the US is unprepared to fight low intensity conflicts. Sections discuss knowledge of the enemy in an LIC environment; training; and structure.

1593. Constantiniu, Florin. "The Notes of a British Secret Agent on the Eve of the Romanian Insurrection of August 1944," Revista de Istorie 35/1 (1982): 161-170, 735-739.

The Romanian insurrection, as told by a British spy, and Hitler's involvement with it.

1594. Cook, Blanche W. "First Comes to Lie: C. D. Jackson and Political Warfare," Radical History Review 31 (1984): 42-71.
　　Deals with the attempt of private citizen C. D. Jackson to stop the influence and progression of communism through political rather than war means.

1595. Cook, Blanche W. "C. D. Jackson: Cold War Propagandist," Covert Action Information Bulletin 35 (Fall 1990): 33-38.
　　Jackson was a White House aide in the Eisenhower administration.

1596. Cook, Don. "On Revealing 'The Last Secret,'" Encounter 45 (July 1975): 80-86.

1597. Cook, Earle F. "Electronic Black Chamber," Army 13/2 (Sepetember 1962): 37-40.
　　Discussion of interceptions of communications during wartime and the need for communications security. Concludes the central role of communications in war and the need to avoid the enemy's intention to use communiques against us. Refers to the Civil War, and World Wars I and II.

1598. Cook, Fred J. "Allen McLane, Unknown Hero of the Revolution," American Heritage 7/6 (October 1956): 74-77, 118-119.
　　Discusses the life and times of an unknown revolutionary war hero. Allen Mclane's work in espionage greatly assisted the rebel fight at Valley Forge. He was present, also, when Washington was burned in the War of 1812.

1599. Cook, Fred J. "J. Edgar Hoover and the FBI," Lithopinion 6/2 (February 1971): 8-15, 58-63.
　　Says that Hoover was immortalized to the point of he became an untouchable autocrat. Discusses Hoover's manipulation of crime statistics; mythology that the FBI played no political favorites; undercover investigations of Martin Luther King, Jr., Robert Kennedy and others; and the corruption of power.

1600. Cooley, John K. "The Libyan Menace," Foreign Policy 42/1 (Spring 1981): 74-93.
　　The author addresses the rise of Quaddafi, CIA protection of Quaddafi, and Quaddafi's control over a substantial portion of the world oil resources. Suggestions are offered to end his control.

1601. Coon, Thomas. "New York City and DIO-3ND in World War II," Naval Intelligence Professionals Quarterly 11/1 (Winter 1995): 7-8.

1602. Cooney, Charles F. "Treason or Tyranny? The Great Senate Purge of '62," Civil War Times Illustrated 18/4 (April 1979): 30-31.

Senator Jesse Bright of Indiana was expelled from the Senate in 1862 for treason in support of the South.

1603. Cooper, Chester L. "The CIA and Decision-making," Foreign Affairs 50/2 (January 1972): 223-236.

A discussion of the intelligence and policy process, especially estimations, in various presidencies from Truman to Nixon.

1604. Cooper, H. H. A. "English Mission," Studies in Intelligence 5/1 (Spring 1961).

A discussion of a Jesuit infiltration mission.

1605. Cooper, H. H. A. "Terrorism and the Intelligence Function," Chitty's Law Journal 24/3 (March 1976): 73-78.

Discusses two problems facing the intelligence community: the role of the spy; and the distinction between intelligence and counterintelligence. Argues for preventative intelligence.

1606. Cooper, H. H. A. "Spychology: The Human Side of the Gentle Art of Espionage," Chitty's Law Journal 29/10 (October 1981): 251-259.

An analysis of the concepts of spies and spying.

1607. Cooper, J. "Deception and Role Playing: On Telling the Good Guys from the Bad Guys," American Psychologist 31 (1976): 605-610.

1608. Cooper, Mary H. "Reforming the CIA: Is the Spy Agency a Dinosaur in Today's World?," CQ Researcher 6 (February 1996): 99-119.

Considers the modern context and usefulness of the Central Intelligence Agency.

1609. Cooper, Rodney H. "Security or Censorship? The Cryptography Controversy," Conflict Quarterly 1/4 (1980): 21-24.

1610. Coox, Alvin D. "L'Affaire Lyushkov: Anatomy of a Defector," Soviet Studies 19 (January 1968): 405-420.

Discusses the defection of G. S. Lyushkov, a Russian general officer and chief of the NKVD to Japan in 1938. The loss of this intelligence officer shocked Stalin, resulting in a direct benefit to the Japanese. The estimate of his real value to Japan remains inconclusive.

1611. Coox, Alvin D. "Flawed Perception and Its Effect Upon Operational Thinking: The Case of the Japanese Army, 1937-1941," Intelligence and National

Security 5/2 (April 1990): 239-254.

The Imperial Japanese Army was rife with deliberate avoidance of the advice of intelligence analysts and officers carried on various biased impressions of US strengths and weaknesses.

1612. Coox, Alvin D. "The Pearl Harbor Raid Revisited," Journal of American-East Asian Relations 3/3 (Fall 1994): 211-227.

One of several articles in this issue on the dynamics of pre and post Pearl Harbor attack. Considers the major intentions of the Japanese navy to bring the US fleet to its knees, which it nearly accomplished, but which also resulted in a significant shift in US military policy.

1613. Copeland, Miles. "The Functioning of Strategic Intelligence," Defense and Foreign Affairs Digest 2-4 (February; March; April 1977): 29-32; 36-38+; 32-35+.

1614. Copeland, Peter A. "Secrecy in the Conduct of United States Foreign Relations: Recent Policy and Practice," Cornell International Law Journal 6/2 (May 1973): 187-214.

Considers three issues pertaining to the secrecy in US foreign relations: (1) secrecy and its authorization in the Constitution; (2) manner in which secrecy is to be supervised; and (3) extent to which the legislative powers of Congress supercede the powers of the executive branch.

1615. Copley, Gregory R. "Forging the Shield: Intelligence Management in the Developing World," Defense and Foreign Affairs Digest 15 (December 1987): 14-21.

1616. Copp, D. S. "Spy Results in Germany's Brandt Resignation," Human Events 34 (1974): 13-17.

1617. Coppersmith, D. "Cryptography," IBM Journal of Research and Development 31 (March 1987): 244-248.

1618. Copson, Raymond W. and Richard P. Cronin. "The 'Reagan Doctrine' and Its Prospects," Survival 29 (January-February 1987): 40-55.

1619. Coquelle, P. "L'espionage en Angleterre Pendant la Guerre de Septs Ans," Revue d'Histoire Diplomatique 14 (1900): 508-533.

1620. Corcoran, William J. "A Multiloop Vigen'ere Cipher with Exceptionally Long Component Series," Cryptologia 18/4 (October 1994): 356-371.

1621. Cordesman, Anthony H. "Syrian-Israeli C^{3}I: The West's Third Front:

Command, Control, Communications and Intelligence Update," <u>Armed Forces Journal</u> (March 1984): 87-90.

Discusses Soviet actions in Syria and the actions which Israel might take to restore the C³I edge.

1622. Corn, David. "Artificial Intelligence," <u>Washington Monthly</u> 27/1 (January-February 1995): 48-50.

A book review essay pertaining to <u>Washington Station: My Life as a KGB Spy in America</u> by Yuri Shvets.

1623. Cornelius, George. "Air Reconnaissance: Great Silent Weapon," <u>U.S. Naval Institute Proceedings</u> 85/7 (July 1959): 35-42.

1624. Corr, Kevin. "The FBI and the Private Practitioner," <u>Illinois Bar Journal</u> 81 (April 1993): 207-211.

1625. Corr, Kevin. "The Role of the FBI Principal Legal Advisor," <u>Journal of the Legal Profession</u> 19 (1994): 157-164.

1626. Corwin, Edward S. "Freedom of Speech and Press Under the First Amendment: A Resume," <u>Yale Law Journal</u> 30/1 (November 1920): 48-55.

Examines the historical foundations for the author's interpretation of the First Amendment in the context of the debate about the espionage and sedition acts passed during World War I.

1627. Cory, John M. "Libraries and the Office of War Information," <u>ALA Bulletin</u> 37 (1943): 38-41.

1628. Coser, Louis. "Dysfunctions of Military Secrecy," <u>Social Problems</u> 11/1 (Summer 1963): 13-22.

Argues that secrecy is used to mask the capabilities of enemies to prevent surprise attacks, but secrecy becomes dysfunctional when misperceptions of individual capabilities rise. Sections discuss military and national power; the factors determining war; new structures of communication; and bargaining under conditions of maximum disclosure.

1629. Costello, John E. "Remember Pearl Harbor," <u>U.S. Naval Institute Proceedings</u> 109/9 (September 1983): 52-62.

A discussion of various dimensions of the disaster, including concessions to Japan, John Doe associates, the deterrent gamble, diplomacy failures, missing war warnings, the cover-up, and the missed clues.

1630. Costello, John E. "Climbing Mount Ni-I-Take," <u>Valley Forge Journal</u> 5/4 (1991): 290-309.

1631. Costeloe, Michael P. "The Mexican Church and the Rebellion of the Polkos," <u>Hispanic American Historical Review</u> 46/2 (May 1966): 170-178.

Discusses the rebellious actions of the Mexican Church in lending money in aid of the Revolution of 1847. Reflects on contents of a secret memorandum.

1632. Costigan, Giovanni. "Treason of Sir Roger Casement," <u>American Historical Review</u> 60 (January 1955): 283-302.

Discusses the prosecution of Casement for high treason, a man described by the prosecutor who had been blinded by hatred for his country. Later executed, Casement believed that his years of service to the Crown merely made him more of an Irishman than a loyalist.

1633. Cote, Maureen. "Translation Error and Political Misinterpretation," <u>Studies in Intelligence</u> 27/4 (Winter 1983): 11-19.

1634. Cote, Maureen. "Veni, Vidi, Vid-Int," <u>Studies in Intelligence</u> 34/3 (Fall 1990).

1635. Cottam, Martha. "The Carter Administration's Policy Toward Nicaragua," <u>Political Science Quarterly</u> 107/1 (Spring 1992): 123-146.

1636. Cottam, Martha and Otwin Marenin. "Predicting the Past: Reagan Administration Assistance to Police Forces in Central America," <u>Justice Quarterly</u> 6/4 (December 1989): 589-618.

Discusses Reagan administration policy to assist Central American police agencies in order to enhance democratic policing. Argues that these efforts have failed in their objective. Mentions the role of the CIA.

1637. Cottam, Richard W. "Revolutionary Iran," <u>Current History</u> 78/453 (January 1980): 12-16; 34-35.

An overview of conditions in Iran that led ultimately to the downfall of the Shah. Refers to the role of the CIA in the assistance to the Shah through the years since 1953.

1638. Cottam, Richard W.; David Schoenbaum; Sharahram Chubin; Theodore H. Moran; and Richard A. Falk. "The United States and Iran's Revolution," <u>Foreign Policy</u> 34 (Spring 1979): 3-34.

Discusses the history and background conditions of rise to power of the Shah of Iran, and the miscalculations of Britain and the United States. Argues that the US underestimated support for Ayatollah Khomeini in the late 1970s combined with the growing internal animosity toward the Shah. Iranians blamed the US for the Shah's rise to power. The US intelligence community failed to report in sufficient detail internal struggles that led to the fall of the Shah.

1639. Cotter, Cornelius P. "Emergency Detention in Wartime: The British Experience," <u>Stanford Law Review</u> 6/2 (March 1954): 238-286.

Discusses the British program for detention of civilians in wartime for national security reasons. Sets forth cautions about the use of such efforts.

1640. Cotter, Cornelius P. and J. Malcolm Smith. "An American Paradox: The Emergency Detention Act of 1950," <u>Journal of Politics</u> 19 (February 1957): 20-33.

Discusses the reasoning and fears that led to passage of the Act, purportedly to enhance internal security against espionage and sabotage. Discusses various complications with the law's enforcement and administration.

1641. Cotter, Richard D. "Notes Toward a Definition of National Security," <u>Washington Monthly</u> 7 (December 1975): 4-16.

Reviewing the work of FBI in national security matters and the Senate Select Intelligence Committee's investigations.

1642. Cottrell, Alvin J. and J. Malcolm Smith. "The Lessons of Korea: War and the Power of Man," <u>Orbis</u> 11/1 (Spring 1958): 39-65.

Discussion of the role of limited wars in American history, and in particular the US efforts to limit the Korean war. Major sections discuss the imposed limitations of the war; the use of Chiang's forces; operations behind the Yalu; the use of atomic weapons; war by truce at Panmunjon; the impact of Korea on Indochina; and Korea and limited war.

1643. Coularthard-Clark, C. D. "Australia's War-Time Security Service," <u>Australian Defence Force Journal</u> 16 (May-June 1979): 22-27.

1644. Coulter, C. S. "Intelligence Service in the World War," <u>Infantry Journal</u> 20 (April 1922): 376-383.

1645. Coumbe, Arthur T. "German Intelligence and Security in Franco-Prussian War," <u>Military Intelligence</u> 14/1 (January 1988): 9-12.

Compares German and French capabilities in the areas of patrols and screens, finding the German capability substantially better than the French.

1646. Countryman, Vern. "The Diminishing Right of Privacy: The Personal Dossier and the Computer," <u>Texas Law Review</u> 49 (May 1971): 837-871.

Computerized personal records under the control of public and private agencies pose control problems defying conventional regulation. Author calls for destruction of those files which serve no public purpose. Discussion of the compiling by federal agencies such as FBI and CIA. Distinguishes between commercial compilers and benevolent compilers.

1647. Courier, Leonard C. "Financial Epitaph for a Spymaster," Studies in Intelligence 27/4 (Winter 1983).
　 Discusses an 18th century spy.

1648. Courier, Leonard C. "A 17th Century English Intelligence Report," Studies in Intelligence 27/2 (Summer 1983).

1649. Courier, Leonard C. "The OSS and the Maginot and Siegfried Lines," Studies in Intelligence 28/2 (Summer 1984).

1650. Courier, Leonard C. "OSS Mission to the Burgundian Maquis," Studies in Intelligence 29/1 (Spring 1985).

1651. Courtney, Jeremiah. "Electronic Eavesdropping, Wiretapping and Your Right to Privacy," Federal Communications Bar Journal 26 (1973): 1-60.
　 Discusses the issue of privacy in the context of increasing federal power to conduct wiretaps. Major sections discuss privacy and the war on crime; the Fourth Amendment and privacy; the Olmstead decision; technology of eavesdropping; various Supreme Court decisions from the 1930s of the 1960s; various legal doctrines; Title III of the Omnibus Crime Control and Safe Streets Act of 1968; national security issues; the FCC's role; and privacy at the crossroads.

1652. Covalucci, Robert J. "CEWI CI: Tactical Counterintelligence within Combat Electronic Warfare and Intelligence," Military Intelligence 10/1 (January-March 1984): 27-33.
　 Identifies and explains the role of counterintelligence in tactical deception.

1653. Cowan, Ralph H. "Artillery-Infantry Intelligence," Combat Forces 5 (September 1954): 46-47.

1654. Cowan, William V. "Kit Carson Scouts," Marine Corps Gazette 53 (October 1969): 30-32.

1655. Cowan, William V. "Melting the Snowman: Communications and the Counternarcotic Threat," Signal 44/4 (April 1989): 27-32.

1656. Cowen, M. L., Jr. "The Military Commission in 1942," Virginia Law Review 29 (1942): 317-328.
　 Major sections discuss the military commission in English history before 1776; military law; military government and martial law; the military commission in American history; jurisdiction of military commission; and the necessity of a trial by military commission.

1657. Cox, Archibald. "Foreword: Freedom of Expression in the Burger Court," Harvard Law Review 94 (1980): 1-73.

A discussion of Supreme Court decisions for 1979 with respect to First Amendment matters. Major sections discuss regulation of content; regulation of time, place, or manner of expression; expressive conduct; conduct affecting publication; financing political campaigns; and conclusions. Refers to CIA and Pentagon Papers cases.

1658. Cox, Arthur M. "CIA and the Evolution of Soviet Military Power," Le Debat 12 (May 1981): 18-25.

Discussion of the subject in French.

1659. Cox, David. "The Aftermath of the Korean Airline Incident: Gathering Intelligence about Intelligence Gathering," Queen's Quarterly 92/1 (Spring 1985): 36-50.

This article deals with the tragedy of the Korean Airlines shoot-down. The aircraft was shot down by the Russians. Evidence, although hotly contested, indicates that it may have been on a spying mission.

1660. Cox, Henry B. "Reasons for Joel Poinsett's Refusal of a Second Mission to South America," Hispanic American Historical Review 43/3 (August 1963): 405-408.

Contains brief observations of Poinsett's memorandum of 1818 on revolutionary circumstances in South America during the Monroe administration.

1661. Cox, Isaac J. "The American Intervention in West Florida," American Historical Review 17/2 (January 1912).

1662. Cox, Isaac J. "The New Invasion of the Goths and the Vandals," Proceedings of the Mississippi Valley Historical Review of the Year 3 (1916).

1663. Cox, Isaac J. "The Border Missions of General George Mathews," Mississippi Valley Historical Review 12/3 (December 1925).

1664. Cox, Richard "Exposing the KGB," Conflict Quarterly 2/3 (Winter 1981): 23-29.

1665. Cox, Sebastian. "A Comparative Analysis of RAF and Luftwaffe Intelligence in the Battle of Britain, 1940," Intelligence and National Security 5/2 (April 1990): 425-443.

Discussion of the organization of German air intelligence, naval intelligence functions, and organizational shortcomings. Argues that intelligence structure is equally important as sources.

1666. Cox, Sebastian. "'The Difference Between White and Black': Churchill, Imperial Politics and Intelligence before the 1941 Crusader Offensive," Intelligence and National Security 9/3 (July 1994): 405-447.

A lengthy discussion of strategic developments in mid-1941, the political effect of such developments in Australia and New Zealand, and the impact on Commonwealth governments. Reflects upon disagreements over intelligence and political distortions of information.

1667. Coyle, Robert E. "Surveillance from the Seas," Military Law Review 60 (Spring 1973): 75-97.

In the context of electronic surveillance by Navy ships during the 1960s, the author discusses the legal problems of surveillance classification of waters and innocent passage; and surveillance as a legal concepts.

1668. Crabb, Cecil, Jr. and Kevin V. Mulcahy. "The National Security Council and the Shaping of U.S. Foreign Policy," International Journal of Intelligence and Counterintelligence 3/2 (Summer 1989): 153-168.

Discusses the role and operations of the National Security Council in the wake of the Iran-Contra hearings. Major topics discussed include a typology of the national security advisory system; roles of national security assistants; Irangate, the NSA as "insurgent"; reform proposals; and lessons of Irangate.

1669. Crabtree, Richard D. "U.S. Policy for Countering Terrorism: The Intelligence Dimension," Conflict Quarterly (Winter 1986).

1670. Craig, Alexander. "Information and Politics: Towards Greater Government Intervention?," International Journal 34/2 (Spring 1979): 209-226.

Discusses government and media relationships centered around the issue of informational access and control. Mentions the Official Secrets Act and the issue of secrecy.

1671. Craig, Julia K. "The Presidential Polygraph Order and the Fourth Amendment: Subjecting Federal Employees to Warrantless Searches," Cornell Law Review 69/4 (April 1984): 896-924.

Analogizes polygraph testing to other forms of governmental invasions of privacy. Concludes that the Fourth Amendment requires the head of a federal agency to obtain a warrant before ordering a polygraph examination of one of his employees.

1672. Craig, Richard B. "Everybody Talks About the War on Drugs...," Orbis 37/1 (Winter 1993): 135-147.

A book review essay concerning 9 books on the war on drugs and related topics, US national policy, and possible complicity of the intelligence community.

1673. Cram, Cleveland C. "Of Moles and Molehunters," Studies in Intelligence 39/5 (1995): 129-137.

The author, a former CIA field officer, developed an extensive review of the literature of counterintelligence for the years 1977 to 1992. This is a summary of a public document available from the Center for the Study of Intelligence at the Central Intelligence Agency. Major sections consider American and Canadian scenes; decline of conspiracism; the British connection; and counterintelligence histories.

1674. Cramer, Myron C. "Military Commissions Trial of the Eight Saboteurs," Washington Law Review 17/4 (November 1942): 247-255.

A lengthy speech given by General Cramer to the annual meeting Washington State Bar Association concerning the legal procedures involved in the trial of German saboteurs tried and convicted in a 2-month period in 1942. Six were electrocuted and two received long prison sentences.

1675. Crane, David M. "Divided We Stand: Counterintelligence Coordination in the Intelligence Community of the United States," Army Lawyer 1995 (December 1995): 26-41.

1676. Crane, Robert D. "The Cuban Crisis: A Strategic Analysis of American and Soviet Policy," Orbis 6/4 (Winter 1963): 528-563.

Major sections discuss events before the crisis; during the crisis; after the crisis; an evaluation of American policy; and a need for a firm policy in the future.

1677. Crangle, Robert D. "Spying, the CIA, and the New Technologies," Ripon Forum 6 (February 1970): 7-14.

1678. Cranston, Alan. "Introduction to S.1: An Official Secrets Act," Criminal Justice Journal 1/1 (Spring 1976): 1-3.

A brief issue introduction containing Senator Cranston's codified views on the wisdom of S.1, and support for Jonathan Fleming's article on the details of the bill. (See this bibliography).

1679. Cranwell, Joseph L., Jr. "Judicial Fine-Tuning of Electronic Surveillance," Seton Hall Law Review 6/2 (Winter 1975): 225-261.

Discusses the history of electronic surveillance law; constitutional standards for Title III of the Safe Streets Act of 1968; statutory standards; conclusions.

1680. Crary, Catherine S. "The Tory and the Spy: The Double Life of James Rivington," William and Mary Quarterly 16/1 (January 1959): 61-72.

A thorough, scholarly account of Rivington's secret life as an important spy in George Washington's sophisticated intelligence system in the American Revolution.

1681. Crawford, Ian C. "FBI v. Abramson and the FOIA: Exemption Seven Shields Political Records," Suffolk University Law Review 17 (Fall 83): 748-775.

A case note discussion of the Freedom of Information Act, appellate and Supreme Court interpretations of Exemption 7 requirements (protection of law enforcement records). The FBI believes that informants do not come forward as often in the years after Exemption 7, thus encouraging need for new law.

1682. Crawford, Robert W. "Call Retreat: The Johnson Administration's Vietnam Policy, March 1967 to March 1968," American Intelligence Journal 16/1 (Spring 1995): 69-77.

1683. Creal, Richard E. "The History of Reconnaissance in World War II," Tactical Air Reconnaissance Digest 2 (February 1968): 14-18.

1684. Crelinsten, R. D. "Terrorism, Counter-Terrorism and Democracy: The Assessment of National Security Threats," Terrorism and Political Violence 1/2 (April 1989): 242-269.

1685. Cremeans, Charles D. "The Agency and the Future," Studies in Intelligence 14/1 (Spring 1970).

1686. Cremeans, Charles D. "Basic Psychology for Intelligence Analysts," Studies in Intelligence 15/4 (Winter 1971): 109-114.

The author's insights into psychological variables that distinguish themselves in the analysis function apart from espionage operations.

1687. Crenshaw, Ollinger. "The Knights of the Golden Circle," American Historical Review 47/1 (October 1941): 23-50.

Details the history of the Knights of the Golden Circle, a secret military organization founded by George Brickley in 1859 to advocate Americanization and annexation of Mexico for the purpose of constructing slave states. Describes the organizational divisions and the demise of the KGC.

1688. Crews, Ed. "Medal of Honor: The U.S. Navy Officer Had Vital Information to Deliver," Military History 7/3 (1990): 16, 68, 70, 72.

Discusses Navy Lieutenant Edouard Izac's mission to provide information on German submarine attack strategies in 1918.

1689. Crile, George, III. "The Fourth Estate: A Good Word for the CIA," Harper's 252 (January 1976): 28-32.

Discusses the CIA and its detractors, including Agee, Phillips, Sturgis and others. Critiques the press presentation of the CIA.

1690. Criley, Richard L. "The Cult of the Informer Revisited: Antiterrorism Policy in the United States," Crime and Social Justice 21-22 (1984): 183-190.

Argues the Reagan administration's reversal of democratic principles, the return to use by the FBI of the political informer, the FBI neutralization COINTELPRO program, and the proposition that the intelligence gatherer equals the agent provocateur.

1691. Critchley, W. Harriet. "Polar Deployment of Soviet Submarines," International Journal 39/4 (1984): 828-865.

This article addresses the rise of the USSR submarine-based nuclear missiles and their arrival in Europe and North America.

1692. Cromer, Gerald. "The Beer Affair: Israeli Social Reaction to a Soviet Agent," Crossroads: An International Socio-Political Journal 15 (1985): 55-75.

An examination of the capture and trial of Israel Beer for treason and the political leaders involved in his betrayal.

1693. Crompton, Rufus. "Georgi Markov--Death in a Pellet," Medico-Legal Journal 48/2 (1980): 51-62.

An address to the Royal Society of Medicine concerning the medical history and forensics related to the alleged KGB-ordered murder of a Bulgarian playwright. Georgi Markov, in 1978.

1694. Croom, Herman L. "The Exploitation of Foreign Open Sources," Studies in Intelligence 13/2 (Summer 1969).

1695. Cronin, Arnold. "V-4 Intelligence Personnel," Naval Intelligence Professionals Quarterly 3/2 (Summer 1987): 7.

1696. Cronin, Thomas E. "A Resurgent Congress and the Imperial Presidency," Political Science Quarterly 95/2 (Summer 1980): 209-237.

Discusses the CIA in connection with congressional action to pass the Hughes-Ryan Amendment regarding congressional approvals of clandestine activities.

1697. Crosby, Ralph D., Jr. "The Cuban Missile Crisis: A Soviet View," Military Review 56 (September 1976): 58-70.

An excellent review of Soviet perceptions of the gains to be realized in nuclear power balance by positioning nuclear weapons in Cuba. Sections include the possible gains, risks and minimization of risks, significant augmentation of risk, and effect of American reactions.

1698. Crosley, Walter S. "The Naval War College, the General Board, and the Office of Naval Intelligence," U.S. Naval Institute Proceedings 39 (September 1913): 965-974.

      An appeal to the maintenance of naval specialists in intelligence for preparation for possible international conflict.

1699. Cross, R. T. "Results of Keeping a Secret," Magazine of American History 25 (1891): 489.

      A one-page summary of Zebulon M. Pike's search for gold in the Southwest, a secret he kept to his death.

1700. Cross, Rupert. "Official Secrets," Lawyer 6 (1963): 31-32.

1701. Crossman, R. H. S. "Psychological Warfare," Journal of the Royal United Services Institute 97 (August 1952): 319-332.

      A brief treatise on the subject, contiued in volume 98 (November 1953): 351-361. Portions of this piece can also be found in Australian Army Journal (June 1953): 528-539.

1702. Crovitz, L. Gordon. "Crime, the Constitution, and the Iran-Contra Affair," Commentary 84/10 (October 1987): 23-28.

      The appointment of the special prosecutor to investigate the diversion of funds to Iran by way of Nicaragua is discussed. Argues the severe impact of this Reagan administration program on the image of the intelligence agencies. Raises the question of the application of regulatory legislation to prohibit such transactions upon the National Security Council.

1703. Crovitz, L. Gordon. "Micromanaging Foreign Policy," Public Interest 100 (Summer 1990): 102-115.

      Major sections discuss George Bush and recent micromanagement; the decline of presidential powers; the War Powers Resolution; and criminalizing politics. Discusses CIA and the Contras.

1704. Crowder, G. "The Security Intelligence Service Amendment Act of 1977 and the State Power to Intercept Communications," Victoria University of Wellington Law Review 9 (February 1978): 145-164.

1705. Crowder, Robert. "An American's Life in Japan Before and After Pearl Harbor," Journal of American-East Asian Relations 3 (Fall 1994).

      One of several articles in this issue to address the dynamics of pre and post Pearl Harbor attack.

1706. Crowe, Sibyl. "The Zinoviev Letter: A Reappraisal," Journal of Contemporary History 10/3 (July 1975): 407-432.

An extensive analysis of events following a letter from the Russian president to the British Communist Party in 1924. Evidence of the letter's authenticity remains suspect. Excellent case study in deception and the vulnerability of intelligence analysts to superficial evidence of credibility.

1707. Crowley, Kathleen M. "Applicability of the Informer's Privilege in the Anti-Surveillance Case," University of Detroit Journal of Urban Law 55/4 (Summer 1978): 1005-1040.

Discusses the nature of the informer problem; judicial tolerance of informer activity; judicial activity toward domestic surveillance; evolution of informer's privilege; and suggestions to improve the informer's privilege analysis.

1708. Crozier, Brian. "The Soviet Presence in Somalia," Conflict Studies 54 (February 1975): 3-19.

The Soviet presence in Somalia was both a climax and a forerunner of events to come. Discusses the Soviet-Somalia Friendship Treaty, Siad government repression methods, Soviet economic aid and advice, and the Soviet naval buildup. Raises questions about the role of American intelligence in estimating the impact of Soviet influence.

1709. Crozier, Brian. "The Surrogate Forces of the Soviet Union," Conflict Studies 92 (February 1978): 1-20.

A discussion of Soviet use of Cuban military forces as terrorists and guerillas, satellite intelligence services, and KGB recruitment of foreign nationals. Discusses Cuban intelligence (DGI).

1710. Cruver, Harry F. "The Air Force Reporting Problem," Air University Review 11/2 (Summer 1959): 80-98.

Considers issues in the Air Force intelligence system.

1711. Cubbage, Thomas L. "German Misapprehensions Regarding Overlord: Understanding Failure in the Estimative Process," Intelligence and National Security 2/3 (July 1987): 114-174.

Discusses German collection and analysis capability; German estimates; roots of failure; surprise; and implications. A detailed article part of a special issue devoted to strategic and operational deception during World War II.

1712. Cubbage, Thomas L. "The Success of Operation Fortitude: Hesketh's History of Strategic Deception," Intelligence and National Security 2/3 (July 1987): 327-346.

A brief account of British Army Colonel Roger F. Hesketh's formula for deception in World War II.

1713. Cubbage, Thomas L. "Westmoreland vs. CBS: Was Intelligence

Corrupted by Policy Demands?," Intelligence and National Security 3/3 (July 1988): 118-180.

As part of a special issue on leaders and intelligence, this article deals with General William Westmoreland's suit against CBS for alleged false statements made in a program about alleged cover-ups of intelligence in the Vietnam war. Discusses the Tet offensive; MACV order of battle; discovery by Sam Adams, CIA analyst; reexamination of the MACV order of battle; the CBS documentary and Westmoreland's claims; testimony of key witnesses; and intelligence and policy demands.

1714. Culenaere, Alphonse. "Cryptophotography," International Criminal Police Review (November 1956): 284-290.

A useful historical piece for those interested in the technological advancements of the 1950s. Provides descriptions of latent image processes, bleaching processes, gelatine tanning processes, and their respective histories.

1715. Culenaere, Alphonse. "A Short History of Microphotography (High-Reduction Photography)," Journal of Forensic Sciences 4 (January 1959).

1716. Cumings, Anne E. "American Concentration Camps: Prospective Challenge to Title II of the McCarran Act," Boston University Law Review 48/4 (Fall 1968): 647-667.

Discusses the McCarran Act; justiciability; and conclusions. Argues that the legal system should introduce a challenge to the McCarran Act, Title II.

1717. Cummins, Light T. "Luciano De Herrera and Spanish Espionage in British St. Augustine," Escribano 16 (1979): 43-57.

An account of Herrera's experiences as a spy in the early 18th century. He was considered a Spanish patriot who spied for the British during the American revolution.

1718. Cummins, Light T. "Spanish Espionage in the South During the American Revolution," Southern Studies 19/1 (Spring 1980): 39-49.

Discusses the extent of British intelligence supplied to Spain regarding American revolutionary strengths. Spanish agents traveled to America as merchants, many of whom became known after the Revolution. Their services provided a basis for new diplomatic relations.

1719. Cummins, Light T. "The Governors of Spanish Colonial Lousiana and Espionage in the Southeastern Borderlands, 1766-1795," Locus 6/1 (1993): 23-37.

1720. Cummings, Richard. "A Diamond Is Forever: Mandela Triumphs, Buthelezi and de Klerk Survive, and ANC on the U.S. Payroll," International Journal of Intelligence and Counterintelligence 8/2 (Summer 1995): 155-177.

An account of the gradual success of the African National Congress and Nelson Mandela to overthrow the apartheid policy and win political victory in South Africa. Discusses the role of the CIA at various stages from the 1960s to the 1980s.

1721. Cummings, Robert. "African and Afro-American Studies Centers: Towards a Cooperative Relationship," Journal of Black Studies 9/3 (March 1979): 291-310.

Within a broader discussion of advances in Afro-American studies, the author suggests that the Central Intelligence Agency has played a significant role in expanding interest in African studies.

1722. Cundiff, Victoria A. "How to Set Up a Trade Secret Protection Program," Intellectual Property Law: An International Analytical Journal 1 (May 1992): 297-307.

1723. Cundiff, Victoria A. "Maximum Security: How to Prevent Departing Employees from Putting Your Trade Secrets to Work for Your Competitors," Santa Clara Computer and High-Technology Law Journal 8 (August 1992): 301-334.

1724. Cunningham, Alden M. "Mexico's National Security," Parameters: Journal of the U.S. Army War College 14/4 (1984): 56-58.

The internal structure of the national security of Mexico is examined, focusing mainly on the maintenance of its stability.

1725. Cunningham, Charles J. "Education for Military Intelligence," Defense Intelligence Journal 2/2 (Fall 1993): 123-134.

Discusses the environment; needs; and the future of military intelligence education.

1726. Cunningham, O. Edward. "In Violation of the Laws of War: The Execution of Robert Cobb Kennedy," Louisiana History 18/2 (1977): 189-202.

Discusses the role of Robert Cobb Kennedy in the Louisiana infantry and his eventual execution before the end of the Civil War. Kennedy was accused of espionage in New York City, denied by Kennedy until his death despite a confession.

1727. Cunliffe, Marcus. "Anticommunism, Anti-Communism, and Anti-Anti-Communism," Reviews in American History 18/3 (1990): 406-410.

A book review essay of Peter Coleman's The Liberal Conspiracy: The Congress of Cultural Freedom and the Struggle for the Mind of Postwar Europe. Mentions the CIA.

1728. Curran, Charles. "The Spy Behind the Speaker's Chair," History Today 18/11 (November 1968): 745-754.

A brief history of the role of Thomas Billis Beach's service as a British spy among the Irish Nationalists.

1729. Curran, John W. "Addiction to American State Trials: Legal Questions in the Trials of the German Saboteurs," Journal of Criminal Law and Criminology 33 (January 1943): 395-396.

Discusses in brief the wartime trial by the military commission of the German saboteurs. Contains the facts of the case and the constitutional and other issues raised by it

1730. Curran, John W. "Lincoln Conspiracy Trial and Military Jurisdiction Over Civilians," Notre Dame Lawyer 27 (November 1933): 27-49.

Reveals the issues discussed at the trial of the Lincoln assassination conspirators, mainly whether civilian government or the military controlled jurisdiction. Defendants argued that the military had no jurisdiction under the Constitution, and that they had a right to a jury trial. Extensive historical discussion of military jurisdiction from 1860 to 1933.

1731. Current, Richard N. "Webster's Propaganda and the Ashburton Treaty," Mississippi Valley Historical Review 34/2 (September 1947): 187-200.

Webster is given credit for his role in the Ashburton Treaty with Britain to affix the northwestern boundary of the US. Mentions the money given to Webster by President Tyler for secret services.

1732. Current, Richard N. "How Stimson Meant to 'Maneuver' the Japanese," Mississippi Valley Historical Review 40 (June 1953): 67-74.

An analysis of evidence suggesting that Henry Stimson and Franklin Roosevelt had hoped to maneuver the Japanese into an attack. Emphasis is given to the controversy surrounding a note in Stimson's diary for November 25, 1941 discussing US intentions to maneuver Japan to attack.

1733. Currer-Briggs, Noel. "Some of Ultra's Poor Relations in Algeria, Tunisia, Sicily and Italy," Intelligence and National Security 2/2 (April 1987): 274-290.

The ineptitude of German signals security in several locations is portrayed through the author's personal experiences in decoding and intercepting messages.

1734. Currie, Catherine. "The Spies from Setauket," Daughters of the American Revolution Magazine 122/9 (1988): 612-615, 698.

A discussion of a spy network and operation in New York during the American revolution.

1735. Currie, James T. "The First Congressional Investigation: St. Clair's Military Disaster of 1791," Parameters: Journal of the U.S. Army War College 20/4 (December 1990): 95-102.

Includes brief discussion of the role of intelligence in the investigation of the St. Clair's expedition.

1736. Curry, Richard O. and F. Gerald Ham. "The Bushwackers' War: Insurgency and Counter-Insurgency in West Virginia," Civil War History 10/4 (1964): 416-423.

1737. Curtis, G. B. "A Study in Elizabethan Typography: A Cipher in The Spanish Masquerade," Baconiana 24 (January 1939): 6-21.

C. L. L'Estrange Ewen claimed that Thomas Lodge planted a cipher in a sonnet titled "The Spanish Masquerado." Allegedly, this was a copy of Bacon's cipher. The author disagrees with the theory that a cipher was planted in Lodge's work.

1738. Curtis, Paul F. "The Intelligence Function," Data 12 (April 1967): 49-51.

1739. Curtis, Richard D. "An Overview of Surface Navy ESM/ECM Development," Journal of Electronic Defense 5/3 (March 1982): 278-283.

1740. Curts, Bob. "Was Admiral Layton Too Hard on Himself? Some Thoughts on Warning and Surprise," Naval Intelligence Professionals Quarterly 3/3 (Fall 1987): 4-5.

1741. Curts, Bob. "U.S. Grant Goes to Shiloh: More Thoughts on Warning and Surprise," Naval Intelligence Professionals Quarterly 5/1 (Winter 1989): 5-8.

1742. Curts, Bob. "The Submarine That Got Away," Naval Intelligence Professionals Quarterly 9/1 (Winter 1993): 17-18.

1743. Curts, Bob. "A Warning That Worked: Napolean's Grab for Three Fleets," Naval Intelligence Professionals Quarterly 9/2 (Winter 1993): 9-12.

1744. Cusack, Thomas R. and Michael D. Ward. "Military Spending in the United States, Soviet Union and the People's Republic of China," Journal of Conflict Resolution 25/3 (September 1981): 429-469.

Discussion of the propensities of the United States, China and the Soviet Union to allocate societal resources to military power. Analytical methods, and the premises on which they are based, are used to evaluate military budgets of each of these super powers.

1745. Cushman, Robert E. "American Movement in War-Time: Civil Liberties,"

American Political Science Review 37 (February 1943):   49-56.

Against the background of World War II, the author discussed red-baiting inside the US government, conscientious objectors, Japanese internment and discrimination against negroes.

1746. Cushman, Robert E.   "The Case of the Nazi Saboteurs," American Political Science Review 36 (December 1942):   1082-1091.

Reviews the events surrounding the arrest and prosecution of fight trained Nazi saboteurs in June, 1942.   One group of four landed at Long Island, New York, while the others landed near Jacksonville, Florida.   Contains a summary of the Supreme Court's decision on the proper role of military tribunals in saboteur cases.

1747. Cushman, Robert E. "Purge of Federal Employees Accused of Disloyalty," Public Administration Review 3/4 (Autumn 1943):   297-316.

Discusses the findings and recommendations of the Dies Committee and the Kerr Committee concerning the expulsion from employment of three men thought to be subversives.

1748. Cushman, Robert E.   "Closing the Gap," Marine Corps Gazette (July 1959):   50-52.

A brief discussion of intelligence collection in the Marine Corps.

1749. Cusick, Michael W.   "Expanding the Government's Capability to Eavesdrop," Loyala University of Chicago Law Journal 15 (Winter 1984): 317-336.

A case note discussion regarding United States v. Yonn, 702 F.2d 1341 (11th Cir. 1983).

1750. Cusins, A. G. T.   "Development of Army Wireless During the War," Journal of the Institution of Electrical Engineers 59/303 (July 1921):   763-770.

For those in search of intelligence advances in World War I, this is a useful description of the role of wireless communications and research into new applications.

1751. Cuthbert, A. R. "The Right to the City: Surveillance, Private Interest and the Public Domain in Hong Kong," Cities 12 (October 1995):   293-310.

1752. Cuthbertson, B. C. "The Strategic Significance of the Northern Cape," Journal of the Royal United Service Institution for Defence Studies 117 (June 1972):   45-48.

1753. Cutler, Lloyd N. "The Right to Intervene," Foreign Affairs 64 (Fall 1985): 96-112.

Attempts to explain to non-scholars the rules that have evolved, current standing, and clarification regarding issues of intervention in foreign entanglements.

1754. Cutler, Robert. "The Development of the National Security Council," Foreign Affairs 34 (April 1956): 440-459.

A general summary of the issues and dynamics involved in the creation of the Council by the National Security Act of 1947. A classic review of this presidential advisory function which also oversees the intelligence function.

1755. Cutler, Robert. "Intelligence As Foundation for Policy," Studies in Intelligence 3/3 (Fall 1959): 59-71.

1756. Cutter, Donald C. "Harbor Entry and Recognition Signals in Early California," California Historical Society Quarterly 49/1 (1970): 47-54.

A discussion of Spanish defenses of California coastline by the use of sound and visual signals. Spain, in protecting the California colony, employed foreign seamen for positions of defense in the Spanish navy. Spain feared such men as it believed they might profit from selling information about ports of entry.

1757. Cuttler, Simon H. "A Patriot for Whom? The Treason of Saint Paul, 1474-75," History Today 37 (January 1987): 43-48.

An examination of the execution of Louis de Luxembourg, Constable of France, for his failed attempt to conquer France.

1758. Cypher, James. "Capitalist Planning and Military Expenditures," Review of Radical Political Economy 6/3 (1974): 1-19.

Useful discussion of the politics and economics of military spending. May be relevant to research on comparative estimating of foreign military powers. Contains sections on macroeconomics of military expenditures, economic growth versus stagnation, and military vs. state and local, and non-military expenditures.

1759. Cyr, Arthur. "Political Development in Britain," Current History 85/514 (November 1986): 366-368, 392.

Discussion of various political events and crises during the Margaret Thatcher government, including several cases of espionage.

1760. Czajkowski, Anthony F. "Techniques of Domestic Intelligence Collection," Studies in Intelligence 3/4 (Winter 1959): 69-83.

Explores the methods of the CIA's Contact Division in the Office of Operations which collected intelligence for some ten years prior to this article's publication inside the US. Article discusses locating and contacting the new source; conducting the first interview; continuing contact; university exploitation; and the alien contact.

1761.   Czinkota,   Michael   R.   "International   Information   for   U.S. Competitiveness," <u>Business Horizons</u> 34/6 (November-December 1991): 86-91.
Explores types of information needed in the international business community and the role of government in international informational collection. Presents study findings on the subject.

1762. Czvak, Istv N. "The Russian Third Section: Outline of a 19th Century National Security Organization," <u>Vil Qtrtnet</u> 2 (1989): 80-93.

D

"Against Germany it was obvious from the start that our work
would have to be of another sort."
(The Secret Surrender, Allen Dulles, p. 22)

1763. Dabelko, David D. and Geoffrey D. Dabelko. "The International Environment and the U.S. Intelligence Community," International Journal of Intelligence and Counterintelligence 6/1 (Spring 1993): 21-42.

Considers the changes that will be expected of the intelligence community in a world of continuing threats, but with fewer resources. Major topics discussed include a redefinition of security; environment as cause of conflict; information requirements; why the intelligence community cannot be responsible for fulfilling all needs; information capabilities; information sharing; current cooperation and information sharing; and intelligence community restructuring.

1764. Dabney, Virginius. "Jack Jouett's Ride," American Heritage 12/1 (January 1961): 56-59.

Discusses exploits of this American hero during and after the American revolution, in particular his actions to save the life of Thomas Jefferson, aid in Kentucky's separation from Virginia, and service in the Kentucky legislature.

1765. Dai, Qing; David E. Apter; Timothy Cheek; Nancy Liu; and Lawrence R. Sullivan. "Wang Shiwei and 'Wild Lilies': Rectification and Purges in the Chinese Communist Party, 1942-1944," Chinese Studies in History 26/2&3 (1992-1993): 3-100; 5-99.

1766. Daiker, Stephen B. "Taking Steps to Quality Customer Lists as Trade Secrets," Florida Bar Journal 66 (October 1992): 22-28.

1767. Dainville, A. de. "Une Resistance Militaire 1940-1944: La Naissance de L'O.R.A. Ses Problemes et son Activite en 1944," Revue Historique des Armees 3 (1974): 11-36.

1768. Dalby, Simon. "Security, Intelligence, the National Interest and the Global Environment," Intelligence and National Security 10/4 (October 1995): 175-197.
    Major sections discuss security after the cold war; environmental challenges; sources of global change; impacts of global change on international security; new concepts of security; new tasks for intelligence agencies; scenarios and the worst case; a new intelligence 'tool kit'; getting policy makers' attention; and a new security agenda?

1769. Dale, Richard. "South Africa and Namibia," Current History 73/432 (December 1977): 209-213, 226.
    A discussion of white supremacy in South African politics. Sections discuss urban Africans, the defense of the realm and the unification of Namibia. Useful in measuring dissent and regime support.

1770. Dalley, Paula. "Freedom of the Press and Government Secrets: The Availability of Prior Restraint Against the Press in the United Kingdom," Harvard International Law Journal 28/1 (Winter 1987): 131-138.
    Discusses an English appellate court decision addressing the publication of information claimed by the government to reveal intelligence information. Compares European and American courts on press freedom. Suggests British intelligence may have suffered significant losses from press revelations.

1771. Dallin, David J. "Operation Kidnap: Berlin's Soviet Underworld," American Mercury 74 (May 1952): 55-62.
    Discusses Soviet use of kidnapping to quiet dissidence. Presents two case studies of kidnappings and suggests that the West should take greater involvement to stop such affairs.

1772. Daly, Judith A. and Stephen J. Andriole. "The Use of Events/Interaction Research by the Intelligence Community," Policy Sciences 12/2 (August 1980): 215-228.
    An application of academic research findings to operational problems of early warning detection. Discusses the use of Early Warning and Monitoring System methods and the transfer of quantitative IR research into operational schemes.

1773. D'Amato, Alfonse M. and Antonia M. Greenman. "The Freedom of

Information Act and the CIA: How S. 1235 Will Enhance Our Nation's Security," Harvard Journal on Legislation 9/2 (Summer 1982): 179-193.

Discusses 5 reasons for enacting S. 1235; sectional analysis of the legislation and conclusions.

1774.   Damrosch, Lori F.   "Politics Across Borders: Nonintervention and Nonenforcible Influence Over Domestic Affairs," American Journal of International Law 83/1 (January 1989): 1-50.

Considers the norm of nonintervention in relations to nonenforcible support for political movements, political parties or political candidates in their states. Asks whether transnational campaign funding violates international law, and whether international law can prohibit states from implementing policies affecting trade, aid or other economic relations when the purpose is to influence the political process.

1775. Damrosch, Lori F. "Covert Operations," American Journal of International Law 83/4 (October 1989): 795-805.

Examines congressional role in covert operations oversight. Concludes that congress has not truly fulfilled its role as partner in military matters, often choosing to take a less dominant role than the Constitution allows, thus resorting to an executive-driven model.

1776. Dana, C. A. "War -- Some Unpublished History," North American Review 153 (August 1891): 240-245.

Relates the account of a man who offered to become a spy for the Confederacy in the Civil War while serving as a Union espionage agent. Discusses his various strategies for reinforcing the Confederate belief in his work for the South.

1777. Danan, James W. "Mr. Woolsey's Neighborhood," Air Force Magazine (April 1994): 44-47.

1778. Daniel, Charles D. "Status and Needs of Army Intelligence, Surveillance and Target Acquisition," Electronic Warfare & Defense Electronics 10 (September 1978): 57, 59-61, 63-66.

1779. Daniel, Donald C. and Katherine L. Herbig. "Proposition on Military Deception," Journal of Strategic Studies 5/1 (March 1982): 155-177.

Factors associated with deception in the military context are discussed in the following sections: nature of deception; process of deception; factors influencing the likelihood of deception; factors that condition success of deception.

1780. Daniels, George E. "An Approach to Reconnaissance Doctrine," Air University Review 33/3 (March-April 1982): 62-69.

Defines and describes the roles and functions of intelligence. Major sections include surveillance and reconnaissance; relationship to intelligence; collection disciplines; objectives of reconnaissance and surveillance; tactical recon as a primary function; tasking of collection resources; and system requirements.

1781. Daniels, Thomas C. "Does the 'One-Party Consent' Exception Effectuate the Underlying Goals of Title III?," Akron Law Review 18 (Winter 1985): 495-514.

Discusses the possibility that restrictions on federal agency wiretapping practices could affect law enforcement objectives. Case analysis of the implications of Boddie v. A.B.C. involving a video-recorded conversation. Argues for the maintenance of the "one party consent" exception to defend against unreasonable government surveillance.

1782. Danish, Ishtiyacue. "Captain Shakespeare (A Spy Traveller)," Hamdard Islamicus 14/4 (1991): 43-57.

1783. Dannenberg, Klaus D. "The Challenge of Technology for Military Intelligence Applications," Journal of Electronic Defense 7 (January 1984): 29-30+.

1784. Dannett, Sylvia G. L. "Rebecca Wright -- Traitor or Patriot?," Lincoln Herald 65/3 (1963): 103-112.

Rebecca Wright served the intelligence interests of General Phil Sheridan when reporting upon the status of forces and equipment in Virginia and other parts of the Confederacy. She was a hero to Sheridan and a traitor to the South.

1785. Darling, Arthur B. "Origins of Central Intelligence," Studies in Intelligence 8/2 (Summer 1964): 55-94.

Each of these articles appeared in the CIA's internal classified journal as condensed versions of the author's chapters in his later published book, The Central Intelligence Agency: An Instrument of Government to 1950 (1990). Variations in the volumes, issues and seasonal dates exist between sources from which citation information was gathered.

1786. Darling, Arthur B. "The Birth of Central Intelligence," Studies in Intelligence 10/1 (Spring 1966).

1787. Darling, Arthur B. "With Vandenburg as DCI: Part I," Studies in Intelligence 12/2 (Summer 1968).

1788. Darling, Arthur B. "With Vandenburg as DCI: Part II," Studies in Intelligence 12/3 (Fall 1968).

1789. Darling, Arthur B. "Central Intelligence Under Souers," Studies in Intelligence 12/4 (Winter 1968).

1790. Darling, Arthur B. "DCI Hillenkoetter: Soft Sell and Stick," Studies in Intelligence 13/4 (Winter 1969).

1791. Dansel, Michael. "Spies: Citizens Beneath All Suspicion," Historama 21 (1985): 20-25.

1792. Darnton-Fraser, H. J. "Napoleon's Head Spy," Westminster 180 (December 1916): 654-659.

1793. Darnton, R. C. "J. P. Brissot, Police Spy," Journal of Modern History 40/2 (1968): 301-327.
    Story of the French Revolution spy, his financial troubles and imprisonment, and his efforts to redeem his good name.

1794. Darr, Kevin H. "DIA's Intelligence Imagery Support Process: Operations Desert Shield/Storm and Beyond," American Intelligence Journal 13/1&2 (Winter-Spring 1992): 43-45.

1795. Darrah, Joan. "1630 CDR Sea Screen Administrative Board," Naval Intelligence Professionals Quarterly 11/3 (Summer 1995): 17-18.

1796. Darron, Robert P. "Early Years of the Marine Corps Remote Sensing Program," Marine Corps Gazette 73 (February 1989): 35-38.

1797. Darron, Robert P. "A Marine in Y1," Naval Intelligence Professionals Quarterly 10/4 (Fall 1994): 7.

1798. Dasbach, Anita M. "U.S.-Soviet Magazine Propaganda: American Illustrated and USSR," Journalism Quarterly 43 (Spring 1966): 73-84.
    Discussion of propagandistic roles of the two magazines, particularly in terms of the construction of favorably impressions. Sections contain content analysis of propaganda themes; subject matter; negative comment; and author's conclusions.

1799. Dascalu, Nicolae. "Aspects of the U.S. Participation in World War II," Revista de Istorie 38/4 (1985): 364-382.
    In Romanian, a discussion of the work of the OSS during the Second World War and OSS activities in connetion with missions in North Africa and Northern Europe.

1800. Dascalu, Nicolae. "Contribution of the Office of Strategic Services

(O.S.S.) to the Victory of the United Nations (1941-1945)," <u>Revista Istorica</u> 1/7-8 (1990): 755-772.

This is the fifth in a series on the subject of OSS operations in Asia. Numbers 1 and 2 in the series are found in volume 1/1, pp. 73-83 and 1/1, pp. 177-186.

1801.   Dash, Samuel. "Katz--Variations of a Theme by Berger," <u>Catholic University Law Review</u> 17 (Spring 1968): 296-315.

Discusses the historical developments in case law concerning wiretapping and eavesdropping.   Includes sections on the Olmstead doctrine; statutory interpretations of wiretapping; nature of bugging; demise of Olmstead; Fourth Amendment standards; and the Berger and Katz cases.

1802. David, Charles. "A World War II German Radio Army Field Cipher and How We Broke It," <u>Cryptologia</u> 20/1 (January 1996): 55-76.

1803. David, E. "The Conspiracy of Cinadon," <u>Athenaeum</u> 67 (1979): 239-259.

1804.   David, Steven R. "Soviet Involvement in Third World Coups," <u>International Security</u> 11/1 (Summer 1986): 3-36.

A detailed analysis of the gains and losses of the Soviet Union in efforts to bring violent overthrow to various Third World governments. Major sections discuss studies of Soviet involvement in coups; Soviet successes in defending regimes against coups; Soviet successes in backing coups; Soviet failures in backing coups; implications for Soviet involvement; and implications for US policy.

1805. Davida, George I. "The Case Against Restraints on Non-Governmental Research in Cryptography," <u>Cryptologia</u> 5/3 (July 1981): 143-147.

1806.   Davidson, Virginia.   "The First Amendment Goes Undercover: A Constitutional Analysis of the Intelligence Identities Act of 1982," <u>Boston University International Law Journal</u> 2/3 (Summer 1984): 495-511.

Examines protected speech and non-protected incitement   standard; overbreadth of the Act; vagueness; alternatives to the Act. Concludes that the Act is both unconstitutional and ineffective.

1807. Davies, Donald W. "The Siemens and Halske T52e Cipher Machine," <u>Cryptologia</u> 6/4 (October 1982): 289-308.

1808. Davies, Donald W. "The Early Models of the Siemens and Halske T52 Cipher Machine," <u>Cryptologia</u> 7/3 (July 1983): 235-253.

A continuation of the earlier piece.

1809. Davies, Donald W. "Sidney Hole's Cryptographic Machine," Cryptologia 8/2 (April 1984): 115-126.

1810. Davies, Donald W. "Charles Wheatstone's Cryptograph and Pletts' Cipher Machine," Cryptologia 9/2 (April 1985): 155-160.

1811. Davies, Donald W. "New Information on the History of the Siemens and Halske T52 Cipher Machines," Cryptologia 18/2 (April 1994): 141-146.

1812. Davies, Donald W. "The Lorenz Cipher Machine SZ42," Cryptologia 19/1 (January 1995): 39-61.

1813. Davies, D. S. "The Treachery Act, 1940," Modern Law Review 4 (January 1941): 217-220.

1814. Davies, H. L. "Military Intelligence in Tribal Warfare on the Northwest Frontier of India," Journal of the United Service Institution of India 63/272 (July 1933): 289-300.
        Persons seeking a copy of this old classic article may wish to write to the United Service Institution of India, Kashmir House, Rajaji Marg, New Delhi, India 110 011. Verify the source organization for any address after 1985.

1815. Davies, Philip H. J. "Organizational Politics and the Development of Britain's Intelligence Producer/Consumer Interface," Intelligence and National Security 10/4 (October 1995): 113-132.
        Considers the problem of how the optical illusion of centralized intelligence emerged in the British service, and how Britain's intelligence machinery has developed a "split personality." Major sections discuss the model; the beginning years; interwar consolidation and wartime expansion; post-war rationalization; and a British intelligence as a consumer-led community.

1816. Davis, Curtis C. "Companions of Crisis: The Spy Memoir as a Social Document," Civil War History 10/4 (1964): 385-400.
        Argues that spy memoirs are contributions to social history, not to diplomatic or military history. Focusses on Civil War spies and indicates that most accounts are overdramatized and exaggerated. Spy memoirs contain some common characteristics.

1817. Davis, Curtis C. "The Civil War's Most Over-Rated Spy," West Virginia History 27/1 (October 1965): 1-9.
        An attempt to correct the record on Belle Boyd's service as a spy for the Confederacy. Finds several factual matters worthy of more careful and critical assessment.

1818. Davis, Curtis C. "'The Pet of the Confederacy' Still? Fresh Findings About Belle Boyd," Maryland Historical Magazine 78/1 (Spring 1983): 35-53.

Explores new evidence of the contributions of Belle Boyd to the cause of the Confederacy. A collection of newly discovered letters provide insights into her work as a spy.

1819. Davis, Curtis C. "In Pursuit of Booth Once More: A New Claimant Heard From," Maryland Historical Magazine 79/3 (Fall 1984): 220-234.

1820. Davis, Curtis C. "A Tale of Two Virginians: Neighborhood Politics in the Lincoln Era," Manuscripts 39 (Spring 1987).

In part, a discussion of William P. Wood (1824-1903), the first chief of the Secret Service.

1821. Davis, Curtis C. "The Craftiest of Men: William P. Wood and the Establishment of the United States Secret Service," Maryland History Magazine 83 (Summer 1988): 11-12.

Wood was the first chief of the US Secret Service from 1865 to 1869.

1822. Davis, Curtis C. "The Old Capitol and Its Keepers: How William P. Wood Ran A Civil War Prison," Records 52 (1989).

Provides some details of William Wood's operation of the Old Capitol Prison during the American Civil War.

1823. Davis, Daniel T. "The Air Role in the War Between the States," Air University Review 27 (July-August 1976): 13-29.

Outlines the activities of professor Thaddeus S. C. Lowe during the Civil War in the area of military applications of balloons. Describes the successes of the balloon corps and the mistake in disbanding the corps following the war.

1824. Davis, Donald R. "Police Surveillance of Political Dissidents," Columbia Human Rights Law Review 4/1 (Winter 1972): 101-141.

Argues that government surveillance of citizens has gone beyond constitutional authority, thus requiring a new balance between warranted and unwarranted activities.

1825. Davis, Earle. "Howard Hunt and the Peter Ward - CIA Spy Novels," Kansas Quarterly 10/4 (1978): 85-98.

A review of espionage fiction from 1966 to 1971 by E. Howard Hunt [David St. John] using the character Peter Ward.

1826. Davis, Edward M. "Police Intelligence and the Right to Privacy," Journal of California Law Enforcement 10/3 (January 1976): 93-95.

1827. Davis, Edward M. "Police Intelligence and the Right of Privacy," Current Municipal Problems 18 (Fall 1976): 159-163.

1828. Davis, Elmer. "OWI Has a Job," Public Opinion Quarterly 7/1 (Spring 1943): 5-14.
    The author was director of the Office of War Information. This is a general description of the OWI's heritage and activities in World War II. Major sections discuss Wilson's classic job; truth, a powerful weapon; home front needs; handling our enemy "news"; other duties; financing war information; four audiences overseas; the importance of short waves; and accomplishments to date.

1829. Davis, Franklin M., Jr. "The Army's Technical Detectives," Military Review 28/5 (May 1948): 12-18.
    Reviews the operations of military intelligence against Germany from 1944 to 1947.

1830. Davis, Franklin M., Jr. "Technical Intelligence and the Signal Corps," Signal 3/6 (July-August 1949): 19-26, 62.

1831. Davis, Gary L. "Electronic Surveillance and the Right of Privacy," Montana Law Review 27/2 (Spring 1966): 173-192.
    Analyzes current (1966) restrictions on electronic surveillance under statute and case law, defines the right to be protected, and explores new approaches.

1832. Davis, Jack. "The Kent-Kendall Debate of 1949," Studies in Intelligence 35/2 (Summer 1991): 37-50.
    Reprinted in 36/5 (1992): 91-103. See item 1834.

1833. Davis, Jack. "Combatting Mindset," Studies in Intelligence 35/4 (Winter 1991): 13-19.
    Reprinted in 36/5 (1992): 33-38. Main sections discuss the inevitability of mind-set in the analytical branches; trade-offs; strategies for combatting mind-set; mind-set enhancement; mind-set insurance; and tradecraft recommendations.

1834. Davis, Jack. "The Kent-Kendall Debate of 1949: Analysis and Policy," Studies in Intelligence 36/5 (1992): 91-103.
    A discussion of Sherman Kent's perspective; Kent's doctrine in 1949; Kendall's perspective; Kendall's doctrine; the question of was there a debate; four decades of doctrine and practice; and producer-consumer relations in the 1990s.

1835. Davis, Jack. "A Policymaker's Perspective on Intelligence Analysis," Studies in Intelligence 38/5 (1995): 7-15.
    The author reflects on his interviews in 1991-1993 with Ambassador

Robert D. Blackwill concerning the requirements for sound intelligence-policy relations. Key sections discuss the transition from mutual ignorance to mutual benefit; what works and what does not; politicization not an issue; intelligence and policy tribes; and final thoughts.

1836. Davis, Jack. "Paul Wolfowitz on Intelligence-Policy Relations," <u>Studies in Intelligence</u> 39/5 (1996): 35-42.

Major sections discuss Wolfowitz's education and background; role in intelligence and policy processes; role in determining what adds value and what does not; debate and uncertainty; analysis as "tools"; objectivity; "bad news" and warning; and the Gulf crisis.

1837. Davis, L. "Six Good Spies," <u>Esquire</u> 83 (June 1975): 123-127.

Discusses six American spies during World War II: Paul Cyr; John Blatnik; Eli Popovich; Mike Burke; Douglas Bazata; Serge Obelensk. Concludes that bravery on the part of these men was remarkable, and they made a difference in the outcome of the war.

1838. Davis, Nathaniel. "The Angola Decision of 1975: A Personal Memoir," <u>Foreign Affairs</u> 57/1 (1978): 109-124.

Arranges the discussion of the case as follows: Three Angolan independence movements; intervention by the US; the author's resignation; interventions by Cuba, Zaire and South Africa; covert action and the CIA program.

1839. Davis, Nathaniel. "U.S. Covert Action in Chile 1971-73," <u>Foreign Service Journal</u> 55 (November 1978): 10-14, 38-39; (December): 11-13, 42.

A detailed review of CIA actions in the coup to oust President Allende of Chile, tracing the US steps from 1971 to 1973. Articulates the various abuses of power by the US, including the CIA. Concludes that the intervention may have changed US-Latin American relations for years to come.

1840. Davis, Raymond. "CORDS: Key to Vietnamization," <u>Soldier</u> 26 (July 1971): 31-34.

1841. Davis, Richard. "Scenario for Snooping: Soviets Picking Silicon Valley Clean," <u>Electronic Warfare/Defense Electronics</u> (May 1978): 22-24.

1842. Davis, Richard. "The Foreign Policymaking Role of Congress in the 1990s: Remote Sensing Technology and the Future of Congressional Power," <u>Congress & the Presidency</u> 19/2 (Autumn 1992): 175-191.

Major sections discuss foreign policy and the Congress; Congress and oversight and remote sensing; role of the intelligence community; and conclusions.

1843. Davis, Richard. "Spying on the Government: The Media, Remote-Sensing Satellites, and U.S. National Security Policy," Political Communication 9/3 (July-September 1992): 191-206.

Argues that the US government controlled and consistently restricted television access via satellites to the Gulf War. Covers types of satellites available for transmissions.

1844. Davis, Robert B. "Changing Roles for MI in the 21st Century," Military Intelligence 16/2 (1990): 32-35.

Argues that the intelligence function continues to play a vital role in treaty monitoring, counterterrorism, and counternarcotics.

1845. Davis, Robert R., Jr. "Buchanian Espionage: A Report on Illegal Slave Trading in the South in 1859," Journal of Southern History 37/2 (1971): 271-278.

Balances the argument that President James Buchanan desired to end the African slave trade to the US. The trading was highly secretive. Benjamin Slocumb was dispatched to the South on a two month espionage mission, later writing a report of his work.

1846. Davis, Robert S., Jr. "The Curious Civil War Career of James George Brown, Spy," Prologue: Quarterly Journal of the National Archives 26/1 (Spring 1994): 17-31.

An extensive discussion of Civil War spying operations. The article is aimed at setting the record straight with respect to the effectiveness of spying operations, including the role of the paid Union spy Brown. Suggests that more historical attention is needed for the Brown escapades.

1847. Davis, Roger H. "Social Network Analysis: An Aid in Conspiracy Investigations," FBI Law Enforcement Bulletin 50 (December 1981): 11-19.

Discusses the techniques and applications of social network analysis, an investigative methodology for mapping degrees and types of influence within a conspiratorial organization. Defines concepts such as social distance, relative influence, and centrality.

1848. Davis, Steven B. "Verification and Compliance for Arms Control," Comparative Strategy: An International Journal 9/4 (1990): 403-413.

1849. Davison, W. Phillips. "Air Force Psychological Warfare in Korea," Air University Quarterly 4 (Summer 1951): 40-48.

1850. Davison, W. Phillips. "Some Trends in International Propaganda," Annals of the American Academy of Political and Social Science 398 (November 1971): 1-13.

Discusses 20th century propaganda; propaganda as a regular function of government; expenses and complexities of propaganda; roles of social scientists; and the goals and uses of propaganda.

1851. Davy, John and Andrew Wilson. "The Secret World War of the Antennae," Atlas 15 (March 1968): 17-19.

1852. Dawidoff, Nicholas. "The Fabled Moe," American Scholar 63/3 (1994): 433-439.
        A critique of the baseball career and espionage travels of Moe Berg, suggesting that Berg was far less important in the spy context than he has been given credit in recent years.

1853. Dawisha, Karen. "The Soviet Union and Czechoslovakia, 1968," Jerusalem Journal of International Relations 3/2-3 (1978): 143-171.
        Discusses Czechoslovakia as a crisis for Soviet decision makers, decision flow, decisional and consultative units, psychological environment of decisions, pattern of information, and outcome.

1854. Dawson, Ed and Andrew Clark. "Divide and Conquer Attacks on Certain Stream Ciphers," Cryptologia 18/1 (January 1994): 25-40.

1855. Dawson, Robert A. "Foreign Intelligence Surveillance Act: Shifting the Balance: The D.C. Circuit and the Foreign Intelligence Surveillance Act of 1978," George Washington Law Review 61 (June 1993): 1380-1429.

1856. Day, Bonner. "The Battle Over Intelligence," Air Force Magazine 61/5 (May 1978): 42-47.
        Advances the argument that political criticism of intelligence abuses produced new demands for increasing the budget and power of the US intelligence community. Concludes that new regulation of the intelligence community has been detrimental to operations and that the community needs strengthening.

1857. Day, Bruce and Mike Martinez. "The Roots of Intellectual Property: Trade Secrets, Patents, Trademarks and Copyrights," Journal of the Kansas Bar Association 60 (January 1993): 30-37.

1858. Deacon, Richard. "Magodwys Forever!: The Present State of the Madoc Controversy," Alabama Historical Quarterly (Spring 1968): 6-17.

1859. Deacon, Richard. "Mossad: Strength Through Intelligence" World & I 1/11 (November 1986): 68-72.

1860. Dean, A. H. "The Pueblo Seizure: Facts, Law, Policy," Proceedings of the American Society of International Law 1969/1 (April 1969): 1-2.

Opening remarks for a panel discussion. Sets forth the American view of the facts of the Pueblo incident. See addresses by G. H. Aldrich and W. E. Butler, cited herein.

1861. Dean, Clyde R. "Critical Intelligence Issues of the 1980's," Signal 35/2 (October 1980): 9-16.

1862. Deane, Hugh. "The Cold War in Tibet," Covert Action Information Bulletin 29 (Winter 1987): 48-50.
Argues that the US intelligence operations in Tibet in support of Tibetan rebels were illegal and immoral.

1863. De Angelis, Sidney M. "The Right of Persons Who Have Been Discharged or Acquitted of Criminal Charges to Compel the Return of Fingerprints, Photographs, and Other Public Records," Temple Law Quarterly 27/4 (Spring 1954): 441-453.
Argues that the use of police records is vital to the intelligence function of local police agencies. Information on suspected criminals should be retained despite that fact that it may be insufficient for proving guilt. Good historical reflection upon the issue prior to many cases in the 1960s and 1970s.

1864. Dearmont, Nelson S. "Federalist Attitudes Toward Governmental Secrecy in the Age of Jefferson," Historian 37/2 (February 1975): 222-240.
Discusses the early post-constitutional period origins of secrecy in the executive branch.

1865. Deavours, Cipher A. "Unicity Points in Cryptanalysis," Cryptologia 1/1 (January 1977): 46-68.

1866. Deavours, Cipher A. "Analysis of the Hebern Cryptograph Using Isomorphs," Cryptologia 1/2 (April 1977): 167-185.

1867. Deavours, Cipher A. "The Kappa Test," Cryptologia 1/3 (July 1977): 223-231.

1868. Deavours, Cipher A. "The Ithaca Connection: Computer Cryptography in the Making," Cryptologia 1/4 (October 1977) 312-317.

1869. Deavours, Cipher A. "Courses in Cryptology at Kean College," Cryptologia 2/2 (April 1978): 134-138.

1870. Deavours, Cipher A. "The Black Chamber: How the British Broke Enigma," Cryptologia 4/3 (July 1980): 129-132.

1871. Deavours, Cipher A. "The Black Chamber: La Methode des Batons," Cryptologia 4/4 (October 1980): 240-247.

1872. Deavours, Cipher A. "The Black Chamber: Shutting Off the Spigot," Cryptologia 5/1 (January 1981): 43-45.

1873. Deavours, Cipher A. "The Black Chamber," Cryptologia 6/1 (January 1982): 34-37.

1874. Deavours, Cipher A. "Interactive Solution of Columnar Transposition Ciphers," Cryptologia 5/4 (October 1981): 247-251.

1875. Deavours, Cipher A. "Helmich and the KL-7," Cryptologia 6/3 (July 1982): 283-284.
     A brief discussion of the illegal sale of the KL-7 crypto system to the Soviets.

1876. Deavours, Cipher A. "Reflections on the "State of the Art," Cryptologia 8/3 (July 1984): 242-245.

1877. Deavours, Cipher A. "Cryptology Courses at Kean College," Cryptologia 11/1 (January 1987): 47-50.

1878. Deavours, Cipher A. "Sois Belle et Tais-toi," Cryptologia 11/3 (July 1987): 162-165.

1879. Deavours, Cipher A. "Interactive Solution of Beaufort Enciphered Text with Overlapping Keys," Cryptologia 12/4 (October 1988): 247-255.

1880. Deavours, Cipher A. "A Ku Klux Klan Cipher," Cryptologia 13/3 (July 1989): 210-214.

1881. Deavours, Cipher A. "Solution of C-35 Texts with Partial Key Overlaps," Cryptologia 14/2 (April 1990): 162-168.

1882. Deavours, Cipher A. "The Autoscriber," Cryptologia 19/2 (April 1995): 137-148.

1883. Deavours, Cipher A. and James Reeds. "The Enigma: Part I; Historical Perspectives," Cryptologia 1/4 (October 1977): 381-391.

1884. Deavours, Cipher A. and Louis Kruh. "The Swedish HC-9 Ciphering Machine," Cryptologia 13/3 (July 1989): 251-265.

1885. Deavours, Cipher A. and Louis Kruh. "The Swedish HC-9 Ciphering Machine Challenge," Cryptologia 14/2 (April 1990): 139-144.

1886. Deavours, Cipher A. and Louis Kruh. "The Turing Bombe: Was It Enough?," Cryptologia 14/4 (October 1990): 331-349.

1887. DeBenedetti, Charles. "The American Peace Movement and the National-Security State, 1941-1971," World Affairs 141 (Fall 1978): 118-129.
    Discusses the role of the Peace Movement in the issue of military preparedness in the months following Pearl Harbor.

1888. DeBenedetti, Charles. "A CIA Analysis of the Anti-Vietnam War Movement: October 1967," Peace and Change 9/1 (Spring 1983): 31-41.
    Discusses the Johnson administration's movement to get the CIA to conduct analysis of the alleged international connections of the US peace movement. Inquiry revealed that no significant connection existed. Discusses the complexity of the peace movement.

1889. Debo, Richard K. "Lockhart Plot or Dzerzhinskiy Plot?," Journal of Modern History 43/3 (September 1971): 413-439.
    An account of the conspiracy to plunge Russia into war against Germany. Lockhart was charged with bribery, destruction of railroads, and conspiracy to kill Lenin. The plot should by renamed.

1890. de Borchgrave, Arnaud. "Senate Bill 391: Amending the National Security Act," Society 19/3 (March-April 1982): 70-81.
    An extensive discussion of the Intelligence Agencies Protection Act of 1981 to prohibit the unauthorized disclosure of information identifying US intelligence officers, agents or informants.

1891. de Borchgrave, Arnaud. "Unspiking Soviet Terrorism," International Security Review 8 (Spring 1982): 3-16.

1892. DeBrandt, Dennis. "Structuring Intelligence for War," Studies in Intelligence 32/1 (Spring 1988).

1893. DeBrandt, Dennis. "Intelligence Rivalries in Wartime," Studies in Intelligence 33/2 (Summer 1989).

1894. DeCandido, GraceAnne A. "FBI Investigated Librarians Who Opposed Library Awareness Program," Library Journal 114 (December 1989): 19-20.
    Discusses newly released information that the Federal Bureau of Investigation probed the backgrounds of many librarians who opposed the "Library Awareness Program." The Program was aimed at soliciting information

about library patrons who checked out certain books or who followed certain flagged patterns. Program was mentioned in the motion picture "Seven."

1895. Decker, John F. and Joel Handler. "Electronic Surveillance: Standards, Restrictions, and Remedies," California Western Law Review 12/1 (Fall 1975): 60-101.

    An account of judicial interpretation of wiretapping prior to 1968, development of modern constitutional standards, legislative restrictions on electronic surveillance.

1896. Decker, Pete. "NILO Vietnam, Parts I and II," Naval Intelligence Professionals Quarterly 8/2&3 (Spring and Summer 1992): 6-11; 5-9.

1897. DeConcini, Dennis. "The Role of U.S. Intelligence in Promoting Economic Interests," Journal of International Affairs 48 (Summer 1994): 39-57.

    The author, a United States senator, argues that the intelligence community should be guided by certain principles in strengthening the international competitive position of US industries. The principles are outlined in support of a policy of intelligence community involvement in economic intelligence.

1898. Decook, P. "The White Lady, 1916-19," Revue Belge d'Histoire Militaire 27/3 (1987): 217-226.

1899. Decorney, Jacques. "Laos: The Forgotten War," Bulletin of the Concerned Asian Scholars 2 (April-June 1970): 21-33.

    Discussion of the author's findings from a trip inside eastern Laos to investigate the secret war in the mountains. Major sections discuss bombings, shelters in the hills, factories, geography, and poverty. Compromise of intelligence documents is mentioned as a concern for the situation.

1900. DeCoster, Bryan D. "OSS Estimate of German Logistics on the Eastern Front, 1941-42," Defense Intelligence Journal 3/1 (Spring 1994): 107-131.

    Major sections cover such topics as the Office of the Coordinator of Information; the German invasion of the Soviet Union; R&A Branch collection sources and methods; R&A Branch estimates of the German supply problem; impact of the R&A Branch estimates; and lessons for present-day intelligence analysis.

1901. Decourdemanche, J. "Note sur Quatre Systemes Turcs de Notation Numerique Secrete," Journal Asiatique 14 (1899): 258-327.

1902. Decter, Moshe. "The Great Deception," American Heritage 12/1 (1961): 73-84.

Discusses the expansion and decline of the role of the Communist Party in America and American society.

1903. Dedijer, Steven. "How to Watch the Watchmen? Parliaments and National Intelligence," Internationella Studier (1977-1978).

Discusses reform efforts in western societies to control the excesses of secret services. Asks questions about intelligence policies and processes.

1904. Dedijer, Steven. "Watching the Watchmen: Parliaments and National Intelligence Services," Bulletin of the Atomic Scientists 34/6 (June 1978): 40-43.

Discusses reform in western societies to control the excesses of secret services. Asks questions about intelligence policies and processes.

1905. Dedijer, Steven. "British Intelligence: The Rainbow Enigma," International Journal of Intelligence and Counterintelligence 1/2 (Summer 1986): 73-90.

Interprets the hidden symbolism and allegories found in the portrait of Queen Elizabeth, completed in 1600. Author finds symbolism in the painting: among others, the rainbow symbolizes intelligence as provided to her by William Cecil, Francis Walsingham, and Robert Cecil.

1906. Dedijer, Vladimir. "Police and Revolutionary Movements: Guide to Infiltration," Comunit 27/169 (1973): 102-115.

Characterizes the spy work of Thomas Beach and Envo Fiselevic. This article is found in an Italian journal; title is approximate.

1907. Dee, Juliet. "Legal Confrontations Between Press, Ex-CIA Agents and the Government," Journalism Quarterly 66/2 (Summer 1989): 418-426.

Describes various methods used by government agencies, such as the CIA, to suppress publication of information believed to be sensitive and contrary to national security interests. Discusses applications of prior restraint, pre-publication review and informal pressures affecting authors.

1908. Dee, Juliet. "Disgorging Benefits and Plugging Dikes: An Analysis of the Legal Arguments Advanced by the United States and the United Kingdom to Stop Former Intelligence Agents from Publishing What They Know," Communication 13/4 (1993): 303-326.

1909. Deeley, Walter G. "A Fresh Look at Purple Dragon," Signal 38/8 (April 1984): 17-24.

A discussion of the National Security Agency's inquiry of signals intelligence in Vietnam and the weaknesses in the security of Air Force communications nets.

1910. Define, William T.   "The Right of Association and Subversive Organizations: In Quest of a Concept," <u>Villanova Law Review</u> 11/4 (Summer 1966): 771-795.

Discusses the origin and definition of the right of association, theories surrounding the concept of right of association, views concerning the application of association, the concept as applied to cases involving subversive organizations, conclusions and predictions.

1911. Deflem, Mathieu. "The Invisibilities of Social Control: Uncovering Gary Marx's Discovery of Undercover," <u>Crime, Law and Social Change</u> 18/1-2 (September 1992): 177-192.

Major sections interpret Marx's book, <u>Undercover</u>: police and the control of behavior as irony; what undercover is, does and can be; social control technologies and the surveillance society; the sociology of social control; and covert control--opiate or inspiration of research.

1912. de Foucault, J. "La Telegraphic Aerienne dans l'Antiquite," <u>Humanites</u> 16 (1943): 111-114.

1913. de Foucault, J. "Correspondance et Messages Secrets," <u>Humanites</u> 18 (1945): 1-6.

1914. Defrasne, J. "The Attitude of the French Command to the Military Repercussions of the Technical and Industrial Revolution from 1919 to 1940: The 'Intelligence' Factor," <u>Revue Internationale d'Histoire Militaire</u> 55 (1983): 185-211.

This article addresses French emergence as a technically and industrially revolutionized country from 1914 to 1940, including the impact of the changes on French society.

1915. Defty, Andrew. "The Future of the British Intelligence Memoir," <u>Intelligence and National Security</u> 10/1 (January 1995): 184-191.

A book review essay covering three books: <u>A Game of Moles</u> by Desmond Bristow and Bill Bristow; <u>Never Judge a Man by his Umbrella</u> by Nicholas Elliott; and <u>With My Little Eye: Observations Along the Way</u> by Nicholas Elliott.

1916. de Graaf, Robert. "Hot Intelligence in the Tropics: Dutch Intelligence Operations in the Netherlands, East Indies During the Second World War" <u>Journal of Contemporary History</u> 22/4 (October 1987): 563-584.

A thorough account of Dutch intelligence against the Japanese in World War II. Details of the organization and operations of the Dutch intelligence service are provided.

1917. de Graaf, Robert. "The Stranded Baron and the Upstart at the Crossroads: Wolfgang zu Putlitz and Otto John," Intelligence and National Security 6/4 (October 1991): 669-700.

      Historical account of the life of spies. Relates the German discovery of its trusted official and the investigation that turned up the espionage activities.

1918. de Graaf, Robert. "From Security Threat to Protection of Vital Interests: Changing Perceptions in the Dutch Security Service, 1945-91," Conflict Quarterly 12/2 (Spring 1992): 11-18.

1919. de Graaf, Robert. "What Happened to the Central Personality Index?," Intelligence and National Security 7/3 (July 1992): 317-326.

      Focusses on the disappearance of the CPI, the backbone of Allied counterintelligence pertaining to names of nazi war criminals and suspects at the end of World War II. Major sections discuss the Deschenes Commission; the Crowcass index; the CPI; Furnival Jones; the Abwehr; the question of possible destruction of the CPI or continued secrecy; and the CPI role in the Anthony Blunt case.

1920. deGraffenreid, Kenneth E. "Tighter Security Needed to Protect U.S. Intelligence," Signal 45/1 (1990): 101-104.

1921. De Gross, Robert. "An Academe's View of the Problem," American Intelligence Journal 4/1 (Summer 1981): 14-16.

1922. De Gross, Robert. "Joint Military Intelligence Training: The DIA Role," Defense Intelligence Journal 2/2 (Fall 1993): 135-142.

      Discusses mobile training; train the trainer; new joint intelligence courses; video teletraining delivery; computer based training; joint regional intelligence training centers; and common core curricula.

1923. DeGrummond, Jane L. "Platter of Glory," Louisiana History 3/4 (1962): 316-359.

1924. De Hoog, John. "Secret War in the Secret Country," Orientations 3 (July 1972): 5-9.

1925. De Jong, Louis. "The 'Great Game' of Secret Agents," Encounter 54 (January 1980): 12-21.

      Discusses the Special Operations Executive "Plan for Holland" in 1940 and the 'Englandspiel' radio transmitter game between the British and Germans. Numerous allied agents were picked up and executed by the Germans as a function of a major failure of operations security. Two theories of the failure are offered.

1926. Delaney, Edward F.   "Sir Henry Clinton's Original Secret Records of Private Daily Intelligence," Magazine of History 4 (1884):   327-342.

1927. DeLaurentis, John M.   "A Further Weakness in the Common Modulus Protocol for the RSA Cryptoalgorithm," Cryptologia 8/3 (July 1984):   242-245.

1928. De la Sierra Fernandez, Luis.   "Pearl Harbor," Revista General de Marina 192/6 (1977):   645-651; 193/8,9 (1977):   169-184; 193/12 (1977):   629-235; 194/2 (1978):   137-150; 194/4 (1978):   403-424.
       This multi-part subject begins with a history of Spanish explorers and sailors who applied their naval skills to the conquest of islands in the South Pacific.   Then it discusses the conflicts between US and Japanese interests in the 1920s and 1930s, moving on to the rapidly escalating tension that resulted in the Pearl Harbor attack.   This is an excellent piece of work containing views not generally discussed by US authors.

1929. Del Carmen, Rolando V. and Joseph B. Vaughn.   "Legal Issues in the Use of Electronic Surveillance in Probation," Federal Probation 50 (June 1986):   60-69.
       Discusses the problem of prison overcrowding which has led to the creation of electronic surveillance systems.   Addresses constitutional issues, in particular the right to privacy, right against self-incrimination, and cruel and unusual punishment.   Favors the continued use of electronic surveillance.

1930. de Leeuw, Karl and Hans van der Meer.   "A Homophonic Substitution in the Archives of the Last Great Pensionary of Holland," Cryptologia 17/3 (July 1993):   225-236.

1931. de Leeuw, Karl and Hans van der Meer.   "A Turning Grille from the Ancestral Castle of the Dutch Stadtholders," Cryptologia 19/2 (April 1995):   153-165.

1932. Deletant, Dennis.   "The Securitate and the Police State in Romania, 1948-64," Intelligence and National Security 8/4 (October 1993):   1-25.
       One of two articles outlining the evolution of the Romanian intelligence service, "Securitate."   Traces the history of the service in post-war Romania, examines the subservience of the service to the Soviets, and charts the relationship of the service to the Party leadership.

1933. Deletant, Dennis.   "The Securitate and the Police State in Romania, 1964-1989," Intelligence and National Security 9/1 (January 1994):   22-49.
       Discusses the removal of opposition to the Ceausescu regime, including the placing of the secret police, the Securitate, under Party control.   Also discusses the annihilation of the professional class and the creation of the submissiveness

demanded by the Ceausescus.

1934. Deletant, Dennis. "The Securitate Legacy in Romania: Who Is in Control?," Problems of Post-Communism 42/6 (November-December 1995): 23-28.

Discusses the problems facing Romania in the post-Soviet years, in particular, the organization of security services, the Securitate's successors, the question of who is watching whom, lingering doubts about the new services, and the question of whether the security services are harming democracy efforts.

1935. Dellums, Ronald W. "Political Repression on the Horizon," National Lawyers Guild Practitioner 38/1 (Winter 1981): 18-22.

Calls attention to bills then before the Congress to weaken controls on the intelligence community.

1936. DeLong, Edward K. "The Activities of the Central Intelligence Agency, at Six Billion Dollars a Year," Computers and Automation 21 (February 1972): 38-40.

Discusses the case and career of Victor Marchetti, former CIA case officer, who published an expose on CIA operations and wasteful military intelligence.

1937. Delorme, Roger. "Twenty Years Later: Stephan Ward's Ghost Rises Again," Histoire Magazina 43 (1983): 56-57.

1938. Delorme, Roger. "Eugene Victor Debs: First and Last Socialist Candidate for the Presidency of the United States," Historama 24 (1986): 61-63.

1939. DeLuca, Arthur J. "G2 and the Atomic Target," Military Review 34 (February 1955): 50-53.

A brief overview of the Army's intelligence role in responding to tactical atomic weapons.

1940. DeLuca, John V. "Shedding Light on the Rising Sun," International Journal of Intelligence and Counterintelligence 2/1 (Spring 1988): 1-20.

A discussion of modern Japan's domestic security agencies, the Japanese Defense Agency, the structure of Japanese foreign policy, and Japanese intelligence bureaucracies. Sections include discussion of the Japanese-American connection; military intelligence; foreign intelligence collection; strategic intelligence and national security; and the future of Japanese intelligence.

1941. Delupis, Ingrid D. "Foreign Warships and Immunity for Espionage," American Journal of International Law 78/1 (January 1984): 53-75.

Keying off the Soviet submarine grounded on Swedish territory in late

October 1981, the author discusses the traditional immunity of armed forces in peacetime, the erosion of immunity, the definition of espionage in international law, the status of foreign spying warships, legal remedies and conclusions.

1942. De Lutiis, Giuseppe. "Control and Secret Services: A Comparison," Democrazia e Diritto 26/2 (March-April 1986): 47-61.

1943. DeMaiziere, Ulrich. "A German View of the Strategic Situation in Central Europe," RUSI and Brassey's Annual, 1977-1978 (1977): 113-123.

1944. DeMarchi, Neil. "League of Nations Economists and the Ideal of Peaceful Change in the Decade of the Thirties," History of Political Economy 23 (1991): 143-178.

1945. Demarest, Geoffrey B. "Tactical Intelligence in Low Intensity Conflict," Military Intelligence 11/4 (1985): 11-20.

1946. Demarest, Geoffrey B. "Espionage in International Law," American Intelligence Journal 14/1 (Autumn-Winter 1993): 75-80.

1947. Dembo, L. S. "Norman Holmes Pearson on H.D.: An Interview," Contemporary Literature 10 (Autumn 1969): 435-446.

1948. Demitriyev, P. "Special Purpose Unit," Soviet Military Review 2 (1980): 41-50.

1949. Demm, Eberhard. "Propaganda and Caricatures in the First World War," Journal of Contemporary History 28/1 (January 1993): 163-192.

1950. De Mowbray, Stephen. "Soviet Deception and the Onset of the Cold War: The British Documents for 1943--A Lesson in Manipulation," Encounter 63/2 (July-August 1984): 16-24.
       Deals with Soviet deception of Western allies and the use of propaganda as an effective deception weapon. Concludes that naivete, idealism, skepticism, realism and Russophobia led to the deception.

1951. Dening, B. C. "The Possibility of Strategical Surprise in Position Warfare," Army Quarterly 10 (July 1925): 287-299.
       Discusses evidence of the hypothesis from World War I, especially 7 major failures to seize strategic surprise.

1952. Dening, B. C. "Notes on Intelligence Training During Maneuvers," Army Quarterly 13 (January 1928): 391-397.

1953. De Ninnd, Sstefania and Gusti Micaela. "The Spigel Case: 20 Years Later," Ponte 39/2 (1983): 131-135.

1954. Dennett, Mark E. "Protecting the FBI's Informants," Harvard Journal on Legislation 19/2 (Summer 1982): 393-408.
       Examines exemption 7(d) of the FOIA which protects FBI informants in terms of current law, proposed amendments, and suggested alternatives.

1955. Denning, Dorothy E. "Wiretapping and Cryptography," IEEE Spectrum 30 (March 1993): 16-17.

1956. Denning, Dorothy E. "The Case of the "Clipper"," Technology Review 98/5 (July 1995): 48-55.
       Discussion of security programs of the National Security Agency.

1957. Denning, Peter J. "Baffling Big Brother," American Scientist 75 (September-October 1987): 464-466.
       Brief discussion of a computer system designed to deny the ability to trace information to a specific person.

1958. Dennis, Anthony J. "Assessing the Risks of Competitive Intelligence Activities Under the Antitrust Laws," South Carolina Law Review 46 (Winter 1995): 263-287.

1959. Dennis, Everette E. "Stolen Peace Treaties and the Press: Two Case Studies," Journalism History 2/1 (1975): 6-14.
       Considers two incidents (Jay's Treaty in 1795 and Treaty of Guadalupe Hidalgo in 1848) as cases of leaked information to the press and the general question of government secrets.

1960. Denniston, A. G. "The Government Code and Cypher School Between the Wars," Intelligence and National Security 1/1 (January 1986): 48-70.

1961. Denniston, Robin. "Three Kinds of Hero: Publishing the Memoirs of Secret Intelligence People," Intelligence and National Security 7/2 (April 1992): 112-125.
       Explores the autobiographies and biographies concerning secret intelligence people, such as, J. C. Masterman; Kim Philby; Donald Maclean; Anthony Blunt; Dusko Popov; Miles Copeland; Patrick Beesley; George Blake; Frederick Winterbotham; E. H. Cookridge; Ladislav Farago; Gordon Welchman; Alan Turing; Anthony Cave Brown, and others.

1962. Denniston, Robin. "Yardley on the Yap," Intelligence and National Security 9/1 (January 1994): 112-122.

Focusses on the relationship between intelligence and diplomacy, specifically in connection with the American Black Chamber and its director, Herbert Yardley. The author addresses Yardley's credibility, and whether or not his achievements depended upon deciphered diplomatic cablegrams.

1963. Denniston, Robin. "Yardley's Diplomatic Secrets," Cryptologia 18/2 (April 1994): 81-127.

1964. Denniston, Robin. "Fetterlein and Others," Cryptologia 19/1 (January 1995): 62-64.
Focusses on the work of E. C. Fetterlin, a Czarist cryptanalyst in the years from the reign of Nicholas II to the late 1920s.

1965. Denniston, Robin. "Diplomatic Eavesdropping, 1922-1944: A New Source Discovered," Intelligence and National Security 10/3 (July 1995): 423-448.
A detailed account of new research on the British eavesdropping practices in the period covered in the title.

1966. DeNoya, Mary. "Washington's Secret Army," Daughters of the American Revolution Magazine 116/2 (1982): 102-105.
A somewhat overstated and laudatory view of the heroics of Washington's intelligence operations.

1967. Dep, A. C. "Espionage and the Great Spy, Wattala Appu," Journal of the Royal Asiatic Society 28 (1993-1994): 1-24.

1968. De Poix, Vincent. "Security and Intelligence," National Defense Magazine 59 (July-August 1974): 35-39.

1969. Der Derian, James. "The (S)pace of International Relations: Simulation, Surveillance and Speed," International Studies Quarterly 34 (1990).

1970. Der Derian, James. "The C.I.A., Hollywood, and Sovereign Conspiracies," Queen's Quarterly 100/2 (Summer 1993): 329-347.
Concludes that the heavy weaponry of the modern spy and crime film has become the central focus of content. This contrasts with the earlier film tradition of focus on the plot and the central characters from Humphrey Bogart to Harrison Ford.

1971. Der Derian, James. "Anti-Diplomacy, Intelligence Theory and Surveillance Practice," Intelligence and National Security 8/3 (July 1993): 29-51.
As part of a special issue devoted to espionage, past, present and future, this article considers the game of names; intelligence theory; the intelligence of

theory; intertextualism and international theory; paranoia of cyberspace; and the future of intelligence intertext.

1972. de Renseignements, Chef. "A Dim View of Women," Studies in Intelligence 6/1 (Spring 1962).

1973. Deriabin, Peter. "The Difficult Intelligence Business," Show: The Magazine of the Arts (March 1964): 36-40.
     A review essay challenging some of the information contained in Allen Dulles' The Craft of Intelligence. Deriabin, a former KGB agent, argues that Dulles was not completely forthcoming about the determination of Soviet espionage.

1974. Deriabin, Peter and T. H. Bagley. "Fedorchuk, the KGB, and the Soviet Succession," Orbis 26/3 (Fall 1982): 611-635.
     An account of Vitaly Fedorchuk's rise in the KGB and the relationship between the KGB, the Communist Party and the military.

1975. Derrett, J. D. M. "Trial of Sir Thomas More," English Historical Review 79/312 (July 1964): 449-477.
     More's trial was a turning point in English constitutional history. Article details his trial for treason. Contains sections on the affair of Standish; the scheme of the trial; arraignment, offer of pardon, and the plea; the evidence for the Crown; the verdict.

1976. de Rudeval, J. Raoult. "The Service of Information: A Practical Study," Infantry Journal 11/1 (July-August 1914).
     This is a translated French article on the subject documents acquisition in the field. Discusses methods employed, the methods of the French information service, the application of data collected in peace time, utilization of local agents and espionage. Part II appears in the September-October issue and discusses information furnished by troops, ruses of war and conclusions.

1977. Deshere, Edward F. "Hypnosis in Interrogation," Studies in Intelligence 4/4 (Winter 1960).

1978. Dershowitz, Allan M. "Wiretaps and National Security," Commentary 53 (January 1972): 56-61.
     Discusses arguments before the Supreme Court regarding the constitutionality of warrantless wiretaps used domestically against organizations and individuals suspected of activities against "national security." Argues that significant abuse has taken place.

1979. Deschamps-Adams, Helene. "An OSS Agent Behind Enemy Lines in

France," Prologue: Quarterly Journal of the National Archives 24/3 (1992): 257-274.

1980. Desmarais, Ralph H. "Military Intelligence Reports on Arkansas Riots: 1919-1920," Arkansas Historical Quarterly 33/2 (1974): 175-191.

Six documents are presented which concern the use of federal troops in Arkansas to quell race riots in 1919 and 1920. Includes the role of intelligence in the race riots.

1981. Desmedt, Yvo G. "The "A" Cipher Does Not Necessarily Strengthen Security," Cryptologia 15/3 (July 1991): 203-206.

1982. d'Esneval, J. "Fonctionnement d'un 2eme Bureau: Le 2eme Bureau de la 4e Armee au Cours de la Periode 18 Au 22 Aout 1914," Revue Militaire Francaise 185 (November 1936): 214-258.

1983. Desnoyers, Charles-Hubert. "Cryptanalytic Essay, Part I, Solution of Problem No. 166," Cryptologia 10/2 (April 1986): 75-95.

Part II is found in Cryptologia 10/3 (July 1986): 158-183.

1984. Despres, Laure. "Estimating USSR Arms Sales by 'Residue Method,'" Revue d'Etudes Comparatives Est-Quest 16/4 (1985): 137-145.

Addresses the sale of arms by the Soviet Union to undeveloped countries, and whether or not there is an increase in volume as reported by the CIA.

1985. DeSola-Pool, Ithiel. "Alexander L. George, Propaganda Analysis: A Study of Inferences Made from Nazi Propaganda on World War II," World Politics 12 (April 1960): 478-485.

Discusses the nature of propaganda analysis resulting from radio transmissions from Nazi Germany. Compares content of information from transmissions taken by the FCC during the war with captured documents revealed at the end of the war. Argues that the methodology of content analysis of propaganda has changed and must continue to change relative to applications in the intelligence field.

1986. DeSola-Pool, Ithiel. "The Necessity for Social Scientists Doing Research for Governments," Background 10 (August 1966): 111-122.

1987. Destler, I. M. "The Nixon System: A Farther Look," Foreign Service Journal 51/2 (1974): 9-14, 28-29.

Suggests that President Richard Nixon's application of secrecy to key decisions also had the effect of undercutting the work of key staffers in the White House.

1988. Destler, I. M. "National Security Advice to U.S. Presidents: Some Lessons from Thirty Years," World Politics 29/2 (January 1977): 143-176.

Discusses the role of the National Security Council since 1947; Nixon's open presidency; lessons of the NSC experience; foreign policy and domestic politics; and the "mid-term system review."

1989. Destler, I. M. "National Security Management: What Presidents Have Wrought," Political Science Quarterly 95/4 (Winter 1980-1981): 573-588.

Discusses fundamental system problems; the national security staff's tendency toward consensus; presidential NSC staffing in practice; and conclusions.

1990. Destler, I. M. "Congress as Boss?," Foreign Policy 42 (Spring 1981): 167-180.

Addresses the rise of congressional power in response to expansion of presidential foreign policy power during the Vietnam War. Discusses the Carter administration's general acceptance of the new exercise of power in Congress, and wonders whether the Reagan administration will be moderated by Congress.

1991. De Toledano, Ralph. "The Noel Field Story," American Mercury 80 (April 1955): 5-8.

1992. Deudney, Daniel and G. John Ikenberry. "The International Sources of Soviet Change," International Security 16/3 (Winter 1991-1992): 74-118.

Major sections consider the Soviet and the alternative strategies in response to internal changes; economic and political environments and their consequences; the cultural, social, and organizational environments; and taproot, timing and international relations theory.

1993. Deutsch, Harold C. "The Historical Impact of Revealing the Ultra Secret," Parameters: Journal of the U.S. Army War College 7/3 (Fall 1977): 16-32.

Emphasizes the pace and degree to which ULTRA became available to western belligerents and influenced the sources of World War II. The same article was published in Cryptologic Spectrum 8/1 (1978): 5-29.

1994. Deutsch, Harold C. "The Influence of Ultra in World War II," Parameters: Journal of the U.S. Army War College 8/4 (December 1978): 2-15.

Refers to ULTRA as the "mother of deception." Discusses order of battle, ULTRA and higher education; Churchill as father and client in chief; processors and clients; influences on operations and strategy; and how much ULTRA affected the outcome of the war.

1995. Deutsch, Harold C. "The American Command: Client of Ultra," Revue d'Histoire de la Deuxieme Guerre Mondiale et des Conflits Contemporains 34/133 (1984): 5-16.

In French, a discussion of decipherment programs and techniques used by British and American forces in World War II.

1996. Deutsch, Harold C. "Clients of Ultra: American Captains," <u>Parameters: Journal of the U.S. Army War College</u> 15/2 (Summer 1985): 55-62.

Author argues that ULTRA and MAGIC code breaking efforts aided significantly the US and Ally leadership position in World War II. Further declassification of records will reap new and different perspectives on their overall contributions.

1997. Deutsch, Harold C. "Commanding Generals and the Uses of Intelligence," <u>Intelligence and National Security</u> 3/3 (July 1988): 194-260.

A detailed analysis of the decisions of American, British and German commanding generals in World War II as to their respective uses of intelligence. The author's focus is on an evaluation of the relationship between these commanders and their intelligence officers.

1998. Deutsch, Harold C. "Sidelights on the Redl Case: Russian Intelligence on the Eve of the Great War," <u>Intelligence and National Security</u> 4/4 (October 1989): 827-828.

Brief consideration of Russian intelligence during World War I and how such intelligence affected the outcome of operations. Mentions the relevance of logistics to intelligence.

1999. Deutsch, Harold C. "The Matter of Records," <u>Journal of Military History</u> 59/1 (January 1995).

2000. Deva, Yashwant. "Signal Intelligence: Concepts, Trends and Issues," <u>Strategic Analysis</u> 14/4 (July 1991): 475-490.

2001. Devillers, Philippe. "From Modus Vivendi to War: On the Capture of Haiphong in the Coup of 19 December 1946," <u>Revue d'Histoire de la Deuxieme Guerres Mondiales et Conflits Contemporains</u> 37/148 (1987): 5-22.

2002. Devine, Robert. "The Cold War and the Election of 1948," <u>Journal of American History</u> 59 (June 1972): 90-107.

2003. DeVoss, James T. "The 'Special' Heritage of the SSO," <u>American Intelligence Journal</u> 6/3 (October 1984): 9, 24-25.

A brief history of the Special Branch and the G-2 Special Security Office during World War II.

2004. De Watteville, H. "Intelligence in the Future," <u>Journal of Royal United Service Institution</u> (August 1926): 478-489.

2005. Dewdney, A. K. "Computer Recreations: On Making and Breaking Codes," Scientific American 259 (October 1988): 144-147.

Discusses technologies for sending and receiving encoded messages in terms of their ancient historical evolution and the more recent Enigma machine. Emphasizes the role of the Polish Bombe in World War II and its impact on modern computer encryption methods.

2006. De Weerd, Harvey A. "Hitler's Plan for Invading Britain," Military Affairs 12 (Fall 1948): 18-26.

2007. De Weerd, Harvey A. "Strategic Surprise in the Korean War," Orbis 6/3 (Fall 1962): 435-452.

Examines factors and assumptions present in the policy making process which led to the surprise attack of June 1950.

2008. De Weerd, Harvey A. "Verifying the SALT Agreements," Army 28 (August 1978): 15-18.

2009. De Weerd, Harvey A. "Churchill, Coventry, and ULTRA," Aerospace Historian 27/4 (December 1980): 227-229.

A critique of several historical accounts relating to the subjects in the title. Concludes that most such accounts may sell books but may not be accurate histories.

2010. Deyling, Robert P. "Judicial Deference and De Novo Review in Litigation Over National Security Information Under the Freedom of Information Act," Villanova Law Review 37 (1992): 67-112.

2011. Diamond, Alan. "Declassification of Sensitive Information: A Comment on Executive Order 11652," George Washington Law Review 41/5 (July 1973): 1052-1071.

Argues that President Nixon's Executive Order 11652 to revise the declassification system made no distinction between review procedures for various documents that had never been declassified. Details of the Order are discussed and weaknesses acknowledged.

2012. Diamond, Sigmund. "Surveillance in the Academy: Harry B. Fisher and Yale University, 1927-1952," American Quarterly 36/1 (Spring 1984): 7-43.

An account of the Yale University's investigation unit headed by H. B. Fisher and aimed at policing moral wrongs on campus (e.g., violence, disorder and drinking). Reveals Fisher's connections with the FBI.

2013. Diamond, Sigmund. "Morality in Government: The Federal Bureau of Investigation in the McCarthy Period," History of Political Thought 7/1 (1986):

167-185.
    Explores some of the critical questions surrounding the unethical practices used by the FBI in controlling political activism during the 1950s.

2014. Diamond, Sigmund. "Compromising American Studies Programs and Survey Research," International Journal of Politics, Culture and Society 6/3 (Spring 1993): 409-415.
    Summarizes the author's concerns and conclusions reflected in his book, Compromised Campus. Other articles in this issue contain analyses and other perspectives.

2015. Diamond, Stuart. "Nuclear Power and the Security Imperative," New York University Review of Law and Social Change 10/2 (Winter 1980-1981): 201-263.
    Surveys governmental and private policies and practices intended to ensure the physical security of the commercial nuclear industry. Emphasizes the unique nature of nuclear power production, which demands intensive protection.

2016. DiBattiste, Carol A. "Air Force Espionage: Two Recurring Issues," Air Force Law Review 32 (1990): 377-394.
    Summarizes the military law of espionage; discusses the recurring issues of right to public trial and access to classified information; offers conclusions.

2017. Dick, C. J. "Catching NATO Unaware: Soviet Army Surprise and Deception Techniques," International Defense Review 19/1 (1986): 21-26.

2018. Dick, James C. "The Strategic Arms Race, 1957-61: Who Opened a Missile Gap?," Journal of Politics 34/4 (1972): 1062-1110.
    Major sections include discussion of the threat; flight tests; deployment; challenge and response?; fiscal year 1959; a second challenge?; the administration and program lead time; second generation; hard facts; intelligence; McNamara; and American initiatives. Concludes that dangerous myths and misconceptions led to the missile buildup.

2019. Dicker, R. J. L. "SURTASS and T-AGOS: A Mobile ASW Intelligence-gathering System," International Defense Review 18/9 (1985): 1489-1492.

2020. Dickerson, Paul and John Rothchild. "The Electronic Battlefield: Wiring Down the War," Washington Monthly 3 (May 1971): 6-14.
    The challenges of the Vietnam war opened many new realms of electronic gadgetry for the Pentagon, creating and expanding many companies in the business of developing electronic hardware for big profits.

2021. Dickinson, Ian S. "Statutory Regulation of the Intelligence Services," Journal of the Law Society of Scotland 39 (August 1994): 298-300.

2022. Dickson, Patricia. "Lieutenant-General William Cadogen's Intelligence Service," Army Quarterly and Defense Journal 108/2 (1978): 161-166.

2023. DiCosmo, Nicola. "Mongolian Topics in the U.S. Military Intelligence Reports," Mongolian Studies 10 (1986-1987): 97-106.

2024. Dieguez, Richard P. "The Grenada Intervention: 'Illegal' in Form, Sound as Policy," New York University Journal of International Law and Politics 16/5 (Summer 1984): 1167-1204.
    Discusses multi-national intervention in Grenada, mechanics of international legal framework, the Reagan administration's assertion of legal justification, and conclusions.

2025. Diffie, Whitfield and Martin E. Hellman. "New Directions in Cryptography," Proceedings of the Institute of Electrical & Electronic Engineers (November 1976): 644-654.

2026. Diffie, Whitfield and Martin E. Hellman. "Privacy and Authentification: An Introduction to Cryptography," Proceedings of the Institute of Electrical & Electronics Engineers 67/4 (March 1979): 397-427.
    An introduction to contemporary cryptography. Contains sections on fundamentals, taxonomy of the study, cryptographic practices, and applications.

2027. Dikshit, R. K. "System of Espionage in the Nitisara of Kamandaka," Journal of Indian History 38 (1959): 627-634.
    An account of activities and role of spies in ancient India. Discusses qualifications, spy network functions, and political diplomacy.

2028. Dillon, Francis R. "Counterintelligence: One Perspective," American Journal of Intelligence 10/2 (Summer-Fall 1989): 37-42.

2029. Dilworth, Richard and Samuel Dash. "A Wire Tap Proposal," Dickinson Law Review 59 (1955): 195-202.
    Argues that more wiretapping legislation can be expected, but the authors wonder how much restriction is necessary. Proposes the use of a warrant upon showing of probable cause. Concludes the need for stringent regulation of wiretaps, but elimination of the means is impractical.

2030. Dimmer, John P., Jr. "Observations on the Double Agent," Studies in Intelligence 6/1 (Winter 1962): 57-72.
    Considers characteristics of double agent handling operations. Majors sections discuss double agent nature and origins; the value of his services; controlling him; assessing his potential; and the do's and don'ts of running the operation.

2031. Din, Gilbert C. "Pierre Wouves D'Arges in North America: Spanish Commissioner, Adventurer, or French Spy," Louisiana Studies 12/1 (1973): 354-375.

2032. Dine, J. C. "How Many is Beaucoup?," Infantry Journal 56 (May 1945): 63-64.

2033. Dingman, Roger. "Reflections on Pearl Harbor Anniversaries Past," Journal of American-East Asian Relations 3 (Fall 1994).

2034. Dinneen, Gerald P. "C^{3}I, An Overview," Signal 33/3 (1978):   10-13.

2035. Dintino, Justin and Frederick T. Martens. "The Intelligence Process: A Tool for Criminal Justice Administrators," Police Chief (February 1979):   60-65.
A discussion of the physical and analytical aspects of domestic police intelligence. Improved police intelligence should improve effectiveness against organized crime.

2036. Dintino, Justin and Frederick Martens. "Enduring Enigma--The Concept of Intelligence Analysis," Police Chief 48/12 (December 1981):   58-64.
Intelligence is the capacity to plan ahead and establish preventive strategies, argue the authors. Argues that new analytical techniques are needed to fight organized crime. Contains sections on organized crime intelligence programs, role of analysis, role of the analyst, strategic and tactical analyst, and implementing the analytical function.

2037. Dintino, Justin and Frederick T. Martens. "Police Intelligence: A Luxury, Necessary Evil, or Managerial Tool," Criminal Justice Journal 1/7 (July 1982): 1-3.
Task of progressive police chief is to give priority to crime problems according to real threats to the community. Intelligence is a managerial tool allowing a police chief to address crime problems in a cost efficient manner.

2038. Dion, Susan. "Pacifism Treated as Subversion: The FBI and the War Resisters League," Peace and Change 9/1 (Spring 1983):   43-54.
Discusses the opposition of the War Resisters League to war and violence. The organization was a target of numerous FBI surveillance operations and attempts to disrupt the organization's activities.

2039. Dionisio, Riccardo R. "Department of Transportation: U.S. Coast Guard Intelligence," Police Chief 42/7 (July 1975):   52-53.
The US Coast Guard's intelligence operations since 1790 are summarized.

2040. Diplock, Kenneth. "Passports and Protection in International Law,"

Grotius Society Transactions 32 (1946): 42-59.

Argues that citizens holding passports have no automatic guarantee of protection in international law. Discusses the origins of the British passport, distinctions between passports, visas and identity cards, and passports and US statutes.

2041. Dippel, John V. H. "Jumping to the Right Conclusion: The State Department Warning on Operation 'Barbarossa,'" International Journal of Intelligence and Counterintelligence 6/2 (Summer 1993): 213-227.

An account of the State Department's acquisition of information on Hitler's plans to invade the Soviet Union.   Major sections discuss the documentation of plans; the movement of information through channels to the US president; the daring nature of the State Department prediction; the international climate; Stalin's studied blindness; and the domestic rift.

2042. DiRosa, Andrew. "U.S. Law Enforcement During World War II," FBI Law Enforcement Bulletin 60/12 (December 1991): 1-6.

2043. Dirschel, Denis. "The Many Faces of Treason," Ukrainian Quarterly 37/4 (1981): 383-391.

Discusses several cases of Soviet espionage in the United States after World War II.

2044. Divine, Robert A. "Eisenhower, Dulles, and the Nuclear Test Ban Issue: Memorandum of a White House Conference, 24 March 1958," Diplomatic History 2/3 (1978): 321-330.

Discusses Eisenhower's efforts to get on-site inspections of nuclear facilities, and the CIA's role in determining that the Soviets had probably suspended testing before US diplomatic efforts began.

2045. Dix, George E. "Undercover Investigations and Police Rulemaking," Texas Law Review 53/2 (January 1975): 203-294.

Discusses the difficulties of police rulemaking for conducting undercover operations, and the lack of judicial lawmaking to improve the situation. Need for more rules is evident.

2046. Dixon, Marlene, et al. "Scapegoating Bulgaria -- The Antonov Tragedy," Crime and Social Justice 23 (1985): i-iv.

An argument in protest of alleged violations of legal and human rights of Sergei Antonov. Purports a CIA disinformation campaign.

2047. Dobel, J. Patrick. "The Honorable Spymaster: John Le Carre and the Character of Espionage," Administration and Society 20/2 (August 1988): 191-215.

Drawing on the characters and dilemmas portrayed in John LeCarre's novels, the author concludes that the work of espionage agents presents nearly impossible barriers to self-maintenance of a moral standard.

2048. Dobry, George. "Wiretapping and Eavesdropping: A Comparative Survey," Journal of the International Commission of Jurists 1/2 (1958): 320-335.

2049. Dockham, John. "A Sharp Look at Sinosovietology," Studies in Intelligence 5/2 (Summer 1961).

2050. Dockry, Kathleen A. "The First Amendment Right of Access to Government-Held Information," Rutgers Law Review 34 (Winter 1982): 292-349.
 An extensive review of case law and statutory law provisions to enable access to government information. Major discusses common law and statutory rights of access; Supreme Court decisions; right of access under Richard Newspapers, Inc. v. Virginia; and implementation of a First Amendment right of access to government information.

2051. Dodenhoff, George H. "The Congo: A Case Study of Mercenary Employment," Naval War College Review 21/8 (April 1969): 44-67.
 Discusses the role of the CIA in combat operations in Kivu Province, purportedly assisting in force training and largely unreported for its central role in combat. Major sections discuss the renegade rebellion; Tshombe's return; the spread of the rebellion; international reaction; the return of the mercenaries; Mobutu's plan; the organization of the forces; and the US State Department's displeasure with the situation.

2052. Doichinova, Elena. "French Intelligence Missions in Bulgaria in the Late 1940's," Voennoistoricheskii Sbornik 57/4 (1988): 109-116.

2053. Dolan, Frances E. "The Subordinate('s) Plot: Petty Treason and the Forms of Domestic Rebellion," Shakespeare Quarterly 43 (Fall 1992): 317-340.

2054. Dominquez, Jorge I. "It Won't Go Away: Cuba on the U.S. Foreign Policy Agenda," International Security 8/1 (Summer 1983): 113-128.
 Suggests 5 themes of control on US-Cuban relations, assuring the "weakness of intelligence," which has been responsible for underestimating Cuban capabilities.

2055. Dommen, Arthur J. "The Attempted Coup in Indonesia," China Quarterly 25 (January-March 1966): 144-170.
 An account of the October 1, 1965 uprising in Jakarta. Mentions the CIA.

2056. Dommen, Arthur J. and George W. Dalley. "The OSS in Laos: The 1945 Raven Mission and American Policy," Journal of Southeast Asian Studies 22/2 (September 1991): 327-346.

Major sections discuss historical background; the first, second, and third contradictions of the missions; arrival in Vientiane; initial confrontations; setting up in Thakhek; and the Raven mission.

2057. Donagan, Barbara. "Atrocity, War Crime, and Treason in the English Civil War," American Historical Review 99 (October 1994): 1137-1166.

2058. Donath, Joap. "A European Community Intelligence Organization," Defense Intelligence Journal 2/1 (Spring 1993): 15-34.

Argues that the European Community requires a strategic intelligence organization comparable to the Central Intelligence Agency, and suggests that such proposed agency be called the European Community Intelligence Organization (ECIO). Major sections discuss the author's reasons for such an organization; comparison of the ECOI with the early years of the CIA; and the EC and its tasks in the EC structure.

2059. Donini, Luigi. "The Cryptographic Services of the Royal British and Italian Navies," Cryptologia 14/2 (April 1990): 97-127.

2060. Donnelly, F. K. "A Possible Source for Nathan Hale's Dying Words," William and Mary Quarterly 42/3 (July 1985): 394-397.

The author suggests that Hale's dying words may have their origins in his Yale University education in the classics, in particular, the influence of John Lilburne.

2061. Donnelly, Frederick. "Linguistic-Terrorism," Conflict Quarterly 1/13 (Winter 1980): 31-35.

2062. Donnelly, Ralph W. "District of Columbia Confederates," Military Affairs 23 (Winter 1959-1960): 12-15.

Briefly summarizes history of the 176th Infantry Regiment, CSA, during the Civil War.

2063. Donnelly, Ralph W. "Formosa Spy," Marine Corps Gazette 52/11 (1968): 91-94.

Discusses the spy work of John Simms, a US Marine Corp officer, on Formosa (new Taiwan) in 1857.

2064. Donnelly, Richard C. "Judicial Control of Informants, Spies, Stool Pigeons, and Agent Provocateurs," Yale Law Journal 60/6 (1951): 1091-1131.

Discusses types of informants and explains the role of each in connection with local police operations and state and federal courts. Asks whether such persons violate Fourth Amendment rights.

2065. Donnelly, Richard C. "Comments and Caveats on the Wire Tapping Controversy," Yale Law Journal 63 (1954): 798-810.

Author, professor of law at Yale, offers a history of wiretapping, Supreme Court case analyses, discussion of the argument that all wiretaps ought to be banned, discussion of the argument that limited wiretaps should be authorized, and conclusion that new legislation was needed.

2066. Donnelly, Richard C. "Electronic Eavesdropping," Notre Dame Lawyer 38 (1963): 667-689.

Discusses the history and development of electronic eavesdropping law, including the case of Olmstead v. U. S., Nardone v. U. S., current conditions and proposals for change in wiretapping practices.

2067. Donnelly, Richard C. "Judicial Control of Secret Agents," Yale Law Journal 76/5 (April 1967): 994-1019.

Considers secret agents, mainly in the domestic police setting, and self-incrimination; secret agents and the Fourth Amendment; and judicial controls for the secret agent.

2068. Donner, Frank J. "The Confession of an FBI Informer," Harper's 245 (December 1972): 54-65.

2069. Donner, Frank J. "Political Intelligence: Cameras, Informers, and Files," Civil Liberties Review 1/3 (Summer 1974): 8-25.

Discussion of the methods of police surveillance and intelligence gathering aimed at domestic groups. Discusses photography as a political weapon; the chilling effects of informers; files and dossiers, and modest proposals for change.

2070. Donner, Frank J. "Investigating the FBI and the CIA," Current 172 (April 1975): 31-37.

2071. Donner, Frank J. "Electronic Surveillance: The National Security Game," Civil Liberties Review 2/3 (Summer 1975): 15-47.

An excerpt from the author's book on political surveillance. This portion provides a brief history of wiretapping in the US, including key cases reviewed and analyzed.

2072. Donner, Frank J. "Let Him Wear a Wolf's Head: What the FBI Did to William Albertson," Civil Liberties Review 3/1 (April-May 1976): 12-22.

An account of the FBI's COINTELPRO disinformation ploy to acquire

William Albertson, a Communist Party of the USA leader, as an informer. Argues the persistent growth of J. Edgar Hoover's intelligence operations in the US between 1934 and 1976.

2073. Donner, Frank J. "How J. Edgar Hoover Created His Intelligence Powers," Civil Liberties Review 3/6 (February-March 1977): 34-51.

Origins and evolution of Hoover's political surveillance system during the presidency of Franklin Roosevelt. Author says that the system was based on an invented presidential assignment and implausible legislative authority.

2074. Donovan, Dolores A. "Informers Revisited: Government Surveillance of Domestic Political Organizations and the Fourth and First Amendments," Buffalo Law Review 33/2 (Spring 1984): 333-388.

Sets forth a modern constitutional interpretations of the problem of government use of informers to infiltrate domestic political groups. Sections discuss the nature of government conduct; the nature of the privacy interest; the informer cases revisited; and the convergence of the First and Fourth Amendments.

2075. Donovan, G. Murphy. "Deciphering Soviet Military Doctrine," Studies in Intelligence 29/2 (Summer 1985).

2076. Donovan, G. Murphy.   "Policy, Intelligence and the Billion-Dollar Petroglyph," Air University Review 37/2 (January-February 1986): 58-71.

Major sections include the corporate personality of policymakers; the intrusions of bias; traditional images of intelligence; the need for a new image of intelligence; and the intelligence phalanx. Argues for an increase in analytical output and less emphasis on gadgetry, and a net improvement in the stature of intelligence analysts.

2077. Donovan, G. Murphy. "Evidence, Intelligence, and the Soviet Threat," International Journal of Intelligence and Counterintelligence 1/2 (Summer 1986): 1-28.

Suggests that improvements in government threat analysis of the Soviet Union should incorporate both an empirical quest and a theoretical quest to enhance the ability of both the intelligence analysts and academics to focus on Soviet theory and doctrine.

2078. Donovan, G. Murphy. "Intelligence Rams and Policy Lions," Studies in Intelligence 30/3 (Fall 1986).

2079. Donovan, G. Murphy.   "Soviet Military Vulnerabilities," Studies in Intelligence 31/1 (Spring 1987).

2080. Donovan, Thomas A. "The CIA Investigation: Asking the Unthinkable?," Foreign Service Journal 52/10 (October 1975): 19-20.
 An examination of the CIA and other intelligence services as seen by the Senate investigation of 1975.

2081. Donovan, Victor R. "Administrative and Judicial Review of Security Clearance Actions: Post Egan," Air Force Law Review 35 (1991): 323-336.
 Considers the implications of the case styled Egan v. Department of the Navy, 108 S. Ct. 818 (1988).

2082. Donovan, William J. "Stop Russia's Subversive War," Atlantic Monthly 181/5 (May 1948): 27-30.
 Former head of the American OSS argues the importance of recognizing the intelligence war, including the infiltration of media sources and the planting of propaganda. Addresses concerns for communist efforts to undermine Germany.

2083. Donovan, William J. "The Needs of the Nation in Intelligence," Naval War College Review 1 (November 1948): 27-35.

2084. Donovan, William J. "Strategic Intelligence in the 'Cold War,'" Naval War College Review 6/1 (1953): 31-42.

2085. Donovan, William J. "Sunrise Reports," Studies in Intelligence 7/1 (Spring 1963).

2086. Donovan, William J. "OSS-NKVD Liaison," Studies in Intelligence 7/2 (Summer 1963).

2086. Donovan, William J. "From Peter to Tito," Studies in Intelligence 9/1 (Spring 1965).

2087. Donovan, William J. "Japanese Feelers," Studies in Intelligence 9/2 (Summer 1965).

2088. Donovan, William J. "Boston Series," Studies in Intelligence 9/4 (Winter 1965).

2089. Doob, Leonard W. "The Utilization of Social Scientists in the Overseas Branch of the Office of War Information," American Political Science Review 41 (August 1947): 649-667.
 Accounts for the types of research activities performed by social scientists in World War II; administrative organization; identification of research personnel; promotion of research; marketing of research; outside obstructions to research; and personnel adjustment.

2090. Doob, Leonard W. "Strategies of Psychological Warfare," Public Opinion Quarterly 13/4 (Winter 1949): 635-644.

Defines and describes the use of information, misinformation, and propaganda in warfare. Key sections discuss the audience's response; present goals, reponses, and tasks; future situations; effects; and the psychological warfare campaign.

2091. Dooner, Patricio. "La Funcion de Inteligencia y los Valores de la Democracia," Estudios Sociales 72 (April-June 1992): 189-192.

Published in Spanish in a Chilean journal.

2092. Doramus, James V. "Cleaning Up a Dirty Business: Resolving the Power of the Executive to Authorize Wiretaps Without Procuring Prior Judicial Approval," American University Law Review 21 (1972): 757-774.

Considers the history of wiretapping in the US; evaluates the scope of the President's wiretap authority; considers the "inherent power" argument with national security justification for wiretaps; restraint on presidential power to wiretap; and considers the relationship between the First and Fourth Amendments.

2093. Dorfman, R. "Choking Off Information Through Prosecution," Quill 73 (December 1985): 8-9.

Comments on the Samuel Loring Morison espionage case. Concerns secret motions filed to keep classified information from the press, but not from the court or the jury. Author characterizes the case as the Loch Ness Monster of First Amendment litigation.

2094. Dorfman, R. "Gags Are No Joke," Quill 75/9 (October 1987): 8-9.

Discusses the case of Louis Brase who lost his security clearance for refusing to answer questions on a government form. Charges the Reagan administration with excessive concern for secrecy and opposed to the position of whistle blowers.

2095. Dorian, Thomas F. and Leonard S. Spector. "Covert Nuclear Trade and the International Nonproliferation Regime," Journal of International Affairs 35/1 (Spring-Summer 1981): 29-68.

Discusses the trade in nuclear weapons technologies by covert means, the markets for such trade, the controls on trade, the role of Israel, and case studies in nuclear arms deals. Suggests that significantly more world attention needs to be brought to the situation.

2096. Dorn, Jacob. "Episcopal Priest and Socialist Activist: The Case of Irwin St. John Tucker," Anglican and Episcopal History 61/2 (1992): 167-196.

2097. Dorn, Peter R. "Improving Intelligence Support To Deployed Marine

Air-Ground Task Forces," American Intelligence Journal 7/2 (September 1985): 7-9.

    This article also appeared in Signal 40 (September 1985): 75-77.

2098. Dornan, Diane. "Isolationism, Internationalism and the Future of U.S. Intelligence," American Journal of Intelligence 13/3 (Summer 1992): 39-46.

2099. Doron, Gideon. "Israeli Intelligence: Tactics, Strategy, and Prediction," International Journal of Intelligence and Counterintelligence 2/3 (Fall 1988): 305-320.

    An overall examination of Israeli intelligence services and their successes and failures. Considers the structure and functions of the Israeli Intelligence System (IIS); components; smaller units; causes of intelligence failures--structure or method?; how to minimize evaluative failures; and conclusions.

2100. Doron, Gideon. "Israel's Mossad," Conflict Quarterly 12/3 (Summer 1992): 71-74.

    A book review essay on Israeli intelligence operations.

2101. Doron, Gideon. "The Vagaries of Intelligence Sharing: The Political Imbalance," International Journal of Intelligence and Counterintelligence 6/2 (Summer 1993): 135-146.

    An assessment of the reasoning and practical limitations of intelligence sharing between intelligence services. Major sections discuss the normality and rationality in intelligence work; scientific methods; illustrations of a few vagaries; and the importance of intelligence sharing.

2102. Doron, Gideon and Martin Sherman. "Free Societies and Their Enemies: An Intelligence Assessment," International Journal of Intelligence and Counterintelligence 8/3 (Fall 1995): 307-320.

    Discusses regime type and international behavior; the choice mechanism of democracies and dictatorships; policy implications; strength recommended; and appendix.

2103. Doron, Gideon and Reuven Pedatzur. "Israeli Intelligence: Utility and Cost-effectiveness in Policy Formation," International Journal of Intelligence and Counterintelligence 3/3 (Fall 1989): 347-362.

    Argues that the formation of Israeli security policy is affected by the juxtaposition of at least four factors: (1) the structure of the intelligence community and the way it transmits information to the policy makers; (2) the personal preferences of the major policy makers and other government leaders; (3) the discrepancy between the civilian and military conceptualizations about security; and (4) the relevance of the intelligence data gathered for policy formation.

2104. Doron, Gideon and Boaz Shapira. "Accountability for Secret Operations in Israel," International Journal of Intelligence and Counterintelligence 4/3 (Fall 1990): 371-382.

Considers accountability for secret intelligence operations in Israel; the process of accountability; empirical case studies of accountability and secrecy; the Pinhas Lavon affair; and the SHABAK affair. SHABAK is an internal intelligence service in Israel.

2105. Doron, Gideon and Gad Barzilai. "The Middle East Power Balance: Israel's Attempts to Understand Changes in Soviet-Arab Relations," International Journal of Intelligence and Counterintelligence 5/1 (Spring 1991): 35-48.

A detailed consideration of the Israeli military intelligence collection and analysis efforts aimed principally at Syria. Discusses the Israel-Soviet relationship, a love-hate bond; the prime Israeli imperative, security; yesterday's regional superpower, the Soviet Union; and conclusions.

2106. Dorondo, Peter J. "For College Courses in Intelligence," Studies in Intelligence 4/2 (Summer 1960).

2107. Dorwart, Jeffrey M. "The Roosevelt-Astor Espionage Ring," New York History 62/3 (July 1981): 307-322.

An account of President Roosevelt's intelligence gathering system and his association with a secret society known as ROOM comprised of men who supplied him with intelligence information.

2108. Dorwart, Jeffrey M. "Citizens Under Military Surveillance," Intelligence and National Security 8/2 (April 1993): 236-237.

A review essay of Army Surveillance in America, 1775-1980 by Joan M. Jensen and Negative Intelligence: The Army and the American Left, 1914-1941.

2109. Dossin, Georges. "Signaux Lumineux au Pais de Mari," Revue d'Assyriologie et d'Archeologie Orientale 25 (1938): 174-186.

2110. Dos Passos, John. "The Conspiracy and Trial of Aaron Burr," American Heritage 17/2 (February 1966): 4-9, 69-84.

A history of the Aaron Burr's rise and fall. Discusses Burr's links with Benedict Arnold's expedition in Quebec in 1775 and his later participation in various conspiracies.

2111. Douglas, Allen and Rachel. "The Lockhart Plot," Executive Intelligence Review (November 1988): 1-15.

2112. Douglas-Hamilton, James. "Ribbentrop and War," Journal of Contemporary History 5/4 (1970): 45-63.

A brief history of Ribbentrop's role as Nazi Foreign Minister and the hostility he stirred with the British before World War II began. Useful in studies of perceptions among enemy government leaders.

2113. Douglass, Joseph D., Jr. "The Growing Disinformation Problem," International Security Review 6/3 (Fall 1981): 333-353.

Argues the possibility of planned Soviet disinformation strategies to manipulate the foreign policies and security postures of several Western nations.

2114. Douglass, Joseph D., Jr. "Soviet Disinformation," Strategic Review 9/1 (Winter 1981): 16-26.

Discusses surprise and disinformation and the Soviet uses of secrecy and deception. Sections discuss alleged mid-1970s shift in Soviet military doctrine; an interview with Ilya Dzhirkvetov; and the need for a concerted effort to counter the disinformation problem.

2115. Douglass, Joseph D., Jr. "Soviet Strategic Deception," Strategic Science (August 1984): 87-99.

Questions the adequacy of US thinking with regard to the Soviet Union's capabilities mainly in economic and military contexts.

2116. Douglass, Joseph D., Jr. and David S. Sullivan. "Intelligence, Warning, and Surprise," Armed Forces Journal International (December 1984): 133-136.

Mainly discusses Soviet preparedness for war and the dimensions of military intelligence needed to target Soviet weaponry. Includes discussion of Soviet military deception.

2117. Douglass, Joseph D., Jr. and Richard Lukens. "The Expanding Arena of Chemical-Biological Warfare," Strategic Review 7 (Fall 1984): 71-80.

2118. Douwes, Dick and Norman N. Lewis. "The Trials of Syrian Isma'ilis in the First Decade of the 20th Century," International Journal of Middle East Studies 21/2 (May 1989): 215-232.

Discusses the treason trials of Isma'ilis, a group proclaiming their Imam resided in Bombay, India.

2119. Dovey, H. O. "The Unknown War: Security in Italy, 1943-45," Intelligence and National Security 3/2 (April 1988): 285-311.

A detailed analysis of British and US secret operations in Italy. Concludes that all operations were effective and all contributed to the overall successes of the war.

2120. Dovey, H. O. "Operation Condor," Intelligence and National Security 4/2 (April 1989): 357-373.

Discusses the German operation Kondor, an espionage operation against the Allies in North Africa. Outlines the operation and the reasons for its success. Argues that no use was made of Kondor books and equipment after the Kondor operatives were captured along with their codes.

2121. Dovey, H. O. "The False Going Map at Alam Halfa," Intelligence and National Security 4/1 (July 1989): 357-373.

A brief article rejecting the premises and conclusions of Professor Michael Handel on the importance of a map in the Alam Halfa battle.

2122. Dovey, H. O. "The Middle East Intelligence Centre," Intelligence and National Security 4/4 (October 1989): 800-812.

Major sections discuss controversies, security summaries, and war diaries. Outlines the organization and structure of the British political intelligence gathering actions in the Middle East and the Balkans in World War II.

2123. Dovey, H. O. "Cheese," Intelligence and National Security 5/3 (July 1990): 176-183.

A brief discussion of the control of agents in an operation known as Cheese. Concludes that the data is not all in on the contribution of Cheese to the war effort.

2124. Dovey, H. O. "Security in Syria, 1941-45," Intelligence and National Security 6/2 (April 1991): 418-446.

Discusses the operations of SIME, Security Intelligence Middle East, concerning Syria, focussed mainly on the Syrian Nationalists.

2125. Dovey, H. O. "Maunsell and Mure," Intelligence and National Security 8/1 (January 1993): 60-77.

Historical analysis of the British intelligence officers Brigadier R. J. Maunsell and David Mure, reflecting upon the documents of their work which reside in the Imperial War Museum. Sections discuss British security in Egypt; agents "Cheese"; assisted migrants; tangled webs, 1941; agent "Stephan"; operation "Condor"; Max Brandli; and personalities.

2126. Dovey, H. O. "The Intelligence War in Turkey," Intelligence and National Security 9/1 (January 1994): 59-87.

Summarizes the measures aimed at stopping the German and Italian conquest of the Balkans. Poor organization of the Germans contributed to German failure in the Balkans, but the effective British deployment of counterintelligence was also a contributing factor.

2127. Dovey, H. O. "The House Near Paris," Intelligence and National Security 11/2 (April 1996): 264-278.

A novel, The House Near Paris, was written by Drue Tartiere, a study of escape networks in Europe in World War II. Discusses the author's experiences in operating safe houses; priests, purses, and photographs; and helpers and their fears.

2128. Dowd, Bob. "Memories of Berlin, 1950-51," Naval Intelligence Professionals Quarterly 7/3 (Summer 1993): 11-12.

2129. Dowd, D. L. "Security and the Secret Police During the Reign of Terror," South Atlantic Quarterly 54 (July 1955): 328-339.
A history of secret police origins in the French Revolution. Major sections discuss the location and description of the French Committee of General Security in 1793; the reign of terror and its misinterpretation; the revolutionary government; the Committee of General Security and the Committee of Public Safety; internal security measures; revolutionary committees; degree of control of various internal security committees; and beliefs concerning the misuse of power.

2130. Dowling, J. L. "Bumper Beepers and the Fourth Amendment," Criminal Law Bulletin 3/4 (July-August 1977): 266-281.
Discusses the use of bumper beeper tracking devices by police intelligence and investigative personnel in the absence of significant clarification of legal authorization. Caution should be exercised in using such devices. Future criminal case law may restrict the use of such devices.

2131. Dowty, Alan. "The U.S. and the Syria-Jordan Confrontation, 1970," Jerusalem Journal of International Relations 3/2-3 (1978): 172-196.
Offers answers to several research questions concerning threat perceptions, information, historical legacy, volume of communications, decisional units, time, probability of war, etc.

2132. Doyle, Michael K. "The U.S. Navy and War Plan Orange, 1933-1940: Making Necessity a Virtue," Naval War College Review 32 (May-June 1980): 49-63.
Describes the plan concerning US confrontation with Japan in the Pacific war. Demonstrates the use of intelligence in planning the US successes in the interpretation of vast quantities of information. Argues for historical analysis of the whole plan and the intelligence it depended on.

2133. Drach, S. M. "Viceroy Joseph's Official Despatches," Transactions of the Society of Biblical Archaeology 6 (1878): 244-248.

2134. Dragonette, Charles N. "The Birth of COMINT," Naval Intelligence Professionals Quarterly 11/2 (Spring 1995): 16.

2135. Draper, G. I. A. D. "The Status of Combatants and the Question of Guerilla Warfare," British Yearbook of International Law 45 (1971): 173-218.

Lengthy discussion of the history of guerilla warfare, the existing law of combatancy re: guerillas, general principles governing irregular combatancy, specific conditions of lawful irregular combatancy, law of hostilities, guerilla fighters in non-international conflicts, and enforcement of measures re: guerillas. Useful in studies of paramilitary operations of intelligence services.

2136. Draper, Hayward L. "Privacy and Police Intelligence Data Banks: A Proposal to Create a State Organized Crime Intelligence System and to Regulate the Use of Criminal Intelligence Information," Harvard Journal of Legislation 14/1 (December 1976): 1-110.

Discusses federal and state funding of organized crime intelligence systems; explores the benefits and inadequacies of these systems; presents a comprehensive statute to regulate the use of criminal intelligence information.

2137. Draper, Theodore. "Battle of the Bulge," Infantry Journal 56 (May 1945): 8-17.

The author's personal recollections of this World War II battle, which was an intelligence failure for the US and a success for the Germans.

2138. Dravis, Michael W. "Storming Fortress Albania: American Covert Operations in Microcosm, 1949-54," Intelligence and National Security 7/4 (October 1992): 425-442.

Major sections discuss the definition of covert operations; joint Anglo-American covert action; other covert actions in Eastern Europe; Albania as target and actions against Albania; and failure of the Albanian operation. Mainly a consideration of US covert operations during the early Cold War period.

2139. Drea, Edward J. "Missing Intentions: Japanese Intelligence and the Soviet Invasion of Manchuria, 1945," Military Affairs 48/2 (April 1984): 66-73.

Discusses Soviet intelligence in Japan immediately after World War II; intelligence failure and firepower deficiencies in the invasion; personnel changes in the Kwangtung army; and the failures of Japanese intelligence due to stereotypical beliefs about the Soviets.

2140. Drea, Edward J. "Ultra and the American War Against Japan: A Note on Sources," Intelligence and National Security 3/1 (January 1988): 195-204.

Argues in an extensive discussion that signal intelligence played an all-important role in General MacArthur's decision to advance rapidly to Hollandia in 1944. Highlights the significance of ULTRA in his decisions to advance.

2141. Drea, Edward J. "Ultra Intelligence and General Douglas MacArthur's Leap to Hollandia, January-April 1944," Intelligence and National Security 5/2

(April 1990): 323-349.

Discusses General Douglas MacArthur's use of signals intelligence to attack and surround the Japanese Eighteenth Army.

2142. Drea, Edward J. "Reading Each Other's Mail: Japanese Communications Intelligence, 1920-1941," Journal of Military History 55/2 (April 1991): 185-205.

An evaluation of American and Japanese capabilities to collect and interpret the diplomatic and military communities in the two decades before Pearl Harbor.

2143. Drea, Edward J. "Were the Japanese Army Codes Secure?," Cryptologia 19/2 (April 1995): 113-136.

2144. Drea, Edward J. "Previews of Hell: Intelligence, the Bomb, and the Invasion of Japan," American Intelligence Journal 16/1 (Spring 1995): 51-57.

A reprint of an article which originally appeared in MHQ: Quarterly Journal of Military History 7/3 (Spring 1995): 74-81.

2145. Drechsler, Karl. "Report #1 of the CIA "Review of the World Situation As It Relates to the Security of the United States"," Militargeschichte 27/1 (1988): 79-85.

2146. Dreifus, C. "'Errors of Enthusiasm,'" Progressive 49 (August 1985): 34-37.

This is an interview with former CIA Director Stansfield Turner.

2147. Drell, Bernard. "Intelligence Research--Some Suggested Approaches," Studies in Intelligence 2 (Fall 1957).

2148. Dreury, Gavin. "The House of Commons and the Security Services," Public Law (Autumn 1984): 370-376.

Discusses the issue of accountability for public services among the Canadian and British intelligence services. Concludes that accountability is a long way off.

2149. Dreury, Gavin. "The Ponting Case - Leaking in the Public Interest," Public Law (Summer 1985): 203-212.

A review of the issues involved in the Ponting case involving allegations of revelation of secret information to the London Times. Case was brought under the British Official Secrets Act of 1911.

2150. Dreyfuss, Robert. "Company Spies: The CIA Has Opened a Global Pandora's Box by Spying on Foreign Competitors of American Companies," Mother Jones 19 (May-June 1994): 16-19, 66-68.

A brief overview of some of the issues involved in the new field of economic intelligence as they apply to CIA's role.

2151. Dreyfuss, Robert. "Tinker, Tailor, Silicon Spy," California Lawyer 16 (May 1996): 36-41+.

2152. Drooz, D. "CIA's Secret Iran Fund," Politics Today 7 (March-April 1980): 10-11.

2153. Dube, Louis J. and Launie M. Ziebell. "The Supreme Court and the "Intelligence Source"," Studies in Intelligence 30/4 (Winter 1986).

2154. Dubin, Laurence M. "Wiretapping: The Federalism Problem," Journal of Criminal Law, Criminology and Police Science 51/6 (March-April 1961): 630-636.
    A case law comment on the subject.

2155. Dudis, John B., Jr. "Electronic Surveillance: New Law for an Expanding Problem," Montana Law Review 32/2 (Summer 1971): 265-278.
    Reviews the history of electronic surveillance law; electronic surveillance in Montana; and the present state of the law regarding surveillance in the US.

2156. Duffield, John S. "The Soviet Military Threat to Western Europe: U.S. Estimates in the 1950s and 1960s," Journal of Strategic Studies 15/2 (June 1992): 208-227.

2157. Duffy, Gloria. "Crisis Mangling and the Cuban Brigade," International Security 8/1 (Summer 1983): 67-87.
    A discussion of the deficiencies in national security leadership, bungling of foreign policy and intelligence reporting and analysis during the 1979 incident.

2158. Duffy, Paul. "From the Soviet Archives: A Secret Document Relating to Canada," Dalhousie Review 72/2 (1992): 184-188.

2159. Dufour, Paul. "'Eggheads' and Espionage: The Gouzenko Affair in Canada," Journal of Canadian Studies 16/3-4 (Fall-Winter 1981): 188-198.
    Discusses the effect that the Gouzenko defector case had on the scientific community, causing loss of its support for the community at home and abroad.

2160. Dugan, James and Carroll Stewart. "Ploesti: German Defenses and Allied Intelligence," Airpower Historian 9 (January 1962): 1-20.

2161. Duggan, James E. "Legal Protection for Computer Programs, 1980-1992: A Bibliography of Law-Related Materials," Hastings Communications and

Entertainment Law Journal 15 (Fall 1992): 211-295.

2162. Duhamel, Peter N. "Minimization: In Search of Standards," Suffolk University Law Review 8 (Fall 1973): 60-84.
    A case note offering a theory that total exclusion of the contents of electronic surveillance should be reserved for cases in which police have conducted indiscriminate "general searches." Considers relevant procedural provisions of Title III; conceptual problems with Title III; and remedial problems with Title III.

2163. Duhamel, Roger. "L'Espionnage et le Renseignement," Action Nationale 72/6 (1983): 529-535.
    This is a French Canadian journal and the approximate translation is, "Espionage and Intelligence".

2164. Dujardin, Jean. "The 'Luc' Network, Summer 1941 to Summer 1942: Aspects of the Problems of Command and Liaison," Cahiers d'Histoire de la Seconde Guerre Mondiale 6 (1980): 33-114.

2165. Duke, David C. "Spy Scares, Scapegoats, and the Cold War," South Atlantic Quarterly 79/3 (Summer 1980): 245-256.
    A brief discussion of the lives and spying activities of two women, Agnes Smedley and Anna Strong. The affiliations of these women with the Communist Party and literary achievements are also discussed.

2166. Dulles, Allen W. "The Secret Challenge," Department of State Bulletin 38 (March 1958): 338-343.
    One of the first directors of the CIA discusses advances in Soviet scientific and technological capabilities. Major sections discuss Soviet technical competence; the impact of Sputnik; the intermediate issues; Soviet subversion and economic penetration; need for technicians from the free world; and long-range significance of Soviet educational advancement.

2167. Dulles, Allen W. "William J. Donovan and the National Security," Studies in Intelligence 3/3 (Summer 1959): 35-41.

2168. Dulles, Allen W. "Intelligence Estimating and National Security: An Address, January 26, 1960," Department of State Bulletin 42 (March 1960): 411-417.

2169. Dulles, Allen W. "Central Intelligence Agency," Business Lawyer 16 (November 1960): 48.

2170. Dulles, Allen W. "The Craft of Intelligence," Harper's 226 (April 1963):

128-174.

2171. Dumbridge, Alex. "C³I," <u>Air Defense Magazine</u> (January-March 1979): 21-26.

2172. Dunbar, Leslie W. "Beyond Korematsu: The Emergency Detention Act of 1950," <u>University of Pittsburgh Law Review</u> 13/2 (Winter 1952): 221-231.
    An analysis of the Internal Security Act of 1950 and the Emergency Detention Act of 1950.

2173. Dunbar, Leslie W. "The First Amendment and the National Security State," <u>Democracy</u> 2/3 (July 1982): 69-79.
    Argues that free speech has been the principle protector of peace in the world, but that the American press has supported consistently the national security justifications of all recent governments in office. Argues that open discourse on national security issues enables discovery of 'mutual trust.'

2174. Duncan, Harry N. "Combat Intelligence for Modern War," <u>Army Information Digest</u> (June 1962): 24-31.

2175. Dunkel, Winfried M. "Nuclear Proliferation--A German View," <u>Military Review</u> 57/11 (November 1977): 49-55.
    Discusses in part the role of intelligence agencies in verifying nuclear weapons in the world and in preventing technological espionage.

2176. Dunlay, Thomas W. "Indian Allies in the Armies of New Spain and the United States: A Comparative Study," <u>New Mexico Historical Review</u> 56/3 (1981): 239-258.

2177. Dunleigh, Lowell M. "Spy at Your Service, Sir," <u>Studies in Intelligence</u> 3/1 (Spring 1959): 81-93.

2178. Dunlop, Richard. "The Wartime OSS," <u>American Legion Magazine</u> 116/6 (June 1984): 15.

2179. Dunn, Christopher. "Judging Secrets," <u>Villanova Law Review</u> 31 (April 1986): 471-523.
    Considers the classification system; the FOIA amendments and the courts; judicial deference explained; demystifying information classification; judicial expertise to review classification decisions; and jurisprudential considerations.

2180. Dunn, Lewis A. "Arms Control Verification: Living with Uncertainty," <u>International Security</u> 14/4 (1990): 165-175.
    A discussion of difficulties involved with arms control verification.

Major sections discuss tough verification challenges; new verification thresholds; getting the verification job done; how little verification confidence is too little?; and future considerations in verification.

2181. Dunn, Peter. "Spies," British Legion Journal 12/10 (April 1933): 339-353.

2182. Dunn, Walter S., Jr. "The 'Ultra' Papers," Military Affairs 42/3 (October 1978): 134-135.
　　　　Discusses a small number of intercepted German messages during World War II and various types of codes used by German intelligence. This collection of "Ultra papers" contained few surprises, but they have enlightened the actions of allied forces.

2183. Dunnigan, B. L.; F. Lewis; and M. Barlow. "The Niagara Cipher--Part I," Cryptologia 14/2 (April 1990): 135-138.

2184. Dunnigan, B. L.; F. Lewis; and M. Barlow. "The Niagara Cipher--Part II," Cryptologia 14/3 (July 1990): 199-203.

2185. Dunning, W. A. "Disloyalty in Two Wars," American Historical Review 24/4 (July 1919): 625-630.
　　　　Discusses disloyalty during the American Civil War and World War I; limitations on Lincoln's statutory or judicial tools for defending against disloyalty; actions to deal with prisoners in the Civil War; the breadth of President Wilson's power in dealing with the problem of disloyalty; and the Espionage Acts of 1917 and 1918.

2186. Dupuy, Jean. "The 1982 CIA Coup in Chad," Covert Action Information Bulletin 36 (Spring 1991): 27-31.

2187. Dupuy, Trevor N. "Pearl Harbor: Who Blundered?," American Heritage 13/2 (February 1962): 64-81.
　　　　Examines the failures in the dissemination of information prior to the Pearl Harbor attack, in particular the failures of naval intelligence and the changes spawned by them.

2188. Durgnat, Raymond. "Spies and Ideologies," Cinema 2 (March 1969): 5-13.

2189. During, F. "Cooperation Between Tanks and Airplanes," Review of Military Literature 15 (June 1935): 36-37.

2190. DuVal, Benjamin S., Jr. "The Occasions of Secrecy," University of

Pittsburgh Law Review 47/3 (Spring 1986): 579-674.

Discusses First Amendment values and the paradox of knowledge; the construction of a taxonomy of the occasions of secrecy; restrictions on the dissemination of knowledge; policy formation with respect to the opinions of government employees; policy implementation; government as information repository; election results; commercial information; restrictions on acquisition of knowledge; patterns of secrecy; and justifications for limiting knowledge.

2191. Dwight, C. Harrison. "Count Rumford: His Majesty Colonel in Carolina," South Carolina Historical Magazine 57 (January 1956): 23-27.

2192. Dworkin, Terry M. "Protecting Private Employees from Enhanced Monitoring: Legislative Approaches," American Business Law Journal 28 (1990): 59-85.

Considers the Employee Polygraph Protection Act of 1988; further lie detector legislation; other forms of enhanced monitoring, and general monitoring privacy legislation.

2193. Dyer, George B. and Charlotte L. "The Beginnings of the United States Strategic Intelligence System in Latin America, 1809-1826," Military Affairs 14/2 (1950): 65-83.

2194. Dyer, George B. and Charlotte L. "Century of Strategic Intelligence Reporting: Mexico, 1822-1919," Geographical Review 44 (January 1954): 49-69.

Considers intelligence gathering in Mexico in these years, including data collection before airplanes.

2195. Dykman, Jackson O. "The Last Twelve Days of Major Andre," Magazine of American History 21 (June 1889): 494-498; 22 (July-August 1889): 49-57, 148-158.

2196. Dykstra, Robert R. "The Continuing War," Civil War History 10/4 (1964): 434-435.

A brief acknowledgment of the Civil War's most noteworthy security breach, the assassination of Abraham Lincoln.

2197. Dziak, John J. "The Action Arm of the CPSU," Problems of Communism (July-August 1981): 53-58.

A book review essay on works which discuss the Soviet KGB. Concludes that a need exists for more research and publication concerning the history and role of the KGB, and that the current works make clear Nikita Khruschev's role in shaping the KGB to be a friendly partner to the Communist Party in the Soviet Union.

2198. Dziak, John J. "Soviet Intelligence and Security Services in the Eighties: The Paramilitary Dimension," <u>Orbis</u> 24/4 (Winter 1981): 771-786.

Accounts for the role and operations of special-purpose troops who, during crisis or war time, would be deployed under the intelligence or security organs of the USSR.

2199. Dziak, John. "Soviet 'Active Measures,'" <u>Problems of Communism</u> 33 (November-December 1984): 66-69.

A book review essay on two works which address Soviet state-sponsored deception as an integral element in Soviet foreign policy. Suggests that, although new works are now available on the subject, much more research and case development is needed.

2200. Dziewanowski, M. K. "Polish Intelligence During World War II: The Case of Barbarossa," <u>East European Quarterly</u> 28/3 (Fall 1994): 381-391.

Attempts to balance the record of contributions of Polish intelligence prior to the German invasion of the Soviet Union in 1941.

E

"...they did not face the reality that Enigma could be broken."
(<u>Seizing the Enigma</u> by David Kahn, p. 279)

2201. Eagle, Kenneth L. "Prior Restraint Enforced Against Publication of Classified Material by CIA Employee," <u>North Carolina Law Review</u> 51 (1973): 865-874.

Discusses the constitutional law applicable to the case of <u>United States v. Marchetti</u> in which the Fourth Circuit Court of Appeals affirmed the issuance of an injunction enforcing a secrecy agreement signed by Marchetti as a condition of employment at CIA.

2202. Eagleburger, Lawrence S. "Unacceptable Intervention: Soviet Active Measures," <u>NATO Review</u> 31/1 (April 1983): 6-11.

Discussion of Soviet intelligence and active measures work in the world, and Soviet intervention in other countries. Sections discuss the large size of the secret Soviet intelligence system; assessing the effect of active measures; the corrosive effect of open political systems; and the need for a persistent response.

2203. Eagles, I. G. "Cabinet Secrets as Evidence," <u>Public Law</u> (Autumn 1980): 263-287.

Extensive discussion of British Cabinet secrecy; rationale for secrecy; what information receives protection; timing of disclosures; and a definition of who may claim the secrecy privilege.

2204. Easterbrook, Frank H. "Insider Trading, Secret Agents, Evidentiary

Privileges and the Production of Information," Supreme Court Review (1981): 309-365.

  Argues that the handling of claims of property or rights of information have different rules. Discusses insider trading and the Chiarella case; secret agents and the Snepp case; evidentiary privileges and the Upjohn case.

2205. Easterbrook, Gregg. "Divad," Atlantic Monthly 262/10 (October 1982): 29-39.

  Argues that the US Army's procurement system was highly defective at the time of purchase of the Division Air Defense (DIVAD) system, competitor to the USSR's radar-directed antiaircraft gun. Implications for the intelligence community are mentioned.

2206. Eaton, Cyrus. "Nixon, the FBI and the CIA," New Humanist 89 (July 1973): 86-88.

  Brief discussion of the role of intelligence agencies in the Watergate affair in the early 1970s. The author relates his personal experiences with surveillance by the FBI and the CIA.

2207. Ebon, Martin. "KGB in Transition: The Bakatin Interregnum," International Journal of Intelligence and Counterintelligence 6/3 (Fall 1993): 327-338.

  An account of the transformation of the Soviet KGB into an intelligence service for the Russian state. Particular attention is given to the role of Vadim Bakatin, the former Interior Minister. Major sections discuss the self-created image of Bakatin; Bakatin's family pressures; Bakatin's life in the Party; political pressures; and the net results of Bakatin's moves to change the KGB in the transition to a post-Soviet Russian state.

2208. Echstein, A. M. "Polybius, Aristaenus, and the Fragment on Traitors," Classical Quarterly 1 (1987): 140-162.

  Historical account refuting other scholarship on the reasons for historian Polybius' discussion of traitors. Authors suggests that it was Polybius who reflected upon the controversial behavior of Aristaenus and the Acheaen League in 198 BC.

2209. Ecker, Janet E. "National Security Protection: The Critical Technologies Approach to U.S. Export Control of High-Level Technology," Journal of International Law and Economics 15/3 (1981): 575-604.

  Discusses use of export controls to protect national security, development of the critical technologies list, Department of Defense involvement in the export licensing process, and assessment of the critical technologies approach to licensing.

2210. Eckhart, K. Gouras. "The Reform of West German Data Protection Law as a Necessary Correlate to Improving Domestic Security," Columbia Journal of Transnational Law 24/3 (1986): 597-621.

A discussion of the basic law of data protection, as contained in the BDSG (the German Federal Data Protection Act); the development of West German privacy law; the implications of merging privacy law and the data protection law; and the impact of changes in BDSG as to limiting security agencies' information gathering.

2211. Eckert, Rainer. "Fascist Information System: Sketch of Reporting Practices of the Gestapo, SD, Provincial Leaders, and Upper-Level Bureaucrats and Jurists, with Consideration of Available Published Sources," Bulletin Faschismus/Zweiter Weltkrieg 1-4 (1990): 67-116.

2212. Eckler, A. Ross. "A Rapid Yes-No Computer-Aided Communicator," Cryptologia 1/4 (October 1977): 326-333.

2213. Edgar, Harold and Benno C. Schmidt, Jr. "The Espionage Statutes and Publication of Defense Information," Columbia Law Review 73/5 (May 1973): 929-1087.

Perhaps the most thorough and detailed examination of the espionage laws ever published up to 1973. A frequently cited piece of substantial research importance.

2214. Edgar, Harold and Benno C. Schmidt, Jr. "Curtiss-Wright Comes Home: Executive Power and National Security Secrecy," Harvard Civil Rights and Civil Liberties Law Review 21 (Summer 1986): 349-408.

Argues that the battle between secrecy and openness in public debate about government operations continues, especially with respect to the power of the president in national security matters. Refers to the Pentagon Papers case, CIA activities as to secrecy contracts, travel restrictions, espionage and theft of information, and lessons from the confusion.

2215. Edmondson, Leslie S. "Espionage in Transnational Law," Vanderbilt Journal of Transnational Law 5/2 (Spring 1972): 434-458.

Discusses the historical changes that have affected the ways by which states have viewed espionage, espionage and the law of war, the law of peace, municipal law and executive power, and conclusions.

2216. Edwards, David. "The Requirements of Cryptography," International Defense Review 17/5 (1984): 48-50.

2217. Edwards, Don. "Too Much Power for the F.B.I.," California Lawyer 3/9 (1985): 11-12.

California Congressman Don Edwards argues that the FBI guidelines on agent investigative conduct are inadequate for defending against abuses of domestic security authority.

2218. Edwards, Don. "Reordering the Priorities of the FBI in Light of the End of the Cold War," St. John's Law Review 65 (Winter 1991): 59-84.
Considers the new roles to be played by the Federal Bureau of Investigation after so many years of involvement in the investigation of persons suspected of communist affiliations.

2219. Edwards, Francis. "Reformation and Excommunication," Contemporary Review 243 (September 1983): 133-136.

2220. Edwards, John C. "Playing the Patriot Game: The Story of the American Defense Society, 1915-1932," Studies in History and Society 1/1 (1976): 54-72.
A history of the activities of the American Defense Society and the National Security League to urge presidents from Wilson to Hoover to control internal and external threats to national security. A good background piece.

2221. Edwards, John L. J. "The Canadian Security Intelligence Act 1984--A Canadian Appraisal," Oxford Journal of Legal Studies 5/1 (Spring 1985): 143-153.
A brief review of the history of Canadian intelligence services followed by a review of the central issues discussed in the McDonald Commission report which ultimately led to the CSIS Act of 1984.

2222. Edwards, John Q. "Pearl Harbor and Midway--Breaking the Secrets," Naval Intelligence Professionals Quarterly 2/2 (Summer 1986): 2-4.

2223. Edwards, John Q. "The 'Y1' Story: Opintel in the Post-WWII Navy," Naval Intelligence Professionals Quarterly 6/3 (Summer 1990): 3-6.

2224. Edwards, Owain. "Espionage, Collection of Violins, and Le Bizzarie Universali: A Fresh Look at William Corbett," Musical Quarterly 73/3 (1989): 320-343.
Articles supports the view that their is little evidence to consider the violinist and composer, Willaim Corbett, a spy, despite the repitition of stories that he was involved in espionage actions. Corbett's alleged involvement in spy work has outlived his music.

2225. Edwards, Steve. "Stalking the Enemy's Coast," Proceedings of the U.S. Naval Institute 118/2 (1992): 56-62.

2226. Eftimiades, Nicholas. "China's Ministry of State Security: Coming of

Age in the International Arena," Occasional Papers and Reprints in Contemporary Asian Studies 2/109 (1992): 1-23.

Article is reproduced in Intelligence and National Security 8/1 (1993): 23-43. Identifies the Peoples' Republic of China national intelligence structure, information objectives, and collection operations. Sections discuss framework for analysis; structure; HUMINT operations; and conclusions.

2227. Egerton, B. "Open Secrets," Progressive 45 (November 1981): 18-19.
A comment on S. M. Christensen's article on electronic intelligence.

2228. Egerton, George. "Diplomacy, Scandal and Military Intelligence: The Craufurd-Stuart Affair and Anglo-American Relations 1918-20," Intelligence and National Security 2/4 (October 1987): 110-134.

Examines the Crauford-Stuart in light of new evidence to make possible a distinction of the elements at the center of the controversy. Concludes that the affair was an important diplomatic incident in Anglo-American relations in 1919. The incident, argues the author, demonstrated hazards of misfired intelligence operations.

2229. Eggert, David S. "Executive Order 12,333: An Assessment of the Validity of Warrantless National Security Searches," Duke Law Journal 1983 (June 1983): 611-644.

Argues that warrantless searches violate the Constitution and exceed presidential authority. Contains sources of presidential national security search authority; discussion of the Fourth Amendment; congressional restrictions; conclusions.

2230. Eggleston, Wilfred. "Report of the Royal Commission on Espionage," Queen's Quarterly 53/3 (August 1946): 369-378.

2231. Egorov, A. "The 90th Anniversary of the Birth of Richard Sorge," Voenno-Istoricheshii Zhurnal 10 (1985): 90-92.

2232. Ehlke, Richard. "Political Surveillance and Police Intelligence Gathering--Rights, Wrongs, and Remedies," Wisconsin Law Review 1 (1972): 175-199.

Discusses legal issues pertaining to surveillance of political action groups and the role of law enforcement in the use of intelligence systems. Argues for administrative oversight of law enforcement intelligence operations. Discusses Anderson v. Sills in the context of containing police surveillance and intelligence gathering methods.

2233. Ehlke, Richard and Harold Relyea. "The Reagan Administration Order on Security Classification: A Critical Assessment," Federal Bar News & Journal

30/2 (February 1983): 91-96.

    Detailed discussion of the evolution of the classification system; presidential executive orders; policy reversal in the Reagan administration; impact of the Freedom of Information Act; and overview.

2234. Eichelberger, Charles B. "Army Future Threat," <u>American Intelligence Journal</u> 11/3 (1990): 13-14.

2235. Eichholz, Armin. "Illustrators: Leszek Wisniewski," <u>Novum Gabrauchsgraphik</u> 56 (August 1985): 54-58.

    Contains several illustrations of Wisniewski, including building trades espionage and satellite espionage.

2236. Eickelman, Dale W. "Kings and People: Oman's State Consultative Council," <u>Middle East Journal</u> 38/1 (Winter 1984): 51-71.

2237. Eickelman, Dale W. and M. G. Dennison.   "Arabizing the Omani Intelligence Services: Clash of Cultures?," <u>International Journal of Intelligence and Counterintelligence</u> 7/1 (Spring 1994): 1-28.

    The author discusses the "practical culture" of political intelligence as applied to the Omani intelligence organization; the Internal Security Service (ISS) in Oman's national security apparatus; the foundation myth of the 1970 coup d'etat; intelligence in the post-1970 "new era"; first steps in Omanization; toward an Islamic" intelligence service; and Oman's next generation.

2238. Eidlin, Fred. "Misperception, Ambivalence, and Indecision in Soviet Policy-Making: The Case of the 1968 Invasion of Czechoslovakia," <u>Conflict: An International Journal</u> 5/2 (1984): 89-117.

2239. Eilan, Arieh.   "Conference Diplomacy," <u>Washington Quarterly</u> 4/4 (Autumn 1981): 24-30.

2240. Einstadter, Werner J. "Asymmetries of Control: Surveillance, Intrusion, and Corporate Theft of Privacy," <u>Justice Quarterly</u> 9/2 (June 1992): 285-298.

2241.   Eisenberg, Robin.   "Constitutional Law - Foreign Intelligence - Determining the Legality of Foreign Electronic Surveillance in Ex Parte Proceeding Is Constitutional (United States v. Belfield 692 F.2d 141 D.C. Cir. 1982)," <u>Suffolk Transnational Law Journal</u> 7 (Fall 1983): 493-512.

    Reviews and analyzes the applications of FISA to the Belfield case. Author concludes that the Belfield court could have resolved the conflict between individual privacy and national security in a more equitable fashion by holding an <u>in camera</u> hearing with the accused and his attorney. Other suggestions are offered.

2242. Eisenberg, Stephen A. J. "Fourth Amendment Practice and the Military Rules of Evidence," Army Lawyer (May 1980): 30-39.

A detailed discussion of the military rules of evidence pertaining to searches, including discussion of wiretapping law as it applies in the military context.

2243. Eisenberg, Stephen A. J. "Hercules Unchained: A Simplified Approach to Wiretap, Investigative Monitoring, and Eavesdrop Activity," Army Lawyer (October 1980): 1-17.

2244. Eizenstat, Stuart E. "Loving Israel--Warts and All," Foreign Policy 81 (Winter 1990-1991): 87-105.

Discussion of the highly intricate internal dynamics of Israel and the relationship between Israel and the US. Considers strains on the relationship in recent times as the political climate takes a turn to the right. Mentions the Jonathan Pollard espionage case.

2245. Ekman, Paul. "Mistakes When Deceiving," Annals of the New York Academy of Sciences 364 (June 1981): 269-278.

2246. Ekman, Paul and W. V. Friesen, "Nonverbal Leakage and Clues to Deception," Psychiatry 1 (1969): 88-105.

2247. Ekman, Paul and W. V. Friesen, "Detecting Deception from the Body or Face," Journal of Personality and Social Psychology 29/3 (1974): 288-298.

Authors conducted an experiment to determine the differences in face and body language. Two hypotheses were constructed concerning deception. Concluded that people disguise the face during deception rather than the body.

2248. Ekmecic, Milorad. "The Austro-Hungarian Secret Service and the May Coup in Serbia, 1903," Istorijski Casopis 32 (1985): 209-232.

2249. Eldridge, Justin L. C. "German Human Intelligence and the Conduct of 'Operation Citadel,'" Military Intelligence 15/1 (January-March 1989): 23-25.

German human intelligence in World War II was less than useful and often conflicting, according to the author. This view contradicts that of Reinhard Gehlen.

2250. Eldridge, Justin L. C. "The Myth of Army Tactical Deception," Military Review 70/8 (August 1990): 67-78.

Reviews the problems associated with an effort to reconstruct a deception planning function.

2251. Eldridge, Justin L. C. "The Blarney Stone and the Rhine: 23rd

Headquarters, Special Troops and the Rhine River Crossing, March 1945," Intelligence and National Security 7/3 (July 1992): 211-241.

The special unit of US Army troops and officers was organized to carry out deceptions missions in the Allied drive across Europe in 1944. Discusses Army unit operations, German intelligence analysis (the OKW), and the German I Fallschirm Army.

2252. Eldridge, Justin L. C. "Defense on the Rhine," Military Intelligence 21/1 (January-March 1995): 38-44.

A brief history of the last days of the Third Reich and the role of human intelligence observations in the German defense of the Rhine River. Recounts the defensive strategies of German General Alfred Schlemm, the setting for the battle, German dispositions, the allied plan, the German operational intelligence picture, Army Group H counterattack, General Schlemm's subordinates, and 21st Army Group estimates.

2253. Eliot, C. W. J. "New Evidence for the Speed of the Roman Imperial Port," Phoenix 9 (1955): 76-80.

2254. Elkins, Dan. "The Critical Role of the Resource Manager in the US Intelligence Community," Defense Intelligence Journal 1/2 (Fall 1992): 205-222.

Discusses the intelligence funding process; the federal budget process; and budgetary aspects of intelligence oversight.

2255. Elkins, Dan. "Follow-Up Article: Intelligence Resource Management," Defense Intelligence Journal 2/1 (Spring 1993): 93-96.

Brief update and correction notes pertaining to the previously cited article in the same journal.

2256. Ellicott, J. M. "Theodorus Bailey Meyers Mason: Founder of the Office of Naval Intelligence," U.S. Naval Institute Proceedings 78 (March 1952): 265-267.

2257. Elliff, John T. "Aspects of Federal Civil Rights Enforcement: The Justice Department and the FBI," Perspectives in American History 5 (1971).

2258. Elliff, John T. "The Attorney General's Guidelines for FBI Investigations," Cornell Law Review 69/4 (April 1984): 785-815.

Discusses the role of the Guidelines; the evolution from internal security to criminal intelligence; domestic security-terrorism investigations; preliminary inquiries; investigations based on advocacy; conclusions.

2259. Elliff, John T. "Two Models of Congressional Oversight," Houston Journal of International Law 11/1 (1988): 149-158.

A paper presented by Elliff for Sven Holmes, general counsel and staff director of the Senate Intelligence Committee which enlightened the lessons of the Iran-Contra affair and the issue of congressional oversight of the intelligence community.

2260. Ellin, Joseph S. "Special Professional Morality and the Duty of Veracity," Business and Professional Ethics Journal 1/2 (Winter 1982): 75-90.

2261. Elliot, A. L. "The Calculus of Surprise Attack," Air University Review 30 (March-April 1979): 56-67.
    Contains three main sections: nature of the problem of surprise; theoretical challenge; and beyond theory--the deployment challenge. The author distinguishes the elements of surprise, then suggests that further study of the topic will yield greater understanding of how the policy community can address uncertainty.

2262. Elliot, Ronald D. "Intelligence Communications in Nonconventional Warfare," Signal 44/3 (1989): 57-63.

2263. Elliot, W. J. "The Military Intelligence Departments of England and Germany in Contrast," United Services Magazine 113 (June 1885): 529-559.

2264. Elliott, Douglas P. "Cloak and Ledger: Is the CIA Funding Constitutional?," Hastings Constitutional Law Quarterly 2/3 (Summer 1975): 717-755.
    Discusses the merits of the William Richardson legal challenge to the constitutionality of CIA secret funding in terms of statutory appropriation and accounting provisions, the CIA exception, legislative history, constitutional mandate and prospects for reform.

2265. Elliott, I. "Listening Devices and the Participant Monitor: Controlling the Use of Electronic Surveillance in Law Enforcement," Criminal Law Review 6 (1982): 327-371.

2266. Elliott, James. "The Freedom of Information Act of 1982 (CTH) and Its Effect on Business Related Information and Confidential Information in the Possession of Commonwealth Agencies," Monash University Law Review 14/3 (September 1988): 186-230.
    Discusses the FOIA of Australia in terms of business secrets implications.

2267. Elliott, John D. "Transitions of Contemporary Terrorism," Military Review 57/5 (May 1977): 3-15.
    Several sections are included: background; what is terrorism?; urban guerilla warfare; transnational terrorism; international terrorism; and conclusions.

Argues that terrorism poses a real threat to the world community, thus indicating the need to develop countermeasures.

2268. Elliott, Richard S. "The Export Administration Act of 1979: Latest Statutory Resolution of the 'Right to Export' Versus National Security and Foreign Policy Controls," Columbia Journal of Transnational Law 19/2 (1981): 255-298.
    Contains an historical overview of export controls, export controls process at work, national security and foreign policy controls under the new act, and conclusions.

2269. Elliott, S. R. "The Canadian Intelligence Corps," Canadian Army Journal 17/2 (1963): 122-127.

2270. Ellis, Mark. "Joel Spingarn's 'Constructive Programme' and the Wartime Antilynching Bill of 1918," Journal of Policy History 4/2 (1992): 134-161.

2271. Ellis, Mark. "'Closing Ranks' and 'Seeking Honors': W. E. B. DuBois in World War I," Journal of American History 79/1 (1992): 96-124.

2272. Ellis, Richard N. "Copper-Skinned Soldiers: The Apache Scouts," Great Plains Journal 5 (1966): 51-67.

2273. Ellis, Stephen. "The Censorship of the Official Naval History of Australia in the Great War," Historical Studies 20/80 (April 1983): 367-382.

2274. Ellis, Wilmot E. "Aerial-Land and Aerial-Maritime Warfare," American Journal of International Law 8/2 (April 1914): 256-273.
    Discusses spherical balloons, dirigible balloons and aeroplanes and the impact of international law on their deployments. An excellent early piece for historical studies of air intelligence.

2275. Ellison, Carl M. "A Solution of the Hebern Messages," Cryptologia 12/3 (July 1988): 144-158.

2276. Ellsworth, Robert F. and Kenneth L. Adelman. "Foolish Intelligence," Foreign Policy 36 (Fall 1979): 147-159.
    Discusses the legacy of failures of the US intelligence system, firestorm of criticism in the 1970s, preconceptions and suggestions for reform.

2277. Elmhurst, Thomas. "Air Reconnaissance: The Purpose and the Value," Journal of the Royal United Service Institution 97 (February 1952): 84-86.

2278. Elsmere, Jane S. "The Trials of John Fries," Pennsylvania Magazine of

History and Biography 103/4 (April 1979): 432-445.
    A case study of the events and issues surrounding Fries' trials for treason following his attempts to orchestrate a rebellion against federal excise taxes.

2279. Elton, G. R. "Anglo-French Relations in 1522: A Scottish Prisoner of War and His Interrogation," English Historical Review 78 (April 1963): 310-316.
    An account of the use of spies by King Henry VIII against the French in 1522. A discussion of the early application of warning intelligence and the need for timely and accurate information.

2280. Elton, G. R. "The Law of Treason in the Early Reformation," Historical Journal 11/2 (1968): 211-236.
    Discusses the use of treason laws in the history of British monarchs. The Treason Act of 1352 empowered the king to intervene when a person attempted to leave the church. Through the years the Act was expanded the power of the crown to act against numerous violations.

2281. Emerson, Paul. "Air Force Intelligence--Tomorrow's Headlines Today," Sergeants 19 (June 1981): 22-26.

2282. Emerson, Steven. "No October Surprise," American Journalism Review (March 1993): 16-23.
    Examines the allegation that the 1980 Carter-Reagan presidential campaign included a conspiracy by the Reagan staff to arrange with Iran to withhold the release of US hostages until after the election. Points to the origins of the allegations and suggests that some media people contrived and manipulated the story.

2283. Emerson, Thomas I. "The Doctrine of Prior Restraint," Law and Contemporary Problems 20/4 (Autumn 1955): 648-671.
    Discusses the development of the doctrine; the case of Near v. Minnesota; the nature of prior restraint and examples of its use; and the US Supreme Court's treatment of prior restraint. Concludes that prior restraint is a difficult problem with few applications where military matters arise.

2284. Emerson, Thomas I. "Freedom of Expression in Wartime," University of Pennsylvania Law Review 116/6 (1968): 975-1011.
    Discusses the limitations on freedom of speech during wartime and First Amendment doctrines that may be applied. Includes discussion of the law of treason; general criticism of war or defense effort; expression specifically urging or advising insubordination or resistance to the draft; other forms of protest; and remedies against harassment or dissent.

2285. Emerson, Thomas I. "The Federal Bureau of Investigation and the Bill of

Rights," Yale Review of Law and Social Action 2/2 (Winter 1971): 169-189.
    Discusses operations of the FBI (functions; ideology; scope of operations; subjects of investigation; kinds of information collected; methods; activities beyond collection of data; public relations); disclosures and leaks; harassment; political influence; relations with state and local police; concentration of power; and various issues related to constitutional and statutory authority.

2286.   Emerson, Thomas I.   "Controlling the Spies," Center Magazine 12/1 (January-February 1979): 60-74.
    Discusses ways to limit the powers of the US intelligence agencies. Several sections are included: the Constitution and the role of the courts; self control; principles of legislation; proposed legislation; other related issues; and conclusions.   Presents arguments on the pros and cons of regulating the intelligence community, but the author prefers more regulation.

2287. Emerson, Thomas I. "National Security and Civil Liberties," Yale Journal of World Public Order 9/1 (Fall 1982): 78-112.
    Explores some of the basic elements in the conflict between national security and constitutional liberties.   Includes discussion of espionage and intelligence organizations. Argues the contradiction between a tightly controlled security system and democracies.

2288. Emerson, Thomas I. "Control of Government Intelligence Agencies--The American Experience," Political Quarterly 53/3 (July-September 1982): 273-291.
    Limited to a discussion of the FBI's domestic intelligence operations and their potential for injury to democracy, if unchecked.   Urges more vigorous congressional oversight of these operations.

2289.   Emerson, Thomas I.   "Control of the Intelligence Agencies," Detroit College of Law Review 1983/4 (Winter 1984): 1205-1208.
    A brief summary of a similarly titled article cited in this bibliography. Limited to principles upon which there ought to be legislative reforms.

2290. Emerson, Thomas I. "Comment" [on Bruce Fein's "Access to Classified Information: Constitutional and Statutory Dimensions"], William and Mary Law Review 26/5 (Special Issue 1985): 845-849.
    Offers five observations of the author's belief that Fein overstated the authority of the executive branch to control determination of the public's right to learn of government secrets, including CIA operations.

2291. Emerson, Thomas I. and David M. Helfeld. "Loyalty Among Government Employees," Yale Law Journal 58/1 (December 1948): 1-143.
    A lengthy and detailed treatise on the subject, containing sections on the development of the current loyalty program; the loyalty program; criteria of

disloyalty; the matter of how great is the actual danger; administrative implications of the loyalty program; constitutional limitations on criteria of disloyalty; procedure; and the experiences of other countries. After the FBI director, J. Edgar Hoover, replied to this article (see this bibliography), the authors offered a "Reply by the Authors," Yale Law Journal 58/2 (February 1949): 412-421, in which they claim that Hoover's remarks were merely an appeal to faith in the FBI.

2292. Emerson, Thomas I.; Michael Krinsky; Jonathan Moore; and Anon M. Buitrago. "National Lawyers Guild v. Attorney General," National Lawyers Guild Practitioner 42/2 (Spring 1985): 33-45.
    Excerpts from the NLG's principal factual papers opposing US Department of Justice motion for summary judgment on matters pertaining to alleged FBI conduct against the NLG. Sections address such issues as FBI discreditation of NLG; FBI neutralization of NLG influence; anonymous mailings; FBI contact with lawyers; media manipulation; and punitive and harassing tax treatment.

2293. Emsley, Clive. "The Home Office and Its Sources of Information and Investigation 1791-1801," English Historical Review 94 (July 1979): 532-561.
    An extensive discussion of the development of Home Office spies and informants in late eighteenth century British government and police circles. Suppression activities against radical movements and suspicious organizations are also discussed.

2294. Emsley, Clive. "The French Police in the 19th Century," History Today 32 (January 1982): 23-27.
    Discussion of the framework within which the police emerged from reorganization after Napolean; the role of the sergeants in restoring confidence; the Revolution of 1848; the major reforms of 1854; and the major concerns of 19th century governments for municipal and judicial policing. Role of intelligence is implied.

2295. Enahoro, Peter. "Did the CIA Kill Lumumba?," Africa (October 1975): 11-13.

2296. Endicott, Samuel C. and Thomas L. Sickinger. "IPB During the Siege of Quebec," Military Review 72/5 (1992): 63-72.

2297. Endicott, Stephen L. "Germ Warfare and 'Plausible Denial': The Korean War, 1952-1953," Modern China 5/1 (January 1979): 79-104.
    A review in detail of the question of whether or not the US used germ warfare in the Korean War, and whether possible use was denied in plausible fashion.

2298. Engel, Roger K. "Intelligence Support for Unified and Specified (U & S) Commands," Signal 39 (September 1984): 47-51.

2299. Engel, Roger K. "Imagery Intelligence for U.S. Military Forces," Signal 41 (September 1986): 53-54+.

2300. Englejohn, Earl D. "For a Standard Defector Questionnaire," Studies in Intelligence 7/2 (Summer 1963).

2301. Engels, Donald. "Alexander's Intelligence System," Classical Quarterly 30 (1980): 327-340.
    Discusses Alexander the Great's intelligence system, grouping his organization of the tasks performed into strategic and tactical intelligence. Argues that few field commanders made better use of intelligence than Alexander, thus yielding his successes in battle.

2302. English, Glenn. "Congressional Oversight of Security Classification Policy," Government Information Quarterly 1/2 (1984): 165-176.
    Discussion of the government classification system for secret information. Sections discuss executive orders; the Freedom of Information Act and security classification; atomic energy restricted data; oversight of classification activity; declassification of one document as a case history; and the need for review of the classification system.

2303. English, Malcolm. "Storm Warning," Air Force Monthly 39 (June 1991): 23-27.

2304. English, Raymond. "A Counterintelligence and Counterterrorism Case: CISPES and the FBI," Harvard Journal of Law & Public Policy 12/2 (Spring 1989): 483-494.
    Discusses the FBI's investigation of the Center for Constitutional Rights FOIA litigation to obtain documents on the CISPES organization; conclusions of the inquiry; proposed safeguards; Senatorial comments; reasons for FBI interest in CISPES; and the debate between standards of "clear and present" or "probable and future."

2305. Enker, Arnold N. "Controls on Electronic Eavesdropping - A Basic Distinction," Israel Law Review 2 (1967): 461-480.

2306. Ennes, James M., Jr. "Israeli Attack on U.S. Ship Reveals Failure of C^3," Electronic Warfare/Defense Electronics 13 (October 1981): 60-62+.

2307. Ennis, Michael E. "Knowing the Enemy," Marine Corps Gazette 68 (September 1984): 46-50.

Discusses the historical significance of military intelligence.

2308. Enthoven, Alain C. and K. Wayne Smith. "What Forces for NATO? And From Whom?," Foreign Affairs 48 (October 1969): 80-89.

Discussion of the issue of conventional use of forces by NATO in contrast to the reported buildup of Warsaw Pact nations. Also discusses nuclear weapons role in NATO. Background piece for studies of the symbolic use of forces and intelligence analysis of capabilities.

2309. Entin, Jonathan L. "United States v. Progressive, Inc.: The Faustian Bargain and the First Amendment," Northwestern University Law Review 75/3 (October 1980): 538-569.

Despite the enormity of the potential consequences of publication of information pertaining to the hydrogen bomb, the author argues, neutral principles of First Amendment adjudication should apply to the most hazardous as well as the most mundane forms of speech.

2310. Ephron, Henry D. "An American Cryptanalyst in Australia," Cryptologia 9/4 (October 1985): 337-340.

2311. Ephron, Henry D. "S.I.S./CB," Cryptologia 14/4 (October 1990): 304-330.

An introduction to the Japanese method of superencipherment in World War II.

2312. Eppenstein, Madelaine and Elizabeth J. Aisenberg. "Radio Propaganda in the Contexts of International Regulation and the Free Flow of Information As a Human Right," Brooklyn Journal of International Law 5/1 (Winter 1979): 154-177.

Major intelligence services produce and monitor radio broadcasts. Broadcasts have legal status in international law. Article examines broadcast propaganda, regulatory machinery and harmful interference, jamming, free flow principles, and practice of states concerning dissemination of information.

2313. Epstein, Edward J. "The War Within the CIA," Commentary 66/2 (August 1978): 35-39.

Charges that investigations of 1975 into the affairs of the CIA originated with leaks by CIA Director William Colby. Colby's intention, it is alleged, was to force counter-intelligence director, James Angleton, to retire so that Colby could enlist Soviet volunteers as US intelligence informants.

2314. Epstein, Edward J. "Disinformation: Or, Why the CIA Cannot Verify and Arms Control Agreement," Commentary 74/1 (July 1982): 21-28.

A discussion of general characteristics and strategies of disinformation and deception. Concludes that Soviet disinformation must have been employed to deceive US analysts concerning Soviet missile capabilities in the early 1960s.

2315. Epstein, Edward J. "Who Killed the CIA?: The Confessions of Stansfield Turner," Commentary 80/4 (October 1985): 53-57.
  A discussion of Stansfield Turner's views on secrecy and the compromise of vital CIA secrets as a function of the system of compartmentation.

2316. Epstein, Edward J. "Secrets from the CIA Archive in Tehran," Orbis 31/1 (Spring 1987): 33-41.
  Discusses public knowledge of espionage activities of the CIA and other agencies; losses of secret data; recruitment of spies and defectors; Soviet provocations; creation of moles; use of diplomatic channels.

2317. Epstein, Fritz T. "Between Compiegne and Versailles: Secret American Military Diplomacy in the Period of the Armistice 1918-19, the Role of Colonel Arthur L. Conger," Vierteljahrshefte fuer Zeitgeschichte 3/4 (1955): 412-445.
  This is an approximate translation of a title to an article in German.

2318. Epstein, Michael A. and Stuart D. Levi. "Protecting Trade Secret Information: A Plan for Proactive Strategy," Business Lawyer 43/3 (May 1988): 887-914.
  Considers security plans aimed at protecting trade secrets and warding off industrial espionage.

2319. Erickson, John. "1941," Survey 44/45 (October 1962): 178-183.

2320. Erickson, John. "The Soviet Response to Surprise Attack: Three Directives, 22 June 1941," Soviet Studies 23 (April 1972): 519-559.
  Major sections discuss the German invasion of the Soviet Union; the directive of June 21 and 22, 1941; the military action; belief that the Soviets knew nothing; Stalin's beliefs; Stalin's actions; the opening of the assault; communication devices; other directives; Stalin's realization; and the change in the operation.

2321. Erickson, William H. "Electronic Eavesdropping--Title III," National Journal of Criminal Defense 5 (Spring 1979): 29-33.
  A discussion of US Supreme Court pronouncements in the 1978-1979 session.

2322. Ericson, Paul G. "The Need for Ethical Norms: A Personal Perspective," Studies in Intelligence 36/5 (Winter 1992): 15-18.
  Published first in Spring 1992 in Studies, the author discusses the need for an ethical code of conduct for operations personnel; ethics and the secret

nature of intelligence; and the need for change.

2323. Ericson, Richard V. "Patrolling the Facts: Secrecy and Publicity in Police Work," British Journal of Sociology 40 (June 1989): 205-226.

Relevant to the realm of domestic police intelligence, this article discusses the role of police in Canadian society in connection with the control of sensitive information about crime and criminals. Major sections consider guardians of symbolic order; public culture; reporters; public knowledge of police and crime; and conclusions.

2324. Erik, N. "Croatia's Special Police," Jane's Intelligence Review 7 (1995): 291-293.

2325. Erik, N. "The Croatian Guards Brigades," Jane's Intelligence Review 10 (1995): 438-442.

2326. Ermann, M. David; Alan M. Horowitz; and William B. Waegel. "Labeling as a Weapon in Interorganizational Conflict: The Congress and the CIA, 1947-1975," Sociological Symposium 24 (Fall 1978): 99-116.

Discusses the efforts of the Congress to label and to defend the Central Intelligence Agency at a time when CIA was under investigation for unlawful actions in domestic and foreign environments. See similar article in this bibliography under the third author's name, William B. Waegel.

2327. Ernst, Maurice C. "Economic Intelligence in CIA," Studies in Intelligence 28/4 (Winter 1984): 1-22.

A detailed history of the emergence and development of economic intelligence within the Central Intelligence Agency. Major sections discuss the phases of development; resources and processes; issues and lessons; and the future of economic intelligence.

2328. Errante, Guido. "The German Intelligence Service During the World War," Cavalry Journal 42 (November-December 1933): 16-18.

A brief recounting of the training employed by German military intelligence.

2329. Erskine, Ralph. "GC & CS Mobilizes 'Men of the Professor Type,'" Cryptologia 10/1 (January 1986): 50-59.

2330. Erskine, Ralph. "U-Boats, Homing Signals and HFDF," Intelligence and National Security 2/2 (April 1987): 324-330.

A brief accounting of the role of homing signals transmitted by German U-boats shadowing convoys. Concludes that the Germans failed to integrate and evaluate the information acquired through signal techniques.

2331. Erskine, Ralph. "Naval Enigma: The Breaking of Heimisch and Triton," Intelligence and National Security 3/1 (January 1988): 162-183.
　　　　Major sections discuss first breaks; CRIBS: The contributions of HUTS 4 and 10; Triton and Enigma M4; and conclusions.

2332. Erskine, Ralph. "U-Boat HF WT Signalling," Cryptologia 12/2 (April 1988): 98-106.

2333. Erskine, Ralph. "A Bletchley Park Assessment of German Intelligence of Torch," Cryptologia 13/2 (April 1989): 135-142.

2334. Erskine, Ralph. "The Soviets and Naval Enigma: Some Comments," Intelligence and National Security 4/3 (July 1989): 503-511.
　　　　A detailed discussion of the data supporting or challenging the time period within which the Soviets made effective use of intelligence from the Enigma machine.

2335. Erskine, Ralph. "Naval Enigma: A Missing Link," International Journal of Intelligence and Counterintelligence 3/4 (Winter 1989): 493-508.
　　　　Discusses the uses of Enigma; the naval Enigma indicator system; Bletchley Park's exploitation of the indicator system; initial breaks into naval Enigma; first benefits of special intelligence; U 110--an assessment; and conclusions.

2336. Erskine, Ralph. "The German Naval Grid in World War II," Cryptologia 16/1 (January 1992): 39-51.

2337. Erskine, Ralph. "Ultra and Some U.S. Navy Carrier Operations," Cryptologia 19/1 (January 1995): 81-96.

2338. Erskine, Ralph and Frode Weierud. "Naval Enigma: M4 and Its Rotors," Cryptologia 11/4 (October 1987): 235-244.

2339. Ervin, Sam J. "Privacy and Government Investigations," University of Illinois Law Forum 1971/2 (1971): 137-153.
　　　　This former Senator from North Carolina discusses his concerns for the need for more checks on executive branch abuse by government investigators, in particular the FBI and the Army.

2340. Ervin, Sam J. "Final Answer: The People in Control," Trial 7/2 (February 1971): 13-16.
　　　　The former senator from North Carolina expresses his views on invasion of privacy by government agents.

2341. Escobar, Christy B. "Nongovernmental Cryptology and National Security: The Government Seeking to Restrict Research," Computer Law Journal 4 (Winter 1984): 573-603.

Outlines the scope of controls the government has over nongovernmental research in cryptology in terms of history of cryptology development, international traffic in arms regulation, statutes and the Constitution.

2342. Escue, Lynne. "Coded Contributions: Navajo Talkers and the Pacific War," History Today 41 (July 1991): 13-20.

Describes the actions of the code talkers in World War II in strengthening protection over military communications in Pacific campaign.

2343. Essick, Richard. "CI Support in LIC," Military Intelligence 11/1 (January-March 1985): 38-39.

A brief analysis of the role of counterintelligence in the environment of Low Intensity Conflict.

2344. Etzold, Thomas H. "The (F) Utility Factor: German Information Gathering in the United States, 1933-1941," Military Affairs 39/2 (April 1975): 77-82.

Discusses the mistakes and miscalculations of German intelligence personnel who operated in the United States during the pre-war years.

2345. Eustace, Harry F. "Special Report: Changing Intelligence Priorities," Electronic Warfare/Defense Electronics 10/11 (November 1978): 35-40, 82.

Discusses CIA/DIA partnership; Defense Intelligence Agency; CIA operations; National Reconnaissance Office; National Security Agency.

2346. Eustis, Frederic A., III. "The Glomar Explorer Incident: Implications for the Law of Salvage," Virginia Journal of International Law 16 (Fall 1975): 177-185.

Considers the legal propriety of deep sea salvage by the US for a ship, the Glomar Explorer. Discusses warship immunity; abandonment of warships; and offers conclusions.

2347. Evancevich, Michael. "Defector Possibilities: Past, Present, Future," Military Intelligence 8/4 (1982): 25-26.

2348. Evangelista, Matthew A. "Stalin's Postwar Army Reappraised," International Security 7 (Winter 1982-1983): 110-138.

Major sections discuss early estimates of Soviet conventional forces; Soviet military capabilities; functions and activities of the Soviet Army; and evaluations of the Soviet conventional threat. Exceptionally useful in analyses of post-war demobilization intentions, capabilities, and potential domestic policy propaganda.

2349. Evans, Allan. "Notes on Qualifications for Government Research as Opposed to Academic Study," Studies in Intelligence 2 (Spring 1958).

2350. Evans, Allan. "Intelligence and Policy Formation," World Politics 12/1 (October 1959): 84-91.
     A book review essay of 3 books: Hilsman's Strategic Intelligence and National Security Decisions; Platt's Strategic Intelligence Production; and Ransom's Central Intelligence and National Security.

2351. Evans, Allan. "Against Footnotes," Studies in Intelligence 8/3 (Fall 1964).

2352. Evans, Allan and R. D. Gatewood. "Intelligence and Research: Sentinel and Scholar in Foreign Affairs," Department of State Bulletin 42 (June 1960): 1023-1027.

2353. Evans, D. L. "USMC Civil Affairs in Vietnam, a Philosophical History," Marine Corps Gazette 52 (March 1968): 40-45.

2354. Evans, Gareth. "Natural Security and Civil Liberties: The Role of the Australian Security Intelligence Organization," Australian Foreign Affairs Record 55 (May 1984): 451-455.

2355. Evans, John W. "Research and Intelligence: The Part They Play in Foreign Policy," Foreign Service Journal 34/3 (March 1957): 24-25, 34, 40.
     An early piece on the State Department's Intelligence and Research function, including organization, products, and policy outcomes.

2356. Evans, Joseph C. "U.S. Business Competitiveness and the Intelligence Community," International Journal of Intelligence and Counterintelligence 7/3 (Fall 1994): 353-362.
     Reviews economic intelligence policy; macroeconomic espionage; economic counterespionage; microeconomic espionage; and proposed alternative roles for the CIA in economic intelligence that would constructively and legally aid US business interests.

2357. Evans, Joseph C. "Berlin Tunnel Intelligence: A Bumbling KGB," International Journal of Intelligence and Counterintelligence 9/1 (Spring 1996): 43-50.
     Major sections discuss appraisals of the tunnel traffic; military matters; gossip; disinformation in the tunnel traffic; the finale--more disinformation; and the permissive, bumbling KGB.

2358. Evans, Katherine W. "National Security and the Press: An Interview with CIA Chief William Casey," Washington Journalism Review 8/7 (July 1986): 14-17.

Reflects the comments offered by CIA direction William Casey on national security and the press. Acknowledges some possible errors of the intelligence community in advising the press, but the press has been culpable in the area of national security secrecy breaches.

2359. Evans, Margaret. "T. Gaston Richelieu and the Publicists: Case--Majeste vs. Reason of Monarchy," Proceedings of the Annual Meeting of the Western Society for French History 12 (1984): 33-39.

An historical case study of treason.

2360. Evans, N. E. "Air Intelligence and the Coventry Raid (1940)," Journal of the Royal United Service Institution 121/3 (September 1976): 66-74.

Argues that it had not been the intention of the British to permit the German Luftwaffe to bomb Coventry to save the ULTRA secret, and there is significant evidence to sustain this view.

2361. Evans, Philip R. "The Case of the Cryptic Communique," Studies in Intelligence 27/1 (Spring 1981).

2362. Everett, Glenn S. "Smiley's Fallen Camelot: Allusions to Tennyson in John LeCarre's Cambridge Circus Novels," Papers on Language & Literature 27 (Fall 1991): 496-513.

2363. Everett, H. W. "The Secret War in the Desert," British Army Review 60 (December 1978): 66-68.

2364. Evron, Yair. "Israel and the Atom: The Uses and Misuses of Ambiguity, 1957-1967," Orbis 17 (Winter 1974): 1326-1334.

Majors sections discuss Israel's strategic postures and doctrines up to 1967; development of the nuclear option; and the October 1973 war. Addresses the issue of security of the Middle East and the role of intelligence gathering in Israel's programs and interests.

2365. Ewing, Alfred W. "Some Special War Work" (Parts I & II), Cryptologia 4/4, 5/1 (October 1980 & January 1981): 193-203, 33-39.

2366. Ewing, Joseph H. "The New Sherman Letters," American Heritage 38/5 (1987): 24-32, 34, 36-37, 40-41.

Contains a complete transcript of letters, previously unpublished, written by General Sherman, thus providing new insights into the man and his views on the vital nature of information in the Civil War.

F

"**Cryptologist Extraordinary, Savant, Mentor, Counselor, Friend**"
(William F. Friedman, cited in The American Magic by Ronald Lewin, p. 143)

2367. Fabel, Robin. "St. Mark's, Apalache and the Creeks," Gulf Coast Historical Review 1/2 (1986): 4-22.

2368. Fagelson, David. "The Constitution and National Security: Covert Action in the Age of Intelligence Oversight," Journal of Law and Politics 5/2 (Winter 1989): 275-347.
     Author discusses constitutional powers and limitations relating to foreign policy and interpretation of them by courts. Explores legal and policy bases for covert operations including political accountability and constitutional considerations. Focusses specifically on covert action of Iran-Contra affair including arms sales and legal and policy effects of the transfers.

2369. Fagen, Leslie G. "The Right to Travel and the Loyalty Oath: Woodward v. Rogers (D.D.C. 1972)," Columbia Journal of Transnational Law 12/2 (1973): 387-400.
     Case note discussion on English common law right to travel; American common law right to travel; modern case law on right to travel; and contribution of Woodward v. Rogers. Beverly Woodward was denied a passport. She refused to sign a passport application oath defending and upholding the US Constitution. Thus, she and others sued to prevent the government from such control on passports. Contains English common law of right to travel, sovereign's right to restrict travel, modern case law, and the applications of law to Woodward v. Rogers.

2370. Fagen, Richard R. "The United States and Chile: Roots and Branches," Foreign Affairs 53/2 (January 1975): 297-313.

A discussion of the dynamics of US-Chilean relations during the Nixon administration, including the role played by the CIA operation to undermine the government of Salvadore Allende. Major sections discuss the Nixon-Kissinger White House; two faces of detente; the Italian-French connection; the hemispheric connection; and Chile, the showcase.

2371. Fagen, Richard R. "Calculation and Emotion in Foreign Policy: The Cuban Case," Journal of Conflict Resolution 10/1 (Summer 1985): 58-95.

Discusses Cuban foreign policy, a derivative of Cuban domestic policy. Argues that Cuban foreign policy is non-heroic and essentially non-aggressive. It is legitimized in Castro's regime and well-supported internally. Useful in analytical studies of the strength of Castro's regime.

2372. Fagone, Peter P. "A Message in Cipher Written by General Cornwallis During the Revolutionary War," Cryptologia 1/4 (October 1977): 392-295.

2373. Fagone, Peter P. "The Solution of a Cromwellian Era Spy Message," Cryptologia 4/1 (January 1980): 1-4.

2374. Fagone, Peter P. "Partial Solutions of Swift's 18th Century Mock Latin Passages," Cryptologia 16/4 (October 1992): 327-338.

2375. Faint, Donald R. "Contingency Intelligence," Military Review 94/7 (July 1994): 59-63.

Discusses eight requirements that have the greatest impact on the success or failure of contingency intelligence.

2376. Fairman, Charles. "The Law of Martial Rule and the National Emergency," Harvard Law Review 55/8 (June 1942): 1253-1302.

Develops the history of martial law in English and American settings; national and state constitutional complexities and martial law; various key decisions limiting martial rule at state and federal levels.

2377. Fajans, Arthur E. "Stronger Safeguards for U.S. Technology," Defense/85 (March 1985): 19+.

2378. Fajans, I. "Ravage Repeat Ravage," Infantry Journal 60 (March 1947): 24-33.

A fictionalized account of a wartime operation carried out by the OSS and its partisan agent.

2379. Falcoff, Mark. "Chile: The Dilemma for U.S. Policy," Foreign Affairs

64/4 (Spring 1986): 833-848.

Discusses the complexities of US-Chilean relations, especially in light of the earlier role of the Central Intelligence Agency in the covert action to remove Salvador Allende. Offers suggestions for future US policy with regard to Chile.

2380. Falcoff, Mark. "Head-Hunting: Assassination As a Policy," National Interest 24 (Summer 1991): 103-105.

Brief consideration of the revival of interest in a policy to allow the national security system an option to consider assassination of foreign leaders. Argues against such a policy.

2381. Falconer, T. "Investigative Report: Industrial Espionage," Canadian Business 63/2 (February 1990): 53-57.

2382. Fak, Viiveke. "Cryptographic Protection of Files in an Automated Office," Cryptologia 7/1 (January 1983): 49-62.

2383. Falk, Richard A. "American Intervention in Cuba and the Rule of Law," Ohio State Law Journal 22 (Summer 1961): 546-584.

Discusses the cold war and the rule of law; the pre-Castro Cuban-American relations from 1498-1898; interventions and provocations 1959-1961; legal doctrines pertaining to nonintervention; and a provisional assessment, including comments on the role of the CIA.

2384. Falk, Richard A. "The Nuremburg Defense in the Pentagon Papers Case," Columbia Journal of Transnational Law 13/2 (1974): 208-238.

Examines the question of whether or not international law should govern matters involving the consummation of international crimes versus the exercise of US national law, with reference to the Pentagon Papers case. Applies the Nuremberg defense to the cases of Daniel Ellsberg and Anthony Russo.

2385. Falk, Richard A. "CIA Covert Action and International Law," Society 12/3 (March-April 1975): 39-44.

Discusses international law in relation to covert operations of the American intelligence community and the CIA; the kindred party system; the international law of human rights; the law of war; double standards; and the rationale for compliance.

2386. Falk, Richard A. "President Gerald Ford, CIA Covert Operations, and the Status of International Law," American Journal of International Law 69/2 (April 1975): 354-358.

This is an editorial comment concerning President Ford's remark regarding covert operations at a September 16, 1974 press conference.

2387. Falk, Richard A. "An Alternative to Covert Intervention," Proceedings of the American Society of International Law 69 (1975): 195-200.

Brief discussion of the author's objections to CIA covert activities aimed at the alteration of the dynamics of self-determination in "target" countries. Identifies five specific objections.

2388. Falk, Richard A. "Beyond Internationalism," Foreign Policy 24 (1976): 65-113.

2389. Falk, Richard A. "The United States and Iran's Revolution: Khomeini's Promise," Foreign Policy 34 (1979): 23-28.

2390. Falk, Stanley L. "The Ambush of Admiral Yamamoto," Navy 6 (April 1963): 32-34.

2391. Falk, Stanley L. "The National Security Council Under Truman, Eisenhower, and Kennedy," Political Science Quarterly 79/3 (September 1964): 403-434.

Argues that the creation of the NSC was a necessary adjunct to presidential decision making in the post-war years, and that it will remain an adaptable organization in national security advice giving.

2392. Falk, Stanley L. "Pearl Harbor: A Bibliography of the Controversy," Naval History (Spring 1988): 55-56.

2393. Falkner, Leonard. "A Spy for Washington: John Honeyman," American Heritage 8/5 (August 1957): 58-64.

The story of John Honeyman's service as a spy in the American revolution, in particular, his role in intelligence prior to the Battle of Trenton.

2394. Falkow, Michele G. "Electronic Surveillance: Protection of Privacy Expectations in Participant Monitoring Cases," Annual Survey of American Law-1984 (Winter 1984): 55-93.

Discusses developments in electronic surveillance law, including state court activism; state court adoption of federal doctrine into state law; state court doctrinal change; and state court dependence on federal law.

2395. Fall, Bernard B. "Reappraisal in Laos," Current History 42 (January 1962): 8-14.

Discusses the author's views on the American policy failure in Laos, based essentially on lack of accurate information, unwillingness of US government to face unpleasant facts, and formulation of decisions on idealistic assumptions. Sections discuss the American stake in Laos; policy rationales; policy polarization; and Geneva talks.

2396.   Fall, Bernard B.   "The Theory and Practice of Insurgency and Counterinsurgency," <u>Naval War College Review</u> (April 1965): 21-38.

Major sections discuss the century of "small wars"; recent and non-so-recent cases; insurgency indications; "revolutionary warfare" in South Vietnam; the erroneous criteria of "success"; and conclusions. Reproduced in the same journal 51/1 (Winter 1998): 46-57.

2397.   Fall, Bernard B.   "Insurgency Indicators," <u>Military Review</u> 46/4 (April 1966): 3-11.

A detailed explanation of the Fall Insurgency Nonmilitary Indicators, developed in the Korean War and applied in the early stages of the Vietnam war. The FINI are measures of the level of area military control over local populations.

2398. Fallows, James. "Putting the Wisdom Back Into Intelligence," <u>Washington Monthly</u> 5/4 (April 1973): 6-18.

Discusses foreign relations and their implications for reforms in the CIA. Suggests changes that should be made in the CIA to improve the Agency's overall collection and analytical processes. Addresses strategic, political and economic intelligence missions. Also discusses some embarrassments and future missions of CIA.

2399. Fallows, James. "Crazies by the Tail: Bay of Pigs, Diem and Liddy," <u>Washington Monthly</u> 6/7 (September 1974): 50-58.

The author traces presidential fears of the truth about international events and conditions which often yield politically dangerous adventures.

2400. Fallows, James. "Murder By the Books," <u>Washington Monthly</u> 8/2 (February 1976): 22-24.

An examination of the potential danger posed to CIA case officers as specific information about their identities is revealed publicly.

2401. Fallows, James. "America's High-Tech Weaponry," <u>Atlantic Monthly</u> (May 1981): 21-33.

Discusses various high technology and top secret technologies of the Air Force Tactical Air Command.

2402. Falt, Olavi. "Collaboration Between Japanese Intelligence and the Finnish Underground During the Russo-Japanese War," <u>Asian Profile</u> 4/2 (June 1976): 205-238.

Extensive discussion of the Japanese intelligence service in the early twentieth century; the Finnish opposition movement; first steps toward collaboration in relation to Russo-Japanese split on diplomatic relations; the Paris conference; the Japanese and Finnish campaigns for independence; and the Portsmouth Treaty and the end of collaboration.

2403. Fancher, Paul T. "Military Intelligence in Armor," Armor 71 (September-October 1962): 44-46.

2404. Farber, Daniel A. "National Security, the Right to Travel, and the Court," Supreme Court Review-1981 (1982): 263-290.

Discussion of passport authority of the executive branch following the case of Haig v. Agee. Agee, former CIA case officer, conducted an anti-CIA campaign, and consequently his passport was revoked under a 1966 State Department regulation.

2405. Farley, M. Foster. "The South Carolina Negro in the American Revolution, 1775-1783," South Carolina History Magazine 79/2 (1978): 75-86.

2406. Farnham, Thomas J. "Moses Y. Beach, Confidential Agent," New England Galaxy 12/2 (1970): 25-32.

2407. Farnsworth, Elizabeth. "Chile: What was the U.S. Role? More Than Admitted," Foreign Policy 16 (1974): 127-141.

Discusses US intelligence intervention by covert action into the government of Salvador Allende. Sections discuss the creation of the crisis; the cutback of US economic credit to create economic pressure; the consequences of the blockade; and the aftermath of the coup.

2408. Faroughy, Ahmad. "Repression and Iran," Index on Censorship 3 (Winter 1974): 9-18.

Explanation of the history of imperial repression in Iran; the role of the printing press in the Iranian revolution; the democracy of the Pahlavai dictatorship; the fall of Mossadegh; and the introduction of the police state.

2409. Farquhar, David M. "The Official Seals and Ciphers of the Yuan Period," Monumenta Serica 25 (1966): 362-393.

2410. Farrar, L. L., Jr. "The Limits of Choice: July 1914 Reconsidered," Journal of Conflict Resolution 16 (March 1972): 1-23.

Major sections discuss competing interpretations of the crisis of 1914; conceptualization of the 1914 crisis; the Austro-Serbian stage; the European stage; and the limits of choice. Relevant to intelligence subjects in the use of situation, system, and decision making analyses to conceptualize a problem, including the option of peaceful settlement.

2411. Farrell, James M. "New England's Cicero: John Adams and the Rhetoric of Conspiracy," Proceedings of the Massachusetts Historical Society 104 (1992): 55-72.

2412. Farson, A. Stuart.   "Schools of Thought: National Perceptions of Intelligence," Conflict Quarterly 9/2 (Spring 1989):   52-104.

Discusses the major types of intelligence writing, including fiction, reports, unofficial documents, unauthorized accounts and media commentaries. Summarizes the writing in the US, United Kingdom, former Soviet Union, Israel, South Africa and Canada.

2413. Farson, A. Stuart.   "Security Intelligence versus Criminal Intelligence," Policing and Society 2/2 (1991):   65-87.

Distinguishes between intelligence for national security and criminal offense purposes, then argues for some controls on the criminal intelligence variety.   Distinction is made within the Canadian situation.

2414. Farson, A. Stuart.   "Criminology, Policing and Intelligence Studies," Conflict Quarterly 12/3 (Summer 1992): 7-29.

Considers the proper and necessary role of intelligence in the study of crime.   Major sections discuss the evolution and modernization of the study of criminology; key issues to be discussed in intelligence studies; politicization of crime; disaggregation of policing; and international police cooperation.

2415. Farson, A. Stuart.   "Oversight of Canadian Intelligence: A Revisionary Note," Public Law (Autumn 1992):   377-385.

Discusses the McDonald Commission; legislative responses; the period since 1984; the government's response; and the Permanent Subcommittee on National Security.

2416. Fatouros, A. A.   "Covert Intervention and International Law," Proceedings of the American Society of International Law 69 (1975):   192-216.

This is a collection of brief papers delivered at the April 1975 meeting of the Society.   A. A. Fatouros was chairman.   Papers were delivered by Richard Falk ("An Alternative to Covert Intervention"); David S. Stern ("Covert Intervention and Third World Ideas"); comments by robert Borosage and Tom Farer.   Reporter was D. Christopher Ohly.

2417. Faurer, Lincoln D.   "Information Security," Signal 38/8 (April 1983):   15.

2418. Faurer, Lincoln D.   "NSA Careers," American Intelligence Journal 6/1 (March 1984).

2419. Faust, Scott A.   "The Seizure and Recovery of the Mayaguez," Yale Law Journal 85 (1976):   794-816.

2420. Faust, Scott A.   "National Security Information Disclosure Under FOIA: The Need for Effective Judicial Enforcement," Boston College Law Review 25

(May 1984): 611-643.

Explores the problems presented by the judiciary's failure to play its proper role in the operation of the FOIA. Discusses the role of the President and the Courts in applying the FOIA to national security information.

2421. Favre, David and Matthew McKinnon. "The New Prometheus: Will Scientific Inquiry Be Bound by the Chains of Government Regulation?," Duquesne Law Review 19 (1981): 651-730.

An extensive discussion of the role of government in regulating all forms of scientific inquiry, in particular access to information concerning scientific findings where national security interests are at stake.

2422. Feder, Stanley A. "FACTIONS and Policon: New Ways to Analyze Politics," Studies in Intelligence 31/1 (Spring 1987): 41-57.

Considers the features and values of two new analytical tools for assessing political phenomena. The FACTIONS model was developed by CIA while Policon was developed privately. Includes analysis of the Corazon Aquino conflict in the Philipines.

2423. Feeney, Harold. "The Bay of Pigs Remembered," Naval Intelligence Professionals Quarterly 4/3 (Fall 1988): 1-4.

2424. Feeney, Harold. "The Night of the White House," Naval Intelligence Professionals Quarterly 11/1 (Winter 1995): 1-4.

2425. Feigl, Hubert. "Intelligence Satellites & Disarmament," Europa-Archiv (1980): 555-563.

2426. Fein, Bruce E. "Regulating the Interception and Disclosure of Wire, Radio, and Oral Communications: A Case Study of Federal Statutory Antiquation," Harvard Journal on Legislation 22 (Winter 1985): 47-96.

Discusses the problem of statutory antiquation by focussing on the application of wiretapping statutes to the interceptions of cordless telephone communications. Argues that obsolete statutes empower the judiciary to make substantial legislative amendments and that Congress should take back control of policy in this area.

2427. Fein, Bruce E. "Access to Classified Information: Constitutional and Statutory Dimensions," William and Mary Law Review 26/5 (Special Issue 1985): 805-844.

Explores executive branch constitutional and statutory powers to prevent the disclosure of classified information to the public, to litigants, and the Congress. Discusses the current scheme of information classification; government interests fostered by secrecy; constitutional values impaired by secrecy; access by

Congress to classified information; and appraisal of statutes and case law.

2428. Fein, Bruce E. "The Constitution and Covert Action," <u>Houston Journal of International Law</u> 11/1 (Fall 1988): 53-68.
Rejects the perspective that Congress can intrude in executive branch use of the CIA to conduct covert actions. Argues the author's view on the correctness of the Reagan administration policy on covert action.

2429. Feis, Herbert. "War Came at Pearl Harbor: Suspicions Considered," <u>Yale Review</u> 45/3 (1956): 378-390.
Argues that classified American and British records may hold more information on the strategies of involvement in the war prior to Pearl Harbor. Finds some credence in the view that President Roosevelt allowed for the vulnerability of the Pacific fleet in order to lure the Japanese into the war.

2430. Feis, William B. "A Union Military Intelligence Failure: Jubal Early's Raid, June 12-July 14, 1864," <u>Civil War History</u> 36/3 (September 1990): 209-225.
Details the origins of the Union's Bureau of Information (intelligence service); Lee's deception strategies; importance of railroad protection; and the restructuring of intelligence. Grant was dissatisfied with the intelligence he was receiving.

2431. Feis, William B. "Neutralizing the Valley: The Role of Military Intelligence in the Defeat of Jubal Early's Army of the Valley, 1864-1865," <u>Civil War History</u> 39/4 (December 1993): 199-215.
Demonstrates the role of intelligence on the battlefield and outlines the prominence of intelligence in the Civil War. Intelligence, argues the author, was responsible for the defeat of the Confederacy.

2432. Feistel, Horst. "Cryptography and Computer Privacy," <u>Scientific American</u> 228/4 (May 1973): 15-23.
An introduction to the various techniques of encryption aimed at the protection of privacy in the computer age. Explores different methods developed by IBM, such as the substitution of the alphabet for numeric variables in a multilayer factorial; the binary cipher format; the hidden password; and the pseudorandom number method.

2433. Feistel, Horst; W. Notz; and J. L. Smith. "Some Cryptographic Techniques for Machine-to-Machine Data Communications," <u>Proceedings of the IEEE</u> 63 (1975): 1545-1554.

2434. Feklisov, A. S. "Klaus Fuchs's Achievements," <u>Voenno-Istoricheskii Zhurnal</u>," 12 (1990): 22-29.

In Russian, this is a Soviet account of the work of Klaus Fuchs, infamous Soviet spy and Russian hero. Article is continued in 13 (1991): 34-43.

2435. Feld, M. D. "Information and Authority: The Structure of Military Organization," American Sociological Review 24 (February 1959): 15-22.

General discussion of military plans drafting and execution, and the inherent secrecy of bureaucratic organizations. Secrecy in military operations is both a precautionary measure and an instrument of power. Information flow is a top-down matter in military organizations.

2436. Feldman, Daniel L. "Constitutional Dimensions of the Iran-Contra Affair," International Journal of Intelligence and Counterintelligence 2/3 (Fall 1988): 381-398.

In the wake of the Iran-Contra scandal, this article focusses on legal and political conditions that appear to have manufactured the devious methods of the Reagan administration to conduct covert actions without maneuvering approval in the Congress. The role and actions of the CIA are discussed extensively.

2437. Feldman, Jan. "Trade Policy and Foreign Policy," Washington Quarterly 8/1 (1985): 65-75.

Concerns the problems hindering improvement of US and USSR trade relations and foreign policies.

2438. Feldman, Miles J. "Toward a Clearer Standard of Protectable Information: Trade Secrets and the Employment Relationship," Intellectual Property Law Review 27 (1995): 477-509.

2439. Feldman, Seth. "The Failure of Intelligence Fifty Years After Pearl Harbor," Queen's Quarterly 99/1 (1992): 20-32.

Argues that intelligence failures associated with the Japanese attack on Pearl Harbor existed on both sides, American and Japanese, and the two countries continue to misread each other in modern times.

2440. Felling, Richard L. "Multidiscipline Hostile Intelligence Service Threat," Military Intelligence 7/4 (October-December 1981): 12-15.

Discusses the goals and tactics of foreign intelligence services in gathering information in the US. Argues for a new multi-disciplinary approach to countermeasures.

2441. Fellwock, Perry. "U.S. Electronic Intelligence: A Memoir," Ramparts 11/2 (August 1972).

2442. Fenyvesi, Charles. "Living with a Fearful Memory: Effects of the Washington, D.C. Siege by Hanafi Muslims," Psychology Today 11 (October

1977): 61-64+.

2443. Ferch,, John A. "Ossification in Organizational Cultures," Studies in Intelligence 34/4 (Winter 1990).

2444. Ferguson, James R. "Scientific and Technological Expression: A Problem in First Amendment Theory," Harvard Civil Rights and Civil Liberties Law Review 16/2 (Fall 1981): 519-560.
　　　　Attempts to apply First Amendment law to the broad category of scientific research. Discusses the problem of scientific knowledge as a form of human expression; applies Supreme Court guidelines to determine constitutional status of scientific expression; and applies standard First Amendment doctrine to restrictions on scientific speech.

2445. Ferguson, James R. "Government Secrecy After the Cold War: The Role of the Congress," Boston College Law Review 34/3 (May 1993): 451-491.
　　　　Major topics include secrecy and democratic values of free speech; the executive-legislative conflict in foreign affairs; the political dimension; the press lobby and other special interest groups; congressional expertise in foreign policy and national security; the Intelligence Identities Protection Act; and conclusions.

2446. Ferling, John E. "Joseph Galloway's Military Advice: A Loyalist's View of the Revolution," Pennsylvania Magazine of History and Biography 98/2 (1974): 171-188.
　　　　Discusses the factors involved in defeating the British during the American Revolution, including the role of intelligence in British military failures.

2447. Ferns, H. S. "This Spy Business: Unprofessional Reflections," Encounter 64/5 (May 1985): 54-61.
　　　　Compares US and Canadian intelligence gathering. Recounts implications of spying by and against the Soviet Union.

2448. Ferraro, Renato. "Il Caso Mayaguez," Revista Marittima 3/4 (1978): 47-58.
　　　　The Mayaguez case is summarized in Italian.

2449. Ferrell, Robert H. "Pearl Harbor and the Revisionists," Historian 17/2 (1955): 215-233.
　　　　Concludes that the mystery of Pearl Harbor remains. Argues that no evidence has been offered to establish that the disaster was anything other than an underestimation of Japanese intentions.

2450. Ferris, John P. "The Real Arthur Brett," Recusant History 18/1 (1986): 34-41.

2451. Ferris, John P. "Whitehall's Black Chamber: British Cryptology and the Government Code and Cypher School, 1919-1929," Intelligence and National Security 2/1 (January 1987): 54-91.

A lengthy and detailed study of the British cryptological advancements in the decade of the 1920s. Concludes that Britain's investments in crypto advances in the interwar years paid off significantly during World War II.

2452. Ferris, John P. "The British 'Enigma': Britain, Signals Security and Cipher Machines, 1906-1946," Defense Analysis 3/2 (June 1987): 153-163.

Discusses the history of cipher machines and the improvements in radio and telegraphic communications after the 1920s; cipher machines and radio communication; the 'emergency only' use of radio due to interception vulnerability; the invention of the Enigma machine for secure transmissions; the American influence on cipher machine advancements; and the expansion of cryptography and cryptanalysis.

2453. Ferris, John P. "The British Army and Signals Intelligence in the Field During the First World War," Intelligence and National Security 3/4 (October 1988): 23-48.

An intensive review of the role of British signals intelligence between 1914-1918. Argues that signals intelligence was not the predominant component of army intelligence in the Great War, but it rendered highly successful service.

2454. Ferris, John P. "From Broadway House to Bletchley Park: The Diary of Captain Malcolm Kennedy, 1934-46," Intelligence and National Security 4/3 (July 1989): 421-450.

Examines the diary of Malcolm Kennedy, a former member of the British Government Code and Cypher School which was written during World War II. Evaluates the diary's historical value to intelligence and incorporates Kennedy's background.

2455. Ferris, John P. "The Intelligence-Deception Complex: An Anatomy," Intelligence and National Security 4/4 (October 1989): 719-734.

Examines the history of using, countering, and making effective the deception tool in any political, social or military event. Uses the Allies' deception campaign in World War II to illustrate the principles.

2456. Ferris, John P. "Before 'Room 40': The British Empire and Signals Intelligence, 1898-1914," Journal of Strategic Studies 12/4 (December 1989): 431-457.

Outlines in great detail the role of signals intelligence in the development of Britain's overall intelligence service.

2457. Ferris, John P. "The British Army, Signals and Security in the Desert

Campaign, 1940-42," Intelligence and National Security 5/2 (April 1990):   255-291.

Extensive discussion of the theory and applications of signals intelligence in the British campaigns in North Africa. Observes that the British system of signals and security did not change before and after 1942.

2458. Ferris, John P. "Ralph Bennett and the Study of Ultra," Intelligence and National Security 6/2 (April 1991): 473-486.

Evaluates the role of ULTRA on policy and war strategies in World War II, concluding that the code breaking work was extraordinary in quality and quantity. Outlines the work of historian Ralph Bennett's work to build the sources of ULTRA's value.

2459. Ferris, John P. and Uri Bar-Joseph. "Getting Marlowe to Hold His Tongue: The Conservative Party, the Intelligence Services and the Zinoviev Letter," Intelligence and National Security 8/4 (October 1993): 100-137.

Develops more evidence concerning the historical debate surrounding the authentication of the Zinoviev letter. Considers circumstances of the letter's publication and the actions of Thomas Marlowe. Contains useful history of the British SIS.

2460. Ferris, John P. and Michael I. Handel. "Clausewitz, Intelligence, Uncertainty and the Art of Command in Military Operations," Intelligence and National Security 10/1 (January 1995): 1-58.

Extensive article that explores connection between intelligence, the conduct of military operations, and the art of command. Major sections discuss intelligence and military operations; intelligence and risk-taking; ULTRA in the Pacific; intelligence and modern war; intelligence and operations and the future of war.

2461. Ferruggia, Michael A. "Balancing the Interests of National Security and Free Speech: A Proposed Modification of the English Approach Suitable for Adoption in the U.S.," Touro Journal of International Law 4 (Spring 1993): 217-249.

A law note that considers government imposition of prior restraint upon publications on information relevant to national security. Evaluates several key US and British cases in which prior restraint was the central issue.

2462. Fesler, Mayo. "Secret Political Societies in the North During the Civil War," Indiana Magazine of History 14/3 (September 1918): 183-286.

Discusses in detail the Knights of the Golden Circle; the Sons of Liberty; the Northwest Confederacy of 1864; and treason trials in Indiana.

2463. Fiadjoe, A. K. "Natural Justice Versus National Security: A Comment on the Case of R. v. Secretary of State for the Foreign and Commonwealth Office and Another, Ex Parte the Council of Civil Service Unions and Others," West Indian Law Journal 8 (October 1984): 220-229.

2464. Fialka, John J. "The American Connection: How Israel Got the Bomb," Washington Monthly 10/10 (January 1979): 50-58.

Discusses American assistance to Israel in the emergence of Israel's nuclear capability; assistance of the NUMEC company and later revelations of NUMEC's role; 'loss' of American uranium in 1962 and 1963 to Israel and role of the oil industry; FBI surveillance of key players; and denials of participation.

2465. Fialka, John J. "Intelligence and Policy: What Is Constant? What Is Changing?," Commentary 45 (June 1994): 16-19.

2466. Fiatal, Robert A. "Minimization Requirements in Electronic Surveillance," (2 parts) FBI Law Enforcement Bulletin 56 (May 1987): 25-30.

Provides guidelines to federal officers concerning electronic surveillance. The term "minimization" cites Katz v. U. S., Berger v. N.Y. and Scott v. U. S. Part II recommends procedures for proper minimization in terms of court cases, which include State v. Tucker, U. S. v. Suquet, U. S. v. Kahn, and U. S. vs. De Palma.

2467. Fichtner, David P. "Taking Arms Against a Sea of Enemies: Danish Politics," Studies in Intelligence 36/5 (Summer 1992): 121-124.

A brief discussion of the boundary dispute between Denmark and Norway. Major sections discuss Denmark's preparations; Norway responds; domestic political problems; succession problems; the government responds; and outlook.

2468. Fielder, Leslie A. "Hiss, Chambers, and the Age of Innocence: Who Was Guilty--and of What?," Commentary 12 (1951): 109-119, 597-598.

2469. Fielder, Richard. "British Propaganda Since World War II: A Case Study," Media, Culture and Society 4 (1982).

2470. Fijnaut, Cyrille. "Political Violence and the Police Response in the Netherlands," Conflict Quarterly 12/4 (Fall 1992): 57-66.

Major sections discuss evolution and scope of political violence in the Netherlands, before and after 1970; response of the government in terms of police action, including domestic intelligence activities; and lessons for the future and for Europe.

2471. Filbert, Brent. "Freedom of Information Act: CIA v. Sims--CIA is Given Broad Powers to Withhold the Identities of Intelligence Sources," University of

Missouri-Kansas City Law Review 54/2 (Winter 1986): 332-343.

Briefs the case in terms of facts, analysis of Sims, section 102 (d)(3) of FOIA, definition of intelligence sources, legislative history, practical necessities of intelligence gathering, range of sources, and confidentiality.

2472. Filby, P. William. "Bletchley Park and Berkeley Street," Intelligence and National Security 3/2 (April 1988): 272-284.

A personal account of the author's in intelligence operations in London during World War II, in particular his work associations with some of the biggest names in GCHQ history.

2473. Filby, P. William. "Floradora and a Unique Break into One-Time Pad Ciphers," Intelligence and National Security 10/3 (July 1995): 408-422.

The author's personal account of his work in the World War II activity to break cipher codes.

2474. Filiberti, Edward J. "The Roots of U.S. Counterinsurgency Doctrine," Military Review 68 (January 1988): 50-61.

Discussion of the counterinsurgency campaign of US Army General J. Franklin Bell in the Philipines in the early twentieth century. This is the first time the US public opinion was mustered in favor of military actions in a foreign land, but Bell's harsh tactics contributed also to the decline of US citizen support for the effort.

2475. Filippelli, Ronald L. "Luigi Antonini, the Italian-American Labor Council, and Cold-War Politics in Italy, 1943-1949," Labor History 33/1 (Winter 1992): 102-125.

Discusses the successes and failures of the American Federation of Labor's efforts to intervene in the reconstruction of Italy after World War II. Useful in studies of linkages between labor unions and the political process, perhaps in studies of covert action.

2476. Filippov, P. "'Bugs and Gas' Operation," International Affairs (USSR) 3 (1982): 108-115.

A Soviet view of accusations made by the US accusing the Soviets of using chemical and toxic weapons in Southeast Asia and in Afghanistan. Discusses US production of similar weapons.

2477. Fillenbaum, S. "Prior Deception and Subsequent Experimental Performance: The 'Faithful' Subject," Journal of Personality and Social Psychology 4 (1966): 532-537.

Reports on experiments into the development of suspicion following acts of deception. Directly applicable to the role of deception in intelligence work.

2478. Finder, Joseph. "The Craft of the Espionage Thriller," Writer 108/6 (June 1995): 9-12.

The author, an experienced and respected writer of non-fiction and fiction, shares his ideas about the craft of espionage novel writing.

2479. Fine, David J. "Federal Grand Jury Investigation of Political Dissent," Harvard Civil Rights and Civil Liberties Law Review 7 (1972): 432-499.

An extensive examination of the topic arguing that the original idea of the grand jury as a protector against oppressive prosecution has been trivialized and investigatory powers have been expanded to a point of making them opposite to their original purpose.

2480. Fink, Gary M. "Labor Espionage," Labor's Heritage 1/2 (1989): 10-35.

2481. Finkelman, Paul. "Abraham Lincoln and American Civil Liberties," Pennsylvania Magazine of History and Biography 116/4 (1992): 513-517.

An essay on the subject.

2482. Finnegan, John P. "U.S. Army Counterintelligence in CONUS - The World War I Experience," Military Intelligence 14/1 (January 1988): 17-21.

Discusses the beginnings of Army CI; the threat; the CI response; the Corps of Intelligence Police; MI-3 and MI-4; the formation of the Army's Military Intelligence Division; the Negative Branch; and criticism and conclusions.

2483. Finnegan, John P. "The Union's Blind Eyes: HUMINT in the Civil War," Military Intelligence 15 (July-September 1989): 38-39.

A very brief summary of the human intelligence operations of the Confederacy. Emphasis is given to limitations of Union General George McClelland's intelligence resources.

2484. Finnie, Richard S. "My Friend Stefansson," Alaska Journal 8/1 (1978): 18-25, 84-85.

2485. Finnie, Wilson. "The Smile on the Face of the Tiger," Northern Ireland Legal Quarterly 41 (Spring 1990): 64-73.

A brief discussion of espionage in Northern Ireland.

2486. Fioravanza, Giuseppe. "The Japanese Military Mission to Italy in 1941," U.S. Naval Institute Proceedings 82 (January 1956): 24-31.

Discussion of the mission to Italy to determine German military efficiency; the questions posed by the Japanese in considering the strengths and weaknesses of the Italian navy; the Italian questions of the Japanese concerning standard procedure and cruising performances; and Japanese concepts on torpedo attacks.

2487. Firth, C. H. "Thomas Scot's Account of His Actions as Intelligencer During the Commonwealth," English Historical Review 12 (1897): 116-126.

2488. Firth, C. H. "Cromwell's Instructions to Colonel Lockhart in 1655," English Historical Review 21 (1906): 742-746.

2489. Fischer, Bernd J. "Resistance in Albania During the Second World War: Partisans, Nationalists and the S.O.E.," East European Quarterly 25/1 (Spring 1991): 21-47.
    Major sections discuss the British and the resistance in World War II from 1939 to 1943; organizations of the resistance; the British decision to commit the S.O.E.; and conclusions.

2490. Fischer, Conan. "The SA (Storm Troopers) of the NSDAP: Social Background and Ideology of the Rank and File in the Early 1930's," Journal of Contemporary History 17/4 (October 1982): 651-670.
    A detailed examination of the role of storm troops in the Nazi hierarchy of the Nazi Party; the mobilization of participants, the SPD and KPD; the separation of views; rank and file records; education of the force; competition; and the drastic change from the KPD to the SA after Hitler's election.

2491. Fischer, Elliot. "Language Redundancy and Cryptanalysis," Cryptologia 3/4 (October 1979): 233-235.

2492. Fischer, Elliot. "A Theoretical Measure of Cryptographic Performance," Cryptologia 5/1 (January 1981): 59-62.

2493. Fischer, Elliot. "Measuring Cryptographic Performance with Production Processes," Cryptologia 5/3 (July 1981): 158-162.

2494. Fischer, Elliot. "The Performance of Hellman's Time Trade-off Against Rotor Ciphers," Cryptologia 6/2 (April 1982): 108-114.

2495. Fischer, Elliot. "Uncaging the Hagelin Cryptograph," Cryptologia 7/1 (January 1983): 89-92.

2496. Fischer, J. "Mr. Truman's Politburo," Harper's 202 (June 1951): 29-36.

2497. Fischer, LeRoy H. "David O. Dodd: Folk Hero of Confederate Arkansas," Arkansas Historical Quarterly 37/2 (1978): 130-146.
    This is an account of the legends and facts pertaining to a confederate spy.

2498. Fishbein, Leslie. "Federal Suppression of Leftwing Dissidence in World

War I," Potomac Review 6 (Summer 1974): 47-68.

2499. Fishel, Edwin C. "A Cable from Napoleon," Studies in Intelligence 2 (Summer 1958).
Discusses an interception of a cable message in 1867.

2500. Fishel, Edwin C. "The Mythology of Civil War Intelligence," Civil War History 10/4 (December 1964): 344-367.
A thorough examination of the myths of Civil War intelligence services of the North and South.

2501. Fishel, Edwin C. "Myths That Never Die," International Journal of Intelligence and Counterintelligence 2/1 (Spring 1988): 27-58.
A reprint of the 1964 article, considered one of the most authoritative briefs of the intelligence services of the Union and the Confederacy. Focusses principally on the myths surrounding Lafayette C. Baker and Allan Pinkerton. Discusses seven fundamental myths, espionage, signal intercepts, visual observations, cavalry reconnaissance, interrogation, newspapers, communications intelligence, and the expansion of mythology.

2502. Fishel, Edwin C. "Pinkerton and McClellan: Who Deceived Whom?," Civil War History 34/2 (June 1988): 115-142.
A careful analysis of Pinkerton's role in advising General McClellan, concluding that Pinkerton was a "sycophantic intelligence officer" who worked for a "neurotic general." McClellan, says the author, deceived himself, and he deceived Pinkerton.

2503. Fishel, Reverdy S. "The Attack on the Liberty: "An Accident?"," International Journal of Intelligence and Counterintelligence 8/3 (Fall 1995): 345-352.
A reconsideration of the question of the accidental nature of the 1967 Israeli attack on the U.S.S. Liberty. Discusses evidence of guilt; two books on the subject and their findings; and the question of motivation.

2504. Fisher, D. E. "From Secrecy to Plagiarism," University of Queensland Law Journal 6/1 (August 1968): 60-83.
Discusses Australian trade secrets law and policy.

2505. Fisher, Louis. "Democracy and Secret Funding," Center Magazine 7/2 (March-April 1974): 54-56.
Provides justifications for secret funding of certain government agencies, in particular the Central Intelligence Agency. Discusses some of the historical precedent for secret funding and considers the need for more congressional oversight.

2506. Fisher, Louis. "Confidential Spending and Government Accountability," George Washington Law Review 47 (January 1979): 347-385.

Examines statutory provisions for secret funding of certain federal agency activities, including activities of the intelligence community and the CIA. Discusses constitutional provisions; judicial interpretations; foreign relations and diplomacy; GAO rulings; other confidential accounts; military appropriations; Atomic Energy Commission; defense appropriations; and payments to domestic informers.

2507. Fisher, Louis. "Foreign Policy Powers of the President and Congress," Annals of the American Academy of Political and Social Science 499 (1988): 148-159.

2508. Fisher, Louis. "How to Avoid Iran-Contras: Review Essay," California Law Review 76/4 (July 1993): 919-929.

An extensive review essay pertaining to The President, the Congress and Foreign Policy by E. Muskie, K. Rush and K. Thompson.

2509. Fisher, S. G. "The Suspension of Habeas Corpus," Political Science Quarterly 3 (September 1888): 454-488.

An old classic on the history of habeas corpus. Habeas corpus was introduced as a protection of citizens against the power of government. Suspension of habeas corpus is given lengthy discussion.

2510. Fishman, Clifford S. "The 'Minimization' Requirement in Electronic Surveillance: Title III, The Fourth Amendment, and the 'Dread' Scott Decision," American University Law Review 28/3 (1979): 315-359.

Discusses Title III of the Omnibus Crime Control and Safe Streets Act of 1968; restrictions on eavesdropping and the use of derivative evidence; minimization provision of the Act applicable to searches, seizures and interceptions; Scott v. U. S.; factors affecting minimization; observations and solutions.

2511. Fishman, Clifford S. "Interception of Communications in Exigent Circumstances: The Fourth Amendment, Federal Legislation, and the United States Department of Justice," Georgia Law Review 22 (1987): 1-87.

Explores the Fourth Amendment and warrantless interception of communication; Title III and court-ordered interceptions; the emergency surveillance provision; the roving intercept provision; comparative practices in Canada, Israel and West Germany; and evaluation and conclusions.

2512. Fishman, Clifford S. "Electronic Tracking Devices and the Fourth Amendment: Knotts, Karo, and the Questions Still Unanswered," Catholic University Law Review 34 (Winter 1985): 277-395.

Discusses beepers (direction finders) and the Fourth Amendment; installation and monitoring procedures; application of the Karo rule and unanswered legal questions; calls for legislation and offers a proposal.

2513. Fisk, Charles E. "The Sino-Soviet Border Dispute: A Comparison of the Conventional and Bayesian Methods for Intelligence Warning," Studies in Intelligence 16/1 (Spring 1972): 53-62.

Following subjects are covered: the conventional method of intelligence warning; the Bayesian method of intelligence warning; a criterion for comparison of probability estimates; the Sino-Soviet experiment; and an evaluation of the Bayesian method.

2514. Fitch, Stephen D. "The FBI Library Awareness Program: An Analysis," Intelligence and National Security 7/2 (April 1992): 101-111.

Appears to justify the FBI's approach to its investigation in the Reagan era of certain university libraries. Major sections discuss the efforts of the Soviets to obtain American scientific data; the sensitive but unclassified issue; controversy over the Library Awareness Program; and the Cuckoo's Egg and the American Library Association.

2515. Fitzgerald, Mary C. "Russian Views on Electronic Signals and Information Warfare," American Intelligence Journal 15/1 (Spring-Summer 1994): 47-48.

2516. Fitzgerald, Peter L. "Executive Agreements and the Intent Behind the Treaty Power," Hastings Constitutional Law Quarterly 2/3 (Summer 1975): 757-771.

Argues that the expansion of executive agreements represents an unconstitutional expansion of executive authority. May be useful in discussions of liaison agreements between US and other intelligence services.

2517. FitzGibbon, Constantine. "'The Ultra-Secret': Enigma in the War," Encounter 44 (March 1975): 81-85.

A book review essay of F. W. Winterbotham's The Ultra Secret, in particular a criticism of the book author's clumsy writing style.

2518. FitzGibbon, Constantine. "Spies, Spies, Spies," Encounter 45 (August 1975): 69-75.

Discusses a British game similar to chess called Attaque used to explore the dangers of espionage and the disposable quality of espionage agent work. Covers the work of Czechoslovak intelligence and definitions of types of spies. Ends with a critique of Miles Copeland's book, The Real Spy World.

2519. FitzGibbon, Thomas N. "Privacy Protection for Programming: Is Modifying Satellite Descramblers a Violation of the Wiretap Law?," Washington

University Law Quarterly 70 (Winter 1992): 231-241.

A brief note reviewing the case of U. S. v. Hux in which the Eighth Circuit concluded that federal wiretap law did not proscribe modification of satellite descramblers to receive encrypted programming. Also reviews holdings in other federal circuits.

2520. Fladeland, Betty. "New Light on Sara Emma Edmonds, Alias Franklin Thompson," Michigan History 47/4 (December 1963): 357-362.

2521. Flanagan, Stephen J. "Managing the Intelligence Community," International Security 10/1 (Summer 1985): 58-95.

Discusses the structure of the intelligence community; the intelligence production cycle in theory and practice; the president's role in managing the community; the director of central intelligence; coordination of the requirement process; the production of national estimates.

2522. Flannery, Christopher. "Intelligence Betrayals," Journal of Contemporary Studies 7/1 (Winter 1984): 45-56.

Reflects upon the intelligence failure in the Granada invasion as an indicator of the need to maintain a strong intelligence service. Cuts in the intelligence resources responsible for the number of hostile agents operating in the US. Reflects upon several espionage cases.

2523. Flannery, John P. "Commercial Information Brokers," Columbia Human Rights Law Review 4/1 (Winter 1972): 203-235.

Discusses the commercial acquisition, storage, retrieval and exchange of private information. Author stresses the need to implement controls upon access to such information.

2524. Fleishman, Joel L. and Arthur H. Aufses. "Law and Orders: The Problem of Presidential Legislation," Law and Contemporary Problems 40/3 (Summer 1976): 1-45.

Detailed discussion of the application of the constitution's mandate of separation of powers to the matter of presidential executive orders. Author concludes that such orders are devices for avoiding conflict with the Congress, but that they tend, with some exceptions, to undermine democratic norms. E. O.'s have served specific ends in the areas of national security and intelligence.

2525. Fleistraman, Avion. "The Symbolic World of 'The Secret Agent,'" English Literary History 32 (1965): 205-211.

2526. Fleming, Jonathan. "The Espionage and Relate Offenses Sections of S.1: Recipe for an Official Secrets Act," Criminal Justice Journal 1/1 (Spring 1976): 5-43.

Argues that S.1 is repressive legislation bordering on an "official secrets act" similar to the British model. Considers the British secrecy law, subchapter C of S.1 on espionage and related offenses, present espionage laws, and anti-leak laws.

2527. Fleming, Thomas. "The Big Leak," Aerospace Historian 38/8 (December 1987): 64-71.

A discussion of the newspaper publication on December 4, 1941, of The Rainbow Five Plan and the various theories of how the leak was accomplished. Refers also to Stevenson's A Man Called Intrepid and infers that Intrepid orchestrated the leak to bring US into the war.

2528. Fleming, Thomas J. "Washington Meets a Test," American Heritage 14/2 (February 1963): 56-59, 79-81.

A brief history of one of George Washington's first intelligence successes in surveilling French forces and equipment in 1754.

2529. Fleming, Thomas J. "The True Story of the Message to Garcia," American Legion Magazine 93/3 (1972): 20-25+.

2530. Fleming, Thomas J. "The Loyalist Americans Who Lost the War," Yankee 40 (April 1976): 96-101, 122-126.

2531. Flemming, R. "CIA Charter: Operating Under the Cloak of Night," Encore 9 (August 1980): 18-19.

2532. Fletcher, Catherine B. "Evolution of the Modern American Spy Novel," Journal of Contemporary History 22/2 (April 1987): 319-331.

Discusses in detail the spy novels of the 1960s, 1970s and 1980s. Notes the changes in the relationships between the superpowers. Observes that the modern novel is more directly related to the real political situation in the world than in previous decades of such work. Examines and comments on the novels of Bickley, McCarry, and Tyler. Argues that the trend had been toward realism in the novel, adding in terrorist threats and technologies in modern novels.

2533. Fletcher, George P. "The Case for Treason," Maryland Law Review 41/2 (Spring 1982): 193-208.

Discusses the historical background of treason, the role of allegiance, the gravamen of treason in thoughts and actions, and lessons from cases of treason.

2534. Fletcher, J. "Intelligence: A Principle of War," Army Journal (December 1969): 3-10.

See next citation.

2535. Fletcher, J. "Intelligence: A Principle of War," Military Review 50/8 (August 1970): 52-57.

Reproduced from Army Journal (Australia), this piece discusses the role of intelligence in warfare. Sections discuss distinctive characteristics; seeking information; variations of principles; morals; reason for principles; concentration and surprise; and experiences of others.

2536. Fletcher, Joseph F. "Mass and Elite Attitudes About Wiretapping in Canada: Implications for Democratic Theory and Politics," Public Opinion Quarterly 53 (Summer 1989): 225-245.

Observes the support for wiretapping by the Canadian elite, a position in opposition to the general attitude ordinary citizens. The articles reveals findings of a study of mass and elite viewpoints on the role of wiretapping in fighting crime, especially white collar crime.

2537. Flexner, James T. "Benedict Arnold: How the Traitor Was Unmasked," American Heritage 18/6 (October 1967): 6-15.

Account of Arnold's plan to deliver West Point to the British and his associations with George Washington. Suggests that Arnold had redeeming qualities aside from his treacherous actions to work against Washington.

2538. Flicke, Wilhelm F. "The Lost Keys to El Alamein," Studies in Intelligence 3/3 (Fall 1959).

2539. Flicke, Wilhelm F. "The Early Development of Communications Intelligence," Studies in Intelligence 3/4 (Winter 1959).

2540. Flore, Romano. "Introduction to Electronic Intelligence," Military Technology 12 (May 1988): 113-114+.

2541. Flores, David A. "Export Controls and the U.S. Effort to Combat International Terrorism," Law and Policy in International Business 13/2 (1981): 521-590.

Discusses scope of the problem of terrorism; status of terrorist acts under international law; evolution of US antiterrorism policy proposals to use export controls to combat terrorism; and conclusions.

2542. Florini, Ann M. "The Opening Skies: Third Party Imaging Satellites and U.S. Security," International Security 13/2 (Fall 1988): 91-123.

An extensive review of the role and operations of satellites owned by private companies and smaller, non-super power countries.

2543. Flowe, Benjamin H., Jr. "An Overview of Export Controls on Transfer of Technology to the U.S.S.R. in Light of Soviet Intervention in Afghanistan,"

North Carolina Journal of International Law and Commercial Regulation 5/3 (Spring 1980): 555-573.

Discusses facts concerning President Carter's embargo, a brief history of Soviet needs for foreign technology, a catalogue of US law governing technology transfer, and US policy objectives.

2544. Floyd, Denis R. "Annotated Bibliography in Conventional and Public Key Cryptography," Cryptologia 7/1 (January 1983): 12-24.

2545. Fluhr, Arthur J. "An "EPIC" Undertaking: El Paso Intelligence Center," Police Chief (June 1979): 56-57.

A brief description of space age technology applied in the war on drugs, illegal aliens and alien smuggling. Discusses primary functions of the EPIC system; operations; and related functions and considerations.

2546. Flyged, J. "Espionage and Sabotage in Sweden During World War II," Sociologisk Forskning 29/3 (1992): 35-53.

2547. Fogel, David. "China: Trial By the Masses," Corrections Magazine 3/4 (1977): 42-44.

Discussion of prison rehabilitation methods in the Peoples' Republic of China upon release of several prisoners, among them some spies from the Chiang Kai-shek era.

2548. Foglesong, David S. "Xenophon Kalamatiano: An American Spy in Revolutionary Russia?," Intelligence and National Security 6/1 (January 1991): 154-195.

Chronicles the life of espionage of an American businessman, Kalamatiano. Major sections discuss his family background; political orientation; recruitment for intelligence service; information gathering activities; his work for the 'Information Service'; travel to Samara; interrogation; trial; and associations with Poole and the Lockhart plot.

2549. Foitzik, Jan. "Revolution and Democracy: Social Democrats' Plans for Wartime Action and Postwar Transition in Germany, 1943-45," Internationale Wissenschaftliche Korrespondenz zur Geschichte der Deutschen Arbeiterbewegung 24/3 (1988): 308-342.

2550. Foley, Timothy D. "The Role of the CIA in Economic and Technological Intelligence," Fletcher Forum of World Affairs 18/1 (Winter-Spring 1994): 135-145.

Lays out several background issues in the CIA's role in economic and technical intelligence; discusses the issue of collect versus not to collect; addresses the question of for whom to collect; and reviews the role of counterintelligence and the problem of foreign economic spying.

2551. Fomin, V. T. "From the History of the Preparation of German Fascist Aggression Against the USSR," Voprosy Istorii 8 (August 1966): 77-87.
     In Russian, a discussion of the German deception plan for Barbarossa.

2552. Fontaine, Roger; Cleto DiGiovanni, Jr.; and Alexander Kruger. "Castro's Specter," Washington Quarterly 3/4 (Autumn 1980): 3-27.
     Argues that the Jimmy Carter administration was ineffective in dealing with Soviet influence in Fidel Castro's Cuba. Draws on documents from several US foreign policy community agencies including the Central Intelligence Agency.

2553. Fontanella, Joseph and Michael R. Rip. "A Window on the Arab-Israeli 'Yom Kippur' War of October 1973: Military Photo-Reconnaissance from High Altitude and Space," Intelligence and National Security 6/1 (January 1991): 15-89.
     Outlines US and Soviet reconnaissance prior to 1973. Major sections discuss reconnaissance in prior conflicts; Soviet photo reconnaissance satellites; deployment of US and Soviet systems; military photo recon and the war.

2554. Fonteneau, General. "French Participation in the War of Independence 1776-80," Revue Histoire des Armees 3/4 (1976): 47-85.

2555. Fontrodena, Mariano. "When the Third Reich Planned to Invade Spain," Historia y Vida 25/291 (1992): 61-67.

2556. Fonzi, Gaeton. "Who Killed JFK?," Washingtonian (November 1980): 157-186.
     The charge is made by the author that CIA's David Atlee Phillips was involved in the Kennedy assassination plot. The author and the magazine were sued.

2557. Foot, Michael R. D. "Was SOE Any Good?," Journal of Contemporary History 16/1 (January 1981): 167-181.
     Establishment and dismantling of the British Special Operations Executive, the SOE-SIS conflicts, SOE operations in World War II, and overall assessment of SOE contributions.

2558. Foot, Michael R. D. "Military Leverage on the 'Secret' Services," Encounter 65 (June 1985): 61-63.
     A brief description of the Special Air Service function in British intelligence; SAS purpose and achievements; the Special Operations Executive (SOE); and the treachery in the Kim Philby espionage case.

2559. Foot, Michael R. D. "Uses and Abuses of Intelligence," Intelligence and National Security 2/1 (January 1987): 184-190.

A review article critically evaluating several books addressing the manner of integration of intelligence into British government in the early twentieth century.

2560. Foot, Rosemary. "The Sino-American Conflict in Korea: The US Assessment of China's Ability to Intervene in the War," Asian Affairs 14/2 (1983): 160-166.

2561. Foot, Rosemary. "New Light on the Sino-Soviet Alliance: Chinese and American Perspectives," Journal of Northeast Asian Studies 10/3 (1991): 16-29.

2562. Ford, Franklin L. "The Twentieth of July in the History of the German Resistance," American Historical Review 51 (Winter 1945-1946): 609-626.

2563. Ford, Franklin L. "Der 20 Juli," Die Amerikanische Rundschau 3/11 (1947): 5-17.

2564. Ford, Harold P. "Piety and Wit: Bad Effects of Covert CIA Activity," America 132 (January 1975): 10-11.

Suggests that covert actions frequently achieve such bad effects that consideration ought to be given to terminating their application in foreign affairs. Reflects upon the detrimental effects of covert action in Chile, arguing that the main element of foreign political action should be overt.

2565. Ford, Harold P. "A Tribute to Sherman Kent," Studies in Intelligence 24/3 (Fall 1980).

Reprinted from an earlier issue of the journal, (Winter 1958): 1-8. An account of the life of Sherman Kent, Yale University student and professor of European history and 19th century French politics.

2566. Ford, Harold P. "The Primary Purpose of National Estimating," Studies in Intelligence 35/3 (Fall 1991).

2567. Ford, Harold P. "The US Government's Experience with Intelligence Analysis: Pluses and Minuses," Intelligence and National Security 10/4 (1995): 34-53.

A summary of the historical events and circumstances that contributed to the emergence and expansion of US intelligence community analytical capabilities. Offers brief conclusions on the future needs of the intelligence analytical staff.

2568. Ford, Harold P. "Thoughts Engendered by Robert McNamara's 'In Retrospect,'" Studies in Intelligence 39/5 (1996): 95-109.

A book review essay on Robert MacNamara's <u>In Retrospect</u>. Sections discuss divided opinions and debates; pressures to intervene; a game of dominoes; McNamara's middle course; private pessimism; the impact of intelligence; skepticism over strategy; the Sigma wargames; upside-down history; widening the war; months of decision; Army resistance; alarming doubts; the fallout from Pleiku; receptivity to CIA judgments; high marks and hindsight; McNamara's lessons; and intelligence officers' lessons.

2569. Ford, James R. "The HP 67/97 Cryptograph," <u>Cryptologia</u> 3/1 (January 1979): 43-49.

2570. Ford, Ronnie E. "Tet Revisited: The Strategy of the Communist Vietnamese," <u>Intelligence and National Security</u> 9/2 (April 1994): 242-286.

Applying new Vietnamese documents, the author examines communist analyses with respect to the Tet offensive. Author concludes that Vietnamese regular forces met their objectives, but local forces did not adapt to the dynamic tactical situation. A different outcome could have been expected had local and regular army forces been adequately fused.

2571. Ford, Ronnie E. "Intelligence and the Significance of Khe Sanh," <u>Intelligence and National Security</u> 10/1 (January 1995): 144-169.

Argues that US intelligence analysts failed to understand North Vietnam's true mindset and intent at either Khe Sanh or in the war in general. Draws on documents obtained from Hanoi to aid his conclusion that Hanoi viewed military power as only one element in a nation's ability to fight. A similar but shortened version of this article appears in <u>American Intelligence Journal</u> 16/2&3 (Autumn-Winter 1995): 63-68.

2572. Ford, Ronnie E. "Secret Army, Secret War, Recent Disclosures and the Vietnam War: The Significance of American 34 Alpha and DESOTO Operations with Regard to the Tonkin Gulf Resolution," <u>Intelligence and National Security</u> 11/2 (April 1996): 364-373.

A book review essay concerning <u>Secret Army, Secret War: Washington's Tragic Spy Operation in North Vietnam</u> by Sedgwick Tourison.

2573. Ford, Thomas R. "Tactical Reconnaissance," <u>Air University Review</u> 12/3 & 4 (Winter 1960 & Spring 1961): 120-129; 78-86.

2574. Forde, H. M. "Strategic Censorship in World War II," <u>Military Review</u> 28/6 (June 1948): 32-36.

2575. Foregger, Richard. "The First Allied Aerial Reconnaissance Over Auschwitz during World War II," <u>Journal of Military History</u> 8 (June 1989): 31-32.

2576. Foreman, Allan. "A Bit of Secret Service History," Magazine of American History 12/4 (1884): 323-331.

2577. Foreman, Gene. "Confidential Sources: Testing the Readers' Confidence," Social Responsibility: Business, Journalism, Law, Medicine 10 (1984): 24-31.
        Offers six principle guidelines for reporters who require the use of confidential sources in order to perform their journalistic assignments. Mentions intelligence matters and the Watergate affair.

2578. Forgus, Silvia P. "Soviet Subversive Activities in Independent Estonia, 1918-1940," Journal of Baltic Studies 23/1 (1992): 29-46.

2579. Forrest, Ian. "This Was Hitler's Spy Squadron," RAF Flying Review 16 (November 1960): 17-18+.

2580. Forsyth, C. "Judicial Review, the Royal Prerogative and National Security," Northern Ireland Legal Quarterly 36 (1985): 25-47.

2581. Forsyth, W. S. and R. Safavi-Naini. "Automated Cryptanalysis of Substitution Ciphers," Cryptologia 17/4 (October 1993): 407-420.

2582. Forsythe, David P. "Democracy, War, and Covert Action," Journal of Peace Research 29/4 (November 1992): 385-395.
        Reviews the litany of American covert actions from the early 1950s to the mid 1980s and offers specific reasons for the resort to such actions to resolve US national security dilemmas.

2583. Fortugno, John P. "Intelligence: A Fleet Learning Deficiency," U.S. Naval Institute Proceedings (January 1985): 123-124.

2584. Forward, John; Rachelle Canter; and Ned Kirsch. "Role-Enactment and Deception Methodologies: Alternative Paradigms?," American Psychologist (August 1976): 595-604.
        Discusses recent conceptualization in role playing and simulation for research applications. Discusses the general inutility of certain types of role playing and deception experiments.

2585. Foster, Caxton C. "Vowel Distribution as a Clue to Vowel Identification," Cryptologia 14/4 (October 1990): 355-362.

2586. Foster, Caxton C. "A Comparison of Vowel Identification Methods," Cryptologia 16/3 (July 1992): 282-286.

2587. Foster, Caxton C. "Secret Musical Codewords," Cryptologia 19/2 (April

1995): 216-220.

2588. Foster, Donald L. "The Man Who Was," Army 33/8 (1983): 55-56.
A brief discussion of British deception plans before the invasion of Sicily in 1943.

2589. Foster, H. Schuyler, Jr. "The Official Propaganda of Great Britain," Public Opinion Quarterly 3 (April 1939): 263-271.
Discusses various applications of British internal propaganda: the milk campaign; physical fitness; air raid precautions; the British Council; and foreign language broadcasts.

2590. Fowler, Robert H. "Was Stanton Behind Lincoln's Murder?," Civil War Times Illustrated 3 (August 1961): 4-23.

2591. Fox, Neil I. "On Technological War," Air University Review 36/1 (November-December 1984): 79-83.
Addresses the subject of intelligence in modern warfare.

2592. Fox, Richard G. "Salisbury Affair: Special Branches, Security and Subversion," Monash University Law Review 5/4 (June 1979): 251-270.
Presents the findings of an Australian investigation into intelligence services. Excellent baseline article for understanding the operations and approaches of the Australian intelligence services.

2593. Francillon, Rene J. "Spying the Earth," Air International (October 1981): 186-187.

2594. Franck, Thomas M. "The Constitutional and Legal Position of the National Security Adviser and Deputy Adviser," American Journal of International Law 74/3 (July 1980): 634-639.
Briefly outlines the legal position, then argues that Congress has an important role in asserting its right to hold inquests into the uses and abuses of executive foreign policy decisions.

2595. Franck, Thomas M. and James J. Eisen. "Balancing National Security and Free Speech," New York University Journal of International Law and Politics 14/2 (Winter 1982): 339-369.
Addresses the issues in U. S. v. Snepp in terms of costs and benefits of the Snepp decision, calibration of the remedies and a proposed new remedy, and conclusions. Calls for legislation to repeal the Snepp decision.

2596. Frank, Larry J. "The United States Navy v. the Chicago Tribune," Historian 42/2 (February 1980): 284-303.

An account of the Tribune's battle with the Navy over allegations by the Navy that publication of US knowledge of Japanese plans to attack Midway Island revealed US capabilities to compromise further Japanese plans. Later it was learned that the censorship of the Tribune had more to do with other publications than the Midway issue.

2597. Frank, Seymour J. "The Conspiracy to Implicate the Confederate Leaders in Lincoln's Assassination," Mississippi Valley Historical Review 40/4 (March 1954): 629-656.
　　　A brief history of the circumstances Secretary of War Edwin Stanton post-war charge that Jefferson Davis and other Southern leaders conspired to assassinate Lincoln.

2598. Frank, Willard C., Jr. "Politico-Military Deception at Sea in the Spanish Civil War, 1936-39," Intelligence and National Security 5/3 (July 1990): 84-112.
　　　Major sections discuss deception and maritime arms traffic; clandestine naval intervention; and conclusions. Concludes that deception depends on a mix of several different factors.

2599. Frankel, M. "My Spy Can Lick Your Spy: Consideration of G. Lonsdale's Spy and the Penkovskiy Papers," Atlantic Monthly 217/4 (April 1966): 103-108.
　　　The author's observations of the Gordon Lonsdale and Oleg Penkovskiy espionage and defection cases.

2600. Franks, C. E. S. "Parliamentary Control of Security Activities," McGill Law Journal 29/2 (March 1984): 326-339.
　　　Considers three views of parliamentary control over security activities: the McDonald Commission; the Federal Government; and the Special Senate Committee on the Canadian Security Intelligence Service.

2601. Franks, C. E. S. "Political Control of Security Activities," Queen's Quarterly 91/3 (Autumn 1984): 565-577.
　　　Discusses reasons why security activities do not fit neatly into democratic societies; the problems of political control of intelligence agencies; and Parliament and the McDonald Commission.

2602. Franks, C. E. S. "The Canadian Parliament and Intelligence and Security Issues," Indian Journal of Political Science 46/1 (January-March 1985): 49-62.

2603. Franks, Renae A. "The National Security Agency and Its Interference With Private Sector Computer Security," Iowa Law Review 72 (May 1987): 1015-1039.
　　　Discussion of the conflict between the National Bureau of Standards and

the National Security Agency over what constitutes sensitive or national security information in the realm of cryptography.

2604. Fraper, P.   "Cabinet Secrecy and War Memoirs," History 70 (October 1985):   397-409.

An account of the problems encountering publishing war memoirs in terms of the 1911 Official Secrets Act, in particular the reports of the Radcliffe Committee of Aivy Councillors on Ministerial Memoirs of 1976.

2605. Fraser, T. G.   "Germany and the Indian Revolution, 1914-18," Journal of Contemporary History 12 (1977):   255-272.

Discussion of the role of foreign dissident groups supported by foreign nations and intelligence organizations in destabilizing potential enemies. Suggests that Germany was perhaps the originator of modern techniques employed in using subversive groups in the revolution in India.

2606. Frazer, Robert W.   "The Ochoa Bond Negotiations of 1865-1867," Pacific Historical Review 11 (December 1942):   397-414.

2607. Fredericks, Brian and Richard Wiersema.   "Battlefield Techint: Support of Operations DESERT SHIELD/DESERT STORM," Military Intelligence 18/2 (April-June 1992):   13-19.

Major sections discuss doctrine; force structure; initial deployment; JCMEC established; Desert Storm; challenges encountered; successes; lessons learned; and recommendations.   Argues for more training of soldiers on identification of enemy equipment.

2608. Freedman, Eric M.   "Freedom of Information and the First Amendment in a Bureaucratic Age," Brooklyn Law Review 49 (1983):   835-855.

This is a constitutional law commentary on FOIA cases in the Second Circuit. Of interest is the discussion of Weberman v. National Security Agency.

2609. Freedman, Joel.   "Minutes of a Secret Caucus Within the Socialist International," World Affairs 147/1 (Summer 1984):   37-42.

The meeting minutes were found in Grenada, including the plan of the Cubans, the Nicaraguans, the El Salvador MNR, the RP of Chile, the PNP of Jamaica and the NJM of Grenada to form a front of resistance against the US.

2610. Freedman, Lawrence.   "The War of the Falkland Islands, 1982," Foreign Affairs 61/1 (Fall 1983):   196-210.

Discusses the invasion of the Falkland Islands by the Argentine forces and the British military response. Good background piece for studies of the role of intelligence in the war.

2611.   Freedman, Lawrence.   "Soviet Active Measures: Distinctions and Definitions," Defense Analysis 1 (1985): 101-110.
Discusses the techniques of political warfare in recorded human history. Argues that the Soviets use secret long term covert political operations to strengthen their goals in overt propaganda.

2612.   Freedman, Lawrence.   "Intelligence Operations in the Falklands," Intelligence and National Security 1/3 (September 1986): 309-335.

2613. Freeman, J. Leiper. "Investigating the Executive Intelligence: The Fate of the Pike Committee," Capitol Studies 5/2 (Fall 1977): 103-118.
Explores the Pike Committee's results from investigations into executive power and Executive Branch use of intelligence services.

2614. French, David. "Spy Fever In Britain, 1900-1915," Historical Journal 21/2 (June 1978): 355-370.
A scholarly examination of espionage in Britain at the turn of the century, including the responses of newspapers and the Parliament.

2615. French, David. "The Origins of the Dardanelles Campaign Reconsidered," History 68/223 (June 1983): 210-224.
A case study of the World War I campaign in which, argues the author, the British government misperceived the power and determination of the Turks.

2616. French, David. "Sir John French's Secret Service on the Western Front, 1914-15," Journal of Strategic Studies 7/4 (December 1984): 423-440.
A detailed accounting of GHQ intelligence in the early phases of World War I. The British learned from their mistakes in World War I and went on to develop a sophisticated intelligence system prior to World War II.

2617. French, David. "Watching the Allies: British Intelligence and the French Mutinies of 1917," Intelligence and National Security 6/3 (July 1991): 573-592.
Discussion of the British analysis of French domestic behavior in World War I. Major sections discuss what British policy makers knew about internal affairs in France and how French policy was made in World War I; the sources held by the British, methods for analyzing information, and impact of British analyses on policy.

2618.   Frenznick, David A.   "The First Amendment on the Battlefield: A Constitutional Analysis of Press Access to Military Operations in Grenada, Panama, and the Persian Gulf," Pacific Law Journal 23 (January 1992): 315-359.
Considers the traditional role of the press in wartime; restrictions on press access to the battlefield, a violation of the First Amendment; and conclusions.

2619. Frickles, Michael D.   "Executive Order 12,356: The First Amendment Right of Government Grantees," Boston University Law Review 64 (March 1984): 447-519.

Examines constitutional basis for a presumption that the federal government may restrict publication of federally funded research. Major sections discuss the Executive Order 12,356; the First Amendment and scientific speech; the constitutionality of the Order; and a proposal for improving constitutional infirmities.

2620. Fried, John H. E.   "War-Exclusive or War-Inclusive Style in International Conduct," Texas International Law Journal 11/1 (Winter 1976):   1-61.

Urges a fundamental distinction between the two concepts in the title, discusses the Vietnam experience, the Mayaguez incident (including dimensions of CIA involvement), fear of repetition of the Pueblo incident, and conclusions.

2621. Friedberg, A. L.   "Britain and the Experience of Relative Decline," Journal of Strategic Studies 10/3 (1987):   331-362.

2622. Friedheim, Eric.   "Welcome to Dulag Luft," Air Force Magazine 28 (September 1945):   16-17, 73.

Contains information on the German methods of interrogation.

2623. Friedlander, Robert A.   "The Mayaguez in Retrospect: Humanitarian Intervention or Showing the Flag?," St. Louis University Law Journal 22 (1978): 601-613.

A summary of the Mayaguez incident in 1975; legal theories of self-help and self-defense in international incidents; humanitarian intervention. A good background piece for studies of national security threats arising without substantial warning at the tactical level.

2624. Friedlander, Robert A.   "Mr. Casey's 'Covert War': The United States, Nicaragua, and International Law," University of Dayton Law Review 10/2 (Winter 1985):   265-293.

Addresses the origins and implications of US involvement in Nicaragua. Asks whether the US is practicing power politics and whether or not the Monroe Doctrine should apply to the controversy.

2625. Friedman, Norman.   "The Falklands War: Lesson Learned and Mislearned," Orbis 26/4 (Winter 1983):   907-940.

The Falklands war is an excellent demonstration of the uses of intelligence and problems associated with the Rapid Deployment Force. Suggests that the British navy won this war in spite of its errors, in particular the casualties it suffered from having no friendly base and vulnerability to air attacks.

2626. Friedman, Richard. "A Stone for Willy Fisher," Studies in Intelligence 30/4 (Winter 1986): 19-30.

'Willy Fisher' was a cover name for one of the Soviet Union's most famous spies, Rudolf Abel.

2627. Friedman, Richard S. "QRT-dora: Epitaph for a Spy," Military Intelligence (December 1981): 58-61.

A history of the espionage activities of Sandor Rado ("Dora"). Rado aided the Soviets against the Nazis before and during World War II.

2628. Friedman, Robert I. "Harvard, the C.I.A. and the Middle East," Present Tense 13/3 (1986): 6-9.

A discussion of the controversy at Harvard over Harvard's acquisition of Central Intelligence Agency funds to hold a conference on Arab and Israeli relations.

2629. Friedman, William F. "Edgar Allen Poe, Cryptographer," American Literature: Journal of Literary History 8/3 (November 1936): 266-280.

This article suggests that Poe was relatively unsophisticated in the realm of cryptography.

2630. Friedman, William F. "Edgar Allan Poe, Cryptographer," American Literature: Journal of Literary History 8/3 (November 1936): 266-280. (Reprinted in Signal Corps Bulletin 97 (July-September 1937): 41-53; "Addendum," 98 (October-December 1937): 54-75.

Discusses Poe's dubbings in cryptography; contains a facsimile of Jefferson's invention of the cylindrical cipher machine.

2631. Friedman, William F. "The Use of Codes and Ciphers in the World War and Lessons to be Learned There From," Signal Corps Bulletin 101 (July-September 1938): 35-48.

2632. Friedman, William F. "The Cryptanalyst Accepts a Challenge," Signal Corps Bulletin 103 (January-March 1939): 24-36.

A discussion of various challenges, including those of John Davys and William Blair.

2633. Friedman, William F. "Jules Verne As Cryptographer," Signal Corps Bulletin 108 (April-June 1940): 70-107.

Provides an analysis of Jules Verne's cryptograms found in three stories.

2634. Friedman, William F. "Information Regarding Cryptographic Systems Submitted for Use by the Military Service and Forms to be Used," Cryptologia 15/3 (July 1991): 247-257.

2635. Friedman, William F. "A Brief History of the Signal Intelligence Service," (Unknown publicly available source; published as a government report in 1942; parts may have appeared in internal Signal Corps journals after World War II).

2636. Friedman, William F. and Charles Mendelsohn. "Notes on Code Words," American Mathematical Monthly (August-September 1932): 394-409.

2637. Friedman, William F. and Elizabeth S. Friedman. "Acrostics, Anagrams and Chaucer," Philogical Quarterly (1959).

2638. Frisbee, John L. "Electronic Warfare: Essential Element of Deterrence," Air Force Magazine 55/7 (1972): 36-41.

2639. Frisbee, John L. "Those National Intelligence Estimates," Air Force Magazine 60/2 (1977): 4.

2640. Fritz, F. "Soviet C2 Information Systems: Theories, Concepts, Evaluations," Signal 43 (December 1988): 35-42.

2641. Fritz, Paul S. "The Anti-Jacobite Intelligence System of the English Ministers, 1715-1745," Historical Journal 16 (June 1973): 265-289.
      The establishment and maintenance of a counter espionage system that was used by the Stuarts against the Jacobites. The success of the system lay in the penetration of the Jacobite organization by a group of vigilant ministers.

2642. Fritchey, Clayton. "The C.I.A. Under Fire," Harper's 233 (October 1966): 37-38+.
      A brief overview of the Central Intelligence Agency as an organization, and something of its early experience with oversight by the Foreign Relations Committee.

2643. Frolik, Jan. "Outline of Organizational Development of State Security Forces of the Corps of National Security, 1949-1989," Sbornik Archivnl ch Pracl 41/2 (1991): 447-510.

2644. Fromkin, David. "Daring Amateurism: The CIA's Social History," Foreign Affairs 75/1 (January-February 1996): 165-172.
      This is a book review essay pertaining to two books on the internal dynamics of CIA: Jeffrey T. Richelson, A Century of Spies: Intelligence in the Twentieth Century; Evan Thomas, The Very Best Men: Four Who Dared: The Early Years of the CIA.

2645. Frucht, K. "We Were a P.W.I. Team," Commentary 1 (January 1946): 69-76.

A personal account of a prisoner of war interrogator and the role he and his team played in learning information essential to the defeat of Hitler.

2646. Fry, Michael G. "On the Track of Treachery - The Assault on Normandy," International Perspectives 18/1 (1989): 3-8.

2647. Fry, Michael G. and Miles Hochstein. "Epistemic Communities: Intelligence Studies and International Relations," Intelligence and National Security 8/3 (July 1993): 14-28.
Considers such topics as intelligence studies; what divides the study of international relations from intelligence status?; and propositions and proposals.

2648. Fry, Michael G. "The Uses of Intelligence: The United Nations Confronts the United States in the Lebanon Crisis, 1958," Intelligence and National Security 10/1 (January 1995): 59-91.
The Lebanon crisis of 1958 is treated in detail. Major sections consider the decision to create the UNOGIL and its consequences; a matter of evidence through intelligence; Hammarskjold, assumptions and goals; Hammarskjold's accomplishments; and conclusions on intelligence matters.

2649. Frye, Alton. "Space Arms Control," Bulletin of the Atomic Scientists 21/4 (1965): 30-33.

2650. Fuchida, Mitsuo. "I Led the Air Attack on Pearl Harbor," U.S. Naval Institute Proceedings 78/9 (September 1952): 939-952.
The author's personal account of his participation in the air attack on Pearl Harbor. Mentions collection of intelligence data in preparation for the attack.

2651. Fuchida, Mitsuo and Masatake Okumiya. "Prelude to Midway," U.S. Naval Institute Proceedings 81/5 (May 1955): 505-513.
The authors' personal recollections of the planning and reasoning of the Japanese attack at Midway. Recognizes the Japanese defeat at Midway was a function of a full alert of the US Navy fleet. The Japanese were unaware of the level of alertness and that their plans had been compromised.

2652. Fukuda, Teizaburo. "A Mistaken War," U.S. Naval Institute Proceedings 94/12 (December 1968): 42-47.
A discussion of the impossibility of Japanese avoidance of World War II. The author had been a naval attache dating back to 1908.

2653. Fukudome, Shigeru. "Hawaii Operation," U.S. Naval Institute Proceedings 82/12 (December 1955): 1315-1331.

2654. Fukuyama, Francis. "Nuclear Shadowboxing: Soviet Intervention Threats in the Middle East," Orbis 25/3 (Fall 1981): 579-605.

    Major sections discuss six threats to intervention; reasons for Soviet caution in the Middle East; intervention threats outside the Middle East; and the past and future. Useful in discussions regarding contingent circumstances of conflict between major powers.

2655. Fulcher, John. "Comes the Teaching Machine," Studies in Intelligence 6/4 (Winter 1962).

2656. Fuld, L. M. "Competitor Intelligence: Can You Plug the Leaks?," Security Management 33/11 (August 1989): 85-87.

    Brief discussion of methods for controlling industrial spying.

2657. Fuller, Graham E. "Intelligence, Immaculately Conceived," National Interest 26 (Winter 1991-1992): 95-99.

    A brief review of the analytical process at the Central Intelligence Agency as carried out by the Directorate of Intelligence (DI).

2658. Fuller, Linda. "Fieldwork in Forbidden Territory: The U.S. State Department and the Case of Cuba," American Sociologist 19/2 (Summer 1988): 99-120.

    Raises several questions about persistent US policy of precluding social scientists and others from freely travelling to Cuba to conduct field research. Mentions various restrictive measures against such travel and the role of the CIA in earlier retaliatory measures against Cuba.

2659. Funk, Arthur L. "American Contacts with the Resistance in France 1940-1943," Military Affairs 34/1 (February 1970): 15-21.

    A detailed accounting of the American Office of Strategic Services organization in Europe beginning in 1942, and the interface between OSS and the British Special Operations Executive.

2660. Funk, Arthur L. "Churchill, Eisenhower and the French Resistance," Military Affairs 45/1 (February 1981): 29-33.

    Discusses Winston Churchill's insistance in 1944 on the matter of aiding the French resistance fighters, including the role of the SOE in the operation. Observes differences between the Churchill and Dwight Eisenhower methods of deploying the SOE.

2661. Funk, Arthur L. "Bibliographical Note on English-Language Books and Documents on Espionage and Secret Operations," Revue d'Histoire de la Deuxieme Guerre Mondiale et des Conflits Contemporains 34/133 (1984): 75-78.

    Discusses the impact and functions of espionage during World War II.

2662. Funk, Roger. "National Security Controls in the Dissemination of Privately Generated Scientific Information," UCLA Law Review 30/2 (December 1982): 405-454.

Discusses the current statutes [espionage statutes; Atomic Energy Act of 1954; Arms Export Control Act of 1976; Export Administration Act of 1979; and Intervention Secrecy Act of 1951] on controls on privately generated scientific information; vagueness, excessive means and prior restraint in national security statutes; abandonment of statutory controls on privately held information; and strategies for reform.

2663. Furash, Edward E. "Industrial Espionage," Harvard Business Review 37/6 (November-December 1959): 6-12; 148-174.

Reports findings of an extensive study of corporate opinions about the existence and practices of industrial spying. Excellent beginning source for those interested in the topic.

2664. Furnas, Wendell J. "'Early Days' of Intelligence Detailing BUPERS," Naval Intelligence Professionals Quarterly 4/1 (Winter 1988): 3-6.

2665. Furnas, Wendell J. "POW, Shanghai, 1942," Naval Intelligence Professionals Quarterly 9/3 (Summer 1993): 5-8.

2666. Furner, J. O. "The Intelligence War," Army Journal (September 1970): 3-8.

2667. Furse, G. A. "Intelligence Services," United Service Magazine 2 (1986): 216.

2668. Fursenko, A. A. "Alexander Hamilton and the British Secret Service," Voprosy Istorii 3 (1966): 210-215.

2669. Furst, Alan. "Autumn Deceptions," Intelligence Quarterly 2/3 (1986): 4-5.

This article attempts to apply the principles of deception in intelligence to the realm of professional football.

2670. Furst, Alan. "The Listeners of World War II," Intelligence Quarterly 3/1 (1987): 1.

A brief acknowledgment of the Navy listening post at Bainbridge Island, Maryland.

2671. Fusca, James. "Space Surveillance," Space/Aeronautics 41 (June 1964): 92-103.

Useful as reference material regarding early days of space surveillance.

2672. Futterman, Stanley N. "Toward Legislative Control of the C.I.A.," New York University Journal of International Law and Politics 4/3 (Winter 1971): 431-458.

Consideration of the legal status and authority of the Central Intelligence Agency, relationship of CIA to the Congress, control over appropriations, limitations on CIA activities, suggestions for greater control, and conclusions.

G

2673. Gabel, Christopher R. "Books on Overlord: A Select Bibliography and Research Agenda on the Normandy Campaign, 1944," Military Affairs 48/3 (July 1984): 144-148.

Offers of list of books and subjects pertaining to Operation Overlord planning and execution and calls for further historical research.

2674. Gabis, Stanley T. "Political Secrecy and Cultural Conflict: A Plea for Formalism," Administration and Society 10/2 (August 1978): 139-175.

Discusses the difficulties of maintaining secrecy in government operations.

2675. Gaddis, John L. "NSC 68 and the Problem of Ends and Means," International Security 4/4 (1980): 164-170.

Discusses the NSC 68 study and the scope of its recommendations on international policies in the Kennedy and Johnson administrations. Argues that policy must be based on verified intelligence rather than personal agendas.

2676. Gaddis, John L. "Comments," [regarding article by Melvyn P. Leffler, "The American Concept of National Security and the Beginnings of the Cold War, 1945-48"] American Historical Review 89/2 (1984): 382-385.

Gaddis argues that Leffler placed too much importance on George

Kennan and the Policy Planning Staff in national security affairs. Sections include discussion of the Policy Planning Staff, budgetary problems, the Soviet threat, and analysis of the international system.

2677. Gaddis, John L. "Expanding the Data Base: Historians, Political Scientists, and the Enrichment of Security Studies," International Security 12/1 (Summer 1987): 3-21.

Argues that the communication channels between policy makers are not always clear and replete with messages. Cites examples from the Nixon presidency, particularly involving the National Security Council and Henry Kissinger. Author argues that there is a disparity between policy makers and academic scholars of foreign affairs in terms of their command over information.

2678. Gaddis, John L. "Intelligence, Espionage, and Cold War Origins," Diplomatic History 13/2 (Spring 1989): 191-212.

Further discussion of the article was published in Diplomatic History 14 (Spring 1990): 199-204. Argues that the "intelligence revolution," beginning in 1945 and the opening of the Cold War, calls for substantially more careful examination in order to provide a complete picture of the role of intelligence in the era. Offers an agenda for future research.

2679. Gaddy, David W. "Gray Cloaks and Daggers," Civil War Times Illustrated 14/4 (July 1975): 20-27.

Discusses the Confederate Secret Service Bureau in terms of its limitations and advantages as a new intelligence organization.

2680. Gaddy, David W. "William Norris and the Confederate Signal and Secret Service," Maryland Historical Magazine 70/2 (Summer 1975): 167-188.

Discusses Norris's efforts as a member of the confederate government, including his various operations to incorporate intelligence tactics into domestic and foreign contexts.

2681. Gaddy, David W. "Secret Communications of a Confederate Navy Agent," Manuscripts 30/1 (Winter 1978): 49-55.

Considers the Naval affairs of the confederate government as they occurred in London and Paris during the last years of the Civil War. Major emphasis is on the use of cyphers.

2682. Gaddy, David W. "Confederate Spy Unmasked: An Afterword," Manuscripts 30 (Spring 1978): 94.

Only two paragraphs in this piece, but it reveals the author's discovery of the name of a Confederate spy by using tombstone records.

2683. Gaddy, David W. "John Williamson Palmer: Confederate Agent,"

Maryland Historical Magazine 83/2 (Summer 1988): 98-110.
        Discusses Palmer's use of deception in his role as spy an propagandist for the Confederacy.

2684. Gaddy, David W. "Reflections on Come Retribution," International Journal of Intelligence and Counterintelligence 3/4 (Winter 1989): 567-573.
        A review essay concerning the book by William A. Tidwell with James O. Hall and David W. Gaddy. The subtitle is "The Confederate Secret Service and the Assassination of Lincoln."

2685. Gaddy, David W. "Rochford's Cipher: A Discovery in Confederate Cryptography," Cryptologia 16/4 (October 1992): 347-353.

2686. Gaddy, David W. "The Cylinder-Cipher," Cryptologia 19/4 (October 1995): 385-391.

2687. Gaj, Krzysztof. "Polish Cipher Machine - LUCIDA," Cryptologia 16/1 (January 1992): 73-80.

2688. Galcotti, M. "Militarizing Russia's Internal Security," Jane's Intelligence Review 9 (1995): 387-388.

2689. Galen, Justin. "Intelligence: The Reagan Challenge," Armed Forces Journal International (January 1981): 72+.
        Useful in studies of changes in intelligence agencies in Reagan era.

2690. Galeotti, Mark. "Razvedchiki - Have the Reconnaissance Troops Regained Their Edge?," Jane's Soviet Intelligence Review 2/1 (November 1990): 490-492.
        Brief discussion of Soviet reconnaissance troop units reinstated in the Afghanistan war.

2691. Galeotti, Mark. "Organized Crime in Moscow and Russian National Security," Low-Intensity Conflict and Law Enforcement 1/3 (1992): 237-252.
        Discusses the expansion of organized crime in the former Soviet Union, and in particular Moscow. Useful article for those studying applications of intelligence concerns to the emerging realm of new forms of international organized crime.

2692. Galich, Iu and N. Kocheshkov. "Naval Strength and the U.S. Space Program," Morskoi Sbornik 4 (1979): 68-71.
        In Russian, this piece discusses the importance of naval communications via satellites to test surface and beneath surface craft. This is an approximate translation of the title.

2693. Galich, Manuel. "Playa Giron from Buenos Aires Twenty Years Ago," Casa de las Americas 21/125 (1981): 54-65.

2694. Gallagher, Kathleen T. "Electronic Surveillance," Georgetown Law Journal 71 (December 1982): 397-417.
This is the 12th annual survey of criminal procedure, 1981-1982 concerning electronic surveillance.

2695. Galagher, Michael G. "Defense of Adverse Actions Against Federal Civilian Employees Occasioned by the Revocation of a Security Clearance," Army Lawyer (June 1983): 18-30.
Discussion of the need for close coordination of managers, personnel officers and attorneys in the defense of adverse actions before the Merit Systems Protection Board.

2696. Gallagher, Edward J., III and Robert M. Hollis. "Federal Decisions on the Constitutionality of Electronic Surveillance Legislation," American Criminal Law Review 11 (1973): 639-694.
An extensive review of Title III to the Omnibus Crime Control and Safe Streets Act of 1968; the original wiretap case in Olmstead v. United States; the effect of prior legislation on electronic surveillance; the modern constitutional standards; legislative responses; the states; the federal courts and the constitutionality of Title III; and judicial controls.

2697. Gallagher, Nancy E. and Dunning S. Wilson. "Suppression of Information or Publisher's Error?: Kermit Roosevelt's Memoir of the 1953 Iranian Counter-coup," Middle East Studies Association Bulletin 15/1 (1981): 14-17.
Discusses the publication problems regarding Roosevelt's book on the coup in Iran, in particular the first edition reference to British intelligence as the British Petroleum Corporation. A revised edition was published that corrected the error to avoid a lawsuit.

2698. Gallagher, Tom. "Reflections on Electronic Deception," American Intelligence Journal 12/1 (Winter 1991): 51-53.

2699. Gallati, Robert R. J. "Legal Aspects of Industrial Espionage," Journal of Security Administration 6/2 (January 1984): 31-40.
Contains overview of the industrial espionage problem and argues for more legal contains on the dissemination of information. The author was a member of the New York State intelligence bureau.

2700. Gallego Serrra, Fermin. "The Greatest Secret of World War II: Station X Uncovered," Historia y Vida 19/217 (1986): 118-125.

2701. Gallina, Charles and John J. Guenther. "C³I in the Marine Corps," Signal 38 (October 1983): 39-40.

2702. Galloway, Alec. "A Decade of U.S. Reconnaissance Satellites," Interavia 27 (April 1972): 376-380.
    A brief discussion of photographic satellites.

2703. Galloway, Russell W., Jr. "The Uninvited Ear: The Fourth Amendment Ban on Electronic General Searches," Santa Clara Law Review 22 (Fall 1982): 993-1026.
    This is one of several articles in this issue which addresses Fourth Amendment issues following Boyd v. United States.

2704. Galnoor, Itzhak. "Government Secrecy: Exchanges, Intermediaries, and Middlemen," Public Administration Review 35/1 (January-February 1975): 32-42.
    Discusses the controversy surrounding the classification of government information. Major sections discuss the information marketplace; practical arrangements for exchanges; the established lobby; the less-established lobby; the non-established lobby; and the unwritten rules of government secrecy.

2705. Galnoor, Itzhak. "The Politics of Public Information," Society 16 (May-June 1979): 20-30.

2706. Galvan, Robert N. "The Role of American Intelligence in the Global Economy," International Journal of Intelligence and Counterintelligence 8/3 (Fall 1995): 353-357.
    A brief argument in favor expanded intelligence community involvement in supporting American business interests. See an opposing viewpoint in the same issue by Larry Valero.

2707. Ganesan, Ravi and Alan T. Sherman. "Statistical Techniques for Language Recognition: An Introduction and Guide for Cryptanalysts," Cryptologia 17/4 (October 1993): 321-366.

2708. Ganesan, Ravi and Alan T. Sherman. "Statistical Techniques for Language Recognition: An Introduction and Guide for Cryptanalysts," Cryptologia 18/4 (October 1994): 289-331.

2709. Ganfield, David R. II. "Protecting Trade Secrets: A Cost-Benefit Approach," Illinois Bar Journal 80 (December 1992): 604-607.

2710. Ganley, Michael. "CIA Sees Soviet Strategic Buildup, But Critics Slam Reports Release," Armed Forces Journal 123/1 (August 1985): 14, 16.
    Focusses on conclusions drawn in a National Intelligence Estimate

claiming a sharp buildup in Soviet nuclear arms. Discusses the political battle between Republicans and Democrats regarding CIA testimony on the subject.

2711. Ganong, Elizabeth A. "Involuntary Confessions and the Jailhouse Informant: An Examination of Arizona v. Fulminante," Hastings Constitutional Law Quarterly 19 (Spring 1992): 911-935.
Discusses history of test used by Supreme Court to determine whether confession is voluntary and admissible, Fifth Amendment due process and right against self-incrimination as it relates to involuntary confessions, the subject case decision, how use of informants can result in involuntary confessions and can lead to unreliable confessions, and summarizes protections provided for defendants under current law.

2712. Gans, Daniel. "Neutron Weapons: Solution to a Surprise Attack?" (Parts I and II), Military Review (January and February 1982): 19-37; 55-72.
Major sections include discussion of weaknesses of forward defenses, implications of modern war, characteristics of fission and ER weapons, war gaming the covering forces, and the Battle of the Black Horse Regiment.

2713. Gantt, Larry O. N., II. "An Affront to Human Dignity: Electronic Mail Monitoring in the Private Sector Workplace," Harvard Journal of Law & Technology 8 (Spring 1995): 345-425.

2714. Garcia, Alfredo. "The Right to Counsel and Informants," Case and Comment 92 (May-June 1987): 21-25.
Considers the problems faced by government investigative agencies when such agencies employ informants. Discusses the deceptive methods used by law enforcement agencies to extract confessions. Analyses several Supreme Court decisions reviewing such methods.

2715. Garcia-Mora, A. "Treason, Sedition and Espionage as Political Offenses Under the Law of Extradition," University of Pittsburgh Law Review 26 (1964): 65-97.
Major sections include discussion of the nature of treason, sedition and espionage under constitutional and statutory laws; treason, sedition and espionage under extradition law; and recent limitations on treason, sedition and espionage as political crimes.

2716. Gardiner, L. Keith. "Dealing with Intelligence-Policy Disconnects," Studies in Intelligence 33/2 (Summer 1989): 1-9.
A discussion of some of the behavioral characteristics of intelligence analysts and policy makers which infect the relationship between the two key parties to the intelligence process.

2717. Gardiner, L. Keith. "Squaring the Circle: Dealing with Intelligence-Policy Breakdowns," Intelligence and National Security 6/1 (January 1991): 141-153.

Considers some of the reasons for communications breakdowns between the intelligence producers and their political clients. Major sections address distinctions between intelligence and policy; personalized processes; failed solutions; cognitive structures; the MBTI method; issue evolution; the role of leadership; liaison links; and presenting the product.

2718. Gardner, M. "On the Practical Uses and Bizarre Abuses of Sir Francis Bacon's Bilateral Cipher," Scientific American 227 (November 1972): 114-118.

Argues that scientists and historians are greatly undecided about Sir Francis Bacon, the inventor of the bilateral cipher system. Evidence of secret messages have been found in the work of Shakespeare, Marlowe, Spencer and Burton.

2719. Gardner, M. "Mathematical Games," American Scientist 237 (August 1977): 120-124.

Discussion of cryptography. Asks whether it will be possible to devise a code that can be encoded and decoded rapidly by a computer without changing the key. His answer is affirmative, by the use of the Caesar cipher.

2720. Gardner, Mary A. "Central and South American Mass Communication: Selected Information Sources," Journal of Broadcasting 22 (Spring 1978): 217-240.

2721. Gardner, Werner W. "Ultra Intelligence Reports to the 6th Army Group," Revue d'Histoire de la Deuxieme Guerre Mondiale et des Conflits Contemporains 34/133 (1984): 53-59.

Concerns the successes of the American and Allied Army Group and their Ultra intelligence program in 1944 and 1945 in the Rhone Valley. This article appears in French and the title appearing here is an approximate translation.

2722. Garfinkel, Steven. "Executive Coordination and Oversight of Security Classification Administration," Government Information Quarterly 1/2 (1984): 157-164.

Argues that the government's control over Top Secret information is under control, although improvements in the system of regulations and instructions could be made.

2723. Garfinkle, Adam M. "The Forces Behind Syrian Politics," Middle East Review 7 (Fall 1984): 5-14.

2724. Garlinski, Jozef. "The Polish Underground State," Journal of Contemporary History 10/2 (April 1975): 219-260.

Major sections discuss the beginning of the underground movement; the rebuilding of a national government in France; the Union for Armed Struggle; the amalgamation of the army groups; political parties; the extermination of the Jews; and education, culture and the press. Discusses the close ties between the British and Polish underground in the passing of intelligence and the conduct of espionage.

2725. Garlinski, Jozef. "Operation 'Friendship,'" Zeszyty Historyczne 76 (1986): 205-207.

This is a summary report of a conference on intelligence, espionage activities and the resistance movements during World War II. The conference was held in Luxembourg in 1985.

2726. Garmire, Bernard L. "A New Methodology for the Miami Police to Combat Organized Crime," Police Chief 38/9 (September 1971): 26-29.

Suggests that a new organized crime investigations unit can be created by combining narcotics, vice and intelligence units for greater effectiveness against organized crime.

2727. Garmon, William T. "The KGB in the United States," Military Intelligence 13/3 (1987): 12-13.

2728. Garn, E. Jake. "The SALT Verification Myth," Strategic Review 7 (Summer 1979): 16-24.

Discusses US monitoring capabilities and argues that those capabilities are marginal at best. Also discusses Soviet methods for concealing weapons developments and various deception activities. Mentions the clandestine ICBM problem.

2729. Garn, E. Jake. "The Suppression of Information Concerning Soviet SALT Violations by the U.S. Government," Policy Review 9 (Summer 1979): 11-32.

Major sections include strategic force deployment, definition of heavy missiles, the ABM Treaty, and the Kamchatka radar deployment. The Soviets, he argues, have repeatedly violated the SALT agreements.

2730. Garner, Lloyd S. "The Air Force Intelligence Service," Air Force Comptroller 17 (January 1983): 17-19.

2731. Garnham, David. "State Department Rigidity: Testing a Psychological Hypothesis," International Studies Quarterly 18/1 (March 1974): 31-39.

Argues that rigidity at the State Department has a psychological basis in the self-selection of foreign service officers and the selection process for characteristics designed to perpetuate the corps.

2732. Garon, Gilles and Richard Outerbridge. "DES Watch: An Examination of the Sufficiency of the Data Encryption Standard for Financial Institution Information Security in the 1990s," Cryptologia 15/3 (July 1991): 177-193.

2733. Garrett, Richard B. "End of a Manhunt," American Heritage 17/4 (April 1966): 40-43, 105.

The capture and death of John Wilkes Booth, assassin of Abe Lincoln, are discussed in detail. Suggests that Booth was killed in contrast to other views of a suicide.

2734. Garrison, Lloyd K. "Some Observations on the Loyalty-Security Program," University of Chicago Law Review 23/1 (Autumn 1955): 1-11.

An address to the April 1955 meeting of the Third National Conference of Law Reviews. Criticizes the Program in terms of the definition of the offense, the sifting of charges, statement of charges, right to confrontation and cross-examination of witnesses, and mixing of prosecutor and judicial functions.

2735. Garrow, David J. "FBI Political Harassment and FBI Historiography: Analyzing Informants and Measuring the Effects," Public Historian 10/4 (Fall 1988): 5-18.

Concludes that human informants for the FBI have formed the most significant elements of its political surveillance substructure. Such informants may have damaged political dissenters but less so than they had originally expected.

2736. Garthoff, Raymond L. "Surprise and Blitzkrieg in Soviet Eyes," RCAF Staff College Journal (1959): 16-29.

2737. Garthoff, Raymond L. "On Estimating and Imputing Intentions," International Security 2/3 (Winter 1977-1978): 22-32.

Analysis of 10 common fallacies in the estimation of intentions of the Soviet military. Examples are given.

2638. Garthoff, Raymond L. "Mutual Deterrence and Strategic Arms," International Security 3/1 (Summer 1978): 112-147.

Major sections consider questions of war and peace in Soviet ideology and policy; military views; mutual deterrence and the Soviet SALT decision; and the maintenance of mutual deterrence. Intelligence is at the heart of the discussion of mutual deterrence treaties.

2739. Garthoff, Raymond L. "Soviet Views in the Interrelation of Diplomacy and Military Strategy," Political Science Quarterly 94/3 (Fall 1979): 391-405.

Major sections included discussion of state policy, military strategy and diplomacy; deterrence; outbreak of war; roles of political and military leadership;

balancing diplomatic and strategic objectives and capabilities.

2740. Garthoff, Raymond L. "American Reaction to Soviet Aircraft in Cuba, 1962 and 1978," Political Science Quarterly 95/3 (Fall 1980): 427-439.
Compares the US reaction to the appearance of MIG 23 fighters in Cuba in 1978 with the discovery in 1962 of offensive missiles. Since MIGs were not considered offensive weapons, the 1978 discovery was not considered a crisis.

2741. Garthoff, Raymond L. "The Meaning of the Missiles," Washington Quarterly 5/4 (1982): 76-82.

2742. Garthoff, Raymond L. "Handling the Cienfuegos Crisis," International Security 8/1 (Summer 1983): 46-66.
Cienfuegos was a crisis of US-Cuba relations in 1970, involving a U-2 overflight that discovered the construction of a Soviet naval facility in the Bay of Cienfuegos. Praises the overflight program and its early warning value.

2743. Garthoff, Raymond L. "Cuban Missile Crisis: The Soviet Story," Foreign Policy 72 (Fall 1988): 61-80.
Discloses new information from the USSR which elaborates upon, and may change, the previous US understanding of Soviet decisions during the missile crisis.

2744. Garthoff, Raymond L. "Commentary: Evaluating and Using Historical Hearsay," Diplomatic History 14/2 (Spring 1990): 223-229.
Author challenges some aspects of the Soviet and American meetings to clarify decision making environment in both countries during Cuban missile crisis.

2745. Garthoff, Raymond L. "Estimating Soviet Military Force Levels: Some Light from the Past," International Security 14/4 (Spring 1990): 93-116.
Major sections include discussions of the 1960 estimate of Soviet force levels; the Soviet force reductions in 1960-61; the contributions from espionage; vagaries of subsequent estimates; estimating force levels and arms negotiations; and current declared Soviet force levels.

2746. Garthoff, Raymond L. "The KGB Reports to Gorbachev," Intelligence and National Security 11/2 (April 1996): 224-244.
Discussion of the nature of the KGB annual reports; the KGB and Gorbachev; role of the KGB; foreign intelligence operations; active measures; counterintelligence; internal security; international ties of the KGB; Perestroika; and concluding observations.

2747. Gartner, Scott S. and Marissa E. Myers. "Body Counts and "Success" in the Vietnam and Korean Wars," Journal of Interdisciplinary History 25/3 (Winter

1995): 377-396.

Discussion of the army's use of a "body count" measure of success in the Korean and Vietnam wars, thus impeding the formulation of an accurate assessment of progress.

2748. Garvey, Jack I. "Repression of the Political Empire--The Underground to International Law: A Proposal for Remedy," Yale Law Journal 90/1 (November 1980): 78-120.

Discussion of the operations and legal principles of foreign secret agents residing in the US who may become national security threats.   Cites the assassination of Orlando Letelier.

2749. Garvin, Tom. "Defenders, Ribbonmen and Others: Underground Political Networks in Pre-Famine Ireland," Past and Present 96 (August 1982): 133-155.

Discusses the underground movement of Daniel O'Connell prior to 1847 in Ireland. Sections include interpretation of ribbonism; defenders and ribbonmen; and evolution of the ribbon tradition.

2750.   Garwin, Richard L.   "Antisubmarine Warfare and National Security," Scientific American 227 (July 1982): 14-25.

Discusses the antisubmarine activities of intelligence, detection, localization and destruction. Argues that mutual survivability in nuclear war depends on the balance of submarine forces.

2751. Gash, Norman. "A Scholar and a Traitor," Policy Review 15 (Winter 1981): 153-160.

Discusses the espionage work of the "fourth man," Anthony Blunt. Mentions a British academy proposal to censure Blunt.

2752. Gasiorowski, Mark J. "The 1953 'Coup d'Etat' in Iran," International Journal of Middle East Studies 19/3 (August 1987): 261-286.

Account of the overthrow of the Mossadegh government in 1953-1954, aided by US intelligence organizations and British encouragement.

2753. Gaskin, Robert. "Flying the U-2," Air Force Magazine 60 (April 1977): 66-71.

2754. Gasque, Aubrey. "Wiretapping: A History of Federal Legislation and Supreme Court Decisions," Southern California Law Quarterly 15 (1963): 593-622.

A brief history of the origins of federal law on wiretapping. Sections on the Nardone decision, changing congressional attitude, third persons not protected, and definition of 'interception.'

2755. Gates, Darryl. "The Enforcement Intelligence Units," California Peace Officer (January-February 1965).

2756. Gates, Robert M. "CIA and the University," Studies in Intelligence 30/2 (Summer 1986).

2757. Gates, Robert M. "The Soviets and SDI," American Intelligence Journal 8/2 (May 1987).

2758. Gates, Robert M. "The CIA and American Foreign Policy," Foreign Affairs 66/2 (Winter 1987-1988): 215-230.
    Argues that there is a general misunderstanding of the role of the CIA in national security management. CIA plays an important role in American foreign policy development. This article was also printed in Studies in Intelligence 31/3 (Fall 1987).

2759. Gates, Robert M. "Unauthorized Disclosures: Risks, Costs, and Responsibilities," American Intelligence Journal 9/2 (Summer 1988): 6-8.
    The former director of the Central Intelligence Agency offers criticisms of government personnel and activities of leakers of classified information, in particular, the sources and methods of intelligence agencies.

2760. Gates, Robert M. "An Opportunity Unfulfilled: The Use and Perceptions of Intelligence at the White House," Washington Quarterly 12/1 (Winter 1989): 35-44.
    Addresses CIA-White House relationships in terms of intelligence assessments and substantive support of the policy process. Concludes that the intelligence community needs to build on past progress and intensify efforts to maintain an intelligence strategy. Article was originally published in classified form in Studies in Intelligence in 1980.

2761. Gates, Robert M. "Statement of Change in the Intelligence Community," American Intelligence Journal 13/1&2 (Winter-Spring 1992): 8-12.

2762. Gates, Robert M. "Intelligence, Democracy, and Freedom," Presidential Studies Quarterly 22/2 (Spring 1992): 231-238.
    The former CIA director's brief speech which outlines the history and uses of intelligence in presidential policy making. Calls for avoiding demobilization of the US intelligence apparatus.

2763. Gates, Robert M. "Guarding Against Politicization: A Message to Analysts," Studies in Intelligence 36/5 (Winter 1992): 5-13.
    Published first in Spring 1992 in Studies, this is the author's address to CIA personnel delivered in the CIA auditorium in March 1992. Offers specific

recommendations on how the management of the analytical process can be improved.

2764. Gauck, Joachim. "Dealing with the Stasi Past," Daedalus 123/1 (Winter 1994): 277-284.

The discovery of records of the East German state intelligence service and what should be done about the former GDR agents and operatives under reunification.

2765. Gaudet, Donna M. "Constitutional Law -- Fourth Amendment -- Electronic Surveillance Authorized Under the Foreign Intelligence Surveillance Act Does Not Violate the Fourth Amendment," Suffolk Transnational Law Journal 14 (Fall 1990): 231-246.

A case note referring to U. S. v. Posey. Argues that the Posey decision properly defers to legislative intent to allow the executive branch discretion in national security cases.

2766. Gautier-Mayoral, Carmen. "Notes on the Repression Practiced by U.S. Intelligence Agencies in Puerto Rico," Revista Juridica de la Universidad de Puerto Rico 52 (Summer 1983): 431-450.

2767. Gavin, William T. "The Secret Life of American Politics," Public Opinion 10/5 (January-February 1988): 2-6.

Discusses views of secrecy and examples of secrecy in American political life. Sections discuss private secrets; campaign secrets; open secrets; official secrets; secret secrets; and dilemmas of secrecy.

2768. Gawada, Stanislaw and Bronislaw Gralak. "German Scholarship in the Service of Anti-Polish Policy from 1918 to 1945," Studia Historyozne 31/3 (1988): 407-423.

2769. Gay, James T. "Some Observations of Eastern Siberia, 1922," Slavonic and East European Review 54/135 (1976): 248-261.

Summarizes an American naval intelligence officer's reports to the State Department.

2770. Gayev, A. "The Noble Chekists," Bulletin [Institute for the Study of the USSR] 22/3 (March 1965): 18-21.

2771. Gazit, Shlomo. "Fraud in Her Majesty's Service," Journal of Strategic Studies 3/2 (June 1980): 217-226.

2772. Gazit, Shlomo. "Estimating and Fortune Telling in Intelligence Work," International Security 4/4 (Spring 1980): 36-56.

A lengthy and exhaustive analysis of the intelligence analytical process, including the traits of good analysts, needed improvements in collection, general and special collections, analytical situations, and outcomes.

2773. Gazit, Shlomo. "Risk, Glory, and the Rescue Operation," International Security Review 6/1 (Summer 1981): 111-135.
A discussion of Israeli rescue missions, the case of the Entebbe raid, and the role of deception and simple strategies.

2774. Gazit, Shlomo. "Intelligence Estimates and the Decision-maker," Intelligence and National Security 3/3 (July 1988): 261-287.
Major sections consider the non-relationship between estimating and fortune telling; a reciprocal relationship between intelligence and decision making; awareness of the need to establish a reciprocal relationship; a two-way relationship; integration in the decision making process; working techniques; and limitations of intelligence.

2775. Gazit, Shlomo. "Intelligence Estimates and the Decisionmaker," Studies in Intelligence 32/3 (Fall 1988).

2776. Geberth, V. J. "Undercover Officer," Law and Order 27/3 (March 1979): 38-43, 46-47, 81.
Discusses the selection and assignment of personnel who work on cases involving organized crime, drug operations, dissident groups and vice.

2777. Geberth, V. J. "Confidential Informants," Law and Order 27/6 (June 1979): 26, 28-30, 32-34, 38-41.
Development and used of confidential informants in local law enforcement.

2778. Gedicks, Al. "Ethnicity, Class Solidarity, and Labor Radicalism Among Finnish Immigrants in Michigan Copper Country," Politics and Society 7/2 (1977): 127-156.
Discusses in part the use of spies and blacklisting to undermine labor organizing efforts among Michigan copper workers in the early part of the twentieth century.

2779. Geelhoed, E. Bruce. "Dwight D. Eisenhower, the Spy Plane, and the Summit: A Quarter Century Retrospective," Presidential Studies Quarterly 17/1 (Winter 1987): 95-106.
Discussion of the downing of the U-2 spy aircraft in 1960 over the Soviet Union. Argues that the incident cost Eisenhower valuable ground in improving relations with the Soviets.

2780. Geiger, George J. "Russia's Aerospace Arsenal: Aircraft, Missiles, and Spacecraft," Aerospace Management 5 (March 1962): 92-110.

A summary of the space and defensive weaponry of the Soviet Union. Particularly useful in historical analyses of the Cuban Missile Crisis of 1962 and US knowledge of Soviet capabilities.

2781. Geis, Gilbert and Colin Goff. "Lifting the Cover from Undercover Operations: J. Edgar Hoover and Some of the Other Criminologists," Crime, Law and Social Change 18/1-2 (September 1992): 91-104.

Outlines totalitarian control of the FBI by J. Edgar Hoover; the FBI and Harry Elmer Barnes; Edwin Sutherland and the FBI; and the Jack Shaw incident. Points out that even criminologists did not escape Hoover's tactics of dossier building and vindictive reprisals for negative comments about the Bureau.

2782. Gelatt, Timothy A. "The New Chinese State Secrets Law," Cornell International Law Journal 22/2 (Spring 1989): 255-268.

Discusses the background of the State Secrets law, applications and negative impact on foreign investment.

2783. Gelb, Leslie H. "Washington Dateline: The Story of a Flap," Foreign Policy 16 (Fall 1974): 165-181.

Argues that the power and integrity of government was negatively affected by an arms control agreement struck with the Soviets that allowed the Soviets to have additional missile platforms not authorized under SALT.

2784. Gelber, Harry G. "Technical Innovation and Arms Control," World Politics 26/4 (July 1974): 509-541.

Suggests that the intelligence community needs to stay abreast of the technical advantages that arise from research and development in the nuclear arms arena.

2785. Gelber, Harry G. "The Hunt for Spies: Another Inside Story," Intelligence and National Security 4/2 (April 1989): 385-400.

Reviews an account of one British intelligence officer's memoirs covering details of capturing spies and other counterintelligence tradecraft. Considers intelligence user reactions and decisions in the absence of CI-supplied information.

2786. Gelber, Harry G. "The Wilderness of Mirrors: More "Inside Stories"," Australian Journal of Politics and History 35/1 (1989): 97-104.

2787. Gellhorn, Ernest. "The Treatment of Confidential Information by the Federal Trade Commission: The Hearing," University of Pennsylvania Law Review 116/2 (December 1967): 401-434.

Describes and analyses public hearings on FTC matters, evidentiary limits of public trials, government secrets and the FTC, and prior statements of a prosecution witness.

2788. Gentry, John A. "The Intelligence Reform Debate," Defense Intelligence Journal 2/1 (Spring 1993): 65-80.

      Discusses the provision of the Intelligence Reorganization Act of 1992; scope of defense intelligence; time horizons; parochialism; the personnel system as hindrance to good intelligence; and recommendations for improvements.

2789. Gentry, John A. "Intelligence Analyst/Manager Relations at the CIA," Intelligence and National Security 10/4 (October 1995): 133-146.

      Describes and assesses the relationship between analysts and their managers in the CIA Directorate of Intelligence. Major sections consider the background of the relationship; key changes in analyst/manager relations; rapid change in the DI 'culture'; an Aldrich Ames in the DI; and can lessons be generalized?

2790. George, Alexander L. "American Policy-Making and the North Korean Aggression," World Politics 7/2 (January 1955): 209-232.

      Examines the effect of strategic planning and estimates of communist intentions and behavior on the to commit American forces to the defense of South Korea. Contains interpretations of the North Korean attack, problems raised by interpretations, reversal of the strategic plan, and event evaluation.

2791. George, Alexander L. "The Case for Multiple Advocacy in Making Foreign Policy," American Political Science Review 66/3 (September 1972): 751-785.

      Discusses prescriptive theories of policy making in complex organizations with particular reference to foreign policy making in the Executive branch. Urges the use of multiple advocacy instead of centralized management to discourage internal dissent about policies.

2792. George, Alexander L. "Propaganda Analysis: A Study of Inferences Made from Nazi Propaganda on World War II," World Politics 12 (April 1960): 478-485.

      Discusses the phases of the Foreign Broadcast Information Service's work to interpret radio traffic from nazi Germany during World War II. Covers the recruitment of leading social scientists, then discusses both failures and successes in the interpretation of indications of German actions. Includes several accounts of the work of the FBIS; compares quantitative and qualitative research methods as applied in this case.

2793. George, B. J. "'The Potent,' 'The Omnipresent Teacher': The Supreme Court and Wiretapping," Virginia Law Review 47/5 (June 1961): 751-797.

Explores the Olmstead wiretapping case; the Nardone case; the second Nardone case; <u>Benanti v. U.S.</u>; the aftermath of Benanti: <u>Pugach v. Dollinger</u>; a tentative analysis of the present problem; and suggested resolutions.

2794. George, James A. "Where the High Flyers Go," <u>Airman</u> 22 (September 1978): 22-31.

2795. George, Joseph, Jr. "Black Flag Warfare: Lincoln and the Raids Against Richmond and Jefferson Davis," <u>Pennsylvania Magazine of History and Biography</u> 115 (July 1991): 291-318.

Considers the thesis that Southern leaders in the Civil War wanted Lincoln dead, thus leading to assassination plots.

2796. George, Kenneth M. "Dark Trembling: Ethnographic Notes on Secrecy and Concealment in Highland Sulawesi," <u>Anthropological Quarterly</u> 66 (October 1993): 230-239.

Discusses results of field research on the role of secrecy among the Sulawesi people in Indonesia.

2797. George, W. L. "Psychology of a Spy," <u>Harper's</u> 135 (June 1917): 92-100.

A classic piece that discussed the use of spies in various endeavors, such as penetration of industry, banking, and commerce. Argues that spies do not fit in the normal mosaic of social life.

2798. Georgia, Scudder. "Agent Radio Operation During World War II," <u>Studies in Intelligence</u> 3/4 (Winter 1959).

2799. Geogiou, George. "A Method to Strengthen Ciphers," <u>Cryptologia</u> 13/2 (April 1989): 151-160.

2800. Geraghty, J. M. "One Face of the Informer--The Approver," <u>University of Queens Law Journal</u> 5 (April 1965): 66-86.

2801. Geraghty, J. M. "Another Face of the Informer--The Police Spy," <u>University of Queens Law Journal</u> 6 (April 1966): 170-190.

2802. Gerald, Rex E. "Portrait of a Community: Joseph De Urrutia's Map of El Paso Del Norte, 1766," <u>American West</u> 3/3 (1966): 38-41.

A brief but fascinating story of the making of the map of fortifications and facilities at Chihuahua, Mexico. Many of the fortifications are in place today.

2803. Gerassi, John. "Pluralism vs. Centralism in Nicaragua: The Sandinistas Under Attack," <u>Scandinavian Journal of Development Alternatives</u> 5 (March 1986): 77-94.

Discusses, in part, the role of the Central Intelligence Agency in attempting to unseat the Sandinistas.

2804. Gerlach, Don R. "Philip Schuyler and 'The Road to Glory': A Question of Loyalty and Competence," New York Historical Society Quarterly 49/4 (October 1965): 341-386.

2805. Gert, Bernard. "The Ethics of Secrecy," Criminal Justice Ethics 4/1 (Winter-Spring 1985): 78-84.
A book review essay of Sissela Bok's Secrets: On the Ethics of Concealment and Revelation (New York: Pantheon, 1982).

2806. Gertz, Bill. "The Secret Mission of NRO," Air Force Magazine (June 1993): 60-63.

2807. Gervasi, T. "Black Ops, 1963 to 1983," Harper's 268 (April 1984): 17+.
The author's list of US covert operations in a 20-year period.

2808. Geschwind, C. N. "The Tale of Hushai the Archite," Studies in Intelligence 13/1 (Spring 1969).

2809. Geselbracht, Raymond H. "The Origins of Restrictions on Access to Personal Papers at the Library of Congress and the National Archives," American Archivist 49/2 (Spring 1986): 142-162.
Access control policies pertaining to donated personal papers housed in the National Archives.

2810. Gewirtz, Paul. "The Courts, Congress, and Executive Policy-Making: Notes on Three Doctrines," Law and Contemporary Problems 40 (Summer 1976): 46-85.
Contains sections on who should make policy; should the delegation be revised?; and the uses of statutory construction. Useful background piece for studies in intelligence policy.

2811. Ghoshal, Sumantra and Seok Ki Kim. "Building Effective Intelligence Systems for Competitive Advantage," Sloan Management Review 28/1 (Fall 1986): 49-58.
Authors emphasize that mere creation of a business intelligence staff does not guarantee collection of timely data, or that available information will reach key decision makers.

2812. Gibbs, William E. "Diaz Executive Agents and United States Foreign Policy," Journal of Inter-American Studies and World Affairs 20/2 (May 1978): 165-190; also in North Dakota Quarterly 45/2 (1977): 36-53.

Discusses the activities of Mexican agents operating in the US to influence policy making during the late 1870s. Based on numerous historical records.

2813. Gibson, Michael T. "The Supreme Court and Freedom of Expression from 1791 to 1917," Fordham Law Review 55/3 (December 1986): 263-333.

An extensive discussion of the subject, reflecting upon sixty cases upon which the Court ruled on First Amendment issues.

2814. Gichon, Mordechai. "Faulty Intelligence," Military Review (December 1962): 38-42.

Answers some questions about the failure of Napoleon's Levant Campaign in 1797.

2815. Gidwitz, Betsy. "Aspects of Soviet International Civil Aviation Policy," Survey 24 (Spring 1979): 19-44.

2816. Giesy, Carl D. "Jurisdictional Limitations on the Foreign Intelligence Surveillance Court," Suffolk Transnational Law Journal 8 (Fall 1984): 259-299.

Discussion of the Carter administration's creation of the FISA court to protect citizen rights and national security operations. Covers the FISA Act, jurisdiction of the FISA court, and concludes that the legislative controls are adequate.

2817. Giffin, Frederick C. "The Death of Walter Krivitsky," Social Science 54/3 (1979): 139-146.

Claims the controversial Soviet defector may have been a victim of foul play. A former member of Soviet military intelligence service, Krivitsky was a key opponent of Stalinist Russia.

2818. Gilad, Tamar and Benjamin. "Business Intelligence--The Quiet Revolution," Sloan Management Review 27/4 (Summer 1986): 53-61.

Describes approaches available to companies eager to implement an intelligence activity. Authors stress that the function relies heavily on complete organizational and management commitment.

2819. Gilbert, James L. "U.S. Army COMSEC in World War I," Military Intelligence 14/1 (January 1988): 22-25.

Majors sections discuss MI-8 and army COMSEC; riverbank and COMSEC training; COMSEC and the AEF; radio intelligence section; security service; and lessons learned.

2820. Gilbert, Lee A. "Patent Secrecy Orders: The Unconstitutionality of Interference in Civilian Cryptography Under Present Procedures," Santa Clara Law

Review 22/2 (Spring 1982): 325-373.

   Discusses the topic in the title. Says that two to three hundred such interferences occur yearly, but appear to be on the decline. Covers the Invention Secrecy Act, relief from procedural problems associated with the Act, and conclusions.

2821. Gill, Peter. "Symbolic or Real? The Impact of the Canadian Security Intelligence Review Committee, 1984-88," Intelligence and National Security 4/3 (July 1989): 550-575.

   Examines the domestic security concerns of Canada. Major sections discuss effective security and democratic rights; resources; mandate; membership; staff and budget; the question of political influences.

2822. Gill, Peter. "Defining Subversion: The Canadian Experience," Public Law (Winter 1989): 617-636.

   Argues lack of definition for "subversion" has provided police and security agencies grounds to legitimate surveillance or otherwise legal political action. Discusses incidents of surveillance operations conducted by Royal Canadian Mounted Police leading to executive inquiries and separation of domestic intelligence functions from RCMP. Examines history of legislative definitions of subversion and changes prompted by findings of McDonald Commission. Also discusses counter subversion.

2823. Gill, Peter. "Reasserting Control: Recent Changes in the Oversight of the UK Intelligence Community," Intelligence and National Security 11/2 (April 1996): 313-331.

   A discussion of information control; evaluating the Glasnost of the major regime; and overall conclusions.

2824. Gillen, John and K. H. Silvert. "Ambiguities in Guatemala," Foreign Affairs 34/3 (April 1956): 469-482.

   Discussion of the overthrow of the Jacobo Arbenz Guzman government in Guatemala in 1954 and ambiguities presented: (1) the new Castillo government is accepted as a creature of the US Department of State; and (2) the new government would like to be perceived as the agent of political democracy.

2825. Gillers, Stephen. "Secret Government and What To Do About It," Civil Liberties Review 1/2 (Winter-Spring 1974): 68-74.

   Distinguishes between "constitutional government" and "national security government." The latter includes the FBI and CIA activities to violate individual liberties. Offers proposals for limitation on these agencies.

2826. Gillis, Peter. "Of Plots, Secret Borrowers and Moles: Archives in Espionage Fiction," Archivaria 9 (Winter 1979-1980): 3-13.

2827.   Gillogly, James J.   "The Beale Cypher: A Dissenting Opinion," Cryptologia 4/2 (April 1980): 116-119.

2828. Gillogly, James J. "Fast Pattern Matching for Word Lists," Cryptologia 9/1 (January 1985): 55-62.
        Discusses the use of fast pattern lists in their applications to simplify entry into difficult cryptograms. Presents an algorithm to reduce the number of comparisons required to produce the final list of matched lists.

2829.   Gillogly, James J.   "Ciphertext-Only Cryptanalysis of ENIGMA," Cryptologia 19/4 (October 1995): 405-413.

2830. Gillogly, James J. "Breaking an Eighteenth Century Shorthand System," Cryptologia 11/2 (April 1987): 93-98.

2831.   Gillogly, James J. and Donald W. Davies.   "The Mysterious Autocryptograph," Cryptologia 8/1 (January 1984): 77-92.

2832. Gilman, Isabel. "Open Air Searches and Enhanced Surveillance in California," Santa Clara Law Review 21/3 (Summer 1981): 779-800.
        Discusses the law and limits of police surveillance activities from aircraft. Includes sections on the Fourth Amendment and the growth of technology, and California searches in the open air.

2833. Gilmore, Allison B. "'We Have Been Reborn': Japanese Prisoners and the Allied Propaganda War in the Southwest Pacific," Pacific Historical Review 64/2 (May 1995): 195-216.

2834. Gilmore, Robert C. "A Matter of Loyalty," Profiles 25 (March 1976): 81-85.

2835. Gimbel, John. "U.S. Policy and German Scientists: The Early Cold War," Political Science Quarterly 101/3 (1986): 433-451.

2836. Gimbel, John. "Project Paperclip: German Scientists, American Policy, and the Cold War," Diplomatic History 14/3 (1990): 343-365.
        Detailed and documented article on the American post-war program to bring German scientists to the US to exploit German scientific and technical know-how for military and industrial purposes. Argues, in part, that the program was not limited to frustrating Soviet advances on scientific or technological fronts, despite pre-war British initiatives aimed precisely at this purpose.

2837. Ginsburgh, Robert N. "Strategy and Airpower: The Lessons of Southeast Asia," Strategic Review 1/2 (1973): 18-24.

2838. Giordano, Robert F. "Army Intelligence Electronic Warfare," Journal of Electronic Defense 10 (October 1987): 33-34.

2839. Girard, Philip. "From Subversion to Liberation: Homosexuals and the Immigration Act 1952-1977," Canadian Journal of Law & Society 2 (1987): 1-27.
An excellent summary of the history of the subject, including sections on homosexuals and the Cold War in the US, the homosexual witch-hunt in Canada, and homosexuals at the border.

2840. Girdner, Bill. "Spy v. Spy," California Lawyer 6 (January 1986): 26-31, 60.
Discusses the perceptions of the spy and the difficulties in making a legal defense for those accused of espionage. Argues that persons accused of espionage have a right to the best defense available.

2841. Girdwood, Roger S. "Burn Bags," Studies in Intelligence 33/2 (Summer 1989).

2842. Girodo, Michael. "Health and Legal Issues in Undercover Narcotics Investigations: Misrepresented Evidence," Behavioral Sciences and the Law 3/3 (1985): 299-308.
Dangers of work in an undercover role, including mental injuries and their long term implications. Includes sections on mental injuries and undercover work, personality disorders and future directions.

2843. Girouard, Richard J. "District Intelligence in Vietnam," Armor 75/6 (November-December 1966): 10-14.

2844. Gish, Donald M. "A Cryptologic Analysis," International Journal of Intelligence and Counterintelligence 6/3 (Fall 1993): 369-388.
A detailed review essay critiquing the underlying assumptions of authors James Rusbridger and Eric Nave in Betrayal at Pearl Harbor: How Churchill Lured Roosevelt into World War II. The reviewer rejects the conspiracy theory on the lack of evidence of the Jn-25 message.

2845. Given, Deam. "A Visit to Vlad," Naval Intelligence Professionals Quarterly 6/2 (1990): 12-14.

2846. Givierge, Marcel. "Questions de Chiffres," Revue Militaire Francaise 36 & 37 (June and July-September 1924): 398-417; 59-78.

2847. Glackin, J. J. "How Secrecy Played Executioner," Bulletin of the Atomic Scientists 31/6 (June 1975): 14-16.
Asks whether Ethel and Julius Rosenberg (atomic spies in the early

1950s) would have been executed if the prosecution had revealed all its information.

2848. Gladwin, Lee A. "Hollywood Propaganda, Isolationism and Protectors of the Public Mind, 1917-1941," Prologue: Quarterly Journal of the National Archives 26 (Winter 1994).

2849. Gladstone, Kay. "British Interception of German Export Newsreels and the Development of British Combat Filming, 1939-1942," Imperial War Museum Review 1/2 (1987): 30-40.

2850. Glantz, David M. "Observing the Soviets: U.S. Army Attaches in Eastern Europe During the 1930s," Journal of Military History 55/2 (April 1991): 153-183.
    An extensive history of attache operations in the Baltic countries as to attache accuracy in reporting upon doctrine, weapons capabilities and purges of the Red Army units.

2851. Glantz, David M. "The Red Mask: The Nature and Legacy of Soviet Military Deception in the Second World War," Intelligence and National Security 2/3 (July 1987): 175-259.
    An extensive and detailed discussion of the topic: general theory of maskirovka; pre-war theoretical views; theory and war experiences; the practice of mashkirovka; reflections on Soviet second world war mashkirovka experiences; and implications for the future.

2852. Glantz, David M. "Soviet Operational Intelligence in the Kursk Operation, July 1943," Intelligence and National Security 5/1 (January 1990): 5-49.
    A detailed and rich account (including maps) of the reorganization and redirection of Soviet military intelligence between the surprise German attack of June 1941 and the Soviet successes in the Kursk operations in 1943. [Bibliographer's note: The opening paragraph of this article briefly discusses the background circumstances of the September 1941 German assault by Guderian's Second Panzer Group in the area near Kiev, a strategic move aimed at striking the rear flanks of the Soviet Army. The surprise attack cost over 600,000 Soviet troops, and many thousands of German soldiers. My wife's grandfather was a young German foot soldier in Guderian's Second Panzer Group. He was killed September 17, 1941 in a small town southwest of Kiev. A German officer's letter to his mother describes his burial site on a farm next to tree, a graphic reminder of the great distance between the place of the foot soldier in war and the intelligence and policy planners.]

2853. Glantz, David M. "Soviet Military Deception in the Second World War," American Intelligence Journal 12/1 (Winter 1991): 21-26.

2854. Glasebrook, Rick. "Flying the North American 0-47 and the Curtiss-Wright 0-52," Aerospace Historian 25/1 (1978): 5-11.
A short history of these two observation aircraft in the interwar years.

2855. Glaser, Daniel and Ronald Watts. "Electronic Monitoring of Drug Dealers on Probation," Judicature 76/3 (October-November 1992): 112-117.

2856. Glasser, Robert D. "Signals Intelligence and Nuclear Preemption," Parameters: Journal of the U.S. Army War College 19/2 (June 1989): 46-56.
Discusses SIGINT as one of the most valuable resources of the intelligence community. Includes sections on Soviet and US SIGINT collection, sources of security breaches, and the SIGINT role in theater and strategic nuclear preemption.

2857. Glassford, William A. "The Balloon in the Civil War," Journal of the Military Service Institution of the United States 18 (March 1896): 255-266.
A classic article for those interested in aerial intelligence gathering history.

2858. Glassford, William A. "Our Army in Aerial Warfare," American Magazine of Aeronautics 2/1 (1908): 18-21.
Another classic in aerial intelligence gathering history.

2859. Glazer, Nathan. "American Values and American Foreign Policy," Commentary 62/1 (July 1976): 32-37.
Argues that America is the only world power to equate national values with foreign policy, seeing itself as a good and strong power. Also argues that the US should base its foreign policy on moral grounds and avoid support for corrupt governments.

2860. Glazov, Yuriy. "The Passing of a Year: The KGB vs. Dissidents," Studies in Soviet Thought 15 (1975): 273-290.

2861. Gleason, Tom. "Culinary Action at the CIA," Studies in Intelligence 35/1 (Spring 1991).
The title reminds us of the other CIA, the Culinary Institute of America.

2862. Gleditsch, Nils P. "National Security and Freedom of Expression: The Scandinavian Legal Battles," Journal of Media Law and Practice (April 1987): 2-5.

2863. Gleditsch, Nils P. "The Treholt Literature: A Study in Polarization," Internasjonal Politikk 52/2 (1994): 275-294.
In Norwegian, this article is one of few scholarly treatments of all the

literature surrounding the Arne Treholt espionage case.

2864. Gleditsch, Nils P. "The Treholt Case: A Review of the Literature," Intelligence and National Security 10/3 (July 1995): 529-538.

An extensive essay that reviews the various theories pertaining to the spying activities of Norwegian Arne Treholt, their implications and results.

2865. Gleditsch, Nils P. and Einar Hgetveit. "Freedom of Information in National Security Affairs: A Comparative Study of Norway and the United States," Journal of Peace Research 21/1 (1984): 17-45.

Compares freedom of information policies in the US and Norway. Offers nineteen possible explanations for the increasing use of the FOIA law in the US in contrast to declining use in Norway. Argues the US is further ahead in openness by comparison with Norway.

2866. Glees, Anthony. "War Crimes: The Security and Intelligence Dimension," Intelligence and National Security 7/3 (July 1992): 242-267.

Discusses the British policy on war crimes; war crimes as a security and intelligence policy in British zone of occupation; the German scientists issue in the British zone of occupation in Germany; ending of war crimes trials and investigations; war criminals in the United Kingdom; operation post report; and conclusions.

2867. Gleichauf, Justin F. "Red Presence in Cuba: The Genesis of a Crisis," Army 29 (November 1979): 34-38.

2868. Gleijeses, Piero. "Ships in the Night: The CIA, the White House and the Bay of Pigs," Journal of Latin American Studies 27/1 (Fall 1995): 1-42.

The author contends that communications gaps between President Kennedy and the CIA aided the advancement of plans toward the failed mission of invasion of Cuba at the Bay of Pigs. As part of his research, the author interviewed Richard Bissell and others concerning CIA's role in Operation PBSUCCESS, the plan to unseat President Arbenz in Guatemala in 1954.

2869. Glendon, William R. "Fifteen Days in June That Shook the First Amendment: A First Person Account of the Pentagon Papers," New York State Bar Journal 65 (November 1993): 24-26+.

A brief discussion of the author's insider perspectives on the infamous Pentagon Papers case, New York Times Co. v. United States, 91 S. Ct. 2140 (1971).

2870. Glennon, Michael J. "The War Powers Resolution Ten Years Later: More Politics Than Law," American Journal of International Law 78/3 (July 1984): 571-581.

Considers the ten-year history of application of the War Powers Act, including the controls on covert actions by the military and the Central Intelligence Agency.

2871. Glennon, Michael J. "Liaison and the Law: Foreign Intelligence Agencies' Activities in the United States," Harvard International Law Journal 25/1 (Winter 1984): 1-42.
Discusses implications of intelligence liaison activities with nations that arrest and torture students engaged in dissident activities while visiting in the US.

2872. Glennon, Michael J. "Two Views of Presidential Foreign Affairs Power: Little v. Barreme or Curtis-Wright?," Yale International Law Review 13/1 (Winter 1988): 5-20.
This brief article, adapted for a speech, concludes: "Arbitrary exercise of power, and the inconsistent danger of autocracy, pose an ever-present danger to democratic processes." Part of the issue in the extent to which intelligence information is the property of the US government, not restricted by the constitutional powers of the President.

2873. Glickman, Dan. "The State of Intelligence: The Chairman's Perspective," American Intelligence Journal 14 (Spring-Summer 1993): 89-92.

2874. Glickman, Dan. "National Security Law," American Intelligence Journal 14/3 (Autumn-Winter 1993-1994): 74-76.

2875. Glickman, Dan. "Intelligence After the Cold War," Kansas Journal of Law and Public Policy 3 (Winter 1993-1994): 142-147.
Considers recent developments regarding espionage, intelligence programs, and national security in the 1990s.

2876. Glickman, S. P. and E. H. Levine. "Use of Microform in Federal Narcotics Intelligence and Law Enforcement," Journal of Micrographics 9/4 (March 1976): 155-159.
Discusses a computer assisted microfiche system used by the Drug Enforcement Agency.

2877. Glushchenko, Anatoli. "U.S. Intelligence 'Covert Operations,'" International Affairs (USSR) 17 (1987): 41-48.

2878. Glynn, Robert B. "L'Affaire Rosenberg in France," Political Science Quarterly 70 (December 1955): 498-521.
Discusses the Rosenberg espionage case from the perspective of the French newspapers and magazines. Sections discuss the arrest and trial; the campaign commencement; the affair crosses the Atlantic; the French line and

campaign; counter-propaganda attempts; and the execution and post-mortem.

2879. Godfrey, E. Drexel, Jr.   "Ethics and Intelligence," Foreign Affairs 56 (April 1978): 624-634.

Addresses the question of whether it is possible for the CIA to distinguish fact and judgment in telling the truth. Argues that national security must be based on truth and avoidance of cover-ups of mistakes.

2880. Godfrey, E. Drexel, Jr.   "Ethics and Intelligence - A Reply," Foreign Affairs 56 (July 1978): 867-875.

A brief reply to the comments of Arthur L. Jacobs. See comments under Jacobs' listing.

2881. Godley, Jeffrey R.   "Administrative Law - Defining CIA's 'Intelligence Sources' as an Exemption to the Freedom of Information Act. CIA v. Sims-471 U.S. 159 (1985)," Western New England Law Review 9/2 (Spring 1987): 333-360.

Discusses in a case note the statutory limits of the FOIA and the CIA's organic statutes, the CIA Act of 1984, the Supreme Court's decision in CIA v. Sims, and analysis of the definition of 'intelligence sources.'

2882. Godson, Roy.   "Intelligence Reform in the United States: The Proposed Charter," World Affairs 143/1 (Summer 1980): 3-19.

Discusses the construction of an effective intelligence capability while ensuring that intelligence agencies do not violate civil liberties. Offers reform proposals.

2883. Godson, Roy.   "Intelligence Requirements for the 1990s," Washington Quarterly 12/1 (Winter 1989): 47-65.

Discusses the major branches of the intelligence process: Analysis, collection, counterintelligence, covert action.

2884. Godson, Roy.   "Intelligence Reorganization," American Intelligence Journal 13/1&2 (Winter-Spring 1992): 25-30.

Testimony of a leading authority on intelligence subjects before House and Senate panels convened to consider reorganization issues in the intelligence community. Argues for a careful and systematic reorganization effort.

2885. Godson, Roy and Richard H. Shultz, Jr.   "Intelligence--The Evaluation of a New Teaching Subject," International Studies Notes 8/3-4 (Fall-Winter 1981-1982): 1-3.

Calls attention to the need to teach intelligence topics, and perhaps entire courses, in connection with studies of foreign policy. Attempts to explain the shortage of such integrated study. Also discusses the work of the Consortium for the Study of Intelligence.

2886. Godson, Roy and Richard H. Shultz, Jr. "Foreign Intelligence: A Course Syllabus," International Studies Notes 8/3-4 (Fall-Winter 1981-1982): 4-16.
A narrative discussion of course content for an intelligence course, including what is intelligence, clandestine collection, counterintelligence, analysis and estimates, covert action, intelligence-policy relationship, relationship between intelligence and democracy, approaches to research and policy studies, etc.

2887. Godson, Roy and Richard H. Shultz, Jr. "Resources on Intelligence," International Studies Notes 8/3-4 (Fall-Winter 1981-1982): 17-18.
A brief discussion of resources, including bibliography of Soviet materials; inventory of bibliographies; House and Senate committees; CIA; declassified documents system; NARA; US military archival records; film and video tapes; ABA sources; and resource centers in the US.

2888. Gold, Alan D. "Wiretaps - Access to Confidential Packet (Canada)," Criminal Law Quarterly 29 (June 1987): 292-295.
Discusses the right of an accused person to acquire access to wiretapped information in Canada.

2889. Goldberg, Arthur J. "Klaus Barbie and the United States Government," Harvard Civil Rights and Civil Liberties Law Review 19/1 (Winter 1984): 1-14.
Author, a former US Supreme Court justice, expresses shock and amazement that Army CIC officers in the post-War II environment could have employed Barbie as a US intelligence informer.

2890. Goldberg, Marc D. "Rapping Ivan's Sticky Fingers," U.S. Naval Institute Proceedings 114 (October 1988): 68-70+.
Methods for capturing Soviet intelligence efforts to steal military technologies are discussed.

2891. Goldberg, Peter A. "The Politics of the Allende Overthrow in Chile," Political Science Quarterly 90/1 (Spring 1975): 93-117.
Discusses the adaptability and decline of Chile's institutions, traditional institutional practices, Allende's taking office as example of institutional adaptability, institutional decay of Allende's power, shifting of basic policies, scope of the conflict, policy changes and responses to policy changes, and Allende's leadership.

2892. Goldberg, William D. "An Examination of the Naming Requirement of Title III in Light of United States v. Donovan -- A Case for Suppression," Villanova Law Review 24/1 (November 1978): 73-90.
Donovan held that Title III's naming requirement violation did not

require the suppression of evidence gathered through electronic surveillance. Discusses the background of the statute, the case law, the case for suppression, shifting the burden of proof, and conclusions. A case note comment.

2893. Golden, Frederic. "Seeing a Conspiracy in the Sky," Discover 5 (December 1984): 8.

2894. Goldman, Patti. "Combatting the Opposition: English and United States Restrictions on the Public Right of Access to Governmental Information," Hastings International and Comparative Law Review 8/3 (Spring 1985): 249-290.
    Contains sections on the effect of political theory on suppression of dissent; constraining opposition to Anglo-American democracies by limitations on public access to governmental information; limitations on public access to information about the judicial process.

2895. Goldschmidt, Maure L. "Publicity, Privacy and Secrecy," Western Political Quarterly 7/3 (September 1954): 401-416.
    Contrasts the two problems of too much publicity and its impact on privacy versus lack of publicity that increases the power of government secrecy. Contains sections on the development of the press, the Internal Security Act of 1950, a Truman Executive Order of September 24, 1951, and the lack of reliable information.

2896. Goldsmith, Andrew. "Political Policing in Canada: The Report of the McDonald Commission and the Security Intelligence Services Act of 1984," Public Law 1985 (Spring 1985): 39-50.
    Discusses the findings and recommendations of the Commission's investigations into the domestic intelligence operations of the R.C.M.P., and the Canadian Security Intelligence Services Act of 1984. Concludes that the Act ignored major contributions of the Commission.

2897. Goldsmith, Michael. "The Supreme Court and Title III: Rewriting the Law of Electronic Surveillance," Journal of Criminal Law and Criminology 74/1 (Spring 1983): 1-171.
    Discusses in exceptional detail the historical origins of Title III, the legislative design, the Supreme Court and the demise of strict enforcement, the after effects of enforcement in lower courts, congressional inaction, executive enforcement and conclusions.

2898. Goldsmith, Michael. "Eavesdropping Reform: The Legality of Roving Surveillance," University of Illinois Law Review (1987): 401-430.
    Roving surveillance is a police practice of monitoring by electronic means the phone conversations of persons traveling in moving vehicles. Argues that this practice should be permitted to continue but there should be some

restrictions on it.

2899. Goldstein, Erik. "Hertford House: The Naval Intelligence Geographical Section and Peace Conference Planning, 1917-1919," Mariner's Mirror 72/1 (February 1986): 85-88.

2900. Goldstein, Erik. "The Foreign Office and Political Intelligence 1918-1920," Review of International Studies 14/4 (October 1988): 275-288.
Major sections discuss the creation of the Political Intelligence Department; the personnel acquired; intelligence gathering; analysis of information; proposing policy options; acceptability of intelligence reports; and the fall of the P.I.D.

2901. Goldstein, Robert. "The Anarchist Scare of 1908," American Studies 2 (1974): 55-75.
Concludes that the negative and seething legacy of the 1908 scare was more intangible than was reflected by the number of people who were beaten, or the number of speaking engagements cancelled, or the articles suppressed by newspapers. Real legacy arose from the increased distrust, suspicion and bitterness between radicals and conservatives, Jews and non-Jews, and immigrants and persons born in the US.

2902. Goldstein, Robert J. "An American Gulag? Summary Arrest and Emergency Detention of Political Dissidents in the United States," Columbia Human Rights Law Review 10/2 (Fall-Winter 1978-1979): 541-573.
Examines the use and planning for summary arrest and emergency detention of persons who appear to threaten domestic safety and welfare. The resort to oppression appears easier and more efficient than the rule of law.

2903. Goldstein, Robert J. "The FBI and American Politics Textbooks," PS 18/2 (Spring 1985): 237-246.
American politics textbooks have failed to tell the real story about FBI abuses of civil liberties. These concerns were raised during the Senate Intelligence Committee hearings in the 1970s.

2904. Goldston, Bruce L. "The Federal Wiretapping Law," Texas Bar Journal 44/4 (April 1981): 382-389.
Accounts for the history of wiretapping since the first federal statute in 1917. Discusses the provisions of Title III of the Omnibus Crime Control and Safe Streets Act of 1968.

2905. Goldston, James A.; Jennifer M. Grayholm; and Robert J. Robinson. "A Nation Less Secure: Diminished Public Access to Information," Harvard Civil Rights and Civil Liberties Law Review 21/2 (Summer 1986): 409-491.

Examines the federal court rulings in U.S. v. Morison and C.I.A. v. Sims relevant to the release of classified information pertaining to national security matters. Argues that suppression of information under the Reagan administration has been the policy marching order.

2906. Goldwater, Barry. "On Covert Action in Chile, 1963-1973," Inter-American Economic Affairs 30 (Summer 1976): 85-95.

An argument in defense of the covert action in Chile. Senator Goldwater found too many other implications of the Allende government's associations with Cuba and the Soviet Union for the US to have take any other course of action.

2907. Goldwater, Barry. "Congress and Intelligence Oversight," Washington Quarterly 6/3 (Summer 1983): 16-21.

Argues that the Church Committee hearings in the 1970s were imposed by the Senate purely for the purpose of disturbing the work of the CIA. Argues for the reduction of oversight by the Congress and the need for more human intelligence.

2908. Goldwater, Barry M., Jr. "Bipartisan Privacy," Civil Liberties Review 1/3 (Summer 1974): 74-78.

Discusses the wide ranging and over-reaching use of the Social Security Number and the potentials for privacy invasions.

2909. Gole, Henry G. "Shadow Wars and Secret Wars: Phoenix and MACVSOG," Parameters: Journal of the U.S. Army War College 21/4 (Winter 1991-1992): 95-105.

A brief review essay covering four books concerned with the Vietnam war program, Phoenix.

2910. Gollin, Alfred M. "England Is No Longer an Island: The Phantom Airship Scare of 1909," Albion 13/1 (Spring 1981): 43-57.

Contains sections on the history of aviation, the air invasion possibilities of the times, and the phantom airship scare. The Brits were fearful of an air invasion by the Germans, worsened by the comments of Arthur Balfour and Maxim Haram.

2911. Gollin, James. "Stirring Up the Past: KAL Flight 007," International Journal of Intelligence and Counterintelligence 7/4 (Winter 1994): 445-463.

Reviews the known facts of the Soviet shootdown of the Korean Airlines jet in 1983; the role of intelligence before and after; the beginning of collaboration; the end product; ABC's of air navigation; what the radar proves; data from the intelligence community; and questions for the intelligence community.

2912. Golomb, Solomon W. "Cryptographic Reflections on the Genetic Code," Cryptologia 4/1 (January 1980): 15-19.

2913. Gooch, John. "Major Mundey, Miss Dwyer and the Dog: An Episode in Passport Control," Intelligence and National Security 3/2 (April 1988): 322-325.
　　An incident in the intelligence topic of tracking the movement of foreign nationals across domestic borders is discussed. Incident involving Major Charles Mundey and his friend Molly Dwyer occurred in 1940.

2914. Good, I. J. "A. M. Turing's Statistical Work in World War II," Biometrika 66/2 (1979): 393-396.

2915. Good, I. J. "Early Work on Computers at Bletchley," Cryptologia 3/2 (April 1979): 65-77.

2916. Good, I. J. "Early Work on Computers at Bletchley," Annals of the History of Computing 1/1 (July 1979): 38-48.
　　A summary of a speech given by the author in 1976 pertaining to early work on computers at England's Bletchley Park. Reflects upon his role in the destruction of German U-boats vital to enemy operations in North Africa.

2917. Good, Jane E. "America and the Russian Revolutionary Movement, 1888-1905," Russian Review 41/3 (July 1982): 273-287.
　　Focusses on activities of four individuals who contributed to fashioning anti-tsarist sentiment in the US: George Kennan; Sergei Kravchinskii Stepniak; Paul Miliukov; Ekaterina Breshko-Breshknovskaia.

2918. Goodboe, Michael E. "A Trained Eye Will See the Spy," Security Management 36/4 (April 1992): 49, 53.

2919. Goodman, Allan E. "U.S. Development Assistance in the Insurgency Environment: Gulliver's Coming Home," Naval War College Review (February 1972): 13-23.

2920. Goodman, Allan E. "Dateline Langley: Fixing the Intelligence Mess," Foreign Policy 57 (Winter 1984-1985): 160-179.
　　Author argues that lack of centralized intelligence collection and analysis is the core problem in the intelligence community. Contains sections on placing the blame for the "intelligence mess", the DCI as policy maker, and replacing the CIA.

2921. Goodman, Allan E. "Reforming U.S. Intelligence," Foreign Policy 67 (Summer 1987): 121-136.
　　Argues that President Reagan asserted too much control over the CIA,

thereby yielding unlawful orders that led to the Iran-Contra scandal. Discusses the background of covert actions, CIA errors in Iran-Contra, problems with covert actions, and suggested reforms.

2922. Goodman, Allan E. "Does Covert Action Have a Future?," Parameters: Journal of the U.S. Army War College 18/11 (June 1988): 74-80.

A review and analysis of various covert actions ordered by presidents from Truman to Reagan. Argues that covert actions in more recent times have produced less information and its overall effectiveness as an intelligence device has declined.

2923. Goodman, Allen E. "Shifting Paradigms, and Shifting Gears: A Perspective on Why There Is No Post-Cold War Intelligence Agenda," Intelligence and National Security 10/4 (October 1995): 3-9.

Points out the continuing roles of the intelligence community and the mission expectations placed on each of the key organizations within the CIA.

2924. Goodman, Allan E. "Testimony: Fact-Checking at the CIA," Foreign Policy 102 (Spring 1996): 180-182.

Some brief observations of the author regarding the need to introduce into CIA analytical work a more regimented fact-checking process, engaged in by analysts who would check each other's work products, and the need for oral briefings to be given at CIA prior to all meetings with policymakers.

2925. Goodman, Allan E. and Bruce D. Berkowitz. "Intelligence Without the Cold War," Intelligence and National Security 9/2 (April 1994): 301-319.

Focusses on revisions the authors believe are needed in the US intelligence process to improve the products and the credibility of the community.

2926. Goodman, Ernest. "The NLG, the FBI and the Civil Rights Movement: 1964--A Year of Decision," National Lawyers Guild Practitioner 38/1 (Winter 1981): 1-17.

Discussion of the National Lawyers Guild role and activities in the early days of the civil rights movement. Major sections discuss the NLG's advancement of civil rights initiatives, monitoring by the FBI, the Selma march and the FBI, and perspectives on the experience.

2927. Goodman, Glenn W., Jr. "Joint Tactical Fusion Program Automating the Processing of Battlefield Intelligence," Armed Forces Journal International (May 1988): 82-84.

2928. Goodman, Grant K. "Dharmapala in Japan, 1913," Japan Forum 5/2 (1993): 195-202.

2929. Goodman, Hirsh and Zeev Schiff. "The Attack on the Liberty," <u>Atlantic Monthly</u> 54/3 (September 1984): 78-84.

Details the attack on the U.S.S. Liberty by pilots of the Israeli Air Force. Contains sections on activities before the attack, the attack, and reparations to the United States.

2930. Goodman, Melvin A. "A Post-Cold War CIA," <u>Foreign Service Journal</u> 70/6 (June 1993): 18-23.

Argues his perspective on the need for significant reform of the Central Intelligence Agency. Major sections discuss politics and intelligence; the problem of "middle-age spread"; oversight of CIA by the Congress; and the need to return to original agency purposes. This author has conducted extensive studies of the CIA's organizational problems.

2931. Goodman, Paul. "The Military Intelligence Organization," <u>Military Review</u> 38/12 (March 1959): 68-72.

A description of an intelligence unit at the division or higher command level by one who headed such units.

2932. Goodman, Richard C. "Privacy and Political Freedom: Applications of the Fourth Amendment to 'National Security Investigations,'" <u>UCLA Law Review</u> 17/6 (June 1970): 1205-1251.

Argues that there is no "national security" exemption from the procedural safeguards of the Fourth Amendment of the United States Constitution. Includes discussion of the Fourth Amendment interests in privacy and political freedom, the development of warrantless national security eavesdropping, the application of the Fourth to national security, and a proposal for accommodation.

2933. Goodwin, Irwin. "East German Sentenced to 8 Years As Spy," <u>Physics Today</u> 38 (May 1985): 79-80.

2934. Goodwin, Irwin. "Physicists Refute Charges That Icons Helped Soviets Build Nuclear Bomb," <u>Physics Today</u> 47 (June 1994): 59-62.

2935. Goodyear, S. F. "Spycatcher?: Field Security as It Was... Perhaps," <u>Army Quarterly and Defense Journal</u> 113/1 (January 1983): 56-61.

The author's personal experiences in the Intelligence Corps during World War II.

2936. Gordeyev, N. "Operational Camouflage in Naval Landing Operations," <u>Voyenna-Istoricheskii Zhurnal</u> (April 1969): 41-51.

An analysis of several US, Japanese and British deceptions during World War II and the Korean War.

2937. Gordeyev, N. "Countering Enemy Intelligence," <u>Morskoi Sbornik</u> 10 (October 1972): 31-35.

Brief discusses in Russian, in this Russian Naval Review, the role of operational camoflage in deception strategies during World War II.

2938. Gordievsky, Oleg. "The KGB Archives," <u>Intelligence and National Security</u> 6/1 (January 1991): 7-14.

Contains a brief sample of the types of documents in the KGB archives in Moscow. Quotes passages concerning KGB operations from some documents.

2939. Gordievsky, Oleg. "The KGB After the Coup," <u>Intelligence and National Security</u> 8/3 (July 1993): 68-71.

A brief essay considering the role and organization of the intelligence service of Russia and the independent states of the former Soviet Union. Sets forth a brief perspective on the future of intelligence organizations and activities of the states' new intelligence organizations.

2940. Gordon, D. Brian. "Use of Civil Satellite Imagery for Operations Desert Shield/Desert Storm," <u>American Intelligence Journal</u> 13/1&2 (Winter-Spring 1992): 39-42.

Covers the use of the system by the Defense Intelligence Agency; uses by the Army, Air Force and Navy; mission to use the system in warfighting.

2941. Gordon, Don E. "Target: The Spoken Word," <u>Army</u> 29/9 (September 1979): 20-21.

A brief discussion of ground communications.

2942. Gordon, Don E. "CEWI Battalion: Intelligence and Electronic Warfare on the Battlefield," <u>Military Intelligence</u> 5 (October-December 1979): 22-28.

2943. Gordon, Don E. "The Electronic Battle," <u>Infantry</u> 70 (May-June 1980): 22-24.

2944. Gordon, Don E. "Does the Corps Need CEWI Battalions?," <u>Marine Corps Gazette</u> 67 (March 1983): 45-49.

2945. Gordon, Don E. "Terrorism - Are We Losing the War?," <u>Journal of Defense & Diplomacy</u> 4/3 (March 1986): 38-44.

Comments on the status and operability of US counterterrorism intelligence.

2946. Gordon, Don E. "Winners and Losers," <u>International Journal of Intelligence and Counterintelligence</u> 1/3 (Fall 1986): 1-24.

Compares competition in a free market with a free market in the realm of business intelligence. Contains sections of the intelligence cycle: directing; collecting; analyzing and processing; dissemination. Discusses relational data bases.

2947. Gordon, Don E. "Private Minnock's Private War," International Journal of Intelligence and Counterintelligence 4/2 (Summer 1990): 199-218.

An account of the events preceding the award of the Legion of Merit to Private Edward Minnock, an intelligence analyst who became the American hero of the 1968 Tet offensive.

2948. Gordon, John D., III. "The Trial of the Officers & Crew of the Schooner 'Savannah,'" Supreme Court Historical Society Yearbook (1983): 31-45.

Discusses the trial of the crew on the Confederate ship 'Savannah.' They were captured by the Union navy.

2949. Gordon, Max. "A Case History of U.S. Subversion: Guatemala, 1954," Science and Society 35 (Summer 1971): 129-155.

A detailed analysis of factors involved in the US covert action to unseat the Jacobo Arbenz government in Guatemala. Contains sections on the US role, the 1944-54 revolution, opposition and counter revolution, Guatemala after Arbenz.

2950. Gordon, Philip L. "Undermining Congressional Oversight of Covert Intelligence Operations: The Reagan Administration Secretly Arms Iran," New York University Review of Law & Social Change 16/2 (1987-88): 229-276.

Discusses historical precedent for the claim of executive privilege in intelligence matters; congressional oversight of intelligence matters; the Iran-Contra affair and prior notice; the invalidity of the Reagan administration's justification to withhold prior notification on weapons sales to Iran; and proposed improvements to oversight of intelligence matters.

2951. Goren, Dina. "Communication Intelligence and the Freedom of the Press. The Chicago Tribune's Battle of Midway Dispatch and the Breaking of the Japanese Naval Code," Journal of Contemporary History 16 (October 1981): 663-690.

Careful treatment of the incident in June 1942 when the Tribune revealed a US breach of Japanese codes, resulting in censorship and prosecution. A good case study analysis for research on secrecy, publication, and wartime.

2952. Gorkov, V. "Reconnaissance, Combat Command and Control Hardware," Aviation and Cosmonautics 11 (November 1985): 42-43.

2953. Gorodetsky, Gabriel. "Churchill's Warning to Stalin: A Reappraisal," Historical Journal 29/2 (1986): 979-990.

Details Winston Churchill's perceptions of a German invasion of the Soviet Union. A useful reference for studies of indications and warnings.

2954. Gorodnichi, N. F. "Little-Known Aspect of ARA Activity in Soviet Russia," Voprosy Istorii 12 (1968): 47-58.

2955. Gorst, Anthony and W. Scott Lucas. "The Other Collusion: Operation Straggle and Anglo-American Intervention in Syria, 1955-56," Intelligence and National Security 4/3 (July 1989): 579-595.
   Major sections discuss the background period, 1945-55; the origins of Operation Straggle, 1955-56; the development of the Straggle operation, March-October 1956. Discusses the Suez Canal crisis of 1956 and the role of American intelligence in providing political pressure.

2956. Gose, Elliott B. "'Cruel Devourer of the World's Light': 'The Secret Agent,'" Nineteenth Century Fiction 15/1 (June 1960): 39-51.
   A literary analysis and vigorous defense of Joseph Conrad's The Secret Agent. Focusses mainly on the author's use of symbolism.

2957. Gotham, Kevin. "Domestic Security for the American State: The FBI, Covert Repression, and Democratic Legitimacy," Journal of Political and Military Sociology 22 (Winter 1994): 203-222.
   A critical examination of the FBI's internal security program known as COINTELPRO.

2958. Gotteri, Nicola. "Le Lorgne d'Idaville and the Intelligence Network of the Ministry of Foreign Affairs During the Russian Campaign, June 1912-March 1913," Revue d'Histoire Diplomatique 103/1-2 (1989): 113-145.

2959. Gottesman, Lawrence P. "The Intelligence Identities Protection Act of 1982: An Assessment of the Constitutionality of Section 601 (c)," Brooklyn Law Review 49/3 (Spring 1983): 479-516.
   Focusses on the constitutionality of the section and asks whether the publication of lawfully obtained information is punishable by act of Congress when the publisher merely has "reason to believe" that such publication would impair or impede foreign intelligence activities. Concludes that the section suffers major constitutional defects.

2960. Gottlieb, Jeff. "Frame-ups," Politics Today 5/3 (May-June 1978): 12-13.
   Brief discussion of the Rosenberg espionage case, emphasizing that the evidence against the two convicted spies was weak.

2961. Gouaze, Linda Y. "Needles and Haystacks: The Search for Ultra in the 1930s (An Excerpt)," Cryptologia 11/2 (April 1987): 85-92.

2962. Gould, William B. "The Right to Travel and National Security," Washington University Law Quarterly 1961 (1961): 334-366.

Concludes that the right to travel abroad is limited and passport controls can intervene where national security is threatened. Summarizes the legislation under consideration at the time.

2963. Goulden, Joseph C. "CIA's Korean Caper: Hans Tofte Leads the Agency to Its First Major Coup," Soldier of Fortune (May 1983).

2964. Goulden, Joseph C. "The Mercenary Life," Intelligence Quarterly 1/2 (July 1985): 1-4.

The author's brief summation of the intrigues surrounding former CIA employee Edwin P. Wilson.

2965. Goulden, Joseph C. "The Rogue of Rogues," International Journal of Intelligence and Counterintelligence 1/1 (Spring 1986): 76-82.

Author disagrees sharply with Walter Pforzheimer on the matter of the negative impact of Edwin P. Wilson's alleged dealings in weapons of death with Libya's leader Muammar Quaddafi. Says that Wilson and others could have escaped all US prosecution efforts with only minimal legal planning, thus calling for tougher, more thorough legislation to deal with merchants of terrorism.

2966. Goulter, Christiana. "The Role of Intelligence in Coastal Command's Anti-Shipping Campaign, 1940-45," Intelligence and National Security 5/1 (January 1990): 84-109.

Concludes that the British anti-shipping campaign against the German naval operations could not have been a success without the employment of five types of intelligence: photographic, agents, diplomatic, ordinary SIGINT, and Enigma.

2967. Gourley, Dudley D. "A Final Solution to the Problem of Organized Crime," Police Chief 39/2 (February 1972): 18.

Argues that organized crime can be attacked by strengthening access to information by the Internal Revenue Service and by creating an economic intelligence group to study economic controls. Useful in studies of the IRS intelligence bureau operations. Few such studies exist.

2968. Gourley, Dudley D. "In Brief: Some Management Problems-The Role of Police Intelligence," Police Chief 40/2 (February 1973): 38.

Argues the importance of altering the police approach to crime from reaction force to action force. Failure by police chiefs to more effectively use information they can gather will ultimately lead to overall failure in intelligence operations.

2969. Gourley, Robert B. "Naval Intelligence and the Internet," Naval Intelligence Professionals Quarterly 11/2 (Spring 1995): 11-12.

2970. Gourley, Robert D. "A War Japan Won With Intelligence," Naval Intelligence Professionals Quarterly 10/3 (Summer 1994): 1-4.

2971. Gourley, Scott R. "Tactical Intelligence Is Key to the AirLand Battle Scenario," Electronic Warfare/Defense Electronics 20 (February 1988): 43-44.

2972. Gourley, Scott R. "Electronic Warfare: Radar Reflectors and Passive Jamming," Jane's Soviet Intelligence Review 2/1 (January 1990): 41.

2973. Gowing, Margaret. "Reflections in Atomic Energy History," Bulletin of the Atomic Scientists 35/3 (1979): 51-54.
    The efforts to secure the design and development of the atomic bomb during World War II caused conflict between scientists in England, France, and the United States.

2974. Grabo, Cynthia M. "Soviet Deception in the Czech Crisis," Studies in Intelligence 14/1 (Spring 1970).

2975. Grabo, Cynthia M. "Deception in the Normandy Invasion," American Intelligence Journal 8/3 (Summer 1987).

2976. Grabo, Cynthia M. "The Watch Committee and the National Indications Center: The Evolution of U.S. Strategic Warning 1950-1975," International Journal of Intelligence and Counterintelligence 3/3 (Fall 1989): 363-385.
    The author characterizes this piece as an unofficial history and a memoir, written without access to original records but with substantial recall of personal involvement, of the Watch Committee at CIA. Major sections discuss the beginnings, 1948-1950; reorganization and the establishment of the National Indications Center; composition of the Watch Committee and the NIC; the sixties, new leaders, new problems; and the decline and demise of the Watch Committee.

2977. Grabo, Cynthia M. "Warning and Deception," American Intelligence Journal 12/1 (Winter 1991): 40-43.
    Addresses the role of warning intelligence regarding military or other hostile attack by a foreign power. Discusses the role of deception and provides several historical examples of the extent to which ingredients of surprise were operative in each event.

2978. Graeber, Doris A. "Executive Decision-Making," Proceedings of the Academy of Political Science 34/4 (1982): 75-87.
    Contains sections on institutional competence and the limitation on

delegation of authority, policies underlying the creation of independent administrative agencies, agency accountability, and variations in agency performance. Useful background piece for studies of intelligence agency accountability.

2979. Graham, Daniel O. "Estimating the Threat: A Soldier's Job," Army 23/4 (April 1973): 14-18.
Discusses the important role of the armed forces in estimating potential enemy strengths and weaknesses. Argues that the decline of US intelligence began after World War II and requires improvements.

2980. Graham, Daniel O. "Fact vs. Fantasy--the Tet Intelligence Imbroglio," Armed Forces Journal International 113/4 (December 1975): 23-24.
An objection to the findings of CIA's Sam Adams with respect to the body counts in Vietnam. Adams' full account appeared in his book, War of Numbers, published in 1994.

2981. Graham, Daniel O. "The Intelligence Mythology of Washington," Strategic Review 4/3 (Autumn 1976): 59-66.
Argues for a revision in our thought processes about the capabilities and weaknesses of the intelligence services of the United States. Contains sections on the myth of the missile gap; bias at CIA; analysis, bias and judgment; and the search for objective bias.

2982. Graham, Daniel O. "The Soviet Military Budget Controversy," Air Force Magazine 59/5 (May 1976): 33-37.

2983. Graham, Katherine. "Secrecy and the Press," Studies in Intelligence 32/4 (Winter 1988).

2984. Graham, Robert A. "Spie Naziste Attorno al Vaticano durante la Seconda Guerra Mondiale," Civilta Cattolica 1 (1970): 21-31.

2985. Granatstein, J. L. "The 'Man of Secrets' in Canada, 1934," Dalhousie Review 51/4 (1971-72): 504-521.
Discusses the experiences of British Lieutenant Colonel Sir Maurice Hankey in shaping British policy toward the Dominions and dependencies. Contains his secret diplomatic writings on military and domestic affairs in Canada.

2986. Granatstein, J. L. "Spies," Queen's Quarterly 89/3 (Autumn 1982): 529-537.
A book review essay focusing in spy cases in Canada and the relatively poor methodology of journalistic studies of espionage.

2987. Granholm, Jennifer M. "Video Surveillance on Public Streets: The Constitutionality of Invisible Citizen Searches," University of Detroit Law Review 64/4 (Summer 1987): 687-713.

Details the funding by Detroit's Mayor Coleman Young for installation of street video cameras to monitor pedestrians and vehicles. Contains sections on arguments against the plan, Fourth Amendment prohibitions, First Amendment prohibitions regarding speech and communication, and charge of no individualized suspicion.

2988. Grant, Jennifer. "Internal Reporting by Investigative Journalists in China and its Influence on Government Policy," Gazette 41/1 (1988): 53-65.

Discusses methods of gathering and reporting of information pertaining to Chinese internal affairs to government agents.

2989. Grant, Natalie. "A Thermidorean Amalgam," Russian Review 22/3 (July 1963): 253-273.

An early study of the case of Ado Birk, Estonian Minister in Moscow from 1922 to 1927, and the role of early Soviet security services.

2990. Grant, Natalie. "The 'Zinoviev Letter' Case," Soviet Studies 19 (October 1967): 264-277.

The interception of a forged letter bearing a Soviet official's signature to the British Communist Party. The letter was one of several forgeries perpetrated by Soviet intelligence.

2991. Grant, Natalie. "Forgery in International Affairs," Foreign Service Journal 47 (May 1970): 31-32, 46.

Soviet forgeries have served as tools of provocation and deceit within the Soviet disinformation program. Discusses the examination of forged materials and the influence a forged document can have.

2992. Grant, Natalie. "Deception on a Grand Scale," International Journal of Intelligence and Counterintelligence 1/4 (Winter 1986-1987): 51-78.

An account of "The Trust," a revolutionary Russian organization on the side of the anti-communists aimed at intelligence gathering and disinformation. Excellent details and historical data relevant to the use of deception on a grand scale.

2993. Grant, Natalie. "The Trust," American Intelligence Journal 12/1 (Winter 1991): 11-15.

The author, a former member of the Russian Section of the American Legation in Riga, Latvia, discusses Soviet espionage in Europe under the cover of "The Trust," a bogus anti-Soviet clandestine organization known as Monarchist Organization of Central Russia.

2994. Gravely, Samuel. "The Ocean Surveillance Information System," Signal (October): 30-36.

2995. Graves, Harold N., Jr. "Propaganda by Shortwave: Berlin Calling America," Public Opinion Quarterly 4 (Spring 1940): 601-619.
Discusses German broadcasts to the US at the beginning of World War II. Broadcasts were intended to alter American attitudes about British intentions.

2996. Gray, Alfred M. "Global Intelligence Challenges in the 1990s," American Intelligence Journal 11/1 (Winter 1989-1990): 3-7.
The author, a decorated member of the Joint Chiefs of Staff, argues for increased intelligence efforts aimed at Third World countries, particularly in relationship to the Marine Corps mission.

2997. Gray, Austin K. "Some Observations of Christopher Marlowe, Government Agent," PMLA: Publications of the Modern Language Association 43/3 (September 1928): 682-700.
The author, a professor at Haverford College, writes about the Privy Council document, June 29, 1587; Marlowe and Roman Catholicism; Rheims and Seminarists; Rheims and Cambridge; students and poets as spies; spies in general; Sir James Crofts; another atheist spy; Marlowe and Newgate; the Baines report, 1593; Richard Cholmely, spy; the King of Scots; Robert Poley, spy; and biography in the plays.

2998. Gray, Colin S. "Gap Prediction and America's Defense: Arms Race Behavior in the Eisenhower Years," Orbis 16 (Spring 1972): 257-274.
Discusses various eras in estimating the arms gap between the US and the Soviet Union, beginning with the influences of the Sputnik I launch and the Gaither Committee report.

2999. Gray, Colin S. "SALT I Aftermath: Have the Soviets Been Cheating?," Air Force Magazine 58 (November 1975): 28-33.

3000. Gray, Colin S. "Moscow Is Cheating," Foreign Policy 56 (Fall 1984): 141-152.
Argues that the executive and legislative branches have been ineffective in estimating and monitoring the degree to which the Soviet Union has cheated on treaties and agreements. Discusses the loss of US credibility with the Soviets and the need for a firm resolve; sets forth suggestions for a "responsible policy."

3001. Gray, Jonathan M. "Operation Mallfinger: Invisible Theatre in a Popular Context," TDR 37 (Winter 1993): 128-142.
Includes discussion of espionage in the context of mass media presentations.

3002. Gray, Paul E. "The University Case Against Secrecy," Technology Review 23/2 (July 1982): 10-12.

Argues the positive and negative implications of government research conducted in universities and the extent to which such research findings should remain secret. Sections discuss the origins of secret university research; government dependence on university research; the compromises that have been made on secrecy in university research; and the balance between the competing arguments.

3003. Gray, Robert C. "Reforming the CIA," Intellect 104 (March 1976): 426-428.

A discussion of the evolution of the CIA, the inadequacies of proposed reforms and the need to delineate CIA activities. Argues that the CIA has been beyond the accountability of Congress for several years.

3004. Greaves, Fielding C. "Intelligence--Key to Victory," Military Review 45/9 (September 1965): 33-38.

3005. Greely, Adolphus W. "Balloons in War," Harper's 101 (June 1900): 33-50.

A lengthy and detailed history of the balloon in warfare as a modern "aeronautical device". Such devices are durable and lend themselves to learning enemy positions and dropping explosives behind enemy lines.

3006. Greely, Adolphus W. "The Signal Corps in War Time," Century Magazine 66 (October 1903): 811-826.

Traces the roots of wartime communications in the US. Refers to the Spanish-American war and the importance of the Signal Corps.

3007. Green, Harold P. "Atomic Energy Information Control," Chicago Bar Record 38/2 (November 1956): 55-62.

An address before the Chicago Bar Association in which the author discusses the implications of extension of the atomic energy information control system (i.e., secrecy enforcement) into private enterprise in a competitive economy.

3008. Green, Harold P. "The Atomic Energy Access Permit Program," George Washington Law Review 25 (1957): 548-567.

Discusses business problems encountered by controls placed on atomic energy information. Outlines the provisions of the Atomic Energy Act of 1954.

3009. Green, Harold P. "The Oppenheimer Case: A Study in the Abuse of Law," Bulletin of the Atomic Scientists 33/7 (September 1977): 12-16, 56-61.

Discussion of the government's information security program, the

Oppenheimer case, and the vendetta against the scientist which was based largely on character assassination. Parallels this case with dynamics of the Watergate affair.

3010. Green, Herbert. "The Citizen Informant," Army Lawyer (January 1982): 1-16.
 Covers the federal system applicability of the Aguilar-Spinelli test; presumptive credibility; corroboration; informant's identity; the military system by comparison; and conclusions.

3011. Green, Jonathan J. "Electronic Monitoring in the Workplace: The Need For Standards," Washington Law Review 52 (March 1984): 438-458.
 Contains sections on electronic eavesdropping, the right of privacy, and wiretapping. Explores the application of Title III of the Omnibus Crime Control and Safe Streets Act of 1968 to the American workplace.

3012. Green, Mary J. "Postmodern Agents: Cultural Representation in Hubert Aquin's Prochain Episode and Yolande Villemaire's Meurtres a Blanc," University of Toronto Quarterly 63 (Summer 1994): 584-597.
 Espionage is discussed in connection with French Canadian literature.

3013. Green, M. L. "Dissemination of Intelligence," Military Review (April 1949): 58-62.
 Argues that intelligence is valueless when it is not disseminated in a timely manner. Different forms of dissemination are discussed.

3014. Green, Murray. "Intelligence for Sale...at the Corner Newsstand," Air Force Magazine 38 (November 1955): 82-86.
 Discusses the amount of sensitive material published in open sources that the Soviets can easily acquire from news magazines and congressional hearings.

3015. Green, Ronald M. "The Ethics of Competitor Intelligence Gathering," Social Responsibility: Business, Journalism, Law, Medicine 18 (1992): 5-20.

3016. Green, William. "The U-2: Facts (and Fiction)," R.A.F. Flying Review 15 (August 1960): 18-22.

3017. Green, William C. "The Historic Russian Drive for a Warm Water Port: Anatomy of a Geopolitical Myth," Naval War College Review (Spring 1993): 80-102.
 Major sections discuss geopoliticians; World War II; the Non-Aggression Pact; wartime conferences; revival of geopolitics; Russian and Soviet views on the value of distant ports; and a dangerous geopolitical myth. Role of intelligence is important in the discussion of distant port planning and strategy.

3018. Greenberg, Irwin. "The Role of Deception in Decision Theory," Conflict Resolution 26/1 (March 1982): 139-156.

Identifies types of deception, goals of deception and examples of deception in international conflicts.

3019. Greenberg, Maurice B. and Richard N. Haas. "Making Intelligence Smarter," International Journal of Intelligence and Counterintelligence 9/2 (Summer 1996): 135-144.

This is an excerpt of a Report of an Independent Task Force sponsored by the Council on Foreign Relations 1996. Major sections discuss the executive summary; improving the product; internal changes; introduction and background; the need for intelligence; collection priorities; setting priorities; improving analysis; economic intelligence clandestine activities; organization; military issues; intelligence and law enforcement; and additional views of participants.

3020. Greene, A. Wilson. "Opportunity to the South: Meade versus Jackson at Fredericksburg," Civil War History 33/4 (December 1987).

3021. Greene, Dorian D. "Ethical Dilemmas Confronting Intelligence Agency Counsel," Tulsa Journal of Comparative & International Law 2 (Fall 1994): 91-108.

Topics under discussion include legal and government ethics, controversies and ethical dilemmas, and national security within the scope of concerns for intelligence agency lawyers.

3022. Greene, Graham and Malcolm Muggeridge. "Reflections on the Character of Kim Philby," Esquire 70 (September 1960): 3-10.

Argues that British spy and defector was working for a cause, not for himself. Contains sections on the British secret service, Philby's beliefs, Philby's disagreeable side, Philby's personality, and Philby's travel to Beirut.

3023. Greene, H. Frances. "Competitive Intelligence and the Information Center," Special Libraries 79 (Fall 1988): 285-295.

3024. Greene, Ward K. "Before James Bond," Studies in Intelligence 26/1 (Spring 1982).

Deals with spy comics.

3025. Greenfield, Gary R. "Yet Another Matrix Cryptosystem," Cryptologia 18/1 (January 1994): 41-51.

3026. Greenfield, James J. "Remedies--Fiduciaries--ConstructiveTrusts-- A CIA Agent's Failure to Submit His Manuscript for Prepublication Review Constitutes a Breach of Fiduciary Duty Warranting the Imposition of a Constructive Trust

Upon Proceeds from the Sale of His Book," <u>University of Cincinnati Law Review</u> 49/3 (Summer 1980): 690-697.

A brief law note regarding the Frank Snepp suit to protect the profits from his book, <u>Decent Interval</u>. Examines the issues of constructive trust versus prior restraint.

3027. Greenidge, A. H. J. "The Conception of Treason in Roman Law," <u>Juridical Review</u> 7 (1895): 228-240.

3028. Greening, Thomas. "The KAL Plane Tragedy Elicits and Clarifies Value Positions," <u>Political Psychology</u> 5/4 (December 1984): 749-751.

The shoot-down of the Korean Airlines jet by Soviet military fighters is a good example of how nations make tradeoff decisions to sacrifice others for their own protection. Emphasizes the notion of the abstract social good.

3029. Greenleaf, Richard E. "The Inquisition in Spanish Louisiana, 1762-1800," <u>New Mexico Historical Review</u> 50/1 (1975): 45-72.

Discusses the issue of the preservation of the state through the imposition of security measures in the historical context of Spanish Louisiana in the late eighteenth century.

3030. Greenough, H. Paul. "Cryptanalysis of the Uncaged Hagelin," <u>Cryptologia</u> 14/2 (April 1990): 145-161.

3031. Greenough, Robert B. "Communist Lessons from the Korean Air War," <u>Air University Review</u> 5/4 (Winter 1952-1953): 22-29.

3032. Greenspan, E. L. "Bill C-157: An Examination of the Exercise of Power," <u>Advocates' Society Journal</u> 2/4 (October 1983): 39-41.

Concerns espionage in Canada and legislative efforts to control it.

3033. Greenspoon, Robert. "U.S. Government Control Over the Export of Scientific Research and Other Technical Data: Holes in the Sieve," <u>Michigan Journal of International Law</u> 16 (Winter 1995): 583-600.

3034. Greenstein, Ruth L. "National Security Restrictions on Research," <u>Wisconsin International Law Journal</u> 2 (1982-1983): 49-58.

Explores the legal practices and implications of restricting US technological outflow to Warsaw Pact nations.

3035. Greenwalt, Kent. "The Consent Problem in Wiretapping and Eavesdropping: Surreptitious Monitoring with the Consent of a Participant in a Conversation," <u>Columbia Law Review</u> 68/2 (February 1968): 189-240.

Contains sections on third party wiretapping, criminal sanctions, and use of civil law: Constitutional decisions; statutes and administrative rules; purposes of and objections to participant monitoring; relevant factors in evaluating instances of participant monitoring; and drawing lines between permitted and prohibited monitoring.

3036. Greenwood, F. Murray. "The Treason Trial and Execution of David McLane," Manitoba Law Journal 20/1 (Fall 1991): 3-14.
    Discussion of eighteenth century anti-treason practices in Canada, in particular the trial of John McLane; the Baconian judiciary; discipline in the Hudson Bay Company; mutiny on the S.S. Beaver and its legacy; and the aftermath of the McLane trial and execution.

3037. Greenwood, Ted. "Reconnaissance and Arms Control," Scientific American 228/2 (February 1973): 14-19.
    A technical discussion of satellite reconnaissance for verifying compliance with SALT I and II.

3038. Greer, Pamela S. "The Suppression Sanction in the Federal Electronic Surveillance Statute," Washington University Law Quarterly 62/4 (Winter 1985): 707-738.
    Examines the background, statutory framework and procedural requirements of Title III of the Omnibus Crime Control and Safe Streets Act of 1968. Also examines judicial use of suppression to sanction violations of the statute. Argues for acceptance of the test as set forth in United States v. Chun.

3039. Gregg, Donald. "Congress and the Directorate of Operations: An Odd Couple?," Studies in Intelligence 23/1 (Spring 1979).

3040. Gregorovic, Miroslav. "The Defense of the Cuban Revolution Against Counterrevolution and Aggression: The Cuban Crisis of 1961-62," Slovansky Prehled 72/1 (1986): 14-26.

3041. Gregory, F. E. C. "Changes in American Systems of Policing Since 1960 - A Selective Analysis," Police Journal 51/4 (October-December 1978): 357-365.
    Extensive discussion of the subject, including role of intelligence in new police organizations.

3042. Gregory, F. E. C. "British Police and Terrorism," Terrorism: An International Journal 5/1-2 (1981): 107-123.
    Discusses police actions against terrorism in England, Scotland and Wales, including the role of intelligence in such operations.

3043. Gregory, F. E. C. "The Indian Police System and Internal Conflicts," Conflict Quarterly 2/1 (Spring 1981): 18-24.

3044. Gregory, Jesse O. "Flak Intelligence Memories," Coast Artillery Journal 91 (May-June 1948): 18-24.

Reflections upon German anti-aircraft defenses in Europe.

3045. Gregory, Thomas W. "Committee in Relation to the Department of Justice," American Bar Association Journal 4/3 (July 1918): 305-316.

The author, then Attorney General of the United States, discusses the limited authority of the Justice Department to prosecute lynching, alien enemies and espionage.

3046. Gregory, Thomas W. "Disloyalty and Treason and Their Punishment as Provided by Federal Law," Washington Law Reporter (1918): 326-328.

3047. Greiner, Bernd. "The Cuban Missile Crisis Reconsidered -- The Soviet View: An Interview with Sergo Mikoyan," Diplomatic History 14/2 (Spring 1990): 205-221.

A conference on the missile crisis offered significantly more information about the background circumstances of the situation than had been available throughout previous studies.

3048. Grell, William F. "A Marine with O.S.S.," Marine Corps Gazette 29 (December 1945): 14-18.

Discusses the author's recollections in the work of the O.S.S. in the French resistance.

3049. Grenier, R. "Movies: Treason Chic," Commentary 79 (January 1985): 61-65.

Evaluates the social context associated with appearance of two British films (An Englishman Abroad; Another Country), and a British author's novel (The Little Drummer Girl, by John LeCarre) subsequently made into film. Argues that treason is a violation of one's culture; persons committing treason are criminals, not heros.

3050. Gretton, Peter. "The Nyon Conference - the Naval Aspect," English Historical Review 354 (January 1975): 103-112.

Discusses aspects relevant to military actions of several nations in the Spanish civil war in the mid-1930s. Mentions the secrets of cryptography in naval patrols in the Mediterranean.

3051. Greve, Karen H. "Graymail: The Disclose or Dismiss Dilemma in Criminal Prosecutions," Case Western Reserve Law Review 31/1 (Fall 1980): 84-131.

Examines theretofore recent cases in which defendants requested US government classified information. Analyzes the advantages and disadvantages of the options available to resolve the dilemma. Concludes that congressional attempts to codify the rules will prove to be cumbersome and inefficient.

3052. Greve, Marcelo A. "The Capture of the USS Pueblo and International Maritime Law," Revista de Marina 6 (1984): 689-694.

3053. Gribnov, A. "Surprise in Combat," Krasnaya Zvezda 11 (January 1974): 2+.

3054. Grieb, Kenneth J. "Reginald Del Valle: A California Diplomat's Sojourn in Mexico," California Historical Society Quarterly 47/4 (1968): 315-328.

3055. Grieco, Joseph M. and Duncan L. Clarke. "National Security Affairs: A Selective Bibliography," Policy Studies Journal 7/1 (1978): 157-165.
        Contains periodical citations on formation of national policy and strategy, defense policy-making, national intelligence and the intelligence community, arms control formulation, Congress and national security policy making, and the American public and national security policy.

3056. Grier, Peter. "The Organization Spook: ... OSS ... Just Another Washington Bureaucracy," Washington Monthly 16/11 (December 1984): 20-23.
        An excellent brief history of the internal operations and bureaucratic responses of the Office of Strategic Services during World War II. Mentions J. Edgar Hoover's concern for the OSS threat to FBI influence. This article was also printed in Studies in Intelligence 29/1 (Spring 1985).

3057. Grier, Samuel L. "Black Pajama Intelligence," Marine Corps Gazette 51 (April 1967): 36-40.

3058. Gries, David D. "The CIA and Congress: Uneasy Partners," Studies in Intelligence 31/2 (Summer 1987).
        An overview of the history of congressional involvement in the intelligence field, beginning with the first Continental Congress and in more modern times the National Security Act of 1947. Major sections discuss the benefits of oversight; basic concerns; and the room for improvement. This article was published in a special edition of declassified CIA documents in Studies in Intelligence 31 (September 1987): 77-84.

3059. Gries, David D. "New Links Between Intelligence and Policy," Studies in Intelligence 34/2 (Summer 1990): 1-6.
        Major sections discuss the growing importance of oral assessments; changing role of written assessments; foreign policy decisionmaking; evolving uses of intelligence; lost opportunities; strengthening intelligence-policy linkages.

3060. Gries, David D. "Intelligence in the 1990s," Studies in Intelligence 35/1 (Spring 1991): 5-11.

A discussion of the need for openness with respect to intelligence community records; openness in perspective; negative aspects of openness; and openness and the future of intelligence.

3061. Gries, David D. "A New Look for Intelligence," Intelligence and National Security 10/1 (January 1995): 170-183.

An accounting of areas of interest in the overhaul of the intelligence community and the Central Intelligence Agency, late 1990s. Major sections discuss: organizational relationships; increasing public accountability; simplifying document classification practices; adjusting core activities; and looking ahead.

3062. Griffin, David E. "The Role of the French Air Force, the Battle of France, 1940," Aerospace Historian 21/3 (1974): 144-153.

3063. Griffith, John. "The Official Secrets Act 1989," Journal of Law and Society 16/2 (Autumn 1989): 273-290.

Considers the reasons for revising the Official Secrets Act of 1911 and particular cases in which information was leaked to the press on matters the British government had hoped to keep secured away of public knowledge.

3064. Griffith, Robert. "The Chilling Effect," Wilson Quarterly 2/3 (Summer 1978): 135-136.

A brief discussion of the McCarran Act, Senator Joe McCarthy, and the 'red menace.' Mentions the expansion of power of the FBI in the 1950s.

3065. Griffen, Rodman D. "The New CIA: Does the Agency Have A Role in the Post-Cold War Era?," CQ Researcher 2 (December 1992): 1073-1095.

An inquiry into the overall effectiveness of CIA during the cold war and speculations about CIA's future roles. Emphasizes the some newer CIA missions in nuclear proliferation, drug trafficking, and terrorism.

3066. Grigulevich, I. R. "The Rosenbergs," Voprosy Istorii 11 (1980): 87-96.

3067. Grimm, Victor E. "Wiretapping: The Federal Law," Journal of Criminal Law, Criminology and Police Science 51/4 (November-December 1960): 441-448.

A case law comment on the subject.

3068. Grinter, Laurence E. "How They Lost: Doctrines, Strategies and Outcomes of the Vietnam War," Asian Survey 15/12 (December 1975): 1114-1132.

Discusses pacification strategy; doctrines, programs and strategies; author analyses of the war; and conclusions.

3069. Griswold, Erwin N. "The Pentagon Papers Case: A Personal Footnote," Supreme Court Historical Society Yearbook (1984): 112-116.

3070. Griswold, Lawrence. "The Congress and Intelligence," Sea Power 19 (June 1976): 31-34.

3071. Grodin, Rachel. "Le Vol d'Information dans la Societe Canadienne," Revue Generale de Droit 20 (June 1989): 235-263.

3072. Grodzins, Morton. "The Basis of National Loyalty," Bulletin of the Atomic Scientists 7/12 (December 1951): 356-362.
        Offers philosophical discussion of functions of loyalty, strands of national loyalty, social impediments to disloyalty, and situations of scientists and loyalty.

3073. Gromley, Charles R. "Discovery Against the Government of Military and Other Confidential Matters," Kentucky Law Journal 43 (1955): 343-356.
        Introduction to the types of of claims involving discovery against government and military agencies; analysis of the problems of government privilege involving immunity and state secrets; and conclusions.

3074. Grondona, Mariano. "Reconciling Internal Security and Human Rights," International Security 3/1 (Summer 1978): 3-16.
        Discusses the balance between internal security and human rights, pointing to the thesis that nations that abuse human rights are "undersecure."

3075. Grossman, C. J. "The McCarran-Walter Act: War Against Margaret Randall and the First Amendment," Crime and Social Justice 27-28 (1987): 220-233.

3076. Grossman, Larry. "Intelligence in the World of Change," Government Executive (March 1992): 11-35.

3077. Groth, Alexander J. "On the Intelligence Aspects of Personal Diplomacy," Orbis 7 (Winter 1964): 833-848.
        Argues that personal diplomacy as a method of gathering intelligence is risky and somewhat incomplete. Refers to personal contacts between Hitler, Stalin and Roosevelt. Contains sections on the policymaker's knowledge, personal contact dynamics, Stalin, diplomacy in Russia, and wartime personal diplomacy.

3078. Groth, Alexander J. and John D. Froeliger. "Unheeded Warnings: Some Intelligence Lessons of the 1930s and 1940s," Comparative Strategy 10/4 (October-December 1991): 331-346.

3079. Grunbaum, W. F. "The British Security Program," Western Political Quarterly 13 (September 1960): 764-779.

Problems faced by the US and the British in standardizing their respective internal security programs, due mainly to the need to balance liberty with security of the state. Contains sections on the evolution of the policy, the mechanics of the program, and the operations of the program.

3080. Gruner, Richard. "Government Monitoring of International Electronic Communications: National Security Agency Watch List Surveillance and the Fourth Amendment," Southern California Law Review 51/3 (March 1978): 429-466.

Discusses NSA's watch list surveillance program, constitutionality of watch lists, standards for judicial warrants for surveillance, and conclusions.

3081. Grunfeld, A. Tom. "The Shanghai Syndrome--Spies and Politics, East and West: A Review Article," Bulletin of Concerned Asian Scholars 22/2 (1990): 64-79.

3082. Grzesinski, Albert and Charles E. Hewitt, Jr. "Hitler's Branch Offices, U.S.A.," Current History (November 1940): 11-13.

Brief discussion of German spies in the US prior to US involvement in World War II.

3083. Grzybowski, Kazimierz. "The Powers Trial and the 1958 Reform of Soviet Criminal Law," American Journal of Comparative Law 9 (1960): 425-440.

Discusses the role of the Powers case in Soviet law as an opportunity for the Soviets to display advances in legal procedure. Contains sections on Powers as a test case, form and substance, the issue of guilt, limits of jurisdiction, and pretrial proceedings and the judicial process.

3084. Guback, Thomas H. "General Sherman's War on the Press," Journalism Quarterly 36/2 (1959): 171-176.

Discusses Sherman's court martial of Thomas W. Knox, a reporter for the New York Herald, for Knox's reporting of the Battle of Vicksburg.

3085. Gubbins, Colin. "Resistance Movements in the War," Journal of the Royal Institute for Defence Studies 92 (May 1948): 210-233.

3086. Gudgel, Edward F. "Intelligence--a New Approach," Signal 26 (June 1972): 69-70.

3087. Gudgin, Peter. "Phantom British Tank Regiments of World War II," Journal of the Royal United Service Institute for Defence Studies 125/3 (September 1980): 64-68.

Discusses the operations of two British tank units in the early phases of the war in the Middle East.

3088. Guelker, Francis. "A Cryptographer's War Memories," Cryptologia 8/3 (July 1984): 203-207.
The personal recollections of the author's experiences in Europe in World War II.

3089. Guenther, Lisa and John Guenther. "The Bowen Collection, One Man's Contribution," American Intelligence Journal 3/1 (Winter 1980).

3090. Guerlac, Henry and Marie Boas. "The Radar War Against the U-Boat," Military Affairs 14/2 (Summer 1950): 99-111.

3091. Guerra, Sandra. "Domestic Drug Interdiction: Finding the Balance," Journal of Criminal Law and Criminology 82 (Winter 1992): 1109-1161.
Critiques shift in police focus toward regulatory style of operations from prior reactive role and examines legal and policy issues raised. Discusses Supreme Court reliance on administrative search doctrine to uphold current methods of investigation. Proposes alternative means of interdiction and issues to be considered in implementation.

3092. Guggenheim, Colette. "The Hiss Affair, An American Dreyfus Affair?," Esprit 1 (1975): 106-112.
Article in French comparing the Alger Hiss case with the infamous 19th century Dreyfus case in France. It suggests that Hiss may have been innocent.

3093. Guida, Richard A. "Protecting America's Military Technology," U.S. Naval Institute Proceedings 110/1 (January 1984): 35-40.
A brief discussion of the fear that the Freedom of Information Act may be responsible for the loss of military secrets.

3094. Guiler, Douglas C. "Evaluating Soviet Military Strength," Studies in Intelligence 34/4 (Winter 1990).

3095. Guill, Manuela. "Strategic Defense Initiative: Defense Against Ballistic Missiles or a Technique of Strategic Deception?," American Intelligence Journal 10/1 (Spring 1989): 10-17.

3096. Guill, Manuela. "Federal Aviation Administration Office of Civil Aviation Security Intelligence," American Intelligence Journal 13/3 (Summer 1992): 29-31.
Explores the mission of the Office of Civil Aviation Security Intelligence (ACI); the Operations Division; Strategic Analysis Division; Sensitive Activities and Law Enforcement Support Division; and Special Evaluation Division.

3097. Guillou, Louis C.; Marc Davio; and Jean-Jacques Quisquater. "Public-Key Techniques: Randomness and Redundancy," Cryptologia 13/2 (April 1989): 167-189.

3098. Gumina,, Paul. "Title VI of the Intelligence Authorization Act, Fiscal Year 1991: Effective Covert Action Reform or Business As Usual?," Hastings Constitutional Law Quarterly 20 (Fall 1992): 149-205.

Provides background of covert action including analyses of what constitutes covert action and argument on issue of executive supremacy in this area. Concludes both Constitution and statutes regarding congressional oversight indicated foreign relations and war powers are shared. Discusses rationale of Title VI as an attempt to prevent future cover-ups, such as Iran-Contra, by requiring enhanced reporting. Considers George Bush's opposition to Title VI on constitutionality; concludes Title VI is constitutional.

3099. Gunabe, Luciano I. "Combat Intelligence in the Peninsula," Philippines Armed Forces Journal 9 (December 1956): 113-117.

3100. Gunter, Michael M. "Foreign Influences on the Kurdish Insurgency in Iraq," Conflict Quarterly 12/4 (Fall 1992): 7-24.

3101. Gunter, Michael M. "Mulla Mustafa Barzani and the Kurdish Rebellion in Iraq: The Intelligence Factor," International Journal of Intelligence and Counterintelligence 7/4 (Winter 1994): 465-474.

Explores the US presence in Iraq in the 1950s; the CIA role in Iraq; reasons for US-Iraqi dependency; Israel's interest; and lessons learned as published in the Pike Committee investigation report.

3102. Gunther, Gerald. "Reflections on Robel: It's Not What the Court Did but the Way That It Did It," Stanford Law Review 20 (1968): 1140-1149.

Robel was a member of the American Communist Party, employed at a defense shipyard. Lower courts found Robel guilty of violating the Subversive Activities Control Act of 1950. The Supreme Court disagreed, arguing that mere membership in the Communist Party was not a violation of law.

3103. Gupta, Karunaker. "How Did the Korean War Begin?," China Quarterly 52 (October-December 1972): 699-716.

Contains sections on the background of the war, outbreak of the war, the rival invasion stories, a question of chronology, the United Nations field observers' report, and conflicting theories on the origins of the war.

3104. Gurko, Leo. "'The Secret Agent'; Conrad's Vision of Megalopolis," Modern Fiction Studies 4/4 (Winter 1958-1959): 307-318.

Accounts for the criticisms Conrad received for the spy novel, The Secret

Agent. Observes the qualities of this classic but controversial work.

3105. Gurov, E. "U.S. Reconnaissance South of the Rio Grande," Mezhdunarodnaia Zhizn' 14/8 (1967): 101-108.

3106. Gurr, Ted R. "War, Revolution, and the Growth of the Coercive State," Comparative Political Studies 21/1 (April 1988): 45-65.
    Discusses the bases of state power, coercion and the growth of state power (including the role of secret police), emergence of militarized and police states, democracies and the uses of coercion, and conclusions.

3107. Gustafson, Thane. "U.S. Export Controls and Soviet Technology," Technology Review (February-March 1982): 34-35.
    Argues that the US is losing vital technological lead to the Soviet Union due to weak export controls.

3108. Gutfield, Arnon. "The Ves Hall Case, Judge Bourquin, and the Sedition Act of 1918," Pacific Historical Review 37 (May 1968): 163-198.
    A study of the role of Montana judge George M. Bourquin in acquitting World War I anti-war activist Ves Hall. Discusses Bourquin's resistance to the pressures of the "super patriots" in their search for traitors and spies.

3109. Gutfield, Arnon. "Western Justice and the Rule of Law: Bourquin on Loyalty in the "Red Scare," and Indians," Pacific Historical Review 65 (February 1996): 85-106.

3110. Guthrie, Larry B. "Legal Implications of the Soviet Microwave Bombardment of the U.S. Embassy," Boston College International and Comparative Law Journal 1/1 (1977): 91-110.
    Contains sections on the question of whether or not there is a prima facie violation of international law resulting from Soviet radiation bombardment, whether or not there are defenses available to the Soviets for their actions, and the remedies available to the US.

3111. Gutman, Richard M. "Combatting Defendants' Obstructionism in the Discovery Process," University of Detroit Journal of Urban Law 55/4 (Summer 1978): 983-1003.
    An overview of obstructionist strategies, including police infiltration of plaintiff's legal team, destruction of documents, delays and incomplete production, gag orders; and reverse discovery.

3112. Gutman, Roy. "Nicaragua: American's Diplomatic Charade," Foreign Policy 56 (Fall 1984): 3-23.
    Discusses the futile US efforts to bring peace to Nicaragua in the early

1980s. Contains sections on diplomatic efforts, the sine quo non of democracy, military pressure, and the question of overthrow or accommodation.

3113. Guy, Jacques B. M. "Statistical Properties of the Two Folios of the Voynich Manuscript," Cryptologia 15/3 (July 1991): 207-218.

3114. Guy, Jacques B. M. "Vowel Identification: An Old (But Good) Algorithm," Cryptologia 15/3 (July 1991): 258-262.

3115. Guzman, Jose R. "The Lallemand Brothers in Texas," Boletin del Archivo General de la Nacion 11/1-2 (1970): 157-187.
     This is an approximate title of an article appearing in Spanish in a Mexican journal.

3116. Gyi, M. "The Unbreakable Language Code in the Pacific Theater of World War II," ETC.: A Review of General Semantics 39/1 (Spring 1982): 8-15.
     Use of the Navajo Indian language during World War II for purposes of encoding secret messages. Discusses Platoon 382, successes, and the honoring of Navajo code talkers.

3117. Gylden, Yves. "De Quelques Systems de Chiffres Synthetiques," Revue Internationale de Criminalistique 1/6-7 (October 1929): 358-373.

3118. Gylden, Yves. "Histoire du Decryptement," Revue Internationale de Criminalistique 2/5 (May 1930): 363-380.

H

"Many spies run desperate risks but are mercenaries at heart--like
well-paid stuntmen, they are only of passing interest."
(Mole by William Hood, p. 11)

3119. Hachey, Thomas E. "American Profiles on Capitol Hill: A Confidential
Study for the British Foreign Office in 1943," Wisconsin Magazine of History
57/2 (1973-1974): 141-153.

Reflects the British interest in the committees of Congress with regard
to committee support for the British in World War II. Includes a reproduced
memo by Isaiah Berlin outlining trade agreements, intervention versus isolation,
and general attitudes toward Britain.

3120. Haefele, Walter R. "General George Washington: Espionage Chief,"
American History Illustrated 24/6 (November-December 1989): 22-27, 69-70.

Characterizes General George Washington's network of spies and
informants during the American Revolution, arguing that military survival
depended upon their efforts.

3121. Haering, George. "How Tactical Air Works," U.S. Naval Institute
Proceedings 108/11 (1982): 60-65.

3122. Hafenmeister, David; Joseph Romm; and Kosta Tsipis. "The Verification
of Compliance with Arms-Control Agreements," Scientific American 252/3
(March 1985): 39-45.

Contains sections on national means of verification, photoreconnaissance, radar systems, and seismometers. Discusses the role of technologies in monitoring the Soviets.

3123. Hafner, Donald L. "Bureaucratic Politics and 'Those Frigging Missiles': JFK, Cuba and U.S. Missiles in Turkey," <u>Orbis</u> 21 (Summer 1977): 307-333.
    Using the Kennedy administration's responses to the Cuban missile crisis and to the matter of missiles in Turkey, this article discusses the president's occasionally difficult relationship with his administrative bureaucrats.

3124. Haftendorn, Helga. "The Security Puzzle: Theory-Building and Discipline-Building in International Security," <u>International Studies Quarterly</u> 35 (1991): 3-17.

3125. Hagaman, H. T. "Marine Corps Intelligence in the 80s," <u>Signal</u> 36 (September 1981): 69.

3126. Hagaman, H. T. "Marine Corps Intelligence," <u>Marine Corps Gazette</u> 66 (January 1982): 50-53.
    Discusses priorities and master intelligence architecture.

3127. Hagan, Frank E. "Espionage As Political Crime? A Typology of Spies," <u>Journal of Security Administration</u> 12/1 (1989): 19-36.
    Argues that espionage largely has been ignored in the realm of criminological studies. Provides typologies of ten spies.

3128. Hagan, John. "The Design of Conrad's 'The Secret Agent,'" <u>English Literary History</u> 22/2 (June 1955): 148-164.
    An excellent analysis and critiques of the classic novel by Joseph Conrad.

3129. Hagen, R. P. "Intelligence Is the Commander's Responsibility," <u>Army</u> 7 (May 1957): 77-80.

3130. Hagens, William J. "The Moss Committee and Freedom of Information," <u>Michigan Academician</u> 4/2 (1971): 205-216.

3131. Haggman, Bertil. "Communist Subversion in the Swedish Armed Forces," <u>Armed Forces and Society</u> 9/1 (Fall 1982): 135-148.
    Includes sections on the background of subversion, the armed revolution, use of the institutions, years of sabotage, Sweden's international role, and concerns for the increase in subversion.

3132. Haggman, Bertil. "Soviet Russian Active Measures in Scandinavia," <u>Ukrainian Review</u> 34/3 (1986): 69-75.
    Discusses Soviet intelligence operations and recruitment of Western

sources in Scandinavia.

3133. Hague, Harlan. "Guides for the Pathfinders: The Indian Contribution to Exploration of the American West," Pacific Historian 26/3 (Fall 1982): 54-63.

A general discussion of the contributions of Indian guides to the settlement of the West. Mentions roles of Indian guides, including interpreting and spying.

3134. Hahn, Walter F. "A National Scandal?," Strategic Review 8 (Spring 1980): 8-9.

Raises the question of whether or not the Soviets violated international biological warfare agreements.

3135. Haight, David. "The Papers of C. D. Jackson: A Glimpse at President Eisenhower's Psychological Warfare Expert," Manuscripts 28 (Winter 1976): 27-37.

3136. Haight, John M., Jr. "Franklin D. Roosevelt, L'Aviation Europeane et la Crise de Munich," Revue d'Histoire de la Deuxieme Guerre Mondial et des Conflits Contemporains 33/132 (1983): 23-40.

This is a rough translation of this title, a piece appearing in a French journal.

3137. Hailback, Kevin S. "IPB in the Third Dimension," Military Intelligence 16/3 (July-September 1990): 36-37.

Discusses the role of military intelligence preparation of the battlefield (IPB). IPB is known as the third dimension of warfare.

3138. Haim, Benjamini. "The Six-Day War, Israel 1967: Decisions, Coalitions, Consequences: A Sociological View," Journal of Strategic Studies 6/3 (September 1983): 64-82.

Contains sections on the decision making processes leading to the war, the Sinai campaign, the occupation of the West Bank, and the war with Syria.

3139. Haines, Herbert. "The Execution of Major Andre," English Historical Review 5 (January 1890): 31-40.

Explores Andre's service as Adjutant General under General Henry Clinton, then later as a spy to verify the intentions of Benedict Arnold in the release of information concerning the West Point post. Describes Andre's capture, his appeal to General Washington, and his execution. Raises the question of whether or not Andre should have been regarded a spy.

3140. Hale, Lisa T. "United States v. Ford (34 F.3d 999 (11th Cir. 1994): The Eleventh Circuit Permits Unrestricted Police Use of Thermal Surveillance on

Private Property Without a Warrant," <u>Georgia Law Review</u> 29 (Spring 1995): 819-847.

3141. Hale, Richard W. "Some Account of Benjamin Thompson, Count Rumford," <u>New England Quarterly</u> 1 (October 1928): 505-531.

3142. Halevy, David and Neil C. Livingstone. "The Ollie We Knew," <u>Washingtonian</u> 22/10 (October 1987): 76-79, 140-158.

3143. Halevy, David and Neil C. Livingstone. "The Last Days of Bill Casey," <u>Washingtonian</u> 23/3 (December 1987): 174-177; 238-245.
    Discusses Casey's intelligence experience, Casey's health problems, the aftermath of Casey's surgery, and Casey's wisdom. A glowing account of Casey's abilities in the field of intelligence.

3144. Haley, J. Frederick. "Reconnaissance at Tarawa Atoll," <u>Marine Corps Gazette</u> 64 (November 1980): 51-55.

3145. Haley, P. Edward. "Legislative-Executive Relations and the United States Intelligence Community," <u>Harvard Journal of Law & Public Policy</u> 12/2 (Spring 1989): 495-507.
    A comprehensive discussion of the development of Executive and Legislative relations on matters concerning the regulation of the intelligence community. Offers insights into the strengths and weaknesses of congressional oversight.

3146. Hall, Benjamin E. "Propaganda After the Cold War: Toward a System of Law," <u>Transnational Law and Contemporary Problems</u> 3/1 (Spring 1993): 249-272.
    Addresses foreign affairs through "public diplomacy"; sources of law on the flow of information; the new world information and communications order; Western intransigence; and responses to propaganda.

3147. Hall, H. "The Foreign Policy Decision-Making Process in Britain, 1934-1935, and the Origins of the Anglo-German Naval Agreement," <u>Historical Review</u> 19 (1976): 477-499.

3148. Hall, Jacquelyn D. "Private Eyes, Public Women: Images of Class and Sex in the Urban South, Atlanta, Georgia, 1913-1915," <u>Atlanta History</u> 36/4 (1993): 24-39.

3149. Hall, James O. "The Spy Harrison," <u>Civil War Times Illustrated</u> 24/2 (February 1986).

3150. Hall, James O. "Hunting the Spy Harrison," <u>Civil War Times Illustrated</u> 24/10 (October 1986): 19-25.

A summary of Henry Harrison's escapades as a spy in the Civil War. Author argues that incorrect conclusions have been drawn about Harrison.

3151. Hall, James P. "Free Speech in Wartime," <u>Columbia Law Review</u> 21 (1921): 526-537.

A classic article containing sections on free speech, practical restraint of free speech, government rule setting, laws regarding free speech, and wartime restrictions on free speech.

3152. Hall, Keith. "Challenges Faced by U.S. Intelligence," <u>American Intelligence Journal</u> 11/3 (Summer-Fall 1990): 1-3.

Comments on the adjustments to new priorities; meeting new requirements; taking advantage of new opportunities; budget realities; expanding options; and the question of optimism for the future.

3153. Hall, Kermit L. "Nu-Oh-Lac: A Cock-and-Bull Story," <u>Reviews in American History</u> 13/1 (1985): 217-221.

Reflections upon espionage during the Civil War, especially in terms of the secret societies. Contains sections on the history of political justice, the Civil War as a Constitutional crisis, secret political societies, and misrepresentation of 'dark lantern' societies.

3154. Hall, Mary T. "False Colors and Dummy Ships: The Use of Ruse in Naval Warfare," <u>Naval War College Review</u> 42/3 (Summer 1989): 52-62.

A discussion of the naval commander's dilemma in using ruses in wartime, yet such use can be a decisive factor in winning a battle. Discusses deception in terms of ruse or perfidy, offers a method for analysis, defines perfidy, accounts for permissible ruses, and ends with an argument that flying false colors and using dummy ships in wartime constitutes perfidy.

3155. Hall, R. Cargill. "Early U.S. Satellite Proposals," <u>Technology and Culture</u> 4/4 (Fall 1963): 410-434.

An excellent summary of the first initiatives by the Army and Navy to advance satellite development immediately following World War II. The satellite development program fell on hard times in the early 1950s, thus allowing the Soviets to orbit the first satellite in 1957. Mentions the plan to use satellites as political and psychological weapons.

3156. Hall, R. Cargill. "Origins and Development of the Vanguard and Explorer Satellite Programs," <u>Airpower History</u> 11/4 (1964): 101-112.

Sections include discussion of scientific interest in astronautics, American satellite studies in the early 1950s, origins of Project Orbiter and Project

Vanguard, the IGY satellite decision, and the Explore project.

3157. Halleck, Henry W. "Military Espionage," <u>American Journal of International Law</u> 5/4 (July 1911): 590-603.

Editor George Davis reported that this article was among General Halleck's papers found after his death in 1872. Its major emphasis was upon the case of Major Andre; is one of the earliest commentaries on the international law aspects of espionage.

3158. Hallett, Robin. "The South African Intervention in Angola, 1975-76," <u>African Affairs</u> 77/308 (July 1978): 347-386.

This article argues that the failure of South Africa to invade Angola and to prevent communist takeover was partly the result of faulty US intelligence reporting.

3159. Halligan, J. "Radio Intelligence and Communications Security," <u>Cryptologia</u> 13/1 (January 1994): 52-55.

3160. Halloran, Bernard F. "Soviet Armor Comes to Vietnam--A Surprise That Needn't Have Been," <u>Army</u> 22/8 (August 1972): 19-23.

Recounts a gross military intelligence failure.

3161. Halperin, John. "Between Two Worlds: The Novels of John Le Carre," <u>South Atlantic Quarterly</u> 79/1 (Winter 1980): 17-37.

An excellent summary of the novels of John Cornwell (AKA: John LeCarre). Argues that LeCarre's novels present the realities of espionage work, containing imperfect characters who are always self-reliant.

3162. Halperin, Morton H. "The Gaither Committee and the Policy Process," <u>World Politics</u> 13/3 (April 1961): 360-384.

Traces and analyzes events leading to the Gaither report on civil defense in the late 1950s. Briefly mentions the CIA. Key sections discuss the drafting, presenting, and the impact of the report; and the public debate.

3163. Halperin, Morton H. "The President and the Military," <u>Foreign Affairs</u> 52/2 (1972): 310-324.

Contains sections on presidential dependency on the bureaucracy, presidents' problems with the military, techniques to improve presidential options, how advice from the military reaches a president and the cabinet, and the decline in the significance of the Secretary of Defense. Relevant to studies of military intelligence.

3164. Halperin, Morton H. "Further Adventures of a Tappee," <u>Civil Liberties Review</u> 1/2 (Winter-Spring 1974): 131-133.

Halperin describes his experiences after discovering he had been wire tapped by the FBI from 1969 to 1971. He was a member of the National Security Council at the time.

3165. Halperin, Morton H. "Clever Briefers, Crazy Leaders, and Myopic Analysts," Washington Monthly 6/7 (September 1974): 42-49.

Argues that the superpowers often retain myopic analysis of the capabilities and intentions of each other with regard to nuclear war. Simplistic decision processes must be replaced with a more sophisticated understanding of the thought processes among and between nations with nuclear weapons.

3166. Halperin, Morton H. "Decision-Making for Covert Operations," Society 12/3 (March-April 1975): 45-51.

Argues that secrecy regarding covert operations hinders public oversight. Reflects upon President Johnson's decision to continue surveillance of North Vietnam, post-World War II covert operations in the People's Republic of China, secrecy and decision making, the choice of covert operations, and the role of the press in feedback to the public.

3167. Halperin, Morton H. "National Security and Civil Liberties," Foreign Policy 21 (Winter 1975-1976): 125-160.

Argues that wiretap information is generally of low value in government investigations, but its chilling effect on constitutional rights is profound.

3168. Halperin, Morton H. "A Balancing Test for Classified Information," Federal Bar News & Journal 38 (1979): 134-140.

Discusses provision 3 of the Freedom of Information Act designed to provide a balancing test for decisions regarding the release of government information. Discusses the development and meaning of the test.

3169. Halperin, Morton H. "The Reform of FBI Intelligence Operations," University of Chicago Law Review 47/3 (Spring 1980): 634-646.

A book review essay in which the reviewer highlights some of John T. Elliff's important domestic intelligence issues. Elliff's book is the same as the title of this essay.

3170. Halperin, Morton H. "Freedom of Information and National Security Affairs: A Comparative Study of Norway and the United States," Journal of Peace Research 20/1 (1983): 1-4.

Contains sections on information and the arms race, the great Atlantic divide, openness and secrecy, historical survey, legal comparison, differences in administrative practices, denial of access, and a comparative perspective on secrecy.

3171. Halperin, Morton H. "Security Classification and the Security System," Government Information Quarterly 1/2 (1984): 117-125.

Argues that Executive Orders regarding secrecy protections for government information have not lessened the amount of secrecy, and they have contradicted the role of the Freedom of Information Act. Contains sections on classification of information by bureaucrats, classification by senior officials, and the FOIA request system.

3172. Halperin, Morton H. "We Need New Intelligence Charters," Center Magazine 18/3 (May-June 1985): 51-53.

Argues that additional inquiry is needed in the area of oversight of the intelligence community, especially with respect to information secrecy.

3173. Halperin, Morton H. "Secrecy and National Security," Bulletin of the Atomic Scientists 41/7 (August 1985): 114-117.

Article decries notion of US government's use of the courts to prevent "leaks" of closely guarded information. Cites trend toward new limits on access to national security information.

3174. Halperin, Morton H. and Daniel N. Hoffman. "Secrecy and the Right to Know," Law and Contemporary Problems 40/3 (Summer 1976): 132- 165.

Argues that Congress must regularize its access and right to national security information and it must restructure the executive classification system. Includes discussion of the legislated classification system (including intelligence information), the role of the courts, proposed new system, and conclusions.

3175. Halperin, Morton H. and Gary M. Stein. "Lawful Wars," Foreign Policy 72 (Fall 1988): 173-195.

A reevaluation of US covert actions and unilateral military action in US foreign policy. Major sections discuss the trouble with secret wars and the foreign affairs power struggle.

3176. Halperin, Morton H. and Jeanne M. Woods. "Ending the Cold War at Home," Foreign Policy 81 (Winter 1990-1991): 128-143.

Accounts for the construction of the national security state infrastructure during the Cold War in America. Suggests that public hearings be held on the domestic impact of secret agencies and laws constructed to defend against the now-defunct Soviet Union.

3177. Halpern, Samuel and Hayden Peake. "Did Angleton Jail Nosenko?," International Journal of Intelligence and Counterintelligence 3/4 (Winter 1989): 451-464.

Discusses the evidence pointing to James Angleton's direct responsibility for having KGB defector Nosenko jailed for over three years while CIA verified his statements. Reflecting on the arguments of Professor Loch Johnson, the authors disagree with certain views on the subject. Major sections discuss support for Johnson's view; support for an alternative view; author's interim decision; primary sources; some first-hand comments; and weight of the evidence.

3178. Hamer, John. "The U.S. Intelligence Community," Skeptic 7 (May-June 1975): 11-15.

3179. Hamilton, Charles V. "America In Search of Itself: A Review Essay," Political Science Quarterly 97 (Fall 1982): 487-493.

3180. Hamilton, James E. "Police Intelligence Units Recommended to Cope with Organized Crime," Police Chief 22 (December 1955): 4-6, 12.
    Defines organized crime and its impact on law enforcement. Offers a strategy of intelligence operations and urges increased intelligence information exchange between departments.

3181. Hamilton, Lee H. "View from the Hill," Studies in Intelligence 31/Special edition (September 1987): 65-76.
    Discussion of the Reagan administration's refusals to consider non-conforming information on the so-called evils of the Sandinista regime in Nicaragua.

3182. Hamilton, Lee H. and Michael H. Van Dusen. "Making the Separation of Powers Work," Foreign Affairs 57 (Fall 1978): 17-39.
    Contains sections on how the Congress acquired more power in the realm of foreign policy, the Constitution's instructions on foreign policy, and suggested improvements in the formulation of foreign policy. Relevant in research of oversight by congressional intelligence committees.

3183. Hamilton, Nancy. "Spy on the Border: Dr. Wolfgang Ebell," Password 32/4 (1987): 159-168.

3184. Hamilton, Nancy. "Spy on the Border: Horst Von Der Goltz," Password 36/3 (1991): 139-148.

3185. Hamilton, W. G. "The Experience of Place in the Spy Novels of John LeCarre," Canadian Geographer 35/4 (Winter 1991): 404-412.

3186. Hamit, Francis. "Taking On Corporate Counterintelligence," Security Management 35/10 (October 1991): 34-35.

3187. Hamlin, Percy. "Aerial Observation, Army of the Potomac," U.S. Air Services 19 (July 1934): 16-19.

3188. Hamm, Michael J. "The Pueblo and Mayaguez Incidents: A Study of Flexible Response and Decision-Making," Asian Survey 17/6 (June 1977): 545-555.

Discusses the "flexible response" policy; the role of intelligence in the Pueblo's mission; political tensions between the US and North Korea; and conclusions.

3189. Hammant, Thomas R. "The Origins of Russian Navy Intelligence," Cryptologia 8/3 (July 1984): 193-202.

This is a translated Russian document on the subject.

3190. Hammer, Carl. "How Did TJB Encode B2?," Cryptologia 3/1 (January 1979): 9-15.

3191. Hammer, Carl. "High-Order Homophonic Ciphers," Cryptologia 5/4 (October 1981): 231-242

3192. Hammer, Carl. "Second Order Homophonic Ciphers," Cryptologia 12/1 (January 1988): 11-20.

3193. Hammer, David L. "Sherlock Holmes: Secret Agent," Baker Street Journal: An Irregular Quarterly of Sherlockiana 36/4 (December 1986): 231-234.

3194. Hammer, James. "Title III and Cordless Telephone Communication: Kansas High Court Approves Warrantless Interception of Residential Cordless Telephone Conversations by Law Enforcement Officials," University of Toledo Law Review 16/1 (Fall 1984): 315-344.

Extensive discussion of Title II controls on police surveillance practices. Argues that the case of State v. Howard, the first case to address the cordless telephone, raised concern for the definition of the cordless as a "wire" or "oral" communication device. Case facts and the appellate decision of the Kansas Supreme Court are included.

3195. Hammer, Paul E. J. "An Elizabethan Spy Who Came in From the Cold: The Return of Anthony Standen to England in 1593," Historical Research 65 (1992): 277-298.

3196. Hammersmith, Jack L. "The U.S. Office of War Information and the Polish Question, 1943-1945," Polish Review 1 (1974): 67-76.

3197. Hammes, T. X. "Sell Intelligence to Your Unit," Marine Corps Gazette 63 (April 1979): 14-15.

3198. Hammond, James D. "The Human Factor in Intelligence," Marine Corps

Gazette 63 (April 1979): 19-20.

3199.   Hammond, N.   "Memories of a British Officer Serving in Special Operations Executive in Greece, 1941," Balkan Studies 23/1 (1982): 127-155.

3200.   Hammond, Paul Y.   "The National Security Council as a Device for Interdepartmental Coordination: An Interpretation and Appraisal," American Political Science Review 54 (December 1960): 899-910.
An overview of the role of the National Security Council, including sections on the origins in the American naval and British cabinet traditions, early practice and appraisal, and NSC structure and operations.

3201.   Hampson, Fen O.   "The Divided Decision-Maker: American Domestic Politics and the Cuban Crises," International Security 8/3 (Winter 1984-1985): 130-165.
Poses the question: "How do domestic politics affect the way decision-makers define a foreign policy crisis?" Contains sections on the controversial view of crisis; the Cuban missile crisis; the Cienfuegos crisis; the Cuban brigade crisis; and implications of the argument.

3202.   Hancock, B. R.   "The New Zealand Security Intelligence Service," Auckland University Law Review 1/2 (1973): 1-34.
Contains sections on the ministerial responsibility and public scrutiny, functions of the security intelligence service, members of the security intelligence service, and the appeals system.

3203.   Hancock, Gus.   "Intelligence Valor in Vietnam," Naval Intelligence Professionals Quarterly 8/2 (Spring 1992): 11.

3204.   Hand, Robert P.   "CG 23 Deception Planning," Military Review 48/9 (September 1967): 44-48.
A comparison of the positive and negative aspects of deception planning.

3205.   Handberg, Roger.   "Know Thy Enemy: Changing Images of the Enemy in Popular Literature," North Dakota Quarterly 53/1 (Winter 1985): 121-127.
Discusses the changes in popular attitudes toward international politics through the use of spy stories, in particular the identification of enemies in such stories. The decline of the spy novel occurred during the 1970s as a function of warming relations between the superpowers.

3206.   Handel, Michael I.   "The Yom Kippur War and the Inevitability of Surprise," International Studies Quarterly 21/3 (September 1977): 461-502.
A theoretical discussion of problems facing intelligence communities and decision makers in their efforts to prevent surprise attack. Discusses three "noise"

levels; offers a case study of the 1973 war; conclusions.

3207. Handel, Michael I. "The Study of War Termination," Journal of Strategic Studies 1/2 (May 1978): 14-26.

3208. Handel, Michael I. "Surprise and Change in International Politics," International Security 4/4 (Spring 1980): 57-85.
Discusses normal and surprise diplomacy, pattern of bilateral diplomatic surprise and stages therein, diplomacy of surprise in different international systems, comparison of military and diplomatic surprise, and costs and benefits of military and diplomatic surprise.

3209. Handel, Michael I. "Numbers Do Count: The Question of Quantity Versus Quality," Journal of Strategic Studies 4/3 (September 1981): 225-270.

3210. Handel, Michael I. "Intelligence and Deception," Journal of Strategic Studies 5/1 (March 1982): 122-154.

3211. Handel, Michael I. "The Study of Intelligence," Orbis 26/4 (Winter 1983): 817-821.
Suggests that the study of intelligence can be divided into three sections: acquisition; analysis; acceptance. Each of these parts of the process is discussed. Research on intelligence topics must continue.

3212. Handel, Michael I. "Intelligence and Crisis Forecasting," Orbis 26/4 (Winter 1983): 817-847.
This is the first article in a forum discussion by several writers on the topic, addressing the role of intelligence in predicting international events. Contains sections on crisis and opportunity forecasting, the unexpected factors, and conclusions.

3213. Handel, Michael I. "Intelligence and Problem of Strategic Surprise," Journal of Strategic Studies 7/3 (September 1984): 229-281.
Discusses intelligence as a force multiplier, surprise in historical perspective, methodological dilemmas and problems of perception, and the politics of intelligence.

3214. Handel, Michael I. "Technological Surprise in War," Intelligence and National Security 2/1 (January 1987): 1-53.
Defines strategic and technological surprise. Discusses different types of technological surprise as an intelligence problem; conditions necessary for the achievement of technological surprise; limits of technological surprise in terms of long and short term costs; countering technological surprise; and conclusions.

3215. Handel, Michael I. "Introduction: Strategic and Operational Deception in Historical Perspective," Intelligence and National Security 2/3 (July 1987): 1-91.

Part of a special issue devoted to deception strategies and policy in the second world war, the author considers topics such as deception in historical perspective; means and methods; attitudes and the environment; the future of deception; can deception be avoided?; deception as a military force multiplier; control of deception operations; and evaluation of the effectiveness of deception.

3216. Handel, Michael I. "The Politics of Intelligence," Intelligence and National Security 2/4 (October 1987): 5-46.

Discusses the narrative techniques of spy novels and the role of secret agents.

3217. Handel, Michael I. "Leaders and Intelligence," Intelligence and National Security 3/3 (July 1988): 3-39.

Covers such topics as the increase in demand for intelligence; civil-military-intelligence relations; dilemmas of leader-intelligence cooperation; the intelligence adviser and the 'education' of of leaders; levels of analysis and the incentive to use intelligence; and brief summaries of the other articles in the issue.

3218. Handel, Michael I. "Methodological Mischief: A Reply to Professor Muller," Intelligence and National Security 4/1 (January 1989): 161-164.

A rebuttal to the observations of Professor Klaus-Jurgen Muller's critique of Handel's article in volume 2/3 (1987).

3219. Handel, Michael I. "Intelligence and Military Operations," Intelligence and National Security 5/2 (April 1990): 1-98.

A general and lengthy introduction to the entire issue's consideration of intelligence and military operations. Sections include discussion of definitions; brief historical period; intelligence uncertainty and the art of war; Clausewitz on uncertainty; uncertainty and the lack of intelligence; military leaders; operations versus intelligence; case studies of battles; and overviews of articles in the issue.

3220. Handleman, Howard. "The Soviet KGB in America," Air Force Magazine 62 (June 1979): 56-61.

Argues that Soviet spying operations have increased and that U.S intelligence community monitoring of agents in the U.S is costly but necessary. Soviet methods of espionage in the US are mentioned, including the use of Cuban agents. A similar article appeared under the title of "KGB Activities in the United States," Air Force Magazine 53 (June 1970).

3221. Handlery, George. "Propaganda and Information: The Case of U.S. Broadcasts to Eastern Europe," East European Quarterly 8/4 (Winter 1974): 391-412.

A comparison of radio broadcasts from Western and Eastern Europe as the data source for concluding that Radio Free Europe serves US markets.

3222. Handlin, O. "Master Spy," Atlantic Monthly 217 (May 1966): 130-131.
Discusses the case of Richard Sorge, who worked as a Soviet spy for the Soviet Union. Relates intelligence blunders.

3223. Handy, Jim. "'The Most Precious Fruit of the Revolution': The Guatemalan Agrarian Reform, 1952-1954," Hispanic American Historical Review 68 (November 1988): 675-705.
Argues that Guatemalan President Jacobo Arbenz failed to control the direction and scope of the agrarian reforms he implemented, thus encouraging outsiders like the United States to perceive that the country was leaning toward communism.

3224. Haneberg, Bob; Dan Laliberte; and Aaron Danis. "Coast Guard Operational Intelligence in an Evolving World," American Intelligence Journal 16/1 (Spring 1995): 39-42.

3225. Hanes, Horace A. "Satellites, Sensors, and Space Specialists--USAF's Space Surveillance Story," Air University Review 16/2 (1965): 2-12.

3226. Hanke, Robert F. "National Technical Means of Verification," Military Engineer 71 (September-October 1979): 308+.

3227. Hanks, Peter. "National Security -- A Political Concept," Monash University Law Review 14/1 (1988): 114-133.
Explores the concept of national security in its linkages with the legal process; assesses ambiguity in the process; reveals the tensions between the values of law and national security; and evaluates legislative initiatives in Australia and Canada. Substantial discussion of Australian intelligence services.

3228. Hannah, Theodore M. "COMINT and COMSEC," Cryptologic Spectrum 2/3 & 2/4 (Summer & Fall 1972): 5-9; 8-11.

3229. Hannah, Theodore M. "Frank B. Rowlett: A Personal Profile," Cryptologic Spectrum (Spring 1981): 4-22.

3230. Hannah, Theodore M. "The Many Lives of Herbert O. Yardley," Cryptologic Spectrum 11/4 (Fall 1981): 4-29.

3231. Hannant, Larry. "Inter-war Security Screening in Britain, the United States and Canada," Intelligence and National Security 6/4 (October 1991): 711-735.
Discusses the civil unrest in Britain, Canada and the US after World War

I and the need for internal civil security via security screening techniques. Conclusions drawn by each of these states was that internal security was needed among teachers, manufacturers, and civil servants.

3232. Hannant, Larry. "Access to the Inside: An Assessment of 'Canada's Security Service: A History,'" Intelligence and National Security 8/3 (July 1993): 149-159.
        Discusses several aspects of the Canadian intelligence service as reflected in a book by Carl Betke and Stan Horrall, Canada's Security Service: An Historical Outline, 1864-1966. Sections of this review essay discuss the origin of the history; content; orientation and bias; and conclusions.

3233. Hannant, Larry. "Fifth-Column Crisis," Beaver 73/6 (1993-1994): 24-28.

3234. Hanne, William G. "From Moscow: South by Southeast," Military Review 56/1 (January 1976): 47-55.

3235. Hanne, William G. "Ethics in Intelligence," Military Intelligence 8/1 (January-March 1982): 6-8.

3236. Hanning, Hugh. "Project Camelot," Atlas 10/4 (October 1965): 229-230.
        Discusses the author's perspectives on Project Camelot, a Defense Department plan to enlist the academic community in the study of the potential for internal war in Latin American countries.

3237. Hanrahan, James P. "Intelligence for the Policy Chiefs," Studies in Intelligence 11/4 (Winter 1967).

3238. Hansen, James H. "RX: Intelligence Communications--Use Acronyms, Allegories, and Metaphors Only as Directed," International Journal of Intelligence and Counterintelligence 2/1 (Spring 1988): 21-26.
        An article devoted to observing the prolific use of acronyms, shorthand expressions, animal metaphors, foreign jargon and computer terms in discussions of intelligence.

3239. Hansen, James H. "The Demise of Lavrenti Beria," Studies in Intelligence 34/2 (Summer 1990).

3240. Hansen, James H. "The Kremlin Follies of 53...The Demise of Lavrenti Beria," International Journal of Intelligence and Counterintelligence 4/1 (Spring 1990): 101-114.
        A brief exploration of the action in the last days of power of the KGB's chief Lavrenti Pavlovich Beria. Major sections offer a narrative portrait of Beria; prelude to confrontation in early 1953; the pre-emptive countercoup; Beria's arrest

and the label of enemy of the people; Beria's execution in December 1953; assessment and implications for today; and 1953 milestones of Beria's rise and fall.

3241. Hanson, Philip. "Estimating Soviet Defence Expenditure," Soviet Studies 30 (July 1978): 403-410.

A review essay pertaining to William T. Lee's book, The Estimation of Soviet Defense Expenditures, 1955-1975.

3242. Hanson, Philip. "Soviet Industrial Espionage," Bulletin of the Atomic Scientists 43 (April 1987): 25-29.

Discusses Soviet dependence on Western military technology and collection methods used to acquire information. Contains sections on the 1940 export restrictions, journalist Thierry Wolton, the KGB T-report, espionage documents, and acquisition of Western technology.

3243. Hanson, Philip. "The CIA, the TsSU and the Real Growth of Soviet Investment," Soviet Studies 34/4 (October 1984): 571-581.

Argues that the CIA estimates of Soviet investment growth are correct. Discusses the equivalency between CIA estimates and estimates produced by the Soviet Central Statistical Administration (TsSU).

3244. Hapack, Joseph T. "Military Intelligence on Polonia in 1918: A Document," Polish American Studies 45/1 (1988): 74-82.

3245. Hardie, Bradford. "Mathematical and Mechanical Methods in Cryptography," Cryptologia 2 (January 1978): 20-27; (April 1978): 101-121.

3246. Hardie, Bradford. "The POTUS-PRIME Connection: Two Notes, Roosevelt, Churchill and Me," Cryptologia 11/1 (January 1987): 40-43.

A report of an American officer who had first-hand connection with the communications between Franklin Roosevelt and Winston Churchill.

3247. Hardt, D. Brent. "The Reagan Administration's Battle for Contra Aid," Fletcher Forum 10/2 (Summer 1986): 259-295.

Reviews the persistence of the Reagan administration to provide aid for "covert" paramilitary operations against the Sandinistas in Nicaragua. Discusses the CIA's role, origins of the Contras, rhetorical diplomacy of Contra aid, and offers conclusions.

3248. Hardy, Bradford. "A Theory of Cryptography," Cryptologia 3/4 (October 1979): 246-247.

3249. Hardy, Timothy S. "Intelligence Reform in the Mid-1970s," Studies in

Intelligence 20/2 (Summer 1976): 1-15.

3250. Hareven, Alouph. "Disturbed Hierarchy: Israeli Intelligence in 1954 and 1973," Jerusalem Quarterly 9 (Fall 1978): 3-19.

Analysis of the people and events involved in the 1954 and 1973 intelligence failures. Argues for protection against manipulative individuals in hierarchies who rely on information, control and feedback.

3251. Hargreaves, Reginald. "For to Deceive," Marine Corps Gazette 43/1 (1959): 36-43.

Describes various forms of deception strategies used by the British, Dutch, French and Americans from Medieval times to the present.

3252. Hargreaves, Reginald. "Spy Out the Land," Marine Corps Gazette 39/9 (1955): 58-62.

A brief overview of the use of spies in the American Revolution, American Civil War and other 20th century periods of conflict.

3253. Harkabi, Yehoshafat. "The Intelligence-Policymaker Tangle," Jerusalem Quarterly 30 (Winter 1984): 125-131.

Argues that intelligence plays an important role in the policy process, but it is often used to justify policy than to shape it. Also argues that an intelligence agency should inform the policy process, not serve merely "warning mechanics." Intelligence reporting problems are discussed.

3254. Harkavy, Robert E. and Stephanie G. Neuman. "The Arms Trade: Problems and Prospects in the Post-Cold War World," Annals of the American Academy of Political and Social Science 535 (September 1994).

3255. Harmon, William E. "Some Personal Observations on the CEWI Concept," Military Intelligence 9/1 (January-March 1983): 4-7.

Comments on the Combat Electronic Intelligence battalion before and after the Vietnam war.

3256. Harnes, Gerald K. "Virginia Hall Goillot: Career Intelligence Officer," Prologue: Quarterly Journal of the National Archives 26/4 (Winter 1994): 249-260.

Virginia Hall was awarded the Distinguished Service Medal of the OSSD for her work in Europe during World War II.

3257. Harp, S. D. "Are Spies Born Secret?," Progressive 45 (February 1981): 11-12.

A brief discussion of the Intelligence Identities Protection Act.

3258. Harper, Gilbert S. "Logistics in Grenada: Supporting No-Plan Wars," Parameters: Quarterly Journal of the U.S. Army War College 20/2 (June 1990): 50-63.

Major sections discuss strategic importance of Grenada; planning; mission and concept of the operation; intelligence; execution; conclusions; and recommendations.

3259. Harper, W. R. and D. H. Harris. "The Application of Link Analysis to Police Intelligence," Human Factors 17/2 (April 1975): 157-164.

3260. Harrington, John H. "Broadcast In Brittany," Infantry Journal 60 (March 1947): 34.

An account of information acquisition by prisoner interrogation in the last days of World War II.

3261. Harrington, Steve. "The Power of the Polygraph," Case and Comment 88/1 (January-February 1983): 3-9.

Sections discuss the accuracy of the polygraph, admissions of guilt, uses of the device by lawyers, and the uncertain future of the device. Relevant to studies of the polygraph in the context of intelligence agencies.

3262. Harris, Barbara. "A Different Kind of Column," Cryptologia 1/1 (January 1977): 17-19.

3263. Harris, Charles H., III. "Witzke Affair: German Intrigue on the Mexican Border 1917-1918," Military Review 59/2 (1979): 36-50.

Maintains that in 1917 allies, acting as German agents, were the reason for the failure of German intelligence against the US from Mexico. Consequently allied counterintelligence kept German agents busy during the remainder of the war.

3264. Harris, Charles H., III and Louis R. Sadler "The 'Underside' of the Mexican Revolution: El Paso, 1912," Americas: Quarterly Review of Inter-American Cultural History 39/1 (1982): 69-83.

Contains sections on the cooperation between US suppliers and Mexico for the supply of arms, ammunition and money for the Mexican revolution. A significant number of spies operated on each side of the border near El Paso, Texas, but the effectiveness of the intelligence systems was doubtful.

3265. Harris, Douglas H. "Development of a Computer-Based Program for Criminal Intelligence Analysis," Human Factors 20/1 (1978): 47-56.

Sections include the criminal intelligence analysis cycle, program development, the organized crime analysis program (OCAP), and preliminary evaluation.

3266. Harris, Elisa D. "Sverdlovsk and Yellow Rain: Two Cases of Soviet Noncompliance?," International Security 11/4 (Spring 1987): 41-95.

Examines the charge by the Reagan administration that the Soviet Union was directly involved in the distribution and use of chemical weapons against civilians in Southeast Asia and whether an outbreak of disease in the Soviet city of Sverdlovsk in 1979 was related to illegal biological warfare. Author concludes that "...neither the chemical warfare charge nor the US explanation for the Sverdlovsk epidemic are supported by the evidence available in the public domain."

3267. Harris, F. W. "Treason in Tudor England: Politics and Paranoia," Law and History Review 5 (Spring 1987): 291-293.

Charges of treason in during the reign of Mary Tudor was a function of paranoia. Author suggests that every era in which treason appears to increase should be evaluated in terms of the paranoia in the society. Incidents of treason must be studied in the context of their times.

3268. Harris, Jeffrey K. "Meeting the Challenge Then, Now and Tomorrow: The National Reconnaissance Office Entering the 21st Century," American Intelligence Journal 16/1 (Spring 1995): 27-32.

3269. Harris, J. P. "British Military Intelligence and the Rise of German Mechanized Forces, 1929-40," Intelligence and National Security 6/2 (April 1991): 395-417.

Examines British intelligence concerning German mechanized forces during the 1930s. Considers deficiencies and failures of British intelligence on such forces, especially in terms of technical data collection.

3270. Harris, Robert N., Jr. "On Applying the 'Mere Evidence' Rule to Government Eavesdropping," University of California Law Review 14 (1967): 1110-1129.

"Mere evidence" is that which is searched or seized by police. It is neither contraband nor tool, nor even a fruit of the crime, even if it is itemized in a warrant. Discusses the First-through-Fourth Amendments rationale, eavesdropping, and conclusions.

3271. Harris, Ruth R. "The 'Magic' Leak of 1941 and Japanese-American Relations," Pacific Historical Review 50/1 (February 1981): 77-96.

Based on released documents, the author provides a more complete analysis of the event cited in the title. She concludes that Magic did not live up to expectations regarding the time and place of planned aggression.

3272. Harris, William R. "March Crisis 1948, Act I," Studies in Intelligence 10/4 (Fall 1966): 1-22.

A discussion of how a cable from Lucius Clay was handled within the CIA and the intelligence community with respect to an allegation by Clay that the Soviets were planning an invasion of Germany. Discusses the procedures for handling the message from Clay and the establishment of Agency precedents.

3273. Harris, William R. "March Crisis 1948, Act II," Studies in Intelligence 11/1 (Spring 1967): 9-36.
A further discussion of the escalation of tensions between the Allied Control Council and the Soviets during March 1948. A second phase was reflected in the Soviet threat to begin searching all baggage aboard trains, which was not carried out, thus ending the March crisis fear of Soviet invasion.

3274. Harrison, E. D. R. "More Thoughts on Kim Philby's My Silent War," Intelligence and National Security 10/3 (July 1995): 514-525.
A continuation of dialogue concerning the work of Soviet spy Kim Philby and his autobiography.

3275. Harrison, Lowell H. "The Aaron Burr Conspiracy," American History Illustrated 13/3 (March 1978): 16-25.
A lengthy discussion of the conditions preceding Burr's arrest and trial on treason charges. Describes Justice John Marshall's conclusion that treason requires an overt act, a factor which was not present, said a later jury, in Burr's acts to plan an invasion of Mexico.

3276. Harrison, Richard A. "Testing the Water: A Secret Probe Towards Anglo-American Co-Operation in 1936," International History Reviews 7/2 (May 1985): 175-234.

3277. Harrison, Richard W. "The Question of Soviet Succession," Journal of Social and Political Studies 4/2 (Summer 1979): 99-122.
Addresses the process of succession in the Brezhnev years, the role of the General Secretary and the problems of succession, the concentration of power, the CPSU Politburo and foreign policy of the post-Brezhnev leadership. Useful for discussions of intelligence analysis of the governmental system and its leaders.

3278. Hart, Roland and Robert H. Sulzen. "Comparing Success Rates in Simulated Combat: Intelligent Tactics vs. Force," Armed Forces & Society 14 (Winter 1988): 273-285.

3279. Harvey, David. "Senate and Security: Addressing the Espionage and Surveillance Threats," Defense Science and Electronics 6 (January 1987): 72-73.

3280. Harvey, Stephen. "The Italian War Effort and the Strategic Bombing of Italy," History 79 (1985): 32-45.

3281. Hasbrook, Edward D. "United States Foreign Policy Through Cloak and Dagger War Operations: Terrorism of Mandate of National Security?," Oklahoma City University Law Review 11 (Spring 1986): 159-205.

Raises the question of domestic law and its implications for controlling covert war. Asks whether international law prohibits covert war operations. Other sections address the use of covert war against terrorism, standards by which to insure justified use of covert war by the US.

3282. Haselkorn, Avigdor. "The Soviet Collective Security System," Orbis 19/1 (Spring 1975): 231-254.

Considers Leonid Brezhnev's plan for a collective security system, including the Warsaw Pact-Middle East subsystem, the Middle-East-Indian subsystem, and the implications of all systems. Relevant to the broad context of Soviet interests in building dependence of other nations.

3283. Haslam, Jonathan. "Political Opportunity to Stalin and the Origins of the Terror in Russia, 1932-1936," Historical Journal 29/2 (1986): 395-418.

Discusses reasons for the terror unleashed by Stalin, the role of the Communist Party, overseas conditions as catalysts to terror, a key to Pravda newspaper article and the League of Nations.

3284. Haslam, Jonathan. "Why Rehabilitate Stalin?," Intelligence and National Security 2/2 (April 1987): 362-368.

A review article discussing issues raised by The Origins of the Great Purges: The Soviet Communist Party Reconsidered, 1933-1938 by J. Arch Getty, and Inside Stalin's Secret Police: NVKD Politics 1936-39 by Robert Conquest.

3285. Haslam, Jonathan. "The KAL Shootdown (1983) and the State of Soviet Air Defense," Intelligence and National Security 3/4 (October 1988): 128-133.

A brief analysis of the incident in terms of the effectiveness of Soviet anti-aircraft defenses.

3286. Haslam, Jonathan. "Stalin's Fears of a Separate Peace, 1942," Intelligence and National Security 8/4 (October 1993): 97-99.

A brief article exploring Stalin's miscalculation regarding the German offensive in 1942. Stalin also misinterpreted the British position in the same year, thus calling into question the kinds of intelligence upon which he based his decisions.

3287. Hassard, John R. G. "Cryptography in Politics," North American Review 128 (March 1879): 315-325.

Discusses in some detail the secret messages used by agents and others in the 1876 political campaign.

3288.   Hastedt, Glenn P.   "Teaching About and Understanding Intelligence Failures," Teaching Political Science 8/2 (January 1981):   163-174.

Argues for an approach to the study of surprise analysis using a discussion of the relationship between intelligence and policy, an intelligence estimation exercise, and a series of related lectures.

3289.   Hastedt, Glenn P.   "Studying the CIA: An Agenda for Research," Conflict Quarterly 4/3 (Summer 1984):   21-38.

Offers a structure within which studies of the Central Intelligence Agency can be studied.   Major sections discuss covert action from normative and tactical perspectives; and intelligence estimating in terms of strategic surprise and threat perception, forecasting literature, and the politicization of intelligence.

3290.   Hastedt, Glenn P.   "The Constitutional Control of Intelligence," Intelligence and National Security 1/2 (May 1986):   255-271.

Discusses problems emanating from the control of intelligence services. Presents the nature of the conflicts between the need for intelligence and the need for constitutional controls.

3291.   Hastedt, Glenn P.   "Controlling Intelligence: The Role of the D.C.I.," International Journal of Intelligence and Counterintelligence 1/4 (Winter 1986-1987):   25-40.

An overview of previous CIA directors (Dulles, McCone, Helms, Casey), the independent mission of CIA and congressional oversight.   Offers five typologies of CIA director loyalty: loyalty to the president; loyalty to the profession; loyalty to causes or zealotry; loyalty to the law; and loyalty to Congress or the public.

3292.   Hastedt, Glenn P.   "Intelligence and the Politics of the New Cold War," Crossroads: An International Socio-Political Journal 25 (1987):   19-30.

Discusses US intelligence gathering systems and the links between foreign and domestic policies.

3293.   Hastedt, Glenn P.   "Intelligence Failure and Terrorism: The Attack on the Marines in Beirut," Conflict Quarterly 8/1 (Winter 1988):   7-22.

Discusses the assumptions often made by policy makers in their employment of intelligence.   Defines the concept of intelligence failure and technical and doctrinal surprise.   Describe events and conditions leading to the bombing of the Marine barracks, then concludes that there were failures of intelligence collection, intelligence processing and intelligence policy application. The blame for the bombing resides at the top of the decision making ladder.

3294.   Hastedt, Glenn P.   "Intelligence and U.S. Foreign Policy: How to Measure Success," International Journal of Intelligence and Counterintelligence 5/1 (Spring

1991): 49-62.

Major sections discuss intelligence and policy evaluation; clarity of policy goals; the measurement of accuracy; and dangers inherent in the accuracy measure. Concludes that accuracy is not the only measure of possible future events.

3295. Hastedt, Glenn P. "Towards the Comparative Study of Intelligence," Conflict Quarterly 11/3 (Summer 1991): 55-72.

Addresses the question of what is to be compared in the study of international intelligence activities; the type of data needed; the comparative framework; the domination of uniqueness or commonality; the intended purposes of such study; and future synthesis.

3296. Hastedt, Glenn P. "CIA's Organizational Culture and the Problem of Reform," International Journal of Intelligence and Counterintelligence 9/3 (Fall 1996): 249-269.

Major sections discuss traditional accounts of Central Intelligence Agency's culture; missing ingredients; charting the development of the CIA's organizational culture; the CIA's founding generation; the John McCone era; the paradigm-extending generation; the mimicking generation; CIA's organizational culture; and CIA, organizational culture and American foreign policy. This author has written extensively on the CIA and its organizational dynamics.

3297. Hasty, David M. "Air Warfare: Tactical Reconnaissance," Journal of Defense & Diplomacy 3/11-12 (1985): 28030.

3298. Haswell, Jock. "The Need to Know," Military Review 56/9 (September 1976): 45-55.

A reprint of an article appearing in British Army Review, August 1975. Briefly outlines the history of British military intelligence.

3299. Haswell, John H. "Secret Writing," Century Illustrated Magazine 85 (November 1912-April 1913): 83-92.

Detailed account of the historical episodes, mainly in the 19th century, of secret writing.

3300. Hatch, Orrin G. "Balancing Freedom of Information with Confidentiality for Law Enforcement," Journal of Contemporary Law 9 (1983): 1-40.

Argues that as government increase emphasis on privatization there is more need for public understanding of activities of government, more confidentiality within government, and greater protection of citizens' rights. Discusses the proposed law, Senate bill 1730, designed to protect confidentiality of government records, especially law enforcement records.

3301. Hattaway, Herman. "Balloons: America's First Air Force," <u>American History</u> 19/4 (June 1984): 24-29.

A brief history of the origins and early development of hydrogen-filled balloons. Discusses military possibilities, the confederacy in the Civil War, aerial observers and early inventors (T. Sobieki, C. Lowe and F. von Zeppelin).

3302. Hauner, Milan. "The Last Game," <u>Middle East Journal</u> 38/1 (Winter 1984): 72-84.

Discusses the "great game," a means of sending secret intelligence agents to infiltrate foreign countries during the 1907 Russian invasion of Afghanistan. Includes sections on Casos Belli Clause, Indian intelligence in Britain and Germany's foreign intelligence.

3303. Haus, Lance. "The Predicament of the Terrorism Analyst," <u>Studies in Intelligence</u> 29/4 (Winter 1985): 13-23.

3304. Hausken, Gary L. "The Value of a Secret: Compensation for Imposition of Secrecy Orders under the Invention Secrecy Act," <u>Military Law Review</u> 119 (Winter 1988): 201-255.

Discusses issue of Fifth Amendment "taking" and whether it applies to secrecy orders imposed upon inventors under Invention Secrecy Act. Includes history of statutes since World War I and effects of World War II, the post war period and other developments. Explains operation of Act and recovery procedures therein.

3305. Haveles, Paul A. "Deception Operations in REFORGER 88," <u>Military Review</u> 70/8 (August 1990): 35-41.

A US Army deception plan during World War II pulled off with less than adequate effectiveness against the German army.

3306. Haver, Richard L. "Intelligence, Radioelectric Combat and the C3 Process," <u>Signal</u> 38 (October 1983): 35-37.

3307. Haver, Richard L. "The Ames Case: Catalyst for a National Counterintelligence Strategy?," <u>Defense Intelligence Journal</u> 4/1 (Spring 1995): 11-18.

Explores the opportunities to create a new CI strategy arising from the Ames espionage case. Major sections explore the shortcomings of US CI programs; the definition of CI; the CI community; impact of the Ames case on the CI community; hostile threats in the year 2000; a strategic concept for CI, its benefits and opportunities.

3308. Hawes, L. A. "The First Two Days: or the Birth of the L. D. V. in Eastern Command," <u>Army Quarterly</u> 50 (1940): 186-187.

3309. Hawker, D. S. "An Outline of the Early History of the Intelligence Corps," Rose and the Laurel 27 (December 1965).

3310. Hawthorn, Tom. "A Bourne-Again Spook," Canadian Dimension 15/8-16/1 (1981): 7-9.
A short discussion of the activities of Canadian's chief of intelligence, Robert Bourne, derived from former colleagues.

3311. Hawthorne, Nathaniel. "Intelligence Office," Democratic Review 14 (1844): 269.
A rare citation from one of America's leading 19th century authors. This is the oldest piece of literature in this collection.

3312. Hayden, Michael V. "Warfighters and Intelligence: One Team--One Fight," Defense Intelligence Journal 4/2 (Fall 1995): 17-30.
Discusses support for the warfighter; the importance of the objective; and case studies of intelligence support in two types of regional wars, Korea and Iraq.

3313. Haydock, Robert, Jr. "Some Evidentiary Problems Posed by Atomic Energy Security Requirements," Harvard Law Review 61 (1948): 468-491.
Discusses criteria for admission of evidence in atomic energy cases involving charges of espionage, and techniques for handling admittedly secret data to assure a fair trial.

3314. Hayhurst, William L. "Trade Secrets: Report of a Federal-Provincial Working Party," Canadian Business Law Journal 12/4 (May 1987): 494-512.

3315. Haynes, John E. and Harvey Klehr. "'Moscow Gold,' Confirmed at Last," Labor History 33/2 (Spring 1992): 279-293.
A discussion of clandestine funding of the American Communist Party. Continued in 35/3 (Summer 1994).

3316. Haynes, Kelly M. "Constitutional Law - Electronic Surveillance in Prison: Are Any Constitutional Rights Violated?," Florida State University Law Review 14 (Summer 1986): 319-332.
Considers the case of State v. Calhoun. Contains sections which discuss the case in relationship to Fourth, Fifth and Sixth Amendment issues as they pertain to the electronic monitoring of prisoners.

3317. Hazelrigg, Lawrence E.. "A Reexamination of Simmel's 'The Secret and the Secret Society': Nine Propositions," Social Forces 47 (1969): 323-330.
A brief overview of the sociological approach to secrecy and social reaction in reflection upon the work of Georg Simmel.

3318. Hazelwood, Leo; John J. Hayes; and James R. Brownell, Jr. "Planning for Problems in Crisis Management: An Analysis of Post-1945 Behavior in the U.S. Department of Defense," International Studies Quarterly 21/1 (1977): 75-106.

Problems incurred by the US Defense Department in the period between 1946 and 1975 can be blamed on faulty analysis and lack of information. Careful study of this period can yield insight into crisis management and improvements in the quality of decisionmaking under crisis conditions.

3319. Head, Sydney W. "African Mass Communications: Selected Information Sources," Journal of Broadcasting 20 (Summer 1976): 381-416.

3320. Heale, Michael J. "Secrets of a Special Relationship," Reviews in American History 16/4 (1988): 630-635.

A review essay of two books: Klaus Fuchs: The Man Who Stole the Atom Bomb by Norman Moss; and Klaus Fuchs: Atom Spy by Robert C. Williams.

3321. Healey, Denis. "The Sputnik and Western Defense," International Affairs (Great Britain) 34/2 (April 1958): 145-156.

Discussion of the obsolescence of the US policy of massive nuclear retaliation as it related to Soviet capabilities and relations with other nations. Could be useful in studying the surprise elements of Sputnik.

3322. Heather, Randall W. "Intelligence and Counter-Insurgency in Kenya, 1952-56," Intelligence and National Security 5/3 (July 1990): 57-83.

Discusses several topics: the Mau-Mau organization; security forces; insurgency; intelligence; surrender negotiations; pseudo gangs; conclusions.

3323. Heck, Caroline. "National Security and the 1st Amendment: The CIA in the Marketplace of Ideas," Harvard Civil Rights and Civil Liberties Law Review 14/3 (Fall 1979): 655-709.

Argues that courts have upheld the constitutionality of CIA prepublication review agreements under governmental interest in national security, but have failed to give adequate attention to the First Amendment and contract issues. Discusses employment restrictions found in national security agencies.

3324. Hedley, John H. "Inside Job," American Journalism Review 16 (January-February 1994): 15.

Brief discussion of espionage activities inside the Central Intelligence Agency.

3325. Hedley, John H. "The CIA's New Openness," International Journal of Intelligence and Counterintelligence 7/2 (Summer 1994): 129-141.

Main topics included are: internal workings; the new office of Public and Agency Information; a new publication, "What's News at CIA"; and changing response.

3326. Hedley, John H. "The Intelligence Community: Is It Broken? How to Fix It?," Studies in Intelligence 39/5 (1996): 11-18.

Transcript of some remarks before the Aspin Commission, subsequently the Brown Commission, to consider the future direction of the intelligence community.

3327. Hedli, Douglas J. "United States Involvement or Non-Involvement in the Hungarian Revolution of 1956," International Review of History and Political Science 11/1 (1974): 72-78.

3328. Heffernan, Richard J. and Dan T. Swartwood. "Trends in Competitive Intelligence," Security Management 37/1 (January 1993): 70-73.

3329. Hefter, Joseph and John R. Elting. "Mexican Spy Company, 1846-1848," Military Collector and Historian 21/2 (1960): 48-50.

3330. Heidehing, Jurgen. "Western Secret Services and the North Chinese Guerillas in World War II," Militargeschechtliche Mitteilungen 1 (1985): 13-136.

3331. Heil, O. and T. S. Robertson. "Toward a Theory of Competitive Market Signaling: A Research Agenda," Strategic Management Journal 12 (1991): 403-418.

Argues that competitor behavior may be influenced by signals sent by competitors in the marketplace. Competitive reactions are often based on signals which precede actions. Sections discuss rationale for competitive market signaling; signal interpretation; reaction to a competitive market signal; and summary.

3332. Heilbrunn, Otto. "Counterinsurgency Intelligence," Marine Corps Gazette 50/9 (September 1966): 49-51.

3333. Heilbrunn, Otto. "Tactical Intelligence in Vietnam," Military Review 48/10 (October 1968): 85-87.

Intelligence in Vietnam was aided by the application of the British special branch system for early warning of impending conditions in battle.

3334. Heilmeier, George H. "Guarding Against Technological Surprise," Air University Review 27/6 (September-October 1976): 2-7.

Discusses technological surprise, prevention of technological surprise, and the future potentials for technological surprise.

3335. Heiman, Grover. "Army: Beep to Bang," Armed Forces Management 16/10 (October 1970): 36-39.

3336. Heiman, Leo. "Israel's Military Intelligence," Military Review 43/1 (January 1963): 79-84.
     Discusses the origins of Israeli intelligence, strengthening of intelligence, merging the intelligence services for future missions, advantages of military intelligence, and infiltrations.

3337. Heiman, Leo. "Guerilla Warfare: An Analysis," Military Review 43/7 (July 1963): 26-36.

3338. Heiman, Leo. "Cloak-and-Dagger Literature Behind the Iron Curtain," East Europe 14/1 (January 1965): 54-56.
     Distinguishes between the purposes of spy novels in the East and the Soviet Union. Observes a major change in Soviet literature in 1961, suggesting that Soviet military intelligence officers can be villains who fail to perform well.

3339. Heiman, Leo. "War in the Middle East: An Israeli View," Military Review 47/9 (September 1967): 56-66.
     Describes conditions and events leading to the Six-Day War, the organization of forces, the Israeli intelligence service, the capture of Soviet missiles, Israeli equipment, strategy and tactics, the human steamroller concept, and the mobilization rate.

3340. Heimark, J. V. "Know Thine Enemy," U.S. Naval Institute Proceedings 85/8 (August 1959): 65-72.
     Discusses the role of naval intelligence at Pearl Harbor, Coral Sea, Midway, Philippine Sea, and in Atlantic anti-submarine warfare.

3341. Heinl, Robert D. "On the Basis of Pacification, Vietnam War Has Been Won," Armed Forces Journal 109 (February 1972): 50-51.

3342. Heinl, Robert D. "Carter's Greatest Challenge: The Soviet Buildup," Sea Power 20 (February 1977): 32-35.

3343. Heitzenrater, Richard. "Decoding Wesley's Diaries," Cryptologia 2/3 (July 1978): 260-264.

3344. Helberg, Claus. "The Vemork Action: A Classic Act of Sabotage," Studies in Intelligence 36/5 (Fall 1992): 81-90.
     These are the reflections of one of the survivors of the raid on Vemork, the location of the German heavy water plant in Norway in 1943, as reproduced from the original 1947 account in the Yearbook of the Norwegian Tourist

Association. Perhaps one of the most daring plots to attack a heavily fortified enemy encampment in modern military history.

3345. Helfeld, D. M. "A Study of Justice Department Policies on Wiretapping," National Lawyers Guild Practitioner 9 (Spring 1949): 57-69.

3346. Helfield, Randa. "Constructive Treason and Godwin's Treasonous Constructions," Mosaic 28 (June 1995): 43-62.
    Concerns treason in literature and the writings of William Godwin.

3347. Helgerson, John. "Truman and Eisenhower: Launching the Process," Studies in Intelligence 38/5 (1995): 65-77.
    Discusses the process of briefing presidents from 1952 to 1992. Major sections discuss the strained relations that complicate arrangements; pre-election briefings; support to the president-elect; the new president as intelligence consumer; briefing Governor Stevenson in 1952; and challenger briefed again in 1956. The author is making a much longer research inquiry into such briefings.

3348. Hellenbroich, H. "Delimitation of West German Police and Intelligence Service Responsibilities in the Field of Preventive Protection of the Nation," Kriminalistik 29/9 (September 1975): 394-396.
    Author discusses distinguishes between the German Police and the intelligence organization known as the Office for the Protection of the Constitution. The roles of each organization are detailed.

3349. Heller, Michael. "Old Lies, New Lies--and Disinformation," Midstream 31/1 (January 1985): 50-54.
    A book review essay of Anatoly Golitsyn's book, New Lies for Old. Accounts for a secret plan of the USSR on disinformation, the KGB's disinformation operations, the deception of non-Soviet countries since 1958, weaknesses in Golitsyn's argument, and the faults in Golitzyn's aim.

3350. Heller, Michael. "Stalin and the Detectives," Survey 211 (Winter-Spring 1975): 160-175.

3351. Heller, Michael. "Disinformation, A Means of Information," Politique Internationale 10 (1980-1981): 237-246.

3352. Heller, Michael. "Krasin-Savinkov: Une Rencontre Secrete," Cahiers du Monde Russe et Sovietique 26/1 (January-March 1985): 63-67.

3353. Hellman, Martin E. "The Mathematics of Public Key Cryptography," Scientific American 241 (August 1979): 146-152, 198.
    A technical discussion of public key cryptographic systems, and

conventional systems, the trapdoor knapsack system and the RSA system. Argues that advances in electronic communications have yielded susceptibility to eavesdropping and forgeries. New crypto systems must be developed to counter these threats.

3354. Helmick, Leah S. "Codes - Fact and Fallacy," American Legion Monthly (August 1937): 18-19, 58.

Discusses the work of Colonel and Mrs. William F. Friedman in the realm of cryptography.

3355. Helms, Richard. "Intelligence in American Society," Studies in Intelligence 11/2 (Summer 1967).

Discusses clandestine services policy intelligence and the 1962 missile crisis, the Cold War, communication intelligence, Kwane Nkrumah, communist insurgencies, and the role of the Central Intelligence Agency. Estimated to be 16 pages in length.

3356. Helms, Richard. "We Believed in Our Work," Studies in Intelligence 27/3 (Fall 1983).

3357. Hemming, Charles C. "A Confederate Odyssey," American Heritage 35/1 (January 1984): 69-84.

Discusses the life of Charles Hemming, in particular his escape from a Union prison and drafting into the Confederate secret service.

3358. Hemphill, John A. "PW and Captured Document Doctrine," Military Review 49/11 (November 1969): 65-71.

Acknowledges that the prisoner of war is a valuable source of intelligence information. Sections include discussion of adequate doctrine, the stability of operations at front lines and rear lines, evaluation of sources, objectives and principles, intelligence support, and specialized operations.

3359. Henderson, F. P. "VMO Squadrons Are Airpower!," Marine Corps Gazette 78/5 (1994): 76-78.

Considers Marine Corps air surveillance missions in World War II and Korea.

3360. Henderson, G. B. "Lord Palmerston and the Secret Service Fund," English Historical Review 53 (July 1938): 485-487.

A brief discussion of the fund following 1848. Concludes that large sums of money were wasted by Palmerston in an effort to rescue two Italians who had been exiled by Portugal. The secret fund used for the maneuver was not under the supervision of the British Parliament.

3361. Henderson, Ian. "Teaching the Dieppe Raid: Some Strategics," History and Social Science Teacher 18/4 (May 1983): 239-241.

Author employs elementary mapwork, film, debate, guest lectures, a machinegun demonstration, and Charlie's 'Glory Box' in his instruction on this important engagement.

3362. Henderson, Robert d'A. "The Future of Ex-Eastern Bloc Intelligence Personnel," Studies in Intelligence 35/2 (Summer 1991).

3363. Henderson, Robert d'A. "De Klerk's Relationship with the South African Intelligence Services," Commentary 15 (November 1991): 2-6.

3364. Henderson, Robert d'A. "South African Intelligence Under de Klerk," International Journal of Intelligence and Counterintelligence 8/1 (Spring 1995): 51-89.

Argues that former South African State President, F. W. de Klerk, had only limited control over his intelligence services, and what little control he had arose from public disclosures of services activities. Major sections discuss the rocky presidential transition; Botha's securocrat establishment; asserting presidential command; intelligence hoax in Namibia; de Klerk's security restructuring; intelligence requirements for political organizations; covert operations and secret funding; and de Klerk's remaining efforts to gain control.

3365. Henderson, Robert d'A. "South African Intelligence Transition from de Klerk to Mandela: An Update," International Journal of Intelligence and Counterintelligence 8/4 (Winter 1995): 471-485.

Discusses the restructuring of South African intelligence; the weakening of the firm grip of the intelligence system; continuing investigations; the ANC in control; controlling third force violence; the amnesty question; and prospects for the future.

3366. Henderson, Wallace D. "Surveillance and Warning," Signal 33/3 (November-December 1978): 39-43.

3367. Hendrick, Burton J. "Worse Than Arnold," Atlantic Monthly 156 (October 1935): 385-395.

Discusses the life and intrigues of Arthur Lee in 1777, in particular, the double agent work Lee performed during the American revolution.

3368. Henhoeffer, William M. "Donovan in Perspective," Studies in Intelligence 27/4 (Winter 1983).

3369. Henhoeffer, William M. "Donovan's Allies in World War I," Studies in Intelligence 30/4 (Winter 1986): 47-53.

3370. Henhoeffer, William M. "'If Donovan Were Here Today,'" Studies in Intelligence 32/3 (Fall 1988).

3371. Henisch, Bridget A. and Heinz K. "Major Andre," Journal of General Education 28/3 (Fall 1976): 237-244.
    A brief discussion of British spy John Andre's experiences as both heroic and villainous. Contains sections on Andre the man of many talents, the capture that immortalized Andre, and American art containing Andre's image.

3372. Henke, Klaus D. "Miscellaneous: Using and Evaluating the Records of the State Security Agency of the Former German Democratic Republic," Vierteljahrshefte fuer Zeitgeschichte 41/4 (1993): 575-587.

3373. Henkin, Louis. "The Right to Know and the Duty to Withhold: The Case of the Pentagon Papers," University of Pennsylvania Law Review 120 (1971): 271-280.
    Explains the lengthy history of the government's right to classify information and to hold it confidential from public consumption. Also observes court rulings upholding the right of the press to publish whatever information it acquires. Difficult questions pertaining the proper balance of interests are posed. The Pentagon Papers case serves as the backdrop for the discussion.

3374. Henkin, Louis. "'A More Effective System' for Foreign Relations: The Constitutional Framework," Virginia Law Review 61/4 (May 1975): 751-776.
    A general essay on the Constitution, responded to by several legal scholars, among them, Richard A. Falk. Falk injects Central Intelligence Agency covert actions as an issue not raised by Henkin.

3375. Hennessy, Peter and Gail Brownfield. "Britain's Cold War Security Purge: The Origins of Positive Vetting," Historical Journal 25/4 (December 1982): 965-974.
    Discusses communist infiltration into Great Britain. Discusses the Gouzenko defection, the espionage of Alan Nunn May and the Canadian atomic project. The British started a screening system for sensitive civil service workers known as "negative vetting," later characterized as feeble and ineffective in ridding the government of spies. A positive purge procedure was installed in 1948.

3376. Hennessy, Peter and Kathleen Townsend. "The Documentary Spoor of Burgess and Maclean," Intelligence and National Security 2/2 (April 1987): 291-301.
    Some brief observations of the authors adding to the insights and documentary evidence of the impact of the British spies Burgess and Maclean.

3377. Hennings, Thomas. "The Wiretapping-Eavesdropping Problem: A Legislator's View," Minnesota Law Review 44 (1960): 813-834.

Contains sections on private wiretapping, law enforcement wiretapping, legality of statutes authorizing wiretapping, wiretapping on the federal level, and the problem of new legislation.

3378. Henry, Fred. "Japanese Espionage and Our Psychology for Failure," U.S. Naval Institute Proceedings 69/5 (May 1943): 639-641.

The military successes of the Japanese early in World War II are attributed to Japan's creation of an intelligence service that collected large amounts of information through espionage.

3379. Henry, Fred. "Japanese Espionage, Foundation for War," U.S. Naval Institute Proceedings 69/10 (October 1943): 1335-1341.

3380. Hensley, John R. "The Brandywine Examples: Case Studies in Industrial Espionage in Early 19th Century Delaware," Delaware History 21/2 (1984): 73-85.

Argues that the DuPont and other large American corporations were substantially successful in conducting trade secrets theft in the nineteenth century.

3381. Hentoff, Nat. "Media Watch: Putting the Gag on CIA Whistle Blowers," Civil Liberties Review 5/2 (July-August 1978): 37-40.

Considers briefly the civil liberties dangers posed by prior restraint of information as addressed in the Marchetti and Snepp cases.

3382. Hentoff, Nat. "A Secret Federal Court," Progressive 44/8 (August 1980): 12-13.

Argues that legislation then pending in Congress would allow government agents to violate the Fourth Amendment protections against unreasonable searches and seizures by seeking approval for such violations from a secret federal court. Raises civil liberties infringement concerns.

3383. Hentoff, Nat. "The Case of the Unlikely Spy," Progressive 50 (February 1986): 22-24.

A brief discussion of the Samuel Loring Morison's 'espionage' case.

3384. Henwood, Doug. "Spooks in Blue," Grand Street 7 (Spring 1988): 212-219.

3385. Henze, Paul B. "The Quest for an Assassin: Mehmet Ali Agca: A Report from Malatya," Encounter 110/5 (May 1983): 9-18.

Describes the author's work to uncover the life and lifestyle of the Pope's attempted assassin, Mehmet Ali Agca. The signs of Agca's future behavior could not be detected as he was a talented person from a good background. Useful for studies of terrorism and intelligence evaluations of potential assassins.

3386. Henze, Paul B. "Origins of the Plot to Kill the Pope," Washington Quarterly 6/4 (Autumn 1983): 3-19.

A proposition that the Soviet Union had sufficient reason to want to assassinate the Pope, thus adding to the conspiracy theory of Mehmet Agca's actions. Reviews a substantial number of details relevant to the plot.

3387. Henze, Paul B. "The Plot to Kill the Pope," Survey 27/118-119 (Autumn-Winter 1983): 2-21.

3388. Henze, Paul B. "Conspiring to Kill the Pope," Problems of Communism 34/3 (May-June 1985): 59-64.

Summarizes evidence to strengthen the view that Bulgaria was behind the plot to kill the Pope. The assassin Mehmet Agca was a 'progressive' in the pay of Bulgaria, and he was previously involved in an assassination as a dress rehearsal for the attempt on the Pope. Also covers the Judge Martella report of 1984 on the plot.

3389. Heppenheimer, T. A. "The Real-Life Search for Red October," Science Digest 94 (April 1986): 44-49+.

3390. Herbeck, Dale A. "Fair Play Did Not Permit Excess: A Critical Review of the Histories of the Espionage Act of 1917," Free Speech Yearbook 26 (1987): 11-27.

3391. Herbeck, Dale A. "New York Times v. Sullivan: Justice Brennan's Beautiful Lie," Free Speech Yearbook 28 (1990): 37-57.

3392. Herbert, Craig S. "Gasbags Preferred," Aerospace Historian 15/2 (1968): 26, 39-51.

3393. Herbig, Daniel and Katherine. "Propositions on Military Deception," Journal of Strategic Studies 5/1 (March 1982): 155-177.

Discusses military deception strategies, two key variants in deception (ambiguity-increasing and misleading), the process of deception, factors influencing the likelihood of deception, and the adaptability of deception.

3394. Herbig, Katherine L. "American Strategic Deception in the Pacific, 1942-44," Intelligence and National Security 2/3 (July 1987): 260-300.

An account of the American buildup for deception efforts after the Pearl Harbor invasion. Discusses Operation Wedlock and the deception in the North Pacific; and persistent organizational struggles.

3395. Herde, Peter. "Pearl Harbor from an Unknown Revisionist Point of View: New Materials About the Background of the Intelligence Service Concerning the Japanese Attack on December 7, 1941," Historiches Jahrbuch 104/1 (1984): 63-112.

An argument, in German, supporting the view that essential information was withheld from military commanders in the months prior to the Pearl Harbor attack.

3396. Herdt, Gilbert. "Secret Societies and Secret Collectives," Oceania 60 (June 1990): 360-381.

Considers cultural and cross-cultural factors in the formation of secret societies and the maintenance of secrecy practices.

3397. Heredia, Hannibal F. "Is There Privacy in the Workplace?: Guaranteeing a Broader Privacy Right for Workers Under California Law," Southwestern University Law Review 22 (Fall 1992): 307-335.

Examines hindrance by state action doctrine private employers face in redressing harms caused by employer monitoring and resolution of issue under state constitutions providing broader protection, as in California. Discusses split in appellate courts and proposes solution for uniformity. Considers applications of concept to surveillance of E-mail.

3398. Herek, Gregory M.; Irving L. Janis; and Paul Huth. "Decision Making During International Crises," Journal of Conflict Resolution 31/2 (June 1987): 203-226.

A study of "high-quality" decision-making procedures versus "defective" decision-making procedures in an attempt to discover the impact of defeats on outcomes. Nineteen international crises since World War II were evaluated. Alternative explanations and implications are offered.

3399. Herken, Gregg. "A Most Deadly Illusion: The Atomic Secret and American Nuclear Weapons Policy, 1945-1950," Pacific Historical Review 49/1 (1980): 51-76.

An extensive analysis of American illusions of total control over the production of nuclear weapons in the post-war period. Discusses some of the post-war espionage cases in connection with defeat of a bill that would have created an all- civilian Atomic Energy Commission.

3400. Herman, Edward S. "U.S. Sponsorship of International Terrorism: An Overview," Crime and Social Justice 27-28 (1987): 1-31.

Major sections discuss power and the semantics of terrorism; the US as terrorist and sponsor of terrorism; mechanisms of support fo state terrorism; and terror outcomes. Mentions US intelligence agencies.

3401. Herman, John. "Agency Africa: Rygor's Franco-Polish Network and Operation Touch," Journal of Contemporary History 22/4 (October 1987): 681-706.

Operation Torch is discussed in light of the role of a Polish spy network's successes in North Africa. Agents in the network passed secret information to the British in Operation Rygor.

3402. Herman, Michael. "Reflections on the Study of Soviet Military Literature," RUSI Journal of Defence Studies 133 (Summer 1988): 79-84.

3403. Herman, Michael. "Intelligence and the Assessment of Military Capabilities: Reasonable Sufficiency of the Worst Case?," Intelligence and National Security 4/4 (October 1989): 765-799.

Major sections discuss intelligence and military power; difficulties in the estimation process; worst-case estimates; reasons for the worst case; management and quality in people; an analytic doctrine; reading the adversary's mind; the challenge of the argument; and net assessment.

3404. Herman, Michael. "Intelligence and Policy: A Comment," Intelligence and National Security 6/1 (January 1991): 229-239.

Addresses the role of intelligence in the policy process. Major sections consider single source and all source intelligence; covert influences; quality of assessment; and a new intelligence agenda. Considers three systems of foreign intelligence gathering and their respective hierarchies and priorities.

3405. Herman, Michael. "Governmental Intelligence: Its Evolution and Role," Journal of Economic and Social Intelligence 2/2 (1992): 91-113.

3406. Herman, Michael. "Intelligence Defectors," Conflict Quarterly 12/3 (Summer 1992): 75-78.

A book review essay.

3407. Herman, Michael. "GCHQ De-Unionisation 1984," Public Policy and Administration 8/2 (Summer 1993): 74-80.

3408. Herman, Michael. "Assessment Machinery: British and American Models," Intelligence and National Security 10/4 (October 1995): 13-33.

A comparison between American and British intelligence assessment frameworks. Major sections discuss top level decision-taking and desiderata; British and American experience up to 1945; post-1945 models; experience elsewhere; a central intelligence organization; big committees and small central groups; intelligence assessors or a bigger college?; the constitutional and administrative context; and practical conclusions.

3409. Herman, Peter C. "Treason in the Manciple's Tale," <u>Chaucer Review</u> 25/4 (1991): 318-328.

3410. Hermann, Robert J. "Advancing Technology: Collateral Effects on Intelligence," <u>American Intelligence Journal</u> 15/2 (Autumn-Winter 1994): 8-11.
      Discusses changes in military techniques; coalition security; and the increased value of open source information.

3411. Herndon, G. Melvin. "Keeping an Eye on the British: William Tatham and the Chesapeake Affair," <u>Virginia Cavalcade</u> 22/1 (1972): 30-39.
      After an attack upon the Chesapeake and the removal of US sailors, Tatham was asked by President Jefferson to conduct reconnaissance operations against British ship movements and cargo.

3412. Herndon, James S. and Joseph O. Baylen. "Col. Phillip R. Faymonville and the Red Army, 1934-1943," <u>Slavic Review</u> 34/3 (September 1975): 483-505.
      Discusses the experiences and implications of the first American military attache to the Soviet Union, Col. Faymonville (1888-1962). The colonel arrived in Moscow in 1934 and provided reports on the Soviet army.

3413. Herold, M. "Fight Against Terrorism in the Federal Republic of Germany," <u>Revue Internationale de Criminologie et de Police Technique</u> 27/1 (January-March 1974): 27-29.
      Discusses the role of German police intelligence in making the arrests of several members of the Baader-Meinhof terrorist group.

3414. Herrick, Robert M. "Where Is the Enemy?," <u>Army</u> 21/6 (June 1971): 46-49.
      Brief discussion of prisoner interrogation and the tracking of prisoner travel by use of maps.

3415. Herring, Jan P. "Building a Business Intelligence System," <u>Journal of Business Strategy</u> 9/3 (May-June 1988): 4-9.
      Brief commentary on industrial espionage versus market analysis and strategy within the context of competition.

3416. Hers, J. F. Ph. "The Rise of the Dutch Resistance: A Memoir," <u>Intelligence and National Security</u> 7/4 (October 1992): 454-472.
      Major sections discuss the student community of 1953-40; the industrial sector; family connections; social, political and religious characteristics; the Wilton-Feyenoord resistance group; the Geuzen group and the Geuzen letter; sabotage; discovery; trial; sentence. Chronicles the ethos, start, structure, and organization of the Dutch resistance.

3417. Hersh, Burton. "Dragons Have To Be Killed," <u>Washingtonian</u> 20/12 (September 1985): 158-161; 192-203.

A detailed account of William Colby's revelations about the CIA's counterintelligence activities in violation of the law. Such operations were run by CIA's counterintelligence head, James Angleton, who was fired by Colby. Alleges that Colby's intention was to bring down Angleton by focussing media attention on illegal operations.

3418. Hersh, Seymour M. "The Angleton Story," <u>New York Times Biographical Service</u> 9 (June 1978): 688-694.

3419. Hersh, Seymour M. "The Price of Power: Kissinger, Nixon, and Chile," <u>Atlantic Monthly</u> 250/6 (December 1982): 31-48.

Includes a discussion of US intelligence involvement in Chile during the Nixon administration.

3420. Hershberg, James G. "Before 'The Missiles of October': Did Kennedy Plan a Military Strike Against Cuba," <u>Diplomatic History</u> 14/2 (Spring 1990): 163-198.

Considers the question of whether or not the Kennedy administration was planning an invasion of Cuba in the months before Soviet missiles were discovered on the island. Substantial discussion of the role of CIA.

3421. Hershey, Amos S. "The International Law of Aerial Space," <u>American Journal of International Law</u> 6/2 (April 1912): 381-388.

Wireless telegraphy, airplanes and balloons changed the nature of international law at the turn of the century. Reports upon the International Law Institute at Ghent in 1906 at which law of aerial space was discussed. Mentions the need to prevent aerial espionage. Useful piece for historical studies.

3422. Herz, John H. "The Fiasco of Denazification in Germany," <u>Political Science Quarterly</u> 63/4 (December 1948): 569-594.

Major sections discuss direct military government control; the law of liberation; amnesties; amendment of 1947; further relaxation of the amendment of 1948; liquidation of the program; and conclusions. Concludes that denazification was a failed effort.

3423. Herz, Martin F. "Some Psychological Lessons from Leaflet Propaganda in World War II," <u>Public Opinion Quarterly</u> 9 (December 1949): 471-486.

The measurement of effectiveness of wartime leaflet propaganda is always difficulty, but there are some ways of reaching a measure: quantity of leaflets found with dead bodies; amount of leaflet information forthcoming during interrogations; revelations by soldiers; surrender information; and enemy command insights. Greatest use of leaflets is against enemy soldiers; least effective use is against enemy civilians.

3424. Herzog, Chaim. "The Middle East War," RUSI Defence Studies Journal 120/1 (March 1975): 3-13.

3425. Heuer, Richards J., Jr. "Cognitive Biases: Problems in Hindsight Analysis," Studies in Intelligence 22/2 (Summer 1978): 21-28.
    A discussion of three cognitive biases affecting the evaluation of intelligence. Major sections discuss experiments; the analyst's perspective; the consumer's perspective; the overseer's perspective; and the question of whether biases can be overcome.

3426. Heuer, Richards J., Jr. "Do You Really Need More Information?," Studies in Intelligence 23/1 (Spring 1979): 15-25.
    Discussion of intelligence analysis: data driven or concept driven? Suggests ways for improving intelligence analyses. Argues for more concept driven analyses via methods of cognitive psychology.

3427. Heuer, Richards J., Jr. "Improving Intelligence Analysis: Some Insights on Data, Concepts, and Management in the Intelligence Community," Bureaucrat 8/4 (Winter 1979-1980): 2-11.
    Argues that the greatest weakness in the intelligence analysis process is the lack of high quality information. Reports on author's experiment to provide increasing levels of information to eight horserace handicappers, finding that judgment did not improve accuracy. Offers two "mental models" that influence analyst judgment: data driven and concept driven. Concludes that the accuracy of the information in the mental model of the analyst is the main factor in assessing correct results.

3428. Heuer, Richards J., Jr. "Analyzing the Soviet Invasion of Afghanistan: Hypotheses from Causal Attribution Theory," Studies in Comparative Communism 13/4 (Winter 1980): 347-355.
    Suggests that the best method for evaluating the event is to reflect upon our own perceptions of the Soviets. US intelligence analysts require close self-examination to determine the perceptions held of the Soviets. Considers both dispositional and situational factors in the conduct of estimating the invasion.

3429. Heuer, Richards J., Jr. "Strategies for Analytical Judgment," Studies in Intelligence 25/2 (Summer 1981).

3430. Heuer, Richards J., Jr. "Strategic Deception and Counterdeception: A Cognitive Process Approach," International Studies Quarterly 25/2 (June 1981): 294-327.
    Author applies research in experimental psychology to strategic and

military deception and counterdeception. Author discovered deception seldom fails when it exploits a target's preconceptions.

3431. Heuer, Richards J., Jr. "Biases in Evaluation of Evidence," <u>Analytical Methods Review</u> (January 1981): 31-46.
This article also appeared in <u>Studies in Intelligence</u> 25/4 (Winter 1981).

3432. Heuer, Richards J., Jr. "Nosenko: Five Paths to Judgment," <u>Studies in Intelligence</u> 31/3 (Fall 1987): 71-101.
A detailed analysis of the Nosenko defection case. Major sections discuss the overview of the case; strategies; and conclusions.

3433. Heurlin, Bertel. "Notes on Bureaucratic Politics in National Security Policy," <u>Cooperation and Conflict</u> 10/4 (1975): 237-259.
Suggests that one method of explaining international politics is through the Bureaucratic Politics Approach (BPA). Accounts for the arguments for and against application of BPA.

3434. Hewig, William, III. "Massachusetts Law - Relaxing the Organized Crime Requirement for Electronic Surveillance: A Carte Blanche for the "Uninvited Ear"?," <u>Western New England Law Review</u> 5 (Spring 1983): 725-761.
A case note referring to <u>Commonwealth v. Jarahek</u> and <u>Commonwealth v. Thorpe</u>.

3435. Hewish, Mark. "ELINT for Strategic and Tactical Applications," <u>International Defense Review</u> (February 1994): 39-43.

3436. Hewitt, Robert L. "The Literary Life," <u>Infantry Journal</u> 60 (June 1947): 37-40.
An account of wartime journalism cranked out by the VIII Corps intelligence personnel responsible for the daily intelligence report.

3437. Heymann, Hans, Jr. "The Intelligence-Policy Relationship," <u>Studies in Intelligence</u> 28/4 (Winter 1984).

3438. Heymont, Irving. "Combat Surveillance," <u>Military Review</u> 38/10 (October 1958): 66-70.

3439. Heymont, Irving. "Commander's Intelligence Priorities," <u>Military Review</u> 39/2 (February 1959): 40-44.
Argues that the Army should revise the essential elements of information for greater intelligence effectiveness in a nuclear environment. Discusses the broadened needs of intelligence and the value of a new concept, the Commander's Intelligence Priorities.

3440. Heymont, Irving. "What Is the Threat?," Military Review 47/4 (April 1967): 47-55.

Argues that threat analysis is an essential ingredient in military research, cost estimates and weapons development analysis.

3441. Hggman, Bertil. "Soviet Russian Active Measures in Scandinavia," Ukrainian Review 34/3 (1986): 69-75.

3442. Hiatt, Blanchard. "Age of Decipherment," Cryptologia 1/2 (April 1977): 101-105.

3443. Hiatt, Blanchard. "'Count Forward Three Score and Ten,'" Cryptologia 1/2 (April 1977): 106-115.

3444. Hibbert, Reginald. "Intelligence and Policy," Intelligence and National Security 5/1 (January 1990): 110-128.

Examines the various ways in which the growth of secret intelligence collection and assessment in the past half-century has affected the process of foreign policy making. A contribution to the Vaughan lecture series at Oxford University in 1989.

3445. Hibbs, Russell S. "The Enemy Within," U.S. Naval Institute Proceedings 111/9 (September 1985): 65-69.

A brief discussion of KGB efforts to penetrate national security, and a damage assessment of losses. Reflects upon the Walker espionage case and the pervasiveness of Soviet spying.

3446. Hicks, Clifford B. "Tales From the Black Chambers: Codes and Ciphers in American History," American Heritage 24 (April 1973): 56-61+.

Argues that cryptographers do not receive credit they deserve, in particular reference to the fact that American cryptographers broke the Japanese codes well before Pearl Harbor, and they had significant information from Japanese radio communications. Develops the history of American secret code experience. Argues that accurate assessment of codes and ciphers is essential to national security.

3447. Hicks, Robert R., Jr. "Assessing Joint Warfighting Capability," American Intelligence Journal 16/1 (Spring 1995): 33-36.

3448. Hiestand, Harry H. "Military Intelligence and Enemy Air Defense," United States Army Aviation Digest 20 (September 1974): 2-3+.

3449. Higginbotham, Donald. "And the Curtain Fell on Yorktown," Studies in Intelligence 25/2 (Summer 1981).

3450. Higgings, Robert. "The Soblen Case," World Today 18 (October 1962): 415-427.

3451. Higgins, Trumbull. "East Wind Rain," U.S. Naval Institute Proceedings 81/11 (November 1955): 1198-1205.
 Discusses the Japanese plans for and reasoning about the attack on Pearl Harbor. Also discusses the optional attack against the Soviet Union.

3452. Higham, Robert. "British Intervention in Greece 1940-1941: The Anatomy of a Grand Deception," Balkan Studies 23/1 (1982): 101- 126.

3453. Higham, Robin D. S. "The Russian Fleet on the Eastern Seaboard, 1863-1864: A Maritime Chronology," American Neptune 20/1 (1960): 49-61.
 Accounts for the approach of the Russian fleet to the Eastern coastline and considers the reasons for such initiative. Suggests that the Russian navy needed to spread out due to heavy losses in the Crimean War, that US ports were perceived to be friendly, and that the Russians needed to "keep tabs" on the British and French navies.

3454. Highland, Harold J. "Censored, A Simulation Exercise," Cryptologia 1/4 (October 1977): 376-377.

3455. Highsmith, Newell L. "Policing Executive Adventurism: Congressional Oversight of Military and Paramilitary Operations," Harvard Journal on Legislation 19/2 (Summer 1982): 327-392.
 Analyzes the ambiguities and loopholes of the War Powers Resolution, and compares it to Title V of the 1980 amendment to the National Security Act of 1947. Argues for the consultation and notification requirements of Title V for controlling such operations.

3456. Hilbert, Lother W. "The Origins of the Military Attache Service in Great Britain," Parliamentary Affairs 13/2 (1960): 329-334.
 A history of British stationing of military officers in Turin, Constantinople and Paris during the Crimean War, and the practice of planting intelligence officers among the attaches. Such practices reinforced the use of attaches in intelligence missions.

3457. Hilbert, Lother W. "The Origins of Military Attache Service in Great Britain," Revue d'Histoire Diplomatique 77 (1961): 155-163.

3458. Hiley, Nicholas P. "The Failure of British Espionage Against Germany, 1907-1914," Historical Journal 26/4 (December 1983): 867-890.
 Discusses Britain's fear of invasion by German and whether or not the Germans could draft a plan of attack in complete secrecy. British intelligence

resources were limited in terms of finances, availability of trained agents, and effective use of information.

3459. Hiley, Nicholas P. "The Failure of British Counter-Espionage Against Germany, 1907-1914," Historical Journal 28/4 (December 1985): 835-862.

Discusses British approaches to controlling espionage by means of stepped up police surveillance of suspected foreign secret agents. Main British concerns were the number of German resident aliens in the country and the resemblances of such persons to German soldiers.

3460. Hiley, Nicholas P. "Counter-Espionage and Security in Great Britain During the First World War," English Historical Review 101/400 (July 1986): 635-670.

Discusses two organizations in the British government for performing counter-espionage activities: a group in the War Office aimed at working against the German, Austrian and Hungarian agents; a "Special Branch of the Criminal Investigation Department" aimed at uncovering and surveilling "suspect organizations." Argues that German agents had difficulty operating in Britain after 1916.

3461. Hiley, Nicholas P. "British Internal Security in Wartime: The Rise and Fall of P.M.S.2, 1915-17," Intelligence and National Security 1/3 (September 1986): 395-415.

Discusses the organization and composition of the counter intelligence groups in existence in August, 1914 in England. Details the origins of certain groups dating as early as 1883. Also includes organizational charts and outlines responsibilities of units, personnel growth and cases.

3462. Hiley, Nicholas P. "The Strategic Origins of Room 40," Intelligence and National Security 2/2 (April 1987): 245-273.

A detailed consideration of the facts pertaining to the origins of the British cryptanalysis function from 1912 to 1914. Argues that several earlier accounts of this history are inaccurate or incomplete. Suggests that the complete story has not yet been told and more research is needed.

3463. Hiley, Nicholas P. "Spying for the Kaiser," History Today 38 (June 1988): 37-43.

Examines pre-war espionage in Britain by German agents before 1918. Argues that paranoia about such spying was warranted due to several actual cases.

3464. Hiley, Nicholas P. "Decoding German Spies: British Spy Fiction, 1908-18," Intelligence and National Security 5/4 (October 1990): 55-79.

British spy fiction in the decade between 1908 and 1918 is discussed in relation to British fears and phobias about Germany. The spy novel of this period, says the author, reflected the subconscious fantasies of adolescents and of insecure middle-class men in a changing British society.

3465. Hiley, Nicholas P. "The Play, the Parody, the Censor and the Film," Intelligence and National Security 6/1 (January 1991): 218-228.

Discusses the real life parody of a play in which Britain is invaded by Germany, and a professional spy network aids invaders from within. Considers the political and intelligence problems posed by the script.

3466. Hiley, Nicholas P. "An Open Secret: Political Accountability and the Changing Role of MI5," Queen's Quarterly 100/2 (Summer 1993): 371-382.

Considers the role and impact of Britain's MI5 spy organization in the definition and administration of national security. Discusses MI5's romantic reputation, new public questions, public accountability, and humorous situations.

3467. Hiley, Nicholas P. and Julian Putkowski. "A Postscript on P.M.S.2," Intelligence and National Security 3/2 (April 1988): 326-331.

Discussion of this World War I domestic intelligence function, including four documents reflecting the investigative informant work of a journalist and officials of the British government.

3468. Hill, Alfred. "Defamation and Privacy Under the First Amendment," Columbia Law Review 76 (1976): 1205-1311.

Contains sections on defamation, invasion of privacy by media defendants, invasion of privacy by non-media defendants, confidentiality, and fiction. A thorough review of the law and procedures relevant to a showing of defamation. Relevant to discussions of confidentiality.

3469. Hill, Herbert. "The CIA in National and International Labor Movements," International Journal of Politics, Culture and Society 6/3 (Spring 1993): 405-407.

A brief argument that CIA backed anti-labor movements in foreign countries and aided suppression of militant unions.

3470. Hill, Kenneth L. "President Kennedy and the Neutralization of Laos," Review of Politics 31 (July 1969): 353-369.

3471. Hill, L. M. "The Two-Witness Rule in English Treason Trials: Some Comments on the Emergence of Procedural Law," American Journal of Legal History 12 (April 1968): 95-111.

Discusses the history of the law of treason in England, including the introduction in the 17th century of various safeguards against unlawful prosecution. The two-witness rule was one such consideration, found to have been a part of English common law practice. The rule has always been contentious.

3472. Hill, Lester S. "Cryptography in an Algebraic Alphabet," <u>American Mathematical Monthly</u> 36 (June-July 1929): 306-312.

A technical discussion of the bi-operational alphabet, including an illustration; determinants in the bi-operational alphabet; normal transformations and the polygraphic cipher systems; an illustration of linear ciphers; and concluding remarks.

3473. Hill, Lester S. "Concerning Certain Linear Transformation Apparatus of Cryptography," <u>American Mathematical Monthly</u> 38 (March 1931): 135-154.

A technical discussion of scales, including an example; scales obtained by algebraic extension of other scales; rational manipulation in a scale; linear transformation in the general range; a fundamental Lemma; regular transformation in J; construction of transformation of the group H; notations and procedure in examples; and three examples.

3474. Hill, Martin R. "It Is Time to Get on with Information Warfare," <u>Defense Intelligence Journal</u> 5/1 (Spring 1996): 25-41.

3475. Hill, R. "Dark Words," <u>Cornhill Magazine</u> 153 (February 1936): 195-205.

Discusses ways by which secret messages have been transmitted.

3476. Hill, Robert A. "The Foremost Radical Among His Race: Marcus Garvey and the Black Scare, 1918-1921," <u>Prologue: Quarterly Journal of the National Archives</u> 16/4 (Winter 1984): 215-231.

An account of the FBI investigations into the World War I activities of black activist Marcus Garvey. Refers to J. Edgar Hoover's role in the case and to the Military Intelligence Division.

3477. Hillenkoetter, Roscoe H. "Using the World's Information Sources," <u>Army Information Digest</u> 3 (November 1948): 3-6.

Admiral Hillenkoetter was director of Central Intelligence Agency in the late 1940s. He describes in general terms the sources of intelligence collectors.

3478. Hillingso, K. G. H. "The Making of National Estimates During the Period of the 'Missile Gap,'" <u>Intelligence and National Security</u> 1/3 (September 1986): 336-356.

3479. Hilsman, Roger, Jr. "Intelligence and Policy-Making in Foreign Affairs," <u>World Politics</u> 5 (October 1952): 1-45.

A classic early scholarly treatment of the interaction between intelligence and the policy process. Discusses the attitudes of operating officials, attitudes of intelligence operators, area of disharmony, possible solutions, and a working model of knowledge.

3480. Hilsman, Roger, Jr. "Internal War--New Communist Tactic," Military Review 42/4 (April 1962): 11-22.

3481. Hilsman, Roger, Jr. "On Intelligence," Armed Forces and Society 8/1 (Fall 1981): 129-143.
    A review essay on 11 books on intelligence and espionage. Distinguishes them in terms of intelligence as information, intelligence as knowledge, intelligence as covert action, intelligence as organization, and the role of intelligence.

3482. Hilsman, Roger, Jr. "Does the CIA Still Have a Role?," Foreign Affairs 74/5 (September-October 1995): 104-116.
    This veteran observer and participant in the intelligence community summarizes the humble beginnings of CIA, addresses some of the popular mythology concerning spies and espionage, considers implications of covert political action, accounts for the implications of new technologies and widely dispersed analytical functions, and points out the embarrassment of riches, and argues for the demise of covert action and espionage in favor of a rise in expenditures for research and analysis.

3483. Hilton, O. A. "Freedom of Press in Wartime, 1917-1919," Southwestern Social Science Quarterly 28/4 (December 1947): 346-361.
    The controls on press freedoms were greatly expanded during World War I, and for some 'super patriots' the tradeoff of individual rights was acceptable. The Post Office of the United States played a role in suppressing the mail of radical groups during the War and as late as 1921.

3484. Hinchly, Ronald H. "National Security in the Information Age," Washington Quarterly 9/2 (Spring 1986): 125-132.
    Major sections discuss the role of information support and its difficulties; information management in the Carter and Reagan administrations; information integration in the Carter and Reagan administrations; the National Security Council and information integration; and decision support aids.

3485. Hinckle, Warren; Sol Sterm; and Robert Scheer. "Michigan State: The University on the Make," Ramparts 4 (April 1966): 11-22.
    This is a popular press resource. May be useful in historical research.

3486. Hinsley, F. H. "British Intelligence in the Second World War: An Overview," Cryptologia 16/1 (January 1990): 1-10.

3487. Hinsley, Harry. "Cracking the Ciphers," Electronics and Power 33 (July 1987): 453-455.

3488. Hirsch, Daniel and William G. Mathews. "The H-Bomb: Who Really Gave Away the Secret?," Bulletin of the Atomic Scientists 46/1 (1990): 22-30.

Offers theory and evidence to argue the claim that the H-bomb secret may have been revealed by the United States by the natural course of testing and atmospheric fallout.

3489. Hirschfeld, Thomas J. "The Toughest Verification Challenge: Conventional Forces in Europe," Arms Control Today 19/11 (January-February 1989): 16-21.

3490. Hitsman, J. Mackay and Desmond Morton. "Canada's First Military Attache: Capt. H. C. Thacker in the Russo-Japanese War," Military Affairs 34/3 (October 1970): 82-85.

A brief history of Thacker's role in gathering specialized information on new weapons and the progress of the war.

3491. Hitt, Jack. "Warning: CIA Censors at Work: A Look at How the Agency Treats Its Old Boys - and Its Cities," Columbia Journalism Review 23/2 (July-August 1984): 44-46.

A popular press resource. May be useful in historical research.

3492. Hittle, J. D. "Marine Corps Battalion Intelligence Service," Marine Corps Gazette 25 (November 1941): 38-39, 145-150.

3493. Hixson, Walter L. "'Red Storm Rising': Tom Clancy Novels and the Cult of National Security," Diplomatic History 17 (Fall 1993): 599-613.

A book review essay and critique of this important national security and military genres of fictional literature.

3494. Hnath, Gary M. and James M. Gould. "Litigating Trade Secrets Cases at the International Trade Commission," AIPLA Quarterly Journal 19 (Summer 1991): 87-122.

A discussion of the subject matter of jurisdiction; parties; domestic inquiry; injury; choice of law; discovery issues; use of foreign proceedings records and decision; and relief.

3495. Hoagland, John. "Changing Patterns of Insurgency and American Response," Journal of International Affairs 25/1 (1971): 120-141.

Discusses mechanisms of insurgency; the changing American view of insurgency; and possible future trends of US security policy in the Third World.

3496. Hoak, Dale. "The Secret History of the Tudor Court: The King's Coffers and the King's Purse, 1542-1553," Journal of British Studies 26/2 (April 1987): 208-231.

3497. Hobar, Basil J. "Ardennes 1944: Intelligence Failure or Deception Success?," Military Intelligence 10/4 (October-December 1984): 8-16.

A history of the military intelligence failures and successes encountered in the December 1944 German breakout at Ardennes. Maps, photos, and conclusions are included.

3498. Hobar, Basil J. "Intelligence Failure at the Bulge," National Guard 38 (December 1984): 24-25.

3499. Hobbing, Enno. "CIA: Hottest Role in the Cold War," Esquire 57 (September 1957): 31-34.

Description of the CIA's organization and something of its activities in recruiting defectors.

3500. Hobbs, J. J. S. "Intelligence in the Field; Current Trends in Organization and in Handling Information," Army Journal (September 1954): 12-15.

3501. Hocking, Jenny. "Counterterrorism as Counterinsurgency: The British Experience," Social Justice 15/1 (Spring 1988): 83-97.

Discusses the main elements of the counterinsurgency strategy: exceptional legislation; intelligence; pre-emptive controls; military involvement in civil disturbances; and media management. Argues that such strategies have negative effects on civil rights.

3502. Hocking, Jenny. "Charting Political Space: Surveillance and the Rule of Law," Social Justice 21/4 (Winter 1994): 66-82.

Considers modern context and roles of intelligence and security services in Britain and Australia.

3503. Hodgden, Louise. "Satellites at Sea: Space and Naval Warfare," Naval War College Review 37/4 (July-August 1984): 31-45.

Accounts for the roles of satellite technology in naval intelligence, including communications, navigation, ocean surveillance, aircraft early warning, and data integration. Discusses Soviet strategies and operations without satellites.

3504. Hodges, David P. "Electronic Visual Surveillance and the Fourth Amendment: The Arrival of Big Brother?," Hastings Constitutional Law Quarterly 3/1 (Winter 1976): 261-299.

Focusses on whether a court may constitutionally authorize the installation of clandestine electronic visual surveillance devices for law enforcement purposes.

3505. Hodges, Theodore B. "Abbot Emerson Smith," Studies in Intelligence 27/4 (Winter 1983).

3506. Hodgson, Earl E., Jr. "United States v. Rathbun: A Fourteen Year Critique," United States Air Force Judge Advocate General Law Review 13 (1971): 224-229.

A brief discussion of the history of federal wiretap legislation from the Olmstead case forward, followed by discussion of the division of federal courts on the issue of consent; United States v. Rathbun is evaluated; conclusions.

3507. Hodgson, Godfrey. "Not for the First Time: Antecedents of the Irangate Scandal," Political Quarterly 58/2 (April-June 1987): 125-138.

Argues that many recent presidents have suffered from "Ramboism" and the ability of staff members to influence them on approaches toward direct action. The Iran-Contra scandal is one of several such incidents in which actions taken by presidents have set aside established agencies of legal means, such as the National Security Council.

3508. Hodkinson, Keith. "Spies, Brain Drains and Allied Problems: Reflections on English Industrial Espionage Law," International Journal of Technology Management 3/1-2 (1988): 87-103.

Considers a variety of topics related to the emergence of British concepts of industrial espionage, such as information secrecy and disclosure; trade secrets; technology transfer; patents and copyrights; and civil and criminal actions against employees for loss of secrets.

3509. Hoefer, Jean M. "They Call Her 'Moses,'" Civil War Times Illustrated 26/10 (1988): 36-41.

3510. Hoeksema, Bruce L. "The President's Role in Insuring Efficient, Economical, and Responsible Intelligence Services," Presidential Studies Quarterly 8/2 (Spring 1978): 187-199.

An argument for reform in order to achieve an effective intelligence service. Argues that the CIA has been hurt by cost cutting and discusses several proposed reforms.

3511. Hoerder, Dirk. "Prussian Agents Among Polish Americans, 1900-1917: A Research Note," Polish American Studies 38/2 (1981): 84-88.

Article has four main purposes: To retrace German agent activity in the United States; to assess Polish speaking agent reports; to comment on a Prussian police official; and to evaluate information concerning Polish Americans.

3512. Hoff, Samuel B. "The CIA: Perspectives on Its Past, Prescription for Its Future," Current World Leaders 36/4 (August 1993): 713-727.

Examines and evaluates the stages of Central Intelligence Agency development since 1947.

3513. Hoffert, Sylvia D. "Madame Loretta Valazquez: Heroine or Hoaxer?," Civil War Times Illustrated 17/3 (1978): 24-31.
　　　Examines the fact or fiction behind Madame Valazquez's claim that she was a spy for the Confederacy, as indicated in her book, "The Woman in Battle."

3514. Hoffman, Bruce. "Right-Wing Terrorism in Europe," Orbis 28/1 (Spring 1984): 16-27.
　　　Discusses cases of right-wing terrorism in Europe in the 1970s and early 1980s, especially in Italy, West Germany and France. Groups participating in such activities are pooling resources. Also discusses role of intelligence organizations.

3515. Hoffman, Bruce. "Intelligence and Terrorism: Emerging Threats and New Security Challenges in the Post-Cold War Era," Intelligence and National Security 11/2 (April 1996): 207-223.
　　　Discusses religious terrorism; the "amateurisation" of terrorism; and the author's overall conclusions about new trends.

3516. Hoffman, Daniel. "Naval Counterintelligence in the 90s: New Way of Doing Things," Naval Intelligence Professionals Quarterly 11/1 (Winter 1995): 5-7.

3517. Hoffman, Jon T. "The Legacy and Lessons of WWII Raids," Marine Corps Gazette 76/9 (1992): 62-65.

3518. Hoffman, P. "The Crypto-Censors," Science Digest 90 (July 1982): 56-60.

3519. Hoffman, Steven A. "Anticipation, Disaster and Victory: India 1962-71," Asian Survey 12/11 (November 1972): 960-979.
　　　Presents a theory that the border war between India and China in 1962 reflected significant weaknesses in Indian civilian intelligence analysis, thereby forcing major improvements in military intelligence to compensate for civilian errors.

3520. Hoffmann, Peter. "Hitler's Personal Security: Gaps and Contradictions," Conflict Quarterly 4/3 (Summer 1984): 56-65.
　　　Major sections of this book summary examine a survey of attacks on Hitler; the bodyguard; security and travel; and serious attempts on Hitler's life.

3521. Hoffmann, Peter. "Peace Through Coup d'Etat: The Foreign Contacts of the German Resistance 1933-1944," Central European History 19 (March 1986): 3-44.

3522. Hoffmann, Peter. "Colonel Klaus von Stauffenberg in the German Resistance to Hitler: Between East and West," Historical Journal 31 (September 1988): 629-650.

Considers and outlines the resistance movement inside Hitler's Germany during World War II, including the movement led by Colonel Klaus von Stauffenberg. Discusses the failure of the movement and the work of the Gestapo to crush the resistance.

3523. Hofmann, Peter A. "The Making of National Estimates During the Period of the 'Missile Gap,'" Intelligence and National Security 1/3 (September 1986): 336-356.

3524. Hogan, David W., Jr. "MacArthur, Stilwell, and Special Operations in the War Against Japan," Parameters: Journal of the U.S. Army War College 25/1 (Spring 1995): 104-115.

Discusses the aristocrat (MacArthur) and the doughboy (Stilwell) in connection with special operations in Burma, China and the Phillipines. Includes discussion of command and control; roles and missions, and contribution to victory. Role of the Office of Strategic Services is mentioned.

3525. Hogg, J. Bernard. "Public Reaction to Pinkertonism and the Labor Question," Pennsylvania History 11 (July 1944): 171-199.

Discusses the over burdening of local sheriff's departments at the end of the nineteenth century, thus inducing employers to seek security protection from the Pinkerton Detective Agency and others. Argues that the use of such private agents, not always permitted under state laws, introduced labor concerns for employee rights versus employer rights to protect property. Includes discussion of agent spying activities.

3526. Hoisinger, David B. "Commmand-Control-Communications Counter-measures and Electronic Warfare," Journal of Electronic Defense 6/3 (March 1983): 51-62.

3527. Holden, B. M., Jr. "Noah Phelps, Father of G-2," Military Review 36/1 (January 1957): 12-14.

3528. Holden, E. S. "The Cipher Despatches," International Review 6 (1879): 405-425.

Analyzes the cipher dispatches of the 1876 presidential election.

3529. Holden-Rhodes, James F. "Unlocking the Secrets: Open Source Intelligence in the War on Drugs," American Intelligence Journal 14/2&3 (Spring-Summer 1993): 67-71.

Considers such topics as OSINT in the third intelligence era, 1989-2010;

"gray area phenomenon" and OSINT, threat and response; counter-drug OSINT application and modeling; and methodology.

3530. Holden-Rhodes, James F. "Kim Revisited: Human Intelligence and Drug Trafficking," American Intelligence Journal 14/1 (Autumn-Winter 1992-1993): 33-36.
Drawing reference to Rudyard Kipling's classic story, Kim, the author discusses new names and faces in the human intelligence game in drug trafficking. Discusses the US intelligence community response; options; and conclusions.

3531. Holding, John D. "Reflections on Igor Gouzenko," Advocates' Society Journal (October 1985): 529-537.

3532. Holland, Max. "After Thirty Years: Making Sense of the Assassination," Reviews in American History 22 (June 1994): 191-209.
Discussion of the John F. Kennedy assassination in the context of American spying operations, the Central Intelligence Agency, the Cold War, and Castro's Cuba.

3533. Hollander, John. "Reflections on Espionage," Queen's Quarterly 100/2 (Summer 1993): 348-356.
Contains some deciphered messages of the master spy "Cupcake."

3534. Holley, Charles. "Israel After Agranat," Middle East 35 (September 1977): 25-33.

3535. Hollinger, David A. "The Confidence Man," Reviews in American History 7/1 (1979): 134-141.
A review essay of Allen Weinstein's study, Perjury: The Hiss-Chambers Case, published in 1978.

3536. Holloway, David. "Soviet Scientists Speak Out," Bulletin of the Atomic Scientists 49/4 (May 1993): 18-19.
Considers the problem of nuclear materials dissemination in the world and the problem of espionage.

3537. Holm, Skip. "Spyplane: The First U-2 Flights," Air Progress Aviation Review (June 1986): 24+.

3538. Holmes, Colin. "Government Files and Privileged Access," Social History 6/3 (1981): 333-350.
Describes British efforts in some parts to reform the Official Secrets Act. A reform law of 1958, amended in 1967, achieved little in the way of new access by the public to government files. Historians argue that a better record of British

history can be written only when more files are released, including files on intelligence matters.

3539. Holmes, Richard. "Anthony Blunt, Gentleman Traitor," Harper's 260 (April 1980): 102-109.

    A summation of the espionage of Anthony Blunt, following on the publication of The Climate of Conspiracy by Andrew Boyle (1979).

3540. Holmes, Wilfred J. "Pearl Harbor Aftermath," U.S. Naval Institute Proceedings 104/12 (December 1978): 68-75.

    Discusses the spirit of the Navy intelligence unit at Pearl Harbor after December 7, 1941, and how the unit's spirit was raised upon arrival of Admiral Chester Nimitz. This is an extract from his book, Double-Edged Secrets.

3541. Holst, Johan J. "What Is Really Going On?," Foreign Policy 19 (Summer 1975): 155-163.

    Argues that the arms race is an example of the action-reaction phenomenon. He argues that the US has misestimated Soviet strategic weapons buildups because we do not know how to estimate the competition.

3542. Holst, Johan J. "Surprise, Signals and Reaction: The Attack on Norway, April 9, 1940--Some Observations," Cooperation and Conflict 1/2 (1966): 31-45.

    Contains observations on prejudice, surprise and strategic intelligence. Modeled after Roberta Wohlstetter's work on Pearl Harbor. Focusses on the images of and expectations of Norwegian officials with respect to how they processed incoming messages.

3543. Holstein, Otto. "The Ciphers of Porta and Vigenere, the Original Undecipherable Code and How to Decipher It," Scientific American 4/4 (October 1921): 332-334.

3544. Holsti, Ole R. "The Belief System and Natural Images: A Case Study," Journal of Conflict Resolution 6/2 (September 1962): 244-252.

    Argues that a person's beliefs affect decisions and reactions to new situations. The more important the decision, the more likely that one may misinterpret changing situations. Reflects upon the beliefs of John Foster Dulles concerning the Soviet Union.

3545. Holsti, Ole R. "Cognitive Dynamics and Images of the Enemy," Journal of International Affairs 21/1 (1967): 16-39.

    Holsti's characterizes a basic theory in the social sciences: an individual responds not only to the 'objective' characteristics of a situation, but also to the meaning a situation has for the individual. He says this also applies to images of the enemy. Reports of a case study of images of the enemy formulated around

John Foster Dulles' "single enemy" view of the Soviet Union.

3546. Holsti, Ole R. "The 'Operational Code' Approach to the Study of Political Leaders: John Foster Dulles' Philosophical and Instrumental Beliefs," Canadian Journal of Political Science 3/1 (March 1970): 123-137.

A rich analysis of John Foster Dulles's philosophical beliefs; his competing views on optimism and pessimism in world situations; his control of historical development; the role of chance in his views; and his instrumental beliefs; and overall conclusions.

3547. Holt, Patricia L. "Female Spy, Male Nurse: Sarah Emma Edmonds Managed to be Both in the Civil War," Military History 5/1 (August 1988): 8, 64-66.

3548. Holter, Darryl. "Labor Spies and Union Busting in Wisconsin, 1890-1940," Wisconsin Magazine of History 68/4 (1985): 243-265.

A discussion of the lengthy fight by unions to get limitations placed on industrial spying and strikebreaking in the period. A 1925 law served to reduce the amount of labor spying.

3549. Holtzappel, Coen. "The 30 September Movement," Journal of Contemporary Asia 9/2 (1979): 216-240.

3550. Holzman, Franklyn D. "Are the Soviets Really Outspending the U.S. on Defense?," International Security 4/4 (Spring 1980): 86-104.

Argues that the CIA has exaggerated the amount the USSR is spending on defense and weapons. The author says that such inflation injures US national security interests.

3551. Holzman, Franklyn D. "Is There a Soviet-U.S. Military Spending Gap?," Challenge 23 (September-October 1980): 3-9.

3552. Holzman, Franklyn D. "Dollars or Rubles: The CIA's Military Estimates," Bulletin of the Atomic Scientists 36/6 (June 1980): 23-27.

A summation of the CIA's methodology to estimate Soviet military capabilities.

3553. Holzman, Franklyn D. "Soviet Military Spending: Assessing the Numbers Game," International Security 6/4 (Spring 1982): 78-101.

Discusses CIA's methods for evaluation total Soviet military spending and certain methodological difficulties.

3554. Holzman, Franklin D. "Politics and Guesswork: CIA and DIA Estimates of Soviet Military Spending," International Security 14/2 (Fall 1989): 101-131.

Argues that CIA and DIA have been biased in their internal evaluations of Soviet military spending. Major sections discuss CIA and DIA methodologies; CIA estimates in constant 1970 ruble prices; CIA estimates and the shift to 1982 prices; evidence contradicting CIA estimates; and an alternative hypothesis. Further correspondence on this topic appears in the same journal 14/4 (1990): 193-198.

3555. Holzman, Franklyn D. "The CIA's Military Spending Estimates: Deceit and Its Costs," Challenge 35/3 (May-June 1992): 28-39.

Argues that the Central Intelligence Agency misrepresented spending gaps between the US and USSR in the cold war. Cost implications are also discussed.

3556. Holzman, Robert S. "The Soldier With Two Sexes," Civil War Times Illustrated 3/9 (1965): 13-14.

3557. Homberger, Eric. "'Uncle Max' and His Thrillers," Intelligence and National Security 3/2 (April 1988): 312-321.

An essay on the British spy thriller author, Maxwell Knight. Some of the Knight novels discussed include Crime Cargo (1934); Gunmen's Holiday (1935); and Contraband (1935). Links Knight's work with many other authors of the 1920s and 1930s.

3558. Homberger, Eric. "English Spy Thrillers in the Age of Appeasement," Intelligence and National Security 5/4 (October 1990): 80-91.

Explores British spy novels in the 1930s. Argues that no serious novel of the decade described the depth and intensity of Hitler's aggression in Europe.

3559. Home, R. W. and Morris F. Low. "Postwar Scientific Intelligence Missions to Japan," Isis 84/3 (1993): 527-537.

Explores in detail the post World War II scientific intelligence survey in Japan conducted in 1946 by Karl T. Compton and Edward L. Moreland.

3560. Homonoff, Howard B. "The First Amendment and National Security: The Constitutionality of Press Censorship and Access Denial in Military Operations," New York University Journal of International Law and Politics 17/2 (Winter 1984): 369-405.

Explores two methods by which the government may maintain secrecy in military operations: censorship and denial of access. Also explores the historical role of the press in military operations and analyzes the law regarding restrictions on the press in wartime.

3561. Hone, Thomas C. and Mark D. Mandeles. "Interwar Innovation in Three Navies: US Navy, Royal Navy, Imperial Japanese Navy," Naval War College Review 40/2 (Spring 1987).

3562. Honey, Martha. "Contra Coverage - Paid for by the CIA," Columbia Journalism Review 25 (March-April 1987): 31-32.

According to the Costa Rican journalist's union the CIA financed journalists in Costa Rica and Honduras to write pro- Contra articles and articles condemning the Sandinistas.

3563. Honts, Charles R. "Interpreting Research on Polygraph Countermeasures," Journal of Police Science and Administration 15/3 (1987): 204-209.

Espionage, argues the author, is a craft that requires extensive training on polygraph countermeasures.

3564. Hood, William. "Unlikely Conspiracy," Problems of Communism 33 (March-April 1984): 67-72.

The author gives specific reasons for challenging the theory that Mehmet Agca shot the Pope in a conspiracy controlled by Bulgarian intelligence.

3565. Hood, William. "Spy Fiction Through Knowledgeable Eyes," International Journal of Intelligence and Counterintelligence 3/3 (Fall 1989): 405-418.

An essay by a veteran of the clandestine world of CIA field operations. The author suggests that the trick in writing intelligence novels is to tell a good story and convey a sense of the atmosphere of the inner world of spying. Characterizes numerous spy novels and offers brief information on the authors' lives.

3566. Hoogenboom, Ari. "Spy and Topog Duty Has Been . . . Neglected," Civil War History 10/4 (December 1964): 368-370.

General McClellan's performance as a field general in the Civil War was negatively affected by Pinkerton's bad estimates of confederate strengths and by poor quality maps. Confederate maps were no better, however.

3567. Hook, Sidney. "An Autobiographical Fragment: The Strange Case of Whittaker Chambers," Encounter 46/1 (March 1976): 78-89.

Examines in some detail the role of Chambers in the trial of State Department employer Alger Hiss. [Hiss was alleged to have been a spy for the Soviets, an allegation that has never been satisfactorily resolved.]

3568. Hook, Sidney. "Intelligence, Morality, and Foreign Policy," Freedom at Issue 25 (April 1976): 23-32.

3569. Hook, Sidney. "The Case of Alger Hiss," Encounter 51/2 (August 1978): 48-55.

Examines how the author of a similar work decided that Alger Hiss was guilty of treason and espionage in spite of Hiss's various denials about the charges.

3570. Hook, Sidney. "David Caute's Fable of 'Fear & Terror': On 'Reverse McCarthyism,'" Encounter 52 (January 1979): 56-64.

An extensive and detailed book review essay of David Caute's book, The Great Fear, regarding Soviet espionage in the US. A sharp criticism of the book.

3571. Hook, Sidney. "The Incredible Story of Michael Straight," Encounter 61/4 (December 1983): 68-73.

The question of ethics in US foreign policy making by intelligence agencies of the government is examined.

3572. Hook, Sidney. "Encounter with Espionage: A Memoir of the Late 1920s," Midstream 31/5 (May 1985): 52-55.

The author describes his early associations with two persons, Silas and Magda, in the 1920s whom he believes were involved with espionage for the Soviet Union.

3573. Hooker, Charles W. "The Deciphering of Cryptograms," Police Journal 1 (October 1928): 621-633.

3574. Hooker, Charles W. "The Jules Verne Cipher," Police Journal 4/1 (January 1931): 107-119.

3575. Hooker, Eileen C. "Nation-Building or Nation-Destroying: Foreign Powers and Intelligence Agencies in Africa," Ufahamu 19/3 (1990): 35-51.

3576. Hooker, Richard D., Jr. "Presidential Decisionmaking and Use of Force: Case Study Grenada," Parameters: Quarterly Journal of the U.S. Army War College 21/2 (Summer 1991): 61-72.

Discusses national security in the Reagan administration; the crisis unfolds in Grenada; chronology of events; and brief comments on intelligence.

3577. Hooper, S. C. "Naval Radiotelegraph in Peace and War," Annals of the American Academy of Political and Social Science 142 (March 1929): 90-94.

The Naval Communication Service complies with the provisions of the 1927 International Radiotelegraph Convention in its efforts to protect the US coastlines and get messages to seamen. Summarizes the international rules of radiotelegraphic communications. Failure to comply with the rules is not espionage per se.

3578. Hoover, J. Edgar. "How the Nazi Spy Invasion Was Smashed," American Magazine 138 (September 1944): 20-21+.

The rounding up of a group of Nazi spies who had landed by boat on US shores early in World War II.

3579. Hoover, J. Edgar. "Hitler's Spying Sirens," American Magazine 138 (December 1944): 40-41+.
The FBI's work to locate domestic spies during World War II.

3580. Hoover, J. Edgar. "The Spy Who Double-Crossed Hitler," American Magazine 141 (May 1946): 23+.

3581. Hoover, J. Edgar. "A Comment on the Article, "Loyalty Among Government Employees," Yale Law Journal 58/2 (February 1949): 401-411.
Hoover used this article to counter charges made by several critiques against the FBI in the November 1948 issue of the Yale Law Review pertaining to alleged agency abuses under the loyalty security program. This is a page-by-page refutation of the article by Thomas I. Emerson and David Helfeld.

3582. Hoover, J. Edgar. "Role of the FBI in the Federal Employee Security Program," Northwestern University Law Review 49 (1954-1955): 333-347.
Major sections included discussion of Executive Order 10450 pertaining to the Federal Employee Security Program, FBI name checks, and FBI full field investigations. Hoover, former, FBI director, discusses the role of the FBI under the Program, justifying it as protection against espionage.

3583. Hoover, J. Edgar. "The Confidential Nature of FBI Reports," Syracuse Law Review 8/1 (Fall 1956): 2-17.
The former director of the FBI argues that the confidence of the public is essential to FBI operations. Discusses the role of informants, intelligence gathering, wiretaps, presidential and departmental orders, and FBI reports.

3584. Hoover, J. Edgar. "The U.S. Businessman Faces the Soviet Spy," Harvard Business Review 42/1 (January 1964): 140-146+.
The former director of the FBI frequently published articles warning of Soviet espionage tactics. This piece warns the business community to be watchful of Soviet interests in US technical secrets. Urges increased plant security and glories in the counter espionage work of the FBI.

3585. Hoover, J. Edgar. "How Red-China Spies on U.S.," Nation's Business 54 (June 1966): 84-88.
Typically, this magazine is considered a publication of the popular press. Due to its popularity, and due to the author's recognition as Director of the FBI, this piece is included for potential reference in research of the writings of J. Edgar Hoover in the 1960s.

3586. Hope, John G. "Surveillance or Collusion? Maxwell Knight, MI5 and the British Fascisti," Intelligence and National Security 9/4 (October 1994): 651-675.
Argues that MI5 had little regard for Fascism, regarding as a potential

danger to public order and national security. Suggest that there is some evidence of collusion between MI5 and the Fascisti, appearing in the career and activities of British agent Charles Maxwell Knight. The article examines the evidence and explores the implications.

3587. Hopkins, Counce. "Pauline Cushman: Actress in the Theater of War," American History Illustrated 19/9 (1985): 20-21.

3588. Hopkins, Joel. "An Interview with Eric Ambler," Journal of Popular Culture 9/2 (1975): 285-293.

3589. Hopkins, Michael F. "A British Cold War?," Intelligence and National Security 7/4 (October 1992): 479-482.
    A review essay evaluating the 1990 books by A. Deighton, Britain and the First Cold War and J. Zametica, British Officials and British Foreign Policy, 1945-1950, and the 1989 book by M. Dockrill and J. W. Young, British Foreign Policy, 1945-1956. Concludes that these works add greatly to the historical account of the Cold War, but mainly from a British viewpoint absent a review of the Russian documents that will come available in the future.

3590. Hopkins, Robert S., III. "COBRA EYE and COBRA BALL: Alaskan Observers," World Air Power Journal 8/1 (Spring 1992): 128-139.

3591. Hopkins, Robert S., III. "An Expanded Understanding of Eisenhower, American Policy and Overflights," Intelligence and National Security 11/2 (April 1996): 332-344.
    Major sections titles include: military overflights, 1945-60; military overflights and delegation of authority; the myth of political sensitivity; and the meaning of intelligence.

3592. Hopkinson, Harry. "An Idiot System for Intelligence," Studies in Intelligence 6/3 (Fall 1962).

3593. Hopple, Gerald W. "Intelligence and Warning: Implications and Lessons of the Falklands Islands War," World Politics 36/3 (April 1984): 339-361.
    Sections include discussion of the central issues of the Falklands war, strategic warning as an analytical perspective, the warning context of the Falklands war, and implications, caveats and lessons. Argues that Britain failed to read the signs of Argentinean aggression.

3594. Horelick, Arnold. "The Cuban Missile Crisis: An Analysis of Soviet Calculations and Behavior," World Politics 16/3 (April 1964): 363-389.
    Majors sections discuss Soviet objectives; Soviet pre-crisis calculations; Soviet crisis calculations; and lessons learned.

3595. Horn, James J. "Did the United States Plan an Invasion of Mexico in 1927?," Journal of Inter-American Studies and World Affairs 15/4 (November 1973): 454-471.

Argues that the Calvin Coolidge administration never seriously considered an intervention in Mexico, and that rumors of such action were founded upon Mexican suspicions and mistrust. Details the evidence to support the view.

3596. Horn, Stanley F. "Dr. John Rolfe Hudson and the Confederate Underground in Nashville," Tennessee Historical Quarterly 22/1 (1963): 38-52.

3597. Hornbein, Majorie. "For the Public Good: The Strange Case of Colorado's Eavesdroppers," Colorado Heritage 3 (1985): 33-38.

Details the first case in Colorado history (1937) in which defendants were tried for eavesdropping by hidden microphones.

3598. Horner, David M. "Special Intelligence in the South-West Pacific Area in World War II," Australian Outlook: Journal of the Australian Institute of International Affairs 32/3 (December 1978): 310-327.

3599. Horowitz, Donald L. "A Harvest of Hostility: Ethnic Conflict and Self-Determination After the Cold War," Defense Intelligence Journal 1/2 (Fall 1992): 137-164.

The author discusses the nature of ethnic loyalties; comparison and conflict; ethnicity and territory; state proliferation and the international system; the quest for amelioration; and ethnicity, self-determination, and international law.

3600. Horowitz, Harold W. "Loyalty Tests for Employment in the Motion Picture Industry," Stanford Law Review 6/3 (May 1954): 438-472.

3601. Horowitz, Irving L. "Michigan State and the CIA: A Dilemma for Social Science," Bulletin of the Atomic Scientists 22/7 (September 1966): 26-29.

A discussion of MSU's associations with the CIA to train Vietnamese counter-insurgency agents, and the dilemmas posed for social science research when the CIA is the funding agency.

3602. Horowitz, Irving L. "Spying and Security: The American Way," Society 12 (March-April 1975): 7-10.

Observes the abuses of the intelligence community, then suggests a national civil rights commission, a clarification of agency jurisdiction, limitations on CIA intelligence gathering, definition of all intelligence functions of government, the use of diplomacy as the dominate factor in policy, removal of secrecy over CIA budget, and restrictions on overseas information gathering by the CIA. This article was reprinted in Current 173 (May 1975): 3-6.

3603. Horowitz, Paul and Page P. Miller. "The Freedom of Information Act: Federal Policy and the Writing of Contemporary History," Public Historian 4/4 (Fall 1982): 87-96.

Discusses the motivations behind the law, passage of the law, main users of the law, criticisms of the use of the law, national security and the FOIA, the 'perceptions' argument against FOIA, modification of the FOIA, monetary costs of the FOIA, historical significance, and problems with FOIA.

3604. Horowitz, Richard. "A Framework for Understanding Intelligence," International Journal of Intelligence and Counterintelligence 8/4 (Winter 1995): 389-409.

Considers issues pertaining to the gap between two opposed views of intelligence: that is an integral element in decision making; that it only rarely assures success on the battlefield and may even be counterproductive.

3605. Horrall, S. W. "The Royal North-West Mounted Police and Labour Unrest in Western Canada, 1919," Canadian Historical Review 61/2 (June 1980): 167-190.

Expresses the view that the Winnipeg general strike in Canada was a seditionist conspiracy which led to the development of the creation of the Royal Canadian Mounted Police. Discussion of the evidence developed by the Canadian government's intelligence services concerning labor organizations and alleged communist influence prior to 1920. Includes historical background to the intelligence services of modern Canada.

3606. Horrall, S. W. "Canada's Security Service: A Brief History," RCMP Quarterly 50 (Summer 1985): 38-49.

3607. Horsford, Cyril. "Spy Satellites and the Law," International Relations 2 (1962): 308+.

3608. Horsford, Cyril. "Treason: The Dark Crime," Medico-Legal Journal 52/2 (Spring 1984): 124-126.

A brief consideration of the legal issues surrounding treason in England. Several cases are included to lay a historical framework.

3609. Horsley, Richard A. "The Sicarii: Ancient Jewish Terrorists," Journal of Religion 59/4 (1989): 435-458.

3610. Horsman, Reginald. "American Indian Policy in the Old Northwest, 1783-1812," William and Mary Quarterly 18/1 (January 1961).

3611. Horton, John. "The Real Intelligence Failure," Foreign Service Journal (February 1985): 22-25.

Concerns the role of intelligence in the policy process, admitting that intelligence agencies are not perfect. Critical of the CIA collection and reporting efforts in months and weeks prior to the Grenada invasion. Suggests need for improving the quality of field reports.

3612. Horton, John. "Mexico, the Way of Iran?," International Journal of Intelligence and Counterintelligence 1/2 (Summer 1986): 91-101.

The Reagan administration's policy toward Mexico was shaped by analogies to Iran's economic, political and social situation of the 1970s. The intelligence community was put on guard by such analogies and the Mexico-as-Iran metaphor was not pursued for its imagined implications for US policy.

3613. Horton, John. "Reflections on Covert Actions and Its Anxieties," International Journal of Intelligence and Counterintelligence 4/1 (Spring 1990): 77-90.

A consideration of the implications of worldwide changes in the political landscape, including the breakup of the Soviet Union, for the Central Intelligence Agency. Offers suggestions about the importance of agency and political leadership to the success of clandestine human intelligence services.

3614. Horvitz, R. "An Intelligent Guide to Intelligence," Whole Earth Review 57 (Winter 1987): 61-69.

A brief summary of the types of information contained in several journals and magazines aimed at intelligence and espionage topics. Includes addresses for each publication.

3615. Hoshen, Joseph; Jim Sennott and Max Winkler. "Keeping Tabs on Criminals," IEEE Spectrum 32 (February 1995): 26-32.

Considers the role of electronics in criminal investigations and espionage. ·

3616. Hosokawa, Bill. "Our Own Japanese in the Pacific War," American Legion Magazine 77/1 (1964): 15-17+.

3617. Hosoya, Chihiro. "Miscalculations in Deterrent Policy: Japanese-U.S., 1938-1941," Journal of Peace Research 5/2 (Summer 1968).

3618. Hougan, James. "A Surfeit of Spies," Harper's 249 (December 1974): 51-67.

Discusses the explosion of the private network of spies who work for commercial organizations. Detailed descriptions of private spy organizations.

3619. Hougan, James. "Pandora's Box: Requests for CIA Information Under the Freedom of Information Act," Harper's 253 (August 1976): 22-24.

Explores the types of requests made under the FOIA for CIA records.

Particular information requests are listed.

3620. Hough, Mike. "The SATBVC and Liberation Movements' Intelligence Services in a Changing South Africa," Strategic Review of Southern Africa: Security and Intelligence in a Post-Apartheid South Africa 14/2 (October 1992).

3621. Houghton, Neal D. "The Cuban Invasion of 1961 and the U.S. Press, in Retrospect," Journalism Quarterly 42/3 (1965): 422-432.
    Discusses the initial image of the press to the Bay of Pigs invasion, the lack of clarity with respect to who was to be blamed for the failure, and misleading statements given by the government and the press in the course of the invasion. Argues that the press has a role in preventing future circumstances like the 1961 invasion.

3622. Houlihan, Michael. "The Part Played by Resistance Movements," History Today 34 (June 1984): 23-46.
    Discusses the role of resistance forces in France and their associations with the American OSS Jedburghs. Also discusses the Yugoslav resistance.

3623. Houn, Franklin W. "Publications As a Propaganda Medium in Communist China," Far Eastern Survey 29 (December 1960): 177-186.
    See also this author's work on the role of the stage in the PRC as a propaganda vehicle in Public Opinion Quarterly 22 (Summer 1959): 222-235.

3624. Hourcle, Laurent R. "Military Secrecy and Environmental Compliance," New York University Environmental Law Journal 2 (July 1993): 316-346.

3625. Houston, Lawrence R. "CIA, the Courts, and Executive Privilege," Studies in Intelligence 17/4 (Winter 1973).
    Estimated to be 4 pages in length.

3626. Houston, Lawrence R. "The CIA's Legislative Base," International Journal of Intelligence and Counterintelligence 5/4 (Winter 1991-1992): 411-415.
    A personal memoir of the establishment of the legislative base of CIA authority and responsibility dating back to service with William Donovan in World War II, followed by the Eberstadt and Lovett committees and creation of the National Security Act.

3627. Howard, J. Woodford, Jr. "Advocacy in Constitutional Choice: The Cramer Treason Case, 1942-1945," American Bar Foundation Research Journal 1986/3 (Summer 1986): 375-413.
    A case study of Cramer v. U. S., a legal milestone in advocacy in the law and the development of modern law of treason in the US. Discusses the role of counsel, litigation strategy and the use of history in constitutional interpretation;

the sources of case law on treason as applied to political crimes cases.

3628. Howard, Matthew. "Spycatcher Downunder: <u>Attorney General for the United Kingdom v. Heinemann Publishers Australia</u>," <u>University of Western Australia Law Review</u> 19 (1989): 158-170.

Considers the Australian High Court's decision in the U.K.'s case against Peter Wright, author of <u>Spycatcher</u>. Provides background to the case; the High Court's decision; and interpretive conclusions.

3629. Howard, Michael. "Military Intelligence and Surprise Attack: The 'Lessons' of Pearl Harbor," <u>World Politics</u> 15/4 (July 1963): 701-711.

This is a review essay of Robert Wohlstetter's book, <u>Pearl Harbor: Warning and Decision</u>. Suggests that the book leaves out certain useful conditions involved in surprise.

3630. Howard, Michael. "Conducting the Concert of Powers," <u>Armed Forces and Society</u> 6/4 (1980): 654-665.

A general discussion of the Henry Kissinger's foreign policy ideas, observations of power in government, and accomplishments in international relations.

3631. Howard, Robert and Kathleen M. Crowley. "Pleading Discovery and Pretrial Procedure for Litigation Against Government Spying," <u>University of Detroit Journal of Urban Law</u> 55/4 (Summer 1978): 931-982.

Article concerns the scope of litigation involving misconduct by local, state and federal intelligence agencies. Sections include discussion of the complaint, scope, grounds, parties, and relief; motions to dismiss; class certification; litigation management; and discovery.

3632. Howard, William L. "Technical Intelligence and Tank Design," <u>Armor</u> 94/1 (January-February 1985): 24-29.

3633. Howard, William L. "Technical Intelligence: The Critical Gap," <u>Military Intelligence</u> 12/1 (January-March 1986): 6-9.

Presents critical overview of US technical intelligence organizations, pointing out the overall lack of direction.

3634. Howard, William L. "The Army's Stepchild--Technical Intelligence," <u>Military Intelligence</u> 15/1 (January-March 1989): 29-32.

Highlights the importance of technical intelligence in the research and development process.

3635. Howe, Herbert M. "The South African Defense Force and Political Reform," <u>Journal of Modern South African Studies</u> 32/1 (1994): 33-38.

3636. Howe, John. "Secret Reports of John Howe, 1808," American Historical Review 17/1 (1911): 70-102; 17/2 (1912): 312-354.
　　　A collection of the British spy's secret papers, as compiled by David W. Parker.

3637. Howe, Russell W. "Asset Unwilling: Covering the World for the CIA," More 8 (May 1978): 20-27.

3638. Howe, Russell W. "Mournful Fate of Mata Hari, the Spy Who Wasn't Guilty," Smithsonian 17/2 (May 1986): 132-134+.
　　　Sections discuss Mata Hari's life before World War I, French intelligence actions, and conclusions.

3639. Howe, Quincy. "At Random: The CIA in France," Atlas 23 (March 1976): 5.
　　　A brief column pertaining to a list of CIA personnel in France, published in the leftist, non-communist magazine Liberation, as reproduced from Counterspy.

3640. Howell, William S. "The North America Broadcast Service of Radio Prague," Quarterly Journal of Speech 55 (October 1969): 247-255.
　　　Discusses an illegal radio station operated out of Prague, Czechoslovakia, the operations of the station, staff and their skills, listenership surveys, music programming, the influence of Western nations, and the role of the station in stretching the bounds of communism through broadcasting.

3641. Howells, William D. "Intelligence in Crises," Studies in Intelligence 27/3 (Fall 1983).

3642. Howlett, J. B. "Analytical Investigative Techniques: Tools for Complex Criminal Investigations," Police Chief 47/12 (December 1980): 42-45.

3643. Howley, Dennis C. "Intelligence, Bureaucracy and the Country Analyst," American Intelligence Journal 6/6 (February 1985): 1-4.

3644. Howley, Dennis C. "Small Unit Leadership in an Intelligence Bureaucracy," American Intelligence Journal 7/2 (September 1985): 17-22.

3645. Howley, Dennis C. "Tailored Training: The Key to Interpretive-Projective Analyses in Current Intelligence," American Intelligence Journal 10/1 (Spring 1989): 18-21.
　　　Emphasizes need for advanced training for analysts and the fact that there are no shortcuts to analytical processes; training is the key; analytical judgment; qualifications and training; rounding out the resource; and tailoring the process.

3646. Howley, Dennis C. "The Crucial Role of the Manager-Leader in Intelligence," <u>American Intelligence Journal</u> 11/3 (Summer-Fall 1990): 37-40.

Considers various organizational dynamics in the conduct of effect defense analysis: role of the manager-leader; the work culture; and leadership in a bureaucracy.

3647. Hoxie, R. Gordon. "The National Security Council," <u>Presidential Studies Quarterly</u> 12/1 (Winter 1982): 108-113.

A descriptive analysis of the Council's origins, the Truman years, the Eisenhower era, the post Eisenhower NSC, and "the future."

3648. Hsia, Tao-tai; Charlotte A. Hambley; and Constance A. Johnson. "Introduction to the State Secrets Laws of the People's Republic of China," <u>China Law Register</u> 2 (Fall 1983): 267-278.

3649. Hoyt, Michael. "The Tampa Media-Espionage Case," <u>Columbia Journalism Review</u> 28 (May-June 1989): 27-31.

3650. Huang, Fu-ch'ing. "Japanese Espionage Agencies in China Before 1894: An Overview of the Le-shan T'ang in Hanchow and the Sino-Japanese Trade Institute in Shanghai," <u>Bulletin of the Institute of Modern History</u> 13 (1984): 305-331.

This article discusses the first attempt by Japan to conduct external intelligence gathering.

3651. Huber, Peter. "The Murder of Ignaz Reiss in Lausanne in 1937: An Example of Stalin's Purges in Foreign Countries," <u>Schweizerische Zeitschrift fuer Geschichte</u> 40/4 (1990): 392-408.

3652. Huber, Peter and Daniel Kunzi. "Paris in the 1930s: Serge Efron and Some NKVD Agents," <u>Cahiers du Monde Russe et Sovietique</u> 32/2 (1991): 285-310.

3653. Huber, Peter W. "The New Competitive Environment," <u>Society</u> 26/5 (July-August 1989): 27-31.

Discusses the growth of electronic intelligence in recent years and the need for new forms of government regulation.

3654. Huchthausen, Peter. "Assignment in Belgrade," <u>Naval Intelligence Professionals Quarterly</u> 9/2 (Spring 1993): 5-8.

3655. Huchthausen, Peter. "Five Years in Russia," <u>Naval Intelligence Professionals Quarterly</u> 10/3 (Summer 1993): 1-4.

3656. Hudson, Manley O.   "The 'Injunction of Secrecy' With Respect to American Treaties," <u>American Journal of International Law</u> 23/2 (April 1929): 329-335.

Argues that all treaties of the US should be published before their ratification.   Discusses Senate Rule 36, "injunction of secrecy"; secrecy with reference to nominations; and suggestions for the future.   Useful in studies of contemporary secrecy of liaison services between intelligence services of the world.

3657. Hufstedler, Evan Y. "Invisible Searches for Intangible Things: Regulation of Governmental Information Gathering," <u>University of Pennsylvania Law Review</u> 127 (June 1979): 1483-1523.

A thorough review of the history of searches under the Constitution. Sections include discussion of the colonial experience, the early history of the Fourth Amendment, the literalist approach, abandoning the trespass doctrine, the mere evidence doctrine, the Fourth Amendment today, and a question of how did we get here and what do we do now.

3658. Hugel, Max.   "Management Techniques for Third World Intelligence Services," <u>Defense and Foreign Affairs Digest</u> 12 (April 1984): 34-35.

3659. Huggins, Martha K. "U.S. Supported State Terror: A History of Police Training in Latin America," <u>Crime and Social Justice</u> 27-28 (1987): 149-171.

Major sections discuss political policing; police training; sources; police training and gun-boat diplomacy; "Good Neighbor" policy and police training in the Roosevelt administration; the role of the FBI; fortifying the national security state in the Truman presidency; police training for counterinsurgency in the Eisenhower administration; intensification of global counterinsurgency in the Kennedy administration; and continued buildup and dismantling in the Johnson and Nixon administrations.

3660. Hugh-Jones, Martin. "Wickham Steed and German Biological Warfare Research," <u>Intelligence and National Security</u> 7/4 (October 1992): 379-402.

Concludes that the German biological warfare test results were far reaching, but the US, British and Canadian tests proved the feasibility and hazards of BW weapons.   Major sections discuss Steed's revelations; reactions and criticisms; how documents reached Steed; British government reaction; Harkey Committee.

3661. Hughes, Graham.   "Agreements for Cooperation in Criminal Cases," <u>Vanderbilt Law Review</u> 45 (January 1992): 1-69.

Considers issues raised by agreements relating to prosecutorial discretion, fairness to defendants, and impact on criminal process. Provides historical picture of such agreements, discretion of prosecutor and means of monitoring same, whether right of fair trial is impinged by such agreements, burdens placed on cooperating witnesses by government enforcement of agreements and procedural concerns relating to appeal and double jeopardy. Useful in analyses of informants.

3662. Hughes, John and A. Denis Clift. "The San Cristobal Trapezoid: Cuban Missile Crisis," Studies in Intelligence 36/5 (Winter 1992): 55-71.

A copyrighted author's analysis of the missile crisis events of 1962: tactical data; strategic warning; two NIEs; Soviet buildup; U-2 missions; SA-2 controversy; focus on San Cristobal; shift in responsibility; evidence of MRBMs; strategic surveillance; seaborne shipments; SS-4s and SS-5s; four key sites;cratology; meeting with Gromyko; SNIEs judgments; the President's decision; low-level missions; the JRC; a bad day; and effective cycle; White House statement; messages from Khrushchev; the US replies; monitoring withdrawal; status reports; paying tribute; monitoring continues; refuting rumors; and briefing the nation.

3663. Hughes, Rupert. "Memories of M.D.I.," American Legion Monthly 18/1 (March 1935): 20-24.

3664. Hughes, Thomas L. "The Fate of Facts in the World of Men," Proceedings of the American Society of International Law 1969/1 (1969): 233-245.

The author, a former director of the Department of State's Intelligence and Research organization, discusses intelligence in terms of theory, psychology and institutional interest.

3665. Huibregtse, P. K. "Psychological Warfare in North Mozambique," NATO's Fifteen Nations 17 (April-May 1972): 28-30.

3666. Huie, William B. "Untold Facts in the Korean Disaster," American Mercury 72/326 (February 1951): 131-140.

Intelligence failure in the first six months of 1950 led to the surprise attack by the North Koreans and the later extension of involvement to China.

3667. Huie, William B. "Who Gave Russia the A-Bomb?," American Mercury 72 (April & May 1951): 413-421, 593-602.

3668. Hulnick, Arthur S. "The Intelligence Producer-Policy Consumer Linkage," Studies in Intelligence 29/4 (Winter 1985).

3669. Hulnick, Arthur S. "The Intelligence Producer-Policy Consumer Linkage: A Theoretical Approach," Intelligence and National Security 1/2 (May 1986): 212-233.

Examines the relationship between those who gather and produce intelligence and those who make policy governing intelligence operations.

3670. Hulnick, Arthur S. "CIA's Relations with Academia: Symbiosis Not Psychosis," International Journal of Intelligence and Counterintelligence 1/4 (Winter 1986-1987): 41-50.

Examines the long term relationship between the CIA and the academic community, suggesting four ways exist to improve the persistently tension-filled association. Discusses the Pike and Church committee hearings on the subject, the DCI's influence and the need to strengthen the relationship.

3671. Hulnick, Arthur S. "Managing Analysis Strategies for Playing the End Game," International Journal of Intelligence and Counterintelligence 2/3 (Fall 1988): 321-343.

Describes and evaluates the many phases in the intelligence analysis production process. Major sections discuss the recent history of CIA's analytical function; control points in production; a matrix model of the production process; management; requirements; tasking; the analytic process; the question of whether the data are adequate; the accuracy of the terms of reference; methodological effectiveness; and the theory versus reality of managing intelligence analysis.

3672. Hulnick, Arthur S. "Determining U.S. Intelligence Policy," International Journal of Intelligence and Counterintelligence 3/2 (Summer 1989): 211-224.

Suggests that the study of intelligence policy should focus on how intelligence policy is formulated, the appropriate players in the formulation process, implementation and control factors, and criteria for evaluation. Major sections discuss the making of US intelligence policy; the core of intelligence; the variety of limitations on the process; and conclusions as to making the system work.

3673. Hulnick, Arthur S. "Political Changes Improve Public Information Access," Signal 45/1 (1990): 105-107.

3674. Hulnick, Arthur S. "Learning About U.S. Intelligence: Difficult But Not Impossible," International Journal of Intelligence and Counterintelligence 5/1 (Spring 1991): 89-99.

Explores in some detail the four basic points of access to and information about the intelligence community for outsiders: the open media; material provided by CIA; the Freedom of Information Act; and the National Archives.

3675. Hulnick, Arthur S. "Intelligence Cooperation in the Post-Cold War Era: A New Game Plan?," International Journal of Intelligence and Counterintelligence 5/4 (Winter 1991-1992): 455-465.

Argues that there is a long history of intelligence sharing between world intelligence organizations and that cooperation is and important part of modern intelligence activity. Major sections discuss competition, not cooperation; the question of whether the US will spy on its friends; political risk analysis; the gauging of competitors; and private intelligence.

3676. Hulnick, Arthur S. "Intelligence Organization: A New Look for a New World," Current World Leaders 36/4 (August 1993): 699-711.
An analytical perspective from a former CIA analyst.

3677. Hulnick, Arthur S. "The Ames Case: How Could It Happen?," International Journal of Intelligence and Counterintelligence 8/2 (Summer 1995): 133-154.
Discussion of the background circumstances of the Aldrich Ames spy case. Provides background on Ames' career; developing problems; relationship with his wife, Rosario; the fox among the chickens; recipe for espionage; beginning of the damage; Soviet errors; throwing the CIA off; Ames in Rome; the hunt for the CIA mole; fatal mistakes; the trap door is sprung; counterintelligence to criminal investigation; and damage assessment.

3678. Hulnick, Arthur S. "The Uneasy Relationship Between Intelligence and Private Industry," International Journal of Intelligence and Counterintelligence 9/1 (Spring 1996): 17-31.
Major sections discuss intelligence and competitiveness; the question of espionage help; alternative assistance; dealing with foreign organized crime; a conference on intelligence in Ottawa, Canada in 1994; and the reduction of ambivalence.

3679. Hulnick, Arthur S. "U.S. Covert Action: Does It Have a Future?," International Journal of Intelligence and Counterintelligence 9/2 (Summer 1996): 145-157.
A brief overview of United States covert action history, and a defense of continued covert action policy under restricted circumstances. Major sections discuss the definition of covert action; lessons of history; current covert action policy; evaluation of covert action; and future covert action policy.

3680. Hulnick, Arthur S. and David W. Mattausch. "Ethics and Morality in United States Secret Intelligence," Harvard Journal of Law & Public Policy 12/2 (Spring 1989): 509-522.
Addresses ethical dimensions for intelligence operations, and moral considerations confronting intelligence officers. A justification for intelligence operations based on the depravity of world conditions.

3681. Humphrey, David C. "Tuesday Lunch at the Johnson White House: A Preliminary Assessment," Diplomatic History 8/1 (Winter 1984): 81-101.
The Tuesday lunch was judged to be the most important foreign policy advisory process of the Johnson administration.

3682. Hunbedt, T. N. "Radar in a Ground Hole," Military Review 27/8 (November 1947): 36-40.

3683. Hundley, Helen. "Tibet's Part in the 'Great Game,'" History Today 43 (October 1993): 45-50.
Includes discussion of British spying operations in Tibet and certain personalities associated with the missions, such as Francis Younghusband, Agvan Dorjiev, and George Nathaniel Curzon.

3684. Hunt, David. "Remembering the Tet Offensive," Radical American 11/6 & 12/1 (1977-1978): 79-96.
A comprehensive review of the background of the offensive surprise attack, the facts of the operation, and the meaning of the offensive. Points out the failure of intelligence.

3685. Hunt, David. "Amphibious Intelligence," Studies in Intelligence 31/3 (Fall 1987).

3686. Hunt, David. "Remarks on 'A German Perspective on Allied Deception Operations,'" Intelligence and National Security 3/1 (January 1988): 190-194.
A critique of Klaus-Jurgen Muller's article (same journal, 1987) on the basis of German strategic thinking in World War II.

3687. Hunt, Linda. "U.S. Coverup of Nazi Scientists," Bulletin of the Atomic Scientists 41/4 (April 1985): 16-24.
Extensive summation of Project Paperclip, a US intelligence project to employ German scientists on sensitive military and space projects following World War II.

3688. Hunt, Richard M. "The CIA Exposures: End of an Affair," Virginia Quarterly Review 45/2 (Spring 1969): 211-229.
Revelations that in 1967 and previous years the CIA was supplying covertly money to various private activities in the US. Several administrations had approved of such violations of congressional intent and statutory law.

3689. Hunter, Alan. "Constitutional Law: Search and Seizure - A Covert Entry Does Not Intrinsically Offend the Fourth Amendment, and Does Not Require Specific and Prior Judicial Authorization," Santa Clara Law Review 20 (Spring 1980): 545-550.
A case note discussion of Dalia v. United States, 441 U.S. 238 (1979).

3690. Hunter, Charles N. "Galahad: Intelligence Aspects," Studies in Intelligence 5/4 (Winter 1961).
A discussion of unconventional warfare in Burma.

3691. Hunter, David H. "Fitting the Pieces Together," Infantry 52 (January-February 1962): 19-21.

3692. Hunter, David H. "The Evolution of Literature on United States Intelligence," Armed Forces and Society 5/1 (Fall 1978): 31-52.

Analysis of the stages of intelligence literature, dividing it into phases: pro-intelligence; anti-intelligence; capstone; and reaction and reform. Observes the constructive value of praise and controversy in the writing about intelligence in democratic societies.

3693. Hunter, Jane. "Out of the Loop--The VP's Office: Cover for Iran/Contra," Covert Action Information Bulletin 33 (Winter 1990): 16-20.

3694. Hunter, Jane. "Covert Operations: The Human Factor," Link 25/3 (August 1992): 1-13.

A book review essay of three books on the subject.

3695. Hunter, Robert. "The CIA: Is it a Department of Dirty Tricks, or an Organization of Fact-Finders? Did It Underwrite the Seizure of Power by the Greek Colonels?," Listener 83 (May 1970): 671-672.

3696. Huntington, Samuel P. "Human Rights and American Power," Commentary 72 (September 1981): 37-44.

Counters the Hans J. Morgenthau argument that the US supported only right wing governments in its foreign policy posture. Contests the view that the CIA should be held accountable for all the evils of foreign policy. Argues for the US policy to be based on strengthening democracies in the world.

3697. Huntington, Samuel P. "American Ideals Versus American Institutions," Political Science Quarterly 97/1 (Spring 1982): 1-37.

Major sections history versus progress in connection with current and future political institutions in their conformity with the "American Creed," part of which concerns a debate over American involvement in other countries. Useful background article for studies of American covert actions and other forms of foreign interventions.

3698. Hurlburt, Arthur S. "Whatever Happened to Counter Intelligence?," Intelligence Quarterly 2/1 (1986): 1-3.

Some observations of a World War II CIC officer.

3699. Hurley, John A. "Humint Revitalization," Military Review 61/8 (1981): 22-29.

A personal account of the use of human intelligence sources in the military.

3700. Hurst, Willard. "Treason in the United States," Harvard Law Review 58/2,3,6 (December 1944; February 1945; July 1945): 226-272; 395-444; 806-857.

A three-part scholarly history: "Treason Down to the Constitution"; "The Constitution"; and "Under the Constitution." Study was requested by the Justice Department in connection with the Supreme Court case in 1944, Cramer v. U.S.

3701. Hurst, Willard. "Historic Background of the Treason Clause of the United States Constitution," Federal Bar News & Journal 6 (April 1945): 305-313.
This is the more recent title of the same publication.

3702. Hurst, Willard. "English Sources of the American Law of Treason," Wisconsin Law Review 1945/3 (May 1945): 315-356.
Examines the English doctrines of treason dating to Edward III in 1350. Sections discuss early English treatises, treatises published in the 18th century, treatises published in the 19th and 20th centuries, and writers on the Constitution.

3703. Hurwitz, Martin. "Perspectives on the 1990s," American Intelligence Journal 11/3 (Summer-Fall 1990): 5-8.
A defense of military intelligence resources at the level of the Unified and Specified Commands. The author has argued for the maintenance of strong intelligence resources to support the military in the field.

3704. Husock, Howard and Anna M. Warrock. "Taking Toshiba Public," Studies in Intelligence 34/2 (Summer 1990).

3705. Huston, J. A. "Communist Intentions National Security Policy," World Affairs 119 (1956): 77-80.
US policy toward the Soviet Union in the cold war era was based on perceived communist intentions, thus making that policy persistently uncertain, shifting and frustrated. New policy should reflect intentions as well as interests and capabilities.

3706. Hutchings, Raymond. "Soviet Defence Spending and Soviet External Relations," International Affairs (Great Britain) 47/3 (July 1971): 518-531.
Considers linking Soviet defence spending and Soviet external relations in order to improve analysis of the economic strength of the Soviet Union.

3707. Hutchinson, Allan C. "Moles and Steel Papers," Modern Law Review 44/3 (May 1981): 320-327.
Considers the implications of the case of British Steel Corp. v. Granada Television, Ltd. having to do with confidentiality versus media access and dissemination.

3708. Hutchinson, Harold R. "Intelligence: Escape from Prisoner's Dilemma," Intelligence and National Security 7/3 (July 1992): 327-334.

Applying the game theory exercise of the "prisoner's dilemma," the author considers two superpowers who must choose between alternative strategies of adopting cooperative or non-cooperative policies. Discusses a resolution to the dilemma and the role of intelligence at various stages.

3709. Hutchinson, John F. "The Nagler Case: A Revealing Moment in Red Cross History," Canadian Bulletin of Medical History 9/2 (1992): 177-190.

3710. Hutchinson, Robert. "Rumor of War: An Information Vendor's View of the Provision of Open-Source in an Unstable World," American Intelligence Journal 14/1 (Spring-Summer 1993): 33-36.

A general discussion of the world situation and the role of open source information to enlighten the intelligence function.

3711. Hutchinson, S. "The Police Role in Counter-Insurgency Operations," RUSI Defense Studies Journal 114 (1969).

3712. Hutt, M. "Spies in France, 1793-1808," History Today 12 (March 1962): 158-167.

Discusses the significance of British secret agent work in France during the time of the Bourbon resurgence. Accounts for the work of the Chouans, a guerilla group in search of British assistance, and the capture of British agent who revealed espionage activities.

3713. Huygens, Etienne. "What Is a Defector?," Intelligence Quarterly 3/1 (1987): 10-13.

3714. Huygens, Etienne. "Defectors from the Tropics," Intelligence Quarterly 3/4 (1988): 10-14.

3715. Huyn, Hans G. "Webs of Soviet Disinformation," Strategic Review 12 (Fall 1984): 51-58.

3716. Huzar, E. "Reorganization for National Security," Journal of Politics 12 (February 1950): 129-152.

A comprehensive review of the reorganization of defense and intelligence organizations under the National Security Act provisions.

3717. Hwang, Byong-Moo. "Misperceptions and the Causes of the Korean War," Revue Internationale d'Histoire Militaire 70 (1988): 197-210.

3718. Hwang, Kelley K. "The Admissibility of Evidence Obtained by

Eavesdropping on Cordless Telephone Conversations," <u>Columbia Law Review</u> 86/2 (March 1986): 323-347.

Discusses Title III of the Omnibus Crime Control and Safe Streets Act of 1968, case law prior and subsequent to enactment of Title III, and congressional power supporting it.   Argues that evidence obtained from eavesdropping in cordless telephone conversations should be inadmissible. Also considers whether Fourth Amendment requires exclusion of same by its own terms as interpreted by courts.

3719. Hyde, Charles C. "The Espionage Act," <u>American Journal of International Law</u> 12/1 (January 1918): 142-146.

Early commentary on the components of the Act and implications for international law. Useful for historical studies of espionage. Note that the entire Act is printed in Supplement I to the <u>American Journal of International Law</u> for 1917, p. 178ff.

3720. Hyde, Charles C. "Aspects of the Saboteur Cases," <u>American Journal of International Law</u> 37 (January 1943): 88-91; 152-171.

Applications of Chief Justice Stone's extended opinion of October 29, 1942 pertaining to the saboteur cases of Quirin, Haupt, Kerling, Burger, Heinck, Thiel and Neubauer. Discusses right of belligerents to employ spies derived from Hague Convention and War Department Rules of Land Warfare. US Supreme Court decision is found on pp. 152-171.

3721. Hyde, Charles K. "Undercover and Underground: Labor Spies and Mine Management in the Early Twentieth Century," <u>Business History Review</u> 60/1 (1986): 1-27.

An examination of the tactics used by company managers to combat and suppress labor activities and union growth.

3722. Hyde, Henry J. "'Leaks' and Congressional Oversight," <u>American Intelligence Journal</u> 9/1 (Summer 1988): 24-27.

Brief remarks concerning the impact of leaks of classified government information on the intelligence community and national security management.

3723. Hyden, John S. "The Sources, Organization, and Uses of Intelligence in the Anglo-Portugese Army, 1808-1814," <u>Journal of the Society for Army Historical Research</u> 62/250-251 (Summer and Autumn 1984): 92-104; 169-175.

I

**"Bond was a world-wide cult and his creator had become
a myth in his own lifetime."**
(The Life of Ian Fleming by John Pearson, p. 346)

3724. Iampol'ski, V. P. "Japanese Secret Services Against the USSR, 1918-45," Voenno-Istoricheskii Zhurnal 11 (1991): 28-37.

3725. Iatskov, A. A. "The Atom and Intelligence," Voprosy Istorii Estestvoznaniia i Tekhniki 3 (1992): 103-134.
Reveals espionage work of the author in World War II in the US to pick up secrets of the American atomic bomb project.

3726. Ibrahim, Saad. "American Domestic Factors and the October War," Journal of Palestine Studies 4/1 (1974): 55-81.
Argues that domestic support or opposition to foreign policy is acquired from public opinion, mass media and special interest groups. Contains sections on American public opinion during the Arab-Israeli conflict, interest and pressure groups, the Jewish community as a base of support for the Zionist lobby, Arab lobbyists, the oil lobby, the media role, and the 1967 and 1973 media coverage.

3727. Ignatius, David. "Dan Schorr: The Secret Sharer," Washington Monthly 8/2 (April 1976): 6-21.
An account of CBS Daniel Schorr's 1975 investigation of Central Intelligence Agency activities and the leak of the Pike Committee report.

3728. Ike, Nobutaka. "Foreign Policy and Decision-Making in Japan 1941," Transactions of the International Conference of Orientalists in Japan 19 (1965): 42-60.

3729. Ikenaga, Cindy S. "Electronic Eavesdropping: Which Conversations Are Protected from Interception?," University of Hawaii Law Review 7 (Spring 1985): 227-237.

Case note referring to State v. Okubo and State v. Lee involving state constitutional protection in electronic eavesdropping cases. Discusses the case facts, constitutional issues, and statutory issues.

3730. Ikuhiko, Hata. "Going to War: Who Delayed the Final Note?," Journal of American-East Asian Relations 3 (Fall 1994).

One of several articles in this issue to address the dynamics of pre and post Pearl Harbor attack.

3731. Ilardi, V. "Crosses and Carets: Renaissance Patronage and Coded Letters of Recommendation," American Historical Review 92 (December 1987): 1127-1149.

This article describes a practice of sending letters of recommendation and favors to officials by using coded letters. The use of a coded letter of recommendation signified a true recommendation such that no applicants receiving such letters were ever denied a job.

3732. Immerman, Richard H. "Guatemala As Cold War History," Political Science Quarterly 95/4 (Winter 1980-1981): 629-653.

Discusses the Guatemalan revolutionary movement; Guatemalan communism and the cold war ethos; the sequence of intervention; consequences in terms of American and Cuban perceptions.

3733. Immerman, Richard H. "Diplomatic Dialings: John Foster Dulles' Telephone Transcripts," Newsletter of the Society for Historians of American Foreign Relations 14/1 (1983): 1-15.

The heavy communication between John Foster Dulles and his brother Allen Dulles, Director of Central Intelligence Agency in the 1950s.

3734. Imwinkelried, Edward J. "United States v. Payner and the Still Unanswered Questions About the Federal Courts' Supervisory Power Over Criminal Justice," National Journal of Criminal Defense 7 (Spring 1981): 1-34.

Discusses the Payner matter in terms of US prosecutorial efforts to reduce the legal barriers to admission of relevant evidence in criminal cases. The facts in the Payner case involved an Internal Revenue Service covert investigation into off-shore deposits of large sums of money.

3735. Ingells, D. J. "Air Tech Intelligence," <u>Skyways</u> 11 (September 1952): 16-18.
A popular press resource, but it may be useful in historical studies.

3736. Ingram, David H. "Fighting Smart" with ACE Intelligence," <u>Marine Corps Gazette</u> (May 1989): 38-39.
Discusses history and modern applications of effective air intelligence.

3737. Ingram, Edward. "Approaches to the Great Game in Asia," <u>Middle East Studies</u> 18/4 (October 1982): 449-457.
Discusses British interests in the Middle East in the nineteenth century, based largely on oil. Mentions Russia's invasion of India. "Great game" was a term introduced by Arthur Connolly. Useful in Middle East analyses and the problem of confusion about foreign policy objectives.

3738. Ingram, George. "The Story of Laura Secord Revisited," <u>Ontario History</u> 57/2 (1965): 85-97.

3739. Ingram, Jack E. "The Origins of NSA," <u>American Intelligence Journal</u> 15/1 (Spring-Summer 1994): 39-41.
A brief history of the National Security Agency.

3740. Inman, Bobby R. "Interview with Bobby R. Inman," <u>Military Electronics and Countermeasures</u> (January 1983).

3741. Inman, Bobby R. "The NSA Perspective on Telecommunications Protection in the Nongovernmental Sector," <u>Signal</u> 33 (March 1979): 6-13; and <u>Cryptologia</u> 3/3 (July 1979): 129-135; and <u>Cryptologic Spectrum</u> (Winter 1979): 1-5.

3742. Innes, Christopher. "Hapgood--A Question of Gamesmanship?," <u>Modern Drama</u> 32 (June 1989): 315-317.

3743. Inouye, Daniel K. "The Senate Select Committee on Intelligence, A Special Report," <u>American Intelligence Journal</u> 1/2 (Winter 1977-1978).
A summary of the report by the former US Senator from Hawaii.

3744. Inquirer [pseud.] "The Practice of a Prophet," <u>Studies in Intelligence</u> 6/3 (Fall 1962): 29-41.
A CIA analyst evaluates the actions and skills of a Soviet spy in Sweden from 1949 to 1951, Ernst Hilding Andersson.

3745. Ioanid, Radu. "The Holocaust in Romania: The IASI Pogrom of June 1941," <u>Contemporary European History</u> 2/2 (1993): 119-148.

3746. Ionov, M. D. "On the Methods of Influencing an Opponent's Decisions," Military Thought 23 (1971): 58-66.

In Russian, but available in translated form, this is a brief discussion of Russian concepts of strategic deception.

3747. Ishio, S. Phil. "The Nisei: Contribution to the Allied Victory in the Pacific," American Intelligence Journal 16/1 (Spring 1995): 59-67.

3748. Ismi, Asad. "United States Policy Towards Vietnam, 1954-1955: The Stabilization of the Diem Government," Vietnam Generation 3/4 (1991): 39-58.

3749. Isnard, Jacques. "Renewing Military Intelligence," Politique Internationale 56 (Summer 1992): 409-416.

In French, this is a discussion of the proposals to make the French intelligence services more useful to the political bodies and leadership.

3750. Israel, Fred L. "Military Justice in Hawaii, 1941-1944," Pacific Historical Review 36/3 (August 1967): 243-267.

In the hours preceding the invasion of Pearl Harbor, the Territorial Governor placed the islands under martial law, a governing status that remained until October 1944. Article discusses the rigors of martial law and domestic security.

3751. Israel, Kenneth. "The Defense Airborne Reconnaissance Office," American Intelligence Journal 15/2 (Autumn-Winter 1994): 61-67.

3752. Ivanchishin, P. "Okhrana Granitsy Sovetskogo Otechestra," Politicheskoe Samoobrazovanie 4 (April 1978): 48-54.

3753. Ivanoff (pseud.). "Anarchists: Their Methods and Organizations," New Review 10 (1894): 9-16.

3754. Ivey, Robert A. "Tough Lessons Learned at JRTC," Military Intelligence 16/2 (April-June 1990): 15-18.

Discusses the role of the Joint Readiness Training Center in the realm of low intensity conflict and the methods of intelligence preparation for the battlefield.

J

**"...in the Intelligence work there is an enormous premium
placed upon going off at half-cock."**
(The Wizard War by R. V. Jones, p. 524)

3755. Jabb (pseud.). "Tales of Intelligence, No. 1: "The Dresden Salt-Cellar,"
Army Quarterly 5 (1922): 111-121.
Tales of French counterintelligence work against the Germans in 1915.

3756. Jablonska-Deptula, Ena. "Church Subject Matter in the Reports of
Mackrott, 1818-1830," Roczniki Humanistyczne 27/2 (1979): 149-187.

3757. Jablonsky, David. "The Paradox of Duality: Adolf Hitler and the Concept
of Military Surprise," Intelligence and National Security 3/3 (July 1988): 55-117.
Addresses two competing mindsets of Hitler in his approach to
warfighting: the direct approach of head-on battles of annihilation; and the
indirect approach of using the legal and polictical systems to gain dominance.
Sections military surprise and decision making in Hitler's regime; technological
surprise; doctrinal surprise; and conclusions.

3758. Jackamo, Thomas J., III. "From the Cold War to the New Multilateral
World Order: The Evolution of Covert Operations and the Customary
International Law of Non-Intervention," Virginia Journal of International Law
32/4 (Summer 1992): 929-977.
Argues that nations will now begin to use less forcible types of covert
actions, such as campaign finances, industrial and economic spying,

counterterrorism, drug interdiction, and prevention of weapons proliferation. Addresses uncertainty in status of traditional law of non-intervention and potential problems raised by any uniform rule on intervention that might be enacted by the United Nations.

3759. Jackson, David. "Individual Rights and National Security," Modern Law Review 20/4 (July 1957): 364-380.
       Considers the United Kingdom's system for internal security protection and compares it with similar programs in other common law nations.

3760. Jackson, Donald. "Zebulon M. Pike 'Tours' Mexico," American West 3/3 (1966): 67-71, 89-93.
       Recounts the history of Pike's travels from St. Louis to Mexico in 1806-1807, a mission which many historians have suggested was intended to spy on Spanish outposts. This article rejects the espionage mission idea.

3761. Jackson, Janko. "A Methodology for Ocean Surveillance Analysis," Naval War College Review 27 (September-October 1974): 71-89.
       A lengthy discussion of the subject.

3762. Jackson, Mark G. "The Court-Martial Is Closed: The Clash Between the Constitution and National Security," Air Force Law Review 30 (1989): 1-20.
       Compares Military Rules of Evidence with the Classified Information Procedures Act with respect to the difficulties posed when military prosecution is initiated for crimes involving classified information.

3763. Jackson, Peter. "France and the Guarantee to Romania, April 1939," Intelligence and National Security 10/2 (April 1995): 242-272.
       Argues that French political and military leadership in the 1930s permitted a policy drift and indecision along the road to World War II. Examines French policy towards Romania and the Franco-British guarantee to Romania. Includes evaluation of French intelligence considerations with respect to Germany's intentions.

3764. Jackson, Wayne G. "Scientific Estimating," Studies in Intelligence 9/2 (Summer 1965).

3765. Jackson, William D. "The Soviets and Strategic Arms: Toward an Evaluation of the Record," Political Science Quarterly 95/2 (Summer 1979): 243-261.
       Major sections include discussion of Soviet strategic weapons policy under Stalin, the evolution of strategic power and policy from 1953 to 1960, the escalation of Soviet strategic effort from 1960 to 1964, Soviet strategic power and policy from 1964 to 1978, the Soviets and SALT, the growth of Soviet strategic

power from 1969 to 1978, and appraisal of recent Soviet strategic behavior.

3766. Jackson, William H., Jr. "Congressional Oversight of Intelligence: Search for a Framework," <u>Intelligence and National Security</u> 5/3 (July 1990): 113-147.

Attempts to clarify the terms and conditions of the debate about oversight; to review the compromises that have arisen through the years of oversight; to address the fluctuations in the purpose of oversight within the evolving intelligence structure and legislative framework.

3767. Jacob, Bonnie. "I Spied," <u>New Dominion</u> 3/4 (1989): 22-29.

A brief story of those who worked for intelligence agencies.

3768. Jacob, Joseph. "Some Reflections on Government Secrecy," <u>Public Law</u> (1974): 25-49.

Reviews problems raised by official and unofficial discussion about governmental secrecy. Discusses Official Secrets Act and methods for handling secrets.

3769. Jacobs, Arthur L. "Should the U.S. Use Covert Action in the Conduct of Foreign Policy?," <u>Freedom at Issue</u> 35 (1976): 13-19.

Discusses covert actions and secrecy in the formation of US foreign policy.

3770. Jacobs, Arthur L. "Ethics and Intelligence--A Reply," <u>Foreign Affairs</u> 5/6 (July 1978): 867-875.

Author disagrees with E. Drexel Godfrey's position that intelligence operational habits induce an "amoral" way of life, and he objects to the need for certain controls on field agents. Too many restrictions, he argues, would lead to agents injury to "national vision." Godfrey's reply is included.

3771. Jacobs, Harold. "Decoy Enforcement of Homosexual Laws," <u>University of Pennsylvania Law Review</u> 112/2 (December 1963): 259-284.

Police use of decoy informants against homosexuals carries certain legal implications. Discusses conduct necessary to establish a criminal homosexual overture; defense arising from the decoy situation; and the problems of proof.

3772.   Jacobs, James.   "An Overview of National Political Intelligence," <u>University of Detroit Journal of Urban Law</u> 55/4 (Summer 1978): 853-876.

Defines political intelligence and its mission to determine the political motivations of private individuals. Explores the origins and development of political intelligence, beginning with World War I and the Red Scare through the anti-Vietnam war movement in the early 1970s.

3773. Jacobs, Michael. "Thatcher and the Increase of State Power in Britain,"

Canadian Dimension 20/2 (1986): 32-35.
    Discusses Thatcher's increased use of British intelligence agencies for domestic surveillance of citizens.

3774. Jaffe, Philip J. "Agnes Smedley: A Reminiscence," Survey 20 (Autumn 1974): 172-179.

3775. Jagerskiold, S. "Swedish Case on the Jurisdiction of States Over Foreigners: Crown v. Von Herder," American Journal of International Law 41 (October 1947): 909-911.
    An espionage case in Sweden at the end of World War II raised once again the question of the limits of jurisdiction of States over their citizens who commit criminal acts in foreign countries.

3776. Jaggers, R. C. "The Assassination of Reinhard Heydrich," Studies in Intelligence 4/4 (Winter 1960).

3777. Jahoda, Marie and Stuart W. Cook. "Security Measures and Freedom of Thought: An Exploratory Study of the Impact of Loyalty and Security Programs," Yale Law Journal 61/3 (March 1952): 295-333.
    Research findings from interviews with 15 faculty members and 70 federal employees, the results of which were to be used in a more extensive research of the topic. Contains a review of loyalty-security procedures in government; perceptions of the loyalty-security program; salience; effects on the climate of thought; social pressures that reinforce the climate of thought; and conditions believed to enhance or inhibit the program.

3778. Jakobsen, Thomas. "A Fast Method for Cryptanalysis of Substitution Ciphers," Cryptologia 19/3 (July 1995): 265-274.

3779. Jakubowicz, Oleg G. "Neural Networks for Intelligence," Signal 43/8 (April 1989): 47-56.
    The application of neural networks in the computer's use in intelligence analysis.

3780. James, Charles D. "Combat Intelligence for Aviation," United States Army Aviation Digest 16/1 (January 1970): 15-18.

3781. James, D. Clayton. "The Other Pearl Harbor," Military History Quarterly 7/2 (Winter 1995).

3782. James, Ralph C. and Estelle James. "The Purge of the Trotskyites from the Teamsters," Western Political Quarterly 19/1 (March 1966): 5-15.
    Major sections discuss the Minneapolis purge; the counterattack in

Detroit; the Trotskyite impact of Hoffa; and conclusions.

3783. James, Raymond C. "The Right to Travel Abroad," Fordham Law Review 42/4 (May 1974): 838-851.
A case note summarizing the law of passports and foreign travel following the case of Bauer v. Acheson.

3784. James, W. "Room 40," University of Edinburgh Journal 22/1 (Spring 1965).

3785. Jameson, C. W.; R. F. Mosemen; and B. J. Collins. "Spy Dust: Detecting a Chemical Tracking Agent," Analytical Chemistry 58 (July 1986): 915-916.

3786. Jameson, Donald F. B. "The Clandestine Battlefield: Trenches and Trends," Strategic Review 11/1 (Winter 1983): 19-28.
A discussion of the comparative features of western and Soviet intelligence services.

3787. Jameson, Donald F. B. "The 'Iran Affair,' Presidential Authority and Covert Operations," Strategic Review 15/1 (Winter 1987): 24-30.

3788. Jameson, Donald F. B. "Robot Spies of the KGB," Signal 44 (December 1989): 79-83.

3789. Jameson, J. Franklin. "St. Eustatius in the American Revolution," American Historical Review 8/4 (1903): 683-703.
Discusses the subtle support by the Dutch for the American revolution via the lower prices the Dutch charged for products going to the Colonies through the island of St. Eustatius in the Northern Caribbean.

3790. Jamieson, Caroline P. "Protecting Proprietary Information in Illinois: A Response to the Illinois Trade Secrets Act from a Drafting Perspective," De Paul Law Review 41 (Spring 1992): 885-925.
Examines protection of trade secrets in Illinois. Sections discuss the history of trade secrets doctrine in the US; the Illinois Trade Secrets Act (ITSA); the purposes of the ITSA; and the ITSA's impact.

3791. Jamieson, George. "The Trial for Treason of James Wilson, July 1820," Juridical Review (March 1994): 50-59.

3792. Jamnig, Peter. "Securing the RSA-Cryptosystem Against Cycling Attacks," Cryptologia 12/3 (July 1988): 159-164.

3793. Jandora, John W. "Threat Parameters for Operations Other Than War,"

Parameters: Journal of the U.S. Army War College 25/1 (Spring 1995): 55-97.
    Discusses operations other than war; three difficult threats; and role of intelligence in such operations.

3794. Jansen, John B. and Stefan Weyl. "Spy at Work: Underground Movement in Germany," Atlantic Monthly 171 (February 1943): 71-77.
    A discussion of the tradecraft of underground work in espionage and resistance organizations, mainly regarding work in Germany.

3795. Jansen, Marc and Ben de Jong. "Stalin's Hand in Rotterdam: The Murder of the Ukrainian Nationalist Yevhen Konovalets in May 1938," Intelligence and National Security 9/4 (October 1994): 676-694.
    An inquiry into the bomb murder of Konovalets, carried out on instructions from Joseph Stalin. Various aspects of the plot are discussed: Who was Yevhen Konovalets?; who was 'Valiukh'?; the Wollweber organization; Pavel Sudoplatov and the murder of Konovalets; and Sudoplatov's further career.

3796. Janov, Gwenellen P. "Electronic Surveillance--The President of the United States Has No Authority to Conduct Wiretaps to Protect Against Domestic Threats to the National Security Without a Judicial Warrant," George Washington Law Review 41 (October 1972): 119-134.
    A case note referring to U. S. v. U. S. District Court for the Eastern District of Michigan and a Supreme Court decision in electronic eavesdropping cases.

3797. Janowitz, Morris. "The Evolution of Civilian Surveillance by the Armed Forces," American Sociologist 6 (August 1971): 254-256.
    A brief history of the escalation of the military role in domestic surveillance.

3798. Jansky, Donald M. "Evolving Government Policy on Cryptography," Signal 35 (August 1981): 67-70.

3799. Jardines, Eliot A. "Lessons from Cuba's Revolutions," Military Intelligence 20/3 (July-September 1994): 34-36.
    Discusses the US role in Cuba, 1868-1959; guerilla warfare; and the uniqueness of the Cuban problem.

3800. Jarrow, James R. "Industrial Espionage? Discovery Within the Rules of Civil Procedure and the Battle for Protective Orders Governing Trade Secrets and Confidential Information," Washburn Law Journal 32 (Spring 1993): 318-325.
    Considers the rules govern the process of discovery of information by plaintiffs in actions that may be expected to divulge sensitive proprietary confidential material. Protections are offered as to what the court may do to

impose protection orders and stiff penalties for violations of orders.

3801. Jarvis, Jeff. "Protecting the Nation's National Security: The Classified Information Procedures Act," Thurgood Marshall Law Review 20 (Spring 1995): 319-347.

Discusses the purpose, scope and procedures of the Classified Information Procedures Act. It is suggested that the law was not entirely useful in such matters as the Iran-Contra affair.

3802. Jasani, Bhupendra and Christer Larsson. "Remote Sensing, Arms Control and Crisis Observation," International Journal of Imaging, Remote Sensing and Integrated Geographical Systems 1/1 (1987): 31-41.

3803. Jauffret, Jean-Charles. "The Army and Algeria in 1954," Revue Historique des Armes 2 (1992): 15-25.

3804. Jefferson, M. "The Tisdall Affair (Great Britain)," Liverpool Law Review 6 (Spring 1984): 188-200.

Account of the delivery of two British secret documents to The Guardian newspaper in 1983. Sarah Tisdall, a clerk in the Foreign Secretary's office, was accused of leaking the documents. She pleaded guilty and received a six-month prison sentence.

3805. Jeffery, Keith. "The British Army and Internal Security 1919-1939," Historical Journal 24/2 (1981): 377-398.

Finds the origins of systematic British military internal security in the World War I period when it was believed that the British police could not control subversiveness and disorder.

3806. Jeffery, Keith. "The Government Code and Cypher School: A Memorandum by Lord Curzon," Intelligence and National Security 1/3 (September 1986): 454-458.

A brief overview of the role and operations of the school.

3807. Jeffery, Keith. "Intelligence and Counter-Insurgency Operations: Some Reflections on the British Experience," Intelligence and National Security 2/1 (January 1987): 118-149.

Discusses coordination; collection; and implementation of counter-insurgency efforts from a British perspective. Concludes that military operations against insurgent or terrorist forces usually may not be truly military efforts, thus calling for special intelligence positioning and focus.

3808. Jeffery, Keith and Eunan O'Halpin. "Ireland in Spy Fiction," Intelligence and National Security 5/4 (October 1990): 92-116.

Explores the themes appearing in Irish spy novels in the twentieth century. Limits the discussion to an impressionistic survey of the treatment of Irish affairs in spy and related fiction. Numerous authors and titles are cited.

3809. Jeffreys-Jones, Rhodri. "Violence in American History: Plug Uglies in the Progressive Era," Perspectives in American History 8 (1974): 465-583.

3810. Jeffreys-Jones, Rhodri. "The Montreal Spy Ring of 1898 and the Origins of 'Domestic' Surveillance in the United States," Canadian Review of American Studies 5/2 (1974): 119-134.
    A detailed discussion of President McKinley's dealings with the Spanish spy threat during the Spanish-American War.

3811. Jeffreys-Jones, Rhodri. "W. Somerset Maugham: Anglo-American Agent in Revolutionary Russia," American Quarterly 28/1 (Spring 1976): 90-106.
    Qualifies and explains Maugham's failure to aid the installation of a pro-western government following the Bolshevik coup in 1917. Author emphasizes the historical significance of Maugham's undercover work.

3812. Jeffreys-Jones, Rhodri. "Review Essay: Weinstein on Hiss," Journal of American Studies 13/1 (March 1979): 115-126.
    Applauds Allen Weinstein's detailed research published in Perjury: The Hiss-Chambers Case (1978) to uncover Alger Hiss' guilt or innocence, but decides that the work has several shortcomings. An exceptionally insightful evaluation of this book.

3813. Jeffreys-Jones, Rhodri. "The Historiography of the CIA," Historical Journal 23/2 (June 1980): 489-496.
    Reviews six new works on the Central Intelligence Agency and provides rich analysis of the organization's historical meaning. See a lengthy discussion of CIA in his book, The CIA and American Democracy.

3814. Jeffreys-Jones, Rhodri. "The Defictionalization of American Private Detection," Journal of American Studies 17/2 (August 1983): 265-274.
    Argues that new scholarship has addressed the world of private detectives. Discusses Frank Morn's history of the Pinkerton Detective Agency in his book, The Eye That Never Sleeps.

3815. Jeffreys-Jones, Rhodri. "The Socio-Educational Composition of the CIA Elite: A Statistical Elite," Journal of American Studies 19/3 (December 1985): 421-424.
    A discussion of the composition of the structure and administrative control within Central Intelligence Agency.

3816. Jeffreys-Jones, Rhodri. "The CIA and the Demise of Anti-Americanism: Some Evidence and Reflexions," European Contributions to American Studies 11 (1986): 121-136.

3817. Jeffreys-Jones, Rhodri. "American Intelligence: A Spur to Historical Genius?," Intelligence and National Security 3/2 (April 1988): 332-337.

   A review article evaluating the contributions of seven major books in the intelligence field: William Blum, The CIA: A Forgotten History; Walter Laqueur, A World of Secrets; Ernest May (ed.), Knowing One's Enemies; John Ranelagh, The Agency; Andrew Sinclair, The Red and the Blue; Wesley K. Wark, The Ultimate Enemy; and Robin W. Winks, Cloak & Gown.

3818. Jeffreys-Jones, Rhodri. "In Search of the Textbook: Recent Overviews of United States Intelligence History Since the Days of the Founding Fathers," Intelligence and National Security 6/4 (October 1991): 750-756.

   A book review essay critiquing the works of Charles D. Ameringer, U.S. Foreign Intelligence: The Secret Side of American History, Nathan Miller, Spying for America: The Hidden History of U.S. Intelligence, and Ernest Volkman and Blaine Baggett, Secret Intelligence: The Inside Story of America's Espionage Empire.

3819. Jeffreys-Jones, Rhodri. "Breaking Other People's Laws," Queen's Quarterly 100/2 (Summer 1993): 438-440.

   A book review essay of Regulating Covert Action: Practices, Contexts, and Policies of Covert Coercion Abroad in International and American Law by W. Michael Riesman and James E. Baker.

3820. Jeffreys-Jones, Rhodri. "Manual Indices and Digital Pathways: Developments in United States Intelligence Biography," Intelligence and National Security 9/3 (July 1994): 555-559.

   A book review essay concerning four information resources on intelligence literature: Neal Peterson, American Intelligence, 1775-1990: A Bibliographical Guide; National Intelligence Book Center, The Electronic Database of the Russell J. Bowen Collection of Works on Intelligence, Security and Covert Activities; CIABASE; and Name Base.

3821. Jelen, George F. "The Defensive Disciplines of Intelligence," International Journal of Intelligence and Counterintelligence 5/4 (Winter 1991-1992): 381-399.

   Discussion of the elements of the intelligence community responsible for defense against the work of foreign intelligence operations. Major sections consider the shared traits of these organizations; counterintelligence; security countermeasures; operations security; offensive versus defensive intelligence; active versus passive intelligence; and the key elements in a single intelligence policy.

3822. Jemnitz, Janos. "The Labor Movement in the United States of America During the Years of the First World War (1914-1917)," <u>Parttorteneti Kozlemenyek</u> 20/2 (1974): 88-128.

3823. Jenero, Kenneth A. and Lynne D. Mapes-Riordan. "Electronic Monitoring of Employees and the Elusive Right to Privacy," <u>Employee Relations Law Journal</u> 18 (Summer 1992): 71-102.

    Discusses types of monitoring used, privacy theories that may be available to employees in trying to limit monitoring, legislative attempts to provide some protection, and how employers may limit exposure to liability. Considers issue in context of both public and private employment.

3824. Jenkins, Brian M. "A U.S. Strategy for Combatting Terrorism," <u>Conflict: An International Journal</u> 3/1-3 (1981): 167-176.

3825. Jenkins, Brian M. "New Modes of Conflict," <u>Orbis</u> 28/1 (Spring 1984): 5-16.

    Discusses conflict short of conventional warfare in the previous nine years. Contains sections on three faces of armed conflict (conventional war; guerilla warfare; terrorism); armed conflict in the postindustrial age; implications.

3826. Jenkins, Ed and Robert H. Brink. "The National Security Council and the Iran-Contra Affair," <u>Georgia Journal of International and Comparative Law</u> 18 (1988): 19-49.

    Argues that the Iran-Contra affair produced a situation in which the NSC was bypassed in favor of direct action by executive branch personnel who were not seen and not accountable.

3827. Jenkins, John A. "Graymail," <u>Student Law Journal</u> 8 (December 1979): 16-20; 42-43.

    Considers facts and issues related to the question of the tradeoff between protecting intelligence secrets and prosecuting fully those who reveal national security information.

3828. Jenkins, Philip. "The Assassins Revisited: Claire Sterling and the Politics of Intelligence," <u>Intelligence and National Security</u> 1/3 (September 1986).

    A review essay challenging the views of Claire Sterling and proposing that her views simply reflect a countervailing political view rather than a view based on balanced scholarship.

3829. Jenkins, Philip. "Terrorism," <u>Intelligence and National Security</u> 3/1 (January 1988): 205-207.

    A brief book review essay of three books on the topic: Christopher Dobson and Ronald Payne, <u>War Without End: The Terrorists - An Intelligence</u>

Dossier; James Adams, The Financing of Terror; and Benjamin Netanyahu (ed.), Terrorism: How the West Can Win.

3830. Jenkins, Philip. "Policing the Cold War: The Emergence of New Police Structures in Europe, 1946-1953," Historical Journal 31/1 (March 1988): 141-158.

A rich discussion of the evolution and expansion of police and intelligence systems in various nations in the early years of the cold war, 1946-1953.

3831. Jenkins, Philip. "Spy Fiction and Terrorism," Intelligence and National Security 5/4 (October 1990): 185-203.

Explores novels about spies and terrorists, novels about terrorism between 1900 and 1920, novels about terrorism after the formation of the Soviet state, terrorism in novels about the Middle East, and novels addressing the radical tradition.

3832. Jenkins, Philip. "Under Two Flags: Provocation and Deception in European Terrorism," Terrorism: An International Journal 11/4 (1988): 275-287.

3833. Jenkins-Smith, Hank C. "Professional Roles for Policy Analysts: A Critical Assessment," Journal of Policy Analysis and Management 2/1 (March 1982): 88-100.

Discusses the methods by which the policy analyst influences a decision outcome. Argues that the environment of the policy analyst is mainly determined by the manner in which the client-analyst relationship and the policy arena fit together. Useful in discussions of the intelligence analyst function.

3834. Jenks, E. "Some Correspondence of Thurloe and Meadowe," English Historical Review 7 (1892): 72-78.

3835. Jenks, E. "Mr. Secretary Thurloe," Macmillan's Magazine 70 (1894): 291-303.

3836. Jenks, William L. "The 'Hutchins' Map of Michigan," Michigan History Magazine 10 (1926): 362.

3837. Jennings, R. Y. "The Caroline and McLeod Cases," American Journal of International Law 32 (1938): 82-99.

Discusses the facts of the Canadian rebellion of 1837 and the dispatch of Britain's minister Ashburton to the US to resolve the matter of the sinking of the ship Caroline and the jailing of McLeod. Legal concerns for the concepts of self-preservation or self-defense.

3838. Jennings, Karen. "Espionage: Anything Goes?," Pepperdine Law Review 14 (March 1987): 647-666.

Discusses prosecution of persons accused of espionage and the factors that are considered in decision to prosecute, including political considerations. Questions what, if any, legal standards should be applied to such cases.

3839. Jensen, Owen E. "Information Warfare: Principles of Third-Wave War," Airpower Journal 8/4 (Winter 1994): 35-44.

3840. Jenson, Richard B. "The International Anti-Anarchist Conference of 1898 and the Origins of Interpol," Journal of Contemporary History 16/2 (April 1981): 323-347.

The Conference met in Rome in 1898 to arrive at a legal definition of anarchism. Discusses the exchange of information between police agencies concerning anarchists and assassins. Mentions the assassination of President McKinley.

3841. Jerian, Nancy A. "Intelligence Agents as Authors: A Comparison of the British Courts' Position on Attorney-General v. Heinemann Publishers and the United States Supreme Court Decision in Snepp v. United States," Loyola of Los Angeles International and Comparative Law Journal 11/2 (1989): 345-376.

This is a comparison of Peter Wright's case concerning the book Spycatcher with the Frank Snepp case over the book Decent Interval. Summarizes the case facts and decisions, outlines the British courts' positions, compares and contrasts the cases, and offers conclusions.

3842. Jernigan, Patricia H. "Army Intelligence Production: Challenge and Commitment," American Intelligence Journal 13/3 (Summer 1992): 71-77.

Discusses historical background of Army intelligence following World War II; production center formation; Army Intelligence Agency operations, communications and automation; reorganization; and assessment of the future threat.

3843. Jerrold, Elbert S. "Why Do We Need the CIA? The Story of Our 'Spy Agency's' Many-Sided Mission," American Legion Magazine 82 (June 1967): 6-11+.

A justification of the CIA in a time of great domestic controversy.

3844. Jervis, Robert. "Cooperation Under the Security Dilemma," World Politics 30/2 (January 1978): 167-214.

Uses two approaches to show when and why security dilemmas arise following an anarchy situation: prisoner's dilemma and the condition in which the defense has the advantage over the offense.

3845. Jervis, Robert. "Deterrence and Perception," International Security 7/3 (Winter 1982-1983): 3-30.

Discusses the dependence of deterrence on perceptions. Contains sections on misperception, credibility, judging the adversary's alternatives, self-deterrence and overconfidence. Useful in discussions of intelligence analysis of threats.

3846. Jervis, Robert. "Hypotheses on Misperceptions," World Politics 20/3 (April 1968): 454-479.

A discussion of the types of misperceptions of other states' intentions which adversaries tend to make. Views intention as a collection of ways by which the state feels it will act when faced with a wide range of future contingencies.

3847. Jervis, Robert. "What's Wrong with the Intelligence Process," International Journal of Intelligence and Counterintelligence 1/1 (Spring 1986): 28-41.

Author emphasizes that the US intelligence system could be organized, directed and operated in exceedingly more efficient ways in order to extract a far greater quantity and quality of analytical material. He says that intelligence services can be worth listening to.

3848. Jervis, Robert. "Intelligence and Foreign Policy: A Review Essay," International Security 11/3 (Winter 1986-1987): 141-161.

A review of Christopher Andrews' and David Dilks' (eds.) The Missing Dimension: Governments and Intelligence Communities in the Twentieth Century and Ernest May's Know One's Enemies: Intelligence Assessment Before the Two World Wars.

3849. Jervis, Robert. "War and Misperception," Journal of Interdisciplinary History 18/4 (Spring 1988): 675-700.

Misperceptions have been the main cause of most wars, and these errors in judging international intentions are not likely to disappear. Offers several historical examples and implications for analysts.

3850. Jervis, Robert. "Strategic Intelligence and Effective Policy," Studies in Intelligence 33/4 (Winter 1989).

3851. Jeszensky, John F. "Send Out the Scouts," Armor 75 (March-April 1966): 42-44.

3852. Jeszenszky, Elizabeth. "The Defense Intelligence Agency: Jointness Is Goodness," American Intelligence Journal 13/3 (Summer 1992): 79-83.

Discusses the background and creation of the Defense Intelligence Agency; DIA struggles; and current mission of DIA.

3853. Johnson, Alexander L. P. "The Foreign Military Press," Infantry Journal 42 (May-June 1935): 279-280.

3854. Johnson, Allan W. "Marine Aviation -- Are We Prepared to Fight in Real Time?," Marine Corps Gazette (May 1989): 40-41.
    Discusses the current Marine Corps air intelligence system.

3855. Johnson, Clarence L. "Development of the Lockheed SR-71 Blackbird," Studies in Intelligence 26/2 (Summer 1982).
    See item 3864. Clarence Johnson, also known as Kelly Johnson, developed the high-flying spy aircraft known as the SR-71.

3856. Johnson, D. H. N. "Military and Paramilitary Activities in and Against Nicaragua," Sydney Law Review 10 (March 1985): 485-502.
    A discussion of the May 1984 ruling by the International Court of Justice ordering the US to extricate itself from military and paramilitary operations in Nicaragua: Background, law and conclusions.

3857. Johnson, E. Clifford. "Electronic Surveillance," Virginia Law Review 66 (March 1980): 297-298.
    A survey of the subject as it applies in Virginia following Cogdill v. Commonwealth, 247 S.E. 2d 392 (Va. 1978).

3858. Johnson, Falk S. "Get That Gun," Intelligence Quarterly 3/4 (1988): 1-3.
    Brief description of the use of radio intelligence in World War II.

3859. Johnson, J. R. "Morgan's Men," Marine Corps Gazette 37 (June 1953): 36-39.

3860. Johnson, J. R. "The Business of Aviation Intelligence," Marine Corps Gazette 39 (February 1955): 22-23.

3861. Johnson, James P. "The Assassination in Dallas: A Search for Meaning," Journal of Psychohistory 7/1 (Summer 1979): 105-121.
    The key to understanding Lee Harvey Oswald's motivations for assassinating President Kennedy lie in Oswald's emotional life, not in the bits of circumstantial evidence which appears so often in the conspiracy theory articles and books. Discusses disinformation.

3862. Johnson, John. "Army Tactical SIGINT and EW," Signal 38/8 (April 1984): 43-52.
    Extensive discussion of military signals intelligence and electronic warfare.

3863. Johnson, George A. "Right to Make a Citizen's Arrest of On-Campus CIA Recruiters," National Lawyers Guild Practitioner 45/2 (Spring 1988): 33-35.
    Summarizes legal position on this matter, which is obvious from the title. Discusses the case law in brief.

3864. Johnson, Kelly. "Development of the Lockheed SR-71 Blackbird," Lockheed Horizons (Winter 1981-82): 1-7.
    See item 3855. Kelly Johnson, also known as Clarence Johnson, developed the high-flying spy aircraft known as the SR-71.

3865. Johnson, Kenneth T. "Developments in Air Targeting: Progress and Future Prospects," Studies in Intelligence 3/2 (Summer 1959).

3866. Johnson, Loch K. "The CIA: Controlling the Quiet Option," Foreign Policy 39 (Summer 1980): 143-153.
    A description of various House investigating committee actions to control the excesses of the intelligence community.

3867. Johnson, Loch K. "The U.S. Congress and the CIA: Monitoring the Dark Side of Government," Legislative Studies Quarterly 5/4 (November 1980): 477-499.
    Examines congressional monitoring of the CIA during 1978, the response of the CIA, oversight responsibilities of committee members, personality and structural influences, and hypotheses for future testing.

3868. Johnson, Loch K. "Seven Sins of Strategic Intelligence," World Affairs 146 (Fall 1983): 176-204.
    Seven sins are: failure to provide policy makers with objective, uninhibited intelligence; disregard of objective intelligence by P/M's; discriminate collection of intelligence; indiscriminate use of covert action; inadequate protection of officers and agents abroad; elimination of counterintelligence; and inadequate accountability in the intelligence chain of command.

3869. Johnson, Loch K. "Decision Costs in the Intelligence Cycle," Journal of Strategic Studies 7/3 (September 1984): 318-335.
    The author discusses three types of information costs in the decision making process: collection costs; intergame costs; and persuasion costs. Argues for less isolation of the analytical community to reduce decision costs.

3870. Johnson, Loch K. "Legislative Reform of Intelligence," Polity 17/3 (Spring 1985): 549-573.
    A look at the changes and transformations of US intelligence operations, caused mainly by new legislation.

3871. Johnson, Loch K. "The CIA and the Media," Intelligence and National Security 1/2 (May 1986): 143-169.
The topic is captured by the title of this piece.

3872. Johnson, Loch K. "Making the Intelligence 'Cycle' Work," International Journal of Intelligence and Counterintelligence 1/4 (Winter 1986-1987): 1-24.
Discusses the phases of the intelligence process and how they apply to the formation of American foreign policy. Argues that the key to good application of intelligence in the decision making process is a receptive audience. Sections discuss planning and direction, collection, types of intelligence, intelligence gathering and processing, production and analysis, the President's Daily Brief and other reports, the National Intelligence Daily, intelligence officers, and intelligence dissemination.

3873. Johnson, Loch K. [Book Review Essay], Conflict Quarterly 7/3 (Summer 1987): 59-63.
A book review essay regarding two volumes in a series of studies by Roy Godson, Domestic Intelligence (1986), and Intelligence and Policy (1986).

3874. Johnson, Loch K. "Mr. Huston and Colonel North," Corruption and Reform 3/2 (1988): 207-234.
Analysis of the Iran-Contra affair and the roles of Colonel Oliver North and the "Huston plan." Contains sections on counterintelligence comes home; the Huston plan recommendations; the President takes a second look; hidden dimension of the Huston plan; lawlessness; exclusion; and conclusions.

3875. Johnson, Loch K. "Intelligence Policy in the Carter and Reagan Administrations: From Reform to Remission," Southeastern Political Review 16 (Spring 1988): 73-104.
Discusses the institutional focus and methodologies of intelligence in each administration; collection and analysis; counterintelligence; the Angleton school; spycatching; the ghosts of the Huston plan, COINTELPRO, and Operation CHAOS; and loopholes.

3876. Johnson, Loch K. "Sentries in the Senate," International Journal of Intelligence and Counterintelligence 2/4 (Winter 1988): 593-601.
A book review essay of Men of Zeal; A Candid Inside Story of the Iran-Contra Hearings by William S. Cohen and George J. Mitchell.

3877. Johnson, Loch K. "Covert Action and Accountability: Decision-Making for America's Secret Foreign Policy," International Studies Quarterly 33/1 (March 1989): 81-109.
The author discusses the ways by which the US decides the use of covert action as a weapon to serve foreign policy interests in relation to other nations.

3878. Johnson, Loch K. "Controlling the CIA: A Critique of Current Safeguards," Harvard Journal of Law & Public Policy 12/2 (Spring 1989): 371-396.

Offers a critique of the safeguards implemented by the Congress to control the excesses of CIA power. Administrative controls include oversights by the NSC, OMB, and internal audits by CIA staff.

3879. Johnson, Loch K. "Strategic Intelligence: An American Perspective," International Journal of Intelligence and Counterintelligence 3/3 (Fall 1989): 299-332.

A lengthy and detailed analysis of the role and functions of American strategic intelligence. Major sections address the purposes of strategic intelligence; the modus operandi of strategic intelligence; distinctiveness of the American experience; commonalities of strategic intelligence; and strategic intelligence in the twenty-first century.

3880. Johnson, Loch K. "Covert Action and American Foreign Policy: Decision Paths for the 'Quiet Option,'" Teaching Political Science 16/2 (Winter 1989): 64-76.

3881. Johnson, Loch K. "Challenges of Strategic Intelligence, Intelligence and National Security 5/3 (July 1990): 215-225.

A book review essay Strategic Intelligence for American National Security, by Bruce D. Berkowitz, The CIA and American Democracy, by Rhodri Jeffreys-Jones, and Surprise Attack: The Victim's Perspective, by Ephraim Kam.

3882. Johnson, Loch K. "The Role of Congress in U.S. Strategic Intelligence," American Intelligence Journal 11/3 (Summer-Fall 1990): 41-45.

Main topics under review include the emergence of intelligence oversight from benign neglect to new oversight; the centrist solution between presidential accountability and legislative review; sticking points; and strengths of legislative oversight.

3883. Johnson, Loch K. "DCI Webster's Legacy: The Judge's Self-Assessments," International Journal of Intelligence and Counterintelligence 5/3 (Fall 1991): 287-290.

A brief analysis of the legacy of CIA's former director, Judge William H. Webster. Considers Webster's responses to media criticisms and Webster's self-evaluation of his service. Reflects the content of the author's interview with Judge Webster.

3884. Johnson, Loch K. "On Drawing a Bright Line for Covert Operations," American Journal of International Law 86/2 (April 1992): 284-309.

Offers suggestions for considering the reasonableness of covert operations, including ethical and practical issues.

3885. Johnson, Loch K. "Smart Intelligence," Foreign Policy 89 (Winter 1992-1993): 53-69.

Author argues that the CIA requires significant realteration of priorities in order to adapt to rapidly changing world conditions facing foreign policy decision makers.

3886. Johnson, Loch K. "The Evolution of CIA Accountability," American Intelligence Journal 16/1 (Spring 1995): 43-46.

Professor Johnson argues that CIA accountability is both necessary and controversial. He observes the persistent tradeoff between giving politically motivated overseers in the Congress too much highly sensitive information subject to compromise versus the threats to abuse of democratic principles in the absence of oversight accountability.

3887. Johnson, Loch K. "Analysis for a New Age," Intelligence and National Security 11/4 (October 1996): 657- 671.

Major sections discuss the perils of analysis, such as determining policy needs; collection barriers; processing; analysis; the demon ambiguity; rising analytic prowess; dissemination and the paradox of rejection; the limits of time and understanding; ideology; relevance; format; marketing; improving the quality of analysis; tasking for collection; and the dependence of analysis on reliable data.

3888. Johnson, Mike. "Cryptology in Cyberspace," Cryptologia 19/4 (October 1995): 392-396.

3889. Johnson, Nelson B. "Intelligence Support to the War on Drugs," Signal 44 (September 1989): 47-50.

3890. Johnson, Nicholas L. "Soviet Satellite Reconnaissance Activities and Trends," Air Force Magazine (March 1981): 90-94.

Discussion of the Soviet reconnaissance aircraft program and restrictions placed on missions by SALT I and II treaties.

3891. Johnson, Nicholas L. "Soviet Military Space Surveillance," Military Engineer 79 (July 1987): 362-367.

3892. Johnson, Richard J. "Zagranichnaia Agentura: The Tsarist Political Police in Europe," Journal of Contemporary History 7/1-2 (January-April 1972): 221-242.

Finds the turning point in the development of the Tsars' secret police system in the political climate of 1881, a time of heightened anti-regime activity. Describes the role and activities of the political police.

3893. Johnson, Robert C. "Spanish Spies in Virginia," History Today 20/5 (1970): 356-365.

History of King Philip III's operation to acquire intelligence concerning a British colony in Virginia in 1607. A rather humorous story of an intelligence mess.

3894. Johnson, Robert H. "The National Security Council: The Relevance of Its Past to Its Future," Orbis 13/3 (Fall 1969): 709-735.

Discusses the evolution of the Council since 1947 and the Nixon administration's efforts to reorganize and revive the Council.

3895. Johnson, S. A. "Junior Marines in Minor Irregular Warfare," Marine Corps Gazette 6 (June 1921): 152-163.

3896. Johnson, Thomas M. "Spy and Counter-Spy," Infantry Journal 43/1 (January-February 1936): 34-38.

An account of G-2-B (intelligence section of the American Expeditionary Force) in World War I. Part II appears in the March-April 1936 issue, pp. 145-150.

3897. Johnson, Thomas M. "Battle Underground, the Work of the C.I.C.," Combat Forces 3 (June 1953): 29-32.

3898. Johnson, Thomas M. "Our Silent Partner in the Secret War Against Communism," American Mercury 91 (September 1960): 3-10.

One of the first pieces of literature of any length to appear on the subject of German spy chief Reinhard Gehlen's work for the US after World War II.

3899. Johnson, Thomas M. "Search for the Stolen SIGABA," Army 12/7 (February 1962): 50-55.

Cryptographic equipment was stolen, then recovered in a French town in the last months of World War II.

3900. Johnson, Thomas M. and R. E. Dupuy. "No Place for Glory Hunters," Army 6 (April 1956): 44-47.

3901. Johnson, Tom. "The Mystery of an Old Japanese Codebook," Cryptologia 19/4 (October 1995): 380-384.

3902. Johnson, William R. "Clandestinity and Current Intelligence," Studies in Intelligence 20/3 (Fall 1976): 15-69.

A lengthy and rich position paper that argues the incompatibility between production of current intelligence and the conduct of espionage. Argues also that the current intelligence process has been degraded by the adoption of journalistic techniques over "real technique of espionage." Major sections discuss how the OSSD won the war; CIA and the sales department; strategic espionage; the role of the office of strategic operations; and liaison operations.

3903. Johnson, William R. "Ethics and Clandestine Collection," Studies in Intelligence 27/1 (Spring 1983): 1-8.

3904. Johnson, William R. "The Elephants and the Gorillas," International Journal of Intelligence and Counterintelligence 1/1 (Spring 1986): 42-56.
        Current intelligence is highly perishable while strategic information has a longer shelf life. Spies break foreign laws as an operating necessity. Espionage is more suited to strategic information than to current information.

3905. Johnson, William R. "Tricks of the Trade: Counterintelligence Interrogation," International Journal of Intelligence and Counterintelligence 1/2 (Summer 1986): 103-113.
        Discusses the unreliability of torture as a means to secure information from a source. Argues that effective interrogation, conducted by professionals, can work on the level of self-control, anxiety and weaknesses of the source. Techniques of interrogation are described.

3906. Johnson, William R. "The Ambivalent Polygraph," International Journal of Intelligence and Counterintelligence 1/3 (Fall 1986): 71-83.
        Discusses the operations of the standard polygraph, but suggests that the device is not useful for three types of individuals or for mass screening of employees. Where personnel have access to the most sensitive information, the device is useful. This article was reprinted in Et Cetera 44/4 (1987): 354-365.

3907. Johnston, Angus J., II. "Disloyalty on Confederate Railroads in Virginia," Virginia Magazine of History and Biography 63/4 (October 1955): 410-426.

3908. Johnston, Francis J. "Henry Skillman, A Confederate Courier," Journal of the Council on America's Military Past 15/4 (1989): 15-23.

3909. Johnston, Henry P. "The Secret Service of the Revolution," Magazine of American History 8/2 (February 1882): 95-105.
        President Washington's allocation of spies to infiltrate enemy lines, communications between secret agents through letters, and the role of Tallmadge after 1776.

3910. Johnston, Henry P. "Colonel Varick and Arnold's Treason," Magazine of American History 8 (November 1882): 717-733.

3911. Johnston, Hugh. "The Surveillance of Indian Nationalists in North

America, 1908-1918," BC Studies 78 (1988): 3-27.

3912. Johnston, Otto W. "British Espionage and Prussian Politics in the Age of Napoleon," Intelligence and National Security 2/2 (April 1987): 230-244.
Suggests that the Prussian correspondence with the Foreign Office contains sufficient evidence of Prissian activist intentions to overthrow Frederick William III; and that there were secret paramilitary covert actions aimed at ridding Germany of Napolean.

3913. Joint Congressional Committee. "The Attack," Foreign Affairs 70/5 (Winter 1991-1992): 156-161.
This is an excerpt from the November 1945 report of the committee investigating the Pearl Harbor attack.

3914. Jonas, Hans. "Reflections on Technology, Progress, and Utopia," Social Research 48/3 (Autumn 1981): 411-455.
A critique of utopian thought, in particular Marxist utopias. Useful in analyses of the dangers of utopian guides to judgment, faith, commitment and perception.

3915. Jones, A. "Walter's Warning," Progressive 46 (June 1982): 14-15.
A commentary on the impact of the Intelligence Identities Protection Act on the Covert Action Information Bulletin.

3916. Jones, C. A. "The World's Most Professional Machine: The Soviet Intelligence Network," Military Review 54 (February 1974): 74-81.

3917. Jones, Cecil B. "Photographic Satellite Reconnaissance," U.S. Naval Institute Proceedings 106/6 (June 1980): 41-51.
A brief overview of satellite intelligence collection systems and their vital role in overall national security.

3918. Jones, David L. "Communist Defection: Its Impact on East-West Relations," Military Review 46/3 (1966): 20-28.
Discusses wholesale defections after World War II, including the defections of high-ranking military and intelligence officials. Emphasis is given to the importance of defection in intelligence work.

3919. Jones, E. "The Psychology of Quislingism," International Journal of Psychiatry 22/1 (1941): 1-6.

3920. Jones, Edgar L. "Fighting with Words," Atlantic Monthly 176 (August 1985): 47-51.
Capitulation of thousands of Japanese soldiers after the invasion of

Okinawa was largely a function of psychological warfare. Use of psychological warfare to produce disquieting thought, propaganda towards the enemy, and the anti-spirit program are also discussed.

3921. Jones, Ernest L. "Our Air Force in the Civil War," National Aeronautic Association Review 3/7 (1925): 100-103, 111.

3922. Jones, Frances I. W. "Treason and Piracy in Civil War Halifax: The Second Chesapeake Affair Revisited," Dalhousie Review 71 (Winter 1991-1992): 472-487.

3923. Jones, Geoffrey and Clive Trebilcock. "Russian Industry and British Business 1910-1930: Oil and Armaments," Journal of European Economic History 11/1 (Spring 1982): 61-103.
        A useful discussion of the topic in analyses of economic conditions in the interwar years.

3924. Jones, Lawrence M. "G-2, Key to Nuclear Target Acquisition," Military Review 43/8 (August 1963): 66-71.
        Target acquisition is the biggest problem in the Army's nuclear weapons intelligence program. Author argues for a total reorganization of the intelligence staff to improve target acquisition.

3925. Jones, P. L. "When Competitors Really Bug You," Security Management 34/12 (December 1990): 44-51.

3926. Jones, Reginald V. "Scientific Intelligence," Journal of the Royal United Service Institute 92 (August 1947): 352-369.
        Discusses the author's experiences in the British intelligence service during World War II, in particular his work with air and scientific intelligence.

3927. Jones, Reginald V. "Scientific Intelligence," Research 9 (September 1956): 347-352.

3928. Jones, Reginald V. "The Theory of Practical Joking--Its Relevance to Physics," Bulletin of the Institute of Physics (June 1957): 193-201.
        Contains a section on human deception which may be useful in studies of deception and surprise.

3929. Jones, Reginald V. "Scientific Intelligence," Studies in Intelligence 6/2 (Summer 1962).
        The author's observations of the role and operations of scientific intelligence in World War II.

3930. Jones, Reginald V. "The Scientific Intelligencer," <u>Studies in Intelligence</u> 6/3 (Fall 1962).

3931. Jones, Reginald V. "The Theory of Practical Joking - An Elaboration," <u>Bulletin of the Institute of Mathematics and Its Applications</u> 11 (1975): 10-17.
    Argues the connection between scientific method and practical joking (contrived incongruity). Major sections of the discussion include incongruity simple; mismatch in scale; irony; incongruity discounted; congruity unexpected; puns and wit; hoaxes; technical spoof in war; success and limitations of physical models; breakdown through change of scale; function of analogy; and mathematical models.

3932. Jones, Reginald V. "Alfred Ewing and "Room 40," <u>Notes and Records of the Royal Society of London</u> 34 (July 1979): 65-90.

3933. Jones, Reginald V. "An Early Epic of ELINT," <u>Journal of Electronic Defense</u> 6/6 (June 1983): 75-76.
    A brief account of a purposeful mission in World War II to fly in close proximity to German aircraft to steal the radar emission.

3934. Jones, Reginald V. "The Intelligence War and the Royal Air Force," <u>Proceedings of the Royal Air Force Historical Society</u> 1 (January 1987).

3935. Jones, Reginald V. "Intelligence and Command," <u>Studies in Intelligence</u> 31/3 (Fall 1987).

3936. Jones, Reginald V. "Intelligence and Command," <u>Intelligence and National Security</u> 3/3 (July 1988): 288-298.
    Discussion of the relationship between the commander and his intelligence organization and some problems within the intelligence organization. Numerous personal reflections upon the author's World War II experiences on these subjects.

3937. Jones, Reginald V. "A Sidelight on Bletchley, 1942," <u>Intelligence and National Security</u> 9/1 (January 1994): 1-11.
    Addresses the organizational problems within the Government Code and Cypher School. Lists three problems: structure, funding, and team spirit.

3938. Jones, Reginald V. "Some Lessons in Intelligence: Enduring Principles," <u>Studies in Intelligence</u> 38/5 (1995): 37-42.
    The author's remarks at a symposium held at CIA headquarters on October 26, 1993. Discusses the scale differences between the present and World War II; experiences in war; channels and linkages; collection and collation; conflicts of priorities; experts and emotions; functions of experts; oversight; the

principle of minimum trespass; and compromise and balance.

3939. Jones, Reginald V.; J. M. Lewis; and Barton Bernstein. "Churchill's Anthrax Bombs: A Debate," Bulletin of the Atomic Scientists 43/9 (November 1987): 42-45.

The authors debate whether or not Churchill intended to use secret biological weapons after 1944.

3940. Jones, S. F. "Russian Imperial Administration and the Georgian Nobility: The Georgian Conspiracy of 1832," Slavonic and East European Review 65 (January 1987): 53-76.

The conspiracy to replace Georgian nobles with Russians after the death of George XII. Useful in studies of conspiracy and revolutions.

3941. Jonson, Ben. "On Spies," Intelligence and National Security 8/4 (October 1993): vii.

A three line poem by the long-deceased classic British author, beginning "Spies, you are lights in state, but of base stuffe...".

3942. Jordan, Don. "Looking In on Us: Surveillance, Surveillance--All Is Surveillance," Environment 19/6 (August 1977): 6-11.

Describes the benefits of remote sensing technologies in the search for oil, explorations, the rain forests, and opium poppy fields. Such technologies should be improved.

3943. Jordan, Kent A. "The Extent of Independent Presidential Authority to Conduct Foreign Intelligence Activities," Georgetown Law Journal 72/6 (August 1984): 1855-1883.

Argues that the president is entrusted primarily by constitutional theory and practice with the intelligence function. Describes types of intelligence activities and examines the constitutional sources for presidential control over the function. Compares presidential and congressional powers.

3944. Jordan, Mark. "Freedom of Information Act: CIA's Right to Nondisclosure Broadened by Liberal Definition of Intelligence Source," Washburn Law Journal 25/3 (Spring 1986): 586-597.

Addresses the case of CIA v. Sims in which the Supreme Court ruled that researchers who worked on the CIA-funded MKULTRA project were intelligence sources within the meaning of section 102 (d)(3) of the National Security Act of 1947. Thus, identities can be withheld.

3945. Jordan, Sandra D. "Classified Information and Conflicts in the Independent Counsel Prosecutions: Balancing the Scales of Justice After Iran-Contra," Columbia Law Review 91/7 (November 1991): 1651-1698.

Addresses balance between a defendant's right to a public trial and government's right to protect matters of national security. Discusses Classified Information Procedures Act (CIPA) and whether or not this law has been successful in preventing defendant's from "graymailing" the government (threatening to divulge secret information in an effort to convince authorities not to prosecute). Concludes CIPA failed in Iran-Contra prosecutions.

3946. Joseph, Paul. "The Politics of 'Good' and 'Bad' Information: The National Security Bureaucracy and the Vietnam War," Politics and Society 7/1 (Spring 1977): 105-126.

Discussion of the quagmire of the Vietnam war; the Marxist interpretation of the war; evidence for the quagmire position; the mining of the Haiphong harbor and the Tet offensive in 1968. Mentions the role and input of the CIA.

3947. Joseph, Ted. "The United States vs. H. Miller: The Strange Case of a Mennonite Editor Being Convicted of Violating the 1917 Espionage Age," Mennonite Life 30/3 (1975): 14-18.

Analyzes the case of Miller's alleged violation of the 1917 Espionage Act. Discusses the lack of procedural justice afforded Miller.

3948. Josephson, Harold. "Ex-Communists in a Crossfire: A Cold War Debate," Historian 44 (November 1981): 69-84.

Asks whether the domestic threat of communism to American institutions was dangerous or as imminent as the anti-communist investigations of the 1950s suggested. Discusses congressional and FBI investigations of ex-communists.

3949. Joshua, Wynfred. "Soviet Manipulation of the European Peace Movement," Strategic Review 11 (Winter 1983): 9-18.

Discusses international fronts, disinformation and forgeries, Soviet financing and the West German Communist Party. Argues that the Soviets have had a purposeful disinformation effort.

3950. Jourard, Sidney M. "Some Psychological Aspects of Privacy," Law and Contemporary Problems 31 (1966): 307-318.

Privacy, says the author, "is an outcome of a person's wish to withhold from others certain knowledge as to his past and present experience and action and his intention for the future." A lack of privacy yields costs in lost health, weaker commitment to society and eventual social stagnation. Argues for a greater step away from conformity toward individuality.

3951. Jourdonnais, Adam. "Intelligence in the New Japan," Studies in Intelligence 7/2 (Summer 1963).

3952. Joyce, John F. "The Privacy Act: A Sword and a Shield But Sometimes Neither," Military Law Review 99 (Winter 1983): 113-167.

Discusses several dimensions of the right of privacy; FOIA and other statutes; factors in the enactment of the Privacy Act; scope and overview of major provisions of the Privacy Act; and various procedural elements of the Privacy Act.

3953. Joyner, Christopher C. "Reflections on the Lawfulness of Invasion," American Journal of International Law 78 (1984): 131-144.

Discusses the international law implications of the invasion of Grenada in October 1983. Good background piece for studies of the role of intelligence prior to intervention in hemisphere conflicts.

3954. Joyner, Christopher C. and Michael A. Guinaldi. "The United States and Nicaragua: Reflections on the Lawfulness of Contemporary Intervention," Virginia Journal of International Law 25/3 (Spring 1985): 621-689.

Discusses the legal issues behind US support for the Contras in Nicaragua, specific treaty instruments, protection of nationals abroad, self-defense in response to armed attack, and the Monroe Doctrine. Looks favorably on US justifications for intervention.

3955. Judd, Stephen G. "The CIA and the University: A Problem of Power," International Journal of Intelligence and Counterintelligence 6/3 (Fall 1993): 339-358.

An analysis of the relationship between the institutions of Central Intelligence Agency and the university. Sections address such issues as institutional inequities in power and knowledge; compromise of the academic process; the problem of information classification; the university and the expansion of executive authority; and the symbolic function of the university in the search for truth.

3956. Juhnke, James C. "John Schrag Espionage Case," Mennonite Life 22/3 (1967): 121-122.

3957. Jukes, Geoff. "The Soviets and Ultra," Intelligence and National Security 3/2 (April 1988): 233-247.

A general review of the conditions under which the Soviets held on to a good measure of cryptanalytic capability during World War II, particularly in connection with Ultra traffic.

3958. Jukes, Geoff. "More on the Soviets and ULTRA," Intelligence and National Security 4/2 (April 1989): 374-384.

Discusses new 'Enigma' evidence that clearly states that not only did the Soviets intercept German ciphers, but they also read German ciphers. Reviews reasons for Soviet secrecy concerning successes against Enigma. Concludes that the Soviets may have deciphered the Enigma codes, given their approach to Germans during the spring 1941 advances.

3959. Jung, John. "Snoopology," Human Behavior 4 (October 1975): 56-59.
        Discusses the differences between naturalistic observation and naturalistic experiments in human research (as performed by psychologists). Poses ethical concerns for forms of intrusive experiments.

3960. Jung, Yook Sang. "Revamping the Korean Intelligence Service: A Viewpoint of the Agency for National Security Planning," International Journal of Comparative and Applied Criminal Justice 18 (Spring-Fall 1994): 197-208.

3961. Junger, Peter D. "Down Memory Lane: The Case of the Pentagon Papers," Case Western Reserve Law Review 23/1 (1971-1972): 3-75.
        Argues that the most powerful check on national defense power is an enlightened citizenry. Reviews the legislative history of the Espionage Act of 1917, Justice Harlon's opinion, the Youngstown Sheet & Tube case, and the New York Times case in the Pentagon Papers matter.

3962. Jurchenko, Daniel A. and Scott R. Gourley. "The Order of Battle Officer," Field Artillery Journal 50 (November-December 1982): 15-17.

K

"A good clandestine intelligence report may have a heavy
ingredient of overt intelligence."
(Strategic Intelligence for American World Policy by Sherman Kent, p. 220)

3963. Kahan, Jerome H. and Anne K. Long. "The Cuban Missile Crisis: A Study of Its Strategic Context," Political Science Quarterly 87 (December 1972): 564-590.

A detailed review of the strategic processes of the US government in the missile crisis. Major sections discuss the buildup to the crisis; evaluation of the crisis; the impact of the crisis on later US and Soviet strategic policies; and policy implications.

3964. Kahn, David. "Number One from Moscow," Studies in Intelligence 5/3 (Fall 1961).

See this author's treatise on codebreaking, The Codebreakers.

3965. Kahn, David. "Modern Cryptology," Scientific American 215 (July 1966): 38-46.

An excellent general history of the twentieth century history of cryptology. Sections discuss codebreaking in history, the definition and application of cryptology, and development of the polyalphabetic systems.

3966. Kahn, David. "Secret Writings: Selected Works on Modern Cryptology," Bulletin of the New York Public Library 73 (May 1969): 315-327.

3967. Kahn, David. "Cryptology and History: Secret Writings for Historians," Maryland Historian 3/2 (Fall 1972): 157-162.
    Suggests fruitful areas of historical research into the role of cryptology in American and European history.

3968. Kahn, David. "World War II History: The Biggest Hole," Military Affairs 39/2 (April 1975): 74-77.
    Argues the need for deeper investigation into codes and alphus, aerial reconnaissance, POW's, espionage and intelligence analysis.

3969. Kahn, David. "The Biggest Bibliography," Cryptologia 1/1 (January 1977): 27-42.

3970. Kahn, David. "The Significance of Codebreaking and Intelligence to Allied Strategy and Tactics," Newsletter of the American Committee on the History of the Second World War 17 (May 1977): 3-4.

3971. Kahn, David. "The Significance of Codebreaking and Intelligence in Allied Strategy and Tactics," Cryptologia 1/3 (July 1977): 209-222.

3972. Kahn, David. "Intelligence and the General Staff," Studies in Intelligence 21/4 (Winter 1977).

3973. Kahn, David. "German Military Eavesdroppers," Cryptologia 1/4 (October 1977): 378-380.

3974. Kahn, David. "Reports from the Reich," Cryptologia 1/4 (October 1977): 371.

3975. Kahn, David. "The Role of Decoding and Intelligence in the Strategy and Tactics of the Allies," Review Histoire Deuxieme Guerre Mondiale 28/111 (1978): 73-85.

3976. Kahn, David. "The Forschungsamt: Nazi Germany's Most Secret Communications Intelligence Agency," Cryptologia 2/1 (January 1978): 12-19.

3977. Kahn, David. "Nuggets from the Archives: Yardley Tries Again," Cryptologia 2/2 (April 1978): 139-143.

3978. Kahn, David. "The Ultra Conference," Cryptologia 3/1 (January 1979): 1-8.

3979. Kahn, David. "A German Consular Cipher," Cryptologia 3/2 (April 1979): 119.

3980. Kahn, David. "The International Conference on Ultra," Military Affairs 43 (April 1979): 97-100.

3981. Kahn, David. "The Futility of It All," Cryptologia 3/3 (July 1979): 158-165.

3982. Kahn, David. "The Geheimschreiber," Cryptologia 3/4 (October 1979): 210-214.

3983. Kahn, David. "Cryptology Goes Public," Foreign Affairs 58/1 (Fall 1979): 141-159.
   The original superstitious world of cryptology has been slowly revealed to the public. Revelations have raised several issues and implications for policy makers.

3984. Kahn, David. "The Market for Encryption," Cryptologia 4/1 (January 1980): 42-44.

3985. Kahn, David. "Problems of the Unbreakable Cipher," Cryptologia 4/1 (January 1980): 36-40.

3986. Kahn, David. "Interviews with Cryptologists," Cryptologia 4/2 (April 1980): 65-70.

3987. Kahn, David. "Nuggets from the Archive: A Null Code at the White House," Cryptologia 4/2 (April 1980): 120-121.

3988. Kahn, David. "Codebreaking in World War I and II: The Major Successes and Failures, Their Causes and Their Effects," Historical Journal 23/3 (September 1980): 617-639.
   An extensive history of codebreaking in the world wars of the twentieth century, especially efforts by the Germans, Russians, Japanese, and British.

3989. Kahn, David. "A Professional's Challenge," Cryptologia 4/4 (October 1980): 238-239.

3990. Kahn, David. "On the Origin of Polyalphabetic Substitution," Isis 71/256 (March 1980): 122-127.
   Summary of the work of Leon Battista Alberti in the development of polyalphabetic code systems and the modern computerization of such systems.

3991. Kahn, David. "Public's Secrets," Progressive 44 (November 1980): 27-31.

3992. Kahn, David. "The Public's Secrets," Cryptologia 5/1 (January 1981):

20-26.

3993. Kahn, David. "German Spy Cryptograms," <u>Cryptologia</u> 5/2 (April 1981): 65-66.

3994. Kahn, David. "An Intelligence Case History: A Defense of Osuga, 1942," <u>Aerospace Historian</u> 28/4 (December 1981): 242-252.
    This is a careful review of military intelligence capabilities of the German Army to predict the Soviet attack in November 1942.

3995. Kahn, David. "Why Germany Lost the Code War," <u>Cryptologia</u> 6/1 (January 1982): 26-31.

3996. Kahn, David. "Churchill Pleads for the Intercepts," <u>Cryptologia</u> 6/1 (January 1982): 47-49.

3997. Kahn, David. "A New Source for Historians: Yardley's Seized Manuscript," <u>Cryptologia</u> 6/2 (April 1982): 115-118.

3998. Kahn, David. "In Memoriam: Georges-Jean Painvain," <u>Cryptologia</u> 6/2 (April 1982): 120-127.

3999. Kahn, David. "The Grand Lines of Cryptology's Development," <u>Computers and Security</u> (November 1982).

4000. Kahn, David. "Cipher Machine Inventor - Boris Hagelin Dies," <u>Cryptologia</u> 8/1 (January 1984): 60-61.

4001. Kahn, David. "World War II's Masterspy: High-Living Nazi Clerk Hans-Thilo Schmidt Delivers for the Allies," <u>Military History</u> 1/1 (August 1984): 14-19, 65.

4002. Kahn, David. "Cryptology and the Origins of Spread Spectrum," <u>IEEE Spectrum</u> 21 (September 1984): 70-80.

4003. Kahn, David. "Undercover for Fifty Years: A Hungarian Volunteer Saves Germany Two Out of Three," <u>Military History</u> 1/2 (October 1984): 8+.

4004. Kahn, David. "Washington's New York Spy Net: Invisible Ink, Dead Drops and a Petticoat Fooled the British," <u>Military History</u> 1/3 (December 1984): 10, 56-60.
    Explains that Abraham Woodhall was the first person called to serve in a spy ring set up at George Washington's request. Includes discussion of invisible ink, dead drops, and a petticoat (signaling device).

4005.   Kahn, David.   "The Annotated The American Black Chamber," Cryptologia 9/1 (January 1985): 1-37.

The author used William Friedman's copy of Herbert O. Yardley's classic book, finding many notes, comments, and corrections, and developed an annotation list for use in a new reading. Verification was also made of numerous outside sources used by Yardley.

4006. Kahn, David. "Chivalry's Dark Secret: Impolite Spy Unhorsed the Ideals of Knighthood," Military History 1/4 (February 1985): 10+.

4007. Kahn, David. "Saboteur Who Shook Manhattan: A Trail of Violence and Grandiose Schemes Across Neutral America," Military History 1/5 (April 1985): 8, 55-57, 63.

Explores the World War I sabotage case at Black Tom Island in the New York harbor. Black Tom was the most important point of munitions supplies to the European war effort. Discussion of intelligence information used to identify the saboteur, Lothar Witzke.

4008. Kahn, David. "Germany's Fraulein Doktor in Antwerp Was an Unusual Spymaster," Military History 2/2 (October 1985): 8, 69-71.

4009. Kahn, David. "From History Doctorate to Spymistress," Military History 2/2 (October 1985): 8, 69-71.

Discusses life of Elizabeth Schragmuller from her doctorate in history to head of military intelligence for the German General Staff. She was the first woman to run an intelligence service.

4010. Kahn, David. "Clausewitz and Intelligence," Journal of Strategic Studies 9/2-3 (June-September 1986): 117-126.

A summation of Clausewitz's concerns for the use of intelligence in war. Suggests that he despised intelligence and classed it negatively among the major factors in military deployment. His theory of intelligence has been invalidated by the role of technology, but his larger points are sustained.

4011. Kahn, David. "The Codebreaker Behind the Footlights," Cryptologia 11/2 (April 1987): 81-84.

4012. Kahn, David. "A Soviet Wiretapping Office," Cryptologia 13/2 (April 1989): 190-195.

4013. Kahn, David. "The Wreck of the Magdeburg," MHQ: The Quarterly Journal of Military History 2/2 (Winter 1990): 97-103.

4014.   Kahn, David.   "Pearl Harbor and the Inadequacy of Cryptanalysis,"

Cryptologia 15/4 (October 1991): 273-294.

4015. Kahn, David. "The Intelligence Failure of Pearl Harbor," Foreign Affairs 70/5 (Winter 1991-1992): 138-152.
An analysis of the role of intercepted messages in the information kitbag of military and executive leaders. Concludes that human errors, not the intelligence system, led to the Pearl Harbor attack. Contains sections on deception, codebreaking, causes, the 'Purple' messages, and recovery.

4016. Kahn, David. "Roosevelt, MAGIC, and ULTRA," Cryptologia 16/4 (October 1992): 289-319.

4017. Kahn, David. "An Enigma Chronology," Cryptologia 17/3 (July 1993): 237-246.

4018. Kahn, David. "The Story of the Hagelin Cryptos," Cryptologia 18/3 (July 1994): 204-242.

4019. Kahn, David. "Woodrow Wilson on Intelligence," Intelligence and National Security 9/3 (July 1994): 534-535.
A brief comment on President Wilson's disdain for spying as an outgrowth of a high moral tone he wished to maintain.

4020. Kahn, David. "The Cryptologic Origin of Braille," Cryptologia 19/2 (April 1995): 151-152.

4021. Kahn, Paul W. "From Nuremberg to the Hague: The United States Position in Nicaragua v. United States and the Development of International Law," Yale Journal of International Law 12/1 (Winter 1987): 1-62.
Discusses the justiciability of state violence, the Hague decision of 1984, the extension of international law to warfare, and self-determination of governance.

4022. Kail, Samuel G. "Combat Intelligence and Counterintelligence," Military Review 36/8 (November 1956): 60-70.
Discusses types of information required, need for terrain details, processing time, and security.

4023. Kairys, David. "The Bill of Attainder Clauses and Legislative and Administrative Suppression of 'Subversives,'" Columbia Law Review 67/8 (December 1967): 1470-1511.
Attempts to show that problems raised by the bill of attainder clauses can be solved by attending to original purposes of such clauses: the use of legislative power to suppress political opposition. Concludes that a proper interpretation of

these clauses prohibits certain oppressive practices of the federal government.

4024. Kairys, David and Julie Shapiro. "Remedies for Private Intelligence Abuses: Legal and Ideological Barriers," New York University Review of Law and Social Change 10/2 (Winter 1980-1981): 233-263.

As part of a symposium on the civil liberties issues attendant to nuclear power development, this piece discusses possible legal remedies for private intelligence abuses. Finds remedies inadequate. Attempts to place the issue in a broader social context. Responses by Jay Peterzell, Frank Donner and a general open discussion.

4025. Kaiser, David. "Conspiracy or Cock-up? Pearl Harbor Revisited," Intelligence and National Security 9/2 (April 1994): 354-372.

A thorough review article addressing issues raised in a book by Henry C. Clausen and Bruce Lee, Pearl Harbor: Final Judgment. Focusses on what Washington knew in 1941, and what was done in response to what was known.

4026. Kaiser, Frederick M. "Oversight of Foreign Policy: The U.S. House Committee on International Relations," Legislative Studies Quarterly 2/2 (August 1977): 255-280.

Examines oversight of the foreign policy apparatus as conducted by the House committee. Author's findings reveal considerable oversight intensity of the Committee. Discusses committee characteristics, partisan composition; policy environment; and legislative perceptions.

4027. Kaiser, Frederick M. "The U.S. Intelligence Community," Society 16/4 (May-June 1979): 31-39.

Discusses the US intelligence community and its positive relations with the public.

4028. Kaiser, Frederick M. "Presidential Assassinations and Assaults: Characteristics and Impact on Protective Procedures," Presidential Studies Quarterly 11/4 (Fall 1981): 545-558.

Discusses the role of the US Secret Service in providing presidential protection and how the Service's procedures have been changed to encourage greater cooperation with federal law enforcement and intelligence agencies.

4029. Kaiser, Frederick M. "Congressional Control of Executive Actions in the Aftermath of the Chadha Decision," Administrative Law Review 36/3 (Summer 1984): 239-276.

Considers Chadha's impact on several agencies of government, including the CIA and the FBI.

4030. Kaiser, Frederick M. "Congressional Rules and Conflict Resolution:

Access to Information in the House Select Committee on Intelligence," Congress & the Presidency 15/1 (Spring 1988): 49-73.

Discusses public law and House rules regarding access to committee information; special authority of House Intelligence Committee; establishing the House Select Committee on Intelligence; Intelligence Authorization Act of 1981; access procedures; impact and consequences; access for noncommittee members; environmental implications; and policy disputes.

4031. Kaiser, Frederick M. "Congressional Oversight of the Presidency," Annals of the American Academy of Political and Social Science 499 (September 1988): 75-89.

Discusses objectives and obstacles; the changing perception and meaning of oversight; oversight in action; and incentives, structures, and conditions.

4032. Kaiser, Frederick M. "A Proposed Joint Committee on Intelligence: New Wine In An Old Bottle," Journal of Law & Politics 5/1 (Fall 1988): 127-186.

Discusses House and Senate Committee on Intelligence; proposals for a joint committee on intelligence; pros and cons of a joint committee on intelligence; characteristics of proposed joint committee on intelligence.

4033. Kaiser, Frederick M. "Origins of Secret Service Protection of the President: Personal, Interagency, and Institutional Conflict," Presidential Studies Quarterly 18/1 (Winter 1988): 101-127.

Draws on unexplored archival and historical records to examine the formal and informal origins of the Secret Service, 1894-1909. Major sections discuss the origins of informal protection, 1894; statutory violations and the impact of two chiefs; developments in the McKinley and Theodore Roosevelt administrations; conflicts surrounding statutory proposals; and rivalry with the Bureau of Investigation.

4034. Kaiser, Frederick M. "The Watcher's Watchdog: The CIA Inspector General," International Journal of Intelligence and Counterintelligence 3/1 (Spring 1989): 55-76.

An overview of the CIA's inspector general function in the oversight process. Major sections discuss the statutory offices of inspector general in various federal agencies; the administrative office of Inspector General in the CIA; proposals surrounding the CIA Office of Inspector General; and concluding observations.

4035. Kaiser, Frederick M. "Impact and Implications of the Iran-Contra Affair on Congressional Oversight of Covert Action," International Journal of Intelligence and Counterintelligence 7/2 (Summer 1994): 205-234.

Discusses phases and implications of the Iran-Contra scandal. Major sections discuss introductory factual circumstances of the affair; the affair itself;

initial congressional inquiries, 1985-1986; follow-up oversight and investigations, 1986-1994; and reasons for change in oversight.

4036. Kaiserling, M. C. W. "Solution to Sirius Music Cipher," Cryptologia 6/3 (July 1982): 282.

4037. Kak, Subhash C. "The Study of the Indus Script: General Script," Cryptologia 11/3 (July 1987): 182-191.

4038. Kak, Subhash C. "The Aryabhata Cipher," Cryptologia 12/2 (April 1988): 113-117.

4039. Kak, Subhash C. "A Frequency Analysis of the Indus Script," Cryptologia 12/3 (July 1988): 129-143.

4040. Kak, Subhash C. "The Vararuchi Cipher," Cryptologia 14/1 (January 1990): 79-82.

4041. Kak, Subhash C. "Indus and Brahmi--Further Connections," Cryptologia 14/2 (April 1990): 169-183.

4042. Kalaris, George and Leonard McCoy. "Counterintelligence for the 1990's," International Journal of Intelligence and Counterintelligence 2/2 (Summer 1988): 179-188.
    Observes four basic functions of counterintelligence and several proposals to improve CI in the 1990s. This article was also printed in Studies in Intelligence 32/1 (Spring 1988).

4043. Kalijarvi, June D. W. and Dan Wallace, Jr. "Executive Authority to Impose Prior Restraint Upon Publication of Information Concerning National Security Affairs: A Constitutional Power," California Western Law Review 9/3 (Spring 1973): 468-496.
    Asks whether the federal executive has independent constitutional authority to impose a non-statutory restraint upon internal government documents. Discusses the First Amendment, the Executive, the balance between secrecy and disclosure, and standards for the future.

4044. Kalisch, Robert B. "Air Force Technical Intelligence," Air University Review 22/5 (July-August 1971): 2-11.
    This is a brief outline of the types of problems faced by the US Air Force technical intelligence personnel, in particular, intelligence concerning aircraft and missile targets.

4045. Kalitka, Peter F. "Counterintelligence: A Law Enforcement Function,"

American Intelligence Journal 8/2 (May 1987).

4046. Kalitka, Peter F. "Knights and Pawns: The Daniloff/Zakharov Case," American Intelligence Journal 8/2 (May 1987).

4047. Kalitka, Peter F. "The Common Denominator," American Intelligence Journal 8/3 (Summer 1987).

4048. Kalitka, Peter F. "Counterintelligence Myths Compromised," American Intelligence Journal 9/1 (March 1988).

4049. Kalitka, Peter F. "To Be Effective, Counterintelligence Double Agent Operations Need to be Centrally Controlled and Directed," American Intelligence Journal 9/3 (Fall 1988).

4050. Kalitka, Peter F. "Centralized Control of Department of Defense Counterintelligence Activities: We Try Again," American Intelligence Journal 11/3 (Summer-Fall 1990): 27-28.
    A brief argument for centralization of the DOD's counterintelligence function, including the development of a national CI doctrine, authorization for centralization, inter-operable data base, monitoring and assisting sensitive technology transfer, and expansion of interface with CIA and FBI.

4051. Kalitka, Peter F. "HUMINT for Hire," American Intelligence Journal 14/1 (Autumn-Winter 1993): 29-31.
    A brief description of the role of human intelligence in the defense environment in the post-Cold War era.

4052. Kallis, Stephen A., Jr. "The Code-O-Graph Cipher Disks," Cryptologia 5/2 (April 1981): 78-83.

4053. Kallis, Stephen A., Jr. "A Child's Garden of Cryptography," Cryptologia 6/4 (October 1982): 368-377.

4054. Kalo, Joseph J. "Deterring Misuse of Confidential Government Information: A Proposed Citizen's Action," Michigan Law Review 72 (1974): 1577-1610.
    Sections discuss misuse of confidential government information and remedies under present law, and proposed citizens action.

4055. Kalshoven, Frits. "'Guerilla' and 'Terrorism' in Internal Armed Conflict," American University Law Review 33/1 (Fall 1983): 67- 81.
    Attempts to add greater precision to distinctions between "guerilla" and "terrorism" as these words apply to conflict inside countries in turmoil. Addresses

questions of international law related to the articles of the 1949 Geneva convention.

4056. Kalugin, Oleg. "Intelligence and Foreign Policy," International Affairs (USSR) (June 1989): 56-66.

This article was also printed in Studies in Intelligence 33/4 (Winter 1989).

4057. Kalven, Harry, Jr. "The Case of J. Robert Oppenheimer Before the Atomic Energy Commission," Bulletin of the Atomic Scientists 10/7 (September 1954): 259-269, 283-286.

A detailed examination of the evidence and issues in the Oppenheimer case.

4058. Kalven, Jamie. "'Yellow Rain': The Public Evidence," Bulletin of the Atomic Scientists 38/5 (May 1982): 15-20.

Attempts to sort out the evidence as to Soviet supplies of chemical weapons in Kampuchea.

4059. Kalven, Jamie. "Security and Secrecy," Bulletin of the Atomic Scientists 38/8 (October 1982): 16-17.

Discusses President Reagan's Executive Order of December 4, 1981 on intelligence activities.

4060. Kamath, P. M. "National Security in the United States: The Organizational Factor," Indian Journal of Public Administration 27/2 (April-June 1981): 318-328.

4061. Kamath, P. M. "Changing Role of the National Security Advisor in the U.S.," Journal of the University of Bombay (1980-1984): 49-53; (1985-1989): 313-323.

An account of the National Security Council during the past thirty-five years and the influences of Truman and Eisenhower on the Council.

4062. Kamenar, Paul D. "Death Penalty Legislation for Espionage and Other Federal Crimes Is Unnecessary: It Just Needs a Little Enforcement," Wake Forest Law Review 24/2 (1989): 881-904.

Argues that the Eighth Amendment does not per se bar imposition of the death penalty in espionage cases; that the Constitution would not bar death penalty for espionage; and that case law decisions leave open the possibility of such a proposal.

4063. Kamenar, Paul D., et al. "Covert Actions in an Open Society - The Persistent Issue," Center Magazine 18/4 (July-August 1985): 10-24.

A discussion of the Reagan administration's policies toward intelligence agencies by several leading scholars in symposium format.

4064. Kamisar, Yale. "The Wiretapping-Eavesdropping Problem: A Professor's View," Minnesota Law Review 44/5 (April 1960): 891-940.
This classic treatise discusses taps, laws and society; ends versus means in eavesdropping; losses in controls over taps in the Olmstead decision; and Fourth Amendment considerations.

4065. Kampf, Herbert A. "The Challenge of Marxist-Leninist Propaganda," Political Communication and Persuasion: An International Journal 4/2 (1987): 103-122.

4066. Kapany, Narinder S. "Fiber Optics," Scientific American (November 1960): 72-81.

4067. Kapchenko, N. "Socialist Foreign Policy and International Relations," International Affairs (USSR) 10 (October 1982): 49- 55.

4068. Kaplan, H. Eliot. "Loyalty Review of Federal Employees," New York University Law Review 23 (1948): 437-448.
Reviews and evaluates the activities of the Loyalty Review Board, concluding that the Board was wasteful of resources and money.

4069. Kaplan, H. J. "Remembering Vietnam," Commentary 84/6 (December 1987): 13-29.
A lengthy reflection on the author's associations with the war in Vietnam and in reference to The Palace File by Nguyen Tien Hun and Jerrold S. Schecter. Brief discussion included on the early CIA evaluation of the quagmire of Vietnam involvement.

4070. Kaplan, David E. "A Snooper's Guide," Bill of Rights Journal 17 (December 1984): 7-12.
Provides a brief outline of what the author estimates are the roles and budgets of the major intelligence agencies of the US government and private industry.

4071. Kaplan, Leonard V. and Susan Bittker. "The Intelligence Network: A Clear and Present Danger," Human Rights 6/2 (Winter 1977): 135-154.
A discussion of two propositions concerning CIA and other department actions to collect intelligence, and the extent to which greater restrictions should be installed in law. Sections discuss covert foreign activities; covert domestic activities; CIA appropriations; and oversight of intelligence agencies.

4072. Kaplan, Matthew N. "Who Will Guard the Guardians? Independent Counsel, State Secrets, and Judicial Review," Nova Law Review 18 (Spring 1994): 1787-1861.

Discusses whether the Congress constitutionally may empower independent counsels to challenge presidential innovations of the state secrets privilege. Considers the various abuses of executive power in this regard and argues that the Congress should be empowered to adjust the balance of power between executive and legislative branches in national security matters.

4073. Kaplan, Robert D. "Greece's Disinformation Daily?," Columbia Journalism Review (November-December 1983): 5-6.

4074. Kaplan, Roger. "The Hidden War: British Intelligence Operations During the American Revolution," William and Mary Quarterly 47/1 (January 1990): 115-138.

Discusses the various methodologies of British spy work during the American revolution. Argues that British intelligence was largely ineffective, but there were some minor successes.

4075. Kaplan, Steven B. "The CIA Responds to Its Black Sheep: Censorship and Passport Revocation--The Cases of Philip Agee," Connecticut Law Review 13/2 (Winter 1981): 317-396.

Examines the backgrounds, holdings, and legal and political significance of federal court responses to CIA's efforts to curtail criticism by its former employees. Considers Agee v. CIA and Agee v. Muskie.

4076. Kaplan, Stephen S. "The Use of Military Force Abroad by the United States Since 1798: An Annotated Bibliography of Unclassified Lists of Incidents Prepared by the U.S. Government," Journal of Conflict Resolution 19/4 (1975): 708-713.

A bibliography of the use and impact of military intervention as part of US foreign policy and intelligence operations.

4077. Kapper, Francis. "Soviet Acquisition of Western Technology," Signal 37 (January 1983): 21-24, 37.

Describes Soviet efforts to acquire western technology, major areas of Soviet interest, methods of acquisition, and projected Soviet needs.

4078. Kaplan, R. "Walter Laqueur at Sixty-Five: Commentary on a World of Secrets and the Terrible Secret," Commentary 82 (1986): 72-75.

Contrast and compares A World of Secrets by Laqueur with The Terrible Secret by the same author, as well as Breaking the Silence by Laqueur and Richard Breitman. The central position is that the uses to which intelligence is put are entirely political, despite the technical or professional characteristics of the "craft of intelligence."

4079. Kapustin, M. "The CIA Against India," <u>International Affairs</u> (USSR) 51 (May 1985): 138-141.

      Summary of the contents of allegations by author P. Parakal that the CIA conducted numerous operations in India due to the nature of Indian foreign policy. Parakal's book on the allegations was published in India.

4080. Kara, Miles L. "The Strategic Intelligence Analyst," <u>Military Intelligence</u> 10/3 (July-September 1984): 10-12.

      Discusses quantum jumps in analysis and the skills needed for successful strategic analysis.

4081. Kara, Miles L. "Counterinsurgency Revisited," <u>Military Intelligence</u> 11/1 (January-March 1985): 34-36.

      Examines the roots of revolution and the ironic position of the first modern "war of liberation" country, the United States.

4082. Karabell, Zachary. "'Inside the US Espionage Den': The US Embassy and the Fall of the Shah," <u>Intelligence and National Security</u> 8/1 (January 1993): 44-59.

      Examines the information details provided to the policy making circles in Washington which appear to show that substantial information was available to the Carter administration to form a different policy toward the Shah. Points out various limitations on the senior policy community's ability to entertain several crises at the same time.

4083. Karabian, Walter. "The Case Against Wiretapping," <u>Pacific Law Journal</u> 1/1 (January 1970): 133-145.

      An argument in terms of the need for privacy; the technology of wiretaps; historical perspectives; and wiretapping following the <u>Katz</u> decision.

4084. Karalekas, Anne. "Intelligence Oversight: Has Anything Changed?," <u>Washington Quarterly</u> 6/3 (Summer 1983): 22-30.

      Reviews congressional efforts to bring oversight to the intelligence community and ponders whether or not such oversight has been effective. Sections discuss charter legislation, vigorous congressional oversight, and covert action. Suggests an even more active role of the Congress in intelligence oversight.

4085. Karas, Thomas H. "Secrecy as a Reducer of Learning Capacity in the U.S. Foreign Policy Bureaucracy," <u>Policy Studies Journal</u> 3/2 (Winter 1974): 162-166.

      A brief argument presenting anecdotal evidence of the negative impact of secrecy in foreign policy processes and outcomes.

4086. Kardong, Abe G. "High, Hot and Headin' Out," Air Force Magazine (December 1971): 49-55.

An interesting prediction that the Cold War was nearly at an end, and that the US and the USSR may well form agreements in the future to help each other.

4087. Karniel, Josef. "Heymann Kiewe: A Jewish Agent of Habsbourg Counterespionage at the Time of Emperor Joseph II," Jahrbuch des Instituts fuer Deutsche Geschichte 14 (1985): 29-74.

4088. Karpinski, Wojciech. "Agents and Exiles: The Okhrana Abroad," Survey 27/118-119 (Autumn-Winter 1983): 41-48.

4089. Kasparek, Christopher and Richard A. Woytak. "In Memoriam Marian Rejewski" and "A Conversation with Marian Rejewski," Cryptologia 6/1 (January 1982): 19-25; 50-60.

4090. Kaspi, Andre. "Le Proces de la CIA," Histoire 70 (1984): 10-21.

A French language article which addresses activities of the CIA, particularly CIA involvement in the US political system and American citizens' liberties.

4091. Kastelic, John W. "Electronic Surveillance," Georgetown Law Journal 73 (December 1984): 334-362.

This issue is the fourteenth annual review of criminal procedure, including Supreme Court and Courts of Appeals holdings on electronic surveillance.

4092. Kathpalia, P. N. "Intelligence: Problems and Possible Solutions," Indian Defence Review (January 1986): 133-135.

4093. Katkov, George. "German Foreign Office Documents on Financial Support to the Bolsheviks in 1917," International Affairs (Great Britain) 32/2 (April 1956): 181-189.

Excellent summary of the role of German Foreign Office documents in a phase of the Russian revolution.

4094. Katovich, Michale; Marion W. Weiland; and Carl J. Conch. "Access to Information and Internal Structures of Partisan Groups: Some Notes on the Iron Law of Oligarchy," Sociological Quarterly 22/3 (Summer 1981): 431-445.

A discussion of the harmony and imbalances in government management, including the use of information systems and the raising of a capable militia.

4095. Katusev, A. F. and V. G. Oppokov. "The Movement That Never

Happened, or the Story of Vlasov's Treason," Voenno-Istoricheskii Zhurnal 4 & 7 (1991): 18-28; 12-20.

4096.   Katz, Alan M.   "Government Information Leaks and the First Amendment," California Law Review 64/1 (January 1976): 108-145.

Analyzes the extent to which the First Amendment protects government employees who give information, and of the press that publishes such information. Also discusses punishment of government employees and conclusions.

4097. Katz, Amrom H. "SALT II and Verification: Adequacy and Advocacy," Military Engineer 71 (September-October 1979): 309-314.

4098. Katz, Barry M. "The Criticism of Arms: The Frankfurt School Goes to War," Journal of Modern History 59/3 (September 1987): 439-478.

Discussion of the coalition between Marxist scholars and the US government during World War II, in particular the Office of Strategic Services. Discusses the participation of Franz Neumann, Herbert Marcuse, and Otto Kirchheimer, all theoreticians of the Frankfurt Institute for Social Research.

4099. Katz, Friedrich. "Germany and Francisco Villa," Historia Mexicana 12/45 (1962): 88-102.

4100. Katz, Samuel M. "Shadow Warriors: Can the Elite Unit That Conquered Entebbe Survive Peace?," B'nai B'rith International Monthly 108 (January-February 1994): 30-32+.

4101.   Katz, Ytzhak and Ygal Vardi.   "Strategies for Data Gathering and Evaluation in the Intelligence Community," International Journal of Intelligence and Counterintelligence 5/3 (Fall 1991): 313-328.

Argues that the failure to correctly evaluate data contributes to misconceptions and misinformation, which in turn results in inappropriate intelligence community reaction. Major sections discuss ideal strategies; data and data interpretation; data distortion and interpretation; meeting between fact and theory; the scientist and the artist and types and strategies; transition between strategies; and conclusions as to specific cases under consideration in the article.

4102. Katzenbach, Nicholas de B. "Information As a Limitation on Military Legislation: A Problem in National Security," International Affairs (Great Britain) 54/8 (October 1954): 196-205.

Discusses the role of secrecy of government information in serving national security interests. Points out tradeoffs in the maintenance of an information secrecy system. Largely a defense of the secrecy systems in Western countries.

4103. Katzenbach, Nicholas de B.   "An Approach to the Problems of Wiretapping," Federal Review of Documents 32 (1963): 107+.

4104. Katzenbach, Nicholas de B. "Foreign Policy, Public Opinion and Secrecy," Foreign Affairs 52/1 (October 1973): 2-19.
       A frequently cited piece by the former Attorney General in the Johnson administration. He asserts a decline in the leadership and credibility of the president related to excesses in foreign policy and national security matters.

4105. Katzman, Jim. "Sea Spy in the Sky," Airman 27 (July 1983): 41-48.

4106. Kaufhold, Edmund. "On the Road to Diego Garcia," Naval Intelligence Professionals Quarterly 11/1 (Winter 1995): 9-11.

4107. Kaufmann, David. "Foreign Technology Division: Unlocking the Secrets of Foreign Aerospace Technology," Contact 26 (May-June 1972): 2-5.

4108. Kauffman, George R. "Intelligence in Heavy Bombardment," Military Review 26/8 (November 1946): 20-28.

4109. Kauppi, Mark V. "Strategic Beliefs and Intelligence: Dominoes and Bandwagons in the Early Cold War," Security Studies 4/1 (Autumn 1994): 4-39.
       Evaluates the analytical products of CIA and the NSC in the years of CIA operations following World War II and the opening of the cold war.

4110. Kauppi, Mark V. "Intelligence Assessments of Soviet Motivations: JIS 80 and Kennan's Long Telegram," Intelligence and National Security 9/4 (October 1994): 603-632.
       Considers the question of how US intelligence assessed the underlying motivations of Soviet foreign policy in the early Cold War period. Major sections discuss the reasoning of military intelligence; the Joint Intelligence Committee and the Joint Intelligence Staff of the Joint Chiefs of Staff; the assessment of motivation; the intelligence report JIS 80 in early 1946; domestic analysis; George Kennan's telegrams; and impact of Kennan's telegrams and JIS 80.

4111. Kawashima, Yasuhide. "Forest Diplomats: The Role of Interpreters in Indian-White Relations on the Early American Frontiers," American Indian Quarterly 13/1 (1989): 1-14.

4112. Kay, Cristobal. "Chile: The Making of a Coup d'Etat," Science and Society 39 (Spring 1975): 3-25.
       Major sections discuss the new character of the working class struggle under the Popular Unity government; the role of the opposition political parties and the Grenios in the making of the coup; and the question of the inevitability

of the coup.

4113.   Kay, David.   "Denial and Deception: Iraq and Beyond," <u>American Intelligence Journal</u> 16/1 (Spring 1995):   79-93.

4114.   Kazmer, Daniel R.   "Comment on Soviet Economic Problems and Technological Opportunities," <u>Comparative Strategy</u> 1/4 (1979):   297-305.

4115.   Kealey, Gregory S.   "The Royal Canadian Mounted Police, the Canadian Security Intelligence Service, the Public Archives of Canada, and the Access to Information: A Curious Tale," <u>Labour/Le Travail</u> 20 (Spring 1988):   199-226.
        The interactions of three Canadian public agencies: the Royal Canadian Mounted Police, the Canadian Security Intelligence Service and the Public Archives of Canada.

4116.   Kealey, Gregory S.   "State Repression of Labour and the Left in Canada," <u>Canadian Historical Review</u> 73/3 (1992):   281-314.

4117.   Kealey, Gregory S.   "The Surveillance State: The Origins of Domestic Intelligence and Counter-Subversion in Canada, 1914-21," <u>Intelligence and National Security</u> 7/3 (July 1992):   179-210.
        Attempts a reconsideration of the origins of the Royal Canadian Mounted Police.   Discusses the dominion police and the RNWMP, 1914-17; the rise and fall of C. H. Cahan, May 1918-January 1919; the re-emergence of the RNWMP, 1919; and the beginning of the end of the dominion police.

4118.   Kealey, Gregory S.   "The Early Years of State Surveillance of Labour and the Left in Canada: The Institutional Framework of the Royal Canadian Mounted Police Security and Intelligence Apparatus, 1918-26," <u>Intelligence and National Security</u> 8/3 (July 1993):   129-148.
        Continuing on the earlier article, this article discusses internal affairs of the RCMP; external relations; and conclusions.

4119.   Kearns, Michael S. and James C. Hammack.   "Present and Future Trends of Imagery Analysis -- From a Cartographer's Viewpoint," <u>American Intelligence Journal</u> 13/1&2 (Winter-Spring 1992):   47-52.
        Discusses the background and role of the Defense Mapping Agency; human cartographic imagery exploitation; remote sensor characteristics; and resolutions.

4120.   Keays, Anne C.   "Software Trade Secret Protection," <u>Software Law Journal</u> 4 (December 1991):   577-595.
        Explores modern trade secrets law as to how the law applies to computer software.   Discusses Restatement of Torts and Uniform Trade Secrets Act;

demonstrates the potential loss of trade secrets protection and remedies for such losses; and examines applications of Restatement and the Act to trade secrets protection in Europe and Japan.

4121. Keefe, Robert. "A Cold War Elegy," Massachusetts Review 24 (Winter 1983): 705-718.
　　　Mentions cold war aerial reconnaissance by the US and the USSR, military intelligence, espionage and the casualties of the cold war.

4122. Keegan, George J. "Concern for Free World Security--Letter to a Friend," Strategic Review 5/2 (1977): 6-11.

4123. Keegan, John. "Jutland," MHQ: The Quarterly Journal of Military History 1/2 (Winter 1989): 110-112.

4124. Keen, M. H. "Treason Trials under the Law of Arms," Transactions of the Royal Historical Society 12 (1962): 95-97.

4125. Kees, Terry S. "Advanced Information Processing and Analysis," American Intelligence Journal 13/3 (Summer 1992): 53-58.
　　　Major topics under consideration are current analytic emphasis at CIA; background and mission of the AIPASG; process and activities; the analysis symposium; challenges; current emphasis and future.

4126. Keesing, Hugo A. "The Defense Intelligence College Comes of Age," Military Intelligence 10/3 (July-September 1984): 26-28.
　　　Explains the history of the DIC, what it offers to the intelligence professional, and how it plans to expand.

4127. Keesing, Hugo A. "Defense Intelligence College: Winning the Silent War," Military Intelligence 12/1 (January-March 1986): 27-28.
　　　Provides an overview of the mission and functions of the DIC. A similar article appeared as "Strategic Intelligence Goes to College: A Look at the Defense Intelligence College Today," American Intelligence Journal 7/3 (January 1986).

4128. Kehm, Harold D. "The Essential Elements of Information and the Intelligence Plan," Military Review 26/6 (June 1946): 51-52.
　　　A brief discussion of EEI in the production of intelligence instructions for the field. Sections discuss the reasons for EEI and the intelligence plan; the use of EEI; and the author's conclusions.

4129. Kehm, Harold D. and Page Smith. "Intelligence Objectives," Military Review 28/5 (May 1948): 53-57

4130. Kellen, Konrad. "War on the Mind: A Commentary," <u>Armed Forces and Society</u> 6/2 (June 1980): 313-325.

A discussion of the mental reactions to warfare, primarily in consideration of World War II and the Vietnam war. Useful in analyses of the psychological strengths and weaknesses of armies.

4131. Keller, Fritz and Elisabeth Hirt. "The CIA As Maecenas; or, How Autonomous Is Autonomous Art?," <u>Zeitgeschichte</u> 13/9-10 (1986): 311-318.

4132. Kelley, Clarence M. "Protecting Our National Community," <u>Judicature</u> 59/4 (November 1975): 192-196.

Text of a speech to the American Judicature Society by a former director of the FBI. Contains general words about the role of the FBI in national security and standards FBI has sought to maintain.

4133. Kelley, Clarence M. "Domestic Industrial Espionage," <u>Security Management</u> 19 (November 1975): 1-3.

The director of the Federal Bureau of Investigation comments on the dangers of industrial spying.

4134. Kelley, Kim L. "The Foreign Intelligence Surveillance Act of 1978," <u>Vanderbilt Journal of Transnational Law</u> 13 (Fall 1980): 719-760.

Explores the constitutional backgrounds, legislative history and content of the Act. Relates the constitutional issues and expands upon possible amendments to FISA. Concludes that the Act clarified a confusing area of law relating to acquisition and control of electronic surveillance activities.

4135. Kelley, Michael F. "The Constitutional Implications of the Mayaguez Incident," <u>Hastings Constitutional Law Quarterly</u> 3/1 (Winter 1976): 301-338.

Argues that President Ford's use of the Navy and the Marine Corps in a military retaliation violated his constitutional and statutory war-making authority. May be useful in studies of National Security Council response, and parallels with Liberty and Pueblo incidents.

4136. Kellman, Steven G. "The Fearful Symmetry of John LeCarre," <u>Georgia Review</u> 37/4 (Winter 1983): 905-911.

A book review essay in consideration of LeCarre's novel, <u>The Little Drummer Girl</u>.

4137. Kellner, Peter. "The Lobby, Official Secrets and Good Government," <u>Parliamentary Affairs</u> 36/3 (Summer 1983): 275-281.

Argues the view that the press should be an adversary of government. Suggests that secrecy of government is enhanced by journalists who are too tight with government agencies. Mentions the Official Secrets Act.

4138. Kelly, G. A. "From Lese-Majeste to Lese-Nation: Treason in Eighteenth Century France," Journal of the History of Ideas 42/2 (April-June 1981): 269-286.

Extensive discussion of the history of treason in France and England. Discusses the ideology of Lese-Majeste under the Bourbons; the concept of Lese-Nation, an offense against the king or other sovereign; the human Lese-Majeste; and the situation of treason after July 1789.

4139. Kelly, George A. "Revolutionary War and Psychological Action," Military Review 40/10 (October 1960): 4-13.

4140. Kelly, John J. "Intelligence and Counter-Intelligence in German Prisoner-of-War Camps in Canada During World War II," Dalhousie Review 48/2 (Summer 1978): 285-294.

A study of the Psychological Warfare Committee set up in Canada to reeducate German prisoners held by the British. The purposes were to reduce the ideological purity of those soldiers who continued to follow Hitlerian doctrines and to reduce the effectiveness of the Gestapo in acquiring a post-war murder squad for prisoners returned to Germany.

4141. Kelly, Joseph B. "Assassination in War Time," Military Law Review 30 (1965): 101-111.

Author reviews the elements of assassination; and killings by assassination and ruses in international and internal conflicts. Offers conclusions.

4142. Kelly, Krysten C. "Warrantless Satellite Surveillance: Will Our 4th Amendment Privacy Rights Be Lost in Space?," John Marshall Journal of Computer & Information Law 13 (Summer 1995): 729-762.

4143. Kelly, Paul X. "Coastal Infiltration and Withdrawal," Studies in Intelligence 7/1 (Spring 1963).

4144. Kelly, Peter A. "Raids and National Command: Mutually Exclusive," Historical Review 60 (April 1980): 19-26.

Discusses the contexts in which two raids were conducted: Sontay and Mayaguez. Argues that the plans for these raids suffered from too much military bureaucracy by ponderous staffs.

4145. Kelly, Ross S. "The Real Stories Behind Those Intelligence 'Failures,'" Army 32 (January 1982): 10-16.

Argues that intelligence failures have more generally been attributed to "failure to use" and/or "failure to believe" on the part of senior decision makers. Information is frequently available, but excessive filtration and interpretation cause narrowing of perspective and options.

4146. Kelly, Stephen D. "Neglect and Trendiness," Defense Intelligence Journal 4/1 (Spring 1995): 91-97.

Argues that the counterintelligence function within the larger intelligence community comes into focus during major espionage cases, such as the case of Aldrich Ames, but the real need is to develop a sustained legal and operational approach to CI. Offers solutions to the problem of non-fit between law and operational regulations.

4147. Kelly, William E. "Soviet Intelligence Since World War II--A Survey of the Literature," New Review of East European History 15/3-4 (March 1976): 67-77.

Focusses on selected works that shed light on the Soviet intelligence apparatus, mainly the KGB. Summarizes the contents of several books on the subject. Considers Soviet espionage; secret police; recruitment; and the goal of intelligence systems.

4148. Kelsey, Rayner W. "The United States Consulate in California," Academy of Pacific Coast History 1/5 (1910).

4149. Kemp, Jack. "International Waterways and Soviet Strategy," Journal of Social and Political Studies 2/4 (Winter 1977): 227-233.

Argues that the Soviets continue to be capable of learning what transpires at every international water passageway. Reflecting upon advanced technologies in the hands of the Soviets, the author discusses the Straight of Gibraltar, the Suez Canal and the Red Sea, the Cape of Good Hope, and the Panama Canal.

4150. Kemp, Percy. "An Eighteenth-Century Turkish Intelligence Report," International Journal of Middle East Studies 16/4 (November 1984): 497-506.

A brief discussion of the subject in terms of general intelligence operations of the Turks; background of Turkish intelligence operations; the Aztec intelligence network; the study of intelligence behavior; the Nizamname-I Misir and its aims and targets.

4151. Kemp, Percy. "The Fall and Rise of France's Spymasters," Intelligence and National Security 9/1 (January 1994): 12-21.

Discusses French intelligence services between the two world wars. The French services were beset with problems, based principally on major political and social changes in French society. Other factors included political weaknesses, scandals and vendettas which underscored the poor foundations left after the Nigerian war.

4152. Kempner, Robert M. W. "The German National Registration System as Means of Police Control of Population," Journal of Criminal Law and Criminology 36/5 (January-February 1946): 362-387.

Synopsis of the situation in Germany during the Nazi regime; the police registration system; other comprehensive registration systems; specialized registration systems; identification papers; and a comparison between the US and German systems.

4153. Kendall, Willmoore. "The Function of Intelligence," World Politics 1/4 (July 1949): 542-552.

A frequently cited and classic review essay on Sherman Kent's own classic book, Strategic Intelligence. The author argues against the then prevailing view of the functions and roles of intelligence service.

4154. Kenden, Anthony. "U.S. Reconnaissance Satellite Programs," Spaceflight 20/7 (July 1978): 243-262.

An extensive report upon American satellite programs, their designs, and their lifespans. Sections include discussion of the beginnings of surveillance, weapons system 117L, Discoverer program, area survey satellites, close-look satellites, "Big Bird" program, Ferrat satellites, sensors, and payoff.

4155. Kennan, George F. "The Sisson Documents," Journal of Modern History 28 (June 1956): 130-154.

Discusses the 1917-18 Committee of Public Information, the official US propaganda organization stationed in Petrograd, Russia. Sections discuss the nature and background of the Sisson documents; evidence as to the authenticity; lack of accord with normal governmental usage; technical aspects; the real origins of the documents; and appendices.

4156. Kennan, George F. "Soviet Historiography and America's Role in the Intervention," American Historical Review 65 (January 1960): 302-322.

Argues that Soviet and Western historians do not differ widely on the early history of Soviet foreign relations. He suggests that each country could benefit from open dialogue on the foreign policy perspectives of other nations. Useful in analyses of covert actions.

4157. Kennan, George F. "Morality and Foreign Policy," Foreign Affairs 64/2 (Winter 1985-1986): 205-218.

Argues that the relationship between moral considerations and American foreign policy introduces several problems and distinctions. Sections discuss US government expected actions in other countries; and positive imperatives. Useful in discussions of interventions into the internal affairs of other nations, perhaps by means of covert action.

4158. Kennan, George F. and John Lukaks. "From World War to Cold War," American Heritage 45/8 (December 1995): 42-44, 50, 52, 54, 56, 58-60, 62, 64-67.

4159. Kennedy, C. "Army Signaling and its Use in War," Journal of the Royal United Services Institution 41 (1897).

One of the earliest serial journal discussions of message encryption security. From the author's perspective, encrypted messages were safe from compromise.

4160. Kennedy, J. de N. "Hard Cases Make Bad Law," Chitty's Law Journal 15 (January 1967): 1-12.

Discusses the defection to Canada of a Soviet cipher clerk, Igor Gouzenko. Topics include the protest by the Soviet embassy, Gouzenko's information, the Soviet intelligence service, the response of the Royal Canadian Mounted Police, and related matters.

4161. Kennedy, P. M. "Imperial Cable Communications and Strategy, 1870-1914," English Historical Journal 86 (1971): 728-752.

Discussion of the insecurity of the British at the end of the nineteenth century in terms of an inability to acquire information about other parts of the world. Sections discuss the invention of the telegraph; the international neutralization pact; the invention of undersea cables by Hicks Beach; the cutting of strategic cables in wartime; and the invention of the wireless telegraph.

4162. Kennedy, Walter P. "The Pattern of an Intelligence Service," Public Administration 26/1 (Spring 1948): 31-36.

A brief discussion of the administrative criteria applicable to organizing an intelligence activity; aims of an intelligence service; mechanics of operation; and physical machinery.

4163. Kennett, Lee. "Charleston in 1778: A French Intelligence Report," South Carolina History Magazine 66/2 (1965): 109-111.

This undated and unsigned report has been determined to have been written in 1778, associated with the fire in Charleston, South Carolina. The letter was written to inform the French Ministry of War of the conditions in Charleston.

4164. Kennett, Lee. "A French Report on St. Augustine in the 1770's," Florida Historical Quarterly 44/1-2 (1965): 133-135.

A brief description of a French officer's report on the fortification at St. Augustine prior to the fall of Charleston and Savannah. The report details the St. Augustine fort; the means of entry into the fort; and the local population.

4165. Kennett, Lee. "French Military Intelligence," Military Affairs (Winter 1965-1966): 201-204.

Evaluation of the French deployment of an intelligence service in the Seven Years War. Considers the two levels of military intelligence; the function of the cavalry; the collation of information; the security of French armies; and the interception of letters from the field.

4166. Kenny, Gerard T. "The 'National Security Wiretap': Presidential Prerogative or Judicial Responsibility?," Southern California Law Review 45/3 (Summer 1972): 888-913.

Argues that the Fourth Amendment permits no exemption for national security wiretaps. Compares the national security wiretap with the traditional rationale for warrantless searches.

4167. Kent, George O. "Pope Pius XII and Germany: Some Aspects of German-Vatican Relations 1933-1943," American Historical Review 70 (October 1964): 59-78.

Explores the relationship between the Nazi Germany and the Vatican. Outlines the apparent advocation of the Nazi "final solution" relative to Jewish population, as reported by Nazi diplomats. Argues that the Pope's fear of Bolshevism outweighed his need to condemn national socialism and fascism. Criticizes the Vatican's inaction as shameful.

4168. Kent, Irving M. "Legal Support Requirements for Civil Affairs Operations in Counterinsurgency," Military Law Review 30 (1965): 112-119.

A basic outline of the civil affairs role in counterinsurgency.

4169. Kent, Irvin M. and Ruth A. Caldwell. "A Stitch in Time," Military Review 48/6 (1968): 69-74.

Discusses United States military intelligence service training of certain foreign intelligence services.

4170. Kent, Robert J. "Wiretapping: Morality and Legality," Houston Law Review 2/3 (Winter 1965): 285-327.

A discussion of the extent and usefulness of wiretapping; efficacy versus morality; the law relevant to wiretapping; and predictions and suggestions.

4171. Kent, Sherman. "Prospects for the National Intelligence Service," Yale Review 36 (September 1946): 116-130.

A careful review of the creation of a centralized intelligence system between 1945 and 1946.

4172. Kent, Sherman. "The Need for An Intelligence Literature," Studies in Intelligence 1/1 (Fall 1955): 1-8.

This classic article argues that the intelligence field had become a profession, thus necessitating the development of a sophisticated literature. See "Late Entries" collection for an additional article by the a same author in the same issue.

4173. Kent, Sherman. "A Crucial Estimate Relived," <u>Studies in Intelligence</u> 8/1 (Spring 1964): 1-18.

This is the author's recognition of his underestimations of Soviet determination to install missile sites and weapons in Cuba in the weeks before the missile crisis of 1962. Reprinted in 36/5 (1992): 111-119. Major sections discuss the estimating machine; the search into uncertainty; the matter of mental set; the data on Cuba; the logic of intent; ways out we did not take; why no revision?; the enemy's viewpoint; the determinants of action; and whence the decisive intelligence?

4174. Kent, Sherman. "Words of Estimative Probability," <u>Studies in Intelligence</u> 8/3 (Fall 1964).

4175. Kent, Sherman. "Death of an Hypothesis," <u>Studies in Intelligence</u> 9/1 (Spring 1965).

4176. Kent, Sherman. "Estimates and Influence," <u>Studies in Intelligence</u> 12/2 (Summer 1968).

Also appeared in <u>Foreign Service Journal</u> 46/5 (April 1969): 16-18, 45.

4177. Kent, Sherman. "Valediction," <u>Studies in Intelligence</u> 12/4 (Winter 1968).

4178. Kent, Sherman. "Allen Welsh Dulles," <u>Studies in Intelligence</u> 13/1 (Spring 1969).

4179. Kent, Sherman. "Estimates and Influence: Some Reflections on What Should Make Intelligence Persuasive in Policy Deliberations," <u>Foreign Service Journal</u> 46/4 (April 1969): 16-18, 45.

A classic article by a former OSS chief of research and analysis. Discusses the credibility of intelligence, the nature of the estimate, the policy welcome, and the defense.

4180. Kent, Sherman. "Elector Lists of France's July Monarchy, 1830-1848," <u>French Historical Studies</u> 7 (Spring 1971): 117-127.

4181. Kent, Sherman. "The Cuban Missile Crisis of 1962: Presenting the Photographic Evidence Abroad," <u>Studies in Intelligence</u> 16/1 (Spring 1972).

4182. Kent, Sherman. "The Yale Report," <u>Studies in Intelligence</u> 17/2 (Summer 1973).

4183. Kenworthy, Eldon. "United States Policy in Central America: A Choice Denied," <u>Current History</u> 84/500 (March 1985): 97-100; 137-138.

Discusses the apparent contradictory policies of the US government in working toward peace in El Savador and Nicargua, including Central Intelligence Agency activities approved by the Reagan administration to undermine the Sandinistas.

4184. Kenyon, Dorothy. "Wiretapping," New York Law Forum 6 (1960): 283-299.

4185. Kerber, Linda K. "The Paradox of Women's Citizenship in the Early Republic: The Case of Martin vs. Massachusetts, 1805," American Historical Review 97 (April 1992): 349-378.
　　　　Includes brief discussion of treason associated with this legal case.

4186. Kerbo, Harold R. "Foreign Involvement in the Preconditions for Political Violence: The World Condition and the Case of Chile," Journal of Conflict Resolution 22 (September 1978): 363-391.
　　　　Discusses the Chilean civil war and the government of Augusto Pinochet. Focus is on the gradual erosion of people's support for Pinochet, based largely on authoritarian policies and massive corruption.

4187. Kerby, Robert L. "American Military Airlift During the Laotian Civil War, 1958-1963," Aerospace Historian 24/1 (November 1977): 1-10.
　　　　US intervention to save civilian lives in Laos is the focus of this article. Discusses a government shakeup and the political aspects of the intervention.

4188. Kercher, David. "Intelligence Production's Future Shock," American Intelligence Journal 16/2&3 (Autumn-Winter 1995): 51-53.

4189. Kermish, J. "The [Warsaw] Ghetto's Two-Front Struggle," Yad Vashem Bulletin 13 (October 1963): 12-15.

4190. Kerr, Sheila. "Familiar Fiction, not the Untold Story," Intelligence and National Security 9/1 (January 1994): 128-135.
　　　　A book review essay of Maclean and Alger Hiss, the Double Whammy. Concludes that the author, Verne Newton, crafted an account that must remain speculative until conclusions about the impact of Maclean and Hiss have been thoroughly tested against credible evidence.

4191. Kerr, Sheila. "The Debate on U.S. Post-Cold War Intelligence: One More New Botched Beginning?," Defense Analysis 10/3 (December 1994): 323-350.

4192. Kerrick, Donald L. "5 Rules for the Intelligence Officer," Military Intelligence 16/4 (1990): 36-37.

4193. Kerstetter, Wayne A. "Terrorism and Intelligence," Terrorism: An

<u>International Journal</u> 3/1 & 2 (1979): 109-115.

A brief analysis of the problem of terrorism and the role of intelligence processes engaged to develop solutions through applications from scientific methods. Emphasizes the role of the analytic process, the heart of intelligence.

4194. Keshen, Jeff. "Cloak and Dagger: Canada West's Secret Police, 1864-1867," <u>Ontario History</u> 79/4 (1987): 353-381.

4195. Kessick, P. D. "Close Gaps in Tactical Intelligence," <u>Marine Corps Gazette</u> 60 (September 1976): 45-46.

4196. Kesting, Robert W. "Espionage During the Texas Revolution," <u>East Texas Historical Journal</u> 30/1 (1992): 22-33.

4197. Ketchum, Richard M. "The Thankless Task of Nicholas Trist," <u>American Heritage</u> 21/8 (August 1970): 12-15, 86-90.

Rich discussion of Trist's role in conducting secret peace talks with Mexico in 1847. Includes discussion of President Polk's use of secrecy in the negotiations.

4198. Keunings, Luc. "The Secret Police in Nineteenth-Century Brussels," <u>Intelligence and National Security</u> 4/1 (January 1989): 59-85.

Major topics considered include: the structures of the police in the 1830s; goals and targeted groups; police methods; and conclusions.

4199. Keyser, F. G. "The Different Systems of Signalling in the Field," <u>Journal of the Royal United Service Institution</u> 37 (1893).

4200. Keyserlingk, Robert H. "The Canadian Government's Attitude Toward Germans and German Canadian's in World War II," <u>Canadian Ethnic Studies</u> 16/1 (September 1984): 16-28.

Discusses immigration policies of Canada and the US during and immediately after World War II. Observes a contradiction in Canadian toleration of German immigration and internment of citizens of Japanese extraction in Canada and the US. Covers the Immigration Act of 1952.

4201. Keyserlingk, Robert H. "'Agents Within the Gates': The Search for Nazi Subversives in Canada During World War II," <u>Canadian Historical Review</u> 66/2 (June 1985): 211-239.

An account of the Canadian government's attempt to suppress the Nazi threat within Canada's borders during World War II.

4202. KGB. "Albania," <u>Intelligence and National Security</u> 7/1 (January 1992): 41-45.

A translated Soviet document produced by the KGB; a discussion of the KGB's intelligence objectives in Albania in the 1970s. Considers Albanian loyalty to China and/or the US.

Also appearing in this issue are other translated documents, as follows:

"The Arctic, the Antarctic and the World's Oceans," 53-65.

The focus of the KGB on the Arctic during the 1970s, particularly in terms of Western oil interests in the area.

"Africa," 66-67.

Argues that the Soviets were losing influence in the sub Saharan region of Africa due to US efforts.

"Asia," 68-81.

Discusses targets of the People's Republic of China in Hong Kong, such as business organizations, foreign missions, British special intelligence services, and Hong Kong scientific institutes. Discusses KGB efforts to collect intelligence on the PRC by way of Hong Kong.

"Ciphers and Counter-Intelligence," 99-121.

Outlines KBG methods for protecting secret cipher services located abroad, and measures to improve counterintelligence for all operations.

"The Federal Republic of Germany (FRG)," 37-40.

Claims that the KGB had operated an effective penetration of the FRG for several years after successes in the United Kingdom were reduced.

"The Middle East," 82-88.

Suggests that Egypt is a secure base from which to run KGB operations. Says the Egyptian intelligence and political systems have been penetrated by the KGB.

"Military Priorities," 14-24.

Refers to the KGB's main global mission during the early 1980s, and its main concerns for its adversaries. Lists questions on which overseas KGB collection operations were to be focussed.

"Residency Priorities: The Case of Denmark," 25-36.

Says that KGB residencies operated against the US, NATO, China, and the host countries.

"The Threat from the 'Main Adversary,'" 122-128.

Discusses the FCD's intensification of counterintelligence against the US, fearing 'ideological sabotage' as the main threat.

"The United States: The 'Main Adversary,'" 1-13.

The determination of the KGB to penetrate the military special services on the basis of their role in US political, strategic, and operational intelligence.

"The Vatican," 46-52.

Suggests that the KGB took an interest in the 'subversive ideology' of the Vatican and stepped up operations to determine any Vatican operations against the Soviet Union.

"Zionism and Israel," 89-98.

Discusses the strong Anti-Semitic sentiments remaining from the Stalin era which leave the KGB with an anti-Zionist agenda. Discusses KGB plans to recruit Jews who may have been disenchanted with the West, and to keep the intelligence on zionist lobbyists in capitalist countries.

4203. Khalilzad, Zalmay. "Soviet-Occupied Afghanistan," Problems of Communism 29 (November-December 1980): 23-40.

4204. Khan, Anwar N. "The Cuban Crisis of 1962 and International Law," Pakistan Horizon 29/4 (1976): 73-84.

4205. Khariton, Yuli and Yuri Smirnov. "The Khariton Version," Bulletin of the Atomic Scientists 49 (May 1993): 20-31.
Detailed consideration of the dynamics of the Soviet atom bomb project, noting the role of espionage in acquisition from the US of design details. The purpose of the article is partly to clear up certain popularly held beliefs about the Soviet efforts to construct an atom bomb and a hydrogen bomb.

4206. Khokhlov, Nikolai. "Cold-Blooded Murder Is Part of Russia's Cold War in the West," American Mercury 79 (September 1954): 144-157.

4207. Khvostov, V. and A. Grylev. "On the Eve of the Great Patriotic War," Kommunist 12 (August 1968): 56-71.
A denial that the Kremlin overlooked warnings of BARBAROSSA in 1941.

4208. Kiele, William A. "A Tensor-Theoretic Enhancemen to the Hill Cipher System," Cryptologia 14/3 (July 1990): 225-233.

4209. Kiely, Stephen J. "Warrantless Electronic Surveillance in Massachusetts," Massachusetts Law Review 67 (Fall 1982): 183-193.
The author, a practicing attorney, discusses the Massachusetts wiretap statute; constitutional limitations and unresolved problems.

4210. Kiger, John. "Federal Governmental Propaganda in Great Britain During the American Civil War," Historical Outlook 19/5 (May 1928).

4211. Killinger, Charles. "Gaetano Salvemini and the American Authorities: Unpublished Federal Bureau of Investigation Documents," Storia Contemporanea 12/3 (1981): 403-439.
A study of Salvemini's associations with the FBI and an assessment of the extent to which he may have collaborated in anti-Fascist policies of the US government.

4212. Killingray, David. "The Maintenance of Law and Order in British Colonial Africa," African Affairs 85/340 (July 1986): 411-437.

Discusses the two pillars of law and order in colonial Africa: authority of administration and collection of revenue. Explores these pillars and the execution of law and order policies in the colonies. Argues that as the balance of power shifted to the African nations, political influences tainted the new police forces. The framework of British-style law and order practices, however, remains in modern Africa.

4213. Killough, J. S. "Internal Security in a Communications Zone," Military Review 30/7 (October 1950): 47-55.

Discusses dynamics of internal security at the beginning of the Korean War, including administration and congressional actions to label certain government employees alleged to have pro-communist sympathies.

4214. Kilpatrick, Larry (pseud.). "Profile of US Intelligence in Southeast Asia," Covert Action Information Bulletin 5 (July-August 1979): 4-9.

4215. Kimbal, Alan. "The Harassment of Russian Revolutionaries Abroad: The London Trial of Vladimir Burtsev in 1898," Oxford Slavonic Papers 6 (1973): 48-65.

4216. Kimball, Day. "The Espionage Act and the Limits of Legal Toleration," Harvard Law Review 33/3 (January 1920): 442-449.

Some brief legal reflections upon the espionage cases prosecuted during World War I.

4217. Kimball, Warren F. and Bruce Bartlett. "Roosevelt and Prewar Commitments to Churchill: The Tyler Kent Affair," Diplomatic History 5/4 (Fall 1981): 291-311.

Discussion of the arrest and prosecution of Tyler Kent in 1940 for violation of the British Official Secrets Act. Examines the media coverage of the case and an article about its implications by Richard Whalen.

4218. Kimery, Anthony L. "CIA: Banking on Intelligence," Covert Action Quarterly 46 (Fall 1993): 55-62.

Argues that the Central Intelligence Agency has been involved in the collection and analysis of economic intelligence for a considerable period of time, probably since its inception. Discusses recent attempts of the CIA to justify further work in this area and points out the corrupting influences of the close associations with industry beneficiaries of CIA work. A footnote indicates that "This article draws on classified U.S. government documents which the author made available to CAQ for verification."

4219. Kincade, William H. "Over the Technological Horizon," Daedalus 110/1 (Winter 1981): 105-127.

Examines technological developments, including intelligence-related items, for the next twenty years, and discusses the implications for devices for force planning and budgeting.

4220. Kinder, Douglas C. "Bureaucratic Cold Warrior: Harry J. Anslinger and Illicit Narcotics Traffic," Pacific Historical Review 50 (May 1981): 169-191.

Argues that Harry Anslinger seized an opportunity to build the Federal Bureau of Narcotics by raising the specter of international importation of drugs. Discusses various sources of drug importation from Italy and the Mafia, China and Japan. Anslinger operated a sophisticated drug intelligence operation which served as the source for his argument and upon which several pieces of state and federal legislation were based.

4221. Kinder, Douglas C. and William O. Walker, III. "Stable Force in a Storm: Harry J. Anslinger and United States Narcotic Foreign Policy, 1930-1962," Journal of American History 72/4 (March 1986): 908-927.

A detailed and rich history of Anslinger's role in establishing and sustaining the Federal Bureau of Narcotics, including his collection and analysis of narcotics intelligence.

4222. King, David E. "Intelligence Failures and the Falklands War: A Reassessment," Intelligence and National Security 2/2 (April 1987): 336-340.

Brief consideration of the the limits of intelligence in relationship to events in the Falklands war.

4223. King, Donald B. "Wiretapping and Electronic Surveillance: A Neglected Constitutional Consideration," Dickinson Law Review 66 (Fall 1961): 17-38.

Presents the basic question pertaining to electronic surveillance; rationale of the Supreme Court in Olmstead; evaluation of the Court's rationale; constitutional rights under Fourth and Fifth Amendments; the balancing of interests; and the answer to the basic question.

4224. King, Donald B. "Electronic Surveillance and Constitutional Rights: Some Recent Developments and Observations," George Washington Law Review 33/1 (October 1964): 240-269.

Discusses changing technology of electronic surveillance; recent legal developments; and the quest for an answer to the question of whether or not there is a right of privacy in the face of surveillance devices.

4225. King, Donald L. "The Legal Status of the Attorney General's 'List,'" California Law Review 44/4 (October 1956): 748-761.

Discusses the position of listed groups, effect of membership in listed groups and conclusions. Numerous internal security programs of the federal government are discussed.

4226. King, Henry R. "Big Brother, the Holding Company: A Review of Key-Escrow Encryption Technology," Rutgers Computer & Technology Law Journal 21 (1995): 224-262.

4227. King, John C. "A Reconstruction of the Key to Beale Cipher Number Two," Cryptologia 17/3 (July 1993): 305-317.

4228. King, John C. "An Algorithm for the Complete Automated Cryptanalysis of Periodic Polyalphabetic Substitution Ciphers," Cryptologia 18/4 (October 1994): 332-355.

4229. King, John C. and Dennis R. Bahler. "An Implementation of Probabilistic Relaxation in the Cryptanalysis of Simple Substitution Ciphers," Cryptologia 16/3 (July 1992): 215-225.

4230. King, John C. and Dennis R. Bahler. "A Framework for the Study of Homophonic Ciphers in Classical Encryption and Genetic Systems," Cryptologia 17/1 (January 1993): 45-54.

4231. King, John C. and Dennis R. Bahler. "An Algorithmic Solution of Sequential Homophonic Ciphers," Cryptologia 18/2 (April 1993): 148-165.

4232. King, Robert D. "Treason and Traitors," Society 26/5 (July-August 1989): 39-48.

A discussion of elements which might be considered in answering such questions as "What makes people betray their country? When is treason justified? What is treason? What are the limits of the claim the state is entitled to make on a citizen's allegiance? Compares characters of treasonous individuals found in novels as well as recent non-fiction accounts.

4233. Kingsley, J. Donald. "Spies and Saboteurs," Current History 2 (August 1942): 426-430.

Discusses contemporaneous cases of espionage and attempted sabotage, evolving from, says the author, a Fascist Fifth Column philosophy.

4234. Kingston, Robert C. "C³I and the U.S. Central Command," Signal 38 (November 1983): 23-25.

4235. Kinnard, Douglas. "Vietnam Reconsidered: An Attitudinal Survey of Army General Officers," Public Opinion Quarterly 39/4 (Winter 1975-1976): 445-456.

Reflects author's survey results of 173 US Army general officers who served in Vietnam from 1965 to 1972 as to the generals' perceptions of media coverage of the war.

4236. Kinnard, Harry W. "Narrowing the Combat Intelligence Gap with STANO [Surveillance, Target Acquisition, and Night Observation] Equipment," Army 19/8 (August 1969): 22-26.
A description of target acquisition equipment deployed in the Vietnam war.

4237. Kinnucan, Paul. "Data Encryption Gurus," Cryptologia 2/4 (October 1978): 371-381.

4238. Kinsley, Michael and Arthur Lubow. "Alger Hiss and the Smoking Gun Fallacy," Washington Monthly 7/8 (October 1975): 52-60.
Urges new consideration of the facts and investigation into the Alger Hiss and Rosenberg cases in light of the scandals of the Nixon administration.

4239. Kintner, William R. "The Men Behind the Intelligence Estimate," Infantry Journal 64/5 (May 1949): 8-9.
The author's characterization of the importance of military intelligence estimation and training of intelligence units.

4240. Kipf, Kari B. "Constitutional Law--Limitations on Police Powers to Conduct Investigatory Stop Based on Anonymous Informant's Telephone Tip," Suffolk University Law Review 25 (Winter 1991): 1252-1259.
Refers to a Massachusetts case, Commonwealth v. Lyons, regarding an informant tip in a drug transaction in which evidence was suppressed as the basis of inadequacy of certification of the informant.

4241. Kirchman, Charles V. "The Message to Garcia: Anatomy of a Famous Mission," Mankind 4/9 (1974): 46-53.
Attempts to clarify the facts in the case of US lieutenant Andrew Rowan's mission to Cuba.

4242. Kirgis, Frederic L., Jr. "Some Comments on Professor Rodes' Draft Convention," Washington and Lee Law Review 39/2 (Spring 1982): 373-376.
A response to Rodes' "On Clandestine Warfare" (see this bibliography). Kirgis' primary criticism is, "In his concern for giving clandestine forces the authority to ply their trade ... he makes their failure to distinguish themselves from noncombatants neither a war crime nor a cause for forfeiture of prisoner-of-war status."

4243. Kirkpatrick, Jeane. "William J. Casey," Studies in Intelligence 31/1

(Spring 1987).

4244. Kirkpatrick, Lyman B., Jr. "Origins, Missions, and Structure of CIA," Studies in Intelligence 2 (Winter 1958).

4245. Kirkpatrick, Lyman B., Jr. "Unrecognized Potential in the Military Attaches," Studies in Intelligence 4/1 (Spring 1960).

4246. Kirkpatrick, Lyman B., Jr. "United States Intelligence," Military Review 41/5 (May 1961): 18-22.

4247. Kirkpatrick, Lyman B., Jr. "Combat Intelligence: A Comparative Evaluation," Studies in Intelligence 5/3 (Fall 1961).

4248. Kirkpatrick, Lyman B., Jr. "The Politics of Communist Confrontation: The Cuban Case History," Naval War College Review 20/7 (March 1968): 30-42.

4249. Kirkpatrick, Lyman B., Jr. "The Politics of Communist Confrontation: The Intelligence Organization," Naval War College Review 20/9 (May 1968): 61-70.
    Discussion of the Russian intelligence system.

4250. Kirkpatrick, Lyman B., Jr. "The Politics of Communist Confrontation: Communism in Latin America," Naval War College Review 20/10 (June 1968): 3-10.

4251. Kirkpatrick, Lyman B., Jr. "The Politics of Communist Confrontation: Communism in Africa," Naval War College Review 21/1 (September 1968): 33-42.
    Evaluates in brief terms the role of communist infiltration in each of the African nations. Covers strategies and popular front movements.

4252. Kirkpatrick, Lyman B., Jr. "The Spy With the Old School Tie," Transaction 6 (January 1969): 57-58.

4253. Kirkpatrick, Lyman B., Jr. "Insurgency: Origins and the Nature of the Beast," Naval War College Review 23/9 (May 1971): 67-75.
    Explores the history and developments in world insurgency movements in the last half of the twentieth century. A lecture given at the Naval War College.

4254. Kirkpatrick, Lyman B., Jr. "Paramilitary Case Study, The Bay of Pigs," Naval War College Review 25/2 (November-December 1972): 32-42.
    Discusses the defects in intelligence thinking which ultimately led to the

US involvement in the Bay of Pigs invasion. Emphasizes the importance of intelligence community education of the policy makers.

4255. Kirkpatrick, Lyman B., Jr. "If You Don't Have a 'Need to Know,' Don't Snoop," Intelligence and National Security 1/1 (Spring 1986).

4256. Kirkwood, R. Cort. "Wall Street and the KGB: A Corporate Connection," International Freedom Review 2/3 (Spring 1989): 29- 39.

4257. Kirschner, Hans-Georg. "On Electronics Warfare of the USA," Dokumentation der Zeit (East Germany) 2 (1971): 22-27.
This is an approximate translation of the German title.

4258. Kirschner, Nancy M. "The Right to Financial Privacy Act of 1978--The Congressional Response to United States v. Miller: A Procedural Right to Challenge Government Access to Financial Records," University of Michigan Journal of Law Reform 13/1 (Fall 1979): 10-52.

4259. Kirshhofer, Kirk H. "Cryptology," International Defense Review 9 (April-August 1976): 281-286, 389-394, 585-590.

4260. Kirsten, Amundsen. "Soviet Submarines in Scandinavian Waters," Washington Quarterly 8/3 (Summer 1985): 111-122.

4261. Kirtley, Jane E. "A Walk Down a Dangerous Road: British Press and Censorship and the Spycatcher Debacle," Government Information Quarterly 5/2 (1988): 117-135.
Considers the three methods used by the Thatcher government to control publication of government information by the press: self-censorship; threat of the Official Secrets Act; and judicial action to punish the press.

4262. Kiselyov, Sergei. "Our Man in Missouri," Bulletin of the Atomic Scientists 49/2 (March 1993): 34-38.

4263. Kisseloff, Jeff. "Nuking the Bill of Rights," Bill of Rights Journal 15 (December 1982): 1-5.

4264. Kissinger, Henry A. "Arms Control, Inspection and Surprise Attack," Foreign Affairs 38/4 (July 1960): 557-575.
Sets forth an argument for vigorous pursuit of arms control negotiations and effective controls to hedge against surprise attacks.

4265. Kitch, Edmund W. "Katz v. United States: The Limits of the Fourth Amendment," Supreme Court Review (1968): 133-152.

A summation of the <u>Katz</u> decision in terms of the Supreme Court's movement to limit government access to private conversations.

4266. Kitchen, Martin. "The German Invasion of Canada in the First World War," <u>International History Review</u> 7/2 (1985): 245-260.
    Discusses German sabotage activities against the Canadians in World War I in an effort to support the central powers.

4267. Kitchens, Allen H. "Crisis in Intelligence: Two Case Studies," <u>Studies in Intelligence</u> 28/3 (Fall 1984).

4268. Kitrinos, Robert W. "International Department of the CPSU," <u>Problems of Communism</u> 33 (September-October 1984): 47-65.
    Major sections discuss the origins of the Department, organizational structure, liaison with foreign communists, identification and other political parties, relations with the KGB, and research institutes.

4269. Kitson, Peter. "Coleridge's Anecdote of John Thelwall," <u>Notes & Queries</u> 32 (September 1985): 345.
    Brief note concerning treason in literature concerning Samuel Coleridge's short tale about John Thelwall.

4270. Kittredge, T. B. "Revelation of Secret Strategic Plans," <u>U.S. Naval Institute Proceedings</u> 81 (1955): 731-740.

4271. Kiyonaga, Bina. "Remembrance of a CIA Wife," <u>Washingtonian</u> 20/6 (1985): 158-162, 206-207.

4272. Klare, Michael T. "Operation Phoenix and the Failure of Pacification in South Vietnam," <u>Liberation</u> 17/9 (May 1973): 21-27.
    Discussion of the CORDS program in Vietnam, "Operation Phoenix." This was a major intelligence and pacification effort in the Vietnam war about which several books and articles have been written.

4273. Klare, Michael T. "Secret Operatives, Clandestine Trades: The Thriving Black Market for Weapons," <u>Bulletin of the Atomic Scientists</u> 44/3 (1988): 16-34.

4274. Klehr, Harvey. "The Strange Case of Roosevelt's 'Secret Agent': Frauds, Fools, and Fantasies," <u>Encounter</u> 59/6 (1982): 84-91.
    Discusses the congressional testimony of Josephine Truslow Adams, who said Adams was the secret messenger between Roosevelt and Communist Party leader Earl Browder. Inquiry by the FBI revealed the total fabrication of the charges and that Mrs. Adams was indeed mentally ill.

4275. Klein, J. K. "The Soviet Espionage System in Germany," <u>Military Review</u> 38 & 39 (1959).

4276. Klein, Z. "The Yom Kippur War: A Surprise on a Trap?," <u>Veyahasim Beinlevmi'im</u> 6 (Autumn 1974): 127-141.

4277. Kleindienst, Richard G. "Wiretapping and Bugging for National Security," <u>Detroit College of Law Review</u> 1986 (Winter 1986): 1035-1059.

An argument in defense of wiretaps for national security purposes. The author, former US Attorney General in part of the Watergate era, recounts some of his experiences in addressing the issue.

4278. Klemperer, Klemens von. "Adam von Trott zu Solz and Resistance Foreign Policy," <u>Central European History</u> 14 (1981): 351-361.

4279. Klen, Michel. "Le Renseignement de l'An 2000," <u>Revue de Defense Nationale</u> 51 (October 1995): 29-43.

Considers French intelligence services and services of other nations in the West in the post-Soviet era. This discussion, in French, summarizes the challenges to be faced by intelligence services in the post cold war era. French intelligence services are given special focus.

4280. Klepikova, Elena and Vladimir Solovyov. "The Secret Russian Party," <u>Midstream</u> 26/8 (October 1980): 12-19.

Discusses the "Secret Russian Party" in the Soviet Union which appears to hold ideas of individual freedom and democracy in the vacuum of communism. Religious values, coupled with growing nationalism, threatens the strength of the Soviet Union. The party is growing and gaining strength.

4281. Klette, Immanuel J. "US Assistance to Venezuela and Chile in Combatting Insurgency, 1963-1964--Two Cases," <u>Conflict</u> 3/4 (1982): 227-244.

4282. Kline, William E. "The INF Treaty," <u>Studies in Intelligence</u> 35/3 (Fall 1991).

4283. Klososvsha, Ninci. "The Master," <u>Kultura</u> 6 (1984): 105-107.

4284. Kloster, Martin G. "The Counterintelligence Operational Concept," <u>Military Intelligence</u> 10/1 (January-March 1984): 6-7.

Inquires into the directions of military counterintelligence in the 1980s.

4285. Klug, Scott. "The Spy Who Was Left Out in the Cold," <u>Regardies</u> 7/6 (February 1987): 110-129.

4286. Knapp, Frank A., Jr. "Style and Stereotypes in Intelligence Studies," Studies in Intelligence 8/1 (Spring 1964).

4287. Knapp, Gary L. "Indicators Development and Correlation," American Intelligence Journal 5/1 (February 1983): 28-29.

4288. Knapp, Michael G. and Timothy B. Hendrickson. "Project Pathfinder: Breaking the Barriers to More Effective Intelligence Analysis," American Intelligence Journal 16/2&3 (Autumn-Winter 1995): 47-50.

4289. Knecht, Richard E. "Participant Eavesdropping and the Right of Privacy: Time to Strike a New Balance," California Western Law Review 8 (1972): 283-300.

     A journal comment on the constitutional basis for challenging participant eavesdropping; United States v. White and the revitalization of On Lee; and suggested approach to participant monitoring as to assumed risk.

4290. Knight, Amy. "Female Terrorists in the Russian Socialist Revolutionary Party," Russian Review 38/2 (April 1979): 139-159.

     Discusses origins of female involvement in terrorism, dating to 1878 and later to the Socialist Revolutionary Party's use of women in campaigns of violence. Ideological commitments kept most women terrorists in violent organizations.

4291. Knight, Amy W. "The Powers of the Soviet KGB," Survey 25 (Summer 1980): 138-155.

4292. Knight, Amy W. "Pyotr Masherov and the Soviet Leadership: A Study in Kremlinology," Survey 26 (Winter 1982): 151-168.

4293. Knight, Amy W. "Andropov: Myths and Realities," Survey 28/1 (Spring 1984): 22-44.

4294. Knight, Amy W. "The KGB's Special Departments in the Soviet Armed Forces," Orbis 28/2 (Summer 1984): 257-280.

     A discussion of the KGB's activities, including activities outside of ordinary intelligence gathering. Discusses the evolution of the special departments during and after World War II, department functions, and recent trends.

4295. Knight, Amy W. "Soviet Politics and the KGB-MVD Relationship," Soviet Union/Union Sovietique 11/2 (1984): 153-181.

     Discusses the use of political positions to gain personal power and legitimacy. Sections discuss the KGB-MVD relationship, the KGB-MVD in the Khrushchev era, the relationship under Brezhnev, and overall Party supervision.

4296. Knight, Amy. "The Party, the KGB, and Soviet Policy-Making," Washington Quarterly 11/2 (Spring 1988): 121-136.

Sections provide discussion of Soviet foreign policy and the KGB before Andropov, Andropov's impact, Chebrikov and Soviet foreign policy, the internal security police, the KGB as a purveyor of information, the KGB and Gorbachev's political reforms, and future trends.

4297. Knight, Amy. "The KGB and Soviet Reform," Problems of Communism 35/5 (September-October 1988): 61-70.

Sections discuss the popular attacks upon the KGB due to methods and activities which contradicted Gorbachev's policy of Glasnost, KGB responses in changing its public image, the balance sheet, and future implications for Gorbachev.

4298. Knight, Amy. "The Fate of the KGB Archives," Slavic Review 52/3 (Fall 1993): 582-586.

Brief discussion of the delivery of KGB files to the repositories of the Russian Federation. Describes the archival records and their political significance.

4299. Knight, Robert. "Harold Macmillan and the Cossacks: Was There a Klagenfurt Conspiracy?," Intelligence and National Security 1/2 (April 1986): 234-255.

4300. Knobelspiesse, A. V. "Captain Stephan Kalman: A Classic Write-in Case," Studies in Intelligence 6/3 (Fall 1962): 1-13.

A discussion of the value and implications of information mailed to intelligence agencies unsupported by the appearance of the writer. One source listed the author's name as a pseudonym.

4301. Knobelspiesse, A. V. "Masterman Revisited: "The Double-Cross System in the War of 1939 to 1945"," Studies in Intelligence 18/1 (Spring 1974).

A review essay of J. C. Masterman's book by the same title. One source listed the author's name as a pseudonym.

4302. Knoll, Erwin. "National Security: The Ultimate Threat to the First Amendment," Minnesota Law Review 66/1 (November 1981): 161-170.

Discusses the national security exception to prior restraint upon information. One of several articles on prior restraint, addressing specifically United States v. Progressive, Inc., and the publication of technical information on nuclear weapons.

4303. Knorr, Klaus. "On the International Implications of Outer Space," World Politics 12/4 (July 1960): 564-584.

Major sections discuss analytical objectives; assumptions; possibility of space race; economic costs and gains; military changes; the balance of deterrence; prestige; sources of conflict; and conclusions.

4304. Knorr, Klaus. "Failures in National Intelligence Estimates: The Case of the Cuban Missiles," World Politics 16/3 (April 1964): 455-467.

Addresses the question of why the intelligence community failed to warn US government decision makers earlier that a Soviet move was distinctly possible, if not probable, instead of estimating its improbability.

4305. Knott, Stephen F. "Thomas Jefferson's Clandestine Foreign Policy," International Journal of Intelligence and Counterintelligence 4/3 (Fall 1990): 325-355.

Accounts for the apparent contradiction between Jefferson's promotion of democratic ideals and his willingness to meddle in the affairs of other countries. Major sections discuss revolutionary beginnings and clandestine diplomacy; secret ways; insurgents and espionage, Jefferson's territorial expansion; Jefferson's clandestine indian policy; Jefferson's "hidden-hand" presidency, to the shores of Tripoli; the question of force or negotiation; conflicting goals; Jefferson's covert legacy; and public secrets.

4306. Knott, Stephen F. "Covert Action Comes Home: Daniel Webster's Secret Operations Against the Citizens of Maine," International Journal of Intelligence and Counterintelligence 5/1 (Spring 1991): 77-87.

Argues that President Tyler and Daniel Webster carried out a blatant abuse of presidential authority when they orchestrated and authorized covert action within US borders. Major sections discuss the factual background; recruiting allies; mysterious resources; executive privilege; and the continuing role of covert action to 1845 as a major tool in executive exercise of authority.

4307. Koch, James R. "Operation Fortitude: The Backbone of Deception," Military Review 92/3 (March 1992): 66-76.

Discusses various military deception strategies of US and German military planners in World War II.

4308. Koch, R. W. "The CIA's Death Valley Albatross," Air Classics 15 (April 1979): 68-73, 98.

4309. Koch, Scott A. "The Role of US Army Attaches Between the World Wars: Selection and Training," Studies in Intelligence 38/5 (1995): 111-115.

Major sections discuss the orphan branch; selection and training; problems at the post; and conclusions.

4310. Koch, Stephen. "Bloomsbury and Espionage," Partisan Review 61 (Winter 1994): 23-45.

Describes the personalities and actions of a group of young British leftist scholars, writers, thinkers, and artists, some of whom later became involved in Soviet espionage against Britain and the West. Note: Account of background contexts pertaining to this group are infrequently seen in books on British espionage, but one exception is an account in Conspiracy of Silence: The Secret Life of Anthony Blunt by Barrie Penros and Simon Freeman.

4311. Kochanski, Martin J. "Remarks on Lu and Lee's Proposals for a Public-Key Cryptosystem," Cryptologia 4/4 (October 1980): 204-207.

4312. Kochanski, Martin J. "A Survey of Data Insecurity Packages," Cryptologia 11/1 (January 1987): 1-15.

4313. Kochanski, Martin J. "Another Data Insecurity Package," Cryptologia 12/3 (July 1988): 165-177.

4314. Koenig, Bruce E. "Enhancement of Forensic Audio Recordings," Journal of the Audio Engineering Society 36 (November 1986): 884-894.

4315. Koenig, Bruce E. "Authenticity of Forensic Audio Recordings," Journal of the Audio Engineering Society 38 (January-February 1990): 3-33.

4316. Koessler, Maximilian. "The International Law on the Punishment of Belligerent Spies: A Legal Paradox," Criminal Law Review 5 (1958): 21-28.

4317. Koffler, Judith S. and Bernett L. Gershman. "The New Seditious Libel," Cornell Law Review 69/4 (April 1984): 816-882.
    Traces the roots of seditious libel in the US and its revival in court decisions in Snepp v. United States, Haig v. Agee and United States v. The Progressive, Inc.

4318. Koh, Harold H. "Why the President (Almost) Always Wins in Foreign Affairs: Lessons of the Iran-Contra Affair," Yale Law Journal 97/7 (June 1988): 1255-1342.
    Argues that the Iran-Contra affair was not a foreign policy oddity. It was, rather, a reflection upon the "chronic dysfunction in the current foreign policy process." Sections discuss how the Iran-Contra investigators failed; why the President always wins in foreign affairs; and the lessons of the Iran-Contra matter.

4319. Koh, Kong Song. "The Need for an Intelligence Unit in the Criminal Investigation Department," Singapore Police Journal (January 1972): 29-42.

4320. Kohler, Robert. "The Intelligence Industrial Base," American Intelligence

Journal 15/2 (Autumn-Winter 1994): 85-91.
    Discusses the role of industry in the technical collection of intelligence. Major sections discuss the role of intelligence; the importance of satellite reconnaissance; the next war; preserving unique programs; and the value of satellite collection.

4321. Koistinen, Paul A. C. "The Spies Within," Reviews in American History 20/2 (June 1992): 264-269.
    A book review essay of Joan M. Jensen's Army Surveillance in America, 1775-1980.

4322. Kolata, Gina B. "Computer Encryption and the National Security Agency Connection," Science 197 (July 1977): 438-440.

4323. Kolata, Gina B. "Cryptography: A New Clash between Academic Freedom and National Security," Science (August 1980): 995-996.

4324. Kolko, Gabriel. "Intelligence and the Myth of Capitalist Rationality in the United States," Science and Society 44/2 (Summer 1980): 130-154.
    Argues that the intelligence process in capitalist countries is blinded by the myth of rationalism, guided essentially by a consensus-seeking approach in which consents and dissents must be integrated.

4325. Kolodziej, Edward A. "The National Security Council: Innovations and Implications," Public Administration Review 29/6 (November-December 1969): 573-584.
    General discussion of the Nixon administration's revision to national security policy through the NSC. Sections discuss operational controls, implications and emerging problems, and options and DOD oversight.

4326. Komer, Robert W. "Clear, Hold and Rebuild," Army 20/5 (May 1970): 16-24.

4327. Komer, Robert W. "Pacification: A Look Back...And Ahead," Army 20/6 (June 1970): 20-29.

4328. Komer, Robert W. "Impact of Pacification on Insurgency in South Vietnam," Journal of International Affairs 25/1 (1971): 48-69.
    Major sections discuss the nature of the "new model" pacification program, 1967-1970; pacification measurement systems; pacification impact on insurgency, and tentative conclusions.

4329. Komorowski, V. "Poland: The Ideology of Counterrevolution," Political Affairs 62/1 (January 1983): 16-21.

4330. Kooken, Don L. "Cryptography in Criminal Investigations," Journal of Criminal Law and Criminology 26/6 (March 1936): 903-919.

Technical discussion of the decipherment of transpositional and substitutional cryptograms in work against criminals.

4331. Kooken, Don L. "Cryptography in Criminal Investigations," Journal of Criminal Law and Criminology 27/7 (May-June 1936): 75-96.

A continuation of the technical discussion in the previous citation.

4332. Kopchinsky, Nicholas L. "An Intelligent Way to Move Intelligence," Signal 39 (September 1984): 57-58.

4333. Kopecky, Susan L. "Dealing with Intercepted Communications: Title III of the Omnibus Crime Control and Safe Streets Act in Civil Litigation," Review of Litigation 12 (Spring 1993): 441-465.

Considers the legality of intercepted messages as evidence, ethical issues, admissibility of evidence gained by interception of oral and wire communication, and risks of civil litigation from interceptions.

4334. Koppel, Ted. "The FBI Wants Better Bugs," Bill of Rights Journal 25 (Winter 1992): 19+.

4335. Korbonski, Stefan. "The True Story of ENIGMA: The German Code Machine in World War II," East European Quarterly 11/2 (Summer 1977): 227-234.

Discusses the Polish history of radio intelligence and cryptography, beginning after Polish independence in 1918. Attempts to correct the historical record to give Poland fair credit for cryptographic innovations.

4336. Korenev, A. P. "The Rights of the Soviet Police and Socialist Legality," Soviet Law and Government 22 (Spring 1984): 81-94.

Describes the agencies of the Ministry of Internal Affairs in the USSR; the rights of the police; verification of citizen documents; the detention of citizens; medical examinations; search; confiscation of objects and documents; and penalties.

4337. Kornbluh, Peter. "The Iran-Contra Scandal: A Postmortem," World Policy Journal 5/1 (Winter 1987-1988): 129-150.

Discussion of the Iran-Contra matter following release of the congressional committee report. Sections include the "commission omission"; congressional complicity; oversight or overlook?; the scourge of covert operations; and recommendations for the next scandal.

4338. Kornblum, Allan N. and Lubomyr M. Jachnycky. "America's Secret

Court: Listening in on Espionage and Terrorism," Judges Journal 24 (Summer 1985): 15-19, 52.

Discusses the Foreign Intelligence Surveillance Act (FISA) in the federal courts, FISA members, and litigating FISA provisions.

4339. Korneev. L. "Cooperation of the Israeli and U.S. Secret Services: 1956-1975," Voenno-Istoricheskii Zhurnal 4 (1978): 73-79.

This article discusses coordination between US and Israeli intelligence services to perform espionage and intelligence missions.

4340. Korostovets, Vladimir. "The Black Cabinet," Contemporary Review 147/3 (1945): 162-165.

Brief comments from a Tsarist diplomat regarding personal experiences in Tsarist Russia.

4341. Korotchenko, I. "Intelligence," Voenno-Istoricheskii Zhurnal 3 (March 1982): 27-31.

A discussion of the topic in Russian.

4342. Kosakowski, Leonard S. "Colonel Friedman: The Man Who Broke Purple," Military Review 93 (April 1993): 74-77.

Discusses the career of William F. Friedman's work on the Purple Code encipherment systems; MAGIC's value; and cryptology after World War II.

4343. Koschwitz, Hansjurgen. "The Hidden Battle: Methods and Strategies of Secret Services for the Manipulation of Foreign Media," Publizistik 33/1 (1988): 71-88.

4344. Koshner, Alan J. "The Founding Fathers and Political Speech: The First Amendment, the Press and the Sedition Act of 1798," Saint Louis University Public Law Review 6 (Fall 1987): 395-417.

Sections discuss the precolonial origins of seditious libel, colonial American theories on freedom of the press and seditious libel, and the founding fathers on seditious libel.

4345. Kosikov, I. A. "Saboteurs of the Third Reich," Novaia i Noveishaia Istoriia 2 (1986): 220-225.

An account of the German intelligence operations during World War II.

4346. Kosinski, L. "Secret German War Sources for Population of East Central Europe and Soviet Union," East European Quarterly 10/1 (Spring 1976): 21-34.

Discusses the pre-war research centers in Nazi Germany which investigated population bases and ethnicities for the purpose of invasion planning. Also discusses sources of statistics used by Nazi researchers.

4347. Kotev, Nikolai. "The Structure, Issues, and Principles of the Work of the British Intelligence Center in Turkey, 1941-42," Voennoistoricheski Sbornik 60/6 (1991): 49-60.

4348. Kotz, Nick. "The Government's Need for Secrecy vs. the Right to Know," Naval War College Review 37/3 (May-June 1984): 36-41.

    An essay on the balance of the equation between the public's right to know and the need for secrecy. Conclusion is drawn that the public's desire for information will always exceed government's willingness to reveal information of a sensitive nature.

4349. Kotze, H. von. "Hitler's Sicherheitsdienst (SD)," Politische Meinung 8/86 (1963).

4350. Koulack, Esther. "'It Could Have Been Any One of Us,'" Canadian Dimension 11/6 (1976): 23-27.

    Argues that political oppression and surveillance in the United States and Canada were reenlivened by the Julius and Ethel Rosenberg spy case.

4351. Kozaczuk, Wladyslaw. "Enigma Solved," Cryptologia 6/1 (January 1982): 32-33.

    A translation of the author's article by Christopher Kasparek.

4352. Kozaczuk, Wladyslaw. "A New Challenge for an Old ENIGMA-Buster," Cryptologia 14/3 (July 1990): 204-216.

4353. Kozar, Paul M. "U.S. Military Technology: The Soviet Perspective," Air University Review 29/3 (March-April 1978): 66-73.

    Suggests that the Soviet view of US technologies is filtered through the lens of contemporary Marxist-Leninist ideology and a unique view of Russia's historical relationship to the West.

4354. Kraemer, Sven F. "The Krasnoyarsk Saga," Strategic Review 18/1 (1990): 25-38.

4355. Krajeck, Kevin. "Policing Dissent: The New Limits for Surveillance," Police Magazine 4/5 (September 1981): 6-11, 14-15, 17-22.

    Extensive discussion of law enforcement intelligence abuses in the realm of domestic security. Particularly good summary of the citizen responses to such abuses and proposals for restricting police intelligence systems.

4356. Kramer, Mark, et al. "Remembering the Cuban Missile Crisis: Should We Swallow Oral History?," International Security 15/1 (1990): 212-218.

    An exchange of correspondence on the oral history dynamics of missile crisis history between Mark Kramer and authors Bruce Allyn, James Blight and David Welch. Major sections discuss the limits of oral history; archival access and critical oral history; and the limits of the knowledge of Soviet participants.

4357. Kramer, Mark. "An Assessment of the Aldrich H. Ames Espionage Case and Its Implications for U.S. Intelligence," International History Review 17 (August 1995): 639-644.

A book review essay pertaining to several new books covering the Aldrich Ames spying case.

4358. Kramer, Paul. "Nelson Rockefeller and British Security Coordination," Journal of Contemporary History 16/1 (January 1981): 73-88.

Reviews the court operations resulting from President Roosevelt's creation of the Office of Coordinator of Commerce and Cultured Relations. The objective was to counter Nazi influence in the US.

4359. Krammer, Arnold P. "Russian Counterfeit Dollars: A Case of Early Soviet Espionage," Slavic Review 30/4 (December 1971): 762-773.

An account of Russian military espionage conducted form 1927 to 1932 by Alfred Tiltin and Nicholas Dozenberg. These spies produced counterfeit dollars in the US and other Western countries.

4360. Krammer, Arnold P. "Technology Transfer As War Booty: The U.S. Technical Oil Mission to Europe, 1945," Technology and Culture 22/1 (January 1981): 68-101.

4361. Krammer, Arnold P. "Japanese Prisoners of War in America," Pacific Historical Review 52/1 (1983): 67-91.

Discusses the three psychological phases of Japanese prisoner experience in interrogation and confinement facilities.

4362. Krammer, Arnold P. "When Stalin Counterfeited American Dollars," American History Illustrated 19/3 (May 1984): 42-49.

4363. Krantz, Kenneth A. "Counterintelligence Support to Joint Operations," Defense Intelligence Journal 4/1 (Spring 1995): 19-27.

Defines counterintelligence and the community of players; asks why CI is different; asks if CI is aimed at helping or hurting; asks if CI can prepare for its role in supporting the commander; and offers brief conclusions.

4364. Kranz, Fred W. "Early History of Riverbank Acoustical Laboratories," Cryptologia 9/3 (July 1985): 240-246.

4365. Krasilovsky, M. William. "Elevating the Role of the Informer: The Value of Secret Information," <u>American Bar Association Journal</u> 40 (July 1954): 603-606

Argues that informers played a vital role in combatting crime and preserving national security. Discusses misprision of felony, penalties for false informers, statutory rewards, prosecution and Qui Tam action, and informers in the modern world.

4366. Krasner, Michael A. "The Decision to Cross the 38th Parallel," <u>Military Review</u> 52/10 (October 1972): 17-26.

Explores the elements of decision making in the Korean war which led to the Truman administration's decision to cross the 38th parallel to unite Korea by force.

4367. Krasno, Jean. "Brazil's Secret Nuclear Program," <u>Orbis</u> 38/3 (Summer 1994): 425-437.

Discusses nuclear motives; nuclear agreements; a brief history of Brazil's nuclear development; how close is Brazil to a bomb?; military autonomy; incentives and disincentives for a bomb; implications for non-proliferation; and US policy implications.

4368. Krass, Allen S. "The Politics of Verification," <u>World Policy Journal</u> 2/4 (Fall 1985): 731-752.

Attitudes of Americans and Soviets pertaining to nuclear arms are discussed, and the extent to which verification of such arms is acceptable.

4369. Krause, Lincoln B. "Insurgent Intelligence: The Guerilla Grapevine," <u>International Journal of Intelligence and Counterintelligence</u> 9/3 (Fall 1996): 219-311.

Major sections discuss the organizational phase; the guerilla warfare phase; the conventioal warfare phase; and a final note.

4370. Krauss, Clifford. "Democracia," <u>Wilson Quarterly</u> 12/1 (January 1988): 119-135.

Discusses the rise and fall of the Sandinistas in Nicaragua following the overthrow of the Somoza government. Also points out the US funding of the Contras by the Reagan administration and the impact the Contras had on the formation of a new government more favorable to US interests.

4371. Kray, Jeff and Pamela Robertson. "Enhanced Monitoring of White Collar Employees: Should Employers Be Required to Disclose?," <u>University of Puget Sound Law Review</u> 15/1 (Fall 1991): 131-170.

Argues for a five-part legal and economic analysis of electronic or other monitoring of white collar employees. Defines the employment contract; discusses legal issues pertaining to employee monitoring; discusses economics of enhanced monitoring; evaluates effects of monitoring in terms of law and economics; and presents proposal for federal legislation.

4372. Krebsbach, Karen. "Competing with the CIA," <u>Foreign Service Journal</u> 73/2 (February 1996): 40-43.

Discusses the role and current objectives of the State Department's Bureau of Intelligence and Research

4373. Kreier, Jesse G. "Electronic Surveillance," <u>Georgetown Law Journal</u> 74 (February 1986): 559-585.

The fifteenth annual survey of criminal procedure on electronic surveillance following decisions in the US Supreme Court and federal Courts of Appeals, 1984-85.

4374. Kreiser, B. Robert. "AAUP Perspectives on Academic Freedom and United States Intelligence Agencies," <u>Journal of College and University Law</u> 19/3 (Winter 1993): 251-257.

A brief discussion of the relationship between the academic and intelligence communities and what that relationship should be watchful of.

4375. Kren, George M. and Leon H. Rappaport. "The Waffen SS: A Social Psychological Perspective," <u>Armed Forces and Society</u> 3/1 (Fall 1976): 87-102.

4376. Krepon, Michael. "Both Sides Are Hedging," <u>Foreign Policy</u> 56 (Fall 1984): 153-172.

Discusses the problems and prospects associated with the deteriorating relationship between the Soviet Union and the US on arms control agreements. Major sections discuss compliance controversies; reciprocal hedging; progressive arms decontrol; easing compliance concerns. Useful in analyses of the role of intelligence in weapons verification.

4377. Krepon, Michael. "CIA, DIA at Odds Over Soviet Threat," <u>Bulletin of the Atomic Scientists</u> 43/4 (May 1987): 6-7.

Jesse Helms charges that CIA analysts have a pro-Soviet bias and DIA analysts inflate the threat to get more money for the Pentagon: "When intelligence yields to consumer pressure it cannot remain credible."

4378. Krepon, Michael. "Spying From Space," <u>Foreign Policy</u> 75 (Summer 1989): 92-108.

Discussion of the use of satellites in clandestine collection in both unsettling and beneficial ways.

4379. Krepon, Michael. "Glasnost and Multilateral Verification: Implications for the U.S. Intelligence Community," <u>International Journal of Intelligence and</u>

Counterintelligence 4/1 (Spring 1990): 47-57.

Discusses the Stockholm Accord as the key break with the past on verification of nuclear weapons; multilateral verification, threat or opportunity?; choices, go with the flow or buck the tide?; cross-connections between openness and multilateralism; implications for the US intelligence community; alternative paths for the US intelligence community; a constructive approach; and the need for openness at home and abroad.

4380. Krestyaninov, V. "CIA Target: Latin America," International Affairs (USSR) 11 (November 1980).

4381. Kriegel, Richard V. "Revolutionary Development," Marine Corps Gazette 51 (March 1967): 34-43.

4382. Krikunov, V. P. "Some Unknown Facts About the Outcome of the Caribbean Crisis," Voenno-Istoricheskii Zhurnal 10 (1990): 33-38.

4383. Krikunov, V. P. "At the Service of Foreign Intelligence Services," Voenno-Istoricheskii Zhurnal 2 (1992): 66-73.

4384. Krinsky, Michael. "Cointelpro Lingers On: National Lawyers Guild v. FBI," National Lawyers Guild Practitioner 43/2 (Spring 1986): 51-54.

Summarizes the allegations and actions of the National Lawyers Guild against investigatory methods of the FBI.

4385. Krivulka, Thomas. "Constitutional Law--Limits of Privacy Expectations Within Seized Electronic Data," Temple Law Review 65/2 (Summer 1992): 645-661.

Refers to a Pennsylvania case, Commonwealth v. Copenhefer, pertaining to police seizure of information and evidence from a defendant's computer system.

4386. Krizman, Bogdan. "The Activities of Archibald Coolidge's American Mission in the South Slav Lands of Former Austria-Hungary 1919," Istorijski Glasnik 1-4 (1962): 111-146.

This is a rough translation of the title, appearing in a Yugoslavian journal.

4387. Kroger, Charles A., Jr. "ELINT: A Scientific Intelligence System," Studies in Intelligence 2 (Winter 1958).

4388. Kronenbitter, Rita T. "The Okhrana's Female Agents, Part I," Studies in Intelligence 9/1 (Spring 1965).

4389. Kronenbitter, Rita T. "The Okhrana's Female Agents, Part II," Studies in

Intelligence 9/2 (Summer 1965).

4390. Kronenbitter, Rita T. "Okhrana Agent Dolin," Studies in Intelligence 10/1 (Spring 1966).

4391. Kronenbitter, Rita T. "Paris Okhrana 1885-1905," Studies in Intelligence 10/2 (Summer 1966).

4392. Kronenbitter, Rita T. "The Sherlock Holmes of the Revolution," Studies in Intelligence 11/3 (Fall 1967).

4393. Kronenbitter, Rita T. "The Illustrious Career of Arkadiy Harting," Studies in Intelligence 11/4 (Winter 1967).

4394. Kronenbitter, Rita T. "Paris Okhrana: Final Phase," Studies in Intelligence 12/2 (Summer 1968).

4395. Kropf, Charles W. "Integrated Operational Intelligence Center (IOIC)," Signal 28 (February 1974): 28-31.

4396. Krotkov, Iurii. "KGB v. Deistvii," Noviy Zhurnal 109 (1972): 190-195.

4397. Kruh, Louis. "Cipher Equipment," Cryptologia 1/1 (January 1977): 69-75.

4398. Kruh, Louis. "Cipher Equipment," Cryptologia 1/2 (April 1977): 143-149.

4399. Kruh, Louis. "Cipher Equipment," Cryptologia 1/3 (July 1977): 255-260.

4400. Kruh, Louis. "MA4210 Alphanumeric Pocket Cipher," Cryptologia 1/4 (October 1977): 334-336.

4401. Kruh, Louis. "The Churchyard Ciphers," Cryptologia 1/4 (October 1977): 372-375.

4402. Kruh, Louis. "The Inventions of William F. Friedman," Cryptologia 2/1 (January 1978): 38-61.

4403. Kruh, Louis. "Who Wrote "The American Black Chamber"?," Cryptologia 2/2 (April 1978): 130-133.

4404. Kruh, Louis. "Cryptology as a Career," Cryptologia 2/2 (April 1978): 164-168.

4405. Kruh, Louis. "Dh-26 Handheld Encryption Unit," Cryptologia 2/2 (April

1978): 172-177.

4406. Kruh, Louis. "A Catalog of Historical Interest" (Parts I, II, & III), Cryptologia 2/3, 2/4, 3/2 (July 1978, October 1978, April 1979): 242-253, 338-349, 78-82.

4407. Kruh, Louis. "A 19th Century Challenge Cipher," Cryptologia 2/4 (October 1978): 334.

4408. Kruh, Louis. "What the Nazis Were Doing," Cryptologia 2/4 (October 1978): 322-323.

4409. Kruh, Louis. "The Deadly Double Advertisement - Pearl Harbor Warning or Coincidence?," Cryptologia 3/3 (July 1979): 166-171.
    A brief discussion of the advertisements of unusual nature that appeared in American magazines in the days before the Pearl Harbor attack.

4410. Kruh, Louis. "CP-III: One Time Cypher Pad Manual Encryption Device," Cryptologia 3/4 (October 1979): 206-209.

4411. Kruh, Louis. "The Day the Friedmans Had a Typo in Their Photo," Cryptologia 3/4 (October 1979): 236-241.

4412. Kruh, Louis. "The CRYPTOMATIC HC-520," Cryptologia 4/1 (January 1980): 5-14.

4413. Kruh, Louis. "Memories of Friedman," Cryptologia 4/1 (January 1980): 23-26.

4414. Kruh, Louis. "The Ciphering System for a 19th Century Challenge Cipher," Cryptologia 4/1 (January 1980): 34-35.

4415. Kruh, Louis. "Reminiscences of a Master Cryptologist," Cryptologia 4/1 (January 1980): 45-50.

4416. Kruh, Louis. "Cipher Equipment: TST-1221," Cryptologia 4/4 (October 1980): 225-229.

4417. Kruh, Louis. "Cipher Equipment: Collins CR-200/220," Cryptologia 5/1 (January 1981): 46-50.

4418. Kruh, Louis. "The Genesis of the Jefferson/Bazeries Cipher Devices," Cryptologia 5/4 (October 1981): 193-207.

4419. Kruh, Louis. "The Navy Cipher Box Mark II," Cryptologia 6/1 (January 1982): 85-93.

4420. Kruh, Louis. "The Mystery of Colonel Decius Wadsworth's Cipher Device," Cryptologia 6/3 (July 1982): 238-247.

4421. Kruh, Louis. "A Basic Probe of the Beale Cipher as a Bamboozlement," Cryptologia 6/4 (October 1982): 378-382.
        Part II of this story is found in Cryptologia 12/4 (October 1988): 241-246.

4422. Kruh, Louis. "Cipher Equipment: The Cryptographic Unit CSI-10," Cryptologia 7/1 (January 1983): 83-88.

4423. Kruh, Louis. "How to Use the German Enigma Cipher Machine: A Photographic Essay," Cryptologia 7/4 (October 1983): 291-296.

4424. Kruh, Louis. "Because of the Freedom of Information Act," Cryptologia 8/1 (January 1984): 75-76.

4425. Kruh, Louis. "Hand-Held Crypto Device SEC-36," and "The Slidex RT Code," Cryptologia 8/2 (April 1984): 112-114; 163-172.

4426. Kruh, Louis. "Cipher Equipment: TST 3336 and TST 9761," Cryptologia 8/3 (July 1984): 278-284.

4427. Kruh, Louis. "The Heraldry of Cryptology," Cryptologia 8/4 (October 1984): 289-301.

4428. Kruh, Louis. "An Armchair View of the Smithsonian Institution Cipher Machine Exhibit," Cryptologia 9/1 (January 1985): 38-51.
        A summary of the exhibition at the Smithsonian of cryptographic machines that have played a special role in the history of the United States.

4429. Kruh, Louis. "The Kryha Liliput Ciphering Machine," Cryptologia 9/3 (July 1985): 252-261.

4430. Kruh, Louis. "Automatic Communications with the SIGABA and the M-294," Cryptologia 9/4 (October 1985): 311-315.

4431. Kruh, Louis. "Early Communications Security in the U.S. Navy," Cryptologia 9/4 (October 1985): 324-330.

4432. Kruh, Louis. "Cryptology and the Law" Parts I-VII," Cryptologia 8/3, 8/4,

9/3, 9/4, 10/2 (July 1984; October 1984; July 1985; October 1985; April 1986; July 1986; October 1986): 246-249; 326-331; 273-285; 348-350; 101-107; 129-133; 248-253.

4433. Kruh, Louis. "The Control of Public Cryptography and Freedom of Speech--A Review," Cryptologia 10/1 (January 1986): 2-9.

This is a review essay pertaining to an article by K. J. Pierce on public key cryptography that appeared in the Cornell International Law Journal (see this bibliography).

4434. Kruh, Louis. "18th Century Shorthand Expert Needed," Cryptologia 10/1 (January 1986): 60-62.

4435. Kruh, Louis. "The Truman Memorandum," Cryptologia 10/2 (April 1986): 65-74.

4436. Kruh, Louis. "An Obscure Cryptographic Device," Cryptologia 11/2 (April 1987): 119-122.

4437. Kruh, Louis. "The Shortsighted View of a Foresighted Admiral," Cryptologia 11/3 (July 1987): 156-159.

A brief account of the communications between Herbert Yardley and Admiral Hooper.

4438. Kruh, Louis. "British Rockex Cipher Machine," Cryptologia 11/4 (October 1987): 245-247.

4439. Kruh, Louis. "Stimson, the Black Chamber, and the 'Gentlemen's Mail' Quote," Cryptologia 12/2 (April 1988): 65-89.

4440. Kruh, Louis. "The Heraldry of Cryptology--Addendum," Cryptologia 13/1 (January 1989): 79-84.

4441. Kruh, Louis. "British-American Cryptanalytic Cooperation and an Unprecedented Admission by Winston Churchill," Cryptologia 13/2 (April 1989): 123-134.

4442. Kruh, Louis. "Tales of Yardley: Some Sidelights to His Career," Cryptologia 13/4 (October 1989): 327-357.

4443. Kruh, Louis. "Why Was Safford Pessimistic About Breaking the German Enigma Cipher Machine in 1942?," Cryptologia 14/3 (July 1990): 253-257.

An account of the codebreaking experiences of Laurence F. Safford, the Navy Department's chief of communications and cryptology organization.

4444. Kruh, Louis. "Unlocking Enigma's Secrets," Cryptologia 14/4 (October 1990): 366-369.
Observations of the Enigma machine exhibit at the Smithsonian Museum in Washington, D.C.

4445. Kruh, Louis. "Military Intelligence Corps Hall of Fame," Cryptologia 15/1 (January 1991): 25-28.

4446. Kruh, Louis. "Sliding Code Device of Unknown Origin," Cryptologia 16/1 (January 1992): 86-88.

4447. Kruh, Louis (ed.). "Army-Navy Collaboration for Cryptanalysis of Enemy Systems," Cryptologia 16/2 (April 1992): 145-164.

4448. Kruh, Louis (ed.). "Strategic Use of Communications During World War II," Cryptologia 16/4 (October 1992): 320-326.

4449. Kruh, Louis. "A 77-Year Old Challenge Cipher Known, Long Cycle Length," Cryptologia 17/2 (April 1993): 172-174.

4450. Kruh, Louis. "The Postal Service Fails to Deliver the Goods," Cryptologia 18/3 (July 1994): 250-252.

4451. Kruh, Louis. "A Pictorial Tour of the National Cryptologic Museum," Cryptologia 18/4 (October 1994): 381-389.

4452. Kruh, Louis. "When a Court Ruled for Bacon Instead of Shakespeare--Temporarily," Cryptologia 19/1 (January 1995): 24-38.

4453. Kruh, Louis (ed.). "Riverbank Laboratory Correspondence, 1919 (SRH-150)," Cryptologia 19/3 (July 1995): 236-246.

4454. Kruh, Louis and Cipher A. Deavours. "The Typex Cryptograph," Cryptologia 7/2 (April 1983): 145-166.

4455. Kruh, Louis and Johnnie Murray. "A Pulp Magazine Cipher," Cryptologia 12/4 (October 1988): 240.

4456. Kruh, Louis and Ralph Erskine. "Yardley Revisited, Again," Cryptologia 13/1 (January 1989): 85-88.

4457. Krulak, Victor H. "Strategic Implications of the Little War," Strategic Review 13/2 (Spring 1985): 31-36.
Discusses the nature of guerilla warfare. Major sections include

discussion of the principles of relative strength and motivation, the pivotal factor of intelligence, self-imposed US constraints, renewed importance of the sanctuary, US support and local command authority, and the battlefield of the visible future.

4458. Kruse, Paul. "A Secret Agent in East Florida: General George Mathews and the Patriot War," Journal of Southern History 18/2 (May 1952).

4459. Krygiel, Annette J. "The Central Imagery Office," American Intelligence Journal 15/2 (Autumn-Winter 1994): 68-71.
　　An overview of the mission and operations of the DoD function known as the Central Imagery Office.

4460. Krygiel, Annette J. "The US Imagery System - Accelerated Architecture Acquisition Initiative," American Intelligence Journal 16/2&3 (Autumn-Winter 1995): 41-46.

4461. Kruskal, Joseph B. "A Trigraph Cipher with a Short Key for Hand Use," Cryptologia 9/3 (July 1985): 202-222.

4462. Kuehl, Daniel T. "Refighting the Last War: Electronic Warfare and the U.S. Air Force B-29 Operations in the Korean War, 1950-53," Journal of Military History 56/1 (January 1992): 87-111.
　　A critical review by the author of the deployment of electronic warfare hardware in the Korean War, reflecting upon certain lessons that should have been learned in World War II.

4463. Kuhn, Arthur K. "The Beginnings of an Aerial Law," American Journal of International Law 4/1 (January 1910): 109-132.
　　Discusses aerial law in the context of international law in times of peace and war, municipal law of private and criminal matters, and conclusions. An excellent early study of law useful for historical writing.

4464. Kulik, Sergei. "The CIA's 'Gigantic Fiasco,'" Aziia i Afrika Segodnia 5 (1982): 16-20.

4465. Kulkov, I. "C.I.A. in the Service of Monopolies and Reaction," International Affairs (USSR) 10 (October 1984): 97-105.
　　A Soviet reaction to the Reagan policies of using intelligence services in service of American corporations and political groups. Sees the CIA as an aggressive tool of capitalism and a "dangerous" institution.

4466. Kullback, Solomon. "Looking Back," Cryptologia 8/4 (October 1984): 337-342.
　　A short discussion of the author's experiences in the War Department in

the decade before World War II.

4467. Kumamoto, Bob. "The Search for Spies: American Counterintelligence and the Japanese American Community 1931-1942," Amerasia Journal 6/2 (Fall 1979): 45-76.

This is a history of the surveillance of Japanese-Americans by US military and civilian intelligence agencies. The history begins with the first fears in the 1920s and ends with the internment program of 1942.

4468. Kunniholm, Bruce. "Commentary," [regarding article by Melvyn P. Leffler "The American Concept of National Security and the Beginnings of the Cold War, 1945-48"], American Historical Review 89/2 (1984): 385-390.

A general summary and evaluation of the remarks of the former Secretary of Defense on national security in the early days of the Cold War.

4469. Kurchatov, A. "U.S. Radio: Propaganda and Espionage," International Affairs (USSR) 10 (October 1971): 73-78.

A Soviet view that radio has been used for spreading propaganda through Radio Free Europe and Voice of America. It amounts to psychological warfare.

4470. Kuroda, Yasumasa. "Young Palestinian Commandos in Political-Socialization Perspective," Middle East Journal 26 (Summer 1972): 253-270.

4471. Kurosawa, K.; T. Ito; and M. Takeuchi. "Public Key Cryptosystem Using a Reciprocal Number with Same Intractability as Factoring a Large Number," Cryptologia 12/4 (October 1988): 225-233.

4472. Kurtz, Michael L. "Lee Harvey Oswald in New Orleans: A Reappraisal," Louisiana History 21/1 (1980): 7-22.

Argues that there are possible links between Oswald's ventures in Cuba and the assassination of Kennedy. Mainly, however, a summary of Oswald's early life and political activism.

4473. Kurtz, Wilbur G. "The Andrews Railroad Raid," Civil War Times Illustrated 5/1 (1966): 8-17, 38-43.

4474. Kushnick, Louis. "Parameters of British American Racism," Race and Class 23/2-3 (Autumn-Winter 1981): 187-206.

Discusses responses to black urban riots in Britain and the US. Includes brief discussion of development of new technologies and expanded intelligence gathering in the US.

4475. Kushnirsky, Fyodor J. "Lessons from Estimating Military Production of the Former Soviet Union," Europe-Asia Studies 45/3 (1993): 483-504.

This journal is the former <u>Soviet Studies</u>. Discusses the instability of the military in the former Soviet Union, and suggests that formal studies of this topic are more important than ever. Argues that liaisons with the Russian military are key to safe cooperation of disarmament and management of nuclear weapons.

4476. Kustovtsev, R. "Illegal Departures from the USSR," <u>Posev</u> 7 (1978): 24-28.

4477. Kutler, Stanley I. "Forging a Legend: The Treason of Tokyo Rose," <u>Wisconsin Law Review</u> 6 (November-December 1980): 1341- 1382.
    A description of the Tokyo Rose case from the initial investigation to final presidential pardon.

4478. Kux, Dennis. "Soviet Active Measures and Disinformation: Overview and Assessment," <u>Parameters: Journal of the U.S. Army War College</u> 15/4 (Winter 1985): 19-28.
    Major sections discuss background of Soviet active measures; organization; political influence operations; media and public opinion influence operations (disinformation); significance of Soviet active measures; and how best to respond.

4479. Kuz'min, I. "Reconnaissance of Atomic Missile Submarines," <u>Morskoi Sbornik</u> 5 (1979): 66-71.
    In Russian, this article discusses use of reconnaissance tactics to observe and to teach contributions of submarines as vital ingredients in national security.

4480. Kuznetsov, Iu. "Confessions of a Former Agent," <u>Aziia in Afrika Segodnia</u> 12 (1986): 21-22.

4481. Kyrychenko, V. P. "Pseudo-Scholarly Research in the Arsenal of the Neocolonialist Politics of US Imperialism in Latin America in the 1970's," <u>Ukrains'kyi Istorychnyi Zhurnal</u> 5 (1986): 112-120.
    This is a rough translation of the title to this piece which appears in Russian.

4482. Kyte, George W. "Francis Marion as an Intelligence Officer," <u>South Carolina Historical Magazine</u> 77/4 (1976): 215-226.

4483. Kyte, George W. "Thaddeus Kosciuszko at the Liberation of Charleston, 1782," <u>South Carolina Historical Magazine</u> 84/1 (1983): 11-21.

4484. Kytka, T. "Description of Methods by Which Secret Communicating May Be Prepared and of the Procedures Employed to Render Them Visible," <u>American Journal of Police</u> 1 (May 1930): 326-331.

L

"American society's hostility to intelligence is a political
fact of life."
(<u>A World of Secrets</u> by Walter Laqueur, p. 326)

4485. La Bella, Charles G. "Foreign Security Surveillance--Balancing Executive Power and the Fourth Amendment," <u>Fordham Law Review</u> 45/5 (April 1977): 1179-1201.

Defines the gap between Fourth Amendment safeguards and national security wiretaps, describes provisions of the Foreign Intelligence Surveillance Act of 1976, then asks whether additional legislation is needed to unfetter the presidential power to conduct foreign surveillance.

4486. Lacey, Edward J. "Game Theory in Intelligence Analysis," <u>American Intelligence Journal</u> 6/3 (October 1984): 20-25.

4487. Lacey, Edward J. "Intel Analysis in Academic Research," <u>American Intelligence Journal</u> 5/1 (February 1983): 12-13.

4488. Lackey, Douglas. "Military Intelligence and the Universities: A Study of an Ambivalent Relationship," <u>Ethics</u> 96 (October 1985): 223-224.

4489. Lackman, Matti. "The Finnish Secret Police and Political Intelligence: Their Methods and Collaborators in the 1920s and 30s," <u>Scandinavian Journal of History</u> 12/3 (1987): 199-219.

4490. Lackman, William. "Future Direction for the United States Imagery System," <u>American Intelligence Journal</u> 14/3 (Autumn-Winter 1993-1994): 31-34.

A paper on trends in user based changes, user expectations, analytical environment, declining resources and joint and combined operations; the challenge for the US imagery system; goals and action plan; architectural path; and organizational path.

4491. Lacouture, John E. "Confidence and ECM Capability: Missing Links in U.S. Air Operations in Lebanon," <u>Defense Electronics</u> 17/3 (March 1985): 113-114, 117-118.

4492. Lacovara, Philip A. "Presidential Power to Gather Intelligence: The Tension Between Article II and Amendment IV," <u>Law and Contemporary Problems</u> 10/3 (Summer 1976): 106-131.

Discusses the intelligence function in our constitutional system, uncertainty in the present state of the law (1976), arguments about presidential prerogatives, substantive standards, use of warrants, limits of judicial power and conclusions.

4493. Laffin, John. "Faithful to Two Flags," <u>World War II Investigator</u> 1/1 (April 1988): 42-44.

A discussion of SOE agent Michael Trotobas, who was known as Capitaine Micel.

4494. Lagemann, John K. "Wild Bill Donovan," <u>Current History</u> 52 (April 1941): 23-25, 55-56.

A lengthy tribute to William J. Donovan, accomplished lawyer and head of the World War II OSS. Donovan is described as a man who could get a person to talk about what he most wanted to hide; and he could judge a person's feelings on any subject.

4495. Lall, Betty G. "Information in Arms Control Verification," <u>Bulletin of the Atomic Scientists</u> 20 (October 1964): 43-45.

4496. Lamant, Pierre L. "The Political Parties and Khmer Resistance As Seen by the French Intelligence Service, 1945-52," <u>Guerres Mondiale et Conflits Contemporains</u> 37/148 (1987): 79-96.

4497. Lamar, William H. "The Government's Attitude Toward the Press," <u>Forum</u> 59 (February 1918): 129-140.

An early analysis of the role and place of the media in international crises, such as the war with Spain, the assassination of Archduke Ferdinand and Duchess Sophie, and the conflict between Germany and Russia. Argues that media influence in the center of these controversies attracted government controls.

4498. Lamb, Chris. "Belief Systems and Decision Making in the Mayaguez Crisis," Political Science Quarterly 99/4 (Winter 1984-1985): 681-702.

A thorough analysis of the beliefs and decision processes during the Ford administration's Mayaguez ship seizure crisis. Major sections include discussion of pre-crisis belief systems, crisis behavior, correcting pre-crisis explanations, and comparative utility of decisions.

4499. Lamb, Mervyn [pseud.]. "On Hazardous Service," Blackwood's Magazine 208-209-210 (1920-1921).

A three-part account of the author's experiences in British intelligence during World War I. The author's real name was Colonel Walter Kirke.

4500. Lambakis, Steven. "Space Control in Desert Storm and Beyond," Orbis 39/2 (Summer 1995): 417-433.

Major topics consider coalition satellite operations; coalition space control; a friendly environment; Iraqi space operations; and space control and future security.

4501. Lambert, William C. "A Very Strange Story," Aerospace Historian 30/1 (1983): 39-49.

4502. Lambie, William K., Jr. "Electronic Surveillance for National Security," Journal of Police Science and Administration 3/3 (September 1975): 346-350.

Reflects the author's testimony of October 2, 1974 before the Subcommittee on Criminal Procedures of the Committee of the Judiciary concerning constitutional protections against threats to national security. He argues that issuance of warrants for national security electronic surveillance impedes the government's legitimate purpose for such surveillance.

4503. Lambrecht, Rainer. "Test Model Guatemala: Overthrow of the Arbenz Government by the CIA in 1954," Militaergeschichte 23/3 (1984): 273-274.

An account of the US overthrow of the Guatemalan government via a policy and series of actions promoting destabilization.

4504. Lammers, Donald. "Fascism, Communism and the Foreign Office," Journal of Contemporary History 6/3 (1971): 66-86.

Discusses how the British Foreign Office struggled to understand the growing regime of fascism and communism in Italy and the Soviet Union, respectively. Argues that foreign policy advisers neglected their duties to discover and discuss some matters of vital concern to national survival.

4505. Lammers, Donald. "From Whitehall After Munich: The Foreign Office and the Future Course of British Policy," Historical Journal 16/4 (1973): 831-856.

Suggests that nine internal documents from the Foreign Office provide insight into the formulation of policy in 1930s Britain.   Argues that Britain remained critical of Germany and her construction of war machinery.

4506. Lammers, Pat and Amy Boyce. "Alias Franklin Thompson: A Female in the Ranks," Civil War Times Illustrated 22/9 (1984): 24-31.
This article discusses how a woman (Emma Edmonds) served during the Civil War as a spy without revealing her gender.

4507. Lanctot, Gustave. "The Scandalous Life of a Forger," Transactions of the Royal Historical Society of Canada 50/1 (1956): 25-48.

4508. Landers, Daniel F. "The Defense Warning System," Defense Intelligence Journal 3/1 (Spring 1994): 21-32.
Discusses the mission, structure, methodology, key participants, successes and failures, and future considerations regarding the DWS.

4509. Landever, Arthur R. "Electronic Surveillance, Computers, and the Fourth Amendment--The New Telecommunications Environment Calls for Reexamination of Doctrine," University of Toledo Law Review 15/2 (Winter 1984): 597-640.
A lengthy discussion of surveillance technology in the context of judicial and administrative controls over its excesses and invasions of privacy.

4510. Landsverk, O. G. "Cryptography in Runic Inscriptions," Cryptologia 8/4 (October 1984): 302-319.

4511. Lane, Ann J. "Recent Literature on the Molly Maguires," Science and Society 30/3 (Summer 1966): 309-319.
Discusses the Molly Maguires, a secret organization in the latter nineteenth century, whose organizational methods were aimed at perpetuation of crimes against Pennsylvania coal companies.   Reviews the literature on the subject, including books by F. P. Dewer and Wayne G. Broch.

4512. Lane, Eric. "Political Surveillance in New York--An Administrative Challenge to Democratic Values," University of Detroit Journal of Urban Law 55/4 (Summer 1978): 1079-1102.
Discusses the 1975 New York investigation and a task force report; New York State Police mandate; the police function; the need for information and crime fighting functions; subversives and dissidents; remedies; and a proposed statute.

4513. Lane, M. "The Diplomatic Service Under William III," Transactions of the Royal Historical Society 10 (1927): 87-109.

4514. Lang, Daniel. "The War's Top Top Secret," Infantry Journal 64/1 (January

1949): 34-39.

Discusses the methods of the Army CIC to protect the Manhattan Project during World War II. This is reprinted from the author's book, Early Tales of the Atomic Age, 1945.

4515. Langan, John P. "Moral Damage and the Justification of Intelligence Collection from Human Sources," Studies in Intelligence 25/2 (Summer 1981): 57-64.

4516. Langan, John P. "National Interest, Morality, and Intelligence," Studies in Intelligence 27/3 (Fall 1983).

4517. Langbart, David A. "'Spare No Expense': The Department of State and the Search for Information about Bolshevik Russia, November 1917-September 1918," Intelligence and National Security 4/2 (April 1989): 316-334.

Discusses the difficulties faced by the Wilson administration, and in particular the US State Department, in securing sufficient good quality information to determine the direction of the Russian revolution and the orientations of revolution leaders.

4518. Langen, Henry E. "Fingerprint Ciphers," Fingerprints and Identification 32 (1951): 15-19, 31.

4519. Langenberg, Donald L. "Secret Knowledge and Open Inquiry," Society 23/5 (July-August 1986): 9-12.

A brief but direct summary of the difficulties imposed on the scientific community by restrictions of scientific communications. Discusses various efforts to address the problem of government information classification.

4520. Langer, John D. "The 'Red General': Phillip R. Faymonville and the Soviet Union, 1917-1952," Prologue: Quarterly Journal of the National Archives 8/4 (Winter 1976): 208-221.

A detailed account of the career and service of Colonel Faymonville as the first military attache to the Soviet Union, later in World War II suspected of disloyalty. This article attempts to set the record straight as to his professional service and his loyalty. Includes photos.

4521. Langer, Walter C. and Sanford Gifford. "An American Analyst in Vienna During the Anschluss: 1936-1938," Journal of the History of Behavioral Sciences 14/1 (1978): 37-54.

4522. Langer, William L. "Scholarship and the Intelligence Problem," Proceedings of the American Philosophical Society 92/1 (March 1948): 43-45.

A brief discussion of the role of scholarly research in intelligence analysis.

4523. Langley, David. "Postscript on the Colonization of the International Trade Union Movement," New Politics 5 (Fall 1966): 66-69.

4524. Langley, Harold D. "Early Diplomatic Couriers," Foreign Service Journal 48/10 (October 1971): 6-10.
Reviews the lengthy history of the State Department's Diplomatic Courier Service, dating in concept from 1783.

4525. Lanier, Gene. "Libraries Invaded by the FBI," Free Speech Yearbook 27 (1989): 68-74.

4526. Lanir, Zvi; Baruch Fischhoff; and Stephen Johnson. "Military Risk-Taking: C^3I and the Cognitive Functions of Boldness in War," Journal of Strategic Studies 11/1 (March 1988): 96-114.
A discussion of C^3I and its values in reducing the fog of battle, making combat decisions more manageable and in improving central control.

4527. Lansdale, Edward G. "Vietnam: Do We Understand Revolution?," Foreign Affairs 43/1 (1964): 75-86.
A perspective on the early stages of the Vietnam War from the vantage point of a former intelligence officer.

4528. Lansing, P. "Freedom to Travel: Is the Issuance of a Passport an Individual Right or a Government Prerogative?," Denver Journal of International Law and Politics 11 (1982): 15-35.
Major sections include discussion of historical aspects of the freedom to travel, the case of former CIA agent Philip Agee, constitutional protection of the right to travel, and multilateral efforts to free travel.

4529. Lapham, Lewis H. "Glass Houses," Harper's 271 (August 1985): 9-10.
A satirical review of the use of surveillance equipment in American society, including use in the illegal trade in industrial and military secrets from one country to another. He questions the net results of all the espionage, suggesting that much government secrecy is all in the name of protecting government errors.

4530. Lapham, Lewis H. "Going South," Harper's 273 (September 1986): 8-9.
A brief but insightful discussion of the CIA's role in the so-called covert action in Nicaragua.

4531. Laqueur, Walter. "The Origins of the Guerilla Doctrine," Journal of Contemporary History 10/3 (July 1975): 341-382.

Addresses concepts of the theorists of small war between 1750 and 1900, and the views of each theorist on the utility and limitations of partisan warfare. Special attention is given to Clausewitz, Scharnhorst, Gneisenau, and Napolean. Intelligence is discussed as part of the small war equation.

4532. Laqueur, Walter. "LeCarre's Fantasies," Commentary 75/6 (June 1983): 62-67.

A lengthy book review essay of authors who have crafted novels about espionage, spies and secret agents. Emphasis is given to the works of John LeCarre and a generations of spy story writers.

4533. Laqueur, Walter. "The Fiction of Intelligence," Policy Review 25 (Summer 1983): 90-96.

4534. Laqueur, Walter. "The Question of Judgment: Intelligence and Medicine," Journal of Contemporary History 10/4 (October 1983): 533-546.

The author, most noted for his work on strengthening intelligence analytical techniques, argues for more study of the parallels between the techniques of medicine and politics. The intelligence community could benefit from greater sensitivity to the medical profession's emphases on signs, symptoms and indications.

4535. Laqueur, Walter. "The Future of Intelligence," Society 23/1 (November-December 1985): 3-11.

A look at US intelligence activities, their roles and conflicts with the CIA actions during the 1970s. (Reprinted in Studies in Intelligence 30/1 (Spring 1986). Major sections discuss secrecy and democracy, active measures/covert operations, and the oversight and evaluation of intelligence.

4536. Laqueur, Walter. "Spying and Democracy of the Future of Intelligence," Current 86/2 (March-April 1986): 25-34.

The author reviews the legacy of distrust between the US CIA and the Soviet KGB during the cold war. Argues in a prescient manner for the eventual collapse of the Soviet Union.

4537. Laqueur, Walter. "Julian Semyonov and the Soviet Political Novel," Society 23/5 (1986): 72-80.

4538. Laqueur, Walter. "How Not To Break the Silence: On the Mystery of the Terrible Secret," Encounter 68 (April 1987): 72-76.

Comments by the author on The Terrible Secret (1980) and Breaking the Silence (1986). The story of Dr. Edward Schulte, a German industrialist who carried covertly Hitler's secrets to the allied powers, is discussed. This was the first report of the Holocaust to the West.

4539. Laqueur, Walter. "New Light on a Murky Affair," Encounter 74 (March 1990): 33-34.

4540. Laqueur, Walter. "LeCarre in Russian Eyes," Commentary 96 (September 1993): 54-55.
    A book review essay concerning LeCarre's novel, The Night Manager.

4541. Lardiere, Eric. "The Justiciability and Constitutionality of Political Intelligence Gathering," UCLA Law Review 30/5 (June 1983): 976-1051.
    Examines a series of law suits in the late 1960s and early in the 1970s challenging the constitutionality of political intelligence gathering on first Amendment grounds. Emphasis is on Supreme Court case, Laird v. Tatum.

4542. Lardner, George, Jr. "The Intelligence Investigations: Congress Cops Out," Progressive 40 (July 1976): 13-17.

4543. Larin, N. "CIA--A Vehicle of International Brigandage and Terrorism," International Affairs (USSR) 6 (June 1984): 72-80.
    Asserts that the CIA continues to fail to provide the US president with accurate information. Discusses the Consortium for the Study of Intelligence as a vehicle for reinstating the popular prestige of the CIA.

4544. Larson, Arthur D. "The Secret Side of War: Anglo-American and German Intelligence in World War II," Journal of Political and Military Sociology 8/1 (Spring 1980): 121-124.
    A book review essay of David Kahn's Hitler's Spies and Anthony C. Brown's Bodyguard of Lies.

4545. Larson, Doyle. "Direct Intelligence Combat Support in Vietnam: Project Teaball," American Intelligence Journal 15/1 (Spring-Summer 1994): 56-58.
    A brief description of a successful air intelligence mission in the Vietnam war in 1972.

4546. Larson, Wendy. "Realism, Modernism, and the Anti-Spiritual Pollution Campaign in China," Modern China 15/1 (January 1989): 37-71.
    A lengthy discussion of one of China's many recent ideological themes, resulting in the label of treason for those who during the 1980s rejected the evolutionist view of political and social forces. A useful piece for those examining case study extensions of the definition of treason.

4547. Lasch, Christopher. "American Intervention in Siberia: A Reinterpretation," Political Science Quarterly 77/2 (June 1962): 205-223.
    Discussion of US involvement in Siberian and two theories of that intervention: Japanese theory; Bolsheviks theory. Sections include discussion of

the expedition to Siberia, the two theories, and opposition.

4548. Lash, J. N. "A Yankee in Gray: Danville Leadbetter and the Defense of Mobile Bay, 1861-1863," Civil War History 37 (September 1991): 197-213.

    Discusses the importance of protecting Mobile against Union military or naval attacks, early in 1861. The Confederate War Department had prepared to build or consolidate an extensive system of fortifications around Mobile Bay. Discusses the use of slaves in construction and espionage associated with the forts.

4549. Lasseter, Victor K. "Tinker, Tailor, Soldier, Spy: A Story of Modern Love," Critique 31 (Winter 1990): 101-111.

4550. Latawski, Paul. "Count Horodyski's Plan 'To Set Europe Ablaze,' June 1918," Slavonic and East European Review 65/3 (July 1987): 391-398.

    Discusses the covert action plan of Jan Horodyski, a Polish intelligence agent, to introduce mass revolution in Austria-Hungary during World War I. The British, having knowledge of the plan, failed to support it due to loss of faith in Horodyski's capabilities.

4551. Latham, Aaron. "Tongsun Park's White House Connection," Esquire 88 (December 1977): 78-90.

    Argues that the CIA should have known about the bribes of American government officials by Park, a Korean lobbyist and spy. Park, says the author, had connections with the CIA.

4552. Latham, Niles. "Desperation in the Middle East Led to Iran-Contra Extremes," Officer 63 (September 1987): 5-10.

4553. Latimer, Thomas K. "U.S. Intelligence and the Congress," Strategic Review 7/3 (Summer 1979): 47-56.

4554. Latour, Charles. "Ocean Reconnaissance from the Sky," NATO's Fifteen Nations 19 (October-November 1974): 34-43.

4555. Latov, P. "U.S. Intelligence and Its Methods," Mezhdunarodnaia Zhizn' 14/9 (1967): 87-96.

4556. Laturno, Gary M. "Presidential Authority to Authorize Investigative Techniques in Foreign Intelligence Investigations," FBI Law Enforcement Bulletin 45 (June 1976): 27-31.

    Sections provide discussion of national security and presidential power, the warrant requirement, and national security wiretap legislation. Argues that presidential power to conduct national security investigations can be limited by Congress and the Supreme Court, but until such legal constraints are imposed, the

President draws his power from the Constitution.

4557. Lauder, George V. and Allan E. Goodman. (Letters to the editor regarding Goodman's article in Foreign Policy, Winter 1984-1985, "Dateline Langley ...") Foreign Policy 58 (Spring 1985): 171-177.

4558. Laurendeau, M. "Police and their Assistants: Police Informers and Undercover Agents," Criminologie 17/1 (1984): 117-125.
   Description of Quebec's law enforcement community's use of informants and undercover agents to gather intelligence information on hard to reach criminal activities.

4559. Laurie, Clayton D. "Black Games, Subversion, and Dirty Tricks: The OSS Morale Operations Branch in Europe, 1943-1945," Prologue: Quarterly Journal of the National Archives 25/3 (Fall 1993): 259-271.
   A detailed history of propaganda of the Office of Strategic Services in the later phases of World War II. Mentions several project names and includes numerous document samples.

4560. Laurie, Clayton D. "The 'Sauerkrauts': German Prisoners of War as OSS Agents, 1944-1945," Prologue: Quarterly Journal of the National Archives 26/1 (Spring 1994): 49-61.
   Activities of German Prisoners of War who were turned around by the Office of Strategic Services during the war and used against Hitler's command system. Includes several photos and documents. Emphasizes the initiatives of OSS director William Donovan and the activities of the OSS Morale Operations Branch.

4561. Lawn, John C. "Intelligence for Illegal Drug Control," American Intelligence Journal 10/2 (Summer-Fall 1989): 51-53.
   A brief summary of the National Narcotics Intelligence System; future developments in the NNIS; policy issues; and conclusions. Author was the administrator of the Drug Enforcement Agency.

4562. Lawrence, Ken. "The Korean Spy Plane: Flight 007 Aptly Named," Covert Action Information Bulletin 20 (Winter 1984): 40-42.

4563. Lawrence, Ken and Ashaki M. Binta. "Mississippi Spies," Southern Exposure 9/3 (1981): 82-86.
   This is a documentary of the Mississippi State Sovereignty Commission, a covert operation formed in 1956 against civil rights activities.

4564. Laursen, Thomas E. "Constitutional Protection of Foreign Travel," Columbia Law Review 81/4 (May 1981): 902-931.

Explores the constitutional protections afforded travel abroad and develops a framework for analyzing the issue of travel restrictions. Reviews relevant Supreme Court decisions. Concludes that courts cannot readily interpret the constitutionality of travel abroad, but foreign travel should be protected indirectly under the First Amendment.

4565. Lavergne, Bernard. "The Capture of the American Spy Ship by the North Koreans," Annee Politique et Economie 41/201 (1968): 68-71.

4566. Lavoie, Chantal. "The Investigative Powers of the Commission with Respect to Business Secrets under Community Competition Rules," European Law Review 17 (February 1992): 20-40.
Considers the legal status of business secrets within the EEC Commission's investigative powers and the debate over conflicting rights to information access.

4567. La Voie, Theresa M. "Challenging 'Covert' Paramilitary Operations in Nicaragua Under the Neutrality Act," Southwestern University Law Review 17 (Fall 1988): 859-887.
Discusses the Neutrality Act, Dellums v. Smith, and Avirgan v. Shackley. Defends the position that the courts should adjudicate a suit for Neutrality Act violations filed against executive officials who may be liable for death or injury to American or foreign citizens in Nicaragua.

4568. La Voy, Diana E. "Foreign Nationals and American Laws," Society 15/1 (1977): 58-64.
Suggests that Congress should become more deeply interested in the activities of foreign intelligence agents in order to protect American citizens from harassment.

4569. Law, Richard F. "Active Countermeasures to Neutralizing the Espionage Threat," American Intelligence Journal 11/2 (Spring 1990): 42-44.
Brief discussion of the motivations to commit espionage; the recognition of espionage cases as a function of alert co-workers, relatives or others; and the Report of the DOD Security Review Commission.

4570. Lawson, John L. "The 'Remarkable Mystery' of James Rivington, 'Spy,'" Journalism Quarterly 35/3 (1958): 317-323, 394.

4571. Lay, James S., Jr. "National Security Council's Role in the U.S. Security and Peace Program," World Affairs 115 (Summer 1952): 33-63.
An early and lengthy discussion of the role of the National Security Council in the Korean War.

4572. Layman, Gene E. "C³CM A Warfare Strategy," Naval War College Review 38/2 (March-April 1985): 31-42.

Major sections include discussion of C³CM within the hierarchy of strategies; a perception of C³CM warfare focused on the enemy's objectives; concentration of efforts on main C³CM objectives; conducting operations under a single integrated tactical plan; and proper balance between centralized and decentralized control.

4573. Layne, Donald Q. and Conrad A. Jorgenson. "Combat Intelligence," Marine Corps Gazette 58 (March 1974): 29-36.

4574. Layton, Edwin T. "American Deciphered Our Code," U.S. Naval Institute Proceedings 105/6 (June 1979): 98-100.

4575. Lazenby, J. F. "Espionage and Treason," Journal of Hellenic Studies 107 (1987): 223-224.

A brief book review essay concerning a book by Andre Gerolymatos: Espionage and Treason: A Study of the Proxenia in Political and Military Intelligence Gathering in Classical Greece.

4576. Leacacos, John P. "Kissinger's Apparat," Foreign Policy 5 (Winter 1971): 3-27.

A reflection upon the operations of the National Security Council during the Henry Kissinger years in the Nixon administration. Includes a section on the types of ambiguities the author believes are found in the then-modern Central Intelligence Agency.

4577. Leach, Raymond J. "Information Support to U.N. Forces," Marine Corps Gazette (September 1994): 49-50.

Discusses intelligence needs of the United Nations military branches.

4578. Leacock, Ruth. "JFK, Business, and Brazil," Hispanic American Historical Review 59/4 (1979): 636-673.

Discusses the Kennedy foreign policy initiatives and concerns regarding business in Brazil and US interests regarding the Goulart administration. One portion of the policy community, headed by William H. Draper, urged the undercutting of Joao Goulart in order to bring the Brazilian government.

4579. Leadbetter, Wyland F., Jr. and Stephen J. Bury. "Prelude to Desert Storm: The Politicization of Intelligence," International Journal of Intelligence and Counterintelligence 6/1 (Spring 1993): 43-54.

Reviews charges by some members of Congress that the CIA 'cooked' assessments on the United Nations' economic sanctions against Iraq prior to the Gulf War. Major sections address the events leading to the charges; CIA assessments and the Congress; media influence; bureaucratic political influences; conclusions and recommendations.

4580. Lear, F. S. "Public Law of the Visigothic Code," Speculum 26 (January 1951): 1-23.

4581. Leary, William M., Jr. "Portrait of a Cold Warrior: Whiting Willauer and Civil Air Transport," Modern Asian Studies 5 (1971): 373-388.
A detailed account of Willauer's experiences in organizing the air defenses and air transport system in China during World War II. Discusses also his post-war work with the Nationalist government.

4582. Leary, William M., Jr. "Aircraft and Anti-Communists: CAT in Action, 1949-52," China Quarterly 52 (December 1972): 654-659.
Considers the development of civil air transport in China in the years cited. The development work was accomplished by Clair L. Chennault and Whiting Willauer. Mentions the Office of Strategic Services (OSS).

4583. Leary, William M., Jr. "CAT at Dien Bien Phu," Aerospace Historian 31/3 (September 1984): 177-184.
An examination of the US Central Intelligence Agency's secret air force, Air America, and Air America's role in the Vietnam War.

4584. Leary, William M., Jr. "Assessing the Japanese Threat: Air Intelligence Prior to Pearl Harbor," Aerospace Historian 34/4 (Winter 1987): 272-277.
Discusses the general awareness of US naval intelligence in 1941 that Japanese planes and pilots were superior to US counterparts. The narrowness of their jobs kept analysts from emphasizing the implications of what they realized.

4585. Leary, William M., Jr. "Robert Fulton's Skyhook and Operation Coldfeet: A Good Pick-Me-Up," Studies in Intelligence 38/5 (1995): 99-109.
A history of the development of an air retrieval system for extraction of mail and secret agents from behind enemy lines in World War II. Major sections discuss CIA involvement in advancing the technology in 1952; the system's inventor, Robert E. Fulton, Jr.; the Skyhook system; human pickups; Operation Coldfeet; problems; the search for NP 8; and valuable intelligence.

4586. Leary, William M., Jr. and William Stueck. "The Chennault Plan to Save China: U.S. Containment in Asia and the Origins of CIA's Aerial Empire, 1949-1950," Diplomatic History 8/4 (Fall 1984): 349-364.
An examination of the CIA's secret airforce, the Civil Air Transport, and its role in fighting Marxist expansionism in China, 1949-1950.

4587. Lebedev, A. "British State Secrets, 30 Years On," International Affairs

(USSR) 4 (April 1985).

4588. Lebow, Richard N. "Misperceptions in American Strategic Assessment," Political Science Quarterly 97/2 (Summer 1982): 187-206.
    A discussion of measures of the strategic balance; CIA versus DOD, how they differ, where they agree; the political naivete of American strategic analysis; and conclusions.

4589. Lebow, Richard N. "Miscalculations in the South Atlantic: The Origins of the Falklands War," Journal of Strategic Studies 6/1 (March 1983): 5-35.
    Discusses the conflict between the Britain and Argentina over sovereignty of the Falkland Islands. Argues that without real intelligence data about the situation, no clear determination of the crisis was possible. Discusses the problem of government self-deception in London and Buenos Aires.

4590. Lebow, Richard N. "The Cuban Missile Crisis: Reading the Lessons Correctly," Political Science Quarterly 98/3 (Fall 1983): 431-458.
    Discusses the missile crisis as an excellent case for generalizing about crisis decision making, theories of bargaining, and the role of nuclear arms in foreign policy. Offers an alternative explanation of brinkmanship.

4591. Lebow, Richard N. "Windows of Opportunity: Do States Jump Through Them?," International Security 9/1 (Summer 1984): 147-186.
    Discussion of the concept of strategic advantage.

4592. Lebow, Richard N. "The Soviet Offensive in Europe: The Schlieffen Plan Revisited?," International Security 9/4 (Spring 1985): 44-78.
    Major topics include Soviet conceptions of military power; the appeal of the offensive; the Schlieffen plan; a defensive strategy for the Warsaw Pact; and conclusions. Includes brief discussion of electronic countermeasures.

4593. Lebow, Richard N. "Was Khrushchev Bluffing in Cuba?," Bulletin of the Atomic Scientists 44/3 (1988): 38-42.

4594. Le Carre, John. "Spying...the Passion of My Time," Queen's Quarterly 100/2 (Summer 1993): 269-272.
    Personal recollections of the infamous teller of spy tales regarding the fiction and realities of espionage during the Cold War period. Argues that the strength of a democracy is mainly in its openness, not its secrecy.

4595. Ledeen, Michael A. "Hiss, Oswald, the KGB and Us," Commentary 65/5 (May 1978): 30-36; (August 1978): 8-10.
    Discusses the possibility that our intelligence services and policy makers may be more correctly assessing the weaknesses of US counterintelligence to KGB

missions.

4596. Ledeen, Michael A. "Fighting Back," Commentary 80 (August 1985): 28-31.
　　Moralistic complaints against covert counter-terrorist action against Soviet sponsored proxies are nothing more than excuses for not fighting back. It's OK to strike military "targets" but its not OK to assassinate Soviet advisors.

4597. Ledeen, Michael A. "Pelton and the Post," American Spectator (August 1986): 31-32.
　　A general discussion of the author's receipt of confidential government files in the Pelton espionage case. Also discusses restriction of press access to government information.

4598. Ledeen, Michael A. and Stephen Bryen. "Decontrol Freaks: The Bush and Clinton Administrations' Unprecedented Giveaway of Secret Military Technology," American Spectator 27 (June 1994): 20-23.

4599. Ledeen, Michael A. and William H. Lewis. "Carter and the Fall of the Shah: The Inside Story," Washington Quarterly 3/2 (Spring 1980): 3-40.

4600. Ledovski, A. M. "The Maoists' Clandestine Contacts with American Diplomacy in 1949," Voprosy Istorii 10 (1980): 75-89.

4601. LeDuc, Don R. "'Free Speech' Decisions and the Legal Process: The Judicial Opinion in Context," Quarterly Journal of Speech 62/3 (1976): 279-287.
　　This article draws upon espionage and obscenity cases as data for examining law as a form of societal communication.

4602. Lee, Bruce. "And I Was There: Bruce Lee Replies," Naval Intelligence Professionals Quarterly 3/1 (Winter 1987): 8-9.

4603. Lee, Eric. "The Eremin Letter: Documentary Proof that Stalin Was an Okhrana Spy?," Revolutionary Russia 6/1 (1993): 55-96.

4604. Lee, Gus C. "Organization for National Security: National Security Council and the Central Intelligence Agency," Public Administration Review 9/1 (1949): 336-344.
　　Contains sections on the National Security Resources Board, the War Council, the Research and Development Board, and the Office of the Secretary of Defense.

4605. Lee, H. P. "The Australian Security Intelligence Organisation--New Mechanisms for Accountability," International and Comparative Law Quarterly

38/4 (October 1989): 890-905.

Overview of legislative controls imposed on the ASIO since 1984. Discusses the British Security Services (MI5); security services of Canada and Australia; and the Inspector-General of Intelligence and Security for the ASIO.

4606. Lee, M. "The Ethos of the Cabinet Office: A Comment on the Testimony of Officials," Public Administration 68/2 (Summer 1990): 238-239.

4607. Lee, Philip. "Canada's Postcard Commandos: Civilians Provide Topographical Data on Enemy or Enemy Occupied Countries," Canadian Geographical Journal 28 (January 1944): 41-45.

A fascinating description of the collection from citizens of postcards of scenes reflecting geographical conditions in enemy-occupied countries. Contains several photos from postcards.

4608. Lee, R. Alton. "New Dealers, Fair Dealers, Misdealers and Hiss Dealers: Karl Mundt and the Internal Security Act of 1950," South Dakota History 10/4 (1980): 277-290.

Gives credit to Senator Mundt for his work to secure passage of the Act.

4609. Lee, William T. "The 'Politico-Military-Industrial Complex' of the U.S.S.R.," Journal of International Affairs 26/1 (1972): 73-86.

Major sections discuss institutional structure for the development and production of weapon systems; forces in the field; doctrine and strategy; and national security budgets and economic consequences.

4610. Lee, William T. "Trends in Soviet Military Spending," Air Force Magazine 60/3 (1977): 84-87.

4611. Lee, William T. "The Soviet Defense Establishment in the 80s," Air Force Magazine 63/3 (March 1980): 100-108.

4612. Lee, William T. "Debate Over U.S. Strategic Forecasts: A Poor Record," Strategic Review 7/3 (Summer 1980): 44-57.

The author, a former intelligence analyst, suggests that Congressman Les Aspin's assessment does not portray accurately the US intelligence community's past performance in the arena of forecasting Soviet weapons development. Argues that CIA misforecasting should be evaluated carefully.

4613. Leek, J. H. "Treason and the Constitution," Journal of Politics 13/4 (November 1951): 604-622.

Considers the views of the constitutional framers on the matter of treason, and some of the case law decisions offering constitutional interpretations.

4614. Lees, Lorraine M. "National Security and Ethnicity: Contrasting Views During World War II," Diplomatic History 11/2 (1987): 113- 125.

Major topics include danger from ethnic communities, wartime agencies, Foreign Nationalities Branch documents, history of nativist outbreaks, Coordinator of Information, internal disagreements in the Foreign Nationalities Branch, the Interdepartmental Committee for Political Warfare.

4615. Lefever, Ernest W. "Can Covert Action Be Just?," Policy Review 12 (Spring 1980): 115-122.

A rationalization for covert actions to serve US foreign policy interests.

4616. Lefever, Ernest W. "Moralism and U.S. Foreign Policy," Orbis 16/2 (Summer 1972): 396-410.

Considers the conflict of views held by realist and idealist theoreticians. Useful in studies of perception and misperception in international conflicts.

4617. Leffler, Melvyn P. "The American Conception of National Security and the Beginnings of the Cold War, 1945-1948," American Historical Review 89/2 (April 1984): 346-381.

The author replies to the perspectives of his earlier article on the State Department's view of American national security. Positively, Leffler argues that the US must continue efforts to analyze the geostrategic, economic, political, technological, ideological, and bureaucratic factors that shape the quest for power.

4618. Leffler, Melvyn P. "Reply" [regarding his article], American Historical Review 89/2 (1984): 391-400.

4619. Legault, Albert. "Nuclear Policy Should Be More Open and Less Ambiguous," International Perspectives 1 (1976): 8-13.

Stresses the reduction of secrecy regarding Canada's assistance to India for nuclear equipment. Also discusses the Nuclear Non-Proliferation Treaty of 1968.

4620. Leggett, George H. "Lenin, Terror and the Political Police," Survey 21/4 (Autumn 1975): 157-187.

4621. Leggett, George H. "Lenin's Reported Destruction of the Cheka Archives," Survey 24/2 (Spring 1979): 193-199.

Discusses Lenin's involvement in the suppression of historical materials through destruction of the Vechecka's archives. The archives contain chronicles of Russian activities, including a recounting of Felix Dzerzhinsky's role in suppression of negative publicity.

4622. Leggett, George H. "The Cheka and a Crisis of Communist Conscience,"

Survey 25 (Summer 1980): 122-137.

4623. Leggett, Robert and Sheldon Rabin. "A Note on the Meaning of the Soviet Defense Budget," Soviet Studies 30/4 (October 1978): 557-566.

A useful analysis of the Soviet defense budget. Contains sections on the implausibility of the budget, defense as an operating budget, and a test of the hypothesis of operating budget. Argues that the defense budget is only an operating budget and its release serves political ends.

4624. Leggett, Robert E. "Measuring Inflation in the Soviet Machinebuilding Sector, 1960-1973," Journal of Comparative Economics 5/2 (June 1981): 169-184.

An analytical discussion of a study aimed at developing a hedonic price index for eight Soviet machine building industries between 1960-1973. Useful in evaluations of military and civilian capabilities.

4625. Lehman, Bruce A. and Timothy A. Boggs. "How Uncle Sam Covers the Mails," Civil Liberties Review 4/1 (May-June 1977): 20-28.

Discussion of the US Postal Service surveillance system, particularly its history, discovery and implementation through the years from the late 19th century to the 1970s.

4626. Lehman, Richard. "Valedictory," Studies in Intelligence 26/2 (Summer 1982).

4627. Lehmberg, Stanford E. "Parliamentary Attainder in the Reign of Henry VIII," Historical Journal 18/4 (1975): 675-702.

This is a detailed revisitation to questions unanswered by earlier studies of the subject of attainder policy in the fifteenth century under King Henry VIII.

4628. Lehn, Major. "Intelligence Under Nuclear Conditions," Military Review 43/8 (August 1963): 72-79.

The use of planning activities to aim intelligence collection toward deeply covered nuclear weapons. Originally published in French in 1962.

4629. Leide, John A. "The Defense Attache System: Challenges and Opportunities for the 1990s," Defense Intelligence Journal 1/2 (Fall 1992): 193-203.

Covers the historical development of the attache system; the DAS today, including operating environment, missions, reporting, representational mission, security assistance, and military advisor; attache selection and training requirements; and new challenges in the world.

4630. Leifland, Leif. "Deception Plan Graffham and Sweden: Another View,"

Intelligence and National Security 4/2 (April 1989): 295-315.

Discusses the implementation of operation Graffham (1943-44) to deliberately mislead German intelligence on allied landings in West Europe. The operation also included the deception of neutral european countries, and most of the deception was carried out through diplomatic channels. Concludes with the German high command war diary which indicated that the deceptions may not have swayed decisions to move troops to Norway. Instead, other possible pieces of intelligence may have been responsible.

4631. Leigh, Ian. "The Security Service, the Press and the Courts," Public Law 1987 (Spring 1987): 12-21.

Considers the legal implications of MI5 abuse of its position and the extent to which the British domestic intelligence service can be brought under control. Discusses telephone tapping and freedom to publish information concerning MI5 abuses.

4632. Leigh, Ian and Laurence Lustgarten. "The Security Service Act 1989," Modern Law Review 52/6 (November 1989): 801-836.

Explores the issue of penetration of MI5 by Soviet intelligence; origins of MI5; functions of MI5; ministerial responsibility and control; Parliamentary controls and accountability; Security Service's powers; remedies for misconduct; and processes for complaints.

4633. Leigh, Monroe. "Passports--Executive Revocation--Delegation of Power," American Journal of International Law 75 (October 1981): 962-963.

A brief summary of Haig v. Agee, 101 S.Ct. 2766 (1981), regarding the power of the Secretary of State to revoke passports on the basis of the Secretary's conclusion about national security matters.

4634. Leighton, Albert C. "Secret Communications Among the Greeks and Romans," Technology and Culture 10/2 (1969): 139-154.

A detailed reflection upon the need for secret messages in Greek and Roman cultures, early means of sending messages, advanced means for short distances, and the decoding of messages.

4635. Leighton, Albert C. "A Papal Cipher and the Polish Election of 1573," Jahrbucher fuer Geschichte Osteuropas 17/1 (1969): 13-28.

4636. Leighton, Albert C. "Further Information on a Paper Cipher of 1573," Jahrbucher fuer Geschichte Osteuropas 19/2 (1971): 239-242.

4637. Leighton, Albert C. "Some Examples of Historical Cryptanalysis," Historia Mathematica 4 (1977): 319-337.

4638. Leighton, Albert C. "The Earliest Use of a Dot Cipher," <u>Cryptologia</u> 1/3 (July 1977): 261-274.

4639. Leighton, Albert C. "The Statesman Who Could Not Read His Own Mail," <u>Cryptologia</u> 17/4 (October 1993): 395-402.

4640. Leighton, Albert C. and Stephen M. Matyas. "The Search for the Key Book to Nicholas Trist's Book Ciphers," <u>Cryptologia</u> 7/4 (October 1983): 297-314.

4641. Leighton, Richard M. "The Planning for Sicily," <u>U.S. Naval Institute Proceedings</u> 80 (1962): 90-101.

4642. Leitenberg, Milton. "The Case of the Stranded Sub," <u>Bulletin of the Atomic Scientists</u> 38/3 (March 1982): 10-13.
　　　　Discusses Soviet submarine grounding as a result of their intelligence gathering intrusions into coastal waters of Sweden.

4643. Leitenberg, Milton. "The Counterpart of Defense Industry Conversion in the United States: The U.S.S.R. Economy, Defense Industry, and Military Expenditure," <u>Journal of Peace Research</u> 16 (March 1979): 263-277.

4644. Lemarchand, Rene. "The CIA in Africa: How Central? How Intelligent?," <u>Journal of Modern African Studies</u> 14/3 (September 1976): 401-426.
　　　　Examines the role of the CIA in Africa in light of recent disclosures of involvement in civil wars, assassinations, and other mischief. Argues that the principle by conducting US policy in Africa should be "common decency and ultimate purpose."

4645. Lembart, Lee. "The Public Cryptography Study Group," <u>Cryptologia</u> 5/2 (April 1981): 118-122.

4646. Lemieux, Vincent and Genevieve Ledoux. "Control of Government Information: The Care of Quebec," <u>Canadian Public Administration</u> 26/3 (1983): 402-419.
　　　　This piece, published in French, is a discussion of government regulations covering access to government information in Quebec.

4647. Lemoine, Jessica L. "The Monitoring of Telephone Conversations on An Extension Held to be a Violation of the Invasion of Privacy Act: <u>Ribas v. Clark</u>," <u>Pepperdine Law Review</u> 13 (December 1985): 249-253.
　　　　Discusses the topic following the case of <u>Ribas v. Clark</u> in which the issue of monitoring conversations by way of extension phones was raised.

4648. Lenczowski, George. "The Arc of Crisis: Its Central Sector," Foreign Affairs 57/4 (Spring 1979): 796-820.

Using a definition of the "Arc," the author examines crisis responses to situations in Turkey, Iran and Pakistan. Relevant to the study of conflict predicates in the Middle East.

4649. Lenczowski, George. "United States Support for Iran's Independence and Integrity, 1945-1959," Annals of American Academy of Political and Social Sciences 401 (May 1972): 45-55.

An interesting view of the occurrences in Iran during the period in title, especially because it contains no information about possible CIA involvement in the Shah's return from exile after the demise of Mossadegh.

4650. Lens, Sidney. "Partners: Labor and the CIA," Progressive 39 (Febrauary 1975): 35-39.

4651. Lens, Sidney. "On the Uses and Abuses of Secrecy," Progressive (March 1980): 46-47.

Argues that secrecy in the US has become a phobic way of life and a subversion to democratic governance.

4652. Lent, John A. "Asian Mass Communications--Selected Information Sources," Journal of Broadcasting 19 (Summer 1975): 321-340.

A selected list of sources pertaining to Asian mass communications, highly useful (but now dated) for those interested in the region. Contains bibliographies, directories, periodicals, and general sources on the topic.

4653. Lent, John A. "Caribbean Mass Communications--Selected Information Sources," Journal of Broadcasting 20/1 (Winter 1976): 111-126.

A description of research which ultimately produced a list of newspapers, periodicals, and journals relevant to the Caribbean region.

4654. Lentner, Howard H. "The Pueblo Affair: Anatomy of a Crisis," Military Review 49 (July 1969): 55-66.

4655. Leo, Richard A. "From Coercion to Deception: The Changing Nature of Police Interrogation in America," Crime, Law and Social Change 18/1-2 (September 1992): 35-60.

Offers a typology of coercive interrogation, including brute physical force, physical torture, deniable coercion, incommunicado interrogation, physical duress, threats of harm; meaning of the third degree; an empirical typology of deceptive interrogation; and the role of professionalism in altering the nature of police interrogation practices.

4656. Leonard, Raymond W. "Studying the Kremlin's Secret Soldiers: A Historiographical Essay on the GRU, 1918-1945," Journal of Military History 56/3 (July 1992): 403-421.

A detailed study of intelligence capabilities of the early and later Soviet military; Soviet military doctrine; mole operations; other operations; and suggestions for further research.

4657. Leonard, Theodore. "Group Target Reporting," Infantry 52 (July-August 1962): 5-7.

4658. Leonberger, Loren B. "War of the Wizards," Airman 14/11 (November 1970): 17-19.

4659. Leopold, G. Vernon. "Cosmic Surveillance by Space-Flight Momentum," Wayne Law Review 6/3 (Summer 1960): 311-339.

Discussion of an evolving concern for space exploration and state security interests; disarmament controls; legal problems; creation of an international cosmic surveillance authority; and various pieces of correspondence on the subject.

4660. LeQueux, W. "Our Strangle-hold on the German Spy System," Canadian Monthly 48 (February 1917): 337-340.

4661. Lerville, Edmond. "Un General Francais Peu Connu le Baron De Kalb, 1721-1780," Revue Histoire des Armees 1 (1986): 78-87.

A brief biographical study of Baron de Kalb's French military service.

4662. Lesce, Tony. "Bugs, Blackmail, Secrets and Spies," International Combat Arms: The Journal of Defense Technology 6 (March 1988): 33-37.

4663. Lesher, Dean. "What Do the Espionage and Sedition Acts Forbid?," California State Bar Journal 17/5 (July-August 1942): 204-213.

Contains discussion of the historical background of the Acts, constitutional considerations, the application of the Acts to World War II, and other war acts.

4664. Leskov, Sergei. "Dividing the Glory of the Fathers," Bulletin of the Atomic Scientists 49/5 (May 1993): 37-39.

Addresses in brief fashion some of the dynamics of controversy between Soviet scientists and Soviet nuclear experts over the Soviet atomic bomb and hydrogen bomb projects.

4665. Leskov, Sergei. "An Unreliable Witness," Bulletin of the Atomic Scientists 50 (July-August 1994): 33-36.

Brief discussion of Soviet scientists and intelligence services.

4666. Lessne, Scott A. "Constitutional Law--International Travel Restrictions and the First Amendment: To Speak or Not to Speak?," Western New England Law Review 4 (Winter 1982): 449-478.

Focusses on the constitutional questions raised by the revocation of Philip Agee's passport for his activities in foreign countries. Asks whether the Supreme Court should have considered the broader context of free speech in connection with travel restrictions.

4667. Lester, Richard. "Secrecy, Patents and Non-Proliferation," Bulletin of the Atomic Scientists 37/5 (May 1981): 35-38.

Argues the difficulties of keeping secrecy over US scientific discoveries.

4668. Leutze, James. "The Secret of the Churchill-Roosevelt Correspondence, September 1939-May 1940," Journal of Contemporary History 10/3 (1975): 465-491.

Argues that there was no evidence to substantiate the claim by spy Tyler G. Kent that President Roosevelt lied to the American people about pre war help given to Britain. Discusses intelligence information exchanges with the British which had the effect of breaking neutrality.

4669. Levchenko, Stanislav. "Inside the Soviet Army," World & I 5 (1990): 108-112.

Major sections include discussion of the Army's role in government, changes made by Mikhail Gorbachev, problems in the Soviet army, and the oncoming death of the communist system. Offers insights into the organization factors relevant to the crumbling of the Army.

4670. Levchenko, Stanislav. "The Once and Future KGB," World & I 6 (March 1991): 82-87.

4671. Levesque, Raymond W. "Counterinsurgency Intelligence," Military Intelligence 12/4 (October-December 1986): 26-30.

Reviews tactical intelligence in guerilla war to include requirements, colletion, and analysis in support of a commander engaged in counterinsurgency operations.

4672. Levesque, Raymond W. "LIC Doctrine and Intelligence," Military Intelligence 13/3 (October 1987): 32-34.

Points out differences between conventional and low intensity conflicts and their impact on intelligence doctrine.

4673. Levi, Edward H. "Confidentiality and Democratic Government," Record of the Association of the Bar of the City of New York 1975 (May-June 1975): 323-335.

The Attorney General of the United States addresses the issue of confidentiality of government records in terms of the tension between the need for organizational secrecy and investigative and discovery needs of the public.

4674. Levin, A. "Shornikova Affair," <u>Slavonic and East European Review</u> 21 (November 1943): 1-18.

4675. Levin, Alexandra L. "Who Hid John H. Surratt, the Lincoln Conspiracy Case Figure?," <u>Maryland Historical Magazine</u> 60/2 (1965): 175-184.
    Describes the activities of a man who had plotted to kidnap Abe Lincoln. When Lincoln was killed, Surratt was found innocent in spite of the evidence. The reasons for his release from responsibility in the assassination plot remain unclear.

4676. Levin, Meyer. "Of Chanah Szenes and Other Secret Agents," <u>Menorah Journal</u> 34 (April 1946): 122-132.

4677. Levin, V. and V. Kolchevsky. "Engineer Camoflage," <u>Soviet Military Review</u> 4 (April 1981): 42-44.

4678. Levin, Walter A. "Britain's Quest for an Ally, 1914-1917," <u>American Intelligence Journal</u> 12/1 (Winter 1991): 16-18.
    A brief discussion of six variables in the process of deceiving the American public to achieve an ally in World War I: organizational capability of British intelligence; penetration of the target (German transmissions of war progress); forces on the ground to conduct the campaign; a sympathetic or predisposed audience; an issue around which to unite; and the ability to counter or discredit opposing views.

4679. Levine, G. "Intelligence as Deception: The Mill on the Floss," <u>PMLA</u> 80 (September 1965): 402-409.

4680. Levine, Jack. "Variable Matrix Substitution in Algebraic Cryptography," <u>American Mathematical Monthly</u> 65 (1958): 170-179.
    A mathematically technical discussion of fixed substitution and two types of variable substitution in cryptography.

4681. Levine, Jack. "Some Elementary Cryptanalysis of Algebraic Cryptography," <u>American Mathematical Monthly</u> 68 (May 1961): 411-418.
    Author defines algebraic cryptography, a process of encipherment which converts a plain message into a cipher message by means of a simultaneous linear congruence, where n is an arbitrary integer.

4682. Levine, Jack. "Corrections for Published Copy of United States

Cryptographic Patents, 1861-1981," Cryptologia 8/2 (April 1984): 161-162.

4683. Levine, Jack and J. V. Brawley. "Some Cryptographic Applications of Permutation Polynomials," Cryptologia 1/1 (January 1977): 76-92.

4684. Levine, Jack and Michael Willet. "The Two-Message in Cipher Text Autokey," (Parts I & II) Cryptologia 3/3 & 3/4 (July & October 1979): 177-186; 220-231.

4685. Levine, Jack and Robert E. Harwig. "Applications of the Drazin Inverse to the Hill Cryptographic System," (Parts I, II, III, IV) Cryptologia 4/2 & 4/3 & 5/2 & 5/4 (April & July 1980; April & October 1981): 71-85; 150-168; 67-77; 213-228.

4686. Levine, Jack and Richard Chandler. "Some Further Cryptographic Applications of Permutation Polynomials," Cryptologia 11/4 (October 1987): 211-218.

4687. Levine, Jack and Richard Chandler. "The Hill Cyptographic System with Unknown Cipher Alphabet But Known Plaintext," Cryptologia 13/1 (January 1989): 1-28.

4688. Levine, Jack and Richard Chandler. "The Two-Message Problem in the Hill Cryptographic System with Unknown Alphabet," Cryptologia 17/1 (January 1993): 1-30.

4689.   Levine, Jeffrey L.   "Judicial Review of Classified Documents: Amendments to the Freedom of Information Act," Harvard Journal on Legislation 12/3 (June 1975): 415-446.
      Examines the relationship between the FOIA and the classification system under E.O. 11652, the textual commitment test, the judicial standards test, substantive in camera review, procedural review, and problems accruing from the relationship. Evaluates the new amendments to the FOIA and the contributions to clarity they will make.

4690. Levine, Nina S. "The Case of Eleanor Cobham: Authorizing History in 2 Henry VI," Shakespeare Studies 22 (1994): 104-121.

4691. Levite, Ariel. "The Role of Intelligence in Israel's Foreign Policy," Defense Analysis 3/2 (Fall 1987): 177-179.
      A brief overview of the missions of Israeli security services and some information about Israeli intelligence in several Middle East events.

4692. Levite, Ariel. "Intelligence and Strategic Surprises Revisited: A Response to Richard K. Betts' 'Surprise, Scholasticism, and Strategy,'" <u>International Studies Quarterly</u> 33/3 (September 1989): 345-349.

The author defends his book, <u>Intelligence and Strategic Surprise</u>, against the critiques of Dr. Richard Betts. He suggests that the orthodox school of surprise theory can be refined and expanded through application of his methodological variations.

4693. Levitin, Samuel. "Equivalence Classes: Toward More Efficient Search," <u>Cryptologia</u> 11/1 (January 1987): 21-28.

4694. Levitt, Geoffrey. "Problems in the Verification and Enforcement of SALT Agreements in Light of the Record of Soviet Compliance with SALT I," <u>Harvard International Law Journal</u> 22 (Spring 1981): 379-404.

Discusses the record of Soviet compliance with SALT I agreements; problems of verification and enforcement; enforcement and verification in the SALT II Treaty; and recommendations.

4695. Levitt, Peter H. "Legality of the Ban on Travel to Iran," <u>Columbia Human Rights Law Review</u> 12/1 (Spring-Summer 1980): 91-112.

Ban on travel to Iran raised two questions: First, whether the President was empowered to prohibit travel to "danger zones;" Second, whether travel restrictions of this nature are constitutionally permissible. Article discusses statutory issues, constitutional issues and conclusions.

4696. Levy, Jack S. "Alliance Formation and War Behavior: An Analysis of the Great Powers, 1495-1975," <u>Journal of Conflict Resolution</u> 25/4 (December 1981): 581-613.

Considers the evolution of "great powers" warfare in long term perspective. Major sections discuss research methods; conceptualization and measurement problems; frequency of great power war; and characteristics of great power war.

4697. Levy, Jack S. "Historical Trends in Great Power War, 1495-1975," <u>International Studies Quarterly</u> 26/2 (June 1982): 278-300.

Considers the evolution of "Great Powers" warfare in long term trends. Major sections discuss research methods; conceptualization and measurement; frequency of great power war; and characteristics of great power war.

4698. Levy, Jack S. "Misperception and the Causes of War: Theoretical Linkages and Analytical Problems," <u>World Politics</u> 34/3 (July 1983): 76-90.

Reviews the literature on misperception, then considers forms of misperception; linkages from misperception to war; conceptual and methodological problems; and conclusions.

4699. Levy, Michael. "The Electronic Monitoring of Workers: Privacy in the Age of the Electronic Sweatshop," <u>Legal Reference Services Quarterly</u> 14 (1995): 5-56.

4700. Levy, Rudolph. "Countering the Terrorist Threat," <u>Military Intelligence</u> 10/4 (October-December 1984): 6-7.
　　　　Outlines the role of intelligence in terrorism counteraction.

4701. Lewellen, Ted C. "State Terror and the Disruption of Internal Adaptations by CIA Covert Actions," <u>Scandinavian Journal of Development Alternatives</u> 9/2&3 (June-September 1990): 47-65.
　　　　Accounts for several CIA covert actions in Third World nations which were followed by periods of harsh internal conditions involving economic and political disruptions.

4702. Lewin, Ronald. "A Signal-Intelligence War," <u>Journal of Contemporary History</u> 16/3 (July 1981): 501-512.
　　　　Argues that signal intelligence, contrary to some historical views, played an extremely important role during World War II. Evidence is offered.

4703. Lewis, Anthony M. "The Blind Spot of U.S. Foreign Intelligence," <u>Journal of Communication</u> 26/1 (Winter 1976): 44-55.
　　　　Explores the question of ethnocentricism in CIA's foreign intelligence reports. Applies examples from the Vietnam War experience.

4704. Lewis, Brenda R. "Even Our Side Hated SOE," <u>Army</u> 32/3 (March 1982): 50-58.
　　　　SOE (Special Operations Executive) was an intelligence and espionage organization that worked closely with underground and resistance forces. The author says that it was a much despised organization for several reasons discussed.

4705. Lewis, Brenda R. "Benedict Arnold: An Epilogue," <u>Army</u> 33/1 (January 1983): 46-52.

4706. Lewis, Edward R., Jr. "The British Spy in Illinois Pharmacy," <u>Pharmacy in History</u> 14/3 (1972): 83-89.

4707. Lewis, Frank W. "The Day of the Dodo," <u>Cryptologia</u> 16/1 (January 1990): 11-12.
　　　　This is a brief account of a spy named "Donald" arrested in the Soviet Union.

4708. Lewis, George H. "Spy Fiction American Style," <u>Journal of Communication</u> 25/4 (1975): 132-137.

Discusses various themes American national characteristics found in espionage fiction published between the 1950s and the 1970s.

4709. Lewis, Jeremy R. T. "Freedom of Information: Developments in the United States," International Journal of Intelligence and Counterintelligence 3/4 (Winter 1989): 465-473.

A brief update on the provisions of the Access to Personal Files Act and Access to Medical Reports Act. Mentions new rules, continuing gaps, policy, and requirements.

4710. Lewis, Jim. "The 'Weeding' of Harold Begbie," Intelligence and National Security 9/1 (January 1994): 50-58.

Discusses the manuscript of journalist Harold Begbie, in which Begbie praises the service of many wireless radio operators of World War I. Four chapters of Begbie's manuscript were missing, as well as chapters on aeronautics and the wireless. Theorizes about the missing information.

4711. Lewis, Jonathan. "National Security and Capital Markets," International Journal of Intelligence and Counterintelligence 6/4 (Winter 1993): 507-517.

Argues for a larger role of the US intelligence community in monitoring signs of possible disruption of formerly centrally planned economies in the transition phases to free market economies. Major sections discuss the role of capital markets in economic development; government intervention; the vulnerable system of newly emergent economies; consequences of failure; capital markets and the clash of civilizations; Islam and capital markets; Iran's power projected; China, looking to stabilize Russian reform?; and the development of a capital markets intelligence base.

4712. Lewis, Kevin N. "Dealing with the Unexpected," Orbis 26/4 (Winter 1983): 839-847.

Argues that the best way to deter, detect, and respond to enemy actions is through the competent gathering and assessment of enemy capabilities via good intelligence work.

4713. Lewis, R. P. W. "The Use by the Meteorological Office of Decyphered German Meteorological Data During the Second World War," Meteorological Magazine 114 (1985): 113+.

4714. Lewy, Guenter. "Can Democracy Keep Secrets?: Do We Need an Official Secrets Act?," Policy Review 26 (Fall 1983): 17-29.

Summarizes the espionage laws of the US, then argues that the laws as currently written fail to preclude leaks of sensitive information.

4715. Li, Chuan-Ming; Tzonelih Hwang; and Narn-Yee Lee. "Conspiracy

Attacks on the Threshold RSA Signature Scheme," Cryptologia 18/4 (October 1994): 372-380.

4716. Li, Wei. "The Security Service for Chinese Central Leaders," China Quarterly 143 (September 1995): 814-827.
Major sections discuss the central security services; political funtions; and conclusions. Contains an organization chart of Beijing-based security institutions.

4717. Liaw, Horng-Twu and Chin-Luang Lei. "An Efficient Password Authentication Scheme Based on a Unit Circle," Cryptologia 19/2 (April 1995): 198-208.

4718. Liberti, Joseph C. "Counterintelligence in Direct Support," Infantry 64/2 (March-April 1974): 39-42.
Discusses prisoner of war interrogations as a weapon of tactical intelligence in the Vietnam war.

4719. Libicki, Martin C. and James A. Hazlett. "Do We Need an Information Corps?," Joint Forces Quarterly 2 (Autumn 1993): 88-97.

4720. Lichtman, A. J. "Tommy the Cork: The Secret World of Washington's First Modern Lobbyist: [T. Corcoran]," Washington Monthly 19 (February 1987): 41-49.
When Truman taped Tommy Corcoran, he gave history a unique look at the beginning of executive branch lobbying, now Washington's major industry.

4721. Licklider, Roy E. "The Missile Gap Controversy," Political Science Quarterly 85/4 (December 1970): 600-615.
Describes the missile gap controversy in the 1950s and reviews the testimony of Senator Cannon, CIA director Allen Dulles, and Defense Secretary Neil McElroy. Offers speculation about Soviet and US missile capabilities and ability to prevent an attack.

4722. Liu, Alan P. L. "Ideology and Information: Correspondents of the New China News Agency and Chinese Foreign Policy Making," Journal of International Affairs 26/2 (1972): 131-145.
Evaluation of the dual role of correspondents for the New China News Agency as both intelligence gatherers and suppliers of information to Western news agencies and to the political hierarchy of China.

4723. Lightbody, Gregg. "'Dezinformatsia'--The Soviet Act of Warring with Words," International Combat Arms: The Journal of Defense Technology (March 1986): 76-79.

4724. Lightbody, Gregg. "The Undercover Spy War," <u>International Combat Arms: Journal of Defense Technology</u> (November 1985): 50-57.

4725. Lilly, J. Robert. "Selling Justice: Electronic Monitoring and the Security Industry," <u>Justice Quarterly</u> 9/3 (September 1992): 493-503.

4726. Lilly, J. Robert; Richard A. Ball; G. David Curry; and Richard C. Smith. "The Pride, Inc. Program: An Evaluation of 5 Years of Electronic Monitoring," <u>Federal Probation</u> 56/4 (December 1992): 42-47.

4727. Lilly, J. Robert; Richard A. Ball; G. David Curry; and John McMulle. "Electronic Monitoring of the Drunk Driver: A Seven-Year Study of the Home Confinement Alternative," <u>Crime & Delinquency</u> 39/4 (October 1993): 462-484.

This is a report of a seven-year study on the home confinement alternative punishment for drunk driving. Electronic monitoring, the authors argue, is the wave of the future, but questions must be raised about the intentions of manufacturers and the threats to individual rights.

4728. Limbert, John. "Nest of Spies: Pack of Lies," <u>Washington Quarterly</u> 5/2 (Spring 1982): 75-82.

An attempt to give closer scrutiny to the seizure of the American embassy in Teheran. Author suggests that a book titled <u>Revelations from the Nest of Espionage</u> is an invaluable first source for explaining who was occupying the embassy and why.

4729. Limoncelli, Gregory. "Clarifying the Authority Delegated to Secretary of State for the Control of Passports: (<u>Haig v. Agee</u>)," <u>Boston College Law Review</u> 24/2 (March 1983): 435-467.

A lengthy case note covering the issues related to the State Department revocation of former CIA employee Philip Agee's passport. Suggests legal territory that a future plaintiff might apply to overcome the Agee ruling.

4730. Linde, Hans. "Courts and Censorship," <u>Minnesota Law Review</u> 66/1 (November 1981): 171-208.

Reviews the development of freedom of the press under state constitutions and the Fourth Amendment; explores the Supreme Court holding in <u>Near v. Minnesota</u>; and considers alternatives in the debate between censorship of laws versus censorship of expression.

4731. Linde, Stephen. "Arms Control--State Department Regulation of Exports of Technical Data Relating to Munitions Held to Encompass General Knowledge and Experience: <u>United States v. Van Hee</u>," <u>New York University Journal of International Law and Politics</u> 9/1 (Spring 1976): 91-112.

Discusses the question resolved by the case: to what extent can unclassified technical data be regulated under the Mutual Security Act of 1954? Includes legislative history, liberalization of export controls in 1969, critique of the Van Hee case, and recommended approach.

4732. Linder, James C. "The Fall of Lima Site 85: The War in Laos," Studies in Intelligence 38/5 (1995): 79-88.

Discusses the details of the CIA war supervision in Laos in 1965 and 1966. Major sections discuss the sensitive TACAN radar facility to monitor North Vietnam; the opium factor; the 1967 campaign; first attacks; defensive vulnerabilities; the lull; casual attitude; evacuation planning; closing in; deferring a decision; sapper attack; evacuation attempt; destroying the site; and postmortem.

4733. Lindsay, Franklin A. "Unconventional Warfare," Foreign Affairs 40/2 (January 1962): 264-274.

Discusses the successes of the Soviet Union in guerilla warfare in Laos and Vietnam; role of secret forces and intelligence; and US development of special forces to respond.

4734. Lindsay, James J. "C³I Challenges for U.S. Special Operations Command," Signal 42 (May 1988): 21-23.

4735. Lindsay, John V. "Inquiry into the Darkness of the Cloak, the Sharpness of the Dagger," Esquire 61 (March 1964): 106-107, 109.

Argues that the Bay of Pigs and the assassination of Diem in South Vietnam have shown that the CIA is overstepping its bounds. Offers an earlier suggestion that the Congress formed a joint committee to check on the CIA, and thereby provided a useful service to the whole intelligence community.

4736. Linebarger, Paul M. "STASM: Psychological Warfare and Literary Criticism," South Atlantic Quarterly 46 (July 1940): 344-348.

Defines STASM: Source, Time, Audience, Subject, and Mission. Presents two assumptions made by psychological warfare analysts, and discusses psychological effects in literary criticism.

4737. Linebarger, Paul M. "Psychological Warfare in World War Two," Infantry Journal 60 (May-June 1947): 36-39, 41-46.

Part I discusses the pre-belligerent stages, the British-German radio war, and ONI and OSS operations. Part II appears in June 1947, 41-46, and discusses the lessons and effects.

4738. Ling, Yu-Long. "A Comparative Study of the Privileges and Immunities of United Nations Member Representatives and Official with the Traditional Privileges and Immunities of Diplomatic Agents," Washington and Lee Law Review 33/1 (Winter 1976): 91-160.

Espionage activities are often carried out under the cover of diplomatic privileges and immunities. This article discusses the law of such privileges and immunities.

4739. Linn, Brian M. "Intelligence and Low-Intensity Conflict in the Phillipine War, 1899-1902," Intelligence and National Security 6/1 (January 1991): 90-114.

Discusses the hyper-critical need for intelligence in irregular/guerilla wars. The need for tactical and strategic intelligence is magnified in this type of conflict, for example the Philippine war of 1899. Suggests that US intelligence was weak in the first two years of conflict, thus illustrating certain consequences.

4740. Linscott, Walt A. "Drainage Patterns and Their Tactical Significance," Marine Corps Gazette (March 1988): 23-24.

Terrain and drainage are discussed as important intelligence concerns.

4741. Linzer, Stephen. "Federal Procedure for Court Ordered Electronic Surveillance: Does It Meet Standards of Berger and Katz?," Journal of Criminal Law and Criminology 60 (1969): 203-214.

Major sections include discussion of the first case on wiretapping (Olmstead), the nature of electronic eavesdropping, Berger v. New York, Katz v. United States, Safe Streets Act of 1968, court orders, time period on interception, and emergency situations.

4742. Lipset, Harold K. "The Wiretapping-Eavesdropping Problem: A Private Investigator's View," Minnesota Law Review 44/5 (April 1960): 873-889.

Discusses restrictions on wiretapping and the use of electronic equipment in the private sector; modern recording equipment; and conclusions.

4743. Lipson, Leon. "An Argument on the Legality of Reconnaissance Satellites," Proceedings of the American Society of International Law 55 (1961): 174-176.

Part of a larger debate on national sovereignty in outer space reconnaissance, this author compares Yuri Gagarin's flight in space with Francis Gary Powers' overflight of the Soviet Union. Argues for more international agreement on inspections and data.

4744. Lipson, Stanley H. "The Matrix Cipher of C. L. Dodgson," Cryptologia 14/1 (January 1990): 28-36.

4745. Lipson, Stanley H. and Francine Abeles. "The Key-vowel Cipher of Charles S. Dodgson," Cryptologia 15/1 (January 1991): 18-24.

4746. Lischer, Tracy K. "U.S. v. Falvey: A Constitutionality Test for Foreign Electronic Intelligence Surveillance," North Carolina Journal of International Law and Commercial Regulation 8/1 (Winter 1982): 77-86.

Discusses several issues and concerns related to the balancing of an individual's right to privacy against the executive branch's need to monitor foreign powers and foreign secret agents.

4747. Lissitzyn, Oliver J. "The Treatment of Aerial Intruders in Recent Practice and International Law," American Journal of International Law 47 (1953): 559-563.

4748. Lissitzyn, Oliver J. "Some Legal Implications of the U-2 and RB-47 Incidents," American Journal of International Law 56/1 (1962): 135-142.

Considers several legal implications of the positions taken by each of the governments affected by the U-2 and RB-47 overflights.

4749. Lissitzyn, Oliver J. "Electronic Reconnaissance from the High Seas and International Law," Naval War College Review 22/2 (February 1970): 26-34.

Concludes that electronic surveillance against coastal states should be resorted to only when analysis reveals that costs are substantially outweighed by benefits.

4750. Litten, Frederick S. "Einstein and the Noulens Affair," British Journal of the History of Science 24/4 (December 1991): 465-467.

4751. Litten, Frederick S. "The Noulens Affair," China Quarterly 138 (June 1994): 492-512.

Explores in detailed fashion the arrest and trial in Shanghai in 1931 of Hilaire Noulens and his wife. The account provides new insights into the conflict between the Soviet Union and China in the 1930s.

4752. Little, Alan M. "The Soviet Propaganda Machine," Department of State Bulletin 25 (1951): 367-370.

4753. Little, Douglas. "Antibolshevism and American Foreign Policy, 1919-1939: The Diplomacy of Self-Delusion," American Quarterly 35/4 (Fall 1983): 376-390.

A useful background article for studies of American domestic intelligence collection. Argues that antibolshevism is the key factor in comprehending American foreign policy.

4754. Little, Douglas. "Cold War and Covert Action: The United States and Syria, 1945-1958," Middle East Journal 44/1 (Winter 1990): 51-75.

Major sections consider US-Syrian relations after World War II; revolving door governments; the Eisenhower years; and conclusions. CIA is mentioned extensively.

4755. Little, Wendell E. "Covert Operations: A Needed Alternative," Air University Review 33 (September-October 1982): 65-70.

A justification for and defense of covert operations as a means of avoiding full scale war. Includes sections on Soviet policies, need for US strategy, the "third option" (covert ops), and issues arising in the 1980s.

4756. Little, Wendell E. "The Intelligence Bookshelf," Air University Review 30 (May-June 1979): 85-91.

A review essay of five books: Secret Intelligence in the Twentieth Century; U.S. Intelligence and the Soviet Strategic Threat; Intelligence, Espionage, Counterespionage and Covert Operations; Spies and All That; and The War Animals.

4757. Litvin, A. L. "VCheka in Soviet Historical Literature," Voprosy Istorii 5 (May 1986): 96-102.

A survey and bibliography of the recent writings about the VCheka.

4758. Lively, James K. "Propaganda Techniques of Civil War Cartoonists," Public Opinion Quarterly 6 (1942): 99-106.

An analysis of Civil War cartoons as to their propaganda intent and value. Includes some cartoon samples.

4759. Livergood, Norman D. "Design Issues in the Simulation of Beliefs in Corporate Intelligence Systems: REALPOLITIK II," International Journal of Man-Machine Studies 39 (July 1993): 99-112.

Discussion of simulation of corporate intelligence practices in Japan and the United States.

4760. Livingston, George D. "Pershing II: Success Amid Chaos," Military Review 50/5 (May 1970): 56-60.

Reflections on the Pershing II intelligence system used in the Vietnam war.

4761. Livingston, George D. "QUILT: A Quantitative Approach to Determining an Enemy's Most Probable Course of Action," Military Review 52/7 (July 1972): 44-53.

QUILT refers to Quantitative Intelligence Analysis Technique. Discusses the use of this technique to determine enemy patterns, assignment of weights to capabilities, and computation of relative frequencies.

4762. Livingston, M. Stanley. "Science and Security," Annals of the American Academy of Political and Social Science (July 1955): 4-12.

An overview of the political and social pressures in American society and the world which led to the creation of the American domestic/government security program in the 1950s.

4763. Livingstone, Neil C. "States in Opposition: The War Against Terrorism," Conflict: An International Journal 3/2-3 (1981): 83-141.

A lengthy and detailed introduction to combatting terrorism and associated problems. Also discusses legal remedies, social reform, high standard of government, strong intelligence capability, harsh punishment, boycotts of other nations, police training, and counter terrorism.

4764. Livingstone, Neil C. "Death Squads," World Affairs 146/3 (Winter 1983-1984): 239-248.

Argues that right and left death squads in Latin America, as encouraged or supported from the US or other nations, were harsh but successful in restoring order and democracy. Such organizations appear to have evolved following the US effort in 1954 to oust Jacobo Arbenz from power in Guatemala.

4765. Livingstone, Neil C. "Oklahoma City: Portent of the Future?," World & I 10 (July 1995): 78-83.

Argues for the reinstatement of domestic surveillance strategies, methods, and capabilities to hedge against terrorism at home.

4766. Lloyd, Ian J. "The Interception of Communication Act 1985," Modern Law Review 49 (January 1986): 86-95.

Discusses the British Act of 1985 regarding the monitoring of citizens' communications and the legal controls necessary to protect individual rights. Also discusses supervision agencies and telephone metering.

4767. Loane, Jabez W., IV. "Treason and Aiding the Enemy," Military Law Review 30 (October 1965): 43-81.

Provides history of treason, constitutional view of treason, development of the federal law, two types of treason, jurisdictional aspects of treason, affirmative defenses, and the military law of treason.

4768. Loatman, R. Bruce and Stephen D. Post. "A Natural Language Processing System for Intelligence Message Analyses," Signal 43/1 (September 1988): 41-45.

4769. Lobban, Richard. "American Mercenaries in Rhodesia," Journal of Southern African Affairs 3/3 (July 1978): 319-326.

Argues that evidence supports the intrusion of US and other mercenary-sponsored organizations in Rhodesia, and that such intrusion is not helpful to US interests. Claims CIA involvement.

4770. Lobe, Thomas. "The Rise and Demise of the Office of Public Safety," Armed Forces and Society 9/2 (Winter 1983): 187-213.

Traces the origins of the OPS to the early 1960s CIA involvement in training foreign police and intelligence organizations, extendign through the Johnson and Nixon administrations to its demise in 1974. Discusses the Vietnam morass; press and congressional criticism of OPS; and internal organizational failures.

4771. Lobel, Jules. "Covert War and Congressional Authority: Hidden War and Forgotten Power," University of Pennsylvania Law Review 134/5 (June 1986): 1035-1110.

Explores the idea of the use of private military forces to infiltrate foreign lands. Such armies are deployed without congressional approval in covert operations for which authority is questionable. Review the history of private armies, their modern use, and legal controls.

4772. Lobel, Jules, et al. "Committee of U.S. Citizens Living in Nicaragua v. Ronald Reagan," National Lawyers Guild Practitioner 44/1 (Winter 1987): 1-7.

Summation of the legal actions of 6 organizations and five individuals who sued for declaratory and injunctive relief against the President, CIA director, and the Secretaries of State and Defense.

4773. Locard, Edmond. "Cryptography in Criminal Matters," International Criminal Police Review 1/2 (October-November 1946): 17.

4774. Locher, James R., III. "Intelligence Support to Special Operations and Low Intensity Conflict," American Intelligence Journal 11/1 (Winter 1989-1990): 13-17.

Presents an historical perspective on low intensity conflict; the response in the 1980s; third world threats; special operations reorganization; Special Operations Forces revitalization; and intelligence challenges.

4775. Lockhart, John M. B. "The Relationship Between Secret Services and Government in a Modern State," RUSI Defence Studies Journal 119 (June 1974): 3-8.

4776. Lockhart, John M. B. "CIA and the Powers of Darkness?," RUSI Defence Studies Journal 120/1 (1975): 82-84.

A book review essay attacking a book on the CIA's ills by Marchetti and Marks.

4777. Lockhart, John M. B. "Sir William Wiseman Bart - Agent of Influence," RUSI Defence Studies Journal 134/2 (Summer 1989): 63-67.

A brief account of the operations of German and British intelligence activities in the United States.

4778. Lockshin, Arnold. "The CIA: Instrument of U.S. Foreign Policy," Political Affairs 54 (May 1975): 30-43.

4779. Lockwood, Jonathan S. "Russia's New Military Doctrine," American Intelligence Journal 14/3 (Autumn-Winter 1993-1994): 61-65.

This article is a reprint of articles appearing in the Washington Post newspaper on September 27, 1992 and December 13, 1992. Contains information on the Polish espionage work for the US by Colonel Ryszard Kuklinski.

4780. Lockwood, Jonathan S. "Sources of Error in Indications and Warning," Defense Intelligence Journal 3/1 (Spring 1994): 75-88.

Discusses four sources of error: enemy; analyst; policymaker; and system.

4781. Lodahl, Jan M. "Verifying SALT," Foreign Policy 24 (Fall 1976): 40-64.

An early analysis of the methods and limitations of verification imposed by the Strategic Arms Limitations Treaty.

4782. Lodge, Juliet and Avi Shlaim. "The U.S. and the Berlin Blockade, 1948-1949," Jerusalem Journal of International Relations 3/2-3 (1978): 51-80.

Discusses the impact of increasing threat, time salience and probability of war on various facets of crisis behavior by decision makers.

4783. Loeb, Robert A. "Eavesdropping in Illinois: The Conflict Between Statutory and Case Law," Illinois Bar Journal 81 (January 1993): 16-21, 43.

Suggests that the Illinois case law appears to permit wiretapping despite statutory law requiring all parties to consent. Sections discuss the split between case and statutory law; appellate interpretations of the Beardsley case; federal jurisdiction principles; law enforcement eavesdropping; technological advances in eavesdropping; and new privacy recognition.

4784. Loeber, Dietrich A. "The Soviet Procuracy and the Rights of the Individual Against the State," Journal of the International Commission of Jurists 1 (Autumn 1957): 59-105.

An extensive, detailed discussion of the agencies of Soviet government responsible by statutes for the protection of individual rights. Mentions investigative agencies.

4785. Loeber, Dietrich A. "Statutes of Agencies with Ministerial Status in the USSR: List of Sources as of 1 July 1982," Review of Socialist Law 8 (December 1982): 359-367.

A list of the agencies in the Soviet Union with ministerial status, including the KGB. See note 4b in this piece for statutory authorities.

4786. Loeffke, Bernard. "The Soviet Union: Perspective of an Army Attache," Parameters: Journal of the U.S. Army War College 10/4 (December 1980): 52-56.

Major sections discuss the social and psychological role of the attache; military mission and training in the Soviet army; and conclusions.

4787. Loescher, Michael S. "New Intelligence Networks Improve Command, Control," Signal 44/12 (August 1990): 45-47.

4788. Loescher, Michael S. "Copernicus Offers a New Center of the Universe," U.S. Naval Institute Proceedings 117/1 (January 1991): 86-93.

4789. Loevinger, Lee. "The Cuckoo's Egg: Tracking a Spy Through the Maze of Computer Espionage," Jurimetrics Journal 31/2 (Winter 1991): 259-264.

A book review essay pertaining to The Cuckoo's Nest: Tracking a Spy Through the Maze of Computer Espionage by Cliff Stoll.

4790. Lofgren, Stig. "Soviet Submarines Against Sweden," Strategic Review 12/1 (Winter 1984): 36-42.

Sections include discussion of Finnish and Norwegian incidents, the penetrated Swedish archipelagoes, the pattern of encroachments, Swedish government's reactions, Soviet motives, the larger context, psychological warfare against Sweden, and basic alternatives for Sweden.

4791. Lomask, Milton. "Benedict Arnold: The Aftermath of Treason," American Heritage 18/6 (October 1967): 17, 84-92.

A history of life for the Benedict Arnold family after Benedict's treasonous actions in the American revolution.

4792. Long, Anne K. and Jerome H. Kahan. "The Cuban Missile Crisis: A Study of Its Strategic Context," Political Science Quarterly 87 (December 1972): 564-590.

Major sections discuss the Crisis, evaluate the Crisis, explore the impact of the Crisis on later US and Soviet strategic policies, and offers policy implications.

4793. Long, D. A. "A Treacherous Quotation: E. M. Forster, Dante and Treason," Encounter 72 (February 1989): 38-40.

4794. Long, G. Allison. "The Biography of A. Francis Arcier (1890-1969)," American Aviation History Society Journal 26 (Summer 1981): 126-142.

4795. Long, John W. "Plot and Counter-plot in Revolutionary Russia: Chronicling the Bruce Lockhart Conspiracy, 1918," Intelligence and National

Security 10/1 (January 1995): 122-143.

Argues that the so-called Lockhart plot, an alleged conspiracy to overthrow of the Soviet Government in 1918, was a newspaper fiction which was carried on for several years by both Soviet and British officials. The entire affair was orchestrated by the secret police, the Cheka, targeted against H. Bruce Lockhart's covert operations in Russia in the years prior to 1918.

4796. Long, Wayne E. "Reorganization: The Revolution in Intelligence," Military Review 57/10 (October 1977): 25-31.

Major sections discuss force orientation and a new process; corps intelligence management system; and current status of intelligence reorganization.

4797. Long, William F., Jr. "Urban Insurgency War Game," Naval War College Review 21/9 (May 1969): 68-72.

Discusses game objectives; type and tempo; game scenario; game situation and events; observers; and participants.

4798. Long, William F., Jr. "Counterinsurgency: Corrupting Concept," U.S. Naval Institute Proceedings 105/4 (1979): 56-64.

4799. Longaker, Richard. "Emergency Detention: The Generation Gap, 1950-71," Western Political Quarterly 27/3 (September 1974): 395-408.

Discusses the Cold War measure, the Emergency Detention Act of 1950, in particular, Title II and the popular indignation it attracts in a nation where there is freedom of the press. Argues vigorously for repeal.

4800. Longfellow, Colleen H. "How to Integrate Computers in Intelligence Analysis: A Guide for Administrators," Criminal Justice Journal 1/9 (September 1982): 1-5.

4801. Longhi, Alain. "Le Secret Dans Les Societes," Analyse et Prevision 18/4-6 (October-December 1974): 541-559.

4802. Longton, Paul A. "Maintenance and Dissemination of Records of Arrest Versus the Right to Privacy," Wayne Law Review 17 (1971): 995-1006.

A case law note following on the decision in Menard v. Mitchell in which defendant Menard's criminal record could be retained by the FBI, said the Court, even though such record depended on police violation of due process. Right to privacy at issue in the case.

4803. Longworth, R. "Reporting From Moscow: Fiction and Secrets," Bulletin of the Atomic Scientists 42 (December 1986): 22-23.

Argues that in choosing Daniloff as a victim of a fabricated Soviet espionage ploy, the Gorbachev leadership sought to intimidate foreign correspondents in the Soviet capital.

4804. Loory, Stuart H. "The CIA Use of the Press: 'A Mighty Wurlitzer,'" Columbia Journalism Review 13/9 (September-October 1974): 9-18.

A history of the use made by CIA of American and foreign reporters, and of the press as an outlet for information the US government wished to have released.

4805. Loory, Stuart H. "CIA's Man in the White House," Columbia Journalism Review 14/9 (September-October 1975): 11-14.

4806. Lopez, Claude-Anne. "The Man Who Frightened Franklin," Pennsylvania Magazine of History and Biography 106/4 (1982): 515-526.

Discusses Peter Allaire and his involvement with Ben Franklin. Allaire was a spy double agent.

4807. Lopez, Claude-Anne. "Benjamin Franklin and William Dodd: A New Look at an Old Cause Celebre," Proceedings of the American Philosophical Society 129/3 (1985): 260-267.

Discusses Ben Franklin's involvement with the Reverend William Dodd. Dodd was later hanged for forgery.

4808. LoPresti, Tony. "Electronic Warfare: The Invisible War," Air Defense Artillery (Summer & Winter 1986): 20-27; 38-42.

4809. Lord, Carnes. "Verification and the Future of Arms Control," Strategic Review 6 (Spring 1978): 24-32.

4810. Lord, Carnes. "Rethinking the NSC Role," Comparative Strategy 6/3 (June 1987): 241-279.

A lengthy and thoughtful analysis of the vital relationship between president and the National Security Council. Argues that the relationship must avoid animosity while it is aimed at building trust.

4811. Los, Maria. "Lustration and Truth Claims: Unfinished Revolutions in Central Europe," Law and Social Inquiry 20 (Winter 1995): 117-161.

4812. Lo Schiavo, N. J. "Law Enforcement Intelligence Unit," Police Chief 62/2 (February 1975): 46, 82.

A discussion of LEIU (Law Enforcement Intelligence Unit) organizations to combat organized crime in the western regions of the US and Canada.

4813. Lossky, Andrew. "Estimates of Enemy Strength," Military Review 27/5 (August 1947): 20-25.

A report on the reflections of enemy strength analysis in North Africa, Sicily and Italy in World War II.

4814. Lotz, Wolfgang and Gerd R. Ueberschr. "The German Postal Service and 20 July 1944," Archiv fuer Deutsche Postgeschichte 1 (1994): 47-52.

4815. Loureiro, Pedro A. "The Imperial Japanese Navy and Espionage: The Itaro Tachibana Case 1941," International Journal of Intelligence and Counterintelligence 3/1 (Spring 1989): 105-121.
    Discusses the facts and investigation of a Japanese naval officer operating in the US in Southern California in 1939 and 1940. Concludes that the 11th Naval District counterintelligence operation against the activities of Itaro Tachibana was successful and informative of Japanese intelligence practices.

4816. Loureiro, Pedro A. "Japanese Espionage and American Countermeasures in Pre-Pearl Harbor California," Journal of American-East Asian Relations 3/3 (1994): 197-210.
    A discussion of the activities of the Office of Naval Intelligence with respect to discovering Japanese navy intentions and capabilities during the decade before the Pearl Harbor attack. One of several articles in this issue on the event of December 7, 1941.

4817. Love, Edmund G. "Deception on the Shuri Line (Okinawa)," Infantry 73/4 (July-August 1983): 14-20.

4818. Lovel, James. "The Price of Silence: Hanging David Dodd," Civil War Times Illustrated 23/7 (1984): 26-31.
    An account for the hanging of 17-year-old David Owen Dodd for spying for the Union during the Civil War.

4819. Lovin, Hugh T. "The Lyndon Johnson Administration and the Federal War on Subversion in the 1960s," Presidential Studies Quarterly 17/3 (Summer 1987): 559-571.
    Brief historical review of the Johnson administration's rejection of the anti-subversion policies and programs of the federal government begun in the early years of the Cold War. Describes the struggle within the Administration and the Congress to keep conservatives from defining the New Left as a subversive organization. Includes internal considerations of CIA views on anti-Vietnam war radicals.

4820. Low, Andrew M. "Post-Authorization Problems in the Use of Wiretaps: Minimization, Amendment, Sealing, and Inventories," Cornell Law Review 61/1 (November 1975): 92-156.
    Defines minimization as a concept, interception problems and scope,

interception techniques, amendments to Title III, sealing, inventories, and conclusions.

4821. Low, Bruce. "Know Thy Enemy, Know Thy Self: Vulnerability Assessment at the AEWC," Journal of Electronic Defense 9 (October 1986): 81-82+.

4822. Lowe, Charles. "About German Spies," Contemporary Review 97 (January 1910): 42-56.
Author offers a harsh and derisive stab at the doomsayer about the infiltration of German spies into pre-war England. Says that there is both hysteria and hypocrisy present in the concerns for German spies.

4823. Lowe, G. E. "Camelot Affair," Bulletin of the Atomic Scientists 22 (May 1966): 44-48.

4824. Lowe, Thaddeus S. "Observation Balloons in the Battle of Fair Oaks," American Review of Reviews 63/2 (1911): 186-190.

4825. Lowenhaupt, Henry S. "Mission to Birch Woods, via Seven Tents and New Siberia," Studies in Intelligence 12/3 (Fall 1968): 1-12.
Discusses CIA targeting of Soviet nuclear plants prior to the overflights of the Soviet Union.

4826. Lowenhaupt, Henry S. "Ravelling Russia's Reactors," Studies in Intelligence 16/3 (Fall 1972): 65-79.

4827. Lowenthal, Mark M. "Intrepid and the History of World War II," Military Affairs 41/2 (April 1977): 88-90.
A brief account of the work of Sir William Stephenson.

4828. Lowenthal, Mark M. "The Intelligence Library: Quantity vs. Quality," Intelligence and National Security 2/2 (April 1987): 368-373.
Some brief observations of the expansion of intelligence literature from 1975 to 1987. Contains several tables of data on the number of books and articles prior to and after 1975.

4829. Lowenthal, Mark M. "Searching for National Intelligence," Studies in Intelligence 31/3 (Fall 1987).

4830. Lowenthal, Mark M. "Searching for National Intelligence: US Intelligence and Policy Before the Second World War," Intelligence and National Security 6/4 (October 1991): 736-749.
Examines questions for national intelligence about strategy, economy, and

diplomacy. Major sections discuss the call for 10,000 aircraft; defense plans for the Western Hemisphere; conflicting assessments; the victory program; and events and conditions just before Pearl Harbor.

4831.   Lowenthal, Mark M.   "Tribal Tongues: Intelligence Consumers, Intelligence Producers," Washington Quarterly 15/1 (Winter 1992): 157-172.
Considers the closeness of relationship between consumers and producers of intelligence, thus introducing substantial probability of nurturing a tribal tongue outcome.

4832.   Lowenthal, Mark M.   "Tribal Tongues: Intelligence Consumers, Intelligence Producers, A Case Study," Studies in Intelligence 36/2 (Summer 1992).
Reprint of the same article as it appeared in Washington Quarterly.

4833.   Lowenthal, Mark M.   "Intelligence Epistemology: Dealing with the Unbelievable," International Journal of Intelligence and Counterintelligence 6/3 (Fall 1993): 319-325.
A brief discussion of analytical methodology concepts and issues related to the epistimology of information classification. Briefly considers the problem of analytical mindsets and the unbelievable.

4834. Lowry, Arthur S. "Who's Listening: Proposals for Amending the Foreign Intelligence Surveillance Act," Virginia Law Review 70/2 (March 1984): 297-337.
Covers the alleged restraints on executive authority to conduct warrantless intelligence searches and surveillances for countering foreign espionage.

4835. Lowry, Lucia M.; C. D. Lowry; and John R. Minor. "The Graveyard Fort: A Disputed Incident in the Life of Count Rumford," Isis 27 (August 1937): 268-285.

4836. Lowry, Richie P. "Toward a Sociology of Secrecy and Security Systems," Social Problems 19/4 (April 1972): 437-450.
Analysis of the role and limits of secrecy in public and private organizations. Secrecy, argues the author, tends to have a propensity to become a latent device for controlling politically sensitive information and individuals. Security systems function to undermine the purposes for which they were originally intended.

4837. Lowry, Richie P. and Dean MacCannell. "Feature Review," Sociological Quarterly 19 (Winter 1978): 152-156.
A book review essay of Philip Agee's Inside the Company; Morton Halperin's The Lawless State; J. C. Masterman's The Double-Cross System in the

War, 1939 to 1945; and Edward Shils' The Torment of Secrecy.

4838. Lucca, Marie J. "The Legality of the U.S. Order to Cut the Staffs of the Soviet Union's Missions to the United Nations," Boston University International Law Journal 6/1 (Spring 1988): 151-178.

  Major sections discuss the history of staff cuts and Soviet retaliatory measures; the legality of the US order; justification of the original US action; and the future and possible resolution.

4839. Lujan, Susan M. "Agnes Meyer Driscoll," Cryptologia 15/1 (January 1991): 47-56.

  A summary of the career of Agnes Driscoll, who spent forty-one years in cryptology. She was a skilled analyst in the dicipherment of systems and codes. This article had been published in Cryptolog 9/5 (1988): 4-6.

4840. Lukes, Igor. "Great Expectations and Lost Illusions: Soviet Use of Eastern European Proxies in the Third World," International Journal of Intelligence and Counterintelligence 3/1 (Spring 1989): 1-13.

  Major sections address issues such as Moscow's approach to the Third World; Soviet deemphasis on support for revolutionary insurgent movements; Eastern European proxies; Moscow's control; Soviet proxies; the USSR and surrogates; and where Moscow-satellite coordination is perfect.

4841. Lukes, Igor. "The Czechoslovak Intelligence Service and Western Reactions to the Communist Coup d'Etat of February 1948," Intelligence and National Security 8/4 (October 1993): 73-85.

  Contains a brief analysis, but full publication of, a document found in the Czechoslovak Foreign Ministry pertaining to Western reactions to the Communist coup in Prague in 1948. The document is published in English, translated by Igor Lukes.

4842. Lukes, Igor. "The GPU and GRU in Pre-World War II Czechoslovakia," International Journal of Intelligence and Counterintelligence 8/1 (Spring 1995): 91-104.

  Drawing from documentary evidence, the author pieces together the pre-war structure of the Czech intelligence organization. Reflects upon the documentary evidence, Lenin's agenda, and the importance of documents in the State Central Archives in Prague. Includes several documents reprinted for research purposes.

4843. Lukes, Igor. "The Birth of a Police State: The Czechoslovak Ministry of the Interior, 1945-48," Intelligence and National Security 11/1 (January 1996): 78-88.

  Discusses events leading to the February coup in Prague, and relying principally on a document concerned with the evolution of the Czech State Security and Intelligence Service.

4844. Lukas, J. Anthony. "Watergate Revisited: Dismantling Cold-War Confidentiality," Civil Liberties Review 2/4 (Fall 1975): 74-81.

Reviews the major arguments in the conflict between confidentiality and disclosure of information retained by government. Discusses the value of leaks in government during the Nixon years.

4845. Lundstrom, John B. "A Failure of Radio Intelligence: An Episode in the Battle of the Coral Sea," Cryptologia 7/2 (April 1983): 97-118.

4846. Lundy, Joseph R. "Police Undercover Agents: New Threat to First Amendment Freedoms," George Washington Law Review 37/3 (March 1969): 634-668.

Discusses the use and shortcomings involved with police undercover operations and techniques. Suggests there is a constitutional framework for controlling such activities; need for legislative action to correct ills of such operations.

4847. Luo, Ergang. "Military Strategies of the Taipings," Fuyin Baokan Ziliao: Zhongguo Jindai Shi 4 (1991): 30-41.

4848. Lupinovich, V. "CIA Diplomacy in Action," International Affairs (USSR) 6 (June 1972): 994-996.

4849. Lupsha, Peter A. "Steps Toward a Strategic Analysis of Organized Crime," Police Chief 47/5 (May 1980): 17-24.

4850. Lupsha, Peter A. "Drug Trafficking: Mexico and Columbia in Comparative Perspective," Journal of International Affairs 35/1 (Spring-Summer 1981): 95-115.

Compares trafficking and control policy in two countries and their impacts on these countries and the United States. Suggests there are weaknesses in a unidimentional policy approach and offers an alternative. Includes reference to intelligence data and role in defining the economic aspects of the international trade in drugs.

4851. Lupsha, Peter A. "Intelligence Policy: Coming in from the Cold," Policy Studies Review 2/3 (1983): 557-559.

A book review essay on four books by Georgetown professor of government, Roy Godson: Intelligence Requirements for the 1980's: Elements of Intelligence; Analysis and Estimates; Counterintelligence; and Covert Action.

4852. Lustgarten, Laurence. "Learning from Peter Wright: A Response to D. C. Watt," Political Quarterly 60 (1989): 222-226.

Considers the book by Peter Wright, Spycatcher as an historical document; the reaction to the book; the role of the courts; and the future of the security services.

4853. Luttwak, Edward N. and Walter Laqueur. "Kissinger and the Yom Kippur War," Commentary 58 (September 1974): 33-40.

A detailed consideration of the role of Henry Kissinger, adviser to President Nixon, in the diplomatic machinations surrounding the October 1973 war.

4854. Luvaas, Jay. "Napoleon's Use of Intelligence: The Jena Campaign of 1805," Intelligence and National Security 3/3 (July 1988): 40-54.

Discusses Napolean's use of strategic intelligence prior to and during the Jena campaign, resulting in "stunning French victories."

4855. Luvaas, Jay. "The Role of Intelligence in the Chancellorville Campaign, April-May, 1863," Intelligence and National Security 5/2 (April 1990): 99-115.

A detailed discussion of the role of intelligence in this American Civil War battle, including the roles of Allan Pinkerton, Major General Joseph Hooker, and aerial balloons.

4856. Luvaas, Jay. "Lee at Gettysburg: A General Without Intelligence," Intelligence and National Security 5/2 (April 1990): 116-138.

Detailed discussion of the impact of little intelligence upon General Lee's ability to wage effective battle during the Gettysburg campaign.

4857. Luzader, John F. "The Arnold-Gates Controversy," West Virginia History 27/2 (January 1966): 75-84.

4858. Lykken, David T. "Detecting Deception in 1984," American Behavioral Scientist 27/4 (March-April 1984): 481-499.

4859. Lynch, Mark H. "Secrecy Agreements and National Security," Government Information Quarterly 1/2 (1984): 139-156.

Argues that secrecy agreements, such as the agreement signed by Frank Snepp at CIA, serve a useful public function and must be enforced. Discusses the Snepp case regarding publication of Decent Interval, cases after Snepp, the S.C.I. agreement, and the classified information agreement.

4860. Lyon, David. "The New Surveillance: Electronic Technologies and the Maximum Security Society," Crime, Law and Social Change 18/1-2 (September 1992): 159-176.

Generalizing from Gary Marx's book, <u>Undercover</u>, the author discusses new forms of societal surveillance practices through computers and other information technologies. Evaluates and applies Marx's term, "maximum security society".

4861. Lyons, Gregory R. "Constitutional Law - Fourth Amendment - Search and Seizure - Title III of the Omnibus Crime Control and Safe Streets Act of 1968 - Electronic Surveillance Covert Entry," <u>Duquesne Law Review</u> 18 (Winter 1980): 351-361.

A review of the Supreme Court decision in <u>Dalia v. United States</u> holding that the Fourth Amendment does not require that a Title III electronic surveillance order include a specific authorization for police to covertly enter the premises described to install a listening device.

M

**"...in peacetime espionage is easy and profitable...in wartime
espionage is difficult and usually unprofitable..."**
(The Double-Cross System... by J. C. Masterman, p. 188)

4862. Macartney, John. "The Defense Intelligence College," American
Intelligence Journal 9/1 (March 1988).

Discussion of the organization and mission of the new multi-service
school for military intelligence personnel.

4863. Macartney, John. "Intelligence: A Consumer's Guide," International
Journal of Intelligence and Counterintelligence 2/4 (Winter 1988): 457-486.

An overview of the structure, function and activities of the intelligence
community. The author says the piece is a "user's manual" aimed at US military
commanders. Sections discuss the intelligence community; intelligence collection;
intelligence products and services; intelligence and policy, customer relations;
classification and compartmentation; limits of intelligence; and tips to commanders
and policymakers on using intelligence.

4864. Macartney, John. "Intelligence and Bureaucratic Politics," Studies in
Intelligence 33/1 (Spring 1989).

4865. MacBride, Sean. "Reflections on Intelligence," Intelligence and National
Security 2/1 (January 1987): 92-96.

An account of intelligence operations and national security as viewed by
the former Irish Minister for External Affairs.

4866. MacCannell, Dean. "Feature Review," <u>Sociological Quarterly</u> 19 (Winter 1978): 152-162.

A book review essay of Agee's <u>Inside the Company</u>; Halperin, et al., <u>The Lawless State: The Crimes of the U.S. Intelligence Agencies</u>; Masterman's <u>The Double-Cross System in the War of 1939-1945</u>; and Shils' <u>The Torment of Secrecy</u>.

4867. MacDonald, C. A. "Economic Appeasement and the German Moderates, 1937-1939," <u>Past and Present</u> 56 (1972): 105-135.

4868. MacDonald, Cheryl. "Canada's Secret Police? Gilbert McMicken, Spymaster," <u>Beaver</u> 71/3 (1991): 44-49.

McMicken was the first chief of Canadian intelligence around the time of the American civil war. Discusses some of his activities in the Western frontier lands.

4869. MacDonald, Norman. "Electronic Surveillance in Crime Detention: An Analysis of Canadian Wiretapping Law," <u>Dalhousie Law Journal</u> 10 (January 1987): 141-166.

Examines wiretapping law in Canada in terms of its history; the Protection of Privacy Act; policy considerations; and future considerations.

4870. MacDonald, Robert J.   "The Silent Column: Civil Security in Saskatchewan During World War II," <u>Saskatchewan History</u> 39/2 (1986): 41-61.

An account of Canada's Saskatchewan's Veterans Civil Security Corps in the Province's experiences in World War II.

4871. Macdonald, Stuart. "Nothing Either Good or Bad: Industrial Espionage and Technology Transfer," <u>International Journal of Technology Management</u> 8/1-2 (1993): 95-105.

A rare lengthy discussion of the complex topic of industrial espionage.

4872. MacDonnell, Francis. "The Search for a Second Zimmermann Telegram: FDR, BSC, and the Latin American Front," <u>International Journal of Intelligence and Counterintelligence</u> 4/4 (Winter 1990): 487-505.

Historical account of the loose alliance between Franklin Roosevelt and British intelligence in 1940-41, allowing the British to operate on US territory. Major sections discuss the origin of the link; the Bolivia coup in July 1941; the Latin American map in October 1941; and conclusions pertaining to what US intelligence learned from the British.

4873. Mache, Wolfgang. "Geheimschreiber," <u>Cryptologia</u> 10/4 (October 1986): 230-242.

4874. Mache, Wolfgang. "The Siemens Cipher Teletype in the History of Telecommunications," Cryptologia 13/2 (April 1989): 97-117.

4875. Machenzie, A. "Fit to be Tied," Quill 73 (July-August 1985): 13-15+.
This article discusses prepublication review requirement covering Department of Defense employees, contractors and those with security clearances. The review requirements covers articles and speeches and it remains in effect for life. A quote capturing the article's theme is: "A leak is unauthorized political discourse."

4876. MacIntosh, J. J. "Ethics and Spy Fiction," Intelligence and National Security 5/4 (October 1990): 161-184.
Discusses four main moral issues: the justification of spying itself; sexism in fictional versions of spying; casual acceptance of murder, torture, deceit, etc.; and the morality of writing, selling, buying and reading literature devoted to such activities.

4877. Mack, Lisa M. "Criminal Law--Voluntary Consent to Wear a Body Wire: Third Circuit Rejects Implicit Threats," Temple Law Quarterly 65 (Spring 1992): 295-307.
Refers to a Pennsylvania case, United States v. Antoon, and the question of voluntariness in wearing a wire recording device in an undercover investigation.

4878. Mackenzie, Angus. "Prior Censorship," Coevolution Quarterly 40 (Winter 1983): 84-88.
Discusses censorship in the United States, the CIA, civil service and US official secrets policy.

4879. Mackenzie, D. B. "The Battalion Intelligence Personnel and Their Training," Journal of the United Services Institution of India (January 1932): 87-91.

4880. MacKenzie, R. B. "Intelligence Starts at the Top," Marine Corps Gazette 57 (July 1973): 40-44.

4881. MacKenzie, R. B. "Intelligence War Game," Marine Corps Gazette 58 (June 1974): 23-29.

4882. Mackenzie, S. P. "Citizens in Arms: The Home Guard and the Internal Security of the United Kingdom 1940-41," Intelligence and National Security 6/3 (July 1991): 548-572.
Examines the reasons and use of the Home Guard in the UK during World War II. Focusses on internal security considerations and personnel problems. The Home Guard was controlled by the War Office.

4883. MacKinnon, Donald W. "The OSS Assessment Program," Studies in Intelligence 23/3 (Fall 1979).

4884. Mackrell, Eileen. "Naval Intelligence at Mid-Career," Naval Intelligence Professionals Quarterly 8/3 (Summer 1992): 1-3.

4885. Mackrell, Eileen. "The Way Ahead at Mid-Career," Naval Intelligence Professionals Quarterly 9/4 (Fall 1993): 4-6.

4886. MacLaren, William G. "NATO C³I Requirements Within the LTDP," Signal 38 (December 1983): 23-24.

4887. Maclaren, John and Nicholas Hiley. "Nearer the Truth: The Search for Alexander Szek," Intelligence and National Security 4/4 (October 1989): 813-826.
        Chronicles the extraordinary life and operations of British spy Alexander Szek. Szek worked in an important German radio station in 1914 and had access to top secret code books. Considers the events leading up to Szek's death. Includes a history of Szek's son, perhaps a more interesting spy.

4888. MacLean, Guy. "Canadians and Secret Operations in the Second World War," Dalhousie Review 62/3 (Autumn 1982): 504-508.
        A book review essay pertaining to two books: Roy MacLaren's Canadians Behind Enemy Lines, 1939-1945; and David Stafford's Britain and European Resistance, 1940-1945.

4889. MacLeish, Roderick, Jr. "The Permissibility of Forcible Entries by Police in Electronic Surveillance," Boston University Law Review 57 (1977): 587-606.
        A law comment on the correctness of the decision in United States v. Agrusa in its treatment of forcible entries in order to effect electronic surveillance. Argues that such entries should be permitted only when the government cannot employ less intrusive methods.

4890. MacLeod, D. Peter. "Treason at Quebec: British Espionage in Canada During the Winter of 1759-1760," Canadian Military History 2/1 (1993): 49-62.
        Discusses a spy network in Quebec that supplied the British with intelligence on the French military.

4891. MacLeod, Roy. "'Full of Honor and Gain to Science': Munitions Production, Technical Intelligence and the Wartime Career of Sir Douglas Mawson, FRS," Historical Records of Australian Science 7/2 (1988): 189-201.

4892. MacMichael, David. "The Other Iran-Contra Cases," Covert Action Information Bulletin 35 (Fall 1990): 52-55.

4893. MacPherson, B. Nelson. "The Compromise of US Navy Cryptanalysis After the Battle of Midway," Intelligence and National Security 2/2 (April 1987): 320-323.

A brief revisitation to the question of whether or not the 1942 Chicago Tribune revelations about Japanese codes caused the enemy to change codes, thus causing additional US naval losses from a wiser enemy naval strategy. Author insists that Tribune publication of sensitive information was damaging to US war progress.

4894. MacPherson, B. Nelson. "Inspired Improvisation: William Casey and the Penetration of Germany," Intelligence and National Security 9/4 (October 1994): 695-722.

An account of significant British assistance to William Casey in organizing, supporting and executing OSS missions against the Germans in World War II. Concludes that OSS would not have been successful in carrying out 102 missions if British insistence upon integrated operations had not been implemented.

4895. MacPherson, B. Nelson. "CIA Origins as Viewed from Within," Intelligence and National Security 10/2 (April 1995): 353-359.

A book review essay concerning three books reflecting CIA internal history: Arthur B. Darling's The Central Intelligence Agency: An Instrument of Government; Ludwell L. Montague's General Walter Bedell Smith as Director of Central Intelligence, October 1950-February 1953; and Michael Warner (ed.), CIA Cold War Records: The CIA Under Harry Truman.

4896. Madden, C. S. and R. T. Hise. "Counter-Intelligence Operations of United States Firms--An Exploratory Study," Akron Business and Economic Review 19/3 (1988): 76-82.

4897. Maddox, Robert J. "Woodrow Wilson, the Russian Embassy and Siberian Intervention," Pacific Historical Quarterly 36/4 (November 1967): 435-448.

Discusses the commitment of US troops in Siberia by President Wilson. Useful in analyses of how administration's interpret foreign events and the information mustered and selectively considered in the decision making process.

4898. Maddox, Tom. "Spy Stories: The Life and Fiction of John LeCarre," Wilson Quarterly 10/4 (Autumn 1986): 158-170.

Provides a brief biographical sketch of LeCarre's life and analyzes the subject's various world views.

4899. Mader, Julius. "Subversion as a Means of the Foreign Policy of the United States," Deutsche Aussenpolitik 7/1 (1962): 92-99.

4900. Madsen, Wayne. "Intelligence Agency Threats to Computer Security," International Journal of Intelligence and Counterintelligence 6/4 (Winter 1993): 413-488.

Major sections discuss networks of intelligence information; penetrations by former KGB/East Block personnel; German penetrations; French penetrations; British penetrations; Eastern European penetrations; American penetrations; Danish penetrations; Norwegian penetrations; Australian penetrations; Israeli penetrations; South African penetrations; Japanese penetrations; Chinese penetrations; actual and possible Iraqi penetrations; Indian penetrations; capabilities of other nations; and desktop surveillance.

4901. Maechling, Charles, Jr. "Our Foreign Affairs Establishment: The Need for Reform," Virginia Quarterly Review 45/2 (1969): 193-210.

Discusses various reform methods to hold the President and Secretary of State accountable for foreign affairs mistakes. Good background piece for the role of intelligence in informing the foreign affairs system.

4902. Maechling, Charles, Jr. "Improving the Intelligence System," Foreign Service Journal 57/6 (June 1980): 10-13, 41-42.

The author, an experienced director of a counter-insurgency program in the Kennedy and Johnson administrations, offers his views on how to improve the quality of intelligence and the public's perception of the role of US international intelligence work.

4903. Maechling, Charles, Jr. "Official Secrets: British Style/American Style," International Journal of Intelligence and Counterintelligence 2/3 (Fall 1988): 359-380.

Discussion of various cases and issues involved in the protection of national security secrets in Britain and the US. Major sections discuss Peter Wright and the Spycatcher case; the Official Secrets Act and other legal remedies; other offenders in Britain; other legal remedies; the political and social context; and official secrets American style.

4904. Maechling, Charles, Jr. "Scandal in Wartime Washington: The Craufurd-Stuart Affair of 1918," International Journal of Intelligence and Counterintelligence 4/3 (Fall 1990): 357-370.

Relates the circumstances of a major scandal in Washington circles during World War I. Major sections discuss the Southern roots of the scandal; the storm center of the affair in Major Charles Kennedy-Crauford-Stuart; the intrigue; the rise and the reprieve; and the details of sexual encounters and espionage that carried international implications.

4905. Maertens, Thomas R. "Tragedy of Errors," Foreign Service Journal 62/8 (September 1985): 24-31.

Argues that the media claims that the KAL 007 plane was a spy plane rely on Soviet disinformation or misinterpretation of the facts. Refers to KGB and the US intelligence roles in this case.

4906. Maertens, Thomas R. "'Shootdown' Shotdown," International Journal of Intelligence and Counterintelligence 1/2 (Summer 1986): 137-145.

A book review essay on R. W. Johnson's book, Shootdown: Flight 007 and the American Connection.

4907. Maffet, Meri W. "Open Secrets: Protecting the Identity of the CIA's Intelligence Gatherers in a First Amendment Society," Hastings Law Journal 32/6 (July 1981): 1723-1775.

Discusses protection offered by current law (1981), prior restraint, punishment, espionage statutes, classified information statutes, protection for CIA agents, and conclusions.

4908. Maghroori, Ray and Stephen M. Gorman. "The Conceptual Weaknesses of American Foreign Policies Toward Authoritarian Third World Allies," Towson State Journal of International Affairs 14/2 (1980): 57-73.

4909. Magill, Lewis M. "Joseph Conrad: Russia and England," Albion 3/1 (1971): 3-8.

4910. Magnus, Roshon L. "Judicial Erosion of the Standard of Public Disclosure of Investigating Records Under the FOIA After FBI v. Abramson," Harvard Law Journal 26/4 (Fall 1983): 1613-1644.

Discusses exemption to FOIA-required disclosure involved in Abramson. Examines FOIA's intended purpose and problem if meant to address this concern, and later judicial development of exemption "seven." Author then considers legislative history of the Act and whether the Supreme Court's decision was appropriate in that context, concluding that none of the statutory construction supports the decision.

4911. Maguire, J. Robert. "The British Secret Service and the Attempt to Kidnap General Jacob Bayley of Newbury, Vermont, 1782," Vermont History 44/3 (1976): 141-167.

Discusses the British plan to kidnap General Jacob Bayley, the founder of Newbury, New York, for his anti-British activities. Covert actions of this kind were performed by the British secret service under the command of Captain Justus Sherwood.

4912. Maguire, Keith. "The Intelligence War in Northern Ireland," International Journal of Intelligence and Counterintelligence 4/2 (Summer 1990): 145-165.

Argues that the failure to gauge the political mood of a population during times of sensitive negotiations can hamper government peace initiatives, as experienced in Northern Ireland. Major sections consider the dual struggle between the Irish Nationalists and the Ulster Unionists; the Ulster Defense Association and the Ulster Freedom Fighters; other terrorist groups; the role of intelligence; British intelligence failures; developing and using intelligence; intelligence requirements; background and recruitment problems; covert action; help from the outside; and the continuation of the intelligence war.

4913. Mahaffey, Fred K.   "C^3I for Automated Control of Tomorrow's Battlefield," Army 29 (March 1979): 26-30.

4914. Maher, Christopher M.   "The Right to a Fair Trial in Criminal Cases Involving the Introduction of Classified Information," Military Law Review 120 (Spring 1988): 83-137.
    Discusses the right to counsel and access to classified information; the right to discovery and the classified information privilege, and the right to a public trial.

4915. Maher, Laurence W.   "The Use and Abuse of Sedition," Sydney Law Review 14 (1992): 287-316.
    Examines the Australian law relevant to sedition: elements of Commonwealth offenses; the case for abolition of the sedition statutes; and reform proposals.   Mentions the US Espionage Acts of 1917 and 1918; the anti-communist era; and the Australian Security and Intelligence Organization.

4916. Maher, Laurence W.   "The Lapstone Experiment and the Beginnings of ASIO," Labour History 64 (1993): 103-118.
    The Lapstone experiment is treated with special attention as a project of the Australian Security Intelligence Organization.

4917. Maher, Laurence W.   "Dissent, Disloyalty and Disaffection: Australia's Last Cold War Sedition Case," Adelaide Law Review 16 (July 1994): 1-77.

4918. Maheu, R.   "Doctor Thomas W. Evans, Dentist and Secret Agent of Napoleon III," Revue Historique des Armees 27/3 (1971): 38-50.

4919. Mahmud, Tayyah.   "Jurisprudence of Successful Treason: Coup d'Etat and Common Law," Cornell International Law Journal 27/1 (Winter 1994): 49-140.
    An extensive review of cases involving charges of treason from 1958 to 1989. Also considers options available to a court when confronted with successful coups d'etat. Offers conclusions.

4920. Mahnken, Thomas G.   "Why Third World Space Systems Matter," Orbis 35/3 (Fall 1991): 563-579.

Extensive, rich discussion of the assets and threats of third world satellite technologies.

4921. Mahoney, Harry T. "The Saga of Xenophon Dmitrivich Kalamatiano," International Journal of Intelligence and Counterintelligence 8/2 (Summer 1995): 179-201.

An account of the espionage work of Kalamatiano, the spy chief of the US State Department's network in Bolshevik Russia during the Russian revolution. Major sections discuss his move to Russia; return to the US; establishment of the network; the Cheka moves in; trial and US response; his self-evaluation; prison term; and return to the US after prison term.

4922. Mahoney, Roger E. "USMC Steps Up in Intelligence," Marine Corps Gazette 64 (January 198): 17-19.

4923. Maicher, Kathleen M. "Inanimate Listening Devices: A Violation of Sixth Amendment Right to Counsel," Loyola University of Chicago Law Journal 14/2 (Winter 1983): 359-390.

This law note considers whether, in light of Sixth Amendment policy and precedent, electronic surveillance activities constitute a violation of the Amendment's right to counsel at all stages of the criminal justice process.

4924. Mainwald, Helga. "On the Intensified U.S. Aggression in Southeast Asia: Laos," Dokumentation der Zeit 22/14 (1970): 23-28.

4925. Maiolo, Joseph A. "'I Believe the Hun Is Cheating': British Admiralty Technical Intelligence and the German Navy, 1936-39," Intelligence and National Security 11/1 (January 1996): 32-58.

The author discusses the apparatus and obstacles to assessment; capital ships; U-boats; and conclusions.

4926. Maisky, I. M. "Dni Ispuytany: Iz Vospominanii Posla," Noviy Mir 12 (December 1964): 160-194.

In Russian, this piece contains memories of Stalin's failure to anticipate BARBAROSSA in 1941.

4927. Major, David G. "Operation 'Famish': The Integration of Counterintelligence into to National Strategic Decisionmaking Process," Defense Intelligence Journal 4/1 (Spring 1995): 29-55.

Argues for the maintenance of a strong counterintelligence strategy. Major sections consider the Reagan administration's CI efforts in operation "Famish"; evolution of the interagency structure; role of the NSC staff; "Famish" operations and implementation; and final and most crucial decisions.

4928. Major, Duncan K. "The Service of Security," Infantry Journal 3/3 (January 1907): 89-94.

Defines field army security protection positions in terms of gaining positions in terms of gaining early information on the enemy: outposts, advance guards, and rear guards.

4929. Majumdar, B. K. "The Role of Secret Service in Ancient India," Proceedings of the Indian History Congress (1956).

4930. Makar, Boshra H. "Transfinite Cryptography," Cryptologia 4/4 (October 1980): 230-236.

4931. Makar, Boshra H. "Application of a Certain Class of Infinite Matrices to the Hill Cryptographic System," Cryptologia 7/1 (January 1983): 63-78.

4932. Malisov, Iu. "Maskirovka delo Vazhoe," Voennaia Vestnik 12 (December 1979).

4933. Mallin, Jay. "Phases of Subversion: The Castro Drive on Latin America," Air University Review 25/1 (November-December 1973): 54-62.

Traces the evolution of Cuba's role in support of Latin American insurgencies. Includes some photos and documents.

4934. Mallison, W. Thomas and Sally V. Mallison. "The Israeli Aerial Attack of June 7, 1981, Upon the Iraqi Nuclear Reactor: Aggression or Self-Defense?," Vanderbilt Journal of Transnational Law 15/3 (Summer 1982): 417-448.

Discusses the legal requirements for self defense in international law, the application of self defense law to the June 7 attack, the United Nations Security Council's deliberations on the matter, and the effects of the attack.

4935. Maland, Charles J. "A Documentary Note on Charlie Chaplin's Politics," Historical Journal of Film, Radio and Television 5/2 (1985): 199-208.

Discusses Chaplin's political ideas as revealed by FBI records recently released.

4936. Malin, Patrick M. "Is Wire Tapping Justified?," Annals of the American Academy of Political and Social Sciences 300 (July 1955): 29-35.

Outlines the extent and mechanics of wiretapping in the US; legal status; values and risks; arguments pro and con; the authors opposition to wiretapping; and minimal safeguards.

4937. Mal'kov, Victor L. "The Office of Strategic Services and von Papen's Peace Initiative in 1943," Novaia i Noveishaia Istoriia 3 (1980): 122-140.

A Russian language history of the OSS role in the peace initiative.

4938. Mal'kov, Victor L. "Secret Reports of the American Military Attache in Moscow on the Eve of the Second World War," Novaia i Noveishaia Istoriia 4 (1982): 101-117.

In Russian, a study of the reports of Soviet military, economic, political and managerial sent from US attache Philip R. Faymonville in the years 1937 and 1938.

4939. Malloy, Michael P. "Developments at the International Court of Justice: Provisional Measures and Jurisdiction in the Nicaragua Case," New York Law School Journal of International and Comparative Law 6 (Fall 1984): 55-91.

Discusses the role of the International Court and its specific concerns in the matter of US intervention in Nicaragua.

4940. Mancini, John. "The OSS Wartime Operations Included Not Only Sabotage and Espionage But the Use of Psychological Tactics," Military History 10/3 (1993): 24-28.

4941. Mandel, Michael. "Discrediting the McDonald Commission," Canadian Forum 61/716 (March 1982): 14-17.

4942. Mandel, Michael. "Freedom of Expression and National Security," University of Western Ontario Law Review 23 (December 1985): 205-209.

Discusses the implications for freedom of expression in the wake of passage of the Canadian Security Intelligence Act (1984). Recounts briefly the discovery of the McDonald Commission on domestic intelligence violations.

4943. Mandel, Robert. "Political Gaming and Foreign Policy Making During Crises," World Politics 29/4 (July 1977): 610-625.

Discusses the distortions of the decision making process during crises, the professional use of political gaming techniques to improve decision making, testing the value of gaming, evaluation results, and applicability of political gaming to research and policy.

4944. Mandel, Robert. "Predicting Overseas Political Instability: Perspectives of the Government Intelligence and Multinational Business Communities," Conflict Quarterly 8 (Spring 1988): 23-46.

4945. Manget, Frederic F. "Presidential War Powers," Studies in Intelligence 31/2 (Summer 1987).

Considers the legal bases for intelligence activities in the executive branch in historical perspective. Major sections cover foreign intelligence operations; constitutional authority to conduct foreign intelligence operations; war powers; and foreign intelligence operations as war. This article appeared in a special issue of Studies in Intelligence 31/Special edition (September 1987): 91-

104.

4946. Manget, Frederic F. "Restitution: A Better Way of Dealing with the Wrongful Appropriation of Classified Government Secrets?," International Journal of Intelligence and Counterintelligence 4/1 (Spring 1990): 23-37.

Argues that the government may have legal recourse against persons who receive and use classified information without authorization through tort litigation strategies. Major sections address types of classified information; trade secrets aspects of classified information; conversion of classified information; restitution; and First Amendment issues.

4947. Manget, Frederic F. "Presidential Powers and Foreign Intelligence Operations," International Journal of Intelligence and Counterintelligence 5/2 (Summer 1991): 131-153.

Raises numerous legal questions about the foundation of authority upon which presidents carry out intelligence objectives. Major sections discuss the nature of foreign intelligence operations; constitutionsal authority to conduct foreign intelligence operations; the War Powers Act; foreign intelligence operations as war; the foreign affairs power; executive power; and execution of laws power.

4948. Manget, Frederic F. "Intelligence and the Rise of Judicial Intervention," Studies in Intelligence 39/5 (1996): 43-50.

Discusses foreign intelligence, counterintelligence, and covert action as considered by the judiciary; official accountability; increasing scrutiny; Congress weighs in; criminal law; the Classified Information Procedures Act; surveillance and the Foreign Intelligence Surveillance Act of 1978; government authorization; civil law; FOIA requests; state secrets privilege; allegations of abuse; and the First Amendment.

4949. Mankiewicz, Frank; John K. Mangum; and Graham B. Moody, Jr. "The Federal Loyalty-Security Program: A Proposed Statute," California Law Review 44/1 (March 1956): 72-93.

An attempt to offer a reform piece of legislation to protect government interests in integrity and security of employees.

4950. Mann, Edward. "Desert Storm: The First Information War?," Airpower Journal 8/4 (Winter 1994): 4-14.

4951. Mann, James. "The Return of the National Security State," Working Papers for a New Society 8/2 (March-April 1981): 27-33.

Argues that the rejuvenation of the US intelligence agencies in the post-Watergate era will make control over their excesses even more difficult in the future.

4952.   Mann, Ronni L.   "Minimization of Wire Interception: Presearch Guidelines and Postsearch Remedies," Stanford Law Review 26/6 (June 1974): 1411-1438.

Legal note examining the wiretap practices of police and propositions for protecting privacy. Discusses minimization perspectives; presearch guidelines for wire or oral communication; and enforcement of minimization.

4953.   Mann, Howard W.   "Security and the Constitution," Current History 29 (October 1955):   236-246.

Describes the role of the courts in holding the integrity of the US Constitution in times of concern for internal security.   Outlines the historical context of the Alien and Sedition Acts of 1798, the concept of clear and present danger, relocation of Japanese-Americans during World War II, and the Smith Act.

4954.   Manning, P. A.   "VMCJ: Marine Composite Reconnaissance Squadron," Marine Corps Gazette 56 (October 1972):   40-43.

4955.   Mansbach, Richard W.   "The Travail of Intelligence Analysis," Studies in Intelligence 27/2 (Summer 1983).

4956.   Mansur, Abdul K. (pseud.).   "The Crisis in Iran: Why the U.S. Ignored a Quarter Century of Warning," Armed Forces Journal International 116 (January 1979):   26-33.

4957.   Manthorpe, Bill.   "The ONI: Moving Into the 21st Century," Naval Intelligence Professionals Quarterly 9/2 (Spring 1993):   1-4.

4958.   Manwaring, Max G. and John T. Fishel.   "Insurgency and Counter-Insurgency: Toward a New Analytical Approach," Small Wars and Insurgencies 3/3 (Winter 1992):   272-310.

4959.   Marbes, Wilhelm.   "Psychology of Treason," Studies in Intelligence 30/2 (Summer 1986):   1-11.

The author, a practicing psychiatrist, describes the characteristics of human motivation and action which can be exploited by the human intelligence officer in the recruitment mode.   He discusses despair, runners and fighters, loyalty, and traits of defectors.

4960.   Marbury, William L.   "The Hiss-Chambers Libel Suit," Maryland Historical Magazine 76/1 (January 1981):   70-92.

Draws from Marbury's personal notes regarding what he learned about Alger Hiss' life and truthfulness in the course of his defense of Hiss.

4961. Marchio, Jim. "Resistance Potential and Rollback: US Intelligence and the Eisenhower Administration's Policies Toward Eastern Europe, 1953-56," Intelligence and National Security 10/2 (April 1995): 219-241.

Addresses a series of questions raised by C. D. Jackson, Special Assistant for Cold War Affairs in the Eisenhower administration, pertaining to intelligence community assessments of conditions in Eastern Europe. Questions considered are: What did intelligence say?; Were assessments available and used by policy makers?; Did intelligence affect policy?; and, what were the key judgments?

4962. Marcum, John A. "Lessons of Angola," Foreign Affairs 54/3 (April 1976): 407-425.

A history and analysis of US foreign policy toward Angola in the 1960s and 1970s. Refers to US and Soviet covert actions and CIA's links with South African security services.

4963. Marcus, Gilbert. "The Veil of Secrecy in South Africa," International Commission of Jurists Review (December 1982): 56-60.

4964. Marcus, Richard L. "The Tudor Treason Trials: Some Observations on the Emergence of Forensic Themes," University of Illinois Law Review 1984/3 (Summer 1984): 675-704.

Author is interested in examining Sir Walter Raleigh's trial for treason in 1603 and the Tudor treason trials in an effort to identify recurrent themes of advocacy.

4965. Marcy, Carl. "The Impact on Secrecy on Congressional Ability to Participate in Foreign Policy Decision Making," Towson State Journal of International Affairs 10/1 (1975): 13-18.

Argues that Congress did not have sufficient access to information regarding foreign policy matters in the 1970s, stressing the Executive Branch's secrecy policies.

4966. Marder, Murray. "Navajo Code Talkers," Marine Corps Gazette (May 1945): 4.

4967. Marenin, Otwin. "United States Aid to African Police Forces: The Experience and Impact of the Public Safety Assistance Programme," African Affairs 85/341 (October 1986): 509-544.

Major sections discuss the US State Department's Office of Public Safety; the goals of public safety assistance; public safety assistance to Sub-Saharan states; the impact of OPS on police forces in Africa; OPS assistance to Zaire; and the failures and lessons of OPS.

4968. Marenin, Otwin. "Policing African States: Toward a Critique,"

Comparative Politics 14/4 (July 1982): 379-396.
    Major sections discuss police and society; the police in African states; and concluding comments.

4969. Marenin, Otwin. "Police Performance and State Rule," Comparative Politics 18/1 (October 1985): 101-122.
    A lengthy and detailed book review essay concerning 9 books relevant to policing the state. Useful for locating books concerned with the domestic role of police and police intelligence functions.

4970. Mares, Antoine. "Les Attaches Militaires en Europe Centrale et la Notion de la Puissance en 1938," Revue Historique des Armees 1 (1983): 60-72.

4971. Margerison, Tom. "Spy in the Sky," Survival 2/5 (September- October 1960): 199-203.

4972. Margoliouth, D. S. "The Use of Cypher in Greek Antiquity," Baconiana 23 (1938): 1-12.

4973. Marino, C. "The Spy Who Loves You," ARMA Records Management Quarterly 24/2 (April 1990): 24-26.

4974. Mark, Eduard. "October or Thermidor?: Interpretation of Stalinism and the Perception of Soviet Foreign Policy in the United States, 1927-1947," American Historical Review 94/4 (October 1989): 937-962.
    Considers in detail the impact of Stalinism on US-Soviet foreign relations in the period.

4975. Mark, Eduard. "The OSS in Romania, 1944-45: An Intelligence Operation of the Early Cold War," Intelligence and National Security 9/2 (April 1994): 320-344.
    Discusses and evaluates the role and effectiveness of American intelligence during the early cold war period. Presents a case study of operations in Romania concerning intelligence and diplomacy, operations management, information sources, dissemination, and effects.

4976. Mark, J. Carson. "The Detection of Nuclear Explosions," Nucleonics 17/8 (August 1959).

4977. Mark, Richard W. "Patent Secrecy Act of 1952," Columbia Journal of Law and Social Problems 15/4 (1980): 359-425.
    Discusses history and present enforcement, constitutional problems posed by the Act, and conclusions. Proposes a rational secrecy policy.

4978. Markmann, C. L. "Hounding GI's in Germany: Work of the Lawyers Military Defense Committee," Progressive 39 (June 1975): 24-26.

4979. Markowitz, Gerald E. and Michael Meeropol. "The 'Crime of the Century' Revisited: David Greenglass' Scientific Evidence in the Rosenberg Case," Science and Society 44/1 (Spring 1980): 1-26.
　　Argues that the Rosenbergs were unjustly executed for alleged espionage. Uses documents received under the FOIA to establish the case for the believed worthlessness of the material used against the Rosenbergs.

4980. Marks, Frederick W., III. "The CIA and Castillo Armas in Guatemala, 1954: New Clues to an Old Puzzle," Diplomatic History 14/1 (Winter 1990): 67-86.
　　Argues that the success of Castillo Armas against the Jacobo Arbenz government was based on Armas's leadership and the confluence of several factors, not simply US contributions. Several factors opposed the Arbenz government.

4981. Marks, Herbert S. "The Atomic Energy Act: Public Administration Without Public Debate," University of Chicago Law Review 15/4 (1948): 839-854.
　　Questions the paucity of public debate on the matter of the Act's creation, attributing much of the problem to the acquiescence to the secrecy imperative.

4982. Marks, Herbert S. and A. B. Trowbridge. "Control of Information Under the Atomic Energy Act of 1954," Bulletin of the Atomic Scientists 11 (1955): 128-132.

4983. Marks, John B. "Intelligence Support to the Air Force: Now and in the Future," Signal 38 (October 1983): 27-30.

4984. Marks, John B. "The Role of Air Force Intelligence," Signal 35 (July 1981): 55.

4985. Marks, John B. "U.S. Air Force Intelligence," Military Intelligence 9/3 (July-September 1983): 4-9, 25.
　　Supplies a complete outline of USAF intelligence departments and respective mission descriptions.

4986. Marks, John D. "On Being Censored," Foreign Policy 15 (Summer 1974): 93-107.
　　As the co-author of the book The CIA and the Cult of Intelligence, Marks argues that the only test of censorship ought to be based on "direct,

immediate and irreparable damage to the nation or its people."

4987. Marks, John D. "How to Spot a Spook," <u>Washington Monthly</u> 6/9 (November 1974): 5-12.
The author reveals names of State Department and CIA personnel in various locations in the world and details methods for identifying such personnel.

4988. Marks, Sally. "'My Name Is Ozymandias': The Kaiser in Exile," <u>Central European History</u> 16/2 (June 1983): 122-170.

4989. Marks, Sally. "Black Watch on the Rhine: A Study in Propaganda, Prejudice, and Prurience," <u>European Studies Review</u> 13/3 (July 1983): 297-334.
The occupation of the Rhineland by the French Army after World War I is discussed. Such occupation led to German complaints against indigenous troops for acts of terror. Propaganda played a role in the exaggeration of some complaints.

4990. Marotta, John J. "Agency Access to Credit Bureau Files: Federal Invasion of Privacy?," <u>Boston College Industrial and Commercial Law Review</u> 12 (1970): 110-129.
Discusses administrative subpoena power for private records, privacy and the Fourth Amendment, proposed federal legislation and conclusions. Suggests a centralized governmental function to supervise information dissemination.

4991. Marre, Jennifer M. "National Security Directive 84: An Unjustifiably Broad Approach to Intelligence Protection," <u>Brooklyn Law Review</u> 51 (Fall 1984): 147-189.
Discusses the controversy surrounding National Security Directive 84 in reaction to <u>Snepp v. United States</u>. Major sections include discussion of national security matters and contractual waiver; First Amendment considerations; separation of powers doctrine; and suggestions for constructing a more constitutionally acceptable form of Directive 84.

4992. Marriott, John. "Satellites," <u>Army Quarterly</u> 107 (July 1977): 291-297.

4993. Marsh, J. M. "The Supreme Court Debates the Law of Treason: Article III, Section 3 of the Constitution," <u>Temple Law Quarterly</u> 19 (January 1946): 306-317.
Discusses the history of the Nazi saboteur case, <u>Cramer v. U. S.</u>, in terms of facts, constitutional requirements; points of disagreement; and conclusions.

4994. Marshall, Eliot. "A Spy Satellite for the Press?," <u>Signal</u> 42/9 (May 1988): 55-60.
Discussion of the cost and national security restrictions on the

development of "Mediasat."

4995. Marshall, J. "CIA Assets and the Rise of the Guadalajara Connection," Crime, Law and Social Change 16/1 (1991): 85-96.

4996. Marshall, James. "The Defense of Public Education from Subversion," Columbia Law Review 51/5 (May 1951): 587-605.

Discussion of academic freedom and its limits; nature of subversion in education; the rights to inquire concerning a teacher's loyalty; oaths; the matter of proof; and the use of school buildings.

4997. Marshall, Robert. "The Atomic Bomb -- and the Lag in Historical Understanding," Intelligence and National Security 6/2 (April 1991): 458-472.

Discusses the long held belief that the atomic bomb had to be dropped to save lives. Examines the reasons for using the bomb in diplomatic terms. Concludes that the final decision was based more on diplomatic than military reasons.

4998. Marshall, S. L. A. "Our Mistakes in Korea," Atlantic Monthly 192 (September 1953): 46-49.

This famous military historian offers insights into the political and military approaches to intervention in Korea, an "acknowledged stalemate" rather than a full war.

4999. Marson, Alain-Gerard. "Background to the American Intervention in Cambodia: Sihanouk's Overthrow," Asian Profile 1/1 (1973): 75-90.

5000. Martella, Dave. "Defending the Land of the Free and the Home of the Fearful: The Use of Classified Information to Deport Suspected Terrorists," American University Journal of International Law and Policy 7 (Summer 1992): 951-993.

5001. Martin, David. "Investigating the FBI," Policy Review 18 (Fall 1981): 113-132.

5002. Martin, David. "Churchill's Yugoslav Blunder: Precursor to the Yugoslav Tragedy," International Journal of Intelligence and Counterintelligence 5/4 (Winter 1991-1992): 417-431.

Discusses British and US support for the Yugoslavian national resistance movement before and during World War II. Major sections consider the switch of support to Josip Tito; the overthrow of Draza Mihailovic; the media, intelligence, and Mihailovic; and British intelligence and press personalities who supported Tito.

5003. Martin, Harry V. "Electronics Remain Keystone to U.S. Intelligence Mission," Defense Electronics 13 (December 1981): 59-81.

5004. Martin, Harry V. and Robert Carroll. "Electronics Companies Combat Increasing Soviet Spying," Defense Electronics 13 (July 1981): 34-35+.

5005. Martin, James K. "Benedict Arnold's Treason As Political Protest," Parameters: Journal of the U.S. Army War College 11/3 (September 1981): 63-74.
　　　Argues that Benedict Arnold reacted to the shortcomings of the Revolution and his treasonous associations with Sir Henry Clinton resulted from personal grievances related to lack of civilian support for the war. His treason, argues the author, was more an act of individual protest.

5006. Martin, John. "The Making of a Nazi Saboteur," Harper's 186 (April 1943): 532-540.
　　　A story of Herbert Haupt, one of eight Nazi saboteurs who landed on the beach in Florida in June 1942, later tried and convicted for treason.

5007. Martin, Joseph W. "What Basic Intelligence Seeks to Do," Studies in Intelligence 14/3 (Fall 1970): 103-113.
　　　Considers the role and function of intelligence doctrine. Major sections discuss criteria of excellence; the question of importance; and improving the product.

5008. Martin, L. John. "Disinformation: An Instrumentality in the Propaganda Arsenal," Political Communication and Persuasion 2/4 (1982): 47-64.
　　　Discusses forms of Soviet and US covert propaganda and their respective intentions to manipulate events.

5009. Martin, Paul H. "Intelligence Support for C^{3}CM Control and Communications Countermeasures," Signal 42 (December 1987): 19-20+.

5010. Martin, Phillip W. "The CIA in Angola: Legacy of War, Miser and Manipulation," Covert Action Information Bulletin 36 (Spring 1991): 41-45.

5011. Martin, Steven J. "Custer Didn't Listen," Military Intelligence 15/2 (April-June 1989): 15-20.
　　　Argues that proper reconnaissance might have saved George Custer's 7th Cavalry. Explores seven major mistakes of Custer's intelligence and reconnaissance actions or inactions.

5012. Martin, Tyrone G. "Let's Use Our Intelligence," U.S. Naval Institute Proceedings 93/11 (November 1967): 56-61.

An argument for beefing up the shipboard intelligence officers awareness. Sections discuss intelligence officer duties, two parts of the intelligence officer, the Office of Naval Intelligence, short-term schools, and the use of photographs by intelligence officers.

5013. Martin, Tyrone G. "The Deflektor Defector," Naval History 4/3 (1990): 33-36.

5014. Martin, Thomas S. "National Security and the First Amendment: A Change in Perspective," American Bar Association Journal 68 (June 1982): 680-685.

Discusses the unresolved questions posed by growing civil litigation designed to control national security violations pursuant to the Espionage Acts, secrecy agreements, prior restraints, passport revocations, etc. Considers the Progressive, Snepp and Agee cases.

5015. Martinez, Eugenio. "Mission Impossible: The Watergate Bunglers," Harper's 249 (October 1974): 50-58.

A member of the Watergate break-in team describes the absurdities of the 1972 mission to burglarize the Democratic National Headquarters, a mission which he claimed was not explained and for which agencies such as the CIA disclaimed all knowledge.

5016. Martinez, P. "A Police Spy and the Exiled Communards, 1871-1873," English Historical Review 97/382 (January 1982): 99-112.

Activities of French intelligence services against French refugees who fled to London in 1871 are discussed.

5017. Martini, John A. "Search and Destroy," American Heritage 43/7 (November 1992): 98-103.

Discusses the US Army's secretive defenses of Alcatraz Island in the San Francisco Bay in 1863-64. Includes several confiscated photos of the era.

5018. Martland, Peter. "The Ohkrana: Guardians of a Recorded Culture," Intelligence and National Security 6/3 (July 1991): 627-628.

Discusses the problem of record privacy concerning Russian and British trade. Suggests that lack of controlling legislation permitted Soviets to commit unethical and illegal business practices.

5019. Martyniuk, Andrew O. "An End to and FBI General Presumption of Confidentiality under Freedom of Information Act Exemption 7(D)," University of Cincinnati Law Review 63 (Fall 1994): 523-563.

5020. Marvel, W. Macy. "Drift and Intrigue: United States Relations with the

Viet-Minh 1945," <u>Millennium: Journal of International Studies</u> 4/1 (1975): 10-27.

This articles discusses, in part, the role of the US Office of Strategic Services in the formulation of policy toward Vietnam immediately before and after World War II.

5021. Marx, Gary T. "Thoughts on a Neglected Category of Social Movement Participant: The Agent Provocateur and the Informant," <u>American Journal of Sociology</u> 80 (1975): 402-442.

Lengthy sociological analysis of agent provocateurs and informants, including backgrounds, motives, ease of entry into a social movement, exposure, movement responses to infiltration, diverse consequences, and justification and legitimization of agents.

5022. Marx, Gary T. "Undercover Cops: Creative Policing or Constitutional Threat?," <u>Civil Liberties Review</u> (July-August 1977): 34-44.

5023. Marx, Gary T. "Ironies of Social Control: Authorities as Contributors to Deviance Through Escalation, Nonenforcement and Covert Facilitation," <u>Social Problems</u> 28/3 (February 1981): 221-246.

Various means applied in law enforcement work to achieve ends, including the ironies of escalation of deviance, nonenforcement, and covert facilitation of law breaking.

5024. Marx, Gary T. "Who Really Gets Stung? Some Issues Raised by the New Police Undercover Work," <u>Crime and Delinquency</u> 28/2 (April 1982): 165-193.

Discusses the limits of undercover investigations, in terms of targets of investigation; stress and supervision; the weaknesses of informers; victimization of third parties; and the potential contributions to crime.

5025. Marx, Gary T. "The New Surveillance," <u>Technology Review</u> 88 (May-June 1985): 42-48.

Discusses the new transactional analysis technologies to track personal histories by computer, devices for surveilling people from long distances, and reconsideration of the concept of privacy.

5026. Marx, Gary T. "The Surveillance Society: The Threat of 1984-Style Techniques," <u>Futurist</u> 19 (June 1985): 21-26.

Discusses police acquisition of information from informers by means of rewards and special electronic sniffers. Discusses the new technology and the law, computer matching and profiling, the mystique of technology, and the bug sniffing briefcase.

5027. Marx, Gary T. "Under-the-Covers Undercover Investigations: Some

Reflections on the State's Use of Sex and Deception in Law Enforcement," Criminal Justice Ethics 4/1 (Winter-Spring 1992): 13-15.

5028. Marx, Gary T. "Commentary," Crime, Law and Social Change 18/1-2 (September 1992): 3-34.

This is a lead article in a collection of papers devoted to the issues raised by Marx's book, Undercover: Police Surveillance in America. It summarizes and comments upon pieces by Richard A. Leo, Alan R. Block, Gilbert Geis and Colin Goff, Jean-Paul Brodeur, Julius Wachtel, David Lyon, Mathieu Deflem. The last piece is reserved for Marx's reflections upon recent developments and enduring issues.

5029. Marx, Gary T. "Some Reflections on Undercover: Recent Developments and Enduring Issues," Crime, Law and Social Change 18/1-2 (September 1992): 193-218.

Considers new applications and developments following publication of the author's book, Undercover. Discusses judicial rulings and legislation which continued to facilitate undercover investigations; the conflict of goals between preventing crime and encouraging it; the fabrication if evidence and exploiting informers; the role of the media in undercover work. Offers some thoughts and enduring tensions in undercover investigations.

5030. Marx, Gary T. and Nancy Reichman. "Routinizing the Discovery of Secrets: Computers as Informants," American Behavioral Scientist 2 (March 1984): 423-445.

Discusses the dependence of police on citizen-supplied information and the role of computers in assisting police investigations. Argues for reforms to improve the crime discovery process through more detailed data searching, matching, profiling, and use of results. Mentions policy and research errors, civil liberties issues, and theoretical implications.

5031. Marx, Gary T. and Nancy Reichman. "Routinizing the Discovery of Secrets: Computers as Informants," Policy Studies Review Annual 8 (1987): 606-632.

Discusses police use of informants as a vehicle for breaching natural privacy arenas in the society for the purpose of controlling crime. Topics include reforms to improve the discovery process, systematic data searching, policy and research implications, and theoretical implications.

5032. Marx, Gary. T. and Sanford Sherigen. "Corporations that Spy on Their Employees," Business and Society Review 60 (Winter 1987): 32-37.

Discusses the use of devices used by companies to form what the authors call the "maximum-security workplace"; argues that advance notice of monitoring should be available to employees.

5033. Marx, Herbert. "The Emergency Power and Civil Liberty in Canada," McGill Law Journal 16/1 (1970): 39-91.

A lengthy discussion of the resort to martial law in Britain, Canada and the US; the emergency doctrine in Canada and the impact of emergency on civil liberties.

5034. Masao, Yamamoto. "Pearl Harbor: An Imperial Japanese Army Officer's View," Journal of American-East Asian Relations (1994): 17-39.

5035. Mascola, Edward G. "Specificity Requirement for Warrants Under the Fourth Amendment--Defining the Zone of Privacy," Dickinson Law Review 73 (1968): 1-43.

Reviews the question and procedures surrounding specificity in police officer development of information for arrest warrants. Major sections include discussion of search warrants for premises and automobiles and eavesdropping under New York and federal laws.

5036. Maslov, P. "The Literature of the Military Operations in the Summer of 1941," Voenno-Istorichesky Zhurnal 9 (September 1966): 187-195.

In Russian, but later translated, this bibliography reflects Russian deficiencies in material and psychological preparation for the German invasion in June 1941.

5037. Maslowski, Peter. "Military Intelligence Sources During the American Civil War: A Time of Transition," Studies in Intelligence 36/2 (Summer 1992).

5038. Mason, M. A. "Beach Intelligence," Washington Academy of Sciences Journal 37 (September 1947): 289-293.

5039. Massey, James L. "An Introduction of Contemporary Cryptology," Proceedings of the IEEE 76 (May 1988): 533-549.

5040. Mast, Charles. "How I Organized French Aid," Miroir de l'Histoire 5/53 (1954): 734-742.

This is an approximate title translation of the title to an article in French.

5041. Masterman, J. C. "The XX Papers," Yale Alumni Magazine and Journal 35 (February 1972): 7-11.

5042. Masters, Barry. "The Ethics of Intelligence Activities," National Security Affairs Forum 24 (Spring-Summer 1976): 39-47.

5043. Masters, James M., Sr. "Minimizing Uncertainty: Marine Corps Intelligence Reorganization and Objectives," Marine Corps Gazette 42 (June

1958): 20-26.

5044. Mathews, David J. "Civilians' Claims That Army's Data Gathering System Works a Chilling Effect on Their First Amendment Rights Held Not to Be Justifiable Controversy Absent Showing of Objective Present Harm or Threat of Future Harm," Villanova Law Review 18/3 (February 1973): 479-491.
    Title captures the major themes of this piece.

5045. Matschulat, Austin B. "Coordination and Cooperation in Counterintelligence," Studies in Intelligence 13/1 (Spring 1969): 25-36.

5046. Matsulenko, Viktor A. "World War II Soviet Camoflage Operations Described," Voenna-Istorich Zhurnal 1 (January 1975): 10-21.

5047. Matsulenko, Viktor A. "Surprise: How It Is Achieved and Its Role," Soviet Military Review 5 & 6 (May-June 1972): 37-39.

5048. Matteson, Robert E. "The Last Days of Ernst Kaltenbrunner," Studies in Intelligence 4/1 (Spring 1960).

5049. Matthews, Joseph B. "The Oppenheimer Story," American Mercury 79 (October 1974): 136-143.
    Presents perspectives of the author on the J. Robert Oppenheimer investigation.

5050. Matthews, Robert A. J. "An Empirical Method for Finding the Keylength of Periodic Ciphers," Cryptologia 12/4 (October 1988): 220-224.

5051. Matthews, Robert A. J. "On the Derivation of a 'Chaotic' Encryption Algorithm," Cryptologia 13/1 (January 1989): 29-41.

5052. Matthews, Robert A. J. "A Rotor Device for Periodic and Random-Key Encryption," Cryptologia 13/3 (July 1989): 266-272.

5053. Matthews, Robert A. J. "The Use of Genetic Algorithms in Cryptanalysis," Cryptologia 17/2 (April 1993): 187-201.

5054. Matthews, W. "Samuel Pepys, Tachygraphist," Modern Language Review 29 (October 1934): 397-404.

5055. Mattingly, Robert E. "'Zdravo, Purvi Americanec,'" Studies in Intelligence 26/1 (Spring 1982).
    Discusses OSS activities in Yugoslavia during World War II.

5056. Mattingly, Robert E. "Who Knew Not Fear," Studies in Intelligence 26/2 (Summer 1982).

5057. Mattingly, Robert E. "Man, You Must Be Lost or Something," Studies in Intelligence 26/3 (Fall 1982).
Discusses OSS activities in France during World War II.

5058. Maurer, John H. and Gordon H. McCormick. "Surprise Attack and Conventional Defense in Europe," Orbis 27/1 (Spring 1983): 107-126.
Discusses the possible nature of unanticipated Soviet attack in Europe and the plans of NATO to minimize such a likelihood.

5059. Maurer, Maurer. "A Delicate Mission: Aerial Reconnaissance of Japanese Islands Before World War II," Military Affairs 26/2 (Summer 1962): 66-75.
Intelligence overflights of Japan prior to World War II to gain information on the military buildup. Flaws of the program of discovery are also discussed.

5060. Maury, John M. "CIA and the Congress," Studies in Intelligence 18/2 (Summer 1974).
Estimated to be 14 pages in length.

5061. Maury, John M. "Intelligence Secrets?," Society 19/3 (March-April 1982): 76-77.
Discusses the strengths and weaknesses of modern technology of intelligence and the importance of protecting intelligence secrets.

5062. Mautner, Martha. "Interviews with Adenauer," Studies in Intelligence 30/3 (Fall 1986).

5063. Maxton, J. "The Judicial Discretion to Exclude Evidence Obtained by Agents Provocateurs," New Zealand Universities Law Review 9 (June 1980): 73-78.
Discusses the question before the House of Lords case of R. v. Sang (1972), 2 All E.R. 1222: whether a judge could exclude evidence obtained by an agent provocateur on the ground that such evidence had been unfairly or improperly obtained.

5064. Maxwell, Elliot E. "The CIA's Secret Funding and the Constitution," Yale Law Journal 84/3 (January 1975): 608-638.
Examines CIA secret funding as potentially unconstitutional. Considers the history of Article I, Section 9, Clause 7 of the US Constitution; purposes of the Clause; government funding of CIA practices; reconciling CIA funding with the Clause, and the national security justification.

5065. Maxwell, Kinera and Roger Reinsch. "The Freedom of Information Act Privacy Exemption: Who Does It Really Protect?," Communications and the Law 7/2 (April 1985): 45-59.

A discussion of the FOIA's privacy exemption to protect individual rights.

5066. May, Ernest R. "The Development of Political-Military Consultations in the United States," Political Science Quarterly 70/2 (June 1955): 161-180.

Discusses the National Security Council as the outcome of a long evolutionary progression of political and military consultations for national security policy. Mentions intelligence information sharing.

5067. May, Ernest R. "The Nature of Foreign Policy: The Calculated versus the Axiomatic," Daedalus 91/4 (Fall 1962): 653-665.

Contains a discussion of the policy conditions before the Korean War in early to mid 1950.

5068. May, Ernest R. "Soldiers and Diplomats: The French Embassy and Franco-Italian Relations, 1935-36," Journal of Strategic Studies 7 (1984): 74-91.

5069. May, Ernest R. "Intelligence: Backing Into the Future," Foreign Affairs 71/3 (Summer 1992): 63-72.

Considers the proposals in the Senate and House to reorganize the intelligence community; the Boren and McCurdy bills. Examines the premises and implications of each proposal. Argues that the legislation will probably not fix the real problem of lack of presidential direction.

5070. May, Ernest R. "Studying and Teaching Intelligence: The Importance of Interchange," Studies in Intelligence 38/5 (1995): 1-5.

The author's keynote address to the Symposium for Teaching Intelligence, held October 1 and 2, 1993 in Washington, D.C. Argues that international relations study and intelligence study must remain integrated in their research considerations.

5071. May, Lowell E. "Centralized Requirements in the DIA," Studies in Intelligence 7/3 (Fall 1963).

5072. Mayer, Thomas F. "A Diet for Henry VIII: The Failure of Reginald Pole's 1537 Legation," Journal of British Studies 26/3 (July 1987): 305-331.

Pole was sent as a diplomat by the Pope. He was secretly instructed to harm Henry VIII. Henry dispatched assassins and organized plots to kill Pole. The mission failed due to Pole's friends on Henry's privy council. Pole's courier, Throck Morton, was a double agent. A historical tale that argues Pole's diplomatic attempts were devious and that espionage tactics were used to pull down Henry VIII in retaliation for divorcing Anne.

5073. Maynard, Douglas H. "Union Efforts to Prevent the Escape of the Alabama," Mississippi Valley Historical Review 41/1 (1954): 41-60.

Detailed account of the Union plans to prevent the confederate ship Alabama from leaving its home port in Liverpool, England. Useful in discussions of covert actions during the Civil War.

5074. Maynard, Douglas H. "Plotting the Escape of the Alabama," Journal of Southern History 20/2 (May 1954): 197-209.

Brief account of covert construction and deployment of naval vessels, constructed in England, to supply the Confederacy in the Civil War.

5075. Maynard, Douglas H. "The Forbes-Aspinwall Mission," Mississippi Valley Historical Review 45/1 (June 1958): 67-89.

An account of President Lincoln's attempts to buy confederate ships in England that were known to have assisted the confederate cause. Useful in discussions of covert actions during the Civil War.

5076. Mayo, Lida. "John Yates Beall: 'The Southern John Brown,'" Virginia Cavalcade 14/4 (1965): 4-9.

5077. Mayton, William T. "Seditious Libel and the Lost Guarantee of a Freedom of Expression," Columbia Law Review 84 (1984): 91-142.

Discusses the historical development of suppression of free speech by charges of seditious libel. One means of such suppression was through the use of police and spies.

5078. Mazer, Cary M. "Treasons, Strategems, and Spoils: Edwardian Actor-Managers and the Shakespeare Memorial National Theatre," Theatre Survey 24 (May-November 1983): 1-33.

5079. Mazour, Anatole G. "Philip R. Faymonville," California Historical Society Quarterly 42 (March 1963): 84-88.

5080. Mazrui, Ali Al'Amin. "Is the Satanic Verses a Satanic Novel?: Moral Dilemmas of the Rushdie Affair," Michigan Quarterly Review 28 (Summer 1989): 347-371.

5081. Mazrui, Ali Al'Amin. "'The Satanic Verses' or a Satanic Novel? Moral Dilemmas of the Rushdie Affair," Alternatives 15/1 (Winter 1990).

Discusses several background issues related to the publication in 1988 of The Satanic Verses by Salman Rushdie. Rushdie was placed under a death threat for his alleged heresy, called a traitor by Islamic religious leaders. Useful piece for influences of religious true beliefs on legal definitions of treason.

5082. McAdams, Richard H. "Tying Privacy in Knotts: Beeper Monitoring and Collective Fourth Amendment Rights," Virginia Law Review 71/2 (March 1985): 297-341.

Examines the basic issues addressed by electronic law, and then criticizes the outcome of the Knotts case. Surveys electronic tracking law, discusses the Fourth Amendment implications of beeper use, and concludes that extensive beeper use threatens privacy interests of society.

5083. McArdle, Paul J. "A Short and Plain Statement: The Significance of Leatherman v. Tarrant County," University of Detroit Mercy Law Review 72 (Fall 1994): 19-47.

Considers Leatherman (113 S. Ct. 1160) an important Supreme Court case in the area of narcotics intelligence unit operations.

5084. McAuliffe, Mary S. "Liberals and the Communists Control Act of 1954," Journal of American History 63 (September 1976): 351-367.

Discusses the liberal and conservative battles in the early 1950s to draft legislation to contain alleged communist influence in the labor movement. Specifically, discusses the Communist Control Act of 1954, the Butler bill and the Humphrey bill.

5085. McAuliffe, Mary S. "Eisenhower, the President," Journal of American History 68/3 (December 1981): 625-632.

A commentary on various recent histories of the Eisenhower administration. Includes comments about Ike's dealings with CIA and use of covert actions.

5086. McBarron, H. Charles and John R. Elting, et al. "Balloon Corps: United States Army, 1861-1863," Military Collector and Historian 28/1 (1976): 16-18.

5087. McBride, Dale R. "Haig v. Agee: A Decisive Victory for Governmental Regulation of Americans in International Travel," California Western International Law Journal 13 (Winter 1983): 144-167.

Discusses the setting of the case of passport controls, the necessity of the freedom to travel, historical right to travel, the court's decision and problems within the Agee analysis.

5088. McCadden, Helen M. "Juan de Miralles and the American Revolution," Americas 29/3 (1973): 359-375.

Outlines the history of George Washington's associations with Juan de Miralles and the assistance rendered to the American Revolution by Spain.

5089. McCaffrey, Hugh. "On the Importance of Secret Intelligence," U.S. Naval Institute Proceedings 106/8 (August 1980): 53-55.

A brief commentary advocating the role of intelligence in decision making processes.

5090. McCain, John S., III. "Proliferation in the 1990s: Implications for U.S. Policy and Force Planning," Strategic Review 17/3 (Summer 1989): 9-20.

5091. McCamant, John F. "Intervention in Guatemala: Implications for the Study of Third World Politics," Comparative Political Studies 17/3 (1984): 373-407.

An assessment of US foreign policy of intervention in the affairs of Guatemala, including the use of the Central Intelligence Agency to overthrow the Arbenz government in 1954.

5092. McCann, Hugh W. "The Secret of Prisoner No. 44451," American Visions 1/4 (1986); 36-41.

This is a brief story about a black intelligence officer who worked in Nazi prison camps during World War II.

5093. McCarn, Davis B. "Developments in Air Targeting: The Damage Assessment Model," Studies in Intelligence 2 (Summer 1958).

5094. McCarthy, Linda S. "'You're From Where and You're Doing What?,'" Studies in Intelligence 31/2 (Summer 1987).

A brief experience of the author, an employee in the Central Intelligence Agency's Historical Collection Library, concerning her trip to the National Archives bookstore to collect items for display on the intelligence aspects of the Constitution's Bicentennial celebration.

5095. McCarthy, Mary. "The National Warning System: Striving for an Elusive Goal," Defense Intelligence Journal 3/1 (Spring 1994): 5-20.

Examines the history of the warning system; current system structure; reasons for warning intelligence failure; the concept of successful warnings; communicating the warning; and alarms, wolves and sheep.

5096. McCarthy, Shaun. "South Africa's Intelligence Reformation," International Journal of Intelligence and Counterintelligence 9/1 (Spring 1996): 63-71.

Major sections discuss guiding principles of new intelligence dispensation; legislative reform; organizational reform; future challenges to the intelligence community; and a new intelligence identity.

5097. McCauley, Nathan E. "The Military Intelligence Profession in the U.S. Army," Military Intelligence 13/3 & 14/1 (October 1987 & January 1988): 14-17,

37; 30-32.

Traces the roots of the MI branch in part I. Explains the impact of the MI Corps on the US Army in part II.

5098. McClean, J. D. "Informers and Agents Provocateurs," Criminal Law Review 1969 (October 1969): 527-538.

5099. McClelland, Charles A. "The Acute International Crisis," World Politics 14 (October 1961): 182-204.

5100. McClelland, Charles A. "Decisional Opportunity and Political Controversy, the Quemoy Case," Journal of Conflict Resolution 6 (September 1962): 201-213.

5101. McClelland, Charles A. "Action Structures and Communication in Two International Crises: Quemoy and Berlin," Background 7 (1964): 201-215.

5102. McClelland, Charles A. "The Anticipation of International Crises: Prospects for Theory and Research," International Studies Quarterly 21 (March 1977): 15-38.

5103. McCleskey, Edward R. "Applying Deception to Special Operations," American Intelligence Journal 12/1 (Winter 1991): 45-50.

Defines special operations missions of SOF units such as Navy SEALS, Army Special Forces, and USAF Special Operations Wings; categories of deception, such as camoflage, disguise, diversion, electronic spoofing, decoying, and cover; and the common threads of past missions among Jewish Nationalists prior to 1948, post-independence Israelis, Palestinian terrorists, US SOF's, Selous Scouts of Rhodesia, and miscellaneous groups.

5104. McColloch, Claude. "The Strange Case of Alger Hiss: A Reply to Lord Jowitt," American Bar Association Journal 40 (March 1954): 199-202; 261-262.

A review essay of Lord Earl Jowitt's book, The Strange Case of Alger Hiss. The reviewer casts an evil eye upon the credibility of the book.

5105. McCollum, James K. "CORDS: Matrix for Peace in Vietnam," Army 32 (July 1982): 48-53.

5106. McCollum, James K. "The CORDS Pacification Organization in Vietnam: A Civilian-Military Effort," Armed Forces and Society 10/1 (Fall 1983): 105-122.

Explores pacification in the early years of the 1950s; escalation in Hanoi and Washington; US pacification without coordination; CORDS formed; and a CORDS province team.

5107. McConaughy, John B. "A Review of Soviet Psychological Warfare," Military Review 40/12 (December 1960): 3-13.

5108. McConnell, J. M. "New World, New Challenges: NSA Into the 21st Century," American Intelligence Journal 15/1 (Spring-Summer 1994): 7-10.

Reflecting on the history of the National Security Agency and encoded communications, the author provides general observations about the future role of NSA.

5109. McCord, James W., Jr. "Watergate and the Intelligence Community," Armed Forces Journal International 110 (August 1973): 57-58.

The FBI failed to acquire critical evidence and to interrogate key witnesses in the weeks following the Watergate breakin due to Justice Department and White House interference.

5110. McCormack, Thelma. "Body Count: The Media and the Revisionist Histories of Vietnam," Studies in Communications 4 (1990): 119-142.

Argues that high US Army officials in the Vietnam war conspired to rig the body count of enemy dead in order to convince the political community that the war was being won. This, according to the author, is the CIA version of the war's disaster. Argues also that the media participated in this revisionist approach.

5111. McCormick, Gordon H. "Surprise, Perceptions, and Military Style," Orbis 26/4 (Winter 1983): 833-839.

Argues that military surprises often follow a failure to assess perceptions and culture of the enemy. Cautions that proper understanding involves consideration of the military style and traditions of the opponent.

5112. McCormick, James M. and Steven S. Smith. "The Iran Arms Sale and the Intelligence Oversight Act of 1980," PS 20 (Winter 1987): 29-37.

An examination of the conflict between the Congress and the President over intelligence oversight, particularly in light of the Iran-Contra matter.

5113. McCormick, William. "Problems of American Scholars in India," Asian Survey 16/11 (November 1976): 1064-1080.

Accounts for the history of foreign scholars in India and the fears of the Indian government that US scholars all work for the Central Intelligence Agency.

5114. McCouch, Grayson M. "'Naming Names': Unauthorized Disclosure of Intelligence Agents Identities," Stanford Law Review 33/4 (April 1981): 693-713.

Using the Agee and Progressive cases as backdrops, this article discusses the US government's information classification system, the failure of the intelligence laws of 1979-80 to improve the classification system, constitutional limits on the disclosure of agents' names, and suggested alternatives.

5115. McCoy, Ron. "Navajo Code Talkers of World War II," American West 18 (1981): 67-73.

5116. McCreary, John F. "Warning Cycles," Studies in Intelligence 27/3 (Fall 1983): 71-79.
 An analysis and evaluation of the warning process.

5117. McCubbins, Mathew D. and Thomas Schwartz. "Congressional Oversight Overlooked: Police Patrols Versus Fire Alarms," American Journal of Political Science 28/1 (February 1984): 165-178.
 A detailed accounting of congressional oversight of the intelligence community, including observations of the role played by Senator Richard Russell in controlling leaks of intelligence information.

5118. McCullough, James and David Gries. "Personal Reflections on Bill Casey's Last Month," Studies in Intelligence 39/5 (1996): 75-91.
 Concludes that CIA director Casey ended his career "...with more of a whimper than a bang." This is a reflective piece on the associations of the authors with director Casey in his final days at CIA.

5119. McCurdy, David. "Glasnost for the CIA," Foreign Affairs 73/1 (January-February 1994): 125-140.
 Major sections discuss coming in from the cold; opening up intelligence; intelligence and economic strength; promoting democracy; operational intelligence; a new approach to intelligence; and first line of defense in the intelligence community.

5120. McDermott, John. "Sir Francis Oppenheimer: 'Stranger Within' the Foreign Office," History 66/217 (June 1981): 199-207.
 A short biography of Sir Francis Oppenheimer and his rise through the ranks of the British Foreign Office to the position of command attache for northern and western Europe. Oppenheimer linked economic with political and strategic issues.

5121. McDermott, Louis M. "Guatemala, 1954: Intervention or Aggression?," Rocky Mountain Social Science Journal 9 (January 1972): 79-88.
 Traces the evolution of US intervention in Guatemala's affairs and government from 1944 to 1954

5122. McDonald, Donald. "Militarism in America," Center Magazine 3/1 (1970): 12-33.
 Argues that the congressional controls on the CIA have been less than

adequate to contain what the author views as an abuse of the original intentions of the National Security Act of 1947.

5123. McDonald, J. Kenneth. "Secrecy, Accountability, and the CIA: The Dilemma of Intelligence in a Democracy," Revue Internationale d'Histoire Militaire 69 (1990): 376-404.

5124. McDonald, Lawrence H. "The Office of Strategic Services: America's First National Intelligence Agency," Prologue: Quarterly Journal of the National Archives 23/1 (Spring 1991): 7-22.

Beginning in the early 1980s, the CIA transferred massive quantities of records to the National Archives and Records Service concerning the activities of the OSS in World War II. General discussion of the Archives records collection on the OSS and the factors related to OSS's bridges to the CIA.

5125. McDonald, Lawrence H. "The OSS: America's First National Intelligence Agency," Special Warfare 6/1 (February 1993): 24-32.

5126. McDonald, Marci. "Would You Believe...Iranian Moderates," Washington Monthly 19/2 (March 1987): 39-45, 47-48, 50.

Discusses the politicization of the Central Intelligence Agency under Reagan: Intelligence estimate of Mexico made gloomier than reality; CIA's intelligence on Iran so poor that CIA had to rely solely on Israeli reports that claimed there were moderates in Iran lobbying for renewed US ties. Casey's reforms of CIA are detailed.

5127. McDougal, Myres S. and Norbert A. Schlei. "The Hydrogen Bomb Tests in Perspective: Lawful Measures for Security," Yale Law Journal 64/5 (April 1955): 648-710.

Considers the legal policy issue surrounding the hydrogen bomb tests; the regime of the high seas; unilateral claims; special deference accorded to claims for security; the hydrogen bomb as a reasonable measure for security; and the future of international agreements.

5128. McDougal, Myres S.; Harold D. Lasswell; and W. Michael Reisman. "The World Constitutive Process of Authoritative Decision," Journal of Legal Education 19/3 & 19/4 (1967): 253-300; 403-437.

A lengthy and scholarly treatment of international law within the context of the decisions made by nation-states and their leaders. Contains discussion of the theory and roles of intelligence in decisionmaking.

5129. McDougal, Myres S.; Harold D. Lasswell; and W. Michael Reisman. "The Intelligence Function and World Public Order," Temple Law Quarterly 46/3 (Spring 1973): 365-448.

An extensive discussion of the theory of intelligence gathering, evaluation and dissemination. Discusses constitutive policies, past performance, processes, conditions and possible developments.

5130. McElroy, David M. "Psyop--The Invisible Battlefield," Military Intelligence 16/3 (July-September 1990): 22-25.

Major sections discuss the role of intelligence in psychological operations; intelligence requirements for PSYOP development; and intelligence dissemination.

5131. McEwen, Michael T. "Intelligence and PSYOP in Terrorism Counteraction," Military Intelligence 10/1 (January-March 1984): 8-10.

Discusses preparation for and reaction to terrorism.

5132. McEwen, Michael T. "Psychological Operations Against Terrorism: The Unused Weapon," Military Review 66/1 (January 1986): 59-67.

Examines methods for reducing the effectiveness of the terrorist by targeting the terrorist and his public organization.

5133. McEwen, Michael T. "A New Terrorism Intelligence Challenge," American Intelligence Journal 8/2 (May 1987).

5134. McGarvey, Patrick J. "The Culture of Bureaucracy, DIA: Intelligence to Please," Washington Monthly 2 (July 1970): 68-75.

Discusses the origins and military leadership of the Defense Intelligence Agency. Argues that the DIA delivers too much information designed to please political bosses, thereby making its evaluations both useless and dangerous.

5135. McGarvey, Patrick J. "Of Spooks and Spies and Daggers: The U.S. Intelligence Community," Government Executive 2 (August 1970): 38-41.

5136. McGehee, F. M., III. "Bribery for National Security," Progressive 42 (March 1978): 7-8.

Discusses the loophole of "national security" rationale through which American corporations participate in overseas bribery. Also discusses the application of the exemption to the CIA and to the CIA's connections with overseas corporation dealings.

5137. McGehee, Ralph W. "CIA: Ignorance is Strength," Bill of Rights Journal 16 (December 1983): 29-31.

Argues that CIA uses prepublication review and claims of national security as means for preventing public knowledge of illegal and embarrassing operations of the agency.

5138. McGehee, Ralph W. "Back in the Saddle Again: A Former CIA Officer Sees a New Binge of Illegal Activity," Progressive 49/8 (August 1985): 32-33.

Discusses the Rockefeller inquiry and congressional investigations into CIA activities to test human subjects with LSD and actions to surveil Robert F. Kennedy and Martin Luther King, Jr. Says that CIA domestic operations remain active.

5139. McGehee, Ralph W. "The Indonesian Massacres and the CIA," Covert Action Information Bulletin 35 (Fall 1990): 56-58.

5140. McGill, G. M. "OSCINT and the Private Information Sector," International Journal of Intelligence and Counterintelligence 7/4 (Winter 1994): 435-443.

Discussion of open source intelligence in terms of information services, such as DIALOG and LEXIS/NEXIS; American information sources; redefining security in a changing world; national security versus the competitive needs of American business; intelligence agencies and private information providers; need for a comprehensive infrastructure for the information superhighway; the increasing the total sum of intelligence; and the costs of public information.

5141. McGowan, William. "Why We Can't Catch More Spies," Washington Monthly 17/6-7 (July-August 1985): 12-18.

An examination of the problems involved in US inability to maintain secret and privileged information.

5142. McGranahan, Donald V. "U.S. Psychological Warfare Policy," Public Opinion Quarterly 10 (Fall 1946): 446-450.

The US avoided use of ideological foundations for its propaganda during World War II in contrast to the Germans, Japanese and Russians. A brief discussion of the contrasts in approaches.

5143. McGrath, James. "The Scientific and Cultural Exchange," Studies in Intelligence 7/4 (Winter 1963).

5144. McGrath, John J. "The KGB Olympics: USSR Fields World-Class Team to Entertain and Entrap the Unwary," Sea Power 23 (May 1980): 25-26+.

5145. McGreevy, Thomas J. "Police Intelligence Operations," Police 8/4 (March-April 1964): 46-52.

5146. McGruther, Kenneth R. "The Role of Perceptions in Naval Diplomacy," Naval War College Review 27/2 (1974): 3-20.

This is a study of how perceptions of opposing military forces and political leadership are constructed, applying the circumstances of the

India-Pakistan war of 1971.

5147. McGurn, William. "The Witness of Whittaker Chambers: A Bitter Hope," Modern Age 28/2-3 (Spring-Summer 1984): 203-207.

The author briefly revisits occurrences in the years after Chambers published his autobiography, Witness.

5148. McHughes, Lee M. "The Hiss Act and Its Application to the Military," Military Law Review 14 (October 1961): 67-107.

Discusses the background and purpose of the Act; provisions and sources for interpretation of the Act; major problems in interpretation; ancillary problems relating to the Act; and the Hiss Act as public policy.

5149. McKay, C. G. "Iron Ore and Section D: The Oxelosund Operation," Historical Journal 29/4 (1986): 975-978.

Discusses a British intelligence mission in 1939 and 1940 to stop the flow of Swedish iron ore to Germany via the Swedish port at Oxelosund.

5150. McKay, C. G. "The Kramer Case: A Study in Three Dimensions," Intelligence and National Security 4/2 (April 1989): 268-294.

Discusses the intensified German effort to collect intelligence through neutral european countries against the US and Britain. Dr. Kramer, a member of the German intelligence community, collected intelligence until the end of World War II from the Swedish capital. There are no complete records on Dr. Kramer's sources and it is not clear how Kramer collected the amount and quality of intelligence.

5151. McKay, C. G. "Whispers in the Dark," Intelligence and National Security 4/2 (April 1989): 401-405.

A book review essay of Fleischhauer Ingeborg's book, Die Chance des Sonderfriedens, Deutsch-Sowjetische Geheimgesprache 1941-1945 concerning a secret peace accord between Russia and Germany during World War II. Hitler's opposition and the German clumsiness in handling the terms caused the failure to complete the agreement. This was a case of backstairs diplomacy.

5152. McKay, C. G. "Our Man in Reval," Intelligence and National Security 9/1 (January 1994): 88-11.

Discusses the intelligence gathered by source BP11 in Reval in 1921. Intelligence concerned Bolshevik subversion against British interests. Source was discredited by using direct intercepts gathered by GC & CS. An attempt to shed new light on this case.

5153. McKay, C. G. "Arvid Damm Makes an Offer," Cryptologia 18/3 (July 1994): 243-249.

5154. McKay, Herbert C. "Notes from a Laboratory," <u>American Photography</u> 60 (November 1946): 38-40, 50.

5155. McKay, Herbert C. "Stereo Photography," <u>U.S. Camera</u> 13 (October 1950): 16.

5156. McKay, Theresa N. "CPL 700.10: 30-Day Limit on Eavesdropping Warrant Begins on Date of Issuance," <u>St. John's University Law Review</u> 60 (Fall 1985): 211-219.

Discusses the statute in the State of New York for issuing warrants to conduct eavesdropping. The case of <u>People v. Paluska</u> raised the question of when the limit on an eavesdropping warrant begins. The Supreme Court held that the warrant's life was no longer than thirty days from issuance, unless a specific date was set by the issuing judge.

5157. McKay, Vernon. "South African Propaganda: Methods and Media," <u>Africa Report</u> 11 (February 1966): 41-46.

An extension of this piece appeared as "The Propaganda Battle for Zambia," <u>Africa Today</u> (April 1966): 18-26 in reference to South Africa.

5158. McKee, W. J. "The Reports Officer: Issues of Quality," <u>Studies in Intelligence</u> 27/1 (Spring 1983): 11-18.

Explores the role and functions of the CIA reports officer. Major sections discuss objectivity; quality versus quantity; speed versus accuracy; security versus use; system versus initiative; and perspective.

5159. McKenzie-Smith, Robert H. "Crisis Decisionmaking in Israel: The Case of the October 1973 Middle East War," <u>Naval War College Review</u> 29/1 (Summer 1976): 39-52.

Major sections include discussion of Israeli political-military doctrine in June 1967; doctrinal outcomes of the June 1967 war; Israel between wars; the 'wolf, wolf' phenomenon; the October 1973 crisis; the decision process; political outcome of the October 1973 war; and possible doctrinal outcomes.

5160. McKinney, Francis F. "The Integrity of Nathanael Greene," <u>Rhode Island History</u> 28/2 (1969): 53-60.

5161. McKinney, Hayes. "Treason Under the Constitution of the United States," <u>Illinois Law Review</u> 12/6 (January 1918): 381-402.

An extensive interpretation of the Constitution's definition of treason against the United States.

5162. McKinney, Hayes. "Spies and Traitors," <u>Illinois Law Review</u> 12/7 (1918): 591-628.

Distinguishes between spies and traitors. Discusses military spies; spies under criminal statutes; traitors under the Constitution; war rebels, war traitors and other so-called war criminals.

5163. McKinnon, Ian J. "Recent Decisions from the Supreme Court of Canada Relating to Electronic Surveillance," Advocate 50 (March 1992): 211-214.

5164. McKnight, Clarence E. "A Nation in Transition: The Role of C³I Systems," Signal 42/8 (April 1988): 55-58.

5165. McKnight, Gerald D. "The 1968 Memphis Sanitation Strike and the FBI: A Case Study in Urban Surveillance," South Atlantic Quarterly 83/2 (1984): 138-156.
    An account of activities leading to the assassination of Martin Luther King and the activities of the FBI following the crime.

5166. McKnight, Gerald D. "A Harvest of Hate: The FBI's War Against Black Youth - Domestic Intelligence in Memphis Tennessee," South Atlantic Quarterly 86 (Winter 1987): 1-21.
    This article asserts that the FBI had become a national police force determined to undermine a militant racial movement the Bureau found repugnant. FBI's COINTELPRO efforts targeted the black group in Memphis known as "The Invaders."

5167. McKnight, Phil. "The Bear Speaks," Naval Intelligence Professionals Quarterly (Spring 1995): 6-7.
    This is a collection of excerpts from a speech by RADM Vladimir M. Federov, Deputy Director of Russian Naval Intelligence.

5168. McLachan, Donald. "Naval Intelligence in the Second World War," Journal of the Royal United Service Institution for Defence Studies 112 (August 1957): 159-162.

5169. McLachlan, Donald. "Will Europe Unite Its Intelligence," Round Table 59/236 (October 1969): 357-359+.
    The subtitle of this piece is "An Acid Test of Sovereignty." Major topics include the Anglo-American relationship; difficulties for all governments; and keeping intelligence out of politics.

5170. McLaughlin, Marsha M. and Suzanne Vaupel. "Constitutional Right of Privacy and Investigative Consumer Reports: Little Brother Is Watching You," Hastings Constitutional Law Quarterly 2/3 (Summer 1975): 773-828.
    Discusses how these private agencies invade privacy, judicial remedies for harms, and proposed legislative controls.

5171. McLaughlin, Richard J. "Confidential Classification of Multi-beam Bathymetric Mapping of the U.S. EEZ: Is a New U.S. Marine Scientific Research Policy in Order?," Ocean Development and International Law 19 (January-February 1988): 1-33.

EEZ refers to the Exclusive Economic Zone. Argues that current US policy fails to effectively influence marine scientific research policies of other coastal states and fails to protect US security and economic interests. Argues for a policy to require data sharing with the EEZ.

5172. McLaughlin, Robert. "Yet Another Machine to Break DES," Cryptologia 16/2 (April 1992): 136-144.

5173. McLennan, A. D. "National Intelligence Assessment: Australia's Experience," Intelligence and National Security 10/4 (October 1995): 72-91.

Major sections consider why intelligence?; secret intelligence; Australia's intelligence tradition; national intelligence; Royal Commission findings; oversight and coordination; the Office of National Assessments; legislative base; assessment boards; current intelligence; access to information; staffing; teething; getting there; director-general; value of intelligence; message and target; crisis reporting; research and briefing; intelligence coordination; SCIS review; and economic intelligence.

5174. McLusky, Robert G. "Federal Nexus in Electronic Surveillance," Washington and Lee Law Review 37 (Spring 1980): 568-577.

Considers the Fourth Circuit holding in Berger v. New York and later cases involving electronic surveillance, especially U. S. v. Duncan. Duncan, a bank president, had electronically eavesdropped on Internal Revenue Service and FBI agents.

5175. McMahon, Deirdre. "'A Transient Apparition': British Policy Towards the de Valera Government," Irish Historical Studies 22/88 (1981): 334-339.

5176. McManus, Doyle. "Dateline Washington: Gipperdammerung," Foreign Policy 66 (Spring 1987): 156-172.

Extensive discussion of the Reagan administration's construction of the Contra resistance fighters in Nicaragua, funded by both US and private money. Role of the Central Intelligence Agency and the administration's structuring of the secret arrangements are discussed.

5177. McMaster, Arthur W. "Soviet Reconnaissance in the Seventies," Military Review 57/9 (September 1977): 64-71.

Describes Soviet reconnaissance doctrine and equipment. Observes the condition of the Soviet tactical intelligence capabilities.

5178. McMillan, Donald J. "Electronic Warfare," Infantry 64/2 (March-April 1974): 33-35.

5179. McMillan, Priscilla J. "The Sudoplatov File: Flimsy Memories," Bulletin of the Atomic Scientists 50 (July-August 1994): 30-33.

A brief consideration of espionage operations involving the Soviet and American atomic bomb projects.

5180. McNamara, Robert M., Jr. "The Problem of Surreptitious Entry to Effectuate Electronic Surveillance: How Do You Proceed After the Court Says 'Yes'?," American Criminal Law Review 15/1 (Summer 1977): 1-28.

Discusses the problem of entry to effect an electronic wiretap and possible solutions to overbroad interpretations of Title III of the Safe Streets Act of 1968.

5181. McNamara, Robert S. "The Military Role of Nuclear Weapons: Perceptions and Misperceptions," Foreign Affairs (Fall 1983): 59-80.

The former Secretary of Defense argues that there is no military role for nuclear weapons. Asserts that US posturing over the military's need for nuclear weapons was a deception which aided US defense policy in the 1960s.

5182. McNamee, Luke. "Naval Intelligence," U.S. Naval Institute Proceedings 50 (September 1924): 1444.

5183. McNeil, Frank. "Intelligence After the Cold War: Meeting the Need for Reform," Foreign Service Journal 69/2 (February 1992): 20-23.

Argues the general points of need for reform in the intelligence community and the Central Intelligence Agency. Sections discuss demystifying intelligence; anti-trust of the intelligence community; saving spies for secrets; intelligent competition between the State Department and CIA analysts; and reduction of CIA clandestine services.

5184. McNulty, Patrick. "Dalia v. United States: The Validity of Covert Entry," Iowa Law Review 65 (June 1980): 931-962.

Discusses electronic surveillance and the Fourth Amendment; the Dalia decision; covert entry and statutory and constitutional requirements; and the constitutionality of covert entry.

5185. McQuillen, William F. "Authorization of Warrantless Wiretapping by the President in National Security Matters Involving Domestic Dissidents," St. Mary's Law Journal 3/1 (Spring 1971): 65-86.

Considers the provisions of FCC Act of 1934 and the Safe Streets Act of 1968; major Supreme Court decisions on wiretapping; electronic surveillance in national security cases; expansion of presidential power in foreign affairs as to the Fourth Amendment; and warrantless wiretapping in internal security matters.

5186. McWilliams, John C. "Covert Connections: The FBN, the OSS, and the CIA," Historian 53/4 (Summer 1991): 657-678.

Author finds linkages between the Federal Bureau of Narcotics, the Office of Strategic Services, and the Central Intelligence Agency.

5187. McWilliams, John C. and Alan A. Block. "All the Commissioner's Men: The Federal Bureau of Narcotics and the Dewey-Luciano Affair, 1947-54," Intelligence and National Security 5/1 (January 1990): 171-192.

Argues that New York Governor thomas Dewey's release from prison in 1946 of gangster Lucky Luciano suggests much larger intrigues between the intelligence community, members of organized crime and the Federal Bureau of Narcotics.

5188. Mead, David. "The Breaking of the Japanese Army Administrative Code," Cryptologia 18/3 (July 1994): 193-203.

5189. Mead, James M. "The Lebanon Experience," Marine Corps Gazette 67 (February 1983): 30-40.

5190. Mealy, Rosemari; Ellen Ray; and Bill Schaap. "Cuba Exposes Massive CIA Operations," Covert Action Information Bulletin 29 (Winter 1988): 36-40.

5191. Meason, James E. "Military Intelligence and the American Citizen," Harvard Journal of Law and Public Policy 12/2 (Spring 1989): 541-567.

Describes the agency activities, duties and legal foundations of military intelligence organization, such as the Defense Intelligence Agency, the National Security Agency, and various intelligence agencies within the military branches.

5192. Meason, James E. "The Foreign Intelligence Surveillance Act: Time for Reappraisal," International Lawyer 24 (Winter 1990): 1043-1058.

Discusses background of the Act's creation; FISA's implementation; statutory details; office practices; track record; author's observations; conclusions.

5193. Medhurst, C. E. H. "Air Intelligence," Flying 31 (September 1942): 141-142+.

5194. Mediansky, F. A. "Anzus: An Alliance Beyond the Treaty," Australian Outlook 38/3 (1984): 178-182.

5195. Medow, Jonathan C. "The First Amendment and the Secrecy State: Snepp v. United States," University of Pennsylvania Law Review 130/4 (April 1982): 775-844.

Discusses the Snepp case in detail, describes the restraints imposed by the secrecy agreements signed by Snepp, examines whether the restraints would apply to private citizens, and considers whether a signature on such agreements violates First Amendment rights.

5196. Medvedev, Zhores. "Andropov: Myth and Realities," Survey 28/1 (Spring 1984): 22-44.

5197. Meek, Terry L. "Navy Intelligence Support to Naval Special Warfare," Naval Intelligence Professional Quarterly 11/4 (Fall 1995): 1-3.

5198. Meier, Heinz K. "Intelligence Operations in Switzerland During the Second World War," Swiss American Historical Newsletter (February 1984): 21-42.

5199. Meigs, Montgomery C. "General M. C. Meigs on the Conduct of the Civil War," American Historical Review 26/2 (January 1921).

5200. Meigs, Montgomery C. "This Must Mean the Philippines," U.S. Naval Institute Proceedings 111 (August 1985): 72-78.

5201. Meijer, Henk and Selim Akl. "Digital Signature Schemes," Cryptologia 6/4 (October 1982): 329-338.

5202. Meijer, Henk and Selim Akl. "Remarks on a Digital Signature Scheme," Cryptologia 7/2 (April 1983): 183-186.

5203. Meinl, Susanne and Dieter Krger. "The Political Path of Friedrich Wilhelm Heinz from Freikorps Fighter to Head of the Intelligence Service of the West German Chancellor's Office," Vierteljahrshefte fuer Zeitgeschichte 42/1 (1994): 39-69.

5204. Meisel, Alan. "Political Surveillance and the Fourth Amendment," University of Pittsburgh Law Review 35/1 (Fall 1973): 53-71.
Traces the origins of the Fourth Amendment as a foundation for a constitutional challenge to political surveillance. Also appraises other remedies and discusses problems of implementation.

5205. Melbourne, Roz M. "Odyssey of the NSC," Strategic Review 2/3 (Summer 1983).

5206. Meldrum, Andrew. "A City on the Front Lines of War," Africa Report 33 (January-February 1988): 59-61.
A brief recognition of issues surrounding espionage in South Africa.

5207. Mellen, Greg. "J. F. Byrne and the Chaocipher - Work in Progress," Cryptologia 3/3 (July 1979): 136-154.

5208. Mellen, Greg. "Graphic Solution of a Linear Transformation Cipher," Cryptologia 5/1 (January 1981): 1-19.

5209. Mellen, Greg. "Rhapsody in Purple: A New History of Pearl Harbor," Cryptologia 6/3 (1982): 193-229; 6/4 (1982): 346-367.
> The author has edited a collection of manuscripts by Captain Laurence F. Safford (later the Navy Department's chief of communications and cryptology) and his colleagues. Papers of Safford were found among papers of Admiral Dundas Tucker.

5210. Mellen, Greg and Lloyd Greenwood. "The Cryptology of Multiplex Systems," Cryptologia 1/1 (January 1977): 4-16.

5211. Melman, Yossi and Dan Raviv. "The Journalist's Connections: How Israel Got Russia's Biggest Pre-Glasnost Secret," International Journal of Intelligence and Counterintelligence 4/2 (Summer 1990): 219-225.
> Historical account of how the Israeli Mossad acquired Nikita Krushchev's April 1956 speech which ended the Stalin era, thus launching the Mossad into international recognition. Major sections discuss East-West competitive scrambling; the role of Isser Harel in the acquisition; the role of a journalist, and of the source of the information; and the US link.

5212. Melnik, Constantin. "A Plea for the Secret Services," Politique Internationale 52 (Summer 1992): 373-381.
> Argues for new support for intelligence services in the era following the demise of the Soviet Union.

5213. Mel'nikov, P. "Operativnaya Maskirovka," Voenno-Istoricheskii Zhurnal (April 1982).

5214. Melosi, Martin V. "National Security Misused: The Aftermath of Pearl Harbor," Prologue: Quarterly Journal of the National Archives 9/2 (Summer 1977): 75-89.
> A discussion of the Roosevelt administration's efforts to cover up the facts and circumstances of Pearl Harbor during the course of World War II. The cover up merely handed the Republican party an issue and delayed the resolution of the matter in the minds of the public.

5215. Melosi, Martin V. "Political Tremors from a Military Disaster: 'Pearl Harbor' and the Election of 1944," Diplomatic History 1/1 (1977): 79-95.
> Argues that the Republicans and their candidate, Thomas E. Dewey, were

hard pressed to find issues to use against President Roosevelt in the campaign of 1944. Republicans were not able to capitalize on the issue of Pearl Harbor because they feared branding as unpatriotic and because they had a difficult time acquiring closely held secret information.

5216. Melosi, Martin V. "The Triumph of Revisionism: The Pearl Harbor Controversy 1941-1982," Public Historian 5/2 (Spring 1983): 87-103.

A thorough review of the positions and writings of several revisionist historians who devoted years of research and publication to uncovering the details of the Pearl Harbor attack. Specific attention is given to Melosi's own work, then to the work of Harry Elmer Barnes, Gordon Prange, and John Toland.

5217. Meltzer, Bernard D. "Required Records, the McCarran Act, and the Privilege Against Self-Incrimination," University of Chicago Law Review 18/4 (Summer 1951): 687-728.

With the McCarran Act provisions concerning the reporting of membership in communist organizations in the background, the author discusses the history of the self-incrimination privilege; the privilege in criminal cases; hearings and investigations; evidence; and the registration provisions of the Act.

5218. Mendelsohn, Charles J. "Blaise de Vigenere and the 'Chiffre Carre,'" American Philosophical Society Proceedings 82/2 (March 1940): 103-129.

Traces the life of Blaise de Vigenere and his creation of a cipher hardly given recognition in the literature.

5219. Mendelson, Charles J. "Cardano on Cartography," Scripta Mathematica 6 (October 1939): 157-168.

5220. Mendenhall, Joseph A. "Lessons of Success Amid Failure," Strategic Review 18/1 (1990): 61-63.

A book review essay of William E. Colby's book, Lost Victory.

5221. Menefee, Seldon C. "Japan's Psychological Warfare," Social Forces 21 (May 1943): 425-436.

5222. Meng, John J. "A Footnote on Secret Aid in the American Revolution," American Historical Review 43/4 (July 1938): 791-795.

A brief historical note concerning the official plans for secret French aid during the American revolution.

5223. Menges, Constantine C. "How Democracies Keep Secrets," Public Opinion 10/5 (January-February 1988): 10-13.

Discusses the raid by the West German Federal Police on the Der Speigel offices on a charge of treason for printing NATO plans. Also discusses secrecy in Britain over strategic information pertaining to the Falklands war.

5224. Menkhaus, David. "Graymail: Constitutional Immunity from Justice?," Harvard Journal on Legislation 18/2 (Spring 1981): 389-427.
Explores the causes of the graymail phenomenon, critiques the Classified Information Procedures Act, and offers an alternative means of eliminating immunity from justice for "graymail" defendants.

5225. Menoher, Paul E., Jr. "Where Do We Go From Here?," American Intelligence Journal 15/1 (Spring-Summer 1994): 11-14.
Discusses the Army SIGINT program known as TROJAN Spirit.

5226. Menoher, Paul E., Jr. "Intel XXI--The Intelligence Vision for Force XXI," American Intelligence Journal 16/2&3 (Autumn-Winter 1995): 35-40.

5227. Menoher, Paul E., Jr. and Patrick B. McNiece. "Army Military Intelligence Strategy for the 21st Century," American Intelligence Journal 15/2 (Autumn-Winter 1994): 17-24.
Describes the Army efforts to introduce advanced planning for the intelligence missions of the 21st century. Sections discuss assessments; assessment tools; new systems; new doctrine; and the approved force structure.

5228. Mercer, Donald L. "Targeting Soviet Forces," Military Review 64/5 (1984): 23-38.

5229. Merillat, Herbert C. "The 'Ultra Weapon' at Guadalcanal," Marine Corps Gazette 66/9 (September 1982): 44-49.
Argues the general impact of the ULTRA codebreaking experience on various US-Japanese engagements, especially Guadalcanal.

5230. Merom, Gil. "Virtue, Expediency and the CIA's Institutional Trap," Intelligence and National Security 7/2 (April 1992): 30-52.
Argues that the attacks on the CIA in the mid-1970s were mainly a function of the struggle between Congress and the 'imperial presidency' over the power to govern. Fundamentally, the author says, the decline of the CIA was a byproduct of the struggle, an 'institutional interest' theory.

5231. Merrick, Ray. "The Russia Committee of the British Foreign Office and the Cold War, 1946-47," Journal of Contemporary History 20/3 (July 1985): 453-468.
Discusses the role of the British Russia Committee in the years 1946-47 in appraising the Soviet threat. Considers recommendations of the Committee for postwar anti-Russian publicity and political action.

5232. Merrills, J. G.   "Right to Respect for Private and Family Life and Correspondence - Article 8 - Application to the Interception of Postal and Telephonic Communications in the Course of a Criminal Investigation - The Meaning of 'In Accordance with Law' and 'Necessary in a Democratic Society' in Article 8(2)," British Yearbook of International Law 55 (1984): 387-391.

5233. Mersky, Peter.   "Vigilante Fadeout," U.S. Naval Institute Proceedings 106/6 (June 1980): 63-69.
     Discussion of the Navy's specialized reconnaissance aircraft.

5234. Mersky, Peter.   "My Dad Made Models," U.S. Naval Institute Proceedings 113/6 (June 1987): 51-53.
     A brief discussion of the intelligence section of the Joint Intelligence Center of the Pacific Ocean Areas during World War II. Discusses the process of creating terrain maps and models, and the end of the terrain model unit.

5235. Mescall, Patrick N.   "A Creature of Compromise: The Establishment of the DIA," International Journal of Intelligence and Counterintelligence 7/3 (Fall 1994): 251-274.
     Discusses the origins and role of the Defense Intelligence Agency against the general backdrop of the erection of the intelligence community in 1947. Discusses the origins of DIA under Secretary of Defense Robert McNamara and the role of the Joint Chiefs of Staff.

5236. Meselson, Matthew S.   "The Search for Yellow Rain," Arms Control Today 16/6 (September 1986): 31-36.
     Based on the experiences of the author, the "yellow rain" controversy was an intelligence interpretation failure at the highest levels of the US government.

5237. Mescheryakov, V.   "Strategic Disinformation in the Achievement of Surprise in the World War II Experience," Military Historical Journal (USSR) 2 (February 1985): 74-80.

5238. Meslin, Brad M.   "Cognitive Decision-Making and Crisis Management," Fletcher Forum 5/2 (Summer 1981): 191-207.
     Major topics include the analytic paradigm; the cybernetic paradigm; the cognitive paradigm; US crisis management and the Iranian crisis; and conclusions. Mentions the CIA and the role of intelligence.

5239. Messegee, J. A., et al.   "Mayday for Mayaguez," U.S. Naval Institute Proceedings 102/11 (1976): 93-111.

5240. Messenger, Charles.   "Adolf Hitler is Alive and Well and Living In ...: Story of the Post-War CIC Investigation into Hitler's Death," World War II

Investigator 1/2 (May 1988): 2-10.

5241. Messenger, Leon C. "The Nanny with the Glass Eye," Studies in Intelligence 29/4 (Winter 1985).

5242. Messenger, Leon C. "The White Lady Intelligence Network," Studies in Intelligence 32/2 (Summer 1988).

5243. Metford, J. C. J. "Falklands or Malvinas?: The Background to the Dispute," International Affairs (Great Britain) 44/3 (July 1968): 463-481.
All who wish to study the intelligence features of the 'Falklands' war of 1982 ought to consider this study of the historical backdrops. Points to the fallacies in the Argentine claims to the 'Malvinas.'

5244. Methven, Bruce E. "First Amendment Standards for Subsequent Punishment of Dissemination of Confidential Government Information," California Law Review 68/1 (January 1980): 83-105.
Argues that the Supreme Court's scheme for protecting confidential government information is ill-conceived because it inhibits revelations of government abuse of power; conflicting interests of government and the public in the free speech area; protections against information leaks; methods for exempting whistleblowers; and problems with the imminent danger test.

5245. Methven, Bruce E. "First Amendment Standards for Subsequent Punishment of Dissemination of Confidential Government Information," Publishing, Entertainment, Advertising and Allied Fields Law Quarterly 19/2 (Fall 1980): 169-141.
See previous listing with same title. Reproduced in this journal by permission.

5246. Methvin, Eugene H. "'Domestic Spying': The Constitutional Imperative," American Spectator (January 1980): 21-23.
Argues the negative implications of new controls on FBI domestic intelligence operations.

5247. Metropolis, N. and E. C. Nelson. "Early Corrupting at Los Alamos," Annals of the History of Computing 4/4 (1982): 348-357.
Although not an intelligence piece, this article may be useful to those interested in the analogy between code construction, technology and computer advancements. Discusses advancements in computers during World War II as applied to the development of the atomic bomb.

5248. Metzdorff, H. A. "The Module Concept of Intelligence Gathering," Police Chief 42/2 (February 1975): 52-58.

Argues that a new method of control and direction can be introduced in the police intelligence organization.

5249. Metzl, Lothar. "Reflections on the Soviet Secret Police and Intelligence Services," Orbis 18/3 (Fall 1974): 917-930.

Argues that John Barron's book, The Secret Work of Secret Soviet Agents, does not reflect complete research into the role and functions of the KGB. Other reports, the author claims, are more accurate.

5250. Meunier, Patrick. "High Speed Intelligence for the Divisional Commander," NATO's Fifteen Nations 22 (October-November 1977): 90-91+.

5251. Mewett, Alan W. "State Secrets in Canada," Canadian Bar Review 63/2 (June 1985): 358-377.

Discussion of a proposal to shift the law governing access to state secrets in Canada from the law of evidence to the substantive law. The question of how to apply federal as opposed to provincial law is raised.

5252. Meyer, Deborah C. "Strategic Satellites: Our Eyes in the Sky, Can They Save the World from Armageddon?," Armed Forces Journal (February 1983): 30-40.

5253. Meyer, Herbert E. "Reinventing the CIA," Global Affairs 7/2 (Spring 1992): 1-13.

5254. Meyer, John J. "Joint Task Force Communications for Command, Control and Intelligence," American Intelligence Journal 14 (Spring-Summer 1993): 73-76.

The author advocates supplementing defense communications with commercial communication systems, a technical variant of the Open Source theme of the American Intelligence Journal.

5255. Meyer, Michael C. "Villa, Sommerfeld, Columbus, and the Germans," Historia Mexicana 28/4 (1979): 546-566.

Discusses the connection between Pancho Villa and the German Spy Sommerfeld as to the theory that the spy promoted Villa's raid on Columbus, Mexico in 1916.

5256. Meyer, Stephen M. "Verification and the ICBM Shell-Game," International Security 4/2 (Fall 1979): 40-68.

Major topics consider the proposed American multiple protective structure (MPS); ICBM survivability in a MPS system; a Soviet MPS system; verification in the MPS environment; monitoring MPS launch production; and other roles for the MPS.

5257. Meyer, Stephen M. "Verification and Risk in Arms Control," International Security 8/4 (Spring 1984): 111-126.

Major sections of this discussion of the complexities of the relationship between arms verification and risk to US national security include monitoring versus verification; early detection versus early warning; signals, false alarms and false warnings; uncertainty versus risk; standards of evidence for compliance or violation; bans, limits and verifiability; and monitoring uncertainty and military risk.

5258. Meyer, Stephen M. "The Soviet Spy Gaps," IEEE Spectrum 23/7 (July 1986): 67-69.

Brief description of Soviet spy satellites; tracking by US communications links; seismic monitoring and the lack of a world wide network; and the open US literature as a boon to the Soviets.

5259. Meyer, Stephen M. "How the Threat (and the Coup) Collapsed: The Politicization of the Soviet Military," International Security 16/3 (Winter 1991-1992): 5-38.

Major topics include the roots of the politicization of the Soviet military; the impact of politicization on the military establishment; implications for Soviet military power; and conclusions.

5260. Meyers, James P., Jr. "'Murdering Heart...Murdering Hand': Captain Thomas Lee of Ireland, Elizabethan Assassin," Sixteenth Century Journal 22/1 (Spring 1991): 47-60.

A detailed account of the treason of Captain Thomas Lee, a mercenary assassin and spy, who opposed England's colonial designs in Ireland.

5261. Meyrowitz, Alan L. "Military Applications of Artificial Intelligence," Signal 38/10 (June 1984): 45-48.

5262. Michael, H. K. "Covert Involvement in Essentially Internal Conflicts: United States Assistance to the Contras under International Law," Vanderbilt Journal of Transnational Law 23 (1990): 539-613.

5263. Michael, James. "Official Secrecy in Britain," Index on Censorship 7/1 (January-February 1978): 9-15.

An overview of several issues raised by the British Parliament's investigation into official secrecy by way of the Franks Commission. Discusses the British version of freedom of information.

5264. Michael, James. "Official Information Law in the United Kingdom," Government Publications Review 10/1 (January-February 1983): 61-70.

Discusses the restrictions of the Official Secrets Act; the problem of leaks and "briefing"; British disclosure laws; and suggestions for change in the law.

5265. Michal, Kristin. "Business Counterintelligence and the Role of the U.S. Intelligence Community," International Journal of Intelligence and Counter-intelligence 7/4 (Winter 1994): 413-427.

     Discusses the debate over economic intelligence; distinctions between economic and industrial intelligence; the roles of other intelligence agencies besides CIA; and disclosure prevention mechanisms.

5266. Michener, John R. "The "Generalized Rotor" Cryptographic Operator and Some of its Applications," Cryptologia 9/2 (April 1985): 97-113.

5267. Michener, John R. "Application of the Generalized Rotor Cryptographic Operator in the Construction of Substitution-Permutation Network Block Codes," Cryptologia 9/3 (July 1985): 193-201.

5268. Michener, John R. "The Use of Complete, Nonlinear, Block Codes for Nonlinear, Noninvertible Mixing of Pseudorandom Sequences," Cryptologia 11/2 (April 1987): 108-111.

5269. Michener, John R. "The Application of Key Dependent and Variable Rotor Sets to Generalized Rotor Cryptographic Systems," Cryptologia 11/3 (July 1987): 166-171.

5270. Michener, John R. "Recent Developments in Electronic Circuitry and Their Effects on the Implementation of Substitution-Permutation Block Code," Cryptologia 12/1 (January 1988): 21-24.

5271. Mickiewicz, Ellen. "The Functions of Communications Officials in the USSR: A Biographical Study," Slavic Review 43/4 (Winter 1984): 641-656.

5272. Micoleau, Charles J. "The 'Secret War': Myths, Morals, and Misconceptions," SAIS Review 9 (Summer 1965): 21-28.

5273. Miedzian, Myzriam. "Real Men, Wimps, and Our National Security," Peace Review 4/3 (Autumn 1992): 4-9.

     Argues that the socialization of males in the United States is in the direction of preferring a fight over a negotiated solution, thus blocking options in the foreign policy process and leading to negative outcomes such as war. Refers to the CIA as part of the masculine-dominated mindset of fight.

5274. Miers, Richard C. "Ambush," Army 9 (February 1959): 34-39.

5275. Mierzejewski, Alfred C. "Intelligence and Strategic Bombing of Germany:

The Combined Strategic Targets Committee," International Journal of Intelligence and Counterintelligence 3/1 (Spring 1989): 83-104.

Detailed accounting of factors involved in the intelligence used to locate sites for British and US bombing missions over Germany. Major sections discuss the creation of the Combined Strategic Targets Committee; the dispute over oil and transportation; the redirection of allied air intelligence; and the Ruhr bombing plan.

5276. Milhalka, Michael. "Soviet Strategic Deception, 1955-1981," Journal of Strategic Studies 5/1 (March 1982): 40-93.

An extensive review of the methods used by the Soviet Union to deceive the West concerning the size and accuracy of its nuclear weapons stockpile.

5277. Mikheyev, Dmitry. "Defectors' Problems in the West," Studies in Intelligence 32/1 (Spring 1988).

5278. Milam, Michael M. "Army Intelligence Production: The AIA Today," Military Intelligence 12/4 (October-December 1986): 22-25.

Explains why the US Army Intelligence Agency was created and addresses its purposes and current status.

5279. Milensky, Edward S. "Arms Production and National Security in Argentina," Journal of Inter-American Studies and World Affairs 22/3 (August 1980): 267-288.

Major sections discuss national security and the need for arms production; threat perceptions and the arms industry; economic base of the defense industry; and arms production in developing nations.

5280. Miles, Sherman. "Pearl Harbor in Retrospect," Atlantic Monthly 182 (July 1948): 65-72.

The author's views on the intelligence aspects of the buildup of Japanese naval forces and its relevance to the attack at Pearl Harbor. He served as Assistant Chief of Staff for Intelligence in the War Department from April 1940 to February 1942.

5281. Milican, Gelman and Stanhope Milican. "Lost Order, Lost Cause," Studies in Intelligence 2 (Winter 1958).

5282. Milivojevic, Marko. "The KGB," Intelligence and National Security 2/2 (April 1987): 341-353.

A book review essay concerning several books on the Soviet intelligence service, KGB: John Barron, KGB Today: The Hidden Hand; Leo Heaps, Thirty Years with the KGB: The Double Life of Hugh Hambleton; Richard H. Schultz and Roy Godson, Dezinformatsia: Active Measures In Soviet Strategy; Anatoliy

Golitsyn, <u>New Lies for Old: The Communist Strategy of Deception and Disinformation</u>; Jay Tuck, <u>High-Tech Espionage: How the KGB Smuggles NATO's Strategic Secrets</u>; and Frantisek August and David Rees, <u>Red Star Over Prague</u>.

5283. Milivojevic, Marko.   "Romania's Intelligence Services: Purges and Politics," <u>Jane's Intelligence Review</u> 1 (1995):   12-14.

5284. Millar, C. M. H.   "Some Escapees and Escapers in the Ancient World," <u>Greece and Rome</u> 5 (1958):   57-61.

5285. Miller, Abraham H.   "Terrorism and Hostage Taking: Lessons from the Iranian Crisis," <u>Rutgers Law Journal</u> 13/3 (Spring 1982):   513-529.
        Discusses the avoidance of terrorist attacks (including the use of intelligence sources and methods), responses to terrorism, and policy implications.

5286. Miller, Abraham H. and Nicholas Damask.   "Thinking About Intelligence After the Fall of Communism," <u>International Journal of Intelligence and Counterintelligence</u> 6/3 (Fall 1993):   257-269.
        A general discussion of possible directions of US intelligence after the fall of the Soviet Union.   Major sections discuss questions raised about the overemphasis upon the predictive value of intelligence; the importance of other indicators of CIA value; the irrelevant debate about CIA's competence; a role for the academy; the need for alternative institutions; and tentative suggestions.

5287. Miller, Anthony P.   "Teleinformatics, Transborder Data Flows and the Emerging Struggle for Information: An Introduction to the Arrival of the New Information Age," <u>Columbia Journal of Law and Social Problems</u> 20/1 (1986): 89-144.
        Explores concepts of telematics, teleinformatics, and transborder data flows; the struggle for information and the role of political power; the technical nature of the info struggle; and various areas in which the struggle is most obvious, such as privacy and national defense.

5288. Miller, A. Ray.   "The Cryptographic Mathematics of Enigma," <u>Cryptologia</u> 19/1 (January 1995):   65-81.

5289. Miller, Arthur R.   "Personal Privacy in the Computer Age: The Challenge in an Information Oriented Society," <u>Michigan Law Review</u> 67 (April 1969): 1089-1246.
        A treatise on the subject including discussion of the cybernetic revolution; threats to personal privacy; efficiency interest; current law on privacy; government handling of personal information; safeguarding computerized information; and a search for a legal framework.

5290. Miller, Arthur R. "The Dossier Society," University of Illinois Law Forum 1971 (1971): 154-167.

Discussion of the author's concerns for the lack of controls on data technologies and computer files. Calls for a framework for establishing protections for the public from intrusions in personal privacy.

5291. Miller, Arthur S. "Watergate and Beyond: The Issue of Secrecy," Progressive 37 (December 1973): 15-19.

5292. Miller, Arthur S. "Carter and the CIA," Progressive 41 (May 1977): 9-10.

5293. Miller, Byron S. "A Law Is Passed--The Atomic Energy Act of 1946," University of Chicago Law Review 15/4 (Summer 1948): 799-821.

Provides a complete history of the origins and development of the Act. Addresses the issue of secrecy within the context of the debate about whether control over nuclear energy production would be civilian or military.

5294. Miller, David W. "007's Analysis of KAL's Flight 007," International Journal of Intelligence and Counterintelligence 1/1 (January 1986): 109-119.

A book review essay of two books: Oliver Clubb, KAL Flight 007: The Hidden Story; and Alexander Dallin, Black Box: KAL 007 and the Super Powers.

5295. Miller, David W. "Cryptanalysis Reexplored," International Journal of Intelligence and Counterintelligence 1/2 (Spring 1986): 136-144.

A book review essay of three books: Thomas Parrish, The Ultra Americans: The U.S. Role in Breaking the Nazi Codes; Robert J. Lamphere and Tom Shachtman, The FBI-KGB War: A Special Agent's Story; and Cipher A. Deavours and Louis Kruh, Machine Cryptography and Modern Cryptanalysis.

5296. Miller, David W. "Weighing the Evidence for the Intelligence Analyst," International Journal of Intelligence and Counterintelligence 6/1 (Spring 1993): 120-130.

A book review essay of David A. Schum's book, Evidence and Inference for the Intelligence Analyst, a two-volume work of over 800 pages on the subject.

5297. Miller, Davina. "Democracy, Dictators and the Regulation of Arms Exports: The UK and Iraq," Intelligence and National Security 9/3 (July 1994): 536-543.

A book review essay covering four books: Chris Cowley, Guns, Lies and Spies: How We Armed Iraq; Paul Henderson, The Unlikely Spy; David Leigh, Betrayed: The Real Story of the Matrix Churchill Trial; and John Sweeney, Trading with the Enemy: Britain's Arming of Iraq.

5298. Miller, Davina. "Intelligence and Proliferation: Lessons from the Matrix

Churchill Affair," Intelligence and National Security 11/2 (April 1996): 193-206.
    Major sections discuss the Scott report; proliferation as an intelligence concern; Matrix Churchill trial; source protection; retrieval and dissemination; intelligence and the decision makers; and the political and economic contexts.

5299. Miller, Donald V. "Ciphertext Only Attack on the Merkel-Hellman Public-key System Under Broadcast Situations," Cryptologia 6/3 (July 1982): 279-281.

5300. Miller, Donald V. "Cryptanalysis of a Two Round Version of DES Using Index Implications," Cryptologia 12/4 (October 1988): 209-219.

5301. Miller, Edwin. "Tactical Deception in World War II," Journal of Electronic Defense 8/10 (October 1985): 91-98.
    Recounts the activities of special army deception troop units in World War II.

5302. Miller, Gerald E. "History of the Office of Policy Coordination," Studies in Intelligence 17/2 (Summer 1973).

5303. Miller, George I. "Observations of Police Undercover Work," Criminology 25/1 (February 1987): 27-46.
    Interviews were conducted with a small sample of undercover police personnel tasked to discover and build files on criminals. Contrasts between the rules and culture of undercover cops and the normal operations of police patrol functions can subject undercover officers to abuses of authority and corruption.

5304. Miller, J. "Nazi Invasion," American History Illustrated 21/7 (November 1986): 42-49.
    A brief discussion of Nazi espionage before and during World War II.

5305. Miller, J. Scott. "Confidential," Washington State Bar News 46 (February 1992): 11-14.

5306. Miller, James E. "The Search for Stability: An Interpretation of American Policy in Italy, 1943-46," Journal of Italian History 1 (Autumn 1978): 264-286.

5307. Miller, James E. "Taking Off the Gloves: The United States and the Italian Elections of 1948," Diplomatic History 7/1 (Winter 1983): 35-55.
    A detailed examination of the US role in covert operations and diplomatic actions to affect the outcome of the Italian election of 1948. Mentions actions and role of the CIA.

5308. Miller, Jay. "U-2R. . . TR-1: Lockheed's Black Ladies," Air International (October 1984): 186-189.

5309. Miller, Judith. "Criminal Negligence: Congress, Chile and the CIA," Progressive 38 (November 1974): 15-19.

5310. Miller, Judith. "CIA Case History: G. Weissmann's Suit," Progressive 40 (December 1976): 8-9.

5311. Miller, Judith. "Gary Weissmann's Catch-22," Progressive 41 (April 1977): 10.

5312. Miller, Kenneth G. "Blueprint for Abduction," Air University Review 29/4 (1978): 31-38.

5313. Miller, Margaret. "The Spy Activities of Dr. Edward Bancroft," Journal of American History 22 (1928): 70-77, 157-170.

5314. Miller, Marshall L. "America Rarely Warms to Soviet Defectors Coming in from the Cold," Armed Forces Journal 124/1 (August 1986): 31-32.

5315. Miller, Marshall L. "How the Soviets Invaded Iran," Armed Forces Journal 124/7 (February 1987): 30-34.

5316. Miller, Matthew. "Ma'am, What You Need Is a New, Improved Hoover," Washington Monthly 20/12 (December 1989): 10-18.
Charges that FBI director William Webster dropped the search for Soviet spies and substituted a search for peace groups and Black and Hispanic FBI agents.

5317. Miller, R. Reuben. "Game Theory and Hostage Taking Incidents: A Case Study of the Munich Olympic Games," Conflict Quarterly 10/1 (Winter 1990): 12-33.

5318. Miller, R. Reuben. "The Bangkok Solution: Peaceful Resolution of Hostage-taking," Intelligence and National Security 10/2 (April 1995): 306-326.
Examines a unique case of hostage-taking: the peaceful conclusion of the attack on the Israeli embassy in Bangkok, Thailand. Major sections discuss the incident stages; framework for bargaining and negotiation; the embassy under siege; and analysis, discussion, and conclusions.

5319. Miller, Robert H. "Letters of Lieutenant Robert H. Miller to His Family, 1861-1862," Virginia Magazine of History and Biography 70/1 (January 1962).

5320. Miller, Robert R. "Californians Against the Emperor," California Historical Society Quarterly 37 (1958): 193-214.

5321. Miller, Robert R. "Gaspar Sanchez Ochoa: A Mexican Secret Agent in the United States," Historian 23/3 (May 1961): 316-329.

Discusses Mexican President Juarez's dispatch of several secret agents to the US in the 1860s to secure financial aid, arms, and military recruits to fight the French. Mexico had been invaded by France under Maximilian's orders.

5322. Miller, Robert R. "Placido Vega: A Mexican Secret Agent in the United States, 1864-1866," Americas 48 (October 1962): 137-148.

5323. Miller, Sally M. "Kate Richards O'Hare: Progression Toward Feminism," Kansas History 7/4 (1984-85): 263-279.

5324. Millet, Stephen M. and Rolf Lepanen. "The Business Information and Analysis Function: A New Approach to Strategic Thinking and Planning," Planning Review 19/3 (May-June 1991): 10-15, 36.

5325. Millett, Richard. "Guatemala's Painful Progress," Current History 85/515 (December 1986): 413-416, 430-431.

Refers to the Central Intelligence Agency's involvement in the overthrow of the Guatemalan government in the 1950s and the successive incidents of internal violence in the country. Argues that some recent progress toward democratization has evolved.

5326. Million, Elmer M. "Political Crimes," Missouri Law Review 5/2 & 5/3 (April and June 1940): 164-192; 293-323.

This is a two-part article. The first part discusses treason as a political crime. Sections include discussion of federal offenses, miscellaneous political offenses, and offenses against neutrality. The second part considers criminal syndicalism and criminal anarchy.

5327. Milner-Barry, P. S. "'Action This Day': The Letters from Bletchley Park Cryptanalysts to the Prime Minister, 21 October 1941," Intelligence and National Security 1/2 (April 1986): 272-276.

5328. Milner-Barry, P. S. "The Soviets and Ultra: A Comment on Jukes' Hypothesis," Intelligence and National Security 3/2 (April 1988): 248-250.

Offers an hypothesis for the sudden improvement in the quality of Soviet intelligence in the spring of 1943, following the fall of Stalingrad and the fall-out of captured Enigma machines.

5329. Milovojevic, Marko. "The KGB," Intelligence and National Security 2/2 (April 1987): 341-353.

A review article discussing issues raised six books on the Soviet intelligence organization, the KGB.

5330. Minattur, Joseph. "Martial Law in the United States," Eastern Journal of International Law 10/2 (April 1978): 52-64.

A brief, simplistic summation of this complex topic. Nonetheless, it is a snapshot taken by an Indian professor. Offers judicial history, suspension of writ of habeas corpus, declarations of martial law, and comments.

5331. Minei, Nicolae. "The Nazi Diplomat and the Drawbacks of 'Unsuitable' Spying," Magazin Istoric 11/7 (1977): 48-51.

This is a brief commentary on the abilities of US counter-intelligence to thwart the espionage work of Hans Thomsen, Nazi spy sent to Washington, D. C. in 1940 by Admiral Canaris and Heinrich Himmler.

5332. Minetree, James L., III. "All-Source Intelligence: A Combat Power Multiplier," Military Review 57/6 (June 1977): 21-27.

Examines how tactical military intelligence operates, past and future. Includes system design graphics.

5333. Minihan, Kenneth A. "Information Dominance: Meeting the Intelligence Needs of the 21st Century," American Intelligence Journal 15/1 (Spring-Summer 1994): 15-19.

Discusses the role and missions of US Air Force intelligence organization units.

5334. Minihan, Kenneth A. "The Defense Intelligence Agency, National and Military Intelligence for the 21st Century," American Intelligence Journal 16/2&3 (Autumn-Winter 1995): 31-34.

5335. Minihan, Kenneth A. "Intelligence and Information Systems Security: Partners in Defensive Information Warfare," Defense Intelligence Journal 5/1 (Spring 1996): 13-24.

5336. Minkkinen, E. O. "Orders to a Secret Agent," Naval Intelligence Professionals Quarterly 7/2 (Spring 1991): 13-14.

5337. Minkkinen, E. O. "'Taylormade' Assignment," Naval Intelligence Professionals Quarterly 8/3 (Summer 1992): 11-12.

5338. Minkkinen, E. O. "Heroin: The Yokosuka Connection," Naval Intelligence Professionals Quarterly 10/3 (July 1994): 5-6.

5339. Minkkinen, E. O. "Of Moles and Men," Naval Intelligence Professionals Quarterly 10/3 (July 1994): 6-7.

5340. Minter, William. "The Limits of Liberal Africa Policy: Lessons from the

Congo Crisis," Trans Africa Forum 2/3 (1984): 27-47.
　　　　CIA activities and their impact on political development of the African nation of Zaire.

5341. Minto, Michael F. "The Criminal Intelligence Squad," Police Chief 42/2 (February 1975): 40-44.

5342. Mintz, Frank P. "Pearl Harbor at Middle Age," Continuity 8 (Spring 1984): 77-85.

5343. Minyailo, V. "The Conference of the State Security Organs," Bulletin (Institute of the Study of the USSR) (September 1959): 21-23.

5344. Miovski, Lourene F. "Freedom of Speech, National Security, and Democracy: The Constitutionality of National Security Directive 84," Washington State University Law Review 12 (Fall 1984): 173-204.

5345. Miranda, Joseph. "Political Warfare: Can the West Survive?," Journal of Social, Political and Economic Studies 10/1 (Spring 1985): 3-24.
　　　　Argues that the values of Western nations in terms of opposition to communism get in the way of effective response to enemies who have quite different values. In essence, the West has not committed to the use of political warfare despite the existence of such agencies as the CIA and its activities. Offers suggestions for strengthening the political warfare capabilities of Western nations.

5346. Miskovsky, M. C. "Impunity of Agents in International Law," Studies in Intelligence 5/1 (Spring 1961).

5347. Mitchel, Steven E. "Classified Information and Legal Research," Law Library Journal 79/3 (Summer 1987): 445-454.
　　　　Traces the development of federal policy in the area of classification procedures as implemented in the Reagan administration. Major sections discuss executive policy in the Nixon and Carter presidencies; Reagan policies; identifying classified documents; and conclusions.

5348. Mitchel, Steven E. "At Home with the FBI: When a Free-Lance Researcher Gets a Soviet Client, a Visit from the FBI Is Sure to Follow," American Libraries 21/11 (December 1990): 1080, 1082.
　　　　A brief description of the author's personal experience in interviewing a man from the Soviet embassy, only then to be visited by the FBI.

5349. Mitchell, Allan. "The Xenophobic Style: French Counterespionage and the Emergence of the Dreyfus Affair," Journal of Modern History 52/3 (September 1980): 414-425.

Argues that the revisionist view of the Dreyfus affair must be considered in the context of xenophobia in France after 1870, not racism. Includes discussion of secret agents, informers, and espionage.

5350. Mitchell, Douglas D. "Fire and Forget?," Journal of Defense & Diplomacy 3/8 (1985): 45-49.
    Discusses the role of intelligence in target selection.

5351. Mitchell, Douglas W. "A Polygraphic Substitution Cipher Based on Multiple Interlocking Applications of Playfair," Cryptologia 9/2 (April 1985): 131-139.

5352. Mitchell, Douglas W. "Nonlinear Key Generators," Cryptologia 14/4 (October 1990): 355-362.

5353. Mitchell, Douglas W. "'Rubik's' Cube As a Transposition Device," Cryptologia 16/3 (July 1992): 250-256.

5354. Mitchell, Douglas W. "A Nonlinear Random Number Generator with Known, Long Cycle Length," Cryptologia 17/1 (January 1993): 55-62.

5355. Mitchell, Fredric. "Lots of Smoke--Little Fire," International Journal of Intelligence and Counterintelligence 1/4 (Winter 1986-1987): 111-118.
    Includes a reprint of an article by Alton Frye, Washington director of the Council on Foreign Relations, which argues for amnesty for US spies. Reports the comments on this proposal from intelligence experts in terms of legal problems, the role of counterintelligence, conditions of amnesty, variations of amnesty, and the pro and con resolutions.

5356. Mitchell, John J. "Government Secrecy in Theory and Practice: 'Rules and Regulations' As an Autonomous Screen," Columbia Law Review 58/2 (February 1958): 199-210.
    A brief summary of the leading cases on government secrecy and then-current legislative activity. Accounts for executive objections and congressional problems with new legislation.

5357. Mitchell, John N. "Wiretapping and Pretrial Detention--Balancing the Rights of the Individual With the Rights of Society," Judicature 53/5 (December 1969): 188-192.
    A rationale for continued use by the Justice Department of wiretaps of organized crime figures on the basis of the belief that the warrant requirements will not invade the privacy of innocent persons.

5358. Mitchell, Lawrence J., III. "Espionage: The Symbiotic Relationship

Between the Central Intelligence Agency and the American Press Corps," Suffolk Transnational Law Journal 11 (Fall 1987): 41-73.

Considers the historical evolution of the journalist-spy; the players; deception; disclosure; the journalist-spy? Nicholas S. Daniloff; and conclusions. Argues that journalists should not cross the line between reporting and agentry for government intelligence organizations.

5359. Mitchell, R. Judson and Teresa Gee. "The Soviet Succession Crisis and Its Aftermath," Orbis 29/2 (Summer 1985): 293-317.

Discusses the succession problems in terms of the historical process of transfer of power, system structure, renewal and realignment, and the prospects of Gorbachev's leadership. The role of the KGB is given substantial consideration.

5360. Mitelman, L. T. "Preface to a Theory of Intelligence," Studies in Intelligence 18/3 (Fall 1974).

5361. Mitev, Dimitur. "General Aleksan dur Protogerov As the Focus of Intelligence Service: British Intelligence Documents on the Revolutionary Acts of General Proto Gerov, 1920-23," Voennoistoricheski Sbornik 60/5 (1991): 155-196.

5362. Mitgang, Herbert. "Garibaldi and Lincoln," American Heritage 25/6 (October 1975): 34-39, 98-101.

A brief history of Abraham Lincoln's efforts to bring Giuseppe Garibaldi to the US to lead Union troops during the Civil War.

5363. Miyazawa, Setsuo. "Scandal and Hard Reform: Implications of a Wiretapping Case to the Control of Organizational Police Crimes in Japan," Kobe University Law Review 23 (1989): 13-27.

5364. Mockler, Robert J. "Strategic Intelligence Systems: Competitive Intelligence Systems to Support Strategic Management Decisionmaking," SAM Advanced Management Journal 57/1 (Winter 1992): 4-9.

Argues that knowledge of one's competition and of the competitive environment are essential ingredients in modern business decision making.

5365. Model, F. Peter. "The Spies Who Came in For the Gold," Wilson Library Bulletin 66 (May 1992): 61-64.

Literature and spying come together in this article.

5366. Moeschl, Wilbur W. "Jet-Speed Intelligence, Part II: Datamation," Air University Review 9/2 (Spring 1957): 78-84.

5367. Moglen, Eben. "Considering Zenger: Partisan Politics and the Legal Profession in Provincial New York," Columbia Law Review 94 (June 1994): 1495-1524.

A detailed analysis of the sedition trial of John Peter Zenger.

5368. Mohan, C. Raja and C. Vishnu Mohan. "The Information Revolution: Issues of Transborder Data Flows," India Quarterly 38/1 (January- March 1982): 1-19.

5369. Moise, Edwin E. "Why Westmoreland Gave Up: Review Article," Pacific Affairs 58/4 (1985-1986): 663-673.

5370. Molina y Vedia, Silvia. "The Case of Chile as a Prototype of Counterrevolutionary Psychological Warfare," Revista Mexicana de Ciencias Politicas y Sociales 23 (October-March 1976-1977): 99-130.

5371. Mollan, Robert. "Smith Act Prosecutions: The Effect of the Dennis and Yates Decisions," University of Pittsburgh Law Review 26/4 (June 1965): 705-747.

Examines the history of prosecutions under the advocacy, organizational and membership clauses of the Smith Act; the Dennis decision; and the Yates decision. Offers conclusions concerning punishable expressions following the Yates decision.

5372. Mollenhoff, C. R. "Britain's Blindfolded Press," Quill 74 (July-August 1986): 24-28.

Recognizes the main obstruction between US and British press access to government data, and it discusses the rigid enforcement practices used to sustain official secrets. Several British court cases are also summarized.

5373. Monaghan, David. "John LeCarre and England: A Spy's-Eye View," Modern Fiction Studies 29 (Autumn 1983): 569-582.

A detailed and rich analysis of the bulk of John LeCarre's novels.

5374. Monahan, Patrick J. "The Regulation of Technical Data Under the Arms Control Act of 1976 and the Export Administration Act of 1979: A Matter of Executive Discretion," Boston College International and Comparative Law Review 6/1 (Winter 1983): 169-197.

Major sections discuss the Arms Export Control Act of 1976; the Export Administration Act of 1979; implications of current controls on technological exports; and analysis. Concludes that selling arms reflects a basic political decision to confer or withhold advantage.

5375. Mondale, Walter F. "Reorganizing the CIA: Who and How," Foreign

Policy 23 (Summer 1976): 53-63.

5376. Monroe, David G. "Constitutional Conception of Treason," Journal of Criminal Law and Criminology 33/3 (September-October 1942): 260-261.
     A brief discussion of the basic constitutional provisions dealing with treason.

5377. Monsagrati, Giuseppe. "Guglielmo Macchia and Mazzinian Ciphers," Bolettino Della Domus Mazziniana 31/1 (1985): 31-62.
     A detailed discussion of the intelligence gathering of the Italian, Guzlielmo Macchia as revealed by secret messages.

5378. Montague, Ludwell L. "Priority National Intelligence Objectives," Studies in Intelligence 5/1 (Spring 1961).

5379. Montague, Ludwell L. "The Origins of National Intelligence Estimating," Studies in Intelligence 16/1 (Spring 1972): 67-78.

5380. Montague, Ludwell L. "The Psychological Strategy Board," Studies in Intelligence 17/2 (Summer 1973).

5381. Monteiro, Alfred, Jr. "Mustering the Force: Cryptologic Support to Military Operations," Defense Intelligence Journal 4/2 (Fall 1995): 67-82.
     Discusses the roles and functions of the National Security Agency; defines terms and roles; examines the military support process; USSS strengths and weaknesses; and the conduct of military support.

5382. Montgomery, George. "The Komsomolets Disaster: Burial at Sea," Studies in Intelligence 38/5 (1995): 43-51.
     Explores the events and circumstances surrounding the sinking of the Russian nuclear attack submarine Komsomolets in 1989 in the Norwegian Sea. Sections discuss the birth of the ship; the sinking; the aftermath; the Russian oceanographic fleet and the Keldysh; the 1991 and 1992 and 1993 surveys to assess the environmental implications of the sinking; and epilogue.

5383. Montminny, George H. "Rapid Transit in Clandestine Intelligence," Studies in Intelligence 14/1 (Spring 1970).

5384. Montross, Lynn. "The Mystery of Pete Ellis," Marine Corps Gazette 38 (July 1954): 30-33.
     A brief review of what was known of the circumstances surrounding the disappearance to Marine Corps spy Pete Ellis.

5385. Montroy, Nancy J. "United States v. Torres: The Need for Statutory

Regulation of Video Surveillance," Journal of Legislation 12 (Spring 1985): 264-274.

Discusses the background facts and litigation in the Torres matter as to television surveillance; policy considerations; and the need for congressional response.

5386. Moor, R. Carl, Jr. "Strategic Economic Intelligence: A Systems Approach," Military Review 56/10 (October 1976): 47-51.

Major sections discuss an overview of the economic system; major subsystems; and strategic estimates. Includes a topical organization of economic intelligence targets.

5387. Moore, Earl E. "Lafayette's Secret Mission to France, 1781," Manuscripts 44/4 (1992): 301-306.

5388. Moore, Frederick L. "Radio Countermeasures," Air University Review 2 (Fall 1948): 57-66.

5389. Moore, John E. "The U.S. Intelligence Community: Its Problems--and Achievements," Navy International 79 (August 1974): 11-12.

5390. Moore, John H. "Getting the Fritz to Talk," Virginia Quarterly Review 54 (Spring 1978): 263-280.

A detailed discussion of interrogation centers in the United States.

5391. Moore, John H. "Richmond Area Residents and the Southern Claims Commission, 1871-1880," Virginia Magazine of History and Biography 91/3 (1983): 285-295.

5392. Moore, John N. "Law and National Security," Foreign Affairs 51/2 (1973): 408-421.

Argues for an expanded application of international law in the key decisionmaking processes of the National Security Council and selected congressional committees.

5393. Moore, John N. "The Secret War in Central America and the Future of World Order," American Journal of International Law 80/1 (1986): 43-127.

Discusses the background of the Central American conflict in Nicaragua; the legal issues in the conflict; recurrent misperceptions; and conclusions about strengthening world order. Includes observations by the CIA.

5394. Moore, Mike. "Lying Well," Bulletin of the Atomic Scientists 50 (July-August 1994): 2.

Very brief commentary on espionage actions pertaining to the atomic bomb project.

5395. Moore, Otis C. "Twenty Years in Space: No Hiding Place in Space," Air Force Magazine 57/8 (1974): 43-48.

Discusses the origins and evolution of the US warning and surveillance network on earth and in space. Also included is a short discussions of the USSR Sputnik I of 1957 and makes to the contemporary Triad Plus One system.

5396. Moore, Preston J. "We Must Learn to Fight a New Kind of War," American Legion Magazine 67 (August 1959): 16-17+.

5397. Moore, Robert G. "Who Goes There? Maritime Surveillance and the Problems of the Coastal Zone," Journal of Defense & Diplomacy 2/10 (October 1984): 43-47.

5398. Moore, Robert G. "C^{3}I for Coastal Security," Journal of Defense & Diplomacy 7/4 (April 1989): 11-15.

5399. Moore, Wilton P. "Union Army Provost Marshals in the Eastern Theater," Military Affairs 26/3 (1962): 120-162.

5400. Moorer, Daniel F., Jr. "What Do You Mean 'The Radio's Down,'" Military Review 75/5 (September-October 1995): 88-93.

Explores the problems of solar flares and disturbances on electronic intelligence operations.

5401. Moorman, Frank. "Enciphering and Deciphering Codes," Scientific American 113/8 (August 1915): 159.

5402. Moorman, Frank. "Code and Cipher in France," Infantry Journal (June 1920): 1039-1044.

This is a summation of the US Army's work in cryptography in France during World War I.

5403. Morabito, Vince. "Public Access to the Records of the Australian Security Intelligence Organisation Under the Archives Act 1983," Sydney Law Review 17 (September 1995): 406-432.

5404. Morales, Nancy. "The National Intelligence Structure," Military Intelligence 10/3 (July-September 1984): 38-39.

Traces the evolution of the US intelligence community from 1947 to the present.

5405. Moran, L. J. "The Uses of Homosexuality: Homosexuality for National

Security," <u>International Journal of the Sociology of Law</u> 19/2 (May 1991): 149-170.

The relationship between homosexuality and the state are traced to Tudor England. Substantial discussion of homosexuals in the spy trade in the Cold War era.

5406. Moran, Richard. "The Origins of Insanity as a Special Verdict: The Trial for Treason by James Hadfield (1800)," <u>Law and Society</u> 19/3 (Summer 1985): 487-519.

Hadfield was tried for treason because he fired a pistol in the direction of King George III in a London theater. He pleaded insanity to the charge of high treason and was acquitted, thereby causing Parliament to pass new laws on insanity.

5407. Moravec, Frantisek. "Operation Uproot," <u>Studies in Intelligence</u> 7/1 (Spring 1963).

Discusses the details of an escape operation of the Czech intelligence service to London.

5408. Morawitz, Wayne L. "Nuclear Proliferation and U.S. Security," <u>Air University Review</u> 28/2 (January-February 1977): 19-28.

5409. Moreland, Allen B. "Congressional Investigations and Private Persons," <u>Southern California Law Review</u> 40/2 (Winter 1967): 189-273.

A treatise on the history and development of congressional investigations as they concern private persons. This article is relevant to cases in the 1950s arising from allegations of communist affiliations.

5410. Morelli, Donald R. and Michael M. Ferguson. "Low-Intensity Conflict: An Operational Perspective," <u>Military Review</u> 64/11 (November 1984): 2-16.

5411. Morgan, Edmund M. "Court-Martial Jurisdiction Over Non-Military Persons Under the Articles of War," <u>Minnesota Law Review</u> 4 (January 1920): 79-116.

Addresses the question of whether non-military persons are subject to trial by court martial. Based on a case of a German spy who had reentered the US in early 1918 to steal information and damage US war equipment.

5412. Morgan, Gerald. "Myth and Reality in the Great Game," <u>Asian Affairs</u> 60/1 (February 1973): 55-65.

5413. Morgan, J. H. "War Treason," <u>Grotius Society</u> 2 (1917): 161-173.

5414. Morgan, Joseph O. and Virginia Prentice. "Third Symposium on Remote

Sensing," Photogrammetric Engineering 32 (January 1966): 98-108.

5415. Morgan, Paul F. "Intelligence Support to Automated Mission Planning and Rehearsal Systems," American Intelligence Journal 13/1&2 (Winter-Spring 1992): 61-64.

  Focusses on issues related to product support, such as mapping, charting and geodesy, imagery products, threat information and accuracy; and the issue of organizational culture in military intelligence.

5416. Morgan, Paul F. "Special Operations Intelligence Systems and Technologies," American Intelligence Journal 15/2 (Autumn-Winter 1994): 25-29.

  General description of the technologies employed in special operations intelligence within Army intelligence. Sections discuss technology requirements; SOF intelligence systems; and future needs.

5417. Morgan, Ted. "The Rosenberg Jury," Esquire (May 1975).

  This author was also known by Sanche de Gramont (pseudonym).

5418. Morgan, Ted. "When the Maquis Stood and Fought," Military History Quarterly 2/2 (Winter 1990): 104-111.

5419. Morgan, William A. "Invasion on the Ether: Radio Intelligence at the Battle of St. Mihiel, September 1918," Military Affairs 51/2 (1987): 57-61.

  An assessment of US Army ability to provide signals intelligence during World War I.

5420. Morgenstern, George. "Asylum for War Criminals, Quislings, and Traitors," British Yearbook of International Law 25 (1948): 382-395.

5421. Morgenthau, Hans J. "To Intervene or Not to Intervene," Foreign Affairs 45/3 (April 1967): 425-426.

  Considers the historical concerns and issues related to international intervention, then applies concerns to such conflicts as the Dominican Republic, Cuba, and Vietnam.

5422. Moriarty, Anthony R. "Abating Military Espionage Problems," International Journal of Intelligence and Counterintelligence 4/4 (Winter 1990): 475-485.

  Considers the questions of why military espionage cases are on the rise and what better methods of personnel security might be employed to reduce such cases. Major sections discuss the problem of so many security clearances; the overall military internal security problem; the spy profile; the investigative process; the polygraph controversy; psychological testing; cost-benefit assessment; and recommendations.

5423. Morison, Samuel E. "Squire Ames and Doctor Ames," New England Quarterly 1 (January 1928): 5-31.

5424. Morison, Samuel E. "The Rising Sun in the Pacific," Foreign Affairs 70/5 (Winter 1991-1992): 153-155.
      This is an excerpt from the History of United States Naval Operations in World War II, Volume III, concerning the Pearl Harbor attack.

5425. Morley, Jefferson and Malcolm Byrne. "The Drug War and 'National Security': The Making of a Quagmire, 1969-1973," Dissent 36/1 (1989): 39-46.

5426. Morley, Morris H. "Toward a Theory of Imperial Policymaking," Journal of Contemporary Asia 11/3 (1981): 333-350.

5427. Morley, Morris and Steven Smith. "Imperial 'Reach': U.S. Policy and the CIA in Chile," Journal of Political and Military Sociology 5/2 (Fall 1977): 203-216.
      A study of the role of US covert politics in Chile between 1970 and 1973. Seeks to find the CIA in the middle of the action and to show how other nations with a history of investment, commercial and financial dependence on the US are susceptible to covert politics.

5428. Morosoff, Peter S. "The Influence of Weather in War," Marine Corps Gazette (March 1988): 21-22.
      Discusses elements in war, such as mud, fog, rain, wind, dust; offers additional reading suggestions.

5429. Morrell, Gordon W. "British Engineers As British Spies: The Metro-Vickers Affair, Moscow 1933," Michigan Academician 23/4 (1991): 325-334.

5430. Morrell, Gordon W. "Redefining Intelligence and Intelligence-gathering: The Industrial Intelligence Centre and the Metro-Vickers Affair, Moscow 1933," Intelligence and National Security 9/3 (July 1994): 520-533.
      Discusses the Metro-Vickers case in connection with the changing conditions of British intelligence gathering following World War I.

5431. Morris, A. J. "And, Is the Kaiser Coming for Tea?," Moirae 5 (1980).

5432. Morris, Benny. "The Birth of the Israeli-Phalange Relationship, 1948-1951," Studies in Zionism (Spring 1984).

5433. Morris, Benny. "The Causes and Character of the Arab Exodus from Palestine: The Israeli Defense Forces Intelligence Branch Analysis of June 1948," Middle Eastern Studies 22/1 (1986): 5-19.

Considers the role of Israeli Defense Forces Intelligence Branch in the Arab exodus from Palestine in 1948-1949.

5434. Morris, Benny. "Operation Dani and the Palestinian Exodus from Lydda and Ramle in 1948," Middle East Journal 40/1 (Winter 1986): 82-109.
Further discussion of military, political, and intelligence actions involved in the Arab exodus in 1948.

5435. Morris, Bernard S. "Communist International Front Organizations: Their Nature and Function," World Politics 9 (October 1956): 76-87.
Provides a brief resume of the role of front organizations in the context of the early cold war era.

5436. Morris, C. Brent. "Fraternal Cryptography: Cryptographic Practices of American Fraternal Organizations," Cryptologia 7/1 (January 1983): 27-36.

5437. Morris, Christopher. "Ultra's Poor Relations," Intelligence and National Security 1/1 (January 1986): 111-122.
A discussion of the breaking of the German naval hand ciphers by the British.

5438. Morris, Edmund. "Archie Roosevelt, Original," Studies in Intelligence 34/3 (Fall 1990).

5439. Morris, Gillian S. "The Ban on Trade Unions at Government Communications Headquarters," Public Law 1985 (Summer 1985): 177-186.
An analysis of the British government's prohibition on service in trade unions at the Government's high security communications center, a vital intelligence function.

5440. Morris, L. P. "British Secret Service Activity in Khorassan, 1887-1908," Historical Journal 27/3 (September 1984): 657-675.
An account of the establishment of a news gathering agency in the Persian Province of Khorassan so that British intelligence could spy on Russia.

5441. Morris, Robert. "The Hagelin Cipher Machine (M-209): Reconstruction of the Internal Settings," Cryptologia 2/3 (July 1978): 267-289.

5442. Morris, Robert; N. J. A. Sloane and A. D. Wyner. "Assessment of the National Bureau of Standards Proposed Federal Data Encryption Standard," Cryptologia 1/3 (July 1977): 281-291

5443. Morris, Roger. "The Aftermath of CIA Intervention," Society 12/3 (March-April 1975): 76-80.

Discusses CIA operations in Brazil, Ecuador, Indonesia, Somalia and Zaire in the 1960s.

5444. Morris, Roger. "The Culture of Bureaucracy: A Rare Resignation in Protest: Nat Davis and Angola," Washington Monthly 7/12 (February 1976): 22-30.

5445. Morrison, Charles D. "Naval Reserve Intelligence Today," Naval Intelligence Professionals Quarterly 11/3 (Summer 1995): 10.

5446. Morrison, David C. "From Iran to Trade to Soviet Intentions, Can Government Intelligence Officers Keep Their Judgments Free of Politics," Government Executive 19 (June 1987): 52-56.

5447. Morrison, John D., Jr. "The Protection of Intelligence Data," Studies in Intelligence 11/1 (Spring 1967): 69-78.

5448. Morrison, P. "Role of Reconnaissance Satellites in the Arms Race," Scientific American 225 (September 1971): 229-230+.

5449. Morton, Louis. "The Japanese Decision for War," U.S. Naval Institute Proceedings 80/12 (December 1954): 1325-1335.

5450. Morton, Louis. "Pearl Harbor in Perspective: A Bibliographical Survey," U.S. Naval Institute Proceedings 81/4 (April 1955): 461-468.

5451. Morton, Louis. "The Decision to Use the Atom Bomb," Foreign Affairs 35/2 (January 1957): 334-353.
A detailed consideration of the use of the atomic bomb. Sections discuss the interim committee of 1939; military considerations; the decision; and the Japanese surrender.

5452. Moser, Don. "The Time of the Angel: The U-2, Cuba, and the CIA," American Heritage 28/6 (October 1977): 4-15.
This piece reviews the evolution of the U-2 aircraft and its role in the Cuban missile crisis, 1962.

5453. Moses, Hans. "The Case of Major X," Studies in Intelligence 18/1 (Spring 1974): 1-24.
The author writes about his role as a double agent in the late 1940s. Techniques of double agent handling are included, such as the approach, the launch of the operation, early stages, security, commitment, initiatives and problems, pressures, meeting, and return to Washington.

5454. Moses, Hans. "The Clandestine Service," Studies in Intelligence 26/2 (Summer 1982).

5455. Moses, Hans. "A Reader's Guide to Espionage: Who's Who and What's What Among Spies, Counterspies, Secret Agents and the Like," World & I 1/11 (November 1986): 17-24.

5456. Moses, Hans. "The Clandestine Service of the Central Intelligence Agency," American Intelligence Journal 14/1 (Autumn-Winter 1992-1993): 81-84.
    Discusses the background history of US clandestine services; current functions in collection, counterintelligence, and special activities; organization in the field, headquarters, personnel, and specialists.

5457. Moses, Morris. "Secrets of a World War II Matchbox Camera," Shutterbug 15/7 (May 1986): 104, 110.

5458. Moskoff, Franklin. R. "Democracy and National Security, Competing Concepts for Canada," Advocates' Society Journal 3/1 (February 1984): 32-40.

5459. Moskoff, William. "CIA Publications on the Soviet Economy," Slavic Review 40/2 (Summer 1981): 269-272.

5460. Moss, Frederick C. "The Effect of the First Amendment on Federal Control of Draft Protests," Villanova Law Review 13 (Winter 1968): 347-369.
    Refers in part to the Espionage Act of 1917.

5461. Moss, Norman. "'Sonya' Explains," Bulletin of the Atomic Scientists 19 (July-August 1993): 9-11.
    A brief account of Ruth Werner's role in Soviet espionage.

5462. Moss, Robert. "The Campaign to Destabilize Iran," Conflict Studies 101 (November 1978): 1-18.

5463. Moss, Robert. "The Cloak-and-Dagger Controversy," International Review 3 (Winter 1974): 19-24, 61.

5464. Motley, James B. "Coping with International Terrorism: The Role of U.S. Intelligence," Harvard International Review 7/6 (May-June 1985): 276-295.

5465. Motley, James B. "International Terrorism: A Challenge for U.S. Intelligence," International Journal of Intelligence and Counterintelligence 1/1 (Spring 1986): 83-96.
    Discusses problems faced by the US and the international community in combatting terrorism. One difficulty for political leaders is acquisition of the

latest intelligence information concerning terrorist organizations. Expansion of US intelligence role in antiterrorism is suggested.

5466. Motley, James B. "Intelligence Requirements: A Contrast in the Conventional Battlefield and the Low Intensity Conflict Environment," Journal of Defense & Diplomacy 6/4 (April 1988): 50-52.

5467. Motley, James B. "U.S. Unconventional Conflict Policy and Strategy," Military Review (January 1990): 3-16.
    Discusses the American political culture; US cultural politics in a hostile world; the Vietnam war's impact on political culture and the American way to war; and future challenges to the use of military force.

5468. Motley, James B. "The Army's Need: A Relevant LIC Environment," International Journal of Intelligence and Counterintelligence 4/3 (Fall 1990): 383-405.
    Detailed discussion of some of the critical analytical problems in determining economic stability of foreign nations, in particular, the Soviet Union. Discusses the causes of CIA error with respect to the Soviet economy; the forecasting problem; the particular needs of US Army planners; the conventional and low-intensity battlefields; the US Army's conceptual problem; intelligence requirements for the conventional battlefield; the LIC environment; and future intelligence requirements.

5469. Mott, Thomas B. "The Organization and Function of a Bureau of Military Intelligence," Journal of the Military Service Institution of the United States 32 (March-April 1903): 184-208.

5470. Motyl, Alexander J. "Policing Perestroika: The Indispensable KGB," Harriman Institute Forum 2 (August 1989): 1-8.
    Discusses the role of the KGB as integral to the Soviet system.

5471. Mount, Graeme S. "Drums Along the St. Mary's: Tensions on the International Border at Sault Ste. Marie," Michigan History 73/4 (1989): 32-36.
    Discusses several conflicts in the border region between 1796 and 1988 which suggest a less than perfect relationship in the area. Includes a discussion of the Fenian espionage movement and German spy activity in World War I.

5472. Mount, Graeme S. "Canada, Spain, and Espionage during the Second World War," Canadian Historical Review 74/4 (December 1993): 566-575.
    Discusses the strained relationship between Canada and Spain late in World War II, tied mainly on investigations of a Spanish consul whom Canada believed was willing to conduct espionage for Japan. Disputes certain theories of the exposure of the consul's activities.

5473. Mourning, Paul W. "Leashing the Dogs of War: Outlawing the Recruitment and Use of Mercenaries," Virginia Journal of International Law 22/3 (Summer 1982): 589-625.

Examines the probable international legal effect of the United Nations proposed convention on mercenaries. Contains historical analysis of the standing of mercenaries, analyzes the draft convention and suggests the form the United Nations treaty might take.

5474. Mowbray, Stephen de. "Soviet Deception and the Onset of the Cold War: The British Documents for 1943--A Lesson in Manipulation," Encounter 62/2 (July-August 1984): 16-24.

An extensive reflection on British Foreign Office files for 1943 to argue the point that the Soviets were capable of deceiving Western intelligence services.

5475. Mowlana, Hamid. "Middle East Mass Communications: Selected Information Sources," Journal of Broadcasting 21/4 (Fall 1977): 497-510.

Contains a short description of the author's content analysis of 1400 studies dealing with international communication in the US. He reduced the collection to 30 references to the Middle East and he includes the 30 in the article.

5476. Moyer, Marc A. "Section 301 of the Omnibus Trade and Competitiveness Act of 1988: A Formidable Weapon in the War Against Economic Espionage," Northwestern Journal of International Law & Business 15/1 (Fall 1994): 178-205.

Considers the Act in the context of industrial espionage and trade secrets theft as part of the overall equation of international trade practices.

5477. Moynihan, Daniel P. "A Spy Story," Freedom At Issue 87 (November-December 1985): 18-21.

The author, a US Senator from New York, argues for controls over Soviet capabilities to electronically surveil telephone calls in the US from Soviet diplomatic buildings.

5478. Muckerman, Joseph E. "The Bay of Pigs Revisited," Military Review 5 (April 1971): 77-85.

5479. Mueller, Jean W. and Wynell B. Schamel. "Teaching with Documents: The First Amendment: The Finished Mystery Case and World War I," Social Education 54 (October 1990): 366-368.

5480. Mueller, John E. "The Search for the 'Breaking Point' in Vietnam: The Statistics of a Deadly Quarrel," International Studies Quarterly (December 1980): 497-519.

5481. Mueller, William B. "Howard Hughes, CIA, and the Incredible Glomar

Explorer," Sea Classics 11 (September 1978): 26-28.

5482. Muggeridge, Malcolm. "Who Betrays Whom?," Twentieth Century 170 (Winter 1962): 118-128.

5483. Muggeridge, Malcolm. "Book Review of a Very Limited Edition," Esquire 67/5 (May 1966): 84.
     Not regarded as a scholarly serial journal, but due to the subject matter and the author's experience in British intelligence and his many novels on espionage, this piece may be useful to researchers.

5484. Muggeridge, Malcolm. "Books: CIA Cultural Penetration," Esquire 68/9 (September 1967): 12, 14, 16.
     Not regarded as a scholarly serial journal, but due to the subject matter and the author's experience in British intelligence and his many novels on espionage, this piece may be useful to researchers.

5485. Muir, Malcolm, J. "Rearming in a Vacuum: United States Navy Intelligence and the Japanese Capital Ship Threat, 1936-1945," Journal of Military History 54/3 (October 1990): 473-485.
     The US intelligence services failed to acquire correct information on the Yamato class of Japanese battleships, and as a consequence suffered unnecessary losses.

5486. Muir, Malcolm J. "A View from the Black Hole," U.S. Naval Institute Proceedings 117/10 (October 1991): 85-86.
     Based on the author's experiences as an Air Force intelligence officer in the Middle East, he suggests that Air Force intelligence remains organizationally isolated from the command system in ways that do not exist in naval intelligence.

5487. Muirhead, M. "Military Cryptography," Journal of the Royal United Service Institution 55/404 (October 1911): 1321-1332.
     Discussion of elements of military cryptography.

5488. Muirhead, M. "Military Cryptography: A Study of the Transposition Cipher System and Substitution Frequency Tables," Journal of the Royal United Service Institution 56/418 (December 1912): 1665-1678.
     Discusses the author's technical insights as he presented them to the US Army Signal Schools.

5489. Mulcahy, Kevin V. "The Bush Administration and National Security Policymaking: A Preliminary Assessment," International Journal of Intelligence and Counterintelligence 4/2 (Summer 1990): 167-180.
     Argues that the Bush administration's national security management style

can be described as managerial, collegial, incremental, and pragmatic. Major sections consider the Bush style; the Bush national security team; decisionmaking at three levels; human relations; moving beyond the Cold War; and final thoughts.

5490. Mulkey, Jesse G. "Marine Air Observer," Marine Corps Gazette 53 (May 1969): 35-37.

5491. Mull, Alexander. "Notes on the Wennerstrom Case," Studies in Intelligence 10/2 (Summer 1966).

5492. Mullahey, Thomas F., Jr. "Counter-Intelligence," Marine Corps Gazette 29 (October 1945): 36-38.

5493. Muller, Klaus-Jurgen. "On the Difficulties of Writing Intelligence History," Studies in Intelligence 30/3 (Fall 1986): 57-62.

5494. Muller, Klaus-Jurgen. "A German Perspective on Allied Deception Operations in the Second World War," Intelligence and National Security 2/3 (July 1987): 301-326.
    An extensive discussion of allied deception and German perception of the Mediterranean strategy; and allied deception and German strategy in Norway. Concludes that deception history is more complicated than we assume, thus calling for more extensive study.

5495. Mulligan, Luciel M. "Hercules Mulligan, Secret Agent," Daughters of the American Revolution Magazine 105/3 (1971): 232-235, 320.

5496. Mulligan, Timothy P. "'According to Colonel Donovan': A Document from the Records of German Military Intelligence," Historian 46/1 (November 1983): 78-86.
    An assessment of German intelligence gathering capabilities in World War II, as viewed by OSS Chief Donovan.

5497. Mulligan, Timothy P. "The German Navy Evaluates Its Cryptographic Security, October 1941," Military Affairs 49/2 (April 1985): 75-79.
    A look at a Germany navy report which posed the probability of its naval code having been commissioned by British intelligence.

5498. Mulligan, Timothy P. "Spies, Ciphers and 'Zitadelle': Intelligence and the Battle of Kursk, 1943," Journal of Contemporary History 22/2 (April 1987): 235-260.
    A detailed discussion of the coded project named Zitadelle, referring to the Battle of Kursk, and the operations of the Soviet espionage ring in Operation Lucy. Soviet success in the Battle of Kursk was directly linked to acquisition of

information from the high ranks of the German command.

5499. Mullin, Chris. "The CIA: Tibetan Conspiracy," Far Eastern Economic Review (September 1975): 30-34.

5500. Mullins, Wayman C. "Stopping Terrorism: The Problems Posed by the Organizational Infrastructure of Terrorist Organizations," Journal of Contemporary Criminal Justice 4/4 (November 1988): 214-228.
   Terrorist organizations differ in organizational design from ordinary organized crime groups, employing a circular and closed design which is difficult for intelligence groups to penetrate.

5501. Mumma, Albert G. "The Alsos Mission," Naval History 3/3 (1989): 51-53.

5502. Munro, Ross H. "Eavesdropping on the Chinese Military: Where It Expects War--Where It Doesn't," Orbis 38/3 (Summer 1994): 355-372.
   Major topics include Taiwan and future war; South China Sea; China's armed forces; relations with the US; Japan, Vietnam, India, Russia; hot spots for regional wars; war on Taiwan and the South China Sea.

5503. Munroe, Kirk W. "Consensual Electronic Surveillance and the Explosive Impact of Sarmiento," Florida Bar Journal 56 (April 1982): 355-358.
   A review of the implications of the Third Circuit's decision in Sarmiento v. State declaring that a private citizen's decision to permit electronic surveillance in the home was unconstitutional if there had been no warrant for such action.

5504. Munson, F. Granville. "The Arguments in the Saboteur Trial," University of Pennsylvania Law Review 91 (1942): 239-252.
   Legal arguments made by federal prosecutors and defense counsel in the trial of eight German saboteurs.

5505. Munson, Margaret R. "MIIDS/IDB: A Look Back and to the Future," American Intelligence Journal 13/3 (Summer 1992): 59-62.
   Discusses the background of the Military Intelligence Integrated Data System in the Defense Intelligence Agency; data base development; data administration; user training; data base production; and the future for tactical users.

5506. Munson, Michael F. "Intelligence Resource Management," American Intelligence Journal 15/2 (Autumn-Winter 1994): 12-16.
   Considers several initiatives as part of the overall reorganization and redirection of the Defense Intelligence Agency. Major sections discuss the common budget framework; the Intelligence Program Support Group; joint

program review; national intelligence needs process; intelligence systems standards and interoperability; joint military intelligence program; intelligence bottoms-up review; security and counterintelligence; and intelligence reserves.

5507. Munton, D. and Don Page. "Planning in the East Block: The Post-Hostilities Problems Committees in Canada 1943-45," International Journal 32 (Winter 1976-1977): 687-726.

5508. Muravchik, Joshua. "The Nicaragua Debate," Foreign Affairs 65 (1986): 366-378.

5509. Muravchik, Joshua. "'Glasnost,' the KGB and the 'Nation,'" Commentary 85/6 (June 1988): 47-49.
    Brief account of an accusation made by Nation magazine that a Russian emigre organization in the United States received federal funds for work alleged to have been associated with American or other intelligence services.

5510. Murdoch, Richard K. "A British Report on West Florida and Louisiana, November 1812," Florida Historical Quarterly 43/1 (1964): 36-51.

5511. Murdoch, Richard K. "Intelligence Reports of British Agents in the Long Island Sound Area, 1814-1815," American Neptune 29/3 (1969): 187-198.

5512. Murfin, Robert. "Intelligence and Communication: Keys to Air-Land Battle 2000," Signal 38 (October 1983): 31-34.

5513. Murillo Jimenez, Hugo. "La Intervencion Nortamericana en Guatemala en 1954: Dos Interpretaciones Recientes," Anuario de Estudios Centroamericanos 11/2 (1985): 149-155.

5514. Murphy, Charles V. "Cuba: The Record Set Straight," Fortune (September 1961): 92-97, 223-235.
    Argues that the Central Intellignence Agency and President John Kennedy were the principal culprits in the Bay of Pigs fiasco.

5515. Murphy, Charles V. "Uncloaking the CIA," Fortune 91 (June 1975): 88-91.

5516. Murphy, David E. "Sasha Who?," Intelligence and National Security 8/1 (January 1993): 102-107.
    A review essay of David Wise's Mole-Hunt... (1992) concerning the lengthy CIA intrigue surrounding Anatoliy Golitsyn's charge that a mole existed in the Agency.

5517. Murphy, James and K. Wayne Smith. "Making Intelligence Analysis Responsive to Policy Concerns," Studies in Intelligence 17/2 (Summer 1973).

5518. Murphy, John B. "Military Intelligence -- The Sphinx," Reserve Officer (July 1932): 7-23.

5519. Murphy, John F. "An International Convention on Invasion of Privacy," New York University Journal of International Law and Politics 8/3 (Winter 1976): 387-433.

Calls attention to the inconsistencies between individual nations on the matter of privacy, and the conflict between state interests and other interests (e.g., domestic order, speech and press, economic, etc.). Points to intrusions of privacy via auditory and visual surveillance in various countries and the public disclosure of private information. Calls for an international convention on privacy.

5520. Murphy, John F. "Clandestine Warfare: Morality and Practical Problems Confounded," Washington and Lee Law Review 39/2 (Spring 1982): 377-379.

A response to Professor Rodes' article in the same journal issue ("On Clandestine Warfare"). Murphy says that Rodes declined "to consider the political obstacles facing those who would need to cope with moral problems of clandestine warfare . . . . [M]orality and politics are inextricably intertwined."

5521. Murphy, John F., Jr. "The Alaskan Mystery Flights," International Journal of Intelligence and Counterintelligence 9/1 (Spring 1996): 97-111.

A brief history of intelligence operations against the Soviet Union in the 1930s, aimed at discovering information about Stalin's warfighting capabilities. Sections discuss suspicions about "Uncle Joe"; strength in the East; golden dreams; recruits; the mystery flights of Colonel Henry "Hap" Arnold; taking pictures; and reaching for an unclear goal.

5522. Murphy, Lisa. "One Small Moment," American History 30/2 (June 1995): 66-71.

This is the story of the Japanese terror balloon and bomb project, Project Fugo. Losing the war in the Pacific, the Japanese military elite decided to develop terror bombs carried by balloons over Northwest states hopefully to distract forces toward homefront protection.

5523. Murphy, Mark. "The OSS-German POW Controversy," Studies in Intelligence 32/1 (Spring 1988).

5524. Murray, Williamson. "ULTRA: Some Thoughts on Its Impact on the Second World War," Air University Review 35/5 (July-August 1984): 52-64.

Explores in detail the role of the ULTRA cryptographic breakthroughs in World War II and their impact in favor of US invasion efforts in 1943 and

1944.

5525. Murray, Williamson. "Appeasement and Intelligence," <u>Intelligence and National Security</u> 2/4 (October 1987): 47-66.

Major sections discuss the problem of perceptions and analysis of intelligence; the problem of analysis and getting it right; and conclusions.

5526. Murtha, John P. "Combat Intelligence in Vietnam," <u>Marine Corps Gazette</u> 52/1 (January 1968): 30-34.

Discusses Marine Corps intelligence operations in Vietnam during 1966 and 1967.

5527. Myer, Charles R. "Viet Cong SIGINT and U.S. Army COMSEC in Vietnam," <u>Cryptologia</u> 13/2 (April 1989): 143-150.

5528. Myers, Harry C. "From 'The Crack Pot of the Frontier': Letters of Thomas and Charlotte Swords," <u>Kansas History</u> 5/3 (1982): 184-213.

5529. Myers, Jennifer S. "Passport Controls: Revocation of Passports for National Security Reasons (<u>Haig v. Agee</u>)," <u>Harvard International Law Journal</u> 23/1 (Spring 1982): 163-170.

Analyzes the Supreme Court decision of major importance concerning the power of the Secretary of State to revoke passports for national security reasons.

5530. Myers, Russell E. "Challenges to the Defense Intelligence Information System Professional," <u>American Intelligence Journal</u> 15/2 (Autumn-Winter 1994): 42-51.

Extensive review of intelligence information systems history and critical challenges. Major sections discuss the DODIIS system; the MIIDS/IDB system; the AMHS system; networking; the JDISS system; and six future challenges.

N

**"I am Nosenko...[t]he bad things you have heard about me
are not true."**
(cited in Cold Warrior by Tom Mangold, p. 205)

5531. Nabbie, Eustace E. "The Alamo Scouts," Studies in Intelligence 3/3 (Fall 1959).
   A story of infiltration in the South Pacific.

5532. Nabbie, Eustace E. "A Small South Pole," Studies in Intelligence 4/3 (Fall 1960).

5533. Nachmani, Amikam. "Generals at Bay in Post-War Palestine," Journal of Strategic Studies 6/4 (December 1983): 72-82.
   Useful in studies of Arab-Israeli conflicts involving intelligence issues.

5534. Nacht, Michael L. "The Delicate Balance of Error," Foreign Policy 19 (Summer 1975): 163-177.

5535. Naftali, Timothy J. "Intrepid's Last Deception: Documenting the Career of Sir William Stephenson," Intelligence and National Security 8/3 (July 1993): 72-99.
   The author lays a foundation for correcting impressions about the life and wartime work of Sir William Stephenson. Concludes that Stephenson and his biographers are equally responsible for furthering myths.

5536. Nagler, Joerg A. "Enemy Aliens and Internment in World War I: Alvo von Alvensleben in Fort Douglas, Utah, A Case Study," Utah Historical Quarterly 58/4 (1990): 388-405.

5537. Nagorski, Zygmunt, Jr. "Soviet International Propaganda: Its Role, Effectiveness, and Future," Annals of the American Academy of Political and Social Sciences 398 (November 1971): 130-139.

5538. Nagy, Alex. "Word Wars at Home: U.S. Response to World War II Propaganda," Journalism Quarterly 67/1 (1990): 207-213.
    A discussion of censorship during the War, including the use of the 1917 Espionage Act and the 1938 Foreign Agents Registration Act. The US Post Office burned several tons of mail shipped in the US under the authorization of Postmaster Frank Walter.

5539. Naimark, Norman M. "Is It True What They're Saying About East Germany?," Orbis 23/3 (Fall 1979): 549-577.
    Explores various aspects of repression of citizens in East Germany, including the role in that repression by the GDR's State Security Service.

5540. Nanda, Ved P. "The Right to Movement and Travel Abroad: Some Observations on the U.N. Deliberations," Denver Journal of International Law and Policy 1/1 (Fall 1971): 109-122.
    A review of the nature and right to movement and travel as recognized in United Nations instruments; scope and implications; difficulties in the implementation of the right; trends in states' practices in recognizing and limiting the right and recommendations.

5541. Nano, F. C. "The First Soviet Double Cross," Journal of Central European Affairs 12 (1952): 236-258.

5542. Napier, F. S. "One Platoon in the Jungle," Soldier 10 (January 1955): 12-13.

5543. Nardelli, F. P. "The Text and the Cipher: Toward the Study of a 'Disturbed' Mode of Transmission," Quellen und Forschungen aus Italienischen Archiven und Bibliotheken 66 (1986): 393-401.
    Discusses a problem involved with the process of deciphering and encoding secret messages, published in Germany.

5544. Nash, Henry T. "The Bureaucratization of Homicide," Bulletin of the Atomic Scientists 36/4 (April 1980): 22-27.
    Discusses this former intelligence analyst's views on how the US planned to kill Soviets by nuclear means without moral revulsion. Approaches the

question of the intelligence analyst's role in nuclear war planning.

5545. Nathan, James A. "The Missile Crisis: His Finest Hour Now," World Politics 27/2 (January 1975): 256-281.

Discusses the missile crisis as the watershed of the cold war, showing American determination and responsibility for the exercise of power in the sphere of American national security interest.

5546. Nathan, James A. "A Fragile Detente: The U-2 Incident Re-Examined," Military Affairs 39/3 (October 1975): 97-104.

Discusses the end of the cold war, the reemergence of the old reflexes, the curious death of detente via the American-Soviet Union U-2 incident, the aborting of the Paris Summit, the strange odyssey of pilot Francis Gary Powers, the strange situation of use of open telephone lines prior to Powers' departure, denouement, and the allegation that the U-2 incident was staged to assist the US in certain international relations contexts.

5547. Nathan, James A. "Dateline Australia: America's Foreign Watergate?," Foreign Policy 49 (Winter 1982-1983): 168-185.

Discusses the evolution of the Central Intelligence Agency and military intelligence activities in Australia, and the implications of such activities for Australian national interests.

5548. Nathan, Reuben S. "Psychological Warfare: Key to Success in Vietnam," Orbis 11/1 (Spring 1967): 182-193.

An outline of psychological warfare applications as part of the overall fabric of the Vietnam war.

5549. Nathanson, Charles E. "The Social Construction of the Soviet Threat: A Study in the Politics of Representation," Alternatives 13/4 (October 1988): 443-483.

Argues that the threat of the Soviet Union was manufactured in the American political rhetoric and actions following World War II. Part of the "script" of the rhetoric included the identification and marginalization of people who sought accommodation between the United States and the Soviet Union.

5550. Nathanson, Nathaniel L. "Freedom of Association and the Quest for International Security: Conspiracy From Dennis to Dr. Spock," Northwestern University Law Review 65 (May-June 1970): 153-192.

Considers the legal history of the concern for international security, especially the Smith Act enforcement actions, the Subversive Activities Control Act, loyalty-security programs, legislative investigations and the contemporary situation in 1970.

5551. Naveh, Hanan and Michael Brecher. "Patterns of International Crises in the Middle East, 1938-1975," Jerusalem Journal of International Relations 2-3 (Winter-Spring 1978): 277-315.

5552. Navrete, F. and L. M. Jacques. "Multi-State Regional Intelligence Project: Filling an Information Void in the Nation's Law Enforcement Network," Police Chief 49/10 (October 1982): 46-49.
    Discusses Regional Organized Crime Information Centers combat the problem of mobile criminals, and the coordination between local, state and federal authorities.

5553. Navrozov, Lev. "What the CIA Knows About Russia," Commentary 66/3 (September 1978): 51-58.
    Author suggests that the US intelligence system is highly vulnerable to deception, especially in areas of economic and defense assessments about the Soviet Union.

5554. Nayameko, R. S. "Fight U.S. Subversion of Trade Union Movement in Africa," African Communist 87 (Fourth Quarter 1981): 56-64.

5555. Nederveen Pieterse, Jan P. "State Terrorism on a Global Scale: The Role of Israel," Crime and Social Justice (1984): 21-22, 58-80.
    Discusses Israel's activities in counterinsurgency, in particular, operations in the West Bank and the Gaza Strip. Mentions intelligence relations between Israel and NATO nations.

5556. Nedzi, Lucien N. "Oversight or Overlook: Congress and the U.S. Intelligence Agencies," Studies in Intelligence 18/2 (Summer 1974).

5557. Needler, Martin C. "Hegemonic Tolerance: International Competition in the Caribbean and Latin America," Caribbean Review 11/2 (Spring 1982): 32-33, 56.
    Discusses several dynamics of political evolution in Latin America, including allegations of CIA mercenary involvement in disrupting pro-communist groups.

5558. Neier, Aryeh. "Adhering to Principle: Lessons from the 1950's," Civil Liberties Review 4/4 (November-December 1977): 26-32.
    Discusses the author's experiences regarding the Federal Bureau of Investigation's investigations of the American Civil Liberties Union activities in the 1950s.

5559. Neier, Aryeh. "FBI Files: Modus Inoperandi," Civil Liberties Review 1/3 (Summer 1974): 50-58.

Challenges the view taken by the FBI that its files are used as aids for investigating crimes and locating criminals. Suggests that the FBI is serving as a major employment and credit checking agency.

5560. Neier, Aryeh. "Surveillance by the FBI," Index on Censorship 10 (April 1981): 42-47.

5561. Neilson, Keith. "'Joy Rides': British Intelligence and Propaganda in Russia, 1914-1917," Historical Journal 24/4 (December 1981): 885-906.
A discussion of the historical involvement of Britain in intelligence missions to Russia, evolving mainly from evaluations of troop movements. Concludes that propaganda and intelligence introduced major difficulties during World War I, and created functional and organizational problems for which there were no pre-war solutions.

5562. Neilson, Keith. "Watching the 'Steamroller': British Observers and the Russian Army Before 1914," Journal of Strategic Studies 8/2 (June 1985): 199-217.
Discusses the British concerns for the unbalancing of power in Europe by the advancements of the Russian military prior to 1914. Major sections discuss Anglo-Russian relations, the common Russian soldier, Russian officers, tactics, defects of the Russian army, and Russian strengths in addressing the flaws of the military.

5563. Neilson, Keith. "Tsars and Commissars: W. Somerset Maugham, Ashenden and the Images of Russia in British Adventure Fiction, 1890-1930," Canadian Journal of History 27/3 (December 1992): 475-500.
An extensive inquiry into the role of Ashenden; or the British Agent in breaking new ground in spy novels in the West.

5564. Nekrasov, V. F. "The Contribution of the Internal Troops to the Cause of Victory of the Soviet People in the Great Patriotic War," Military Historical Journal 9 (September 1985): 29-35.
The title appearing here is an English translation. The article appears in Russian.

5565. Nekrich, A. M. "Labyrinths of the Secret War," Novaiia i Noveishaia Istoriia 10/1 (1966): 122-131; (3): 107-114.
This is an approximate title translation for an article appearing in a Russian language journal.

5566. Nel, Phillip R. "Soviet African Diplomacy and the Role of the International Department," African Insight 12 (1982): 132-141.

5567. Nelsen, Harvey.   "The U.S. Intelligence Budget in the 1990's," International Journal of Intelligence and Counterintelligence 6/2 (Summer 1993): 195-203.

Raises questions about the future of the intelligence community budget in years following the disappearance of the Soviet Union. Major sections discuss categories of allocation; openness to view; President Bush and the intelligence budget; military intelligence; and challenges for CIA director Robert Gates.

5568. Nelson, Anna K.   "Mission to Mexico-Moses Y. Beach, Secret Agent," New York Historical Society Quarterly 59/3 (July 1975): 227-245.

A summation of Beach's activities as a secret agent appointed by President James Polk. His service contributed to ending the war with Mexico.

5569. Nelson, Anna K. "Secret Agents and Security Leaks: President Polk and the Mexican War," Journalism Quarterly 52/1 (Spring 1975): 9-14, 98.

Details the author's of Polk in ending the war with Mexico, including the use of secret agents.

5570. Nelson, Anna K. "The 'Top of Policy Hill': President Eisenhower and the National Security Council," Diplomatic History 7/3 (1983): 307-326.

A detailed history of the national security advice, including intelligence, given to President Eisenhower and the National Security Council.

5571. Nelson, Anna K. "President Truman and the Evolution of the National Security Council," Journal of American History 72/2 (September 1985): 360-378.

Discusses Harry Truman's implementation of the National Security Council concept introduced by former Secretary of Defense James V. Forrestal, the reasoning for the council in the unification of the armed services and the intelligence function, and the Truman charge to the National Security Council.

5572. Nelson, Dick and Julie Koenen-Grant.   "A Case of Bureaucracy 'in Action': The U.S. Embassy in Moscow," International Journal of Intelligence and Counterintelligence 6/3 (Fall 1993): 303-318.

A case study to describe events in the extraordinary effort to build a new embassy in Moscow. Major sections address the traditional status of embassies; embassies and intelligence; negotiating new embassy sites; Nixon and Detente; commencing construction; security problems in Moscow; public attention to the issue; the end of the Cold War; and a retrospective.

5573. Nelson, Gaylord. "How to Stop the Snooping," Progressive 37/8 (August 1973): 14-16.

Brief history of investigative and surveillance activities of the US government and the author's proposals for restraining the excesses of government snooping.

5574. Nelson, Gaylord. "'National Security' and Electronic Surveillance: The Need for Corrective Legislation," Intellect 103 (January 1975): 230-233.

5575. Nelson, Gaylord. "Warrantless Bugs: The Invisible Pests," Trial 11 (March-April 1975): 64-65+.
     Summary of the major Supreme Court cases which developed a tradition of opposition to the dangers of wiretaps. Major sections include discussion of Fourth Amendment protection, taps and the executive branch, wiretap abuses, and proposals for change.

5576. Nelson, Harold W. "Intelligence and the Next War: A Retrospective View," Intelligence and National Security 2/1 (January 1987): 97-117.
     Extensive analysis of images of intelligence before 1914; the transformation of operational intelligence in the first world war; images of military intelligence between the world wars; and intelligence and the next war since 1945.

5577. Nelson, P. B. "Only the Well-Guided Will Succeed," Military Review 33 (November 1953): 29-36.

5578. Nesbit, Robert F. "Catching Up with Pomfret, Vermont: An Examination of Intelligence Dissemination Architectures," American Intelligence Journal 15/2 (Autumn-Winter 1994): 30-36.
     Outlines a strategic direction and context for intelligence dissemination technologies and methodologies. Major sections discuss the push and pull methodologies; the question of which methods are best; require architecture migration; dealing with information-rich environments; and conclusions.

5579. Nesse, Janet M. "United States v. Progressive, Inc.: The National Security and Free Speech Conflict," William and Mary Law Review 22/1 (Fall 1980): 141-160.
     Explores the history of litigation regarding prior restraints on the press and explains an important precedent decision. Concludes that the Court improperly applied the Atomic Energy Act of 1954 and diminished the scope of the First Amendment right of free speech.

5580. Nesson, Charles R. "Aspects of the Executive's Power Over National Security Matters: Secrecy Classification and Foreign Intelligence Wiretaps," Indiana Law Journal 49/3 (Spring 1974): 399-421.
     Focusses on two specific inherent executive powers central to the Ellsberg case: secrecy classification and foreign intelligence wiretapping. Concludes that a need exists for federal courts and the Congress to control both powers.

5581. Neu, Charles E. "Understanding the CIA," <u>Reviews in American History</u> 19/1 (1991): 128-135.

A book review essay of four books: John Ranelagh's <u>The Agency</u>; Trumbell Higgins's <u>The Perfect Failure</u>; Rhodri Jeffreys-Jones' <u>The CIA and American Democracy</u>; and Loch Johnson's <u>America's Secret Power</u>.

5582. Neumann, William L. "United States Aid to the Chilean Wars of Independence," <u>Hispanic American Historical Review</u> 27/2 (May 1947).

5583. Neuse, Steven M. "Teaching Political Science with Chillers and Thrillers," <u>Teaching Political Science</u> 7/2 (January 1980): 153-167.

Suggests that political science courses can reach student interest through use of crime and espionage novels to stimulate interest in political concepts and life.

5584. Neveu, Erik. "SAS, CIA et KGB," <u>Histoire</u> 84 (1985): 26-29.

Argues that all three intelligence services are involved in the South African system of apartheid.

5585. Neville, C. J. "The Law of Treason in the English Border Counties in the Later Middle Ages," <u>Law and History Review</u> 9/1 (Spring 1991): 1-30.

5586. Newberry, Jane L. "Political Question Doctrine and Conduct of Foreign Policy," <u>Harvard International Law Journal</u> 25/2 (Spring 1984): 433-441.

This is a brief comment on two appellate cases dealing with the political question doctrine of the Reagan administration policy in Central America. Both cases enlighten the subject of the President's authority to deal with foreign policy mattes, including the conduct of covert action.

5587. Newell, Art. "Semper Sandstorm," <u>Naval Intelligence Professionals Quarterly</u> 3/3 (1987): 5-6.

Reflections upon the Navy's Office of Naval Intelligence in the Gulf war.

5588. Newell, Clayton R. "Improving IEW (Intelligence and Electronic Warfare) Coordination," <u>Military Review</u> 63/12 (December 1983): 24-27.

Discusses coordination of electronic warfare intelligence among military branches, and the need for even more coordination in the future.

5589. Newman, David and Tyll Van Geel. "Executive Order 12,333: The Risks of a Clear Declaration of Intent," <u>Harvard Journal of Law & Public Policy</u> 12/2 (Spring 1989): 433-447.

Addresses the issue of crafting a policy to prohibit assassination of foreign officials, and a proposal to declare such a policy in order for American foreign policy to be unambiguous. Discusses constitutional law questions;

international law perspectives; a US declaratory policy and its reasoning; and a game theory perspective on American declaratory policy.

5590. Newman, James R. "The Control of Information Relating to Atomic Energy," Yale Law Journal 56/5 (May 1947): 769-802.

A discussion of information controls and scientific progress where secrecy is involved; the statutory policy on secrecy; mechanics of the control system; the problem of intent; procedural provisions of Section 10; the information section and the Espionage Act; and reconciling the Atomic Energy Act and the Espionage Act.

5591. Newman, Robert P. "Communication Pathologies of Intelligence Systems," Speech Monographs 42/4 (Winter 1975): 271-290.

5592. Newman, Robert P. "Clandestine Chinese Nationalism Efforts to Punish Their American Detractors," Diplomatic History 7/3 (Summer 1983): 205-222.

An examination of the FBI's role in discrediting American officials who opposed the Chiang Regime in Nationalist China (Taiwan).

5593. Newman, Robert P. "Red Scare in Seattle, 1952: The FBI, the CIA, and Owen Lattimore's 'Escape,'" Historian 48/1 (November 1985): 61-81.

An account of the Cold War hysteria in 1952 and the impact of its seriousness on the court case of Harry A. Jarvinen.

5594. Ney, Virgil. "Bibliography on Guerilla Warfare," Military Affairs 29 (Fall 1960): 146-149.

Citations for over 120 items, mainly books, but including articles, reports and government documents.

5595. Nhlanhla, Joe. "The Modalities of Combining the SATBVC and Liberation Movements' Intelligence Services in a Changing South Africa," Strategic Review for Southern Africa: Security and Intelligence in a Post-Apartheid South Africa 14/2 (October 1992).

5596. Nhlanhla, Joe. "The Transformation of Military Intelligence and Special Forces: Toward an Accountable and Transparent Military Culture," South African Defence Review 12 (1993).

5597. Niblack, Albert. "Proposed Day, Night Fog Signals for the Navy with Brief Description of the Ardois Night System," U.S. Naval Institute Proceedings (1891).

5598. Nicholas, Jack D. "The Element of Surprise in Modern Warfare," Air University Review 8/3 (Summer 1956): 3-20.

5599. Nicholls, Mark. "Sir Walter Ralegh's Treason: A Prosecution Document," English Historical Review 110/438 (September 1995): 902-924.

  Revisits the role of Sir Walter Ralegh (or Raleigh) in various conspiracies in the early seventeenth century. Includes a document essential to the author's argument.

5600. Nichols, David. "The Hidden Truth About Secrecy in Government," Public Opinion 10/5 (January-February 1988): 7-9, 59.

  Discusses the contemporary secrecy debate, ideological origins of openness, recovering the hidden truth about secrecy, secrecy and the separation of power, and secrecy and good government.

5601. Nichols, John S. "La Prensa: The CIA Connection," Columbia Journalism Review 27 (July-August 1988): 34-35.

  La Prensa is a Mexican newspaper.

5602. Nichols, Kenneth D. "In the Matter of J. Robert Oppenheimer: Findings and Recommendations," Bulletin of the Atomic Scientists 10 (September 1954): 271-274.

  Discusses the factors considered in Oppenheimer's clearance removal proceedings; Oppenheimer's contributions in World War II; clearance granting in 1943; basis for clearance under the Atomic Energy Act and Executive Order 10450; security findings; and Oppenheimer's value to atomic energy or related programs.

5603. Nichols, W. Thomas. "Before Reforming the 'Intelligence Community,' What Questions Must Be Asked?," Freedom At Issue 35 (1976): 20-23.

  An examination of the various intelligence services in the US government and the role of Congress and President in oversight of intelligence agencies.

5604. Nicolson, Harold. "Intelligence Services: Their Use and Misuse," Harper's 215 (November 1957): 12-20.

  Considers sources of intelligence, official and unofficial. Much intelligence in military matters can be obtained by secret service methods despite the existence of human error. Official sources are better for political matters.

5605. Nickerson, H. "Force Recon--by Land, Sea, and Air," Marine Corps Gazette 43 (February 1959): 44-48.

5606. Nielsen, Don. "Task Force 157 Born Twenty Years Too Soon...," American Intelligence Journal 14/1 (Autumn-Winter 1993): 23-27.

5607. Nielsen, Harald. "The German Analysis and Assessment System," Intelligence and National Security 10/4 (October 1995): 54-71.

Discusses the German intelligence services, their history, their legal basis, their tasks and their means and methods; and cooperation between the services; and situation assessment at the political level.   Contains several current organizational charts of the German intelligence services.

5608. Nigra, Le Roy. "Little Man: Surumato Susio in the Japanese Intelligence Service," Infantry Journal 59 (July 1946): 14-17.

5609. Nikitin, N. and S. Petrov. "The Secret War of American Imperialism," Voenno-Istoricheski Zhurnal 2 (1980): 59-64.

5610. Nikolaieff, A. M. "Secret Causes of German Successes on the Eastern Front," Coast Artillery Journal (September-October 1935): 373-377.
Discusses the breaking of the Russian code messages by the Austrian intelligence service during World War I. Reproduced in Signal Corps Bulletin 91 (July-August 1936).

5611. Nikoloric, Leonard A. "The Government Loyalty Program," American Scholar 19/3 (Summer 1950): 285-298.

5612. Niksch, Larry A. "U.S. Troop Withdrawal from South Korea: Past Short-comings and Future Prospects," Asian Survey 21/3 (March 1981): 325-341.

5613. Nimmer, Melville B. "National Security Secrets and Free Speech: The Issues Left Undecided in the Ellsberg Case," Stanford Law Review 26 (January 1974): 311-333.
Explores the statutory and constitutional status of penalties for the disclosure of official secrets and reflects upon government assertions and provable claims in the Ellsberg "Pentagon Papers" case.

5614. Nincic, M. "Can the U.S. Trust the U.S.S.R.?," Scientific American 254/4 (April 1986): 33-41.

5615. Nippel, W. "Policing Rome," Journal of Roman Studies 74 (1984): 20-29.
Discusses public order functions of the aediles, a government function in charge of supervision of markets, cleaning, maintenance, repairs, accessibility of streets and other places, and policing. The police function was run like a military unit.

5616. Nish, Ian. "Japan and Its Impact on South-east Asia," Intelligence and National Security 9/4 (October 1994): 753-758.
A book review essay pertaining to five books which indirectly bear on the subject of intelligence and national security: J. E. Dreifort, Myopic Grandeur: The Ambivalence of French Foreign Policy in the Far East, 1919-45; R. J.

Aldrich, <u>The Key to the South: Britain, the United States, and Thailand during the Approach of the Pacific War, 1929-42</u>; A. Gilcrist, <u>Malaya, 1941: The Fall of a Fighting Empire</u>; P. Elphick and M. Smith, <u>Odd Man Out: The Story of the Singapore Traitor</u>; and P. Bates, <u>Japan and the British Commonwealth Occupation Force, 1946-52</u>.

5617. Nitoburg, E. L.   "An Act of Banditry Against Grenada," <u>International Affairs</u> (USSR) (Fall 1984): 63-70.

5618. Nitoburg, E. L.   "Grenada: Bol'Shaia Lozh' I Razboi Vachintona," <u>Voprosy Istorii</u> (1985): 107-119.
    An account of the US invasion of Grenada, including discussion of CIA involvement.   The translation of the title is "Grenada: Washington's Great Treachery."

5619. Nitze, Paul.   "Deterring Our Deterrent," <u>Foreign Policy</u> (Winter 1976): 195-210.
    Discusses the policy of maintaining strategic offensive forces sufficient to carry out retaliation in case of attack.

5620. Nitze, Paul.   "The Development of NSC 68," <u>International Security</u> 4/4 (1980): 170-176.
    Discusses the vulnerability of Europe, US reliance upon nuclear weapons against the Soviet threat, budget problems that led to the creation of NSC 68, Soviet capabilities, and the procedural steps to institute NSC 68.

5621. Noakes, John A.   "A 'New Breed of Detective': The Rise of the FBI Special Agent," <u>Studies in Law, Politics, and Society</u> 14 (1994): 25-42.

5622. Nocera, Joseph.   "The Art of the Leak: From Judas Iscarist to Greg Schneider," <u>Washington Monthly</u> 11/5-6 (July-August 1979): 17-25.
    Discusses the use of the leak as a method for controlling the press, pushing a point or guiding a policy outcome.

5623. Nocera, Joseph.   "Le Couvert Blown: William Colby en Francais," <u>Washington Monthly</u> 12 (November 1980): 11-19.
    An essay concerning Frank Snepp's book, <u>Decent Interval</u>, and Snepp's publication of the work without approval of the Central Intelligence Agency. Discusses changes made to the book prior to publication and the author's charge that Snepp was framed by the government in an effort to ruin credibility. The profits from this book's sale were seized by the government by court ruling.

5624. Nodacker, Milton.   "Intelligence and Deception Factors in the Battle of El Alamein," <u>Military Intelligence</u> 14/1 (January 1988): 26-29.

Analyzes the contributions of intelligence and the extensive use of deception operations in the North African campaign in World War II.

5625. Noether, Emiliana P. "'Morally Wrong' or 'Politically Right'?: Espionage in Her Majesty's Post Office, 1844-45," Canadian Journal of History 22/1 (April 1987): 41-57.

A detailed account of the circumstances of the post office espionage case beginning in 1844. The case began when Guiseppi Mazzini, exiled Italian revolutionary, complained that his mail had been opened and compromised in England.

5626. Noonan, Robert W., Jr. "'Lightning-Look'--Intelligence Interoperability," Military Review 62/1 (January 1982): 43-51.

Summary of field exercises held in the Republic of Korea using division surveillance and electronic warfare.

5627. Norberg, Arthur L. "High-Technology Calculation in the Early 20th Century: Punched Card Machinery in Business and Government," Technology and Culture 31/4 (1990): 753-779.

5628. Noren, J. H. "Statistical Reporting in the States of the Former USSR," Post-Soviet Geography 35/1 (January 1994): 13-37.

5629. Noren, J. H. and R. Watson. "Interrepublican Economic Relations After the Disintegration of the USSR," Soviet Economy 8/2 (April-June 1992): 89-129.

Useful in analyses of intelligence assessments of the USSR in the era.

5630. Norman, Lloyd H. "Westmoreland's J-2," Army 17/5 (May 1967): 21-25.

General William Westmoreland's chief of intelligence was General Joseph McChristian. This laudatory piece recounts some of McChristian's work in Vietnam.

5631. Norman, Michael. "Intelligence in NATO Forward Strategy," RUSI Defence Studies Journal (March 1969): 59-65.

5632. North, Robert. "Perception and Action in the 1914 Crisis," Journal of International Affairs 21 (1967): 103-122.

Examines the strains of conflict between nations in World War I, emphasizing the difficult nature of measuring perceptions and fears. Major sections discuss the outbreak of war in 1914; German perceptions of inadequate strength; German perceptions of British, French and Russian intentions; Russian mobilization; approaching the "upper limits"; and content analysis of perceptions and actions.

5633. Northridge, A. R. "B-29's Against Coke Ovens," <u>Studies in Intelligence</u> 9/2 (Summer 1965).

5634. Northridge, A. R. "Pearl Harbor: Estimating Then and Now," <u>Studies in Intelligence</u> 9/3 (Fall 1965).

5635. Northridge, A. R. "The Selectively Reluctant Informant," <u>Studies in Intelligence</u> 11/2 (Summer 1967).
    Discussion of intelligence targets in Bangkok, Thailand.

5636. Nortrup, Jack. "Nicholas Trist's Mission to Mexico: A Reinterpretation," <u>Southwestern Historical Quarterly</u> 71/3 (January 1968): 321-346.
    An extensive and rich new analysis of Nicholas Trist's work in the consummation of the Treaty of Guadalupe Hidalgo with Mexico during the presidency of James Polk.

5637. Norton, Douglas M. "The Open Secret: The U.S. Navy in the Battle of the Atlantic, April-December 1941," <u>Naval War College Review</u> 26/4 (January-February 1974): 63-83.
    Provides an earlier example of the conflict between the President and the Congress over warmaking powers. Discusses the significance of political relationships between the Executive and Legislative branhes in the US Congress with respect to formal relations with Great Britain in 1941.

5638. Norton, John H. "Russia, China, and Insurgency," <u>Naval War College Review</u> 23/2 (October 1970): 53-68.
    Addresses Communist theory, strategy, and tactics in relation to insurgency. Includes consideration of the divergent approaches to this subject taken by the Soviet Union and the Peoples Republic of China.

5639. Notz, Frank P. "The Future Intelligence Training Environment," <u>Naval Intelligence Professionals Quarterly</u> 9/3 (Summer 1993): 9-10.

5640. Notz, Frank P. "Some Thoughts on Joint Intelligence Training," <u>Defense Intelligence Journal</u> 2/2 (Fall 1993): 167-176.
    The author offers a series of observations on the question of how training should be accomplished without creating new bureaucracies.

5641. Notz, Frank P. "The Culture of Naval Intel: Some Thoughts on the Way Ahead," <u>Naval Intelligence Professionals Quarterly</u> 9/4 (Fall 1993): 1-4.

5642. Notz, Frank P. "The Joy of Naval Intelligence," <u>Naval Intelligence Professionals Quarterly</u> 10/4 (Fall 1994): 12-13.

5643. Notz, Frank P. "The Foundation of Naval Intelligence," Naval Intelligence Professionals Quarterly 11/3 (Summer 1995): 7-9.

5644. Nowak, John E. "Using the Press Clause to Limit Government Speech," Arizona Law Review 30 (Winter 1988): 1-50.
        An essay devoted to the problem of government speech and whether the press clause of the First Amendment can be interpreted to establish principles for restricting government information to the public. Discusses press clause values; prior Supreme Court decisions on the press clause; and use of the press clause to limit government speech.

5645. Nowak, Leonard G. "Division Intelligence Left in the AirLand Battle's Dust?," Military Review 67/11 (November 1987): 52-59.
        Reviews the current status of divisional intelligence units and how such units may more effectively contribute to the future of the Army mission.

5646. Nuechterlein, Donald E. "The Concept of 'National Interest': A Time for New Approaches," Orbis 23/1 (Spring 1979): 73-92.
        Definition of national interest in terms of the homeland, economic well-being, favorable world order, and promotion of values; use of the National-Interest matrix; definition of vital interest; and using the matrix as a planning tool.

5647. Nufer, Harold F. "Four Momentous Events in 1971-72: Catalysts for Reform of the National Security Classification System," Air University Review 28/5 (July-August 1977): 56-63.
        Discusses the executive branch use of secrecy as a national security shield; the Pentagon Papers case and court decisions; Senator Mike Gravel's entrance to the controversy; the role of columnist Jack Anderson; and declassification efforts since 1971.

5648. Nunn, Kenneth B. "The Legality of Covert Action Under Contemporary International Law," La Raza Law Journal 1/2 (Spring 1984): 139-167.
        Lengthy discussion of covert action; a working definition; covert action in Chile; status of covert action under traditional international law; law of the United Nations; and the case of US intervention in Nicaragua.

5649. Nurik, Lester and Robert M. Barrett. "Legality of Guerilla Forces Under the Laws of War," American Journal of International Law 40/3 (July 1946): 563-583.
        Discusses the Brussels Conference; the Hague regulations; the necessity of government of some kind; the Mexican war and the peace treaty of 1848; Mexico in 1865; the US Civil War; the Franco-German war; the Philippine insurrection; the South African war; and World War II.

5650. Nyameko, R. S. "U.S. Bid to Derail South African Trade Union Movement," African Communist 92 (First Quarter 1983): 33-37.

5651. Nye, Joseph S., Jr. "Peering into the Future," Foreign Affairs 73 (July-August 1994): 82-93.

5652. Nye, Wilbur S. "The U.S. Military Telegraph Service," Civil War Times Illustrated 7/7 (1968): 28-34.
      Discussion of the introduction of telegraph services during the Civil War, and the ability of experts to tap into communications.

5653. Nypaver, Stephen, III. "Issues Raised in the Prosecution of an Undercover Fence Operation Conducted by the U.S. Army Criminal Investigation Command," Army Lawyer (April 1982): 1-17.

O

"Oshima...A monument ought later to be erected in his honor..."
(cited in Hitler's Japanese Confidant by Carl Boyd, p. 18)

5654. Oakes, Guy. "The Cold War Ethic: National Security and National Morale," International Journal of Politics, Culture and Society 6/3 (Spring 1993): 379-404.
  Considers the Berlin Crisis; the Soviet atomic bomb; national security and national will; and the propaganda of moral reform.

5655. Oakes, James L. "Judge Gurfein and the Pentagon Papers," Cardozo Law Review 2 (1980): 5-14.
  Discusses leaks of information from the Pentagon in 1971. Federal judge Murray Irwin Gurfein's role in attempts to halt publication of the Pentagon Papers in the New York Times.

5656. Oakes, James L. "The Doctrine of Prior Restraint Since the Pentagon Papers," University of Michigan Journal of Law Reform 15/3 (Spring 1982): 497-519.
  Major sections discuss the Pentagon Papers case facts; preserving the doctrine against prior restraint; specific case examples; prior restraint and the national security exception; and the cases of Marchetti, Snepp and The Progressive.

5657. Oakley, Howard T. "The Riverbank Publications on Cryptology," Cryptologia 2/4 (October 1978): 324-330.

5658. Oakley, Phyllis. "Intelligence and Research in the Department of State," American Intelligence Journal 13/3 (Summer 1992): 21-24.

Discusses INR's role in the intelligence community; INR's three main contributions to foreign policy; INR organization; regional and functional analysis; and coordination.

5659. Oaks, Robert F. "Philadelphia in Exile: The Problem of Loyalty During the American Revolution," Pennsylvania Magazine of History and Biography 96/3 (July 1972): 298-325.

A history of the exiled Quakers during the American revolution and the role of loyalty during the period.

5660. O'Brian, John L. "Uncle Sam's Spy Policies: Safeguarding American Liberty During the War," Forum 61 (April 1919): 407-416.

During World War I, every person was considered a spy chaser, and third attitude was engendered by propaganda about enemies. Emphasis was given to German aliens and immigrants. Wrongs were committed by "amateur detectives."

5661. O'Brian, John L. "Loyalty Tests and Guilt by Association," Harvard Law Review 61 (1948): 592-611.

An annual address to the 71st meeting of the New York Bar Association (1948) with particular emphasis on democratic societies attempted to ferret out foreign agents while preserving democratic principles.

5662. O'Brien, F. W. "Swiss Law and Subversive Groups," Northern Ireland Legal Quarterly 18 (September 1967): 302-312.

5663. O'Brien, Kevin A. "Interfering with Civil Society: CIA and KGB Covert Political Action During the Cold War," International Journal of Intelligence and Counterintelligence 8/4 (Winter 1995): 431-456.

Discusses origins and goals of the CIA and KGB; implementation of CIA and KGB policies; assessment of success; and conclusions.

5664. O'Brien, Kevin A. "South Africa's Evolving Intelligence and Security Structures," International Journal of Intelligence and Counterintelligence 9/2 (Summer 1996): 187-232.

An extensive and detailed discussion of the topic. Major sections discuss South Africa's national security; new structure of the RSA intelligence community; issues impacting on the new intelligence environment; transitional developments; and the prevailing optimism.

5665. O'Brien, Michael J. "Hercules Mulligan, Confidential Agent of George Washington in New York During the Revolution," Journal of the American Irish Historical Society 26 (1927): 96-104.

5666. O'Brien, Rita C. and G. K. Helleiner. "The Political Economy of Information in a Changing Economic Order," International Organization 34/4 (Autumn 1980): 445-470.

Discusses new text styles for moving information in the post-industrial era; changes in the environment of politics; multilateral bargaining; construction of information interdependence; remote satellites; and governmental issues in information dissemination.

5667. O'Broin, Leon. "Dave Neligan, 'The Spy in the Castle,'" Irish Sword 15/61 (1983): 271-276.

An account of David Neligan's Irish police spying activities.   He attempted to break into the British Intelligence system.

5668. O'Callaghan, D. "The Enemy in Our Midst," Nineteenth Century (October 1919).

5669. Occhiogrosse, Paul F. "The Shin Beth Affair: National Security Versus the Rule of Law in the State of Israel," Loyala of Los Angeles International and Comparative Law Journal 11/1 (1989): 67-116.

Summarizes the role of the Shin Beth (Israel's secret internal police) in anti-terrorism.   Discusses the petitions to the Supreme Court, preliminary developments, the Supreme Court decision, analysis and criticism of the decision, post-decision developments, and recommendations for reform.

5670. Occleshaw, M. E. "The 'Stab in the Back'--Myth of Reality?," RUSI Defence Studies Journal 130 (September 1985): 49-54.

5671. O'Connell, Edward P. and John T. Dillaplain. "Nonlethal Concepts: Implications for Air Force Intelligence," Airpower Journal 8/4 (Winter 1994): 26-34.

5672. O'Connell, Gerald F. "Administrative Law - Freedom of Information Act - An Agency's Unpublished Time of Request Cutoff Date for Searching Its File for Records Requested Under the Freedom of Information Act Is Invalid As Unreasonable Unless Exceptional Circumstances Are Shown; All Records in an Agency's Possession, Whether Created by the Agency Itself or by Another Agency, Are 'Agency Records,'" University of Cincinnati Law Review 52 (Summer 1983): 921-935.

Discusses at length the lawsuit brought by former Central Intelligence Agency employee Ralph McGehee to acquire records held by the CIA regarding the religious cult tragedy in Jonestown, Guyana.

5673. O'Connell, Jerome A. "Radar and the U-Boats," U.S. Naval Institute Proceedings 89 (1963): 53-65.

5674. O'Connor, Luke. "The Inclusion-Exclusion Principle and its Applications to Cryptography," Cryptologia 17/1 (January 1993): 63-79.

5675. O'Connor, Raymond G. "Truman: New Powers in Foreign Affairs," Australian Journal of Politics and History 25/3 (1979): 319-326.

5676. O'Daniel, Victor. "Archbishop John Hughes, American Envoy to France (1861)," Catholic Historical Review 3/3 (October 1917).

5677. O'Dea, Anna and Samuel A. Pleasant. "The Case of John Honeyman: Mute Evidence," Proceedings of the New Jersey Historical Society 84/3 (July 1966): 174-181.

5678. Odeen, Phillip A. "Organizing for National Security," International Security 5/1 (Summer 1980): 111-129.
        Discusses the roles of the national security advisor and the National Security Council staff; planning for crises and conflict; and coordination of security policy.

5679. O'Dell, G. W. T. "We Now Have a New Breed of O-2," Marine Corps Gazette 63 (April 1979): 15-16.

5680. Odierna, Lori K. "Criminal Law--In re Motion to Unseal Electronic Surveillance Evidence (990 F.2d 1015 (8th Dir. 1993)): Third Party Access to Government-Acquired Wiretap Evidence," Western New England Law Review 17 (1995): 371-405.

5681. Odom, William E. "Who Controls Whom in Moscow?," Foreign Policy 19 (Summer 1975): 109-123.

5682. Odom, William E. "Staying Ahead in MI Tactical Revolution," Army 32 (October 1982): 174-176+.

5683. Odom, William E. "American Intelligence: Current Problems in Historical Perspective," American Intelligence Journal 9/1 (Summer 1988): 21-23.
        Brief observations of the former director of the National Security Agency concerning the impact of leaks of classified information on the intelligence community.

5684. O'Donnell, James. "Albania's Sigurimi: The Ultimate Agents of Social Control," Problems of Post-Communism 42/6 (November-December 1995): 18-22.
        Reviews the practices of the Albania security services under Soviet KGB domination.

5685. O'Donnell, John. "CIA: Intelligence or Ignorance?," <u>American Mercury</u> 85 (July 1957): 118-120.

A brief discussion of the CIA in the last years of Allen W. Dulles as director. Generally regarded as a popular press publication.

5686. O'Donnell, Thomas A. "Illumination or Elimination of the "Zone of Twilight": Congressional Acquiescence and Presidential Authority in Foreign Affairs?," <u>University of Cincinnati Law Review</u> 51/1 (1982): 95-116.

5687. O'Donnelly, Duque and Hugo Estrada. "Secrecy: Requisite for the Expedition Against England in 1588, Part II," <u>Revista de Hiseria Naval</u> 2/7 (1984): 63-74.

A rare discussion of secrecy in the Latin American historical context.

5688. Oelrich, Ivan. "The Changing Rules of Arms Control Verification: Confidence Is Still Possible," <u>International Security</u> 14/4 (Spring 1990): 176-184.

The author considers the most significant change in arms control verification to be the means for achieving verification, particularly with respect to conventional arms.

5689. Ofri, Arie. "Crisis and Opportunity Forecasting," <u>Orbis</u> 26/4 (Winter 1983): 821-828.

Considers the role and contributions of research in the decisionmaking processes applicable to crisis and opportunity assessments.

5690. Ofri, Arie. "Intelligence and Counterterrorism," <u>Orbis</u> 28/1 (Spring 1984): 41-52.

Discusses United States methods for countering terrorism and the political objectives of terrorism. Also contains recommendations for fighting terrorism.

5691. Ogata, R. Craig. "Understanding Corporate Deviance: The Case of Industrial Espionage," <u>Journal of Security Administration</u> 6/2 (January 1984): 17-29.

Comments on the issues involved in the Hitachi industrial espionage case of 1982. Offers a theory of industrial espionage.

5692. Oglesby, Carl. "The Secret Treaty of Fort Hunt," <u>Covert Action Information Bulletin</u> 35 (Fall 1990): 8-16.

5693. Ognev, Grigori. "Propaganda and Men's Good Will," <u>Soviet Literature</u> 12 (December 1978): 157-161.

5694. O'Halpin, Eunan. "Sir Warren Fisher and the Coalition, 1919-1922," <u>Historical Journal</u> 24/4 (1981): 907-928.

As part of the larger discussion of Fisher's reorganization of the British Treasury, there is discussion of inquiries into expenditures of the Secret Service Branch.

5695. O'Halpin, Eunan. "The Secret Service Vote and Ireland, 1868-1922," Irish Historical Studies 23 (November 1983): 348-353.

5696. O'Halpin, Eunan. "Intelligence Fact and Fiction," Intelligence and National Security 2/4 (October 1987): 168-171.
This is a review article concerning Nigel West's GCHQ: The Secret Wireless War, 1900-1986 and Phillip Knightley's The Second Oldest Profession.

5697. O'Halpin, Eunan. "Intelligence and Security in Ireland, 1922-45," Intelligence and National Security 5/1 (January 1990): 50-83.
Major sections consider intelligence organization in the civil war; army intelligence, 1923-38; the police special branch; techniques; Anglo-Irish security liaison; the Communist movement; British intelligence in Ireland, 1922-38; security organization and liaison, 1938-45; the Axis legations in Dublin; signals intelligence; German-IRA cooperation; British intelligence in Ireland, 1939-45; and conclusions.

5698. Olcott, Martha B. "The Basmachi or Freeman's Revolt in Turkestan 1918-1924," Soviet Studies 33/3 (July 1981): 352-369.
A detailed discussion of the Soviet takeover of Central Asia after World War II and the resistance movements that formed in response.

5699. O'Leary, Jeffrey. "Surprise and Intelligence: Towards a Clearer Understanding," Airpower Journal 8/1 (Spring 1994): 34-51.
Discusses the nature, definition, and potential for strategic surprise; historical overview of intelligence and surprise; and conclusions and recommendations.

5700. Oliver, S. P. "Military Espionage in France," Bibliography Facsimiles Quarterly 187 (April 1898).
A rare bibliographic discussion from the late nineteenth century.

5701. Oliver, Kay. "Analyzing Economic Intelligence," Studies in Intelligence 36/1 (Spring 1992): 23-27.

5702. Olmsted, Kathryn. "'An American Conspiracy': The Post-Watergate Press and the CIA," Journalism History 19/2 (1993): 51-58.

5703. Olney, Claude W. "The Secret World of the Industrial Spy," Business and Society Review 64 (Winter 1988): 28-32.

Emphasizes corporate espionage and the use of advanced technologies to obtain trade secrets and other proprietary information.

5704. Olsen, Frank H. "Great Hoaxes," Infantry 59/6 (November-December 1969): 44-47.
Brief accounts of famous deception plans of the Civil War and World War II.

5705. Olsmith, Edwin S., Jr. "Midway Revisited," Signal 31 (November-December 1976): 36-39.

5706. Olson, Mancur, Jr. "The Economics of Target Selection for the Combined Bomber Offensive," Journal of the Royal United Service Institution 107 (November 1962): 308-314.

5707. O'Meara, Richard L. "Applying the Critical Jurisprudence of International Law to the Case Concerning Military and Paramilitary Activities in and Against Nicaragua," Virginia Law Review 71/7 (October 1985): 1183-1210.
Adopts David Kennedy's view of the 'critical' approach to legal analysis of international relations. Describes the proceedings of the case in the title at the International Court of Justice and applies critical theories to the legal arguments. Supports the Kennedy view that "international law discourse is a conversation without content."

5708. O'Meara, Stephen P. "On Getting Wired: Considerations Regarding Obtaining and Maintaining Wiretaps and Bugs," Creighton Law Review 26 (April 1993): 729-749.
Addresses four areas of concern with respect to government electronic surveillance: (1) exhaustion of other methods of investigation; (2) achievement of the objectives of electronic surveillance; (3) minimizing authorized surveillance; and (4) sealing the product of electronic surveillance.

5709. Omestad, Thomas. "Psychology and the CIA: Leaders on the Couch," Foreign Policy 95 (Summer 1994): 105-122.
An analysis of CIA reports concerning the psychological strengths and weaknesses of foreign leaders, such as Jean-Bertrand Aristide, Kim Jong Il, Vladimir Zhirinovsky and others. Sections discuss the reach from biography to psychoanalysis, the sources of information and expertise involved in leader analysis, sources outside the intelligence community, and the problem of tabloid profiling.

5710. Onate, Benjamin F. "What Did Truman Say About CIA?," Studies in Intelligence 17/3 (Fall 1973): 9-11.

5711. Onate, Benjamin F. "Catch-as-Catch-Can Operations," Studies in Intelligence 20/4 (Winter 1976): 27-29.
A field case officer discusses his improvisations.

5712. O'Neal, John R. "The Rationality of Decision Making During International Crisis," Polity 20/4 (Summer 1988): 598-622.
Following in the genre of research on international crises, this article suggests that policy officials set up procedures for national decision making for addressing crises. Values held by such officials and their staffs are a central factor in international relations.

5713. O'Neill, James E. "Secrecy and Disclosure: The Declassification Program of the National Archives and Records Service," Prologue: Quarterly Journal of the National Archives 5/1 (Spring 1973): 43-45.
A brief statement of the progress of the National Archives to declassify documents in the public interest.

5714. Oney, Earnest R. "The Eyes and Ears of the Shah," Intelligence Quarterly 1/4 (February 1986): 1-3.

5715. Ong, Chit C. "Major General William Dobbie and the Defence of Malaya, 1935-38," Journal of Southeast Asian Studies 17/2 (September 1986): 282-306.
A study of British failure to plan for attack on Singapore.

5716. Onsky, S. "The USA-Latin America: A Difficult Dialogue," International Affairs (USSR) 7 (1974): 72-81.
Describes from a Soviet perspective the 4th Session of the Organization of American States' General Assembly. Mentions Central Intelligence Agency efforts to unify all Latin American armies and the support of the United States for "ultra-reactionary militaries."

5717. Oommen, B. J. and J. R. Zgierski. "Breaking Substitution Cyphers Using Stochastic Automata," IEEE Transactions on Pattern Analysis and Machine Intelligence 15 (February 1993): 185-193.

5718. Oppenheim, A. C. "The Eyes of the Lord," Journal of the American Oriental Society 88/1 (January-March 1968): 173-180.
Discusses the formation and development of intelligence services in China during the time of the emperors. God, according to accounts, sent angels to earth to find the sinners and to report activities to Him. Establishes the earliest forms of intelligence in recorded history.

5719. Oppenheim, Jerrold. "The Coaxial Wiretap: Privacy and the Cable," Yale Review of Law and Social Action 2/3 (Spring 1972): 282-288.

Discusses legal concerns for invasions of privacy through breaches of cable systems.

5720. O'Reilly, James T. "Regaining a Confidence: Protection of Business Confidential Data Through Reform of the Freedom of Information Act," Administrative Law Review 34/2 (Spring 1982): 263-313.

A comprehensive review of the problem of business secrets protection under the FOIA. Sections discuss the search for a standard; the right to notice prior to agency disclosure; airing the submitter's objections; the question of introducing to a court documents other than submitter's letters; recommendations.

5721. O'Reilly, James T. "Advisors and Secrets: The Role of Agency Confidentiality in the Federal Advisory Committee Act," Northern Kentucky Law Review 13/1 (1986): 27-49.

Discusses confidentiality problems with advisory committees in the Executive Branch. Major sections include protectability of members' input to an agency; protectability of agency documents going to advisers; the special case of business information; the role of the press; the role of perceptions.

5722. O'Reilly, Kenneth. "A New Deal for the FBI: The Roosevelt Administration, Crime Control, and National Security," Journal of American History 69/3 (December 1982): 638-658.

The evolution of the FBI to a crime fighting organization during the Roosevelt administrations. Gradual evolution of the FBI into significant domestic intelligence role.

5723. O'Reilly, Kenneth. "The FBI and the Origins of McCarthyism," Historian 45/3 (May 1983): 372-393.

A look at FBI and its involvement with the origins of McCarthyism.

5724. O'Reilly, Kenneth. "The Roosevelt Administration and Legislative-Executive Conflict: The FBI vs. the Dies Committee," Congress & Presidency 10/1 (Spring 1983): 79-88.

5725. O'Reilly, Kenneth. "The FBI and the Civil Rights Movement During the Kennedy Years--From the Freedom Rides to Albany," Journal of Southern History 54/2 (May 1988): 201-232.

A detailed exploration of the Federal Bureau of Investigation's inquiries and intelligence operations employed during the 1960s civil rights movement during the presidency of John Kennedy.

5726. Orentlicher, Diane F. "Snepp v. United States: The CIA Secrecy Agreement and the First Amendment," Columbia Law Review 81/3 (April 1981): 662-706.

An extensive discussion of the United States Supreme Court case which denied to Frank Snepp, former Central Intelligence Agency case officer and author of Decent Interval, profits resulting from alleged violation of a secrecy oath. Discusses prior restraint and public employment, CIA prepublication review procedures and a suggested less restrictive alternative. The profits of this book were seized by the government.

5727. Orfield, Lester B. "Wiretapping in Federal Criminal Cases," Texas Law Review 42/7 (October 1964): 983-1005.

A comprehensive review of federal wiretapping law. Covers pre-1928 wiretapping; the Olmstead decision as a turning point case; the Federal Communications Act; admissibility in federal cases; and various criminal justice procedures relevant to wiretaps.

5728. Organ, J. W. "Counter-C^3 Targeting Procedures," Marine Corps Gazette (September 1981): 49-53.

Proposes a 10-step program for integrating counter-C^3 targets into a commander's plan for fire support.

5729. Orionova, Galina. "Escape from Boredom: A Defector's Story," Atlantic Monthly (November 1980): 42-50.

The author's defection from the Soviet Union, based on her severe disappointment with the Soviet system and society.

5730. Orlov, Alexander. "Ghastly Secrets of Stalin's Powers," Life (April 1953): 10-12, 115-123 (April 6); 160-162, 164, 166, 168, 170 (April 13); 142-144, 146, 148, 150, 153, 154, 156, 159 (April 20); 145-146, 148-152, 157-158, (April 20).

This magazine is considered a popular press publication, but in view of the unique aspects of Orlov's public appearance, having lived in hiding in the US from 1938 to 1953 of a high Soviet intelligence officer, the material may prove useful in research of defectors. Orlov was the highest ranking intelligence operative of the Soviet intelligence system to defect up to 1953.

5731. Orlov, Alexander. "The Theory and Practice of Soviet Intelligence," Studies in Intelligence 7/1 (Spring 1963).

5732. Ormerod, David and David Ward. "The Bond Game," London Magazine 5/2 (1965): 41-55.

Generally considered a popular press publication.

5733. Ornstein, Jacob. "The Articulation of Babel," Studies in Intelligence 4/3 (Fall 1960).

Discussion of language training.

5734. Orton, J. Douglas and Jamie L. Callahan. "Important 'Folk Theories' in Intelligence Reorganization," International Journal of Intelligence and Counterintelligence 8/4 (Winter 1995): 411-429.

Major sections discuss management structures referenced by the Senate's 1992 reorganization hearings; rise of the Ames case in early 1994; emergence of the Aspin Commission in September 1994; resignation of James Woolsey in December 1994; formalization of the Aspin Commission in January 1995; and extension of momentum past the Commission in February 1995.

5735. Osborn, Earl D. "An Argument Against Espionage," Bulletin of the Atomic Scientists 38/6 (June 1982): 69.

The title speaks for the contents. A call for "no more espionage."

5736. Osborne, Brian. "New Players--Same Game," Queen's Quarterly 100/2 (Summer 1993): 415-420.

A book review essay concerning Peter Hopkirk's book, The Great Game: The Struggle for Empire in Central Asia.

5737. Oseth, John M. "Intelligence Controls and the National Interest," Parameters: Journal of the U.S. Army War College 11/4 (December 1981): 34-42.

Major sections discuss the problem of intelligence in a democracy; national security as a focal point; protecting citizens from intrusive government; American ideals, adherence to constitutional design; and future prospects.

5738. Oseth, John M. "Intelligence and Low-Intensity Conflict," Naval War College Review 37/6 (November-December 1984): 19-36.

Considers the intelligence challenges in low-intensity conflict; pre-commitment support; support for security assistance missions; support for US forces engaged in combat; impediments to meeting the challenge; and general prescriptions for application.

5739. O'Shaughnessy, Gary W. "Air Force HUMINT," American Intelligence Journal 14/1 (Autumn-Winter 1992-1993): 17-20.

A basic discussion of human intelligence; scientific and technical intelligence; foreign material acquisition; targeting; plans and intentions; cost; Air Force HUMINT; organization; and future.

5740. O'Shea, Cornelius. "A Framework for the Study of Deception," American Intelligence Journal 12/1 (Winter 1991): 34-39.

Provides a survey of some of the deception literature and coherence to the various aspects of military deception. Covers cognitive processes; categories, levels and fields; decision-making, planning and implementation; signals/noise; and the target environment and deception application.

5741. Osmundson, Anthony D. "Fourth Amendment Application to Semi-Public Areas: Smayda v. United States," Hastings Law Journal 17/4 (May 1966): 835-842.

A case note on the Ninth Circuit decision in Smayda involving clandestine surveillance by police of public rest rooms.

5742. Ostrom, Charles W., Jr. and Robin F. Marra. "U.S. Defense Spending and the Soviet Estimate," American Political Science Review 80/3 (September 1986): 819-842.

An intricate and detailed discussion of US and Soviet defense spending models, including the assumptions upon which the models are based.

5743. O'Sullivan, Gerry. "Acid Tests," Humanist 51 (March-April 1991): 35.

Brief comments on the Central Intelligence Agency and the use of psychotropic drugs and LSD.

5744. Oswald, Alison L. "William Frederick Friedman: A Pictorial Essay," Cryptologia 16/3 (July 1992): 257-264.

Numerous photographs of the legendary cryptologist.

5745. O'Toole, George. "Harmonica Bugs, Cloaks, and Silver Boxes: Eavesdropping in Post-Watergate America," Harper's 250 (June 1975): 36-39.

Discusses various applications and implications of eavesdropping devices.

5746. O'Toole, G. J. A. "Our Man in Havana: The Paper Trail of Some Spanish War Spies," IQ: Intelligence Quarterly 2/2 (1986): 1-3.

5747. O'Toole, George J. A. "Benjamin Franklin: American Spymaster or British Mole?," International Journal of Intelligence and Counterintelligence 3/1 (Spring 1989): 45-53.

Asks and answers a series of questions about Ben Franklin's role in the American revolution: Was the Hell Fire club an instrument of the British secret service?; Was Benjamin Franklin a member of the Hell Fire Club?; Was Franklin an agent of the British secret service?; and, did Franklin have his own highly-placed agents in London?

5748. O'Toole, George J. A. "Kahn's Law: A Universal Principle of Intelligence?," International Journal of Intelligence and Counterintelligence 4/1 (Spring 1990): 39-46.

Offers an interpretation of a principle put forth by author David Kahn: emphasizing the offensive tends toward a neglect of intelligence. Major sections discuss the value of Kahn's law; starting the secret service; other examples; and exceptions to the rule.

5749. Ott, Bill. "Quick Bibs: Spy Novels in the 90s," <u>American Libraries</u> 23 (May 1992): 416.

A brief recognition of selected espionage novels of the 1990s.

5750. Ott, Melvin. "Shaking Up the CIA," <u>Foreign Policy</u> 93 (Winter 1993-1994): 132-151.

Considers several issues involved in the production of intelligence analysis by the CIA's Directorate of Intelligence. In particular, considers problems of bureaucratization, organizational design, communications with policy makers, and politicization.

5751. Oudes, Bruce. "The CIA and Africa," <u>Africa Report</u> 19/4 (July 1974): 49-52.

Discusses CIA operations in Africa as described by the Marchetti and Marks book, <u>The CIA and the Cult of Intelligence</u>.

5752. Oursler, Fulton, Jr. "Secret Treason," <u>American Heritage</u> 42/8 (August 1991): 52-68.

5753. Outerbridge, Richard. "Cryptographic Features of the UNIX Operating System," <u>Cryptologia</u> 6/3 (July 1982): 253-257.

5754. Outerbridge, Richard. "A Pedagogical Cipher," <u>Cryptologia</u> 6/4 (October 1982): 339-345.

5755. Outerbridge, Richard. "DEA and LUCIFER Available on COMPUSERVE," <u>Cryptologia</u> 9/3 (July 1985): 238-239.

5756. Outerbridge, Richard. "Some Design Criteria for Feistel-Cipher Key Schedules," <u>Cryptologia</u> 10/3 (July 1986): 142-156.

5757. Outerbridge, Richard. "Cadbury Code Confidential," <u>Cryptologia</u> 10/4 (October 1986): 225-226.

5758. Overton, David W. "The DI 10 Years After Reorganization: Stresses, Successes, and the Future," <u>Studies in Intelligence</u> 36/5 (Spring 1992): 45-54.

Major sections consider the invention of the 1981 Directorate of Intelligence reorganization at CIA; 1982-84 and getting beyond the words; the path to today; the age of ADP; costs and benefits; looking ahead; and applying lessons from the past.

5759. Overy, Richard J. "The German Pre-War Aircraft Production Plans: November 1936-April 1939," <u>English Historical Review</u> 90/357 (October 1975): 778-797.

A detailed history of the development of the German Luftwaffe before 1939, including the structure of German aircraft production planning.

5760. Overy, Richard J. "German Air Strength 1933 to 1939: A Note," Historical Journal 27/2 (June 1984): 465-471.
Argues that German air strength was grossly exaggerated, and that exaggeration resulted from weak data and the complexities of German aircraft production. Useful in analyses of the dynamics of inaccuracy in estimating war production efforts.

5761. Owen, Stephen T. "Eavesdropping at the Government's Discretion: First Amendment Implications of the National Security Eavesdropping Power," Cornell Law Review 56/1 (November 1970): 161-170.
Discusses the deterrent effect of potential eavesdropping on freedom of expression, the overbreadth of Section 2511(3) and conclusions regarding wiretapping.

5762. Owen, Tom. "Forensic Audio and Video: Theory and Applications," Journal of the Audio Engineering Society 36 (January-February 1988): 34-41.
Includes discussion of forensic audio and video applications in espionage detection and investigation.

5763. Owens, Ira C. "Revolution in MI," Army (October 1992): 165-167.
Part of a continuing series of articles on Army intelligence changes.

5764. Owens, Ira C. "Intelligence: A Decisive Edge," Army (October 1993): 172-174, 176, 178.
Part of a continuing series of articles on Army intelligence changes.

5765. Owens, Ira C. "Army Intelligence in Transition," American Intelligence Journal 14/3 (Autumn-Winter 1993-1994): 17-20.
Part of a continuing series of articles on Army intelligence changes.

5766. Owens, Mackubin T., Jr. "Arms Control: Tracking Soviet Violations," Journal of Contemporary Studies 6 (Fall 1983): 101-113.

5767. Owens, Robert L. "Intelligence: The Police Dimension," Military Police Journal 16 (September 1966): 7-9, (October 1966): 18-21.

5768. Owsley, Frank L., Jr. "British and Indian Activities in Spanish West Florida During the War of 1812," Florida Historical Quarterly 46/2 (1967): 111-123.
Discusses the British loss of control over Florida, including the British intelligence blunders during the War of 1812.

5769. Owsley, Harriet C. "Henry Shelton Sanford and Federal Surveillance Abroad, 1861-1865," <u>Mississippi Valley Historical Review</u> 48/2 (September 1961): 210-228.

     Sanford was Abraham Lincoln's minister to Belgium who devised a spy system to aid the Union in the Civil War.

5770. Oxford, Edward. "World of Mirrors," <u>American History Illustrated</u> 24/10 (October 1989): 34-45.

     Considers the plot to assassinate President John F. Kennedy in terms of the theory of the lone assassin, Lee Oswald, versus conspiracy theory involving several other players such as the CIA.

5771. Oxford, Edward. "Intrigue in the Islands," <u>American History Illustrated</u> 26/3 (March 1991): 50-66.

5772. Oxford, Edward. "Prelude in the Pacific," <u>American History Illustrated</u> 26/4 (April 1991): 52-58, 60-63.

5773. Oxford, Edward. "Our Greatest Land Battle," <u>American History Illustrated</u> 30/2 (February 1995): 52-61.

     Discusses the World War II Battle of the Bulge, including the intelligence aspects. Contains photographs.

P

"...and that his name was Penkovsky."
<u>(The Spy Who Saved the World</u>
by Jerrold Schecter and Peter Deriabin, p. 420)

5774. Pacepa, Ion M. "The Defector's Story," <u>Washingtonian</u> 21/3 (December 1985): 168-183.

Examines the Zweibon decision regarding Fourth Amendment warrant requirements for executive-ordered wiretaps in national security cases.

5775. Packard, Wyman H. "The Naval Attache," <u>U.S. Naval Institute Proceedings</u> 91/4 (March 1965): 130-133.

Discusses the roles of naval attaches in foreign countries, communications with other nation navies, arrangements for clearances for US ships, and naval advisor to embassy personnel.

5776. Packard, Wyman H. "A Briefing on Naval Intelligence," <u>All Hands</u> 591 (April 1966): 12-18.

5777. Packard, Wyman H. "Intelligence and the Navy," <u>Naval Review</u> (1968): 202-217.

Argues that the Navy has the leading intelligence service among all the armed services. Major sections address questions of who participates in Navy intelligence, who receives the products of naval intelligence, and complaints about the value of naval intelligence.

5778. Packard, Wyman H. "The History of the ONI," <u>Naval Intelligence Professionals Quarterly</u> 3/3 (Fall 1987): 2-3; 4/1 (Winter 1988): 6-11; 4/2 (Spring 1988): 3-6; 4/3 (Fall 1988): 8-12.

5779. Packard, Wyman H. "The Origin of Naval Intelligence Professionals," <u>Naval Intelligence Professionals Quarterly</u> 5/3 (Fall 1989): 17-18.

5780. Padover, Saul K. "Japanese Race Propaganda," <u>Public Opinion Quarterly</u> 7 (Summer 1943): 191-204.
    Views Japanese propaganda techniques in the context of increasing national and racial cleavages throughout the world. Major sections discuss Japanese claims to world domination; Britain and America as scapegoats; bait for Filopinos; China as a special puzzle; India for Indians; Palestine for Arabs; and democracy as antidote.

5781. Padover, Saul K. "Psychological Warfare," <u>Headline Series</u> 86 (March-April 1951): 3-56.

5782. Pady, Donald S. and Laura S. Kline. "Finger Counting and the Identifications of James VI's Secret Agents," <u>Cryptologia</u> 4/3 (July 1980): 140-149.

5783. Page, C. D. "We Put Intelligence to Work," <u>National Guard</u> 9 (December 1955): 5-6.

5784. Page, Don. "Tommy Stone and Psychological Warfare in World War Two: Transforming a POW Liability into an Asset," <u>Journal of Canadian Studies</u> 16/3-4 (Fall-Winter 1981): 110-120.

5785. Page, Helena P. "Long-Range Forecasting in the Pentagon," <u>World Today</u> 38/7-8 (July-August 1982): 275-281.
    Difficulties in Defense Department forecasting and planning have altered the manner of evaluation. Defense categorizes "future worlds" in four subgroups: World A (muted bi-polarity); World B (super-power conflict); World C (super-power cooperation); World D (devolution of power).

5786. Pahl, Thomas L. "The Dilemmas of a Civil Libertarian: Francis Biddle and the Smith Act," <u>Journal of the Minnesota Academy of Science</u> 34 (1967).

5787. Pahl, Thomas L. "The G-String Conspiracy, Political Reprisal or Armed Revolt? The Minnesota Trotskyite Trial," <u>Labor History</u> 8/1 (Winter 1967): 30-52.
    Considers the applications of the Smith Act of 1940 as a weapon against the Socialist Workers Party in Minneapolis and St. Paul, Minnesota.

5788. Paige, Byron. "Make the Most of Your Prisoners," Military Review 22/10 (October 1942): 44-45.

Discusses the most effective methods for acquiring information from prisoners of war.

5789. Paige, Emmett, Jr. and Frank B. Horton, III. "Intelligence & Technology: A New Era, Introductory Remarks," American Intelligence Journal 15/2 (Autumn-Winter 1994): 6-7.

An overview of the entire issue devoted to intelligence and technology. Discusses three challenges to military intelligence: demands generated by the international system; constraints imposed by the resource environment; and opportunities offered by technological change.

5790. Paine, Christopher. "Admiral Inman's Tidal Wave," Bulletin of the Atomic Scientists 38/3 (March 1982): 3-6.

Discusses then incoming deputy director of CIA Inman's approach to the relationship between science and national security.

5791. Paine, Christopher. "Secrets," Bulletin of the Atomic Scientists 38/4 (April 1982): 11-16.

An abstract of his book on the subject. A detailed survey of the Reagan administration's efforts to narrow the public's access to information about government actions in the name of national security.

5792. Paine, Lynn S. "Corporate Policy and the Ethics of Competitor Intelligence Gathering," Journal of Business Ethics 10/6 (June 1991): 423-436.

Discusses the growth of competitor intelligence gathering; the darker side of gathering intelligence; ethics and the competitor orientation of strategy; questionable methods of acquiring intelligence; the dearth of corporate guidance; and the risks of corporate silence.

5793. Painter, Jonathan W. "A Judicial Approach to Executive Foreign Affairs Powers: The Road Not Taken in Regan v. Wald," Boston College International and Comparative Law Journal 8/1 (Winter 1985): 181-204.

Discusses inherent foreign affairs powers of the executive, Youngstown Sheet & Tube Co. v. Sawyer, development of the tests for implied presidential powers, effect of the President's failure to follow procedure, and analysis of options open to a court in resolving the situation posed by Wald.

5794. Palay, Marc. "The Fourth Amendment and Judicial Review of Foreign Intelligence Wiretapping: Zweibon v. Mitchell," George Washington Law Review 45/1 (November 1976): 55-99.

A case note in consideration of charges by the Jewish Defense League that the Justice Department wiretapped JDL headquarters without a warrant, thereby violating the Fourth Amendment. Government asserted a right to tap based on presidential power to conduct foreign affairs.

5795. Paleski, Z. "Psychological Aspects of Surprise," Voyennaya Mysl 7 (1971): 102-109.

5796. Palmer, Bruce, Jr. "US Intelligence and Vietnam," Studies in Intelligence 28/5 (1984): 33-47.

A report on the US Army's dissent on the extent of North Vietnamese commitment to carry on the Vietnam war. This was a special edition of the journal. Articles in this edition have not been listed by the Central Intelligence Agency among declassified items available for public access.

5797. Palmer, Robert E. "The Confrontation of the Legislative and Executive Branches: An Examination of the Constitutional Balance of Powers of the Attorney General," Pepperdine Law Review 11 (1984): 331-389.

Within the broader discussion of the topic, this case note observes areas within which presidents have claimed executive privilege to control information.

5798. Palmer, Stephanie. "Tightening Secrecy Law: The Official Secrets Act of 1989," Public Law (Summer 1990): 243-256.

Emphasizes the selective enforcement of the Official Secrets Act and proposals to fix the problems associated with fair enforcement.

5799. Paltsits, Victor H. "The Use of Invisible Ink for Secret Writing During the American Revolution," Bulletin of the New York Public Library 39 (May 1935): 361-364.

5800. Panizzi, A. "Post-Office Espionage," North British Review 2 (1844): 257-295.

This is one of the oldest article in this collection. See also item by Nathaniel Hawthorne, same year. It considers the scandal in the British Post Office over allegations by exiled Italian revolutionary Guiseppe Mazzini that mail had been opened and compromised.

5801. Pannoni, Gregory A. "Overthrow of Allende: An Analysis of U.S. Involvement," Towson State Journal of International Affairs 13/2 (Spring 1979): 97-115.

5802. Panoff, Kyrill. "Murder on Waterloo Bridge: The Case of Georgi Markov," Encounter 53 (November 1979): 15-21.

Suggests that Georgi Markoff was murdered in 1978 by Bulgarian intelligence agents for his participation in exposing the ills of Bulgaria through Radio Free Europe.

5803.   Paone, Rocco M.   "Soviet Policy in Southern Africa," American Intelligence Journal 5/2 (July 1983).

5804.   Paone, Rocco M.   "China's Seapower," American Intelligence Journal 6/2 (July 1984).

5805.   Paone, Rocco M.   "Strategic Minerals in Southern Africa," American Intelligence Journal 6/3 (October 1984).

5806.   Paone, Rocco M.   "The Soviet Union and Espionage: An Overview," American Intelligence Journal 7/1 (June 1985): 18-22.

5807.   Paone, Rocco M.   "The New Chinese Navy--Is It Blue Water Yet?," American Intelligence Journal 7/3 (January 1986).

5808.   Papandreou, Andreas.   "Greece: An American Problem," Massachusetts Review 12/4 (1971): 655-671.

5809.   Papandreou, Andreas.   "The Takeover of Greece," Monthly Review 24 (December 1972): 13-22.
        Reflects the author's perspectives on US initiatives to influence the direction of internal affairs in Greece following World War II. Includes some discussion of the CIA efforts to establish an intelligence service.

5810.   Papenfuse, Edward C., Jr.   "Economic Analysis and Loyalist Strategy During the American Revolution: Robert Alexander's Remark on the Economy of the Peninsula or Eastern Shore of Maryland," Maryland History Review 68/2 (1973): 173-195.
        The title captures the main topics, but the piece includes mention of the successes of the loyalist intelligence network for acquiring information.

5811.   Paquet, C.   "Le 2e Bureau en Campagne," Revue Militaire Francaise 22 & 23 (1923 and 1924): 83-102; 181-201.

5812.   Parish, John C.   "Intelligence Work at First Army Headquarters," Historical Outlook 11/6 (June 1921): 213-217.
        The author, an experienced military intelligence officer, describes training and practices of intelligence personnel during World War I.

5813.   Park, Choon-Ho.   "The 50-Mile Military Boundary Zone of North Korea," American Journal of International Law 72/4 October 1978): 866-874.
        Discusses in part North Korea's reasoning regarding the extension of her territorial waters to defend against invasion and espionage.

5814. Park, E. "A Phantom Division Played a Role in Germany's Defeat," Smithsonian 16 (April 1985): 138-140+.

A history of the US 603rd Engineer Camouflage Battalion, 23rd headquarters Special Troops.

5815. Parker, Daniel M. "The Empty Cockpit," U.S. Naval Institute Proceedings 110/8 (1984): 38-44.

5816. Parker, Frederick D. "The Unsolved Messages of Pearl Harbor," Cryptologia 15/4 (October 1991): 295-313.

5817. Parker, John. "What Lies Behind the Modesty of Interpol?," Eastern Journal of International Law 3/3 (October 1971): 239-242.

From the formation of Interpol in 1946 the organization has gathered a sizeable mythology. This article attempts to set the record straight by laying out Interpol's constitution, brief representative cases, organization and operations. Police forces of 106 countries contribute to Interpol.

5818. Parker, Julius. "US Army Intelligence Center and School--Meeting the Tactical Intelligence Needs of Commanders in the Field," American Intelligence Journal 9/1 (March 1988).

5819. Parker, R. B. "The June War: Whose Conspiracy?," Journal of Palestine Studies 31/4 (Summer 1992): 5-21.

A summary of the significant conspiracy theories regarding the June 1967 Arab-Israeli war.

5820. Parker, Reginald. "The Right to Go Abroad: To Have and To Hold a Passport," Virginia Law Review 40/7 (November 1954): 853-874.

A discussion of freedom of emigration and immigration in their historical contexts; emigration and democratic theory; current US State Department policy; legality of the State Department position; and the inadequacy of statutory basis for US government policy.

5821. Parker, Richard B. "Prisoners of a Concept: Cultural Myopia and the Role of Education," Air University Review 32/2 (January-February 1981): 52-58.

Covers the formation of the Israeli Agranat Commission to inquire into misconceptions of the Egyptians prior to the 1967 war which led to surprise attack. Discusses the nature of misconceptions in the Israeli intelligence functions and the lessons to be learned from the Israeli failures and repairs to intelligence operations.

5822. Parker, Richard B. "Working With the Soviets: Expectations and Warnings," Air University Review 32/6 (September-October 1981): 98-102.

Discusses the difficulties the Soviets had in maintaining strong relationships and influence in Third World countries. Explores the case of Egyptian-Soviet arms sales, Soviet inflexibility, failure of Soviet cultural acceptance, and the demise of Soviet influence in Egypt.

5823. Parker, Russell D. "Historical Interpretations of the Spanish Intrigue in Tennessee: A Study," East Tennessee Historical Society's Publications 58-59 (1986-1987): 39-62.

5824. Parkinson, Russell J. "United States Signal Corps Balloons, 1871-1902," Military Affairs 24/4 (Winter 1960-1961): 189-202.

5825. Parks, Wallace. "Secrecy and the Public Interest in Military Affairs," George Washington Law Review 26/1 (October 1957): 23-77.
      Argues that open government should serve as the general principle upon which exceptions to the principle are carefully made and with appropriate safeguards. Discusses civil and military relations, military decisions, and public affairs; and the uses and limits of information security.

5826. Parrish, Michael E. "Cold War Justice: The Supreme Court and the Rosenbergs," American Historical Review 82/4 (October 1977): 805-842.
      This article provides new analysis of the Rosenberg case and addresses issues raised, and the conflict resulting from litigation.

5827. Parrish, Michael E. "Justice Douglas and the Rosenberg Case: A Rejoinder," Cornell Law Review 70/6 (August 1985): 1048-1057.
      The author counters the criticisms of his article on the subject (see previous citation). Agrees that Justice Douglas was neither the villain nor the hero of the Rosenberg espionage case.

5828. Parrot, Bruce. "Technological Progress and Soviet Politics," Survey 2 (Spring 1977-1978): 39-60.

5829. Parrow, Kathleen A. "Neither Treason Nor Heresy: Use of Defense Arguments to Avoid Forfeiture During the French Wars of Religion," Sixteenth Century Journal 22 (Winter 1991): 705-716.

5830. Parry, Clive. "Legislatures and Secrecy," Harvard Law Review 67/5 (March 1954): 737-785.
      Lengthy and detailed essay on the interplay between the executive and legislative branches in democratic societies with emphasis on British security practices before and during World War II. Major sections discuss the doctrine of privilege as a security device; and the Official Secrets Act.

5831. Parry, D. L. L. "Clemenceau, Caillaux and the Political Use of Intelligence," Intelligence and National Security 9/3 (July 1994): 472-494.

Argues that the rise of George Clemenceau resulted from a manipulation of discontent in 1917, thus casting Joseph Caillaux as a villain and Clemenceau as hero. Civilian and military intelligence services in France supplied journalists and politicians with information necessary to introduce the hero and the villain to public attention.

5832. Parry, Robert and Peter Kornbluh. "Iran-Contra's Untold Story," Foreign Policy 72 (Fall 1988): 3-30.

Argues that the Reagan Administration mislead the American people about the leftist revolution in El Salvador and Nicaragua for the purpose of reshaping perceptions about America's role in Central America.

5833. Parsons, Charles J. "G-2 Operations in Combat," Military Review 26/7 (July 1946): 24-26.

Recounts the work of the 102d Infantry Division intelligence unit in World War II. Covers operations, organization, attached teams, scouting and patrolling, public relations, terrain studies, maps and map issue, and cavalry reconnaissance.

5834. Parsons, Lynn H. "The Mysterious Mr. Digges," William and Mary Quarterly 22/3 (July 1965): 486-492.

Considers the questions and circumstances surrounding the role of Thomas A. Digges in the American revolution. Benjamin Franklin believed Digges was a double agent for the British, but George Washington supported Digges.

5835. Paschall, Rod. "Marxist Counterinsurgencies," Parameters: Journal of the U.S. Army War College 16/2 (Summer 1986): 2-15.

Discusses the Marxist counterinsurgency era of the 1980s. Dispels myths about insurgencies and examines specific examples in Angola, Mozambique, Ethiopia, Afghanistan, Kampuchea, and Nicaragua.

5836. Passas, Nikos. "Structural Sources of International Crime--Policy Implications from the BCCI Affair," Crime, Law and Social Change 20/4 (December 1993): 293-309.

5837. Paschall, Rod. "Special Operations in Korea," Conflict 7/2 (1987): 155-178.

A detailed examination of partisan operations in Korea.

5838. Paschall, Rod. "Deception for St. Mihiel: 1918," Studies in Intelligence 32/3 (Fall 1988).

5839. Paschall, Rod. "Deception for St. Mihiel, 1918," Intelligence and National Security 5/3 (July 1990): 158-175.

Discusses an intended deception plan by an American staff officer in World War I to redirect German forces.

5840. Pate, John R., Jr. "The Role of Secrecy in the Conduct of Foreign Policy," Proceedings of the American Society of International Law 66/4 (September 1972): 61-78.

Report of a roundtable of April 27, 1972, including remarks by Bayless Manning, Max Frankel, Phil Goulding, Carl Marey, Harry McPherson, and audience questions. A dialogue on secrecy's positive and negative features.

5841. Patel, Dorab. "The Spycatcher Cases," Civil Justice Quarterly 10 (April 1991): 170-181.

5842. Pateman, Ray. "Intelligence Agencies in Africa: A Preliminary Assessment," Journal of Modern African Studies 30/4 (1992): 569-585.

Argues that all African states have established state security and intelligence apparatuses, often with substantial outside assistance.

5843. Paterson, Thomas G. "The Historian as Detective: Senator Kenneth Keating, the Missiles in Cuba, and His Mysterious Sources," Diplomatic History 11/1 (Winter 1987): 67-70.

An examination of information supplied by Senator Keating concerning the Cuban missile crisis of 1962.

5844. Paterson, Thomas G. "Commentary: The Defense-of-Cuba Theme and the Missile Crisis," Diplomatic History 14/2 (Spring 1990): 249-256.

Discusses American underestimation of the extent of Soviet military involvement in Cuba prior to the missile crisis. Sections discuss the defense-of-Cuba theme; economic coercion; and defensive measures.

5845. Paterson, Thomas G. and William J. Brophy. "October Missiles and November Elections: The Cuban Missile Crisis and American Politics, 1962," Journal of American History 73/1 (June 1986): 87-119.

Discusses campaign politics in early 1962; the Cuban issue before October 16; October 16-22; October 23-28; October 29 to November 6 (election day); and the outcome of the Senate and House races.

5846. Patrick, Angie. "Criminal Law--Search and Seizure--Use of a Pen Register May Be a Search Within the Purview of Article I, Section 9 of the Texas Constitution," St. Mary's Law Journal 26 (1995): 643-671.

Considers the case of Richardson v. State and the use of the pen register device in consideration of constitutional protections on search.

5847. Patrick, Louis S. "The Secret Service of the American Revolution," Journal of American History 1 (1907): 497-508.

Recounts the life and secret service activities of Colonel Henry Ludington, 1739-1817.

5848. Patrick, Stephen B. "The Ardennes Offensive: The Battle of the Bulge, December 1944," Strategy and Tactics 37 (1973): 4-21.

A useful analysis of this classic case study in intelligence failure.

5849. Paul, Roland A. "Laos: Anatomy of an American Involvement," Foreign Affairs 49 (April 1971): 533-547.

Discusses the intensification of American involvement in Laos in 1966 to reduce the influence of the Soviets in the area. Asks about the obligations of American involvement and the secrecy of American intrusion.

5850. Paulu, Burton. "Eastern European Mass Communications: Selected Information Sources," Journal of Broadcasting 22 (Winter 1978): 107-130.

This is a bibliography of mass media coverage of Eastern Europe in the cold war era.

5851. Paust, Jordan J. "The Seizure and Recovery of the Mayaguez," Yale Law Journal 85/6 (May 1976): 774-806.

Discusses the international legal implications of the US recovery of the Mayaguez. Analyzes the right of a coastal state to seize and search merchant vessels, obligations of Cambodia to use peaceful means to settle international disputes, and the role of legal advisers in the Ford administration.

5852. Paust, Jordan J. "International Law and Control of the Media: Terror, Repression and the Alternatives," Indiana Law Journal 53/4 (Summer 1978): 621-678.

Major sections include discussion of the stake of international legal policies; the suspect and unlawful patterns of state practice; and alternatives to governmental control.

5853. Paust, Jordan J. "More Revelations About Mayaguez (And Its Secret Cargo)," Boston College International and Comparative Law Review 4/1 (Spring 1981): 61-76.

Major sections discuss the plaintiff's use of international law; location of the ship; appearance of the ship; the secret cargo; and prior knowledge of hostilities. The main issue in the case was the legality of governmental actions.

5854. Paust, Jordan J. "Is the President Bound by the Supreme Law of the Land?--Foreign Affairs and National Security Reexamined," Hastings Constitutional Law Quarterly 9 (Summer 1982): 719-772.

Addresses the question in the title through the issue of the President's right to control both access to and content of public information. Considers the executive function of the operation of the intelligence system.

5855. Pavlenko, N. "Documents on Pearl Harbor," Voenno-Istoricheskii Zhurnal 1 (January 1961): 85-105.

5856. Pavlicek, Larry. "Developing a Counterintelligence Mind-Set," Security Management 36/4 (April 1992): 54-56+.

5857. Paxson, Alan R. "Castles, Canals, and Colonial Cabins," Studies in Intelligence 28/1 (Spring 1984).

5858. Payne, Douglas W. "The Mantos' of Sandanista Deception," Strategic Review 13/2 (Spring 1985): 9-20.
        Discusses the political and military organization used by the Sandinista de Liberacion Nacional (FSLN) in Nicaragua. Sections discuss the revolutionary seedbeds of the FSLN; the manto of Sandino; the Christian manto; the Ortega manto; the Ortega brothers and FSLN training abroad; the manto of the "Group of Twelve"; Pastora and the Social Democratic manto; prelude to the final offensive; the manto of the Junta; manto of the disjointed FSLN; and the Sandinista model of successful Latin revolution.

5859. Payne, H. C. "Theory and Practice of Political Police During the Second Empire in France," Journal of Modern History 30/1 (March 1958): 14-23.
        Analyses the theory of political police and discusses the role of political police in the Second Empire. Accounts for three different meanings of the police to the French people. Argues that the most successful innovation relevant to the political police of the period was the creation of the Gendarmerie, a force of many thousands of police within the Army stationed throughout the country.

5860. Payne, Walter A. "The Guatemalan Revolution, 1944-1954: An Interpretation," Pacific Historian 17 (Spring 1973): 1-32.

5861. Payton, Gary D. "Soviet Military Presence Abroad: The Lessons of Somalia," Military Review 59/1 (January 1979): 67-77.
        Discusses Soviet military presence in Somalia from 1963 to 1977. Sections discuss the full circle of Soviet military assistance; expansion of Berbera facilities; dedication to Marxism; Somali nationalism; destabilization; Cuban surrogates; Indian Ocean posture; demilitarization talks; treaties; and lessons learned.

5862. Payton, Gary D. "Joint Intelligence Training in the US Air Force," Defense Intelligence Journal 2/2 (Fall 1993): 177-184.

Discusses the modern context of joint and multiservice training; organization; and joint training initiatives.

5863. Peake, Cyrus H. "History's Role in Intelligence Estimating," Studies in Intelligence 3 (Winter 1959).

5864. Peake, Hayden B. "Harry S. Truman on CIA Covert Operations," Studies in Intelligence 25/1 (Spring 1981).

5865. Peake, Hayden B. "More About Harry Truman on CIA Covert Operations," Studies in Intelligence 25/2 (Summer 1981).

5866. Peake, Hayden B. "The Apostle in Seat 4-F," Studies in Intelligence 28/4 (Winter 1984).

5867. Peake, Hayden B. "SIGINT Literature: World War II to the Present," American Intelligence Journal 15/1 (Spring-Summer 1994): 88-92.
    A review essay of major works in signals intelligence, beginning with John Buchan's classic eight-volume work published in 1922.

5868. Peake, Hayden B. "Intelligence Satellites: A Bibliographic Launchpad," American Intelligence Journal 15/2 (Autumn-Winter 1994): 58-60.
    A book review essay on the collection of books devoted to discussion of intelligence satellites and fixed wing aircraft.

5869. Peake, Louis A. "Andrew Summers Rowan and the Message from Garcia," West Virginia History 44/3 (1983): 227-240.
    Discusses Rowan's mission to Cuba during the early days of the Spanish-American War to report the rebel leader Garcia's equipment and supply needs.

5870. Pearce, E. "London Commentary, 'The Soft-Handed Authoritarians,'" Encounter 567. (November 1986): 30-32.
    This is a commentary decrying the Official Secrets Act as overly restrictive to the point of absurd. Also, provides a critique of the historical accuracy of the BBC movie, "The Mocled Mutineer." Article states that historical records will not be discoverable for thirty-one more years.

5871. Pearce, Robert. "Espionage in Africa: The Case of the Duchess. The Capture of the Italian Ship, the Duchessa d'Aosta, by the British during the Second World War," Historical Journal 26/2 (June 1983): 423-430.
    A brief, but detailed, summary of the role of espionage and counterespionage in African states during World War II. Refers to the Special Operations Executive (SOE) and Duchesa d'Aosta.

5872. Pearsall, Richard E. and Richard C. Wheeler. "Combat Information: The Key Force Multiplier," Signal 34 (October 1979): 45-47.

5873. Pearson, Frederic S. and R. E. Doerga. "The Netherlands and the 1940 Nazi Invasion," Jerusalem Journal of International Relations 3/2-3 (1978): 25-50.
      Discusses the use of information, distortion of information, decision makers, options, constraints, consensus, structure and other factors which led to the invasion.

5874. Pearson, Peter K. "Cryptanalysis of the Ciarcia Circuit," Cryptologia 12/1 (January 1988): 1-10.

5875. Pease, Donald E. "Leslie Fiedler, the Rosenberg Trial, and the Formulation of an American Canon," Boundary 2 17 (Summer 1990): 155-198.

5876. Pebbles, C. "The Guardians," Spaceflight (November 1978): 381-385.

5877. Pechan, Bruce L. "The Collector's Role in Evaluation," Studies in Intelligence 5/2 (Summer 1961): 37-47.
      An experienced field case officer explains aspects of the human intelligence collection process. Major sections discuss the determination of probability; determination of significance; collector capabilities; and collector limitations.

5878. Peck, K. "A Court That Never Says No," Progressive 48 (April 1984): 13-17.
      A brief discussion of the US Foreign Intelligence Surveillance Court created to oversee and judge the need for government electronic surveillance operations.

5879. Peck, K. "Strange Bedfellows," Progressive 48 (November 1984): 11-12.
      The work of the American Civil Liberties Union to exempt the CIA's operational files from the F.O.I.A.

5880. Peck, Winslow. "U.S. Electronic Espionage: A Memoir," Ramparts 11/2 (August 1972): 45+.

5881. Peckham, Howard H. "British Secret Writing in the Revolution," Michigan Alumnus Quarterly Review 44/15 (February 1938): 126-131.

5882. Peebles, Curtis L. "Satellite Photograph Interpretation," Spaceflight (October 1982): 161-163.

5883. Peel-Shaw, Alan; Bob McCrie; and Rainer von zur Muklen. "Vetting-

Techniques in Britain, the USA and Germany," International Security Review 19 (September-October 1982): 36-44.

Discusses the techniques for screening new and veteran employees in order to reduce the possibility of dishonesty and/or disloyalty.

5884. Peers, William R. "Guerilla Operations in Northern Burma," Military Review 28/6 (June 1948): 11-13.

5885. Peers, William R. "Intelligence Operations of OSS Detachment 101," Studies in Intelligence 4/2 (Summer 1960).

5886. Peet, Richard C. "Interview: Maj. Gen. Edward G. Lansdale," Journal of Defense & Diplomacy 1/4 (1983): 53-54, 64.

5887. Peled, Benjamin. "I.D.F. Air Force," Revue Internationale d'Historie Militaire 42 (1979): 181-188.

5888. Pelz, Stephen E. "When Do I have Time to Think? John F. Kennedy, Roger Hilsman, and the Laotian Crisis of 1962," Diplomatic History 3/2 (Spring 1979): 215-229.

Involvement in Laos in 1962, John Kennedy's use of a task force to study the situation, Hilsman's proposal to send the Seventh Fleet to the Gulf of Siam; decision to establish a neutralization agreement.

5889. Pemberton, Ian C. B. "The British Secret Service in the Champlain Valley During the Haldimand Negotiations, 1780-1783," Vermont History 44/3 (1976): 129-140.

5890. Pemberton, W. B. "Intrepidity of Father Robertson," Blackwood's Magazine 283 (May 1958): 329-346.

The exploits of Father James Robertson, an intelligence agent operating in Germany during World War II.

5891. Pencak, William. "Samuel Adams and Shays's Rebellion," New England Quarterly 62/1 (March 1989): 63-74.

A detailed consideration of Adams' leadership during the 1786 Shays rebellion, including the manner in which he considered various threats to the national government.

5892. Pendergass, J. T. "Cryptanalytic Use of High-Speed Digital Computing Machines," Cryptologia 17/2 (April 1993): 124-147.

5893. Penney, Walter. "Grille Reconstruction," Cryptologia 1/2 (April 1977): 195-201.

5894. Percival, Harold P. "Lost Armies II -- Destruction Due to Defective Intelligence Service," Army Quarterly (January 1929): 319-328.

5895. Percy, M. O. "Air-Ground Intelligence Cooperation," Military Affairs (November 1948): 49-53.

5896. Perham, John. "The Great Game of Corporate Espionage," Dun's Review (October 1970): 30-33, 93-94, 96.
   A brief overview of the problems associated with containing corporate theft of internal secrets. Several case examples are cited. Role of corporate internal security is discussed.

5897. Perkins, James A. "Administration of the National Security Program," Public Administration Review 13/2 (Spring 1953): 80-86.
   Examines the characters and roles of individuals given authority under the National Security Act of 1947, and reviews the organizational limitations of each of the major national security activities.

5898. Perkins, Matthew W. "Foreign Intelligence Surveillance -- Civil Actions and the Foreign Intelligence Surveillance Act: You Can Knock But You Can't Come In, American Civil Liberties Union of Southern California v. Barr, 952 F.2d 457 (D.C. Cir. 1991)," Suffolk Transnational Law Review 16/2 (Spring 1993): 807-821.
   A case comment on the American Civil Liberties Union litigation alleging government violations of the Foreign Intelligence Surveillance Act of 1978.

5899. Perle, Richard. "Technology and the Quiet War," Strategic Review 11/1 (1983): 29-35.

5900. Perle, Richard. "The Eastward Technology Flow: A Plan of Common Action," Strategic Review 12/1 (Spring 1984): 24-32.

5901. Perlmutter, Amos. "The Covenant of War," Harper's 248/1485 (February 1974): 51-61.
   A discussion of the characteristics and intelligence failures of the October 1973 Israeli war with Egypt.

5902. Perlmutter, Amos. "Israel's Fourth War, October 1973: Political and Military Misperceptions," Orbis 19/2 (Summer 1975): 434-460.
   Raises and discusses several critical observations regarding the failures of the Israeli policy makers--"inner circle." Offers a framework for understanding their misperceptions, and conclusions.

5903. Perlo, V. "CIA Propaganda Bombshell," New World Review 32 (1964): 13.

5904. Perr, Irwin N. "Religion, Political Leadership, Charisma, and Mental Illness: The Strange Story of Louis Riel," Journal of Forensic Sciences 37 (March 1992): 574-584.

5905. Perroots, Leonard H. "Defense Intelligence As a Force Multiplier," Defense/86 6 (November-December 1986): 32-36.

5906. Perroots, Leonard H. "New Approaches to C³ Interoperability on the Intelligence Community," Signal 43/1 (September 1988): 31-34.
  Discusses the movement toward interoperability, intelligence support, security levels and hindrances to interoperability.

5907. Perroots, Leonard H. "The DIA Response to Terrorism," American Intelligence Journal 10/1 (Spring 1989): 5-9.
  A brief overview of the terrorist responses of the Defense Intelligence Agency.

5908. Perry, Geoffrey E. "Russian Hunter-Killer Satellite Experiments," Military Review 58/10 (October 1978): 50-57.
  Considers this Soviet technological concern. Sections discuss the mystery of the weapon; the speculation; repetition of experiments; the 1971 series; and the US reaction.

5909. Perry, Mark. "The Secret Life of an American Spy," Regardie's (February 1989): 78-99.
  Material may be useful to espionage researchers, but this publication is not generally accepted as a scholarly journal. This publication is recognized for its good writing and inside-the-beltway perspectives.

5910. Perry, Mark. "The Case Against William Webster," Regardie's (January 1990): 90-95.
  Controversy surrounding the CIA director. See previous citation as to this publication source.

5911. Perry, M. O. "Air-Ground Intelligence Cooperation," Military Review 28/11 (November 1948): 49-54.
  Discusses the imperative of exchange of information between air and ground reconnaissance elements.

5912. Perry, Victor. "Israeli Intelligence Services Over the Years," Midstream 34 (May 1988): 34-36.

5913. Perry, William. "Fallows Fallacies," International Security 6/4 (Spring 1982): 174-182.

A book review essay concerning James Fallows' book, National Defense.

5914. Perry, William J. "Advanced Technology and Arms Control," Orbis 26/2 (Summer 1982): 351-359.

Summarizes the role and application of US nuclear weapons with respect to SALT I and II agreements. Suggests that all forms of nuclear war no longer make sense since technologies have countered each option on all sides. Useful background piece for studies of weapons assessment.

5915. Perry, William J. "Desert Storm and Deterrence," Foreign Affairs 70/4 (1991): 66-82.

Discusses the role of intelligence and warfighting technologies associated with the Gulf war.

5916. Perry-Mosher, Kate E. "The Rock Island P.O.W. Camp," Civil War Times Illustrated 8/4 (1969): 28-36.

5917. Perschetz, Martin L. "Domestic Intelligence Informants, the First Amendment and the Need for Prior Judicial Review," Buffalo Law Review 26/1 (Fall-Winter 1976): 173-208.

Argues for prior judicial review of the decision by police agencies to use informants, especially when they are used in intelligence gathering.

5918. Persico, Joseph E. "Casey's German Gamble," MHQ: The Quarterly Journal of Military History 3/1 (Autumn 1990): 70-77.

Discusses World War II espionage activities of CIA director William Casey.

5919. Perventsev, V. V. "From the History of Russian Consular Services in the 18th Century," Voprosy Istorii 8 (1985): 163-167.

5920. Pesken, Joan. "Ruse and Representations: On Children's Ability to Conceal Information," Developmental Psychology 28 (January 1992): 84-89.

A formal study of childrens' ability to conceal information or to misinform between the ages of three and five. May be useful in studies of deception, secrecy, and misinformation.

5921. Pessen, Edward. "The Rosenberg Case Revisited: A Critical Essay on a Recent Scholarly Examination," New York History 65/1 (January 1984): 82-102.

An extensive book review essay of Ronald Radosh's and Joyce Milton's The Rosenberg File: A Search for the Truth. Argues that there are numerous flaws in this work.

5922. Peter, Fritz W. "Stimmen die Angaben der CIA Doch?," Politische Studien 32/258 (July-August 1982): 405-413.
    Rough translation: "Are Statements of the CIA Really Correct?"

5923. Peter, Lawrence T. "Operation Desert Storm: Naval Intel in Riyadh," Naval Intelligence Professionals Quarterly 7/3 (Summer 1991): 1-2.

5924. Peter, Lawrence T. "Naval Intelligence at Mid-Career," Naval Intelligence Professionals Quarterly 8/3 (Summer 1992): 1-3.

5925. Peter, Lawrence T. "The Way Ahead at Mid-Career," Naval Intelligence Professionals Quarterly 9/4 (Fall 1993): 4-6.

5926. Peters, Ralph. "Information Is Not Intelligence," Army 36 (January 1986): 34-37.

5927. Peters, Ralph. "Intelligence Failures and the Limits of Logic," Parameters: Journal of the U.S. Army War College 17/1 (Spring 1987): 43-50.
    Argues that the intelligence system, especially the analytical function, should be increased, not decreased, in order to avoid even more intelligence failures.

5928. Peters, Ralph. "Age of Fatal Visibility," Military Review 68/8 (August 1988): 49-59.
    Discusses counterintelligence objectives in the context of 1980s military intelligence operations.

5929. Peters, Steve. "The Murder of Col. Joseph M. Bounds, Eleventh Texas Cavalry, Young's Regiment, C.S.A.," Texana 12/1 (1974): 56-60.
    Discusses the lives of two Civil War soldiers and their involvement in espionage activities.

5930. Petersen, Glenn. "Kanengamah and Pohnpei's Politics of Concealment," American Anthropologist 95/2 (June 1993): 334-352.
    Discusses the sociology of concealment; ambiguities in politics and language; the Kanengamah and truth and politics; leadership, truth, and power; and the politics of concealment.

5931. Petersen, John L. "Forecasting: It's Not Impossible," Defense Intelligence Journal 3/2 (Fall 1994): 37-46.
    Reflects on the basic concerns of forecasting: information collection; predetermined events; wild cards; critical issues; scenarios; and common opportunities and hazards.

5932. Petersen, Phillip A. "American Perceptions of Soviet Military Power," Parameters: Journal of the U.S. Army War College 7/4 (Winter 1977): 71-82.

Discusses the roots of the debate in intelligence and policy circles over actual Soviet military power; Team A and Team B; the Collins controversy; the character of the debate; crucial elements of the underlying policy preferences; the evidence; images and beliefs about military power and security.

5933. Peterson, Arthur G. "Departmental Strategic Intelligence," Military Intelligence 10/3 (1984): 40-42.

5934. Peterson, Forrest S. "The Three Blackbirds," Naval Aviation Museum Foundation 7/2 (Fall 1986): 34-42.

A discussion of the high-flying X-15 tests in the 1950s. Test results were relevant to U-2 spy aircraft testing.

5935. Peterson, Hans J. "The Dieppe Raid in Contemporary German View," American Review of Canadian Studies 13/1 (Spring 1983): 65-78.

Discusses the failures in the American, Canadian and British attack on Dieppe in 1942, thereby elevating German sensitivity to potential invasion along the French coast. German news media made a laughing stock out of Winston Churchill. Suggests that Churchill's plan of attack at Dieppe was urged by the Soviets.

5936. Peterson, John H. "Info Wars," U.S. Naval Institute Proceedings 119/5 (1993): 85-92.

5937. Peterson, Marilyn B. and R. Glenn Ridgway. "Analytical Intelligence Training," FBI Law Enforcement Bulletin 59/5 (May 1990): 13-17.

Considers topics in the field of intelligence analysis, analysis in academia, analytical course development, pitfalls of teaching analysis, future developments, and standards.

5938. Peterson, Michael L. "The Church Cryptogram: To Catch a Tory Spy," American History Illustrated 24/6 (November-December 1989): 36-43.

Discusses a short cryptogram intercepted during the American Revolution and placed in George Washington's hands. A female messenger revealed the name of the sender, Dr. Benjamin Church, Jr. Church was later proven to be a British spy.

5939. Peterson, Neal H. "Intelligence and US Foreign Policy, 1945-1954," Studies in Intelligence 28/4 (Winter 1984): 67-78.

5940. Peterson, Neal H. "Intelligence Literature of the Cold War," Studies in Intelligence 32/4 (Winter 1988).

Note: An author with a similar name, Neal H. Petersen, produced a prize-winning bibliography on intelligence literature, <u>American Intelligence, 1775-1990</u>, Regina Books, 1992.

5941. Peterson, Paul M. "Civilian Demonstrations Near the Military Installation: Restraints on Military Surveillance and Other Intelligence Activities," <u>Military Law Review</u> 140 (Spring 1993): 113-178.

Examines legal implications of domestic intelligence collection under circumstances of military post demonstrations. Considers historical background; existing regulatory guidance; statutory analysis; and analysis of proposed regulatory changes.

5942. Peterson, Trev V. "The National Security Exception to the Doctrine of Prior Restraint: United States v. Progressive, Inc.," <u>University of Nebraska Law Review</u> 60/2 (1981): 400-415.

Provides facts in the Progressive case; analysis of injunctive relief under common law, injunctive relief under the Atomic Energy Act, comparative harm, and implications for the prior restraint doctrine.

5943. Peterson, William J. "The Importance of PSYOPS and Intelligence in LIC," <u>Military Intelligence</u> 13/3 (1987): 31.

5944. Peterzell, J. "Can You Name That Agent?," <u>Columbia Journalism Review</u> 23 (November-December 1984): 46-47.

A review of the Intelligence Identities Protection Act. The Act's major strength is its prohibition against printing the names of US foreign intelligence agents.

5945. Peterzell, J. "Can the CIA Spook the Press?," <u>Columbia Journalism Review</u> 25 (September-October 1986): 29-34.

A discussion of tactics and measures used by CIA Director William Casey and General William E. Odom of the National Security Agency to prevent publication of details concerning the Ronald Pelton and William Bell espionage cases.

5946. Petit, D. Pastor. "An Exceptional Spy: Hans T. Schmidt," <u>Historia y Vida</u> 24/277 (1991): 117-124.

5947. Petit, D. Pastor. "A Major Soviet Spy Ring: The Impact of the Red Orchestra," <u>Historia y Vida</u> 25/297 (1992): 4-11.

5948. Petras, James F. "Guerilla Movements in Latin America," <u>New Politics</u> 6 (Spring 1967): 80-94.

5949. Petras, James F. "The CIA, Frei, and the Junta," New Politics 11 (Fall 1976): 25-35.

5950. Petras, James F. "Chile: Crime, Class Consciousness, and the Bourgeoisie," Crime and Social Justice 7 (Spring-Summer 1977): 14-22.
    Argues that bourgeoisie perpetuated political assassinations, physical assaults, illegal para-military groups, lockouts, sabotage and riots to bring down the Allende government. Discusses the role of the CIA from the author's perspective.

5951. Petras, James F. "Political Economy of State Terror: Chile, El Salvador, and Brazil," Crime and Social Justice 27-28 (1987).

5952. Petrov, G. "CIA's Testing Ground in Guatemala," International Affairs (USSR) 10 (October 1983): 109-116.
    A Soviet view of American's rape of the Republic of Guatemala over land interests; US backing of the Somoza regime; the expansion of the guerilla movement; and Guatemala as puppet state of the US.

5953. Petrov, I. and V. Chernyavsky. "U.S. Intelligence and Foreign Policy," International Affairs (USSR) 10/10 (October 1964): 34-39.

5954. Petrov, S. "The Achievement of Surprise in the L'vov-Sandomierz Operation," Voenno Istoricheskii Zhurnal 7 (July 1974): 33-36+.

5955. Petrow, Stefan. "The Rise of the Detective in London, 1869-1914," Criminal Justice History: An International Annual 14 (1994): 91-108.
    Historical assessment of the emergence of detectives in the Metropolitan Police Force. Among other aspects of this history is mention of the detective's role in uncovering espionage.

5956. Petrusenko, V. "The CIA and Imperialist Propaganda," International Affairs (USSR) 4 (April 1980): 97-107.
    A Soviet view of the role of the CIA in American foreign relations.

5957. Petrusenko, V. "U.S. Intelligence: A Weapon of Foreign Policy Expansion," International Affairs (USSR) 5 (May 1981): 93-102.
    A Soviet view of CIA operations in the international arena, mainly on reflection upon controversies surrounding the Agency in the 1970s.

5958. Petrusenko, V. "The CIA Steps Up Subversive Activities," International Affairs (USSR) 10 (October 1982): 102-108.
    A Soviet view of the CIA and international intrigue.

5959.   Petrusenko, V.   "The CIA and Shaping of U.S. Foreign Policy," International Affairs (USSR) 14 (May 1986): 95-103.
More of the same, as in earlier articles.

5960. Pettee, George S. "Faults and Errors in World War II," Infantry Journal 59 (October 1946): 27-34.
This is part I of a series of documents on World War II intelligence failures. Part II is found in the November 1946 issue, 31-33; Part III is found in the December 1946 issue, 32-33.

5961. Pettee, George S. "Strategic Intelligence," Infantry Journal 59 (December 1946): 32-33.

5962.   Pettee, George S.   "Future of American Secret Intelligence," Public Administration Review 7/2 (1947): 129-131.

5963.   Pfaelzer, Marianna R. and Allan D. Bersin.   "The Police and Public Disorder Intelligence: The Los Angeles Experience," Crime Prevention Review 2/4 (July 1975): 1-8.
Reviews briefly court decisions on police collection of intelligence, leaning the direction of increasing oversight and restrictions.

5964.   Pfautz, James C.   "Combat Intelligence Support for Tactical Air Operations," Signal 39 (September 1984): 43-45.

5965.   Pfeiffer, Jack B.   "Adlai Stevenson and the Bay of Pigs," Studies in Intelligence 27/3 (Fall 1983).
A paper on the perspectives of Stevenson declassified in 1994 and available at the National Archives. Includes the view that CIA approved of Stevenson's remarks regarding the cover story for the Bay of Pigs operation.

5966. Pfeiffer, Jack B. "OSS Propaganda in Europe and the Far East," Studies in Intelligence 28/3 (Fall 1984).
Not listed by the Central Intelligence Agency in the collection of declassified articles released for public access.

5967. Pforzheimer, Walter L. "Letters to the President," Studies in Intelligence 9/4 (Winter 1965).
Letters of Rose O'Neil Greenhow, the most notorious spy of the Civil War confederacy.

5968. Pforzheimer, Walter L. "Code Breaking--The Ultra Story," Marine Corps Gazette 64/7 (July 1980): 76-80.

5969. Pforzheimer, Walter L. "Remarks," Houston Journal of International Law 11/1 (Fall 1988): 143-148.

The author's observations concerning "Irangate" and the role of legislative oversight of covert actions are offered.

5970. Pfost, Donald R. "Reagan's Nicaraguan Policy: A Case Study of Political Deviance and Crime," Crime and Social Justice 27-28 (1987): 66-87.

Argues the position that the Reagan administration's policies toward Nicaragua violated domestic and international law, thus making such actions political crimes. Attempts to document representative cases, including criminal acts and laws violated. Mentions the CIA.

5971. Phares, Walid. "The Intelligence Services in Lebanon During the War of 1975-1990," International Journal of Intelligence and Counterintelligence 7/3 (Fall 1994): 363-381.

Discusses the background of the Lebanese conflict; Lebanon's intelligence services before the war; foreign intelligence involvement in the 1975 war; wartime Lebanese intelligence; the militia's intelligence; and the intelligence puzzle of Lebanon during the war period.

5972. Phelan, George R. "Introduction to Command Intelligence," Naval War College Review 6/4 (December 1953): 31-56.

5973. Phenenger, Michael E. "Tactical Intelligence: How Do Agents Fit In?," Military Intelligence 10/3 (1984): 30-31.

5974. Phillips, A. H. "Cipher for Secrets," Technology Review 42/8 (June 1940): 321+.

Discusses espionage by means of ciphers and codes.

5975. Phillips, David A. "Final Act in the Theater of the Absurd," Retired Officer (April 1976): 26-29.

Reflections by the author on his career in the Central Intelligence Agency.

5976. Phillips, David A. "Old Boys Never Talk--Until Now," Washingtonian (October 1979): 65-70.

A summation of the memoirs of several former Central Intelligence Agency personnel.

5977. Phillips, David A. "CIA Boosts Intelligence Role Using High-Tech Electronics," Electronic Warfare/Defense Electronics 14/2 (December 1982): 54-66.

5978. Phillips, David A. "Soviet Threats ... Internal or External?," Electronic Warfare/Defense Electronics 15 (October 1983): 120-127.

5979. Phillips, David A. "The Toughest, Deadliest Hombre (OSS Colonel Carl Eifler)," 40/4 Retired Officer (April 1984): 26-31.
A brief history of Eifler's work in Burma as commander of Office of Strategic Services Detachment 101.

5980. Phillips, David A. "The Great White Case Officer," International Journal of Intelligence and Counterintelligence 1/1 (Spring 1986): 97-102.
Reflections by the author upon Allen Dulles' persistent defense of the importance of the CIA. Characterizes anonymously several insiders who had first-hand knowledge of the CIA in Dulles' time.

5981. Phillips, David A. "'Goodbye, Mr. President,'" "'Enjoy Your Retirement, Director,'" International Journal of Intelligence and Counterintelligence 1/2 (Summer 1986): 127-132.
The author compiled a series of reflections on former director's of the CIA from interviews and secondary sources. Much of the information emanates from the author's luncheon meetings with other former intelligence officers at a French restaurant, "Chez Espionage" (pseud.) in the Washington, D.C. area.

5982. Phillips, David A. "Some Truth, Some Untruth, Some Half-Truth," International Journal of Intelligence and Counterintelligence 1/3 (Fall 1986): 109-114.
More reflections of former intelligence officers, based on the private luncheons at "Chez Espionage."

5983. Phillips, David A. "Stalking the Great Spy Novel," World & I 1/11 (November 1986): 60-63.

5984. Phillips, David A. "The Walker Family Revisited, Phillip Agee Returns," International Journal of Intelligence and Counterintelligence 1/4 (Winter 1986-1987): 133-139.
Comments and observations on intelligence officer reactions to the Walker spy case and the proposed return to the United States of former Central Intelligence Agency case officer Phillip Agee.

5985. Phillips, David A. "CIA-Bashing Time Again: Covert Action Is the Blunt Instrument," International Journal of Intelligence and Counterintelligence 2/1 (Spring 1988): 115-121.
More reflections of the author, based on his regular luncheons with former intelligence officers at "Chez Espionage."

5986. Phillips, David A. "Intelligence Is No Laughing Matter," International Journal of Intelligence and Counterintelligence 2/2 (Summer 1988): 267-272.
     The final collection of reflections of the author, based on his regular luncheons with former intelligence officers at "Chez Espionage." He died shortly after this article went to press.

5987. Phillips, Jacqueline. "State and Federal Constitutional Safeguards Against the Use of Consensual Electronic Surveillance," Southern University Law Review 10 (Fall 1983): 133-146.
     This is a case note following State v. Reeves, 427 So. 2d 410 (La. 1983).

5988. Phillips, Lester H. "Canada's Internal Security," Canadian Journal of Economics and Political Science 12 (February 1946): 18-29.
     Major sections discuss the defense of Canadian security regulations; amendments and revisions to regulations; protection of essential services and areas; control of communications and safeguarding of information; the subversive press; and the subversive literature.

5989. Phillips, Lester H. "Preventive Detention in Canada," Canadian Forum 26 (June 1946): 56-57.

5990. Phillips, William. "In and Out of the Underground: The Confessions of Whittaker Chambers," American Mercury 74 (June 1952): 92-99.
     Considers the ideas and intrigues of informer Whittaker Chambers.

5991. Pichot-Duclos, Jean. "Economic Intelligence, Weapon of the Post-Cold War Period," Defense Nationale 49 (December 1993): 83-104.

5992. Pick, Winslow. "U.S. Electronic Espionage: A Memoir," Ramparts (August 1972): 41-44.
     Not generally considered a scholarly source, yet the article stirred significant controversy to merit mention here for possible research application.

5993. Pickering, James H. "Enoch Crosby, Secret Agent of the Neutral Ground: His Own Story," New York History 47/1 (1966): 61-73.
     Exploits of Enoch Crosby and his service as a spy for the American cause in the American Revolution. Draws from Crosby's writings in 1832 about his experiences.

5994. Piedra, Alberto M. "Chile," Strategic Review 3 (Winter 1975): 25-38.

5995. Pierce, K. J. "Public Cryptography, Arms Export Controls, and the First Amendment: A Need for Legislation," Cornell International Law Journal 17/1 (Winter 1984): 197-236.

Major sections discuss the emergence of the public cryptography industry and federal attempts to control the industry; prepublication control by enforcing international traffic in arms regulations; ITAR lacks procedural protections for prior restraint finding; the national security exception; and a legislative proposal.

5996. Pierce, P. N. "The Unsolved Mystery of Pete Ellis," Marine Corps Gazette 46/2 (February 1962): 34-40.
This is a brief biography of Colonel Ellis' life and times as a spy against Japan.

5997. Pierson, Markus. "Love and Espionage," Southwest Art 20 (August 1990): 63.

5998. Pierson, William W. "The Committee on the Conduct of the War," American Historical Review 23/4 (April 1918).
A brief historical discussion of this important agency of World War I.

5999. Piggott, F. S. G. "Intelligence at an Army Headquarters in the Western Front During the Last Phase of the Great War," Army Quarterly (January 1925): 234-244.

6000. Piggot, Francis J. C. "Verification: Intelligence or Inspection?," Disarmament 6 (June 1965): 18-20.

6001. Pike, Frederick B. "Guatemala, the United States, and Communism in the Americas," Review of Politics 17 (April 1955): 233-243.

6002. Pike, John. "Spies in the Skies: The National Reconnaissance Office and the Intelligence Budget," Covert Action Quarterly 50 (Fall 1994): 48-56.
Major sections discuss secrecy and the intelligence budget; the NRO as a normally reclusive organization; inside the NRO; cameras in space and imaging intelligence; radio eavesdropping via signals intelligence; wide area surveillance; the NRO budget; and NRO reorganization.

6003. Pike, John. "Uncloaked Daggers: CIA Spending for Covert Operations," Covert Action Quarterly 51 (Winter 1994-1995): 48-55.

6004. Pilant, Lois. "Achieving State-of-the-Art Surveillance," Police Chief 60/6 (June 1993): 24, 26+.

6005. Pilchen, Saul M. and Benjamin B. Klubes. "Using the Classified Information Procedures Act in Criminal Cases: A Primer for Defense Counsel," American Criminal Law Review 31 (Winter 1994): 191-214.

6006. Pilecki, Chris A. "After Perestroika: A New Improved Communist Threat?," Military Intelligence 16/4 (1990): 27-28.

6007. Pilon, Juliana G. "Moscow's U.N. Outpost," Ukrainian Quarterly 40/2 (1984): 127-143.
     An account of possible Soviet use of the United Nations headquarters for unethical means of influencing developing nations.

6008. Pinck, Dan. "Getting to Mrs. Nestor's Farm: A Secret Agent in Wartime China," Encounter 71/2 (July-August 1988): 15-21.
     The author's personal reflections on his activities as a secret agent in China from 1942 to 1946.

6009. Pinck, Dan. "Beyond the Veil," Encounter 72 (April 1989): 39-42.
     A book review essay concerning Bob Woodward's book on the director of CIA, William Casey, Veil. Also remarks on Iran-Contra, journalism in politics and the CIA.

6010. Pine, Shawn M. "Deficiencies in Military Counterintelligence: A View from the Field," International Journal of Intelligence and Counterintelligence 8/2 (Summer 1995): 221-227.
     A former US Army CI officer offers a critiques of miltary CI capabilities, in particular, the work of the 902nd MI Group, headquartered in San Antonio, Texas. Major sections discuss the history of the 902nd; the irrational rationale for reorganization; the personnel merry-go-round; and a negative prognosis.

6011. Pine, Shawn M. "CISOC: The Army's Counterintelligence Special Operations Concept," International Journal of Intelligence and Counterintelligence 9/1 (Spring 1996): 81-96.
     Discussion of the CISOC structure; Fort Hood blues; the generic CISOC; left out in the cold; and fixing the CISOC mess.

6012. Pineau, Roger. "0723, 7 December 1941," Naval Intelligence Professionals Quarterly 7/4 (Fall 1991): 1-3.

6013. Pineau, Roger. "A Code Break and the Death of Admiral Yamamoto," Naval Intelligence Professionals Quarterly 5/2 (Summer 1989): 3-5.

6014. Pineau, Roger. "A Code Break and the Death of Admiral Yamamoto (Encore)," Naval Intelligence Professionals Quarterly 9/4 (Fall 1993): 15-16.

6015. Pineau, Roger. "The Death of Admiral Yamamoto," Naval Intelligence Professionals Quarterly 10/4 (Fall 1994): 1-5.

6016. Pinkerton, Robert A. "Detective Surveillance of Anarchists," North American Review 173/5 (November 1901): 609-617.

The son of Allen Pinkerton describes the principles of surveillance, politics in surveillance, and dealing with anarchists.

6017. Pinkerton, Roy H. "The Role of Intelligence in Policy-Making," Military Review 46/7 (July 1966): 40-51.

6018. Pinkerton, William A. "The Bolshevik Problem in America," Detective 35 (May 1919).

6019. Pinto, Oreste. "The Secrets of Super Spies," Science Digest 35 (May 1954): 57-62.

A brief account of the author's experiences and reflections upon the life of a double agent during and after World War II. Includes tradecraft.

6020. Piot, Charles D. "Secrecy, Ambiguity, and the Everyday in Kabre Culture," American Anthropologist 95/2 (June 1993): 353-370.

Discusses the role of secrecy in the daily life of the Kabre of northern Togo; and proposes an interpretation of the need for secrecy in this culture.

6021. Pipes, Daniel. "Terrorism: The Syrian Connection," National Interest 15 (Spring 1980): 15-29.

6022. Pipes, Daniel. "Dealing with Middle Eastern Conspiracy Theories," Orbis 36/1 (Winter 1992): 41-56.

Argues for new careful attention to conspiracy theories; act defensively; discourage the conspiracy mentality; and on special occasions exploit such theories.

6023. Pipes, Richard. "Why the Soviet Union Thinks It Could Fight and Win a Nuclear War," Commentary 64/7 (July 1977): 24-31.

Title summarizes contents. Also appeared in Air Force Magazine 60/9 (1977): 54-66.

6024. Pipes, Richard. "Team B: The Reality Behind the Myth," Commentary 82/4 (October 1986): 25-40.

A discussion of the author's experiences with the estimative process under the Team A, Team B competition.

6025. Pipes, Richard. "What To Do About the CIA," Commentary 99/3 (March 1995): 36-43.

An assessment of the CIA's internal and community problems, and an evaluation of what needs to change in order to accommodate new expectations of the national security structure. Major sections consider triumphs and fiascos; mirror-imaging; political interference; and what can be done.

6026. Pisano, Vittorfranco S. "Clandestine Operations in Italy: The Bulgarian Connection," Conflict Quarterly 4/1 (Winter 1984): 28-38.
        A brief summary of official investigations into Bulgarian intelligence collection and human intelligence operations in Italy in the early 1980s.

6027. Pisarev, Iu. A. "Russian Intelligence Service Activity and the Secret Serb Organization Black Hand," Novaia i Noveishaia Istoriia 1 (1993): 23-35.

6028. Pitler, Robert. "Eavesdropping and Wiretapping - The Aftermath of Katz and Kaiser," Brooklyn Law Review 34 (1968): 223-246.
        A review of the case law made in Katz v. United States and People v. Kaiser in terms of the role of electronic surveillance. Defends such surveillance, especially in organized crime investigations.

6029. Pittman, J. "Behind the Facade of U.S. Democracy," World Marxist 19 (Fall 1976): 20-28.

6030. Place, Richard. "The Self-Deception of the Strong: France on the Eve of the War of the League of Augsberg," French Historical Studies 6 (Fall 1970): 459-473.
        An account of French intelligence and planning failures regarding German capabilities prior to the Rhineland invasion in 1688.

6031. Place, T. Harrison. "British Perceptions of the Tactics of the German Army, 1938-1940," Intelligence and National Security 9/3 (July 1994): 495-519.
        Argues that the British military took less than full advantage of opportunities presented by the German invasion of Poland in 1939. Outlines various inadequacies of the British Expeditionary Forces as to materials, doctrine, politics, diplomatic position, and communications relative to German ground tactics.

6032. Plamondon, Ann L. "A Comparison of Official Secrets and Access to Information in Great Britain and the United States," Communications and the Law 16 (June 1994): 51-68.

6033. Planche, Joseph B. "2+5 = Effective Intelligence," Infantry 56 (July-August 1966): 48-51.

6034.   Plaschka, Richard G.   "Treason, Revolt, and Our Historical Consciousness," Cesky Casopis Historicky 89/5&6 (1991): 777-786.

6035. Platt, Alan and Robert Leonardi.   "American Foreign Policy and the Postwar Italian Left," <u>Political Science Quarterly</u> 93/2 (Summer 1978): 197-215.

6036. Platt, F. Jeffrey.   "The Elizabethan "Foreign Office"," <u>Historian</u> 56/4 (Summer 1994): 725-740.
    A history of the foreign office function during the reign of Elizabeth in the late sixteenth century. Examines the work of Elizabeth's three principal foreign secretaries: Sir William Cecil; Sir Francis Walsingham; and Sir Robert Cecil.

6037. Platt, Washington.   "The Nine Principles of Intelligence," <u>Military Review</u> 36/2 (February 1957): 33-36.
    Principles based on Clausewitz's <u>On War</u>, especially exploitation of sources, significance, cause and effect, spirit of the people, trends, and degree of certainty.

6038. Platt, Washington.   "Forecasting in Strategic Intelligence," <u>Military Review</u> 37/5 (May 1957): 42-49.
    The problems associated with intelligence prediction are reviewed in this short article.

6039. Platt, Washington.   "Strategic Intelligence vs. Combat Intelligence," <u>Officer</u> 33/9 (September 1957): 8-9, 21.
    Observations of the contrasts between strategic and tactical intelligence. Sections discuss newcomers to strategic intelligence; former combat officers faced with strategic problems; practical conclusions drawn from study; and the academic worker in strategic intelligence.

6040. Platt, Washington.   "National Character: A Vital Element in Foreign Intelligence," <u>Military Review</u> 39/8 (August 1959): 13-19.
    Regards national character as the mind and spirit of the people. Comprehension of the national character is important to intelligence evaluation. Includes a discussion of the failure of Hitler to understand the American and British characters prior to World War II.

6041. Platt, Washington.   "Platt's Law," <u>Studies in Intelligence</u> 13/3 (Fall 1969).
    Rules for editing intelligence reports.

6042. Playfair, Emma.   "Israel's Security Needs in the West Bank, Real and Contrived," <u>Arab Studies Quarterly</u> 10/4 (1988): 406-423.

6043. Plehwe, R. and R. Wettenhall.   "Reflections on the Salisbury Affair - Police-Government Relations in Australia," <u>Australian Quarterly</u> 51/1 (March 1979): 75-91.

Discusses changes made in the Australian police after the firing of the police commissioner Harold Salisbury. Discusses the relationship between the police and the Australian Security Intelligence Service.

6044. Pless, Laurance D. "Snepp v. United States--Short Shrift for the Prior Restraint Doctrine," North Carolina Law Review 59/2 (January 1981): 417-427.
      Sets forth the case law relevant to the Supreme Court's decision in Snepp v. United States regarding constructive profits from secretly published book without prior approval.

6045. Ployakov, A. "Accuracy of Information," Soviet Military Review 3 (March 1981): 20-21.

6046. Pocalyko, Michael N. "25 Years After the Blink," U.S. Naval Institute Proceedings 113 (September 1987): 41-47.

6047. Podhoretz, Norman P. "Making the World Safe for Communism," Commentary 61 (April 1976): 31-41.
      A discussion of conservative and liberal approaches and contradictions in the post-World War II world of anti-communism. Very useful for comprehending the limits of ideology in a complex debate about the use of force to control other governments. Mentions political assassinations.

6048. Poirier, Robert G. "The Katyn Enigma: New Evidence in a 40-Year Riddle," Studies in Intelligence 25/1 (Spring 1981).
      Discussion of the event, including such topics as mass graves, monument to the massacre, intelligence imagery of Katyn Woods, strength of the Red Army, POW camps and aerial photographs. Estimated to be 12 pages in length.

6049. Polden, Patrick. "John Reeves as Superintendent of Aliens," Journal of Legal History 3/1 (May 1982): 31-51.
      A history of Reeve's role in the domestic surveillance and control of aliens in the early 19th century in England.

6050. Polenberg, Richard. "Franklin Roosevelt and Civil Liberties: The Case of the Dies Committee," Historian 30/2 (February 1968): 165-178.
      Discusses the politics of the Dies Committee, named after Texas Congressman Martin Dies, used to pillory the Roosevelt administration in the late 1930s on the belief that internal security was at stake.

6051. Polenberg, Richard. "Progressivism and Anarchism: Judge Henry D. Clayton and the Abrams Trial," Law and History Review 3 (Fall 1985): 397-408.
      Study of the 1918 case of Jacob Abrams and others concerning the distribution of two leaflets opposed President Wilson's intervention in Russia.

6052. Polgar, Tom. "Defection and Redefection," <u>International Journal of Intelligence and Counterintelligence</u> 1/2 (Summer 1986): 29-42.

Discusses the aversion of Russian leaders toward permitting citizens to talk with foreigners. Russians use the defector channels to the US to introduce confusion and to achieve counterintelligence objectives.

6053. Polgar, Tom. "The Intelligence Services in West Germany," <u>International Journal of Intelligence and Counterintelligence</u> 1/4 (Winter 1986-1987): 79-96.

Observes the persistent compromises of West German intelligence. Discussion of the origins of such compromises in German history.

6054. Poliakov, Leon. "Spy of God," <u>Commentary</u> 40 (August 1965): 67-70.

A brief summary of the experiences of Kurt Gerstein, the "spy for God", in World War II Nazi Germany.

6055. Polis, Richard I. "European Needs and Attitudes Towards Information Security," <u>Cryptologia</u> 12/4 (October 1988): 234-239.

6056. Polk, James H. "Reflections on the Czechoslovakian Invasion, 1968," <u>Strategic Review</u> 5/1 (Winter 1977): 30-37.

6057. Pollard, J. A. "Words Are Cheaper Than Blood: The Overseas O.W.I. and the Need for a Permanent Propaganda Agency," <u>Public Opinion Quarterly</u> 7 (Fall 1945): 283-304.

6058. Pollitt, Ronald. "The Abduction of Doctor John Story and the Evaluation of Elizabethan Intelligence Operations," <u>Sixteenth Century Journal</u> 14/2 (Spring 1983): 131-156.

Extensive discussion of Queen Elizabeth I's employment of covert intelligence operations in the Crown's overall efforts to counteract its enemies.

6059. Pollitt, Ronald. "From Ambassador to Prison Spy," <u>Studies in Intelligence</u> 29/2 (Summer 1985).

6060. Pollock, William W. "Electronic Warfare: Communications Intelligence," <u>Journal of Defense & Diplomacy</u> 4/5 (May 1986): 25-27.

6061. Polmar, Norman and Thomas B. Allen. "The Crypto Bandits," <u>Air Force Magazine</u> 72/6 (June 1989): 89-92.

Brief discussion of the role played by US traitors in supplying the Soviet Union with substantial communications secrets; leaks from the US Navy; vulnerable equipment; Soviet shopping for information; and Soviet deployment of quiet submarines.

6062. Polmar, Norman and Thomas B. Allen. "The Decade of the Spy," U.S. Naval Institute Proceedings 115/5 (1989): 104-109.
     Espionage during the 1980s.

6063. Polmar, Norman and Thomas B. Allen. "The Bombs of August," American History 30/2 (June 1995): 34-41, 72-76.
     A detailed discussion of the American atomic bomb project and the high level of secrecy surrounding its development.

6064. Pompa, Victor. "Managerial Secrecy: An Ethical Examination," Journal of Business Ethics 11/2 (February 1992): 147-156.
     Discusses a prima facie case against management secrecy; a hypothetical case situation; justification for secrecy; and collective justification.

6065. Ponyatovsky, K. "Modern Science in the Service of the NKVD," Ukrainian Quarterly 8 (Autumn 1952): 347-351.
     Discusses the Soviet secret police methods for extracting information by using Pavlov's technique of "nervism," starvation to poison the nervous system.

6066. Pool, Ithiel De Sola. "Content for Analysis Purposes: Alexander George's Propaganda Analysis: A Study of Inferences Made from Nazi Propaganda in World War II," World Politics 12/3 (April 1960): 478-485.
     A book review essay and discussion of problems of content analysis research, the approaches of Alexander George, propaganda as a purposeful strategic activity, qualitative versus quantitative research techniques, and contingency analysis.

6067. Popchock, Barry. "His Lordship," Civil War Times Illustrated 27/5 (1988): 22-27, 44.
     Discusses the American Civil War spy Pryce Lewis who conducted his work in disguise on the side of the Union. Later, Lewis became a detective with the Pinkerton Detective Agency.

6068. Pope, Samuel. "The Study of Intelligence," RUSI Defence Studies Journal 128/3 (September 1983): 58-59.

6069. Pope, Samuel. "Diversion: An Unrecognized Element of Intelligence?," Defense Analysis 3/2 (June 1987): 133-151.
     Extensive discussion of the concept of diversion, including forms of diversion; Soviet use of diversion in theory and practice; and conclusions.

6070. Popli, M. L. "What Ails Our Intelligence System?," Indian Defence Review (January 1991): 61-65.

6071. Popli, M. L. "National Intelligence Assessments and Estimates: Whither Our Joint Intelligence Committee?," Indian Defence Review (October 1991): 26-28.

6072. Popplewell, Richard. "The Surveillance of Indian Revolutionaries in Great Britain and on the Continent, 1903-14," Intelligence and National Security 3/1 (January 1988): 56-76.

Details British intelligence and investigative operations aimed at Indian revolutionaries in London during the period. Discusses the work of Bombay's superintendent of police, Sir John Arnold Wallinger, who was responsible for substantial inquiry into the Indian conspirators.

6073. Popplewell, Richard. "British Intelligence in Mesopotamia, 1914-16," Intelligence and National Security 5/2 (April 1990): 139-172.

Discusses intelligence in the World War I battle between British and Turkish forces, in particular, the weaknesses in British signals intelligence and status of forces. Argues that British weaknesses were attributed to poor organization and agent personnel shortages.

6074. Popplewell, Richard. "Themes in the Rhetoric of KGB Chairmen from Andropov to Kryuchkov," Intelligence and National Security 6/3 (July 1991): 513-547.

Examines public relations aspects of the KGB in the world of Glasnost. The KGB had a mission to improve the image of the USSR and of the KGB. Discusses KGB rhetoric in terms of self-promotion of power.

6075. Popplewell, Richard. "'Lacking Intelligence': Some Reflections on Recent Approaches to British Counter-Insurgency, 1900-1960," Intelligence and National Security 10/2 (April 1995): 336-352.

A book review essay of five books which address in different ways British counter-insurgency: David M. Anderson and David Killingray (eds.), Policing and Decolonisation: Nationalism, Politics and the Police, 1917-65; Michael J. Cohen and Martin Kolinsky (eds.), Britain and the Middle East in the 1930s: Security Problems, 1935-39; Peter Heehs, The Bomb in Bengal: The Rise of Revolutionary Terrorism in India, 1900-1910; Peter Hopkirk, On Secret Service East of Constantinople; and Thomas R. Mockaitis, British Counterinsurgency 1919-60.

6076. Porch, Douglas. "French Spies and Counter-Spies," Intelligence and National Security 2/1 (January 1987): 191-195.

A book review essay concerning two books on the subject.

6077. Porch, Douglas. "French Intelligence and the Fall of France 1930-40," Intelligence and National Security 4/1 (January 1989): 28-58.

The French military commanders and intelligence officers overestimated the capabilities of the German military and political leaders. Some of this, according to the author, hinged on a French feeling of moral inadequacy, French intelligence organization, and a philosophy that overlooked the role of intelligence.

6078. Porch, Douglas. "French Intelligence Culture: A Historical and Political Perspective," Intelligence and National Security 10/3 (July 1995): 486-511.

Seeks to answer several critical questions concerning the history, current conditions, and future modes of operation of the French intelligence services. Major sections address the character of the French secret services; organization; and future of the services.

6079. Porteous, Samuel D. "Economic Espionage: New Target for CSIS," Canadian Business Review 20/4 (Winter 1993): 32-34.

A brief look at the work of the Canadian Security and Intelligence Service to contain intelligence missions by foreign governments and groups to steal Canadian economic or technological information.

6080. Porteous, Samuel D. "Spook Speak," Foreign Service Journal 71/3 (March 1994): 38, 40-41.

Discusses the difficulties associated with bringing US corporations into a serious conversation about the extent and types of economic espionage carried out by foreign companies against US companies.

6081. Porteous, Samuel D. "Economic Espionage: Issues Arising from Increased Government Involvement with the Private Sector," Intelligence and National Security 9/4 (October 1994): 735-752.

Contains definitions of terms in the general realm of economic espionage, such as economic security, economic intelligence, economic espionage, industrial espionage, and sharp practices; international incidents pertaining to economic espionage; and issues for consideration in the near future.

6082. Porteous, Samuel D. "Economic/Commercial Interests and the World's Intelligence Services: A Canadian Perspective," International Journal of Intelligence and Counterintelligence 8/3 (Fall 1995): 275-306.

Discusses the role of in the analyses of world economic conditions. Major sections discuss related services to government officials; intelligence and economic and commercial interests; Canadian capabilities; a warranted role review; several useful appendices containing case studies.

6083. Porter, Bernard. "The Freiheit Prosecutions, 1881-1882," Historical Journal 23/4 (1980): 833-856.

Discusses British trials for anarchists in the period.

6084. Porter, Bernard. "The Historiography of the Early Special Branch," Intelligence and National Security 1/3 (September 1986): 381-394.

6085. Porter, Bernard. "Secrets from the Edge," Intelligence and National Security 9/4 (October 1994): 759-763.
    A book review essay covering three books on the British secret services: Brian Crozier, Free Agent: The Unseen War 1941-1991; Gary Murray, Enemies of the State; and Her Majesty's Stationery Office, The Security Service.

6086. Porter, Kenneth W. "Negroes and the East Florida Annexation Plot, 1811-1813," Journal of Negro History 30/1 (January 1945).

6087. Porter, Kenneth W. "The Seminole-Negro Indian Scouts, 1870-1881," Southwestern Historical Quarterly 55 (1951-1952): 358-377.
    A fascinating history of United States scouts who were a mixture of runaway slaves and Seminole indians, who operated on both sides of the Rio Grande River in the 1870s and 1880s.

6088. Porter, Lanning M. "Operational Intelligence in the U.S. Army," Military Intelligence 12/4 (October-December 1986): 31-36.
    Discusses several military actions at the level of war. Outlines the peculiar characteristics of intelligence associated with these actions.

6089. Porter, W. C. and W. G. von Platen. "Reconnaissance in COIN," Air University Review 15/3 (March-April 1964): 64-68.
    Considers the advancements in aerial reconnaissance against Viet Cong forces. Includes photos.

6090. Portnoi, I. L. "Provocation of the U.S. Warships in the Odessa Seaport, 1922," Istoricheskii Arkhiv 6 (1960): 183-185.
    This is an approximate title for this article in Russian.

6091. Posen, Barry R. "Measuring the European Conventional Balance: Coping with Complexity in Threat Assessment," International Security 9/3 (Winter 1984-1985): 47-88.
    Describes the problem of NATO force defense against the Warsaw Pact nations; NATO vs. Pact doctrine; factors inn thorough balance assessment; limitations of model-building; assigning values in the Attrition-FEBA Expansion model; and lessons of the model.

6092. Possony, Stefan T. "Organized Intelligence: The Problem of the French General Staff," Social Research 8 (May 1941): 213-237.
    The collapse of the French General Staff in 1940, says the author, was the direct result of a failure to organize the work of intelligence.

6093. Possony, Stefan T. "Open Skies, Arms Control, and Peace," Air Force 47/3 (1964): 71-72.

6094. Possony, Stefan T. "U.S. Intelligence at the Crossroads," Orbis 9/3 (Fall 1965): 587-612.

Discusses intelligence estimates, estimations of Soviet intentions, the influence of American "Mensheviks" and Thomas W. Wolfe's approach to Soviet military and political strategy. Useful in discussions of United States intelligence estimations of the Soviet Union's intentions.

6095. Possony, Stefan T. "HVA (Haupt Verwaltung Aufklaerung): A Revolutionary Intelligence Service," Defense and Foreign Affairs Digest 7 (April 1979): 42-43.

6096. Post, Jerrold M. "Aging Communist Leaders: Psychological Considerations," Studies in Intelligence 23/1 (Spring 1979).

6097. Post, Jerrold, M. "Critical Time Junctures in the National Estimative Process," Studies in Intelligence 26/1 (Spring 1982).

6098. Post, M. D. "German War Ciphers," Everybody's Magazine 38 (June 1918): 28-34.

A classic article from the World War I cipher experience.

6099. Postbrief, Sam. "Departure from Incrementalism in U.S. Strategic Planning: The Origins of NSC-68," Naval War College Review 33/2 (March-April 1980): 34-57.

Reexamines the Truman administration's national security planning apparatus before and during the Korean war. A thorough investigation of the details of policy approaches to NSC-68.

6100. Poteat, George H. "The Intelligence Gap: Hypotheses on the Process of Surprise," International Studies Notes 3/3 (Fall 1976): 4-8.

6101. Potter, David. "A Treason Trial in Sixteenth-Century France: The Fall of Marshal du Biez, 1549-51," English Historical Review 105 (July 1990): 595-623.

Explores in detail the circumstances of the treason trial of du Biez, emanating from the seriousness by which the French considered the actions of surrendering a fortress without due cause.

6102. Potter, Elmer B. "Admiral Nimitz and the Battle of Midway," U.S. Naval Institute Proceedings 102/7 (1976): 60-68.

6103. Potter, Elmer B. "The Crypt of Cryptanalysts," <u>U.S. Naval Institute Proceedings</u> 109/8 (August 1983): 52-56.

A brief discussion of the information sources used by the Navy to determine the characteristics of the Japanese fleet before it arrived at Midway in June 1942.

6104. Potter, Elmer B. "Admiral Nimitz and His Use of Secret Intelligence in the Pacific," <u>Revue d'Histoire de la Deuxieme Guerre Mondiale et des Conflits</u> 34/133 (1984): 29-42.

An examination of the effectiveness of US intelligence operations for providing information prior to the Battle of Midway.

6105. Potter, Luther L., Jr. and Jack R. Donovan. "Tactical Intelligence," <u>Military Intelligence</u> 8/3 (July-September 1982): 4-8.

Outlines the organization and activities of battalion and division relationships in the tactical intelligence environment.

6106. Potter, William. "Perception and Misperception in U.S.-Soviet Relations," <u>Problems of Communism</u> 29/2 (1980): 68-71.

The strains of US and Soviet relations are associated with misperceptions held and reinforced by each country.

6107. Poullada, Leon B. "Afghanistan and the United States: The Crucial Years," <u>Middle East Journal</u> (Spring 1981): 178-190.

Historical discussion containing major sections which address the formative period, 1919-1942; the years of opportunity, 1942-1953; the critical years, 1953-1956; the problem of military aid; and conclusions. Brief mention of the CIA.

6108. Pound, Roscoe. "The Military Telegraph in the Civil War," <u>Massachusetts Historical Society Proceedings</u> 66 (1942): 185-283.

6109. Poveda, Tony G. "The FBI and Domestic Intelligence: Technocratic or Public Relations Triumph?," <u>Crime and Delinquency</u> 28/2 (April 1982): 194-210.

Argues that domestic intelligence operations in the J. Edgar Hoover FBI served essentially organizational and public relations functions.

6110. Poveda, Tony G. "The Rise and Fall of FBI Domestic Intelligence Operations," <u>Contemporary Crises: Crime, Law and Social Policy</u> 6/2 (April 1982): 103-118.

Domestic intelligence of the FBI rises and falls within the total context of the political economic environment in the US. A useful evaluation of the organizational changes in the FBI from 1908 to 1982.

6111. Poveda, Tony G. "Effects of Scandal on Organizational Deviance - The Case of the FBI," Justice Quarterly 2/2 (June 1985): 237-258.

A comparison of two perspectives on organizational deviance: how disclosures of organizational power are related to scandal, and the impact of scandal on organizational deviance. Focus is on the FBI as an organization, and the methods of the study rely on newspaper articles from 1950 to 1982.

6112. Powe, Marc B. "Which Way for Tactical Intelligence After Vietnam?," Military Review 54/9 (September 1974): 48-56.

Discusses military intelligence organization problems.

6113. Powe, Marc B. "The History of American Military Intelligence: A Review of Selected Literature," Military Affairs 39/3 (October 1975): 142-145.

Focusses primarily upon books about American military intelligence history while arguing that historian's need to look more closely at the progress made by military intelligence.

6114. Powe, Marc B. "American Military Intelligence Comes of Age," Military Review 55/12 (December 1975): 17-30.

Discusses the key contributions of Ralph H. Van Deman for creating the first complete US intelligence system.

6115. Powe, Scot. "Espionage, Leaks, and the First Amendment," Bulletin of the Atomic Scientists 42/6 (June-July 1986): 8-10.

Discussion of Samuel Loring Morison's prosecution under the espionage law. Morison leaked US satellite photos to a British magazine, Jane's Defence Weekly.

6116. Powell, Dave. "Unraveling the Web of Computer Espionage," American Intelligence Journal 14/2&3 (Spring-Summer 1993): 83-88.

Discusses the author's experiences in sniffing out the experts on computer espionage; global espionage by computer; the disappearance of information on networks; and common sense protection against information theft.

6117. Powell, E. Alexander "The Remarkable American Count," American Heritage 7/12 (December 1956): 74-77, 98-100.

Discusses the work of Benjamin Thompson, also known as Count Rumford, especially his role and life during the American revolution.

6118. Powell, Geoffrey. "John Buchan's Richard Hannay," History Today 37 (August 1987): 32-39.

John Buchan (1875-1940) authored several modern espionage novels and short stories. He found inspiration for the novel The Thirty Nine Steps (1915) in the exploits in Southwest Africa of a secret service agent named William Edmond

Ironside (1880-1959). Ironside played an important role in British espionage in what is now Namibia.

6119. Powers, Richard G. "J. Edgar Hoover and the Detective Hero," <u>Journal of Popular Culture</u> 9/2 (1975): 257-278.

　　The author's early study of Hoover's ability to sell himself and the FBI as defenders of law and order, thus entering the popular culture as the detective hero. See the author's recent book, <u>Secrecy and Power</u>.

6120. Powers, Richard G. "The Attorney General and the G-Man," <u>Southwest Review</u> 62/4 (Fall 1977): 329-346.

　　A discussion of the first movie about the work of the Federal Bureau of Investigation, <u>G-Men</u>. The film was opposed by the Attorney General, Homer Cummings.

6121. Powers, Richard G. "One G-Man's Family: Popular Entertainment Formulas and J. Edgar Hoover's F.B.I.," <u>American Quarterly</u> 30/4 (Fall 1978): 471-492.

　　A thorough analysis of J. Edgar Hoover's manipulation of movies, magazines, comic strips and radio regarding the FBI's role in crime fighting. Useful in discussions of propaganda, organization myth making and domestic crime threats.

6122. Powers, Thomas. "Inside the Department of Dirty Tricks," <u>Atlantic Monthly</u> 244/2 (August 1979): 33-64.

　　The author's adaptation of discussions about covert actions found in his book, <u>The Man Who Kept the Secrets</u>, pertaining to CIA's former director Richard Helms.

6123. Powers, Thomas. "The Government Is Watching: Is There Anything the Police Don't Want to Know?," <u>Atlantic Monthly</u> 230 (October 1972): 51-63.

　　Suggesting possible applications of George Orwell's novel <u>1984</u>, the author points to examples of reasonable suspicions concerning government spying on citizens. Referring to various cases of domestic and other forms of government spying, reforms and protections are proposed.

6124. Powers, Thomas. "How to Retire at 45," <u>Notre Dame Magazine</u> (February 1982): 27-29.

　　The author interviewed former Central Intelligence Agency case officer Ralph McGehee.

6125. Powers, Thomas. "How the Bomb Was Kept from Hitler," <u>Atlantic Monthly</u> 100 (May 1990): 26-29.

6126. Poyo, Gerald E. "Key West and the Cuban Ten Years," Florida Historical Quarterly 57 (January 1979).

6127. Poyourow, Robert L. "Title III and National Security Surveillances," Boston University Law Review 56/4 (July 1976): 776-802.
    Discusses national security surveillances in the wake of Zweibon v. Mitchell; Title III of the Safe Streets Act of 1968 and the Keith decision; and an analysis of the issues presented in Zweibon.

6128. Prados, John. "High-Flying Spies," Bulletin of the Atomic Scientists 48/7 (September 1992): 11-12.
    A brief account of military aircraft and intelligence collection operations.

6129. Prados, John. "The Warning That Left Something to Chance: Intelligence at Tet," Journal of American-East Asian Relations 2/2 (1993): 161-184.

6130. Prados, John. "Woolsey and the CIA," Bulletin of the Atomic Scientists 49/6 (July-August 1993): 33-38.

6131. Prados, John. "The Spies at the Bottom of the Sea," MHQ: Quarterly Journal of Military History 6/2 (Winter 1994): 38-47.
    A reasonably detailed account of the salvage operations in 1945 aimed at recovering a critical Japanese naval vessel downed off the Phillipine Islands in 1944, thus leading to significant understanding of Japanese tactics in naval warfare.

6132. Prados, John. "US Intelligence and the Japanese Evacuation of Guadalcanal, 1943," Intelligence and National Security 10/2 (April 1995): 294-305.
    An account of the Japanese Imperial Navy's successful evacuation of Guadalcanal, one of the worst Allied intelligence failures of the Pacific War.

6133. Pratt, Fletcher. "A Plea for Ciphers," U.S. Naval Institute Proceedings 59/363 (May 1933): 692-696.

6134. Pratt, Fletcher. "How Not to Run a Spy System," Harper's 195 (September 1947): 241-246.
    One of the few voices that opposed the centralization of intelligence after World War II.

6135. Pratt, Gerald D. "Diplomatic Immunity--Foreign Nationals Employed by the United Nations are not Afforded the Same Degree of Immunity as Foreign Diplomats; Seizure of Illegally Obtained National Security Information from a Foreign Minister did not Violate his Right to Diplomatic Immunity: United States

v. Enger, 472 F. Supp. 490 (D.N.J. 1978)," Denver Journal of International Law and Policy 9/1 (Winter 1980): 148-152.

Reports the facts, issues, law and holding in the case. Enger was charged with espionage and conspiracy to commit espionage following a Federal Bureau of Investigation-United States Navy coordinated counterintelligence operation. Enger claimed a legal defense of diplomatic immunity, but the court rejected this position.

6136. Pratt, Lawrence. "Anglo-American Naval Conversations on the Far East of January 1938," International Affairs (Great Britain) 47/4 (October 1971): 745-763.

Historical study of the communications between the United States and England regarding plans for US involvement in a war with Japan, some of which were made in 1936+.

6137. Presseisen, Ernst L. "Prelude to 'BARBAROSSA': Germany and the Balkans, 1940-1941," Journal of Modern History 32/4 (September 1960): 359-370.

6138. Prestel, Robert L. "TQ at NSA," American Intelligence Journal 15/1 (Spring-Summer 1994): 43-45.

Brief discussion of the application of Total Quality Management at the National Security Agency.

6139. Preston, Joseph W. "Just Cause--Intelligence Support to Special Operations Aviation," Military Intelligence 16/3 (July-September 1990): 16-18.

Discusses the role of the 1989 mission of the 160th Special Operations Aviation Group in 'Just Cause' in Panama. Includes emphases on reconnaissance and target analysis.

6140. Preston, William, Jr. "In Security's Name," Progressive 43 (May 1979): 55-56.

6141. Prestwich, J. O. "The Treason of Geoffrey de Mandeville," English Historical Review 103 (April 1988): 283-317.

A case study of the twelth century treason of de Mandeville.

6142. Preuss, Lawrence. "International Law and German Legislation on Political Crime," Grotius Society 20 (1935): 85-105.

Discussion of the increase of political crime from World War I to 1934, political crime in post-war Germany, the position of foreigners under the German law of political crime, the law of treason and espionage, German law and the territorial principle, and the German law of high treason.

6143. Price, Alfred. "The Radio War," R.A.F Flying Review 18 (June 1963): 25-27+.
Describes British and German radar systems employed in World War II.

6144. Price, Byron. "Governmental Censorship in Wartime," American Political Science Review 36/5 (October 1942): 837-849.
Argues that censorship is offensive and dangerous in a democracy, but most accept the notion of wartime applications of information controls. Discusses mail and press censorship and describes the role of President Roosevelt's Office of Censorship.

6145. Price, Hugh. "Another View of the New Zealand Security Intelligence Service," Political Science 31/1 (July 1979): 65-68.
A comment/discussion, largely negative, in response to Professor W. T. Roy's article (see this bibliography), suggesting that Roy's account is fragmentary and descriptive.

6146. Price, James. "Our Man in the Torture Chamber: The Novels of Ian Fleming," London Magazine 2/4 (1962): 67-70.

6147. Price, Robert. "Further Notes on Anecdotes on Spread-Spectrum Origins," IEEE Transactions on Communications 31 (January 1983): 85-97.

6148. Price, Robert. "A Conversation with Claude Shannon: One Man's Approach to Problem Solving," Cryptologia 9/2 (April 1985): 167-175.

6149. Price, Thomas J. "The Changing Image of the Soviets in the Bond Saga: From Bond-Villains to 'Acceptable Role Partners,'" Journal of Popular Culture 26/1 (Summer 1992): 17-37.
Major sections discuss society, popular fiction and spy stories; the Bond saga as industry; Bond villains, conspiracies and the role of the Soviets; and the Bond saga as history.

6150. Price, Thomas J. "Popular Perceptions of an Ally: "The Special Relationship" in the British Spy Novel," Journal of Popular Culture 28 (Fall 1994): 49-66.

6151. Prince, James. "Is There a Role for Intelligence in Combating Terrorism?," Conflict: An International Journal 9/3 (1989): 301-318.

6152. Pringle, Peter. "Yellow Rain: The Cost of Chemical Arms Control," SAIS Review 5/1 (1985): 151-162.

6153. Prior, Leon O. "Nazi Invasion of Florida," Florida Historical Quarterly

49/2 (October 1970): 129-139.

Recounts the Nazi espionage and sabotage mission to Florida in World War II in terms of objectives, goals, the arrival, the capture and the trials.

6154. Pritchett, Diane T. "The Syrian Strategy on Terrorism: 1971-1977," Conflict Quarterly 8 (Summer 1988): 27-48.

6155. Probst, Reed R. "Clausewitz on Intelligence," Studies in Intelligence 29/3 (Fall 1985).

6156. Probst, Reed R. "Intelligence as a Force Enhancer," Studies in Intelligence 31/4 (Winter 1987).

6157. Probst, Reed R. "Triage in Intelligence," Studies in Intelligence 34/1 (Spring 1990).

6158. Pronay, Nicholas and Philip M. Taylor. "'An Improper Use of Broadcasting': The British Government and Clandestine Radio Propaganda Operations Against Germany During the Munich Crisis and After," Journal of Contemporary History 19/3 (July 1984): 357-384.

Discusses the British use of radio propaganda in September 1938 in violation of rules of the League of Nations and without any net positive impact on the German will to proceed with plans for conflict in Europe.

6159. Propas, Frederic L. "Creating a Hard Line Toward Russia: The Training of State Department Soviet Experts, 1927-1937," Diplomatic History 8/3 (Summer 1984): 209-226.

6160. Propp, Kenneth. "Export Controls: Restrictions on the Export of Critical Technologies," Harvard International Law Journal 22/2 (Spring 1981): 411-418.

Briefly explains the US Defense Department's list of Initial Militarily Critical Technologies which identifies items that potential adversaries might acquire to harm US national security interests. Mentions certain constitutional challenges to the authority to issue and guard the list's secrecy.

6161. Prouty, L. Fletcher. "The Secret Team and the Games They Play," Washington Monthly 2/3 (May 1970): 11-19.

Author discusses his personal experiences in CIA and the methods used by CIA to secure its position in the national security policy community.

6162. Prouty, L. Fletcher. "An Inside Look: Watergate and the World of CIA," Ramparts 12 (October 1973): 21-23.

Generally considered a popular press resource, but the author's book, The Secret Team (1973) attracted considerable public controversy.

6163. Pruden, Russell and Thomas C. Mendenhall. "The Yale Collection of War Literature," Yale University Library Gazette 17 (July 1942): 14-20.
   A useful bibliographic discussion.

6164. Pryce-Jones, David. "Agents of Influence," Commentary 99/4 (April 1995): 53-56.
   Brief discussion of the Guardian newspaper's role relationship to espionage and propaganda in Britain.

6165. Pryor, Frederic L. "On Reading My Stasi Files," National Interest 38 (Winter 1994-1995): 74-82.
   The author applied to the German government to read the file the East German Stasi intelligence service had prepared on him during his time in Germany more than thirty years ago. His purpose was to come to terms with his past and the reasoning behind the Stasi records of his work and activities.

6166. Ptak, Michael J. "Commercial Torts -- Trade Secrets -- Arkansas Extends Trade Secret Protection to Customer Lists under the Arkansas Trade Secrets Act," University of Arkansas at Little Rock Law Journal 14 (Summer 1992): 693-716.
   Discusses the historical development of Arkansas trade secrets law; reasoning of the Arkansas Supreme Court in Allen v. Johar, Inc.; and analysis and significance of Allen.

6167. Puderbaugh, Richard T. "Elegant Writing in the Intelligence Services," Studies in Intelligence 16 (1972).
   This piece is found in a special edition to Studies.

6168. Puderbaugh, Richard T. "Elegant Writing - Report Number Two," Studies in Intelligence 17/2 (Summer 1973).

6169. Pugh, Michael. "Legal Aspects of the Rainbow Warrior Affair," International & Comparative Law Quarterly 36 (July 1987): 655-669.
   Argues that there was a contravention of international law when French military security (DGSE) personnel sank the British-registered Rainbow Warrior in the Auckland Harbour in 1985.

6170. Pughe, George A. "The Dust That Isn't There," Studies in Intelligence 2 (Spring 1958).
   Refers to Soviet publications in the Library of Congress.

6171. Pulaski, Charles A., Jr. "Authorizing Wiretap Applications Under Title III: Another Dissent to Giordano and Chavez," University of Pennsylvania Law Review 123/4 (April 1975): 750-821.
   Major sections include introductions to each case; wiretap authorization

procedures in the two cases; the suppression sanction; the nature of institutionalized deception; misreliance on ex post facto government affidavits.

6172. Punke, H. H. "Secret Diplomacy and American Democracy," Social Studies 47 (1956): 83-88.
　　　Argues that American secret diplomacy mitigates against strong popular participation in the affairs American government.

6173. Purdy, Chip. "Foreign Intelligence Surveillance Act: Unconstitutional Warrant Criteria Permit Wiretapping if a Possibility of Terrorism," San Diego Law Review 17/4 (July 1980): 963-977.
　　　Discussion of the warrant criteria established in the Foreign Intelligence Surveillance Act of 1978 as applied to persons who may be international terrorists. Author concludes that the criteria are unconstitutional under the Fourth Amendment.

6174. Pursell, Caroll W., Jr. "Thomas Digges and William Pearce: An Example of the Transit of Technology," William and Mary Quarterly 21 (1964): 551-560.

6175. Purvis, Thomas L. "The Aftermath of Fort William Henry's Fall: New Jersey Captives Among the French and Indians," New Jersey History 103/3-4 (1985): 68-79.

6176. Putnam, George W. "Patriots Who Were Not Soldiers," Magazine of History 40 (February 1914): 73-87.

6177. Putney, Diane T. "Reflections on Intelligence and History," American Intelligence Journal 13/3 (Summer 1992): 85-87.
　　　Author argues that primary sources in the intelligence field are the key to good history, and that good intelligence history can be written to inform the policy process.

6178. Puttick, Keith. "Interception of Communications Act," New Law Journal 135 (September 1985): 912.

6179. Puzder, Andrew. "The Fourth Amendment and Executive Authorization of Warrantless Foreign Security Surveillance," Washington University Law Quarterly 1978/2 (Spring 1978): 397-430.
　　　A case law note on the subject.

6180. Pyle, Christopher H. "CONUS Intelligence: The Army Watches Civilian Politics," Washington Monthly 1/12 (January 1970): 4-16.
　　　Discusses the US Army intelligence operations to surveil and report on activities of dissident political groups. Includes discussion of Army needs for the

information; Army authority; the program's impact; and what can be done to resolve the conflict over the investigations.

6181. Pyle, Christopher H.   "CONUS Revisited: The Army Covers Up," Washington Monthly 2/5 (July 1970): 49-58.

Discusses the US Army's continued spying escapades in civilian politics in the US. Details the Army plans and operations for internal intelligence work against individuals and groups.

6182. Pyle, Christopher H. "Spies Without Masters: The Army Still Watches Civilian Politics," Civil Liberties Review 1/3 (Summer 1974): 38-49.

Discusses the motives, operations and results of Army surveillance of US citizens. Especially useful are observations about the weakness of civilian controls over military intelligence.

6183. Pyle, Christopher H. "The Invasion of Privacy," Proceedings of the Academy of Political Science 34/4 (1982): 131-142.

Discusses the historical evolution of invasions of privacy since 1890 and argues the case that the FBI abused its authority by harassing political dissidents.

6184. Pyper, Robert. "Sarah Tisdall, Ian Willmore, and the Civil Servant's 'Right to Leak,'" Political Quarterly 56/1 (January-March 1985): 72-81.

Describes the events of leaks of government information in the cases of Sarah Tisdall and Ian Willmore. Defends the need for government secrecy but suggests that new controls must be employed to encourage more secrecy when moral issues are at stake.

Q

"...an enemy places some obstacle or similar thing
between the sender and the addressee..."
(Qalqashandi, cited in The Code-Breakers by David Kahn, p. 95)

6185. Quade, Vicki. "Graymail Law Challenged in Two CIA Cases," American Bar Association Journal 68 (October 1982): 1209-1210.

Brief discussion of Edwin Wilson's case to force the CIA to reveal information to test the Classified Information Procedures Act of 1982.

6186. Quam, Ed. "Intelligence Restructuring: The European Command Perspective," Defense Intelligence Journal 1/1 (Spring 1992): 55-60.

A brief consideration of the intelligence mission in the US European Command (EUCOM).

6187. Quandt, William B. "Soviet Policy in the October Middle East War, Part I," International Affairs [Great Britain] 53/3 (July 1977): 377-389.

First of two parts. Discusses the background of Soviet Middle East policy after 1967; political differences and the Soviet supply of arms; question of Soviet foreknowledge; and Soviet policy during the war.

6188. Quandt, William B. "Soviet Policy in the October Middle East War, Part II," International Affairs [Great Britain] 53/4 (October 1977): 587-603.

Second of 2 parts. Picks up with the deterioration of the military situation on the Syrian front after October 9. Discusses talks on ceasefire, Soviet weapons deliveries, negotiations in Moscow and conclusions and lessons.

6189.   Quartararo, Rosaria.   "Il Canale Segreto di Chamberlain," <u>Storia Contemporanea</u> 8 (1976).

6190.   Quesenberry, John M.   "SIGINT in World War II: Personal Reminiscences of an Intercept Operator in China," <u>American Intelligence Journal</u> 15/1 (Spring-Summer 1994): 59-65.
     The personal experiences of the author in China during World War II.

6191.   Quester, George H.   "On the Identification of Real and Pretended Communist Military Doctrine," <u>Journal of Conflict Resolution</u> 10 (June 1966): 172-179.

6192. Quester, George H. "Missiles in Cuba, 1970," <u>Foreign Affairs</u> 49/3 (April 1971): 493-506.
     Considers indicators and issues associated with new Soviet efforts to position missiles in Cuba.

6193. Quester, George H. "The Guerilla Problem in Retrospect," <u>Military Affairs</u> 39/4 (1975): 192-196.

6194. Quibble, Anthony. "The Eastern Front at the Turning Point," <u>Studies in Intelligence</u> 6/3 (Fall 1962).
     Discusses German logistics in 1941.

6195. Quibble, Anthony. "Alias George Wood," <u>Studies in Intelligence</u> 10/4 (Winter 1966): 69-90.
     A study of counterespionage techniques.

6196. Quibble, Anthony. "Roderick 'Steve' Hall," <u>Studies in Intelligence</u> 11/3 (Fall 1967): 45-78.
     A discussion of OSS agent Hall's work and his Alpine tragedy during World War II.

6197. Quigg, Philip W. "Open Skies, Open Space," <u>Foreign Affairs</u> 37/1 (March 1958): 95-106.
     An economist's perspective on the free frontier of space and the need for defining through the United Nations the uses of space for intelligence purposes.

6198. Quigley, John. "Missiles with a Message: The Legality of the United States Raid on Iraq's Intelligence Headquarters," <u>Hastings International and Comparative Law Review</u> 17 (Winter 1994): 241-274.
     Major topics consider the evidence of an Iraqi plot; requirements for self defense in international law; and several fact questions that bear on the international legal issues; and conclusions.

6199. Quin, James F. and John E. Holman. "Intrafamilial Conflict Among Felons Under Community Supervision: A Examination of the Co-Habitants of Electronically Monitored Offenders," Journal of Offender Rehabilitation 16/3&4 (1991): 177-192.

6200. Quinn, Frank; Leaf Rich; and Richard A. Berglund. "Insurgency and Counterinsurgency in Eastern Europe," Defense Intelligence Journal 3/2 (Fall 1994): 75-103.

    Extensive discussion of East European turmoil; insurgency and counterinsurgency in the region; Hungary; Poland; Slovakia; Czech Republic; and overall analysis and conclusions.

6201. Quint, Peter E. "The Separation of Power Under Carter. United States v. Snepp-595 F.2d 926 (4th Cir. 1979); Haig v. Agee-453 U.S. 280 (1981); Narenji v. Civiletti-617 F.2d 745 (D.C. Cir. 1979); United States v. Humphrey-456 F. Supp. 51 (E.D. Va. 1978); United States v. Hung-629 F.2d 9098 (4th Cir. 1980)," Texas Law Review 62 (February 1984): 785-891.

    A case note summation of the cases mentioned in the title and the relevance of these cases to national security policymaking. Some of these cases pertain to the CIA.

6202. Quintanilla, Hector, Jr. "The Investigation of UFOs," Studies in Intelligence 10/3 (Fall 1966): 95-110.

6203. Quisquater, Jean-Jacques and Yvo G. Desmedt. "Chinese Lotto As An Exhaustive Code-Breaking Machine," Computer 24 (November 1991): 14-22.

R

"The man whose life was so full of mystery would probably himself
have wished it to end where it began--in mystery."
(Reilly: Ace of Spies by Robin Bruce Lockhart, p. 220)

6204. Raab, Stephen S. "A Midnight Ride," Civil War Times Illustrated
(March-April 1994).

6205. Ra'anan, Uri and Richard H. Shultz, Jr. "Oral History: A Neglected
Dimension of Sovietology," Strategic Review 15/2 (Spring 1987): 58-70.

6206. Raat, William D. "The Diplomacy of Suppression: Los Revoltosos,
Mexico, and the United States, 1906-1911," Hispanic American Historical Review
56/4 (1976): 529-550.
　　　　Suggests that an espionage system was established by the US and Mexico
to counteract the activities of Los Revoltosos aimed at overthrowing President
Diaz. Discusses the espionage system, the Cananco strike, implications of the
"regeneracion" editors, aid of detective agencies, and Francisco Madero's success.

6207. Raat, William D. "U.S. Intelligence Operations and Covert Action in
Mexico, 1900-47," Journal of Contemporary History 22/4 (October 1987):
615-638.
　　　　This article details the establishment and maturation of intelligence
operations conducted by the US in Mexico, especially covert actions. It chronicles
the roles of the FBI, OSS and State Department and it discusses aspects of the
Leon Trotsky assassination.

6208. Rabe, Stephen G. "Eisenhower and the Overthrow of Rafael Trujillo," Conflict Quarterly 6/1 (Winter 1986): 34-44.

Using declassified sources, discusses Eisenhower administration's fear that Trujillo had become a menace to hemispheric security, thus bringing it to consider violent means of deposing him.

6209. Rabe, Stephen G. "The Clues Didn't Check Out: Commentary on 'The CIA and Castillo Armas,'" Diplomatic History 14/1 (Winter 1990): 87-95.

Argues that the historian is obligated to carefully examine all sources of information on a subject before making judgments about the unfolding of an event.   The author is particular critical of Frederick Marks' writing on the overthrow of the Arbenz government in Guatemala, preferring the works of Blanche Cook, Richard Immerman, Stephen Kinzer, Stephen Schlesinger and Bruce Wood.

6210. Rabe, Stephen G. "Eisenhower Revisionism: A Decade of Scholarship," Diplomatic History 17/1 (Winter 1993): 97-115.

6211. Rabinowitch, Eugene. "Atomic Spy Trials: Heretical Afterthoughts," Bulletin of the Atomic Scientists 7/5 (May 1951): 139-142.

Asks how important were atomic spy activities; was there too little or too much secrecy? Also discusses disillusionment, the future, and criminal sentences for espionage.

6212. Rabinowitz, Victor. "The Rosenberg Case and United States Policy," Science and Society 31 (Winter 1967): 67-73.

Author summarizes the book on the Rosenberg espionage case by the Schneir's, suggesting that the prosecution's main witness had doubtful credibility, the evidence discredits the prosecution's witness, and the conviction was based on a sketch of the atomic bomb rather than a more sophisticated rendition.

6213. Rabson, John. "All Are Well at Boldon: A Mid-Victorian Code System," Cryptologia 16/2 (April 1992): 127-135.

6214. Rabson, John and Hugo Rabson. "The War Office HK POW Cypher System," Cryptologia 14/1 (January 1990): 53-60.

6215. Race, Jeffrey. "Vietnam Intervention: Systematic Distortion in Policy-Making," Armed Forces & Society 2 (Spring 1976): 377-396.

6216. Radosh, Ronald. "The Teacher as Scholar-Spy: The CIA and the Academy," Change 8/7 (August 1976): 38-42, 64.

Argues that universities should not be exploited by the CIA for purposes of research or recruitment of faculty. Major sections include discussion of the

CIA presence in academia, the relationship between the CIA and scholars, and separating the CIA from universities.

6217. Radu, Michael L. "Romanian Involvement in Colonial Angola," South African Journal of African Affairs 9/3&4 (1979): 151-154.
A rare glimpse at this African nation's intrigues.

6218. Radu, Michael S. "Terror, Terrorism, and Insurgency in Latin America," Orbis 28/1 (Spring 1984): 27-41.
Discusses patterns and methods of terrorism in Latin America; some sociological aspects of Latin American terrorism; universities and violence; the Church and violence; terrorists and terrorism; terrorism and guerilla warfare; and terrorism and terror.

6219. Raeff, Mark. "The Well-Ordered Police State and the Department of Modernity in Seventeenth-and Eighteenth-Century Europe: An Attempt at a Comparative Approach," American Historical Review 80/5 (December 1975): 1221-1243.
Discusses the expansion of the state's role in the economic, social and cultural aspects of european life. Notes the internal development of countries, including the statutory and administrative expansion of the police function. Useful in discussions of the role of police in domestic development.

6220. Raezer, Thomas A. "Needed Weapons in the Army's War on Drugs: Electronic Surveillance and Informants," Military Law Review 116 (Spring 1987): 1-65.
Major sections include discussion of electronic surveillance, consensual interceptions and the wired informant, nonconsensual surveillance, informants, recruiting and rewarding, using "reverse stings," and protection of informants. Focusses on military intelligence of the drug problem.

6221. Rahmathullah, B. "Indo-U.S. Politics: An Analysis," Indian Journal of Politics 12/3 (1978): 227-236.
A discussion of the political change in India and the relationship of India to the United States. Discusses the legacies and actions of certain American presidents, such as President Franklin D. Roosevelt's correspondence with Prime Minister Winston Churchill on British intentions concerning the colony of India, and later, President Jimmy Carter's decision to proclaim the Indian Ocean as a demilitarized zone.

6222. Raimondi, Guiseppe and Rudolfo Rufino. "Capabilities and Vulnerabilities in the Evaluation of Military Information," Military Review 39/10 (October 1959): 96-101.

6223. Ramesh, R. S.; G. Athithan; and K. Thiruvengadam. "An Automatic Approach to Solve Simple Substitution Ciphers," Cryptologia 17/2 (April 1993): 202-218.

6224. Ramsay, A. M. "A Roman Postal Service Under the Republic," Journal of Roman Studies 10 (1920): 79-86.
Major sections include discussion of the Roman road system, the use of the inscription, and reasons for the lapse of the postal system. Concludes that a sophisticated system of postal communication existed before Augustus.

6225. Ramsay, A. M. "The Speed of the Roman Imperial Post," Journal of Roman Studies 15 (1925): 60-74.
Argues that the Roman message and intelligence system emphasized the certainty of arrival within a reasonable and calculable time over the speed of delivery. Discusses historical development of the system. Useful in historical discussions of intelligence transmission.

6226. Ramsay, Jack. "My Case Against the RCMP," Maclean's (July 1972): 19-23, 58, 60, 62, 65-66, 68-69, 73-74.
Argues that the Royal Canadian Mounted Police (RCMP) is more interested in perceptions of its police functions than in the pursuit of justice. The decline in morale through the years has led to less effectiveness in the RCMP's police work. Major sections discuss discipline by fear, RCMP rules, injustice, inspections, statistics, morale, favorites, frustration, image, and change.

6227. Ramsay, Logan C. "The 'Ifs' of Pearl Harbor," U.S. Naval Institute Proceedings 76 (1950): 364-371.

6228. Ramsbotham, David. "Analysis and Assessment for Peacekeeping Operations," Intelligence and National Security 10/4 (October 1995): 162-174.
Intelligence assessment in the context of United Nations and NATO operations is discussed. Major sections consider the nature of preventive action; conflict resolution; post conflict reconstruction or peace rebuilding; and conclusions.

6229. Ramsey, R. W. R. "German Espionage in South America 1939-45," Army Quarterly and Defence Journal 118/1 (January 1988); 55-59.
Discusses Abwehr activities in Latin America. The Abwehr was directed by Admiral Wilhelm Canaris.

6230. Ranard, Donald L. "The Korean CIA in the USA," Worldview 19/11 (November 1976): 19-21.
A brief discussion of the activities operations of the Korean Central Intelligence Agency conducted inside the US.

6231. Randall, James G. "The Newspaper Problem in Its Bearing Upon Military Secrecy During the Civil War," American Historical Review 23/2 (January 1918): 303-323.
     A thorough discussion of the impact of newspaper revelations upon military actions in wartime. Concludes that military interference in freedom of the press was minimal and voluntary restraint by the press was more significant.

6232. Randall, James G. "The Blundering Generation," Mississippi Valley Historical Review 27/1 (June 1940).

6233. Randall, Willard S. "Mrs. Benedict Arnold," MHQ: Quarterly Journal of Military History 4/2 (Winter 1992): 80-89.
     See also this author's full biography of Benedict Arnold.

6234. Randle, Devin D. "What Really Happened to Gary Powers and His U-2," Air Classics 15 (April 1979): 64-67.

6235. Randolph, Norris. "Our Man in Weston," New England Monthly (July 1985): 14-16.

6236. Random, R. A. "Intelligence as a Science," Studies in Intelligence 2 (Spring 1958).

6237. Rankin, Karl L. "Communist Insurgency in Greece," Naval War College Review (September 1962): 1-22.

6238. Rankin, Murray J. "National Security: Information, Accountability, and the Canadian Security Intelligence Service," University of Toronto Law Journal 36/3 (Summer 1986): 249-285.

6239. Rankin, Murray J. "The Security Intelligence Review Committee: Reconciling National Security with Procedural Fairness," Canadian Journal of Administrative Law and Practice 3 (1988): 73-97.

6240. Ransom, Harry H. "Strategic Intelligence and Foreign Policy," World Politics 27/1 (October 1974): 131-146.
     A discussion of new information revealing the impact of intelligence gathering on the process of domestic and foreign policy making.

6241. Ransom, Harry H. "Congress and the Intelligence Agencies," Proceedings of the Academy of Political Science 32/1 (1975): 153-166.
     Discusses the difficulties encountered from 1947 to the mid-1970s in bringing more accountability to US intelligence agencies.

6242. Ransom, Harry H. "The Uses (and Abuses) of Secret Power," <u>Foreign Service Journal</u> 52/9 (March 1975): 15-18, 29-30.

An assessment of assumptions that guide intelligence gathering and analysis in the perpetual conflict between democratic principles and national security.

6243. Ransom, Harry H. "Secret Intelligence Agencies and Congress," <u>Society</u> 12/3 (March-April 1975): 33-38.

Discusses the on-going conflict between executive and legislative branches over secrecy of national security information. Argues that the original concept of the CIA did not include a dual purpose agency of collection/analysis and covert operations.

6244. Ransom, Harry H. "The Uses (and Abuses) of Secret Power: Toward Re-Shaping the Intelligence Community," <u>Worldview</u> 18/5 (May 1975): 11-18.

Evaluates a series of assumptions about the role of the American intelligence community in national security. Assumptions concern such matters as the need for the Central Intelligence Agency, the control of CIA activities, the supervision of covert actions, the role of Congress in oversight, press disclosures and the CIA, and the relationship between domestic turmoil and CIA activities.

6245. Ransom, Harry H. "Congress and Reform of the CIA," <u>Policy Studies Journal</u> 5/4 (Summer 1977): 476-480.

Discusses the evolution of oversight of the intelligence community in the Congress, limited somewhat by the failure of the House of Representatives to create an investigating committee for intelligence affairs. The author offers explanations for the House's failure to act immediately to introduce intelligence oversight.

6246. Ransom, Harry H. "Being Intelligent About Secret Intelligence Agencies," <u>American Political Science Review</u> 74/1 (March 1980): 141-148.

The author identifies the sources of public knowledge about the CIA, including the books by former insiders, activist groups, whistle-blowers, congressional committee reports and government documents. All such insights provide only minimal exploration of the inside world of the CIA.

6247. Ransom, Harry H. "Strategic Intelligence," <u>Proceedings of the Academy of Political Science</u> 34/4 (1982): 153-164.

Discusses the effects of increased technological advancements on the intelligence gathering apparatuses of the US.

6248. Ransom, Harry H. "Review Essay," <u>American Political Science Review</u> 80 (1986): 985-991.

6249. Ransom, Harry H. "Essay: Information and Action," <u>Studies in Intelligence</u> 31/1 (Spring 1987).

6250. Ransom, Harry H. "The Intelligence Function and the Constitution," <u>Armed Forces and Society</u> 14/1 (Fall 1987): 43-63.
A discussion of the roles played by the President and the Congress in directing and controlling the intelligence function since World War II. The article tries to demonstrate the permissive/restrictive role of Congress over the Executive branch.

6251. Rapoport, David. "Fear and Trembling: Terrorism in Three Religious Traditions," <u>American Political Science Review</u> 78/3 (September 1984): 658-677.

6252. Raskin, Marcus G. "A Short Account of International Student Politics and the Cold War with Particular Reference to the NSA, CIA, etc.," <u>Ramparts</u> (March 1967): 29-39.
Generally considered a popular press publication.

6253. Raskin, Marcus G. "Democracy Versus the National Security State," <u>Law and Contemporary Problems</u> 40/3 (Summer 1976): 189-220.
Argues that the state secrets system of the US has been deformed to the menace of it citizens, thus posing a danger to world civilization. Discusses the national security state as a ballast for US supremacy, the use of the national security state to undermine law, and imperialism as a self-justifying instrument of domestic policy in the national security state.

6254. Raskin, Marcus G. "'JFK' and the Culture of Violence," <u>American Historical Review</u> 97/2 (April 1992): 486-499.
Referring to Oliver Stone's movie, "JFK", the author discusses the culture of violence that produced such events as the attempted assassination of Fidel Castro, the Vietnam War, and American covert actions. Argues that government records must be unsealed in order to fully understand the methods for perpetuating the culture of violence.

6255. Raskin, Marcus G. and Robert L. Borosage. "National Security and Official Accountability: Can We Return to Government Ruled By Law?," <u>Vital Issues</u> 23 (September 1973): 1-4.

6256. Rasmussen, William K. "Joint Military Intelligence Training: Understanding the Army Perspective," <u>Defense Intelligence Journal</u> 2/2 (Fall 1993): 149-166.
Discusses the challenge and joint environment of Army training; the intelligence battlefield; conditions for a joint intelligence training program; joint intelligence training opportunities; training limitations and consensus.

6257. Rathbone, Richard. "Police Intelligence in Ghana in the Late 1940s and 1950s," Journal of Imperial and Commonwealth History 21/3 (1993): 107-128.
A rare glimpse of the circumstances in this African country in the era.

6258. Rathmell, Andrew. "Copeland and Za'im: Re-evaluating the Evidence," Intelligence and National Security 11/1 (January 1996): 89-105.
Discusses evidence of the Syrian coup of 1949 as carried out by Colonel Husni al-Za'im with the support of the CIA. Major sections discuss the background of the coup; Za'im's coup; the US and Za'im; and an exaggerated conspiracy theory. Refers to the controversy surrounding Miles Copeland in this matter.

6259. Rathom, J. R. "Germany's Plots Exposed: The German Spy System from the Inside," World's Work 35 (February 1918): 394-415.
A classic article which describes the channels of German communications into parts of the US by means of wireless codes and messages. Sections include discussion of personalities and events, such as Von Bernstorff, Von Papen, Boy Ed, the night of the Lusitania sinking, a wireless episode, how plots were first detected, how the traps were laid, and the men who did the work.

6260. Ratliff, Michael. "Joint Doctrine, Service Intelligence and Support to the Warfighter," Defense Intelligence Journal 4/2 (Fall 1995): 45-65.
Major sections discuss the significance of doctrine for naval intelligence; the need to extend joint intelligence doctrine; why service intelligence was neglected in joint doctrine; the intelligence system and process; the customer's need to understand; core capabilities of service intelligence centers; and inputs and outputs.

6261. Ratliff, William. "Cuba Por Dentro: El MININT," Journal of Inter-American Studies in World Affairs 36/1 (Spring 1994): 212-215.
A book review essay of a book with the same title by Juan A. Rodriguez Menier.

6262. Ratner, Margaret. "The Subcommittee on Security and Terrorism: New Threat to Civil Liberties," Covert Action Information Bulletin 12 (April 1981): 32-34.

6263. Raub, S. A. "Command, Control, and Communication Countermeasures," Marine Corps Gazette (June 1984): 56-62.
Discusses the three essential ingredients in tactical intelligence.

6264. Rau, James P. "Government Secrecy Agreements and the First Amendment," American University Law Review 28/3 (Spring 1979): 395-426.
Examines the use of government secrecy agreements, First Amendment

standard of reasonableness, the application of the reasonableness standard to prepublication review provisions, the doctrine of prior restraint, and the necessity for express presidential or congressional authority for prepublication review agreements.

6265. Raufer, Xavier. "Middle East Terrorism: Rules of the Game," Political Warfare (Fall 1991): 1-13.

6266. Raufer, Xavier. "Gray Areas: A New Security Threat," Political Warfare (Spring 1992).

6267. Rauh, Joseph L., Jr. "Nonconfrontation in Security Cases: The Greene Decision," Virginia Law Review 45/7 (November 1959): 1175-1190.
       Overview of the establishment of the Loyalty Review Board and the problem of FBI insistance on strict confidentiality of investigatory records in loyalty cases. Considers the implication of the nonconfrontation principle in terms of abuse of due process rights.

6268. Rauh, Joseph L., Jr. and Daniel H. Pollitt. "Restrictions on the Right to Travel," Case Western Reserve Law Review 13/1 (December 1961): 128-146.
       Addresses individual control on right to travel; area control; and implications of State Department restrictions on constitutional rights.

6269. Rauh, Joseph L., Jr. and James C. Turner. "Anatomy of a Public Interest Case Against Case the CIA," Hamline Journal of Public Law and Policy 11 (Fall 1990): 307-363.
       Considers facts and issues in the case of Orlikow v. U. S. (682 F. Supp 77). Public interest litigation and national security in reference to the Central Intelligence Agency are given focus.

6270. Ravenal, Earl. C. "Secrecy, Consensus and Foreign Policy: The Logic of Choice," Towson State Journal of International Affairs 10/1 (1975): 1-12.
       This article compares the secrecy of the Richard Nixon administration in foreign policy matters with secrecy of such matters in the Gerald Ford White House. The style of Henry Kissinger is stressed as a source of secrecy techniques and policies.

6271. Ravey, John. "Strike-Breaking: A Canadian Problem," Canadian Labour 17/10 (1972): 9-11.

6272. Rawles, James W. "U.S. Military Upgrades Its Battlefield Eyes and Ears-- Tactical Intelligence Assets Remain a High Priority," Electronic Warfare/Defense Electronics 20/2 (February 1988): 56-58+.

6273. Rawles, James W. "Soviet SIGINT Platforms Range from Trawlers to Consulates," Electronic Warfare/Defense Electronics 20/2 (February 1988): 89-90+.

6274. Rawles, James W. "The Army Intelligence School," Electronic Warfare/Defense Electronics 20/8 (August 1988): 77-80.

6275. Rawles, James W. "Keeping a Watchful Eye on the Border," Electronic Warfare/Defense Electronics 20/9 (September 1988): 82-90.
    Use of surveillance satellites to control drug importation from Mexico.

6276. Rawnsley, Gary D. "Cold War Radio in Crisis: The BBC Overseas Services, the Suez Crisis and the Hungarian Uprising," Historical Journal of Film, Radio and Television 16/2 (1996): 197-219.

6277. Ray, Ellen and William Schaap. "Grenada--No Bishop, No Revo: US Crushes Caribbean Jewel," Covert Action Information Bulletin 20 (Winter 1984): 3-24.

6278. Rayfield, Donald. "The Death of Paolo Iashvili," Slavonic and East European Review 68/4 (October 1990): 631-664.
    An account of the Soviet purges of Georgian writers in 1937, among such writers was Paolo Iashvili, who committed suicide in the courtroom of his secret police accusers. Iashvili had been labeled a spy by Lavrenti Beria's informers.

6279. Raymond, Raymond J. "The Marshall Plan and Ireland, 1947-52," Irish Studies 4 (1985): 295-328.

6280. Raymond, Raymond J. "David Gray, the Aiken Mission, and Irish Neutrality 1940-41," Diplomatic History 9/1 (Winter 1985): 55-57.

6281. Rayner, Mary. "Law, Politics, and Treason in South Africa," Human Rights Quarterly 8/3 (August 1986): 471-486.
    Review of case studies of treason trials in South Africa from the 1950s to 1986. Author is disturbed by the evolving use, misuse and abuses of treason's original meaning.

6282. Raynor, William C. "Police Intelligence," Police Chief 42/2 (February 1975): 18.
    A short description of a topic requiring significantly more research attention.

6283. Reardon, Jacqueline. "Espionage Law--First Amendment--Applying the Espionage Statutes to Press Leaks, United States v. Morison, 844 F.2d 1057,"

Suffolk Transnational Law Journal 13 (Fall 1989): 455-467.
        A brief student note on the Espionage Act of 1917 in light of the case of U. S. v. Morison.

6284. Reaves, Lynne. "Squashing Bugs: John DeLorean, Judge Laurie Beat Stings," American Bar Association Journal 70 (October 1984): 30.
        A brief summary of the maneuvers of John DeLorean to frustrate capture and prosecution on drug charges by means of code talking. Undercover surveillance by video camera is a useful tool in law enforcement work, but it has limitations as demonstrated in this case.

6285. Reber, Jan R. "The Essence of Espionage," Assets Protection (Spring 1975): 7.

6286. Reber, John J. "Pete Ellis: Amphibious Warfare Prophet," U.S. Naval Institute Proceedings 103/11 (November 1977): 53-64.
        An account of Ellis' contributions to naval history, including some discussion of intelligence work.

6287. Redlinger, Lawrence J. and Sunny Johnston. "Secrecy, Informational Uncertainty, and Social Control," Urban Life 8/4 (January 1980): 387-397.
        An introductory article to an entire issue devoted to the effects of secrecy and information control on individuals and society. Provides a brief theoretical backdrop to the articles in the issue.

6288. Reed, Caroline. "D-Day Propaganda," History Today 34 (June 1984): 27-30.
        Describes US propaganda actions in World War II, in particular the dropping of leaflets prior to D-Day in June 1944. Observes the French resistance to leaflet drops and the types of leaflets that were eventually dropped behind German lines.

6289. Reed, George L. "Voices in the Sand: Deception Operations at the NTC (National Training Center)," Armor 97 (September-October 1988): 26-31.

6290. Reed, John F. "Spy Chief to Army Chief," Valley Forge Journal 5/3 (1991): 165-194.
        A lengthy discussion of the American revolution and espionage.

6291. Reeds, James. "'Cracking' a Random Number Generator," Cryptologia 1/1 (January 1977): 20-26.

6292. Reeds, James. "Rotor Algebra," Cryptologia 1/2 (April 1977): 186-194.

6293. Reeds, James. "Solution of Challenge Cipher," Cryptologia 3/2 (April 1979): 83-95.

6294. Reeds, James. "William Friedman's Transcription of the Voynich Manuscript," Cryptologia 19/1 (January 1995): 1-23.

6295. Reedstrom, E. Lisle. "Rescue at Death Island," Old West (Summer 1994): 24-29.
   An account of Major George A. Forsyth's civilian reconnaissance scouts against the Cheyenne and Sioux tribes in 1870s West.

6296. Rees, David. "The Crisis in United States Intelligence," Conflict Studies 114 (December 1979): 1-16.
   Essentially an argument in favor of rebuilding the intelligence community for its role in national security. Sections discuss the growth and evolution of the twentieth century American intelligence system; F.B.I. counterintelligence; CIA operations 1947-1974; covert operations; CIA's Achilles heel; popular pressures; new curbs on CIA; congressional oversight procedures; and the continuing threat from world conditions.

6297. Rees, John and Louise. "A Bumper Harvest of Spies," World & I 1/11 (November 1986): 38-59.

6298. Rees, Tom and J. C. Smith. "Telephone Tappery -- Interception of Communications Act of 1985, S.9: Admissibility of Evidence Obtained by Interception," Criminal Law Review (August 1992): 580-582.

6299. Regan, Priscilla M. "Privacy, Government Information, and Technology," Public Administration Review 46/6 (November-December 1986): 629-634.
   Considers the meaning of privacy and its impact on computers; statutes developed for individuals to investigate the records kept on them by government; linkages between computer records systems; and policy questions regarding individual liberties. Useful in weighing the balance between privacy and the necessity for government information gathering.

6300. Regnard, Henri. "L'URSS et le Renseignement Scientifique, Technique et Technologique," Defense Internationale 39 (December 1983): 107-121.

6301. Regnard, Henri. "Theft of Western Technology: The Soviets Have Built a Complex System to Acquire Western Technology," Journal of Defense & Diplomacy 2/4 (April 1984): 44-48, 64.

6302. Regnard, Henri. "Eastern Europe Serves the Soviet Union by Gathering Intelligence in the West," Deutsche Aussenpolitik 38/4 (1987): 356-364.

6303. Regnard, Henri. "Soviet Gains from Intelligence Gathering in the West," Deutsche Aussenpolitik 38/3 (1987): 231+.

6304. Reich, Robert C. "Re-examining the Team A-Team B Exercise," International Journal of Intelligence and Counterintelligence 3/3 (Fall 1989): 387-403.

A revisitation to Central Intelligence Agency director George Bush's program in 1976 to open Soviet military capability analysis to a competitive outside group of scholars and Soviet Union specialists. Contains a history of the A-team B-team creation; the reasons for installing the competitive analysis exercise; the media response; the Senate response; effects on analysis; and outlook.

6305. Reid, Brian H. "Another Look at Grant's Crossing of the James, 1864," Civil War History 39/4 (December 1993).

6306. Reilly, Tom. "Jane McManus Storms: Letters from the Mexican War, 1846-1848," Southwestern Historical Quarterly 85/1 (July 1981): 21-44.

Considers various aspects of Storms' writings, including coverage of various secret missions of the U.S government to bring about a peace treaty with Mexico.

6307. Reinke, E. "Classical Cryptography," Classical Journal 58/3 (December 1962): 113-121.

6308. Reisman, W. Michael. "Covert Action," Yale Journal of International Law 20 (Summer 1995): 419-425.

This author and James Baker published a book titled Regulating Covert Action: Practices, Contexts, and Policies of Covert Coercion Abroad in International and American Law. This brief article summarizes some of their main arguments.

6309. Reitz, James T. "The Soviet Security Troops--The Kremlin's Other Armies," Soviet Armed Forces Review Annual 6 (1982): 279-327.

6310. Rejewski, Marian. "An Application of the Theory of Permutations in Breaking the Enigma Cipher," Applicationes Mathematicae 16/4 (1980): 543-559.

6311. Rejewski, Marian. "How Polish Mathematicians Deciphered the Enigma," Annals of the History of Computing 3/3 (July 1981): 213-234.

A personal view of the work of the Polish Cipher Bureau from 1932 to 1939 as mathematicians who worked to decipher the codes of the military version of the Enigma. The author participated in the decipherment project.

6312. Rejewski, Marian. "Mathematical Solutions of the Enigma Cipher," Cryptologia 6/1 (January 1982): 1-18.
   Translation by Christopher Kasparek.

6313. Rejewski, Marian. "Remarks on Appendix 1 to British Intelligence in the Second World War by F. H. Hinsley," Cryptologia 6/1 (January 1982): 75-83.

6314. Rekenthaler, Douglas A. "Satellite Surveillance: New Policy Issues?," Journal of Defense & Diplomacy 3/9 (1985): 15-19.

6315. Relyea, Harold C. "Information, Secrecy, and Atomic Energy," New York University Review of Law and Social Change 10/2 (Winter 1980-1981): 265-298.
   Concerns primarily the availability of information about atomic power. Focuses on the evolution of atomic energy information regulation in the US and the implications such regulation has on the rights and liberties of citizens.

6316. Relyea, Harold C. "Shrouding the Endless Frontier--Scientific Communication and National Security: Considerations for a Policy Balance Sheet," Government Information Quarterly 1/1 (1984): 1-14.

6317. Relyea, Harold C. "Increased National Security Controls on Scientific Communication," Government Information Quarterly 1/2 (1984): 177-207.

6318. Relyea, Harold C. "National Security and Freedom of Security," Journal of Media Law and Practice 5/3 (1984): 97-116.
   Discusses national security and the right of public access to government-held information. The authority to retain national security information is held by the President. Also, the piece discusses the range of the President's discretionary power in this regard.

6319. Relyea, Harold C. "National Security and Information," Government Information Quarterly 4 (1987): 11-28.

6320. Relyea, Harold C. "The Coming of Secret Law," Government Information Quarterly 5/2 (1988): 97-116.
   A detailed discussion of the early publication of law in American history; the rise of the administrative state; the rise of the national security state; and conclusions regarding the problem of secret law.

6321. Relyea, Harold C. and Tom Riley. "Freedom of Information Developments Around the World: A Symposium," Government Publications Review 10/1 (January-February 1983): 1-95.
   Several articles in this issue address the matter of freedom of information. These authors wrote an introductory essay.

6322. Rempel, David G. and Abe Dueck. "Mennonite Medics in Russia during World War I," Journal of Mennonite Studies 11 (1993): 149-161.

6323. Renshaw, Patrick. "International Workers of the World and the Red Scare 1917-1924," Journal of Contemporary History 3/4 (1968): 63-72.

Thorough review of the role of the IWW labor organization in pre-World War I actions to organize all wage workers; government actions to counter IWW efforts. Discusses criminal actions against the IWW's.

6324. Repington, Charles C. "The Airship Menace," Blackwood's Magazine 188 (July-December 1910): 3-13.

A classic article on intelligence from airships of the early twentieth century.

6325. Reske, Charles F. "Project ALPHA, Behind Closed Doors with Mondo Bravo: The 'True' Story of the U.S. Naval Security Group by Someone Who Lived It," Naval Intelligence Professionals Quarterly 4/2 (Summer 1988): 11-13.

6326. Retter, Charles T. "Cryptanalysis of a Maclaren-Marsaglia System," Cryptologia 8/2 (April 1984): 97-108.

6327. Retter, Charles T. "A Key-Search Attack on Maclaren-Marsaglia Systems," Cryptologia 9/2 (April 1985): 114-130.

6328. Reuss, Martin. "In Memorium: The First Berlin Crisis," Military Review 59/5 (1979): 30-38.

6329. Reuter, Frank T. "'Petty Spy' or Effective Diplomat: The Role of George Beckwith," Journal of the Early Republic 10/4 (Winter 1990): 471-492.

6330. Revel, Jean-Francois. "The Secret-Service Malaise," Encounter (July-August 1988): 34-37.

6331. Rey, Julio A. "Revolution and Liberation: A Review of Recent Literature on the Guatemalan Situation," Hispanic American Historical Review 38/2 (1958): 239-255.

A book review essay of several books dealing with US intervention in the alleged communist conspiracy in Guatemala in 1954. Very useful analyses of the variety of perspectives published in English and Spanish.

6332. Rey, Lucien. "The Revolution in Zanzibar," New Left Review 25 (May-June 1964): 29-32.

One of few articles on this topic.

6333. Rezneck, Samuel. "The Early History of the Parliamentary Declaration of Treason," English Historical Review 42 (October 1927): 497-513.
Discusses the significance of the statute of treason of 1352 and the statute's implications for treason law in later centuries.

6334. Rezneck, Samuel. "Constructive Treason by Words in the Fifteenth Century," American Historical Review 33 (1928): 543-552.
Explains that in the fifteenth century spoken words were sufficient to convict a person of treason. Discusses two false premises: the presumed existence of a mysterious common law doctrine of treason by words; and the 1352 statute's alleged proscription against treason by words. Spoken words were usually accompanied by other actions.

6335. Rhee, Will. "Comparing U.S. Operations Kingpin (1970) and Eagle Claw (1980)," International Journal of Intelligence and Counterintelligence 6/4 (Winter 1993): 489-506.
Evaluates the rescue missions in 1970 and 1980, respectively the mission to return American POWs from Vietnam, and the mission to free hostages held by Iran following the Iranian siege of the US embassy. Provides a summary of the two missions; compares the two missions; discusses the common problems of the missions; and concludes that the record of success is spotty.

6336. Rhinehart, James M. "Covert Action in High Altitudes," Studies in Intelligence 20/1 (Spring 1976).
Discusses covert action in Tibet.

6337. Rhodes, Benjamin D. "A Prophet in the Russian Wilderness: The Mission of Consul Felix Cole at Archangel, 1917-1919," Review of Politics 46/3 (1984): 388-409.
An account of the activities of Felix Cole, American vice-consul at Archangel in 1918, and Cole's views on the need for American intervention in the months prior to the Bolshevik Revolution.

6338. Rhodes, J. F. Holden and Peter A. Lupsha. "Horsemen of the Apocalypse: Gray Area Phenomenon and the New World Disorder," Low Intensity Conflict and Law Enforcement (August 1993): 212-222.

6339. Rhodes, Robert P. "Electronic Surveillance, Organized Crime, and Civil Liberties," Policy Studies Journal 6 (1978): 419-424.
An observation of the balance that must be maintained between the effectiveness of electronic surveillance devices and civil liberties.

6340. Riccardelli, Richard F. "The Information and Intelligence Revolution," Military Review 75/5 (September-October 1995): 82-87.

6341. Riccardelli, Richard F. "News from the Front: Warfighter Intelligence and Combat Operations," Defense Intelligence Journal 4/2 (Fall 1995): 31-44.

Discusses the September 1994 Army Operation 'Uphold Democracy' in Haiti and associated intelligence support activities.

6342. Riccardi, J. Lee. "The German Federal Data Protection Act of 1977: Protecting the Right to Privacy?," Boston College International and Comparative Law Review 6/1 (1983): 243-271.

Discusses the background and development of German law protecting privacy and the creation of the BDSG organization to regulate personal data collection. Concludes that the BDSG and statutory protections then current were more effective than in previous years to protect individual rights.

6343. Rice, Danton B. "Criminal Law: Informant Bugging - When Is a Private Conversation Really Private?," Washburn Law Journal 24 (Winter 1985): 376-385.

A case note following State v. Roudybush 686 P.2d 100 (Kan. 1984).

6344. Rice, Howard C. "James Swan: Agent of the French Republic, 1794-1796," New England Quarterly 10 (September 1937): 464-486.

An account of the activities of James Swan, official purchasing agent for the French government in the years discussed, during the French revolution.

6345. Rich, George H. "The Espionage Act and Certainty in Statutory Offenses Relating to National Defenses," George Washington Law Review 10/2 (December 1941): 198-207.

Reviews the espionage cases of Gorin v. U. S. and Salich v. U. S., both occurring in 1941.

6346. Rich, W. T. "Pearl Harbor: History and Implications," Military Intelligence 7/1 (January-March 1981): 47-51.

6347. Richard, Eric L. "'Unleashing' the Intelligence Community," American Bar Association Journal 69 (July 1983): 906-910.

Discusses the Reagan administration's sharp increase in the number of orders for electronic surveillance. Concludes that the increases are more symbolic than real in terms of investigative value.

6348. Richards, Henry. "The Chilean Tragedy," Center Magazine 9 (November 1976): 9-14.

6349. Richards, Ian. "The Invisible Prime Factor," American Scientist 70 (March 1982; July-August 1982): 176-179; 351-352.

A mathematical discussion of such topics as "the ancient theorem" of code breaking, public key codes, and conclusions about certain "unbroken" codes. Useful in advanced discussions of cryptography.

6350. Richards, Pamela S. "Gathering Enemy Scientific Information in Wartime: The OSS and the Periodical Reproduction Program," Journal of Library History 16/2 (1981): 253-264.

6351. Richards, Pamela S. "Information Science in Wartime," Journal of the American Society of Information Science 39 (1988): 301-306.

6352. Richardson, Laurel. "Secrecy and Status: The Social Construction of Forbidden Relationships," American Sociological Review 53/2 (April 1988): 209-219.

Discusses how status and secrecy affect the social construction of secret, forbidden, intimate relationships. Reflects intensive interviews with 65 single women involved with married men. Concludes that secrecy protects the interests of the powerful.

6353. Richardson, Renee. "The Arctic Curtain Opens," Naval Intelligence Professionals Quarterly 8/4 (Fall 1992): 2-5.

6354. Richardson, Seth W. "The Federal Employee Loyalty Program," Columbia Law Review 51/5 (May 1951): 546-563.

Discusses controversy and operations of the loyalty program during the Truman administration and thereafter.

6355. Richelson, Jeffrey T. "The Satellite Data System," Journal of the British Interplanetary Society 37/5 (1984): 226-228.

Suggests that the SDS has several intelligence gathering objectives, not all of which can be known due to secrecy of the program. Discusses functions, characteristics, launches, and secrecy.

6356. Richelson, Jeffrey T. "The Keyhole Satellite Program," Journal of Strategic Studies 7/2 (June 1984): 121-153.

An analysis of the space reconnaissance program of the US and its role in national security. Contains a special discussion of Discovery 14.

6357. Richelson, Jeffrey T. "Old Surveillance, New Interpretations," Bulletin of the Atomic Scientists 42/2 (February 1986): 18-23.

"Revised estimates" of Soviet strategic capabilities often reflect analysis of earlier rather than new data. New analysis is based on new methodologies or assumptions. Includes details of warhead yield analysis, silo hardening, and SS-19 warhead counting.

6358. Richelson, Jeffrey T. "U.S. Intelligence and Soviet Star Wars," <u>Bulletin of the Atomic Scientists</u> 42 (May 1986): 12-14.

This article claims that "Star Wars" is a necessary US response to a vigorous Soviet space-based defense effort which must be examined in the light of earlier misleading intelligence predictions of Soviet strategic programs. Also, discusses the overestimation of Soviet weapons from 1957 to 1986.

6359. Richelson, Jeffrey T. "Monitoring the Soviet Military," <u>Arms Control Today</u> 16/7 (October 1986): 14-19.

Discusses national technical means for collecting intelligence on Soviet nuclear testing, ABM launches and other forms of weapons testing.

6360. Richelson, Jeffrey T. "Military Intelligence -- SPOT is Not Enough," <u>Bulletin of the Atomic Scientists</u> 45 (September 1989): 26-27.

Major sections include discussion of aerial reconnaissance, intelligence sharing arrangements, commercial satellite systems, and military reconnaissance image satellites.

6361. Richelson, Jeffrey T. "The Calculus of Intelligence Cooperation," <u>International Journal of Intelligence and Counterintelligence</u> 4/3 (Fall 1990): 307-323.

Discusses the nature of intelligence cooperation between various intelligence services, in particular the BRUSA (British-US Communications Intelligence Agreement of 1943. Major sections discuss types of international cooperation; potential benefits and costs; and the effects of world change.

6362. Richelson, Jeffrey T. "Task Force 157: The US Navy's Secret Intelligence Service, 1966-77," <u>Intelligence and National Security</u> 11/1 (January 1996): 106-145.

Major sections discuss origins; mission, structure, and personnel; collection operations to 1975; the weather channel; the new DNI and disestablishment; the task force surfaces in 1977; and final observations.

6363. Richelson, Jeffrey T. "The Future of Space Reconnaissance," <u>Scientific American</u> 264/1 (January 1996): 38-44.

6364. Richman, David. "The CIA Silences a Whistle-Blower," <u>Human Rights</u> 10/1 (Winter 1982): 24-27, 48-52.

Discusses the legal reasoning involved in the case against Frank Snepp for publication of his book, <u>Decent Interval</u>, without CIA authorization.

6365. Richman, Steven M. "Voices That Go Bump in the Night: Conflicting Rights Under the Wiretap Statutes," <u>Seton Hall Legislative Journal</u> 11 (Summer 1987): 171-199.

Examines legislative and judicial attempts to address the broader issues of the obligations of non-law enforcement people who intentionally or inadvertently intercept electronic data through the operation of a radio or other non-intrusive equipment.

6366. Richmond, Irwin. "Pauline Cushman: A Personality Profile," Civil War Times Illustrated 7/10 (1969): 38-44.

6367. Richter, Michael. "A Note on Public-Key Cryptosystems," Cryptologia 4/1 (January 1980): 20-21.

6368. Ricks, John A. "'De Lawd' Descends and Is Crucified: Martin Luther King, Jr., in Albany, Georgia," Journal of Southwest Georgia History 2 (Fall 1984): 1-17.

6369. Rider, Mary M. "Images of Propaganda: World War I and World War II Posters," Queen City Heritage (Fall 1983): 31-36.

6370. Rielly, John E. "The American Mood: A Foreign Policy of Self-Interest," Foreign Policy 34 (Spring 1979): 74-86.
　　Reviews public opinion data on various foreign policy issues, among them the question of the role of the CIA in work inside other countries.

6371. Riemann, Robert H. "The Challenge of Glasnost for Western Intelligence," Parameters: Journal of the U.S. Army War College 20/4 (December 1990): 85-94.
　　Covers the impact of "Glasnost" in the West; what historical precedent tells us; the challenges of Glasnost for Western intelligence organizations; and the impact on Western intelligence and its implications.

6372. Riesman, David. "Civil Liberties in a Period of Transition," Public Policy 3 (1942): 33-96.
　　A lengthy discussion of the role of civil liberty policy in overall public policy. Major sections discuss the testing of limits of civil liberties; the clear and present danger test; war as a distinctive criterion; the belief in civil liberties test; the test of "violent overthrow of government"; the background of American views; the need for a new orientation; and the road into public policy concerning civil liberties.

6373. Riggs, Robert B. "Of Spies and Specie," Military Review 42 (August 1962): 13-21.
　　Discussion of the intelligence tactics used by the Continental and British armies in the American Revolution. Considers George Washington's intelligence doctrine, his analyses of conditions, and internal security systems.

6374. Riggs, Robert B. "Kinesthetic Warfare--Made for the Future," Military Review 45/9 (1965): 13-19.

6375. Rigney, Daniel. "Secrecy and Social Cohesion," Society 16/4 (May-June 1979): 52-55.

A general discussion of secrecy in organizations and society. Sections discuss the nature of security discipline; impersonal mechanisms of secrecy; expressive and instrumental functions of secrecy; malfunctions and breakdowns; intellectual skills; and the historical context of secrecy.

6376. Riley, John W., Jr. "Opinion Research in Liberated Normandy," American Sociological Review 12/6 (December 1947): 698-703.

A sociological study of attitudes following the June 6, 1944 landing of allied troops at Normandy, France. Includes reactions to allied landings; contact with allied troops; criticism of allied troops; and post-D-Day civilian problems.

6377. Riley, John W., Jr. and Leonard S. Cottrell, Jr. "Research for Psychological Warfare," Public Opinion Quarterly 21/1 (Spring 1957): 147-158.

Suggests the uneven development of research for psychological warfare as a function of simplistic questions of failure to address complex questions of human motivation and interaction.

6378. Riley, Morris. "British Intelligence Manipulates the News," Counterspy 8/1 (September-November 1983): 30-32.

6379. Riley, To. "Freedom of Information Acts: A Comparative Perspective," Journal of Media Law and Practice 3/2 (1982): 245-252.

This article compares levels and types of accessibility of the public to secret military information in several Western countries.

6380. Rill, Gerhard. "Pietro Giuliani: Details and Background of a Betrayal, 1524-26," Mitteilungen des Oberoestereichischen 14 (1984): 27-45.

A description of Giuliani's espionage activities in Spain, France, and the Habsburg Empire while serving in the court of Emperor Charles V.

6381. Rinaldi-Dimitriou, Gail A. "The Korean Airliner Incident of 1983: Can the U.S. Obtain Redress from the U.S.S.R.?," San Fernando Valley Law Review 13 (1985): 37-56.

Considers the undisputed and disputed facts (including minor role of intelligence); international law; individual claims on a municipal level; factors the US should consider in an international claim; and legal redress against the USSR.

6382. Rinaldo, Richard J. "The Tenth Principle of War," Military Review 67/10 (October 1987): 55-62.

The 10th principle is information, an addition to the Army's basic principles of war.

6383. Ringe, Donald A. "The American Revolution in American Romance," American Literature: Journal of Literary History 49/3 (1977): 352-365.
Evaluates the writing of several authors who attempted to capture the atmosphere of the American Revolution throughout the novel. Compares the work of John Neal (Seventy-Six) with the works of James Fennimore Cooper (The Spy), and others.

6384. Rinskopf, Elizabeth R. "Intelligence Oversight in a Democracy," Houston Journal of International Law 11/1 (Fall 1988): 21-30.
Discusses the basis of oversight of intelligence activities; the operations of the legislative oversight process; and the role and effectiveness of the Foreign Intelligence Surveillance Act.

6385. Rinskopf, Elizabeth R. "Intelligence Law Challenges in the New World," American Intelligence Journal 13/3 (Summer 1992): 33-37.
A discussion of intelligence challenges and the need for intelligence lawyers in the new world; transnational issues and their implications; weapons proliferation and economic competitiveness; role of lawyers in protecting classified information; and lawyers and covert action.

6386. Riordan, Jim. "The Strange Story of Nikolai Starostin, Football and Lavrentii Beria," Europe-Asia Studies 46/4 (1994): 681-690.
An interesting tale of the intersection between these characters. Beria was head of Stalin's KGB. This journal is the former Soviet Studies.

6387. Riordan, Theodore F. "Contract Law - Totten Doctrine - Judicial Sabotage of Government Contracts for Sabotage Services, Guong v. United States 860 F.2d 1063," Suffolk Transnational Law Journal 13/2 (Spring 1990): 807-817.
Considers litigation by Vu Duc Quong against the CIA to recover money owed as a function of a contract for services in Vietnam. An American Civil War case of secret espionage served as the principle under which Quong could not recover from the US government.

6388. Riosa, Aloeo. "Angelo Tasca from the Phoney War to the "Other Resistance"," Annali della Fondazione Giangiacomo Feltrinelli 24 (1985): 191-217.

6389. Rip, Michael R. "Military Photo-Reconnaissance during the Yom Kippur War: A Research Note," Intelligence and National Security 7/2 (April 1992): 126-132.
Briefly reviews new information relating to the importance of aerial and

satellite reconnaissance activities during the Yom Kippur War.

6390. Rip, Michael R. and David P. Lusch. "The Precision Revolution: The Navstar Global Positioning System in the Second Gulf War," <u>Intelligence and National Security</u> 9/2 (April 1994): 167-241.
    Overview of satellite systems; GPS frequencies and codes; GPS timing signals and errors; measures of error; system accuracy; access to GPS signals; jamming of GPS signals; millimeter accuracy; deployment of GPS in the Persian Gulf; the use of GPS in Desert Storm; aerial operations; air breathing missiles; air to surface missiles; ground forces; maritime operations; and present and future military uses.

6391. Rip, Michael R. and David P. Lusch. "The Navstar Global Positioning System in Operation Desert Storm: A Research Note," <u>Intelligence and National Security</u> 10/2 (April 1995): 327-335.
    Reports updated information on the performance of the Navstar system from an earlier article in the same journal. Contains substantial technical information regarding this intelligence advantage in the Gulf War.

6392. Rip, Michael R. and Joseph F. Fontanella. "A Window on the Arab-Israeli 'Yom Kippur' War of 1973: Military Photo-Reconnaissance from High Altitude and Space," <u>Intelligence and National Security</u> 6/1 (January 1991): 15-89.
    An extensive inquiry into the photo reconnaissance work of them War of 1973. Major sections discuss high altitude and space reconnaissance of prior conflicts; Soviet and US photo reconnaissance satellites; development of Soviet recon systems; and phote reconnaissance operations during the War.

6393.   Ripley, S. Dillon.   "Incident in Siam," <u>Yale Review</u> (Winter 1947): 262-276.
    A World War II case study of a secret plan and underground activities to evacuate POW's from Japanese prison camps. Role of the OSS is mentioned.

6394. Rippy, J. Fred. "Britain's Role in the Early Relations of the United States and Mexico," <u>Hispanic American Historical Review</u> 7/1 (February 1927).

6395. Riposte, Ralph. "New Anachronism," <u>Studies in Intelligence</u> 2 (Summer 1958).

6396. Rislakki, Jukka. "What Is Worth Spying on in Finland?," <u>Politiikka</u> 25/3 (1983): 199-209.

6397. Ristovic, Milan. "Conflicts Among Intelligence Groups of Yugoslav Government-in-Exile in Turkey Between 1941 and 1943," <u>Voyaistoryski Glasnik</u> 35/2 (1984): 153-170.

6398. Ritter, Gerhard. "Die Ausenpolitischen Hoffnungen der Verschworer des 20 Juli 1944," Merkur 3 (November 1949): 1121-1138.

6399. Ritter, Terry. "Substitution Cipher with Pseudo-Random Shuffling: The Dynamic Substitution Combiner," Cryptologia 14/4 (October 1990): 289-303.
Part II is found in Cryptologia 15/1 (January 1991): 1-17.

6400. Ritter, Terry. "The Efficient Generation of Cryptographic Confusion Sequences," Cryptologia 15/2 (April 1991): 81-139.

6401. Ritter, Terry. "Estimating Population from Repetitions in Accumulated Random Samples," Cryptologia 18/2 (April 1994): 155-160.

6402. Rivest, Ronald L. "'Forwards and Backwards' Encryption," Cryptologia 4/1 (January 1980): 30-33.

6403. Rivest, Ronald L. "Statistical Analysis of the Hagelin Cryptograph," Cryptologia 5/1 (January 1981): 27-32.

6404. Rivest, Ronald L. and Adi Shamir. "How to Expose An Eavesdropper," Communications of the ACM 27 (April 1984): 393-395.

6405. Rivkin, David B., Jr. "Covert Action: Is It Justified? Should a Democratic Government Keep Secrets from Its Citizens?," American Legion Magazine 124/3 (March 1988): 24-25, 62-63.
A brief defense of covert action, including discussion of benefits to national security, concealing disagreements, obstacles, public opinion, and legality.

6406. Rivkin, David B., Jr. "Intelligence Oversight and Congress: Practical and Constitutional Imperatives," Houston Journal of International Law 11/1 (Fall 1988): 31-45.
Discusses popular and legal concerns for the effectiveness of congressional oversight of intelligence operations, aimed at greater concerns for congressional exercise of constitutional powers.

6407. Roach, J. Ashley. "Ruses and Perfidy: Deception During Armed Conflict," University of Toledo Law Review 23 (Winter 1992): 395-420.
Examines rules established by international law covering ruses and perfidy in war, on land, at sea, and in the air. Major sections discuss deceptions; protective signs and symbols; protective signals; misuse of signs, signals and symbols; and spies.

6408. Robb, Gary C. "Police Use of CCTV Surveillance: Constitutional Implications and Proposed Regulations," University of Michigan Journal of Law

Reform 13/3 (Spring 1980): 571-602.

Evaluates the constitutionality of closed circuit television (CCTV) searches; private security applications of television technology; US Constitution's Fourth Amendment issues; and proposed regulations on law enforcement CCTV systems.

6409. Robb, Stephen C. "Marine Corps Signals Intelligence "The Warfighter's Force Multiplier," American Intelligence Journal 15/1 (Spring-Summer 1994): 25-29.

Discusses the task environment, the target environment, current capability, and strategy for the future.

6410. Robbins, Peggy. "Allan Pinkerton's Southern Assignment," Civil War Times Illustrated 15/9 (1977): 6-11, 44-47.

This is an account of Pinkerton's work in the South in 1861 to acquire information about attitudes, morale, military posts and population. Reviews the collection of information acquired by Pinkerton during his spying actions in the South in the summer of 1861.

6411. Roberts, Adam. "The CIA: Reform Is Not Enough," Millennium: Journal of International Studies 6/1 (Spring 1977): 64-72.

An overview of the issues connected with reforming the Central Intelligence Agency.

6412. Roberts, Kenneth. "Bullying and Bargaining: The United States, Nicaragua, and Conflict in Central America," International Security 15/2 (Fall 1990): 67-102.

Major topics include US policy in Nicaragua, competing explanations; bilateral interaction; regional cooperation and the Contadora negotiations; the Arias treaty and the assertion of autonomy; and conditions for a negotiated settlement. Role of the CIA is mentioned on several occasions.

6413. Robertson, Kenneth G. "The Sociology of Spying," Reviewing Sociology 2/3 (Summer 1982): 4-12.

This is a book review essay of several books on then current intelligence studies. Apart from observing general content, the author emphasizes conflicts arising from intelligence services secrecy.

6414. Robertson, Kenneth G. "Intelligence, Terrorism and Civil Liberties," Conflict Quarterly 7/2 (Spring 1987): 43-62.

Major sections include the nature of terrorism; definition of intelligence; intelligence and terrorism; intelligence; law enforcement and terrorism; and intelligence and civil liberties. Concludes three main principles must be applied in employing intelligence to fight terrorism.

6415. Robertson, Kenneth G. "Editorial Comment: An Agenda for Intelligence Research," Defense Analysis 3/2 (Fall 1987): 95-101.

A brief introduction to the entire issue devoted to papers on intelligence topics. Observes the strong influences of history and political science on the advancements made in the study of intelligence.

6416. Robertson, Kenneth G. "Intelligence Requirements for the 1980's," Intelligence and National Security 2/4 (October 1987): 157-167.

A review article discussing issues raised by the seven volumes edited by Roy Godson on intelligence requirements.

6417. Robertson, Kenneth G. "Accountable Intelligence - The British Experience," Conflict Quarterly 8/1 (Winter 1988): 20-33.

6418. Robertson, Kenneth G. "Canadian Intelligence Policy: The Role and Future of CSIS," International Journal of Intelligence and Counterintelligence 3/2 (Summer 1989): 225-248.

Extensive discussion of the Canadian Security and Intelligence Service. Major sections discuss basic themes in Canadian intelligence policy; the role of intelligence; Canadian national security policy; an eye on the United States; the management of intelligence; the mechanisms of intelligence policymaking; and the future of CSIS.

6419. Robertson, Kenneth G. "Terrorism: Europe without Borders," Terrorism: An International Journal 14 (1991): 105-110.

6420. Robinett, Paul M. "Reflections on the Role of the Intelligence Officers," Military Review 32/8 (November 1952): 29-32.

A brief discussion of the need for military intelligence officer training, development and integrated duty assignments of such officers with other staff officers.

6421. Robins, Philip. "A Watch from the Sky," Flying Review International 21 (February 1966): 333-336.

6422. Robinson, Bill. "The Fall and Rise of Cryptanalysis in Canada," Cryptologia 16/1 (January 1992): 23-38.

6423. Robinson, Clarence A., Jr. "Fighting the War on Drugs," Signal 44/12 (December 1989): 34-40.

6424. Robinson, Clarence A., Jr. "Essential C^3I Offers Payoff for Big Ticket Investments," Signal 45/1 (January 1990): 20-25.

6425. Robinson, D. "Our Comic-Opera Spy Set-Up," <u>American Legion Magazine</u> 50 (February 1951).

6426. Robinson, Daniel J. and David Kimmel. "The Queer Career of Homosexual Security Vetting in Cold War Canada," <u>Canadian Historical Review</u> 75/3 (1994): 319-345.
Addresses the issue of potential security risks believed to be posed to Canadian national security by civil service employees during the 1950s and 1960s. Discusses actions of various investigative agencies of the government that collected and processed information, some of which was used to make primitive profiles of homosexuals. Useful in studies of personnel security programs.

6427. Robinson, D. F. "The Threat to Liberty and the Role of Intelligence-Gathering in Its Defence," <u>Army Quarterly and Defence Journal</u> 108 (October 1978): 409-416.

6428. Robinson, Douglas H. "Zeppelin Intelligence," <u>Aerospace Historian</u> 21/1 (March 1974): 1-7.
Describes German air intelligence in World War I.

6429. Robinson, Glen O. "Access to Government Information: The American Experience," <u>Federal Law Review</u> (1976): 35-61.
Discusses the evolution of the FOIA in terms of its revolutionary character, the issues and controversies, implementation and enforcement, and effects and perceptions. Contains a section on executive secrets: national security and law enforcement.

6430. Robinson, June. "The United States Balloon Corps in Action in Northern Virginia During the Civil War," <u>Arlington Historical Magazine</u> 8/2 (1986): 5-17.
Discusses the Corps' service from 1861 to 1863. The Corps served as a reconnaissance unit.

6431. Robinson, J. R. "Radar Intelligence and the Dieppe Raid," <u>Canadian Defence Quarterly</u> 20/5 (1991): 37-43.

6432. Robinson, Linda. "Wrong Numbers: Disconnecting the Cordless Telephone from the Right of Privacy," <u>Criminal Justice Journal</u> 13/1 (Winter 1991): 101-114.

6433. Robinson, Sheryl. "The Gulf War from Tel Aviv," <u>Studies in Intelligence</u> 35/5 (Winter 1991): 1-3.
Briefly explores author's personal experiences of the first Scud missile attack; the war of nerves; the routine aspects; and scary situations. She says she still jumps at the sound of sirens.

6434. Robinson, Thomas R. "Treason in Roman Law," Georgetown Law Journal 8/1 (December 1919): 14-31.

Discusses criminal relations with the enemy, attacks on the form of government, breaches of duty by governmental officials and priests, breaches of duty by citizens, breaches of religious duties by citizens, and attacks on representatives of the state.

6435. Robinson, Thomas R. "Treason in Modern Foreign Law," Boston University Law Review 2/1-2 (January-April 1922): 34-36; 98-113.

A comparative study of treason law in France, Belgium, Japan, Sweden, Italy, Chile, Germany and Turkey.

6436. Robinson, William J. "Spies and Snipers," World's Work 32 (July 1916): 347-352.

A discussion of the increase in the number of spies in the World War I era. Discusses the capture of a German spy and other cases of the period. A classic.

6437. Roby, Sheryll. "ASD (C^3I) Reorganization," American Intelligence Journal 13/3 (Summer 1992): 25-28.

Discusses the role of the principal Department of Defense deputy for intelligence; the intelligence program support group; and various divisions of the Advance Systems Directorate function.

6438. Rochet, Jean. "Infiltration and Misinformation," Histcrama 17 (1985): 20-22.

6439. Rochford, James M. "Police Intelligence and Organized Crime Enforcement," Police Chief 42/2 (February 1975): 47-49.

An outline of the role and functions of the Chicago organized crime intelligence unit.

6440. Rochlin, Robert S. "Observation Satellites for Arms Control Inspection," Journal of Arms Control 1 (1963): 224-227.

6441. Rockman, Bert A. "Mobilizing Political Support for U.S. National Security," Armed Forces & Society 14/1 (1987): 17-41.

Explores topics such as domains of national security policy; mass opinion in foreign policy; consensus and conflict in policy making; the role of institutions; presidential popularity; and conclusions.

6442. Rockwell, Brad. "Domestic Covert Actions and the Need for National Security Qui Tam Prosecutions," American Journal of Criminal Law 16/2 (Winter 1989): 207-268.

Considers the character and scope of covert actions; preventing domestic covert actions through regulation; qui tam prosecutions; and conclusions.

6443. Rodes, Robert E., Jr. "On Clandestine Warfare," Washington and Lee Law Review 39/2 (Spring 1982): 333-372.

Offers a typology of clandestine operations and countermeasures; discussion of the laws of warfare; criticizes current laws of warfare. Distinguishes between questions pertaining to "legitimacy of cause" (jus in bello) and questions of "legitimacy of the cause itself" (jus ad bellum). Sets forth a draft convention on clandestine warfare.

6444. Rodgaard, John A. "Japanese Midget Submarines at Pearl Harbor," Naval Intelligence Professionals Quarterly 11/2 (Spring 1995): 1-3.

6445. Rodgaard, John A., et al. "The Fifth Submarine," American Intelligence Journal 15/2 (Autumn-Winter 1994): 77-78.

A team of imagery analysts (author and co-authors, Carol Lucas, Tim Hosek and Dewey Houck) give close examination to the photo evidence of Japanese use of midget submarines during the attack on Pearl Harbor.

6446. Rodman, Burton. "The Intelligent 27," Cavalry Journal 44/189 (1935): 31-36.

6447. Rodman, David. "Against Fishel: Another Look at the Liberty Incident," International Journal of Intelligence and Counterintelligence 9/1 (Spring 1996): 73-80.

Major sections discuss research on the Liberty incident; the alleged motive for the Israeli attack; the attack on the Liberty; the Loftus-Aarons account; the author's alleged misuse of the term "anti-semitism"; and the burden of proof.

6448. Rodman, Peter W. "The NSC System: Why It's Here to Stay," Foreign Service Journal 69/2 (February 1992): 24-26.

Discussion of the modern context of the National Security Council and its role in advising presidents.

6449. Roe, P. C. "See It--Report It," Marine Corps Gazette 37 (March 1953): 40-45.

6450. Rogers, Charles C. "Naval Intelligence," U.S. Naval Institute Proceedings 9/5 (1887): 659-692.

This very old piece describes European military intelligence organizations. Further, it describes the newly formed organization, the US Navy's Office of Naval Intelligence. A classic and detailed article, this is one of the oldest pieces in this collection.

6451. Rogers, Henry H. "Scientific Intelligence in Modern Warfare," Military Review 28/2 (May 1948): 27-31.

An outline of concepts and terms employed in scientific intelligence.

6452. Rogers, Henry H. "The Role of Electronics in Warfare," Military Review 29/7 (July 1949): 23-27.

A brief discussion of how the military explains the electromagnetic spectrum concept to field personnel.

6453. Rogers, Robert S. "Treason in the Early Empire," Journal of Roman Studies 49 (1959): 90-94.

A reply to the critique of the author's book, Criminal Trials and Criminal Legislation.

6454. Rogers, William L. "An International Police Force," American Journal of International Law 37 (1943): 305-308.

Argues that an international police force to preserve peace is impracticable. The rule of the balance of power should be applied instead.

6455. Rogers, William P. "The Case for Wire Tapping," Yale Law Journal 63 (April 1954): 792-798.

The former Attorney General of the United States in the Eisenhower administration offers a defense for the use of wiretapping devices and operations, but there is need for new legislation to control such matters.

6456. Roggeman, Yves. "Remarks on the Auto-Correlation Function of Binary Periodic Sequences," Cryptologia 10/2 (April 1986): 96-100.

6457. Rogin, Michael. "'Make My Day!': Spectacle As Amnesia in Imperial Politics," Representations 29 (1990): 99-123.

Considers the concept of public spectacle in connection with Ronald Reagan's use of a Clint Eastwood line in a 1983 movie in relation to the covert action in the Iran-Contra affair.

6458. Rohrbach, Hans. "Mathematical and Mechanical Methods in Cryptography," Cryptologia 2/1 (January 1978): 20-37.

6459. Rohbach, Hans. "Report on the Decipherment of the American Strip Cipher O-2," Cryptologia 3/1 (January 1979): 16-26.

6460. Rohwer, Jurgen. "La Radiotelegraphie: Auxiliare du Commandement dans la Guerre Sous-marin," Revue d'Histoire de la Deuxieme Guerre Mondiale 28 (January 1968): 41-66.

6461. Rohwer, Jurgen. "Communication Technology and the Attack on Pearl Harbor," Revue International d'Histoire Militaire 27 (1968): 324-332.
A Rand Corporation study which concluded that US intelligence did not evaluate closely enough Japanese codes and code systems before World War II.

6462. Rohwer, Jurgen. "'Special Intelligence' und die Vernichtung der 'Scharnhorst,'" Marine Rundschau 74 (1977).

6463. Rohwer, Jurgen. "Special Intelligence und die Geleitungsteuerung im Herbst 1941," Marine Rundschau 75 (November 1978): 711-719.

6464. Rohwer, Jurgen. "Ultra and the Battle of the Atlantic: The German View," Cryptologic Spectrum 8/1 (Winter 1978): 5-29.
An argument that the British were capable of learning German plans only partially through decryption of German codes, using other methods such as direction finding and traffic analysis when they were blind.

6465. Rohwer Jurgen. "'Ultra', XB-Dienst, and 'Magic': A Comparison of Their Roles in the Battle of the Atlantic and the War in the Pacific," Marine Rundschau 76/10 (1979): 637-648.
A comparison of the effectiveness of the United States, British, and German intelligence gathering and codebreaking systems and the roles of systems of codebreaking during World War II.

6466. Rohwer, Jurgen. "The Influence of Allied Wireless Codebreaking During the Second World War," Quarterly Journal of Contemporary History 23 (July 1979): 525-570.
In German, this piece interprets the Allied work to break codes employed by Axis forces.

6467. Rokke, Ervin J. "Restructuring Air Force Intelligence," American Intelligence Journal 14/3 (Autumn-Winter 1993-1994): 21-24.
Argues that the world is changing and so must the Air Force. Briefly outlines the current intelligence structure in the Air Force hierarchy.

6468. Rolo, Charles T. "The Strategy of War by Radio," Harper's (November 1940): 640-649.

6469. Rolya, William I. "Intelligence, Security, and Electronic Warfare," Signal 32 (March 1978): 15-17.

6470. Rolya, William I. "INSCOM: Who Are We? Where Have We Been?," Journal of the U.S. Army Intelligence Command 2 (October-November 1978): 15-19.

6471. Romerstein, Herbert. "The Role of Forgeries in Soviet Active Measures," Survey: A Journal of East and West Studies 30/3 (October 1988): 106-120.

An historical account of Soviet use of disinformation documents, especially forgeries, dating such actions to 1918. Develops examples of forgeries and the modern context of forgery detection by the CIA.

6472. Romine, B. Harl. "Intelligence Data for Tactical Commanders," American Intelligence Journal 15/1 (Spring-Summer 1994): 30-38.

Extensive technical explanation of state-of-the-art intelligence data dissemination since the Desert Storm conflict.

6473. Romlein, J. W. "What Situation?," Military Review 33 (November 1953): 3-6.

6474. Rona, Thomas P. "Information Warfare: An Age Old Concept with New Insights," Defense Intelligence Journal 5/1 (Spring 1996): 53-68.

Major sections discuss the concept and functions of information warfare; information warfare aimed at decisions at all levels; a broader perspective on information warfare; and challenges and opportunities.

6475. Ronner, M. J. and C. E. Dolejs. "Sensors: Extending the Battlefield," Marine Corps Gazette 65 (July 1981): 56-85.

6476. Rondot, Philippe. "Of the Right Use of Intelligence Services," Politique Internationale 85 (Autumn 1979): 171-181.

Discusses the purpose of and necessity for secret intelligence agencies in the wake of increasing intelligence operations in the West.

6477. Rood, H. "Defeating the German Spy System in America," Century Magazine 96 (July 1918): 423-430.

6478. Roon, Ger van. "Count Moltke As Expert in International Law at the Army Supreme Command," Vierteljahashefte fuer Zeitgeshichte 18/1 (1970): 12-61.

6479. Rose, J. H. "A British Agent in Tilsit," English Historical Review 16 (1901): 712-718.

6480. Rose, G. T. "Terrorists Are Coming," Politics Today 5 (July 1978): 22-26+.

6481. Rosefielde, Steven. "The Illusion of Material Progress: The Analytics of Soviet Economic Growth Revisited," Soviet Studies 43/4 (1991): 597-611.

Details the areas of the gap between what Soviet economists present as the estimates of economic growth and what the CIA has traditionally estimated. Considers Soviet statistics on national income and production.

6482. Rosello, Victor M. "Clausewitz's Contempt for Intelligence," Parameters: Journal of the U.S. Army War College 21/1 (Spring 1991): 103-114.

Majors sections of this article argue that Clausewitz did not appreciate intelligence reports due to the high error factor often appearing. Also considers the sophistication of Napoleanic intelligence; weaknesses of Napoleanic intelligence; Jomini on intelligence; and Clausewitzian intelligence or information.

6483. Rosello, Victor M. "Operation JUST CAUSE: The Divisional MI Battalion, the Nonlinear Battlefield, and AirLand Operations--Future," Military Intelligence 17/3 (July-September 1991): 28-31.

Describes intelligence organizational problems during the Army invasion of Panama in 1989. One of few pieces on this operation.

6484. Rosen, Benson and J. Stacy Adams. "Organizational Boundary Roles: Information Gatekeeping and Transmission," Journal of Applied Social Psychology 4/4 (October-December 1974): 375-384.

Examines factors involved in the severity of influence administered to subordinate information gatekeepers who are guilty of covering up and concealing or distorting information.

6485. Rosen, Jacob. "Captain Reginald Hall and the Balfour Declaration," Middle East Studies 24/1 (1988): 56-67.

6486. Rosenau, William. "A Deafening Silence: U.S. Government Policy and the Sigint Facility at Lourdes," Intelligence and National Security 9/4 (October 1994): 723-734.

Discusses the Russian Sigint monitoring facility located southwest of Havana, Cuba which is capable of intercepting commercial and government telephone communications in the US and between the US and Europe. Sections discuss capabilities of the Lourdes complex; Lourdes and US policy; Sigint versus COMSEC; and conclusions.

6487. Rosenbaum, Ron. "The Shadow of the Mole: Two Superpowers, Three Master Spies, Four False Defectors, Five Schools of Mole Lore, and Seven Types of Ambiguity," Harper's 267 (October 1983): 45-60.

Offers the theory that the CIA is operated from within by a KGB mole.

6488. Rosenberg, Bernard. "CIA, DIA, FBI--And 50 More!" Dissent 22/4 (Fall 1975): 311-315.

Argues that the power and budgets of numerous intelligence agencies form a threat to the privacy of citizens.

6489. Rosenberg, Bruce A. "James Fenimore Cooper's The Spy and the Neutral Ground," ATQ 6 (March 1992): 5-16.

6490. Rosenberg, Bruce A. "Cooper's The Spy and the Popular Spy Novel," ATQ 7 (June 1993): 115-125.

6491. Rosenberg, David A. "American Atomic Strategy and the Hydrogen Bomb Decision," Journal of American History 66/1 (June 1979): 62-87.
A detailed consideration of the national security issues associated with Harry Truman's decision to proceed with hydrogen bomb research.

6492. Rosenberg, David A. "'A Smoking Radiation Ruin at the End of Two Hours': Documents on American Plans for Nuclear War with the Soviet Union, 1954-1955," International Security 6/3 (Winter 1981-1982): 3-38.
Introduces and comments upon two recently declassified documents that present plans for nuclear war in the first years of the Eisenhower administration.

6493. Rosenberg, David A. "Classified History Declassified: The Uses and Abuses of Top Secret Scholarship," Reviews in American History 9/3 (September 1981): 407-413.
A book review essay of the multi-volume book, The History of the Joint Chiefs of Staff and the Korean War, by authors J. F. Schnabel, K. W. Condit and R. J. Watson.

6494. Rosenberg, David A. "The Origins of Overkill: Nuclear Weapons and American Strategy, 1945-1960," International Security 7/3 (Spring 1983): 3-71.

6495. Rosenberg, David A. "Being 'Red': The Challenge of Taking the Soviet Side in War Games at the NWC," Naval Intelligence Professionals Quarterly 4/2 (Summer 1988): 6-8.

6496. Rosenberg, David A. "Being 'Red': The Challenge of Taking the Soviet Side in War Games," Naval Intelligence Professionals Quarterly 4/3 (Fall 1988): 15-17.

6497. Rosenberg, David A. "Being 'Red': The Challenge of Taking the Soviet Side in War Games at the Naval War College," Naval War College Review 41/1 (Winter 1988): 81-93.
Outlines the history of naval intelligence war-gaming strategies and the change in philosophy in the 1970s to introduce an opposition team to eliminate "mirror imaging" of the enemy.

6498. Rosenberg, Joseph L. "Irish Conscription: 1941," Eire-Ireland 14/1 (1979): 16-25.

6499. Rosengarten, Adolph G., Jr. "The Bulge: A Glimpse of Combat Intelligence," Military Review 41/6 (June 1961): 29-33.
Discusses the role and operations of Army intelligence prior to the Battle of the Bulge. Brief discussions of the Siegfried Line, Operation Grief, German reserves and the final stages of the battle.

6500. Rosengarten, Adolph G., Jr. "With ULTRA From Omaha Beach to Weimar, Germany--A Personal View," Military Affairs 42/3 (October 1978): 127-133.
This is an account of the author's personal experiences in military intelligence during World War II, especially his work in deciphering secret German codes.

6501. Rosenheim, Shawn. "The King of 'Secret Readers': Edgar Poe, Cryptography, and the Origins of the Detective Story," ELH 56/2 (1990): 375-400.
Poe's interest in cryptography and secret writing influenced the emergence of the nineteenth century detective novel.

6502. Rosenthal, Alan. "Film at War," Film Library Quarterly 7 (Spring 1974): 7-12.
This is an account of the role of film in pictorial representation of the Arab-Israeli War in 1967. Useful in studies of photo and map intelligence.

6503. Rosenthal, Joel. "The Problem of Covert Action in a Democracy," Ethics and International Affairs (Spring 1989): 1-3.

6504. Rosenthal, Paul C. and Robert S. Grossman. "Congressional Access to Confidential Information Collected by Federal Agencies," Harvard Journal on Legislation 15/1 (December 1977): 74-118.
Argues that the constitutional underpinnings upon which congressional requests for information rest should preclude information suppliers, executive officials, or the judiciary from blocking information requests on grounds of confidentiality.

6505. Rosenzweig, Margaret L. "The Law of Wiretapping," Cornell Law Quarterly 33/1 (June and September 1947): 514-555; 73-98.
A two-part study of wiretapping law conducted for the New York State Bar Association. Provides a history of the law of wiretapping in federal and state courts. Outlines the decision in the Olmstead case and summarizes the provisions of US Code, Section 605, of the Federal Communications Act. Covers the law of wiretapping in the states; the law of wiretapping in New York state; and analysis of considerations supporting the conflicting views as to the practice of wiretapping.

6506. Rositzke, Harry. "America's Secret Operations: A Perspective," Foreign Affairs 53/2 (January 1975): 334-351.

A historical study of US intelligence operations since World War II, including the organization and objectives of the Central Intelligence Agency.

6507. Rositzke, Harry. "The KGB's Broadening Horizons," Problems of Communism 24 (May 1975): 43-45.

6508. Roskill, Stephen W. "Lord Hankey--The Creation of the Machinery of Government," RUSI Defence Studies Journal 120/3 (1975): 10-18.

6509. Ross, Bill. "Space Support to the Warrior: The Intelligence Professional's Responsibility," American Intelligence Journal 15/2 (Autumn-Winter 1994): 72-76.

Major sections discuss the need for doctrine; the need for training; space based systems; and a summary of the requirements for adequate space support for ground troops.

6510. Ross, C. D. "Forfeiture for Treason in the Reign of Richard II," English Historical Review 71 (October 1956): 560-575.

Forfeiture was introduced as a penalty for high treason. Discusses the Statute of Richard II and the reinstatement of the common law to permit wives to sue for their inheritance when husbands were found guilty of treason. Forfeiture was a tactic of the Crown against the land-owning class.

6511. Ross, Irwin. "The Master Spy Who Almost Got Away: Swedish Air Force Colonel Wennerstrom," Harper's 229 (December 1964): 47-54.

Argues that the loss of Stig Wennerstrom to the Russians had the same educational lessons in espionage tradecraft as the Hiss case in the US. Wennerstrom gave the Russians the Draken J-35 aircraft locator system.

6512. Ross, Joel and Douglas Naquin. "High-Intensity Annoyance," Studies in Intelligence 34/1 (Spring 1990).

6513. Ross, Thomas B. "Spying in the United States," Society 12/3 (March-April 1975): 64-71.

Discussion of the National Security Act of 1947, domestic intelligence in the United States, expansion of CIA power, and proposed congressional oversight.

6514. Rostow, Walter W. "The Beginnings of Air Targeting," Studies in Intelligence 7/4 (Winter 1963).

Addresses strategic bombing direction from London in World War II.

6515. Rostow, Walter W. "Waging Economic Warfare from London: The Enemy Objective Unit," Studies in Intelligence 35/5 (Winter 1991): 73-79.

This piece is based on the author's July 1991 essay at the National Archives in 1991, drawing on his World War II in the Enemy Objectives Unit of the OSS. Major sections discuss doctrine; three bureaucratic battles; EOU in perspective; and some final observations.

6516. Rosswurm, Steven and Toni Gilpin. "The FBI and the Farm Equipment Workers: FBI Surveillance Records as a Source for CIO Union History," Labor History 27/4 (1986): 485-505.

This article addresses the FBI procedures for obtaining information on union activities and the process for public access to such files.

6517. Rostow, Eugene V. "Great Cases Make Bad Law: The War Powers Act," Texas Law Review 50/5 (May 1972): 833-900.

Reviews in detail the provisions of the War Powers Act, especially the historical origins. Briefly mentions the national security power of the Secretary of State to control foreign travel.

6518. Roth, John R. "Criminal Procedure - Electronic Tracking Devices and the Fourth Amendment," Wayne Law Review 30 (Spring 1984): 1151-1167.

This is a case note following United States v. Knotts, 103 S. Ct. 1081 (1983).

6519. Rothfels, Hans. "The German Resistance in Its International Aspects," International Affairs (Great Britain) 34 (1958): 477-489.

6520. Rothrock, John. "Information Warfare: Time for Some Constructive Skepticism?," American Intelligence Journal 15/1 (Spring-Summer 1994): 71-76.

Addresses several issues within the broad topic of information warfare, such as thrust versus vector; means versus objectives; challenging questions; a prism through which to consider information warfare; information warfare employment and doctrine; the offensive sphere; the protective sphere; and the competitive-use-of-information sphere.

6521. Rothschild, M. "Central Employment Agency: Students Respond to the CIA Rush," Progressive 48/2 (February 1984): 18-21.

Recruitment activities on college campuses by the CIA. Puts a positive face on CIA recruiting in the early 1980s.

6522. Rothschild, M. "Who Killed Manuel Buendia?," Progressive 49 (April 1985): 18-23.

A Mexican official's assassination which has never been thoroughly investigated as to its possible international connections.

6523. Rotmistrov, P.   "On the Role of Surprise in Contemporary War," Voennaya Mysl 2 (February 1955).

6524. Rottenberg, Simon.   "The Clandestine Distribution of Heroin, Its Discovery and Suppression," Journal of Political Economy 76/1 (1968):   78-90.

Discusses the organization of clandestine enterprise of converting opium into morphine, then into heroin; the market for the service of police inaction; and the allocation of police resources.   A detailed evaluation of the options and incentives operating in the drug trade.

6525. Roucek, J.   "The Role of Spying in International Relations," International Review of History and Political Science 2/1 (1974):   120-132.

6526. Rouleau, E.   "Double Life of Eli Cohen," Atlas 10/1 (July 1965):   10-12.

A brief exploration into the life and expionage work of Eli Cohen, hanged as a spy in Damascus in 1965.

6527. Rourke, Francis E.   "Administrative Secrecy: A Congressional Dilemma," American Political Science Review 54/3 (September 1960):   684-694.

Discusses executive-legislative conflict over issues related to the withholding of information in the legislative process.

6528. Rourke, Francis E.   "Executive Fallability: Presidential Management Styles," Administration and Society 6/2 (1974):   171-197.

The author argues that Richard Nixon's presidency introduced exceptionally negative consequences for using secrecy as a management tool in the executive branch.

6529. Rourke, Francis E.   "Style of Presidential Secrecy," Towson State Journal of International Affairs 10/1 (1975):   19-26.

Presidents since 1945 have each carried out of variety of foreign policy secrecy policies.   This article emphasizes the styles of John Kennedy and Lyndon Johnson.

6530. Rourke, Francis E.   "Bureaucratic Autonomy and the Public Interest," American Behavioral Scientist 22/5 (May-June 1979):   537-546.

Within the larger discussion of the political changes aimed at making federal agencies more politically responsive, this article discusses the CIA as an agency feared for its secrecy and low public accountability.

6531. Roush, Maurice D.   "The Halet Evaluation System," Military Review 49/9 (1969):   10-17.

Discusses local military intelligence collection in Vietnam.

6532. Route, Leslie B., Jr. and John F. Bratzel. "Origins: U.S. Intelligence in Latin America," Studies in Intelligence 29/4 (Winter 1985).

6533. Rowan, Andrew S. "My Ride Across Cuba," McClure's Magazine 11 (August 1898): 372-379.

6534. Rowat, Donald C. "How Much Administrative Secrecy?," Canadian Journal of Economics and Political Science 31/4 (November 1965): 479-498.

6535. Rowat, Donald C. "The Problem of Administrative Secrecy," International Review of Administrative Science (1966).

6536. Rowen, Henry S. "Reforming Intelligence: A Market Approach," American Intelligence Journal 14/3 (Autumn-Winter 1993-1994): 49-54.
    Considers the market for intelligence; the analogy of large, multinational firms; the reasoning for the current organization; and the need to empower the users.

6537. Rowles, James P. "U.S. Covert Operations Against Nicaragua and Their Legality Under Conventional and Customary International Law," University of Miami Inter-American Law Review 17 (Spring 1986): 407-508.
    Major sections of this extensive discussion include: why international law matters; US covert operations against Nicaragua; the World Court case; international law and the legality of US covert operations; US threats to use force; US intervention in the internal affairs of Nicaragua; and US actions and the principle of peaceful settlement of international disputes.

6538. Roy, W. T. "Cloak and Dagger in Fantasyland: The S.I.S. Debate in New Zealand," Political Science 30/2 (December 1978): 97-105.
    Traces the growth of the New Zealand secret services, considers the sources of public concern with the services, and evaluates the extent of impact of public concerns on new control legislation.

6539. Royster, Charles. "The Nature of Treason: Revolutionary Virtue and American Reactions to Benedict Arnold," William and Mary Quarterly 36/2 (April 1979): 163-193.
    Discusses in detail Arnold's defection to the British in 1775. Describes Arnold's heroics in Canada and his motivations for money and a promotion.

6540. Rubanov, V. "From the 'Cult of Secrecy' to the Information Culture," Soviet Law and Government 28 (Summer 1989): 6-23.
    An interesting critique of the overextension of the Soviet secrecy system to the detriment of the goals of socialist development. Argues that the overextension of secrecy alienates people from their government; cites the work

in the US and Britain to reduce the amount of secrecy in government. Reproduced in Soviet Review 30/5 (September-October 1989): 18-35.

6541. Rubenstein, Alan D. "Minimization and the Fourth Amendment, New York Law Forum 19 (1974): 861-881.

A case note addressing electronic surveillance minimization and the relative successes of Title III of the Safe Streets Act of 1968.

6542. Rubenstein, Diane. "Publish and Perish: The Expurgation of French Intellectuals," Journal of European Studies 23 (March-June 1993): 71-99.

Includes brief discussion of French treason trials during World War II.

6543. Rubenstein, Henry. "DC Power and Cooling Towers," Studies in Intelligence 16/3 (Fall 1972): 81-86.

Discusses advances in US assessment of the Soviet nuclear weapons program in the early 1960s, in particular, the new information gathered regarding tritium and lithium production.

6544. Rubin, Alfred P. "Some Legal Implications of the Pueblo Incident," International and Comparative Law Quarterly 18/4 (October 1969): 961-970.

Discusses issues of international law suggested by the behavior of North Korean and US officials, general implications of the case, the twelve-mile limit, the concept of innocent passage, and confusions raised by negotiations.

6545. Rubin, Alfred P. "Impact of the Pueblo Incident in International Law," Oregon Law Review 49/1 (December 1969): 1-12.

A brief background on the Pueblo incident involving the capture of this navy vessel by North Korea in 1968. Discusses general implications; the law of the twelve-mile limit; the doctrine of innocent passage; and some confusing elements of the case. (See previous citation for Rubin. Published in both places by agreement).

6546. Rubin, Alfred P. "Sunken Soviet Submarines and Central Intelligence: Laws of Property and the Agency," American Journal of International Law 69/4 (October 1975): 855-858.

Brief discussion of the international law implications of the CIA's Glomar Explorer project to raise a Soviet submarine from the ocean floor.

6547. Rubin, F. "Security Concerns of the USSR and the Other Warsaw Treaty Organization Countries," RUSI Defence Studies Journal 128 (September 1983): 35-40.

6548. Rubin, F. "The Hungarian Military Intelligence and Security Services," RUSI Defence Studies Journal 129/4 (December 1984): 59-64.

6549. Rubin, Frank. "Multiplex Ciphers," <u>Cryptologia</u> 2/2 (April 1978): 152-160.

6550. Rubin, Frank. "Computer Methods for Decrypting Random Stream Ciphers," <u>Cryptologia</u> 2/3 (July 1978): 215-231.

6551. Rubin, Frank. "Solving a Cipher Based on Multiple Random Number Streams," <u>Cryptologia</u> 3/3 (July 1979): 155-157.

6552. Rubin, Frank. "Cryptographic Aspects of Data Compression Codes," <u>Cryptologia</u> 3/4 (October 1979): 202-205.

6553. Rubin, Frank. "Decrypting a Stream Cipher Based on J-K Flip Flops," <u>Cryptologia</u> 5/1 (January 1981): 51-57.

6554. Rubin, Frank. "Foiling the Known-Plaintext Attack," <u>Cryptologia</u> 10/4 (October 1986): 217-222.

6555. Rubin, Frank. "Foiling the Exhaustive Key-Search Attack," <u>Cryptologia</u> 11/2 (April 1987): 102-107.

6556. Rubin, Frank. "The Cryptographic Uses of Post Tag Systems," <u>Cryptologia</u> 12/1 (January 1988): 25-33.

6557. Rubin, Frank. "Comments on 'Cryptanalysis of Knapsack Ciphers Using Genetic Algorithms,'" <u>Cryptologia</u> 15/2 (April 1994): 153-154.

6558. Rubin, Frank. "The Quadratic and Double Quadratic Residue Ciphers," <u>Cryptologia</u> 19/3 (July 1995): 274-284.

6559. Rubin, Frank. "Message Authentication Using Quadratic Residues," <u>Cryptologia</u> 19/4 (October 1995): 397-404.

6560. Rubin, Mitchell S. "The FBI and Dissidents: A First Amendment Analysis of Attorney General Smith's 1983 FBI Guidelines on Domestic Security Investigations," <u>Arizona Law Review</u> 27 (Spring 1985): 453-476.
　　　　Major sections include discussion of a comparison of the Smith guidelines with the Levi guidelines; FBI authorizations under the Smith guidelines; intelligence gathering at peaceful public demonstrations; and FBI use of informants.

6561. Rubner, Michael. "President Reagan, the 1973 War Powers Resolution, and the Invasion of Grenada," <u>Political Science Quarterly</u> 100/4 (Winter 1985-1986): 627-647.

Considers the various consultations regarding the application of the War Powers Act to the proposed intervention in Grenada; reporting and triggering the sixty-day clock; and implications and conclusions.

6562. Rubottom, R. Richard. "Latin America: Revolution or Evolution as the Answer to Insurgency," <u>Naval War College Review</u> 16/10 (June 1963): 17-25.

6563. Rudd, Hughes. "My Escape from the CIA," <u>Harper's</u> 223 (October 1961): 43-47.

A tale about the author's recruitment into service for the Central Intelligence Agency. Years later he became a respected and well known television reporter.

6564. Rudenstine, David. "The Pentagon Papers Case (New York Times v. United States, 91 Sup.Ct. 2140): Recovering Its Meaning Twenty Years Later," <u>Cardoza Law Review</u> 12 (June 1991): 1869-1913.

An extensive discussion of the issues and implications of the publication of the so-called Pentagon Papers in the New York Times newspaper.

6565. Ruddy, Francis S. "Permissible Dissent and Treason," <u>Criminal Law Bulletin</u> 4/3 (1968): 145-159.

Discusses the British origins of the legal principles of treason; distinction between conspiring to levy war and actual acts of war; adherence to the enemy as a state of mind; acts which give comfort to the enemy; the mens rea requirement for treason; and overt acts.

6566. Ruehsen, Moyara de Moraes. "Operation 'AJAX' Revisited: Iran, 1953," <u>Middle East Studies</u> 29/3 (July 1993): 467-486.

6567. Ruetten, Richard T. "General Douglas MacArthur's 'Reconnaissance in Force': The Rationalization of a Defeat in Korea," <u>Pacific Historical Review</u> 36 (1967): 79-93.

A critique of the command leadership of General Douglas MacArthur prior to the Chinese counteroffensive of November 25, 1950. Argues that, contrary to popular opinion and official record, General MacArthur chose to ignore vital intelligence information prior to the battle which cost thousands of casualties.

6568. Ruffner, Kevin C. "CORONA and the Intelligence Community: Declassification's Great Leap," <u>Studies in Intelligence</u> 39/5 (1996): 61-69.

Discusses the declassification of CIA documents pertaining to project CORONA, the satellite surveillance of Cuba and the Soviet Union in the early 1960s.

6569. Ruffley, Mary J. "Criminal Law - Electronic Surveillance - The Fourth Amendment Does Not Prohibit Per Se a Covert Entry Performed for the Purpose of Installing Otherwise Legal Electronic Bugging Equipment and Does Not Require that a Title III Electronic Surveillance Order Include a Specific Authorization of Covert Entry for Installation Purposes," University of Detroit Journal of Urban Law 57 (Spring 1980): 588-614.

A case note pertaining to Dalia v. U. S.; considers historical framework; analysis of the Dalia decision; and interprets post-Dalia practical effects.

6570. Ruggles, Richard and Henry Brodie. "An Empirical Approach to Economic Intelligence in World War II," Journal of the American Statistical Association 42 (March 1947): 72-91.

A classic discussion of methods used by the Economic Warfare Division of the American Embassy in London to analyze German war equipment production using captured weapons.

6571. Ruggles, Richard P.; John de J. Pemberton, Jr.; and Arthur R. Miller. "Symposium: Computer Data Banks and Individual Privacy," Minnesota Law Review 53/2 (December 1968): 211-245.

A symposium on the subject addressing the needs and values of data banks; the dangers, legal aspects and remedies of computer data bank violation; and proposals and requirements for solutions.

6572. Ruhl, Robert K. "Raid at Son Tay," Airman 19 (August 1975): 24-31.

A brief summary of the intelligence dimensions and military operations at Son Tay, Vietnam.

6573. Ruiz Marrero, Carmelo. "La CIA y su Rol en el Mundo Contemporaneo," Revista de Ciencias Sociales 29/1-2 (January-June 1990): 189-245.

Published in Spanish in a Puerto Rican journal.

6574. Ruland, Christoph. "Realizing Digital Signatures with One-Way Hash Functions," Cryptologia 17/3 (July 1993): 285-300.

6575. Rule, James B., et al. "Documentary Identification and Mass Surveillance in the United States," Social Problems 31/2 (December 1983): 222-234.

Examines six of the most common personal identification items used in the United States to conduct domestic surveillance of people: Social Security numbers; driver's licenses; credit cards; birth certificates; passports; and bank books.

6576. Rule, John C. "Gathering Intelligence in the Age of Louis XIV," International History Review 14/4 (1992): 732-752.

6577. Rundquist, E. A. "The Assessment of Graphology," <u>Studies in Intelligence</u> 3/3 (Summer 1959).

6578. Runyon, James C. "Naval Intelligence Organizations in Washington, D.C.," <u>Naval Intelligence Professionals Quarterly</u> 7/3 (Summer 1991): 18-19.

6579. Runzheimer, Juergen. "Der Veberfall auf den Sender Gleiwitz im Jahre 1939," <u>Vierteljahrhefte Fuer Zeitgeschichte</u> 10 (1962): 408-426.

6580. Rusbridger, James. "Naval Intelligence: Lessons in Security from the Pacific During World War II," <u>Navy International</u> 90/3 (March 1985): 167-170.

6581. Rusbridger, James. "The Sinking of the 'Automedan' and the Capture of the 'Nankin': New Light on Two Intelligence Disasters in World War II," <u>Encounter</u> 64/5 (May 1985): 8-14.
  Details the British loss of Cabinet materials, plans, etc. to the Germans and the Japanese (via the capture of the Automedan) which ultimately led to Pearl Harbor.

6582. Rusbridger, James. "Winds of Warning: Mythology and Fact About ENIGMA and Pearl Harbor," <u>Encounter</u> 66/1 (January 1986): 6-13.
  Argues that most interpretations of cryptanalysis during World War II overlook the cooperation of, and information exchanges between, the US, Britain, and Holland regarding the Far East situation. Discusses the influence of radio on cryptanalysis, the enigma machine, the enhancement of the enigma for Japanese transmissions, exchanges of information, and the reasons for Pearl Harbor as a surprise.

6583. Rusbridger, James. "Between Bluff, Deceit, and Treachery: The Story of Henri Dericourt and an SOE Disaster in France," <u>Encounter</u> 66 (May 1986): 5-13.
  Details Britain's covert espionage operations during World War II and subsequent failure in France due to lack of coordination and resistance from MI6, MI6, the SIS and the Royal Air Force.

6584. Rush, Myron. "A Neglected Source of Evidence," <u>Studies in Intelligence</u> 2 (Summer 1958).

6585. Rushford, Gregory G. "Making Enemies: The Pike Committee's Struggle to Get the Facts," <u>Washington Monthly</u> 8/5-6 (July-August 1976): 42-53.
  Examines the degree of conflict between the executive and legislative branches in the course of investigation by the House Select Committee on Intelligence Activities into the mid-1970s activities of the various intelligence services.

6586. Russell, Charles A. and Robert E. Hildner. "Intelligence and Information Processing in Counterinsurgency," Air University Review 24/5 (July-August 1973): 46-56.

Discusses the focus of counterinsurgency, the importance of counterinsurgency, dossier building, and the basic principles and features of intelligence and information of the Air Force Office of Special Investigations.

6587. Russell, Conrad. "Theory of Treason in the Trial of Strafford," English Historical Review 80 (January 1965): 30-50.

Discusses the 1352 treason statute, the evidence necessary under the statute, the lasting implications of the statute, and the dangers posed by the interpretation of the Strafford case that could lead to civil war.

6588. Russell, E. Neil. "EW Canada--Looking Back, Looking Ahead," Journal of Electronic Defense 9/7 (July 1986): 49-51.

Describes Canadian electronic warfare in the latter part of World War II.

6589. Russell, Frank S. "The Intelligence Department," Blackwood's Magazine (May 1900): 725-733.

Discusses the criticisms of the intelligence department in England between the 1850s and 1900, the then-current situation in the South Africa campaign, and the problem of unheeded information.

6590. Russell, Peter H. "The Proposed Charter for a Civilian Intelligence Agency: An Appraisal," Canadian Public Policy 9/3 (September 1983): 326-337.

Discusses Bill C-157 to establish the Canadian Security Intelligence Service (CSIS), some of the critical issues surrounding its creation, the scope of CSIS authority, methods of investigation, and controls.

6591. Russell, Richard L. "CIA: A Cold War Relic?," International Journal of Intelligence and Counterintelligence 8/1 (Spring 1995): 11-20.

An overview of issues and questions raised in the course of considering the role of CIA in the foreign policy process. Major sections address CIA's support to foreign policy; potential areas for reform; and CIA's unique niche.

6592. Russett, Bruce. "Pearl Harbor: Deterrence Theory and Decision Theory," Journal of Peace Research 2 (1967): 89-105.

Argues that the Japanese decision to go to war was made over a long period of time and as a result of numerous incremental decisions. Uses decision theory, discusses Japan's perceptions of US commitment, and calls for a revision of general deterrence theory.

6593. Russo, Alan M. "Intelligence Gap," Infantry 61 (September-October 1971): 20-22.

6594. Rutan, Gerald F. "The Canadian Security Intelligence Service: Squaring the Demands of National Security with Canadian Democracy," Conflict Quarterly 5/4 (Fall 1985): 17-30.

Discussion of the Canadian intelligence services in the aftermath of a national commission investigation into the activities of the Royal Canadian Mounted Police. New establishment of the intelligence service.

6595. Ryan, David H. "United States v. Marchetti and Alfred A. Knopf, Inc. v. Colby (509 F.2d 1362): Secrecy 2; First Amendment 0," Hastings Constitutional Law Quarterly 3/4 (Fall 1976): 1073-1105.

CIA's efforts to seek an injunction to stop publication by author and former CIA employee Victor Marchetti, and a publisher's suit against former CIA director William Colby. Outlines the cases, discusses the CIA secrecy agreement, the application of First Amendment standards to the publication of secret information, and the procedure for prepublication review based on a test for only damaging information.

6596. Ryan, Joseph F. "The Inspector General of the Canadian Security Intelligence Service," Conflict Quarterly 9/2 (Spring 1989): 33-51.

Little information is available concerning the work of the Canadian Intelligence Service Inspector General, argues the author. This article focuses on the role and functions of the IG office. Major sections discuss historical background; role and functions; current operations of the IG; the IG's review programme; the IG and liaison with the CSIS; and comparative analysis.

6597. Ryan, Joseph F. "Review of the Canadian Security Intelligence Service: A Suitable Model for the United Kingdom?," Intelligence and National Security 5/3 (July 1990): 200-206.

A review of the Parliament's views on the CSIS reforms of 1984; additional reform proposals of 1989; and the need for more reforms in the future.

6598. Ryan, Julie; John Woloschek; and Barry Leven. "Complexities in Conducting Information Warfare," Defense Intelligence Journal 5/1 (Spring 1996): 69-82.

The authors discuss the information war in a practical sense; strategic information warfare; bounding information warfare; the elements of information warfare attack; intelligence support to information warfare; determining the effectiveness of information warfare; and modeling in support of information warfare.

6599. Ryan, Terry. "Imagery Intelligence Reform: Is It Time?," American Intelligence Journal 13/1&2 (Winter-Spring 1992): 19-24.

Considers the changing strategic environment; emerging technologies; lack of interoperability; lack of strategy; and dwindling resources.

6600. Ryan, T. M. "Criminal Law--Violation of Espionage Act of 1917," <u>Notre Dame Lawyer</u> 20 (September 1944): 97-98.

Considers the case of <u>Hartzel v. U. S.</u>, 64 Sup.Ct. 1233.

6601. Ryan, William F. "The Genesis of the Techno-Thriller," <u>Virginia Quarterly Review</u> 69 (Winter 1993): 24-40.

Discusses politics, technology and espionage in literature through the novels of Tom Clancy and Stephen Coonts.

6602. Rychetnik, Joe. "Both Old-Fashioned Skulduggery and Brave Fighting Lay Behind the U.S. Acquisition of California," <u>Military History</u> 11/5 (1994): 20, 24, 86-88.

A brief but rare account of the military intelligence work of Archibald Gillespie in the war with Mexico in 1846.

6603. Ryland, Walter H. "Police Surveillance of Public Toilets," <u>Washington and Lee Law Review</u> 23/2 (Fall 1966): 423-432.

Police surveillance of public toilets served to discover consensual sexual activity, but it raised Fourth Amendment concerns. Discusses <u>Smyada v. United States</u>, the reasonableness of a search, and the right to privacy.

S

**"...many of the objects of espionage are symbolic or conventional
rather than realistic."**
(The Torment of Secrecy by Edward Shils, p. 220)

6604. Saaty, Thomas L.; Luis G. Vargas; and Amos Barzilay. "High-Level Decisions: A Lesson from the Iran Hostage Rescue Operation," Decision Sciences 13/2 (April 1982): 185-198.
Explores the factors influencing decision makers' final decisions, especially tangible and intangible factors. Poses an analytical hierarchy and process model and applies the model to the Iran hostage case.

6605. Sabin, Edward P. "Threat Inflation: U.S. Estimates of Soviet Military Capability," Peace & Change 14/1 (1989): 191-202.

6606. Sabin, Lynn W. "Employment of Sensors," Marine Corps Gazette 73 (February 1989): 30-35.

6607. Sabin, Margery. "The Community of Intelligence and the Avant-Garde," Raritan 4/3 (Winter 1985).

6608. Sabine, David B. "Pinkerton's 'Operative': Timothy Webster," Civil War Times Illustrated 12/5 (1973): 32-38.
This is a brief history of union spy Timothy Webster and Webster's eventual execution.

6609. Sachse, William L. "Our Naval Attache System: Its Origins and Developments to 1917," U.S. Naval Institute Proceedings 72 (May 1946): 661-672.

The creation of the Office of Naval Intelligence in 1882 is outlined, including establishment of the mission, objectives, and legislative recognition.

6610. Sadler, Lori M. "Improving National Intelligence Support to Marine Corps Expeditionary Forces," American Intelligence Journal 13/3 (Summer 1992): 49-51.

Discusses the recent historical changes in the Marine Corps intelligence capabilities; essential elements of basic encyclopedic data, secure communications, and flexible national capabilities; and the role and needs of the Marine Air Ground Task Forces.

6611. Saerchinger, C. "Radio, Censorship and Neutrality," Foreign Affairs 18 (1940): 337-349.

6612. Safford, L. F. "The Functions and Duties of the Cryptography Section, Naval Communications: From the Archives," Cryptologia 16/3 (July 1992): 265-281.

6613. Safran, Nadav. "The War and the Future of Arab-Israeli Conflict," Foreign Affairs 52/2 (January 1974): 215-237.

Discusses the wars of 1967 and 1973 between Arabs and Israelis, including implications for intelligence aspects.

6614. Safran, Nadav. "Trial by Ordeal: The Yom Kippur War, October 1973," International Security 2/2 (Fall 1977): 133-170.

Offers especially insightful discussion on the prelude to the war, surprise through self-deception, initial forces and deployments, the course of the war, the war at sea, and the aftermath.

6615. Sagan, Scott D. "Lessons of the Yom Kippur Alert," Foreign Policy 36 (Fall 1979): 160-177.

Discusses the misleading and contradictory lessons of the October War and argues that decisions in time of crises should be made on intuition and foresight, not on ambiguous facts and lessons.

6616. Sagan, Scott D. "Nuclear Alerts and Crisis Management," International Security 9/4 (Spring 1985): 99-139.

Considers crisis management within the context of three case examples: May 1960 DEFCON 3 alert; October 1962 Cuban missile crisis; and October 1973 DEFCON 3 alert. Role of intelligence is discussed in each case.

6617.   Sagan, Scott D.   "The Origins of the Pacific War," Journal of Interdisciplinary History 18/4 (Spring 1988): 893-922.
   Discusses phases of progression toward war beginning in 1938.

6618. Sagdeev, Roald. "Russian Scientists Save American Secrets," Bulletin of the Atomic Scientists 49 (May 1993): 32-36.
   Brief summary the espionage operations of the Soviets as to the US atomic bomb project and the Soviet-crafted hydrogen bomb.

6619.   Sakkas, Peter E.   "Espionage and Sabotage in the Computer World," International Journal of Intelligence and Counterintelligence 5/2 (Summer 1991): 155-202.
   A detailed discussion of vulnerabilities of computers to attacks by 'hackers' and others bent on compromising or destroying data. Major sections discuss viruses; Trojan Horses; logic bombs; genetic-based viruses; worms; trapdoors; brief review of computer penetrations; targets; industrial and foreign espionage; the talent pool for computer espionage; employers of the talent pool; covert and intelligence activities; technical background; defenses against attacks; disaster/contingency centers; and psychological and cost barriers.

6620. Salans, Carl F. and Richard A. Frank. "Passports and Area Restrictions," Stanford Law Review 20/5 (May 1968): 839-857.
   A comprehensive examination of State Department and judicial decisions on passport controls arising from the Staughton Lynd case of travel to North Vietnam in 1966.

6621. Sale, Richard. "Carter and Iran: From Idealism to Disaster," Washington Quarterly 3/4 (Autumn 1980): 75-87.
   Major sections discuss the new orthodoxy of foreign policy in the Carter years; the Mondale-Aaron domination; human rights policy; Iran and identifying the opposition to the Shah; and accounting for American poor performance. Mentions the CIA.

6622.   Sale, Sara L.   "Admiral Sidney W. Souers and President Truman," Missouri Historical Review 86/1 (October 1991): 55-71.
   Discusses in detail the relationship between Souers and President Truman. Souers was Truman's "intelligence gatherer," and he served as director of central intelligence in 1946.

6623. Salisbury, Alan B. "Beyond BETA: Tactical Intelligence Fusion Systems in Transition," Signal 38 (October 1983): 19-21.

6624. Salisbury, Harrison E. "A Comment on Theoharis' Unanswered Question," Government Publications Review 10/3 (1983): 257-261.

Remarks upon the work and methods of Athan Theoharis to discover records relating to the operations of the Federal Bureau of Investigation.

6625. Salisbury, Johnson A. "Criminal Procedure--Foreign Intelligence Surveillance Act of 1978: A New Charter for Electronic Intelligence Gathering," North Carolina Law Review 58/1 (October 1979): 171-188.
Discusses the Act as a means for providing an exclusive charter for conducting electronic surveillance aimed at gathering foreign intelligence information.

6626. Salmon, John. "'A Mission of the Most Secret and Important Kind': James Lafayette and American Espionage in 1781," Virginia Cavalcade 31/2 (1981): 78-85.
The story of Lafayette's double agent work in 1781. Discusses clandestine collection methods directed at British headquarters.

6627. Salmon, Patrick. "British Plans for Economic Warfare Against Germany 1937-1939: The Problem of Swedish Iron Ore," Journal of Contemporary History 16/1 (January 1981): 53-72.
Argues the close connection between Swedish iron ore and German steel production was linked directly to other major factors in the outbreak of World War II in Europe.

6628. Salmon, Vincent. "Security by Masking," Journal of the Acoustical Society of America 79 (June 1986): 2077-2078.

6629. Salter, John R., Jr. "Reflections on Ralph Chaplin, the Wobblies, and Organizing in the Save the World Business - Then and Now," Pacific Historian 30/2 (1986): 4-19.

6630. Salton, George L., et al. "Trends in Protected Communications," Signal 33 (August 1979): 85-95.
Several experts discuss the trends in encoded communication links and systems.

6631. Saltzburg, Stephen A. "National Security and Privacy: Of Governments and Individuals Under the Constitution and the Foreign Intelligence Surveillance Act," Virginia Journal of International Law 28/1 (Fall 1987): 129-155.
Concludes that the FISA and the Foreign Intelligence Surveillance Court are constitutionally sound and provide adequate protections under the Fourth Amendment.

6632. Samford, John A. "The Intelligence Necessary to the Formulation of a Sound Strategy," Studies in Intelligence 2 (Fall 1957).

6633. Samia, F. G. "The Norwegian Connection: Norway (Un)willing Spy for the U.S.," Covert Action Information Bulletin (June 1980): 4-9.

6634. Samson, George. "Japan's Fatal Blunder," International Affairs (Great Britain) 24 (October 1948): 543-554.

Considers the question of whether or not Japan's decision to attack the US in 1941 was a justifiable risk in the circumstances in which it was made. Considers Japanese intelligence estimates of various US capabilities.

6635. Samuels, Linda B. and Bryan K. Johnson. "The Uniform Trade Secrets Act: The States' Response," Creighton Law Review 24/1 (1990-1991): 49-98.

Discusses highlights of trade secrets law; definitions; injunctive relief; damages; attorneys' fees; preservation of secrecy; statute of limitations; effect on other law; uniformity of application and construction; severability; and time of taking effect.

6636. Samuelson, Nancy B. "Revolutionary War Women and the Second Oldest Profession," Minerva: Quarterly Report on Women and the Military 7/2 (1989): 16-25.

6637. Samuelson, Nancy B. "Employment of Female Spies in the American Civil War," Minerva: Quarterly Report on Women and the Military 7/3-4 (1989): 57-66.

6638. Sanborn, Paul J. "The Battle of Brandywine: An Intelligence Evaluation of General George Washington's Tactical Operations During the Battle Along the Brandywine, 11 September 1777," American Intelligence Journal 16/2&3 (Autumn-Winter 1995): 69-80.

A rich analysis of the operations, containing sections addressing background and preliminaries; an intelligence view of Washington's deployment; critical American weaknesses; Washington's plan and preparations; the American intelligence breakdown; and the battle unfolds.

6639. Sancho, Justo. "Enumeration of Multivariable Decipherable Boolean Functions," Cryptologia 11/3 (July 1987): 172-181.

6640. Sandeen, Eric J. "Anti-Nazi Sentiment in Film: 'Confessions of a Nazi Spy' and the German-American Bund," American Studies 20/2 (Fall 1979): 69-81.

A discussion of the 1938 film in the context of the evolution of domestic intelligence investigations by the FBI preceding World War II.

6641. Sander, Alfred D. "Truman and the National Security Council, 1945-1947," Journal of American History 59/2 (September 1972): 369-388.

Outlines the political reasons for creation of the National Security Council and the original roles of the Council. Truman was supplied with information by the Council prior to the Korean war.

6642. Sanders, A. "Does Professional Crime Pay?: A Critical Comment on Mack," Modern Law Review 40/5 (September 1977): 553-560.

Mainly a critique of the methodology of Mack's book on professional criminals, wherein Mack relied upon police intelligence personnel to identify a list of professional criminals for purposes of study. This author rejects Mack's methods.

6643. Sanders, Neill F. "Henry Shelton Sanford in England April-November, 1861: A Reappraisal," Lincoln Herald 77/2 (1975): 87-95.

This is a discussion of Sanford's service as a union minister and intelligence officer to gather information on confederate shipping sources.

6644. Sanders, Neill F. "'Unfit for Consul?': The English Consulates and Lincoln's Patronage Policy," Lincoln Herald 82/3 (1980): 464-474.

6645. Sanders, Neill F. "'When a House Is on Fire': The English Consulates and Lincoln's Patronage Policy," Lincoln Herald 83/1 (1981): 579-591.

Lincoln's appointments of various consulates to Ireland served as intelligence agents to collect information on British supplies to the Confederacy.

6646. Sanders, Neill F. "Cotton, Lard and Rebels: James Osborn Putnam As Lincoln's Le Havre Consul," Lincoln Herald 88/4 (1986): 157-169.

6647. Sanders, Sylvia. "Data Privacy: What Washington Doesn't Want You to Know," Reason 12/9 (1981): 24-37.

6648. Sandler, Susan F. "National Security Versus Free Speech: A Comparative Analysis of Publication Review Standards in the United States and Great Britain," Brooklyn Journal of International Law 15 (1989): 711-757.

Explores the espionage statutes 793, 794, and 798. Major sections address the statutes and free speech; Great Britain's Official Secrets Act and free speech; and a comparison between US and British secrets law.

6649. Sandman, Joshua H. "Analyzing Foreign Policy Crisis Situations: The Bay of Pigs," Presidential Studies Quarterly 16/2 (Spring 1986): 310-316.

The author concludes that Kennedy's weakness was in the area of communications between and among government and non-government advisors. He should also have regarded the adversary, the implications for US allies, international law and the moral position of the US.

6650. Sanford, William V. "Evidentiary Privileges Against the Production of Data Within the Control of Executive Departments," <u>Vanderbilt Law Review</u> 3/1 (1949): 73-98.

Suggests that the Executive branch receives substantial information in the course of its business that can be highly useful to litigants in civil and criminal matters, especially information about national security, communications from informers, military and diplomatic secrets. The problem of Executive privilege is discussed and the use of the federal courts to determine Executive privilege to withhold information.

6651. Sanger, Grant. "Freedom of the Press or Treason?," <u>U.S. Naval Institute Proceedings</u> 103 (September 1977): 96-97.

6652. Sanger, Richard H. The Age of Sociopolitical Change," <u>Naval War College Review</u> (October 1969): 3-16.

Addresses the topic of insurgency.

6653. Sangmauh, Egya N. "Eisenhower and Containment in North Africa, 1956-1960," <u>Middle East Journal</u> 44/1 (Winter 1990): 76-91.

Discusses US perceptions and strategy; the Tunisian arms crisis; the "Good Offices" mission; and conclusions. Mentions the Central Intelligence Agency.

6654. Sannes, Erling N. "'Queen of the Lecture Platform': Kate Richards O'Hare and North Dakota Politics, 1917-1921," <u>North Dakota History</u> 58/4 (1991): 2-19.

6655. Santiago, George. "Intelligence Support to Civilian Law Enforcement," <u>Military Intelligence</u> 21/1 (January-March 1995): 5-11.

Reviews approaches and procedures for assistance between the Puerto Rico Army National Guard and civilian law enforcement in various drug interdiction missions. Analyzes Puerto Rico's situation using low-intensity conflict, mission phases, and the imperatives of LIC.

6656. Santoni, Alberto and Theodor Fuchs. "The Influence of Ultra on the War in the Mediterranean," <u>Marine-Rundschau</u> 78/9 (1981): 503-512.

A look at the effectiveness of the British intelligence system at deciphering German and Italian naval codes during World War II.

6657. Santos, Richard G. "Juan Nepomuceno Seguin, Texan Spy in the North-East Mexican Command," <u>Humanitas</u> 17 (1976): 551-567.

A detailed account of the escapades of Juan N. Seguin, an Hispanic Texan spy.

6658. Sapp, Edwin G. "Decision Trees," Studies in Intelligence 18/4 (Winter 1974).

6659. Sapp, Stephen L. "Private Interceptions of Wire and Oral Communication Under Title III: Rethinking Congressional Intent," American Journal of Criminal Law 16/2 (Winter 1989): 181-206.
    Analyzes the problem of private interceptions; overview of Title III and whether or not interceptions occur within the meaning of Title III; criminal or tortious interception; and judicially-created exceptions.

6660. Sarchett, Barry W. "Unreading the Spy Thriller: The Example of William F. Buckley, Jr," Journal of Popular Culture 26/2 (Fall 1992): 127-140.
    Considers the themes and perspectives found in various modern spy thrillers with emphasis on Buckley's character, "Blackford Oakes."

6661. Sarotte, Mary E. "Spying Not Only on Strangers: Documenting Stasi Involvement in Cold War German-German Negotiation," Intelligence and National Security 11/4 (October 1996): 765-779.
    Major sections discuss the Erfurt talks and the Kassel meetings involving Willy Brandt; "Aufklarung," or reconnaissance, of the German-to-German negotiations; involvement in the German-to-German negotiations; the riddle of the "Koran"; and conclusions.

6662. Sarraille, William. "Constitutional Law: National Security Limits on First Amendments Rights," Howard International Law Journal 28/2 (1987): 465-472.
    Discusses the decision of a US Court of Appeals upholding a statute prohibiting protests within five hundred feet of an embassy.

6663. Sarty, Roger. "Intelligence and Air Forces in the Battle of the Atlantic, 1943-1945," Acta 2 (1991): 149-158.

6664. Sasso, Claude R. "Scapegoats or Culprits: Kimmel and Short at Pearl Harbor," Military Review 63/12 (December 1983): 28-47.
    Reviews the investigations of the Pearl Harbor attack, the work of and replacement of Admiral Kimmel's predecessor, conflicts between Admiral Kimmel and General Short, and the belief that an attack would occur at Guam or the Philippines due to too many plausible explanations.

6665. Sassoon, George T. "The Application of Sukhotin's Algorithm to Certain Non-English Languages," Cryptologia 16/2 (April 1992): 165-173.

6666. Saunders, David. "Vladimir Burtsev and the Russian Revolutionary Emigration (1888-1905)," European Studies Review 13/1 (January 1983): 39-62.
    Discusses the arrest and conviction of Burtsev in 1897 for advocating the

murder of Nicholas II. Includes discussion of the reasons why Burtsev's writings offended the government; Burtsev's rationale; and the opinions of Burtsev's Russian contemporaries.

6667. Saunders, Eric F. "Electronic Eavesdropping and the Right to Privacy," Boston University Law Review 52 (Fall 1972): 831-847.
Examines the background of a third-party electronic eavesdropping case, U. S. v. White; revisits the Katz decision; questions whether or not the White case was the correct resolution to case law conflicts; and raises other considerations pertaining to private communications.

6668. Saville, Gordon P. "Electronics in Air Defense," Signal 4 (September-October 1949): 5-7.

6669. Savon, Herve. "Cuba 1962: The Possible Interpretations of a Nuclear Crisis," Revue de Defense Nationale 27/7 (1971): 1102-1122.

6670. Savory, Reginald J. O. "The Invasion Scare of 1755-1756," Army Quarterly and Defence Journal (October 1970): 64-69.

6671. Sawyer, Steve. "'Rainbow Warrior': Nuclear War in the Pacific," Third World Quarterly 8 (October 1986): 1325-1326.

6672. Sax, Brian M. "Judicial Recruiting of Overbroad Statutes: Protecting the Freedom of Association From Scales to Robel," California Law Review 57/1 (January 1969): 240-261.
Considers the development of free association as an independent constitutional right, rewriting overbroad statutes, and conclusions.

6673. Sax, Samuel W. and Avigdor Levy. "Arab-Israeli Conflict Four: A Preliminary Assessment," Naval War College Review 26 (January-February 1974): 7-16.
Discusses mistakes at the political and military levels; intelligence services; Israel's tactical unpreparedness; quantitative compensation for qualitative gaps; and the war at sea.

6674. Sayer, John. "Art and Politics, Dissent and Repression: The Masses Magazine Versus the Government, 1917-1918," American Journal of Legal History 32 (January 1988): 43-78.
Discusses the background of The Masses, its beginning in 1911 as a publication aimed at blending art and politics, and the civil case against the publication in 1917; the criminal trials in 1918; and the aftermath from 1918 to 1919.

6675. Sayigh, Rosemary. "The Mukharabat State: A Palestinian Woman's Testimony," Journal of Palestine Studies 14/3 (1985): 18-31.

An account of the experiences of a woman who was arrested, interrogated and imprisoned by the military police in Lebanon. Her husband's alleged role in espionage is also mentioned.

6676. Sayle, Edward F. "A Short Tour Through the History of Intelligence," Studies in Intelligence 25/1 (Spring 1981).

This item is not listed in the collection of declassified articles made available for public access by the Central Intelligence Agency.

6677. Sayle, Edward F. "Chronology of a Deception," Studies in Intelligence 25/2 (Summer 1981).

Discussion of the role of intelligence in the Battle of Yorktown during the American revolution.

6678. Sayle, Edward F. "Project Termination with a Change of Administration," Studies in Intelligence 25/4 (Winter 1981).

Discusses 18th-century covert actions.

6679. Sayle, Edward. F. "A Tribute to Some Unsung Heroes," Studies in Intelligence 26/2 (Summer 1982).

A brief history of spies in the American revolution.

6680. Sayle, Edward F. "George Washington: Manager of Intelligence," Studies in Intelligence 27/4 (Winter 1983).

6681. Sayle, Edward F. "The Historical Underpinnings of the U.S. Intelligence Community," International Journal of Intelligence and Counterintelligence 1/1 (Spring 1986): 1-27.

An excellent, sweeping sketch of the history of United States intelligence policy and operations. Emphasizes the ad hoc nature of American spy services and how the United States has struggled to balance values of openness in democracy with the secrecy demands of clandestine affairs between competitive nations.

6682. Sayle, Edward F. "Nuggets from Intelligence History," International Journal of Intelligence and Counterintelligence 1/2 (Summer 1986): 115-126.

Provides a brief account of Confederate President Jefferson Davis' efforts to apply economic intelligence in the Civil War throughout the cotton trade.

6683. Sayle, Edward F. "Espionage in the American Tradition," World & I 1/11 (November 1986): 25-29.

6684. Sayle, Edward F. "The Framers on the Realities," Studies in Intelligence 31/2 (Summer 1987).

Discusses the early American history of intelligence and the debates by the Constitution's framers over the role of secrecy. Includes sections on the intelligence practitioners among the framers; secrecy under discussion; the president and "secrecy under despatch"; counterintelligence; intelligence funding; and the president as manager of intelligence. Reproduced in a special issue of Studies in Intelligence 31 (September 1987): 1-7.

6685. Sayle, Edward F. "The Deja Vu of American Secret Diplomacy," International Journal of Intelligence and Counterintelligence 3/2 (Fall 1988): 399-406.

This is an editor's note which finds historical bases for presidential conduct of secret diplomatic arrangements dating to the George Washington administration.

6686. Scalingi, Paula L. "Intelligence Community and Arms Control," Signal 44 (September 1989): 31-35.

6687. Scalingi, Paula L. "Intelligence Community Cooperation: The Arms Control Model," International Journal of Intelligence and Counterintelligence 5/4 (Winter 1991-1992): 401-410.

Brief article remarking upon reorganization efforts within the Central Intelligence Agency. Major sections discuss multi-mission single-issue cooperative mechanisms; impediments to cooperation between major intelligence centers; the arms control model; arms control cooperation today; and prospects for change.

6688. Scalingi, Paula L. "U.S. Intelligence in an Age of Uncertainty: Refocusing to Meet the Challenge," Washington Quarterly 15/1 (Winter 1992): 147-156.

Considers the new world order and the US intelligence community; intelligence requirements; reorganization issues; and the need for flexibility.

6689. Scalingi, Paula L. "Proliferation and Arms Control," Intelligence and National Security 10/4 (October 1995): 149-161.

A summary of the critical analytical challenges facing those responsible for monitoring nuclear proliferation in the world; methods for meeting the challenges; and conclusions.

6690. Scanlan, Margaret. "Philby and His Fictions," Dalhousie Review 62/4 (Winter 1982-1983): 533-553.

Lengthy critique of Soviet spy Kim Philby's autobiography and its links with numerous fictional works, such as John LeCarre's The Looking Glass War.

6691. Scanlon, Charles. "A Strategy to Maximize Military Human Intelligence," American Intelligence Journal 14/1 (Autumn-Winter 1992-1993): 9-16.

Argues that HUMINT offers direct insights into the plans and intentions of adversaries. Major sections discuss an orientation to the new emerging threats; concentration on warfighting requirements; the need for a supportive, streamlined management structure; and increasing capabilities at the operator level.

6692. Schachte, W. L., Jr. "NISCOM Counterintelligence Strategy for the 1990's," American Intelligence Journal 10/2 (1989): 43-45.

Emphasizes the focus of Naval Intelligence on investigation; operation; initiatives; and security countermeasures.

6693. Schachter, Oscar. "The Legality of Pro-Democratic Intervention," American Journal of International Law 78/3 (July 1984): 645-650.

Comments on the subject in response to a paper in the same issue by W. Michael Reisman.

6694. Schad, Mildred. "Police Liability for Invasion of Privacy," Cleveland-Marshall Law Review 16/3 (September 1967): 428-434.

Discusses the pre-Mapp decision remedy for illegal searches, defenses, damages, invasion of privacy by federal agents, and value of the tort remedy.

6695. Schaefer, Edward F. "A Simplified Data Encryption Standard Algorithm," Cryptologia 20/1 (January 1996): 77-84.

6696. Schaefer, Scott. "Spies for Hire: Ex-Spooks Offer Civilians A Private CIA," Soldier of Fortune 20 (July 1995): 53-55+.

6697. Schakne, Robert. "Chile: Why We Missed the Story," Columbia Journalism Review 19 (March-April 1976): 60-62.

Argues that American reporters failed to convey US intervention activities, that is, covert action, in Chile due to only brief trips to the country and inadequate communications with embassy personnel, military attaches, and economic mission personnel. Mentions the role of the CIA in the covert action.

6698. Schaller, Michael. "American Air Strategy in China, 1939-1941: The Origins of Clandestine Air Warfare," American Quarterly 28/1 (1976): 3-19.

A history of the orchestration of influential individuals and interest groups in the effort to aid the Chinese Nationalist plans for attacking Japan in 1940-1941 period. Private pilots were used in the development of the plans and the entire effort was a forerunner of later clandestine air operations.

6699. Schaller, Michael. "SACO! The United States Navy's Secret War in China," Pacific Historical Review 44/4 (November 1975): 527-553.

SACO is an acronym for Sino-American Cooperation Association, an American naval unit entirely under Chinese control in the early years of World War II. The unit provided Chinese Nationalists with aid and training designed to support Chiang Kai-shek's anti-communist forces. The position of the OSS is discussed briefly.

6700. Schanzer, Steven T. "INTELINK--An Information Strategy," American Intelligence Journal 15/2 (Autumn-Winter 1994): 37-41.
Examines the development of the INTELINK system, a key factor in interoperability of information systems for intelligence support. Contains an organization chart of the Intelligence Systems Board and a prospectus on the future of INTELINK.

6701. Schapiro, Leonard. "The General Department of the Central Committee of the C.P.S.U.," Survey 21/3 (Summer 1975): 53-65.

6702. Schapiro, Leonard. "The International Department of the CPSU: Key to Soviet Policy," International Journal 22 (Winter 1976-1977): 41-58.
Discusses the role of the International Department in policy making, and in overseeing all military and social activities. Covers the role within the CPSU; role in foreign embassies; and the role in foreign policy.

6703. Schaub, Jeffrey L. "The 'Zakharov-Daniloff Affair,'" the Diplomatic Expulsions of October 1986, and the Hostile Espionage Threat Facing the United States of America," Brooklyn Journal of International Law 14/1 (1988): 109-145.
Major sections discuss the chronology of the Zakharov-Daniloff affair and the 1986 diplomatic expulsions; the hostile espionage threat; prior US efforts to cope with the hostile espionage threat; goals and results of the American expulsion orders; and the international legal framework.

6704. Schauer, Frederick. "Fear, Risk, and the First Amendment: Unraveling the 'Chilling Effect,'" Boston University Law Review 58/5 (November 1978): 685-732.
A reexamination of "chilling effect" doctrine in terms of behavioral assumptions; the inability to quantify or test assumptions about chilling effects; components of chilling effect doctrine; applications of the doctrine in case law; revisitation of the doctrine of prior restraint; and consideration of whether or not the behavioral consideration is necessary.

6705. Schauer, Margery and Frederick. "Law as the Engine of State: The Trial of Anne Boleyn," William and Mary Law Review 22/1 (Fall 1980): 49-84.
Discusses the relationship between law and state trials, concluding that the execution of Anne Boleyn was a matter serving the political interests of King Henry VIII rather than a matter of law and justice.

6706. Scheer, George F. "The Sergeant Major's Strange Mission," <u>American Heritage</u> 26/6 (June 1975): 26-29.

> Discusses a plan devised to kidnap Matthew Arnold, spy and traitor.

6707. Scheffer, David J. "U.S. Law and the Iran-Contra Affair," <u>American Journal of International Law</u> 81 (July 1987): 696-723.

> Major sections include discussion of regulations of the sale of arms to Iran; regulations of military assistance to the Contras; and administration of intelligence activities. Discusses NSD 159 and its controversies.

6708. Scheibe, Karl E. "The Psychologist's Advantage and Its Nullification: Limits of Human Predictability," <u>American Psychologist</u> 33 (1978): 869-881.

> Argues that prediction of human conduct and experience is possible within three modes: sagacity, authority and control, and acumen. Refers to the tools of information management: mirrors, masks, lies, and secrets.

6709. Scheips, Paul J. "Signaling at Port Huron, 1863," <u>Civil War History</u> 2 (1956): 106-113.

6710. Scheips, Paul J. "Union Signal Communications: Innovation and Conflict," <u>Civil War History</u> 9/4 (December 1963): 399-421.

> Discusses the emergence and roles of the US Army Signal Corps and the US Military Telegraph during the Civil War.

6711. Schell, Roger R. "Computer Security: The Achilles' Heel of the Electronic Air Force?," <u>Air University Review</u> 30/2 (January-February 1979): 16-33.

> Considers what makes computers a security problem; computer security alternatives; security kernel technology; and policy recommendations.

6712. Schellenberg, Walter. "Memoirs," <u>Novaia i Noveishaia Istoriia</u> 5 (1991): 174-199.

> The author's selective memoirs of his years in Hitler's SS.

6713. Schelling, Thomas C. "Surprise Attack and Disarmament," <u>Bulletin of the Atomic Scientists</u> 15/10 (1959): 413-418.

6714. Schelling, Thomas C. "Arms Control: Proposal for a Special Surveillance Force," <u>World Politics</u> 13/1 (1960): 1-18.

> Discusses underlying premises for arms control; nature of the contingency; pre-emptive instability; aggravating factors; irreversible destabilization; unilateral actions; positive-evidence concept; scheme and resources; and how to get started.

6715. Schelling, Thomas C. "Thinking About Nuclear Terrorism," <u>International Security</u> 6 (Spring 1982): 61-77.

Emphasizes the ease of access to nuclear weapons and the fear that terrorists will acquire and use such weapons in the future; safeguards against non-national weapons; strategies for terrorist use; and encouragement for nations to combine efforts to preclude terrorist access to nuclear weapons.

6716. Schemmer, Benjamin F. "Strategic C^3: The Satellite Arena--20 years After Sputnik," <u>Armed Forces Journal International</u> 116/2 (February 1978): 18-30.

6717. Schemmer, Benjamin F. "Is C^3 America's Achilles Heel?," <u>Armed Forces Journal International</u> 117/9 (September 1979): 16-26.

Comments on the importance of C^3I; presidential communications with strategic forces; the poor quality of our C^3 system; the need for updating our system; and various details how the system can be improved.

6718. Schemmer, Benjamin F. "U.S. Needs More Rockets to Launch Vital National Security Satellites," <u>Armed Forces Journal International</u> 118/7 (July 1980): 38-41.

6719. Schemmer, Benjamin F. "Former DIA Director Urges that Four-Star Should Head All Military Intelligence," <u>Armed Forces Journal International</u> 127/7 (July 1988): 24.

6720. Schemmer, Benjamin F., et al. "The Slow Murder of the American Intelligence Community," <u>Armed Forces Journal International</u> 116/3 (March 1979): 50-54.

A critique of the management and operations of the CIA under the directorship of Stansfield Turner. Argues that there is an overemphasis on technical means.

6721. Schiavo, N. J. L. "Law Enforcement Intelligence Unit," <u>Police Chief</u> 42/4 (February 1975): 46-82.

Reflects upon the regional intelligence units established in California in the 1950s, and the organization of several police departments across state lines that have formed LEIU's (Law Enforcement Intelligence Units). A main objective of these units was surveillance of organized crime.

6722. Schick, Alan. "Passports-Revocation-Implicit Congressional Approval of Passport Revocation" (Haig v. Agee), <u>Suffolk Transnational Law Journal</u> 6 (Spring 1982): 197-207.

Author reviews Phillip Agee's attempt to acquire a passport on the basis of the Secretary of State's power to revoke such passports where the Secretary has determined that such issuance could cause serious damage to United States national security.

6723. Schick, Joseph S. "With the 849th SIS, 1942-45," Cryptologia 11/1 (January 1987): 29-39.

6724. Schiefer, H. B. "The Possible Use of Chemical Warfare Agents in Southeast Asia," Conflict Quarterly 2/2 (Summer 1982): 32-41.
　　　　Major sections include discussion of the US charges; doubts with respect to US charges; Canadian interest in the reports; general situation in February 1982; interviews with victims of alleged chemical attacks; and the results of the study.

6725. Schiffman, Maurice K. "Technical Intelligence in the Pacific in World War II," Military Review 31/1 (January 1952): 42-48.
　　　　Discusses the formation of technical intelligence in World War II; operations; captured enemy equipment; unity of command; and technical intelligence in the future.

6726. Schimmelpenninck, David C. van der Oye. "Russian Military Intelligence on the Manchurian Front, 1904-05," Intelligence and National Security 11/1 (January 1996): 22-31.
　　　　Reflects on Russian military intelligence through use of recently released records of the Tsarist Archive of Russian Military History in Moscow.

6727. Schlafly, Phyllis. "Faulty Intelligence Is Dangerous to Our Defense," Daughters of the American Revolution Magazine 113/5 (May 1979): 474-477.
　　　　Claims US intelligence is allowing SALT negotiations to deceive policymakers about Soviet nuclear arms. Mentions CIA analysis of the situation.

6728. Schleifmann, Nurit. "Provocateurs and Revolutionaries: The Okhrana and Burtsev," Survey 27/118-119 (Autumn-Winter 1983): 22-40.

6729. Schlesinger, Arthur M., Jr. "The Oppenheimer Case," Atlantic Monthly 194/4 (October 1954): 29-36.
　　　　The author probes the accusations made against J. Robert Oppenheimer, nuclear scientist; the statements of the other scientists; statements of David Griggs; the anti-communist attitudes of the times; and the term "substantial defects of character."

6730. Schlesinger, Arthur M., Jr. "Congress and the Making of Foreign Policy," Foreign Affairs 51/1 (Fall 1972): 78-113.
　　　　A sweeping, detailed history of Congress and foreign policy, including several events related to international intrigues.

6731. Schlesinger, Arthur M., Jr. "How to Control the CIA," Current 174 (July 1975): 12-15.

> A reprinted article.

6732. Schlesinger, Arthur M., Jr. "The Ike Age Revisited," Reviews in American History 11/1 (1983): 1-11.

> A review essay noting the strength of Dwight Eisenhower's popularity over time. Discusses the Eisenhower diaries; Eisenhower's views on military action and intelligence; and problems for Eisenhower's legacy.

6733. Schlesinger, Arthur M., Jr. "A Democrat Looks at Foreign Policy," Foreign Affairs 66/2 (Winter 1987-1988): 263-283.

> Argues that the Reagan administration unnecessarily heightened tension with the Soviet Union, resorting to covert actions and military spending as foreign policy vehicles. Offers suggestions for a democratic president in creating more cooperation rather than hostility, and mentions the oversight of the CIA.

6734. Schlesinger, Stephen. "Cryptanalysis for Peacetime: Codebreaking and the Birth and Structure of the United Nations," Cryptologia 19/3 (July 1995): 217-235.

6735. Schlesinger, Thomas O. "Obligations of the Prisoner of War," Military Review 50/12 (December 1970): 80-85.

> Techniques of interrogating prisoners of war are discussed by examples of situations in World War II.

6736. Schmeidel, John. "My Enemy's Enemy: Twenty Years of Co-operation between West Germany's Red Army Faction and the GDR Ministry of State Security," Intelligence and National Security 8/4 (October 1993): 59-72.

> Reviews the state of the evidence concerning the relationship between the Red Army Faction and the East German Ministry of State Security. Sections discuss the first generation contacts and the founding of Department XXII; Stasi penetration of the RAF command; and training for assassination attacks.

6737. Schmid, Richard. "Denazification: A German Critique," American Perspective 2/5 (October 1948): 231-242.

6738. Schmidt, Annesley K. "Electronic Monitors," Federal Probation 50 June 1986): 56-59.

> The implications and case law associated with the use of electronic monitoring during probation supervision of adjudicated offenders.

6739. Schmidt, Carl T. "The Need for Economic Intelligence," Military Review 27/6 (September 1947): 36-40.

6740. Schmidt, Carl T. "G-2, Army of the Potomac," Military Review 28/4 (July 1948): 45-56.

Discusses the intelligence effort of the field army in the Civil War; the role of Allen Pinkerton in General McClellan's "secret service"; and the role of George Sharpe in the Bureau of Military Information.

6741. Schmidt, Carl T. "Economic Intelligence in a Theater of Operations," Military Review 30/1 (January 1950): 39-43.

6742. Schmidt, Dana A. "The Kurdish Insurgency," Strategic Review 2 (Summer 1974): 51-58.

Discusses the minority status of the Kurds; Kurdish history; revolts led by Mullah Mustafa Barzani; insurgency in Iraq; and the uncertainty of prospects for the Kurds.

6743. Schmitt, Gary J. "Congressional Oversight of Intelligence," Studies in Intelligence 29/2 (Spring 1985).

6744. Schmitt, Gary J. "The Rule of Law and 'Perfect Secrecy,'" Houston Journal of International Law 11/1 (Fall 1988): 255-262.

Argues that the gradual encroachment of Congress in the president's foreign affairs authority carries significant implications in the intelligence area.

6745. Schneider, Alan N. "Ian and I," Naval Intelligence Professionals Quarterly 3/3-6/1 (Fall 1987-Fall 1989): 13-14; 16-17; 1-2; 4-7; 8-10; 7-9; 9-12.

This series appeared in Fall 1987, Winter 1988, Summer 1988, Fall 1988, Winter 1989, Summer 1989, and Fall 1989. This is a limited biography of the intelligence escapades of the author during World War II and his association with Ian Fleming, the author of several novels on the character James Bond.

6746. Schneider, Alan N. "James Bond's Alter Ego," Naval Intelligence Professionals Quarterly 6/4 (Fall 1990): 11-13.

6747. Schneider, Alan N. "My Name Is Fleming--Ian Fleming," Naval Intelligence Professionals Quarterly 6/1 (Winter 1990): 7-9.

6748. Schneider, Alan N. "The Longest Day: 6 June 1944," Naval Intelligence Professionals Quarterly 10/2 (Spring 1994): 1-4.

6749. Schneidman, Whitney W. "Diplomacy, Intelligence, and Portugal's Revolution," Studies in Intelligence 33/2 (Summer 1989).

6750. Schneir, Sharon L. "The Eastern District of New York Rejects Constitutional Challenges to the Foreign Intelligence Surveillance Act of 1978

(United States v. Falvey 540 F. Supp. 1306 (E.D.N.Y. 1982))," Brooklyn Journal of International Law 10 (Winter 1984): 193-217.

The Falvey Court was the first constitutional test of the Foreign Intelligence Surveillance Act, resulting in the view that the F.I.S.A has successfully balanced Fourth Amendment protections with national security interests. Discusses facts of the Falvey case, F.I.S.A applications, Fourth Amendment interpretations regarding electronic surveillance, and conclusions.

6751. Schneir, Walter and Miriam. "The G-Men and the H-Bomb," Progressive 47 (September 1983): 28-30.

A criticism of the FBI investigation into the allegations surrounding the Rosenberg-Sobell espionage case.

6752. Schoch, Magdaline and Jean Barbey. "Offenses Against the French State Committed Abroad," Journal of the American Institute of Criminal Law and Criminology 31 (July 1940): 188-198.

A translated piece (by Dr. Magdaline Schoch) that considers punishable acts; prosecution in French courts and conclusions regarding prosecutions. Translation by Jean Barbey. Includes mention of loyalty and national interests.

6753. Schoeman, Ferdinand. "Undercover Operations: Some Moral Questions About S.804," Criminal Justice Ethics 5/2 (Summer-Fall 1986): 16-22.

Discusses worrisome scenarios in the intimate relationships that are violated during undercover investigations. Addresses the problem of Fourth Amendment concerns and privacy rights of suspects; the distinction between intimate and non-intimate relationships; and value of trust and loyalty in relationships.

6754. Schoenbaum, David. "The United States and Iran's Revolution: Passing the Buck(s)," Foreign Policy 34 (1979): 14-20.

Discusses the collapse of Iran as functions of intelligence failures and political reporting. The political community failed to take responsibility for US ties to the Shah and to defense security assistance through arms sales. US dependence on oil and arms sales led to a denial of Iranian internal unrest.

6755. Schoenberg, David. "Kapitza, Fact and Fiction," Intelligence and National Security 3/4 (October 1988): 49-61.

Discusses the professional life and intrigues surrounding Soviet nuclear physicist Peter Kapitza. Discusses the fact and fiction surrounding Kapitza's experiences.

6756. Schofield, B. B. "The Defeat of the U-Boats During World War II," Journal of Contemporary History 16/1 (January 1981): 119-129.

Provides details of the Allied efforts to counteract the U-boat threats to shipping in World War II. Relevance of intelligence gathering and analysis is mentioned.

6757. Schooling, J. Holt. "Secrets in Cipher: From Ancient Times to Late-Elizabethan Days," Pall Mall Magazine 8/33 (January 1896): 119-129.

A series of 4 articles before the turn of the twentieth century on the history and applications of secret messages.

6758. Schooling, J. Holt. "Secrets in Cipher: From Late-Elizabethan Days to Mid-Stuart Times," Pall Mall Magazine 8/34 (February 1896): 245-256.

6759. Schooling, J. Holt. "Secrets in Cipher: From the Times of Charles II to the Second George," Pall Mall Magazine 8/35 (March 1896): 452-462.

6760. Schooling, J. Holt. "Secrets in Cipher: From the Time of George II to the Present Day," Pall Mall Magazine 8/36 (April 1896): 608-618.

6761. Schooling, J. Holt. Francis Bacon's Bi-Lateral Cypher: A Report," Pall Mall Magazine 26 (April 1902): 484-489.

A discreditation of the work of Elizabeth Gallup's cipher analysis of Bacon.

6762. Schorr, Daniel. "A Chilling Experience: The White House, the FBI, and Me," Harper's 246 (March 1973): 92-97.

The investigation of CBS newsman Daniel Schorr is the central focus of this piece. The investigation commenced in August 1971, launched mainly as retaliation by the Nixon administration for the author's reporting of events during the Watergate scandal.

6763. Schorr, Daniel. "The FBI and Me," Columbia Journalism Review 13 (November-December 1974): 8-14.

Discusses abuse of domestic intelligence gathering, in particular the author's encounter with the FBI. Covers the denied information, the cover story, and the extensiveness of the Schorr investigation.

6764. Schorr, Daniel. "The Daniel Schorr Affair--A Reply," Columbia Journalism Review (July 1976): 48-49.

The author takes up his defense in arguing that some of his press colleagues are less interested in a serious exploration of the issues in the world of intelligence than they are in mulling over personalities. Schorr seeks a more sincere inquiry into the issue of the public's right to know.

6765. Schorr, Daniel. "Are CIA Assets a Press Liability?," More 8 (February 1978): 18-23.

6766. Schorreck, Henry F. "The Role of COMINT in the Battle of Midway," Cryptologic Spectrum 5/3 (Summer 1975): 3-11.

6767. Schraeder, Peter J. "Speaking With Many Voices: Continuity and Change in U.S. Africa Policies," Journal of Modern African Studies 29/3 (1991): 373-412.

A detailed discussion of routine situations and bureaucratic politics; crisis management and the high politics of White House involvement; extended crisis situations and domestic politics; patterns and process in perspective; and the future of US-Africa policies. Mentions CIA several times.

6768. Schramm, R. R. "Organized Crime: A Canadian Approach," Police Chief 55 (January 1988): 32-34.

Discusses Canadian enforcement practices since the 1960s, including the use of intelligence units.

6769. Schroeder, Gertrude. "Soviet Reality Sans Potemkin," Studies in Intelligence 12/1 (Spring 1968): 43-51.

The author travelled and worked for CIA in the Soviet Union in 1967 on an assignment to learn about the realities of everyday Soviet life.

6770. Schuchard, Marsha K. "Blake's 'Mr. Femality': Freemasonry, Espionage, and the Double-Sexed," Studies in Eighteenth-Century Culture 22 (1992): 51-71.

6771. Schultz, Donald E. "Kennedy and the Cuban Connection," Foreign Policy 26 (Spring 1977): 57-64, 121-139.

Evaluates the notion that President Kennedy was assassinated on instructions from Fidel Castro. Observes the weaknesses in the evidence and in the theory.

6772. Schultz, James B. "Defeating Ivan with TEMPEST," Defense Electronics 15 (June 1983): 64-65+.

6773. Schultz, James B. "NSA and Industry Experience TEMPEST Growing Pains," Defense Electronics 16 (June 1984): 190+.

6774. Schultz, Robert. "More Than Wages: Twin Cities Theater Workers' Control Struggles," Minnesota History 53/8 (1993): 323-333.

6775. Schultz, Sigrid. "Invasion Lies," Collier's 63 (March 1944): 11-12+.

This is a popular magazine piece of rare content on German propaganda before and during World War II. Not considered traditional scholarship, but certainly worthy of mention here.

6776. Schulz, Ann T. "Iran: The Descending Monarchy," Current History 76/443 (January 1979): 5, 33-34.

Addresses the manner in which the Shah of Iran planned reforms in his country, which were considered too little too late and based too heavily on military rather than domestic needs.

6777. Schulzinger, Robert D. "The Colossus at Work," Reviews in American History 112/4 (1984): 589-594.

An overview of the US and the CIA and its intervention policy used to overthrown the Guatemalan government.

6778. Schurer, H. "Karl Moor: German Agent and Friend of Lenin," Journal of Contemporary History 5/2 (1970): 131-152.

Discusses Karl Moor's associations with Lenin; Moor's deception of Lenin through false reports; German trust of Moor; and Moor's principle role in espionage for Germany and Austria.

6779. Schuyler, Michael. "The Bitter Harvest: Lyndon B. Johnson and the Assassination of John F. Kennedy," Journal of American Culture 8/3 (1985): 101-109.

6780. Schwabe, Klaus. "U.S. Secret War Diplomacy, Intelligence, and the Coming of the German Revolution in 1918: The Role of Vice Consul James McNally," Diplomatic History 16 (Spring 1992): 175-200.

An extensive discussion of the interplay between diplomacy and intelligence in the pre-World War I period.

6781. Schwantes, Carlos A. "Farmer-Labor Insurgency in Washington State: William Bouck, the Grange, and the Western Progressive Farmers," Pacific Northwest Quarterly 76/1 (January 1985): 2-11.

6782. Schwantes, Carlos A. "The Ordeal of William Morley Bouck, 1918-1919: Limits to the Federal Suppression of Agrarian Dissidents," Agricultural History 59/3 (1985): 417-428.

6783. Schwartau, Winn. "'Defense in Depth' for Information Systems Survival," International Journal of Intelligence and Counterintelligence 8/2 (Summer 1995): 229-234.

Discusses the defensive goals of information systems security efforts; the protection of information systems; and the future of the defense-in-depth concept.

6784. Schwartz, Charles. "A New Graphical Method for Encryption of Computer Data," Cryptologia 15/1 (January 1991): 43-46.

6785. Schwartz, Harry. "The Spy Who Came in from the Cold War," Saturday Review of Literature 49 (January 1966): 36-38.

A popular literature piece of significant value on the observations of espionage in literature in the 1960s. Not considered scholarship in the traditional sense but it is a useful period piece given the popularity of LeCarre novels and the James Bond films of the decade.

6786. Schwartz, Helene E. "Oversight of Minimization Compliance Under the Foreign Intelligence Surveillance Act: How the Watchdogs Are Doing Their Jobs," Rutgers Law Journal 12/3 (Spring 1981): 405-511.

Provides an overview of the F.I.S.A., discusses executive oversight, examines types of electronic and human surveillance, considers judicial and congressional oversight, includes appendices containing official government documents.

6787. Schwartz, Herman. "Electronic Eavesdropping--What the Supreme Court Did Not Do," Criminal Law Bulletin 4/2 (1968): 83-89.

Supreme Court decisions are more suggestive rather than they are definitive, in particular, the decisions concerning electronic surveillance. Considers the decisions in Berger, Katz, and Lopez. The author fears that the Court will allow eavesdropping to extend beyond what has already been permitted by statute.

6788. Schwartz, Herman. "The Legitimation of Electronic Eavesdropping: The Politics of "Law and Order," Michigan Law Review 67 (1967): 455-510.

Considers some constitutional issues raised by wiretapping and eavesdropping and particular problems with the actual procedures carried out by police. Sections discuss nonparticularized searches; and anticipated extent of legalized eavesdropping. Questions the need for so much electronic surveillance.

6789. Schwartz, Herman. "Six Years of Tapping and Bugging," Civil Liberties Review 1/3 (Summer 1974): 26-37.

Discusses the implications of wiretapping and bugging and argues that they should be used only under extraordinary circumstances. Offers statistics and contemplates legislative proposals.

6790. Schwartz, Leonard E. "Manned Orbiting Laboratory--For War or Peace?," International Affairs (Great Britain) 43/1 (January 1967): 51-64.

Discusses the Johnson administration's decision in 1965 to develop the MOL. Says that the US decision was based on intelligence reports that the Soviets were already at work on a similar system. Perhaps this is a useful article for comparisons between rationales and intelligence evidence between MOL and SDI.

6791. Schwartz, Louis B. "On Current Proposals to Legalize Wiretapping," University of Pennsylvania Law Review 103/2 (November 1954): 157-167.

A general discussion of the proposals, including discussion of the failure to show need for wiretapping legislation, the dangers of wiretapping versus other police surveillance methods, the clarification of which crimes should be covered by wiretapping, necessary statutory safeguards, and tapping with one party permission.

6792. Schwartz, Stephen. "Comandos: The CIA and Nicaragua's Contra Rebels," Commentary 93/4 (April 1992): 60-61.

A book review essay concerning Sam Dillon's book by the same title.

6793. Schwartz, Stuart B. "The Voyage of the Vassals: Royal Power, Noble Obligations, and Merchant Capital Before the Portugese Restoration of Independence, 1624-1640," American Historical Review 96/3 (June 1991): 735-762.

Among the complex discussions of social, political and religious dynamics surrounding the end of feudalism and the rise of the Spanish and Portugese states, some discussion is had on accusations of treason against the Jews in the fall of Salvador de Bahia in Portugal.

6794. Schwartzschild, Leopold. "The Unexpected Capture of Hess in a British 'Secret Service' Trap," Voenno-Istoricheskii Zhurnal 5 (1991): 37-42.

6795. Schwartzman, Robin B. "Fiscal Oversight of the Central Intelligence Agency: Can Accountability and Confidentiality Coexist?," New York University Journal of International Law and Politics 7/3 (Winter 1974): 493-544.

Examines the CIA funding process and explores means to increase congressional control over CIA funding without damaging CIA functions. Discussion includes the role of executive agencies, role of oversight committees, Congress as a whole, the Office of Management and Budget and Treasury, the oversight process, differences in the system, the question of constitutional law and the CIA budget, and recommendations.

6796. Schwarz, F. A. O., Jr. "Intelligence Activities and the Rights of Americans," Record of the Association of the Bar of City of New York 32 (January-February 1977): 43-52.

A general discussion of domestic intelligence activities of the CIA and FBI, including discussion of the facts, general lessons, and resolutions with respect to the COINTELPRO operations.

6797. Schweizer, Peter. "The Growth of Economic Espionage: America Is Target Number One," Foreign Affairs 75/1 (January-February 1996): 9-15.

Argues that the theft of industrial secrets from US high technology firms is the wave of the future of international espionage. Suggests that US policy makers and corporations should face directly the threats by economic espionage, but rejects the idea of intelligence community involvement in such activities as spying on other nations for economic protection.

6798. Schwien, Edwin E. "An Intelligence Case History," Infantry Journal 43 (September-October 1936): 408-417.

A detailed account of the work of the intelligence sections of the French 42nd Division in World War I in 1914.

6799. Schwien, Edwin E. "Intelligence Training Within the Cavalry Regiment," Cavalry Journal (September-October 1938).

6800. Schweitzer, Nicholas. "Bayesian Analysis for Intelligence: Some Focus on the Middle East," International Interactions 4/4 (June 1978): 247-264.

Discusses the innovation of Bayesian and Delphi analytical tools used in the CIA's Office of Political Analysis with some success. This article was published in Studies in Summer 1976.

6801. Schwoerer, Lois G. "William, Lord Russell: The Making of a Martyr, 1683-1983," Journal of British Studies 24/1 (January 1985): 41-71.

William Lord Russell's trial and execution is discussed. Also discussed is Russell's later status as a Whig martyr.

6802. Sciaroni, Bretton G. "The Theory and Practice of Executive Branch Intelligence Oversight," Harvard Journal of Law & Public Policy 12/2 (Spring 1989): 397-432.

Discusses the origins of executive branch intelligence oversight; creation and evolution of oversight in contemporary terms; the role of the President's Oversight board in the Reagan administration; executive oversight and the Iran-Contra affair; missed opportunities of the Congress in Iran-Contra investigation; and recommendations.

6803. Sciaroni, Bretton G. "Boland in the Wind: The Iran-Contra Affair and the Invitation to Struggle," Pepperdine Law Review 17/2 (1990): 379-427.

Considers the origins of the President's Intelligence Oversight Board; the question of legislative coverage of the activities of the National Security Council; and the question of whether the Boland amendments altered the separation of powers doctrine.

6804. Scott, Hugh. "Wiretapping and Organized Crime," Howard Law Journal 14/1 (Winter 1968): 1-28.

Argues that bugging and wiretapping members of organized crime are the most effective surveillance methods against conspiracies. Discusses the threat of organized crime, techniques against criminal activity, appropriate legislation, Johnson administration proposals, and amendments concerning the use of surveillance devices.

6805. Scott, Kenneth. "New Hampshire Tory Counterfeiters Operating from New York City," New York Historical Society Quarterly 34 (January 1950): 31-57.

6806. Scott, Kenneth. "Tory Associators of Portsmouth," William and Mary Quarterly 17/4 (October 1960): 507-515.
    An historical note regarding the fifty-nine men who signed a document in support of British protection of the Governor of Portsmouth, New Hampshire in 1775. Lists the names of the men who signed.

6807. Scott, Len. "The Spy Who Wanted to Save the World," Intelligence and National Security 8/4 (October 1993): 138-146.
    A book review essay concerning The Spy Who Saved the World (1992) by Jerrold Schecter and Peter Deriabin. Book considers the Soviet spy and defector Oleg Penkovskiy.

6808. Scott, Len and Steve Smith. "Lessons of October: Historians, Political Scientists, and Policy-Makers and the Cuban Missile Crisis," International Affairs (Great Britain) 70/4 (October 1994): 659-684.
    The authors call into question the wisdom of the policy and operational decisions involved in missile crisis of 1962. Draws on newly available archival materials. Considers implications for current and future policy. Challenges previous historical conclusions.

6809. Scott, Paul R. "The Birth of the 2's: Combat Intelligence in the American Expeditionary Force," Military Intelligence 6/3 (July-September 1980): 25-26.

6810. Scott, Peter D. "The United States and the Overthrow of Sukarno, 1965-1967," Pacific Affairs 58/2 (Summer 1985): 239-264.
    Explores the CIA's role and activities in the covert action in Indonesia; the US and the Indonesian army's mission; the US moves against Sukarno; the US support for Sukarno before the Gestapu; and the CIA's operation in 1965.

6811. Scott, Peter D. "How Allen Dulles and the SS Preserved Each Other," Covert Action Information Bulletin 25 (Winter 1986): 4-14.

6812. Scott, Peter D. "Contragate: Reagan, Foreign Money, and the Contra Deal," Crime and Social Justice 27-28 (1987): 110-148.
    Argues that experienced conspirators and international funds, intervening illegally yet again in the American electoral process, account for Ronald Reagan's

unwavering commitment to the Nicaraguan contra organization. Mentions the Central Intelligence Agency.

6813. Scott, S. K. "Police Operational Intelligence: The Key to Survival," Enforcement Journal 10/4 (1971): 20-21.

6814. Scott, S. R. "The Official Information Act 1982: The Beginning of a New Era; Ministerial Veto," 6 Ottawa Law Review (1985): 139-157.

6815. Scott, William F. "The Face of Moscow in the Missile Crisis," Studies in Intelligence 10/1 (Spring 1966).

6816. Scoular, Robert F. "Wiretapping and Eavesdropping: Constitutional Developments From Olmstead to Katz," St. Louis University Law Journal 12 (1968): 513-549.
     Discusses the history of wiretapping legislation and case law; current case law tests of electronic eavesdropping; the Katz and Berger decisions; the Omnibus Crime Control and Safe Streets Act of 1968; and conclusions.

6817. Scouten, James W. "The States, the Federal Constitution, and the War Protesters," Cornell Law Review 53/3 (February 1968): 528-542.
     A brief analysis of Vietnam War protests and federal investigative and surveillance authorities.

6818. Scoville, Herbert, Jr. "Policing a Nuclear Test Ban," Studies in Intelligence 3/1 (Winter 1959).

6819. Scoville, Herbert, Jr. "Verification of Nuclear Arms Limitations: An Analysis," Bulletin of the Atomic Scientists 26 (October 1970): 6-12.

6820. Scoville, Herbert, Jr. "The Technology of Surveillance," Society 12/3 (March-April 1975): 58-63.
     Argues the efficiency of technological intelligence over the politically sensitive nature of human intelligence.

6821. Scoville, Herbert, Jr. "Is Espionage Necessary for Our Security?," Foreign Affairs 54/3 (April 1976): 482-496.
     Discusses the misuse of power in the exercise of the intelligence community in clandestine operations. Oleg Penkovsky, says the author, gave data to the US which tended to confirm existing analyses of that technical means of verification were necessary and reliable.

6822. Scuro, Daniel P. "Votre Secrets, Monsieur?," Security Management 36/10 (October 1992): 35-36+.

6823. Seabury, Paul. "The Moral Purposes and Philosophical Bases of American Foreign Policy," Orbis 20/1 (Spring 1976): 3-14.

A lengthy discussion of the debate between moralists and realists on the issue of foreign policy objectives. Useful in discussions of covert action and clandestine collection.

6824. Seabury, Paul. "Hymn to the Mole," International Journal of Intelligence and Counterintelligence 2/4 (Winter 1988): 577.

The author adapts his 7-verse poem from the work of William Cowper and Bishop Reginald Heber.

6825. Seagle, William. "The American National Police: The Dangers of Federal Crime Control," Harper's 169 (November 1934): 751-761.

Discusses the rise of the National Crime Commission and its role in expanding federal involvement in crime control. Mentions the FBI and the FBI intelligence function.

6826. Seagrave, S. and R. A. Jones. "From China with Love," Esquire 65 (January 1966): 42-47+.

Generally considered a popular press publication.

6827. Seagraves, R. W. A. "NILO--The Naval Intelligence Liaison Officer in Vietnam," U.S. Naval Institute Proceedings 94/12 (December 1968): 145-146.

Naval intelligence officers formed a network of operations in Vietnam in connection with Army field units.

6828. Seaman, Mark. "SOE in France: An Account of the Work of the Special Operations Executive in France 1940-1944," Defense Analysis 3/2 (Fall 1987).

The title captures the subject matter of this article.

6829. Seaman, Mark. "The War's Worst Traitor," World War II Investigator 1/5 (August 1988).

6830. Seaman, Mark. "Founding Father? Sir Colin Gubbins and the Origins of SOE," Intelligence and National Security 11/2 (April 1996): 360-363.

A book review essay of Gubbins and SOE by Peter Wilkinson and Joan B. Astley.

6831. Seaquist, Larry. "Defense Intelligence in a Disorderly World," Defense Intelligence Journal 1/1 (Spring 1992): 31-54.

Opens with a discussion of the changes in the world condition that call for a new security climate; the new regional defense strategy; the innovative practice of intelligence; the strategic level and the national policy making arena; sources and methods; and quality defense intelligence professionals.

6832. Searle, Lynn S. "The 'Administrative' Search from Dewey to Burger: Dismantling the Fourth Amendment," Hastings Constitutional Law Quarterly 16 (1989): 261-290.

6833. Sears, L. "Security and Liberty," American Scholar 20/2 (Spring 1951): 137-149.
Focusses on the labeling of "communists"; right to a fair trial; government jobs and espionage; and several cases in which government agents were overzealous in their snooping and reporting. Asks five questions concerning the balance of the relationship between civil liberties and government power.

6834. Sears, Louis M. "Slidell and Buchanan," American Historical Review 27/4 (July 1922): 709-730.
Discusses the relationship between John Slidell, commissioner to Mexico, and Secretary of State James Buchanan. Slidell passed on information to Buchanan, only later to work for Jefferson Davis and the Confederacy.

6835. Sears, Louis M. "Nicholas P. Trist: A Diplomat With Ideals," Mississippi Valley Historical Review 11 (June 1924): 85-98.

6836. Sears, Stephen W. "The Curious Case of General McClellan's Memoirs," Civil War History 34/2 (June 1988).

6837. Sears, Stephen W. "The Last Word on the Lost Order," MHQ: Quarterly Journal of Military History 4/3 (Spring 1992).

6838. Sears, Stephen W. "The Most Extraordinary and Astounding Adventure of the Civil War," Civil War Chronicle (Fall 1992): 25-37.

6839. Secrest, Donald; Gregory Brunk; and Howard Tamashiro. "Moral Justification for Resort to War with Nicaragua: The Attitudes of Three Elite Groups," Western Political Quarterly 44/3 (September 1991): 541-559.
Major sections discuss attacks on the just war theory; research design; elite agreement with just war design; cognitive structure; ideology and support for military intervention, and discussion.

6840. Seddon, Nicholas. "ASIO and Accountability," Australian Quarterly 54/4 (Summer 1983): 362-381.

6841. Seed, Geoffrey. "A British Spy in Philadelphia, 1775-1777," Pennsylvania Magazine of History and Biography 85/1 (January 1961): 3-37.
A detailed account of the role of Gilbert Barkly as a British spy in Philadelphia during the American revolution. Includes numerous letters pertaining to his intelligence work.

6842. Seegers, Annette. "South Africa's National Security Management System, 1972-1990," Journal of Modern African Studies 29/2 (June 1991): 253-273.
     Discusses the role of intelligence services within the broader concerns for the total national security system of South Africa.

6843. Seegers, Annette. "Current Trends in South Africa's Security Establishment," Armed Forces and Society 18/2 (Winter 1992).

6844. Seeley, Thomas D., et al. "Yellow Rain," Scientific American 253/3 (1985): 178+.
     This article is a good place to begin research on this controversial mystery, a mixture of science and international politics.

6845. Seh, Robert H and John P. Lang. "Intelligence Support in NATO: An Operator's Overview," Journal of Electronic Defense 5 (May 1982): 51-54.

6846. Seiderman, Paul. "Pacification: A Winning Combination That Came Too Late?," Armed Forces Journal International (January 1977): 24-25.

6847. Seitz, John L. "The Failure of U.S. Technical Assistance in Public Administration: The Iranian Case," Public Administration Review 40/5 (September-October 1980): 407-413.
     Discusses the AID program in concert with CIA's assistance to Iranian Secret Police, the SAVAK.

6848. Selig, Michael. "United States v. Motion Picture Film The Spirit of '76: The Espionage Case of Producer Robert Goldstein (1917)," Journal of Popular Film and Television 10/4 (1983): 168-174.

6849. Sella, Amnon. "Barbarossa: Surprise Attack and Communication," Journal of Contemporary History 13/3 (July 1978): 555-583.
     Historical study of the uses of deception.

6850. Sella, Amnon. "Patterns of Soviet Involvement in Local War," Journal of the Royal United Services Institute for Defence Studies 224 (June 1979): 53-56.

6851. Selmer, Ernst S. "The Norwegian Modifications of the Siemens and Halske T52 Cipher Machines," Cryptologia 18/2 (April 1994): 147-149.

6852. Selth, Andrew. "Politically Motivated Violence in the Southwest Pacific," Terrorism and Political Violence 4/3 (Autumn 1992): 51-63.

6853. Semerjian, Evan Y. "Proposals on Wiretapping in Light of Recent Senate Hearings," Boston University Law Review 45/2 (Spring 1965): 216-248.

An extensive discussion of the dangers of wiretapping, constitutional considerations, shortcomings of Senate hearings, and the nature of authorization to wiretap. Concludes that new regulatory laws are needed to protect privacy.

6854. Seng-wen, Ch'en. "The Chinese Communist Investigation System," <u>Issues and Studies</u> 8 (August-September 1972): 50-59, 66-70.

6855. Senja, Jan. "The East Bloc Spy - der Web: A Sticky Network Links the Intelligence Agencies of the East Bloc with the KGB," <u>World & I</u> 1/11 (November 1986): 73-79.
Discusses the two Soviet intelligence organizations, KGB and GRU and their spy networks in Warsaw Pact nations.

6856. Seraile, William. "Ben Fletcher, I. W. W. Organizer," <u>Pennsylvania History</u> 46/3 (1979): 213-232.
Discusses Fletcher's alleged violation of the Selective Service Act and Espionage Act, and President Roosevelt's pardon in 1933.

6857. Sergeev, Feodosii M. "The Road of American Strategic Intelligence," <u>Voenno-Istoricheskiy Zhurnal</u> 5 (May 1966): 49-60.
This is an approximate title for an article appearing in a Russian language journal.

6858. Sergeev, Feodosii M. "American Intelligence After the Catastrophe at Pearl Harbor," <u>Novaia i Noveishaia Istoriia</u> 11/3 (1967): 114-126.
Discusses CIA's involvement in the overthrow of Chile's Salvador Allende in 1973. The piece is based on journalistic reports and argues that the Allende overthrow reflected US policy and history.

6859. Sergeev, Feodosii M. "The History of American Intelligence," <u>Voprosy Istorii</u> 6 (1970): 118-133; 7: 126-137.
This is an approximate title for an article appearing in a Russian language journal.

6860. Sergeev, Feodosii M. "American Intelligence: Conspiracy, Subversive Activity, and Espionage," <u>Novaia i Noveishaia Istoriia</u> 1,2,3 (1971): 93-106; 2: 112-125; 3: 122-134.
This is an approximate title for an article appearing in a Russian language journal.

6861. Sergeev, Feodosii M. "The Role of the CIA in the Military Fascist Coup in Chile," <u>Novaia i Noveishaia Istoriia</u> 3 (1977): 91-102; 4: 101-116.
A two part Soviet history of US intelligence from the 19th century to the post World War I era. A comparative view, but errors abound.

6862. Sergeev, Feodosii M. "The Failure of Operation Overflight," <u>Novaia i Noveishaia Istoriia</u> 4 (1980): 110-122; 5: 107-126.

The two-part article discusses the circumstances, from a Soviet perspective of shoot-down of Francis Gary Powers (U-2 incident) and a summation of Powers training before the controversial overflight.

6863. Sergeev, Feodosii M. "Operation Guatemala, 1954," <u>Voprosy Istorii</u> 8 (1981): 101-114.

A Russian language journal.

6864. Sergeev, Feodosii M. "America's Secret Path to the Vietnam War," <u>Novaia i Noveishaia Istoriia</u> 3 (1985): 134-157.

A Russian language journal.

6865. Sergeev, Feodosii M. "The Nazi Intelligence Service and the USSR: The Tukhachevski Affair and the Zeppelin Operation," <u>Novaia i Noveishaia Istoriia</u> 1 (1989): 114-132.

This is an approximate title for an article appearing in a Russian language journal.

6866. Sereisky, Jean E. "Benedict Arnold in New Brunswick," <u>Atlantic Advocate</u> 8 (1963): 33-43.

6867. Sereno, Renzo. "Psychological Warfare, Intelligence, and Insight," <u>Psychiatry</u> 13/2 (May 1950): 266-273.

6868. Sergeyev, Fyodor. "Operation Ajax," <u>International Affairs</u> (USSR) 8 (August 1987): 105-115.

A Soviet perspective on the US intervention into Iran in the early 1950s and the overthrow of Mossadegh. Offers CIA motives, oil cartel interests, and the joint efforts to overthrow the regime between Britain and the US.

6869. Serino, Rosemarie. "Espionage Prosecutions in the United States," <u>Catholic University Law Review</u> 4/1 (January 1954): 44-51.

Briefly summarizes the legal issues in several espionage cases, in particular the Ethel and Julius Rosenberg case. Cites several Supreme Court decisions use in evaluation of the legal position of the Rosenbergs.

6870. Sernaque, Santos A. S. and Maria T. M. Rodriguez. "El Delito de Traicion a la Patria (Terrorismo) en Peru," <u>Revista de Derecho Puertorriqueno</u> 33 (December 1993): 93-118.

6871. Sessions, Gene. "Espionage in Windsor: Clarence H. Waldron and Patriotism in World War I," <u>Vermont History</u> 61/3 (1993): 133-155.

6872. Sessions, William S. "The Evolving Threat: Meeting the Counterintelligence Challenges of the 1990s: A Strategic Issue Facing Our Nation," American Intelligence Journal 10/2 (Summer-Fall 1989): 19-23.

6873. Sessions, William S. "Counterintelligence Challenges in a Changing World," FBI Law Enforcement Bulletin 60/9 (September 1991): 1-4.

6874. Seters, Deborah Van. "Hardly Hollywood's Ideal: Female Autobiographies of Secret Service Work, 1914-45," Intelligence and National Security 7/4 (October 1992): 403-424.
  Discusses autobiographies of female secret service agents. Sheds light on operations and female involvement in a male dominated field of intelligence during World War I and II. Dispels stereotypes and presents the feminine voice in intelligence activities.

6875. Settel, A. "Seven Nazis Were Hanged: The Diary of a Witness," Commentary 29 (May 1960): 369-379.
  A recounting of the trial and eventual hangings of seven Nazi war criminals. Includes the author's thoughts at the time, since he was a member of the public relations team for US High Commissioner.

6876. Sevin, Dieter. "Operation Scherhorn," Military Review 46/3 (March 1966): 35-43.
  Recounts a successful deception plan of the Soviets to occupy the time of German intelligence during World War II.

6877. Seybolt, Peter J. "Terror and Conformity: Counterespionage Campaigns, Rectification, and Mass Movements, 1942-1943," Modern China 12/1 (January 1986): 39-73.
  Discusses China's internal struggles between Nationalist and Communist political forces before and during World War II. Intensive efforts were expended by the Communists to clean out of the party the dissidents, spies and traitors.

6878. Seymour, George D. "The Last Days and Valiant Death of Nathan Hale," American Heritage 15/3 (April 1964): 50-51.
  A brief account of the last days before Nathan Hale was executed for treason by the British in September 1776.

6879. Seymour, Whitney N., Jr. "Press Paranoia: Delusions of Persecution in the Pentagon Papers Case," New York State Bar Journal 66 (February 1994): 10-12+.

6880. Shackelford, George G. "Benedict Arnold in Richmond, January, 1781," Virginia Magazine of History and Biography 60/4 (October 1952): 591-599.

Discusses the capture of Arnold in Richmond in 1781. Includes a bibliographical note regarding the Arnold collections in various libraries.

6881. Shafir, Shlomo. "The View of a Maverick Pacifist and Universalist: Rabbi Abraham Cronbach's Plea for Clemency for Nazi War Criminals in 1945," American Jewish Archives 42/2 (1990): 146-154.
Discusses in detail the role of Cronback in the defense of Julius and Ethel Rosenberg, and his most controversial defense of Nazi war criminals.

6882. Shahak, I. "The Israeli Myth of Omniscience: Nuclear Deterrence and Intelligence," American-Arab Affairs 36 (Spring 1991): 95-103.
Evaluates Israeli intelligence services as to their efficiency and effectiveness in the Gulf war.

6883. Shain, Russell E. "Hollywood's Cold War," Journal of Popular Film 3 (Fall 1974): 334-350.

6884. Shalom, Stephen R. "International Lawyers and Other Apologists: The Case of the Cuban Missile Crisis," Polity 12/1 (1979): 83-109.
The author takes issue with a book by Abram Chayes, The Cuban Missile Crisis: International Crisis and the Role of Law, arguing that some international lawyers had become apologists for US government intervention in Cuba. Discusses the official and unofficial cases of the crisis; the role of lawyers; moderation and prudence; necessity and proportionality; and international organizations.

6885. Shamburgh, David L. "China's National Security Research Bureaucracy," China Quarterly 110 (June 1987): 276-294.
Discussion of China's more holistic approach to assessing national security, that is, her comprehensive analytical approach when considering relations between the state and diplomatic postures. Intelligence is mainly regional area studies instead of more topical approaches in the West.

6886. Shambaugh, David L. "China's America Watchers," Problems of Communism 37/3-4 (May-August 1988): 71-94.
China's America watching activities occur on four levels: inside the Ministry of Foreign Affairs; inside private institutions of independent research; inside university departments; and inside national research associations and scholarly societies.

6887. Shank, Gregory. "Contragate and Counterterrorism," Crime and Social Justice 27-28 (1987): i-xxvii.
This is an introductory essay to the entire issue devoted to the subject of "contragate." Discusses contragate and the Reagan doctrine; state terrorism in the

Americas; state terrorism in the Middle East; domestic political fallout; and conclusions. Mentions the CIA.

6888. Shank, Gregory. "Counterterrorism and Foreign Policy," <u>Crime and Social Justice</u> 27-28 (1987): 33-65.

Major sections discuss writing the songs the world sings; criminalization of dissent; legislative action; punishing crime and terrorism; NSDD 138 and Israeli "counterterrorism methods"; and the politics of war and state terrorism in politics.

6889. Shankman, Arnold. "Freedom of the Press During the Civil War: The Case of Albert D. Boilean," <u>Philadelphia History</u> 42/4 (1975): 305-315.

Amidst the discussion of Boilean's exploits is brief discussion of the origins of congressional treason legislation.

6890. Shannon, Claude E. "Communication Theory of Secrecy Systems," <u>Bell System Technical Journal</u> 28 (1949): 656-715.

6891. Shapira, Yoram. "The 1954 Guatemala Crisis," <u>Jerusalem Journal of International Relations</u> 3/2-3 (1978): 81-116.

Outlines the development of the crisis in terms of stages corresponding to the changing threat perceptions of the Guatemalan decisional elite. Attempts to answer research questions concerning decision making in crisis situations.

6892. Shapiro, Alexander H. "Political Theory and the Growth of Defensive Safeguards in Criminal Procedure: The Origins of the Treason Trials Act of 1696," <u>Law and History Review</u> 11 (Fall 1993): 215-255.

6893. Shapiro, Ira S. "Civil Liberties and National Security: The Outlook in Congress," <u>Intellect</u> 105 (February 1977): 230-233.

Discusses congressional approaches to oversight for intelligence community operations. Major sections discuss the creation of the Senate Intelligence Committee; fighting the backlash; S.3197, national security electronics surveillance; and S.1 and criminal justice reforms.

6894. Shapiro, Ira S. "The Foreign Intelligence Surveillance Act: Legislative Balancing of National Security and the Fourth Amendment," <u>Harvard Journal on Legislation</u> 15/1 (December 1977): 119-204.

Extensive discussion of the history of national security wiretapping, national security wiretap legislation and the Fourth Amendment, the standard of probable cause, dangers of a non-criminal standard, departure from <u>in</u> <u>camera</u> review, and inadequacies of the existing laws.

6895. Shapiro, Saul B. "Citizen Trust and Government Cover-up: Refining the

Doctrine of Fraudulent Concealment," Yale Law Journal 95/7 (June 1986): 1477-1499.

Major sections include: fraudulent concealment and the government; the government as a trusted defendant; constitutional rights are threatened by government concealment; and employing the trusted defendant standard.

6896. Shaplen, Robert. "Our Involvement in Laos," Foreign Affairs 48/3 (April 1970): 478-493.

Discusses differences in historical detail between Vietnam and Laos; North Vietnamese exploitation of Laos during the war; US role in Laos' defense; and CIA actions in Laos. Calls for more oversight by Congress in covert actions.

6897. Sharbach, Sarah E. "A Woman Acting Alone: Louise Olivereau and the First World War," Pacific Northwest Quarterly 78/1-2 (1987): 32-40.

6898. Sharfman, Peter. "Intelligence Analysis in the Age of Electronic Dissemination," Intelligence and National Security 10/4 (October 1995): 201-211.

Considers three consequences of movement in the direction of electronic dissemination of intelligence products: the replacement of the 'push' architecture by a 'pull' architecture; the impact of rapid dissemination of intelligence analyses; and changes in the organizational environment for analysis.

6899. Sharman, Jackson R., III. "Covert Action and Judicial Review," Harvard Journal of Law and Public Policy 12/2 (Spring 1989): 569-609.

A case note observing the tensions between the Executive and Legislative branches over covert operations, thus encouraging the Judiciary to take a more active role in determining the parameters of intervention. Refers to several important cases which established judicial review of covert actions.

6900. Sharp, Alan. "Quelqu'un nono ecoute?: French Interception of German Telegraphic and Telephonic Communications during the Paris Peace Conference, 1919: A Note," Intelligence and National Security 3/4 (October 1988): 124-127.

Argues that the Germans did not intend to use phones for important communications during the period. They used an encoded system of communication.

6901. Sharp, Arthur G. "Spy Without Visible Cause," Military History 9/6 (1993): 14, 87-91.

6902. Sharpe, K. E. "The Real Cause of Irangate," Foreign Policy 68 (Fall 1987): 19-41.

An aberrationist versus legalist discussion of Irangate, citing Watergate and secret bombings in Cambodia as examples of an imperialist presidency, promulgated by the National Security Act.

6903.   Sharpe, Kenneth E.   "Intelligence vs. Covert Action: The CIA and Democracy," World Outlook (Winter 1989):   173-187.
Major sections include discussion of three kinds of covert action; morality of covert action; serving the national interest; does covert action work?; why the secrecy about covert action?; and does covert action protect constitutional rights?

6904.   Sharpe, Sybil.   "Covert Police Operations and the Discretionary Exclusion of Evidence," Criminal Law Review 1994 (November 1994):   793-804.

6905.   Sharron, Marc.   "The Fall of the House of Ngo: A Case History," Institute of Applied Psychology Review 4 (Summer 1964):   83-92.

6906.   Shatalov, V. and L. Shishov.   "U.S. Use of Outer Space for Military Purposes," Voenno-Istoricheskii Zhurnal 10 (1984):   66-74.
In Russian, this article assesses US advancements in space technology and its continued use in the area of intelligence operations. Title here is only an approximation.

6907.   Shattuck, John H.   "Tilting at the Surveillance Apparatus," Civil Liberties Review 1/3 (Summer 1974):   59-73.
A review of several cases brought by civil liberties lawyers to dismantle the political surveillance system. Contains an extensive citation list of such cases through 1974.

6908.   Shattuck, John H.   "Uncovering Surveillance," Trial 11 (January-February 1975):   40-41+.
Recounts the expansion of government involvement in the use of surveillance technologies to locate and convict enemies of government. Discusses the litigation response to such actions; the identification of a theory under which to litigate; and the difficulties of the discovery process.

6909.   Shattuck, John H.   "National Security Wiretaps," Criminal Law Bulletin 11/1 (January-February 1975):   7-28.
Discusses the ACLU's general opposition to wiretapping; national security wiretapping practices; and imposing legislative controls for procedural controls on wiretapping.

6910.   Shattuck, John H.   "National Security a Decade After Watergate," Democracy 3/1 (Winter 1983):   56-71.
Suggesting that the Reagan administration use of civil liberties abuses has a long history, major sections discuss the concept of 'national security'; civil rights dangers; origins of 'national security'; and foreign ties. Makes reference to CIA and other intelligence organizations.

6911.   Shattuck, John H.   "In the Shadow of 1984:   National Identification Systems, Computer-Matching, and Privacy in the United States," Hastings Law Journal 35/6 (July 1984):   991-1005.

Discusses the diminishing right of privacy; the overall privacy problem in the US; the proposal to introduce a computerized national identification system, which the author believes will affect immigration and civil liberties; and proposed methods for computer matching.

6912.   Shattuck, John H.   "Federal Restrictions on the Free Flow of Academic Information and Ideas," Government Information Quarterly 3/1 (1986):   5-29.

A detailed critique of the weaknesses of the Freedom of Information Act.

6913.   Shattuck, John H.   "Secrecy on Campus," Journal of College and University Law 19/3 (Winter 1993):   217-226.

Major topics include identifying and protecting university missions in relation to externally sponsored research, an overt operation; balancing university missions with national security interests; and conclusions.

6914.   Shaw, M. Richard.   "British Intelligence and Iran," Counterspy 6/3 (May-June 1982):   31-33.

6915.   Shchetinin, Valentin.   "Economic Aspects of International Security," International Affairs (USSR) 10 (1986):   100-106.

A consideration of the Jamaican economy and how intelligence about that country is collected from the most curious sources.

6916.   Sheafer, Edward D., Jr.   "Managing the Intelligence Deluge," Signal (September 1984).

6917.   Sheafer, Edward D., Jr. "Navy HUMINT," American Intelligence Journal 14/1 (Autumn-Winter 1992-1993):   21-22.

A brief synopsis of the role of Navy human intelligence.

6918.   Sheafer, Edward D., Jr. "A Case Study of Total Quality Leadership at the Office of Naval Intelligence," American Intelligence Journal 14/3 (Autumn-Winter 1993-1994):   35-40.

Describes the origins, development and current status of the Office of Naval Intelligence Total Quality Leadership program.   Discusses the management of change; focus on business processes; TQL begins to flourish; opportunities for improvement; the bottom line; and the rewards.

6919.   Shearer, Oliver V., III and Steven E. Daskal.   "The Desert 'Electronic Warfare' Storm," Military Technology 15/9 (September 1991):   21-28.

6920. Shearing, Clifford D. "Policing South Africa: Reflections on Botha's Reforms," Canadian Journal of Sociology 11/3 (1986): 293-307.

6921. Shebelskie, Michael R. "The Major Nicholson Incident and the Norms of Peacetime Espionage," Yale Journal of International Law 11/2 (Spring 1986): 521-544.
    Summarizes the facts and legal issues involved in the Soviet sentry killing of a military attache, Major Arthur Nicholson. Outlines the conflicting claims, the conflicting conceptions of lawful actions of Nicholson; and the outcome of the case.

6922. Shed, A. "A Patriot for Whom? Colonel Redl and a Question of Identity," History Today 36 (July 1986): 9-14.
    Discusses the leaking of Austrian military secrets to Russia on the eve of World War I by Austrian Chief of Counterintelligence. Colonel Redl's homosexuality was partly the cause of his recruitment. Upon Redl's discovery as he lay dying of syphilis, Redl committed suicide.

6923. Sheehan, Catherine F. "Opening the Government's Electronic Mail: Public Access of National Security Council Records," Boston College Law Review 35/5 (September 1994): 1145-1201.
    Considers the developments of the Executive Order of the President, the National Security Adviser, and the National Security Council; statutes governing government records; cases interpreting the records statutes; the Armstrong case; and suggestions for a definitive resolution of the status of NSC records.

6924. Sheen, Henry G. "The Disintegration of the German Intelligence Services," Military Review 29 (June 1949): 38-41.
    A short discussion of the internal struggles of the Nazi intelligence services that eventually led to their demise.

6925. Sheen, Henry G. "A Cloak for 'Overload,'" Military Review 29 (February 1950): 20-25.

6926. Sheffy, Yigal. "Stratagem and Deception in the Third Battle of Gaza," Maarachot IDF Journal 302-303 (March-April 1986): 56-61.
    In Hebrew, this is a brief history of the role of strategic deception in the 1917 British Palestine campaign in Gaza.

6927. Sheffy, Yigal. "Institutionalized Deception and Perception Reinforcement: Allenby's Campaign in Palestine," Intelligence and National Security 5/2 (April 1990): 173-238.
    Discussion of two major deception operations during the British campaign in World War I in Egypt and Palestine. Major sections discuss the British

operations and intelligence; deception objectives and implementation; Turkish reaction to the deceptions; the deception story; conclusions.

6928. Sheffy, Yigal. "Unconcern at Dawn, Surprise at Sunset: Egyptian Intelligence Appreciation Before the Sinai Campaign, 1956," <u>Intelligence and National Security</u> 5/3 (July 1990): 7-56.

An extensive study of the Sinai campaign. Major sections discuss Nasser's appreciation of the situation before nationalization of the Suez Canal; Israeli-Egyptian contacts; the Egyptian view of Israel's military objectives; the Egyptian estimate of the military balance of power; the second stage between August-October 1956; military threat from the west and north; the Israeli deception plan; and the final days and the Egyptian response.

6929. Sheffy, Yigal. "Shorshei Hahavatzelet: Hamodiin BaYishuv 1918-1947," <u>Intelligence and National Security</u> 9/2 (April 1994): 380-382.

A book review essay of professor Yoav Gelber's book by the same title, remarking that this book stands apart in its description and analysis of Israeli intelligence services. The book considers these services in the Jewish community in Palestine during the period.

6930. Sheldon, Rose M. "The Roman Secret Service," <u>Intelligence</u> Quarterly 1/2 (July 1985): 7-8.

6931. Sheldon, Rose M. "Toga and Dagger," <u>Signal</u> (September 1985): 55-57.

6932. Sheldon, Rose M. "Byzantine Counterintelligence and the Bulgarians," <u>Intelligence Quarterly</u> 1/4 (February 1986): 3-4.

6933. Sheldon, Rose M. "Tradecraft in Ancient Greece," <u>Studies in Intelligence</u> 30/1 (Spring 1986): 39-47.

6934. Sheldon, Rose M. "Tinker, Tailor, Caesar, Spy," <u>American Intelligence Journal</u> 7/4 (June 1986): 3-5.

6935. Sheldon, Rose M. "Hannibal's Spies," <u>International Journal of Intelligence and Counterintelligence</u> 1/3 (Fall 1986): 53-70.

Innovation and guile were two noteworthy characteristics of intelligence operations in ancient times. Hannibal brought the Roman empire to near disaster through his application of "dirty tricks."

6936. Sheldon, Rose M. "The Ill-Fated Trojan Spy," <u>Studies in Intelligence</u> 31/1 (Spring 1987): 35-39.

Reprinted in <u>American Intelligence Journal</u> 9/3 (Fall 1988).

6937. Sheldon, Rose M. "Tradecraft in Ancient Greece," International Journal of Intelligence and Counterintelligence 2/2 (Summer 1988): 189-202.

This article had appeared in Studies in Intelligence 30/1 (Spring 1986). A discussion of how the ancient Greeks practiced the art of "strategemata" or strategies of war, including the sending of secret messages and the use of intelligence to protect city-states.

6938. Sheldon, Rose M. "Spying in Mesopotamia," Studies in Intelligence 33/1 (Spring 1989): 7-12.

6939. Sheldon, Rose M. "The Spartacus Rebellion: A Roman Intelligence Failure?," International Journal of Intelligence and Counterintelligence 6/1 (Spring 1993): 69-84.

A study of the army of rebellious slaves that controlled the southern part of Italia, commencing rebellion in the first century B.C. Major sections discuss the Spartacus revolt; the final act of Spartacus in 71 B.C.; how the Romans handled crises. Comments on the inadequacy of Roman intelligence collection.

6940. Sheldon, Rose M. "Spies and Mailmen and the Royal Road to Persia," American Intelligence Journal 14/1 (Autumn-Winter 1992-1993): 37-40.

Discusses the relationship between intelligence and communications to national security in recorded history. Includes sections on the Persian Empire; the "Eye of the King"; the Persian royal post; the Angaroi; and the fire post.

6941. Shell, E. R. "High Technology: Back in the Bottle?," Technology Review 8/3 (August-September 1981): 76-77.

Discusses the evolution of the debate over the National Security Agency's controls over public key cryptographic systems.

6942. Shelley, Louise I. "The Soviet Militsiis: Agents of Political and Social Control," Policing & Society 1/1 (1990): 39-56.

Discusses the four stages of development of the Soviet militsiia; the organization structure; the militsiia profession; and functions and operations of the militsiia.

6943. Shelton, William H. "What Was the Mission of Nathan Hale?," Journal of American History 9 (April-June 1915): 269-289.

A classic article on this important American spy in General George Washington's espionage rings.

6944. Shepard, S. J.; P. W. Sanders; and C. T. Stockel. "The Quadratic Residue Cipher and Some Notes on Implementation," Cryptologia 17/3 (July 1993): 264-284.

6945. Sheridan, Thomas I., III. "Electronic Intelligence Gathering and the Omnibus Crime Control and Safe Streets Act of 1968," Fordham Law Review 49 (1976): 331-354.

Discusses Title III of the Safe Streets Act of 1968, regarding electronic surveillance; safeguards against overuse of the statute, such as particularization, time provisions, minimization requirements, record keeping, warehousing information, and notice. Concludes that Title III restrictions will not affect national security or law enforcement efforts.

6946. Sherman, Lawrence W. "Chartering the FBI--and Implications for Local Police Departments," Criminal Law Bulletin 16/1 (January-February 1980): 53-58.

Briefly reviews the need for an FBI charter, shows what the proposed charter does and does not do, and considers the application of the FBI charter to local police department.

6947. Sherman, Richard B. "Presidential Protection During the Progressive Era: The Aftermath of the McKinley Assassination," Historian 46 (November 1983): 1-20.

Discusses legislation to make the assassination of a president a federal crime; contradictions of protection of the president; roles of the Secret Service and the District of Columbia police; and Secret Service protection of the president-elect.

6948. Sherman, Richard B. "The President and the People: Presidential Protection Procedures, 1901-1933," Prologue: Quarterly Journal of the National Archives 18/4 (April 1986): 233-239.

A comprehensive account, richly illustrated with photography, of the US Secret Service from 1901 to the present. Expresses concern for the increasing violation of the President from public access.

6949. Sherr, James. "Change and Continuity in the Former KGB," Janes Intelligence Review 5/3 (March 1993): 110-111.

6950. Sherr, James. "Cultures of Spying," National Interest 38 (Winter 1994-1995): 56-62.

Considers the role and defenses for intelligence services in the post Cold War era. Major sections discuss the US technological base for intelligence; the ability and justifications for conducting human intelligence against "friendly" countries; intelligence in modern Russia; and the business of intelligence.

6951. Sherr, James. "Russia's Federal Security Services," Jane's Intelligence Review 8 (1995): 339-342.

6952. Sherr, James. "The New Russian Intelligence Empire," Problems of Post-Communism 42/6 (November-December 1995): 11-17.

Reviews the current status of the Russian Federation's security services and considers some of the implications for these services in the overall advancement of the Russian state.

6953. Sherrin, P. M. "Spanish Spies in Victoria, 1898," BC Studies 36 (1977-1978): 23-33.

Discusses Spanish espionage actions against the US in the war of 1898, including US monitoring and popular reactions within the US. Gives attention to an intelligence operation in Victoria, British Columbia.

6954. Sherry, Norman. "The Greenwich Bomb Outrage and 'The Secret Agent,'" Review of English Studies 18 (November 1967): 412-428.

Compares the true account of the Greenwich bombing with Joseph Conrad's account in The Secret Agent. Discusses possible reasons for the bomb detonation; aspects of the investigation; possible objectives of the anarchist; and the police plot versus the anarchist plot.

6955. Sheymov, Victor. "Tower of Secrets," U.S. Naval Institute Proceedings (October 1993): 37-44.

6956. Shieber, Benjamin M. "Electronic Surveillance, the Mafia, and Individual Freedom," Louisiana Law Review 42/4 (Summer 1982): 1323-1372.

Major sections include: structure and operations of organized crime; restrictions on individual freedom by organized crime; safeguards protecting individual freedom against invasion by organized crime; what organized crime does to overcome law enforcement limitations on its activities; the essential nature of electronic surveillance; and objections to law enforcement use of electronic surveillance.

6957. Shillingsburg, Miriam J. "Simms' Benedict Arnold: The Hero As Traitor," Southern Studies 17/3 (1978): 273-289.

Discusses William G. Simms' theory of art; Simms' use of historical sources to write about Arnold and Arnold's wife's role in the espionage; Simms' creative liberties; new characters; and following tradition.

6958. Shils, Edward. "Privacy: Its Constitution and Vicissitudes," Law and Contemporary Problems 31/2 (Spring 1966): 281-306.

A sociological perspective on the dynamics of privacy.

6959. Shimada, Koichi. "Japanese Naval Air Operations in the Philippine Invasion," U.S. Naval Institute Proceedings 81/1 (January 1955): 1-17.

Covers the Japanese plan of war against the US and Britain in the

Philippines in anticipation of the failure of diplomatic resolution. Sections discuss attack preparations; zero fighters; reconnaissance; finalities; submarine movements; and first attack days.

6960. Shimanovskij, V. "U.S. Methods of Foreign Propaganda," Mezhdunarodnaia Zhizn' 14/6 (1967): 102-106.

6961. Shimansky, A. "Concerning the Achievement of Strategic Surprise in the Preparation for the Summer-Fall Campaign of 1944," Voenno-Istoricheskiy Zhurnal 6 (1968): 17-28.
· A rough translation of this title for an article appearing in a Russian language journal.

6962. Shiozaki, Hiroaki. "British-American Relations Before the Pacific War: The Role of Sir William Wiseman," Shigaku Zasshi 90/2 (1981): 57-82.
This is an approximate translation of the title for an article appearing in this Japanese language journal.

6963. Shiriaev, B. A. "The United States of America - Organizer of the Invasion of Cuba in April 1961," Vestnik Leningradskogo Universiteta 20 (1966): 153-156.
This is an approximate translation of a Russian language journal article title.

6964. Shlaim, Avi. "Failures in National Intelligence Estimates: The Case of the Yom Kippur War," World Politics 28/3 (April 1976): 348-380.
Discusses the topics of strategic surprise, the Agranat Report, the psychological roots of surprise, safeguards, and institutional reform.

6965. Shlaim, Avi. "The Lavon Affair," Middle East International 76 (October 1977): 12-14.

6966. Shlaim, Avi. "Hisni' Za'im and the Plan to Resettle Palestinian Refugees in Syria," Journal of Palestine Studies 15/4 (Summer 1986): 68-80.

6967. Shlaim, Avi and R. Tanter. "Decision Process, Choice, and Consequences," World Politics (July 1978): 483-516.
Discusses the Arab-Israeli war of attrition in 1973; the decision to bomb Egypt; the decision to halt the bombing based on Soviet intervention; the cost in options once the Soviets took up interior defense of Egypt; and the four decision tasks underlying national security policy: search, revision, evaluation, and choice.

6968. Shloss, Leon. "DOD Security: The New Look," Government Executive 1 (October 1969): 44-46.

6969. Shmuel, J. "The Imperative of Criticism: Intelligence Review," Maarachot IDF Journal 2/3 (1985): 62-69.

6970. Shoenberg, David. "Kapitza, Fact and Fiction," Intelligence and National Security 3/4 (October 1988): 49-61.
Discusses the life and work of Peter Kapitza, the alleged father of Soviet atomic bomb, alleged master spy of the 1930s in Cambridge, and the alleged chief adviser to Stalin on nuclear physics. The author considers the facts and the myths surrounding Kapitza's life.

6971. Shoham, Uri. "The Israeli Aerial Raid Upon the Iraqi Nuclear Reactor and the Right of Self-Defense," Military Law Review 109 (1985): 191-223.
Argues that Israel satisfied the self-defense requirements in international law before carrying out the raid on the reactor at Baghdad. Contains information regarding the content of intelligence which suggested the validity of the progress of the Iraqis in nuclear production.

6972. Shoop, Julie G. "Electronic Monitoring: Is Big Brother at the Office?," Trial 28 (January 1992): 13-16.
A brief discussion of the electronic monitoring of employees through computer and telephone communications. Discussion of business calls versus personal calls; health effects; and legislative proposals for change.

6973. Short, K. R. M. and Richard Taylor. "Soviet Cinema and the International Menace, 1928-1939," Historical Journal of Film, Radio and Television 6/2 (1986): 131-159.

6974. Showers, D. M. "0723, 7 December 1941," Naval Intelligence Professional Quarterly 7/4 (Fall 1991): 1-3.

6975. Showers, D. M. "The Codebreakers in the Basement," Naval Intelligence Professional Quarterly 8/2 (Spring 1992): 3-5.

6976. Showers, D. M. "The 'Y1' Story: Opintel in the Post-WW I Navy," Naval Intelligence Professional Quarterly 5/3 (Fall 1989): 1-5.

6977. Showers, D. M. "ULTRA: The Navy's First COMINT Weapon," Intelligence Professionals Quarterly 10/2 (Spring 1994): 8-10.

6978. Showers, D. M. "ULTRA: The Navy's COMINT Weapon in the Pacific," American Intelligence Journal 15/1 (Spring-Summer 1994): 49-53.
A brief discussion of ULTRA in the Pacific in World War II and the author's experiences in fleet intelligence operations.

6979. Shryock, Richard W. "The Intelligence Community Post-Mortem Program 1973-1975," Studies in Intelligence 21/3 (Fall 1977).

6980. Shugrue, Richard E. "Wiretapping in Nebraska. (Annual Survey of Nebraska Law)," Creighton Law Review 19/2 (Spring 1986): 194-235.

Argues that government can be authorized to invade privacy through the Fourth Amendment, in particular through the use of wiretapping. Covers wiretap legislation, federal test cases, and Nebraska case law.

6981. Shukiar, Herbert J. "Tactical Intelligence Analysis Challenges for the 80s," Signal 36 (October 1981): 37-40.

6982. Shuldiner, David. "'In Praise of Molly's Sons': Ballads and Legends About an Irish Secret Society," Folklore & Mythology Studies 7 (Spring 1983): 52-62.

Discussion of the relationships secret societies, such as the Molly Maguires, to history.

6983. Shulgin, Basil. "How I Was Hoodwinked by the Bolsheviks," Slavonic Review (March 1928): 505-519.

The author's frustrations in publishing articles in Russia, and his desire to return to Russia to finish his work. Refers to a secret anti-Bolshevik organization known as "Alphabet." The author published a book titled The Three Capitals.

6984. Shulman, David. "Ciphers and Their Solutions," Police Journal 25 (July-August 1939).

6985. Shulman, David. "An Unknown Cipher Disk," Cryptologia 8/2 (April 1984): 187-190.

6986. Shulman, Mark R. "The Rise and Fall of American Naval Intelligence, 1882-1917," Intelligence and National Security 8/2 (April 1993): 214-226.

Argues that although the Office of Naval Intelligence was at first a promising organization, it was reduced to dual roles of librarian and propagandist for "Blue Water" navalists, and this condition continued until World War I.

6987. Shulsky, Abram N. "Intelligence and Arms Control Policy," Comparative Strategy 6/2 (1987): 145-164.

Discusses the functions of verification of nuclear weapons; the verification process; response policy; unilateral verification; SALT I; agreements with Russia; and the change in focus toward more technical features of arms control.

6988. Shulsky, Abram N. "The Iran-Contra Affair and the Intelligence Oversight Process," Houston Journal of International Law 11/1 (1988): 245-255.

Discusses congressional interest in legislation to force the president to give prior notice of covert action plans; arguments in favor of prior notice; arguments against prior notice.

6989. Shulsky, Abram N. "Intelligence and Arms Control Policy," Teaching Political Science 16/2 (Winter 1989): 47-54.

6990. Shulsky, Abram N. and Gary J. Schmitt. "The Future of Intelligence," National Interest 38 (Winter 1994-1995): 63-73.

Considers the future of counterintelligence at CIA in the wake of the Aldrich Ames espionage case; the larger points with respect to the continued need for refocussed human intelligence; the question of need for centralization of the intelligence community and the proposal to decentralize certain functions. Argues for a separate human intelligence agency.

6991. Shultz, Richard H., Jr. "Coercive Force and Military Strategy: Deterrence Logic and the Cost-Benefit Model of Counterinsurgency Warfare," Western Political Quarterly 32/4 (1979): 444-466.

Major sections include discussion of counterinsurgency strategy from a cost-benefit perspective; model specification; operationalization of the strategy in Vietnam, 1965-68; strategy misspecification; exogenous factors; endogenous factors; and answers the question of the inevitability of failure.

6992. Shultz, Richard H., Jr. "The Role of External Forces in Third World Conflicts," Comparative Strategy 4/2 (1983): 79-111.

A detailed consideration of the factor of external forces in creating opportunities for Third World country instability. Sections cover conditions of internal political conflict; Soviet perspective on internal conflict; nature of conflict and the dimensions of power; changes in the correction forces and opportunities in the Third World; intelligence and special activities programs; overt and covert propaganda; arms and logistical support; military-political training and adversary assistance; internal security training and assistance; and unconventional conflict and US opinions.

6993. Shultz, Richard H., Jr. "Soviet Use of Surrogates to Project Power into the Third World," Parameters: Journal of the U.S. Army War College 16/3 (August 1986): 32-42.

Major sections discuss surrogates and strategy; case studies in the Caribbean, Central America, the Middle East; and conclusions.

6994. Shultz, Richard H., Jr. "Covert Action and Executive-Legislative Relations: The Iran-Contra Crisis and Its Aftermath," Harvard Journal of Law &

Public Policy 2/2 (Spring 1989): 449-482.
   Discusses in exceptionally detailed fashion the congressional legislative reactions to the Iran-Contra matter; defines covert action; offers American perspectives on covert action; discusses covert action and post-World War II US foreign policy; and summarizes the impact of legislation after the Iran-Contra crisis.

6995. Sibbet, Daniel B. "MASINT: Intelligence for the 1990s," American Intelligence Journal 11/3 (1990): 23-26.
   Discusses the role of Measurements and Signals Intelligence in the changing world of intelligence; the new realities in treaty monitoring, economic warfare; war on drugs, and counter stealth; and the difference between MASINT and IMINT and SIGINT.

6996. Sibbet, Daniel B. "Intelligence and Verification," American Intelligence Journal 12/3 (Autumn 1991): 47-52.
   Discusses verification within the arms control process; treaty monitoring; collection in support of treaty monitoring; the operational dilemma; fig leaf collection, or collection of real intelligence through treaty monitoring; and challenges for the collection manager.

6997. Sibbet, Daniel B. "Commercial Remote-Sensing: Open Source Imagery Intelligence," American Intelligence Journal 14/2&3 (Spring-Summer 1993): 37-40.
   Contains a brief history of collection of intelligence from the air dating to World War I; data uses in environmental change and government applications; the kinds of sensors now in place; and multispectral imagery systems as open source intelligence.

6998. Sibert, Edwin L. "Operation Portrex," Studies in Intelligence 4 (Fall 1960).
   Discusses the Vieques war game.

6999. Sibraa, Kerry W. "National Security-Parliamentary Scrutiny of Security and Intelligence Services in Australia," Parliamentarian 68/3 (July 1987): 120-127.

7000. Siegel, Jennifer. "British Intelligence on the Russian Revolution and Civil War -- A Breach at the Source," Intelligence and National Security 10/3 (July 1995): 468-485.
   A perspective on the subject, keying off the circumstances surrounding the affairs of Robert Bruce Lockhart, consul-general in Moscow just prior to the Revolution's outbreak.

7001. Sidle, Winant. "The Public's Right to Know," <u>U.S. Naval Institute Proceedings</u> 111/7 (July 1985): 37-43.

Concludes that the public does have a right to know, but it is not an absolute right. Particularly discusses the role of the press in national security controversies.

7002. Siers, Donna B. "The Anatomy of Defense Strategy in an Espionage Case," <u>Criminal Law Bulletin</u> 23 (July-August 1987): 309-322.

The author, a trial consultant in numerous civil and criminal applied her experience to conducting a mock trial as a rehearsal for the jury selection in the espionage case of Richard Craig Smith. Offers a methodology for building a defense jury profile.

7003. Sigal, Leon V. "Official Secrecy and Informal Communication in Congressional-Bureaucratic Relations," <u>Political Science Quarterly</u> 90/1 (Spring 1975): 71-92.

Discusses three channels of informal communication, "secrets" and "official secrets," the atomic bomb appropriations secret, bombing of Cambodia 1969-70, communications and bureaucratic tactics, conclusions.

7004. Sigaud, Louis A. "Mrs. Greenhow and the Rebel Spy Ring," <u>Maryland Historical Magazine</u> 41/3 (September 1946): 173-198.

7005. Sigaud, Louis A. "More About Belle Boyd," <u>Lincoln Herald</u> 64/4 (1962): 174-181.

7006. Sigaud, Louis A. "William Boyd Compton: Belle Boyd's Cousin," <u>Lincoln Herald</u> 67/1 (1965): 22-33.

7007. Siggelakis, Susan J. "Advocacy on Trial," <u>American Journal of Legal History</u> 36 (October 1992): 499-516.

Discussion of Department of Justice cases brought in the 1950s under the Smith Act and the Subversive Activities Control Act.

7008. Sigler, Jay A. "Freedom of the Mails: A Developing Right," <u>Georgetown Law Journal</u> 54/1 (Fall 1965): 30-54.

Contains a valuable history of postal censorship concerns, United States Postal Service mail control procedures, mail covers, and conclusions.

7009. Sigmund, Paul E. "The 'Invisible Blockade' and the Overthrow of Allende," <u>Foreign Affairs</u> 52/2 (January 1974): 322-340.

Includes brief discussion of CIA role in the overthrow of the Salvador Allende government in Chile.

7010. Sigmund, Paul E. "Chile: What Was the U.S. Role? Less Than Charged," Foreign Policy 16 (1974): 142-156.

This is a counter argument to that which was offered by Elizabeth Farnsworth as to the cutoff of American aid to Chile prior to 1973. Critiques the role of the scholar in careful examination of the evidence; the issue of Chile's moratorium on payment of foreign debt; allegations about the blockade proposal; and reasons for the coup.

7011. Sigmund, Paul E. "The CIA in Chile," Worldview 19/4 (April 1976): 11-17.

Discusses the 1973 coup in Chile; early CIA involvement; plans for the coup; whether or not CIA made a difference in the outcome; and Senate conclusion that CIA was not involved in any significant way with the 1973 coup.

7012. Sigurdson, Jon and Patricia Nelson. "Intelligence Gathering and Japan: The Elusive Role of Grey Intelligence," International Journal of Intelligence and Counterintelligence 5/1 (Spring 1991): 17-34.

Discusses the importance of grey intelligence, primarily information about technological research and the organizations that produce it, in the overall development of Japan. Major sections discuss electronics in Japan; intelligence as a tool for strategic understanding; elusive information; Japanese intelligence gathering; gathering intelligence on Japan; the Extreme Ultrahigh Vacuum project and its actors; the technological landscape; and non-high-tech companies.

7013. Silas, Faye A. "Death for Spies? Walker Trials Prompt Debate," American Bar Association Journal 71 (December 1985): 18-19.

A brief discussion of the congressional legislation insisting upon the creation of a death penalty for espionage in response to the Walker espionage case.

7014. Silbert, Jeffrey M. "An Analysis of the Newly Adopted Fingerprint Law for Brokerage Firms," Criminology 9/2-3 (1971): 207-220.

White collar crime in the securities industry attracted the attention of the New York legislature in the creation of a fingerprint requirement for all employees on the stock exchanges. The New York State Identification and Intelligence System is the repository for all such prints. Controversies concerning privacy invasion have sprung up around the system.

7015. Silver, Arnold M. "Questions, Questions, Questions: Memories of Oberursel," Intelligence and National Security 8/2 (April 1993): 199-213.

A personal account of the author's work with the 7077th European Command Intelligence Center in Germany at the end of World War II. The Center's purpose was to interrogate POWs. Describes the Center's organization and operations, and its implications for future intelligence work on defectors.

7016. Silver, Brenda R. "Woman As Agent: The Case of LeCarre's <u>Little Drummer Girl</u>," <u>Contemporary Literature</u> 28/1 (Spring 1987): 14-40.
    Author characterizes women and men in the literature of espionage, focussing on LeCarre's novel.

7017. Silver, Daniel B. "The CIA and the Law: The Evolving Role of the CIA's General Counsel," <u>Studies in Intelligence</u> 25/2 (Summer 1981).

7018. Silver, Daniel B. "The Uses and Misuses of Intelligence Oversight," <u>Houston Journal of International Law</u> 11/1 (1988): 7-19.
    Argues that oversight of intelligence services has a proper role, but there have been occasions in which oversight has been abused. Sections discuss democratic values and misuses of intelligence oversight; intelligence activities; a proposed definition of intelligence oversight; and the present state of oversight.

7019. Silver, Edward S. "The Wiretapping-Eavesdropping Problem: A Prosecutor's View," <u>Minnesota Law Review</u> 44/5 (April 1960): 835-889.
    Sections discuss the problems of private wiretapping; the number of wiretaps; the safeguards surrounding court orders; police corruption; the myths about gambling; and the need for law enforcement tapping. Argues for more restrictions on public and private wiretapping.

7020. Silverberg, Marshall. "The Separation of Powers and Control of the CIA's Covert Operations," <u>Texas Law Review</u> 68 (February 1990): 575-622.

7021. Silverstein, Marc. "After the Fall: The World of Graham Greene's Thrillers," <u>Novel</u> 22 (Fall 1988): 24-44.

7022. Simakov, E. "Operatwnaya Maskirovka V.V.C.V. Nastuplinviz Opratisyz," <u>Voenno-Istoricheskiy Zhurnal</u> 2 (February 1977): 19-26.

7023. Simchenkov, P. M. "Achievement of Secrecy in the Experience of the Great Patriotic War," <u>Voenno-Istoricheskiy Zhurnal</u> 6 (1986): 17-24.
    Discusses the methods by which the Soviets protected their secret operations during the World War II.

7024. Simmel, Georg. "The Sociology of Conflict," <u>American Journal of Sociology</u> 9 (1904): 490-525.
    An extensive discussion of the role of secrecy in social conflict, perhaps one of the first sociological considerations of the topic. Translated by Albion Small. The most essential piece of early scholarship on the topic of secrecy.

7025. Simmons, Edwin H. "The Secret Mission of Archibald Gillespie," <u>Marine Corps Gazette</u> 52/11 (1968): 60-67.

7026.   Simmons, Gustavus J.   "Cryptology: The Mathematics of Secure Communication," Mathematical Intelligencer 1/4 (1979): 233-246.

7027.   Simmons, Gustavus J.   "How to Insure that Data Acquired to Verify Treaty Compliance Are Trustworthy," Proceedings of the IEEE 76 (May 1988): 621-627.

7028.   Simmons, Gustavus J.   "Scanning the Issue of Cryptology," Proceedings of the IEEE 76/5 (May 1988).

7029.   Simmons, Isabel.   "The Unbreakable Code," Marine Corps Gazette 55/11 (November 1971): 59.

A very brief discussion of the Navajo Indian code talkers of World War II fame.

7030.   Simmons, Robert R.   "Lifting Bob Woodward's Veil," International Journal of Intelligence and Counterintelligence 2/2 (1988): 273-279.

A book review essay on Woodward's book, Veil.

7031.   Simmons, Robert R.   "Intelligence Policy and Performance in Reagan's First Term: A Good Record or Bad?," International Journal of Intelligence and Counterintelligence 4/1 (Spring 1990): 1-22.

An evaluation of the Reagan administration's intelligence policy organization and execution. Major sections discuss key questions, methodology, and sources; the reinstatement of the President's Foreign Intelligence Advisory Board; executive orders; the Agent Identities Protection Act; the Freedom of Information Act; and covert action.

7032.   Simon, J. E. S.   "Evidence Excluded by Considerations of State Interest," Cambridge Law Journal (1955): 62-79.

Reflects upon the issue of state interest in securing government information against release, in particular, information relating to national security.

7033.   Simon, Paul.   "Is America Tongue-Tied?," Academe: Bulletin of the American Association of University Professors 69/2 (1983): 9-12.

7034.   Simon, Sheldon W.   "The Pueblo Incident and the South Korean Revolution in North Korea's Foreign Policy: A Propaganda Analysis," Asian Forum 2 (Summer 1970): 201-214.

Analysis of the propaganda of the North Koreans after the release of Pueblo crew in January 1969. Discusses North Korean foreign policy; espionage and the relations between North Korea and the Soviet Union; war preparation; unification; the South Korean "revolution"; and North Korean intelligence operations.

7035. Simon, Walter G. "The Evolution of Treason," <u>Tulane Law Review</u> 35/4 (June 1961): 669-704.

Discusses the lengthy British and American history of the law of treason; punishment for treason; treason in Spain; treason and politics; Anglo-Saxon history of treason and succeeding legislation; later history of treason.

7036. Simonyan, R. G. "CIA: The Back-Stage Manager," <u>Soviet Military Review</u> 8 (August 1976): 44-47.

7037. Simonyan, R. G. "Intelligence When Preparing for and Conducting Front Offensive Operations," <u>Voenno Istoricheskiy Zhurnal</u> 12 (December 1977): 1-10.

7038. Simpson, Brian. "The Criminal Proceedings Act and the Sheraton Raid (Australia)," <u>Legal Service Bulletin</u> 9 (August 1984): 194-196.

7039. Simpson, John. "Falling for a Warsaw-Pact Dame," <u>Harper's</u> 274 (June 1987): 58-62.

The author recounts his experiences with Eastern European intelligence services, meeting a beautiful female spy, and the British security service MI5.

7040. Simpson, Keith. The German Experience of Rear Area Security on the Eastern Front, 1941-45," <u>RUSI Journal for Defence Studies</u> 121/4 (December 1976): 39-46.

Discussed the relative ineffectiveness of German rear area protection against the advancing Russian army.

7041. Sims, Charles. "Over the Fence," <u>Flying Review International</u> 23 (August 1968): 445-446+.

7042. Sims, John C. "Triangulating the Boundaries of the Pentagon Papers," <u>William and Mary Bill of Rights Journal</u> 2 (Winter 1993): 341-453.

Considers the implications of the Pentagon Papers case well after the Supreme Court holding in 1971 (<u>New York Times Co. v. United States</u>, 91 S. Ct. 2140 (1971).

7043. Sims, Rebecca. "Operatives and S&L's: The CIA and Financial Institutions," <u>Covert Action Information Bulletin</u> 35 (Fall 1990): 43-48.

Discusses the long history of Central Intelligence Agency involvement with financial institutions and banking scandals. Describes the early CIA banks; First National Bank of Maryland; the Palmer National Bank; the Indian Springs State Bank; the Aurora Bank; Sunshine State Bank; and Hill Financial and Vision Banc Savings. Points to links between these banks, the CIA and organized crime activities.

7044. Sinclair, Betty. "Behind the Scenes in Ulster," World Marxist Review 17 (August 1974): 123-128.

7045. Sinclair, Robert S. "Communication to the Editor: On 'Cognitive Biases,'" Studies in Intelligence 23/1 (Spring 1979).

7046. Singer, J. David. "Threat Perception and the Armament-Tension Dilemma," Journal of Conflict Resolution 11/1 (March 1958): 90-105.
Major sections include discussion of the national security dilemmas of escalation of threat perceptions: the perils of "para bellum"; the question of cause or effect; threat perception and the decision makers; and an examination of alternatives.

7047. Singh, Jasjit. "Reconnaissance, Surveillance and Target Acquisition," Strategic Analysis (January 1986): 1026-1058.

7048. Singh, S. N. "Why India Lags Behind," Nineteenth Century 70 (October 1911): 739-752.

7049. Singerman, Robert. "The American Career of the Protocols of the Elders of Zion," American Jewish History 71/1 (1981): 48-78.

7050. Sinnigen, William G. "The Officium of the Urban Prefecture in the Late Roman Empire," Papers and Monographs of the American Academy of Rome 17 (1957).

7051. Sinnigen, William G. "Two Branches of the Late Roman Secret Service," American Journal of Philology 80/3 (July 1959): 238-254.
Outlines the development of the two secret service departments in the last years of the Roman empire: Schola agentum in rebus, and schola notariorum. Discusses their organization, function and uses, and personnel.

7052. Sinnigen, William G. "The Roman Secret Service," Classical Journal 57/2 (1961): 65-72.

7053. Sinnigen, William G. "The Origins of the Frumentarii," Memoirs of the American Academy of Rome 27 (1962): 211-224.

7054. Sinnigen, William G. "Three Administrative Changes Ascribed to Constantius II," American Journal of Philology 83 (1962): 369-382.

7055. Sinnigen, William G. "The Chiefs of Staff of the Later Roman Secret Service," Byzantinische Zeitschrift 57 (1964): 78-105.

7056. Sinnigen, William G. "Administrative Shifts of Competence Under Theodoric," Traditio 21 (1965): 456-467.

7057. Sissons, D. C. S. "More on Pearl Harbor," Intelligence and National Security 9/2 (April 1994): 373-379.
    A careful review article concerning a book by James Rusbridger and E. Nave, Betrayal at Pearl Harbor: How Churchill Lured Roosevelt into World War II. The reviewer doubts there was a conspiracy on a grand scale; rather, more of a grand error on a small scale which he says the book illustrates.

7058. Siwundhala, Hulme T. "White Ideologies and Non-European Participation in the Anglo-Boer War, 1899-1902," Black Studies 15/2 (December 1984): 223-234.
    A brief account of the internal dynamics of the Boer War, including the role of spies and traitors.

7059. Sked, Alan. "A Patriot for Whom? Colonel Redl and a Question of Identity," History Today 36 (July 1986): 9-14.
    Study of the espionage activities of Colonel Alfred Redl in Austria in 1913. Redl was blackmailed into becoming a Russian spy following Russian intelligence discovery that he was gay. Sections include discussion of the Vienna military investigation, the execution of Redl, and the investigation of Redl.

7060. Skene, Melvin. "The Secret Eye: The Spy in Literature the Evolution of Espionage Literature - A Survey of the History and Development of the Spy and Espionage Novel," Pacific Quarterly 3/1 (January 1978): 11-26.
    A useful overview of the genre of spy literature.

7061. Skousen, W. Cleon. "The Intelligence Unit," Law and Order 14/6 (June 1966): 68-73.
    Useful in studies of American domestic intelligence in the 1960s.

7062. Skousen, W. Cleon. "The National Network of Police Intelligence Units," Law and Order 14/7 (July 1966): 10-14.

7063. Slackman, Michael. "The Orange Race: George S. Patton, Jr.'s Japanese-American Hostage Plan," Biography 7/1 (Winter 1984): 365-375.

7064. Slade, Jimmie L. "AirLand Battle Doctrine and the Intelligence Officer," American Intelligence Journal 6/3 (October 1984): 3-9.

7065. Slater, Jerome. "Apolitical Warrior or Soldier-Statesman: The Military and the Foreign Process in the Post-Vietnam Era," Armed Forces and Society 4/1 (Fall 1977): 101-118.

Discussion of two models of military professionalism: apolitical warrior versus soldier-statesman. Briefly mentions the role of domestic intelligence in the model of soldier-statesman.

7066. Slayman, Andrew. "Civil War Espionage," Archaeology 48 (May-June 1995): 18+.

7067. Slayton, Barney F. "'War in the Ether': Soviet Radio-Electronic Warfare," Military Review 60/1 (January 1980): 56-67.
Examines Soviet army electronic warfare doctrine and capabilities in preparation for the next war. Major sections discuss organization; tactics; and training.

7068. Slights, William W. E. "The Play of Conspiracies in Volpore," Texas Studies in Literature and Language: A Journal of the Humanities 27/4 (Fall 1988): 369-389.
Discusses conspiracy and secrecy in Volpore.

7069. Sloan, Stephen. "Clandestine Collection in an Open Society: The Problem of Reconciliation," Intercollegiate Review 19/1 (Fall 1983): 55-59.

7070. Sloan, Stephen. "Developing a Proactive Approach to Crisis Management: Command Post Exercises and the Crucial Role of the Intelligence Function," Security Journal 2/1 (January 1991): 2-17.
Discusses the role of positive intelligence can play in organizations that must deal with crisis situations. Argues that such organizations should develop an initial threat assessment, build a scenario, disseminate information, conduct command post exercises, and engage in an after action review.

7071. Slocum, Winthrop. "Uncovering Japan's Technical Secrets," Military Review 29/6 (June 1949): 17-26.

7072. Slomanson, William R. "Civil Actions Against Interpol: A Field Compass," Temple Law Quarterly 57/3 (1984): 553-599.
Considers the nature and role of INTERPOL as an international organization; INTERPOL operations in the US, including its relations with the CIA and FBI; INTERPOL as a civil defendant; and a review of problems in selecting the proper court for civil actions against INTERPOL.

7073. Slonim, Scott. "Reports As Spies? Controversy Brews," American Bar Association Journal 66 (May 1980): 550-551.
A brief note reflecting upon CIA director Stansfield Turner's policy of using reporters overseas to acquire information for the CIA.

7074. Slotnick, Michael C. "The Anathema of the Security Risk: Arbitrary Dismissals of Federal Government Civilian Employees and Civilian Employees of Private Contractors Doing Business with the Federal Government," University of Miami Law Review 17/1 (Fall 1962): 10-50.

Discussion of the federal government's security program for civilian employees; the program's application to private contractor employees; federal government civilian employees and private contractor employees in the courts.

7075. Slusser, Robert M. "The Budget of the OGPU and Special Troops from 1923-4 to 1928-9," Soviet Studies 10/4 (April 1959): 375-383.

Presents factual data concerning the security police budget and establishes a context for study of the OGPU on the basis of budgetary allocations.

7076. Slusser, Robert M. "Recent Soviet Books on the History of the Secret Service," Slavic Review 24/1 (March 1965): 90-98.

Reviews collections of books on the early stages of the Soviet secret police.

7077. Slusser, Robert M. "Recent Soviet Books on the History of the Secret Service," Slavic Review 32/4 (December 1973): 825-828.

This is part II of the earlier review essay. Considers nine books and documents aimed at uncovering the history of Soviet secret police.

7078. Smelser, Marshall. "George Washington and the Alien and Sedition Acts," American Historical Review 59/2 (January 1954): 322-334.

A brief history of the congressional creation of these emergency statutes. Major sections discuss the history of the statutes; the Jay Treaty; and the XYZ affair. Argues that significant evidence existed in the early years of the nation to indicate a French conspiracy and plot to seize control of the US, thus attracting Washington's support for the Acts.

7079. Smigel, Stanley E. "Some Views on the Theory and Practice of Intelligence Collection," Studies in Intelligence 2/2 (Spring 1958).

7080. Smiley, Alfred A. "Intelligence Analysis in LIC," Military Intelligence 16/3 (July-September 1990): 32-33.

Discusses the need for intelligence analysis in all military operations. Argues the complex requirements for analysis in low-intensity conflicts.

7081. Smirnov, Iu. and V. G. Ushakov. "Moscow Chekists in the Defense of the Capital, 1941-42," Voenno-Istoricheskiy Zhurnal 1 (1991): 10-13.

7082. Smith, Anthony. "The 'Spycatcher' Case," Law Institute Journal 61 (July 1987): 690+.

7083. Smith, Baxter. "New Evidence of FBI 'Disruption' Program," Black Scholar: Journal of Black Studies and Research 6/1 (1975): 43-48.

Asserts that the FBI spied on Black political organizations in the 1960s and 1970s.

7084. Smith, Bethania M. "Civil War Subversives," Journal of the Illinois Historical Society 45/3 (Autumn 1952): 220-240.

Discusses the Knights of the Golden Circle, an underground group having its origins in the 1850s in the Caribbean.

7085. Smith, Bradley F. "Admiral Godfrey's Mission to America, June/July 1941," Intelligence and National Security 1/3 (September 1986): 441-450.

7086. Smith, Bradley F. "A Note on the OSS, Ultra, and World War II's Intelligence Legacy for America," Defense Analysis 3/2 (Fall 1987): 184-189.

A brief discussion of President Harry Truman's direction of the abolishment of OSS and the plans for reconfiguration of national intelligence. Mentions the role of the Bureau of the Budget in crafting the demise of OSS.

7087. Smith, Bradley F. "Sharing Ultra in World War II," International Journal of Intelligence and Counterintelligence 2/1 (Spring 1988): 59-72.

Examines the World War II transmissions of British special intelligence information called 'Ultra.' Suggests that numerous bits of intelligence insight gained from Ultra were passed to the Soviets throughout the War, and sharing of intelligence with the US was usually associated with joint missions.

7088. Smith, Bradley F. "An Idiosyncratic View of Where We Stand on the History of American Intelligence in the Early Post-1945 Era," Intelligence and National Security 3/4 (October 1988): 111-123.

A brief overview of the types of documents available for historical mining in the areas of domestic and foreign intelligence. Argues that sources are few in number, but more are coming into the historical market regularly. Also argues for more historical research on particular subjects.

7089. Smith, Bradley F. "The Road to the Anglo-American Intelligence Partnership," American Intelligence Journal 16/2&3 (Autumn-Winter 1995): 59-62.

A brief history of the gradual cooperation between the British and the Americans on the construction of their respective intelligence services, mainly in the twentieth century through World War II.

7090. Smith, Bruce L. "Democratic Control of Propaganda Through Registration and Disclosure," Public Opinion Quarterly 6 (1942): 27-40.

A wartime discussion of the probable effects of a "gag" law; the principle of disclosure; the McCormack and Voorhis Acts; previous laws on registration and disclosure; and administrative enforcement of registrations.

7091. Smith, Charles L. "Soviet Maskirovka," Airpower Journal 2/1 (Spring 1988): 28-39.

7092. Smith, Chester L. "Trends in Covert Applications of Electrotechnology," IEEE Technology and Society 10 (Summer 1991): 15-21.

7093. Smith, David E. "John Wallis As a Cryptographer," Bulletin of the American Mathematical Society 24 (1917): 83-96.

7094. Smith, Dean. "The Zimmermann Telegram, 1917," American History Illustrated 13/3 (1978): 28-37.
        A thorough but brief history of this classic piece of World War I intelligence history.

7095. Smith, E. D. "Was the Monastery at Cassino Bombed?," Army Quarterly 118 (July 1969): 220-224.
        Discussion of a possible tactical intelligence blunder.

7096. Smith, Esmond D., Jr. "Ultra and the Walker Case," Studies in Intelligence 32/4 (Winter 1988).

7097. Smith, Esmond D., Jr. "ULTRA and the Walkers," U.S. Naval Institute Proceedings 115/5 (1989): 110-119.

7098. Smith, Edmond D., Jr. "A Naval Intelligence Strategy," Naval Intelligence Professionals Quarterly 5/1-5/2 (Summer and Winter 1989): 1-3; 5-7.
        A series of two articles on the authors views on the subject of reorganization of naval intelligence.

7099. Smith, Esmond D., Jr. "The Security Dilemma," Naval Intelligence Professional Quarterly 5/3 (Fall 1989): 13-16.

7100. Smith, Esmond D., Jr. "The Spies Among Us: Trends in Military Espionage," Naval Intelligence Professionals Quarterly 7/1 (Winter 1991): 1-4.

7101. Smith, Esmond D., Jr. "Security and the Ames Case: An Assessment," Naval Intelligence Professionals Quarterly 11/4 (Fall 1995): 4-8.

7102. Smith, E. Timothy. "The Fear of Subversion: The United States and the Inclusion of Italy in the North Atlantic Treaty," Diplomatic History 7/2 (Spring 1983): 139-155.

Discusses the US need to include Italy in the Western bloc of nations out of fear of Soviet fifth column movements in the late 1940s.

7103. Smith, Evan B. "Open Government in the United States and Canada: Public and Press Access to Information," Canadian-U.S. Law Journal 9 (1985): 113-136.

Comparative analysis of constitutional and statutory rights of access to government information (including Canada's Access to Information Act of 1983) and access to government meetings.

7104. Smith, F. B. "British Post Office Espionage, 1844," Historical Studies 14 (April 1970): 189-203.

Discusses Guiseppe Mazzini's allegations that the British Post Office conducted or sponsored espionage against diplomatic mail. Mazzini was the exiled Italian revolutionary later involved in the Italian revolution of 1860.

7105. Smith George. "Union Propaganda in the American Civil War," Social Studies 35/1 (January 1944).

7106. Smith, G. G. "The Clandestine Submarines of 1914-15: An Essay in the History of the North American Triangle," Canadian Historical Association Annual Report (1963): 194-203.

7107. Smith, Gregory K. "The Independent Counsel in the Iran/Contra Affair: Why Gordon Liddy Went to Jail, and Oliver North Went to Disneyland," American Criminal Law Review 29 (Summer 1992): 1261-1299.

7108. Smith, Hugh. "Intelligence and UN Peacekeeping," Survival 36/3 (Autumn 1994): 174-192.

Discusses the international context in which intelligence is gathered for the United Nations. The UN is an organization with "no enemies of the kind national intelligence thrives on..."

7109. Smith, James M. "Federalist 'Saints' Versus the 'Devil of Sedition': The Liberty Pole Cases of Dedham, Massachusetts, 1798-1799," New England Quarterly 28/2 (June 1955): 198-215.

Discusses the role of liberty poles in the Democratic-Republican resistance to policies of the Federalists in the years following the American revolution, and the trials for sedition that surrounded liberty pole erections in New England.

7110. Smith, Jim. "The Freedom of Information Act of 1966: A Legislative History Analysis," Law Library Journal 74 (1981): 231-280.

Discusses the rationale for the Act, the background in the Administrative

Procedure Act of 1946, the Administrative Code bills of the 84th Congress, the "Housekeeping Statute" Amendment of 1958, a codification of the FOIA 1966. Argues that the intention of the Act was to eliminate vague language in earlier laws to permit more public disclosure.

7111. Smith, Joseph B. "The CIA in Vietnam: Nation-Builders, Old Pros, Paramilitary Boys, and Misplaced Persons," Washington Monthly 9/12 (February 1978): 22-31.
A former CIA employee, Smith discusses the CIA's role in South Vietnam in the early days of the Vietnam war. Major sections discuss the conventional wisdom about the escalation of US involvement, the liberals in the CIA, and Smith's inclinations.

7112. Smith, Joseph B. "Life Without Badges: The Cost of Cover in the CIA," Washington Monthly 10/3 (May 1978): 44-48.
Some personal observations of the author, an experienced CIA official, reflecting upon then-current changes at CIA.

7113. Smith, Joseph B. "Sic Semper Politico Petroleum," Washington Monthly 12/2 (March 1980): 38-39.
A brief inset commentary pertaining to Thomas Powers' book, The Man Who Kept the Secrets.

7114. Smith, Kevin B. "Combat Information Flow," Military Review 69/4 (April 1989): 42-54.
Explores obstacles and the limits of human capabilities in the process of gathering information useful to commanders in airland battle planning.

7115. Smith, Lacey B. "English Treason Trials and Confessions in the Sixteenth Century," Journal of the History of Ideas 15/4 (October 1954): 471-498.
Extensive discussion of treason trials in Tudor England, especially under Henry VIII, and confessions extracted from defendants.

7116. Smith, Lawrence D. "Secret Messages Vital in War," Science Digest 14 (July 1943): 15-20.

7117. Smith, Lloyd W. "U.S. Marine Intelligence," Military Intelligence 9/3 (July-September 1983): 10-15.
Supplies a complete outline of US Marine Corps intelligence organizations and respective missions.

7118. Smith, Louis A., III. "Pennsylvania's Constitutional Right of Privacy: A Survey of Its Interpretation in the Context of Search and Seizure and Electronic Surveillance," Duquesne Law Review 31 (Spring 1993): 557-586.

Analysis of case law in Pennsylvania regarding electronic surveillance, followed by presentation of hypothetical cases and how Pennsylvania law might apply.

7119. Smith, Lyn. "Covert British Propaganda: The Information Research Department, 1947-1977," Millennium: Journal of International Studies 9/1 (1980): 67-83.

Examines available evidence on covert British post-war propaganda and the modern context of propaganda in the United Kingdom.

7120. Smith, Margaret C. "How Margaret Chase Smith Would Monitor the CIA," Freedom at Issue 35 (1976): 11-13.

The title captures the contents in terms of controlling the president's use of CIA for covert actions.

7121. Smith, Michael J. "Ethics and Intervention," Ethics & International Affairs 3 (1989): 1-26.

7122. Smith, Paul A., Jr. "Propaganda: A Modernized Soviet Weapons System," Strategic Review 11/3 (Summer 1983): 65-70.

7123. Smith, R. Hudson. "Secrets from the Rock," Blackwood's Magazine 312 (January 1976): 108-122.

Discusses British, German and Spanish intelligence gathering on Gibraltar in World War II. Effectiveness of the British intelligence missions is main focus.

7124. Smith, Raymond W. "Don't Cut Signal Telegraph," Civil War Times Illustrated 15/2 (1976): 18-28.

This article describes the role of telegraphy in the Civil War.

7125. Smith, R. Jack. "Colonel Lawrence K. White," Studies in Intelligence 25/4 (Winter 1981).

The collection of declassified titles available for public access does not list this article.

7126. Smith, Richard A. "Business Espionage," Fortune 53 (May 1956): 118-126.

Very few articles appeared on this subject in the 1950s.

7127. Smith, Richard B.; Reuben B. Robertson, et al. "National Security, Law Enforcement, and Business Secrets Under the Freedom of Information Act," Business Lawyer 38/2 (February 1983): 707-739.

An edited transcript of a program presented by the American Bar Association in August 1982. Focus was on problems of handling national security, business secrets and law enforcement information. The question of FOIA applications to the CIA was discussed at length.

7128. Smith, Richard H. "The First Moscow Station: An Espionage Footnote to Cold War History," International Journal of Intelligence and Counterintelligence 3/3 (Fall 1989): 333-346.

 Explores the Dusko Popov defection case; the William Hood version of the Popov story; the Peer DeSilva version; Edward Ellis Smith; Smith in Moscow and Smith returns home; and the final days of Smith's life.

7129. Smith, Richard K. "The Violation of the 'Liberty,'" U.S. Naval Institute Proceedings 104/6 (June 1978): 62-79.

 The Israeli attack upon the Liberty in 1967 is interpreted as a purposeful act to stop US reporting of Israeli successes on the war with Egypt.

7130. Smith, Robert F. "A Note on the Origins of the CIA's Covert Action Capability," Historian 48/2 (February 1986): 225-230.

 This article focuses on how NSC 10/2 came to be created, thus expanding CIA's capabilities to carry our covert actions. Cites protection of Venezuelan oil threat as the reason for the executive directive.

7131. Smith, Robert M. "Spies Against Labor: Industrial Espionage Agencies, 1855-1940," Labor's History 5/2 (1993): 64-77.

7132. Smith, Thomas T. "The Bodden Line: A Case-study of Wartime Technology," Intelligence and National Security 6/2 (April 1991): 447-457.

 Chronicles the story behind the British cypher efforts in Section V. The German operation Bodden dealt with technology breakthroughs. Section V began efforts to decrypt Bodden. Argues that war and technology always go together.

7133. Smith, Truman. "An American Estimate of the German Air Force," Airpower Historian (April 1963).

7134. Smith, Wayne S. "A Trap in Angola," Foreign Policy 62 (Spring 1986): 61-74.

 Contains, in part, an analysis of CIA's involvement in the 1975 attempt by the Ford administration to secretly underwrite a coalition government under the Alvor agreement.

7135. Smith, William F. "Intelligence and National Security," World Affairs Journal 1 (Spring 1982): 23-32.

 A discussion of the history of intelligence, guidelines for intelligence agencies, the role of intelligence officers, the problem of selling secrets, effects of spy infiltration, countering espionage, improving intelligence without endangering the American public. Appears also in <u>Vital Speeches of the Day</u> 51/22 (September 1985): 677-680.

7136. Smith, William F. "F.B.I. Guidelines: A Responsible Balance," <u>California Lawyer</u> 3/2 (February 1985): 11, 75-76.

The former Attorney General argues that the FBI guidelines to control conduct of investigations in cases involving ordinary crimes, racketeering and domestic security will not harm citizen lawful activities.

7137. Smith, W. Thomas. "Confederate Secret Service Disc," <u>North South Trader</u> 11/6 (1975): 16-19.

7138. Smyth, Denis. "Screening 'Torch': Allied Counter-Intelligence and the Spanish Threat to the Secrecy of the Allied Invasion of French North Africa in November 1942," <u>Intelligence and National Security</u> 4/2 (April 1989): 335-356.

Argues that the allied invasion of North Africa in 1942 was successful because of security, not deception. Discusses the use of double agents versus security and its relevance in North Africa. Concludes with a discussion of methods for keeping the Spanish in the dark and the contributions of these methods to the success of Operation Torch.

7139. Smyth, Denis. "<u>Our Man in Havana</u>, Their Man in Madrid: Literary Invention in Espionage Fact and Fiction," <u>Intelligence and National Security</u> 5/4 (October 1990): 117-135.

Discusses the prescience of Graham Greene's novel, <u>Our Man in Havana</u>, in relation to the Spanish spy Angel Alcazar de Velasco.

7140. Smyth, Howard M. "The Ciano Papers: Rose Garden," <u>Studies in Intelligence</u> 13/1 (Spring 1969).

Estimated to be 62 pages in length. Lengthy discussion of Galeazzo and Edda Ciano, Benito Mussolini's son-in-law and wife, respectively. Galeazzo was hanged for treason in 1944 while his wife, Edda, escaped to Switzerland. See a recent book by Evan Thomas, <u>The Very Best Men: Four Who Dared: The Early Years of the CIA</u> for a little bit of the Ciano papers story.

7141. Smythe, Donald. "The Ruse at Belfort," <u>Army</u> 22/6 (June 1972): 34-38.

Discusses US intelligence deceptions at St. Mihiel in World War I.

7142. Smythe, Tony. "Britain's Civil Liberties--An Official Secret," <u>Civil Liberties Review</u> 1/1 (Fall 1973): 162-178.

7143. Snider, L. Britt. "The New (And Largely Unappreciated) Legal Framework for U.S. Intelligence," <u>American Intelligence Journal</u> 14/3 (Autumn-Winter 1993-1994): 77-80.

A brief discussion of legal issues relative to intelligence, in particular, the Boren/McCurdy bills; the development of new legislation; and the new statutory framework.

7144. Snow, Edward, J. "Soviet Propaganda and the Neutron Bomb Decision," Political Communication and Persuasion 1/3 (1981): 257-268.

7145. Snowe, Olympia J. "The Moscow Embassy: A Study in Congressional Response to Crisis," Journal of Legislation 16 (1989): 35-46.
Discussion of the complexities surrounding the Soviet penetration of the security of the American embassy in Moscow. Provides an overview of the problem; security problems at the embassy; congressional response; and conclusions. Includes US-USSR agreement on diplomatic security.

7146. Snyder, Frank M. "Command and Control and Uncertainty," Naval War College Review 32/2 (March-April 1979): 109-113.
Two themes are discussed: (1) that command and control helps commanders reduce or resolve uncertainties; (2) that some uncertainties are created by the command and control system.

7147. Snyder, Robert E. "Margaret Bourke-White and the Communist Witch Hunt," Journal of American Studies 19/1 (April 1985): 5-25.
A discussion of Ms. White's experiences as a Time-Life photographer, and the accusations by the FBI that she had engaged in communist activities.

7148. Snyder, Samuel S. "Computer Advances Pioneered by Cryptologic Organizations," Annals of the History of Computing 2/1 (January 1980): 60-70.
Offers a chronology of National Security Agency "firsts" in technology. Discusses early magnetic drum research; Atlas I and II computers; Abner computer; Bogart computer; and others such as Solo, Harvest and Lighting; summary of NSA's impact on the computer industry.

7149. Sobel, David. "The NSA's Clipper Proposal," Covert Action Quarterly 46 (Fall 1993): 50-54..
Discusses the controversy surrounding the National Security Agency's development of a new computer chip known as "Clipper", which the author's suggests is an attempt by the intelligence community "to restrict the development and dissemination of effective civilian cryptography..."

7150. Sobota, Lenore. "Unexploded Bomb: The Progressive (U. S. v. The Progressive, 467 F.Supp. 990) and Prior Restraint," Southern Illinois University Law Journal 1980/2 (June 1980): 199-223.
Examines the constitutionality of the Atomic Energy Act's secrecy provisions in light of the Progressive case. Discusses doctrine of prior restraint.

7151. Sofaer, Abraham D. "Executive Power and the Control of Information: Practice Under the Framers," Duke Law Journal 1977 (March 1977): 1-57.

Outlines the long term problem of freedom of information in the US; the Federalist period and the release of records; information practices under Thomas Jefferson; and secrecy as a tool of expansion as first applied by President Monroe.

7152. Sofokidis, Jeanette H. "A Close Look at the CIA," American Education 4/5 (May 1968): 2-4.

7153. Sohr, Raul. "Un Debate Poco Inteligente Sobre las Actividades de Intengencia," Mensaje 41/409 (June 1992): 201-202.

7154. Sokolski, Henry D. "Fighting Proliferation With Intelligence," Orbis 38/2 (Spring 1994): 245-260.

Discusses proliferation of nuclear weapons; the need to rethink policy and intelligence reasoning; a new paradigm of proliferation; and intelligence requirements.

7155. Sokolski, Henry D. "Will There Be an Arms Trade Intelligence Deficit?," Annals of the American Academy of Political and Social Science 535 (September 1994).

7156. Solarz, Stephen J. "When to Intervene," Foreign Policy 63 (Summer 1986): 20-39.

Considers insurgencies with merit; Cambodian perils; Reagan's real goal; and drawing the line on covert actions.

7157. Soley, Lawrence and Sheila O'Brien. "Clandestine Broadcasting in the Southwest Asian Peninsula," International Communication Bulletin 22 (Spring 1987): 13-19.

Discusses the background of clandestine broadcasting in Europe during World War II then moves up to the 1960s era of the Voice of the People of Thailand, a clandestine station of the Communist Party of Thailand. Also discusses Voice of America operations in Thailand.

7158. Solomon, Joel and Robert Prigo. "Eavesdropping with Laser," American Journal of Physics 55 (April 1987): 381.

7159. Solomon, Kenneth I. "The Short Happy Life of Berger v. New York," Chicago-Kent Law Review 45/2 (Fall-Winter 1968-69): 123-142.

A brief discussion of the eavesdropping issue, suggesting that electronic surveillance is constitutionally acceptable. Acceptance began with the Berger case by defining the limits of police electronic surveillance actions.

7160. Solov'ev, V.   "Zionism--A Weapon of International Imperialism and Aggression," Voenno-Istoricheskiy Zhurnal 12 (December 1983): 44-51.

7161. Solovyov, Vladimir. "Knowing the KGB," Partisan Review 49/2 (1982): 167-183.
    The author reflects upon his ambivalence toward, and his anger with, the Soviet KGB. At one time he was a KGB collaborator.

7162.   Somit,   Albert.   "Theory   and   Practice   of   Insurgency   and Counterinsurgency," Naval War College Review 15 (October 1962): 44-56.

7163. Sommers, Marilyn B. "Law Enforcement Intelligence: A New Look," International Journal of Intelligence and Counterintelligence 1/3 (Fall 1986): 25-40.
    Offers three forms of law enforcement analyses: crime, investigative, and strategic. Discusses each type of analysis and concludes that the most useful insights come from strategic analysis.

7164. Sondermann, Fred A. "The Concept of National Interest," Orbis 21/1 (Spring 1977): 121-138.
    An analysis of the perplexing concept of national interest. Particularly useful in discussions of covert action and clandestine collection.

7165. Sonnenfeldt, Helmut. "Implications of the Soviet Invasion of Afghanistan for East-West Relations," Atlantic Community Quarterly 18/2 (Spring 1980): 184-192.
    Discusses defensive motivations; the effect of detente; the constant effort required; and the dangerous occurrence in 1968. Reprinted from NATO Review 2 (1980).

7166. Soper, Karl. "Getting Serious About Restructuring Intelligence," Naval Intelligence Professionals Quarterly 12/1 (Winter 1996): 1-3.

7167.   Sorkin, Michael. "The FBI's Big Brother Computer," Washington Monthly 4/7 (September 1972): 24-30.
    Asks whether Congress will look the other way when it allows continuation of the national data bank of FBI's dreams. Argues for controls on FBI records.

7168. Soto, Pedro J. "Fiction or Reality: Testimony of an Author in Crisis," Caribbean Review 9/3 (Summer 1980): 15, 45.

7169. Souers, Sidney W. "Policy Formulation for National Security," American Political Science Review 43/3 (June 1949): 534-543.

An outline of the origins of the National Security Council as an instrument of foreign policy. Major sections discuss the background of the NSC; Council composition; problems of the Council; and policy development.

7170. Soyster, Harry E. "The Changing Nature of the American Spy," <u>American Journal of Intelligence</u> 10/2 (Summer-Fall 1989): 29-32.

A discussion of the eras and personalties involved with traitorous behavior.

7171. Sparks, David S. "General Patrick's Progress: Intelligence and Security in the Army of the Potomac," <u>Civil War History</u> 10/4 (December 1964): 371-384.

Discussion of Civil War intelligence organization under General Patrick; effectiveness of Patrick's organization; how Patrick's brigade joined with General Pope; Patrick's reassignment; conflict with other intelligence organizations; Patrick's proudest moment and the end of his career.

7172. Sparks, Kenneth R. "Selling Uncle Sam in the Seventies," <u>Annals of the American Academy of Political and Social Sciences</u> 398 (November 1971): 113-123.

A discussion of problems within the US Information Agency and the need to reorganize US propaganda efforts.

7173. Sparrow, Elizabeth. "The Alien Office, 1792-1806," <u>Historical Journal</u> 33/2 (June 1990): 361-384.

Discussion of the direction of secret agents from the British Alien Office, the first administrative office for the British secret service between 1793 and 1806.

7174. Sparrow, Elizabeth. "The Swiss and Swabian Agencies, 1795-1801," <u>Historical Journal</u> 35/4 (December 1992): 861-884.

Considers the British organization aimed at conducting covert financial bribery of the Swiss government. Also discusses French infiltration, controlled mainly by the British.

7175. Sparrow, Malcolm K. "Network Vulnerabilities and Strategic Intelligence in Law Enforcement," <u>International Journal of Intelligence and Counterintelligence</u> 5/3 (Fall 1991): 255-274.

Major sections discuss the need for strategic analysis; relevance of network analysis; link analysis; structural analysis; network vulnerabilities; applications of centrality; role equivalence and applications; weak ties; and characteristics of criminal networks.

7176. Specht, Max H. "Forward Interrogation," <u>Infantry Journal</u> 54 (January 1944): 14-16.

Experiences of an intelligence officer with prisoner interrogation in North Africa during World War II.

7177. Spector, Leonard S. "Strategic Warning and New Nuclear States," <u>Defense Intelligence Journal</u> 3/1 (Spring 1994): 33-52.

Discusses the history and expansion of nuclear proliferation; the changed proliferation context; and states which appear from intelligence reports to suggest new proliferation concerns.

7178. Spector, Robert D. "Irony As Theme: Conrad's 'The Secret Agent'," <u>Nineteenth-Century Fiction</u> 13/1 (1958): 69-71.

7179. Spector, Ronald H. "The Twilight of the Secret Agent," <u>Armed Forces and Society</u> 7/2 (Summer 1981): 657-660.

7180. Spector, Ronald H. "Allied Intelligence and Indochina, 1943-1945," <u>Pacific Historical Review</u> 51/1 (February 1982): 23-51.

Discusses the role of intelligence activities in advising President Roosevelt of the situation in Vietnam in relation to the Japanese war effort.

7181. Spector, Ronald H. "Does Intelligence Make Any Difference?," <u>Reviews in American History</u> 14/3 (September 1986): 449-453.

A review essay concerned with Ernest R. May's edited studies, <u>Knowing One's Enemies: Intelligence Assessment Before the Two World Wars</u> (Princeton, 1985). Author suggests that historians have been slow in coming to appreciate intelligence information as relevant to larger studies.

7182. Speer, Paul D., Jr. "Iceland or Bust," <u>Naval Intelligence Professionals Quarterly</u> 5/2 (1989): 16-17.

7183. Speers, Michael F. "A Biased State," <u>Intelligence Quarterly</u> 3/2 (1987): 1-4.

7184. Speers, Michael F. "Trouble in Intensive Care," <u>Intelligence Quarterly</u> 4/3 (1989): 1-6.

An account of activities of a foundation that aids defector resettlement.

7185. Speers, Michael F. and Nigel West. "Conspiracy Buffs Unite: Epstein vs. Shevchenko," <u>Intelligence Quarterly</u> 1 (October 1985): 1-2.

7186. Speier, Hans. "Treachery in War," <u>Social Research</u> 51/1-2 (Spring-Summer 1984): 243-265.

An extensive analysis of the transition in the role of espionage and treason in the evolution of limited warfare to total wars.

7187. Speigel, Steven L. "Israel As the Strategist Asset," Commentary 75/6 (1983): 51-55.

7188. Spell, Lota M. "The Anglo-Saxon Press in Mexico, 1846-1848," American Historical Review 38 (October 1932): 20-31.

7189. Spence, Richard B. "Sidney Reilly in America, 1914-1917," Intelligence and National Security 10/1 (January 1995): 92-121.

An account of the mysterious travels of Sidney Reilly, especially Reilly's connections with several US business interests with stakes in the economic gains from european warfare. Concludes that Reilly was driven mainly by pride and vindictiveness, but he was an effective secret agent with a crooked and rotten side.

7190. Spencer, Jack H. "Brigades on Line," Military Intelligence 15/4 (1989): 11-13.

A very brief discussion of military intelligence operations in Germany.

7191. Spenser, Jay P. "The Flight Against Evil," Air & Space/Smithsonian 2/5 (1987-88): 74-82.

7192. Sperry, F. M. "Strategic Intelligence--an Introduction," Military Review 27/7 (October 1947): 16-22.

7193. Spetrino, David A. "AIDS Disinformation," Studies in Intelligence 32/4 (Winter 1988).

7194. Spex, Milton. "How to Steal Government Secrets," Washington Monthly 10/11 (February 1979): 54-60.

Weaknesses in defense contractor security programs are pointed out.

7195. Spicer, Prescott M. "Tactical Reconnaissance for Atomic Commanders," Air University Review 8/4 (Fall 1956): 39-50.

7196. Spiegel, Andrew B. "Putting Human Rights Into Your Private Practice," Human Rights 10 (Winter 1982): 38-39, 43-45, 48.

Reflects upon the adequacy of regulatory oversight and law in connection with CIA and FBI surveillance practices. Discusses Reagan administration policies with respect to policy on spying and the handling of classified documents.

7197. Spiegel, Steven L. "U.S. Relations with Israel: The Military Benefits," Orbis 30/3 (1986): 475-497.

7198. Spiller, Roger J. "Some Implications of ULTRA," Military Affairs 40/2 (April 1976): 49-53.

Addresses several basic questions regarding the effectiveness of the ULTRA operations during World War II, such as the impact on the progress of the war and the value to the British Expeditionary Force in the Battle of France.

7199. Spiller, Roger J. "Assessing Ultra," Military Review 59/8 (August 1979): 13-23.

Discusses the role of ULTRA in the outcome of the Second World War, and calls for reassessment of historical findings.

7200. Spillman, Richard. "Cryptanalysis of Knapsack Ciphers Using Genetic Algorithms," Cryptologia 17/4 (October 1993): 367-377.

7201. Spillman Richard; Mark Janssen; Bob Nelson; and Martin Kepner. "Use of a Genetic Algorithm in the Cryptanalysis of Simple Substitution Ciphers," Cryptologia 17/1 (January 1993): 31-44.

7202. Spirito, Leonard A. and Marc B. Powe. "Military Intelligence: A Fight for Identity," Army 26 (May 1976): 14-21.

7203. Spjut, R. J. "Defining Subversion," British Journal of Law and Society 6 (Winter 1979): 254-261.

A brief discussion of subversion in British constitutional law; the threat to the state; and conclusions.

7204. Spritzer, Ralph S. "Electronic Surveillance By Leave of the Magistrate: The Case in Opposition," University of Pennsylvania Law Review 118/2 (December 1969): 169-201.

Discusses the law of electronic surveillance from the Olmstead case forward. Major sections discuss the transition from trespass to electronic invasion; the contributions of Katz v. U. S.; the role of Congress; seizures of tangible objects and incriminatory statements; and in security and foreign intelligence.

7205. Squires, J. Duane. "Aeronautics in the Civil War," American Historical Review 42/4 (July 1937): 652-669.

A discussion of the purposes of balloons in the Civil War. Includes brief background on the architect of ballooning the War and the significance of balloons in the general advance of the technology of military operations.

7206. Staar, Richard F. "The High-Tech Transfer Offensive of the Soviet Union," Strategic Review 17 (Spring 1989): 32-39.

7207. Stacy, Thomas G. "The Constitution in Conflict: Espionage Prosecutions, the Right to Present a Defense, and the State Secrets Privilege," University of Colorado Law Review 58/2 (Spring 1987): 177-254.

Examines and criticizes the attempt in the Richard Craig Smith espionage case to resolve the issue of classified document access by statutory or common law. Also discusses standards which must be applied in espionage cases by the government or the defendant.

7208. Stacy, William R. "Matter of Fact, Matter of Law, and the Attainder of the Earl of Strafford," American Journal of Legal History 29/4 (October 1985): 323-348.

Reflects upon the arguments for and against the outcome of a classic treason case involving the Earl of Strafford in 17th century Britain. Argues that both law and the administration of justice remain subject to criticism as to the outcome.

7209. Stacy, William R. "Richard Noose and the Use of Parliamentary Attainder in the Reign of Henry VIII," Historical Journal 29 (March 1986): 1-15.

Henry VIII and his ministers used parliamentary attainder to destroy their political enemies and to deny enemies all due process.

7210. Stafford, David A. T. "The Detonator Concept: British Strategy, SOE and European Resistance After the Fall of France," Journal of Contemporary History 10/2 (April 1975): 185-217.

Considers the origins of Britain's entrance into the war with Germany in 1939, and the advancements of secret service organizations in furtherance of Britain's interests from 1939-1941.

7211. Stafford, David A. T. "Britain Looks at Europe, 1940: Some Origins of S.O.E.," Annales: Canadian Journal of History 10/2 (August 1975): 231-248.

Focusses on the British Special Operations Executive organization as a representative symbol of British attitudes towards Europe after the fall of France in 1940.

7212. Stafford, David A. T. "SOE and British Involvement in the Belgrade Coup d'Etat of March 1941," Slavic Review 36/3 (September 1977): 399-419.

An extensive discussion of British intelligence operations in the Balkans in the late 1940s.

7213. Stafford, David A. T. "'Ultra' and the British Official Histories: A Documentary Note," Military Affairs 42 (February 1978): 29-31.

A brief commentary on the public release of documents pertaining to the 'Ultra' communications of World War II. The first documents were released in 1977.

7214. Stafford, David A. T. "Spies and Gentlemen: The Birth of the British Spy Novel, 1893-1914," Victorian Studies 24/4 (Summer 1981): 489-509.

A detailed accounting of the emergence of the British spy novel against the backdrop of numerous intrigues and cases of espionage in Europe in the 1890s.

7215. Stafford, David A. "Conspiracy and Xenophobia: The Popular Spy Novels of William le Queux, 1893-1914," Europa-Archiv 3/3 (1982): 163-185.

7216. Stafford, David A. "John Buchan's Tales of Espionage: A Popular Archive of British History," Annales: Canadian Journal of History 18/1 (April 1983): 1-21.
　　　Discusses Richard Hannay as secret agent in Buchan's spy novels.

7217. Stafford, David A. "'Intrepid': Myth and Reality," Journal of Contemporary History 22/2 (April 1987): 303-317.
　　　Discusses the role and activities of Sir William Stephenson, a British spy during World War II.

7218. Stafford, David A. "The Fantasies Behind the Door: In Search of Stasi," Queen's Quarterly 100/2 (Summer 1993): 357-370.
　　　Reflects the author's visit to the files of the former East German secret police, the Stasi. Suggests that the files reveal many indicators of a regime that operated on surveillance and intrigue, now eliminated by the joining of the former two Germanies.

7219. Stafford, Debra D. "'Secret Trials': A Defense Perspective," Army Lawyer (April 1988): 24-35.

7220. Stafford, Edward P. "I'm Sorry, Monsieur, But We Cannot Trust the U.S. Government," U.S. Naval Institute Proceedings 106 (July 1980): 104-106.

7221. Stanchfield, John B. "The Peril of Espionage," North American Review 203 (June 1916): 830-840.
　　　An argument for increasing defenses against espionage in the US during World War I.

7222. Stanford, Norman. "Shadows in the Night," Marine Corps Gazette 47 (February 1963): 44-48.
　　　The role of rumors in warfare is given brief account.

7223. Stanford, Phil. "Watergate Revisited," Columbia Journalism Review 24 (March-April 1986): 46-49.
　　　According to Jim Hougan's book, Secret Agenda, the CIA planted Hung, McCord (both ex-CIA personnel) to spy on sexual activities in the White House. It charges that the break-in was a sabotaged operation designed to uncover a

call-girl ring. Draws on FBI documents which state that no bugs were found at Watergate.

7224. Stanislav, Jan. "Military and Political Questions Concerning the Allies' Assistance in Preparing an Uprising on Czech and Slovak Territory, 1942-44: The Beginning of the Slovak National Uprising," Historicky Casopis 41/2 (1993): 143-160.

7225. Stanley, Gerald. "Justice Deferred: A Fifty-Year Perspective on Japanese-Internment Historiography," Southern California Quarterly 74/2 (1992): 181-206.

7226. Stanley, Richard L. "Intelligence Preparation of the Battlefield--A Systematic Approach," American Intelligence Journal 7/3 (January 1986).

7227. Stanton, George. "Defense Against Communist Interrogation Organizations," Studies in Intelligence 13/3 (Fall 1969): 49-74.
    Major sections discuss the importance of techniques of preparation; handling the arrest process; the interrogation; some general rules; combatting environmental influences; combatting arguments; warning; coping with interrogator tricks; propaganda exploitation; and penitentiary, escape, and release.

7228. Stanton, Michael. "The Secret Sentinels: Careers in Intelligence," Occupational Outlook Quarterly 29 (Fall 1985): 2-14.

7229. Stares, Paul B. "Space and U.S. National Security," Journal of Strategic Studies 6/4 (December 1983): 31-48.
    Discusses the impact and benefits of developments and growth of the US military space program as part of national defense.

7230. Stares, Paul B. "New Trends in Satellite Reconnaissance," Defense Analysis 3/2 (June 1987): 180-181.
    A brief observation of the new role of reconnaissance satellites as part of the warfighting capabilities of the US and the Soviet Union. Suggests that the new role may alienate widespread acceptance of satellites.

7231. Starnes, John. "Canadian Internal Security: The Need for a New Approach, a New Organization," Canadian Defense Quarterly 9/1 (Summer 1979): 21-26.

7232. Starnes, John. "Canadian Security: Counter-intelligence," International Perspectives (September-October 1984): 23-26.
    Argues that the Canadian Security Intelligence Service was created to prevent Soviet exploitation of Canada's free society.

7233. Starnes, John. "A Canadian Secret Intelligence Service?," International Perspectives: A Canadian Journal of World Affairs (July-August 1987): 6-9.

7234. Starnes, John. "Why I Write Spy Fiction," Intelligence and National Security 5/4 (October 1990): 204-211.
The author explores the development of his interest in spy novels, later publishing five novels, some of which reflected his experience in the Canadian Intelligence Corps.

7235. Starr, Frederick S. "Mapping Ancient Roads in Anatolia," Archaeology 16 (1963): 162-169.

7236. Starr, Richard F. "The Warsaw Treaty Organization," Current History 86/523 (November 1987): 357-360, 387-389.
Discusses the internal intrigues between the Warsaw Treaty Organization and the Soviet Union, suggesting that the Soviets often undermine the work of the WTO, sometimes through espionage and the exploitation of ethnic factors.

7237. Starunin, A. I. "Operational Surprise," Voennaia Mysl 3 (March 1941): 27-35.
In Russian, discusses Germany's surprise attacks in Poland and France.

7238. Stavrianos, Lefton S. "The Greek National Liberation Front (EAM): A Study in Resistance Organization and Administration," Journal of Modern History 24/1 (1952): 42-55.

7239. St. Clair, Diane. "Bibliography on Repression," Black Scholar 12/1 (1981): 85-90.
Among numerous topics listed are titles pertaining to domestic intelligence capers against radical groups in the 1960s.

7240. Stead, Philip J. "The Roman Police," Police Studies 6/4 (Winter 1983-84): 3-7.

7241. Steadman, Michael J. "Industrial Espionage: What You Don't Know Can Hurt You," Business and Society Review 76 (Winter 1991): 25-32.
Discussion of business intelligence methods conducted by foreign governments and foreign companies against US firms.

7242. Stearns, Richard G. and W. Dennis Shaul. "Modern Dilemma: Two Views of the NSA-CIA Crisis by Present and Former NSA Officers," Mademoiselle 65 (August 1967): 232-233+.
A popular press article, not generally considered scholarship. However, the content is useful and reasonably credible for research and publication purposes.

7243. Stebbins, Robert A. "Putting People On: Deception of Our Fellowman in Everyday Life," Sociology and Social Research 59/3 (April 1975): 189-200.

Addresses the general nature of interpersonal deception from the perspective of social psychology.

7244. Stech, Frank J. "Self-Deception: The Other Side of the Coin," Washington Quarterly 3/3 (Summer 1980): 130-140.

Reviews and challenges the theory of Roberta Wohlstetter concerning the signals-noise problem in deception analysis and warfare. The author's main concern is for the problem of "fearful thinking."

7245. Steed, H. Wickham. "Aerial Warfare: Secret German Plans," Nineteenth Century and After 116/7 (1934): 1-16.

This is a two-part article on the subject. Part II is found in 116/9 (1934): 331-339.

7246. Steele, George P. "Warnings from the South Atlantic," Orbis 26/3 (Fall 1982): 573-578.

Reaffirmation of the role of British intelligence in the 1982 Falklands war is part of this brief summary.

7247. Steele, Lisa J. "Waste Heat and Garbage: The Legalization of Warrantless Infrared Searches," Criminal Law Bulletin 29 (January-February 1993): 19-39.

Inquires into the use of infrared sensors to locate enclosed greenhouses use to grow and process illegal narcotics. Analyses U. S. v. Penny-Feeney and asks whether warrantless infrared searches are constitutional under the Fourth Amendment.

7248. Steele, Richard W. "The Pulse of the People: Franklin D. Roosevelt and the Gauging of American Public Opinion," Journal of Contemporary History 9/4 (October 1974): 195-216.

Discusses Roosevelt's sensitivity to public opinion and the methods he used to gather information about the public mood.

7249. Steele, Richard W. "Franklin D. Roosevelt and His Foreign Policy Critics," Political Science Quarterly 94/1 (Spring 1979): 15-32.

Major topics discuss the small groups of selfish men; the isolationist "fifth column"; manipulation of the media; FDR and wartime dissent; and conclusions.

7250. Steele, Richard W. "Fear of the Mob and Faith in Government in Free Speech Discourse, 1919-1941," American Journal of Legal History 38/1 (January 1994): 55-83.

Discusses the expansion of the free speech movement after World War

I and the subsequent concerns for free speech in the 1930s rise of fascism. Mentions the Roosevelt administration's efforts in the late 1930s to control the weapons of counter-subversion. Mentions the FBI in this context.

7251. Steele, Robert D. "Intelligence in the 1990's: Recasting National Security in a Changing World," American Intelligence Journal 11/3 (Summer-Fall 1990): 29-36.

Discusses the changing nature of international threats in terms of six challenges to national security in the 1990s: meeting needs of public programs; indications and warnings of revolutionary change; new theory and methods of counterintelligence; developing an information technology strategy; establishing a responsive requirements system; and realigning resources in an era of change.

7252. Steele, Robert D. "Applying the 'New Paradigm': How to Avoid Strategic Intelligence Failures in the Future," American Intelligence Journal 12/3 (Autumn 1991): 43-46.

Discusses the sins of strategic intelligence, the relationship between intelligence analysts and policy makers, and the relationship between defense intelligence and "national knowledge management."

7253. Steele, Robert D. "Intelligence Support to Expeditionary Planners," Marine Corps Gazette 95 (September 1991).

7254. Steele, Robert D. "The National Security Act of 1992," American Intelligence Journal 13/1&2 (Winter-Spring 1992): 31-37.

Summary of the provisions of the Boren/McCurdy bills in the Senate and House. Outlines the components of the bills in terms of organizational proposals, analysis initiatives, human intelligence initiatives, DOD departmental initiatives, defense agency initiatives, and operational adjustments.

7255. Steele, Robert D. "A Critical Evaluation of U.S. National Intelligence Capabilities," International Journal of Intelligence and Counterintelligence 6/2 (Summer 1993): 173-194.

Sections discuss evaluation of strategic and operational intelligence capabilities; tactical and technical capabilities; and US intelligence analysis process.

7256. Steele, Robert D. "National Intelligence and Open Source: From School House to White House," American Intelligence Journal 14/2&3 (Spring-Summer 1993): 29-32.

Discussion of the new role and applications of open source intelligence. Argues for the creation of four new capabilities within the executive branch: a Center for the Exploitation of of Open Sources; National Knowledge Foundation; Office of Multi-Special Imagery; and National Open Source Architecture.

7257. Steele, Robert D. "ACCESS: The Theory and Practice of Competitor Intelligence," Journal of the Association for Global Strategic Information (July 1994).

7258. Steele, Robert D. "Reinventing Intelligence: Holy Grail or Mission Impossible?," International Journal of Intelligence and Counterintelligence 7/2 (Summer 1994): 199-203.

Summarizes the author's various earlier suggestions for improving intelligence collection and analysis, and a more current statement of where the community should go in the future.

7259. Steele, Robert D. "The Importance of Open Source Intelligence to the Military," International Journal of Intelligence and Counterintelligence 8/4 (Winter 1995): 457-470.

Argues that OSCINT is a force multiplier. Major sections discuss open source applications in the military; the information continuum; national approaches to OSCINT; advantages and disadvantages; obstacles to military exploitation of open sources; opportunities for advantages; and the role of the military reserve.

7260. Steele, Robert D. "Private Enterprise Intelligence: Its Potential Contribution to National Security," Intelligence and National Security 10/4 (October 1995): 212-228.

Argues that in the near future the private sector will be doing most of the espionage and gathering of open source intelligence (OSCINT). Discusses OSCINT and the changing threat; OSCINT and the consumer; OSCINT and the changing definitions of national security; and conclusions.

7261. Stehlin, Stewart. "Germany and a Proposed Vatican State, 1915-1917," Catholic Historical Review 60 (October 1974): 400-415.

7262. Steigerwalt, A. K. "The NAM and the Congressional Investigations of 1913: A Case Study in the Suppression of Evidence," Business History Review 34/3 (1960): 335-344.

A brief segment in the history of the National Association of Manufacturers and links with federal agent.

7263. Stein, Arthur S. "When Misperception Matters," World Politics 34/4 (July 1982): 502-526.

A first step toward a theory of misperception. Focusses on the actor's misperception of another's intentions. Concludes that misperception does not always affect an actor's choices or determine the outcome.

7264. Stein, J. "Honorable Men," Progressive 44 (September 1980): 14-15.

7265. Stein, J. "Moles," Progressive 45 (April 1981): 12-13.

A brief discussion of newspaper accounts in the matter of S. R. Weissman's suit against the C.I.A.

7266. Stein, J. "Campus Hijinks," Progressive 45 (September 1981): 14-15.

Commentary on the Max Hugel-William Casey connection for business dealings and the politics of the C.I.A.

7267. Stein, J. "Naming Names," Progressive 45 (December 1981): 14.

What can result from identifying intelligence officer names.

7268. Stein, Janice G. "'Intelligence' and 'Stupidity' Reconsidered: Estimation and Decision in Israel, 1973," Journal of Strategic Studies 3/2 (September 1980): 147-177.

Contains topical headings: fooling the intelligent; the logic of strategic argument; deterrence, defense and miscalculated escalation; estimation and decision; intelligence and stupidity reconsidered.

7269. Stein, Janice G. "Military Deception, Strategic Surprise, and Conventional Deterrence: A Political Analysis of Egypt and Israel, 1971-73," Journal of Strategic Studies 5/1 (March 1982): 94-121.

Discussion of the Egyptian plans to invade Israel on two occasions before the 1973 war and Israeli intelligence analysis on Egyptian capabilities.

7270. Stein, Janice G. "The 1973 Intelligence Failure: A Reconsideration," Jerusalem Quarterly 24 (Summer 1982): 41-54.

Discusses three Israeli intelligence estimates, followed by a wider discussion of the principal explanations of surprise. Concludes that the limits of the intelligence process are the principal obstacles to accurate and timely warning.

7271. Stein, Janice G. "Building Politics into Psychology: The Misperception of Threat," Political Psychology 9/2 (June 1988): 245-268.

Argues for including considerations of politics into the overall assessment of threat perceptions in international conflicts. Major sections consider errors as they are treated as mediating variables; and the impact of political and strategic variables.

7272. Stein, Janice G. "Intelligence and Political Leadership in Israel," Queen's Quarterly 100/2 (Summer 1993): 407-414.

A book review essay of two books: Israel's Secret Service by Ian Black and Benny Morris; and Every Spy a Prince by Dan Raviv and Yossi Melman. Considerations of the successes and failures of Israeli intelligence services are offered.

7273. Stein, Janice G. and Michael Brecher. "Image, Advocacy and the Analysis of Conflict: An Israeli Case Study," Jerusalem Journal of International Relations 1 (Spring 1976): 33-58.

7274. Stein, Ralph M. "Laird v. Tatum: The Supreme Court and a First Amendment Challenge of Military Surveillance of Lawful Civilian Political Activity," Hofstra Law Review 1 (1973): 244-275.
    Explores issue in Laird and considers possible Supreme Court error in the matter of denial of testimony by political activists; whether military surveillance abridged First Amendment rights; and the implications of Laird in future challenges to government surveillance.

7275. Steinbach, Peter. "The Red Orchestra: Fifty Years Afterward," Zeitschrift fuer Geschichtswissenschaft 41/9 (1993): 771-780.

7276. Steinberg, Blema S. "Goals in Conflict: Escalation, Cuba, 1961," Canadian Journal of Political Science 14/1 (1981): 83-105.
    Discusses United States and Soviet Union steps in the escalation of the Cuban missile crisis of 1962. An excellent piece for those who wish to research the relationship between perceptions, intelligence and international conflict.

7277. Steinberg, Gerald. "The Ultimate Battleground: Weapons in Space," Technology Review (October 1981).

7278. Steinberg, Julien. "The Case of the Nervous Spy," American Mercury 72 (June 1951): 706-717.
    Discusses the Soviet espionage work of Andrei Schevchenko. This is part III of four parts published before and after this issue. Generally considered a popular press publication.

7279. Steinberg, Leonard. "Covert Wars and Presidential Power: Judicial Complicity in a Realignment of Constitutional Power. (Symposium: the Bicentennial of the Constitution) Crockett v. Reagan-720 F.2d 1355 (D.C. Cir. 1983); Sanchez-Espinoza v. Reagan-770 F.2d 202 (D.C. Circ. 1985)," Hastings Constitutional Law Quarterly 14 (Spring 1987): 683-714.
    Examines the constitutional allocation of war and war-related foreign policy powers, and judicial complicity in increasing the concentration of power in the presidency. Reviews cases of foreign and military intervention in Central America; discusses relevant constitutional law; procedural mechanisms used by the judiciary; and applications of law to Central American cases.

7280. Steinberg, Steve. "A Student's View of Cryptography in Computer Science," Communications of the ACM 34 (February 1991): 15-17.

7281. Steiner, Barry H. "Policy Organization in American Security Affairs: An Assessment," Public Administration Review (July-August 1977): 357-367.

7282. Steiner, Barry H. "American Intelligence and the Soviet ICBM Build-up: Another Look," Intelligence and National Security 8/2 (April 1993): 172-198.
     Reexamines a series of errors in the National Intelligence Estimates (NIE's) which projected military forces of the Soviet Union quantitatively five years into the future. Considers the implications of force estimations for the current stage of cooperation between Russia and the US.

7283. Steiner, James E. "Disguised Inflation in Soviet Industry: A Rejoinder," Journal of Comparative Economics 7/4 (December 1983): 449-451.
     The author has attempted to convince another analyst that the USSR economy contains a factor of disguised inflation, owed mainly to the machine-building and metalworking industries.

7284. Steiner, James E. and Franklyn D. Holzman. "CIA Estimates of Soviet Military Spending," International Security 14/4 (Spring 1990): 185-198.
     A debate by correspondence with the journal over the respective methods of each author in estimating Soviet defense spending. A useful colloquy on the subject.

7285. Steinhaus, Richard Z. "Treason, A Brief History with Some Modern Applications," Brooklyn Law Review 22 (1956): 254-277.
     Reflects upon the origins of the law of treason from the Roman era, the English Treason Act of 1351 and applications in World Wars I and II. Discusses the legal concerns for allegiance, jurisdiction and venue, overt acts, problems of the prosecution, and conclusions.

7286. Steinhauser, Thomas C. "A Winning Team: How the NMCC Works," Armed Forces Journal 109 (May 1972): 48-49.
     A brief description of the National Military Command Center.

7287. Steinhauser, Thomas C. "In Support of a Stronger U.S. Military Intelligence Community," Signal 39 (September 1989): 21-22.

7288. Steinitz, Mark S. "The U.S. Propaganda Effort in Czechoslovakia, 1945-48," Diplomatic History 6/4 (Fall 1982): 359-386.
     Explores the wartime Office of War Information (OWI) and its post-war successor, the US Information Service.

7289. Steinwall, Susan D. "Appraisal and the FBI Files Case: For Whom Do Archivists Retain Records?," American Archivist 49/1 (1986): 52-63.
     Discusses the attempts of activists and social scientists to obtain valuable

historical papers from the FBI before FBI destroyed them simply because the agency deemed them non-valuable.

7290. Stella, Tomas. "Cerro Maravilla: Injustice in Puerto Rico," Caribbean Review 9/3 (Summer 1980): 12-15, 44-45.

7291. Stenberg, Richard R. "President Polk and the Annexation of Texas," Southwestern Social Science Quarterly 14/4 (March 1934): 333-356.
   A detailed account of President James Polk's methods of achieving annexation of Texas in 1845, including the role of American secret agents.

7292. Stenberg, Richard R. "The Failure of Polk's War Intrigue of 1845," Pacific Historical Review 4/1 (March 1935): 39-69.
   A detailed consideration of covert actions conducted by Polk in the seizure of Texas lands down to the Rio Grande River.

7293. Stenberg, Richard R. "President Jackson and Anthony Butler," Southwest Review 22 (July 1937).

7294. Stenberg, Richard R. "Polk and Fremont, 1845-1846," Pacific Historical Review 7/1 (September 1937).

7295. Stenberg, Richard R. "President Polk and California: Additional Documents," Pacific Historical Review 10/2 (June 1941).

7296. Stengers, Jean. "La Guerre des Messages Codes, 1930-1945," Histoire 31 & 33 (February & April 1981): 19-31; 100-101.

7297. Stengers, Jean. "Une Histoire Des Services De Renseignements Britanniques," Revue Belge de Philologie et d'Histoire 65/4 (1987): 826-842.
   French observations of the history of British intelligence organizations.

7298. Stenning, Philip C. "Some Reflections on Accountability in the Ministry of the Solicitor General of Canada," Optimum, The Journal of Public Sector Management 24/2 (Fall 1993).

7299. Stenseth, D. "The New Russia: CIS and the Future," Security Dialogue 23/3 (September 1992): 19-26.

7300. Stephan, Paul B., III. "The Central Intelligence Agency: Present Authority and Proposed Legislative Change," Virginia Law Review 62/2 (March 1976): 332-383.
   Explores the history of Central Intelligence Agency's legal authority and examines restrictions on its activities within the US in light of President Ford's

domestic intelligence executive order; also examines CIA's authority to conduct foreign activities.

7301. Stephan, Robert W. "Smersh: Soviet Military Counterintelligence during the Second World War," Journal of Contemporary History 22/4 (October 1987): 585-614.

A comprehensive review of the evolution of SMERSH, a Soviet intelligence and counterintelligence unit, and its role in the contemporary Soviet military hierarchy. Uses US Army declassified files of intelligence reports on Soviet counterintelligence activities in World War II.

7302. Stephens, Thomas W. "Bureaucracy, Intelligence, and Technology: A Reappraisal," World Affairs 139/3 (Winter 1976-1977): 231-243.

A rich explanation of the role and limits of technology in the intelligence decision making process. Useful in studies of the organization of intelligence agencies and the conditions of secrecy management which dominate decision processes.

7303. Stephenson, Orlando W. "The Supply of Gunpowder in 1776," American Historical Review 30/2 (January 1925): 271-281.

7304. Stepniak, S. "The Dynamite Scares and Anarchy," New Review 6 (1892): 530-535.

7305. Sterling, David L. "In Defense of Debs: The Lawyers and the Espionage Case," Indiana Magazine of History 83/1 (March 1987): 17-42.

A focus on the defense strategies in the case of Eugene Debs, notorious radical of the early twentieth century.

7306. Stern, David S. "Covert Intervention and Third World Ideas," Proceedings of the American Society of International Law 69 (1975): 200-216.

Comments regarding a panel discussion on covert actions, including views of the CIA role by Robert Borosage and Tom Farer.

7307. Stern, E. "Information Management and the Whiskey on the Rocks Crisis," Cooperation & Conflict: Nordic Journal of International Politics 27/1 (March 1992): 45-96.

Evaluates the role of information in crisis situations in relationship to the case of the "Whiskey on the Rocks" crisis in 1981.

7308. Stern, Laurence. "The Daniel Schorr Affair: A Morality Play for the Fourth Estate," (and reply by Schorr) Columbia Journalism Review 15 (May and July 1976): 20-25; 48-49.

A journalistic commentary concerning Schorr's leak of the Pike Report to the Village Voice editor Clay Falker. Discusses, in part, the potential that Congress had for a legal case against Schorr. Schorr's reply followed.

7309. Stern, Philip. "The Loyalty Program: A Case for Termination," Washington Monthly 1/10 (November 1969): 32-41.
   Argues for elimination of the federal government's loyalty and security program, suggesting that the program has deeply invaded personal privacy.

7310. Stern, Robert L. "The Rosenberg Case in Perspective -- Its Present Significance," Journal of Supreme Court History (1990): 79-92.
   Consideration of various legal issues in the espionage case of Ethel and Julius Rosenberg, Rosenberg v. U. S., 73 S.Ct. 1152.

7311. Stern, Sol. "A Short Account of International Student Politics and the Cold War with Particular Reference to the NSA, CIA, Etc.," Ramparts 5 (March 1967): 29-38.
   The title of this piece provides outline of contents. Article was reprinted in Ramparts 7 (1969): 87-97.

7312. Stern, W. B. "'Exterior Treason': A Study in Comparative Criminal Law," University of Chicago Law Review 6 (December 1938): 77-91.
   Reviews the laws of treason in comparative context between Continental European statutes and Anglo-American law.

7313. Sternat, Christian M. "Assassination as a Means of Intervention: The Death of Lumumba--The Rule of Amin," Case Western Reserve Journal of International Law 10/1 (Winter 1978): 197-221.
   Observes the background of Patrice Lumumba, US assassination plans including the CIA role, moral action and rationalization, assassination and international law, treaty applications, Idi Amin Dada, signs of Amin's misrule and rationale for elimination, conclusions.

7314. Sternberg, Richard H. "Covert Entry in Electronic Surveillance: The Fourth Amendment Requirements," Fordham Law Review 47 (November 1978): 203-222.
   Contends that there are three Fourth Amendment requirements for covert entry in addition to requirements pertaining to surveillance itself. Reviews the reasonableness requirement; probable cause and presearch justification of reasonableness; express warrant authorization for covert entry; and conclusions.

7315. Steury, Donald P. "Naval Intelligence, the Atlantic Campaign and the Sinking of the Bismarck: A Study in the Integration of Intelligence into the Conduct of Naval Warfare," Journal of Contemporary History 22/2 (April 1987): 209-233.

Argues that sinking the Bismarck resulted from a combination of a German command factors and a British intelligence success. Apparently German naval intelligence centers were not intended for sustained naval confrontation.

7316. Stevens, Guy. "Microdot Images in History, Espionage and Technology," Photographic Journal 128 (June 1988): 256-262.
     Discusses the role of microphotography in intelligence gathering.

7317. Stevens, Halbert F. "Information Dominance: The New High Ground," Defense Intelligence Journal 5/1 (Spring 1996): 43-52.

7318. Stevens, Jennie A. and Henry A. Marsh. "Surprise and Deception in Soviet Military Thought" (Parts I and II), Military Review 62/6 & 7 (June and July 1982): 2-11; 24-35.
     Discusses Soviet deception strategies as vehicles for surprise attack. Discusses and evaluates four categories of Soviet deception and their applications.

7319. Stevens, John A. "Benedict Arnold and His Apologist," Magazine of American History 9/3 (March 1880): 181-191.

7320. Stevens, J. W. and D. W. MacKenna. "Assignment and Coordination of Tactical Units," FBI Law Enforcement Bulletin 58/3 (March 1989): 2-9.
     Survey findings regarding the application of tactical units in local police departments, including a review of other assignments carried out by such units including intelligence work.

7321. Stevens, Paul S. "Room to 'Maneuver': Some Policy Issues in the Iran-Contra Affair," Houston Journal of International Law 11/1 (Fall 1988): 159-168.
     Discussion of the reorganization of the National Security Council staff following the Iran-Contra affair.

7322. Stevens, Peter F. "Early Disinformation Campaign," Military History 9/2 (1993): 12, 16, 94-96, 98.

7323. Stevens, Sayre. "SAM Upgrade Blues," Studies in Intelligence 18/2 (Summer 1974).

7324. Stevens, Thomas F. "Cryptology From the Sea," American Journal of Intelligence 15/1 (Spring-Summer 1994): 21-24.
     A brief discussion of the Navy cryptologic community.

7325. Stevenson, Russell B., Jr. "Protecting Business Secrets Under the Freedom of Information Act: Managing Exemption 4," Administrative Law Review 34/2 (Spring 1982): 207-261.

Detailed discussion of the overview of law governing the release of business information under the Freedom of Information Act; protecting private information in the hands of the government; organizational factors; agency practices and procedures; reverse-FOIA litigation; and remedies.

7326. Steward, Lee H. "Intelligence Support to Military Civic Action in Low-Intensity Conflict," Military Intelligence 16/3 (July-September 1990): 34-35.

Argues that military civic action, if used effectively, utilizes existing assets to reduce many of the social and economic problems that contribute to LIC.

7327. Stewart, Gordon M. "What Is a Generalist?," Studies in Intelligence 2/2 (Summer 1958).

7328. Stewart, James G. "Looking Into the Dirty Laundry," Intelligence and National Security 11/1 (January 1996): 154-157.

A book review essay of Ann Woolner's Washed In Gold: The Story Behind the Biggest Money-Laundering Investigation In US History.

7329. Stewart, John F. "Military Intelligence Operations in Low-Intensity Conflict: An Organizational Model," Military Review 68/1 (January 1988): 17-27.

Discusses LIC and military operations principles; the role of MI in LIC; implications for MI architecture and doctrine; MI design parameters; three model sets; and MI needs in LIC.

7330. Stewart, John F. "Intelligence Strategy for the 21st Century," Military Review 75/5 (September-October 1995): 74-81.

7331. Stewart, Nina. "In Transition: Counterintelligence and Security Countermeasures in the Information Age," American Intelligence Journal 13/3 (Summer 1992): 11-16.

Addresses the direction of the Department of Defense on matters of counterintelligence and security countermeasures. Sections discuss the structural framework; the vision; acknowledging complaints; facing the issues with flexibility; forging partnerships; managing change; nurturing excellence; and protecting the infrastructure.

7332. Stewart, R. D. "Criminal Intelligence: A Need for a Properly Structured System," Police College Magazine 14/1 (1976): 31-37.

Discusses the role and operations of regional police intelligence units in Britain.

7333. Stewart, Richard A. "Rommel's Secret Weapons: Signals Intelligence," Marine Corps Gazette 74 (March 1990): 51-55.

7334. Stewart, Richard W. "Crossing the Rhine and the Irrawaddy," Military Review 69/8 (August 1989): 74-83.

7335. Stewart, W. Cassell. "The Pinkerton-Maroney Investigation," Alabama Review 35/3 (July 1982): 163-171.

7336. St. George, Andrew. "How Does It Feel to be Bugged, Watched, Followed, Hounded and Pestered by the CIA," Esquire 83 (June 1975): 118-122, 168.
Generally considered a popular press publication.

7337. St. George, Brian [pseud.]. "Mervyn Lamb's Diary, (Part II)," Army Quarterly and Defence Journal 109/4 & 110/1 (1979 & 1980): 14-18; 31-37.
The unknown author writes about Lamb's (General Sir Walter Kirke) experiences in World War I as Director of British Military Intelligence.

7338. Stickgold, Marc. "Yesterday's Paranoia Is Today's Reality: Documentation of Police Surveillance of First Amendment Activity," University of Detroit Journal of Urban Law 55/4 (Summer 1978): 877-929.
Discusses the background of police monitoring of political speech in light of the Benkert v. Michigan State Police case; identifies intelligence operations of specific police departments with regard to political activities. Provides background on empirical study and analytical discussion. Offers conclusions about police justification versus police product; and judicial attitudes.

7339. Stielow, Frederick J. "Librarian Warriors and Rapprochement: Carl Milam, Archibald MacLeish, and World War II," Libraries and Culture 25/4 (1990): 513-533.
Summarizes Milam's life and work at the American Library Association. Discusses MacLeish and the library as cultural weapon; rapproachement between Milam and MacLeish; wartime activities (including intelligence work); and conclusions.

7340. Stiles, R. Bradford. "Environmental Law and the Central Intelligence Agency: Is There a Conflict Between Secrecy and Environmental Compliance?," New York University Environmental Law Journal 2 (July 1993): 347-350.

7341. Stinson, J. Whitla. "Some Consideration Governing Title VI of the Espionage Act," University of Pennsylvania Law Review 77 (January 1929): 369-381.
Discusses the section of the Espionage Act concerned with seizure, detention, and forfeiture of arms or munitions of war or other articles. Concludes that the Act is broadly applicable to all trade in munitions.

7342. Stinson, Steven A. "The Federal Bureau of Investigation: Its History, Organization, Functions and Publications," Government Publications Review 6/3 (1979): 213-240.

The title describes the essential content.

7343. St. James, Dana J. "The Legality of Antisatellites," Boston College International and Comparative Law Review 3/2 (Summer 1980): 467-494.

Examines ASAT weaponry in terms of definitions, development, and their impact in war and peace. Contains an analysis of the international law as it relates to ASATs.

7344. St. John, Peter. "King's Two Coexisting Natures," International Perspectives: A Canadian Journal of World Affairs (July-August 1975): 58-60.

The author offers observations of Canadian Prime Minister W. L. M. King's two competing mindsets regarding intelligence matters.

7345. St. John, Peter. "Canada's Accession to the Allied Intelligence Community 1940-45," Conflict Quarterly 4/4 (Fall 1984): 5-21.

Major sections discuss development of British security coordination; operational intelligence and cryptograhy; the examination unit and Vichy; and post-war operations.

7346. St. Mark, J. J. "Wolfe Tone's Diplomacy in America: August-December 1795," Eire-Ireland 7 (1972): 10-11.

7347. Stober, Michael. "The Limits of Police Provocation in Canada," Criminal Law Quarterly 34 (May 1992): 290-348.

7348. Stockbridge, J. C. "The Case of Major Andre," Magazine of American History 3/12 (December 1879): 739-742.

7349. Stockdale, James B. "Communicating Without Technology," Signal 34 (October 1979): 26-30+.

A brief outline of the US prisoner of war situation following the Vietnam war.

7350. Stockinger, Edwin. "Five Weeks at Phalane," Studies in Intelligence 17/1 (Spring 1973): 11-19.

Discusses CIA's role and operations in Laos during the Vietnam war.

7351. Stockman, David A. "The Wrong War? The Case Against National Energy Policy," Public Interest 53 (Fall 1978): 3-44.

Discusses in part the Central Intelligence Agency's role in international economic conditions, in particular, the size and stability of oil production.

7352. Stockwell, John. "The CIA and the Violent Option," Africa 85 (September 1978): 52-54.

7353. Stockwell, John. "A C.I.A. Trip--from Belief, to Doubt, to Despair," Center Magazine 12/5 (September-October 1979): 18-29.
This former CIA field officer served in Africa in the 1960s. He describes his feelings of rejection of CIA values and CIA operations.

7354. Stoertz, Howard, Jr. "Monitoring a Nuclear Freeze," International Security 8/4 (Spring 1984): 91-110.
Major sections discuss general considerations in monitoring through US intelligence collection systems; monitoring implications of the House freeze resolution; measures to improve monitoring confidence; and issues of the adequacy of verification.

7355. Stohl, Michael. "Review Essay: The International Network of Terrorism," Journal of Peace Research 20/1 (1983): 87-94.
A book review essay of Claire Sterling's book, The Terror Network, and Edward Herman's book, The Real Terror Network.

7356. Stokes, Dillard. "How to Insure Security in Government Service: Past Failures and Present Remedies," Commentary 17 (January 1954): 25-36.
Reviews events in the early 1950s concerning the loyalty and security programs of the US, including the spy hysteria of the era. Argues that new procedures are necessary to spare the innocent and trap the guilty.

7357. Stokes, Louis. "A Joint Intelligence Committee--the Wrong Approach," American Intelligence Journal 9/1 (Summer 1988): 28-29.
Brief remarks on the impact of leaks of classified information on the intelligence community, particularly with respect to alleged leaks coming from members of the congressional committees.

7358. Stoler, Margaret G. "Benjamin Church: Son of Liberty, Tory Spy," American History Illustrated 24/6 (November-December 1989): 28-35.

7359. Stolfi, Russel H. S. "Barbarossa Revisited: A Critical Reappraisal of the Opening Stages of the Russo-German Campaign (June-December 1941)," Journal of Modern History 54/1 (March 1982): 27-46.
A detailed account of Adolph Hitler's direction of war in the Soviet Union in the late summer and fall of 1941.

7360. Stoll, Cliff. "Stalking the Wily Hacker," Communications of the ACM 31 (May 1988): 484-497.

7361. Stoll, Cliff. "The Cuckoo's Egg," <u>PC Computing</u> (September 1989): 112-119.

Decription of the author's work to catch a major international computer thief. Continued in later editions. Continued in a later issue. See also the author's book, <u>The Cuckoo's Egg: Tracking a Spy Through the Maze of Computer Espionage</u>.

7362. Stone, G. R. "The Scope of the Fourth Amendment: Privacy and the Public Use of Spies, Secret Agents, and Informers," <u>American Bar Foundation Research Journal</u> 1/4 (1976): 1193-1271.

Discusses the case law developments applicable to police department deployment of undercover agents.

7363. Stone, Geoffrey R. "Surveillance and Subversion: The FBI's Secret War," <u>Reviews in American History</u> 8/1 (March 1980): 134-138.

A review essay pertaining to Athan Theoharis' <u>Spying on Americans: Political Surveillance from Hoover to the Huston Plan</u>.

7364. Stone, Geoffrey R. and Nancy S. Stone. "Intelligence as Governance," <u>Reviews in American History</u> 9/2 (June 1981): 270-274.

A book review essay of Frank Donner's book, <u>The Age of Surveillance</u>.

7365. Stone, Helena M. "Another Look at the Sisson Forgeries and Their Background," <u>Soviet Studies</u> (January 1985): 90-102.

In taking another look at the Sisson forgeries (accusing the Bolsheviks of receiving funds from the Germans), the papers are a result of someone's effort to provide hard evidence for "nebulous current rumors".

7366. Stone, William L. "Schuyler's Faithful Spy: An Incident in the Burgoyne Campaign," <u>Magazine of American History</u> 2 (1878): 414-419.

7367. Stoppard, Tom. "Double Agents: Espionage and the Uncertainty Principle," <u>Sciences</u> 29 (September-October 1989): 36-37.

7368. Storch, R. D. "The Plague of the Blue Locusts: Police Reform and Popular Resistance in Northern England, 1840-57," <u>International Review of Social History</u> 20 (1975): 61-90.

An excellent history of the implantation of police systems in Northern England in the 1840s.

7369. Stout, Neil R. "The Spies Who Went Out in the Cold," <u>American Heritage</u> 23/2 (February 1972): 52-55, 100-103.

An account of a bumbled espionage mission of two British officers, DeBirniere and Browne, in Worcester, Massachusetts in 1775.

7370. Stout, Neil R. "Excerpts From John Howe's 'Smuggler's Journal,'" Vermont History 40/4 (Autumn 1972): 262-270.

An account of Howe's spying work during the American revolution and his work as a smuggler at the age of sixty.

7371. Stover, William J. and Mark Pedry. "Covert Activities of the Central Intelligence Agency: An Implement of American Foreign Policy," International Review of History and Political Science 16/4 (November 1979): 1-24.

7372. Stowe, R. F. "Diplomatic and Legal Aspects of Remote Sensing," Photogrammetric Engineering and Remote Sensing 42/2 (1976): 177-180.

7373. Strachey, J. St. L. "Political Spies," Bibliography Quarterly 177 (July 1893): 235-264.

7374. Stradling, R. A. "Spanish Conspiracy in England, 1661-1663," English Historical Review 87 (1972): 269-286.

Discusses the conduct and actions of Spanish spies in England in the mid-17th century. Spain had hoped for a revolution in England.

7375. Strasser, Gerhard F. "The Noblest Cryptologist: Duke August, the Younger of Brunswick-Luneburg (Gustavus Selenus) and His Cryptological Activities," Cryptologia 7/3 (July 1983): 193-217.

7376. Stratton, Ray E. and August C. Jannarone. "Toward a Strategic Targeting Doctrine for Special Operations Forces," Air University Review 36/5 (July-August 1985): 24-29.

Major sections consider targeting for deterrence in low intensity conflicts; targeting for containment; and challenges. Contains photos.

7377. Stratton, Roy O. "Navy Guerilla," U.S. Naval Institute Proceedings 89/7 (July 1963): 83-87.

7378. Strauss, Christopher E. "Search! Extending the Intelligence Preparation of the Battlefield," Field Artillery Journal 51 (January-February 1983): 50-53.

7379. Strauss, Herbert M. "Marine Corps Intelligence in an Expeditionary Era: Meeting the Challenge of Change," American Intelligence Journal 14/3 (Autumn-Winter 1993-1994): 25-29.

Contains a discussion of Marine Corps perspectives on intelligence; the Marine Corps role in the national military strategy; Corps intelligence and the roadmap for the future; recasting the Corps' intelligence paradigm; and the readiness of the Corps intelligence function.

7380. Strausz-Hupe, Robert. "Soviet Psychological Strategy," U.S. Naval Institute Proceedings 87 (June 1961): 22-28.

7381. Strawn, Susan. "Spy v. Spy: The Reliance on Authority in National Security Cases," American Journal of Criminal Law 15 (Fall-Winter 1987-88): 161-193.
    Detailed consideration of the issues involved in United States v. Barker, 514 F.2d 208, 546 F.2d 940.

7382. Street, Harry. "State Secrets -- A Comparative Study," Modern Law Review 14/2 (April 1951): 121-135.
    The laws of state secrets in England and the US are compared. Considers the concept of the public interest and some proposals for reform.

7383. Strickland, Lee S. "The CIA Meets the American Public," Studies in Intelligence 33/1 (Spring 1989).
    Discusses Freedom of Information Act requests submitted to and processed by CIA.

7384. Strickland, Stephan and Theodore Vallance. "Classified Research: To Be or Not To Be?," Educational Record (Summer 1967): 224-235.

7385. Stripp, Alan J. "Breaking Japanese Codes," Intelligence and National Security 2/4 (October 1987): 135-150.
    The author's historical inquiry into the British signals intelligence efforts to crack Japaneses and other Oriental code systems. Discusses the work in Delhi against Japanese intelligence, and the work in Abbottabad. Contains an appendix, a typical Japanese code system.

7386. Strohm, Gary D. "Electronic Intelligence vs. Terrorism," Military Intelligence 13/1 (March 1987): 24-27.
    Examines some of the ways in which intelligence and enforcement agencies are using computer technology to combat terrorism.

7387. Strong, Frank R. "Fifty Years of 'Clear and Present Danger': From Schenck to Brandenburg -- and Beyond," Supreme Court Review (1969): 41-80.
    Acknowledging the fiftieth anniversary of the 'clear and present danger' test of the First Amendment's limits, the author reviews various case law decisions which have advanced the test and deepened its significance.

7388. Strong, J. Thompson. "Covert Activities and Intelligence Operations: Congressional and Executive Roles Redefined," International Journal of Intelligence and Counterintelligence 1/2 (Summer 1986): 63-72.
    Argues that covert operations are fundamentally foreign policy options

and that intelligence agencies do not establish such policy but only execute it. Congress has an important constitutional role in monitoring covert operations.

7389. Strong, J. Thompson. "Tilting with Machiavelli: Fighting Competitive Espionage in the 1990s," International Journal of Intelligence and Counterintelligence 7/2 (Summer 1994): 161-174.

Discusses a collection of American failures to perceive and act upon threats posed by international competitive espionage against US corporations. Identifies the National Security Threat List developed by the Attorney General.

7390. Strong, Robert A. "October Surprise," Intelligence and National Security 8/2 (April 1993): 227-235.

A review essay of October Surprise by Barbara Honegger, Casey by Joseph Persico, and October Surprise by Gary Sick.

7391. Strother, French, "Fighting Germany's Spies," World's Work 35-36 (March, April, May, June, July, August, September 1918): 513-528; 652-669; 78-102; 143-153; 303-317; 393-401; 542-552).

7392. Strout, Cushing. "The Oppenheimer Case: Melodrama, Tragedy, and Irony," Virginia Quarterly Review 40 (1964): 268-278.

A consideration of some of the tangential issues pertaining to the J. Robert Oppenheimer case in the 1950s.

7393. Strout, Cushing. "Reconsidering the Rosenbergs: History, Novel, Film," Reviews in American History 12 (September 1984): 309-321.

Extensive analysis of books and films on to the Rosenberg spy case.

7394. Struve, Gleb; V. Shulgin; and S. Voytsekhouskiy. "New Materials About 'Trust,'" Novjy Zhurnal 125 (1975): 194-214.

7395. Stuart, Edwin C. "The Organization and Functions of a Bureau of Military Intelligence," Journal of the Military Service Institution of the United States 32 (March-April 1903): 158-183.

7396. Stuart, Meriwether. "Samuel Ruth and General R. E. Lee: Disloyalty and the Line of Supply to Fredericksburg, 1862-1863," Virginia Magazine of History and Biography 71/1 (January 1963): 35-109.

A detailed account of Ruth, Confederate superintendent of transportation, and Ruth's role in conveying intelligence to the Union between 1863 and 1865.

7397. Stuart, Meriwether. "Colonel Ulric Dahlgren and Richmond's Union Underground, April 1864," Virginia Magazine of History and Biography 72/2 (April 1964): 152-204.

Discusses in detail the role of Dahlgren's espionage work in Virginia and Dahlgren's execution in March 1864.

7398. Stuart, Meriwether. "Operation Sanders: Wherein Old Friends and Ardent Pro-Southerners Prove to Be Union Secret Agents," Virginia Magazine of History of Biography 81/2 (April 1973): 157-199.
Discusses Arnold Harris' plan to kidnap Confederate spy George Sanders.

7399. Stuart, Meriwether. "Of Spies and Borrowed Names: The Identity of Union Operatives in Richmond Known As 'The Phillipses' Discovered," Virginia Magazine of History and Biography 89/3 (July 1981): 308-327.
This is an investigation into Civil War spy techniques.

7400. Stuart, Meriwether. "Dr. Lugo: An Austro-Venetian Adventurer in Union Espionage," Virginia Magazine of History and Biography 90/3 (July 1982): 339-358.
Lugo was a Union spy. He successfully infiltrated confederate hierarchy. He was convicted, sentenced to execution, but returned to Union control.

7401. Stuart, Graham H. "Safeguarding the State Through Passport Control," Department of State Bulletin 12 (June 1945): 1066-1070.
A brief discussion of nationality and citizenship problems; enforcing neutrality regulations; and passport regulation.

7402. Stubblebine, Albert N. "C^3I for Automated Focus on Intelligence Picture," Army 29 (March 1979): 33-34.

7403. Studeman, William O. "Teaching the Grunt to Dance: Contradictions and Opportunities in Open Source Information within the Intelligence Community," American Intelligence Journal 14 (Spring-Summer 1993): 11-18.
A detailed exploration of the role and opportunities for extending applications of open source information in the intelligence community. Includes discussion of a plan to create an integrated community open source architecture.

7404. Studnicky, Lawrence J., III. "Constitutional Law: Authority of Secretary of State to Revoke Passports (Agee v. Muskie)," Harvard International Law Journal 22 (Winter 1981): 187-194.
An analysis of the Agee case before the Supreme Court decision.

7405. Stueck, William. "The Soviet Union and the Origins of the Korean War," World Politics 28/4 (July 1976): 622-635.
A book review essay regarding issues taken up by Robert R. Simmons in The Strained Alliance: Peking, P'yongyang, Moscow and the Politics of the Korean Civil War.

7406. Stulberg, Barry A. "State Secrets Privilege: The Executive Caprice Runs Rampant," <u>Loyola of Los Angeles International and Comparative Law Journal</u> 9 (Spring 1987): 445-479.

Argues that the federal judiciary has abdicated its role in balancing the competing interests at stake in the matter of the state secrets privilege, thus creating a shield against governmental liability in cases brought to discover state secrets.

7407. Stupach, Ronald J. and D. C. Booher. "Guerilla Warfare: A Strategic Analysis in the Superpower Context," <u>Journal of Southeast Asia and the Far East</u> 1 (November 1970): 181-196.

7408. Sturges, Gerald. "The House Report on Public Cryptography," <u>Cryptologia</u> 5/2 (April 1981): 84-93.

7409. Sturtevant, Mary K. "Congressional Oversight of Intelligence: One Perspective," <u>American Intelligence Journal</u> 13/3 (Summer 1992): 17-20.

Contains rare insights into workings of the Senate Select Committee on Intelligence and its unique vantage point for intelligence oversight. Considers effect on work of Committee and staff; and work best done by the Committee.

7410. Subrahmanyam, K. "An Integrated Approach to Reconnaissance, and Target Acquisition," <u>Strategic Analysis</u> (January 1988): 1018-1025.

7411. Suecc, W. "Weber Antike Geheimschreibenmethoden und ihr Nachleben," <u>Philologus</u> 32 (1912): 142-175.

Loosely translated, this piece discusses Max Weber's antique secret writing method and its continued applications.

7412. Sulc, Lawrence B. "The Soviet Union's Cut-Throat Soldiers," <u>World & I</u> 1/11 (November 1986): 103-111.

7413. Sulc, Lawrence B. "Counter-Terrorism--First Line, Last Line," <u>Terrorism: An International Journal</u> 11 (1988): 241-245.

7414. Sulc, Lawrence B. "The President Needs the PFIAB," <u>World & I</u> (July 1989): 136-140.

7415. Sullivan, Brian R. "'A Highly Commendable Action': William J. Donovan's Intelligence Mission for Mussolini and Roosevelt, December 1935-February 1936," <u>Intelligence and National Security</u> 6/2 (April 1991): 334-366.

Examines the intelligence gathering operations, both military and diplomatic, of William Donovan. Suggests that the accounts of this period are little more than mythical concerning Donovan's actions.

7416. Sullivan, David S. "A SALT Debate: Continued Soviet Deceptions," Strategic Review 7/4 (1979): 29-38.

7417. Sullivan, David S. "Lessons Learned from SALT I & II: New Objectives of SALT III," International Security Review 6/3 (Fall 1981): 355-386.
    Discusses Soviet deception in the first two SALT negotiations, giving the Soviets a clear advantage.

7418. Sullivan, Francis C. "Wiretapping and Eavesdropping: Review of the Current Law," Hastings Law Journal 18/1 (November 1966): 59-87.
    Discusses background and development of wiretapping law; electronic eavesdropping; non-electronic eavesdropping; and conclusions. Applies federal and New York law.

7419. Sullivan, Joseph W. "'A Giant of Embodied Conscience': Joseph M. Coldwell and the Socialist Party in Rhode Island," Rhode Island History 50/4 (1992): 117-129.

7420. Sullivan, Robert E. and Nancy E. Bader. "The Application of Export Control Laws to Scientific Research at Universities," Journal of College and University Law 9 (Fall 1982): 451-467.
    Discusses recent restrictions on scientific exchanges; authority for government actions; International Traffic in Arms Regulation; Executive Order 12356 on classification of information; contract terms; and proposals for a more cooperative policy.

7421. Sullivan, William H. "Dateline Iran: The Road Not Taken," Foreign Policy 40 (Fall 1980): 175-186.
    Considers the background factors in the fall of the Shah of Iran, including the role of the national security adviser.

7422. Sulzberger, A. O., Jr. "Papers Disclose Allies' Edge in Knowing German Codes," Cryptologia 3/1 (January 1979): 51-53.
    A reprint of a newspaper article concerning documents located in the National Archives and Records Administration (NARA), Washington, D.C.

7423. Sumantra, Goshal and D. Eleanor Westly. "Organizing Competitor Analysis Systems," Strategic Management Journal 12 (1991): 17-31.

7424. Summers, Harry G. "Yomping," Military Review (March 1984): 4-16.
    A summary of the battles of the Falklands war, including sections on the beachhead at San Carlos Water, the battle of Goose Green, yomping to Port Stanley, arrival of the Army's 5th infantry brigade, and the final assault. Mention is made of intelligence leaks and tactical surprise factors.

7425. Summers, J. "South Australian Government and the Police," <u>Politics</u> 14/1 (May 1979): 101-108.

Discusses the linkages between local and national police administration and oversight in Australia. Mentions the intelligence function of the South Australian Police Special Branch as to their role in monitoring persons and organizations considered to be special security risks.

7426. Sundarem, Gowri S. "Some Current C³I Concepts and Programs," <u>International Defense Review</u> 13/7 (1980): 1036-1042.

A brief overview of command, control, and intelligence concepts and programs.

7427. Sundaram, Gowri S. "US Military Space Programs: Emphasis on Survivability," <u>International Defense Review</u> 17/8 (August 1984): 1019-1030.

Discusses a proposal to establish a unified space command. Includes discussion of launch vehicles, communications, navigation systems, space surveillance and defense, and new technologies.

7428. Sunder, John E. "British Army Officers on the Santa Fe Trail," <u>Bulletin of the Missouri Historical Society</u> 23/2 (1967): 147-157.

7429. Sundquist, Eric J. "'Witness' Recalled," <u>Commentary</u> 86/6 (December 1988): 57-63.

A book review essay of Whittaker Chambers's autobiography, <u>Witness</u>. Concludes that the book is "one of the most remarkable philosophical and literary documents of our age."

7430. Sunstein, Cass R. "Government Control of Information. (Symposium: New Perspectives in the Law of Defamation)," <u>California Law Review</u> 74 (May 1986): 889-926.

Explores equilibrium theory in the context of the need for secrecy versus the goal of ensuring an informed citizenry. Discusses the Jeffersonian model of free expression; secrecy and disclosure; current approach to government controls; two problems in First Amendment theory; and conclusions. Includes discussion of CIA employees and <u>Snepp v. U. S.</u>

7431. Suppiger, Joseph E. "Private Lincoln and the Spy Battalion," <u>Lincoln Herald</u> 80/1 (1978): 46-49.

7432. Surette, Raymond. "Video Street Patrol: Media Technology and Street Crime," <u>Journal of Police Science and Administration</u> 13 (March 1985): 78-85.

Discusses a street video surveillance program in Dade County, Florida in the early 1980s. Includes program description; pre-program factors; operations; and assessment.

7433. Susser, Peter A. "Electronic Monitoring in the Private Sector: How Closely Should Employers Supervise Their Workers?," Employee Relations Law Journal 3/4 (Spring 1988): 575-598.

Discusses current monitoring practices; worker stress and computer pacing; privacy protections; legislative provisions and litigations.

7434. Sutherland, Arthur E., Jr. "British Trials for Disloyal Association During the French Revolution," Cornell Law Quarterly 34/3 (Spring 1949): 303-330.

Drawing on the backdrop of public interest in subversion and espionage against the US, the author finds similar concerns reflected in British trials for disloyal association during the French revolution.

7435. Sutherland, Arthur E., Jr. "Freedom and Internal Security," Harvard Law Review 64/3 (January 1951): 383-416.

Reflecting upon the Internal Security Act of 1950 as oppressive legislation, the author considers law relevant to communist organizations, treason, espionage and sabotage. Contains observations of the reasoning behind President Truman's veto of the legislation and the congressional override.

7436. Suvenirov, O. F. "The People's Commissariat for Defense and the NKVD in the Prewar Years," Voprosy Istorii 6 (1991): 26-35.

7437. Suvorov, Viktor. [pseud.]. "GUSM: The Soviet Service of Strategic Deception," International Defense Review 18/8 (September 1985): 1235-1240.

The author was a GRU officer. He discusses the role of the GUSM as the main directorate in the Soviet military for strategic deception.

7438. Suvorov, Viktor. [pseud.]. "Spetsnaz: The Soviet Union's Special Forces," Military Review 44/3 (March 1984): 30-46.

An extensive review of Soviet special attack forces. An earlier version appeared in International Defense Review 16 (September 1983): 8+.

7439. Swan, Guy C., III, et al. "Scott's Engineers," Military Review 63/3 (March 1983): 61-68.

A brief history of General Winfield Scott's engineer forces in the war with Mexico, 1846-1847, including the role of the engineers in reconnaissance and mapping.

7440. Swanberg, W. A. "Was the Secretary of War a Traitor?," American Heritage 14/2 (February 1963): 34-37, 96-97.

Addresses the question of whether or not President Buchanan's Secretary of War, John A. Floyd, should be considered a traitor in historical perspective, a traitor to the Union cause.

7441. Swanberg, W. A. "The Spies Who Came in From the Sea: Eight Germans Who Landed on Long Island and Florida Coasts in June 1942," American Heritage 21/3 (April 1970): 66-69, 87-91.

Discusses the capture and trial of eight Nazi saboteurs who landed on the shores of Florida in 1942, captured by the FBI.

7442. Swahn, Johan. "International Surveillance Satellites: Open Skies for All?," Journal of Peace Research 25 (Spring 1988): 229-244.

Considers the background of satellite surveillance; proposals for international surveillance satellites; the concept of open skies; and a variety of implications for such satellites, such as economics and law.

7443. Swanson, Alan H. "Wiretapping: The State Law," Journal of Criminal Law, Criminology and Police Science 51/5 (January-February 1961): 534-544.

A case law comment on the subject.

7444. Swanson, Roger F. "The United States As a National Security Threat to Canada," Military Review 51/1 (January 1971): 69-76.

Major topics include Canada's national interest; reasons for Canada's insecurity; foreign domination; strategic-economic impact; Canadian geography; and existing dissimilarities.

7445. Swartout, Robert, Jr. "American Historians and the Outbreak of the Korean War: An Historigraphical Essay," Asia Quarterly 1 (1979): 65-77.

7446. Swartz, David. "Redirecting the CIA," Foreign Service Journal 73/2 (February 1996): 24-31.

Acknowledges the clash of operational philosophies between the Central Intelligence Agency and the Department of State. Argues that the CIA should be kept out of policymaking and that the position of the ambassador should be elevated in the policy process.

7447. Swearingen, Ben E. "Hitler's Family Secret," Civilization (March-April 1995).

7448. Sweetman, Bill. "Out of the Black: Secret Mach 6 Spy Plane," Popular Science 242 (March 1993): 56-63, 98, 100-101.

7449. Swenson, Russell G. "The Warning and Crisis Support Functions in Regional Joint Intelligence Centers," Defense Intelligence Journal 1/1 (Spring 1992): 81-94.

Historical background of civilian and military intelligence analyst functions; strategic warning from intelligence; intelligence information handling for crisis support; and the future of joint intelligence centers.

7450. Swenson, Russell G. "The Elements of Intelligence Readiness," <u>Defense Intelligence Journal</u> 3/1 (Spring 1994): 53-74.

Major sections define intelligence readiness and discuss the link to information strategy, military capability, and strategic warning. Also discusses a framework for intelligence readiness; the stretch to information strategy; credible multiplication of military capability; and reassuring intelligence readiness.

7451. Swift, Eben F. "Aggressor in Action," <u>Infantry Journal</u> 60 (September 1947): 23-25.

An account of intelligence activities in the November 1946 maneuvers at Camp Pendleton, CA.

7452. Swindler, William F. "Seditious Aliens and Native 'Seditionists,'" <u>Supreme Court Historical Society Yearbook</u> (1984): 12-19.

7453. Swire, James B. "Eavesdropping and Electronic Surveillance: An Approach for a State Legislature," <u>Harvard Journal on Legislation</u> 4/1 (December 1966): 23-54.

A detailed discussion of the evolution of eavesdropping and electronic surveillance; the role of the state legislature; and proposals for changing the law to accommodate competing interests.

7454. Swietek, Ryszard. "In the Service of Polish Intelligence in North and South America, 1941-45," <u>Przeglad Historyczny</u> 79/3 (1988): 539-572.

7455. Sykes, Lynn and Dan Daves. "The Yield of Soviet Strategic Weapons," <u>Scientific American</u> 256/1 (January 1987): 29-37.

7456. Sylvester, John, Jr. "Will Candor Survive the Leaking Ship of State?," <u>Foreign Service Journal</u> 52/6 (1975): 15-16, 32.

Discusses the implications of weak secrecy and information security practice in government.

7457. Syrett, David. "German U-Boat Attacks on Convoy SC118: 4 February to 14 February 1943," <u>American Neptune</u> 44/1 (Winter 1984): 48-60.

7458. Syrett, David. "The Secret War and the Historians," <u>Armed Forces and Society</u> 9/2 (Winter 1983): 293-328.

Discusses the methods used by historians to report intelligence operations of World War II.

7459. Syrett, David. "Weather-Reporting U-Boats in the Atlantic, 1944-45: The Hunt for the U-248," <u>American Neptune</u> 52/1 (Winter 1992): 16-24.

7460. Syrett, David. "Communications Intelligence and the Sinking of the U-1062: 30 September 1944," Journal of Military History 58/4 (October 1994): 685-698.

Explores the role of communications intelligence by the US Navy to hunt and sink one U-Boat, U-1062, a vessel assigned to the allied blockade between the Far East and Europe.

7461. Szajkowski, Zosa. "Double Jeopardy - The Abrams Case of 1919," American Jewish Archives 23/1 (April 1971): 6-32.

Discusses radicals and their prosecutions during the anti-Bolshevik period after World War I in the US.

7462. Szamuely, George. "The Intellectuals & the Cold War," Commentary 88/6 (December 1989): 54-56.

Discusses CIA support and funding for leftist journalists and scholars in the 1940s and 1950s. Considers arguments of Peter Coleman's book, The Liberal Conspiracy.

7463. Szamuely, Tibor. "The Elimination of the Opposition Between the Sixteenth and Seventeenth Congresses of the CPSU," Soviet Studies 17/3 (January 1966): 318-338.

Discussion of the second Soviet revolution, 1929-1934.

7464. Szanton, Peter and Graham Allison. "Intelligence: Seizing the Opportunity," Foreign Policy 22 (Spring 1976): 183-215.

Argues for a major restructuring of the intelligence community, including the division of the CIA into two organizations. Argues to place analysis and estimates in a second agency, to reconsider the role of covert action and other matters.

7465. Szasz, Ferenc M. "Peppermint and Alsos," MHQ: Quarterly Journal of Military History 6/3 (1994): 42-47.

During the invasion of Europe on June 6, 1944, the operations Peppermint and Alsos provided important reconnaissance information on nuclear poisons and technical insights from German nuclear scientists.

7466. Szulc, Tad. "Inside the American Intelligence Establishment: Guess Who's Trying to Be Henry Superspy," Washingtonian 9 (March 1974): 54-57, 99-100, 102-106.

7467. Szulc, Tad. "Politicization of CIA," Skeptic 7 (May-June 1975): 17-20.

7468. Szulc, Tad. "CIA's Electric Kool-Aid Acid Test: LSD Experimentation," Psychology Today 11 (November 1977): 92+.

A popular magazine article, not generally considered scholarship, but the contents addresses a topic only rarely discussed in print media in the time.

7469. Szulc, Tad. "The NSA--America's $10 Billion Frankenstein," Penthouse 7 (November 1977): 55+.

A popular magazine article, not generally considered scholarship, but the contents addresses a topic only rarely discusses in the times, namely the alleged budget of the National Security Agency.

7470. Szulc, Tad. "I Spy, You Spy," Washingtonian 14/2 (February 1978): 97-107.

A discussion of the espionage activity of the US government in Washington, D.C.

T

"I kept one or more boats continually employed in crossing the Sound on this business."
(Benjamin Tallmadge, cited in <u>Major John Andre</u> by Robert Hatch, p. 111)

7471. Taft, Philip. "The I.W.W. in the Grain Belt," <u>Labor History</u> 1/1 (Winter 1960): 53-67.

> Discusses the International Workers of the World struggle to organize the United States grain belt before 1920. Also mentions the Palmer Raids. Useful in studies of labor spying.

7472. Taft, Philip. "The Federal Trials of the IWW," <u>Labor History</u> 3/1 (Winter 1962): 57-91.

> Major sections discuss the hostile atmosphere of opinion; the Chicago trial; the Sacramento trial; the Wichita trial; and the struggle for amnesty.

7473. Takerer, Keith M. "The Mail from Budapest," <u>Studies in Intelligence</u> 2/3 (Fall 1958).

> Discusses a Czech counterintelligence operation.

7474. Talamus, Ann. "FBI Targets Arab-Americans," <u>Covert Action Information Bulletin</u> 36 (Spring 1991): 4-8.

7475. Talbott, Strobe. "Scrambling and Spying in SALT II," <u>International Security</u> 4/2 (Fall 1979): 3-21.

> Discusses the complexities of interaction between nuclear weapons

control verification strategies, diplomacy and technology. Offers conclusions concerning the Brezhnev-Carter correspondence.

7476. Talmon, J. L. and Ze'er Katz. "The Lavon Affair--Israeli Democracy at the Crossroads," New Outlook 4 (March-April 1961): 23-32.

7477. Tamanaha, Brian Z. "A Critical Review of the Classified Information Procedures Act," American Journal of Criminal Law 13 (Summer 1986): 277-328.
 Discusses the application of the Act to the "graymail" problem (i.e., criminal defendants who threaten to disclose classified information at trial). Includes discussion of background of the Act; substitutions ex parte; state secrets privilege; and proposals for CIPA modification. Discusses cases involving CIA personnel.

7478. Tamburini, Filippo. "Testaments of Don Enrico Tozzoli, 28 December 1843-6 to December 1852," Revista di Storia della Chiesa in Italia 39/1 (1985): 118-138.

7479. Tames, Richard. "Laurence of Arabia," British Heritage 6/5 (1985): 24-33.

7480. Tanenhaus, Sam. "Hiss: Guilty as Charged," Commentary 95/4 (April 1993): 32-37.

7481. Tanhan, George K. and Dennis J. Duncanson. "Some Dilemmas of Counterinsurgency," Foreign Affairs 48/1 (October 1969): 113-122.
 Addresses counterinsurgency issues in the context of the Vietnam war.

7482. Tanksley, David M. "C²: Finding the Middle Ground," Military Review 65/11 (November 1985): 52-55.
 Proposes the author's philosophy on the need for expanding command and control by grafting intelligence on the C^2 function.

7483. Tanter, Raymond. "International Crisis Behavior: An Appraisal of the Literature," Jerusalem Journal of International Relations 3 (Winter-Spring 1978): 340-374.

7484. Tanzer, Marc. "Foiling the New Corporate Spy," Security Management 36/9 (September 1992): 38-42.

7485. Taplin, Winn L. "Deep Black and Shades of Gray," International Journal of Intelligence and Counterintelligence 2/1 (1988): 132-135.
 This is a book review essay of William Burrow's Deep Black.

7486. Taplin, Winn L. "Six General Principles of Intelligence," International Journal of Intelligence and Counterintelligence 3/4 (Winter 1989): 475-492.

Principles discussed: intelligence derives from international conflict or rivalry; conduct or use of intelligence involves secrecy; clandestine collection of information is the fundamental activity of intelligence; truth must be the basis of intelligence; intelligence in a vacuum is of no value; tardy intelligence is of no value; special activities must involve native knowledge of the national groups toward which they are directed.

7487. Tarschys, D. "Secret Institutions in Russian Government: A Note on Rosenfield's Knowledge and Power," Soviet Studies (1985): 525-534.

A survey of nearly three dozen secret and special institutions in pre-revolutionary Russian, falling into two main categories: predecessors of the nuclear security service; and aides who had given policy advice and who had administered assistance to the sovereign. Managing repression and managing the economy were inseparable. Elements in the dictator's struggle for political survival.

7488. Tauber, Eliezer. "The Capture of the NILI Spies: The Turkish Version," Intelligence and National Security 6/4 (October 1991): 701-710.

An account of the NILI spy network, a Jewish group that worked on behalf of British intelligence in the Middle East during World War I. Discusses NILI's first contact with the British and the subsequent capture of members by the Ottoman security authorities. Observes that the exclusion of the Ottoman perspective leaves the account incomplete.

7489. Taubitz, D. M. "National Security Versus the Right to a Passport (Haig v. Agee)," Detroit College of Law Review 1982 (Winter 1982): 945-967.

In depth discussion of Haig v. Agee with respect to the 1979 revocation of former CIA employee Agee's passport. Sections discuss right to travel and passport law; right to criticize the CIA and maintain a passport; and conclusions. Concludes that Supreme Court decision to withhold Agee's passport was correct in view of national security implications.

7490. Tavra Chacura, Alexander. "The Assault and Seizure of Pisaqua: Critical Analysis of Intelligence," Revista de Marina 1 (1986): 92-97.

7491. Tayler, John M. "In Queen Victoria's Secret Service," Studies in Intelligence 29/4 (Winter 1985).

7492. Taylor, A. J. P. "Through the Keyhole," New York Review 10 (February 1972): 14-18.

The author, an acclaimed British historian, argues that intelligence most often fails to produce anything of value.

7493. Taylor, Alan. "Fenimore Cooper's America," <u>History Today</u> 46/2 (February 1996): 21-27.

  The author of <u>The Spy</u> is discussed in the context of several of his writings as the first great American novelist. Brief discussion is offered concerning the first spy novel.

7494. Taylor, Blaine. "Ambush in Hostile Skies," <u>Military History</u> 5/1 (1988): 42-49.

  This is a report of an interview with Rex T. Barker, the officer who shot down Japanese Admiral Isoroku Yamamoto.

7495. Taylor, Cortlandt M. "The Role of Intelligence in the Air Force," <u>Signal</u> 36 (January 1982): 62.

  A very brief overview.

7496. Taylor, Edmond. "Cult of the Secret Agent," <u>Horizon</u> 17 (Spring 1975): 4-13.

7497. Taylor, Herbert G., Jr. "The Tactical Army of Counterintelligence," <u>Military Intelligence</u> 10/1 (1984): 46-48.

7498. Taylor, I. A. "Informers of Ninety-Eight," <u>North America</u> 166 (May 1898): 522-534.

7499. Taylor, Jack H. "Wohlstetter, Soviet Strategic Forces, and NIE's," <u>Studies in Intelligence</u> 19/1 (Spring 1975): 1-8.

  A formal recognition that Albert Wohlstetter had properly interpreted the US under-assessment of Soviet weapons buildup in the 1960s and 1970s for publication in the National Intelligence Estimates. See Wohlstetter's articles in this bibliography.

7500. Taylor, Joe G. "Slavery in Louisiana During the Civil War," <u>Louisiana History</u> 8/1 (Winter 1967): 27-33.

  A brief discussion of the subject, including the use by the Union army of Louisiana informers among the slave population.

7501. Taylor, Michael D. "The Exposed Flank of National Security," <u>Orbis</u> 18/4 (Winter 1975): 1011-1022.

  Offers several proposals for remedying deficiencies in the national security structure, especially reinforcing the civil flank of national security.

7502. Taylor, Philip B., Jr. "The Guatemalan Affair: A Critique of United States Foreign Policy," <u>American Political Science Review</u> 50/3 (September 1956): 787-806.

Argues that the US policy toward poorer countries like Guatemala was predatory to the point of potential incitement of warfare. Major sections discuss Latin country views of the US; historical background of the Guatemalan involvement; US views of the situation; and how the US and Latin American countries solved the problem.

7503. Taylor, Philip M. "'If War Should Come': Preparing the Fifth Arm of Total War, 1935-1939," Journal of Contemporary History 16 (January 1981): 27-51.
Discusses the state of confusion that existed in the British war planning efforts in the six years before actual fighting with Germany, including interdepartmental rivalries.

7504. Taylor, Robert P. "The Military Laser," American Intelligence Journal 6/1 (March 1984): 25-29.

7505. Taylor, Robert W. "Terrorism and Intelligence," Defense Analysis 3/2 (June 1987): 165-176.
Discusses the role of intelligence analysis in relation to terrorism; problems in the collection of and analysis of information (e.g., maintaining basic freedoms and civil rights; the political terrorist as a new breed; terrorism and state sponsorship; terrorism and the media; and organizational weaknesses and lack of coordination; and recommendations for the future.

7506. Taylor, Rufus L. "Command and the Intelligence Process," U.S. Naval Institute Proceedings 86/8 (August 1960): 27-39.

7507. Taylor, Rufus L. "The Importance of Intelligence to the Nation and the Navy," Navy 9 (September 1966): 18-23.

7508. Taylor, Rufus L. "An Oral History: Remembrances of VADM Rufus L. Taylor," Naval Intelligence Professionals Quarterly 6/2 (Spring 1990): 1-6.

7509. Taylor, Stan A. "Intelligence and National Security Power," Studies in Intelligence 31/3 (Fall 1987).
A review essay and bibliography of several books on strategic intelligence.

7610. Taylor, Telford, et al. "The Crisis in Intelligence Gathering," Columbia Journal of Law and Social Problems 12/4 (Fall 1976): 451-487.
A panel discussion: Taylor as moderator and panelists, Roger Hilsman, Frederick A. O. Schwarz, Jr. and Paul C. Warnke. Discussion of the cures for intelligence excesses or perceived excesses.

7511. Taylor, Theodore C. "Tactical Concentration and Surprise--In Theory," Naval War College Review 38/4 (July-August 1985): 41-51.

Considers the lessons of the English engineer, Frederick William Lancaster, in military theory and mathematical expressions of military fighting strengths. Contains mathematical calculations for hedging against surprise.

7512. Tebrich, Spencer. "Human Scent and its Detection," Studies in Intelligence 5/1 (Spring 1961).

7513. Tefft, Stanton K. "The Politics of Secrecy," Society 16/4 (1979): 60-67.

The author argues that secrecy, when considered through the ages, has more negative than positive outcomes. His case evidence extends from ancient times to present.

7514. Teichroew, Allan. "Military Surveillance of Mennonites in World War I," Mennonite Quarterly Review 53/2 (1979): 95-127.

Reveals evidence of a purposeful US government effort to surveil this pacifist organization and the effort to imply that the group was pro-German.

7515. Teller, Edward. "The Feasibility of Arms Control and the Principle of Openness," Daedalus 89 (Fall 1960): 781-799.

Major topics consider the relationship between arms control and peace; the Third World; the spread of nuclear weapons; the question of control; methods of detection; and the principle of openness.

7516. Tellis, Ashley J. "AEWC&C Aircraft for Pakistan: Choices and Alternatives," Asian Affairs: An American Review 14/1 (1987): 20-35.

Discusses the (then) proposed US sale to Pakistan of Airborne Early Warning Command and Control planes as well as the controversy stemming from such a proposal.

7517. Temple, Harry. "Deaf Captains: Intelligence, Policy, and the Origins of the Korean War," International Studies Notes 8/3-4 (Fall-Winter 1981-1982): 19-23.

Discusses Truman's NSC-68 report of the National Security Council and its impact on developments leading to the Korean War.

7518. Tenev, Jovi. "Electronic Eavesdropping in Great Britain and the United States," Boston College International and Comparative Law Journal 1/1 (1977): 321-336.

Provides a comparative analysis of the two nations' policies on eavesdropping. Discusses evidence doctrine; adjustments of the doctrine; electronic eavesdropping and evidentiary norms; and conclusions.

7519. Tennant, Peter. "Swedish Intelligence in the Second World War," Intelligence and National Security 2/2 (April 1987): 354-361.

A book review essay concerning Wilhelm M. Carlgren's book, Svensk Underrattelsetjanst 1939/45. The book's author concluded that the Swedish intelligence organization was generally ineffective during World War II.

7520. Tennant, Peter. "How We Failed to Buy the Italian Navy," Intelligence and National Security 3/1 (January 1988): 141-161.

A personal account of the author's experiences as a press attache in Stockholm as part of the effort to negotiate the defection of the Italian navy. Considers espionage under Swedish law in connection with several intrigues surrounding wartime relations between Sweden and Italy.

7521. Tenniswood, Theodore H. "The Coordination of Collection," Studies in Intelligence 8/2 (Spring 1964): 50-57.

7522. Tepfers, V. "The Soviet Political Police Today," East and West 1 (1954): 42-49.

A useful article for research on the Soviet police of the Stalin era.

7523. Terechow, William. "The Soviet Atlas as a Source," Studies in Intelligence 10/1 (Spring 1966).

7524. Terrill, Richard J. "Organization of Law Enforcement in the Soviet Union," Police Studies 12 (Spring 1989): 18-24.

Discusses various factors which support the maintenance of a centralized police force in the Soviet Union.

7525. Terry, Thomas M. "Administrative Law--Passports May Not Be Revoked for National Security and Foreign Policy Reasons Without Congressional Authorization (Agee v. Muskie)," Notre Dame Lawyer 56 (February 1981): 508-514.

Examines Agee v. Muskie and precedent-setting cases addressing the authority of the government to remove passports. Argues that the national security rationale should not be used to restrict a person's right to travel abroad.

7526. Tettenborn, A. M. "Secrets, Well-Meaning Moles and Courts," Company Law 5 & 6 (July 1984; March 1985): 191-192; 89-90.

7527. Thayer, Russell. "Dirigible Balloons for War Purposes," Journal of the Military Service Institution of the United States 7 (1886): 177-194.

This is one of the earliest known technical discussions of the role of balloons in warfare.

7528. Thelen, Friedrich. "Post-Cold War Spies: Cloak and Stagger?," European Affairs (May-June 1991).

7529. Theodorou, Jerry. "Political Risk Reconsidered," International Journal of Intelligence and Counterintelligence 6/2 (Summer 1993): 147-172.
Major sections discuss the emergence of political risk analysis; the definition of political risk; negativity in the political risk equation; a proposed methodology for the study of political risk; and theoretical issues.

7530. Theoharis, Athan G. "From the Cold War to Watergate: National Security and Civil Liberties," Intellect 103 (October 1974): 20-26.
Major focus is on the Nixon administration and civil liberties; the cold war and illegal surveillance; the Coplon case; the Eisenhower years; and the 1960s.

7531. Theoharis, Athan G. "Classification Restrictions and the Public's Right to Know: A New Look at the Alger Hiss Case," Intellect 104 (September-October 1975): 86-89.
Key sections discuss the discovery of the typewriter; other troubling questions; the actions of the House Un-American Activities Committee; the Weinstein suit; and classification and abuse of power.

7532. Theoharis, Athan G. "The FBI's Stretching of Presidential Directives, 1936-1953," Political Science Quarterly 91/4 (Winter 1976-1977): 649-672.
Argues that presidential directives from 1936 to 1953 encouraged the Federal Bureau of Investigation to expand its domestic intelligence capabilities beyond legal authority.

7533. Theoharis, Athan G. "The Decline of an Anti-Colonial Tradition: Official Attitudes Towards Revolutions During the Cold War Years," Journal of the Hellenic Diaspora 4/3 (1977): 14-23.

7534. Theoharis, Athan G. "Public or Private Papers?: The Arrogance of the Intelligence Community," Intellect 106 (October 1977): 118-120.
Major themes consider public officials and the destruction of their papers; Federal Bureau of Investigation record-keeping procedures; and the arrogance of intelligence officials.

7535. Theoharis, Athan G. "The Truman Administration and the Decline of Civil Liberties: The FBI's Success in Securing Authorization for a Preventive Detention Program," Journal of American History 64/4 (March 1978): 1010-1030.
Suggests that President Truman may not have known about the variety of ways the Federal Bureau of Investigation made and enforced its own internal security policy.

7536. Theoharis, Athan G.   "The Current Proposal to Repeal the FOIA Legislation: An Historian's Legal Nightmare," Judges Journal 19 (Spring 1980): 22-24, 42-44.

Brief discussion of FBI Charter Act of 1979 and a small section giving FBI the option of destroying certain records or sending records to the National Archives. Asks whether FBI should be granted such discretion in light of certain questionable and illegal actions of FBI personnel.

7537. Theoharis, Athan G.   "The Presidency and the Federal Bureau of Investigation: The Conflict of Intelligence and Legality," Criminal Justice History: An International Annual 2 (1981): 131-160.

A discussion of the scrutiny of the FBI for its alleged willful acts to mislead Congress as to its activities.

7538. Theoharis, Athan G.   "FBI Surveillance During the Cold War Years: A Constitutional Crisis," Public Historian 3/1 (Winter 1981): 4-14.

Discusses the Federal Bureau of Investigation's role against alleged dissident groups with little or no regard for the constitutional rights of those affected.

7539. Theoharis, Athan G.   "FBI Files, the National Archives and the Issue of Access," Government Publications Review 9/1 (January-February 1982): 29-36.

Argues that Federal Bureau of Investigation's long-standing violation of privacy rights necessitates historical research of the FBI records, and he suggests that the National Archives has failed to perform adequately in furtherance of historical inquiries into FBI behavior.

7540. Theoharis, Athan G.   "The Freedom of Information Act and the Intelligence Agencies," Government Publications Review 9/1 (January-February 1982): 37-44.

Challenges intelligence agency claims for exempting files from discovery under the Freedom of Information Act. Argues that congressional is less than adequate because committees do not have available independent historical research capabilities.

7541. Theoharis, Athan G.   "The CIA and the New York Times: An Unanswered Question," Government Publications Review 10/3 (1983): 257-261.

Surveys a mysterious connection between CIA psychological warfare official Joseph Bryan III and New York Times officials in 1951. Argues for additional research on the relationship between the CIA and the media and CIA and FBI.

7542. Theoharis, Athan G. "FBI Surveillance: Past and Present," Cornell Law Review 69/4 (April 1984): 883-894.

A brief history of FBI surveillance of political dissidents from 1940 to 1984, based on papers acquired under the Freedom of Information Act.

7543. Theoharis, Athan G.   "Researching the Intelligence Agencies: The Problem of Covert Activities," Public Historian 6/2 (Spring 1984):   67-76.

Discusses the difficulties faced by the public in using the FOIA to gain access to FBI and CIA records. An uninformed public cannot easily counteract agency activities to which it might object.

7544. Theoharis, Athan G.   "The FBI and the American Legion Contact Program," Political Science Quarterly 100/2 (Summer 1985): 271-286.

Chronicles the American Legion's involvement with the FBI during World War II as well as the Legion's establishment of an information-gathering system.

7545. Theoharis, Athan G.   "The FBI and the Politics of Surveillance, 1908-1985," Criminal Justice Review 15/2 (Autumn 1990):   221-230.

A history of FBI domestic intelligence operations from 1908 to the mid-1980s, arguing that all such operations were self-justifying. Contains evidence of numerous abuses of authority.

7546. Theoharis, Athan G. and Elizabeth Meyer.   "The 'National Security' Justification for Electronic Eavesdropping: An Elusive Exception," Wayne Law Review 14/3 (1968): 749-771.

Contains thorough analysis of several arguments against use of electronic eavesdropping, in particular, in cases involving national security. Reviews history of wiretap policy and offers a proposal to limit use.

7547. Tholl, Claire K. "Major Andre Is Still With Us," North Jersey Highlander 7/3 (1971): 3-8.

7548. Thom, M. I. "The Evolution of C^{3}I," International Defense Review 13/7 (1980): 1033-1035.

7549. Thom, William G.   "The Challenge of Analyzing African Military Capabilities," American Intelligence Journal 7/1 (June 1985): 1-9.

7550. Thomann, Charles E. "The National Intelligence Act of 1980," American Intelligence Journal 3/1 (Winter 1980): 8-34.

Lengthy analysis of this late Carter administration statute.

7551. Thomas, A. J. "The Organization of American States and Subversive Intervention," Proceedings of the American Society of International Law 55 (1961): 19-24.

Reflections upon the rise to power of Cuba's Fidel Castro in 1959. The author considers the policies of the Organization of American States with respect to subversive intervention in Latin American states.

7552. Thomas, Andy. "British Signals Intelligence After the Second World War," Intelligence and National Security 3/4 (October 1988): 103-110.

A brief discussion on the location of some of the records of British SIGINT, and the types of information that require consideration for a full appreciation of the British, Canadian and US cooperation. Concludes that there is no open organized archive of all the records on SIGINT.

7553. Thomas, Charles W. "Combat Intelligence for the Deep Attack," Military Review 63/4 (April 1983): 42-51.

Outlines electronic combat systems capability at the battalion level, and points to future capabilities.

7554. Thomas, David T. "Foreign Armies East and German Military Intelligence in Russia 1941-45," Journal of Contemporary History 22/2 (April 1987): 261-301.

Discusses the mobility of German intelligence to provide necessary and important information on the Soviet army capabilities before the Nazi attack on Russia in 1941.

7555. Thomas, Evan. "Wayward Spy," Civilization 2/2 (September-October 1995): 36-45.

A fairly detailed discussion of the career of former CIA official and planner of the Bay of Pigs mission, Richard Bissell.

7556. Thomas, Evan. "Gaining Access to CIA's Records," Studies in Intelligence 39/5 (1996): 19-23.

The author's personal recollections and observations about his access to various CIA classified documents. Concludes that it would be wise for CIA to open up many early files in order to lay to rest the widely held view that the Agency is hiding "...terrible secrets--that do not exist!"

7557. Thomas, G. Guy. "Soviet Radio Electronic Combat and the U.S. Navy," Naval War College Review 35/4 (July-August 1982): 16-24.

Discusses the topic in terms of exploitation, deception, denial, and destruction.

7558. Thomas, G. Guy. "Warfare in the Fourth Dimension--Is the Navy Ready for It? How Can the Navy Prepare for It?," Naval War College Review 36/1 (January-February 1983): 16-23.

Discusses electronic warfare strategies and war game play.

7559. Thomas, Hugh. "The U.S. and Castro, 1959-1962," American Heritage 29/10 (October-November 1978): 26-35.

A thorough summary of the actions leading to Castro's complete self-installation as the Marxist ruler of Cuba. Discusses CIA involvement.

7560. Thomas, J. "Class, State, and Political Surveillance: Liberal Democracy and Structural Contradictions," Insurgent Sociologist 11-12 (Summer-Fall 1981): 47-58.

7561. Thomas, Jack E. "E.O. 12333--Analysis and Facts," American Intelligence Journal 4/4 (September 1982): 13-16.

7562. Thomas, Jack E. "The Leakage of Classified Information: A Significant National Security Problem," American Intelligence Journal 9/1 (Summer 1988): 15-19.

Summarizes recommendations by various committees regarding leaks of classified government information; offers suggestions for solution.

7563. Thomas, Jack E. "Reorganization of Intelligence Activities in the Office of the Secretary of Defense," American Intelligence Journal 14/3 (Autumn-Winter 1993-1994): 41-47.

Author's remarks concerning progressive steps to reorganize intelligence activities of the Office of Secretary of Defense from March 1977 to 1994.

7564. Thomas, Louis. "Geographic Intelligence," Studies in Intelligence 7/3 (Fall 1963).

7565. Thomas, Martin. "The Massingham Mission: SOE in French North Africa, 1941-1944," Intelligence and National Security 11/4 (1996): 696-721.

A discussion of the Algeria-based Massingham mission of the Special Operations Executive (SOE), and the author's attempt to assess the mission in light of newly released records. Discusses the interrelationship between the OSS and the British SOE.

7566. Thomas, Paul G. "Secrecy and Publicity in Canadian Government," Canadian Public Administration 19/1 (Spring 1976): 158-164.

A review essay concerning the Canadian Privy Council Office report of April 1974 entitled "The Provision of Government Information" by D. F. Wall. Report was requested by the Trudeau government in response to a series of information leaks.

7567. Thomas, Ronald C., Jr. "Influences on Decisionmaking at the Bay of Pigs," International Journal of Intelligence and Counterintelligence 3/4 (Winter 1989): 537-548.

Discusses relevant previous research; formulation prior to getting on the agenda; momentum from below; other political influences; the CIA fills the decision void; the National Security Council discussions; and conclusions.

7568. Thomas, Rosamund M. "The British Official Secrets Acts 1911-1939 and the Ponting Case," Criminal Law Review (August 1986): 491-510.

7569. Thomas, Rosamund M. and Laurence Lustgarten. "Espionage and Secrecy," British Journal of Criminology 33 (Spring 1993): 302-303.
A book review essay.

7570. Thomas, Stafford T. "On the Selection of Directors of Central Intelligence," Southeastern Political Review 9/1 (Spring 1981): 1-59.

7571. Thomas, Stafford T. "Assessing Current Intelligence Studies," International Journal of Intelligence and Counterintelligence 2/2 (Summer 1988): 217-244.
Focussing on the study of Western, especially US intelligence services, the author aims to introduce a clearer view of intelligence epistemology. Major sections address concerns for description; policy prescription; normative prescription; and explanation.

7572. Thomas, Stafford T. "Presidential Styles and DCI Selection," International Journal of Intelligence and Counterintelligence 7/2 (Summer 1994): 175-194.
Applying his criteria for evaluating the selection of directors of central intelligence, the author discusses constants in the decision equation; variables; DCI positional considerations; and examples of DCI types.

7573. Thomas, William C. "Understanding the Objectives of Terrorism," American Intelligence Journal 16/2&3 (Autumn-Winter 1995): 54-58.
Sections discuss terrorist objectives; recognition; intimidation; coercion; insurgency support; provocation; and using tools.

7574. Thompson, Edmund R. "INSCOM: To Move More Intelligence Faster Up the Line," Army 27 (October 1977): 125-126+.
A brief discussion of the role and activities of the Army's Intelligence and Security Command.

7575. Thompson, Edmund R. "Critical Intelligence Issues of the '80's," Signal (October 1980): 11-12.
A brief summary of the issues.

7576. Thompson, Edmund R. "Army Intelligence at Yorktown: Catalyst to Victory," Military Intelligence 7/3 (July-September 1981): 44-47.

Discusses the spirit of victory, the Yorktown campaign, the role of intelligence operations, strategic deception, tactical deception, secret messages and signals, and conclusions.

7577. Thompson, Edmund R. "Intelligence in Yorktown," Defense/81 (October 1981): 25-28.

7578. Thompson, Edmund R. "George Washington, Master Intelligence Officer," American Intelligence Journal 6/2 (July 1984): 3-8.

7579. Thompson, Edmund R. "Sleuthing the Trail of Nathan Hale," Intelligence Quarterly 2/3 (October 1986): 1-4.

7580. Thompson, Edmund R. "Document Sheds New Light on 'General Gage's Informers,'" Intelligence Quarterly 5/3 (October 1989): 8-10.

7581. Thompson, Edmund R. "George Washington: A Master of Deception," American Intelligence Journal 12/1 (Winter 1991): 7-10.
    Offers some brief observations on the tactical and strategic deceptions George Washington used to good effect during the American Revolution. Sections discuss tactical, operational and strategic deception.

7582. Thompson, George R. "Development of the Signal Corps Field Telegraph 1861-1863," Signal 12 (1958): 28-34.

7583. Thompson, Jerry D. "Drama in the Desert: The Hunt for Henry Skillman in the Trans-Pecos, 1862-1864," Password 37/3 (1992): 107-126.

7584. Thompson, Kenneth W. "American Foreign Policy: Values Renewed or Discovered," Orbis 20/1 (Spring 1976): 123-135.
    Offers numerous suggestions about how to incorporate values in the mid 1970s foreign policy dialogue.

7585. Thompson, Michael. "Thoughts Provoked by 'The Very Best Men': The Need for Integrity," Studies in Intelligence 39/5 (1996): 25-34.
    A review essay on the issues and circumstances that served as the backdrop for Evan Thomas' book, The Very Best Men. Sections discuss covert action; need for examination; the starting point; serious shortcomings of the DDO; the Bays of Pigs situation; assassination attempts; negative influence; esprit de corps; costs of devious conduct; and insistence on integrity.

7586. Thompson, Patrick A. "Wiretapping--Power of the US Attorney-General to Authorize Wiretapping Without Judicial Sanction," Kentucky Law Journal 60 (1971): 245-252.

Outlines the facts of the case, problems created by wiretapping's infringement on personal privacy, the case law precedents of relevance, and the decision of the courts in Bivens.

7587. Thompson, W. A. "Scouting with Mackenzie," Journal of the U.S. Cavalry Association 10 (1897): 429-433.

7588. Thornberry, Cedric H. R.. "The Soblen Case," Political Quarterly 34/2 (April 1963): 162-173.
Considers the circumstances of Robert Soblen's emigration to the US before World War II and his subsequent conviction for espionage. Further considers the specific factions involved in asylum, deportation, and extradition as they are involved in the case.

7589. Thornberry, Cedric H. R. "Dr. Soblen and the Alien Law of the United Kingdom," International and Comparative Law Quarterly 12 (1963): 414-474.
Discusses English law on admission and expulsion of aliens; political asylum in Britain since World War II; the Soblen case before the courts; and some conclusions and suggestions for reform.

7590. Thornborough, Gayle. "The Count in the Kitchen," American Heritage 4 (Summer 1953): 6-9.

7591. Thorne, Peter. "Andrew Thorne and the Liberation of Norway," Intelligence and National Security 7/3 (July 1992): 300-316.
The author draws on his father's 1951 Report on the Liberation of Norway and the surrender of German forces in 1945. Major sections discuss the leitmotif and favoring factors; order of battle problems; the revised plan for Norway; the Eisenhower version; planning for a Wehrmacht resistance; guessing the Lillehammer enigma; Swedish uncertainties; doomsday; and envoi.

7592. Thornley, I. D. "Treason by Words in the Fifteenth Century," English Historical Review 32 (1917): 556-561.

7593. Thornley, I. D. "Treason Legislation of Henry VIII," Transactions of the Royal Historical Society 11 (1917): 87-98.

7594. Thornley, I. D. "The Act of Treason, 1352," History 6 (1921): 106-108.

7595. Thornton, Zane. "Community Progress in Information Handling," Studies in Intelligence 11/4 (Winter 1967).

7596. Thorson, S. J. and D. A. Sylvan. "Counterfactuals and the Cuban Missile Crisis," International Studies Quarterly 26 (December 1982): 539-571.

7597. Thun-Hohenstein, Romedio G. von. "Engagement of Agents in Albania: A Failed Commando Undertaking in the Cold War," Damals 21/1 & 2 (1989): 2-17; 115-130.

7598. Thurbon, M. T. "The Origins of Electronic Warfare," Journal of the Royal United Service Institution for Defence Studies 122 (1977): 56-73.
        A discussion of electronic warfare dating from the American Civil War the "Phoney War" in Europe.

7599. Thurlow, Richard C. "British Fascism and State Surveillance, 1934-45," Intelligence and National Security 3/1 (January 1988): 77-99.
        Provides a brief historical overview of the Fascist movement in Britain and the intelligence efforts to undermine and control the direction of the movement's work. Concludes that this case study offers furtile ground for future consideration of the limits of freedom in British society.

7600. Thurlow, Richard C. "Internment in the Second World War," Intelligence and National Security 9/1 (January 1994): 123-127.
        A review essay of F. Lafitte's book, The Internment of Aliens, and A. W. Brian Simpson's In the Highest Degree Odious.

7601. Thurston, Samuel F. "Central Intelligence Agency and the New York Times," Computers and Automation 20 (July 1971): 51-57.

7602. Tice, Brian P. "U.S. Air Force Operations and Intelligence: Getting It Together," Airpower Journal 1/3 (Summer 1987): 31-33.
        Offers briefly some proposals for improving "jointness" in intelligence support for the Air Force mission.

7603. Tidwell, William A. "Horrible Thought," Studies in Intelligence 2/4 (Winter 1958).
        A discussion of the inertia in the estimative intelligence process.

7604. Tidwell, William A. "Notes on the CRITIC System," Studies in Intelligence 4 (Spring 1960).

7605. Tidwell, William A. "A New Kind of Air Targeting," Studies in Intelligence 11/4 (Winter 1967).

7606. Tidwell, William A. "Confederate Expenditures for Secret Service," Civil War History 37/3 (September 1991): 219-231.
        Discusses Confederate espionage efforts in the context of the Confederacy's expenditures of four times as much money in gold than the Union. Mentions the role of Jefferson Davis in ordering the expenditures.

7607. Tierno, R. "That You May Live," <u>Infantry School Quarterly</u> 42 (January 1953): 68-77

7608. Tighe, Eugene F., Jr. "The Change and the Challenge," <u>Photogrammetric Engineering and Remote Sensing</u> 45/7 (1979): 949-955.

7609. Tighe, Eugene F., Jr. "Military Intelligence," <u>Defense/81</u> (March 1981): 2-9.

7610. Tighe, Eugene F., Jr. "View from the Top: Interview with Admiral Bobby Inman: Intelligence Should Be the Front Line of Defense," <u>Military Electronics and Countermeasures</u> 9/1 (1983): 4-12.

7611. Tighe, Eugene F., Jr. "Narrowing the Industry-Intelligence Community Gap," <u>Signal</u> (September 1984).

7612. Tighe, Eugene F., Jr. "Protection U.S. Security," <u>Signal</u> 40/1 (September 1985): 83-84.

7613. Tighe, Eugene F., Jr. "Imagery and Reconnaissance: Reminiscences," <u>American Intelligence Journal</u> 13/1&2 (Winter-Spring 1992): 81-85.
     Some personal recollections of the author pertaining to his extensive service in military intelligence, in particular, his work during and following World War II in the new field of photo reconnaissance.

7614. Tillman, Barrett. "Hellcats Over Truk," <u>U.S. Naval Institute Proceedings</u> 103/3 (1977): 63-71.

7615. Timbers, Edwin. "Legal and Institutional Aspects of the Iran-Contra Affair," <u>Presidential Studies Quarterly</u> 20 (Winter 1990): 31-40.
     Major sections include discussion of the Boland Amendment, provisions of the United Nations Charter, the objectives of arms sales to Nicaragua, the Tower Commission, and the failure of the system.

7616. Timm, Eric M. "Countersabotage--A Counterintelligence Function," <u>Studies in Intelligence</u> 7/1 (Spring 1963).
     An essay on the role of countersabotage in wartime.

7617. Tirshwell, Eric. "Victim or Villain? Considering the 'Pollard Affair,'" <u>Congress Monthly</u> 56/5 (1989): 17-18.

7618. Tittenhofer, Mark A. "The Rote Drei: Getting Behind the 'Lucy' Myth," <u>Studies in Intelligence</u> 13/2 (Summer 1969).

7619. Tobenkin, Elias. "Boris Savinkov: The Conversion of the Soviets' Most Spectacular Foe," Current History (December 1924): 392-393.

7620. Tobias, Carl. "Elevated Pleading in Environmental Litigation," U.C. Davis Law Review 27 (Winter 1994): 357-374.
    Considers issues in the Supreme Court case, Leatherman v. Tarrant County Narcotics Intelligence & Coordination Unit, 113 S. Ct. 1160 (1993).

7621. Toensing, Victoria. "Congressional Oversight: Impending the Executive Branch and Abusing the Individual," Houston Journal of International Law 11/1 (Fall 1988): 169-176.
    Argues that there is cause for alarm concerning abuses of the congressional oversight of intelligence activities.

7622. Toffler, Alvin. "Washington's Electronic Eavesdroppers," Coronet 45 (January 1959): 88-93.
    This article is published in a popular press magazine not normally considered scholarly, but the author is a well recognized and respected sociologist who has contributed to interpretations of technological advancement and its implications for social change.

7623. Toffler, Alvin. "Moscow's Dark Cloud," World Monitor 4/7 (July 1991): 29-36.

7624. Toffler, Alvin and Heidi Toffler. "Powershift: The World's Most Dangerous Brain Drains," International Journal of Intelligence and Counterintelligence 5/3 (Fall 1991): 329-332.
    These popular authors offer brief remarks with respect to the possibilities for the relocation of Soviet nuclear weapons and the whereabouts of KGB officers in a post-Soviet world. Fears are expressed concerning the possibility of nuclear weapons and former KGB "brains" appearing in the military and economic wars of the future.

7625. Tolbert, Emory J. "Federal Surveillance of Marcus Garvey and the U.N.I.A.," Journal of Ethnic Studies 14/4 (Winter 1987): 25-46.
    Discusses J. Edgar Hoover's efforts to discredit and oppress the Black Nationalist movement of Marcus Garvey and the Universal Negro Improvement Association.

7626. Tolles, Frederick B. "Unofficial Ambassador: George Logan's Mission to France, 1798," William and Mary Quarterly 7 (January 1950): 3-25.
    Pertains to Dr. George Logan's trip to France, perhaps as a member of a conspiracy associated with French underground actions in the US.

7627. Tolley, Kemp. "Stop, Look, and Listen," U.S. Naval Institute Proceedings 93 (April 1967): 58-65.

7628. Tomaselli, Ruth E. "Inkathagate: Covert Funding--Overt Violence," Covert Action Information Bulletin 38 (Fall 1991): 39-43.

A brief and limited examination of the covert security forces of the South African Inkatha Zulu organization operating against the African National Congress in the 1980s.

7629. Tomlinson, James E. "Foreign Counterintelligence: An FBI Priority," FBI Law Enforcement Bulletin 60/9 (September 1991): 10-14.

7630. Tomlinson, William B. "Chinese Industry from the Air," Studies in Intelligence 11/1 (Spring 1967).

7631. Tonkovich, Emil A. "The Use of Title III Electronic Surveillance to Investigate Organized Crime's Hidden Interests in Gambling Casinos," Rutgers Law Journal 16 (Spring-Summer 1985): 811-829.

Discusses application of Title III in the Department of Justice "hidden interest" case against Nick Civella and other Kansas City associates of organized crime.

7632. Toole, Wycliffe D., Jr. "Military Cover and Deception vs. Freedom of Information," U.S. Naval Institute Proceedings 101/12 (December 1975): 18-23.

Argues that military cover and deception are not always the marks of political deceit. The military requires the use of secrecy in its decisions making explanations. FOIA, it is argued, has become and easy resource for "enemy planners."

7633. Topol, David H. "United States v. Morison (844 F.2d 1057 (1988): A Threat to the First Amendment Right to Publish National Security Information," South Carolina Law Review 43 (Spring 1992): 581-615.

7634. Topol, M. L. "A License to Kill," Voenno-Istoricheskii Zhurnal 11 (1990): 48-62.

7635. Topping, Aileen M. "'A Free Facetious Gentleman,' Jean Savy, Double Agent?," Florida Historical Quarterly 56/3 (1978): 261-279.

Examines the historical evidence pertaining to Jean Savy's work as a double agent for Spain and England.

7636. Tordella, Louis W. and Edwin C. Fishel. "A New Pearl Harbor Villain: Churchill," International Journal of Intelligence and Counterintelligence 6/3 (Fall 1993): 363-369.

A book review essay concerning Betrayal at Pearl Harbor: How Churchill Lured Roosevelt into World War II by James Rusbridger and Eric Nave.

7637. Torrey, Gordon and Donald Avery. "Postal Forgeries in Two World Wars," Studies in Intelligence 4 (Summer 1960).

7638. Toru, Watanabe. "1991: American Perceptions of the Pearl Harbor Attack," Journal of American-East Asian Relations 3 (Fall 1994).

7639. Toscano, Mario. "Machiavelli" Views World War II Intelligence," International Journal of Intelligence and Counterintelligence 1/3 (Fall 1986): 41-52.

This is a reprinted article by the late historian Toscano, illustrating the point that information must not only reach the decision maker but it must also be accepted as valid. Uses the negotiations leading to the German-Soviet pact of 1939 as a case in point.

7640. Tovar, B. Hugh. "The Not-So-Secret War, or How State-CIA Squabbling Hurts U.S. Intelligence," Studies in Intelligence 25/1 (Spring 1981): 43-49.

The author, an experienced operator at CIA, documents the failures of collaboration between CIA and the State Department in the years following the fall of the Shah of Iran.

7641. Tovar, B. Hugh. "Thoughts on Running a Small War," International Journal of Intelligence and Counterintelligence 1/3 (Fall 1986): 85-93.

Recognizes that American presidents always confront the possibility of intervention in foreign conflicts, and that the CIA is suited for continuing covert paramilitary business where necessary.

7642. Tovar, B. Hugh. "Vietnam Revisited: The United States and Diem's Death," International Journal of Intelligence and Counterintelligence 5/3 (Fall 1991): 291-312.

Considers competing intellectual views regarding the role of Diem's assassination in the general context of strong US commitment to total involvement in Vietnam after 1963. Considers several aspects of the buildup of involvement in the time, including entrance of the CIA in the decision equation.

7643. Tovar, B. Hugh. "The Indonesian Crisis of 1965-1966: A Retrospective," International Journal of Intelligence and Counterintelligence 7/3 (Fall 1994): 313-338.

Discusses the coup d'etat by Indonesian communists, an event which surprised academics in terms of the strength and determination of the rebel forces. Major sections discuss the weak Indonesian military; Suharto's Indonesia; the intelligence scene; the question of genocide; the role of the BBC; the question of surprise; the military relationship; the myth of the Generals' Council; the Gestapu affair; the question of an intelligence failure; the counter-coup; destruction of the Communist Party; and declassification of LBJ Library documents.

7644. Towe, Thomas E.   "A Growing Awareness of Privacy in America," Montana Law Review 37/1 (Winter 1976): 39-89.
      Among several privacy issues, the author discusses President Ford's Commission on Intelligence Activities (Rockefeller).

7645. Tower, John G. "Congress Versus the President: The Formulation and Implementation of American Foreign Policy," Foreign Affairs 60/2 (Winter 1981-1982): 229-246.
      Presents numerous arguments regarding the conflict over foreign policy decision making, including the role of Congress in containing the intelligence community.

7646. Townsend, Elias C. "EEIs in Combat Intelligence," Army 6 (May 1956): 46-47.

7647. Townsend, Robert E.   "Deception and Irony: Soviet Arms and Arms Control," American Intelligence Journal 14/2&3 (Spring-Summer 1993): 47-53.
      Examines a highly successful deception operation by the Soviet Union against US intelligence, and the successful use of open source intelligence to uncover the plot. Covers the Shelepin deception plan of 1959; the plan's impact; and Soviet access to the intelligence process.

7648. Townshend, Charles. "The Irish Republican Army and the Development of Guerilla Warfare, 1916-1921," English Historical Review 94/371 (April 1979): 318-345.
      A detailed explanation of the circumstances under which Irish rebels perfected guerilla warfare in the years considered.

7649. Trachtenberg, Marc. "The Influence of Nuclear Weapons in the Cuban Missile Crisis," International Security 10/1 (1985): 137-163.
      Major topics discuss the role of nuclear arms in the missile crisis of 1962; the balance of resolve; the American side in the strategic balance; the Soviet side; and conclusions. Mentions the CIA role and input.

7650. Trachtenberg, Marc. "White House Tapes and Minutes of the Cuban Missile Crisis: Ex-Com Meetings in October 1962," International Security 10/1 (1985): 164-203.
      An outline of some critical documents relevant to the circumstances of the missile crisis negotiations and resolution. Mentions role and input of the Central Intelligence Agency.

7651. Trachtenberg, Marc. "Commentary: New Light on the Cuban Missile Crisis?," Diplomatic History 14/2 (Spring 1990): 241-247.

Discussion of the changes in the conventional views of the Crisis ("battle of blunders") to a new view of effective crisis management. Role of U-2 overflights is mentioned.

7652. Trafton, Robert T. "NMITC--An Update," Naval Intelligence Professionals Quarterly 4/1 (January 1988): 14-16.

A brief overview of the Navy and Marine Corps Intelligence Training Center (NMITC).

7653. Trafton, Robert T. "Drug Interdiction Training at the Navy and Marine Corps Intelligence Center (NMITC)," American Intelligence Journal 11/1 (Winter 1989): 19-23.

An overview of the drug interdiction program of the US Navy; legal foundation for interdiction; training; and organizational interaction with other law enforcement groups.

7654. Trager, Frank N. "The National Security Act of 1947: Its Thirtieth Anniversary," Air University Review 29/1 (November-December 1977): 2-15.

A general discussion of the creation of the national defense system, including the intelligence component. The organizational provisions of the Act are outlined, including provision for the Central Intelligence Agency.

7655. Trager, Frank N. "Burma in 1977: Cautious Changes and a Careful Watch," Asian Survey 18/2 (February 1978): 142-152.

Mentions the treason trials in Burma, a state under significant change in economic and political arenas.

7656. Trainor, B. E. "Recon Operations in Southeast Asia, 1970-1971," Marine Corps Gazette 70 (May 1986): 54, 59.

7657. Trainor, James L. "What Role Can Unmanned Satellites Play in Tactical Warfare?," Armed Forces Management 12/3 (December 1965): 66-67.

7658. Travers, David. "The Permanent Intelligence Committees of the United States Congress and Effective Oversight of Covert Operations," Defense Analysis 3/2 (June 1987): 182-184.

A brief overview of the role of congressional oversight committees after the Iran-Contra scandal was revealed.

7659. Traynor, William L. "The Political War in Vietnam," Marine Corps Gazette 51 (August 1967): 24-27.

7660. Trefousse, Hans L. "Failure of German Intelligence in the United States, 1935-1945," Mississippi Valley Historical Review 42/1 (June 1955): 84-100.

　　Discusses in detail the German espionage activities in the United States during World War II. The author argues that this work was largely ineffectual in benefitting Hitler.

7661. Tregle, Joseph G., Jr. "British Spy Along the Mississippi: Thomas Hutchins and the Defenses of New Orleans, 1773," Louisiana History 8/4 (1967): 313-327.

　　An account of Hutchins' espionage escapades in Louisiana in 1773 and the unforeseen results.

7662. Trengrouse, W. M. "The Ninja," Studies in Intelligence 9/1 (Spring 1965).

　　A discussion of the Ninja in medieval Japan.

7663. Trepper, Leopold. "The Big Game: Memoirs of the Director of the Red Orchestra," Novaia i Noveishaia Istoriia 1 (1990): 163-170.

　　The author, whose true name is Leiba Domb, wrote a personal account of his work as head of the Soviet Union's spy network, Red Orchestra, early in World War II.

7664. Treverton, Gregory F. "Reforming the CIA," Millennium: Journal of International Studies 5/3 (Winter 1976-1977): 312-317.

　　Discusses congressional inroads into controlling intelligence operations, presidential actions, a proposal for structural division of the CIA, and a call to reform the CIA as soon as possible.

7665. Treverton, Gregory F. "Covert Action: From "Covert" to Overt," Daedalus 116/2 (Spring 1987): 95-123.

　　Drawing on the Tower Commission Report on CIA involvement in the Iran-Contra Affair, the author discusses CIA's new conservatism and compares CIA actions in Bay of Pigs, Guatemala, Chile and Iran-Contra.

7666. Treverton, Gregory F. "Covert Action and Open Society," Foreign Affairs 65/5 (Summer 1987): 995-1014.

　　Details CIA covert actions from 1950-1966. A similar piece to one published in Daedalus 116 (Spring 1987): 95-123.

7667. Treverton, Gregory F. "Imposing a Standard: Covert Action and American Democracy," Ethics and International Affairs 3 (1989): 27-43.

　　Major sections include discussion of covert intervention cases, covert action guidelines, the congressional buddy system, weaknesses in congressional oversight of covert actions, and limits on congressional imposition of standards.

7668. Treverton, Gregory F. "Covert Intervention in Chile, 1970-1973," <u>Studies in Intelligence</u> 35/4 (Winter 1991).

7669. Treverton, Gregory F. "Estimating Beyond the Cold War," <u>Defense Intelligence Journal</u> 3/2 (Fall 1994): 5-20.
        Reports on the work of the National Intelligence Council, an advisory group to the Director of Central Intelligence. Major sections discuss responses to the changed world; estimating as a process; estimating well; the craft of estimating; and relevance and objectivity.

7670. Treves, Tullio. "Military Installations, Structures, and Devices on the Seabed," <u>American Journal of International Law</u> 74/4 (October 1980): 808-857.
        Discusses the functions and importance of military objects on the seabed, the evolving legal framework, peaceful purposes, internal and territorial waters, archipelagic waters, and the international seabed area.

7671. Trevor-Roper, Hugh. "The Philby Affair: Espionage, Treason, and Secret Services," <u>Encounter</u> 30/4 (April 1968): 3-26.
        An extensive consideration of the Kim Philby espionage work for the Soviet Union in the years 1941-1951. Extensive discussion of Philby's impact on Western intelligence operations.

7672. Tribe, Laurence H. and David H. Remes. "Some reflections on <u>The Progressive Case</u>: Publish <u>and</u> Perish?," <u>Bulletin of the Atomic Scientists</u> 36/3 (March 1980): 20-24.
        Discusses the government's case against the editor of <u>The Progressive</u> as to the alleged release of classified nuclear information.

7673. Trice, Robert H. "The American Elite Press and the Arab-Israeli Conflict," <u>Middle East Journal</u> 33/3 (Summer 1979): 304-325.
        Describes the elite American press; general trends in editorial attention and support, 1966-1974; editorial opinion on Arab-Israeli issues; differences among American prestige newspapers; and conclusions.

7674. Trickey, F. David. "Constitutional and Statutory Bases of Governors' Emergency Powers," <u>Michigan Law Review</u> 64/2 (December 1965): 290-307.
        A study of state constitutional and statutory emergency power provisions aimed at evaluating the sources and scope of emergency powers. Concludes that governors have extremely broad power in emergency situations.

7675. Trilling, Diana. "A Memorandum on the Hiss Case," <u>Partisan Review</u> 17/5 (May 1950): 484-500.
        A thorough review of the issues involved in the allegations against Alger Hiss.

7676. Trimble, T. Ridgeway. "'Damn Rascal,'" Maryland Historical Magazine 79/2 (1984): 142-144.

Provides an account of Samuel B. Davis' spy activities during the Civil War and his near-execution for such activities.

7677. Tritten, James J. "A Sea Change for Naval Intel: Adjusting to New Realities," Naval Intelligence Professionals Quarterly 10/2 (Spring 1994): 5-7.

7678. Troth, Robert S. "Intelligence Professionals," American Intelligence Journal 9/1 (March 1988).

7679. Trotter, David. "The Politics of Adventure in the Early British Spy Novel," Intelligence and National Security 5/4 (October 1990): 30-54.

Discusses the emergence and development of the British spy novel in the late nineteenth century and early twentieth century. Major sections discuss the contrast between real intelligence and caricature intelligence; and consider terrorists in novels, spies, the novels of William le Queux and E. Phillips Oppenheim, the novels of the "frontiersmen," and the novels of Richard Hannay.

7680. Troup, Miller. "The Element of Surprise in War," Cavalry Journal (March-April 1938): 104-109.

7681. Troy, Thomas F. "Donovan's Original Marching Orders," Studies in Intelligence 17/2 (Summer 1973): 39-69.

7682. Troy, Thomas F. "The Coordinator of Information and British Intelligence: An Essay on Origins," Studies in Intelligence 18/1 (Spring 1974).

This article was published in a special supplement edition of the CIA's inside journal.

7683. Troy, Thomas F. "Truman on CIA," Studies in Intelligence 20/1 (Spring 1976).

Discussion of Truman's role in the transitions from OSS to CIA, including discussion of William Donovan, OSS, JCS, CIG, ONI, JIS, JIC, military intelligence, and CIG. Estimated to be 18 pages in length.

7684. Troy, Thomas F. "Knifing of the OSS," International Journal of Intelligence and Counterintelligence 1/3 (Fall 1986): 95-108.

The rise and fall of William J. Donovan, OSS chief in World War II, is recounted. Includes discussion of the enemies made by Donovan who eventually sank his ship for any future assignments in the intelligence realm. Discusses new evidence in the Park report and the Hopkins calendar.

7685. Troy, Thomas F. "The Information War," World & I 1/11 (November

1986): 14-16.

7686. Troy, Thomas F. "The Quaintness of the U.S. Intelligence Community: Its Origins, Theory and Problems," International Journal of Intelligence and Counterintelligence 2/2 (Summer 1988): 245-266.

    Considers the growth of United States intelligence services; the CIA as the better mousetrap; the afterthought of the intelligence community; what is suggested by the name of the community; community realities; what to do with the DCI; and considerations of the future.

7687. Troy, Thomas F. "The British Assault on J. Edgar Hoover: The Tricycle Case," International Journal of Intelligence and Counterintelligence 3/2 (Summer 1989): 169-209.

    Sets forth a defense of J. Edgar Hoover's "Tricycle" defection case (Dusko Popov). Major sections consider the indictment of Hoover by critics; Troy's rebuttal; an outline of the critical writings on the case; evidence for Troy's argument; unfriendly defense witnesses; cross examining the defense witnesses; and summing up for the defense.

7688. Troy, Thomas F. "The "Correct" Definition of Intelligence," International Journal of Intelligence and Counterintelligence 5/4 (Winter 1991-1992): 433-454.

    The author offers a firm argument for his definition of intelligence, suggesting also that many other definitions fail to provide sufficient grasp of the intelligence realities that must be incorporated in a definition.

7689. Troy, Thomas F. "Writing History in CIA: A Memoir of Frustration," International Journal of Intelligence and Counterintelligence 7/4 (Winter 1994): 397-411.

    A personal account of the author's work inside and outside the Central Intelligence Agency as an "official" recorder of the history of William Donovan. Major sections discuss Intrepid; the Cunningham Fellowship; busted hopes; a vicious circle; a horn of plenty; enter Bill Casey; and epilogue.

7690. Truby, J. David. "Pesky Ships of the Air: Lincoln Was Impressed, but Petty Squabbles Brought Down the Union Balloons," Military History 4/4 (February 1988): 8, 58-61.

7691. Trudell, Jereen. "The Constitutionality of Section 793 of the Espionage Act and Its Application to Press Leaks," Wayne Law Review 33 (Fall 1986): 205-228.

    Major sections discuss the enactment and application of the Espionage Act; application of Section 793 to press leaks; the due process vagueness challenge; the void-on-its face challenge; and application to other leak cases. Considers the application to U. S. v. Morison.

7692. Trumpener, Ulrich. "War Premeditated? German Intelligence Operations in July 1914," Central European History 9/1 (March 1976): 58-85.

Relying on new sources of information, this is a history of German army intelligence services during the July crisis in 1914. Attempts to provide a new perspective on the Prussian army leadership.

7693. Trusen, Olaf. "Secret Service" (2 parts), Western Monats 168-169 (August & September 1940): 609-613; 13-18.

7694. Tsanacas, Demetri. "The Transborder Data Flow in the New World Information Order: Privacy or Control," Review of Social Economy 43/3 (1985): 357-370.

An analysis of problems caused by the international transfer of information by businesses. Also discusses attempts by governments to regulate data flows.

7695. Tsinev, G. "Military Counterintelligence History Reviewed: Reprinted from Kommunist Vooruzhennyke Sil, December 1978," Translations of U.S.S.R. Military Affairs 1421 (March 1979): 1-9.

7696. Tsipis, Kosta. "Arms Control Pacts Can Be Verified," Discover 8/4 (April 1987): 78-93.

A review of the developments in arms control verification by the US and the Soviet Union. Various technologies for verification are discussed, and the gaps in these technologies are revealed.

7697. Tsvigun, Semun K. "Regarding the Intrigues of Imperialistic Intelligence Agencies," Kommunist 14 (September 1981): 88-99.

7698. Tsvigun, Semun K. "Subversive Acts--Imperialism's Weapon," Kommunist 13 (March 1980): 109-119.

7699. Tsypkin, Mikhail. "The Soviet Military: Glasnost Against Secrecy," Problems of Communism 40/3 (May-June 1991): 51-66.

7700. Tuatay, Susan L. "Passports--Regulation Allowing Revocation of Passports for National Security or Foreign Policy Reasons Held Invalid," Texas International Law Journal 16/1 (Winter 1981): 141-149.

A brief discussion of the Agee case in the stages before the ruling by the Supreme Court.

7701. Tucker, Dundas P. "Rhapsody in Purple: A New History of Pearl Harbor," (Parts 1 & 2), Cryptologia 6/3, (July 1982; October 1982): 193-228; 346-367.

7702. Tucker, Jonathan B. "Strategic Command-and-Control Vulnerabilities: Dangers and Remedies," Orbis 26/4 (Winter 1983): 941-963.

7703. Tugwell, Maurice. "The New McCarthyism," Conflict Quarterly 1/1 (Summer 1980): 33-34.

7704. Tugwell, Maurice. "Understanding Propaganda," Conflict Quarterly 1/3 (Fall 1980): 9-17.

7705. Tunkel, Victor. "Industrial Espionage: What Can Be Done?," Denning Law Journal (1993): 99-112.

7706. Tuohy, Ferdinand. "Trojan Horse, 1940 Model: Chronicle from Europe," Atlantic Monthly 166 (July 1940): 58-64.
	An outline of "Fifth Column" activities in various European countries, as reported to Atlantic in May 1940.

7708. Turack, Daniel C. "Freedom of Movement and the International Regime of Passports," Osgoode Hall Law Journal 6 (December 1968): 230-245.

7709. Turack, Daniel C. "Freedom of Transnational Movement: The Helsinki Accord and Beyond," Vanderbilt Journal of Transnational Law 11/1 (Fall 1978): 585-608.
	Discusses the Helsinki review conference at Belgrade; German reaction to the accord; Soviet reaction to the accord; general assessment of the first conference; and post-Belgrade practices. A useful background piece for studies of transnational movement of people.

7710. Turk, Austin T. "Organizational Deviance and Political Policing," Criminology 19/2 (August 1981): 231-250.
	Argues that there are structural sources of organizational deviance in organizations that perform political policing. Argues for more oversight of the intelligence and federal police organizations.

7711. Turkoly-Joczik, Robert L. "Eisenhower's Laotian Adventure," Military Intelligence 13/3 (October 1987): 6-10.
	Discusses US Army covert operations in Laos during the late 1950s and early 1960s. Examines the Eisenhower administration's role in such missions.

7712. Turnbaugh, Roy. "The FBI and Harry Elmer Barnes: 1936-1944," Historian 42/3 (1980): 385-398.
	Harry Barnes was sharply critical of FBI failures to pursue organized criminals. And for that position, and his opposition to US entry into World War II, he was investigated by the FBI and threatened with prosecution for sedition.

This article is an excellent study of how J. Edgar Hoover influenced the thinking of his own investigators to the point of nearly trivial concerns about speeches and statements not followed by actions.

7713.   Turner, Barry A.   "The Organizational and Interorganizational Development of Disasters," <u>Administrative Science Quarterly</u> 21 (September 1976): 378-396.

7714.   Turner, Barry A.   "Research Note: A Comment of the Nature of Information in Channels of Observation," <u>Cybernetica</u> 20/1 (1977):   39-42.

7715.   Turner, Frederick J.   "Genet's Attack on Louisiana and Florida," <u>American Historical Review</u> 3 (1898).

7716.   Turner, Michael A.   "Understanding CIA's Role in Intelligence," <u>International Journal of Intelligence and Counterintelligence</u> 4/3 (Fall 1990): 295-305.
    Major sections discuss the nature of intelligence; the intelligence community; Director of Central Intelligence as intelligence community chief; functions of the Central Intelligence Agency; oversight of covert action; and the difficult role of CIA.

7717.   Turner, Michael A.   "Issues in Evaluating U.S. Intelligence," <u>International Journal of Intelligence and Counterintelligence</u> 5/3 (Fall 1991): 275-285.
    Discusses the need for terminological precision; intelligence at the institutional level and at the working level; warning intelligence; monitoring; and forecasting.

7718.   Turner, Michael A.   "CIA-FBI Non-Cooperation: Cultural Trait of Bureaucratic Inertia?," <u>International Journal of Intelligence and Counterintelligence</u> 8/3 (Fall 1995):   259-273.
    A discussion of the Central Intelligence Agency and Federal Bureau of Investigation administrative cultures.   Major sections discuss the problems of agency interaction as raised by the Aldrich Ames spy case; a critique of CIA; judging CIA's culture; culture as a positive organizational trait; ambiguities in the law; the separate but equal issue; what has and will be done to correct the situation.

7719.   Turner, Michael A.   "Setting Analytical Priorities in U.S. Intelligence," <u>International Journal of Intelligence and Counterintelligence</u> 9/3 (Fall 1996): 313-327.
    Major sections discuss the basic premise; the context of analytical agenda setting; agenda-setting through interactions; and implications.   Contains an interesting collection of three models of the analytical process interactions.

7720. Turner, Ralph. "The Development of Invisible Writing With Sulphocyanic Acid," Journal of Criminal Law and Criminology 32 (1941-1942): 257-258.

A brief description of laboratory techniques used to bring out words on a piece of blank paper in a 1938 case, thus suggesting a new technique for discovering secret writing. [Note: The author had the great pleasure of meeting professor Turner, a forensics expert and well repected teacher now deceased, at his home near his campus at Michigan State University in 1979.]

7721. Turner, Robert F. "The Constitution and the Iran-Contra Affair: Was Congress the Real Law Breaker?," Houston Journal of International Law 11/1 (Fall 1988): 83-142.

Major sections discuss analytical approaches to the separation of foreign affairs powers; the need for secrecy; executive privilege; congressional control over presidential staff; the question of congressional dishonesty; the Boland amendment; and policy observations.

7722. Turner, Robert F. "Coercive Covert Action and the Law," Yale Journal of International Law 20/2 (Summer 1995): 427-449.

This is a detailed book review essay on Regulating Covert Action: Practices, Contexts, and Policies of Covert Coercion Abroad in International and American Law by W. Michael Reisman and James E. Baker. Major sections discuss a definition of covert action; the international rules of the game; Nicaraguan covert action and the 'Paramilitary Activities' case; a new democracy norm in international law?; democracy, democide and peace; constitutional separation of powers; and the President's Intelligence Oversight Board.

7723. Turner, Robert F. "The CIA's Nicaragua 'Murder Manual': A Sandinista Dirty Trick?," International Journal of Intelligence and Counterintelligence 9/1 (Spring 1996): 33-41.

A brief analysis of the circumstances leading to the publication of a document that was presumed to represent the CIA's covert action to train Contras to assassinate government officials. Based on the author's interviews with all the basic participants (except Edgar Chamorro), the conclusion is drawn that the publication of the manual was a Sandinista "dirty trick."

7724. Turner, Stansfield. "The State of Intelligence and Foreign Policy," Signal 33 (August 1979): 37-40.

This is a formal banquet address given on June 20, 1979.

7725. Turner, Stansfield. "The CIA and National Security," Naval War College Review 37/3 (May-June 1984): 4-11.

Discusses CIA accomplishments in the US national security arena and congressional oversight controls for checking excesses.

7726. Turner, Stansfield. "The Stupidity of 'Intelligence': Mishandling of 1979 Report Concerning Soviet Troops in Cuba," <u>Washington Monthly</u> 18/1 (February 1986): 29-33.

Discusses the Soviet combat brigade in Cuba, from the author's book, <u>Secrecy and Democracy: The CIA in Transition</u>. The brigade's presence in Cuba was not a new development and Kennedy agreed to its presence in the early 1960s. This fact was not become known at the time due to unwillingness and lack of cohesion between elements of the intelligence community.

7727. Turner, Stansfield. "Intelligence and Secrecy in an Open Society," <u>Center Magazine</u> 19/2 (March-April 1986): 2-17.

Discusses the methods used by CIA to maintain secrecy of its operations. The author's paper is followed by questions and answers in a symposium on the subject.

7728. Turner, Stansfield. "Intelligence for a New World Order," <u>Foreign Affairs</u> 70/4 (Fall 1991): 150-166.

The author argues that intelligence should now be aimed at evaluations of economic and political conditions in the world, and there should be a single director of central intelligence for conducting the business of integrated intelligence. Reorganization of the intelligence community should be a priority.

7729. Turner, Stansfield and George Thibault. "Countering the Soviet Threat in the Mediterranean," <u>U.S. Naval Institute Proceedings</u> 103/7 (1977): 25-32.

7730. Turner, Stansfield and George Thibault. "Intelligence: The Right Rules," <u>Foreign Policy</u> 48 (Fall 1982): 122-138.

Proper intelligence gathering and analysis are functions of a competent NSC review, congressional oversight, public debate, and the charter of the intelligence community.

7731. Tuthill, Don. "Operational Planning, Pre-Pueblo," <u>Naval Intelligence Professionals</u> 4/3 (Fall 1988): 13-14.

7732. Tuthill, Don. "Tonkin Gulf, 1964," <u>Naval Intelligence Professionals Quarterly</u> 4/1 (Winter 1988): 19-21.

7733. Tuttle, Andrew C. "Secrecy, Covert Action, and Counterespionage: Intelligence Challenges for the 1990s," <u>Harvard Journal of Law & Public Policy</u> 12/2 (Spring 1989): 523-540.

Secrecy opposes values of an open society. Congressional investigations of covert CIA operations made such operations political and public. CIA has responsibility for overseas counterespionage. Concludes that First Amendment protections will probably not be violated by leaks of sensitive information.

7734. Tuttle, Andrew C. "The Fourth Amendment and Espionage," American Intelligence Journal 11/2 (Spring 1990): 40-41.
    A brief argument on the need to have the support of the Congress and the federal courts in the apprehension of persons who commit espionage.

7735. Tvaruzek, Bretislav. "The Abwehr in the Protectorate of Bohemia and Moravia, 1939-44," Historie a Vojanstvl 42/3 (1993): 110-141.
    This article is continued in 42/4 (1993): 95-119.

7736. Twining, David T. "The KAL Incident," Military Intelligence 10/3 (July-September 1984): 7-9.
    Examines the downing of the Korean Air Lines plane and lessons for military intelligence professionals and planners.

7737. Twining, David T. "Soviet Strategic Culture--The Missing Dimension," Intelligence and National Security 4/1 (January 1989): 169-187.
    A review essay examining the methodological and epistemological attributes of Soviet strategic culture as a means for improving intelligence analysis. Major sections discuss the myth of Soviet strategic supremacy and culture avoidance; quantitative/qualitative tension; the Team A-Team B experiment; the search for context; the role, relevance and impact of political culture; and strategic culture--the missing dimension.

7738. Twomey, David P. "Employer Monitoring of Telephone Calls and Electronic Mail: Staying Within the Employer Exceptions Under Federal Law," North Atlantic Regional Business Law Review 28 (Spring 1995): 119-125.

7739. Tyler, Ronnie C. "An Auspicious Agreement Between a Confederate Secret Agent and a Governor of Northern Mexico," American West 9/1 (1972): 38-43, 63.

7740. Tyron, James L. "International Organization and Police," Yale Law Journal 25/7 (May 1916): 513-535.
    Discussion of the concept of an international army and navy to enforce international law and peace.

7741. Tyson, James L. "Target America: The Influence of Soviet Propaganda on U.S. Media," Strategic Review (Winter 1982): 70-73.
    A brief overview of a book by the same author with nearly the same title. Argues that the US appears ineffective in neutralizing the impact of Soviet propaganda.

U

"The U-2 Program was the CIA's greatest coup."
(Ike's Spies by Stephen Ambrose, p. 267)

7742. Ulam, Adam B. "LeCarre - Tired of the West," Orbis 34/1 (Winter 1990): 103-106.
A review essay reflecting Ulam's generally negative views of John LeCarre's The Russia House.

7743. Ulam, James M. "The Hearsay Rule: Are Telephone Calls Intercepted by Police Admissible to Prove the Truth of Matters Impliedly Asserted?," Mississippi College Law Review (Spring 1991): 349-367.

7744. Ullman, Richard H. "At War with Nicaragua," Foreign Affairs 62/1 (Fall 1983): 39-58.
Details issues and controversies involved in US intervention in the Nicaraguan revolution.

7745. Ullman, Richard H. "The Covert French Connection," Foreign Policy 75 (Summer 1989): 3-33.
Discusses systematic US and French cooperation in terms of US covert assistance to the French nuclear forces. Major sections discuss freezing out France and new relations in the 1970s; unwrapping the physics package; delivering the package; scientific assistance; and questions about Soviet knowledge of assistance.

7746. Ullmann, Donald F. "HUMINT in the Military," <u>American Intelligence Journal</u> 14/1 (Autumn-Winter 1992-1993): 71-73.

A brief overview of the subject in terms of the battlefield context. Contains two figures on the theater campaign plan and the operational continuum.

7747. Ulsamer, Edgar. "The Soviet Juggernaut: Racing Faster than Ever," <u>Air Force Magazine</u> 59 (March 1976): 56-58+.

7748. Ulsamer, Edgar. "Military Intelligence: Streamlined, Centralized, Civilianized," <u>Air Force Magazine</u> 59/8 (August 1976): 26-30.

An analysis of the reorganization of the US intelligence community.

7749. Ulsamer, Edgar. "Moscow's Misinformation Pays Off," <u>Air Force Magazine</u> 61 (November 1978): 88-90.

7750. Ulunian, Artem. "The Special Branch of the Russian Police: Greece and Turkey Through Intelligence Eyes," <u>Revolutionary Russia</u> 5/2 (1992): 209-217.

7751. Underhill, L. K. "Jurisdiction of Military Tribunals in the United States Over Civilians," <u>California Law Review</u> 12 (January and March 1924): 75-98; 159-178.

Aims at discovering the extent of jurisdiction of tribunals of the US land and naval forces and other jurisdictions over persons engaged in civil matters. Sections discuss military law; persons subject and not subject to military law; various types of military courts and courts-martial practices; military government; and martial law.

7752. Ungar, Sanford J. "The FBI File," <u>Atlantic Monthly</u> 235 (April 1975): 37-52.

Subtitle is "Men and Machinations in the Court of J. Edgar Hoover." Discusses FBI internal practices and the role of Cartha DeLoach and William C. Sullivan as deputy directors of the Bureau.

7753. Ungar, Sanford J. "Intelligence Tangle: The CIA and the FBI Face the Moment of Truth," <u>Atlantic Monthly</u> 237 (April 1976): 31-42.

Discusses the controversies surrounding domestic intelligence activities of the CIA and FBI in the 1970s. Major sections discuss what has been learned; how the jungle grew; how the situation worsened; and what can be done to improve the situation.

7754. Ungar, Sanford J. "J. Edgar Hoover Leaves the State Department," <u>Foreign Policy</u> 28 (Fall 1977): 110-116.

Discussion of the case of Francis Knight, a State Department Passport Office employee who developed administrative and personality characteristics similar to the FBI Director, J. Edgar Hoover. Knight aggrandized her power in the files she maintained, but ultimately she was relieved of her duties.

7755. Ungar, Sanford J. "The Growing Threat to Government Secrecy," Technology Review (February-March 1982): 30-35.

7756. Ungeheuer, F. "Spies by the Thousands: Report from Germany," Harper's 242 (June 1971): 26-29.
 A discussion of the espionage capers between East and West Germany, how spies conducted business between the countries, and the consequences of capture. Suggests that espionage had become an expected practice in each country.

7757. Unna, Warren. "CIA: Who Watches the Watchmen?," Harper's 216 (April 1958): 46-53.
 Describes the role of CIA in national security decision making processes, and considers the need for congressional oversight.

7758. Unrath, Walter J. "A Matter of Hindsight: Army Clandestine Intelligence Operations and the Klaus Barbie Affair," American Intelligence Journal 14/1 (Autumn-Winter 1992-1993): 47-51.
 A personal account of the author to clarify and extend the inquiry into the Department of Justice investigation of the Klaus Barbie cooperation with US intelligence following World War II.

7759. Unsinger, Peter C. "Three Intelligence Blunders in Korea," International Journal of Intelligence and Counterintelligence 3/4 (Winter 1989): 549-561.
 Discusses the background situation in 1950 just prior to the North Korean attacks to the south; the NK invasion; the question of whether the Chinese army would intervene; Chinese surprise attacks; positional warfare; behind the lines; and acquiring intelligence behind the lines.

7760. Unsinger, Peter C.; Thomas J. Rosa; and Michael E. Miller. "Utilizing the Entire Criminal Act Continuum to Deter and Detect Crime: Sherlock Holmes, You've Misled Us! Vidocq, Come Home, All is Forgiven!," Crime Prevention Review 4/3 (April 1977): 8-12.
 Examines the criminal process in terms of information theory: the view that signals are emitted by criminals and picked up by informant receivers and the police. Argues that Vidocq, a shady French detective, used an early form of information theory application in his criminal and detective enterprises.

7761. Upham, George B. "Burgoyne's Great Mistake," New England Quarterly 3 (1930): 657-680.

7762. Upshur, Giles. "The US Naval Attache," Naval Intelligence Professionals Quarterly 9/1 (Winter 1993): 9-11.

7763. Ushakov, V. A. and V. Ia Shestapalov. "Who Masterminded the 1953 Coup in Iran?," Voprosy Istorii 4 (1980): 181-186.
This is an approximate translation of this title to an article in Russian.

7764. Usowski, Peter S. "John McCone and the Cuban Missile Crisis: A Persistent Approach to the Intelligence Policy Relationship," International Journal of Intelligence and Counterintelligence 2/4 (Winter 1988): 547-576.
A detailed review of the role of CIA director John McCone in the Cuban Missile Crisis of 1962. Explores differences between the traditionalists and the activists in the intelligence realm; McCone and President Kennedy; the missiles in Cuba; getting the facts; McCone's suspicions; honeymoon cables; solid proof; McCone's view vindicated; Rusk's blunders; McNamara's ban; decisions at the top; maneuvering and anticipating; CIA and the crisis; and assessing McCone.

7765. Usowski, Peter S. "Photo Intelligence and Public Persuasion," Studies in Intelligence 34/1 (Spring 1990).

7766. Usowski, Peter S. "Intelligence Estimates and US Policy Toward Laos, 1960-63," Intelligence and National Security 6/2 (April 1991): 367-394.
Examines the impact of the CIA's intelligence estimates on US policy towards Laos during the Kennedy administration. CIA's political intelligence was important to the formation of US policy toward Laos, favoring anti-communist groups.

7767. Utley, Beverly. "Brave Women: Distaff Side of the Revolution," American History Illustrated 3 (1968): 10-18.

7768. Utley, Harold H. "The Tactics and Techniques of Small Wars," Marine Corps Gazette 18 (August 1933): 44-48.

7769. Uyeda, Clifford I. "The Pardoning of 'Tokyo Rose': A Report on the Restoration of American Citizenship to Iva Ikuko Toguri," Amerasia Journal 5/2 (1978): 69-93.
A lengthy account of the involvement of the author and others in the vigorous pursuit of a pardon for "Tokyo Rose's" treason conviction. Also discusses organizational politics of the effort, which resulted in a pardon by President Carter in 1977.

V

"...the treachery about which Congress did not know."
(Secret History of the American Revolution by Carl Van Doren, p. 432)

7770. Vaill, George D. "Only One Life, But Three Hangings," American Heritage 24/8 (August 1973): 100-101.
Nathan Hale statue on the campus of Yale University is given brief discussion.

7771. Vaillancourt, John P. "Edward Bancroft (@Edwd. Edwards), Estimable Spy," Studies in Intelligence 5/1 (Winter 1961): 53-67.
A case study of British penetration of Ben Franklin's Paris mission written by a CIA case officer.

7772. Vaisse, Maurice. "L'evolution de la Fonction d'Attache Militaire en France au XXe Siecle," Relations Internationales 32 (1982): 507-524.

7773. Valcourt, Richard R. "Controlling U.S. Hired Hands," International Journal of Intelligence and Counterintelligence 2/2 (Summer 1988): 163-178.
Author argues that CIA collaboration with drug dealers in Asia and Latin America in the general cold war against communism raises the means-ends question for the future of intelligence. Also discusses the Reagan policies to allow top level association with sleazy arms dealers and dictators. Closes with his views on what is to be done and breaking the bonds of such easy solutions to more profound intelligence concerns.

7774. Valcourt, Richard R. "Conspiracy for Democracy," International Journal of Intelligence and Counterintelligence 4/1 (Spring 1990): 119-129.
    This is a review essay of Peter Coleman's The Liberal Conspiracy.

7775. Valenta, Jaroslav. "Additions and Corrections on the Role of Prague in the Tukhachevski Affair," Vierteljahrshefte fuer Zeitgeschichte 39/3 (1991): 437-445.

7776. Valenta, Jiri. "Soviet Decisionmaking and the Czechoslovak Crisis of 1968," Studies in Comparative Communism 8/1-2 (Spring-Summer 1975): 155-168.

7777. Valenta, Jiri. "The Soviet Invasion of Afghanistan: The Difficulty of Knowing Where to Stop," Orbis 24/2 (Summer 1980): 201-218.
    A discussion of the reasons for the Soviet attempts to expand control over Afghanistan during the 1970s. Major sections discuss the historical setting; coups, intrigues and insurgency; Islamic fundamentalism and Soviet Muslims; strategy and foreign policy; decisionmaking in the Kremlin; Karmal in Kabul; and lessons and implications.

7778. Valenta, Jiri. "From Prague to Kabul: The Mode of Soviet Invasions," International Security 5/2 (Fall 1980): 114-141.
    Considers Soviet perceptions of instabilities and failing reliabilities; security considerations; strategic considerations; contrasts between Czechoslovakia and Afghanistan; decision-making; the Soviet debate; Soviet risk assessment; planning the invasion and the coup; military doctrine and strategy; and deception, deployment, and coup.

7779. Valenta, Jiri. "Soviet Use of Surprise and Deception," Survival 24/2 (March-April 1982): 50-61.
    Discusses Soviet deception practices and strategic surprise since 1945. Suggests that a real test of these practices can only come from an attack on NATO countries.

7780. Valentine, L. L. "Sue Mundy of Kentucky," Register of the Kentucky Historical Society 62/3 & 62/4 (1964): 175-205, 278-306.

7781. Valeriote, Francis M. "Judicial Authorization for Wiretap: An Illusory Protection," Ottawa Law Review 12 (Winter 1980): 215-226.

7782. Valero, Larry. "The Role of American Intelligence in the Global Economy," International Journal of Intelligence and Counterintelligence 8/3 (Fall 1995): 359-362.
    A brief argument in opposition to extended involvement of the intelligence community in the international business interests of the US.

7783. Valliere, John E. "Disaster as Desert One: Catalyst for Change," Parameters: Quarterly Journal of the U.S. Army War College 22/3 (Autumn 1992): 69-82.

Discusses military mission failure in 1980 to rescue hostages in Tehran. Major sections discuss the planned opertion; prologue; recrimination, blame, and catalyst; operational security and command and control; and mission plan review.

7784. Valiulis, Maryann G. "The "Army Mutiny" of 1924 and the Assertion of Civilian Authority in Independent Ireland," Irish Historical Studies 23/92 (1983): 354-366.

7785. Valpey, Virginia. "Elegant Writing in the Clandestine Services III," Studies in Intelligence 21/1 (Spring 1977).

7786. Van Antwerp, William M. "Get It While It's Hot," Infantry Journal 60 (May 1947): 41-41.

A personal account of intelligence gathering against the Japanese in World War II.

7787. Van Atta, Dale. "God and Man at the CIA," Washingtonian (December 1983): 108-111.

7788. Van Bemmelen, J. M. "Did Lee Harvey Oswald Act Without Help?," New York University Law Review 40 (May 1965): 466-476.

Argues that no evidence exists to substantiate a conspiracy in the Kennedy assassination, but the Warren Commission could have conducted a more extensive investigation.

7789. Van Boven, H. Lee. "Electronic Surveillance in California: A Study in State Legislative Control," California Law Review 57 (1969): 1182-1256.

Addresses the legislative response to invasion of privacy by means of electronic devices. Examines California legislation. Major sections discuss the context and background of legislation; federal and state developments outside of California; substantive prohibitions under California law; electronic surveillance for law enforcement purposes; participant monitoring; and sanctions and remedies.

7790. Van Cleve, George W. "The Constitutionality of the Solicitation or Control of Third-Country Funds for Foreign Policy Purposes by United States Officials without Congressional Approval," Houston Journal of International Law 11/1 (Fall 1988): 69-81.

Argues that the president can solicit funds from private sources from third countries to advance his foreign policy, but the president cannot spend such funds without congressional approval; and analysis of the Constitution's appropriations clause.

7791. Van Cleave, William R. "The U.S. and Israel: A New Crisis," <u>Global Affairs</u> 7/2 (Spring 1992): 36-55.

7792. Vandam, A. D. "Spy-mania and the Revanche Idea in France," <u>Fortnightly</u> 70 (September 1898): 396-409.

7793. Vanderbrook, Michael. "UNCTAD V: Intelligence Support at a Major International Economic Conference," <u>Studies in Intelligence</u> 24/1 (Spring 1980): 47-56.
    Addresses the organization and operation of the intelligence support structure that aided the US delegation to the United Nations Conference on Trade and Development. This article is not listed among documents declassified by the Central Intelligence Agency for public access.

7794. Vandenbroucke, Lucien S. "Anatomy of a Failure: The Decision to Land at the Bay of Pigs," <u>Political Science Quarterly</u> 99/3 (Fall 1984): 471-491.
    Argues that the models applied by Professor Graham Allison in his extensive evaluation of the Kennedy administration's foreign policy decisionmaking assumptions are fundamentally useful, but the analyses could be enhanced with insights from cognitive theory.

7795. Vandenbroucke, Lucien S. "The 'Confessions' of Allen Dulles: New Evidence on the Bay of Pigs," <u>Diplomatic History</u> 8/4 (Fall 1984): 365-380.

7796. Van Der Kroef, Justus M. "Origins of the 1965 Coup in Indonesia: Probabilities and Alternatives," <u>Journal of Southeast Asian Studies</u> 3/2 (September 1972): 277-298.
    A richly detailed account of the 1965 coup, including descriptions of the complex interactions between individuals and groups.

7797. Van Der Kroef, Justus M. "The 1965 Coup in Indonesia: The CIA's Version," <u>Asian Affairs: An American Review</u> 4/2 (1976): 117-131.

7798. Vander Meer, William E. "VISTA (Very Intelligent Surveillance and Target Acquisition) -- A View of the Future," <u>Journal of Electronic Defense</u> (October 1982): 47-48.

7799. van der Meulen, Michael. "The Book Cipher System of the Wehrmacht," <u>Cryptologia</u> 19/3 (July 1995): 247-260.

7800. van der Meulen, Michael. "Werftschluessel: A German Navy Hand Cipher System--Part I," <u>Cryptologia</u> 19/4 (October 1995): 349-364.
    Part II is found in 20/1 (January 1996): 37-54.

7801. van der Oye, David C. Schimmelpinninck.
See Schimmelpinninck, David C. van der Oye

7802. Vandewalle, Dirk. "Qadhafi's 'Perestroika': Economic and Political Liberalization in Libya," Middle East Journal 45/2 (Spring 1991): 216-231.
Discussion of the internal dynamics of Libyan society and the power of Muammar Qadhafi. Refers to treason.

7803. Vandiver, James V. "Acquisition and Disposition of Police Front Line Information," Journal of Police Science and Administration 2/3 (September 1974): 288-296.
Use of tactical intelligence and information by Police Organizations.

7804. Van Dyke, John. "Miss Menzies Wishes the Record to be Complete" (reprint), New Jersey History 85/3-4 (1967): 217-224.

7805. Van Edgerton, F. "The Carlson Intelligence Mission to China," Michigan Academician 9/4 (1977): 419-432.

7806. Van Hoek, Kees. "The Leyds Memoirs," Dalhousie Review 19 (April 1939).

7807. Van Hollen, Christopher. "The Tilt Policy Revisited: Nixon-Kissinger Geopolitics and South Asia," Asian Survey 20/4 (April 1980): 339-361.
Argues that the Kissinger advice to Richard Nixon to tilt policy in favor of Pakistan during the Bangladesh conflict was unhelpful to US interests in the region. Includes information contained in a CIA report.

7808. Van Natta, Thomas F. "New Names for Old Ideas--Intelligence Planning," Military Review 28/10 (October 1948): 57-62.

7809. Van Natta, Thomas F. "The Commander and G-2," Military Review 30/8 (August 1950): 41-44; 30/10 (October 1950): 35-37.

7810. Van Patten, Jonathan K. "Magic, Prophesy, and the Law of Treason in Reformation England," American Journal of Legal History 27/1 (January 1983): 1-32.
Major sections discuss the law of treason from Edward III to Henry VIII; magic and prophesy--politics on the margin as seen by the center; and the symbolic struggle for supremacy.

7811. Van Seters, Deborah. "'Hardly Hollywood's Ideal': Female Autobiographies of Secret Service Work, 1914-45," Intelligence and National Security 7/4 (October 1992): 403-424.

Accounts of female secret service agents in World Wars I and II tend to suggest that women can work well within the context of espionage operations. Accounts, says the author, give voice to the female role in intelligence.

7812. Van Tyne, Claude H. "French Aid Before the Alliance of 1778," American Historical Review 31 (October 1925): 20-40.

7813. Van Winkle, Daniel. "John Champe: The Story of a Patriot Spy," Americana 17 (July 1923): 310-314.

7814. Vanzant, Neil C. "The Beachcomber and the Beachhead," U.S. Naval Institute Proceedings 101/6 (June 1975): 64-71.
A recollection of the mission of the Joint Intelligence Center to collect strategic intelligence by a variety of means during World War II.

7815. Vargas, Kevin J. "What Ever Happened to Tactical Intelligence?," Military Review 42/10 (October 1962): 15-20.

7816. Varon, Benno W. "Sidney Reilly, Who Almost Undid the Bolsheviks," Midstream 31/1 (January 1985): 34-37.
An essay in review of the 12-part British film concerning the life and espionage work of Sidney Reilly.

7817. Vasendin, N. and N. Kuznetsov. "Modern Warfare and Surprise Attack," Voyennaia Mysl' 6 (1966).

7818. Vasilev, P. "On Operational-Strategic Deception in World War II," Voenna Istoicheskii Zhurnal 3 (1962): 41-52.

7819. Vaughan, A. O. "Some Scouts--but Not Scouting," Longman's Magazine (February 1904): 227-241.
A very early commentary on military intelligence.

7820. Vaughan, Doug. "No More Mr. Nice Guy: The CIA and Economic Intelligence," Covert Action Quarterly 46 (Fall 1993): 4-8.
Argues that the Central Intelligence Agency purposely uses the issue of economic intelligence to expand its budget and redefine the Agency mission.

7821. Vaughan, Doug. "French Bull: Spies for Profit and Glory," Covert Action Quarterly 46 (Fall 1993): 46-49.
Discusses US concern for the economic espionage intrigues of the French, in particular the alleged participation in espionage in the computer industry by the French corporation Groupe Bull.

7822. Vaughn, Bruce. "The Use and Abuse of Intelligence Services in India," Intelligence and National Security 8/1 (January 1993): 1-22.
 Surveys the development of India's intelligence agencies and discusses their operations in terms of performance. Contains some history and organization structure. Sections discuss Bangladesh; Sri Lanka; Pakistan; and Fiji.

7823. Vaughn, Stephen. "Prologue to Public Opinion: Walter Lippmann's Work in Military Intelligence," Prologue: Journal of the National Archives 15/3 (Fall 1983): 150-163.
 Lippman served as an officer in military intelligence during World War I. He formulated his skepticism about public opinion as a result of his service in writing propaganda documents and interrogating prisoners.

7824. Vaughn, Stephen. "Spies, National Security, and the State 'Inertia Projector': The Secret Service Films of Ronald Reagan," American Quarterly 39/3 (Fall 1987): 355-380.
 An extensive review and analysis of Ronald Reagan's anti-subversion films and the use of films in general to hype national security concerns.

7825. Vaultier, Roger. "Espionage et Contre-espionage au Temps de Louis XIV," Revue Histoire des Armees 12 (1956): 17-22.

7826. Vella, Carolyn M. and John J. McGonagle, Jr. "Competitive Intelligence: Plugging Information Voids," Mergers and Acquisitions 21 (July-August 1986): 43-48.

7827. Verhoeyen, Etienne. "The 'Marc' Information Network, 1942-1944, Part I," Cahiers/Bijdragen 14 (1991): 1-60.

7828. Verhoeyen, Etienne. "'Honorable Correspondents': Belgian Citizens and 'Allied' Information Services During the Period of Neutrality, September 1939-May 1940," Revue Belge d'Histoire Militaire 29/6 & 29/7 (1992): 449-462; 511-535.

7829. Verma, O. P. "Espionage in Kautilya's Arthasastra," Indian Historical Quarterly 36 (1960).

7830. Vermaat, J. A. Emerson. "Moscow Fronts and the European Peace Movement," Problems of Communism 31 (November-December 1982): 43-56.

7831. Vernam, G. S. "Cipher Printing Telegraph Systems for Secret Wire and Radio Telegraphic Communications," Journal of the American Institute of Electric Engineers 45 (February 1926): 109-115.
 This is a discussion of the Vernam principle.

7832. Verne, Newton. "The Spy Who Came to Dinner," Washingtonian 20 (October 1984): 95-96, 100-108.

7833. Vernon, Graham D. "Soviet Combat Operations in World War II: Lessons for Today?," Military Review 60/3&4 (March and April 1980): 30-40; 42-50.

Part I discusses the Russian front; Russian commanders; and Russian soldiers. Part II discusses combat operations and intelligence.

7834. Vernon, Laurens M. "Eavesdropping in New York: 1968 Legislation," Syracuse Law Review 20/3 (Spring 1969): 601-627.

Discusses legislation for the year 1968 concerning eavesdropping. Major sections discuss the background and effect of Berger v. New York; federal legislation; and practical problems under current law.

7835. Vertzberger, Ya'acov. "India's Border Crisis with China, 1962," Jerusalem Journal of International Relations 3/2-3 (1978): 117-142.

Stresses the exceptional importance of accumulation and processing of information by decision makers charged with the responsibility to respond to international crises. Responses to research questions concerning threat, time and probability of war are addressed.

7836. Vertzberger, Ya'acov. "Bureaucratic Organizational Politics and Information Processing in a Developing State," International Studies Quarterly 28/1 (March 1984): 69-95.

7837. Viator (pseud.). "The Turkish Revolution," Fortnightly Review 90 (September 1908): 353-368.

7838. Vick, Alan J. "Post-Attack Strategic Command and Control Survival: Options for the Future," Orbis 29/1 (Spring 1985): 95-117.

Addresses the question of how the C^3I system can survive an initial nuclear attack, reconstitute and move on to prosecuting a retaliatory strike. Discusses system overview, vulnerability, counter C^3I targeting and escalation, survivability and action.

7839. Vidich, Arthur J. "Intelligence Agencies and the Universities: Further Implications of the Thesis Advanced by Sigmund Diamond in 'Compromised Campus,'" International Journal of Politics, Culture and Society 6/3 (Spring 1993): 365-378.

Major sections discuss the transition from traditional to modern espionage; the professionalization of espionage; Hoover's FBI; the OSS at Harvard University; and conclusions.

7840. Viksne, J. "The Yom Kippur War in Retrospect," <u>Army Journal</u> 324 (May 1976): 25-28.

7841. Villard, Harry S. "CIA in Embryo: Our Spies in North Africa," <u>Foreign Service Journal</u> 56 (June 1979): 24-28, 34.

Discusses US spies in North Africa during World War II, most of whom were not trained for their duties, did not speak Arabic and were unfamiliar with Moslem religion and culture.

7842. Villmoare, Adelaide H. "Normal and Abnormal Justice in America: Reflections on the Rule of Law and American Politics," <u>Polity</u> 13/2 (1980): 300-311.

A book review essay on the rule of law and politics in the American criminal justice system. Mentions the rule of law as understood by journalists to include the free acquisition of information.

7843. Viorst, Milton. "The Mafia, the CIA, and the Kennedy Assassination," <u>Washingtonian</u> 11 (November 1975): 113-118.

Discusses the interconnections between these three elements.

7844. Visvanathan, Shiv. "The Glasnost Spy," <u>Alternatives</u> 15/1 (Winter 1990): 83-96.

The author accounts for the shifting themes and styles in the spy novels of the glasnost era of the 1980s.

7845. Vivian, Francis. "The Capture and Death of Major Andre," <u>History Today</u> 7/12 (December 1957): 813-819.

7846. Vizgin, V. P. "The Role of Intelligence, 1941-1946: Material from the Russian Archives of the Foreign Intelligence Service," <u>Voprosy Istorii Estestvoznaniia i Tekhniki</u> 3 (1992): 97-103.

Discusses the acquisition of US atomic bomb secrets during World War II by Soviet intelligence agents operating inside the US and focussing attention on the Los Alamos project area.

7847. Vogel, Daniel S. "Inside a KGB Cipher," <u>Cryptologia</u> 14/1 (January 1990): 37-51.

7848. Voinovich, Vladimir. "Incident at the Metropol," <u>Kontinent</u> 5 (1975): 51-97.

7849. Volkman, Ernest. "Dust on the Plains of Siberia," <u>Military Science and Technology</u> 1/2 (1981): 77-82.

7850. Volkman, Ernest. "The Gaps That Never Were," <u>Military Science and Technology</u> 1/3 (1981): 61-67.

7851. Volkman, Ernest. "God and Ice Water: The Problem With American Intelligence," <u>Military Science and Technology</u> 1/1 (1981): 54-57.

7852. Volkman, Ernest. "Intelligence at Sea," <u>Military Science and Technology</u> 1/6 (1981): 83-87.

7853. Volkman, Ernest. "Intelligence Redux: Kissinger's Coup," <u>Military Science and Technology</u> 1/5 (1981): 58-63.

7854. Volkman, Ernest. "Intelligence to Please: The ABM," <u>Military Science & Technology</u> 1/4 (1981): 61-65.

7855. Volkman, Ernest. "A Proposal for Reform," <u>Military Science and Technology</u> 2/1 (1982): 66-71.
    An argument in favor of significant changes in the intelligence community.

7856. Volkman, Ernest and Robert Shrum. "The Cuba Syndrome," <u>Politics Today</u> (November-December 1979).

7857. Volmer, Louis. "East Europe's Espionage and Terrorism Maze," <u>International Freedom Review</u> 4/1 (1990): 5-28.

7858. Voltaggio, Frank, Jr. "Origins of ECM in the Air Force," <u>Journal of Electronic Defense</u> 5/6 (June 1982): 34-35.

7859. Voltaggio, Frank, Jr. "The Archangel Is Illuminated," <u>Journal of Electronic Defense</u> 7/2 (February 1984): 24, 68.

7860. Voltaggio, Frank, Jr. "Out in the Cold--Early ELINT Activities of the Strategic Air Command," <u>Journal of Electronic Defense</u> 10/11 (November 1987): 127-140.

7861. Voorhis, Jerry L. "Germany and Denmark, 1940-1943," <u>Scandinavian Studies</u> 44 (Spring 1972): 171-185.

7862. Vorbach, Joseph E. "The Law of the Sea Regime and Ocean Law Enforcement: New Challenges for Technology," <u>Ocean Development and International Law</u> 9/3-4 (1981): 323-333.
    Apart from the general topic, this piece mentions some technological applications for transmitting information regarding coastal enforcement matters.

7863. Voss, Frederick S. and James G. Barber. "Pinkerton Brought Law and Order--19th Century Style," <u>Smithsonian</u> 12/5 (May 1981): 60-68.

No self-respecting bibliography of intelligence would be complete without an article about one of America's leading, and partly mythological, intelligence operatives, Allen Pinkerton. This is an article about Pinkerton's exploits.

7864. Vosseller, Aurelius B. "Science and the Battle of the Atlantic," <u>Yale Review</u> 35/4 (June 1946): 667-681.

Article was written in collaboration with Glenn Nixon. Discusses the author's experiences regarding the role of scientific information and technologies in US naval warfare against U-boats.

W

"No doubt future historians will continue to argue the pros and cons
of the value of secret information."
(The Ultra Secret, by F. W. Winterbotham, p. 3)

7865. Waagenaar, Sam. "Mata Hari," Intelligence and National Security 2/4
(October 1987): 172-179.
This is a review article concerning Russell W. Howe's Mata Hari - The
True Story.

7866. Wachtel, Julius. "From Morals to Practice: Dilemmas of Control in
Undercover Policing," Crime, Law and Social Change 18/1-2 (September 1992):
137-158.
Discusses the tradeoffs between truth and consequences in undercover
work; the undermining of social convention about the evil-doers and the righteous;
some practical ways to mitigate the negative effects of undercover work;
dilemmas of control; and the need for a more informed public policy on
undercover operations.

7867. Wackwitz, Donald N. "Jet-speed Intelligence, Part I: Tools of
Command," Air University Review 9/2 (Spring 1957): 71-77.
See Part II under Wilbur W. Moeschl.

7868. Wade, Nicholas. "Decoding the NSA's Right to Know," Civil Liberties
Review 5 (January-February 1979): 76-78.
Concerns the issue of private initiatives to construct cryptographic

systems and codes and the extent to which the National Security Agency wishes for such initiatives to be suppressed.

7869. Wade, Warren L. "The Hollywood Star, the Double Agent, and Me," Naval Intelligence Professionals Quarterly 8/3 (Summer 1992): 9-10.

7870. Wade, William. "Participant Monitoring Freed from Warrants," Detroit College of Law Review 1992 (Fall 1992): 909-932.
Discusses electronic surveillance under conditions of approval by one party to the telephone conversation.

7871. Wade, William W. "The Man Who Stopped the Rams," American Heritage 14/3 (March 1963): 18-25, 78-81.
Discusses the information gathering activities of Thomas Dudley. Dudley tracked ships built in Liverpool and destined for the Confederacy.

7872. Wadham, John. "The Intelligence Services Act of 1984," Modern Law Review 57/6 (November 1994): 916-927.
This article summarizes the legislative history and key provisions of the Act. Major sections discuss the history of various intelligence acts; the 1994 Act; and conclusions as to the importance of the Act in creating legislative oversight of the SIS and the GCHQ.

7873. Waegel, William B.; M. David Ermann; and Alan M. Horowitz. "Organizational Responses to Imputations of Deviance," Sociological Quarterly 22/1 (Winter 1981): 43-55.
Argues that organizations like the Central Intelligence Agency have developed advanced methods for warding off labels of unlawful or deviant behavior through exploitation of resources of third parties that support CIA.

7874. Waghelstein, John D. "Che's Bolivian Adventure," Military Review 59/8 (August 1979): 39-48.
Detailed consideration of Cuban revolutionary Che Guevara's exploits in Bolivia in the mid 1960s. Contains photos.

7875. Wagner, Donald C. "An All-Source Collection Management Process," Defense Intelligence Journal 2/1 (Spring 1993): 81-92.
Discusses the intelligence collection management process; the current process and interoperability; an all-source approach; an example of an all-source strategy development; a combined all-source management process; and conclusions.

7876. Wagner, J. Richard. "Congress and Canadian-American Relations: The Norman Case," Rocky Mountain Social Science Journal 10/3 (1973): 85-92.

Author discusses Herbert Norman's role in espionage case investigated by the US Congress. Norman was a Canadian diplomat.

7877. Wagner, J. Richard and Daniel J. O'Neill. "The Gouzenko Affair and the Civility Syndrome," American Review of Canadian Studies 8/1 (Spring 1978): 31-42.

7878. Wagner, Louis C. "Modernizing the Army's C³I," Signal 43 (January 1989): 29-31+.

7879. Waite, James L. "Scandinavia--The Weak Northern Flank of NATO," Journal of Social, Political and Economic Studies 10/4 (Winter 1985): 407-427.

A discussion of the importance of Sweden to the northern flank of the NATO defenses in light of Soviet efforts to undermine the strengths of the alliance. Includes discussion of espionage activities in Sweden.

7880. Wald, Patricia M. "The Freedom of Information Act: A Short Case Study in the Perils and Paybacks of Legislating Democratic Values," Emory Law Journal 33/3 (Summer 1984): 649-683.

A brief history of the FOIA, its fortunes in the 1970s and early 1980s, and the FOIA's critical role in American life. Sections discuss legislative history and background; applications of the Act; the 1974 Amendments; the costs of the Act; and suggestions for change. Intelligence agencies are mentioned.

7881. Walden, Jerrold L. "The CIA: A Study in the Arrogation of Administrative Powers," George Washington Law Review 39/1 (October 1970): 66-104.

Major sections discuss the creation of the CIA; how the CIA operates; the legislative history and foreign policy; who is watching the CIA?; to whom is the CIA responsible?; and conclusions. Argues for new legislative controls over CIA operations.

7882. Walden, Jerrold L. "Proselytes for Espionage: The CIA and Domestic Fronts," Journal of Public Law 19/2 (1970): 179-207.

A detailed discussion of the extent of Central Intelligence Agency employment of private individuals, groups, and organizations to serve the interests of the Agency for propaganda purposes. Major sections discuss colleges and universities; National Student Association; other private organizations; and labor organizations.

7883. Waldrop, Bill. "A Question of Ethics: Is It Proper for a Law Firm to Hire a Private Eye to Tail a Bank Examiner?," California Lawyer 12 (February 1992): 17-19.

Private investigators and the spy business.

7884. Walker, C. Lester. "China's Master Spy," Harper's 193 (August 1946): 162-169.

Inquires about China's Bureau of Investigations and Statistics and its leadership. Includes a biographical sketch of the BIS's leader, Tai Li, and accounts of the organization's work against the Japanese in World War II and service under the Chiang regime.

7885. Walker, C. P. "Police Surveillance by Technical Devices," Public Law (1980): 184-217.

Addresses legal concerns in England for the use of technical eavesdropping devices by police. Major sections discuss recent cases; admissibility of evidence; application in police work; and pro and con arguments in use of technical surveillance devices.

7886. Walker, David A. "OSS and Operation Torch," Journal of Contemporary History 22/4 (October 1987): 667-679.

Based on recently declassified documents this account centers on planning and execution of Operation Torch. Points out OSS role and its failures, that is, Bill Donovan's inexperience, as well as the inexperience of North African vice-consuls in assessing French army strengths in North Africa.

7887. Walker, James. "The Secret Service Under Charles II and James II," Transactions of the Royal Historical Society 15 (1932): 226-235.

7888. Walker, John K. "Covert Searches Under Warrant," Search and Seizure Law Reporter 14 (November 1987): 161-166.

7889. Walker, Lewis B. "Life of Margaret Shippen, Wife of Benedict Arnold," Pennsylvania Magazine of History and Biography 24,25,26 (1900-1902): 257-266, 401-429; 20-46, 145-190, 189-302, 452-497; 71-80, 224-244, 322-334, 464-468.

A series account of Margaret "Peggy" Shippen and her intimate involvement in the espionage of her husband, Benedict Arnold, despite the family's denial of the circumstances.

7890. Walker, Neil. "Spycatcher's Scottish Sequel," Public Law 1990 (Autumn 1990): 354-371.

Considers the issues involved in a Scottish case involving the publication of a book, Inside Intelligence (Lord Advocate v. The Scotsman Publications, Ltd.), by Anthony Cavendish. Argues that the criminal law was less effective than the civil law in such matters.

7891. Walker, Samuel. "Controlling the Cops--A Legislative Approach to Police Rulemaking," University of Detroit Law Review 63/3 (Spring 1986): 361-391.

Argues for a systematic and legislatively driven movement toward police rulemaking that would contain the worst kinds of police abuses of civil liberties. Among the concerns for police rulemaking is police intelligence operations and police corruption.

7892. Walker, Steven. "National Defense Area," Army Lawyer (October 1981): 8-15.

7893. Walker, Warren S. "The Prototype of Harvey Birch," New York History 37 (1956): 399-413.

7894. Walker, William O., III. "Drug Control and National Security," Diplomatic History 12/2 (Spring 1988): 187-199.

7895. Walker, William O., III. "Drug Control and the Issue of Culture in American Foreign Relations," Diplomatic History 12/4 (Fall 1988): 365-382.

7896. Walkin, Jacob. "Some Contrasts Between the Tsarist and Communist Political Systems," New Review of East European History 15 (March 1976): 55-66.

7897. Wallace, Robert. "The Barbary Wars," Smithsonian 5 (January 1975): 82-91.
    Historical account of Algerian capture of US merchant ships and blackmail of the US government for the return of the crews, followed by President Jefferson's appeals to Congress to use the Navy. Discusses the dynamics of the conflict, the nature of the war, and the US victory in Tripoli. Most relevant to the intelligence field is the discussion of the testing of Arab myths about the US will to engage.

7898. Wallace, William. "How Frank Was Franks?," International Affairs (Great Britain) 59/3 (Summer 1983): 453-458.
    A book review essay of Falkland Island Review: Report of a Committee of Privy Counsellors Chairman: The Rt Hon. The Lord Franks. Cmnd 8787 (1983). Considers input of the Joint Intelligence Committee.

7899. Wallach, Evan J. "Executive Powers of Prior Restraint Over Publication of National Security Information: The U.K. and the USA Compared," International and Comparative Law Quarterly 32 (April 1983): 424-451.
    Carefully defining prior restraint, national security and the executive; recognizes differences exercised in the US and the UK regarding prior restraint; discusses the history of prior restraint law.

7900. Wallach, John P. "'I'll Give It to You on Background': State Breakfasts," Washington Quarterly 5/2 (Spring 1982): 54-60.

7901. Waller, John H. "The Double Life of Admiral Canaris," International Journal of Intelligence and Counterintelligence 9/3 (Fall 1996): 271-289.

Major topical sections discuss the players in the game; taking chances; chief of the Abwehr; the conspirators; the shadow putsch; the black orchestra; operation Felix; the killing of Heydrich; tricks of the trade; plotting against Hitler; Hitler fires Canaris; the failed assassination; Hitler's retaliation; and the unmasking of Canaris.

7902. Waller, J. Michael. "Russia's Security and Intelligence Services Today," Naval Intelligence Professionals Quarterly 9/4 (Fall 1993): 7-8.

A very brief overview.

7903. Waller, J. Michael. "Organized Crime and the Russian State: Challenges to U.S.-Russian Cooperation," Demokratizatsiya: Journal of Post-Soviet Democratization 2/3 (Summer 1994): 364-383.

In a lengthy and detailed discussion of the impact of organized crime in Russia, the author describes the history and role of Russian intelligence services engaged in work against organized crime. Urges caution by United States policy makers in the association between United States intelligence and law enforcement agencies and similar Russian organizations in order for the United States to avoid embarrassment through possible support of a criminal gang.

7904. Waller, J. Michael. "The KGB Legacy in Russia," Problems of Post-Communism 42/6 (November-December 1995): 3-10.

Discusses the former Soviet Union's intelligence service and the extent to which that service is embedded in the Russian culture. Major sections address the failure to uproot the KGB; the former KGB today; the transition to democratic politics; the movement of former KGB personnel into business ventures; reform proposals; and the implications for the West.

7905. Waller, J. Michael and Victor J. Yasmann. "Russia's Great Criminal Revolution: The Role of the Security Services," Journal of Contemporary Criminal Justice 11/4 (November 1995): 276-297.

Discusses the role and competency of Russian intelligence services in the post-communist era. Argues that such services are highly unreliable and institutionally part of the problem of modern Russia. Describes the structure and players in the intelligence services in substantial detail.

7906. Waller, John. "The Myth of the Rogue Elephant Interred," Studies in Intelligence 22/2 (Summer 1978).

7907. Waller, John H. "Master of Disguise," Military History 8/4 (1991): 77-91.

7908. Waller, R. "Libyan Threat Perception," Jane's Intelligence Review 9 (1995): 407-410.

7909. Wallich, Paul. "Quantum Cryptography," Scientific American 260 (May 1989): 28+.

7910. Wallich, Paul. "Tap Dance: Keeping Communications Networks Safe for Bugging," Scientific American 266 (June 1992): 115-116.

7911. Wallington, Peter. "The Public Order Act: Some Implications for the Policing of Industrial Disputes," Criminal Law Review (May 1987): 180-191.

7912. Wallner, Paul F. "Open Sources and the Intelligence Community: Myths and Realities," American Intelligence Journal 14/2&3 (Spring-Summer 1993): 19-24.
     Discusses the meaning of open source intelligence; quality of open source intelligence in the intelligence community; the tradition of using open sources; consumers and customers; and the management organization for effective use of open sources.

7913. Wallop, Malcolm. "Soviet Violations of Arms Control Agreements: So What?," Strategic Review 2 (Summer 1978): 17-28.

7914. Wallop, Malcolm. "U.S. Covert Action: Policy Tool or Policy Hedge?," Strategic Review 12/3 (Summer 1984): 9-16.

7915. Wallop, Malcolm. "Congressional Perspective: Intelligence for a Purpose," Comparative Strategy 14 (1995): 421, 423-424.

7916. Walls, William and Lynwood Metts. "The Changing Role of Intelligence: Perspectives from the Pacific Theater," Defense Intelligence Journal 1/1 (Spring 1992): 61-74.
     Contains sections that consider joint intelligence centers in the Pacific; the Pacific today; the birth of the Joint Intelligence Center Pacific Ocean Areas; and lessons of JICPOA.

7917. Walser, Ray. "A World War I Tale," Foreign Service Journal 71/2 (February 1994): 28-40.
     Considers the question of whether or not US ambassador David R. Francis consorted with a Russian spy as a Wilson appointee in Moscow in 1916-1917. Refers extensively to Somerset Maugham's novel, Ashenden.

7918. Walsh, James P. "The Death of John Birch--Documented," Wisconsin Magazine of History 58/3 (1975): 209-218.

Discusses the killing of John Birch by Chinese communist soldiers in mid-1945. Draws on declassified documents to characterize Birch's Air Force intelligence work in China.

7919. Walsh, Michael L. "OPSEC in History," Military Intelligence 7/4 (1981): 6-11.

Security during the American Revolution is the topic of this brief article.

7920. Walt, Steven. "The Reconnaissance of Security Studies," International Studies Quarterly 35 (1991): 7-11.

7921. Walter, Charles W. "Interposition: The Strategy and Its Uses," Naval War College Review 22 (June 1970): 72-84.

Discusses a strategy of placing forces between the opponent and the objective, that is, putting ships in the path of the opponent as the British did against the Russians in the Great Northern War of 1719. Use of psychological deception strategies is also discussed.

7922. Walter, George. "Secret Intelligence Services," Military Review 44/8 (August 1964): 91-98.

7923. Walters, Ronald W. "The Clark Amendment: Analysis of U.S. Policy Choices in Angola," Black Scholar: Journal of Black Studies and Research 12/4 (July-August 1981): 2-12.

A Black perspective on the Angolan issue; US intervention in Angola, including CIA operations; the Clark amendment; and the central issue of US relations with Angola.

7924. Walters, Rudolph B. "Airborne Long Range Input or ALRI," Air Force Review 15/4 (1964): 60-65.

7925. Walters, Vernon A. "Gen. de Gaulle in Action," Studies in Intelligence 18/4 (Winter 1974): 39-44.

This article is reprinted in Studies in Intelligence 38/5 (1995): 123-127. It contains General Walters' trip report of his attendance at the Four Power 1960 Summit Conference in Paris, a formal meeting between President Dwight Eisenhower, Charles de Gaulle, British Prime Minister MacMillan, and Nikita Khrushchev. The conference was conducted in the shadow of the American U-2 overflight of the Soviet Union.

7926. Walters, Vernon A. "Thirty-Five Years in Intelligence," Studies in Intelligence 20/2 (Summer 1976).

A speech given at Camp Richie upon General Walters' retirement as CIA's DDCI. Estimated to be 15 pages in length.

7927. Walters, Vernon A. and Robert M. Gates. "Dedicating the Berlin Wall Monument: Tribute to the Long Watch," Studies in Intelligence 36/5 (1992): 39-43.

This is a speech by Ambassador Vernon Walters and Robert M. Gates, given on December 18, 1992, at a ceremony dedicating the CIA's Berlin Wall Monument.

7928. Walton, Frank L. "The Ride of Colonel Rufus Putnam," Yonkers Historical Bulletin 14/1 (1967): 10-13.

7929. Walton, H. D. "Some Recent Advances in Police Technology," Medical Science and Law 22 (January 1982): 2-15.

7930. Walton, R. D. "Feeling for the Jugular: Japanese Espionage at Newcastle 1919-1926," Australian Journal of Politics and History 32/1 (1986): 20-38.

Discusses Japanese spying in New South Wales in the 1920s.

7931. Walton, R. D. "Japanese Espionage: Australia, 1888-1931," Journal of the Australian War Memorial 11 (October 1987): 37-46.

7932. Wandres, J. "Peace Without Hiroshima," Naval Intelligence Professionals Quarterly 9/3 (Summer 1993): 18-19.

7933. Wandres, J. "John Ford, Intelligence Photographer," Naval Intelligence Professionals Quarterly 10/3 (Summer 1994): 8-9.

7934. Wandycz, Piotr S. "Colonel Beck and the French: Roots of Animosity," International History Review 3/1 (January 1981): 115-127.

7935. Wang, Y. C. "Tu Yueh-Sheng (1888-1951): A Tentative Political Biography," Journal of East Asian Studies 26 (May 1967): 433-455.

7936. Wangborg, Manne. "Some Problems of Measuring Military R & D," International Social Science Journal 35/1 (1983): 47-59.

Discusses the difficulties a social scientist or analyst encounters when investigating the level of military research and development. Accurate assessments of R & D are affected by varying terminology, definitions of terms, secrecy, budget practices, and currency rates.

7937. Wannall, W. Raymond. "Setting Straight the FBI's Counterintelligence Record," World & I (January 1987): 167-177.

7938. Wannall, W. Raymond. "The FBI: Perennial Target of the Left," Journal of Social, Political and Economic Studies 13/3 (Fall 1988): 279-299.

Argues that the American political left is well organized and directed at undermining the FBI's traditional internal security role.

7939. Wannall, W. Raymond. "The FBI's Domestic Intelligence Operations: Domestic Security in Limbo," International Journal of Intelligence and Counterintelligence 4/4 (Winter 1990): 443-474.

A detailed discussion of the FBI's domestic intelligence role. Major sections discuss the historical basis for FBI's DI jurisdiction; new intelligence duties; domestic intelligence defined; implementation of Franklin Roosevelt's directive; Attorney General Robert Kennedy; the Levi guidelines and their impact; the William Smith guidelines; the question of investigating subversion; calls for intelligence gathering; Church committee instructions followed by congressional oversight; need to restore DI activities; and action to restore DI operations.

7940. Warburton, Albert E., III. "The Total Military Intelligence Officer: Intelligence Systems Managers," Military Review 60/4 (April 1980): 27-41.

Outlines the Office of Personnel Management System intelligence specialities and military intelligence officer profiles, and recommendations for changes in the intelligence officer rank structure.

7941. Ward, Compton E. "Subversive Insurgency--An Analytical Model," Naval War College Review 20/12 (September 1967): 3-25.

7942. Ward, Francis K. "Siamese Dusk," Blackwood's Magazine 255 (May 1944): 309-321.

7943. Ward, James R. "The Role of Intelligence in National Defense," Daughters of the American Revolution Magazine 114/8 (1980): 1000-1002.

A brief overview of the role of intelligence in wars from the American revolution to World War II.

7944. Ward, James R. "The Activities of Detachment 101 of the OSS," Special Warfare (October 1993): 14-21.

7945. Ward, R. H. "Terrorist Connection--A Pervasive Network," Police Studies 8/4 (Winter 1985): 189-197.

The nature of terrorism requires that a constant flow of intelligence must be acquired by all types of police departments. Proposes the expansion of local police department computer facilities to take in more information about terrorist groups. Intelligence operations can be strengthened through computers, despite limited budgets.

7946. Ward, Robert E. "The Inside Story of the Pearl Harbor Plan," U.S. Naval Institute Proceedings 77 (December 1951): 1271-1283.

Discusses the planning of the Pearl Harbor attack, training and preparations, the strike and the aftermath.

7947. Ward, Robert J. "LIC Strategy," Military Intelligence 11/1 (January-march 1985): 52-60.

Contains an extensive study of Army low intensity doctrine and the role of the military intelligence advisor in foreign internal defense operations.

7948. Ward, William and Martin T. Orne. "The Physiological Detection of Deception," American Scientist (July-August 1982): 407-409.

Discusses field polygraph testing; question of what evokes a physiological response; problem of decreasing detectability, individual differences; and problem of differences in social characteristics between examiner and examinee.

7949. Waring, Ronald. "The Problems of Security Within NATO," NATO's Fifteen Nations 8 (December 1963-January 1964): 22-25; 9 (April-May 1964): 94-96.

7950. Wark, Wesley K. "British Intelligence on the German Air Force and Aircraft Industry, 1933-1939," Historical Journal 25/3 (September 1982): 627-648.

Suggests that there were four periods during which intelligence about the German air force discerned growth and development: 1933-35 ('secrecy' period); 1935-36 ('honeymoon' period); 1937-38 ('blindness' period); and 1938-39 ('war scares and war' period).

7951. Wark, Wesley K. "Baltic Myths and Submarine Bogeys: British Naval Intelligence and Nazi Germany, 1933-1939," Journal of Strategic Studies 6/1 (March 1983): 60-81.

The failures of British naval intelligence, especially the misjudgment of the possibility of war in Europe, are discussed. Emphasis is given to failure to evaluate German capabilities.

7952. Wark, Wesley K. "Military Attache in Berlin: General Sir Frank Noel Mason-Macfarlane," Military History 12 (1984): 136-144.

7953. Wark, Wesley K. "For Services Rendered: Leslie James Bennett and the RCMP Security Service," Conflict Quarterly 4/4 (Fall 1984): 57-59.

A brief book review essay of a book by John Sawatsky with a book title captured in the title of this article.

7954. Wark, Wesley K. "In Search of a Suitable Japan: British Naval Intelligence in the Pacific Before the Second World War," Intelligence and National Security 1/2 (May 1986): 189-211.

7955. Wark, Wesley K. "Williamson Murray's Ware," Intelligence and National Security 1/3 (September 1986).

7956. Wark, Wesley K. "British Intelligence and Small Wars in the 1930s," Studies in Intelligence 30/3 (Fall 1986).

7957. Wark, Wesley K. "Coming in from the Cold: British Propaganda and Red Army Defector, 1945-1952," International History Review 9/1 (February 1987): 48-72.

Between 1945 and 1952, British propaganda produced increasing levels of Russian defectors, and it was necessary for the British Army on the Rhine to establish a special branch for processing defectors. The Information Research Department (IRD) performed the task with distinction.

7958. Wark, Wesley K. "'Great Investigations': The Public Debate on Intelligence in the US After 1945," Defense Analysis 3/2 (Fall 1987): 119-132.

Considers the political expressions of concern for the creation of the intelligence community in the years after World War II. Includes evidence from various press accounts of the premises upon which the political community constructed the United States intelligence structure following passage of the National Security Act of 1947.

7959. Wark, Wesley K. "British Intelligence and Small Wars in the 1930's," Intelligence and National Security 2/4 (October 1987): 67-87.

Discussion of operations of British intelligence during the Spanish Civil War and other small wars, recognizing British analytical biases which limited perspectives on the Italians and Japanese. See item 7956.

7960. Wark, Wesley K. "Cryptographic Innocence: The Origins of Signals Intelligence in Canada in the Second World War," Journal of Contemporary History 22/4 (October 1987): 639-665.

The story of the birth of Canadian SIGINT, 1939-present is revealed. Mention is made of the UK-USA SIGINT Pact of 1947 entered into by Canada in the process of building a SIGINT capability.

7961. Wark, Wesley K. "Three Military Attaches at Berlin in the 1930's: Soldier-Statesman and the Limits of Ambiguity," International History Review 9/4 (November 1987): 586-611.

Major sections discuss the military attaches and British foreign policy; Colonel Andrew Thorne; Colonel F. E. 'Boots' Hotblack; Colonel Frank Noel Mason-Macfarlane; and decision making by the British military elite. The British attache system was an important element in British intelligence against the Germans.

7962. Wark, Wesley K. "From Frontier to Foreign Intelligence: The Evolution of Military Intelligence in Canada," <u>Armed Forces and Society</u> 16/1 (Fall 1989): 77-98.

Discusses the organizations of Canadian military intelligence.

7963. Wark, Wesley K. "Beyond the Missing Dimensions: The New Study of Intelligence," <u>Canadian Journal of History</u> 24/1 (April 1989): 82-89.

This is a review essay in which the reviewer examines the contributions of 3 books to the emergent field of intelligence studies: <u>Intelligence and International Relations, 1900-1945</u> by Christopher Andrew and Jeremy Noakes; <u>Intelligence and Strategic Surprise</u> by Ariel Levite; and <u>Cloak and Gown: Scholars in the Secret War, 1939-1961</u> by Robin Winks.

7964. Wark, Wesley K. "Something Very Stern: British Political Intelligence, Moralism and Strategy in 1939," <u>Intelligence and National Security</u> 5/1 (January 1990): 150-170.

Discusses the role of political intelligence in 1939 Britain in transitioning the foreign policy from moralisms to moral outrage and the eventual declaration of war against Germany and Italy.

7965. Wark, Wesley K. "Fictions of History," <u>Intelligence and National Security</u> 5/4 (October 1990): 7-16.

An introductory essay containing observations of the beginnings and development of spy fiction. Discusses the history of retailing spy fiction, and spying futures. Highlights the other articles in the issue.

7966. Wark, Wesley K. "In Never-Never Land?: The British Archives on Intelligence," <u>Historical Journal</u> 35/1 (1992): 195-203.

7967. Wark, Wesley K. "Introduction: The Study of Espionage: Past, Present, Future?," <u>Intelligence and National Security</u> 8/3 (July 1993): 1-14.

An overview of the entire issue devote to the subject. Contains the author's perspectives on intelligence studies and a brief summary of each of the pieces in the issue.

7968. Wark, Wesley K. "The Intelligence Revolution and the Future," <u>Queen's Quarterly</u> 100/2 (Summer 1993): 273-290.

Raises and considers questions pertaining to the world's intelligence networks and the relative needs for information. Discusses the transition in espionage activities in the next century and the impact of change on the collection and analytical functions. See item 7968.

7969. Wark, Wesley K. "The Intelligence Revolution and the Future," <u>Studies in Intelligence</u> 37 (1994): 11-15.

This article is not listed among the collection of declassified items by the Central Intelligence Agency.

7970. Wark, Wesley K. "'Our Man in Riga': Reflections on the SIS Career and Writings of Leslie Nicholson," Intelligence and National Security 11/4 (October 1996): 625-644.

The author looks in on Leslie Nicholson's career in MI6, in particular with respect to his account of his work in Riga in his memoir British Agent, the first memoir of an MI6 insider.

7971. Warner, Geoffrey. "The United States and Vietnam 1945-65 Part I: 1945-54" and ". . . Part II: 1954-1965," International Affairs (Great Britain) 48/3 & 48/4 (September and October 1972): 379-394; 593-615.

A two-part study occasioned by the publication of the Pentagon Papers. Pt. I discusses Ho Chi Minh's support from the O. S. S., the emergence of the domino theory, and conditions for intervention by Eisenhower. Pt. II opens with the US policy toward the Far East as presented in the National Security Council, August 20, 1954. Moves on to the French withdrawal to Spring 1956, the Kennedy administration's problems with Diem in 1963, Johnson's bombing of the North in 1965 and conclusions.

7972. Warner, Geoffrey. "The United States and the Fall of Diem: The Coup that Never Was," Australian Outlook 28 (December 1974): 245-258; 29 (April 1975): 3-17.

7973. Warner, John S. "The Watchdog Committee Question," Studies in Intelligence 19/2 (Summer 1976).

7974. Warner, John S. "The Marchetti Case: New Case Law," Studies in Intelligence 20/1 (Spring 1977): 1-12.

7975. Warner, John S. "National Security and the First Amendment," Studies in Intelligence 27/1 (Spring 1983).

7976. Warner, John S. "Commentary on 'Intelligence Gathering and the Law,'" Studies in Intelligence 27/1 (Summer 1983).

7977. Warner, John S. "Where Secrecy Is Essential," Studies in Intelligence 31/2 (Summer 1987).

Argues that secrecy is rational in certain social and political institutions in American society. Major sections discuss intelligence and secrecy of funding during the revolutionary war; the Framers' view of secrecy; congressional enactments; judicial decisions; congressional action; and conclusions. This article appeared in a special issue of Studies in Intelligence 31 (September 1987): 45-64.

7978. Warner, Michael. "The Creation of the Central Intelligence Group," Studies in Intelligence 39/5 (1996): 111-120.

A discussion of the early years of planning for a central intelligence community. Major sections discuss the years from war to peace; the Truman initiative; controversy and compromise; and small beginnings.

7979. Warner, Michael. "Origins of the Congress of Cultural Freedom, 1949-50," Studies in Intelligence 38/5 (1995): 89-98.

A redacted version of a larger classified draft study maintained at CIA headquarters. Major sections discuss a March 1949 conference in New York; Sidney Hook and others at the conference; covert action prospect; disappointment in Paris; considering Berlin; an ideal organizer; enthusiastic response; and dramatic opening. Another version appeared in volume 38 (Summer 1994): 29-38.

7980. Warner, R. G. M. "The Joint Photographic Intelligence Centre," Roundel 15 (October 1963): 22-26.

7981. Warner, William T. "International Technology Transfer and Economic Espionage," International Journal of Intelligence and Counterintelligence 7/2 (Summer 1994): 143-160.

A discussion of the commitments to and methods of state-initiated activities to acquire economic and military technologies. Discusses the intelligence work in this area by the US, France, Japan, and Russia.

7982. Warnke, Allen E. "The Secret Wars: A Guide to Source in English," American Journal of International Law 77 (July 1983): 717-718.

This is a book review of a 3-volume bibliography by Myron J. Smith, Jr.

7983. Warren, Charles. "What Is Giving Aid and Comfort to the Enemy?," Yale Law Journal 27/3 (January 1918): 327-347.

Argues a view of treason as words alone at minimum. Includes general discussion of the legal principles of the law of treason.

7984. Warren, Charles. "Spies and the Power of Congress to Subject Certain Classes of Civilians to Trial by Military Tribunal," American Law Review 53 (March-April 1919): 195-228.

Studies of World War I espionage concepts should include this article.

7985. Warren, Earl. "Governmental Secrecy: Corruption's Alley," American Bar Association Journal 60/5 (1974): 550-552.

Discusses the internal problems of secrecy of public purpose and the fact that disclosure of secrets is a major concern of government.

7986. Warren, Kirk S. "United States v. Knotts: The Electronic Beeper and the Unwary Traveler," Ohio Northern University Law Review 10 (Summer 1983): 549-582.

Discusses the use of beepers as tracking devices. In Knotts, the Supreme Court upheld the use of beepers as acceptable accessories in police work. Knotts involved a drug manufacturing conspiracy and the transportation of drug paraphernalia across state lines.

7987. Warren, Samuel D. and Louis D. Brandeis. "The Right to Privacy," Harvard Law Review 4/5 (December 1890): 193-206.

The first article ever to appear in a law journal on the subject. Presents the concept and legal principles involved in privacy. A classic introduction to the topic.

7988. Warren, Ward. "Politics, Presidents, and DCI's," International Journal of Intelligence and Counterintelligence 8/3 (Fall 1995): 337-344.

The new Curator of the Historical Intelligence Collection for the Central Intelligence Agency discusses succession of directors of central intelligence (DCI's) through the years since 1947; the political picks; the non-politicals; and the barristers.

7989. Warrock, Anna M. and Howard Husock. "Taking Toshiba Public," Studies in Intelligence 34/2 (Summer 1990).

7990. Warsocki, Michael L. "Intelligence Within Operational Art," Military Review 75/2 (March-April 1995): 44-49.

Author cautions that as we accelerate intelligence and communications integration we must ensure leaders effectively employ operational art to achieve strategic aims.

7991. Warth, Robert D. "The Palmer Raids," South Atlantic Quarterly 48 (1949): 1-11.

Discussion of Attorney General A. Mitchell Palmer's obsession with communist conspiracies, and his campaign to root out alleged communists and radicals. Cites several statistics of the raids and discusses opposition to his methods by Louis Post.

7992. Wasemiller, A. C. "The Anatomy of Counterintelligence," Studies in Intelligence 13/1 (Spring 1969): 10-24.

7993. Washburn, Patrick S. "J. Edgar Hoover and the Black Press in World War II," Journalism History 13/1 (1986): 26-33.

An account of the FBI's activities concerning the Black press and suspected illegal activities and alleged ties with the American Communist Party.

7994. Wasserman, Benno. "The Failure of Intelligence Predictions," Political Studies 8/2 (June 1960): 156-169.

Examines the official notions of intelligence and knowledge, the way in which intelligence functions and knowledge are sought, and the sort of knowledge which is obtained by intelligence and which underlies foreign policy.

7995. Wasserstein, Bernard. "Chasing a Chameleon: Trebitsch Lincoln," History Today 38 (April 1988): 10-16.

Lincoln, a missionary, failed MP, counter-revolutionary, and Buddhist abbot, is tracked through a series of secret lives and international intrigue in the early twentieth century. Apparently, Lincoln was a double-agent and patriot.

7996. Wasserstein, Bernard. "Secrets of Old Shanghai," Republican China 16/1 (1989): 74-81.

7997. Waters, A. B. "The Price of Intelligence," Marine Corps Gazette 38 (July 1954): 34-43.

7998. Waters, Maurice. "Special Diplomatic Agents of the President," Annals of the American Academy of Political and Social Sciences 307 (September 1956): 124-130.

Discusses the history of special diplomatic agents; common use of special agents; foreign affairs work; Harry Hopkins as a special agent; and advantages and disadvantages of special agents.

7999. Waters, R. S. "Possible Results Had Modern Air Reconnaissance Existed in 1914," Journal of the Royal United Service Institute 78 (1933): 44-59.

Draws conclusion that the existence of air reconnaissance in the early stages of World War I would have altered significantly the immediacy and organization of battles.

8000. Waters, W. Davis. "Deception in the Art of War: Gabriel Rains, Torpedo Specialist of the Confederacy," North Carolina Historical Review 66 (January 1989): 25-60.

8001. Watkins, Arthur V. "War By Executive Orders," Western Political Quarterly 4/4 (December 1951): 539-549.

Discusses national and international legal aspects of the Korean War. Asserted that the President bypasses the Constitution and the Congress. May be useful in case studies relevant to the Korean War.

8002. Watkins, John. "Action Off the Isle De Batz, 9 June 1944: From H.M.S. Ashanti," Mariner's Mirror 78/3 (1992): 307-326

8003. Watson, Bruce W. "Intelligence and Academe: A Third View," <u>American Intelligence Journal</u> 2 (January 1982): 19-23.

8004. Watson, Joel F. "The Japanese Evacuation and Litigation Arising Therefrom," <u>Oregon Law Review</u> 22/1 (December 1942): 46-59.
Discusses historical precedents for application of 'military necessity' to the internment of 113,000 persons of Japanese ancestry following the Pearl Harbor attack. Covers briefly case taking shape in the federal courts over the issue of internment.

8005. Watson, H. Lee. "Congress Steps Out: A Look at Congressional Control of the Executive," <u>California Law Review</u> 63/4 (July 1975): 983-1094.
Considers the legislative roles of Congress; Congress in the eyes of the Framers; and the constitutionality of non-legislating congressional action. A useful background piece for consideration of congressional oversight of the intelligence community.

8006. Watson, Vera. "Spy in the Committee of Public Safety," <u>History Today</u> 9 (October 1959): 672-680.
Discusses the British penetration of the French Committee of Public Safety, supplying the British with reports and other documents. Executions were held to clean out the spies, but the espionage continued. More research is needed.

8007. Watson, Vera. "Plot to Assassinate Pitt," <u>History Today</u> 10 (September 1960): 641-646.
Explains the attempt to assassinate William Pitt and King George III. Discusses research methods concerning assassination plots; Pitt's plans to outwit and deceive his assassination plotters; and the capture and sentencing of the plotters.

8008. Watson, W. C. "Arnold's Retreat After the Battle of Valcour," <u>Magazine of American History</u> 6/6 (June 1881): 414-417.
Brief summary of events surrounding Benedict Arnold's mission to Valcour Island in New York during the American revolution.

8009. Watson, W. R. "The S-2's Crystal Ball," <u>Marine Corps Gazette</u> 36 (June 1952): 34-37.

8010. Watt, D. Cameron. "The Anglo-German Naval Agreement of 1935: An Interim Judgement," <u>Journal of Modern History</u> 28 (1956): 155-175.

8011. Watt, D. Cameron. "Foreign Affairs, the Public Interest and the Right to Know," <u>Political Quarterly</u> 35 (April-June 1963): 121-136.
A general discussion of the public accessibility to government papers on

foreign affairs. Sections include discussion of the British 50-year rule change; the role of the historian in society; throttling the flow of information; the increasing interest in foreign affairs; official obscurantism; the Lord Chancellor's powers; the defense of secrecy; the disadvantages of concealment; the 'public interest' myth; the historical section of the Cabinet; present day needs; and the demand for change.

8012. Watt D. Cameron. "Intelligence Studies: The Emergence of the British School," Intelligence and National Security 3/2 (April 1988): 338-341.

A book review essay of Intelligence and International Relations 1900-1945, edited by Christopher Andrew and Jeremy Noakes.

8013. Watt, D. Cameron. "Fall-out from Treachery: Peter Wright and Spycatcher," Political Quarterly 59 (April-June 1988): 206-218.

An evaluation of the evidence against the British security and intelligence services presented in Wright's book. Discusses 'dirty tricks'; the role of the security services; assessing Wright's evidence; and the future of the security services.

8014. Watt, D. Cameron. "Francis Herbert King: A Soviet Source in the Foreign Office," Intelligence and National Security 3/4 (October 1988): 62-82.

Discusses the King case espionage case in the Foreign Office in the mid-1930s. Covers the intrigues in British, German and Soviet intelligence operations to breach communications systems and correspondence.

8015. Watt, D. Cameron. "Learning from Peter Wright: A Reply," Political Quarterly 60 (1989): 237-238.

A brief response to a critique by Laurence Lustgarten (see this bibliography).

8016. Watt, D. Cameron. "An Intelligence Surprise: The Failure of the Foreign Office to Anticipate the Nazi-Soviet Pact," Intelligence and National Security 4/3 (July 1989): 512-534.

Examines the reasons for the British failure to anticipate the Nazi-Soviet non-aggression pact. He points to confused, misled, presumptive, and sporadic intelligence reports of the developing conditions leading to the Pact.

8017. Watt, D. Cameron. "Intelligence and the Historian: A Comment on John Gaddis's "Intelligence, Espionage and Cold War Origins," Diplomatic History 14/2 (Spring 1990): 199-204.

Written in response to another historian's article that bemoans the difficulties historians have in researching intelligence topics, Watt discusses his own difficulties and disagrees with popular hardships for historians.

8018. Watt, D. Cameron. "Critical Afterthoughts and Alternative Historico-Literary Theories," Intelligence and National Security 5/4 (October 1990): 212-225.

The author offers some overview reflections upon several articles devoted to spy fiction in this issue of the Journal.

8019. Watt, D. Cameron. "The Sender der deutschen Freiheitspartei: A First Step in the British Radio War Against Nazi Germany," Intelligence and National Security 6/3 (July 1991): 621-626.

Examines the daily operations of British radio intelligence and propaganda. Compares German and British radio styles and content, and focusses on how the different operations were viewed by there political leaders.

8020. Watt, D. Cameron. "Research Notes," Intelligence and National Security 11/1 (January 1996): 146-153.

The author's discovery of some new information revealed in the Sir Anthony Eden files regarding Sir Robert Vansittart.

8021. Watt, E. F. B. "Bombs and Bundles," Canadian Forces Sentinel 8/3 (1972): 14-18.

8022. Watts, Philip. "Celine's Defense: Introduction," South Atlantic Quarterly 93 (Spring 1994): 521-529.

Concerns the treason trial of French citizen and alleged collaboratist Louis F. Celine.

8023. Way, Peter. "Shovel and Shamrock: Irish Workers and Labor Violence in the Digging of the Chesapeake and Ohio Canal," Labor History 30/4 (1989): 489-517.

8024. Way, Rosemary C. "The Law of Police Authority: The McDonald Commission and the McLeod Report," Dalhousie Law Journal 9 (1985): 683-723.

8025. Wayner, Peter. "A Redundancy Reducing Cipher," Cryptologia 12/2 (April 1988): 107-112.

8026. Wayner, Peter. "Mimic Functions," Cryptologia 16/3 (July 1992): 193-214.

8027. Wayner, Peter. "Strong Theoretical Stegnography," Cryptologia 19/3 (July 1995): 285-299.

8028. Wead, Frank W. "Air Intelligence: Gathering and Disseminating All Battle Data," Flying 32 (February 1943): 163-164.

8029. Weaver, Bill. "Kentucky Under Fire: Admiral Kimmel and the Pearl Harbor Controversy," Filson Club History Quarterly 57/2 (April 1983): 151-174.

8030. Webb, James H., Jr. "The Cultural Attache: Scholar, Propagandist, or Bureaucrat?," South Atlantic Quarterly 71 (Summer 1972): 352-364.
    Addresses the role of cultural attache, including duties to collect information for reporting to intelligence agencies.

8031. Webb, Guy P. "Machines and the Chinese Name," Studies in Intelligence 5/1 (Winter 1961).

8032. Webb, William A. "A Public-Key Cryptosystem Based on Complementing Sets," Cryptologia 16/2 (April 1992): 177-181.

8033. Weber, Ralph E. "James Lovell and Secret Ciphers During the American Revolution," Cryptologia 2/1 (January 1978): 75-88.

8034. Weber, Ralph E. "Joel R. Poinsett's Secret Mexican Dispatch Twenty," South Carolina Historical Magazine 75 (April 1974): 67- 77.
    A detailed review of the messages to the American minister in Mexico during the 1820s.

8035. Weber, Ralph E. "As Others Saw Us," Studies in Intelligence 31/2 (Summer 1987).
    An extensive compilation of letters, reports and newspaper articles summarizing some of the key issues for an intelligence officer who may have been observing the evolution of events during the American Revolution and the debate over the proposed Constitution. This piece was reprinted in a special issue of Studies in Intelligence 31 (September 1987): 9-44.

8036. Weber, Ralph E. "A Masked Dispatch," Cryptologia 14/1 (January 1990): 374-380.
    This leading historian of cryptologia discusses the coded messages to John Jay from Robert Livingston.

8037. Weber, Ralph E. "America's First Encrypted Cable: Seward's Other Folly," Studies in Intelligence 36/5 (Winter 1992): 105-109.
    Discusses the development of a new cipher for the State Department, beginning in 1866. Major sections discuss security concerns for the first code; costly communications; a historic document; the cost; more trouble; a new code; lower tariffs; stalemate; and paying up for cable messages sent by the government.

8038. Weber, Ralph E. "Seward's Other Folly: The Fight Over America's Encrypted Cable," Cryptologia 19/4 (October 1995): 321-348.

8039. Webster, William H. "Sophisticated Surveillance--Intolerable Intrusion or Prudent Protection?," Washington University Law Quarterly 63 (February 1985): 351-364.

Transcript of author's memorial lecture at Washington University, St. Louis, in 1985. He argues that controlled and authorized wiretapping is an inappropriate measure in the interests of national security.

8040. Webster, William H. "Sophisticated Surveillance - Intolerable Intrusion or Prudent Protection?," Detroit College of Law Review (Winter 1986): 1179-1191.

Addresses the controversies surrounding police sources of information, including informants, electronic surveillance and undercover agents. Argues that such methods are popularly acceptable in the face serious public safety concerns.

8041. Webster, William H. "With Fidelity to the Constitution," Studies in Intelligence 31/2 (Summer 1987).

These are formal remarks of the former CIA director at a meeting of the Institute of Judicial Administration on August 8, 1987 in San Francisco, California. Considers the major role of intelligence; implementing foreign policy; and the oversight committees. This article appeared in a special issue of Studies in Intelligence 31 (September 1987): 85-90.

8042. Webster, William H. "Address: The Role of Intelligence in a Free Society," University of Miami Law Review 43/1 (September 1988): 155-164.

Part of a symposium issue on the presidency, Congress and foreign policy, this is a summary of the author's views on the subject. Argues that trust is the key ingredient in the relationship between CIA and the Congress.

8043. Webster, William H. "The Hostile Threat in the 1990's," American Intelligence Journal 10/2 (Summer-Fall 1989): 15-18.

Contains brief remarks of the CIA director on the hostile threats faced by the US from Soviet intelligence operations.

8044. Webster, William H. "The Intelligence Community's Mission in Today's World," Signal 44 (September 1989): 37-39.

Discusses covert operations, increasing demands, countering threats, and budget constraints. Mentions the new Counternarcotics Center and the Counterintelligence Center.

8045. Webster, William H. "The Intelligence Community's Mission in Today's World," Military Logistics (September 1989): 17-24

8046. Webster, William H. "New Challenges for Intelligence: The Problems of Terrorism and Narcotics," World Outlook 10 (Winter 1989): 162-172.

Argues for closer coordination and cooperation between intelligence and law enforcement agencies in order to have a greater impact on the problems of terrorism and the drug trade.

8047. Webster, William H. "The Role of the CIA in the New World Order," West's Federal Rules Decisions 141 (July 1992): 679-688.

8048. Wechsler, James A. "The Decline of J. Edgar Hoover," Progressive (January 1965): 12, 16-17.

8049. Wedge, Bryant. "Khrushchev At a Distance--A Study of Public Personality," Trans-action 5/10 (1968): 24-28.

8050. Wedge, Bryant. "International Propaganda and Statecraft," Annals of the American Academy of Political and Social Sciences 398 (November 1971): 36-43.
Discusses the power of new forms of communication and the ability of these forms to change public opinion, and inform and persuade in ways never before possible. Consequences and implications of global communications are discussed, followed by a call to bring more freedom to the world through technologies of communication.

8051. Weeks, Albert L. "When the Russians Discovered Cosmos," Military Science and Technology 6 (1982): 64-71.
Briefly outlines the launching of the Russian Sputnik in October 1957, the characterization of Sputnik as a large medicine ball, and a future projection of space warfare.

8052. Weeks, Albert L. "The KGB: A Key Player in Kremlin Politics?," Journal of Defense and Diplomacy 7/10 (October 1989): 68-74.

8053. Weeks, Albert L. "Yeltsin's Monopoly of the Security Organs," American Intelligence Journal 14/3 (Autumn-Winter 1993-1994): 55-59.
Explains and evaluates the organizational changes in Russian intelligence services after the breakup of the former Soviet Union. Major sections discuss the increasing police power; the post-Red October; Yeltsin's incorporation of security offices; and future scenarios.

8054. Weeks, Charles J. "Juggernaut or Buffoon? Americans Observe the Soviet Navy, 1917-1941," Proceedings and Papers of the Georgia Association of Historians 5 (1984): 62-67.
A look at the US naval intelligence account of the Soviet naval effectiveness and the inability of the Soviet Navy to accurately assess their strength.

8055. Weems, Miner L. "Propaganda As an Instrument of Foreign Policy," Southern Quarterly 4/2 (1966): 144-158.

8056. Wege, Carl A. "Assad's Legions: The Syrian Intelligence Services," International Journal of Intelligence and Counterintelligence 4/1 (Spring 1990): 91-100.
Covers the structural characteristics of the Syrian organs of the State under Hafez al-Assad; the military component; the non-military component; terrorism; interaction of the security organs; and conclusions.

8057. Wege, Carl A. "The Syrian Socialist Party: An Intelligence Asset?," International Journal of Intelligence and Counterintelligence 7/3 (Fall 1994): 339-352.
Discusses the Syrian security environment; the nature of Syrian security operations; the SSNP political organization as an operational asset; the praetorian state and the operational assets in a divided house; and the ongoing danger of internal conflict.

8058. Wegner, Daniel M.; Julie D. Lane; and Sara Dimitri. "The Allure of Secret Relationships," Journal of Personality and Social Psychology 66 (February 1994): 287-300.

8059. Wei, George. "Surreptitious Takings of Confidential Information," Legal Studies 12 (November 1992): 302-331.

8060. Weil, H. M. "Domestic and International Violence Forecasting Approach," Futures 6 (June 1974): 477-485.

8061. Weimer, Daniel. "The Shady World of Corporate Espionage," Technology Review (December 1988): 22-24.
A brief overview of a complex topic.

8062. Weinbaum, Marvin G. "War and Peace in Afghanistan: The Pakistani Role," Middle East Journal 45/1 (Winter 1991): 71-85.
Discusses several critical factors in the Afghanistan resistance toward the Soviet Union in terms of Pakistan's role. In particular, mention is made of the Pakistan intelligence service connections with the United States Central Intelligence Agency.

8063. Weinberg, Steve. "The Mob, the CIA, and the S&L Scandal," Columbia Journalism Review 29 (November-December 1990): 28-35.
A popular press article of some length and depth worthy of research attention.

8064. Weinberg, Sydney. "What to Tell America: The Writers' Quarrel in the Office of War Information," Journal of American History 55/1 (June 1968): 73-89.

A thorough inquiry into the policies and operations of the World War II Office of War Information and the controversy over official propaganda about the war's progress and public imagery.

8065. Weiner, Myron. "India's New Political Institutions," Asian Survey 16/9 (September 1976): 898-901.

Discusses briefly four new Indian government organizations: the centralized intelligence organization; the prime minister's secretariat; the Youth Congress; and the central government police forces.

8066. Weiner, Myron. "Security, Migration, and Conflict in South Asia," Defense Intelligence Journal 1/2 (Fall 1992): 165-192.

Major sections discuss migration and state security; international population movements in South Asia; political refugees from repressive regimes; unwanted migrants; the impact of migration on the security and stability of South Asian states; and the institutional framework for policies.

8067. Weiner, Nella F. "Fermi? He Didn't Even Tell His Wife," Bulletin of the Atomic Scientists 50 (July-August 1994): 3.

Brief discussion of Enrico Fermi's secrecy concerning the atomic bomb project.

8068. Weiner, Tim. "The Dark Secret of the Black Budget," Washington Monthly 19/4 (1987): 31-35.

A discussion of the "black budget" projects in the Reagan administration. Such projects are directed by CIA, NSA, or military organizations and have budgets that are concealed in the budgets of other departments of government.

8069. Weinert, Richard P. "Federal Spies in Richmond," Civil War Times Illustrated 3/10 (1965): 28-34.

8070. Weinstein, Allen. "Reappraisals: The Alger Hiss Case Revisited," American Scholar 41 (Winter 1971): 121-132.

A summary of the author's book on the question of Alger Hiss's alleged espionage work, in particular, Hiss's association with Whittaker Chambers.

8071. Weinstein, Allen. "The Symbolism of Subversion: Notes on Some Cold War Icons," Journal of American Studies 6/2 (August 1972): 165-179.

8072. Weinstein, Allen. "Nixon v. Hiss: The Story Nixon Tells and the Other Story," Esquire (November 1975): 73-75+.

Major sections include discussion of Richard Nixon's resignation from the presidency; the Hiss case and how it began; the investigation of Hiss; Nixon, his advisors and the House UnAmerican Activities Committee; the reopening of the investigations; and breaking the case. Fundamentally, an extract of the author's book on the subject.

8073. Weinstein, Allen. "Nadya--A Spy Story ... Conversation in Jerusalem," Encounter 48 (June 1977): 72-79.
Discusses the memoirs of the Ulanovskaya family and their service in Soviet intelligence. Covers the types of missions in their World War I and their eventual capture.

8074. Weinstein, John M. "Nonmilitary Threats to Soviet National Security," Naval War College Review 38/4 (July-August 1985): 28-40.
Major sections discuss Soviet economic and agricultural vulnerabilities; Soviet demographic vulnerabilities; and political and ideological vulnerabilities.

8075. Weinstein, Sidney T. "The Role of Counterintelligence in the Next Decade," American Journal of Intelligence 10/2 (Summer-Fall 1989): 33-36.
Accounts for the historical role of counterintelligence and offers observations on the current and future threats that call for counterintelligence advancements.

8076. Weir, Andrew; Jonathan Bloch; and Pat Fitzgerald. "Sun Sets Over the Other Empire," Middle East (October 1981): 39-42.
Discusses British SIS covert operations in the Middle East in the 1950s and 1960s.

8077. Weir, Leslie D. "Soviet Publicists Talk About US Intelligence," Studies in Intelligence 4/2 (Summer 1960).

8078. Weisberger, B. A. "The Great Arrogance of the Present Is to Forget the Intelligence of the Past," American Heritage 41 (September-October 1990): 96-102.
This is an interview with Ken Burns. Although it is not directly on the point of intelligence operations or services, its broader context is relevant to the study of intelligence history. Burns remarks on the implications of his film, The Civil War, the reflection upon lessons of the past.

8079. Weisenbloom, Mark. "Teaching Defense Intelligence Organization," Defense Intelligence Journal 1/1 (Spring 1992): 95-104.
Discusses historical overview; structural-functional overlay; and the need to integrate historical overview with the structural-functional overlay.

8080. Weiser, Benjamin. "A Question of Loyalty," American Intelligence Journal 14/1 (Autumn-Winter 1992-1993): 61-70.

Demonstrates the scope and importance of Colonel Ryszard Kuklinski's contributions to avoiding nuclear holocaust in Europe. Kuklinski, a Polish military intelligence official, provided the US with a large quantity of sensitive intelligence information that aided efforts against Soviet intrigues in the 1970s.

8081. Weiss, Bernard L. "Keys to Success in C^3I," Signal 36 (August 1982): 52-54.

8082. Weiss, Gus W. "The Life and Death of Cosmos 954," Studies in Intelligence 22/1 (Spring 1978).

8083. Weiss, Gus W. "The Farewell Dossier," Studies in Intelligence 39/5 (1996): 121-126.

· Major sections discuss Soviet science and technology espionage; US computer export policy; strong suspicions and skepticism; presidential interest; the defection of Colonel Vetrov; interest in technology transfer; a deception operation; and National Security Directive 75.

8084. Weiss, Philip. "The Quiet Coup, U. S. v. Morison: A Victory for Secret Government," Harper's (September 1989): 54-65.

Reflects upon the US government's case against Daniel Ellsberg in the 1971 revelations of the Pentagon Papers to the New York Times. Then discusses the case of Samuel Loring Morison's leak of the KH-ll satellite photos to Jane's Defense Weekly. The Morison case was a test of the government's ability to expand criminal penalties for alleged violations of the classification system.

8085. Weiss, Robert P. "Private Detective Agencies and Labor Discipline in the United States, 1855-1946," Historical Journal 29/1 (March 1986): 87-107.

Argues that private detectives served the crime fighting interests of American corporations, thus having a major impact on industrial relations and trade unionism in the years considered.

8086. Weissman, Neil. "Regular Police in Tsarist Russia, 1900-1914," Russian Review 44/1 (January 1985): 45-68.

A lengthy discussion of regular and secret police of the era.

8087. Weissman, Stephan R. "CIA Covert Action in Zaire and Angola: Patterns and Consequences," Political Science Quarterly 94/2 (Summer 1979): 263-286.

A review of Central Intelligence Agency covert actions in Zaire and Angola during the 1960s, concluding that such actions did not prove useful to US foreign policy interests in the region.

8088. Weland, James. "Misguided Intelligence: Japanese Military Intelligence Officers in the Manchurian Incident, September 1931," Journal of Military History 58/3 (July 1994): 445-460.

Discusses in detail the successes of Japanese intelligence in the years leading up to the 1931 Manchurian conflict. Major sections discuss the intelligence service; covert operations; intelligence officers; and the flawed service.

8089. Welch, David A. "Propaganda and Indoctrination in the Third Reich: Success or Failure?," European History Quarterly 17/4 (October 1987): 403-422.

Discusses problems and perspectives of interpretation; the organization of Nazi propaganda; Nazi propaganda themes, 1933-1939; and conclusions.

8090. Welch, David A. "Intelligence Assessment in the Cuban Missile Crisis," Queen's Quarterly 100/2 (Summer 1993): 421-437.

An overview of the major documents now available to intelligencers concerning the Cuban missile crisis of 1962. Refers to intelligence gathering and the CIA.

8091. Welch, David A. and James G. Blight. "The Eleventh Hour of the Cuban Missile Crisis: An Introduction to the ExComm Transcripts," International Security 12 (Winter 1987-1988): 5-29.

An analysis of decision making during the Cuban Missile Crisis based on newly released records of the Executive Committee of the National Security Council ("ExComm"). Role of CIA personnel is included.

8092. Welch, Jasper. "Promoting the Defense Budget: Some Intelligence Issues," Armed Forces Journal (December 1984): 44, 46.

Important policy and ethical issues are involved in the promotion of the defense budget. Subtopics discuss promotion of the budget by Defense Secretary McNamara; defense annual reports; intelligence work; appointment of Team B; CIA publications; Freedom of Information Act; and issues in the defense budget.

8093. Welch, Edwin W. "Classified Information and the Courts," Federal Bar Journal 31/4 (Fall 1972): 360-377.

Discusses Executive Order 11652 and the classification of information; classified information before "Courts of Equity"; classified information before civil and criminal courts; and problems peculiar to court martial practice.

8094. Welchman, Gordon. "From Polish Bomba to British Bombe: The Birth of Ultra," Intelligence and National Security 1/1 (January 1986): 71-110.

8095. Weller, Geoffrey R. "The Canadian Security Intelligence Service Under Stress," Canadian Public Administration 31/2 (Summer 1988): 279-302.

8096. Weller, Geoffrey R. "Accountability in Canadian Intelligence Services," International Journal of Intelligence and Counterintelligence 3/2 (Fall 1988): 415-441.

Discusses various elements in the overall reform of the Canadian intelligence services, including the intelligence structure; duties; the communications security establishment; the history of accountability; misconduct and the demand for reform; reform measures; and the consequences of reform.

8097. Weller, Jac. "Wellington's Asset: A Remarkably Successful System of Intelligence," Military Review (June 1962): 10-14.

8098. Weller, Jac. "Military Aspects of the Palestinian Collapse," Military Review 53/7 (1973): 56-67.

Discusses the failure of Palestinian guerrillas in the war of 1967, and the successes of the Israeli Defense Force in collecting information on the guerrillas. Sections include discussion of the Israeli military plan; IDF internal security; and retaliation.

8099. Weller, Robert. "Rear Admiral Joseph N. Wegner USN (Ret.) and the Naval Cryptologic Museum," Cryptologia 8/2 (1984): 14-16.

8100. Wellington, Joseph A. "In Camera Hearings and the Informant Identity Privileges Under Military Rule of Evidence 507," Army Lawyer (February 1983): 9-16.

8101. Wells, C. Bradford. "A SIRA Team in Retrospect," Studies in Intelligence 5/3 (Summer 1961).

8102. Wells, Samuel F., Jr. "The Lessons of the War," Wilson Quarterly 2/3 (Summer 1978): 119-126.

A review of the lessons and memories of the Korean War, particularly the increase in military preparedness to block communist aggression. Argues that limited war can be considered successful by contrast to the protracted situation in Vietnam.

8103. Wells, Samuel F., Jr. "Sounding the Tocsin: NSC 68 and the Soviet Threat," International Security 4/1 (Fall 1979): 116-158.

Discussion of Harry Truman's defense budget ceiling after NSC 68 in April 1950; State Department call for increased efforts and tougher diplomacy with the Soviets; and a final assessment of NSC 68.

8104. Welzenbach, Donald E. "Observation Balloons and Reconnaissance Satellites," Studies in Intelligence 30/1 (Spring 1986): 21-28.

Discusses secret US intelligence plans to overfly the Soviet Union with balloons in the 1950s. This article is not listed among declassified items released for public access by the Central Intelligence Agency.

8105. Welzenbach, Donald E. "Science and Technology: Origins of a Directorate," Studies in Intelligence 30/2 (Summer 1986): 13-26.

A history of the origins and development of the Central Intelligence Agency's Directorate of Science and Technology. The Directorate opened for business in 1963. This article is not listed among declassified items released for public access by the Central Intelligence Agency.

8106. Welzenbach, Donald E. and Nancy Galyean. "Those Daring Young Men and Their Ultra-High-Flying Machines," Studies in Intelligence 31/3 (Fall 1987): 103-115.

A discussion of U-2 overflights of Murmansk, Soviet Union. This article is not listed among declassified items released for public access by the Central Intelligence Agency.

8107. Wenger, Beth S. "Radical Politics in a Reactionary Age: The Unmaking of Rosika Schwimmer, 1914-1930," Journal of Women's History 2/2 (Fall 1990): 66-99.

An account of the political life of Rosika Schwimmer, a peace activist who was at one point called a German spy.

8108. Wennerhold, R. "Criminal Solicitation - Danger for the Unwary Undercover Investigator," Police Chief (August 1977): 13-19.

An activity in which intelligence and investigative skill are required assets

8109. Wentworth, John. "Wentworth Geneology--The Hitherto Unknown Councilor Paul," New England Historical and Geneological Register 42 (1888): 170-172.

8110. Werner, A. "Most Mysterious Manuscript: Who Wrote It?," Horizon 3 (January 1963): 4-9.

A summary of the history of cryptography, then consideration of a valuable manuscript acquired in 1912, allegedly drafted during the sixteenth century by Roger Bacon. Cryptographer William Friedman was the last person to attempt to decipher the manuscript. Discusses Bacon, Jesuit Athanasius Kircher, professor William R. Newbold, and similarities with De Materia Medica from the first century.

8111. Werner, James. "Secrecy and Its Effect on Environmental Problems in the Military: An Engineer's Perspective," New York University Environmental Law Journal 2 (July 1993): 351-359.

8112. Wertheim, W. F. "Whose Plot? New Light on the 1965 Events," Journal of Contemporary Asia 9/2 (1979): 197-215.
Discusses the conspiracy to oust Indonesian President Sukarno.

8113. Weschler, James. "How to Rid the Government of Communists," Harper's 195 (1947): 438-443.

8114. Wessel, Gerhard. "The BNDD - the External Secret Services of the Federal Bureau of Germany," Beitrage zur Konfliktfor Schung 15/2 (1985): 5-23.

8115. West, Lois A. "US Foreign Labor Policy and the Case of Militant Political Unionism in the Phillipines," Labor Studies Journal 16/4 (Winter 1981): 48-75.
Argues that the Phillipine labor force has been manipulated by and association of the AFL-CIO and the American Central Intelligence Agency, thus contributing to Phillipine nationalism and the suppression of dissent.

8116. West, Nigel. "Australian Intelligence Literature," Intelligence Quarterly 1/2 (July 1985): 9-14.

8117. West, Nigel. "Canadian Intelligence Literature: Gouzenko and the RCMP," Intelligence Quarterly 2/3 (April 1986): 15-16.

8118. West, Nigel. "The Defector Syndrome: A British Perspective," American Intelligence Journal 8/2 (May 1987).

8119. West, Rebecca. "Whittaker Chambers," Atlantic Monthly 189/6 (June 1952): 33-39.
Considers the dimension of Chambers' personality, as reflected in Chambers' book, Witness.

8120. West, Rebecca. "Doctor Stephen Ward Returns," Esquire 62 (September 1964): 138+.
Dr. Ward was a Soviet spy. Discusses his relationship with Christine Keeler; his background and relationship with the Soviets; plans of blackmail; Keeler's part in the plot; and the trial of Ward.

8121. Westermann, W. L. "On Inland Transportation and Communication in Antiquity," Political Science Quarterly 43 (1928): 364-387.

8122. Westin, Alan F. "The Wire-Tapping Problem: An Analysis and a Legislative Proposal," Columbia Law Review 52/2 (February 1952): 165-208.
Discussion of Section 605 of the Federal Communications Act referring to wiretapping evidence; reflection upon legal history form the Olmstead case of

1928 to Section 605; Section 605 to the Nardone case; the Goldstein and Goldman cases; the situation in 1951; state legislation and court decisions; guides for legislative action; and a proposed wiretap act.

8123. Westin, Alan F. "Libertarian Precepts and Subversive Realities: Some Lessons Learned in the School of Experience," Commentary 19 (1955): 1-9.

Detailed consideration of the weaknesses of the libertarian perspective on civil liberties during McCarthy era. Discussion of the Federal Loyalty Program and the use of the US Constitution's Fifth Amendment as a defense against questions of loyalty.

8124. Westney, D. Eleanor. "The Emulation of Western Organizations in Meiji Japan: The Case of the Paris Prefecture of Police and the Keishi-cho," Journal of Japanese Studies 8/2 (Summer 1982): 307-342.

The Japanese adapted the French police system to their own culture, organizing with national security and information leaks in mind. Major sections include discussion of the selection of the model; the emulation of the model; departures from the model; a view forty years later; the impact on the environment; and the Keishi-cho as a case of organizational development.

8125. Westover, J. G. "A Civil War Secret Service Code," Journal of Southern History 8 (November 1942): 556-557.

This piece contains a reproduction of a code used by Confederate General Merriwether J. Thompson.

8126. Westwood, James T. "A Contemporary Dilemma: The Impact of Intelligence Operations on Foreign Policy," Naval War College Review 29/4 (Spring 1977): 86-92.

Draws on several historical cases to make the point that proper direction and control of intelligence analysis is critical to the policy process.

8127. Westwood, James T. "The USSR's SLOC Program," Naval Intelligence Professionals Quarterly 3/2 (Summer 1987): 5-6.

8128. Westwood, James T. "Soviet Electronic Warfare: Theory and Practice," Jane's Soviet Intelligence Review 1/9 & 1/10 (September and October 1989): 386-391; 443-446.

A summary of Soviet electronic warfare devices, organization and operations.

8129. Wexler, Jodi. "The Rainbow Warrior Affair: State and Agent Responsibility for Authorized Violations of International Law," Boston University International Law Journal 5 (Fall 1987): 389-412.

Discusses the case; the international legal issues arising from the case; the road to arbitration; the United Nations Secretary-General's arbitration ruling as to its validity and binding force; and conclusions.

8130. Wexler, Mark N. "Conjectures on the Dynamics of Secrecy and the Secrets Business," Journal of Business Ethics 6 (August 1987): 469-480.

8131. Weyl, Nathaniel. "A Labyrinth of Treason," Midstream 31/6 (1985): 54-57.

Discusses the penetration of the British MI5 and MI6 intelligence organizations; a comparison between British, American and Soviet intelligence agents; and an overview the design of the American counterintelligence system. Argues that Britain has been more susceptible to communist penetration than the American system.

8132. Weyrauch, Walter O. "Gestapo Informants: Facts and Theory of Undercover Operations," Columbia Journal of Transnational Law 24/3 (Summer 1986) 553-596.

Article details the standards and forms a collaboration, including inducements to collaborate (e.g., circumstantial threats versus monetary rewards). Types of confidential collaborators are examined: citizens of neutral countries, enemy citizens living in Germany, Germans with anti-Nazi sentiments on record, and persons tainted for ethnic or religious reasons. The fate of collaboration, reasons for continued secrecy, and typology of the non-collaborator are discussed.

8133. Whaley, Barton. "Codeword Barbarossa," Esquire 80 (December 1973): 106-108+.

This is a summary of the author's book on the subject. Argues that the German deception of the Russians depended on Stalin's failure to heed warnings from allies. Stalin came to appreciate the value of intelligence from the Barbarossa event.

8134. Whaley, Barton. "Covert Rearmament in Germany 1919-1939: Deception and Misperception," Journal of Strategic Studies 5/1 (March 1982): 3-27.

A summary of the author's monograph. Effective use of deception by the German's to cover up progress in rearmament and manipulation of the British.

8135. Whaley, Barton. "Toward a General Theory of Deception," Journal of Strategic Studies 5/1 (March 1982): 177-192.

Offers a preliminary general theory of deception as a teaching tool and as an analytical tool. Offers a typology of perception as a complex interaction of misperception and self-deception.

8136. Whatley, Frederick W. "Snepp v. United States," Cleveland State Law Review 30 (Spring 1981): 247-293.

This is a case comment concerning the background of Snepp; the CIA secrecy contract; the information the CIA can protect; methods of information control; criminal prosecution; the damages resulting from the constructive trust; and punitive damages.

8137. Wheatcroft, S. G. "On Assessing the Size of Forced Concentration Camp Labour in the Soviet Union," Soviet Studies 33/12 (April 1981): 265-295.

A study of the size of forced labor in the Soviet Union. Sections discuss the errors in Steven Rosefielde's assessment as to Rosefielde's material evidence; the Rosefielde circumstantial evidence; and the link between evidence and conclusion.

8138. Wheatley, Dennis. "Deception in World War II," Journal of the Royal United Services Institute for Defence Studies 121/3 (September 1976): 87-88.

The author intended only a short statement to correct an impression left in Anthony Cave Brown's book, Bodyguard of Lies, concerning the operations of the British deception unit known as the London Controlling Station.

8139. Wheeler, Daniel D. "Problems with Chaotic Cryptosystems," Cryptologia 13/3 (July 1989): 243-250.

8140. Wheeler, Daniel D. "Problems with Mitchell's Nonlinear Key Generators," Cryptologia 15/4 (October 1991): 355-363.

8141. Wheeler, Daniel D. and Robert A. J. Matthews. "Supercomputer Investigations of a Chaotic Encryption Algorithm," Cryptologia 15/2 (April 1991): 140-152.

8142. Wheeler, Douglas L. "In the Service of Order: The Portuguese Political Police and the British, German, and Spanish Intelligence, 1932-1945," Journal of Contemporary History 18/1 (January 1983): 1-26.

Given limited files and documentation on the political police, the author contains his analysis to the relationship between the chief decision makers and the police, relations with British espionage operations against the Germans, and to the main functions of the police.

8143. Wheeler, Douglas L. "Secrecy, Intelligence Literature and History," American Intelligence Journal 7/4 (June 1986).

8144. Wheeler, Douglas L. "Global Intelligence Resources," American Intelligence Journal 11/1 (Winter 1989-1990): 8-12.

The author estimates the number of intelligence service personnel the world over, determining the number to be approximately 2,156,000, not counting informants. Includes brief discussion of implications of global human resources.

8145. Wheeler, Douglas L. "The Archives of Portugal: A Guide to an Intelligence Treasure Trove," International Journal of Intelligence and Counterintelligence 4/4 (Winter 1990): 539-550.

Discusses the Portugese archives and libraries in general; the five major government archives of Portugal; and a conclusion that the Portugese files contain many surprises with respect to intelligence operations.

8146. Wheeler, Douglas L. "Spy Mania and the Information War: The Hour of the Counterspy 1914/1915," American Intelligence Journal 14/1 (Autumn-Winter 1992-1993): 41-45.

A brief account of counterespionage systems in place prior to the outbreak of World War I in Britain and Germany.

8147. Wheeler, Mark. "The SOE Phenomenon," Journal of Contemporary History 16 (July 1981): 513-519.

A review essay of three historical studies of the British Special Operations Europe program to overthrow occupied Europe during World War II.

8148. Wheelwright, Julie. "Poisoned Honey: The Myth of Women in Espionage," Queen's Quarterly 100/2 (Summer 1993): 291-309.

Argues that there are many myths surrounding the service of women in espionage work. Author attempts to correct the record by discussing several aspects of female involvement demonstrating more positive and contributing characteristics.

8149. Whelan, Charles M. "Passports and Freedom of Travel: The Conflict of a Right and a Privilege," Georgetown Law Journal 41/1 (November 1952): 63-90.

Discusses the common right of freedom of travel and the growth of the American law of passports. Concludes that the Secretary of State has discretionary power to revoke passports and whether such discretion should and will be reviewed by the federal courts.

8150. Whetten, Lawrence and Michael Johnson. "Military Lessons of the Yom Kippur War," World Today 30/3 (March 1974): 101-109.

Discusses primarily the air and ground war lessons.

8151. Whitaker, Paul and Louis Kruh. "From Bletchley Park to Berchtesgaden," Cryptologia 11/3 (July 1987): 129-141.

Events involved in a mission to Germany in mid-1945 to discover cryptologic capabilities.

8152. Whitaker, Reginald. "Origins of the Canadian Government's Internal Security System, 1946-1952," Canadian Historical Review 65/2 (June 1984): 154-183.

Discussion of Canada's development of security services to counter the loss of state secrets during the early years of the cold war. Canada took steps to avoid the problems of the US during the McCarthy era, turning over investigative powers to contain subversive activities to the RCMP. Despite its good work, Canada suffered losses due to spies in the government. Canada's system is given an overall stamp of success.

8153. Whitaker, Reginald. "Official Repression of Communism During World War II," Labour/Le Travail: Journal of Canadian Labour Studies 17 (Spring 1986): 135-166.

8154. Whitaker, Reginald. "Return to the Crucible," Canadian Forum (November 1986): 11-28.

8155. Whitaker, Reginald. "The Politics of Security Intelligence Policy-making in Canada: I 1970-84," Intelligence and National Security 6/4 (October 1991): 649-668.
Examines the politics of security intelligence policy making, comparing the Canadian methods with those of the British and the US. Draws on the need for public accountability concerning security intelligence operations, and notes that unless there is a major public scandal there is virtually no accountability for the intelligence user or sources of information.

8156. Whitaker, Reginald. "Security and Intelligence in the Post-Cold War World," Socialist Register (1992): 111-130.

8157. Whitaker, Reginald. "The Politics of Security Intelligence Policy-making in Canada: II 1984-91," Intelligence and National Security 7/2 (April 1992): 53-76.
Second of a two-part article which traces the reforms of the Canadian Security Intelligence Service (CSIS). This article traces the record of the new system and the effectiveness of new instruments of accountability in the CSIS Act of 1984.

8158. Whitaker, Reginald. "Apprehended Insurrection? RCMP Intelligence and the October Crisis," Queen's Quarterly 100/2 (Summer 1993): 383-406.
Accounts for the excesses of the Canadian intelligence operations of the Royal Canadian Mounted Police when the War Measures Act was applied to an alleged internal security crisis in October 1970. The author's study of RCMP intelligence work was made possible through the Access to Information statute.

8159. Whitaker, Reginald. "The 'Bristow Affair': A Crisis of Accountability in Canadian Security Intelligence," Intelligence and National Security 11/2 (April 1996): 279-305.

Major sections consider the Security Intelligence Review Committee as watchdog or lapdog; bureaucratic advice to the government; ministerial guidelines on human sources; the parliamentary committee; the SIRC report; the handling of the media; some shortcomings of the SIRC report; the Preston Manning file; the Tory dimension; and the Parliament falters.

8160. White, James. "Subversive Activities Legislation--The Supreme Court's Supervisory Role," University of San Francisco Law Review 1 (1966): 207-216.

Reviews earlier decisions pertaining to subversive activities and bill of attainder. Then, reviews recent decisions, such as Apthaker v. Secretary of State and Brown v. U. S.

8161. White, Jeffrey B. "Some Thoughts on Irregular Warfare," Studies in Intelligence 39/5 (1996): 51-59.

Major sections discuss implications for intelligence; operational environment; changes in political geography; cultural and physical aspects; an emerging issue regarding ecological information; importance of history; ethnic and religious factors; modern and irregular warfare; organization; technology; logistics; direction; doctrine; decisive battle; soldiers and warriors; allies and accomplices; segregation and integration; balance sheet; intelligence considerations; specialists and generalists; and collection needs.

8162. White, Leonard D. "The Loyalty Program of the United States Government," Bulletin of the Atomic Scientists 7/12 (December 1951): 363-366, 382.

Reports on the origins of loyalty, loyalty during World War II, loyalty boards, role of the Federal Bureau of Investigation and the results of the loyalty programs.

8163. White, Mark J. "Belligerent Beginnings: John F. Kennedy on the Opening Day of the Cuban Missile Crisis," Journal of Strategic Studies 15/1 (March 1992).

8164. White, Ralph K. "Propaganda: Morally Questionable and Morally Unquestionable Techniques," Annals of the American Academy of Political and Social Sciences 398 (November 1971): 26-35.

8165. White, Ralph K. "Misperception in the Arab-Israeli Conflict," Journal of Social Issues 33 (Winter 1977): 190-221.

Discusses the factors leading to misperceptions; how each side failed to understand the other's beliefs; the focus on the future rather than the past to find ground for negotiation; and the role of the US in negotiations.

8166. White, Ralph K. "Empathy as an Intelligence Tool," International Journal of Intelligence and Counterintelligence 1/1 (Spring 1986): 57-75.

Intelligence services, like national policy makers, must develop and apply empathy for actual or potential enemies in order to prepare more realistic estimates of capabilities and intentions. Definitions and historical examples are supplied, as well as methods for achieving empathy.

8167. White, R. Murray. "Scouting," National Review (May 1903): 474-479. This is a British publication.

8168. White, Stephen and Ol'ga Kryshtanovskaya. "Public Attitudes Toward the KGB: A Research Note," Europe-Asia Studies 45/1 (1993): 169-176.
Considers the organization and control of the KGB; and the KGB in public life. This journal is the former Soviet Studies.

8169. White, Tracy M. "The Heat Is On: The Warrantless Use of Infrared Surveillance to Detect Indoor Marijuana Cultivation," Arizona State Law Journal 27 (Spring 1995): 295-309.
Major sections discuss the factual basis of the Drug Enforcement Agency's investigation of Joseph Pinson by using infrared technology; the Eighth Circuit's holding in the case; the Ninth Circuit's probable ruling; and conclusions as to the use of FLIR surveillance technology to detect indoor cultivation of marijuana.

8170. White, Welsh S. "Regulating Prison Informers Under the Due Process Clause," Supreme Court Review (1991): 103-142.
Discusses the extent to which the due process clause of the US Constitution may impose restraints on prison informers who participate in eliciting incriminating statements from other prisoners. Sections discuss the cases prior to Fulminante; the Fulminante decision; other possible approaches to the due process clause; and conclusions.

8171. White, William. "The Microdot: Then and Now," International Journal of Intelligence and Counterintelligence 3/2 (Summer 1989): 249-270.
A history of the microdot, 1839-1989; a history of microphotography; the information age; and Soviet shortcomings.

8172. Whiting, Allen S. "New Light on Mao; Quemoy 1958: Mao's Miscalculations," China Quarterly 62 (1975): 263-270.
Mao Tse Tung's use of propaganda and ploys to entice the United States into conflict in defense of Quemoy and Matsu during the administration of Dwight Eisenhower.

8173. Whitlock, Duane L. "The Silent War Against the Japanese Navy," Naval War College Review 48/4 (Autumn 1995): 43-52.

8174. Whitman, John. "On Estimating Reactions," Studies in Intelligence 9/2 (Summer 1965).

Estimated to be 6 pages in length.

8175. Whitmore, George D. "The Role of Photogrammetry in an 'Open Skies' Program," Photogrammetric Engineering 2/3 (1958): 376-382.

8176. Whitmore, S. B. "The Truth About the Coventry Air Raid," Journal of the Royal Artillery 109/2 (September 1982): 149-155.

8177. Whitridge, Arnold. "Beaumarchais and the American Revolution," History Today 17/2 (1967): 98-103.

A French covert action by King Louis XVI and Caron di Beaumarchais to set up a secret business to fund arms shipments to the American colonists to fight the British. The intervenor was Silas Deane, who had authorization from the revolutionary congress to deal with the French.

8178. Whitton, John B. "War by Radio," Foreign Affairs 19 (April 1941): 584-596.

8179. Whitton, John B. "Cold War Propaganda," American Journal of International Law 45 (January 1951): 151-153.

8180. Whitton, John B. "Subversive Propaganda Reconsidered," American Journal of International Law 55 (January 1961): 120-122.

Briefly discusses President Eisenhower's proclamation of "Captive Nations Week" in terms of the international law norm against the use of subversive propaganda.

8181. Whitton, John B. "Hostile International Propaganda and International Law," Annals of the American Academy of Political and Social Sciences 398 (November 1971): 14-25.

Discusses four types of propaganda: subversive; defamatory; wartime; and private.

8182. Wicker, Tom. "The Undeclared Witch-Hunt," Harper's 239 (November 1969): 108-110.

A story about the Defense Department's revocation of the security clearance of Benning Wentworth, considered a national security threat due to his declared homosexuality. Discusses wiretapping abuses in the Nixon era.

8183. Wickham, John A., Jr. "C^{3}I as a Force Multiplier," Signal 42/8 (April 1988): 21-22.

8184. Wickham, John A., Jr. "Booming Espionage," Signal 44/4 (December 1989): 21-22.

8185. Wiegley, Roger D. "The Recovered Sunken Warship: Raising a Legal Question," U.S. Naval Institute Proceedings 105/1 (January 1979): 26-32.
A discussion of the legal entanglements of locating sunken ships on the high seas. Intelligence aspects of Project Jennifer are described.

8186. Wiener, Frederick B. "The Greed of Benedict Arnold: Siren Call to Treason," Army 24/5 (May 1974): 43-47.

8187. Wiesel, G. "INPOL--The West German Police Information System," Police Studies 2/4 (Winter 1980): 22-35.
A substantial summary of the West German intelligence data base known as the Joint Electronic Information System (INPOL).

8188. Wiggins, Florence R. "The Long Vigil of Mary Feake Roe," Daughters of the American Revolution Magazine 110/3 (1976): 312-313.
An account of Roe's activities during her marriage to William Roe, a Revolutionary war spy from 1777-1786.

8189. Wigmore, John H. "Abrams v. U. S.: Freedom of Speech and Freedom of Thuggery in Wartime and Peace-Time," Illinois Law Review 14/8 (March 1920): 539-561.
Argues that the two dissenting opinions in Abrams represented poor law and poor policy from which several negative implications may result.

8190. Wilcox, C. De. W. "The Ethics of Major Andre's Mission," New York State Historical Association Proceedings 15 (1916): 126-137.

8191. Wilcox, E. H. "Miasoyedoff's Treachery," Fortnightly 108 (August 1917): 267-276.

8192. Wilds, Thomas. "How Japan Fortified the Mandated Islands," U.S. Naval Institute Proceedings 81 (April 1955): 401-407.

8193. Wiley, Edward. "The National Cryptologic School," Signal 44 (December 1989): 115-116.

8194. Wilhelm, Richard. "The Story of Shipboard EW Integration," Journal of Electronic Defense 10/3 (March 1987): 53-60.
A discussion of shipboard elecronic defense systems advancements after 1967.

8195. Wilkes, Owen and Nils P. Gleditsch. "NAROL--An Early Attack Assessment System," Intelligence and National Security 2/2 (April 1987): 331-335.

A brief extract of a larger piece on the role of the LORAN-C military navigation system, including consideration of its role in early warning intelligence.

8196. Wilkey, Malcolm R. "S-2, Division Artillery," Field Artillery Journal 33/9 (September 1943): 699-700.

Describes the job of the artillery division's intelligence function.

8197. Willard, B. L. "Investigations and Naval Intelligence: 1945-1965," Naval Intelligence Professionals Quarterly 7/1 (Winter 1991): 8-11.

8198. Willard, Richard K. "Law and the National Security Decision-Making Process in the Reagan Administration," Houston Journal of International Law 11/1 (Fall 1988): 129-142.

Discusses the Reagan administration's approach to law and the national security process, 1981-82; the anti-leak effort in 1982-84; the Iran-Contra decision making process, 1985-86; and speculations about the future of NSDD-84.

8199. Willard, Richard K.; Daniel Rapaport; Ford Rowan; and Allen Weinstein. "Democracy versus Secrecy: Should the United States Have An Official Secrets Act? Suppressing Leaks: Is Polygraph Testing Acceptable in a Democracy?," Center Magazine 17/5 (September-October 1984): 59-64.

Willard proposes an official secrets act for the US and the use of polygraph testing to root out leaks; Rapaport opposes polygraph testing for national security purposes; Rowan rejects the notion of an official secrets act; and Weinstein opposes an official secrets act and polygraph testing.

8200. Willbourn, Dorothy. "Constitutional Law--Power of the Court to Review Jurisdiction in Military Commissions," Illinois Bar Journal 31 (1943): 216-221.

8201. Willes, E. W. "Criminal Intelligence Service Canada," Police Chief 38/9 (September 1971): 18-19.

Canadian law enforcement agencies have formed a national intelligence network to fight organized crime.

8202. Willhelm, Sidney M. "The Rise of State Rule: An Exploratory and Interpretive Essay," Catalyst 9 (1977): 1-58.

A polemic in which the author argues, among other eccentric views, that the CIA was the only institution of the US government holding the "state" together. Sections provide the cast of this piece: "Capital's economic demise"; militarization vs. capital"; "CIA vs. capital"; "Domestic instability"; and "Probing the power struggle among state's agencies of social control."

8203. Williams, C. "Crime Intelligence and Australian Policing," Pacific Defence Reporter 7/8 (February 1981): 27-30.

Proposes the creation of an Australian Bureau of Criminal Intelligence for collection, evaluation and distribution of accurate information to local police bureaus. Discusses the use of such agencies at the national government level in other countries.

8204. Williams, C. "Congressional Oversight of Covert Actions: The Public's Stake in the Forty-Eight Hour Rule," Harvard Journal of Law and Public Policy 12 (1989): 285-301.

Discusses the initial congressional response to the Iran-Contra matter and the Senate's attempt to reach and accommodation with the Administration; the Senate's reaction to Administration policy; the forty-eight hour rule as a public policy issue; the nature and need for covert actions; the subjection of covert actions to checks and balances; and the Executive branch rejoinders.

8205. Williams, C. O. G. "Contained Terrorist Incidents in Australia: Police or Military Problem?," Australian Defence Force Journal 28 (May-June 1981): 54-62.

8206. Williams, David. "Sowing the Wind: The Deportation Raids of 1920 in New Hampshire," Historical New Hampshire 34/1 (Spring 1979): 1-31.

An excellent accounting of the events surrounding the Palmer red scare raids. Useful as a background piece on early 20th century domestic intelligence.

8207. Williams, David. "They Never Stopped Watching Us: FBI Political Surveillance, 1924-1936," UCLA History Journal 2/1 (Spring 1981): 5-28.

An account of J. Edgar Hoover's alleged perpetual violation of Attorney General Stone's edict regarding domestic surveillance in the years 1924 to 1936.

8208. Williams, David. "The Bureau of Investigation and Its Critics, 1919-1921: The Origins of Federal Political Surveillance," Journal of American History 68/3 (December 1981): 560-579.

Argues that the FBI's surveillance of dissidents began with World War I as a result of presidential and congressional acceptance of J. Edgar Hoover's effective work.

8209. Williams, Edward B. "The Wiretapping - Eavesdropping Problem: A Defense Counsel's View," Minnesota Law Review 44 (1960): 855-871.

Discusses the long term problem with wiretapping in the years after the invention of the telephone. Separate discussions of the wiretapping problem and the eavesdropping problem, followed by recommendations for controls by legislation.

8210. Williams, Edward G. "A Note on Fort Pitt and the Revolution on the Western Frontier," Western Pennsylvania History Magazine 60/3 (1977): 265-276.

Discusses espionage activities at Fort Pitt between 1776 and 1782. This piece is related to others by the author in the previous issue of the Magazine.

8211. Williams, George. "Intelligence and Book Learning: A Comprehensive Survey of Public Sources on Secret Activities," Choice 16 (November 1979): 1125-1138.

A lengthy book review essay concerning numerous books on the history and contemporary operations of the intelligence community.

8212. Williams, H. C. "Some Public-Key Crypto-Functions as Intractable as Factorization," Cryptologia 9/3 (July 1985): 223-237.

8213. Williams, J. R. and L. L. Guess. "The Informant: A Narcotics Enforcement Dilemma," Journal of Psychoactive Drugs 13/3 (Summer 1981): 235-245.

8214. Williams, James A. "Intelligence Support to NATO," Signal 38/4 (December 1983): 87-90.

8215. Williams, James A. "The Intelligence Workforce," American Intelligence Journal 6/1 (March 1984).

8216. Williams, James A. "INCA: The Issues and Opportunities," Signal 39 (September 1984): 25-26.

8217. Williams, James A. "The Last Hope of First Promise," Intelligence Quarterly (July 1986): 4-5.

8218. Williams, James A. "What Next for Military Intelligence?," American Intelligence Journal 8/3 (Summer 1987).

8219. Williams, James A. "Intelligence for the Future: Roadmap or Puzzle?," Defense Intelligence Journal 2/1 (Spring 1993): 3-14.

A discussion of current needs for sophisticated and advanced intelligence.

8220. Williams, John. "Official Secrecy in England," Federal Law Review 3 (1968): 20-25.

8221. Williams, R. C., Jr. "Amphibious Scouts and Raiders," Military Affairs 13/3 (Fall 1949): 150-157.

Several types of underwater and surveillance units in World War II are discussed.

8222. Williams, Robert W. "Commanders and Intelligence: The Growing Gap," Army 22 (December 1972): 21-24.

8223. Williams, Robert W. "Surprise: The Danger Signals," Army 24 (April 1974): 10-16.

8224. Williams, Robert W. "Commanders and Surprise," Studies in Intelligence 26/3 (Fall 1982): 9-19.
   This article is not listed among items declassified by the Central Intelligence Agency for public access.

8225. Williamson, Charles A. "Special Operations Intelligence," American Intelligence Journal 11/3 (1990): 15-17.

8226. Williamson, John A. and William D. Lacier. "The Twelve Days of England," U.S. Naval Institute Proceedings 106/3 (1980): 76-83.
   How the US Navy uses codebreaking in anti-submarine engagement.

8227. Willoughby, Charles A. "Espionage and the American Communist Party," American Mercury 88 (January 1959): 117-123.
   This former major general discusses activities of Soviet spies, mainly the work of spy Richard Sorge and his work as a reporter and associate of Agnes Smedley. Also discusses Steve Nelson, the American version of Sorge, who was trained at the Lenin School in Moscow.

8228. Willoughby, Charles A. "Khrushchev and the Flight to Sverdlovsk," American Mercury 91 (August 1960): 34-43.
   Discusses clandestine Soviet intelligence operations in the United Nations during the Khrushchev era. Discusses intelligence operations in Czechoslovakia, capture of a Soviet agent in Switzerland, and the U-2 spy plane incident.

8229. Willoughby, Malcolm. "The Beach Pounders," U.S. Naval Institute Proceedings 8/3 (1957): 818-828.
   The Coast Guard's beach patrols are discussed in connection with their role in anti-sabotage and anti-espionage during the Second World War.

8230. Wills, Garry. "The Kennedy Imprisonment: The Prisoner of Toughness," Atlantic Monthly 261/2 (February 1982): 52-66.
   This is the second in a series of articles on the Kennedy administration. This part discusses the planning and execution of the Bay of Pigs operation in 1961.

8231. Wills, Garry. "The Unconstitutional Presidency," European Contributions to American Studies 15 (1988): 44-49.

8232. Wilsnack, Richard W. "Information Control: A Conceptual Framework for Sociological Analysis," Urban Life 8/4 (January 1980): 467-499.

One of several articles in this issue devoted to the sociological analysis of secrecy and information control. Major sections discuss control processes; espionage; secrecy; persuasion; evaluation; the relationships between control processes; counteracting processes; collaboration; hypotheses; and the social context of information control.

8233. Wilson, Charles M. "The Hit-and-Run Raid," American Heritage 12/5 (May 1961): 29-31.

Details the circumstances of the Confederacy's plans to steal money, horses and weapons from a Vermont town during the Civil War. Covers the account from the arrival of secret agents to the robbery, ending with a description of a meeting be townspeople and the robbers after the war.

8234. Wilson, Craig L. "Intelligence Training," Signal (September 1984): 14-16.

8235. Wilson, David. "Courses in Cryptology--Cryptanalysis Course Down Under," Cryptologia 2/1 (January 1978): 9-11.

8236. Wilson, David. "Littlewood's Cipher," Cryptologia 3/2 (April 1979): 120-121.

8237. Wilson, David. "Littlewood's Cipher Part II: A Method of Solution," Cryptologia 3/3 (July 1979): 172-176.

8238. Wilson, David A. "National Security Control of Technological Information," Jurimetrics Journal 25 (Winter 1985): 109-129.

Argues for fewer restrictions on university level research and development in the realm of advancements in technology.

8239. Wilson, James. "Dieppe: Vindication," Army Quarterly and Defence Journal 124/1 (1994): 68-72.

Attempts to vindicate the intelligence failures of the Dieppe raid of 1942 by arguing that lives were saved in the 1944 Normandy invasion.

8240. Wilson, James G. "Chaining the Leviathan: The Unconstitutionality of Executing Those Convicted of Treason," University of Pittsburgh Law Review 45/1 (Fall 1983): 99-179.

Demonstrates why the Constitution should be interpreted to require an additional protection against use of capital punishment in treason cases unless aggravated murder is proven by the government.

8241. Wilson, James H. "A Staff Officer's Journal on the Vicksburg Campaign," Journal of the Military Service Institution of the United States 43 (1908): 93-109, 261-275.

A classic article for reference in all research on Civil War intelligence.

8242. Wilson, James Q. "Bugging, Break-Ins and the FBI," Commentary 65/6 (June 1978): 52-58.

Discusses domestic surveillance activities of the FBI with particular reference to the 1978 indictment of three former FBI agents for alleged violations of federal laws.

8243. Wilson, James Q. "The Changing FBI--The Road to Abscam," Public Interest 59 (Spring 1980): 3-14.

The author defends the FBI's investigations of white collar crimes, such as ABSCAM, as having a long and legitimate foundation in congressional approval.

8244. Wilson, Lavalette. "Andre's Landing Place at Haverstraw: A Mooted Question Settled," Magazine of American History 13/2 (February 1885): 173-176.

8245. Wilson, Samuel V. "American Intelligence and the Tricentennial," Studies in Intelligence 20/3 (Fall 1976).

Author's speech delivered at the Association of Former Intelligence Officers meeting in Reston, Virginia. Estimated to be seven pages in length.

8246. Wilson, Thomas R. "Joint Vocational Intelligence Training," Defense Intelligence Journal 2/2 (Fall 1992): 143-148.

Discusses the Army's joint military intelligence training program in terms of challenges, the intelligence battlefield; conditions for joint training; JIT opportunities, limitations and consensus.

8247. Wilt, Alan F. "The Intelligence Wave," Air University Review 31/4 (May-June 1980): 114-118.

A book review essay of three books on intelligence by authors David Kahn, Patrick Beesly and Vernon Walters; their observations of World War II in public mind and an inside look at the German Army.

8248. Wiltz, John E. "The MacArthur Hearings of 1951: The Secret Testimony," Military Affairs 39 (December 1975): 167-173.

Discusses the portions of the hearings held at a high point of executive branch concern for the decisions made by MacArthur at the outset of the Korean War. Also discusses the possibility of a war with the Soviet Union if Chiang Kai-shek were permitted to become involved.

8249. Wimsatt, W. K., Jr. "What Poe Knew About Cryptography," <u>PMLA: Publications of the Modern Language Association of America</u> 58/3 (September 1943): 754-779.

A rich study of Poe's blend of the detective story and literary cryptograms.

8250. Winchester, J. "Aerial Reconnaissance in Peace and War," <u>NATO Fifteen Nations</u> 8/4 (May 1963): 90-99.

8251. Winchester, Karen A. and James W. Zirkle. "Freedom of Information and the CIA Information Act," <u>University of Richmond Law Review</u> 21 (Winter 1987): 231-302.

Major sections consider FOIA exemptions; Executive Orders; the Vaughn Index; the Glomar response; the CIA Information Act of 1984 and its purpose; and legislative history. Limitations of the FOIA with respect to CIA records are observed.

8252. Windmiller, Marshall. "A Tumultuous Time: OSS and Army Intelligence in India, 1942-1946," <u>International Journal of Intelligence and Counterintelligence</u> 8/1 (Spring 1995): 105-124.

A rich examination of OSS operations in India during World War II. Major topics include, getting established in India in early 1942; relations with the British; relations among the Americans; the Chinese problem; OSS interest in Indian politics; the women of Research and Analysis; planning for postwar intelligence; the Russian menace, and contrasting agendas.

8253. Windham, Michael C. "Intelligent Preparation of the Battlefield," <u>Field Artillery Journal</u> 55 (March-April 1987): 17-20.

8254. Wingo, Harvey. "A 2020 Vision of Visual Surveillance and the Fourth Amendment," <u>Oregon Law Review</u> 71 (Spring 1992): 1-46.

Sets forth a hypothetical Supreme Court decision in the year 2020 pertaining to evidence regarding a crime required by means of a night vision surveillance device that could see through walls. Discusses relevant case law, beginning with <u>Katz</u>.

8255. Winkel, Brian J. "Why Cryptologia," <u>Cryptologia</u> 1/1 (January 1977): 1-3.

The new editor of this new journal explains the rationale for the journal's creation.

8256. Winkel, Brian J. "Poe Challenge Cipher Finally Broken," <u>Cryptologia</u> 1/1 (January 1977): 93-96.

8257. Winkel, Brian J. "Word Ways, A Journal Worth Going Your Way," Cryptologia 1/3 (July 1977): 232-234.

8258. Winkel, Brian J. "Poe Challenge Cipher Solutions," Cryptologia 1/4 (October 1977): 318-325.

8259. Winklemann, Ray. "Defense Against Electronic Espionage," Defense Systems Review 3/4 (1985): 59-68.

8260. Winkler, Peter. "The Advent of Cryptology in the Game of Bridge," Cryptologia 7/4 (October 1983): 327-332.

8261. Winks, Robin W. "'Whodunit?': Canadian Society As Reflected in Its Detective Fiction," American Review of Canadian Studies 17/4 (Winter 1987-1988): 373-381.
    Discusses the expansion of the Canadian-written detective and spy novel, and the techniques used by Canadian writers to appeal to a world market for such works.

8262. Winks, Robin W. "The Wise Man of Intelligence," Foreign Affairs 73/6 (November-December 1994): 144-149.
    A book review essay concerning Peter Grose's Gentleman Spy: The Life of Allen Dulles.

8263. Winokur, Scott. "The Spying Game," California Lawyer 13 (December 1993): 64+.

8264. Winston, Emanuel A. "Vital Intelligence: A National Right," Midstream 33 8/4 (June-July 1987): 9-10.
    Justifies Jeffrey Pollard's spying activities for Israel concerning Iraqi gas, chemical and biological warfare, Soviet arms shipments to Arab countries. Pakistan's A-bomb plans, US assessments of PLO activities, Libyan air defenses, and Soviet fleet movements in the Mediterranean. Author argues that United States intelligence liaison actions withheld this information from Israeli intelligence.

8265. Winternitz, Robert and Martin Hellman. "Chosen-Key Attacks on a Block Cipher," Cryptologia 11/1 (January 1987): 16-20.

8266. Winters, Frank. "Vietnam Pearl Harbor," Saga 37/3 (December 1968): 14-17.
    Author suggests that vital intelligence information regarding the Tet offensive was ignored by policy makers.

8267. Winters, Jim. "Tom Dooley, the Forgotten Hero," Notre Dame Magazine (May 1979): 10+.

8268. Winterton, George. "The Concept of Extra-Constitutional Executive Power in Domestic Affairs," Hastings Constitutional Law Quarterly 7/1 (Fall 1979): 1-46.

Examines the concept of extra-constitutional executive power in domestic affairs, discusses problems raised by such power, and considers whether or not the concept should be recognized by the law. Considers various national security applications and cases.

8269. Winterton, M. J. "Collation of Crime Intelligence with Regard to Chinese Triads in Holland," Police Journal 54/1 (January-March 1981): 34-57.

Discusses the history and emergence of Chinese Triads in Amsterdam, Holland and the value of intelligence gathering in countering Triad moves. Excellent information on the operations of these organized crime gangs.

8270. Wirbel, L. "Somebody's Listening--There's a Computer on the Line," Progressive 44 (November 1980): 16-19+.

Discussion of the National Security Agency's mission to intercept, decode and analyze messages of other governments; the NSA and domestic surveillance; the high technology of the NSA; and links between NSA and other agencies. Concludes that vigilance over the security of the computers as well as civil liberties must be maintained.

8271. Wirtz, James J. "The Intelligence Paradigm," Intelligence and National Security 4/4 (October 1989): 829-837.

Discusses the definitions, need for, and construction of an intelligence paradigm. Argues that experience is the mother of invention, who contributes to the paradigm, the paradigm, and the future direction of thinking. Also considers failure of the paradigm and reasons for failure.

8272. Wirtz, James J. "Deception and the Tet Offensive," Journal of Strategic Studies 13/2 (June 1990): 82-98.

Argues that the Tet offensive was a more purposeful vehicle of North Vietnamese deception than has been accepted by most historians, many of whom suggest that the effort was merely intended to alter American popular opinion of the war.

8273. Wirtz, James J. "Miscalculation, Surprise and American Intelligence After the Cold War," International Journal of Intelligence and Counterintelligence 5/1 (Spring 1991): 1-16.

Considers the phenomena of miscalculation and surprise in a post-Cold War world in which Third World nations must now be more closely judged as potential adversaries. Major sections discuss challenges to the new world order; the new contexts of miscalculation and surprise; and miscalculation in the Gulf war. This article was reprinted in <u>Studies in Intelligence</u> 35/2 (Summer 1991).

8274. Wirtz, James J. "Intelligence to Please?: The Order of Battle Controversy During the Vietnam War," <u>Political Science Quarterly</u> 106/2 (Summer 1991): 239-263.

An extensive analysis of the Vietnam war debate between CIA and military analysts over the implications of the Enemy Order of Battle reports pertaining to the North Vietnamese Army. Includes discussion of Sam Adams and the CIA skeptics and resolves that the paper war in Washington and Saigon overrode the war in the field.

8275. Wirtz, James J. "Constraints on Intelligence Collaboration: The Domestic Dimension," <u>Defense Analysis</u> 8/3 (December 1992): 247-259.

8276. Wirtz, James J. "Constraints on Intelligence Collaboration: The Domestic Dimension," <u>International Journal of Intelligence and Counterintelligence</u> 6/1 (Spring 1993): 85-99.

Surveys various intelligence relationships that emerged since World War II; describes how cooperative arrangements can leave the US intelligence community vulnerable to external threats and internal criticism; analyzes why and when the American public can tolerate domestic intelligence operations; and draws conclusions about how the end of the Cold War will introduce a new era of domestic recrimination in the US.

8277. Wise, David. "Cloak and Dagger Operations: An Overview," <u>Society</u> 12/3 (March-April 1975): 26-33.

Argues that covert domestic activities of the CIA are dangerous features of democratic life.

8278. Wise, David and Thomas B. Ross. "Cloaking the Dagger: The Invisible Government," <u>Commentary</u> (March 1965): 87-89.

This is a book review essay pertaining to the Wise and Ross study of the CIA, <u>The Invisible Government</u>.

8279. Wise, James E., Jr. "Operation Pastorius," <u>Naval Intelligence Professionals Quarterly</u> 5/2 (Summer 1989): 12-14.

8280. Wise, James E., Jr. "The Reluctant Spy Willie Colepaugh," <u>Naval Intelligence Professionals Quarterly</u> 5/3 (Fall 1989): 18-19.

8281. Wise, Sherwood E. "A Moment in My Eternity," <u>Military Review</u> 5/1 (June 1988): 24-26.

A discussion of the decoding of the Japanese agreement to surrender.

8282. Wise, James E., Jr. "Hapless Spy Oskar Mantel," <u>Naval Intelligence Professionals Quarterly</u> 6/1 (Winter 1990): 13-14.

8283. Wisner, Frank G. "On 'Craft of Intelligence,'" <u>Studies in Intelligence</u> 8/4 (Winter 1964).

A book review essay of <u>Craft of Intelligence</u> by CIA director Allen W. Dulles.

8284. Wittenberg, Eric J. "The Practitioner's Guide to Ohio Covenant Not to Compete and Trade Secrets Law in the Post-Employment Context," <u>Ohio Northern University Law Review</u> 18 (Fall 1992): 833-876.

8285. Wittenberg, Ernest. "The Thrifty Spy on the Sixth Avenue El," <u>American Heritage</u> 17/1 (January 1966): 60-64, 100-101.

A brief summary of American military counterintelligence against Germany in 1915. Sections discuss Germany's biggest spy ring; the German plan to cripple the US; the Secret Service on the German's trail; and the downfall of the spy ring.

8286. Wittner, Lawrence S. "The Truman Doctrine and the Defense of Freedom," <u>Diplomatic History</u> 4/2 (1980): 161-187.

8287. Wittner, Lawrence S. "When CIA Hearts Were Young and Gay: Planning the Cold War (Spring 1945)," <u>Peace and Change</u> 5/2-3 (1978): 70-76.

The evolution of the OSS to the CIA during the early days of the cold war; the response by the US intelligence community to the rise of the Soviet Union; the American national security problem of balancing forces in Europe and concerns for the loss of Japan.

8288. Witze, Claude. "Our Answer to Future Threats: Action or Reaction?," <u>Air Force and Space Digest</u> 48 (May 1965): 37-42.

8289. Wixson, Andrew. "Portrait of a Cuban Refugee," <u>Studies in Intelligence</u> 8/2 (Summer 1964).

Probably a sensitive article appearing in this CIA-controlled journal. Citation was located in secondary source.

8290. Woelk, Steven E. and Ed McCaul. "Spy Ship's Cruise Into Disaster," <u>Military History</u> 11/4 (1994): 62-69, 88, 90.

Discusses the experiences of author Woelk on board the USS Pueblo spy ship when it was captured in 1968.

8291. Woff, Richard. "The Border Troops of the Russian Federation," <u>Jane's Intelligence Review</u> 7/2 (February 1995): 70-73.

8292. Wohlforth, William C. "The Perception of Power: Russia in the Pre-1914 Balance," <u>World Politics</u> 39/3 (April 1987): 353-381.
    Majors sections consider estimation of the pre-war balance; perceptions of the powers; perceived versus estimated power; and the perceived balance of the war.

8293. Wohlstetter, Albert. "Legends of the Strategic Arms Race, Part I: The Driving Engine," <u>Strategic Review</u> 2/4 (Fall 1974): 67-92.
    Considers that precise outcomes to the hazards of nuclear war can be calculated and, therefore, analyzed before and as an alternative to actual nuclear war. Subtopics include building a national defense; war games; calculated predictions.

8294. Wohlstetter, Albert. "Is There a Strategic Arms Race?," <u>Foreign Policy</u> 15 (Summer 1974): 3-20.
    Defines the arms race and suggests the parameters of considering the condition of an arms race. Introduces three elements of models useful in evaluating a condition of an arms race: realistic assessment of Soviet objectives; responses to crises; and tradeoffs contemplated. Warns against overestimation Soviet threat potentials.

8295. Wohlstetter, Albert. "Rivals, But No Race," <u>Foreign Policy</u> 16 (Fall 1974): 48-81.
    An extensive and classic treatment of analytical problems of overestimating the enemy's capabilities, in this case Soviet strategic forces. Subtopics include the debate over Soviet estimates; quality versus quantity; the quantitative spiral; offensive and defensive budgets; net effect of qualitative change; and the question of whether or not there is an arms race.

8296. Wohlstetter, Albert. "Optimal Ways to Confuse Ourselves," <u>Foreign Policy</u> 20 (Fall 1975): 170-198.
    Argues that the US has a long history of overestimating the Soviet threat, part of which is understandable and some of which is useful to our national security interests. Distinguishes between arms race and arms competition.

8297. Wohlstetter, Albert. "Legends of the Strategic Arms Race, Part II: The Uncontrolled Upward Spiral," <u>Strategic Review</u> 3/1 (Winter 1975): 71-86.
    An extension of his article in 1974, covering overestimation of nuclear arms, quality versus quantity, and the concept of 'overkill.' Argues that more is not always better.

8298. Wohlstetter, Albert. "Racing Toward or Ambling Back?," Survey 22/3-4 (1976): 163-217.

This article argues that the US has actually underestimated Soviet forces and has, accordingly, permitted a decrease in defense spending since the 1960s.

8299. Wohlstetter, Roberta. "Cuba and Pearl Harbor: Hindsight and Foresight," Foreign Affairs 43/4 (July 1965): 691-707.

Using a model of intelligence failure and strategic surprise set forth in her book, Pearl Harbor: Warning and Decision, the author compares the Pearl Harbor event with the Bay of Pigs decisional process, 1961. She concludes that plenty of information had been available to avoid failure.

8300. Wohlstetter, Roberta. "The Pleasures of Self-Deception," Washington Quarterly 2/2 (Autumn 1979): 54-63.

How victim nations often deceive themselves, especially between wars; how perceptions are shaped by negotiations.

8301. Wolf, Charles, Jr. "Insurgency and Counterinsurgency: New Myths and Old Realities," Yale Review 55/2 (Winter 1967): 225-241.

Challenges the doctrine that popular attitudes and support play the decisive role in enabling insurgent movements to emerge and to evolve into wars of liberation. May be useful for studies of covert action.

8302. Wolf, James B. "Asian and African Recruitment in the Kenya Police, 1920-1950," International Journal of African Historical Studies 6/3 (1973): 401-412.

8303. Wolf, John B. "Police Intelligence--Focus for Counter-Terrorist Operations," Police Journal 49/1 (January-March 1976): 19-27.

Argues that intelligence systems can and should be developed to counter the activities of terrorists. Discusses some aspects of how this might be accomplished.

8304. Wolf, John B. "Analytical Framework for the Study and Control of Agitational Terrorism," Police Journal 49/3 (July-September 1976): 165-171.

8305. Wolf, John B. "Anti-Terrorism: Operations and Controls in a Free Society," Police Studies 1/3 (September 1978): 35-41.

Discusses the nature and organization of several terrorist groups and the necessary intelligence operations which must be maintained to counter such groups.

8306. Wolf, John B. "Enforcement Terrorism," Police Studies 3/4 (December 1981): 45-54.

Discussion of several internation groups organized to introduce agitational terrorism. Includes some discussion of military intelligence organizations in several parts of the world used to conduct terrorist acts.

8307. Wolf, Louis. "William Joseph Casey: The 'Cyclone' Moves in at Langley," Covert Action Information Bulletin 12 (April 1981): 28-31.

8308. Wolf, Louis. "Government Manipulation and Distortion of History," Vietnam Generation 5/1-4 (1994): 175-181.
Suggests that much more is to be gained in historical research by considerations of how officials in the White House, the CIA, and the military establishments viewed the Laotian dimension of the Vietnam war.

8309. Wolf, Robert A. "Electronic Surveillance: Foreign Intelligence-Wiretapping of an Alien Spy for Foreign Intelligence Purposes Does Not Violate Communications Act of 1934 or Fourth Amendment," New York University Journal of International Law and Politics 8/3 (Winter 1976): 479-520.
Discusses the Butenko decision, the Communications Act of 1934, the Fourth Amendment, a framework for judicial analysis and conclusions. Includes discussion of surveillance of groups (Zweibon v. Mitchell); surveillance of suspected leakers of classified information (Halperin v. Kissinger); surveillance of suspected spies and aliens; and surveillance of embassies and diplomats.

8310. Wolfe, Alan. "The Anatomy of Oppression," Social Policy 2/4 (November-December 1971): 44-50.
Argues that repression of dissident political groups in America is accomplished by various means, including the use of police intelligence and espionage.

8311. Wolfe, Thomas W. "Obstacle Course for Attaches," Studies in Intelligence 4/2 (Summer 1960): 71-77.
The author draws on his experience as an attache to discuss methods for countering Soviet personnel distractions to the observation of essential facilities.

8312. Wolfers, Arnold. "The Pole of Power and the Pole of Indifference," World Politics 4/1 (October 1951): 39-63.
A classic consideration of the contrasts between realist and idealist views of world powers.

8313. Wolfers, Arnold. "National Security as an Ambiguous Symbol," Political Science Quarterly 67/4 (December 1952): 481-502.
Argues that foreign policy guided by national security interest is often presented as a panacea for effective international relations, but which can be deceptive in guiding the fullness of foreign affairs.

8314.   Wolff, Robert L.   "William Leonard Langer," Proceedings of the Massachusetts Historical Society 89 (1977): 187-195.

A brief account of the life and work of this noteworthy analyst who served with distinction in the early years of the Central Intelligence Agency.

8315. Wolfson, N. "Trade Secrets and Secret Trading," San Diego Law Review 25/1 (January-February 1988): 95-124.

8316. Wolpin, Miles D. "Egalitarian Reformism in the Third World vs. the Military: A Profile of Failure," Journal of Peace Research 15 (Spring 1978): 89-107.

Concludes that economic conditions in underdeveloped countries will probably remain the same unless military organizations are neutralized; socialism will be the reform of choice in the disillusioned countries. CIA and foreign secret police involvement in forced reforms are likely to fail when they run counter to economic and other forces already operating in underdeveloped nations.

8317. Wolseley, Garnet J. "The Intelligence Department," Studies in Intelligence 7/3 (Fall 1963).

8318. Wong, J. N. "The Progress of Pinyin," Studies in Intelligence 5/4 (Winter 1961).

8319. Wonus, M. C. "The Case of the SS-6," Studies in Intelligence 13/2 (Spring 1969).

8320. Wood, Bryce. "Self-Plagiarism and Foreign Policy," Latin American Research Review 3 (Summer 1968): 184-191.

8321. Wood, Bryce. "The End of the Good Neighbor Policy: Changing Patterns of U.S. Influence," Caribbean Review 11/2 (Spring 1982): 25-27, 54.

Argues that Franklin Roosevelt's Good Neighbor Policy has ended with CIA involvement in the Guatemala coup of 1953, attempts to oust Fidel Castro from Cuba, and intervention in Nicaragua.

8322. Wood, Chester C. "The Flow of Strategic Intelligence," U.S. Naval Institute Proceedings 59/9 (September 1933): 1296-1304.

Reflecting upon the incursions between the Germans and the British in early phases of World War I, this classic article evaluates the information available through traffic analysis on naval force strengths.

8323. Wood, Chester C. "The Military Aspects of the National Estimate," Naval War College Review 14/7 (1962): 1-19.

8324. Wood, Gordon. "Conspiracy and the Paranoid Style: Causality and Deceit in the Eighteenth Century," William and Mary Quarterly 39 (July 1982): 401-441.

A detailed and rich exploration of several basic questions concerning the origins of the American revolution, perhaps evolving from the psyches of leaders of the respective combatants.

8325. Wood, Horace E. "Terrorism and MAC Operations: The Intelligence Connection," Airlift Operations Review 3 (October-December 1981): 16-20.

8326. Wood, Sidney E. "VQ-1 in Vietnam," American Intelligence Journal 15/1 (Spring-Summer 1994): 54-55.

An excerpt of an article in the Naval Intelligence Professionals Quarterly 9/4 (Fall 1993): 13-14, in which the author describes personal experiences in intelligence in the Vietnam war.

8327. Woods, Carl J. "An Overview of the Military Aspects of Security Assistance," Military Law Review 128 (Spring 1990): 71-113.

Discusses historical background of military assistance; present goals; elements of military security assistance; constraints on assistance; trends; and recommendations.

8328. Woods, Donald H. "Improving Estimates that Involve Uncertainty," Harvard Business Review 44/4 (1966): 91-98.

8329. Woods, Randall B. "Conflict or Community? The United States and Argentina's Admission to the United Nations," Pacific Historical Review 46/3 (1977): 361-386.

A thorough review of Argentina's admission to the United Nations. Sections include discussion of the Franklin Roosevelt administration and the Good Neighbor Policy; Argentina and it Axis ties; the reversal of the US policy toward Argentina's admission based heavily on American investors interests; nations against Argentina's admission; and the Soviet role in the admission.

8330. Woodward, Bob. "A Journalist's Perspective on Public Disclosures," American Intelligence Journal 9/2 (Summer 1988): 9-14.

The author of Veil, a book about CIA director Bill Casey, responds to questions concerning his views on public disclosure of sensitive government information in the intelligence context. Interview format.

8331. Woodward, Rachel. "Establishing Europol," European Journal on Criminal Policing and Research 1/4 (Winter 1993): 7-33.

Discusses establishment of national drug intelligence units in European Community nations to identify drug traffickers.

8332. Woolf, Leonard S. "Espionage, Security, and Liberty," Political Quarterly 27/2 (April-June 1956): 152-162.

With the Robert Oppenheimer case as a backdrop, this article discusses Soviet espionage plans through MVD; US national security; counter-espionage; and the penalty for betrayal. Also refers to the case of a Russian couple given political asylum for turning over to the Australian government certain important Russian documents. Points to Oppenheimer and Petrov as recruited Soviet agents.

8333. Woolsey, R. James; Doyle Larson; and Linda Hall. "Honoring Two World War II Heroes," Studies in Intelligence 38/5 (1995): 27-36.

Contains the remarks of each of the authors at a ceremony at CIA headquarters on October 27, 1993 in honor of the contributions to intelligence work of Reginald V. Jones and Jeannie de Clarens.

8334. Worland, Rick. "The Cold War Mannerists: The Man from U.N.C.L.E. and TV Espionage in the 1960s," Journal of Popular Film and Television 21/4 (Winter 1994): 150-161.

Considers the role of American television in purveying images of Soviet and US spies in the Cold War era.

8335. Wormald, Jenny. "Gunpowder, Treason and Scots," Journal of British Studies 24/2 (1985): 141-168.

An examination of the British Gunpowder plotters of 1605 and the events leading up to their treasonous actions.

8336. Worthing, Sharon L. "Government Surveillance of Religious Organizations," Journal of Church and State 23 (Autumn 1981): 551-563.

8337. Woytak, Richard A. "The Origins of the Ultra-Secret Code in Poland, 1937-1938," Polish Review 23/3 (1978): 79-85.

A brief discussion of the polish work to break the Enigma code, which eventually yielded the "Ultra" code.

8338. Woytak, Richard A. "A Conversation with Marian Rejewski," Cryptologia 6/1 (January 1982): 50-57.

8339. Woytak, Richard A. "Colonel Kowalewski and the Origins of Polish Code Breaking and Communication Interception," East European Quarterly 21/4 (Winter 1987): 497-500.

A brief discussion of the code breaking work of a Polish military officer, Jan Kowalewski.

8340. Woytak, Richard A. "Polish Military Intelligence and Enigma," East European Quarterly 25/1 (March 1991): 49-57.

A brief history of Polish military intelligence work between the two wars.

8341. Wozniuk, Vladimir. "A Note on the Politics of Collaboration," <u>Conflict: An International Journal</u> 8/4 (1988): 285-294.

Distinguishes between collaborationist and treasonous behaviors as types of betrayal. Selects cases during World War II to demonstrate the distinction.

8342. Wraga, Richard. "Trest," <u>Vozrozhdenie</u> 7 (January 1950): 114-135.

Author was also known as Ryszard Niezbrzycki, who emigrated from Russia in the 1920s. Article concerns political deception in the developmental stages of the Soviet Union.

8343. Wraga, Richard. "Cloak and Dagger Politics," <u>Problems of Communism</u> 10/2 (March-April 1961): 56-59.

Discusses methods used by secret services, such as the KGB, to provoke and manipulate authorities in the world. Considers limited competence of Western intelligence services in the use of information concerning the Soviet security services. Research references may be entirely inconclusive on this position, however.

8344. Wrage, Stephen D. "A Moral Framework for Covert Action," <u>Fletcher Forum</u> 4/2 (Summer 1980): 234-244.

Offers a moral argument for covert action interventions in opposition to the anti-moralist viewpoints.

8345. Wriggins, Howard. "Political Outcomes of Foreign Assistance: Influence, Involvement, or Intervention," <u>Journal of International Affairs</u> 22/2 (1968): 217-230.

Discusses the three 'I's': influence, involvement and intervention; military assistance as intervention; political intervention.

8346. Wright, Christopher C. "Robert W. Thew (1927-1989): His Life and Work," <u>Warship International</u> 28/1 (1991): 9-13.

8347. Wright, D. G. "The Great War, Government Propaganda and English 'Men of Letters' 1914-16," <u>Literature and History</u> 7 (1978): 70-100.

8348. Wright, E. "A Patriot for Whom?: Benedict Arnold and the Loyalists," <u>History Today</u> 36 (October 1986): 29-35.

Arnold, it is argued, was intelligent and successful as a battle commander. When he joined the rebel cause in 1775, he was a traitor to Britain, but by 1780 he had become a British spy. Thus, he purged the original betrayal. The author suggests he was a man who was uncertain about his loyalties.

8349. Wright, George W. "Toward a Federal Intelligence Memory," Studies in Intelligence 2/3 (Summer 1958).

8350. Wright, George. "Dreyfus Echo: Justice and Politics in the Fourth Republic," Yale Review 48 (March 1959): 354-373.
    Provides a background history of the French Dreyfus Affair, including the collateral cases of two soldiers, Turpin and Labruse, and Rene Hardy. The cases involves treason and national security leaks.

8351. Wright, Jeffrey W. "Intelligence and Economic Security," International Journal of Intelligence and Counterintelligence 5/2 (Summer 1991): 203-221.
    Major sections discuss intelligence in support of commerce; national security implication of world economic changes; promoting and protecting the economy in a changing world; information and intelligence; giving intelligence to business; the Department of Defense role in economic intelligence; counterintelligence; and the future of economic intelligence.

8352. Wright, Lacy. "John Paul Vann: Portrait of an Activist," Foreign Service Journal 50/3 (1973): 15-16, 30-32.
    A portrait of John Paul Vann's life and his service in the Vietnam war. Discusses his friends, adventures in Vietnam, colleagues, and difficulties with the US government policy makers. Generally applauds his thinking about the progress of the war and his beliefs.

8353. Wright, Quincy. "National Security and International Police," American Journal of International Law 37 (1943): 499-502.

8354. Wright, Quincy. "World Intelligence Center," Journal of Conflict Resolution 1 (1957): 93-97.
    Proposal to create an intelligence center in which global problems could be addressed by the world's greatest minds.

8355. Wright, Quincy. "Subversive Intervention," American Journal of International Law 54/3 (July 1960): 521-535.
    Discusses the international law implications of President Eisenhower's declaration of "Captive Nation's Week" in 1959.

8356. Wright, Quincy. "Legal Aspects of the U-2 Flight," American Journal of International Law 54 (October 1960): 836-854.
    An excellent early assessment of the law of overflight as it pertained to U-2 flights over the Soviet Union.

8357. Wright, Quincy. "Intervention and Cuba in 1961," Proceedings of the American Society of International Law 55 (1961): 2-19.

Examines international law implications of intervention in Cuba in 1961. Draws out many points of international law and precedent, and explores the available public information on CIA involvement.

8358. Wright, Quincy. "The Cuban Quarantine," American Journal of International Law 57/3 (July 1963): 546-565.

An excellent review of the events which led to the quarantine, such as US aerial surveillance, and the threats of the Soviets. Discusses the quarantine policy, the Pacific blockade, territorial integrity and political independence, authority of the OAS, and necessary defenses.

8359. Wright, Quincy. "Escalation of International Conflict," Journal of Conflict Resolution 9 (December 1965): 434-449.

A discussion of how some international conflicts escalate rapidly while others dissipate; the prediction of such conflicts is mostly based on educated guess; and international law questions are rarely important in the middle of conflicts.

8360. Wriston, Henry M. "Presidential Special Agents Diplomacy," American Political Science Review 10 (1916): 481-490.

Discusses President Wilson's use of agents in Mexico in terms of constitutional principles. Author says that secrecy needs, promptness and avoidance of diplomatic compromises have legitimated the presidential use of special agents.

8361. Wrong, D. H. "After the Cuban Crisis," Commentary 35 (January 1963): 29-33.

Argues that a protracted invasion of Cuba would only have demoralized the Cuban people. Discusses Soviet missiles, possible moves against Castro, and unlikely possibility of American invasion.

8362. Wubben, H. H. "The Maintenance of Internal Security in Iowa, 1861-1865," Civil War History 10/4 (1984): 401-415.

8363. Wunderlin, Clarence E., Jr. "Paradox of Power: Infiltration, Coastal Surveillance, and the United States Navy in Vietnam, 1965-68," Journal of Military History 53/3 (July 1989): 275-289.

Operations of the US Navy in coastal surveillance and interdiction are discussed in historical and applied terms relative to the Vietnam war.

8364. Wyckoff, T. "War By Subversion," South Atlantic Quarterly 59 (Winter 1960): 35-46.

Considers the third possibility to scenarios of World War II, war by subversion. Considers subversion versus aggression; Kissinger's theory of massive retaliation; nationalism; and economic aid to underdeveloped countries.

8365. Wylie, Alexander C. "Intelligence's Role in Counterterrorism," <u>Military Police Journal</u> 11 (Spring 1984): 15-20.

8366. Wyllys, Rufus. "The East Florida Revolution of 1812-1814," <u>Hispanic American Historical Review</u> 9/4 (November 1929).

8367. Wyrwa, Tadeusz. "Intelligence Gathering and Politics in Polish-French Relations Prior to 1939," <u>Zeszyty Historyczne</u> 67 (1984): 203-214.

8368. Wyrwa, Tadeusz. "Pre-1939 Relations Between French and Polish Intelligence Services," <u>Revue d'Etudes Comparatives Est-Ouest</u> 22/4 (December 1991): 131-136.

8369. Wyrsch, James R. and Anthony P. Nugent, Jr. "Missouri's New Wiretap Law," <u>Journal of the Missouri Bar</u> 48 (January-February 1992): 21-24.

8370. Wyzanski, Charles E., Jr. "The Open Window and the Open Door: An Inquiry Into Freedom of Association," <u>California Law Review</u> 35/3 (September 1947): 336-351.
        This is the text of a lecture by the author delivered September 11, 1947 before the State Bar of California on the nature and limits of freedom of association.

X

**"R&A and X-2 had one interest in common...
the theory of intelligence."**
(<u>Cloak & Gown</u> by Robin Winks, p. 323)

8371. Xydis, Stephen G. "Coups and Countercoups in Greece 1967-1973 (with Postscript)," <u>Political Science Quarterly</u> 89/3 (Fall 1974): 507-538.
   Explores the main political events in Greece from 1967 to 1973; the impact of no-party authoritarianism; Western Europe and the Greek regime; American involvement and reaction, including the role of American and British intelligence organizations; durability of no-party authoritarianism; relaxation of military authoritarianism; aborted movement toward representative government; Greek regime and the Communist Party states; and the question of Greek return to democracy in 1974.

Y

"There's nothing we can do, Yardley.
The top side simply won't have it. Don't see how
we can get along without you." "Oh, you'll manage, I replied"
(The American Black Chamber by Herbert Yardley, pp. 371-372)

8372. Ya'ari, Ehud. "Al-Fatah's Political Thinking," New Outlook 11 (November-December 1968): 20-33.
      Useful examination of this terrorist groups thought processes, perhaps insightful for those interested in transitions in political thoughts from the 1960s to succeeding decades.

8373. Ya'ari, Ehud. "Behind the Terror," Atlantic Monthly (June 1987): 18-22.
      Discusses the history, operations, and philosophy of a little-publicized terrorist group in Syria. Mentions the role of Western intelligence services.

8374. Yagisawa, Masahiro. "A New Method for Realizing Public-Key Cryptosystem," Cryptologia 9/4 (October 1985): 360-372.

8375. Yankelunas, Edward P. "The Power of the Executive to Restrict the International Travel of American Citizens on National Security and Foreign Policy Grounds," Buffalo Law Review 30/4 (Fall 1981): 781-814.
      Discusses the conflict between the right to free international travel and the need for the government to regulate international travel for national security and foreign policy reasons. Discusses the "right," passport regulation, and the cases of Zemel v. Rusk and Haig v. Agee.

8376. Yap, Key Chong. "Culture-Bound Reality: The Interaction Epistemology of Chang Tung-Sun," East Asian History 3 (1992): 77-120.
Study of Chang Tung-Sun's life, writings, work and eventual trail on charges of treason.

8377. Yankovich, V. "The Origins of Russian Navy Communications," Cryptologia 8/3 (July 1984): 194-197.
Discussion, as translated by T. R. Hammant, of Soviet naval communications strategies and techniques.

8378. Yardley, Herbert O. "Achievements of Cipher Bureau: MI-8 During the First World War," Cryptologia 8/1 (January 1984): 62-74.

8379. Yardley, Herbert O. "ASIO and the Hope Report," Legal Service Bulletin 9 (June 1984): 142-143.

8380. Yarnell, Allen. "Eisenhower and McCarthy: An Appraisal of Presidential Strategy," Presidential Studies Quarterly 10 (1980): 90-98.

8381. Yates, D. M. and W. Russell. "On-Line Retrieval for a Local Police Intelligence Unit," Police Research Bulletin 16 (October 1970): 5-12.
A British police research service offers a plan for an on-line information system to link crimes, persons, and persons-crimes.

8382. Yates, David E. "Return to Vietnam," Naval Intelligence Professionals Quarterly 11/3 (Summer 1995): 1-6.

8383. Yeh, Wen-hsin. "Dai Li and the Liu Geqing Affair: Heroism in the Chinese Secret Service During the War of Resistance," Journal of Asian Studies 48/3 (August 1989): 545-562.
Discussion of Dai Li's motivational work as head of the Republic of China's military intelligence branch during the War of Resistance under Japanese occupation.

8384. Yelton, David K. "British Public Opinion, the Home Guards, and the Defense of Great Britain, 1940-1944," Journal of Military History 58/3 (July 1994): 461-480.

8385. Yeosock, John J. "Army Operations in the Gulf Theater," Military Review 71/9 (September 1991): 2-15.

8386. Ye Savkin, V. "Surprise," Military Review 54/4 (April 1974): 84-91.
Argues that nuclear weapons increase the implication of surprise in international relations. Mobility and readiness are the keys to countering surprise.

8387. York, Herbert F. and G. Allen Greb. "Strategic Reconnaissance," Bulletin of the Atomic Scientists 33/4 (April 1977): 33-41.

Calls attention to the fact that decisions made in choosing a weapons system have depended on the evolution of technology.

8388. York, Neil L. "Clandestine Aid and the American Revolutionary War Effort: A Re-Examination," Military Affairs 43/1 (1979): 26-30.

A discussion of clandestine supply of munitions during the Revolution, in particular the supplies sent from France. Also characterizes the accounts of other authors who have discussed this subject. Concludes that the supplies were essential to the progress of the revolution for the cause of the Americans.

8389. Yoshikawa, Takeo and Norman Stanford. "Top Secret Assignment," U.S. Naval Institute Proceedings 86/12 (December 1960): 27-39.

An account of a Japanese ensign who participated in the Pearl Harbor raid, in particular, the officer's espionage work in Hawaii.

8390. Yost, Charles W. "The Arab-Israeli War: How It Began," Foreign Affairs 46/2 (January 1968): 304-320.

A summary of the circumstances leading to the 1967 Arab-Israeli war, including aspects of diplomatic failures and the Israeli preemptive strike against the unprepared Egyptian air force.

8391. Yost, Charles W. "The Instruments of American Foreign Policy," Foreign Affairs 50/1 (October 1971): 59-68.

An interesting and useful support article for understanding the methods of some presidents in drafting and managing foreign affairs policies. Presents Franklin Roosevelt's method for planting his supporters in the State Department to overcome any resistance to his policies, then discusses developments following the establishment of the National Security Council.

8392. Young, David M. "Security and the Right to Know," Military Review 44/8 (August 1964): 46-53.

8393. Young, George. "The Mystery of Surcouf," Bermudian Magazine 54/2 (March 1983): 24-25, 30-35.

8394. Young, Jay T. "US Intelligence Assessment in the Changing World: The Need for Reform," Intelligence and National Security 8/2 (April 1993): 125-139.

Reviews the various areas of the analytical process and product requiring reform initiatives and implementation. Major sections consider products and processes; the DI's problems; problems in the intelligence community; reforming the CIA; the bigger picture; and seizing the moment.

8395. Young, John W. "The Foreign Office, the Quai d'Orsay and the Case of the Russian Bomb, June 1953," Intelligence and National Security 1/3 (September 1986): 451-453.

8396. Young, John W. "Great Britain's Latin American Dilemma: The Foreign Office and the Overthrow of 'Communist' Guatemala, June 1954," International History Review 8/4 (November 1986): 572-592.

Discusses the overthrow of the Arbenz government in Guatemala in 1954, and the support of the British government for Arbenz. Mentions the role of the US bombing of a British ship as a function of the US blockade, emerging in strained relations between Britain and the US.

8397. Young, P. L. "America's Mysterious 'Space Base' Down Under," Progressive 44 (July 1980): 31-33.

Commentary on intelligence collection activities of a technical nature in Pine Gap, Australia.

8398. Young, Raymond W. "The Aerial Inspection Plan and National Sovereignty," George Washington Law Review 24 (April 1956): 565-589.

Considers the Dwight Eisenhower plan for "open skies" which permitted the US and the USSR to conduct free aerial reconnaissance o nuclear facilities. Sections discuss disarmament through aerial inspections; traditional air sovereignty; the US position on air sovereignty; international conferences; and impact of disarmament on air space sovereignty.

8399. Young, Robert. "Revolutionary Terrorism, Crime, and Morality," Social Theory and Practice 4 (Fall 1977): 287-320.

8400. Young, Robert J. "Spokesmen for Economic Warfare: The Industrial Intelligence Centre in the 1930's," European Studies Review 6/4 (1976): 473-489.

A discussion of the Centre's role in the collection, interpretation and communication of all industrial intelligence relating to foreign military potential. This was a secret agency of great importance to the preparation of the British military plans.

8401. Young, Robert J. "French Military Intelligence and the Franco-Italian Alliance, 1933-1939," Historical Journal 28/1 (March 1985): 143-168.

Addresses a summary assessment of the work of French military intelligence, including questionable interpretation/analysis. Also discusses liaison activities between France and Italy.

8402. Young, Robert J. "The Use and Abuse of Fear: France and the Air Menace in the 1930's," Intelligence and National Security 2/4 (October 1987): 88-109.

A detailed discussion of the preparedness and weaknesses of French air capability during the interwar years. Considers also what German intelligence knew about French capabilities.

8403. Young, Rowland L. "Freedom of Information ... Law Enforcement," American Bar Association Journal 68 (August 1982): 1002-1003.

A brief summary of the Supreme Court holding in Federal Bureau of Investigation v. Abramson.

8404. Young, Stephen B. "Westmoreland v. CBS: The Law of War and the Order of Battle Controversy," Parameters: Journal of the U.S. Army War College 21/4 (Winter 1991-1992): 74-94.

Discusses background of the order of battle situation in Vietnam; complex status of enemy forces; General Westmoreland's allegations under the law of war; and the order of battle controversy and reference to a CIA study of enemy casualties. This article is an abridgement of a similar article in the Vanderbilt Journal of Transnational Law 21/2 (1988): 219-279.

8405. Young, T. R. "Underground Structures of the Democratic State," Mid-American Review of Sociology 8/2 (Winter 1983): 67-80.

Underground organization structures in democratic societies are explained from a sociological perspective. Domestic intelligence forces are used to run covert operations against such structures in order to maintain the disjunction between democracy in public life and inequality in private life.

8406. Young, Wayland. "Verification," Disarmament and Arms Control 2 (Summer 1964): 342-352.

8407. Younger, Irving. "Congressional Investigations and Executive Secrecy: A Study in the Separation of Powers," University of Pittsburgh Law Review 20 (June 1959): 755-784.

Major sections include discussion of selected case of executive secrecy, lessons of the cases, scope of doctrine, bases for invocation of the doctrine, executive secrecy and political tactics, executive secrecy and the courts, and executive secrecy and democratic politics.

8408. Younger, Irving. "Was Alger Hiss Guilty?," Commentary 60 (August and December 1975): 23-37; 4+.

This is a two-part analysis of the case and follow-up discussion.

8409. Yu, Maochun. "OSS in China: New Information About an Old Regime," International Journal of Intelligence and Counterintelligence 7/1 (Spring 1994): 75-96.

Building on the mystery surrounding the documentary of the OSS in

China, the author aims the inquiry in different directions by using the National Archives records,, considering the British connections with OSS and records of the SOE, inquiring into interservice rivalries, and considering the OSS culture with respect to China.

8410. Yuval, Gideon. "How to Swindle Rabin," <u>Cryptologia</u> 3/3 (July 1979): 187-190.

Z

**"...the Zimmermann telegram was only a pebble on the long road
of history. But a pebble can kill a Goliath..."**
(The Zimmermann Telegram by Barbara Tuchman, p. 195)

8411. Zacharias, Ellis M. "What Is Wrong with Our Spy System?," Real 2/2
(1953): 14-17, 78-81.

8412. Zacharias, Ellis M. "What Should the New Administration Do About
Psychological Warfare?," Foreign Policy Bulletin 32 (March 1953): 4-6.

8413. Zacharias, Fred C. "Rethinking Confidentiality," Iowa Law Review 74/2
(January 1989): 351-411.
　　　　　Discussion of confidentiality principles in the lawyer-client relationship.
May be useful in general analyses of secrecy in varying organizational and
relational contexts.

8414. Zagare, Frank C. "The Geneva Conference of 1954: A Case of Tacit
Deception," International Studies Quarterly 23/3 (1979): 390-411.
　　　　　An interpretation of a game or abstract model can be used to evaluate the
structure and outcomes of deception. Includes description of player preferences,
decision rules, and dynamics of play.

8415. Zagel, James. "The State Secrets Privilege," Minnesota Law Review 50
(1965-1966): 875-910.
　　　　　Discusses military and diplomatic secrecy in terms of their conflicts with

litigants who cannot acquire information in their own defense. Contains sections on the issues involved, definitions of state secrets, role of the court, the privilege in specific types of litigation and recent trends.

8416. Zak, William J., Jr. "Sixth Amendment Issues Posed by the Court-Martial of Clayton Lonetree," American Criminal Law Review 30 (Fall 1992): 187-214.
    A case note in consideration of the right to counsel issues associated with the espionage case of Marine Corporal Clayton Lonetree.

8417. Zaloga, Steven J. "The Tank Gap Data Flap," International Security 13/4 (Spring 1989): 180-187.
    This is a review and evaluation of an article in the Summer 1988 issue of the same journal by authors Malcolm Chambers and Lutz Underseher, "Is There a Tank Gap?: Comparing NATO and Warsaw Pact Tank Fleets." Useful in understanding analytic problems in arms inventory estimations.

8418. Zaloga, Steven J. "The Missiles of October: Soviet Ballistic Missile Forces During the Cuban Crisis," Journal of Soviet Military Studies 3/2 (June 1990): 307-323.
    Extensive discussion of US intelligence efforts to collect advanced information on missiles in Cuba, and Soviet failure to hide missiles from US detection.

8419. Zalewski, Cynthia M. "In Re Grand Jury Investigation: Does the Informer's Privilege Exist within the Grand Jury Setting?," University of Toledo Law Review 23 (Spring 1992): 645-662.
    Addresses whether or not the City of Detroit and the witness should have been entitled to use the informer's privilege. Covers background of the case; statement of the case involving alleged corruption in the Detroit Police Department; case analysis; and conclusions.

8420. Zaritski, B. E. "The U.S. and Leftist Forces in Western Europe, 1943-49," Voprosy Istorii 6 (1983): 66-79.

8421. Zaslavsky, Victor and Yuri Luryi. "The Passport System in the USSR and Changes in Soviet Society," Soviet Union/Union Sovietique 6 (1979): 137-153.
    A rare glimpse at techniques for Soviet citizen internal control.

8422. Zasloff, Joseph. "Laos: The Forgotten War Widens," Asian Survey (January 1970): 65-72.

8423. Zawackaka, E. "Raciborzanki in the Foreign Service of the Home Army," Slaski Kwzrtalnik Historyozny Sob'tka 39/3 (1984): 365-385.

8424. Zdanowski, Henryk. "A Government Apparatus for Cold War," Nowe Drogi 21/223 (1967): 67-80.

This is an approximate translation of the title to an article in Polish.

8425. Zeidenstein, Harvey G. "The Reassertion of Congressional Power: New Curbs on the President," Political Science Quarterly 93/3 (Fall 1978): 393-409.

Major sections discuss varieties of restrictions on presidential actions; termination or continuation of emergency authority; consultation with the Congress before military operations; Senate confirmation of OMB heads; presidential reports to Congress; CIA reports to congressional committees; mandate for committee disclosure of classified information; committee oversight and scenarios for the future.

8426. Zellick, Graham J. "Telephone Tapping," Public Law (Summer 1981): 147-149.

Discusses British law on telephone tapping.

8427. Zellick, Graham J. "Secrets, Moles, Ministers and Judges," Public Law (Summer 1984): 173-177.

A case comment on Secretary of State for Defence v. Guardian Newspapers, Ltd. concerning leaked government information. Comments on the rationale of the Canadian government's case against Sarah Tisdale, a government employee convicted of leaking national security information to The Guardian. Discusses Sec. 10, Contempt of Court Act of 1981 and the rights of the press.

8428. Zellick, Graham J. "National Security, Official Information and the Law," Contemporary Review 249 (October 1986): 189-196.

This article evaluates statutes governing national security and government information in Great Britain.

8429. Zellick, Graham J. "Spies, Subversives, Terrorists and the British Government: Free Speech and Other Casualties," William and Mary Law Review 31 (Spring 1990): 773-821.

Detailed and extensive discussion of four British statutes: the Interception of Communications Act of 1985; the Official Secrets Act 1989; the Security Service Act 1989; and the Prevention of Terrorism Act 1989.

8430. Zgorniak, Marian. "Les Preparatifs Allemands d'Attaques Contre la Pologne (1939) d'Apres les Informations du Deuxieme Bureau d'Etat-major," Revue d'Histoire de la Deuxieme Guerre Mondiale 77 (January 1970): 41-54.

8431. Zhai, Qiang. "Transplanting the Chinese Model: Chinese Military Advisers and the First Vietnam War, 1950-54," Journal of Military History 57/3 (October 1993): 689-714.

Major sections discuss the recognition of the Democratic Republic of Vietnam; the border campaign; the Northwest campaign; the siege of Dien Bien Phu; and conclusions.

8432. Zheng, Jianshun. "The Problem of Treason in the Opium War," Fuyin Baokan Ziliao: Zhongguo Jindai Shi 10 (1991): 46-51.

8433. Zhukor, V. "Space Espionage, Plans and International Law," International Affairs (USSR) (1960): 53-57.

8434. Zhukov, V. "The Secret 'Nisei G-2,'" Voenno-Istoricheskiy Zhurnal 2 (February 1965): 120-123.
This is an approximate translation of a title to an article in a Russian language journal.

8435. Ziegler, David W. "Yellow Rain: An Analysis That Went Awry?," International Journal of Intelligence and Counterintelligence 2/1 (Spring 1988): 91-113.
A study of the errors of commission among US intelligence analysts in the investigation of alleged Soviet use of toxic warfare ('yellow rain') in Southeast Asia during the late 1970s and early 1980s. Five elements of evidence are analyzed for their respective contributions to the myth of USSR use of toxic weapons. Case study of the limitations on analytical objectivity.

8436. Ziemke, Earl F. "Operation Kreml: Deception, Strategy, and the Fortunes of War," Parameters: Journal of the U.S. Army War College 9/1 (March 1979): 72-83.
A discussion of the importance of deception in warfare. Operation KREML and Operation BLAU were Hitler's deception strategies against the Russians in 1941.

8437. Zimmerman, Peter D. "Photos from Space: Why Restrictions Won't Work," Technology Review 91 (May-June 1988): 47-53.
Concerns photo images from satellites. Argues that the press can misinterpret satellite photos, leading to damaged US relations with other countries.

8438. Zimmerman, Peter D. "From the SPOT Files: Evidence of Spying," Bulletin of the Atomic Scientists 45 (September 1989): 24-25.
A brief discussion of the SPOT commercial intelligence program.

8439. Zimring, Fred R. "Notes and Documents: Cold War Compromises--Albert Barnes, John Dewey, and the Federal Bureau of Investigation," Pennsylvania Magazine of History and Biography 108/1 (1984): 87-100.

An examination of the collaboration between the FBI and anti-communist liberals, such as Dewey and Barnes, and the strange coalition's attacks on left-wing liberals.

8440. Zindar, John M. "The Tactical Intelligence Officer in LIC," Military Intelligence 11/1 (January-March 1985): 46-47.
Outlines the massive concerns and responsibilities of an S2 in the low intensity conflict environment.

8441. Zinman, Toby S. "Blizintsy/Dvojniki Twins/Doubles Hapgood/Hapgood," Modern Drama 34 (June 1991): 312-321.

8442. Zinnes, Dina A. "A Comparison of Hostile Behavior of Decision-Makers in Simulated and Historical Data," World Politics 18 (April 1966): 474-502.

8443. Zive, Gregg W. "Prior Restraint and the Press Following the Pentagon Papers Cases--Is the Immunity Dissolving?," Notre Dame Lawyer 47/4 (April 1972): 927-958.
Explains why the press has enjoyed preferential treatment in the area of prior restraints on publication or communications. Asks whether or not the victory in the Papers cases helped or hindered prior restraint protection.

8444. Zivich, Edward M. "Intelligence Story in Three Parts," Studies in Intelligence 9/3 (Fall 1965).

8445. Zlotnick, Jack. "Bayes' Theorem for Intelligence Analysis," Studies in Intelligence 16/1 (Spring 1972): 43-52.
Explores the Bayesian approach to probability analysis; the life span of evidence; causal evidence; catchall hypotheses; false evidence; and the research promise.

8446. Zoll, Donald A. "The Press and the Military: Some Thoughts After Grenada," Parameters: Journal of the U.S. Army War College 14/1 (Spring 1984): 26-34.
Discusses the author's views on the role of the press in warfare, and in particular in the Grenada invasion.

8447. Zorpette, Glenn. "Breaking the Enemy's Code," IEEE Spectrum 24 (September 1987): 47-51.

8448. Zuber, Richard I. "Domestic Eavesdropping and Wiretapping: Admissibility of Intercepted Communications," Colorado Lawyer 21 (March 1992): 455-462.

8449. Zubok, Vladislav M. "Spy vs. Spy: The KGB vs. the CIA, 1960-1962," Cold War International History Project Bulletin 4 (Fall 1994): 22-33.

Major sections discuss the KGTB reports to Khrushchev; the hunt for Allen Dulles; the crisis in Berlin and in the KGB; and scorpions in a bottle.

8450. Zuckerman, Fredric S. "Vladimir Burtsev and the Tsarist Political Police in Conflict, 1907-14," Journal of Contemporary History 12/1 (January 1977): 193-219.

8451. Zuckerman, Fredric S. "Political Police and the Revolution: The Impact of the 1905 Revolution on the Tsarist Secret Police," Journal of Contemporary History 27/2 (April 1992): 279-300.

8452. Zunno, Frank A. "NYSIIS and NEOCIS," Police Chief 38/9 (September 1971): 31-32.

A brief discussion of the two information/intelligence systems of the six-state region in the Northeast to monitor organized crime.

8453. Zunno, Frank A. "Let's Put Intelligence in Perspective," Police Chief 38/9 (September 1971): 46-47.

A brief discussion of the history and then current operations of police intelligence. Argues for more staff definition of the intelligence function in police organizations.

8454. Zutz, Robert. "The Recapture of the S. S. Mayaguez: Failure of the Consultation Clause of the War Powers Resolution," New York University Journal of International Law and Politics 8/3 (Winter 1976): 457-478.

Addresses the content, scope and deficiencies of the War Powers Act in terms of the Act's relationship to consultation obligations of the President. May be useful in studies of the Pueblo incident, international terrorism, or secrecy and the presidency.

Author Unknown

"Major Martin was ready to go to war."
(The Man Who Never Was, by Ewen Montagu, p. 96)

Note to user: With the exception of a few names subsequently linked to articles published in the Central Intelligence Agency internal journal, Studies in Intelligence, authors of articles in this collection could not be determined. Since the sequence of numbers was established in 1997, numerical reassignment of all numbers to accommodate a small number of CIA articles lacking author names was not possible. However, the collection identified as **Late Entries: Section I** contains author names and other citation information discovered by late 1998 for items 8473, 8474, 8475, 8488, 8491, 8493, 8521, 8523, 8531, 8532, 8592, 8593, 8598, 8610, 8615, 8620, 8635, 8637, 8639, 8655, 8664, 8670, 8674, 8679, 8682, 8695.

Each item in this collection is listed according to the first major word in the title. In some cases, citations reflect declassified documents which appeared in serial journals; other cases suggest authorship by editors or editorial staff. Some law journals disallow author attribution for articles written by law students.

8455. "513 MI Group, INSCOM's Newest Element," INSCOM Journal (September 1982): 9-12.

8456. "A 1943 OSS Analysis of 'The Russo-Czech Alliance,'" East European Quarterly 19/1 (March 1985): 113-118.
　　　　Originally, this was a secret document produced by OSS, now declassified. It pertains to an alliance of Russians and Czechs in World War II.

8457. "Access to Official Information: A Neglected Constitutional Right," Indiana Law Journal 27/2 (Winter 1952): 209-230.

Discusses freedom of information of national security and other information in the context of newspaper access. Cites several international and US efforts to gag the press from access to such information. Argues that no standard for government concealment policy has been established.

8458. "Aerial Reconnaissance," Data: Magazine of Military RDT&E Management 10 (April 1965): 7-41.

8459. "Air Combat Intelligence," Flying 35 (October 1944): 123-124.

8460. "Air Force Technical Applications Center," Air Force Magazine 66/5 (May 1983): 134-137.

Discusses the role of this organization in the detection of nuclear events in the atmosphere, underground, and in space.

8461. "All-Out Intelligence Training," Infantry Journal 62 (April 1948): 68-69.

A personal recollection of intelligence escapades on October 11, 1944 in France.

8462. "A Look at Codes and Ciphers," FBI Law Enforcement Bulletin 36/1 (January 1967): 17-20.

8463. "Albert Einstein," Studies in Intelligence 24 (1980).

A brief biographical sketch. Not listed by the Central Intelligence Agency among articles declassified for publication.

8464. "Alien Enemies and Japanese-Americans: A Problem of Wartime Controls," Yale Law Journal 51/8 (June 1942): 1316-1323.

An excellent contemporaneous discussion of the "alien" enemy problem and the issues of legal authority of the President to intern those considered to be threats to internal security. Concludes that loyalty must be determined in each individual case, not on the basis of membership in a racial or cultural group.

8465. "Anderson v. Sills: The Constitutionality of Police Intelligence Gathering," Northwestern University Law Review 65/3 (July-August 1970): 461-485.

Discusses three issues: (1) Whether plaintiffs had "standing" to challenge Attorney General's memo and security reports; (2) whether police intelligence gathering plan was unconstitutional; and, (3) whether court's injunction was designed to aid law enforcement compliance.

8466. "Argentine Decision--The Use of Force," American Intelligence Journal 6/2 (July 1984): 20-24.

8467. "The Attorney General and Aliens: Unlimited Discretion and the Right to Fair Treatment," Yale Law Journal 60 (1951): 152-160.

8468. "Authority of Secretary of State to Determine Standards for Issuance of Passports," Fordham Law Review 27/3 (Autumn 1958): 426-429.
Brief case note as a reflection upon Kent v. Dulles, 357 U.S. 116 (1958), holding that the Secretary of State does not have the authority to deny a passport on the basis of alleged communist membership or affiliation, nor on the basis of a refusal to execute a non-communist affidavit.

8469. "Authority of Secretary of State to Revoke Passports for National Security of Foreign Policy Reasons: Haig v. Agee," Minnesota Law Review 66/4 (April 1982): 667-686.
Case comment regarding issue in article's title. Resolves that the Secretary of State has overly broad discretionary power to revoke or deny passports. Calls for congressional action to remove the potential for abuses and considerations of constitutional questions.

8470. "The Authority of Washington on the West Is No Longer Discussed," Annee Politique et Economic 40/200 (1967): 330-332.

8471. "Automation Aids Intelligence," Armed Forces Management (July 1962): 64+.

8472. "Battle Order of World Espionage," United Nations World 3 (June 1949): 31-33.

8473. "Beaumarchais..." See "Late Entries," item 8816.

8474. "Beyond Webster..." See "Late Entries," item 9976.

8475. "A Bible Lesson..." See "Late Entries," item 8960.

8476. "Black Ops 1963-1983," Harper's (April 1984): 17-20.
Discusses 45 major and minor covert activities of the CIA from 1963 to 1983, noting that the majority belong in the paramilitary category.

8477. "Bibliography of Cryptography," American Mathematical Monthly 50 (May 1943): 345-346.

8478. "Bonn--Spy Target No. 1," German International 23/4 (1979): 12-17.

8479. "Books and Ideas," Air University Review 1 (1959).
A continuing column providing source materials for intelligence studies.

8480. "Breaking and Entering into Private Premises to Effect Electronic Surveillance," Dalia v. United States," Maryland Law Review 39/4 (1980): 754-807.

Summarizes the facts and issues in Dalia; the legal background including constitutional framework, statutory framework; potential sources of authority for covert entry, and reasonableness of forcible entry under the Fourth Amendment.

8481. "Breaking the Code," Electronics & Wireless World 94 (May 1988): 518.

8482. "British-German Radio War," Infantry Journal (May-June 1947): 36-39, 41-46.

8483. "The Brown Commission and the Future of Intelligence," Studies in Intelligence 39/5 (1996): 1-9.

A transcript of a roundtable discussion on March 1, 1996 among Commission members Ann Caracristi, L. Britt Snider, Douglas Horner, Brendan Melley, Kevin Scheid, and William Kvetkas.

8484. "Can You Hear Me Mr. President?," Canadian Dimension (Canada) 9/6 (1973): 27-37.

This article examines the scandal of the Watergate affair, including the dimension of political spying. Reviews the context of political espionage in the Nixon administration and emphasizes recruitment of former CIA members, the ITT affair, and slush funds.

8485. 'Captain Courageous.' "All-out Intelligence Training: Need for Some Men with Basic Intelligence," Infantry Journal 62 (April 1948): 68-69.

8486. "The Central Intelligence Agency: Present Authority and Proposed Legislative Change," Virginia Law Review 62/2 (March 1976): 332-382.

An extensive discussion of the legislative and case law foundations of the Central Intelligence Agency. Useful in studies of controversies around the Agency in the 1970s.

8487. "Certain Aspects of Operational Intelligence Reconnaissance," Journal of Soviet Military Studies 2/2 (June 1989): 288-303.

Describes in some detail the operations of the Soviet military intelligence organizations in World War II.

8488. "CETA: Chinese..." See "Late Entries," item 8791.

8489. "Chiapas Uprising," Covert Action Quarterly (Spring 1994): 34-48.

Raises a question as to possible CIA involvement in the revolutionary movement in Chiapas, Mexico.

8490. "Chile - What Was the U.S. Role?," Foreign Policy 16 (Fall 1974): 126-156.

8491. "Chinese Growth Estimates..." See "Late Entries," item 8760.

8492. "CIA and Academe," Studies in Intelligence 27/4 (Winter 1983).
Not listed by the Central Intelligence Agency among declassified articles released to the public.

8493. "The CIA and the Law..." See "Late Entries," item 10039.

8494. "CIA Assassination Plots in Latin America," Current History 70/413 (February 1976): 79-89.
Excerpts, say the anonymous authors, of the November 1975 Senate Select Committee on Intelligence report on US involvement in assassination plots.

8495. "CIA Censors Hispanic Art," Latin American Art 5/4 (Winter 1994): 75-76.

8496. "CIA e Realta Internationale," Revista di Studi Politici Internazionali 43/1 (January-March 1976): 3-7.

8497. "CIA: No Comment on Anything," Fortune 48 (July 1953): 36+.

8498. "CIA Roundtable," Washington Quarterly (Autumn 1978): 26-39.

8499. "The CIA, the FBI, and the Media: Excerpts From the Senate Report on Intelligence Activities," Columbia Journalism Review 15 (July-August 1976): 37-42.
The title captures the contents: straight excerpting and abridgment of selected sections of Book I: Foreign and Military Intelligence; and Book II: Intelligence Activities and the Rights of Americans.

8500. "Citizen's Arrest of CIA Recruiters: The Buck Stops Here," National Lawyers Guild Practitioner 42/2 (Spring 1985): 61-64.
This is a summation of charges by Brown University students as they made citizens' arrests of Central Intelligence Agency recruiters, November 26, 1984.

8501. "Civil Liberties and National Security: A Delicate Balance," Northwestern University Law Review 68/5 (November-December 1973): 922-941.
Discusses government methods through time to justify civil liberties infringements when "national security interests are invoked. Discusses treason, advocacy and incitement, wartime offenses and restricted information.

8502. "Clandestine Police Surveillance of Public Toilets Held to be Unreasonable Search," Columbia Law Review 63/5 (May 1963): 955-961.

A note on then recent developments following a case known as Bielecki v. Superior Court, 57 Cal.2d 602, 371 P.2d 288, 21 Cal.Rep. 552 (1962).

8503. "The Code-Breaking Computers of 1944," IEEE Proceedings 140 (May 1993): 237-248.

The title captures the subject matter. This piece is located in part A, Science, Measurement and Technology.

8504. "Codes and Ciphers for Combined Air-Amphibian Operations," Cryptologia 8/2 (April 1984): 181-186.

8505. "Codes and Secret Inks in War," Fingerprint and Identification 22/12 (June 1941): 3-6, 18-20.

8506. "Comint in the Russian Navy, WW I," Cryptolog (May 1976): 1-4.

A rare topic of historical concern.

8507. "Concerning Espionage and Social Courtesy," Studies in Intelligence 10/2 (Summer 1966).

8508. "Conduct Proscribed as Promoting Violent Overthrow of the Government," Harvard Law Review 61/7 (July 1948): 1215-1224.

Discusses then existing legislation in state and federal governments, constitutional limitations, conduct proscribed as advocacy (organization, individual), proscription of membership, and conclusions.

8509. "The Congo, 1960: State Terrorism and Foreign Policy," Harper's 269 (October 1984): 52-56.

8510. "Congress May Delegate Its Legislative Authority to Impose Passport Area Controls," Minnesota Law Review 50 (1965-1966): 977-984.

This is a case comment on Zemel v. Rusk, 381 U.S. 1 (1965) concerning the Secretary of State's authority to impose area restrictions on passports, and whether any such restriction were constitutional.

8511. "Congress Reserves Option to Reorganize Intelligence," Signal (August 1992): 32-34.

8512. "Congressional Oversight of Intelligence Operations: A Panel," American Society of International Law Proceedings 82 (1989): 21-25.

A panel session on the subject with remarks by William G. Miller, Daniel B. Silver, Frederick P. Hitz, Bernard F. McMallon and Phillip Cherry.

8513. "Congressional Wiretapping Policy Overdue," <u>Stanford Law Review</u> 2/4 (July 1950): 744-762.

Summarizes treatment of wiretapping by courts, Congress, and the executive departments; proposed congressional revision; conclusions. Argues that, although difficult to achieve, the Congress should make law to establish boundaries of tapping and to provide the machinery of wiretapping supervision.

8514. "Constitutional Law - Clandestine Surveillance of Public Toilet - Not an Unreasonable Search," <u>Vanderbilt Law Review</u> 19/3 (June 1966): 945-951.

Intelligence is gathered in the strangest locations, but not always with social approval. A relevant article for studies of domestic spying or invasion of privacy.

8515. "Constitutional Law: Resolving Conflict Between the Right to Travel and Implementation of Foreign Policy," <u>Duke Law Journal</u> 1966/1 (Winter 1966): 233-247.

A review and analysis of the Supreme Court's decision in <u>Zemel v. Rush</u> upholding a geographic passport restriction on travel to Cuba. The Court did not consider how future passport cases would be analyzed and it failed to address criminal sanctions to regulate foreign travel.

8516. "Constitutional Law: Saboteurs and the Jurisdiction of Military Commissions," <u>Michigan Law Review</u> 41 (1942): 481-486.

8517. "Constitutional Law - Search and Seizure - No Fourth Amendment Implications Raised by the Monitoring of an Electronic Tracking Device Installed in a Car Traveling onto Private Property from a Public Roadway," <u>William Mitchell Law Review</u> 10 (Winter 1984): 319-331.

A case note following the decision in United States v. Knotts, 103 S. Ct. 1081 (1983).

8518. "Contra Aid Files Unsealed: Judge Rules Administration Acknowledge Covert Aid Publicly, Disclosure Couldn't Harm National Security," <u>News Media and the Law</u> 9 (Summer 1985): 35-36.

8519. "Control, Communications and Intelligence Update," <u>Armed Forces Journal</u> (March 1984): 87-90.

Emphasizes the role of intelligence in the Middle East, especially in the conflict between Syria and Israel. Contains sections on Assad of Syria; Soviet actions in Syria, including goals and intentions; and changes since the June 1982 war.

8520. "Controversy Over Legislative Limitations on Covert US Intelligence Operations: Pro and Con," <u>Congressional Digest</u> 59/5 (May 1980): 129-160.

8521. "The Coordinator of Information..." See "Late Entries," item 10190.

8522. "The Counterrevolutionary Apparatus of the United States: The Chilean Offensive," Casa de las Americas 16/92 (1975): 3-28.

8523. "The Creation of the KGB," Institute for the Study of the U.S.S.R. Bulletin 1 (July 1954): 13-15.

8524. "Crime and Cryptology," FBI Law Enforcement Bulletin 39/4 (April 1970): 13-14.

8525. "Criminal Law--Espionage--Transmission to Germany Prior to Declaration of War of Information Gathered from Nonconfidential Sources Held Not in Violation of Espionage Act of 1917," Harvard Law Review 59 (April 1946): 617-619.
　　　　Case note in consideration of U. S. v. Heine, 151 F.2d 813.

8526. "Criminal Registration Ordinances--Police Control Over Potential Recidivists," University of Pennsylvania Law Review 103/1 (October 1954): 60-112.

8527. "The Current Program for an Intelligence Literature," Studies in Intelligence 1/1 (September 1955): 9-12.
　　　　The editors of this then-new CIA internal journal discussed their intentions to set a new course regarding the development of a literature for the intelligence field.

8528. "Daty Zhizni i Deiafel'nosti A. M. Gor'kogo. S. Predisloviem E. Cherniavskogo," Krasnyi Arkiv 5/78 (1936): 23-84.
　　　　In Russian, refers to dates in the life of Alexey M. Peshkov (Gorky), and may include substantial insights into the operations of the secret police in various reigns of 19th and 20th century Tsars.

8529. "A Deception Case Study," Journal of Soviet Military Studies 1/2 (June 1988): 262-275.
　　　　A careful discussion of the deception to cover the Demiansk operation in 1942.

8530. "Deception in War," Military Review (November 1958): 92-97.

8531. "Decision Trees." See "Late Entries," item 9981.

8532. "Declassification..." See "Late Entries," item 9117.

8533. "Defense Intelligence Rigs for Varied Global Roles," <u>Signal</u> (August 1992): 35-36.

8534. "Denial of Federally Aided Housing to Members of Organizations on the Attorney General's List," <u>Harvard Law Review</u> 69/3 (January 1956): 551-559.
A brief analysis of the issue surrounding a provision in the Housing Act of 1937 which refuses occupancy to any person on the Attorney General's subversives list. Discusses constitutionality of the Gwinn Amendment, due process, freedom of speech and assembly, and the use of the AG's list.

8535. "Disinformation: War With Words," <u>Air Force Magazine</u> (March 1982): 85-89.

8536. "Documents on CIA Surveillance of CCAs," <u>Bulletin of Concerned Asian Scholars</u> 14/3 (July-September 1982): 62-63.
Allegedly a "CIA domestic intelligence" document revealing a report of surveillance of the Committee of Concerned Asian Scholars.

8537. "Eavesdropping and the Constitution: A Reappraisal of the Fourth Amendment Framework," <u>Minnesota Law Review</u> 50/2 (October 1965): 378-414.
Discusses problems posed by eavesdropping, present treatment under the Fourth Amendment, proposed constitutional rationale, and offers conclusions in defense of the Fourth Amendment application of the issue.

8538. "Eavesdropping on Electromagnetic Radiation Emanating from Video Display Units: Legal and Self-Help Responses to a New Form of Espionage," <u>Criminal Law Quarterly</u> 32 (March 1990): 253-259.

8539. "Echeloned Positive Communication," <u>Intelligence and National Security</u> 3/4 (October 1988): 156.
A poem, allegedly written by CIA employee at some unidentified time and discovered by professor Lawrence Freedman. Reflects upon the IIM, NIE's, DDI and DCI.

8540. "Economic Espionage," <u>Commentary</u> 32 (May 1993).

8541. "Electronic Intelligence Gathering and the Omnibus Crime Control and Safe Streets Act of 1968," <u>Fordham Law Review</u> 44 (November 1975): 331-354.

8542. "Electronic Reconnaissance in Vietnam," <u>International Defense Review</u> 5 (August 1972): 358-362.

8543. "Electronic Security Command: A Major Command," <u>Air Force Magazine</u> (May 1982): 94-95.

A brief outline, including an organization chart, of the ESC--a unit of 12,000 people.

8544. "Electronic Surveillance, Criminal Law in the Ninth Circuit: Recent Developments," Loyola of Los Angeles Law Review 13/3 (June 1980): 611-616.
Summarizes United States Court of Appeals, Ninth Circuit cases addressing covert entry to install eavesdropping equipment, naming conversants in warrants, necessity for wiretap, pen registers, and failure to follow agency regulations.

8545. "Electronic Surveillance, District of Columbia Court of Appeals Decisions," Howard Law Journal 23/2 (Spring 1980): 184-196.
Summarizes case decisions in the D.C.C.A. regarding electronic surveillance.

8546. "Electronic Surveillance, Title III and the Requirement of Necessity," Hastings Constitutional Law Quarterly 2 (Spring 1975): 571-618.

8547. "Electronic Warfare History, World War II," Electronic Warfare/Defense Electronics 4 (Summer & Fall 1972): 20+; 20-22+.

8548. "Elegant Writing in the Clandestine Services," Studies in Intelligence 24/3 (Fall 1980): 75-79.
Not listed by the Central Intelligence Agency among declassified articles for public access. May be erroneous citation. See other articles on the same subject by Richard T. Puderbaugh, and by Virginia Valpey.

8549. "Elements of CIA Style," Harper's 270 (January 1985): 16-19.
An excerpt of an anti-Sandinista manual which was at issue in the Reagan administration's covert activities in Nicaragua.

8550. "English Treachery Act, 1940," Journal of Criminal Law and Criminology 31 (January 1941): 615.
This is a one-paragraph summation of the Act, which provided for the death penalty for treachery and acts related to treason.

8551. "Espionage on the Homefront," FBI Law Enforcement Bulletin 60 (December 1991): 3.
A brief account of the Federal Bureau of Investigation's role in espionage investigations in the United States.

8552. "The Evolution of Military Intelligence," Military Review (September 1946): 75-79.

8553. "An Examination of U.S. Prisoners of War," Infantry Journal 15/3 (September 1918): 249-250.

This is a German intelligence officer's report of June 17, 1918 of a US Marine trooper captured in France.

8554. "Executive Privilege and the Freedom of Information Act: The Constitutional Foundation of the Amended National Security Exemption," Washington University Law Quarterly 1976/4 (Fall 1976): 609-666.

Outlines the administrative procedures in the Freedom of Information Act; discussed the state secrets privilege in common law of evidence and suggests its use by courts in making decisions about executive privilege. Considers the President's constitutional privilege to refuse disclosure.

8555. "Experiences of An Interrogation Officer," Blackwood's Magazine 263 (February 1948): 113-120.

8556. "Falklands War Pressured British EW Development," Defense Electronics 17/1 (January 1985): 56-57, 59-62.

8557. "Feature Review" Sociological Quarterly 19/1 (Winter 1978): 152-162.

This is a review essay on six books on intelligence services and secrecy.

8558. "The Fiduciary Duty of Former Government Employees," Yale Law Journal 90/1 (November 1980): 189-215.

Discusses policies in the regulation of post-government employment, the Ethics in Government Act, proposals concerning fiduciary duty for former government employees, and conclusions.

8559. "The First Amendment Right to Gather State-Held Information," Yale Law Journal 89/5 (April 1980): 923-939.

Argues that the right to gather information held by the government is found in the First Amendment, and that government regulation of the right must be narrow and nondiscriminatory.

8560. "The First SR-71 High Altitude Reconnaissance Photos Ever Made Public," Armed Forces Journal International 113 (July 1976): 20-23.

Brief discussion of the capabilities of the SR-71 aircraft.

8561. "Five Lessons For America in the Powers Trial and Its Aftermath," Air Force Magazine 43/10 (October 1960): 37-41.

8562. "FOIA Exemption 7 and Broader Disclosure of Unlawful FBI Investigations," Minnesota Law Review 65/6 (July 1981): 1139-1168.

Observes provisions of FOIA Exemption 7; then discusses "unlawful"

FBI investigations, and offers a suggested approach to resolve Exemption 7 problems.

8563. "The Foreign Intelligence Surveillance Act and Standards of Probable Cause: An Alternative Analysis," Georgetown Law Journal 80 (February 1992): 843-871.

8564. "Foreign Intelligence Surveillance Act: Legislating a Judicial Role in National Security Surveillance," Michigan Law Review 78 (June 1980): 1116-1152.
    Discusses the legal history of national security surveillance, the provisions of FISA, the constitutionality of FISA, and conclusions. Generally argues that FISA has been sustained because it was crafted to account for the balance between Fourth Amendment rights and executive authority to gather foreign intelligence.

8565. "Foreign Security Surveillance and the Fourth Amendment," Harvard Law Review 87/5 (March 1974): 976-1000.
    Discusses the justification of a foreign security exception to the warrant requirement following Katz v. United States and United States v. United States District Court.

8566. "The Fort Monmouth Investigations," Bulletin of the Atomic Scientists 10/6 (June 1954): 225-226.
    Discusses the investigations into Senator Joseph McCarthy's allegations that spies were at work at Fort Monmouth engineering laboratory.

8567. "Freedom and the Intelligence Function; Symposium," Center Magazine 12 (March 1979): 45-60.

8568. "Freedom of Information: CIA Can Keep Secret Almost Anything; FOIA Proposals Reintroduced in Congress; Privacy Exemption Can Be Overcome; Legislative Records on Line, But Costs are High," News Media and the Law 9 (Spring 1985): 30-39.

8569. "From the Archives: Examples of Intelligence Obtained From Cryptanalysis," Cryptologia 7/4 (October 1983): 315-326.

8570. "From the Archives: Codes and Ciphers For Combined Air-Amphibian Operations," Cryptologia 8/2 (April 1984): 181-186.

8571. "From Azeff to Agca," Survey 118/119 (Autumn-Winter 1983): 1-89.
    A collection of articles concerning espionage, intrigue and assassination from the days of the Ohkrana to the attempted assassination of Pope John Paul II.

8572. "From OSS With Love: The Rise of a Testing Method," Psychology Today (December 1978).

8573. "From Private Places to Personal Privacy: A Post-Katz Study of Fourth Amendment Protection," New York University Law Review 43/5 (November 1968): 968-987.
    Discusses the development of the scope of the Fourth Amendment protection for open and closed places, non-trespass intrusions, Katz v. United States, right to privacy, justifiable reliance on privacy and conclusions.

8574. "The Future of the Russian Security Service," Jane's Intelligence Review (September 1992): 396-398.

8575. "A Good Man is Hard to Find," Fortune (March 1946): 92-95, 217-223.
    Describes Office of Strategic Services training at an estate in Northern Virginia. Discusses psychological training and personnel screening for clandestine work of OSS. This article is published in a traditionally popular press magazine, but the information is considered valuable for research purposes.

8576. "Government Information and the Rights of Citizens," Michigan Law Review 73/6 (May-June 1975): 971-1340.
    An extensive journal staff project covering access to government information and increasing privacy of citizens. Covers classification system, executive privilege, FOIA, state open-records laws, open-meeting laws, state privacy laws, federal law of privacy and Privacy Act of 1974.

8577. "Government Interceptions of Attorney-Client Communications," New York University Law Review 49 (1974): 87-109.
    Discusses need for secure communications; judicial treatment of government interceptions; and proposed solution.

8578. "Government Privilege Against Disclosure of Official Documents," Yale Law Journal 58 (May 1949): 993-998.

8579. "Governmental Investigations of the Exercise of First Amendment Rights: Citizens' Rights and Remedies," Minnesota Law Review 60/6 (June 1976): 1257-1288.
    Discusses First Amendment rights which may be violated by governmental investigations, remedies for covert governmental investigations that violate civil rights, and conclusions as to the need for congressional limitations.

8580. "Have We An Intelligence Service?," Atlantic Monthly 84 (April 1948): 66-70.
    A critique of the weaknesses of American intelligence service in the post

World War II period, and some implications for succeeding years. This article is published in a tradionally popular magazine, but the information is considered valuable for research purposes.

8581. "He Sleeps Alone: Career of Alfred Redl," Blackwood's Magazine 253 (June 1943): 412-417.

8582. "High-Tech Big Brother," Scientific American 254 (January 1986): 60+.
A discussion of electronic surveillance technology.

8583. "Historical Intelligence Documents: CIA's Early Days," Studies in Intelligence 38/5 (1995): 117-122.
Contains three documents of historical import: minutes of the Director of Central Intelligence's staff meeting on 23 September 1947 establishing the Central Intelligence Agency; final issue of the Daily Summary, dated 20 February 1951, for President Harry S. Truman; and a note from Truman to DCI Bedell Smith.

8584. "How Our Man in Tehran Brought Down a Demagogue: The CIA vs. Mohammed Mossedegh," Esquire 91 (June 1975).
While this publication is not ordinarily given status as a journel, the subject matter and the depth of coverage warrant inclusion. This article is published in a tradionally popular magazine, but the information may have value in historical research.

8585. "HACK the 'Chilling Effect': The Dombrowski Rational Applied," Rutgers Law Review 21/4 (Summer 1967): 679-713.
Discusses House Un-American Activities Committee created in 1938. Sections include the powers of congressional investigating committees, the Dombrowski case, applications of the Dombrowski rationale, and the question of vagueness.

8586. "The Illegality of Eavesdropping--Related Break-Ins: United States v. Finazzo and United States v. Santora," Harvard Law Review 92 (1982): 919-930.
Discusses two decisions in light of Title III of the Omnibus Crime Control and Safe Streets Act of 1968.

8587. "Imperialist Subversion in Africa," African Communist 84 (First Quarter 1981): 84-86.
A review of Dirty Work: The CIA in Africa, edited by Ellen Ray, W. Schaap, K. van Meter and L. Wolf.

8588. "Indonesian Walking Papers," Grand Strategy 2/6 (1982): 9-10.
Alleges that the Natuna Islands have been the targets of Soviet espionage

for purposes of escalating land disputes between the Soviets and the Indonesians.

8589. "Insuring Against Abuse of Diplomatic Immunity," Stanford Law Review 38/6 (July 1986): 1517-1547.

8590. "Intelligence: The Making or Breaking of India's Singh Administration," Defence and Foreign Affairs (August 1990).

8591. "Intelligence and Policy: The On-Going Debate," Studies in Intelligence 24/4 (Winter 1980): 9-15.
    Not listed by the Central Intelligence Agency among declassified articles for public access.

8592. "Intelligence Reform..." See "Late Entries," item 9370.

8593. "Intelligence for Economic..." See "Late Entries," item 8735.

8594. "Intelligence: Yesterday, Today, and Tomorrow," Journal of the U.S. Army Intelligence and Security Command 1 (October 1977): 6-16.

8595. "Internal Security Act of 1950," Columbia Law Review 51/5 (May 1951): 606-660.
    Discussion of the congressional findings leading to the Internal Security Act; registration; sedition; aliens; emergency detention; and constitutionality issues.

8596. "Internal Security: Establishment of a Canadian Security Intelligence Service--Canadian Security Intelligence Service Act, ch. 21, 1984, Can. Stat.," Harvard International Law Journal 26 (Winter 1985): 234-249.

8597. "Invasion of Privacy: Use and Abuse of Mail Covers," Columbia Journal of Law and Social Problems 4/2 (July 1968): 165-177.
    One of the first formal articles containing scholarly analysis of the mail cover issue. Contains statistics of mail covers for 1964 and court decisions.

8598. "The Investigation of UFOs." See "Late Entries," item 9898.

8599. "The Invisible War," Politica Internationale 15/5 (May 1987): 49-137.
    Contains articles by several authors on matters of international trafficking in drugs, terrorism, and intelligence services.

8600. "Italy: Threat Assessment," Terrorism 2 (1979): 283-296.
    Discusses efforts of Italian police to address criminal and terroristic activities, and limited resources of police against the magnitude of the problems.

8601. "Japanese Naval Intelligence," ONI Review 1 (July 1946): 36-40.

8602. "John S. Mosby," Civil War Times Illustrated 4/7 (July 1965): 4-7, 49-54.
A summary of the military exploits of the confederate scout and guerilla whose "cunning and daring made each of his Rangers worth 20 ordinary soldiers." Mosby is credited with providing intelligence that made possible the victory at Second Manassas during the American Civil War.

8603. "Judicial Control of Secret Agents," Yale Law Journal 76/5 (April 1967): 994-1019.
Discusses the Supreme Court cases which address controls on use of police informers: Hoffa v. United States, Osborn v. United States, and Lewis v. United States. Includes a discussion of secret agents and the Fourth Amendment.

8604. "Judicial Review of Military Surveillance of Civilians: Big Brother Wears Modern Army Green," Columbia Law Review 72/6 (October 1972): 1009-1047.
Title captures the content. Discusses barriers to judicial review, limitations on the scope of domestic intelligence, and conclusions. This is a case note.

8605. "Judicial Review of the Right to Travel: A Proposal," Washington Law Review 42/3 (April 1967): 873-901.
Discusses background of the "right to travel," the nature of the right, toward a theory of the right, a comparison of class and area restrictions, and a proposed standard for judicial review.

8606. "The Latief Case: Suharto's Involvement Revealed," Journal of Contemporary Asia 9/2 (1979): 248-250.
Discusses the scandals and conspiracies in the 1965 Indonesian coup to unseat President Sukarno.

8607. "Lawrence R. Houston Receives National Security Medal," Studies in Intelligence 18/2 (Summer 1974).
Estimated to be 6 pages in length. A biographical sketch written by the journal editors.

8608. "Legal Aspects of Reconnaissance in Airspace and Outer Space," Columbia Law Review 61/6 (June 1961): 1074-1102.

8609. "Legal Techniques for Protecting Free Discussion in Wartime," Yale Law Journal 51/5 (March 1942): 798-819.

8610. "Leon Trotsky." See "Late Entries," item 9555.

8611. "Lesson in Military Intelligence," <u>Field Artillery Journal</u> 31/8 (August 1941): 584-588.

A pictorial/photo collection of German soldiers and what can be learned from such photos.

8612. "Loyalty and Private Employment: The Right of Employers to Discharge Suspected Subversives," <u>Yale Law Journal</u> 62 (May 1953): 954-984.

8613. "Marcuse Cop-Out or Cop?," <u>Progressive Labor</u> 6/6 (February 1969): 61-66.

Discusses the work of the Marxist, later New Left, philosopher Herbert Marcuse in service of intelligence efforts in Worled War II.

8614. "The Media and the CIA," <u>Government Publications Review</u> 10/3 (1983): 257-261.

8615. "Michael Collins..." See "Late Entries," item 9380.

8616. "The Middle East War," <u>Armed Forces Journal International</u> 111 (January 1974): 33-38.

8617. "The Military and State Secrets Privilege: Protection for the National Security or Immunity for the Executive?," <u>Yale Law Journal</u> 91/3 (January 1982): 570-589.

Discusses the imbalance in favor of government secrecy in the need-for-information versus secrecy relationships between individuals and society. Suggests a set of alternative procedures to improve the balance.

8618. "The Military Applications of Remote Sensing by Infrared," <u>Proceedings of the Institute of Electrical and Electronic Engineers</u> (January 1975).

8619. "Military Censorship," <u>Field Artillery Journal</u> 33/6 (June 1943): 437-439.

Discusses the importance of censorship in war in order to avoid communication of vital information. Contains bibliography of six books on cryptography, including Herbert Yardley's <u>The American Black Chamber</u>.

8620. "Military-Economic Estimating: A Positive View," <u>Studies in Intelligence</u> 10/3 (Fall 1966).

Estimated to be 6 pages in length. Author may be Julie O. Kerlin.

8621. "The Military Library," <u>Military Affairs</u> 8 (1945).

8622. "Mr. Robertson of Ratisbon," <u>Blackwood's Magazine</u> 252 (October 1942): 232-236.

8623. "Napoleon as Forger," <u>Canadian Bankers Association Journal</u> 9 (1901).

8624. "The National Security Agency and Its Interference with Private Sector Computer Security," <u>Iowa Law Review</u> 72 (May 1987): 1015-1039.
    Analyzes two issues regarding executive authority over civilian cryptography: whether the President of the United States may reassign control over civilian government and computer standards in the face of express congressional delegation of the same authority; and whether NSA may go beyond the limits of Bureau of Standards regulation in controlling even private sector computer security.

8625. "National Security and Civil Liberties--Part Two: 'Covert Actions in an Open Society,'" <u>Center Magazine</u> (July-August 1985): 9-24.

8626. "National Security and the Amended Freedom of Information Act," <u>Yale Law Journal</u> 85/2 (December 1975): 401-422.
    Discusses the (b)(1) exemption of the amended FOIA, E.O. 11652, the courts and executive classification abuses. Offers suggestions as to improving the (b)(1) exemption to reduce widespread abuses of information classification.

8627. "National Security and the Public's Right to Know: A New Role for the Courts Under the Freedom of Information Act," <u>University of Pennsylvania Law Review</u> 123/6 (June 1975): 1438-1473.
    Discusses the scope of judicial review of classified documents, the judicial response to FOIA amendments, and the appropriateness of judicial review as to political questions, need for secrecy in foreign affairs, agency expertise and judicial competence.

8628. "The National Security Interest and Civil Liberties," <u>Harvard Law Review</u> 85/6 (April 1972): 1130-1326.
    A lengthy and thorough examination of criminal punishment and speech, restriction on international travel, loyalty tests, information security of government documents, executive secrecy, secrecy enforcement, covert government surveillance via electronics and informers, and emergency powers of the executive.

8629. "National Security, Law Enforcement and Business Secrets Under the Freedom of Information Act," <u>Business Lawyer</u> 38/2 (February 1983): 707-739.
    This is an edited transcript of three sections of an ABA meeting in San Francisco in August, 1982 addressing the topics in the title. Panelists included Richard B. Smith (Chairman), Ruben B. Robertson (Co-chairman), William H. Webster, Stanley Sporkin, Floyd Abrams, Morton Halperin, Jonathan C. Rose, William F. Kennedy, Alan Morrison, and Thomas Susman. Discusses national security and law enforcement exemptions to FOIA and business secrets and law enforcement exemption.

8630. "Navajo Code Talkers Return," Marine Corps Gazette 59 (January 1975): 5.

8631. "New Jersey Electronic Surveillance Act," Rutgers Law Review 26/3 (Spring 1973): 617-646.

8632. "NMIA Interviews Admiral Inman," American Intelligence Journal 4/4 (September 1982): 6-12.
      National Military Intelligence Association discussions with Admiral Bobby Inman, Director of the National Security Agency.

8633. "Nongovernmental Cryptology and National Security: The Government Seeking to Restrict Research," Computer/Law Journal 4 (Winter 1984): 573-603

8634. 'Oak Leaf' [pseud.]. "A Look at G-2," Infantry Journal 58 (April 1946): 19-21.

8635. "On Optimism." See "Late Entries: Section I," item 10106.

8636. "On the Way to Securing a World Position?: Japan's Intelligence Agencies and Their Objectives," Japan Quarterly 29/2 (April-June 1982).

8637. "The Operational Potential..." See "Late Entries: Section I," item 9251.

8638. "The Oppenheimer Case," Bulletin of the Atomic Scientists 10/5 (May 1954): 173-191.
      A lengthy discussion of the government's case against J. Robert Oppenheimer, including the role of intelligence agencies in gathering information.

8639. "The OXCART Story." See "Late Entries: Section I," item 9697.

8640. "The Passing of Charlemagne," Recruiters' Bulletin 6 (December 1919).
      Discussion of intelligence operations and the use of disguise in the US Marine insurgency in Haiti.

8641. "Passport Denial As a Security Measure," Minnesota Law Review 43/1 (1958): 126-137.
      Discusses passports policy of the State Department, the Constitution and the right to travel, and conclusions.

8642. "Passport Denied," State Department Practice and Due Process," Stanford Law Review 3/2 (February 1951): 312-324.
      Discusses the history of the passport problem in the US, the question of a right to leave and reenter the US, the validity of the "right v. privilege" concept,

a proposed approach, and the balancing of interests as applied to the issuance of passports.

8643. "Passport Refusals for Political Reasons: Constitutional Issues and Judicial Review," Yale Law Journal 61/2 (February 1952): 171-203.
Discusses cases of passport denials, procedures for passport refusals, the problem of judicial review, and the constitutionality of State Department policies.

8644. "The Pentagon and the October War," Journal of Palestine Studies 4/1 (Autumn 1974): 179-181.
Contains remarks by Admiral Thomas H. Moorer made in a May 3, 1974 speech to the Navy League regarding the subject. Comments included observations about strategic surprise.

8645. "Plugging the Leak: The Case for a Legislative Resolution of the Conflict Between the Demands of Secrecy and the Need for an Open Government," Virginia Law Review 71 (June 1985): 801-868.

8646. "Police Infiltration of Dissident Groups," Journal of Criminal Law, Criminology and Police Science 61/2 (June 1970): 181-194.
Discussion of the cases in which decisions were rendered under the First and Fourth Amendments, and in connection with the 'right to privacy.' Includes legal remedies and conclusions.

8647. "Political Spies," Quarterly Review 177 (July-August 1893): 235-237.

8648. "Present and Proposed Standards for Foreign Intelligence Electronic Surveillance," Northwestern University Law Review 71/1 (March-April 1976): 109-133.
Discusses safeguards at the time, judicially-imposed warrant requirements, advisability of a statutory warrant requirement for foreign intelligence electronic surveillance, and constitutionality of proposed legislation.

8649. "The Press Under Post Office Censorship," Current History 7 (November 1917): 235-238.

8650. "Prevention of Espionage and Leakage of Information," Infantry Journal 15/2 (August 1918): 146-148.
This is a short instruction in 12 lessons as to how infantry troops can prevent intelligence leaks, and the importance of troop ability to recognize one's own intelligence agents.

8651. "Prior Restraints in the Military," Columbia Law Review 73/5 (May 1973): 1089-1119.

Concerns prior restraint on military personnel censorship practices, the approval procedures, regulation of intra-military distribution, approval of extra-military publications.

8652. "Privacy and Efficient Government: Proposals for a National Data Center," Harvard Law Review 82/2 (December 1968): 400-417.
Reviews the Kaysen Task Force report on the storage and retrieval of federal statistics, the concept of a data center, conflict with privacy concerns, and proposals to balance efficiency with privacy.

8653. "Privacy, Defamation, and the First Amendment: The Implications of Time, Inc. v. Hill," Columbia Law Review 67/5 (May 1967): 926-952.
Discusses libel, privacy and the First Amendment prior to the Time case. Discusses the Hill arguments and Dr. Meiklejohn's theory of the First Amendment, implications of the case of Time v. Hill and conclusions.

8654. "Private Intelligence As to the American Army," Magazine of American History 10,11,12,13,14 (October 1883-August 1884).
A serial reproduction of original documents on private intelligence reports of the American Revolution, recorded in 1781. The original reports are stored in the New York Public Library.

8655. "The Problem of Chinese..." See "Late Entries: Section I," item 9807.

8656. "Production of Combat Intelligence," Infantry Journal 64/2 (February 1949): 24-26.
Excerpt of an Army training film on the operations of a G-2 section. Transcript of the film segment.

8657.   "Project on Secrecy and Openness in Scientific and Technical Communication," Cryptologia 8/2 (April 1984): 109-111.

8658. "The Protective Principle of Extraterritorial Jurisdiction: A Brief History and an Application of the Principle to Espionage as an Illustration of Current United States Practice," Boston University International Law Journal 6 (Fall 1988): 337-359.
A detailed discussion of United States v. Zehe, 601 F. Supp. 196.

8659. "The Pseudo-Gang," Studies in Intelligence 24/4 (Winter 1980): 39-43.
Presumed subject is tactics used against the Mau Mau. Not listed by the Central Intelligence Agency among declassified articles for public access.

8660. "Psychological Warfare in Korea: An Interim Report," Public Opinion Quarterly 15 (Spring 1951): 65-75.

8661. "Reconnaissance and Special Duty Aircraft," <u>Air Force Magazine</u> (May 1979): 124-126.

8662. "Reconnaissance and Surveillance," <u>Data: Magazine of Military RDT&E Management</u> 12 (April 1967): 11-63.

8663. "The Red Army in the Opinion of the Abwehr, July 1941," <u>Ukrains'kyi Istoryohnyi Zhurnal</u> 7 (1990): 114-120.

8664. "Re-examining our Perceptions..." See "Late Entries: Section I," item 9599.

8665. "Reform in the Classification and Declassification of National Security Information: Nixon Executive Order 11,652," <u>Iowa Law Review</u> 59/1 (October 1973): 110-143.
Discusses the E. O. by way of a brief survey of classification history, description and sectional analysis, and conclusions.

8666. "Report of the Public Cryptography Study Group," <u>Cryptologia</u> 5/3 (July 1981): 130-142.

8667. "The Responsibility and Authority of the Secretary of the Navy for the Oversight of Intelligence Activities Under the Operational Code of a Joint Forces Commander," <u>Naval Law Review</u> 42 (1995): 167-188.

8668. "Right of Association Extended to Curtail Harassment of Political Associations Through Criminal Investigations," <u>Utah Law Review</u> 1969 (April 1969): 383-395.
Discusses the right of association as applied in <u>Pollard v. Roberts</u>.

8669. "The Right of the Press to Gather Information," <u>Columbia Law Review</u> 71/5 (May 1971): 838-864.
Would be useful in analyses of the media as 'intelligence agents,' especially in cases similar to the Pentagon Papers/Daniel Ellsberg matter. May be useful to compare journalist techniques with those of the intelligence community members.

8670. "The Role of the Consultant..." See "Late Entries: Section I," item 10122.

8671. "The Role of Employer Practices in the Federal Industrial Personnel Security Program--A Field Study," <u>Stanford Law Review</u> 8/2 (March 1956): 234-260.
Considers the ISP as published in executive orders and types of security clearances; the program in action; and conclusions.

8672. "Sabotage in Portsmouth: Story of James Hill and the Dockyard Fires of 1776," Blackwood's Magazine 256 (August 1944): 103-109.

8673. "'The Sand Reckoner': ONI Vignettes," Naval Intelligence Professionals Quarterly 3/2 (1987): 11-14.

8674. "Secrecy and Intelligence..." See "Late Entries: Section I," item 9543.

8675. "Secret Files: Legitimate Police Activity or Unconstitutional Restraint on Dissent?," Georgetown Law Journal 58/3 (February 1970): 569-590.
    Discusses the New Jersey experience in the prevention and control of civil disorders, balancing societal interests, state interest, nexus between state interest and imposed restriction, constitutional limits on police investigative power, and recommendations.

8676. "Secret Intelligence, 1777: Two Documents," Huntington Library Quarterly 24 (1960-1961): 233-249.

8677. "Secret Service Papers of John Howe," American Historical Review (October 1911 and January 1912).

8678. "Security Group in China, 1928 through 1945," Cryptologia 7/2 (Winter 1986): 1-36.

8679. "The Shorthand of Experience." See "Late Entries: Section I," item 9167.

8680. "Shredded Knapsack," Scientific American 252 (January 1985): 56-57.

8681. "The Significance and Effects of Surprise in Modern War," History, Numbers, and War 1 (Spring 1977): 3-15.

8682. "Singapore's People's Association." See "Late Entries: Section I," item 9526.

8683. "Soviet Atomic Espionage," Bulletin of the Atomic Scientists 7/5 (May 1951): 143-148.
    Discusses the cases of Klaus Fuchs, Bruno Pontecorvo, Allen Nunn May, David Greenglass and Harry Gold. Points out the failures of British counter-intelligence.

8684. "Soviet Espionage (Latin America)," Military Review 41 (June 1961): 18-19.
    A brief glimpse at a topic about which there is little good research.

8685. "Soviet Organs of State Security in the Years of the Great Patriotic War," Voprosy Istoriy (May 1965): 20-39, 219-220.
Discusses, in Russian, deception tactics of the NKGB against German intelligence between 1940 and 1944.

8686. "Soviet Reform," Washington Quarterly 11 (Spring 1988): 119-168.

8687. "Spies Are Us," Discover 10 (March 1989): 10.

8688. "Spies in Disarray," Africa (January 1982): 33-35.

8689. "The Spy Business in Ottawa," Canadian Forum 26 (April 1946): 3-7.

8690. "Spycatcher, Ex-Spies and Publication: A Comparison of Two Governments' Responses to the Release of Confidential Information," Columbia-VLA Journal of Law & the Arts 14 (Winter 1990): 233-259.

8691. "The Spy System in Europe," Beadle's Monthly: A Magazine of To-day 1 (January-June 1866): 80-84.
This is the second oldest citation in the total collection.

8692. "The Spy That Came Out of the Computer," German International 23/8 (1979): 14-17.
Discusses the use of computer records by the West German intelligence and police organizations. Concerns for citizen rights are raised.

8693. "Spying and Slandering: An Absolute Privilege for the CIA Agent?," Columbia Law Review 67/4 (April 1967): 752-772.
Considers the legal issues in the case of Heine v. Raus. A CIA agent was sued because of defamatory utterance. Revelation of his identity attracted an invocation of the "state secrets privilege".

8694. "Staff for the Cold War: A Programme for Their Training," Roundtable 46 (September 1956): 330-336.

8695. "The Standardization of Foreign..." See "Late Entries: Section I," item 9506.

8696. "State's Intelligence Chief, Ray S. Cline: Intangible Merchandise," Government Executive 2 (December 1970): 34.

8697. "State Secrets Law," China Law Reporter 2/4 (Fall 1983): 271-278.
This is a literal English translation of the state secrets law.

8698. "The Statue of Nathan Hale," <u>Studies in Intelligence</u> 17/3 (Fall 1973). Estimated to be 3 pages in length.

8699. "Strategic Surprise in Korea," <u>Orbis</u> 6 (1962): 435-444.

8700. "Successes and Failures of the German Cryptography Services in World War II," <u>Revue d'Histoire de la Deuxieme Guerre Mondiale et des Conflits</u> 34/133 (1984): 65-73.

8701. "The Supreme Court and the Espionage Act of 1917," <u>Lawyers Guild Review</u> 4 (June-July 1944): 27-29.

8702. "A Survey of the More Important (Coded) Anglo-American Plans (Operations) and Allied Conferences in World War II," <u>Vojnoistorijski Glasnik</u> 21/3 (1970): 259-266.
This Yugoslavian piece contains discussion of allied military plans during World War II.

8703. "Sword Invisible: Cromwell's Secret Service Organization," <u>Blackwood's Magazine</u> 253 (May 1943): 363-368.

8704. "Tapping Telephones and Opening Letters," <u>Criminal Law Review</u> (1957): 502-510.
A brief history of the legal analogy between phone taps and mail openings; draws on legislative history of the sixteenth, seventeenth, and eighteenth centuries.

8705. "A Technical Intelligence Officer in Burma," <u>Military Review</u> 26 (January 1947): 69-73.
This piece contains a British intelligence officer's account of his experiences in Burma during World War II. Also appears in the <u>Journal of United Service Institution of India</u>.

8706. "Technique of Soviet Interrogation," <u>World Today</u> 5 (April 1949): 145-153.

8707. "Tempest Comes in from the Cold?," <u>Electronics and Power</u> 33 (July 1987): 424.

8708. "Their Shadows Before: Japanese Fishers in the Bay of Bengal," <u>Blackwood's Magazine</u> 251 (April 1942): 277-284.

8709. Horatio [pseud.] "There Are More Things In National Estimates," <u>Studies in Intelligence</u> 21/3 (Fall 1977): 37-38.

8710. "These Men Run the CIA," Esquire 65 (May 1966): 84-85, 166+.

This article appears in a popular magazine, but the subject matter and the paucity of reflection on the CIA in the mid-1960s encourages citation here. It may be useful to students and researchers looking in on the historical development of CIA management.

8711. "Through the Looking Glass," Journal of Palestine Studies 4/2 (Winter 1975): 143-154.

8712. "Trade Secret Misappropriation: A Cost-Benefit Response to the Fourth Amendment Analogy," Harvard Law Review 106 (December 1992): 461-478.

8713. "Treason in Legal History," Law Times 161 (February 1926): 115-116.

Discusses the British history of treason dating to 1351. Treason was the first criminal act to receive statutory definition, but its concept dates before the first law. A defense using the 1351 law was applied in a case in 1917, Rex v. Casement, 115. L.T. Rep. 267.

8714. "Trial of Joshua Hett Smith for Complicity in the Conspiracy of Benedict Arnold and Major Andre," Historical Magazine 10/Supplement (1866): 1-5, 33-38, 65-73, 97-105, 128-138.

An old and valuable account of the circumstances surrounding the American revolutionary war spy work of Arnold, Andre, and Smith, a New York loyalist and landowner later acquitted of charges. This is one of the oldest pieces cited in this bibliographic collection.

8715. "U-2 and Its Repercussions," Dissent 7/3 (Summer 1960): 313-314.

An early article on this spy aircraft immediately following the overflight of the Soviet Union by Francis Gary Powers.

8716. "Umbrellas, Loops, and Tractors," Cryptologic Spectrum (Summer 1980): 4-14.

8717. "The Unexpected Capture of Hess in a Trap Set by British Intelligence," Voenno-Istoricheskii Zhurnal 5 (1990): 62-64.

8718. "United Nations Employees Not Accorded Diplomatic Immunity in Case of Espionage; Recapture of Stolen Classified Information from Diplomat Does Not Violate Diplomatic Immunity," Vanderbilt Journal of Transnational Law 12/4 (Fall 1979): 1031.

This is a brief case analysis of a situation involving two Soviet citizens employed at the United Nations who were arrested and indicted for espionage, then deported. Soviets officials argued diplomatic immunity, but failed to convince the court.

8719. "United States Air Force Security Service: A Major Air Command," <u>Air Force Magazine</u> (May 1973): 98-99.
A basic description of this organization as an intelligence function.

8720. "The United States Constitution in Its Third Century: Foreign Affairs--Special Issue," <u>American Journal of International Law</u> 83 (October 1989): 713-900.

8721. "United States of America v. Oliver L. North," <u>National Lawyers Guild Practitioner</u> 46/3 (Summer 1989): 65-96.
This is a legal document containing admissions of the US government, which the government did not wish to have entered in the trial record of Oliver North. Roles of the CIA and DOD are considered and placed in evidence.

8722. "Universities and the Intelligence Community," <u>Academe</u> (February 1979): 15-18.

8723. "U.S. Electronic Espionage, a Memoir: An Interview with a Former NSA Analyst," <u>Ramparts</u> 11 (August 1972): 35-50.
Generally considered a popular press publication, but its subject matter may have value in research of the controversies surrounding the National Security Agency of the times.

8724. "U.S. Intelligence and Vietnam," <u>Studies in Intelligence</u> 28/5 (1984).
The title refers to the entire issue of this CIA internal journal. All articles in this special issue were classified and not yet released for public access.

8725. "U.S. Intelligence Performance in Central America," <u>Inter-American Economic Affairs</u> 36/4 (Spring 1983): 91-98.
Summarizes the contents of a 1982 House Permanent Select Committee on Intelligence report on the title's topic. Contains objections to findings reflected in the report.

8726. "The Use of Balloons in the War Between Italy and Turkey," <u>American Journal of International Law</u> 6/2 (April 1912): 485-487.
Reports upon the use of balloons to drop bombs on Turkish forces killing or injuring 14 persons. Summarizes the First Hague Convention on the launching of explosives from balloons. Useful piece for historical studies.

8727. "'Vietnam II': CIA in Nicaragua," <u>Human Rights</u> 11 (Winter 1983): 9-13.

8728. "Wallenberg: A Lingering Tragedy of World War II," <u>Studies in Intelligence</u> 25/2 (Summer 1981).

Estimated to be 9 pages in length. Not listed by the Central Intelligence Agency among articles declassified for public access.

8729. "Warrantless Electronic Surveillance of Dissident Domestic Organizations under the National Security Exception," Valparaiso University Law Review 5/3 (Spring 1971): 651-666.

A case comment on United States v. Sinclair in which defendants were indicted for conspiring to bomb the CIA office in Ann Arbor, MI. The issue was whether the US Attorney General could authorize warrantless wiretaps of dissident domestic organizations. Article discusses the national security discrepancy, domestic organizations versus foreign powers, and conclusions.

8730. "What Constitutes Wire-Tapping? (United States v. Lewis)," Illinois Law Review 45/5 (November-December 1950): 689-692.

The decision in the title held that one party to a telephone conversation may consent to a third party listener such that the information obtained is admissible in the federal courts.

8731. "Who Is the New Chief of the American Secret Service?," Deutsche Aussenpolitik 10/6 (1965): 724-725.

A brief article on CIA director Richard Helms.

8732. "Wiretapping and Electronic Surveillance--Title III of the Crime Control Act of 1968," Rutgers Law Review 23/2 (Winter 1969): 319-388.

An extensive and detailed examination of federal eavesdropping law, the national security provision, and conclusions.

8733. "You and Me and the RCMP," Canadian Dimensions 13/3 (1978): 3-8.

Discusses the RCMP's security service through as developed from an interview with the author of S: Portrait of a Spy: RCMP Intelligence - The Inside Story.

Late Entries

"the rascal must have his belly ripped up"
(cited in <u>Spies and Spymasters</u>, Jock Haswell, 1977, p. 15)

Note to user: Following are citations added after July 1997 and through December 1, 1998. They are arranged alphabetically in two sections. **Section I, Late Entries** contains items **8734** (Abarinov, Vladimir) through **10324** (Zwieg, Ronald). **Section II, Late Entries** contains items **10325** (Amuchastegui, Domingo) through **10369** (Yesin, V. I. and Yu. V. Grekov).

Late entry citations by author also include items for which no author was identified. A special circumstance concerns a small number of citations to articles appearing in the CIA's internal classified journal, <u>Studies in Intelligence</u>. The Late Entries collection includes some author names and article citation details for items appearing in the Author Unknown collection. Some names were withheld from a 1992 listing of CIA publications for reasons of national security, then published later in 1998 through CIA's web page or other sources. Some author names continue to be unknown, but the article citations appear here. Additional information about these articles, and other publications of the CIA, may be acquired from CIA's Center for the Study of Intelligence, Washington, D.C. 20505.

Section I, Late Entries:

8734. Abarinov, Vladimir. "More Troubled Waters in the KGB Archives," <u>Demokratizatsiia: Journal of Post-Soviet Democratization</u> 11/2 (1992): 41+.

8735. Abrahamson, Sherman R.   "Intelligence for Economic Defense," <u>Studies in Intelligence</u> 8/1 (Spring 1964).

8736. "Act to Punish Acts of Interference with the Foreign Relations, the Neutrality, and the Foreign Commerce of the United States, to Punish Espionage, and Better to Enforce the Criminal Laws of the United States, and for Other Purposes," <u>American Journal of International Law</u> 11/Supplement (October 1917): 178-198.

8737. Adams, Anna.   "Karl Bregenzer: Missionary Martyr-Spy," <u>Journal of Church and State</u> 37/1 (1995): 121-133.
    A brief and reasonably detailed account of Bregenzer's work for the Moravian church in Nicaragua in the 1920s, including his alleged espionage work for the US Marine Corps during the occupation in 1928 and succeeding years.

8738. Adler, Allan.   "Unclassified Secrets," <u>Bulletin of the Atomic Scientists</u> 41/3 (March 1955): 26-28.
    Discusses the conflicts between statutes which severely limit public information about problems in the departments of defense and energy.

8739. Adler, Patricia A. and Peter Adler.   "The Irony of Secrecy in the Drug World," <u>Urban Life</u> 8/4 (January 1980): 447-465.
    Discusses the principles and methods of undercover police who work in narcotics enforcement.

8740. Afanas'ev, Iurii N.   "The Case of the Russian Archives: An Interview with Iurii N. Afanas'ev," <u>Slavic Review</u> 52/2 (Summer 1993): 338-352.
    An interview conducted in 1993 at the University of Michigan concerning the condition of the Russian archives, including references to files of the KGB.

8741. Africa, Sandy.   "The Role, Prospects and Expectations of the TBVc Intelligence Services During an Interim Government Period," <u>Strategic Review for Southern Africa: Security and Intelligence in a Post-Apartheid South Africa</u> 14/2 (October 1992): 89-90.

8742. "Agent Provocateur and Abuse of Process," <u>Journal of Criminal Law</u> 60 (August 1996): 298-300.

8743. Ahern, Charles R. "Yo-Yo Story: An Electronics Analysis Case History," <u>Studies in Intelligence</u> 5/4 (Winter 1961).

8744. Aitchison, Danae J. "Unacceptable Risk or Unacceptable Rhetoric? An Argument for a Quasi-Suspect Classification for Gays Based on Current Government Security Clearance Procedures," <u>Journal of Law & Politics</u> 7 (Fall

1990): 133-176.

Considers dimensions of <u>Dubbs v. CIA</u> (866 F.2d 1114) and <u>High Tech Gays v. Defense Industrial Security Clearance Office</u> (895 F.2d 563).

8745. Albini, Joseph L. and Julie Anderson. "Whatever Happened to the KGB?," <u>International Journal of Intelligence and Counterintelligence</u> 11/1 (Spring 1998): 26-56.

Major sections discuss organizational alterations; the new oligarchy; the political elite-nomenklatura; hoodlums rising; the KGB's mission; the linkages; criminal infiltrations of government; the banking scams; private security services; contract killings; the ambiguous legal design; the espionage offensive; symbiosis and political intrigue; the crime and corruption campaign; the political crisis of 1993; Chechnya and further reorganization; changes in foreign intelligence; Middle East operations; economic espionage; the domestic situation; banks and money-laundering; active measures; and the Chekist legacy.

8746. Albright, David and Mark Hibbs. "Iraq's Nuclear Hide-and-Seek," <u>Bulletin of the Atomic Scientists</u> 47/7 (September 1991): 14-23.

8747. Aldrich, Richard J. "OSS, CIA, and European Unity," <u>Diplomacy & Statecraft</u> (1995).

8748. Aldrich, Richard J. "More on Stalin's Men: Some Recent Western Studies of Soviet Intelligence," <u>Intelligence and National Security</u> 11/3 (July 1996): 593-605.

A book review essay pertaining to four works: Stephen Koch, <u>Double Lives: Stalin, Willi Munzenberg and the Seduction of the Intellectuals</u>; Jenny Rees, <u>Looking for Mr. Nobody: The Secret Life of Gorowny Rees</u>; V. E. Tarrant, <u>The Red Orchestra: The Soviet Spy Network Inside Nazi Europe</u>; and Anthony Cave Brown, <u>Treason in the Blood: H. St. John Philby, Kim Philby and the Spy Case of the Century</u>.

8749. Aldrich, Richard J. "Anglo-American Intelligence Co-operation and the "Special Relationship During the Cold War," <u>Review of International Studies</u> (1998).

8750. Aldrich, Richard J. "American Intelligence and the British Raj: The OSS, the SSU and India, 1942-1947," <u>Intelligence and National Security</u> 13/1 (Spring 1998): 132-164..

Major sections discuss Office of Strategic Services and anti-colonialism; OSS, India and Roosevelt, 1942; secret service treaties and liaison missions; OSS and Office of War Information in India 1943-44; OSS and British security in India; OSS, India and the post-war world; and transfers of power.

8751. Alegi, Gregory. "Balbo e il Riarmor Clandestino Tedesco. Un Episodio Segreto della Collaborazione Italo-Tedesco," Storia Contemporanea 23/2 (1992): 307-317.

8752. Aleksin, V. "Oni Pogibli na Boevom Postu," Morskoi Sbornik 12 (1992): 12-14.
    A rough translation of this Russian language article: "They Died on Military Duty."

8753. Alexander, Martin S. "Safes and Houses: William C. Bullitt, Embassy Security and the Shortcomings of the US Foreign Service in Europe Before the Second World War," Diplomacy & Statecraft 2/2 (July 1991): 187-210.

8754. Alexander, Martin S. "Introduction: Knowing Your Friends, Assessing Your Allies--Perspectives on Intra-Alliance Intelligence," Intelligence and National Security 13/1 (Spring 1998): 1-17.
    The author concludes that spying on one's friends can be just as important to national security as spying on enemies. Major sections discuss trends in intelligence history; intelligence on allies, a neglected sub-field; conceptual problems; secret special relationships; methodological problems; case studies; and the relevance of knowing your friends.

8755. Alexander, Martin S. and William J. Philpott. "The Entente Cordiale and the Next War: Anglo-French Views on Future Military Cooperation, 1928-1939," Intelligence and National Security 13/1 (Spring 1998): 53-84.
    Major sections discuss the 1920s and the predominant imperial security; Franco-British liaison in the 1920s; sources of intelligence, 1930-35; British distrust of France and moves toward staff talks; British anxiety about the condition of France; staff talks begin; improved information, uncoordinated strategies, 1937-38; British worry about France, winter 1938-39; rebuilding the entente, January-September 1939; and conclusions about unspoken assumptions and inadequate intelligence.

8756. Allard, Kenneth. "Information Operations in Bosnia: A Preliminary Assessment," American Intelligence Journal 17/3&4 (1997): 55-58.
    Major sections summarize operations in Bosnia; perception versus reality; command and control; use of information; media and public affairs; communications; automation; and support to the warfighter.

8757. Allen, G. R. G. "A Ghost from Gallipoli," Royal United Services Journal 58/630 (May 1963).

8758. Allen, Edward L. "The Assessment of Communist Economic Penetration," Studies in Intelligence 3 (Winter 1959).

8759. Allen, Edward L. "The Validity of Soviet Economic Statistics," Studies in Intelligence 4/2 (Summer 1960).

8760. Allen, Edward L. "Chinese Growth Estimates Revisited," Studies in Intelligence 7/1 (Spring 1963).

8761. Allen, Robert L. "The Role of Interindustry Studies in Economic Intelligence," Studies in Intelligence 2 (Fall 1957).

8762. Allen, Thomas B. "Twilight Zone at the Pentagon," MHQ: The Quarterly Journal of Military History 2/2 (Winter 1990): 52-65.
    Discusses in significant detail the activities of war game planners and analysts in the early years of the Vietnam war. Discussion focusses on the war games known as SIGMA-I and SIGMA-II.

8763. Almarez, Felix D., Jr. "Governor Manuel de Salcedo of Hispanic Texas," Texana 6/1 (1968): 12-31.

8764. Alvarez, David. "Faded Lustre: Vatican Cryptography, 1815-1920," Cryptologia 20/2 (1996): 97-131.

8765. Alvarez, David. "No Immunity: Signals Intelligence and the European Neutrals, 1939-1945," Intelligence and National Security 12/2 (April 1997): 22-43.
    Sections discuss the operations of the allies, such as Spain, Portugal, Turkey, Switzerland, Sweden, the Vatican State, Ireland, other allies, and diplomatic bags; axis approaches; and conclusions regarding SIGINT operations.

8766. Ambrose, Stephen E. "The Secrets of Overlord," MHQ: The Quarterly Journal of Military History 1/4 (Summer 1989).

8767. American Association of University Professors. "Cryptographic Research and NSA: Report of the Public Cryptography Study Group," Academe 67/6 (December 1981): 358-382.

8768. Amerikanskiy Turist [pseud.]. "A Note on Casual Intelligence Acquisition," Studies in Intelligence 2 (Summer 1958).

8769. Anderson, Dwayne. "Yesterday's Weapons Tomorrow," Studies in Intelligence 9/3 (Fall 1965).

8770. Anderson, Dwayne. "On the Trail of Alexandrovsk," Studies in Intelligence 10/4 (Winter 1966).

8771. Anderson, Martha B. "Handwriting Analysis in Intelligence Operations," Studies in Intelligence 20/4 (Winter 1976).

8772. Andre, Louis E. "Intelligence Production: Towards a Knowledge-Based Future," Defense Intelligence Journal 6/2 (Fall 1997): 35-45.

Writing from a perspective that analytic activity "...turns information into intelligence," major sections discuss the knowledge-based future; how we reach the future of the analytic realm; the shape of a knowledge-based construct; and the keys to modernization.

8773. Andreas, W. "Italien und der Anfang der Neuzeitlichen Diplomatie," Historische Zeitschrift 168 (1942): 259-284.

In German, translated: "Italy and the Beginning of the Newly Developed Diplomacy."

8774. Andrew, Christopher. "Introduction to the 'ISOS Years': Madrid 1941-3," Journal of Contemporary History 30/3 (July 1995): 355-358.

A brief overview of the life and significance of Kenneth Benton to British wartime intelligence work in Spain.

8775. Andrew, Christopher. "Conclusion: An Agenda for Future Research," Intelligence and National Security 12/1 (January 1997): 224-233.

This is an overview reflection upon several articles in this issue, addressed primarily to the need for further exploration of the Central Intelligence Agency's origins.

8776. Andriole, Stephen J. and Robert A. Young. "Towards the Development of An Integrated Crisis Warning System," International Studies Quarterly 21/1 (March 1977): 107-150.

Major sections consider the components of an integrated crisis warning system; components of the prototype crisis warning system; and components of the second stage prototype crisis warning system. Contains an excellent collection of references on modeling decisions in crisis warning.

8777. Angelicchio, M. J. "Agent Hazard in the Super-Het," Studies in Intelligence 7/3 (Fall 1963).

8778. Anglin, Douglas G. "The Life and Death of South Africa's National Peacekeeping Force," Journal of Modern African Studies 33/1 (March 1995): 21-52.

Discusses genesis of the force; mandate; composition; command; training; cohesion; deployment; denouement; and assessment. Mentions police and other security services.

8779. Ankerbrand, John. "What to Do with Defectors," Studies in Intelligence 5/3 (Fall 1961).

8780. "Appendix 4, Camera Data: Corona," Photogrammetric Engineering & Remote Sensing 61 (June 1995): 718.
    Additional data concerning the Corona spy satellite program.

8781. Arango, Carlos R. "Counterintelligence vs. Insurgency," Studies in Intelligence 12/1 (Spring 1968).

8782. Arango, Carlos R. "Insurgent Counterintelligence," Studies in Intelligence 12/ (Winter 1968).

8783. Arias Bonet, J. A. "Los Agentes in Rebus: Contribucion as Estudio de la Policia en al Bajo Imperio Romano," Anuario Historia Derecho Espan 27-28 (1957-1958): 197-219.

8784. Arness, Stephen M. "Paper Mills and Fabrication," Studies in Intelligence 2 (Winter 1958).

8785. Arnold, Tom; John F. Lynch; and Paul Vanslyke. "Protecting the Corporate Information Jewels," Patent Law Review 8 (1976): 12-58.
    Major sections discuss the common information leaks; and plugs for information leaks.

8786. "An Article on the Art of Intelligence Analysis," Studies in Intelligence 30/3 (Fall 1986).
    This article is not listed among the collection of declassified items by the Central Intelligence Agency for public access.

8787. Ash, Lawrence N. "Wilderness Guide: Intelligence for the Commander in Bosnia," Naval War College Review 49/3 (Summer 1996): 30-41.
    Major sections discuss military operations other than war (MOOTW); support tot he operational commander; support to MOOTW; support to multinational operations; and the intelligence community as wilderness guide.

8788. Ashby, LeRoy. "Frank Church Goes to the Senate," Pacific Northwest Quarterly 78 (January-April 1987): 17-31.

8789. Atkins, Don and George Crawford. "Reprogramming Brilliant Weapons: A New Role for MASINT," American Intelligence Journal 17/3&4 (1997): 45-47.
    Discusses scenario XXX; brilliant munitions; and MASINT reprogramming.

8790. Ayoob, Mohammed. "Between Self-Determination and Intervention: The Third World's Sovereignty Dilemma," <u>Defense Intelligence Journal</u> 5/2 (Fall 1996): 71-96.

Major sections discuss privileging state over nation; the problematic reassertion of ethno-national self-determination; state making and group rights; self-determination without secession; the role of the international community; and conclusions.

8791. Babcock, Fenton. "CETA: Chinese-English Translation Assistance," <u>Studies in Intelligence</u> 17/1 (Spring 1973): 63-69.

See item 8488. Author not determined at the time this citation was originally discovered.

8792. Backscheider, Paula R. "Robert Harley to Daniel Defoe: A New Letter," <u>Modern Language Review</u> 83/4 (October 1988): 817-819.

Daniel Defoe served as an undercover agent for British Secretary of State Robert Harley in the early years of the eighteenth century, travelling to Scotland to report on local attitudes and events pertaining to the Treaty of Union. This is a brief article, including the text of the letter to Defoe. Defoe's code name was "Alexander Goldsmith."

8793. Baclawski, Joseph A. "The Best Map of Moscow," <u>Studies in Intelligence</u> Unclassified edition (1997): 111-114.

This is the story of how the CIA developed a complete and accurate map of Moscow to fill an intelligence gap.

8794. Baker, Bob. "Warning Intelligence: The Battle of the Bulge and the NVN Easter Offensive," <u>American Intelligence Journal</u> 17/3&4 (1997): 71-79.

Compares characteristics of the Battle of the Bulge in 1944 with the Easter Offensive in Vietnam in 1972, particularly in terms of command assumptions; the weakest link; command, control and communications; weather and terrain; surprise; and intelligence.

8795. Baker, W. R. "The Easter Offensive of 1972: A Failure to Use Intelligence," <u>Military Intelligence</u> 24/1 (January-March 1998): 40-42, 60.

Discusses the background of the South Vietnamese Easter offensive in 1972; reluctance to use intelligence; C^2 problems; and the failure to use HUMINT.

8796. Bailey, Mary and Gordon Torrey. "Intelligence in the Ecological Battle," <u>Studies in Intelligence</u> 14/3 (Fall 1970).

Considers the ecological implications of locusts.

8797. Bailey, R. Kevin. "'Did I Miss Anything?': Excising the National Security Council from FOIA Coverage," <u>Duke Law Journal</u> 46 (April 1997):

1475-1517.

Major sections discuss the NSC and the Iran-Contra affair; FOIA coverage of Executive Branch agencies; and counterpoints to the Armstrong VII decision in other FOIA developments in 1996.

8798. Baird, Matthew. "Introduction" [first issue], Studies in Intelligence 1 (Fall 1955).

This is an introductory essay to the first issue of Studies, the Central Intelligence Agency's internal classified journal. Despite the absence of external refereed vetting, articles found in this journal are subjected to critical evaluation by top people in the intelligence field. In future years, access to declassified articles will permit important scholarly review of the extent to which the internal vetting process permitted publication of significant works which advanced knowledge of intelligence concepts, practices, research, and theory, relative to the times and circumstances.

8799. Baldwin, Charles S., IV. "Protecting Confidential and Proprietary Commercial Information in International Arbitration," Texas International Law Journal 31 (Summer 1996): 451-494.

Major sections discuss confidentiality rules of selected arbitral institutions; provisions for confidentiality in arbitration agreements; additional proactive confidentiality methods; ability of arbitrators and national courts to order and enforce provisional remedies preserving confidentiality; confidentiality issues presented by multi-party proceedings; ability of arbitrators to order discovery; choice of law; case law concerning enforcement of confidentiality of commercial arbitration in subsequent legislation; and nature of award and final order of arbitral tribunal.

8800. Bale, Jeffrey M. "The Ultranationalist Right in Turkey and the Attempted Assassination of Pope John Paul II," Turkish Studies Association Bulletin 17 (April 1991): 1-63.

8801. Ball, Desmond. "Signals Intelligence in China," Jane's Intelligence Review 7/8 (August 1995): 365-370.

8802. Ball, Desmond. "Over and Out: Signals Intelligence (Sigint) in Hong Kong," Intelligence and National Security 11/3 (July 1996): 474-496.

Major sections discuss Kuomintang SIGINT activity; post-war re-establishment of British SIGINT activity; US SIGINT operations; staff problems at the Little Sai Wan station; the Hong Kong station and the Chinese invasion of Vietnam, February 1979; closure of the Little Sai Wang station, 1982; the aerial farm at Tai Mo Shan; project Kittiwake and the Stanley Fort satellite station, Chung Hom Kok; and closure of Chung Hom Kok, 1993-1995.

8803. Ball, Desmond. "SIGINT Strengths Form a Vital Part of Burma's Military Muscle," Jane's Intelligence Review 10/3 (March 1998): 35-41.

Explores beginnings; the massacre of people in Rangoon; the SPDC; the high command; the intelligence and security establishment; the DDSI; the SIGINT organization; Burma's SIGINT capabilities; monitoring the insurgents; foreign SIGINT; maritime surveillance; telecommunications; EW capabilities; monitoring and jamming HF radio broadcasts; and conclusions.

8804. Banisar, David. "Big Brother Goes High Tech," Covert Action Quarterly (Spring 1996): 6-10.

8805. Banks, Leo W. "The Lady Is a Spy," Arizona Highways 72/3 (March 1996): 32-35.

Brief commentary on topics including actors; espionage in the Civil War, and personal profiles.

8806. Bannerman, Christopher. "Forward Looking Infrared Radar and the Fourth Amendment," QLR 16/4 (Winter 1997): 419-444.

Key sections of this article discuss the history of the Fourth Amendment and the modern balancing test; arguments favoring warrantless FLIR utilization and arguments against such use; and conclusion that thermal surveillance does not breach Fourth Amendment protections. This journal was formerly titled Bridgeport Law Review. This issue is dedicated to this author, who was killed in a head on auto crash shortly after the piece was drafted.

8807. Baras, Victor. "Beria's Fall and Ulbricht's Survival," Soviet Studies 27/3 (July 1975): 381-395.

An excellent summary of the circumstances by which Walter Ulbricht survived the post-Stalin changes in the face of challenges by the head of the Soviet secret police, Lavrenti Beria, who was probably assassinated in June 1953.

8808. Barclay, Michael. "Trade Secrets: How Long Shall An Injunction Last?," UCLA Law Review 26 (October 1978): 203-233.

Major sections discuss an overview of trade secret litigation; historical trends; the modern trend; calculation of the injunctive period; non-disclosed trade secrets and the problem of continuing secrecy; and conclusions.

8809. Barcroft, Peter A. "Chile--Criminal Jurisdiction--Prosecution of Officials of Secret Service for Assassination of Former Ambassador to United States," American Journal of International Law 90 (April 1996): 290-296.

A summation of the circumstances of legal action in Chile to bring to justice the architects of the assassination of Orlando Letelier, former ambassador of Chile to the US. The Chilean Secret Service (DINA) was implicated in the murder.

8810. Bar-Joseph, Uri. "State-Intelligence Relations in Israel: 1948-1996," Journal of Conflict Studies 17/2 (Fall 1997): 133-156.

Historical perspectives are discussed concerning the relationship between Israel's intelligence services and the internal politics and policies of the Israel government.

8811. Bar-Joseph, Uri. "A Bull in a China Shop: Netanyahu and Israel's Intelligence Community," International Journal of Intelligence and Counterintelligence 11/2 (Summer 1998): 154-174.

Major sections discuss the removal of barriers between the US and Israel intelligence; the political setting; the security connections; poor advice; suspecting the elite; the tenuous relationship and dynamics of internal mistrust; the intelligence response to political pressure; upholding professionalism; hedging and dodging; and upholding the tradition.

8812. Barkun, Michael. "Millenarian Groups and Law Enforcement Agencies: The Lessons of Waco," Terrorism and Political Violence 6/1 (1994): 75-95.

A review of the processes by which the US government investigative agencies involved in the siege at Waco overestimated and misinterpreted the intentions and capabilities of David Koresh's Davidian movement. Useful in analyses of domestic intelligence and terrorism events.

8813. Barnett, Roger W. "Information Operations, Deterrence, and the Use of Force," Naval War College Review 51/2 (Spring 1998): 7-19.

Major sections discuss information operations; US readiness for deterrence of information attack; and deterrence for information operations.

8814. Baroze, Osnat. "The Historical Archives of Aaronsohn House," Cathedra 59 (1991): 181-187.

8815. Barron, Edwin S. "Analyst in a Helicopter," Studies in Intelligence 22/2 (Summer 1978).

8816. Bass, Streeter. "Beaumarchais and the American Revolution," Studies in Intelligence 14/1 (Spring 1970): 1-18.

8817. Bast, Carol M. "Eavesdropping in Florida: Beware a Time-Honored But Dangerous Pastime," Nova Law Review 21 (Fall 1996): 431-465.

Discusses rationale for taping; eavesdropping cases and the federal law; the Florida law; Florida's constitutional privacy provisions; and two-party consent.

8818. Bast, Carol M. and Joseph B. Sanborn, Jr. "Not Just Any Sightseeing Tour: Surreptitious Taping in a Patrol Car," Criminal Law Bulletin 32 (March-April 1996): 123-133.

Major sections discuss controls on interception of oral communications; conversations in a patrol car; implications and concerns of police car taping; and conclusions.

8819. Baugher, Thomas R. "Swans Swimming in the Sewer: Legal Use of 'Dirty Assets' by CIA," International Journal of Intelligence and Counterintelligence 9/4 (Winter 1996-1997): 435-471.

Considers the "Alpirez affair"; the FBI's problems; extrapolating CIA guidelines from the FBI's guidelines; deducing contents of the classified guidelines; reasoning behind the guidelines assumption; disadvantages of using only "clean" assets; legal pathways; the FBI's guidelines; effectiveness of the guidelines; proposed CIA guidelines; comments on the guidelines; other benefits of the guidelines; and the reality of abhorrence.

8820. Baxter, Morris, Jr. and Curtiss L. "CHURCHWAY, SNOOPY, MAD, et al.," Studies in Intelligence 18/1 (Spring 1974).

8821. Baxter, Sylvester. "Reconnaissance to Florence and Queen Creek," Journal of the Southwest 37/4 (1995): 625-634.

A copy of a report by the author Baxter on his reconnaissance mission in Arizona in 1888 in which accounts are given of the conditions of geographical features and artifacts of the area.

8822. Becker, Joseph. "Comparative Survey of Soviet and US Access to Published Information," Studies in Intelligence 2 (Fall 1957).

8823. Becker, Joseph. "Computer - Capabilities, Prospects, and Implications," Studies in Intelligence 4/3 (Fall 1960).

8824. Becton, Wendell R. and Elwood R. Maunder. "Military Forestry in France After 1944," Forest History 16/3 (1972): 38-43.

8825. Bedarida, Francois. "L'Histoire de la Resistance et l'Affaire Jean Moulin," Cahiers de l'Institut d'Histoire du Temps Present 27 (1994): 155-164.

8826. Beesly, Patrick. "Das 'Operational Intelligence Centre' der Britischen Admiralitat im Zweiten Weltkrieg," Marine-Rundschau 73 (1976): 147-164, 368-383.

See other articles by this author in the B Section. He has published extensively on US naval intelligence topics. Similar articles by this author appeared in English as follows: "Operational Intelligence Centre, Naval Intelligence Division 1939-1945," Naval Review 63/1 (July 1975): 224-235; 63/2 (October 1975): 314-324; 64/3 (January 1976): 44-52.

8827. Begoum, F. M. "You and Your Walk-In," Studies in Intelligence 6/1 (Spring 1964).

8828. Begoum, F. M. "Observations on the Double Agent," Studies in Intelligence 6/4 (Winter 1964).

8829. Beinin, Joel. "Nazis and Spies: Representations of Jewish Espionage and Terrorism in Egypt," Jewish Social Studies 2/3 (Spring-Summer 1996): 54-84.
    Sections discuss the Arab-Israeli war of 1948 and the "discovery" of Egyptian Nazism; Operation Susannah, discourse and the official Egyptian story; the international campaign for the defendants; after the executions; marginalizing the "heroes of the affair"; and can the perpetrators of Operation Susannah speak?

8830. Bekrenev, L. K. "Operational Contacts," Studies in Intelligence 9/4 (Winter 1965).

8831. Beller, Patrick R. "The Life and Work of Stephan Haller," Studies in Intelligence 3 (Summer 1959).

8832. Bennett, Edward W. "Intelligence and History from the Other Side of the Hill," Journal of Modern History 60 (June 1988): 312-337.
    A lengthy and rich book review essay referring to five significant book-length studies of intelligence operations and history.

8833. Bensinger, Gad J. "Operation Greylord and Its Aftermath," International Journal of Comparative and Applied Criminal Justice 12/1&2 (1988): 111-118.

8834. Bentley, Stewart. "The Dutch Resistance and the OSS: Of Market-Garden and Melanie," Studies in Intelligence Unclassified edition (Spring 1998): 105-120.
    Major sections discuss the stirring of resistance; initial operations; the underground press; slow growth; major resistance organizations; the Eindhoven and Nijmegen undergrounds; OSS involvement; Melanie moves ahead; operation Market-Garden; intelligence failure; carrying on; and undeserved obscurity. Contains several photographs of the operations. This article appears in the unclassified and unnumbered issue of the CIA's internal journal.

8835. Benton, Kenneth. "The ISOS Years: Madrid 1941-3," Journal of Contemporary History 30/3 (1995): 359-410.
    An account of the German Abwehr's intelligence operations in Spain in the years mentioned. Major sections discuss this autobiography of World War II intelligence work in Spain: Vienna 1937-38; Riga 1938-40; Bletchley Park 1940-41; unwanted tasks; walk-ins; and Kim Philby.

8836. Bentwich, N. "Espionage and Scientific Invention: Spies in War and Peace, and the Use of New Inventions," Journal of the Society of Comparative Legislation 1 (1910): 243-260.

8837. Ben-Zvi, Abraham. "Intention, Capability and Surprise: A Comparative Analysis," Journal of Strategic Studies 13/4 (December 1990): 19-40.

8838. Ben-Zvi, Abraham. "Perception, Misperception and Surprise in the Yom Kippur War: A Look at the New Evidence," Journal of Conflict Studies 15/2 (Fall 1995): 5-29.

8839. Ben-Zvi, Abraham. "The Dynamics of Surprise: The Defender's Perspective," Intelligence and National Security 12/4 (October 1997): 113-144.
    Major sections discuss the study of surprise; perceptions of intentions; case studies; the Pearl Harbor attack; the outbreak of the Chinese-Indian border war; the outbreak of the Yom Kippur war; and conclusions.

8840. Berend, Dennis. "The Last Days of the FBIS Mediterranean Bureau," Studies in Intelligence 18/4 (Winter 1974).

8841. Beres, Louis R. "Confronting Nuclear Terrorism," Hastings International and Comparative Law Review 14/1 (Fall 1990): 129-154.
    Major sections discuss the identification of terrorists; identifying the threat; behavioral strategies for identifying the adversary; behavioral strategies at the international level; forms and effects in nuclear terrorism; identifying the preemption option; and redefining national interests.

8842. Beres, Louis R. "Israel and Anticipatory Self-Defense," Arizona Journal of International and Comparative Law 8 (1991): 89-99.
    An overview of the general principles applicable to Israel's right to anticipatory self-defense.

8843. Beres, Louis R. "Israel, Force and International Law: Assessing Anticipatory Self-Defense," Jerusalem Journal of International Relations 13/2 (1991): 1-14.

8844. Beres, Louis R. "A Palestinian State and Israel's Nuclear Strategy," Crossroads: An International Socio-Political Journal 31 (1991): 97-104.

8845. Beres, Louis R. "After the Gulf War: Israel, Preemption and Anticipatory Self-Defense," Houston Journal of International Law 13/2 (Spring 1991): 259-280.
    Discusses historical background of self-defense in international law; contemporary Israel and its right of self-defense; and conclusions.

8846. Beres, Louis R. "Israel, Palestine and Regional Nuclear War," <u>Bulletin of Peace Proposals</u> 22/2 (June 1991): 227-234.

8847. Beres, Louis R. "A Palestinian State: Implications for Israel's Security and the Possibility of Nuclear War," <u>Bulletin of the Jerusalem Institute for Western Defense</u> 4/3 (October 1991): 3-10.

8848. Beres, Louis R. "The Question Palestine and Israel's Nuclear Strategy," <u>Political Quarterly</u> 62/4 (October-December 1991): 451-460.
Considers Israel's willingness to use nuclear weapons; further considerations of Israeli deterrence and pre-emption options; countervalue or counterforce; and jurisprudential and strategic considerations.

8849. Beres, Louis R. "After the Gulf War: Israel, Palestine and the Risk of Nuclear War in the Middle East," <u>Strategic Review</u> 19/4 (Fall 1991): 48-55.

8850. Beres, Louis R. "Striking 'First': Israel's Post-Gulf War Options Under International Law," <u>Loyola of Los Angeles International and Comparative Law Journal</u> 14/1 (November 1991): 1-24.
Major topics discuss Arab-Israeli hostilities; Israel's current position; Israel's future security; dangers resulting from not striking first; and conclusions.

8851. Beres, Louis R. "The Permissibility of State-Sponsored Assassination During Peace and War," <u>Temple International and Comparative Law Journal</u> 5/2 (1991): 231-249.
Major topics of discussion include assassination where no state of war exists; assassination where a state of war exists; assassination as a means of law enforcement; assassination as anticipatory self-defense against terrorism; and conclusions.

8852. Beres, Louis R. "After the SCUD Attacks: Israel, 'Palestine,' and Anticipatory Self-Defense," <u>Emory International Law Review</u> 6/1 (Spring 1992): 71-104.
Examines the tactical dimensions of the threat posed to Israel by a Palestinian state and the legal dimension of Israel's use of anticipatory self-defense.

8853. Beres, Louis R. "Victims and Executioners: Atrocity, Assassination and International Law," <u>Cambridge Review of International Affairs</u> (Winter-Spring 1993).

8854. Beres, Louis R. "Israel, Iran and Prospects for Nuclear War in the Middle East," <u>Strategic Review</u> 21/2 (Spring 1993): 52-60.

8855. Beres, Louis R. "Preserving the Third Temple: Israel's Right to Anticipatory Self-Defense Under International Law," <u>Vanderbilt Journal of Transnational Law</u> 26/1 (April 1993): 111-148.

Major topics of discussion include the justification for preemptive measures; the effects of Palestinian independence; Israel's nuclear strategy; and conclusions.

8856. Beres, Louis R. "Israel and its Enemies," <u>Society</u> 30/5 (July-August 1993): 68-77.

8857. Beres, Louis R. "Israel's Security in the 90's," <u>Midstream</u> 39/9 (December 1993): 2-4.

A brief discussion of the Israeli experience with the gap that sometimes exists between intelligence and policy, and the dangers posed to Israeli national security.

8858. Beres, Louis R. "The United States and Nuclear Terrorism in a Changing World: A Jurisprudential View," <u>Dickinson Journal of International Law</u> 12/2 (Winter 1994): 327-366.

Major topics include identification of the terrorists and their organizations; recognizing the threat; recognizing the adversary by applying behavioral strategies; behavioral strategies at the international level; identifying forms and effects in nuclear terrorism; identifying the preemption option; and conclusions. See similar article in <u>Hastings International and Comparative Law Review</u>, Fall 1990, listed above.

8859. Beres, Louis R. "On International Law and Nuclear Terrorism," <u>Georgia Journal of International and Comparative Law</u> 24/1 (Spring 1994): 1-36.

Major sections discuss who the terrorists are; the threat; behavioral strategies to identify the adversary; recognizing forms and effect in nuclear terrorism; evaluating the preemption option; and redefining national interests. See similar items above.

8860. Beres, Louis R. "The Meaning of Terrorism--Jurisprudential and Definitional Clarifications," <u>Vanderbilt Journal of Transnational Law</u> 28/2 (March 1995): 239-249.

8861. Beres, Louis R. "The Meaning of Terrorism for the Military Commander," <u>Comparative Strategy: An International Journal</u> 14/3 (July-September 1995): 287-299.

8862. Beres, Louis R. "Assassination and the Law: A Policy Memorandum," <u>Studies in Conflict and Terrorism</u> 18 (October-December 1995): 299-315.

8863. Beres, Louis R. "On Assassination of Terrorists," <u>Midstream</u> 42/3 (April 1996): 2-3.

A brief justification of the use of assassination as a self-defense practice, as argued by this author on many other occasions.

8864. Beres, Louis R. "Getting Beyond Nuclear Deterrence: Israel, Intelligence and False Hope," <u>International Journal of Intelligence and Counterintelligence</u> 10/1 (Spring 1997): 75-90.

Major sections discuss disclosure versus "deliberate ambiguity"; and beyond nuclear deterrence and preemption options and conventional deterrence.

8865. Beres, Louis R. "Preventing the Ultimate Nightmare: Nuclear Terrorism Against the United States," <u>International Journal of Intelligence and Counterintelligence</u> 10/3 (Fall 1997): 333-342.

Major sections consider strategic questions; terrorism's quality; pain into power; and asking the right questions.

8866. Beres, Louis R. and Zalman Shoval. "On Demilitarizing a Palestinian 'Entity' and the Golan Heights: An International Law Perspective," <u>Vanderbilt Journal of Transnational Law</u> 28/1 (January 1995): 1-13.

8867. Beres, Louis R. and Yoash Tsiddon-Chatto. "Reconsidering Israel's Destruction of Iraq's Osiraq Nuclear Reactor," <u>Temple International and Comparative Law Journal</u> 9/2 (Fall 1995): 437-440.

A brief overview of the legal issues involved in the Israeli military strike against the Osiraq reactor. This is a rejoinder to a critique by John Quigley which appears on pp. 445-449.

8868. Berkley, George. "For a Board of Definitions," <u>Studies in Intelligence</u> 9/2 (Summer 1965).

8869. Berkowitz, Bruce D. "Information Age Intelligence," <u>Foreign Policy</u> 103 (June 1996): 35-50.

Major sections discuss the current approach to intelligence reform; an alternative agenda for reform; and a new model for intelligence.

8870. Berkowitz, Bruce D. "Reform of the Intelligence Community," <u>Orbis</u> 40/4 (Fall 1996): 653-663.

A discussion of published studies by government and private research groups on reforming the intelligence community.

8871. Berkowitz, Bruce D. "Information Technology and Intelligence Reform," <u>Orbis</u> 41/1 (Winter 1997): 107-118.

Raises concerns for the intelligence community's ability to develop, manage, and organize technology to improve information systems contributions to intelligence in the post-cold war world. Major sections discuss the price of technology; the impact of the information revolution; producing intelligence in the information age; intelligence assets in the information age; and conclusions.

8872. Bernhard, Nancy E. "Clearer the Truth: Public Affairs Television and the State Department's Domestic Information Campaigns, 1947-1952," Diplomatic History 21/4 (Fall 1997): 545-567.

8873. Bernstein, Barton J. "'In the Matter of J. Robert Oppenheimer,'" Historical Studies in the Physical and Biological Sciences 12/2 (1982): 195-252.
A lengthy analysis of the Oppenheimer security investigation by the FBI and the various intrigues associated with government actions against the nuclear scientist. Major sections discuss the origins of the case; movement toward a hearing; the hearing testimony; the findings which labeled Oppenheimer a "security risk"; and the meanings of the case.

8874. Bernstein, Barton J. "The Oppenheimer Loyalty-Security Case Reconsidered," Stanford Law Review 42 (July 1990): 1383-1484.
A detailed review and consideration of the accusation by William L. Borden that J. Robert Oppenheimer was "more probably than not" a Soviet spy. Major sections discuss Oppenheimer's life and wartime work on the H-bomb; the growth of suspicions about Oppenheimer; the Eisenhower administration's Oppenheimer problem; the hearing; Oppenheimer and the question of security risk; and conclusions.

8875. Bernstein, Merrick D. "'Intimate Details': A Troubling New Fourth Amendment Standard for Government Surveillance Techniques," Duke Law Journal 46 (1996): 575-610.

8876. Berry, Marion. "Violation of the Queen Consort or Wife of the Eldest Son: Twentieth Century Treason?," Criminal Law Journal 19 (December 1995): 332-334.

8877. Best, Antony. "'Straws in the Wind': Britain and the February 1941 War-Scare in East Asia," Diplomacy & Statecraft 5/3 (November 1994): 642-665.

8878. Best, Antony. "Constructing an Image: British Intelligence and Whitehall's Perception of Japan, 1931-1939," Intelligence and National Security 11/3 (July 1996): 403-423.
A study of British intelligence efforts aimed at Japan, mainly from the Mukden incident in 1931 to 1939. Argues that Britain's assessments of Japan were largely erroneous, due mainly to a kind of policy complacency.

8879. Best, Antony. "'This Probably Over-Valued Military Power': British Intelligence and Whitehall's Perception of Japan 1939-41," Intelligence and National Security 12/3 (July 1997): 67-94.

A detailed analysis of the issue of Britain's complacency in applying solid intelligence information in the policy process concerning Japan's military capabilities and intentions.

8880. "Bestiary of Intelligence Writing," Studies in Intelligence 26/3 (Fall 1982).

This item is not listed among the collection of declassified items by the Central Intelligence Agency for public access.

8881. Betts, Richard K. "Intelligence Warning: Old Problems, New Agendas," Parameters: US Army War College Quarterly 28/1 (Spring 1998): 26-35.

Discusses "factual-technical" warning, which depends on comprehensive collection activities; "contingent-political" warning, which depends on data analysis; and new circumstances referring to old problems of surprise and warning.

8882. Beyer, Gregg A. "Human Rights Monitoring and the Failure of Early Warning: A Practitioner's View," International Journal of Refugee Law 2/1 (January 1990): 56-82.

Discusses the case of the Issaks of Somalia; the United Nations Group of Governmental Experts; uniform systematic human rights monitoring and reporting; bridging human rights monitoring and government-NGO action; and conclusions and recommendations.

8883. "Bibliography of Recent Soviet Books and Articles," Studies of Intelligence 10/1 (Spring 1966).

8884. Bienen, Henry. "Self-Determination and Self-Administration in the Former Soviet Union," Defense Intelligence Journal 5/2 (Fall 1996): 27-46.

Major sections discuss historical legacies; ethnic fragmentation; models of national integration; self-determination and self-administration; a commonwealth of independent states?; self-administration as an alternative; conclusions.

8885. Biles, Jack I. "Winnie Verloc: Agent of Death," Conradiana 13/2 (1981): 101-108.

An interpretation of a major character in Joseph Conrad's The Secret Agent.

8886. Bimfort, Martin T. "A Definition of Intelligence," Studies in Intelligence 2 (Fall 1958).

8887. Birch, D. J. "Incriminating Remarks Made by Defendant to an Undercover Police Officer--Applicability of Paragraph C:11.13 of the P.A.C.E. Code of Practice--Whether Admissible If Paragraph C:11.13 Breached," Criminal Law Review (May 1997): 348-349.

Refers to circumstances in the United Kingdom.

8888. Bittker, Boris I. "The World War II German Saboteurs' Case and Writs of Certiorari Before Judgment by the Court of Appeals: A Tale of Nunc Pro Tunc Jurisdiction," Constitutional Commentary 14 (Winter 1997): 431-451.

Major sections discuss the Supreme Court's jurisdiction to entertain petitions for habeas corpus; oral argument in the saboteur cases, the first day; certiorari before judgment below--jurisdiction in the nick of time; and conclusions.

8889. Black, Marcia and Robert S. McPherson. "Soldiers, Savers, Slackers, and Spies: Southeastern Utah's Response to World War I," Utah Historical Quarterly 63/1 (1995): 4-23.

8890. Blacker, L. V. S. "Wars and Travels in Turkestan, 1918-1920," Journal of the Central Asian Society 9 (1922): 4-20.

8891. Blake, Jeff D. "Ernest L. Wilkinson and the 1966 BYU Spy Ring: A Response to D. Michael Quinn," Dialogue 28/1 (1995): 163-172.

Addresses the question of who was responsible for initiating the spying activities, suggesting the Wilkinson was the culprit. Aims to correct impressions of the author, D. Michael Quinn. See Quinn's reply in same journal, pp. 173-177.

8892. Blake, Kellee G. "Aiding and Abetting: Disloyalty Prosecutions in the Federal Civil Courts of Southern Illinois, 1861-1866," Illinois Historical Journal 87/2 (1994): 95-108.

Explores the disloyalty prosecutions during the Civil War, finding only one case of treason and a variety of other charges in the Southern District of Illinois.

8893. Blanche, Ed. "Israeli Intelligence Agencies Under Fire," Jane's Intelligence Review 10/1 (January 1998): 18-23.

Discusses intelligence failures; the debacle in Amman, Jordan; an Israeli Mossad operation in collapse; King Hussein's fury; Arafat weakened; and the Meschaal mystery.

8894. Blassingame, John. "The Selection of Officers and Non-Commissioned Officers of Negro Troops in the Union Army, 1863-1865," Negro History Bulletin 30/1 (1967): 8-11.

Useful in studies of ethnic diversity in military intelligence operations of the Civil War.

8895. Blewett, Robert. "Why Is Jonathan Pollard Still in Prison?," <u>Midstream</u> 42/5 (June-July 1996): 31-32.
     The author's opinions regarding the Jonathan J. Pollard espionage case are offered.

8896. Bloch, Gilbert. "'L'Affaire Ciceron': Espionnage ou 'Intox'?," <u>Guerres Mondiales et Conflits Contemporains</u> 45/177 (1995): 21-30.
     A reflection on the Cicero affair, a World War II espionage case involving German spying on the British ambassador in Turkey.

8897. Blockley, R. C. "Internal Self-Policing in the Late Roman Administration: Some Evidence from Ammianus Marcellinus," <u>Classica et Medievalia</u> 30 (1969): 403-419.

8898. "Blown Away? The Bill of Rights After Oklahoma City," <u>Harvard Law Review</u> 109 (June 1996): 2074-2091.
     Major sections discuss what will be and what might have been with respect to the Antiterrorism and Effective Death Penalty Act of 1996 (AEDPA); terrorism and the Constitution; and conclusions.

8899. Blum, Richard. "Espionage and the University," <u>Cambridge Review</u> 105 (July 1984): 143-148.

8900. Blum, William. "Hit List," <u>Covert Action Quarterly</u> 46 (Fall 1993): 9.
     A single page listing of what the author alleges to be a collection of people targeted for assassination aided by US intelligence agencies. Raises the question of possible justification for retaliation.

8901. Bogardus, Anneke-Jans. "Prelude to Operation Overlord: The Air Campaign," <u>Military Review</u> 74/3 (1994): 64-66.
     A very brief account of the air aspects of the Normandy invasion. Useful in studies of air campaigns and intelligence operations in general, and in historical assessments of enemy production losses.

8902. Bogert, Fred. "Cantonment in the Clove, 1776-1777," <u>North Jersey Highlander</u> 7/3 (1971): 9-18.

8903. Bogue, Joy R. "American Liaison Groups," <u>Military Review</u> 27/4 (April 1947): 61-64.
     Brief discussion of intelligence liaison activities with the Chinese during World War II.

8904. Boifeuillette, Louis. "Letter from a Staff Agent," <u>Studies in Intelligence</u> 7/3 (Fall 1963).

8905. Boifeuillette, Louis. "A Staff Agent's Second Thoughts," Studies in Intelligence 11/4 (Winter 1967).

8906. Boissier-Sporn, Monique. "Precepts for Covert Action," National Security Studies Quarterly 3 (Winter 1997): 51-59.

8907. Bonacich, Phillip. "Secrecy and Solidarity," Sociometry 39/3 (September 1976): 200-208.
     Argues that groups in Prisoner's Dilemma-like situations that cannot sanction noncooperators will be more cohesive and will have stronger norms against noncooperation than will groups in which a noncoopator can be identified. A highly quantitative and theoretical piece which may find application in research on informers and other areas where Prisoner's Dilemma logic is relevant.

8908. Bonet, J. A. Arias. "Los Agentes in Rebus: Contribucion al Estudio de la Policia en al Banjo Imperio Romano," Anuario Historia Derecho Espan 27-28 (1957-1958): 197-219.

8909. Borel, Paul A. "On Processing Intelligence Information," Studies in Intelligence 3 (Winter 1959).

8910. Boretsky, Michael. "The Tenability of the CIA's Estimates of Soviet Economic Growth," Journal of Comparative Economics 11 (December 1987): 517-542.

8911. Boretsky, Michael. "CIA's Queries About Boretsky's Criticism of Its Estimates of Soviet Economic Growth," Journal of Comparative Economics 14/2 (June 1990): 315-326.

8912. Bosch, John C. "Caught in the Middle in Beirut," Studies in Intelligence 21/1 (Spring 1977).

8913. Boskey, Charles. "A Justice's Papers: Chief Justice Stone's Biography and the Saboteur's Case," Supreme Court Historical Society Quarterly 14 (1993): 10-15, 20.

8914. Bovey, John. "The Golden Sunshine," Virginia Quarterly Review 51/1 (1975): 53-70.

8915. Bowden, Tom. "Bloody Sunday--a Reappraisal," European Studies Review 2/1 (1972): 25-42.
     Discusses the events of November 21, 1920 in Dublin, Ireland, known as Bloody Sunday, including discussion of the underground intelligence system of the Irish Republican Army leader Michael Collins.

8916. Bowman, M. E. "The 'Worst' Spy: Perceptions of Espionage," American Intelligence Journal 18/1&2 (1998): 57-62.

Attempts to place various espionage cases in perspective. Discusses briefly the cases of the Walkers; Lonetree; Wu-Tai Chin; Pelton; Pollard; Miller; Ames; Nicholson; Pitts; the institutional problem; and the fallout of espionage.

8917. Brabourne, Martin L. "More on the Recruitment of Soviets," Studies in Intelligence 9/4 (Winter 1965).

Few articles discuss this subject.

8918. Bradshaw, Russell. "To Russia: One Way," Aerospace Historian 25/4 (1978): 198-205.

8919. Braga, Anthony A.; Lorraine A. Green; David L. Weisburd, et al. "Police Perceptions of Street Level Narcotics Activity: Evaluating Drug Buys as a Research Tool," American Journal of Police 13/3 (1994): 37-58.

8920. Brand, David L.; Paul J. Bryson; and Alfredo Lopez, Jr. "Intelligence Support to the Logistician in Somalia," Military Intelligence 20/4 (October-December 1994): 5-8.

Discusses the role and operations of the 507th Corps Support Group (CSG) Airborne in Somalia in 1993. Identifies other support intelligence and police units.

8921. Brandwein, David S. "Telemetry Analysis," Studies in Intelligence 8/3 (Fall 1964).

8922. Brandwein, David S. "Interaction in Weapons R&D," Studies in Intelligence 12/4 (Winter 1968).

8923. Brandwein, David S. "The SS-8 Controversy," Studies in Intelligence 13/2 (Summer 1969).

8924. Brandwein, David S. "Confessions of a Former USIB Committee Chairman," Studies in Intelligence 18/2 (Summer 1974).

8925. Brcak, Nancy and John R. Pavia. "Racism in Japanese and U.S. Wartime Propaganda," Historian 56/4 (1994): 671-684.

Demonstrates the cartoon characterizations that both the Japanese and the Americans used to deposit images of the enemy in popular culture documents, such as magazines and newspapers.

8926. Breitmen, Richard. "American Rescue Activities in Sweden," Holocaust and Genocide Studies 7/2 (Fall 1993): 202-215.

Discusses the work of Herschel Johnson, the American Minister to Sweden, in association with the Office of Strategic Services.

8927. Breytenbach, W. J. "Security and Intelligence Structures in 'New' South Africa with Special Reference to Regionalism within the Context of the Federal/Unitary Debate," Strategic Review for Southern Africa: Security and Intelligence in a Post-Apartheid South Africa 14/2 (October 1992): 29-30.

8928. Brigane, David V. "Credentials - Bona Fide or False?," Studies in Intelligence 4/4 (Winter 1960).

8929. Brockmiller, John. "Psywar in Intelligence Operations," Studies in Intelligence 5/2 (Summer 1961).

8930. Brower, Philip M. "The U.S. Army's Seizure and Administration of Enemy Records Up to World War II," American Archivist 26/2 (1963): 191-207.

8931. Brown, Donald C. "On the Trail of Hen House and Hen Roost," Studies in Intelligence 13/1 (Spring 1969).

8932. Brown, Donald C. "Another View of S&T Analysis," Studies in Intelligence 19/2 (Summer 1975).
    A perspective on the Central Intelligence Agency's Science and Technology Directorate.

8933. Brown, George C. "With the Ambulance Service in France: The Wartime Letters of William Gorham Rice, Jr., Part III," Wisconsin Magazine of History 65/2 (1981-1982): 103-119.

8934. Brown, Kathryn E. "The Interplay of Information and Mind in Decision-Making: Signals Intelligence and Franklin D. Roosevelt's Policy-Shift on Indochina," Intelligence and National Security 13/1 (Spring 1998): 109-131.
    Major sections discuss a brief history of Franklin Delano Roosevelt's policy and policy changes toward Indochina; Roosevelt's mind; Roosevelt's decision-making apparatus; Roosevelt's signals intelligence on Indochina; independence movements; Western European collusion; the Soviet Union; China; and why Roosevelt's policy toward Indochina changed.

8935. Brown, Richard G. "Anti-Soviet Operations of Kwantung Army Intelligence, 1939-1939," Studies in Intelligence 4/1 (Spring 1960).

8936. Brown, Richard G. "Anti-Soviet Operations of Kwantung Army Intelligence, 1940-1941," Studies in Intelligence 6/1 (Spring 1962).

8937. Brown, William S. "Technology, Workplace Privacy and Personhood," Journal of Business Ethics 15 (November 1996): 1237-1248.

Discusses the development of the workplace privacy concept; technology and workplace privacy; privacy and personhood; and a proposed theoretical construct of workplace privacy.

8938. Brugioni, Dino A. and Robert F. McCort. "British Honors for Lundahl," Studies in Intelligence 19/1 (Spring 1975).

Brief discussion of the intelligence award given to Arthur C. Lundahl, founder of the Central Intelligence Agency's National Photographic Interpretation Center.

8939. Brunot, Patrick. "Le Controle Parlementaire des Politiques de Renseignment," Defense Nationale 53 (Fall 1997): 55-63.

8940. Bryan, Ferald J. "Joseph McCarthy, Robert Kennedy, and the Greek Shipping Crisis: A Study of Foreign Policy Rhetoric," Presidential Studies Quarterly 24/1 (1994): 93-104.

Considers the success of the McCarthy investigations committee, and in particular the work of staff counsel Robert Kennedy, in undermining trade between Greece and other US allies during the Korean War.

8941. Bungert, Heike. "The OSS and Its Cooperation with the Free Germany Committees, 1944-45," Intelligence and National Security 12/3 (July 1997): 130-144.

Attempts to apply findings from recently released OSS records with documents from the East German archives in order to describe the origins of the Free Germany committees and cooperation of OSS with various committee organizations in Europe.

8942. Buntin, John. "Cops and Spies," Government Executive (April 1996): 40.

8943. Burke, James. "Seven Years to Luna 9," Studies in Intelligence 10/2 (Summer 1966).

8944. Burke, James D. "The Missing Link," Studies in Intelligence 22/4 (Winter 1978).

8945. Burr, William. "Avoiding the Slippery Slope: The Eisenhower Administration and the Berlin Crisis, November 1958-January 1959," Diplomatic History 18/2 (1994): 177-205.

A useful analysis of National Security Council decision making practices during the Eisenhower administration.

8946. Burrows, Quentin. "Scowl Because You're On Candid Camera: Privacy and Video Surveillance," Valparaiso University Law Review 31 (Summer 1997): 1079-1139.

Discusses the history of the right to privacy; analysis of foreign counterparts and the American experience; the state laboratories; and a proposal to curtail video surveillance.

8947. Burrows, William E. "Beyond the Iron Curtain," Air & Space 9/3 (1994): 26-35.

Describes the Cold War reconnaissance overflights of the Soviet Union in search of Soviet radar facilities.

8948. Burtness, Paul S. and Warren U. Ober. "Secretary Stimson and the First Pearl Harbor Investigation," Australian Journal of Politics and History 14/1 (1968): 24-36.

8949. Burton, Shirley, J. "The Espionage and Sedition Acts of 1917 and 1918: Sectional Interpretations in the United States District Courts of Illinois," Illinois Historical Journal 87/1 (1994): 41-50.

Considers the implications of several federal court prosecutions and convictions for espionage and sedition which occurred in the State of Illinois in the years mentioned. Research analysis yielded conclusions with respect to variations in the application and interpretations of these laws.

8950. Butow, R. J. C. "Marching Off to War on the Wrong Foot: The Final Note Tokyo Did Not Send to Washington," Pacific Historical Review 63/1 (1994): 67-79.

Discusses implications and circumstances of the text of an undelivered draft diplomatic note from the Japanese government to President Roosevelt outlining the Japanese perception of the impasse that had been reached in the negotiations to avoid war.

8951. Cable, James. "The Geneva Conference on Indochina," Histoire, Economie et Socit 13/1 (1994): 63-75.

In French, this article considers background dynamics of negotiations among British and French diplomats to resolve the conflict in Vietnam in 1954. Useful in analyses of covert actions and other events leading to American involvement in later years.

8952. Cahn, Anne H. and John Prados. "Team B: The Trillion Dollar Experiment," Bulletin of the Atomic Scientists 49 (April 1993): 22-31.

Provides a useful and detailed history of the outside group of experts that were invited to second-guess the CIA in 1976 on the assessment of Soviet military strengths, spending, and intentions. Resolves that the effort was largely wasted.

8953. Cain, John W. "Technical Factors in Aerospace Photography," <u>Studies in Intelligence</u> 6/3 (Fall 1962).

8954. Camp, Damon D. "Out of the Quagmire After Jacobson v. United States: Towards a More Balanced Entrapment Standard," <u>Journal of Criminal Law and Criminology</u> 83/4 (Winter 1993): 1055-1097.
Discusses the concept of the undercover "sting" operation and the dynamics of the entrapment defense. Major sections discuss the world of stings; entrapment as a defense to conduct; subjective and objective approaches to entrapment; the case for reformation; potential solution; and conclusions.

8955. Campbell, Kenneth. "Access to European Community Official Information," <u>International and Comparative Law Quarterly</u> 46 (January 1997): 174-180.

8956. Campbell, Kenneth J. "General Eisenhower's J-2: Major General Kenneth Strong, British Army Intelligence," <u>American Intelligence Journal</u> 17/3&4 (1997): 81-83.
This a brief biographical sketch reflecting General Strong's career in intelligence and the author's explanations of his success.

8957. Campbell, Kenneth J. "Major General Charles A. Willoughby: General MacArthur's G-2," <u>American Intelligence Journal</u> 18/1&2 (1998): 87-91.
An edited and abbreviated version of a longer article not yet published concerning Willoughby's service. Sections discuss the war in the Pacific; Willoughby's estimates; occupation of Japan and the detour into counterintelligence; the Korean war; and conclusions.

8958. Campbell, Kenneth J. and Robert Cosgriff. "Admiral Bobby Ray Inman: A Study in Intelligence Leadership," <u>American Intelligence Journal</u> 17/1&1 (1996): 85-90.
Discusses Inman's background and early career; directorship of Naval Intelligence; leadership style; leadership methods and organizational relationships; leadership talents; and conclusions.

8959. Caraccilo, Dominic J. "A Leavenworth Nightmare: The Battle of Buna," <u>Periodical: Journal of America's Military Past</u> 21/1 (1994): 40-56.
Outlines in substantial detail the events of the New Guinea battle of Buna, including weaknesses in allied support, intelligence reporting, and battle preparation.

8960. Cardwell, John M. "A Bible Lesson on Spying," <u>Studies in Intelligence</u> 22/3 (Fall 1978): 59-63.

8961. Carew, Anthony. "The American Labor Movement in Fizzland: The Free Trade Union Committee and the CIA," Labor History 39/1 (1998): 25-42.

Reflecting on the recently published Jay Lovestone and Irving Brown papers, it is possible to argue that the AFL Free Trade Union Committee was heavily financed by the Central Intelligence Agency between 1949 and 1958. The Committee provided substantial cover for CIA information gathering operations in these years.

8962. Carleton, Alfred. "The Syrian Coup d'Etat of 1949," Middle East Journal 4/1 (January 1950): 1-11.

Discusses the social, economic, and political cross currents in the Syrian internal revolt in March 1949. Mentions changes in organizational assignment of the police and gendarerie.

8963. Carlson, Michael T. "Glimpse into the History of Secret Writing," Studies in Intelligence 20/3 (Fall 1976).

8964. Carment, David. "Australian Communism and National Security, September 1939-June 1941," Royal Australian Historical Society Journal 65 (March 1980): 246-256.

8965. Carne, Greg. "Thawing the Big Chill: Reform, Rhetoric and Regression in the Security Intelligence Mandate," Monash University Law Review 22 (September 1996): 379-431.

8966. Carpentier, Patrick L. "Security as an Intelligence Community Concern," Studies in Intelligence 10/3 (Fall 1966).

8967. Carr, Caleb. "The Man of Silence," MHQ: The Quarterly Journal of Military History 1/3 (Spring 1989).

8968. Carr, Fergus. "The New Security Politics in Europe," International Journal of the Sociology of Law 24/4 (December 1996): 381-398.

8969. Carter, Chip. "At Home with the General," Civil War Times Illustrated 30/6 (1992): 10, 12-13.

8970. Carter, P. B. "Evidence Obtained by Use of Covert Listening Device," Law Quarterly Review 113 (July 1997): 468-480.

Refers to circumstances in the United Kingdom reflecting on the implications of the July 1996 case of R. v. Khan (Sultan) and the proposals to create statutory protection in the area of law enforcement use of covert listening devices.

8971. Cartwright, Jeffrey S. "Aviation Intel Isn't Ops," <u>U.S. Naval Institute Proceedings</u> (November 1996): 45-47.

8972. Carus, P. "Treatment of Spies," <u>Open Court</u> 26 (December 1912): 759-762.

8973. Casey, William J. "Memorial Ceremony," <u>Studies in Intelligence</u> 27/2 (Summer 1983).
Reflections on the memorial ceremony held for the victims of the Beirut bombing of the US embassy.

8974. Casler, Lawrence. "Images of Conrad's Father in <u>The Secret Agent</u>," <u>International Fiction Review</u> 16/1 (1978): 39-41.
An interpretation of Joseph Conrad's early spy novel.

8975. Cassidy, David. "Controlling German Science, I: U.S. and Allied Forces in Germany, 1945-1947," <u>Historical Studies in the Physical and Biological Sciences</u> 24/2 (1994): 198-235.
Consult later volume and issue for continuation of this piece.

8976. Castagna, Michael J. "Virtual Intelligence: Reengineering Doctrine for the Information Age," <u>International Journal of Intelligence and Counterintelligence</u> 10/2 (Summer 1997): 180-195.
Majors sections consider the intelligence revolution; constraints of the Gulf War syndrome; toward virtuality; broadening the analytical perspective; hierarchical to networked; and inexpensive overwhelming force; overcoming the Gulf War syndrome; augmenting combat power along the continuum of conflict; intelligence dividend; and overcoming the vestiges of yesteryear.

8977. Castaldo, Clive. "France Divided: The Dreyfus Affair," <u>Modern History Review</u> 7/1 (1995): 22-26.

8978. Cecchini, Bianca M. "'L'Infame' Chelotti, Bargello Fiorentino: Abusi e Prevaricazioni di un Funzionario di Polizia Nella Toscana Leopoldina (1772-1783)," <u>Rassegna Storica Toscana</u> 38/1 (1992): 43-63.

8979. Chaillot, Cynthia and Gabriel Marquardt. "Before the Farm," <u>Studies in Intelligence</u> 23/4 (Winter 1979).

8980. Champion, Brian. "A Review of Selected Cases of Industrial Espionage and Economic Spying, 1568-1945," <u>Intelligence and National Security</u> 13/2 (Summer 1998): 123-143.
Attempts to place modern charges of rampant industrial idea theft in historical perspective by examining some classic recorded circumstances in which

nations and companies stole the vital secrets of others.

8981. Chance, J. F. "John de Robethon and the Robethon Papers," <u>English Historical Review</u> 13 (1898): 55-70.

8982. Chandlee, John D. "Scooping the Soviet Press," <u>Studies in Intelligence</u> 6/4 (Winter 1962).

8983. Chapman, Robert D. "You Gotta Know When to Hold," <u>International Journal of Intelligence and Counterintelligence</u> 11/2 (Summer 1998): 221-239.
      This is a book review essay concerning <u>"One Hell of a Gamble"</u>: <u>Khrushchev, Castro and Kennedy 1958-1964</u> by Alexandr Fursenko and Timothy Naftali. The reviewer served as a CIA operations officer on many covert actions, including actions against Cuba. Comments on the lack of thorough analysis of the early days of Fidel Castro's pursuit of power in Cuba.

8984. Chase, Ernest. "Intelligence Yield from ECE," <u>Studies in Intelligence</u> 7/1 (Spring 1963).

8985. Chase, John D. "South of Thirty," <u>U.S. Naval Institute Proceedings</u> 93/4 (1967): 30-39.

8986. Cheung, Y. H. "The Economics of Industrial Espionage: A Game Theory Approach," <u>Journal of International Business Studies</u> (1997): forthcoming.

8987. Chiarella, Louis A. and Michael A. Newton. "'So Judge, How Do I Get That FISA Warrant?': The Policy and Procedure for Conducting Electronic Surveillance," <u>Army Lawyer</u> 1997 (October 1997): 25-36.
      Major sections discuss the importance of counterintelligence; what is the Foreign Intelligence Surveillance Act of 1978?; how one obtains a FISA court order; and conclusions.

8988. "Chinese Security Regulations: NCNA," <u>Studies in Intelligence</u> 22/2 (Summer 1978): 39-40.
      Discussion of People's Liberation Army security regulations, Chinese Communist Party Central Committee and the military commission. This is a report.

8989. Chorley, Lord. "Inquest in the Rosenberg-Sobell Case," <u>Modern Law Review</u> 33 (March 1970): 121-130.
      This is a book review essay of <u>Invitation to an Inquest</u> by Walter and Miriam Schneir, pertaining to the espionage cases of Julius and Ethel Rosenberg, and of Morton Sobell.

8990. Christensen, Charles R. "An Assessment of General Hoyt S. Vandenberg's Accomplishments as Director of Central Intelligence," Intelligence and National Security 11/4 (Fall 1996): 754-764.

Discusses background of Vandenberg's selection; Vandenberg's accomplishments and legacy. Concludes that his contributions played a pivotal role in bridging between William Donovan's OSS and Walter Bedell Smith's CIA.

8991. Christoph, James B. "A Comparative View: Administrative Secrecy in Britain," Public Administration Review 35/1 (January-February 1975): 23-32.

8992. Chronomaniac [pseud.]. "Geo-Time and Intelligence," Studies in Intelligence 9/2 (Summer 1965).

8993. Churchill, Ward. "The Bloody Wake of Alcatraz: Political Repression of the American Indian Movement During the 1970s," American Indian Culture and Research Journal 18/4 (1994): 253-300.

Details of the FBI's actions against the American Indian Movement in the Oglala Sioux occupation of Alcatraz Island in 1969 and 1970. Useful in domestic intelligence analyses of the period.

8994. "The CIA Canoe Pool," Studies in Intelligence 28/1 (Spring 1984).

This article is not listed among the collection of declassified items by the Central Intelligence Agency for public access.

8995. Cilliers, Jakke. "Rethinking South African Security Architecture," African Defence Review 20 (December 1994): 22-233.

8996. "Civil Liberty and Civil War: The Indianapolis Treason Trials," Indiana Law Journal 72 (Fall 1997): 927-937.

Contains portions of the trial transcript.

8997. Clark, Keith. "On Warning," Studies in Intelligence 9/4 (Winter 1965).

A reflection on warnings about coups d'etat.

8998. Clark, Keith. "Notes on Estimating," Studies in Intelligence 11/2 (Summer 1967).

8999. Clark, Michael T. "Economic Espionage: The Role of the United States Intelligence Community," Journal of International Legal Studies 3 (Summer 1997): 253-299.

9000. Clark, Phillip S. "Aspects of Soviet Photoreconnaissance Satellite Programme," Journal of the British Interplanetary Society 36 (1983): 169-184.

9001. Clarke, G. H. "Joseph Conrad and His Art," <u>Sewanee Review</u> 30 (July 1922): 258-276.

An extensive analysis and critique of Joseph Conrad's novels, including <u>Secret Agent</u>.

9002. Clarke, Walter and Robert Gosende. "'Keeping the Mission Focused': The Intelligence Component in Peace Operations," <u>Defense Intelligence Journal</u> 5/2 (Fall 1996): 47-69.

Major sections discuss doctrine; new missions, new roles; intervention, sovereignty, and self-determination; the humanitarian battlefield and defining the enemy; military issues for intervention and supporting the command; principles for future peace operations; and proposed international intervention doctrine.

9003. Clayton, James D. "The Other Pearl Harbor," <u>MHQ: The Quarterly Journal of Military History</u> 7/2 (Winter 1995).

9004. Cleminson, F. R. "Ongoing Monitoring and Verification: Learning from IAEA/UNSCOM Experience in Iraq," <u>Korean Journal of Defense Analysis</u> 7/1 (Summer 1995): 129-154.

9005. Clift, A. Denis. "Dinkum Oil," <u>Defense Intelligence Journal</u> 6/2 (Fall 1997): 79-91.

This is the text of an address by the author given at the Patterson School of Diplomacy and International Commerce, University of Kentucky, in September 1997. Issues under discussion include the continuing need for the development of a literature in the intelligence field.

9006. Clift, A. Denis. "Safecrackers: The Past, Present and Future of US Intelligence," <u>Defense Intelligence Journal</u> 7/1 (Spring 1998): 107-126.

This the text of a speech given at the Georgia Institute of Technology in April 1998. Major sections consider deception, mindset and illusion; science and technology; additional human dimensions; and the next generation of intelligence professionals.

9007. Clodfelter, Mark. "Pinpointing Devastation: American Air Campaign Planning Before Pearl Harbor," <u>Journal of Military History</u> 58/1 (1994): 75-101.

Emphasizes the role of the American air warfare plan to strike consistently at German targets of industrial production of the implements of war. Argues that the policy was fundamentally correct in its expected and actual outcomes.

9008. Coblenz, Michael. "The Economic Espionage Act of 1996," <u>Washington State Bar News</u> 51 (September 1997): 25-27+.

9009. CODIB Task Team VI. "R & D for Intelligence Processing," Studies in Intelligence 10/1 (Spring 1966).

9010. Cogan, Charles G. "In the Shadow of Venona," Intelligence and National Security 12/3 (July 1997): 190-195.

A book review essay concerning two works: John F. Neville's The Press, the Rosenbergs, and the Cold War, 1995; and John E. Haynes' Red Scare or Red Menace, 1996.

9011. Cogan, Charles G. "From the Politics of Lying to the Farce at Suez: What the US Knew," Intelligence and National Security 13/2 (Summer 1998): 100-122.

The author says that this article seeks to outline a definitive view of what the US knew about the Suez invasion plan in 1956. Majors sections discuss the background of the event; American intelligence capabilities; signs of a plot; American reactions; and the polemic over warning.

9012. Coggins, Margaret H.; Marisa R. Pynchon; and Joel A. Dvoskin. "Integrating Research and Practice in Federal Law Enforcement: Secret Service Applications of Behavioral Science Expertise to Protect the President," Behavioral Sciences and the Law 16 (Winter 1998): 51-70.

9013. Cohen, Fred. "Miranda and Police Deception in Interrogation: A Comment on Illinois v. Perkins," Criminal Law Bulletin 26/6 (1990): 534-546.

Major sections discuss the Perkins case and what it was and was not about; and the author's observations of the Illinois court decision. Useful in research on informants.

9014. Cohen, J. and J. Ettinger. "Monitoring Telephone Lines in the Workplace," Practical Lawyer 38 (1992): 25-33.

9015. Colby, William E. "Intelligence in the 1980s," Studies in Intelligence 25/1 (Spring 1981).

See item 1541.

9016. Cole, Timothy M. "Congressional Investigation of American Foreign Policy: Iran-Contra in Perspective," Congress & the Presidency 21/1 (1994): 29-48.

A detailed critique of the congressional approach to the Iran-Contra scandal during the Reagan administration, in particular, assessment of the potential for overreach of the oversight role of the Congress in the investigation of international controversies. Useful conceptual analyses for studies of the intelligence dimensions of the event.

9017. Collins, J. Foster. "The Debate Continues: The CIA in Indonesia: The Scholars vs. the Professionals, No U.S. Intrigue," International Journal of Intelligence and Counterintelligence 10/2 (Summer 1997): 222-226.

A book review essay on a book by Audrey and George McT Kahin on subversion in Indonesia. Discusses the magnitude of intervention; putting the blame on Washington; and covert support to the dissidents.

9018. Collins, J. Foster and B. Hugh Tovar. "Sukarno's Apologists Write Again," International Journal of Intelligence and Counterintelligence 9/3 (Fall 1996): 337-357.

An extensive book review essay of Audrey R. Kahin and George McT. Kahin's Subversion as Foreign Policy: The Secret Eisenhower and Dulles Debacle in Indonesia.

9019. Combs, Arthur. "The Path Not Taken: The British Alternative to U.S. Policy in Vietnam, 1954-1956," Diplomatic History 19/1 (1995): 33-57.

Considers various intrigues between British and American diplomats and policy makers with respect to the 1956 elections in Vietnam.

9020. "Communication with the Editor(s)," Studies in Intelligence.

Numerous letters and commentaries have appeared in the CIA's internal classified journal through the years since 1955. The CIA's list of declassified items in this category is available on the internet at http://www.odci.gov/csi, or by writing to the CIA's Center for the Study of Intelligence. Some of these items may have substantive value to researchers, but they are too numerous to list here.

9021. Compos, Don. "The Interrogation of Suspects Under Arrest," Studies in Intelligence 2 (Summer 1958).

9022. Conrad, Earl. "I Bring You General Tubman: Sesquicentennial of Harriet Tubman's Birth," Black Scholar 1/3-4 (1970): 2-7.

9023. Cooper, R. and A. Schwartz. "Can Big Brother Legally Watch What You Are Doing?: An Examination of Workplace Surveillance and the Laws that Govern It," New Jersey Lawyer 158 (1994): 28-32.

9024. Convery, Jane. "Keeping Secrets--Beyond Confidentiality and the Criminal Law?," Communications Law 1 (August 1996): 149-154.

9025. Cook, Blanche W. "Presidential Papers in Crisis: Some Thoughts on Lies, Secrets, and Silence," Presidential Studies Quarterly 26/1 (Winter 1996): 285-292.

Discusses the veils of secrecy that continue to permeate the policies governing revelation of presidential papers despite various laws and policies to open all records for historical examination.

9026. Cook, Don. "The Yorktown Strategem," MHQ: The Quarterly Journal of Military History 7/1 (Autumn 1995): 8-17.
     An overview of the Yorktown battle and the deception methods employed by the French military.

9027. Cooper, H. H. "English Mission," Studies in Intelligence 5/1 (Spring 1961).

9028. Cooper, John C. "Self-Defence in Outer Space," Spaceflight (September 1962): 164.

9029. Cooper, John C. "Current Developments in Space Law," Spaceflight (July 1963): 136.

9030. Copeland, Miles. "The Game of Nations: The Amorality of Power Politics," Studies in Intelligence 14/1 (Spring 1970): 107-112.

9031. Coppi, Hans. "Die "Rote Kapelle" im Spannungsfeld von Widerstand und Nachrichtendienstlicher Tatigkeit: Der Trepper Report vom Juni 1943," Vierteljahrsheft fuer Zeitgeschichte 44/3 (1996): 431-458.

9032. Corgan, James X. and Michael A. Gibson. "Geological Exploration in East Tennessee: Gerard Troost's Travels in 1834," Tennessee Historical Quarterly 54/2 (1995): 140-153.
     A reasonably detailed account of the travels of Troost and his reconnaissance mission through Eastern Tennessee in the spring of 1834. Useful in historical analyses of reconnaissance methodology.

9033. Coriden, Guy E. "The Intelligence Hand in East-West Exchange Visits," Studies in Intelligence 2 (Summer 1958).

9034. Coriden, Guy E. "Report on Hungarian Refugees," Studies in Intelligence 2 (Winter 1958).
     Discusses unrest in Hungary and the handling of escapees.

9035. Cornick, Martyn. "The BBC and the Propaganda War against Occupied France: The Work of Emile Delavenay and the European Intelligence Department," French History 8/3 (September 1994): 316-332.
     Summarizes research on the BBC's European Intelligence Service and the French Intelligence Service to turn French public opinion to British and Free Franch advantage. Contains edited interview with Emile Delavenay, who was assistant director of European Intelligence for the BBC.

9036. Corscadden, Paul H. "DDI/New York," Studies in Intelligence 13/3 (Fall 1969).

9037. Corscadden, Paul H. and H. Lawrence Sandall. "The CIA Operations Center," Studies in Intelligence 19/3 (Fall 1975).

9038. Cortesi, Lawrence. "Capturing the U-505," American History Illustrated 29/1 (1994): 46-53.
  The capture of the German U-505 in 1944 advantaged US military analysts in the acquisition of German technical achievements in torpedo development and codes and ciphers relevant to naval warfare.

9039. Cossins, Anne. "Revisiting Open Government: Recent Developments in Shifting the Boundaries of Government Secrecy under Public Interest Immunity and Freedom of Information Law," Federal Law Review 23 (1995): 226-276.
  Issues under consideration include freedom of information and privileges and immunities under Australian law.

9040. Coutts, J. A. "Bugging Private Premises," Journal of Criminal Law 61 (February 1997): 75-77.
  Refers to circumstances in the United Kingdom.

9041. Cowey, Ross. "More on the Military Estimates," Studies in Intelligence 19/2 (Summer 1975).

9042. Cowey, Ross. "The Future Market for Finished Intelligence," Studies in Intelligence 20/4 (Winter 1976).

9043. Cozzetto, Don A. and Theodore B. Pedeliski. "Privacy and the Workplace: Future Implications for Managers," Review of Public Personnel Administration 16 (Spring 1996): 21-31.
  Considers a variety of issues related to the role and implications of electronic and other devices aimed at employee monitoring.

9044. Crabtree, Susan. "Mata Hirees," Insight 13/19 (May 1997): 14-18.
  A brief discussion of roles, successes, and promotion restrictions for women in the Central Intelligence Agency.

9045. Crawford, Chester C. "The Polygraph in Agent Interrogation," Studies in Intelligence 4/2 (Summer 1960).

9046. Crawford, John W., Jr. "Passing Rickover's Muster," Naval History 6/1 (1992): 35-38.

9047. Crawford, Kimberly A. "A Constitutional Guide to Use of Cellmate Informants," FBI Law Enforcement Bulletin 64 (December 1995): 18-23.
    Discusses the Fifth amendment self-incrimination rule; due process; and the Sixth amendment's right to counsel provision.

9048. Cray, Robert E., Jr. "The John Andre Memorial: The Politics of Memory in Gilded Age New York," New York History 77/1 (1996): 204-231.

9049. Crockett, R. B. "The Foreign Office News Department and the Struggle Against Appeasement," Historical Research 63 (February 1990): 73-85.

9050. Crossman, R. H. S. "The Hiss Case," Political Quarterly 24/4 (October-December 1953).
    A summary of the key issues and evidence in the Alger Hiss case of alleged espionage activities.

9051. Crouch, Thomas W. "Frederick Funston of Kansas: His Formative Years, 1865-1891," Kansas Historical Quarterly 40/2 (1974): 177-211.

9052. Crown, David. "Political Forgeries in the Middle East," Studies in Intelligence 22/ 1 (Spring 1978).

9053. Cummings, Robert M. "Some Aspects of Trade Secrets and Their Protection: The Public Domain and the 'Unified Description' Requirement," Kentucky Law Journal 54 (1966): 190-205.
    Outlines the theory of trade secret protection and outlines the state of the law at the time. Proposes further trade secrets protection legislation.

9054. Curriden, Mark. "Miffed Over a Mole: Controversy Erupts Over a Lawyer-Informant Who Continued to Practice Law After Admitting a Felony," ABA Journal 83 (May 1997): 36-38.

9055. Currie, David P. "The Constitution in the Supreme Court: The Second World War," Catholic University Law Review 37 (Fall 1987): 1-13.

9056. Currie, James T. "Iran-Contra and Congressional Oversight of the CIA," International Journal of Intelligence and Counterintelligence 11/2 (Summer 1998): 185-210.
    A discussion of the Central Intelligence Agency's oversight exemptions; breaches of confidence; the question of timing; the Iran-Contra affair was years in the making; dealing with the Mullahs; helping on the sly; the lid comes off; informing the public; tangling with Bush; significant improvements; and trying the barely possible.

9057. Currier, Prescott. "My 'Purple' Trip to England in 1941," <u>Cryptologia</u> 20/3 (1996): 193-201.

9058. Cushman, Robert E. "Ex Parte Quirin et al.--The Nazi Saboteur Case," <u>Cornell Law Review</u> 28 (1942): 54-65.
  Summarizes the events and legal circumstances relevant to the trials of eight nazi saboteurs who entered the US illegally in 1942 and were captured by the military and the FBI.

9059. Daffini, Carole. "Der Fall Marteau," <u>Comparativ</u> 4/3 (1994): 144-148.

9060. Dahms, John A. "Shepherding a Soviet Tour," <u>Studies in Intelligence</u> 9/1 (Spring 1965).

9061. Dalleo, Peter T. "Thomas McKean Rodney: U.S. Consul in Cuba: The Havana Years, 1825-1829," <u>Delaware History</u> 22/3 (1987): 204-218.

9062. Danelski, David J. "The Saboteurs' Case," <u>Journal of Supreme Court History</u> 61 (1996).
  Refers to the Nazi saboteur cases of 1942, <u>Ex Parte Quirin</u> and others.

9063. Darnsley-Stuart-Stephens, C. de B. "Secret Service in Germany," <u>English Review</u> 19 (March 1915): 475-489.

9064. Darnsley-Stuart-Stephens, C.de B. "Wolves in Sheep's Clothing," <u>English Review</u> 22 (March 1916): 236-247.

9065. Darnsley-Stuart-Stephens, C.de B. "Concerning Secret Agents," <u>English Review</u> 22 (April 1916): 336-345.

9066. Das, Dilip K. "Impact of Antiterrorist Measures on Democratic Law Enforcement: The Italian Experience," <u>Terrorism: An International Journal</u> 13/2 (1990): 89-98.

9067. Daugherty, William J. "A First Tour Like No Other," <u>Studies in Intelligence</u> Unclassified edition (Spring 1998): 1-45.
  This is a lengthy personal account of the author's experiences as a new CIA case officer in Iran in the spring of 1979 when Iranian students and revolutionaries toppled the Shah's government and seized the American embassy. He discusses his background prior to assignment in Tehran; historical perspective on the situation in Iran; and a series of observations about the circumstances of his capture, interrogation, and events during captivity for fourteen months. This article is published in the 1998 unnumbered and unclassified issue of the CIA's internal journal.

9068. Davids, Karel. "Openness or Secrecy? Industrial Espionage in the Dutch Republic," Journal of European Economic History 24/2 (1995): 333-348.

Major sections discuss openness of knowledge in the 17th century context; secrecy and espionage; a policy of openness in the Dutch Republic; from openness to secrecy; and conclusions.

9069. Davies, Philip H. J. "Intelligence Scholarship as All-Source Analysis: The Case of Tom Bower's The Perfect English Spy," Intelligence and National Security 12/3 (July 1997): 201-207.

A book review essay of the book mentioned in the title, and a subtitle of Sir Dick White and the Secret War, 1935-90. The book was published in London in 1995.

9070. Davis, Bruce E. and Jacob H. Stillman. "A Supplement to the Survey of Military Justice," Military Law Review 12 (1960): 219+.

Includes consideration of military rules pertaining to espionage or treason in the military context.

9071. Davis, Euan G. "A Watchman for All Seasons," Studies in Intelligence 13/1 (Spring 1969).

9072. Davis, Euan G. and Cynthia M. Grabo. "Deception," Studies in Intelligence 17/1 (Spring 1973).

9073. Davis, Jack. "Bridging the Intelligence-Policy Divide," Studies in Intelligence Unclassified edition (1994): 7-16.

9074. Davis, Michael. "Do Cops Really Need a Code of Ethics?," Criminal Justice Ethics 10/2 (1991): 14-28.

9075. Davis, Richard G. "Pointblank vs. Overlord: Strategic Bombing and the Normandy Invasion," Air Power History 41/2 (1994): 4-13.

A study of the bombing history of US forces in 1944, especially the concentration of effort on German manufacturing plants, in the months preceding the secret June 1944 Overlord mission to invade Europe via Normandy.

9076. Davison, Stanley R. "A Century Ago: The Tortuous Pursuit," Montana 27/4 (1977): 2-19.

9077. Day, Dwayne A. "Corona: America's First Spy Satellite Program, Part I," Quest (Summer 1995): 9-12.

9078. Day, Dwayne A. "Corona: America's First Spy Satellite Program, Part II," Quest (Fall 1995): 32-33.

9079. Dearth, Douglas H.   "Failed States: An International Conundrum," Defense Intelligence Journal 5/2 (Fall 1996): 119-130.

　　　　Major sections discuss the nation and the state; what is a failed state and why do they fail?; does it matter if states fail?; what can be done about failed states?; the history of state failures; the future of the state system; and the range of possible solutions.

9080. D'Echauffour, Gabriel M.   "Non-Electronic Agent Communications," Studies in Intelligence 13/3 (Fall 1969).

9081. Dedring, Juergen. "Early Warning and the United Nations," Journal of Ethno-Development 4/1 (July 1994): 98-104.

9082. Deery, Phillip. "Cold War Victim or Rhodes Scholar Spy?," Overland 147 (Winter 1997).

　　　　Discusses in some length the file of Czechoslovak secret agent Jan Milner.

9083. de Graaff, Robert.   "Accessibility of Secret Service Archives in the Netherlands," Intelligence and National Security 12/2 (April 1997): 154-160.

　　　　This is a research note on the subject, including a useful bibliography of sources, particularly with respect to examining operations of the Dutch security services.

9084. de Graaff, Robert and Cees Wiebes.   "Intelligence and the Cold War Behind the Dikes: The Relationship Between the American and Dutch Intelligence Communities, 1946-1994," Intelligence and National Security 12/1 (January 1997): 41-58.

　　　　Major sections discuss the present situation; Dutch internal security; liaison activities with other services; the foreign intelligence service; the Petersen affair; the botched IDB mission to Kiev; continued cooperation; and conclusions.

9085. de Jensen, Lamar. "The Spanish Armada: The Worst-Kept Secret in Europe," Sixteenth Century Journal 19 (Winter 1988): 621-641.

9086. Della-Giustina, John E. "Intelligence in Peace Operations: The MID in Cuba, 1906-1909," Military Intelligence 20/4 (October-December 1994): 18-22.

　　　　A brief history of the Military Intelligence Division in Cuba. Major sections discuss MID history; the first and second interventions; intelligence from Cuba; end of the intervention; aftermath; and lessons learned.

9087. de Lombares, Michel. "L'Affaire Dreyfus: Apercu General, Apercus Nouveaux," Revue de Defense Nationale 25 (1969): 1125+.

9088. Demarest, Geoffrey B. "Espionage in International Law," <u>Denver Journal of International Law and Policy</u> 24 (Spring 1996): 321-348.

See a significantly shorter article with same title in item 1946 of this bibliography. Following introductory observations and definitions, major sections discuss international espionage law; today's collection environment; and conclusions.

9089. DeMars, William. "Waiting for Early Warning: Humanitarian Action After the Cold War," <u>Journal of Refugee Studies</u> 8/4 (December 1995): 390-410.

9090. Denece, Eric. "Pour un Conseil National de Securite," <u>Revue de Defense Nationale</u> 51 (November 1995): 29-35.

9091. Denevoise, John. "Soviet Defector Motivation," <u>Studies in Intelligence</u> 2 (Fall 1958).

9092. Denning, Dorothy E. and Dennis K. Branstad. "A Taxonomy for Key Escrow Encryption Systems," <u>Communications of the ACM</u> 39/3 (March 1996): 34-40.

Discusses components in terms of user security component; key escrow component; and data recovery component. Includes a table displaying a summary of characteristics of key escrow encryption systems and approaches.

9093. Denniston, Robin. "'Yanks to Lunch'--An Early Glimpse of Anglo-American Signals Intelligence Co-operation, March, 1941," <u>Intelligence and National Security</u> 11/2 (April 1996): 357-359.

A very brief interpretation of a document reflecting British and American cooperation in signals intelligence in 1941.

9094. Depaulo, Bella M.; Miron Zuckerman; and Robert Rosenthal. "Humans As Lie Detectors," <u>Journal of Communication</u> 30 (1980): 129-139.

Examines how people detect deception, how they think they detect deception, and whether the two processes correspond to each other. Includes an excellent collection of references to research on deception at the individual level.

9095. Deschamps-Adams, Helene. "An OSS Agent Behind Enemy Lines in France," <u>Prologue: Quarterly Journal of the National Archives</u> 24/3 (1992): 257-274.

9096. Dessants, Betty A. "Ambivalent Allies: OSS' USSR Division, the State Department, and the Bureaucracy of Intelligence Analysis, 1941-1945," <u>Intelligence and National Security</u> 11/4 (October 1996): 722-753.

Following on analysis of William Langer's 1945 report to OSS head, William J. Donovan, on problems associated with the end of World War II, the author examines the patron-client relationship between the State Department and the OSS Research and Analysis Branch during 1942-1945.

9097.   De Sverac.   "Relations Entre les USA et les Republiques Latino-Americaines," Revue Militaire Generale 3 (1971): 293-310.
Roughly translated from the French, this title concerns the relationship between the US and countries in Latin America.

9098.   Detmer, Jamie.   "Counterintelligence," Insight 13/19 (May 1997): 12-14.

9099.   Deutch, Miguel.   "The Property Concept of Trade Secrets in Anglo-American Law: An Ongoing Debate," University of Richmond Law Review 31 (March 1997): 313-369.
Major sections discuss methodology; "In Rem Right" or "Proprietary Right"; aims of protecting trade secrets and the In Rem concept; compatibility of the 'Right' in a trade secret with the In Rem model; and conclusions about the In Rem right.

9100.   Deutsch, James I.   "'I Was a Hollywood Agent':   Cinematic Representations of the Office of Strategic Services in 1946," Intelligence and National Security 13/2 (Summer 1998): 85-99.
Discusses background circumstances of the Hollywood production of three films about the OSS following World War II. Suggests that although the War Department was perturbed about some of the information that had been revealed to the Hollywood producers, the intelligence establishment likely benefitted from the films' depictions.

9101.   deVera, Arleen. "Without Parallel: The Local 7 Deportation Cases, 1949-1955," Amerasia Journal 20/2 (1994): 1-25.
A study of enforcement actions against cannery farm workers during the period mentioned through provision of the Internal Security Act and the Immigration and Naturalization Act. Useful in historical studies of domestic intelligence and alleged subversion.

9102.   De Vito, Michael A. and Stuart M. Flamen.   "'Flir'ting with Danger: A Fourth Amendment Analysis of Infrared Imaging," St. John's Journal of Legal Commentary 10 (Summer 1995): 651-672.
A discussion of the Forward Looking Infrared Device (FLIR) and Fourth amendment privacy protection. Major sections discuss FLIR technology; whether the use of FLIR constitutes a search; and a new proposed test.

9103.   Diamant, Lincoln.   "Skinners: Patriot 'Friends' or Loyalist Foes?," Hudson Valley Regional Review 4/2 (1987): 50-61.

9104. Diamond, Arlyn. "A Legacy," Massachusetts Review 16/3 (1975): 588-591.

9105. Diamond, John M. "Problems and Prospects in U.S. Imagery Intelligence," National Security Studies Quarterly 3 (Spring 1997): 21-48.

9106. Di Bartolomeo, Lisa. "Criminal Law--Government Not Entitled to Restitution for Sting Operations Under the Victim and Witness Protection Act," Suffolk University Law Review 29 (Fall 1995): 903-908.

9107. Divine, Robert A. "Alive and Well: The Continuing Cuban Missile Crisis Controversy," Diplomatic History 18/4 (1994): 551-560.
    An extensive book review essay concerning several trade press book-length studies of the records of actions during the Cuban missile crisis in 1962.

9108. Dmitrichev, Timour F. "Conceptual Approaches to Early Warning--Mechanisms and Models: A View from the United Nations," International Journal of Refugee Law 3/2 (1991): 264-271.
    Major sections discuss the purposes, needs and objectives of the Office for Research and Collection of Information; and the organization and 268 indicators in the ORCIDATA system.

9109. Dobriansky, Lev E. "A Man and Patriot," Ukrainian Quarterly 25/3 (1969): 204-218.
    The entire issue is dedicated to the life and work of professor Roman Smal-Stocki.

9110. Dockham, Patricia R. "A Plea for Continuity in Intelligence Production," Studies in Intelligence 23/4 (Winter 1979).

9111. Dockrill, M. L. "The F.O. and Chatham House, 1919," International Affairs (Great Britain) 56 (1980): 665-672.

9112. Dodd, A. H. "The Spanish Treason, the Gunpowder Plot, and the Catholic Refugees," English Historical Review 53 (1938).

9113. Doerfer, Gordon L. "The Limits of Trade Secret Law Imposed by Federal Patent and Antitrust Supremacy," Harvard Law Review 80 (1967): 1432-1462.
    Discusses the significant Supreme Court cases in Sears and Compco in the area of trade secrets law; the law of trade secrets; the law of patents; trade secrets, patent policy, and Sears; and trade secrets and the antitrust rationale.

9114. Doel, Ronald E. and Allan A. Needell. "Science, Scientists, and the CIA: Balancing International Ideals, National Needs, and Professional Opportunities,"

Intelligence and National Security 12/1 (January 1997): 59-81.
    Major sections discuss intelligence and the postwar organization of military R&D; planning scientific intelligence; establishing an Office of Scientific Intelligence; covert science and CIA medical research; and conclusions.

9115. Doherty, Robert M. "I'm Just a Coal Miner's...Lawyer: Local Diplomacy and the U-2 Incident," Proteus 13/1 (1996): 15-18.

9116. Donley, Michael; Cornelius O'Leary; and John Montgomery. "Inside the White House Situation Room: A National Nerve Center," Studies in Intelligence Unclassified edition (1997): 7-13.
    Discusses mission, organization, and functions of the situation room; essential relationships; support to the NSC; intelligence support to policymakers; interagency connections; comparisons with other Washington-area centers; and implications for leadership.

9117. Donnalley, Gail F. "Declassification in an Open Society," Studies in Intelligence 18/3 (Fall 1974): 11-18.
    Discussion of the President's Executive Order on declassification and the FOIA's impact on CIA.

9118. Donovan, Michael. "National Intelligence and the Iranian Revolution," Intelligence and National Security 12/1 (January 1997): 143-163.
    A detailed analysis of the author's perspective that the CIA failed grossly to properly evaluate the fall of the Shah's regime in 1978, and that the failure of analysis had deep historical roots in the Agency.   Other agencies and governmental institutions are also implicated.

9119. Dovey, H. O. "The Eighth Assignment, 1941-1942," Intelligence and National Security 11/4 (October 1996): 672-695.
    An account of Brigadier Dudley Clarke's World War II assignments in Cairo during this period, as discussed in the following major sections: a period of experimenting; defeat and victory; and conclusions.

9120. Dovey, H. O. "The Eighth Assignment, 1943-1945," Intelligence and National Security 12/2 (April 1997): 69-90.
    A continuation of the previous item, with major sections under consideration as follows: 'A' force at sea; 'A' force in North Africa; operation Barclay's impact; the Italian armistice; deception plan Boardman; operation Capricorn and mischief; operation Lemons and operation Savages; Italian channels; degrees of success; and closing down.

9121. Dower, John. "Science, Society, and the Japanese Atomic-Bomb Project During World War Two," Bulletin of Concerned Asian Scholars 10/2 (April

1978): 41-54.

A detailed history of the plans and evolution of Japan's atomic bomb project. Contains a lengthy introduction to the subject and sections on early inquiries; the Committee of Experts; the NI Project; and the search for uranium.

9122. Downie, J. A. "Defoe the Spy," British Society for Eighteenth-Century Studies 9 (June 1976): 17-18.

9123. Downie, J. A. "'Mistakes on All Sides': A New Defoe Manuscript," Review of English Studies 27 (1976): 431-437.

9124. Downie, J. A. "Secret Service Payments to Daniel Defoe, 1710-1714," Review of English Studies 30/120 (November 1979): 437-441.

Discusses Defoe's work in establishing an intelligence system, travelling to Scotland on several occasions from 1706-1712, and establishing cover names of Alexander Goldsmith and Claude Guilot.

9125. Drave, C. R. "Production at Small Posts," Studies in Intelligence 5/3 (Fall 1961).

9126. Dreyfuss, Robert. "Orbit of Influence: Spy Finance and the Black Budget," American Prospect (March-April 1996): 30-36.

Discusses the associations between the American aerospace and defense industrial establishment and the intelligence agencies that use electronic equipment.

9127. Drexler, Robert W. "Sent by President James K. Polk to End the War with Mexico, Nicholas Trist Soon Embarked on His Own Agenda," Military History (February 1998): 10-12; 78.

Brief discussion of Trist's plans for ending the war that deviated from the plans of Polk.

9128. Duckworth, Barbara A. "The Defense of HUMINT Service: Preparing for the 21st Century," Defense Intelligence Journal 6/1 (Spring 1997): 7-13.

Discusses the issues facing Defense Humint Service; the future of DoD Humint; and needs for future service.

9129. Dudziak, Mary L. "Josephine Baker, Racial Protest, and the Cold War," Journal of American History 81/2 (1994): 543-570.

A detailed consideration of the racial protest actions of a popular singer in the 1950s era of anti-Communist crusades against African-Americans who spoke out unhesitatingly about American domestic racism. Useful in historical studies of domestic intelligence activities aimed at dissidence.

9130. Duncan, K. C. "Geographic Intelligence," Studies in Intelligence 3 (Spring 1959).

9131. Dunham, Alton. "Leading a Diverse Workforce into the 21st Century," Defense Intelligence Journal 7/1 (Spring 1998): 89-105.
Defines diversity in terms of the current and future intelligence cadre; why diversity?; the basis of diversity; the legal requirements of diversity; barriers to diversity in the workplace; implementing diversity; and managing diversity.

9132. Dunnington, Colin and Clive Norris. "A Risky Business: The Recruitment and Running of Informers by English Police Officers," Police Studies 19/2 (1996): 1-23.
Major sections discuss recruitment and the manufacture of motivation; instrumental strategies; informational strategies; affective strategies; running with risk-officer protection strategies; running with risk-informer protection strategies; and discussion.

9133. Dunslerville, L. C. "Military Mission to North-west Persia, 1918," Journal of the Central Asian Society 8/2 (1921): 79-88.

9134. Dupont, Steven N. "The Copyright and Trade Secret Protection of Communication Software: Placing a Lock on Interoperability," John Marshall Journal of Computer & Information Law 13 (October 1994): 17-41.

9135. "Du Renseignement," Defense Nationale 54 (January 1998): 7-58.
Several articles in this issue consider various aspects of French intelligence services, both military and civilian.

9136. Eagle, Roderick L. "The Secret Service in Tudor Times," Contemporary Review 215 (December 1969): 302-304, 326.
A brief glimpse into the secret service work of Sir Francis Walsingham, Queen's Secretary of State, from 1587-1590.

9137. Eagleton, Terry. "Resources for a Journey of Hope: The Significance of Raymond Williams," New Left Review 168 (March-April 1988): 9-10.
An obituary to this author of espionage novels. See a major investigation into his novels in Bruce Robbins (ed.), Intellectuals: Aesthetics, Politics, Academics. Minneapolis: University of Minnesota, 1990, pp. 273-290.

9138. Earle, Rebecca. "Information and Disinformation in Late Colonial New Grenada," Americas: A Quarterly Review of Inter-American Cultural History 54/2 (October 1997): 167-184.
Discusses the role of the spoken word versus the written word in the social construction of rumor in colonial and independence-era New Grenada.

9139. Earling, William. "Design for Jet-Age Reporting," Studies in Intelligence 4/1 (Spring 1960).

9140. East, Sherrod. "In Memoriam, Jesse Steiwer Douglas, 1909-1965," American Archivist 28/4 (1965): 611-612.

9141. Easterby, J. H. "Captain Langdon Cheves, Jr., and the Confederates Silk Dress Balloon," South Carolina Historical and Geneological Magazine 45 (January 1944): 1-11.
    This article is continued in 45 (April 1944): 99-110.

9142. Earthart, Robert S. and Peter A. Lupsha. "Proactive Intelligence to Combat Organized Crime: Rocky Mountain and Sunbelt States Combat Organized Crime," Police Chief 48/11 (November 1981): 29-31.

9143. Ebersole, J. F. "Skimmer Ops," U.S. Naval Institute Proceedings 100/7 (1974): 40-46.

9144. Ecklund, George. "Guns or Butter Problems of the Cold War," Studies in Intelligence 9/3 (Fall 1965).

9145. Eckman, Paul and Wallace V. Friesen. "Nonverbal Leakage and Clues to Deception," Psychiatry 32 (1969): 88-106.
    Major sections discuss definitions of deception at the individual level; dimensions of deceptive situations; sending capacity, external feedback, and internal feedback; and illustrative experiments.

9146. Eckman, Paul and Wallace V. Friesen. "Detecting Deception from the Body or Face," Journal of Personality and Social Psychology 29 (1974): 288-298.
    Reflects findings of a study aimed at two hypotheses concerning differences between the face and body when people employ deception. Discusses methodology, results, discussion of results, and need for further research.

9147. Edbrook, C. D. "Principles of Deep Cover," Studies in Intelligence 5/1 (Spring 1961).
    A rare early discussion of tradecraft principles.

9148. Edelstein, Jonathan I. "Anonymity and International Law Enforcement in Cyberspace," Fordham Intellectual Property, Media & Entertainment Law Journal 7 (Autumn 1996): 231-294.

9149. Edgette, Judith. "Domestic Collection on Cuba," Studies in Intelligence 7/3 (Fall 1963).

9150. Editor(s). <u>Studies in Intelligence</u>.
        Various editors have contributed introductory commentaries, essays, or statements through the years, some of which have been declassified and available to the public. Some of these items contain substantive information that may have value in research and publication on intelligence topics. A list of declassified <u>Studies</u> articles is available on the internet: http://www.odci.gov/csi.

9151. Edwards, Francis S. J. "Still Investigating Gunpowder Plot," <u>Recusant History</u> 21 (1993).

9152. Edwards, Philip K. "The President's Board: 1956-1960," <u>Studies in Intelligence</u> 13/2 (Summer 1969).

9153. Eisenberg, Stephen A. J. "Graymail and Gray Hairs: The Classified and Official Information Privileges Under the Military Rules of Evidence," <u>Army Lawyer</u> (March 1981): 5-18.

9154. Eisenhower, Dwight D. "From the CIA Cornerstone Ceremonies," <u>Studies in Intelligence</u> 4/4 (Winter 1960).
        This item contains the remarks of President Eisenhower at the ceremonies dedicating the new CIA's headquarters at Langley, Virginia.

9155. Eisenstadt, Michael. "The Iraqi Armed Forces Two Years On," <u>Jane's Intelligence Review</u> (March 1993): 121-127.

9156. Ekirch, Arthur A., Jr. "Eisenhower and Kennedy: The Rhetoric and the Reality," <u>Midwest Quarterly</u> 17/3 (1976): 279-290.

9157. Eliav, Mordechai. "Involvement of German and Austrian Diplomats in Palestine, 1917," <u>Cathedra</u> 48 (1988): 90-124.

9158. Eliot, Frank. "Moon Bouce Elint," <u>Studies in Intelligence</u> 11/1 (Spring 1967).

9159. Elison, Larry M. and Deborah E. "Comments on Government Censorship and Secrecy," <u>Montana Law Review</u> 55 (Winter 1994): 175-208.
        Detailed review of right to know laws and the concepts and issues surrounding freedom of information.

9160. Elkes, Martin C. "LAMS Story," <u>Studies in Intelligence</u> 19/2 (Summer 1975).

9161. Ellenport, Samuel. "American Foreign Policy and Mass Democracy," <u>American Scholar</u> 36/4 (1967): 589-593.

9162. Elliott, Kim A. "Too Many Voices of America," Foreign Policy 77 (Winter 1989): 113-131.

A discussion of the then-current operations of the Voice of America, including relocation of sites to lower operating costs and to preclude jamming.

9163. Ellis, Kenneth L. "British Communications and Diplomacy Since 1844," Society of Archivists Journal 4 (April 1973): 592-595.

Discusses in brief some aspects of spying in Britain after 1844.

9164. Ellis, Mark. "J. Edgar Hoover and the 'Red Summer' of 1919," Journal of American Studies 28/1 (1994): 39-59.

A study of Hoover's conduct of investigations into African-American dissident organizations leading up to and including several riots in the summer of 1919. Useful in historical studies of domestic intelligence against alleged dissident groups.

9165. Ellis, Mark S. "Purging the Past: The Current State of Lustration Laws in the Former Communist Bloc," Law and Contemporary Problems 59 (Autumn 1996): 181-196.

Lustration laws apply to the screening and prosecution of former communist leaders, candidates for office, and selected public officials. They depend on the information contained in files of secret police organizations, such as the KGB and the STASI. This article reviews the status of lustration laws in several former Soviet states.

9166. Elton, G. R. "Informing for Profit: A Sidelight on Tudor Methods of Law-Enforcement," Cambridge Historical Journal 11(1953): 149-167.

9167. Elzweig, Thomas F. "The Shorthand of Experience," Studies in Intelligence 3/2 (Spring 1959): 31-45.

Discussion of actions applied to the recruitment of intelligence agents, particularly Czech handling of a German walk-in.

9168. Engeljohn, Earl D. "Half a Million Wanted Persons," Studies in Intelligence 7/2 (Summer 1963).

9169. Eriksson, Par. "Intelligence in Peacekeeping Operations," International Journal of Intelligence and Counterintelligence 10/1 (Spring 1997): 1-18.

Major sections discuss conflicts and peacekeeping in the 1990s; intelligence in peace support operations today; intelligence and the credibility of the peacekeeping units; intelligence and the troops of contributing nations; intelligence process adapted to peacekeeping operations; UN peacekeeping methods; processing and analysis; frameworks for creating patterns; indicators and concepts; dissemination; and overcoming intelligence absence.

9170. Ergetowski, Ryszard. "Karol Forster w Swietle Korespondencji z J. I. Kraszewskim," <u>Przeglad Polonijny</u> 19/3 (1993): 147-162.

9171. Ernst, Anna-Sabine. "Between 'Investigative History' and Solid Research: A Reorganization of Historical Studies About the Former German Democratic Republic," <u>Central European History</u> 28/3 (1995): 373-395.

   Major sections discuss arguments and interests; the new research institutions in Berlin-Brandenburg; and conclusions. Briefly discusses records on the GDR intelligence agency, the Stasi.

9172. Erskine, Ralph. "Naval Enigma: An Astonishing Blunder," <u>Intelligence and National Security</u> 11/3 (July 1996): 468-473.

   Major sections discuss naval enigma keying methods; Sud and double encipherment; breaking Sud; and conclusions.

9173. Erskine, Ralph. "Churchill and the Start of the Ultra-Magic Deals," <u>International Journal of Intelligence and Counterintelligence</u> 10/1 (Spring 1997): 57-74.

   This expert on the Ultra secrets explores new territory. Following are major sections of this article: first steps toward cryptanalytic cooperation; the Sinkov mission; Churchill enters the picture; and extraordinary foresight.

9174. Erskine, Ralph. "Eavesdropping on 'Bodden': ISOS v. the Abwehr in the Straits," <u>Intelligence and National Security</u> 12/3 (July 1997): 110-129.

   According to the abstract, this article describes "British efforts during the Second World War to counter an Abwehr ship-reporting organization in the Straits of Gibraltar, known as the 'Bodden' line, which employed advanced infra-red equipment for night observation purposes." Major sections discuss the history of Bodden; Naval Intelligence Directorate alarm; Bodden and the Torch convoys; and conclusions.

9175. Erskine, Ralph. "When a Purple Machine Went Missing: How Japan Nearly Discovered America's Greatest Secret," <u>Intelligence and National Security</u> 12/3 (July 1997): 185-189.

   A research note on the implications of the loss of the American capability to decipher Japanese Foreign Office codes when a machine turned up missing in a war zone in 1942.

9176. Erwin, Robert. "Oppenheimer Investigated," <u>Wilson Quarterly</u> 18/4 (1994): 34-45.

   Summarizes J. Robert Oppenheimer's life and work, including his achievements in World War II; the security clearance review; and the award of the Fermi prize in physics in 1963.

9177. Eustace, Denys. "La Montee en Puissance de la Gendarmarie," <u>Defense Nationale</u> 51 (December 1995): 51-57.

9178. Evans, Charles L. "U.S. Export Control of Encryption Software: Efforts to Protect National Security Threaten the U.S. Software Industry's Ability to Compete in Foreign Markets," <u>North Carolina Journal of International Law & Commercial Regulation</u> 19 (Summer 1994): 469-490.

9179. Expatriate [pseud.]. "Reminiscences of a Communications Agent," <u>Studies in Intelligence</u> 2 (Fall 1958).

9180. Eysturlid, Lee W. "'An Opportunity to Show Their Epaulets and Feathers': The South Carolina Militia During the First Secession Crisis, 1848-1851," <u>Armed Forces & Society</u> 20/2 (1994): 303-316.
    The title captures the contents fairly well. This study will find application in investigations of 19th century domestic intelligence activities, particularly advanced by military organizations.

9181. Faint, Donald R. and Robert M. Gearhart. "Special Operations Intelligence: Meeting 21st Century Challenges," <u>American Intelligence Journal</u> 17/3&4 (1997): 23-26.
    Major sections discuss Special Operations Forces (SOF); priorities; dissemination; emerging technologies; and the challenge.

9182. Fairley, Douglas. "D Notices, Official Secrets and the Law," <u>Oxford Journal of Legal Studies</u> 10/3 (1990): 430-440.

9183. Faligot, Roger. "The Plot to Unseat Qaddafi," <u>Middle East</u> (August 1981): 32-36.

9184. Faligot, Roger. "Les Agents de la Chine Nouvelle," <u>Politique Internationale: Revue Trimestrille</u> (Winter 1996-1997): 429-437.
    Discusses Chinese intelligence services in the current context of information warfare.

9185. Farndon, Stanley B. "The Interrogation of Defectors," <u>Studies in Intelligence</u> 4/2 (Summer 1960).

9186. Farnham, Barbara. "Roosevelt and the Munich Crisis: Insights from Prospect Theory," <u>Political Psychology</u> 13/2 (1992): 205-235.
    A discussion of the theory of frame change in association with the German Munich crisis during Franklin Roosevelt's administration of the US-Nazi Germany war. Useful in analyses of perceptions and surprise.

9187. Fauth, James J. "Adversary Agent Radios," <u>Studies in Intelligence</u> 10/4 (Winter 1966).

9188. Featherstone, James W. "Cloud Nine: A Problem in Intelligence Production," <u>Studies in Intelligence</u> 13/3 (Fall 1969).

9189. Feifer, George. "The Berlin Tunnel," <u>MHQ: The Quarterly Journal of Military History</u> 10/2 (Winter 1998): 62-71.
The story of CIA's project to tunnel under the East-West border in Berlin, Germany in 1953. The architect of the plan was CIA station chief Bill Harvey. The tunnel project was eventually spotted by the Soviets, an effort aimed at compromising Soviet communications systems.

9190. Feintuck, Mike. "Government Control of Information: Some British Developments," <u>Government Information Quarterly</u> 13/4 (1996): 345-359.

9191. Feldman, Martha S. and James G. March. "Information in Organizations as Signal and Symbol," <u>Administrative Science Quarterly</u> 26 (June 1981): 171-186.
Discusses theories and illustrations of the role of information in organizations. Sections discuss information and organizational choice; information incentives, gossip, and misrepresentation; information as symbol and signal; the dynamics of symbols; and conclusions about organizational choice and excess supply of information.

9192. Fels, William B. "A Union Military Intelligence Failure: Jubal Early's Raid, June 12-July 14, 1864," <u>Civil War History</u> 36/3 (1990): 209-225.

9193. Ferrill, Arther. "The Second-Oldest Profession," <u>MHQ: The Quarterly Journal of Military History</u> 3/1 (Autumn 1990).

9194. Ferris, John P. "'Worthy of Some Better Enemy?': The British Estimate of the Imperial Japanese Army 1919-41 and the Fall of Singapore," <u>Canadian Journal of History</u> 28/2 (August 1993): 223-256.
Discusses the historical accounts and associated evidence for the humiliating defeat of the British military in Malaya, caused mainly by gross deficiencies in intelligence estimates of the Imperial Japanese Army.

9195. Ferris, John P. "'Indulged in All Too Little'?: Vansittart, Intelligence and Appeasement," <u>Diplomacy & Statecraft</u> 6/1 (March 1995).

9196. Ferris, John P. "Coming in from the Cold: The Historiography of American Intelligence, 1945-1990," <u>Diplomatic History</u> 19/1 (Winter 1995): 87-115.

A detailed outline of the stages of evolution of US intelligence throughout the Cold War era. Provides an excellent overview of the organizations, personalities, and events of the era and provides numerous reference notes to other useful works. Suggests that substantially more work is required of historians and others to piece together the history of American intelligence during the period.

9197. Fialka, John J. "Stealing the Spark: Why Economic Espionage Works in America," Washington Quarterly 19/4 (Autumn 1996): 175-189.

Major sections discuss the shrinking dream; losing America's "crown jewels"; friends and neighbors; inventors and thieves; and litigation without end.

9198. Fialka, John J. "While America Sleeps," Wilson Quarterly 21/1 (Winter 1997): 48-63.

Key subjects under discuss include industrial espionage, trade secrets concepts and practice, competitive intelligence, and national security issues.

9199. Fichtner, David P. "Intelligence Assessment in the Peloponnesian War," Studies in Intelligence Unclassified edition (Fall 1994): 59-64.

Presents a controversial view of the subject.

9200. Fields, Thomas J. "Thinking About Defense Humint for the Future," Defense Intelligence Journal 6/1 (Spring 1997): 63-70.

Major sections discuss what is needed; why more Humint is needed; and challenges to be faced.

9201. Findley, Paul. "The Middle East Angle of the Pollard Case," Washington Report on Middle East Affairs 15 (May-June 1996): 18, 103.

This is not a refereed journal, but the piece is considered worthy of mention since it provides a useful update to the controversial Pollard espionage case. Contains insights into the Israeli and US sentiments toward spy Pollard.

9202. Finer, Sydney W. "The Kidnapping of the Lunik," Studies in Intelligence 11/4 (Winter 1967).

9203. Finn, Peter and Daniel McGillis. "Public Safety at the State Level: A Survey of Major Services," Journal of Police Science and Administration 17/2 (1990): 133-146.

Discusses data and results of a survey of police functions, including investigative and intelligence functions.

9204. Fischer, Ben B. "'One of the Biggest Ears in the World': East German SIGINT," International Journal of Intelligence and Counterintelligence 11/2 (Summer 1998): 142-153.

Major sections discuss the pride of Maennchen; widespread operations; call home with discretion; valuable results; overcoming barriers; an unrevealed hand; and the cause that failed. Includes an outline of the HA III organization.

9205. Fischer, Joseph R. "Cut From a Different Cloth: The Origins of U.S. Army Special Forces," New England Journal of History 51/1 (1994): 2-23.

A useful history of the idea and implementation of the special forces units which had their origins in World War II OSS operations, followed by postwar covert actions.

9206. Fishel, Edwin C. "Military Intelligence 1861-63, Part I," Studies in Intelligence 10/1 (Summer 1966).

9207. Fishel, Edwin C. "Military Intelligence 1861-63, Part II," Studies in Intelligence 10/3 (Fall 1966).

9208. Fishel, Edwin C. "Civil War Intelligence: A New Perspective on Command Decisions," American Intelligence Journal 17/1&2 (1996): 79-84.

Discusses first Bull Run and the "phony war"; second Bull Run; Antietam campaign; Fredericksburg; Chancellorsville; Richmond; Richmond campaign; and the intelligence balance.

9209. Fitzpatrick, James K. "The Supreme Court's Bipolar Approach to the Interpretation of 18 U.S.C. 1503 and 18 U.S.C. 2232(c)," Journal of Criminal Law and Criminology 86/4 (Summer 1996): 1383-1410.

Considers aspects of these statutory provisions concerning wiretaps as taken up in United States v. Aguilar. Major sections discuss the history of the sections; facts and procedural history; summary and opinions; analysis of the Supreme Court decision; and conclusions.

9210. Fitz-Simons, Daniel E. "Francis Marion the 'Swamp Fox': An Anatomy of a Low-Intensity Conflict," Small Wars and Insurgencies 6/1 (1995): 1-16.

A detailed consideration of Marion's strategies and tactics learned from the Cherokee indians prior to the American revolution. Useful in studies of the transfer of learning how to conduct various intelligence tactics from indians to white military strategists and leaders.

9211. Flanagan, Julie A. "Restricting Electronic Monitoring in the Private Workplace," Duke Law Journal 43 (April 1994): 1256-1281.

9212. Flemer, Sherman W. "Soviet Intelligence Training," Studies in Intelligence 3/4 (Winter 1959).

9213. Fletcher, Katy. "Evolution of the Modern American Spy Novel," Journal

of Contemporary History 22/2 (April 1987): 319-331.
Suggests several reasons for the rise of the modern spy novel. Mentions several novels, and novelists who represent the approaches and perspectives of novel writing in recent times.

9214. Flood, Michael. "Nuclear Sabotage," Bulletin of the Atomic Scientists 32/8 (1976): 29-36.

9215. Flooks, Henry. "Chinese Defections Overseas," Studies in Intelligence 9/3 (Fall 1965).

9216. Flynn, Michael T. "Intelligence Must Drive Operations," Infantry 87/3 (July-December 1997): 28-33.
A summary of the role of military intelligence in field planning and operations.

9217. Flynn, Richard. "Estimating Soviet Gold Production," Studies in Intelligence 19/3 (Fall 1975).

9218. Flynn, Sean M. "A Puzzle Even the Codebreakers Have Trouble Solving: A Clash of Interests Over the Electronic Encryption Standard," Law and Policy in International Business 27 (Fall 1995): 217-246.

9219. Foot, Michael R. D. "Reflections on SOE," Manchester Literary and Philosophical Society Memoirs and Proceedings 111 (1968-1969): 87-96.

9220. Forbush, Ramsey; Gary Chase; and Ronald Goldberg. "CIA Intelligence Support for Foreign and National Security Policy Making," Studies in Intelligence 20/1 (Spring 1976).

9221. Ford, Christopher A. "Watching the Watchdog: Security Oversight in the New South Africa," Michigan Journal of Race & Law 3 (Fall 1997): 59-110.
This article is one of several in the issue in a symposium on constitution making in South Africa.

9222. Ford, Corey. "'Our German Wehrmacht Is Being Stopped by a Shadow,'" American Heritage 21/2 (1970): 56-57, 85-92.

9223. Ford, Harold P. "The U.S. Decision to Go Big in Vietnam," Studies in Intelligence 29/1 (Spring 1985): 3-11.
Escalation of the war in Vietnam proceeded along lines of reasoning that determined the best policy was to severely punish North Vietnam despite the apparent loss of political stability in the South. Several in the CIA believed that the punishment approach was probably wrong due to the indigenous nature of

enemy strength. Reports also on the process followed in the war game known as SIGMA-I.

9224. Ford, Harold P. "William Colby: Retrospect," <u>Studies in Intelligence</u> Unclassified edition (1997): 1-5.

A dedicatory essay in honor of the late William Colby, former director of the Central Intelligence Agency. Recognizes the high points of Colby's career and some of the criticisms he encountered during his final years at CIA. Mr. Colby died in a boating accident.

9225. Ford, Harold P. "Why CIA Analysts Were So Doubtful About Vietnam," <u>Studies in Intelligence</u> Unclassified edition (1997): 85-95

Discusses various advantages of the analytical staff in viewing the circumstances of the advancing stages of the Vietnam war; areas of doubt; what analysts were up against; classic analytic hazards; and illustrative quotations.

9226. Forster, H. A. "Summary Dealing with Spies," <u>American Law Review</u> 51 (July 1917): 587-590.

9227. Forster, H. A. "Military Jurisdiction Over Spies and Sympathizers," <u>American Legal News</u> 28 (1917): 25.

9228. Fortmann, Michel and David G. Haglund. "Public Diplomacy and Dirty Tricks: Two Faces of United States "Informal Penetration" of Latin America on the Eve of World War II," <u>Diplomacy & Statecraft</u> 6/2 (1995): 536-577.

9229. Framingham, Richard. "Career Trainee Program, GRU Style," <u>Studies in Intelligence</u> 10/3 (Fall 1966).

9230. Fraumann, Edwin. "Economic Espionage: Security Missions Redefined," <u>Public Administration Review</u> 57 (1997): 303-308.

Major sections consider the scope of the problem of economic espionage; conducting economic espionage by intrusive and nonintrusive methods; economic espionage activities; economic espionage across countries; role of federal agencies in protecting US interests; statutory protection; and private sector initiatives to counter economic espionage.

9231. Fredman, Jonathan M. "Covert Action, Loss of Life, and the Prohibition on Assassination: Policy and Law," <u>Studies in Intelligence</u> Unclassified edition (1997): 15-25.

Major sections discuss the end of assassination as an instrument of US policy; the prohibition and related policies; the experience since 1976; four major categories; lethal operations directly risking loss of life; lethal operations indirectly risking loss of life; nonlethal operations directed at identifiable persons; nonlethal operations not directed at identifiable persons; and conclusions. An erratum is published in the spring 1998 unclassified and unnumbered issue, pp. 119-120.

9232. Freedman, Lawrence. "The CIA and the Soviet Threat: The Politicization of Estimates, 1966-1977," Intelligence and National Security 12/1 (January 1997): 122-142.

      An article in five major sections which addresses the formulation and application of National Intelligence Estimates regarding Soviet military and nuclear capabilities during the period.

9233. Freedman, Lawrence. "Powerful Intelligence," Intelligence and National Security 12/2 (April 1997): 198-202.

      A book review essay of Michael Herman's Intelligence Power in Peace and War (1996).

9234. Freeman, J. F. "A New Source for Figures on Soviet Military Output," Studies in Intelligence 6/2 (Spring 1962).

9235. Freeman, Laurie N. "U.S. Canadian Information Sharing and the International Antitrust Enforcement Assistance Act of 1994," Georgetown Law Journal 84 (December 1995): 339-371.

      Regarding antitrust enforcement practices, major sections discuss access to information and confidentiality in the US; access and confidentiality in Canada; US-Canadian enforcement cooperation; International Antitrust Enforcement Assistance Act; and various imbalances that make the Act less than successful.

9236. French, William J. "The Scott Amendment to the Patent Revision Act: Should Trade Secrets Receive Federal Protection," Wisconsin Law Review (1971): 900-921.

      Discusses an overview of trade secret law; the Sears, Compco, and Lear cases; section 301 of the Scott amendment; and conclusions.

9237. Freshwater, J. L. "Policy and Intelligence: The Arab-Israeli War," Studies in Intelligence 13/4 (Winter 1969).

9238. Freudenrich, L. Ben. "An Arcane Art of Necrology," Studies in Intelligence 21/2 (Summer 1977).

9239. Fricke, Graham L. "The Eureka Trials," Australian Law Journal 71 (January 1997): 59-69.

      Addresses issue of jury role in treason trials in Australia.

9240. Friedberg, Aaron L. "Science, the Cold War, and the State," Diplomatic History 20/1 (1996): 107-118.

A review essay which may be useful in studies of the relationship between scientists and the production of secret weapons.

9241. Friedman, Hal M. "The Beast in Paradise: The United States Navy in Micronesia, 1943-1947," Pacific Historical Review 62 (May 1993): 173-195.
A useful background piece on American post-war efforts to gain strategic influence, perhaps even control, in the Indonesian region. Discusses economic and racial dimensions in the region.

9242. Friedman, Hal M. "Modified Mahanianism: Pearl Harbor, the Pacific War, and Changes to U.S. National Security Strategy in the Pacific Basin, 1945-1947," Hawaiian Journal of History 31 (1997): 179-204.
Argues the extreme impact of the Pearl Harbor attack on the American policies toward Asia and in terms of general orientation to national security planning.

9243. Friedman, Hal M. "The 'Bear' in the Pacific? US Intelligence Perceptions of Soviet Strategic Power Projection in the Pacific Basin and East Asia, 1945-1947," Intelligence and National Security 12/4 (October 1997): 75-101.
A richly detailed analysis of the subject containing sections as follows: the context; the 'Bear' in the Pacific?; and assessment.

9244. Froomkin, A. Michael. "It Came From Planet Clipper: The Battle Over Cryptographic Key 'Escrow,'" University of Chicago Legal Forum (1996): 15-50.

9245. Frost, David. "An Interview with Richard Helms," Studies in Intelligence 25/3 (Fall 1981).

9246. Fryxell, Alma. "Psywar by Forgery," Studies in Intelligence 5/4 (Winter 1961).
Reflections on Soviet psychological warfare.

9247. Fu, H. L. and Richard Cullen. "National Security Law in China," Columbia Journal of Transnational Law 34/2 (1996): 449-468.
An overview of the topic containing major sections in which the following subjects are discussed: background; structure and application of national security law in China; accountability; and conclusions.

9248. Fuller, Kenneth C.; Bruce Smith; and Merle Atkins. "'Rolling Thunder' and Bomb Damage to Bridges," Studies in Intelligence 13/3 (Fall 1969).

9249. Funk, Arthur L. and Carole Bquin. "Les Americains et les Britanniques dans la Liberation de la Corse," Guerres Mondiales et Conflits Contemporains

44/174 (1994): 7-21.

In French, the title of this piece is roughly translated as "The Americans and the British in the Liberation of Corsica."

9250. Gabriel, Richard A. "Lessons of War: The IDF in Lebanon," Military Review 64/8 (August 1984): 47-65.

An analysis of the Israeli Defense Force performance in the war of 1973 with Lebanon in terms of tactics; armor; infantry; artillery; medical care; engineers; logistics; and the cost of the war.

9251. Gafford, Richard. "The Operational Potential of Subliminal Perception," Studies in Intelligence 2 (Spring 1958).

Estimated to be 5 pages in length.

9252. Garofalo, Nicholas R. "Present and Future Capabilities of OTH Radars," Studies in Intelligence 13/1 (Spring 1969).

9253. Gale, David D. "United States v. Ozar: The Eighth Circuit Gives the FBI a Key," Creighton Law Review 29 (April 1996): 1278-1321.

Concerns a case in which electronic surveillance was used, and which eventually was challenged in the US Court of Appeals. Major sections discuss the background of warrantless searches; analysis of the holding in US v. Ozar.

9254. Galeotti, Mark. "Russia's Internal Security Forces--Does More Mean Better?," Jane's Intelligence Review 6 (June 1991): 271-272.

9255. Ganguly, Sumit. "Deterrence Failure Revisited: The Indo-Pakistani War of 1965," Journal of Strategic Studies 13/4 (December 1990): 76-85.

9256. Gannon, Michael. "Reopen the Kimmel Case," U.S. Naval Institute Proceedings 120 (1994): 51-56.

For those who maintain a deep interest in the circumstances surrounding the firing of Admiral Kimmel, and the later testimony given to the investigating committee of Congress on alleged failures of Kimmel's actions before the Pearl Harbor attack, this article adds new wrinkles. Asserts that evidence against Kimmel cannot be produced to establish failure to properly conduct reconnaissance missions to defend Pearl Harbor.

9257. Garcia, Thomas R. "Federal Courts--In re United States--Should Federal Magistrates Be Delegated the Authority to Approve Electronic Surveillance Applications?," Western New England Law Review 18 (Winter 1996): 271-303.

9258. Gardiner, S. R. "Two Declarations of Garnet Relating to the Gunpowder Plot," English Historical Review 3 (1888).

9259. Garrett, Clarke. "The Strange Career of Junius Frey: Utopian Dreamer or Austrian Spy?," Proceedings of the Annual Meeting of the Western Society for French History 20 (1993): 167-175.

9260. Garrett, G. P. "Free Speech and the Espionage Act," Journal of the American Institute of Criminal Law and Criminology 10 (May 1919): 71-75.

9261. Garst, Ronald D. and Max L. Gross. "On Becoming an Intelligence Analyst," Defense Intelligence Journal 6/2 (Fall 1997): 47-59.
Sections discuss some general thoughts; the knowledge base; information, the raw material of analysis; analytical skills; presentation skills; educating the analyst; intelligence training; and the need to maintain a commitment to the analyst.

9262. Garthoff, Raymond L. "Some Observations on Using the Soviet Archives," Diplomatic History 21/2 (Spring 1997): 243-257.
Major sections discuss the Soviet decision to deploy missiles in Cuba; the question of nuclear weapons in Cuba; tactical nuclear weapons and pre-delegated authority for deployment; shootdown of the U-2; the Fomin-Seali back channel; Dobrynin, Robert Kennedy and the Jupiters in Turkey; the Cordier ploy; Castro's call for Soviet nuclear preemption; and how close was the world to nuclear catastrophe.

9263. Gasser, William R. "Aerial Photography of Agriculture," Studies in Intelligence 11/3 (Fall 1967).

9264. Gates, Robert M. "The Prediction of Soviet Intentions," Studies in Intelligence 17/1 (Spring 1973).

9265. Gates, Robert M. "Le Renseignement, la Communaute Internationale, et le Nouveau Desorde Mondial," Defense Nationale 52 (April 1996): 152-160.

9266. Gazit, Shlomo. "Intelligence and the Peace Process in Israel," Intelligence and National Security 12/3 (July 1997): 35-66.
Major sections consider an introduction to the three phases of the peace process (prior to negotiation; in support of negotiations; and post-agreement); intelligence needs in the future agreement; and personal impressions with respect to intelligence and the peace process.

9267. Gelber, Yoav. "The Activities of the Jewish Agency's Political Department in Egypt, 1944-48," Cathedra 67 (1993): 24-53.

9268. Gemmer, Karl H. "Police and Crime Control in the Federal Republic of Germany," New York Police Studies 1/1 (1978): 55-61.

9269. Gentry, John A. "Knowledge-Based 'Warfare': Lessons from Bosnia," American Intelligence Journal 18/1&2 (1998): 73-80.

Major sections discuss operation Joint Endeavor; knowledge-based failures; failure to learn from UNPROFOR; lack of preparation of personnel; dysfunctional personnel policies; inept information gathering; disregard for non-military information sources; poor analytic abilities; inability to use open-source information; self-imposed communications constraints; problems of people; incomplete IFOR information campaign; and lessons of the Bosnian experience.

9270. George, Theodore A. "Calculation of Soviet Helicopter Performance," Studies in Intelligence 3 (Fall 1959).

9271. Gerard, John. "Traditional History and the Spanish Treason of 1601-1603," Month 87 (1896).

9272. Geschwind, C. N. "Wanted: An Integrated Counterintelligence," Studies in Intelligence 7/2 (Summer 1963).

9273. Geschwind, C. N. "Counterintelligence Interrogation," Studies in Intelligence 9/4 (Winter 1965).

9274. Ghirardo, Diane Y. "'Citta Fascista': Surveillance and Spectacle," Journal of Contemporary History 31/2 (April 1986): 347-372.

A discussion of fascist propaganda and domestic security in the 1920s and 1930s.

9275. Gibbs, David N. "Secrecy and International Relations," Journal of Peace Research 32/2 (1995): 213-228.

An inquiry into American covert action in the Congo in the early 1960s. Alleges misdeeds by the Central Intelligence Agency. Useful in analyses of intelligence organizations in Africa during the Eisenhower and Kennedy years.

9276. Gibson, Dirk C. "A Quantitative Description of FBI Public Relations," Public Relations Review 23 (Spring 1997): 11-30.

9277. Gibson, T. A. "A Teutonic Knight," Army Quarterly 87 (October 1963): 77-86.

Discusses the life and career of Nazi intelligence officer Klaus von Stauffenberg.

9278. Gilcher-Holtey, Ingrid. "Menschenrecht oder Vaterland? Die Formierung der Intellektuellen in der Affare Dreyfus," Berlin Journal of Sociology 7/1 (1997): 61-70.

In German, this is a discussion of various dimensions of the espionage charges brought against the French military officer Alfred Dreyfus.

9279. Gill, Peter. "'Sack the Spooks': Do We Need an Internal Security Apparatus?," Socialist Register (1996).

9280. Gillispie, Charles C. "Science and Secret Weapons Development in Revolutionary France, 1792-1804: A Documentary History," Historical Studies in the Physical and Biological Sciences 23/1 (1992): 35-192.
　　　　A detailed and rich discussion of the relationship between scientists and their patrons in the 19th century. Particularly useful in studies of advancements in intelligence collection pertaining to new weapons of war.

9281. Gingrich, Gerry. "The Agile Mind of Leadership," Defense Intelligence Journal 7/1 (Spring 1998): 67-77.
　　　　Argues that new thinking and leadership in intelligence organizations requires intuition, creativity, and ingenuity. Major sections discuss old or new ways of thinking about variables in the problem's simplicity or complexity; linear or nonlinear thinking; and universal or specific thinking.

9282. Gioumau, Walter H. "Good Old Days - 'You Are on Your Own,'" Studies in Intelligence 15/4 (Winter 1971).

9283. Girling, John. "Agents of Influence," Australian Outlook 38 (August 1984): 111-114.

9284. Girodo, Michel. "Symptomatic Reactions to Undercover Work," Journal of Nervous and Mental Disease 179 (1991): 626-630.

9285. Glancy, Dorothy. "The U.S. Crime of Trade Secret Theft," European Intellectual Property Review 1 (July 1979): 179-182.

9286. Glenn, John M. "Father of the Green Berets," Military History (February 1998): 50-56.
　　　　An interview with Aaron Bank, who took the first steps to create a covert action and guerilla force command as part of the Office of Strategic Services in World War II.

9287. Glynn, Sean and Alan Booth. "The Public Records Office and Recent British Economic Historiography," Economic History Review 32/3 (August 1979): 303-315.
　　　　Remarks on the caution necessary in conducting research using state papers of the Public Records Office. May be useful as a reference in research on intelligence records.

9288. Goldberg, Stanley. "Racing to the Finish: The Decision to Bomb Hiroshima and Nagasaki," Journal of American-East Asian Relations 4/2 (1995): 117-128.

Alleges, through interpretations of various archival documents, that a central motivation for dropping atomic weapons on the two locations was fear that a congressional investigation might have been launched to probe the justification for the Manhattan project. Useful in analyses of roles played by intelligence and technical advisers to presidents, in particular, the biases carried into the decision making process.

9289. Goldstein, Erik. "British Peace Aims and the Eastern Question: The Political Intelligence Department and the Eastern Committee, 1918," Middle East Studies 23/4 (1987): 419-436.

9290. Goldstein, Erik. "New Diplomacy and the New Europe at the Paris Peace Conference of 1919," East European Quarterly 21/4 (1988): 393-400.

9291. Goldwasser, Katherine. "After Abscam: An Examination of Congressional Proposals to Limit Targeting Discretion in Federal Undercover Investigations," Emory Law Journal 36/1 (1987): 75-147.

Major sections discuss existing limitations on federal undercover targeting discretion; legislative recommendations for regulating federal undercover targeting discretion; critique of the House and Senate committee recommendations; and conclusions.

9292. Goode, Matthew. "'Obey the Law and Keep Your Mouths Shut': German Americans in Grand Rapids During World War I," Michigan History 78/2 (1994): 18-23.

Discusses the duplicity involved in the protection of civil rights and civil liberties of German-American citizens in the months preceding US involvement in World War I. Useful in analyses of the cross currents of justice administration in connection with national security under strains of potential domestic espionage of sabotage by groups perceived to maintain loyalties to an external enemy.

9293. Goodell, Thaxter L. "Cratology Pays Off," Studies in Intelligence 8/3 (Fall 1964).

9294. Goodman, Allan E. "Anatomy of PRM-8," Studies in Intelligence 21/4 (Winter 1977).

9295. Goodman, Allan E. "The Future of Intelligence," Intelligence and National Security 11/4 (October 1996): 645-656.

The author discusses the current situation with US intelligence community reforms; the institutional response; ahead, the changing paradigms;

finding the right stuff; and intelligence role and organization for the twenty-first century.

9296. Goodman, Melvin A. "Ending the CIA's Cold War Legacy," Foreign Policy 106 (Spring 1997): 128-143.

9297. Gora, Joseph M. "The Day the Presses Stopped: A History of the Pentagon Papers Case," Cardoza Law Review 19 (March 1998): 1311-1328.

9298. Gordenker, Leon. "Early-Warning of Disastrous Population Movement," International Migration Review 20 (Summer 1986): 170-189.
    An analysis of existing and potential early warning facilities in man-made disasters which induce forced movement of people. Sections discuss the nature of early warning; using early warning; organizing for early warning; receivers of early warning; the political tinge of early warning; and conclusions.

9299. Gordievsky, Oleg. "New Memoirs from Moscow," Intelligence and National Security 11/3 (July 1996): 586-605.
    A book review essay of nine books, most published in Russian.

9300. Gordon, Don E. "The CEWI Battalion: A Tactical Concept That Works," Military Review 60/1 (1980): 2-12.

9301. Gorman, Paul F. "Measuring the Military Balance in Central Europe," Studies in Intelligence 23/4 (Winter 1979).

9302. Goss, Porter J. "Intelligence Authorization Act Report," American Intelligence Journal 17/3&4 (1997): 7-13.
    The chairman of the House Permanent Select Committee on Intelligence summarizes the scope of the Committee review; Committee findings and recommendations; shortfalls in all-source intelligence analysis; collection and downstream processing imbalance; clandestine HUMINT planning and funding; technical investments: overhead collection; intelligence system interoperability; declassification; national drug intelligence architecture; and overall perspective on the intelligence budget and committee intent.

9303. Gotanda, John Y. "Glomar Denials Under FOIA: A Problematic Privilege and a Proposed Alternative Procedure of Review," University of Pittsburgh Law Review 56 (Fall 1994): 165-168.
    Explores the problems associated with an agency's employment of a "Glomar denial" of an FOIA request. Major sections discuss overview of the FOIA; procedures for reviewing an agency's determination of privilege; privacy Glomarization; and alternative procedures.

9304. Goulter-Zervoudakis, Christina. "The Politicization of Intelligence: The British Experience in Greece, 1941-1944," Intelligence and National Security 13/1 (Spring 1998): 165-194.

A detailed and rare study of the role of SOE intelligence gathering activities in Greece during World War II, including discussion of the complexities of SOE entanglements with resistance groups of all political persuasions.

9305. Gourley, Robert D. "Intuitive Intelligence," Defense Intelligence Journal 6/2 (Fall 1997): 61-75.

Discusses a definition of intuition; current research; six proposed changes to the way analysts approach their positions and roles; and conclusions. An attachment to this article addresses intelligence assessment games.

9306. Gowing, Philip D. "Discovery! The Secret of Brunei Bay," Air Power History 42/1 (1995): 30-39.

An account of the author's photographic reconnaissance work to develop evidence of a Japanese amassing of naval vessels in the weeks following losses suffered in the Leyte Gulf battle.

9307. Goworek, Tomasz. "The U.S. Army Air Service's First Air-to-Air Victim May Have Arranged His Own Capture," Military History 11/4 (1994): 10-16.

An account of the US Air Service victories in the air over France in the early stages of World War I. One of the pilots had been involved in actions to bring about his own defection, a man who later became a Polish spy under cover of a career in the post war airplane business.

9308. Grabo, Cynthia M. "Strategic Warning: The Problem of Timing," Studies in Intelligence 16/1 (Spring 1972).

9309. Grabski, Andrzej F. "Nowe Raporty Szpiega," Przeglad Historyczny 82/3&4 (1991): 481-495.

In Polish, this is the author's account of espionage adventures.

9310. Graham, James. "Intelligence and Peacekeeping: Definitions and Limitations," Peacekeeping & International Relations 24 (November 1995): 3-9.

9311. Grant, Natalie. "The Russian Section, a Window on the Soviet Union," Diplomatic History 2/1 (1978): 107-115.

9312. Grant, Sam and Peter C. Oleson. "Breast Cancer Detection Research: Dual Use of Intelligence Technologies," Studies in Intelligence Unclassified edition (1997): 27-34.

Major sections discuss breast cancer national action plan; request for assistance, referring to the cooperation of the Central Intelligence Agency with the

National Information Display Laboratory (NIDL); technologies of interest; partnerships; NIDL background; intelligence community interest; and conclusions.

9313. Gravalos, Mary E. O.   "The Pitfall of a Latin Quirk," Studies in Intelligence 7/3 (Fall 1963).
> Reflections on wishful reporting.

9314. Gravalos, Mary E. O.   "A Good Trip," Studies in Intelligence 13/2 (Summer 1969).

9315. Graves, Harold N., Jr.   "Lord Haw Haw of Hamburg," Public Opinion Quarterly 4 (September 1940): 429-450.
> Discusses the espionage work of William Joyce.

9316. Gray, Colin S. "Three Visions of Future War," Queen's Quarterly 103/1 (Spring 1996): 35-48.
> Discusses the visions: information warfare and the information revolution; anarchy and the clash of civilizations; and the second nuclear age proliferation of nuclear weapons.

9317. Gray, William A. "Crystal Balls and Glass Bottles," Studies in Intelligence 12/1 (Spring 1968).

9318. Green, Harris. "Experience in War: Cloak-and-Dagger in Salzburg," MHQ: The Quarterly Journal of Military History 9/3 (Spring 1997).

9319. Green, Harold P. "The Unsystematic Security System," Bulletin of the Atomic Scientists 11 (April 1955): 118-121, 164.
> A discussion of the Cold War security system in the Atomic Energy Commission. Sections discuss the elements of the system; the early security measures; control of AEC data; proliferation of security statutes; Executive Orders; standards of security risk; E.O. criteria; AEC criteria; and the lack of affirmative requirements in the present standard.

9320. Greenlaw, Paul S. and Cornelia Prundeanu.   "The Impact of Federal Legislation to Limit Electronic Monitoring," Public Personnel Management 26 (Summer 1997): 227-244.

9321. Greenslade, Rush V. "Rubles Versus Dollars," Studies in Intelligence 6/4 (Winter 1962).

9322. Greenslade, Rush V. "CIA Meets the Press," Studies in Intelligence 13/1 (Spring 1969).

9323.   Greenslade, Rush V.   "The Many Burdens of Defense in the Soviet Union," Studies in Intelligence 14/3 (Fall 1970).

9324.   Greer, Kenneth E.   "Corona," Studies in Intelligence 17/Supplement (Spring 1973):   1-37.
A special report within CIA on the first US spy satellites.   A recent book on the subject was written by Curtis Peebles, The Corona Project: America's First Spy Satellites (Annapolis: Naval Institute Press, 1997).

9325.   Greer, Steven.   "Supergrasses and the Legal System in Britain and Northern Ireland," Law Quarterly Review (April 1986):   198-249.
Considers the role of police informers in Great Britain and Northern Ireland.

9326.   Grevling, Katharine.   "Undercover Operations: Balancing the Public Interest?," Law Quarterly Review 112 (July 1996):   401-403.
Reviews the circumstances in two drug case appeals in British courts, R. Latif and R. v. Shahzad.

9327.   Gries, David D.   "Openness at CIA," Cosmos 3 (1993):   25-29.

9328.   Gries, David D.   "Opening Up Secret Intelligence," Orbis 37/3 (Summer 1993):   365-372.
This author, a former CIA analyst, argues for a new openness policy and he attempts to place openness in perspective of recent history.   Also discusses openness and negative aspects, and considerations for the future.

9329.   Gries, David D.   "Commentary," Studies in Intelligence Unclassified edition (1996):   93-94.
The author's additional remarks pertaining to an article by James McCullough (see this bibliography) regarding CIA director Bill Casey's final month in office in late 1986.

9330.   Griffiths, J. A. G.   "The Official Secrets Act," Journal of Law and Society 16/2   (1989):   273-290.

9331.   Grimstead, Patricia K.   "Russian Archives in Transition: Caught Between Political Crossfire and Economic Crisis," American Archivist 56/4 (Fall 1993):   614-663.
A detailed report on the condition of the Soviet historical archives by an expert on the subject.   Major sections discuss the role of the State archival service in Russia; access and use; financial catastrophe; commercialization; politics and public views on outsider access; and reference facilities and information needs.

9332. Grinstein, Joseph. "Jihad and the Constitution: The First Amendment Implications of Combating Religiously Motivated Terrorism," Yale Law Journal 105 (March 1996): 1347-1381.

Major sections discuss religiously motivated terrorism within the borders of the United States; the hallowed constitutional position of religious belief; the view that the United States Supreme Court's inflexible definition of belief hampers group religious freedoms; placing limits on government's power; and conclusions.

9333. Grondona, L. St.Clare. "Sidelights on Wilton Park," Royal United Services Institution Journal 115 (December 1970): 34-37.

Discusses interrogation centers.

9334. Grosmere, Ellen. "An All-Purpose Data Handling System," Studies in Intelligence 7/2 (Summer 1963).

9335. Grossman, Joel B. "The Japanese American Cases and the Vagaries of Constitutional Adjudication in Wartime: An Institutional Perspective," Hawaii Law Review 19 (Fall 1997): 649-691.

9336. Grunden, Walter E. "Hungnam and the Japanese Atomic Bomb: Recent Historiography of a Postwar Myth," Intelligence and National Security 13/2 (Summer 1998): 32-60.

A lengthy analysis of the factors that contributed to the emergence and persistence of the myth that the Japanese had successfully tested a nuclear weapon in the last days of World War II. Major sections discuss the Snell story and postwar US intelligence investigations; Hungnam, heavy water, and the NZ-factory; and the exploded myth and recent historiography.

9337. Grundmann, William R. "Reshaping the Intelligence Production Landscape," Defense Intelligence Journal 6/2 (Fall 1997): 23-33.

Sections discuss organizational change; functional change; analytical community challenges; steps to shape the environment; and conclusions.

9338. Guensber, Gerold. "Abwehr Myth: How Efficient Was German Intelligence in World War II?," Studies in Intelligence 21/3 (Fall 1977).

9339. "Guerre de l'Information et Intelligence Economique et Strategique," Armement (December 1997-January 1998): 4-160.

The issue contains several articles, mostly in French, which are focused on information's role in war and intelligence in the larger strategic context.

9340. Guffey, Cynthia J. and Judy F. West. "Employee Privacy: Legal Implications for Managers," Labor Law Journal 47 (November 1996): 735-745.

Major sections discuss federal employee privacy statutes; privacy implications under common law; workplace issues regarding privacy and employee records; privacy and employee performance; electronic monitoring and surveillance; and arrests in the workplace.

9341. Guisnel, Jean. "Services Secrets: La Guerre de l'Information," Politique Internationale: Revue Trimestrille (Winter 1996-1997): 339-352.

9342. Gunter, Michael M. "Political Instability in Turkey during the 1970s," Conflict Quarterly 9 (Winter 1989): 63-77.

9343. Gunter, Michael M. "Susurluk: The Connection Between Turkey's Intelligence Community and Organized Crime," International Journal of Intelligence and Counterintelligence 11/2 (Summer 1998): 119-141.
Major sections consider the unlikely entourage; a cabal for crime; earlier revelations; parliamentary investigation; people and plans; further fallout; few prospects for change; and the Kutlu Savas report.

9344. Gutfield, Arnon. "Western Justice and the Rule of Law: Bourquin on Loyalty, the 'Red Scare,' and Indians," Pacific Historical Review 45/1 (February 1996): 85-106.
A discussion of the career and decisions of federal district judge George Bourquin, particularly regarding Red Scare and American Indian cases.

9345. Guzman, Jose R. "Privateering Activities in the Gulf of Mexico," Boletin del Archivo General de la Nacion 11/3-4 (1970): 355-452.
This is an approximate translation of the title appearing in a Spanish language journal in Mexico.

9346. Gyimah-Boadi, E. "Self-Determination and Politics in Africa After the Cold War," Defense Intelligence Journal 5/2 (Fall 1996): 97-118.
Major sections discuss African domestic politics and the post-World War II and Cold War era; external assaults on African state sovereignty and self-determination at the end of the Cold War; the domestic consequences of changing international norms and practices; the resurgence of intra-state demands for self-determination and the new frontiers of African politics; patterns of domestic politics in Africa; and what is to be done?

9347. Haberstich, Art. "The Mariner as Agent," Studies in Intelligence 10/4 (Winter 1966).

9348. Hablas, Charles E. "Biographic Collection Programs," Studies in Intelligence 13/2 (Summer 1969).

9349. Hackett, Kevin O. "Entrapment, DeLorean and the Undercover Operation: A Constitutional Connection," John Marshall Law Review 18/2 (1985): 365-405.

Major sections discuss entrapment and its progeny; the rise and fall and resurrection of the due process doctrine; the undercover operation and the right to privacy; and conclusions regarding the DeLorean case.

9350. Haeck, Louis. "Aspects Juridiques de Certaines Utilisations Militaires de l'Espace," Annals of Air and Space Law 21/1 (1996): 65-97.

9351. Hager, Nicky. "Exposing the Global Surveillance System," Covert Action Quarterly (Winter 1996-1997): 11-17.

9352. Haines, Gerald K. "Virginia Hall Goillot: Career Intelligence Officer," Prologue: Quarterly Journal of the National Archives 26/4 (1994): 248-260.

A detailed review of the career of Goillot in intelligence missions for the Office of Strategic Services during World War II, and later service for the Central Intelligence Agency. Useful in analyses of the role of women in intelligence and espionage.

9353. Haines, Gerald K. "CIA's Role in the Study of UFOs, 1947-90," Studies in Intelligence Unclassified edition (1997): 67-84.

Major sections discuss background issues; early concerns, 1947-52; the Robertson panel, 1952-53; the 1950s and fading CIA interest; CIA's U-2 and OXCART as UFOs; the 1960s and declining CIA interest during period of rise in controversy; the 1970s and 1980s and the UFO issue refuses to die. See also item 8598 for an earlier treatment of the subject.

9354. Haines, Gerald K. "The CIA's Own Effort to Understand and Document its Past: A Brief History of the CIA History Program, 1950-1995," Intelligence and National Security 12/1 (January 1997): 201-223.

Major sections discuss the early years; the Dulles years; the renewed efforts in the 1960s; major expansion; problems in the 1970s; abolishment; renewed interest in the 1980s; problems again after the death of William Casey; revitalization in the 1990s; and conclusions.

9355. Hajek, Lester. "Target: CIA," Studies in Intelligence 6/1 (Winter 1962): 29-55.

Lengthy reflections on a Soviet defamation and propaganda campaign. Mentions the Hohenlohe papers, Francis Gary Powers, and the U-2 aircraft used to overfly the Soviet Union.

9356. Halamish, Aviva. "American Volunteers in Illegal Immigration to Palestine, 1946-1948," Jewish History 9/1 (1995): 91-106.

A study of the movement of thousands of Jewish survivors of the

Holocaust to Palestine during the period mentioned, an operation sponsored by and aided by the Israeli foreign intelligence service, the Mossad.

9357. Hall, Arthur R. "Landscape Analysis," Studies in Intelligence 11/2 (Summer 1967).

9358. Hall, Keith R. "Leading Intelligence in the 21st Century: The Role of Satellite Reconnaissance," Defense Intelligence Journal 7/1 (Spring 1998): 7-24.

Discusses the early years of satellite reconnaissance work; creation of the National Reconnaissance Office; expanding role; the post-Cold War transition; responding to the new environment; from reconnaissance to surveillance; information superiority; the Jeremiah panel; technical alliances; the role of satellite reconnaissance in the 21st century; and information dominance challenge.

9359. Hall, R. Cargill. "The Eisenhower Administration and the Cold War: Framing American Astronautics to Serve National Security," Prologue: Quarterly Journal of the National Archives 27 (Spring 1995): 59-70.

Major sections discuss the Cold War and American astronautics; space missions and legal principles; and the space program organized for Cold War. Contains photographs of the key players in the space program, including CIA director Allen Dulles.

9360. Hall, R. Cargill. "Strategic Reconnaissance in the Cold War from Concept to National Policy, 1945-1955," Prologue: Quarterly Journal of the National Archives 28 (Summer 1996): 107-125.

9361. Halliday, John D. "Censorship in Berlin and Vienna during the First World War: A Comparative View," Modern Language Review 83/3 (July 1988): 612-626.

Examines the organizations involved in censorship actions in Berlin and Vienna in World War I, particularly with respect to legal and judicial control by police, prosecutors, and the military.

9362. Halpern, Samuel. "Revisiting the Cuban Missile Crisis," Society for Historians of American Foreign Relations Newsletter 24/4 (1993): 17-24.

9363. Hamilton, Francis M., III. "Should 'Clean Hands' Protect the Government Against s. 2525 Suppression Under Title III of the Omnibus Crime Control and Safe Streets Act of 1968?," Washington and Lee Law Review 53 (Winter 1996): 1473-1512.

A summary of the law of Title III and its applications in several recent wiretapping surveillance cases. Useful in domestic surveillance research involving law enforcement.

9364. Hamilton, Henry and John O. Smykla. "Guidelines for Police Undercover Work: New Questions About Accreditation and the Emphasis of Procedure Over Authorization," Justice Quarterly 11/1 (March 1994): 135-151.

A survey of one hundred large police departments in the US to explore the dynamics of police undercover operations and procedural controls on such operations.

9365. Hamilton, Peter. "Industrial Secrets and Crime," Royal Society of Arts Journal 118 (February 1970): 125-134.

9366. Hammant, Thomas R. "Communications Intelligence and Tsarist Russia," Studies in Intelligence 22/2 (Summer 1978).

9367. Hammant, Thomas R. "Soviet COMINT and the Civil War, 1918-1921," Studies in Intelligence 23/2 (Summer 1979).

A translation of a Soviet officer's article: "The Organization and Combat Use of Radio Intelligence during the Civil War," Journal of Military History 11 (1972), published in Moscow, USSR.

9368. Hansen, James R. "The Big Balloon," Air & Space 9/1 (1994): 70-77.

A brief account of Project Echo, a communications satellite program for reconnaissance by means of communications satellites.

9369. Hapak, Joseph T. "Military Intelligence on Polonia in 1918: A Document," Polish American Studies 45/1 (1988): 74-82.

9370. Hardy, Timothy S. "Intelligence Reform in the Mid-1970's," Studies in Intelligence 20/2 (Summer 1976).

9371. Harknett, Richard J. "Information Warfare and Deterrence," Parameters: US Army War College Quarterly 26/3 (Autumn 1996): 93-107.

Discusses the context of information warfare; netwar, cyberwar, and the strategy of deterrence; deterrence and cyberwar; deterrence and netwar; and conclusions.

9372. Harlow, Bryce and Kenneth W. Thompson. "Richard Nixon: The Man and the Political Leader," Miller Center Journal 1 (1994): 81-97.

An analysis of the great contradictions in Richard Nixon's personality and thought processes which may be useful in studies of the many domestic intelligence operations executed during the Nixon administration.

9373. Harris, David A. "Superman's X-Ray Vision and the Fourth Amendment: The New Gun Detection Technology," Temple Law Review 69 (Spring 1996): 1-60.

Major sections discuss the new gun detection technology; three ways police can use gun detectors; fitting gun detectors into the Fourth Amendment; using gun detectors within the framework of Terry v. Ohio; and the conflict between the technology and new statutes permitting the carrying of concealed weapons.

9374. Harris, James R. "Admiral Kimmel and Pearl Harbor: Heritage, Perception, and the Perils of Calculation," Filson Club History Quarterly 68/3 (1994): 379-417.

An extensive analysis of Kimmel's naval career and orientation to interpretations of enemy capabilities and intentions in the years prior to the Pearl Harbor attack.

9375. Harris, John H. "The Rolt Memorial Lecture, 1984: Industrial Espionage in the Eighteenth Century," Industrial Archaeology Review 7/2 (1984): 127-138.

An insightful lecture by a well-recognized industrial historian, the author observes that industrial espionage was a common practice in the eighteenth century, and the techniques of information acquisition have application in modern times.

9376. Harris, J. R. "French Industrial Policy Under the Ancien Regime and the Pursuit of the British Example," Histoire, Economie et Socit 12/1 (1993): 93-100.

9377. Harrison, Mark. "Soviet Economic Growth Since 1928: The Alternative Statistics of G. I. Khanin," Europe-Asia Studies 45/1 (1993): 141-167.

9378. Hart, John L. "Pyotr Semyonovich Popov: The Tribulations of Faith," Intelligence and National Security 12/4 (October 1997):44-74.

A detailed consideration of the Soviet spy Popov, with particular emphasis on his personality and motivations.

9379. Hartch, Gregory B. "Wrong Turns: A Critique of the Supreme Court's Right to Travel Cases," William Mitchell Law Review 21 (Winter 1995): 457-484.

Major sections review the history of the right to travel; the Rehnquist Court and the right to travel's vanishing act; and a workable definition of the right to travel.

9380. Hartline, Martin C. and M. M. Kaulbach. "Michael Collins and Bloody Sunday," Studies in Intelligence 13/4 (Winter 1969).

Estimated to be 6 pages in length.

9381. Hartness, William M. "Aspects of Counterinsurgency Intelligence," Studies in Intelligence 7/3 (Fall 1963).

9382. Hartse, Caroline M. "The Emotional Acculturation of Hutterite Defectors," Journal of Anthropological Research 50/1 (1994): 69-85.
   Useful most likely in analyses of defection from a cause or religious group, this is a study of the defection of Hutterites to a Protestant faith.

9383. Hash, Paul E. and Christina M. Ibrahim. "E-Mail, Electronic Monitoring, and Employee Privacy," South Texas Law Review 37 (June 1996): 893-910.

9384. Haslam, Jonathan. "The British Communist Party, the Comintern and the Outbreak of War, 1939: 'A Nasty Taste in the Mouth,'" Diplomacy & Statecraft 3/1 (1992): 147-154.

9385. Haslam, Jonathan. "Russian Archival Revelations and Our Understanding of the Cold War," Diplomatic History 21/3 (Spring 1997): 217-228.

9386. Hata, Ikuhito. "Going to War: Who Delayed the Final Note?," Japan Echo 19 (Spring 1992): 53-65.
   Discusses the draft note considered in the article by R. J. C. Butow, see above citation.

9387. Hatch, David A. "Venona: An Overview," American Intelligence Journal 17/1&2 (1996): 71-77.
   Discusses the background of the National Security Agency project aimed at declassification of certain cryptologic records; the cryptologic problem; exploitation; contents; Soviet personalities and organizations; covernames; Soviet tradecraft; sources of information; atomic espionage; and the Rosenbergs.

9388. Hathaway, Robert M. "Suez, the Perfect Failure: A Review Essay," Political Science Quarterly 109/2 (1994): 361-366.
   A book review essay of two books on the Suez Canal crisis in 1956: Keith Kyle, Suez; and William R. Louis and Roger Owen, Suez 1956: The Crisis and Its Consequences.

9389. Hatzenbeuhler, Max A. "Scandinavians as Agents," Studies in Intelligence 15/4 (Winter 1971).

9390. Havill, Adrian. "Line of Fire," Washingtonian 32/11 (November 1994): 72-74.
   Reviews the circumstances of the shooting incident in front of CIA headquarters in Langley, Virginia.

9391. Haydock, Michael D. "This Means War!," American History (January-February 1998): 42-50; 62-63.
   Offers perspectives on the circumstances which led up to the sinking of

the battleship Maine in 1898. Includes several photographs.

9392. Haywood, O. G., Jr. "Military Decisions and Game Theory," Operations Research 4 (1954): 365-385.

Analyzes two battle situations in World War II (the Rabaul-Lae convoy, and the Avranches-Gap), and develops the analogy between existing military doctrines and the "theory of games" proposed by J. von Neumann.

9393. Hedley, John H. "Secrets, Free Speech, and Fig Leaves," Studies in Intelligence Unclassified edition (Spring 1998): 75-83.

The author, chairman of the Central Intelligence Agency's Publication Review Board, explains the internal practices and reasoning behind the publications review process for current and former CIA personnel who seek publication release of their writings. The article appears in the unclassified and unnumbered issue of the CIA's internal journal. Sections discuss the basic requirements of CIA's Publications Review Board practices; the fact that reviews are not optional; the two tracks of CIA's review process; the definitional changes; the Clarridge precedent; the rise in book publication; and the new era and challenges.

9394. Heffter, Clyde R. "A Fresh Look at Collection Requirements," Studies in Intelligence 4/3 (Fall 1960).

9395. Heiberg, Marianne. "Insiders/Outsiders: Basque Nationalism," European Journal of Sociology 16 (Spring 1975): 169-193.

9396. Helmore, P. W. and E. B. Edwards. "Air Operations in Vietnam: I and II," Royal United Service Institution Journal 112/645 (1967): 16-31.

9397. Helms, Richard M. "In Memoriam: R. Adm. Sidney W. Souers," Studies in Intelligence 17/1 (Spring 1973).

9398. Helms, Richard M. "Strategic Arms Limitation and Intelligence," Studies in Intelligence 17/1 (Spring 1973).

9399. Helsper, Charles H. "Periodic Reports by Industrial Groups as Sources of Intelligence Information," Studies in Intelligence 2 (Spring 1958).

9400. Henderson, Robert D'A. "Armed and Dangerous--the Memories of Ronnie Kasrils," Journal of Conflict Studies 15/2 (Fall 1995): 162-165.

A brief reflection on the South African revolutionary leader, Ronnie Kasrils, and the work to stir an internal war in opposition to the South African government.

9401.   Henderson, Robert D'A.   "Operation Vula Against Apartheid," International Journal of Intelligence and Counterintelligence 10/4 (Winter 1997-1998): 418-455.

A discussion of the plan of South African insurrectionists to orchestrate an internal war against the South African government, a plan known as operation Vula. Major sections discuss the discovery of Vula; significance of operation Vula; Southern Africa in the 1980s; ANC debates its military failure; Vula's communist leadership; recruiting foreign activists, 1986-1988; going into action, 1988-1990; the new playing field in 1990; the reaction of the South African State Security from mid-1990 to mid-1991; questions still outstanding; an appraisal; and a sub-state intelligence venture.

9402.   Herbert, David L. and V. Lee Sinclair, Jr.   "The Use of Minors As Undercover Agents of Informants: Some Legal Problems," Journal of Police Science and Administration 5/2 (1977):   185-192.

Reviews the law enforcement practice of using juveniles as undercover agents or informants; penal sanctions; permissible and prohibited uses of juveniles in drug investigations; and conclusions.

9403. Herbst, Jeffrey. "Potential US Responses to the Crisis of Sovereignty and Self-Determination," Defense Intelligence Journal 5/2 (Fall 1996): 9-26.

Sections discuss the crisis in sovereignty and self-determination; promoting intellectual fluidity; promoting organizational fluidity; doctrine of intervention; new forms for self-determination; and changing viability of nations.

9404.   Herman, Isadore.   "Estimating Aircraft Performance," Studies in Intelligence 6/2 (Winter 1962).

9405.   Herman, Michael.   "Antipodean Dilemmas," Intelligence and National Security 12/4 (October 1997): 215-222.

This is a book review article and critique of Nicky Haer's book, Secret Power: New Zealand's Role in the International Spy Network.

9406.   Herndon, Booton.   "Corpses Thawing in Springtime: The Bulge Revisited," Virginia Quarterly Review 71/2 (1995): 338-352.

Consideration is given to the circumstances of strategy and preparation in the months before the intelligence and operational blunders of the German breakout in the Battle of the Bulge.

9407.   Hershey, Robert.   "Commercial Intelligence on a Shoestring," Harvard Business Review (September-October 1980): 22-26.

Methods are discussed by which small companies can open an internal function to keep tabs on competitors. Major sections discuss making a start; buying information; the do-it-yourself approach; structuring management; benefits of size; and editor's observations.

9408. Heuer, Richards J., Jr. "Cognitive Biases: Problems in Hindsight Analysis," Studies in Intelligence 22/2 (Summer 1978): 21-28.

9409. Heymann, Stephen P. "Legislating Computer Crime," Harvard Journal on Legislation 34/2 (Summer 1997): 373-391.
    Major sections discuss the importance of distinguishing real needs for new legislation from efforts to reopen old debates; areas in which computer technology renders obsolete established substantive criminal laws; issues of criminal procedure that require revisiting, including cryptography and the Fifth Amendment; and the need for new investigative tools.

9410. Hilden, Leonard. "Conditioned Reflex, Drugs and Hypnosis in Communist Interrogations," Studies in Intelligence 2 (Spring 1958).

9411. Hillman, Donald E. and R. Cargill Hall. "Overflight: Strategic Reconnaissance of the USSR," Air Power History 43/1 (1996): 28-39.

9412. Hindley, Meredith. "Negotiating the Boundary of Unconditional Surrender: The War Refugee Board in Sweden and Nazi Proposals to Ransom Jews," Holocaust and Genocide Studies 10/1 (Spring 1996): 52-77.

9413. Hindley, Meredith. "The Strategy of Rescue and Relief: The Use of OSS Intelligence by the War Refugee Board in Sweden, 1944-45," Intelligence and National Security 12/3 (July 1997): 145-165.
    Discusses the War Refugee Board arrival in Stockholm; the Baltic rescue program; ransom negotiations with Himmler; the Norwegian rescue program; and implications of the WRB and OSS partnership.

9414. Hinman, Edward M. "The Interpretation of Soviet Press Announcements of "Cosmos" Satellite Launchings," Studies in Intelligence 13/2 (Summer 1969).

9415. Hinsley, Harry. "The Counterfactual History of No ULTRA," Cryptologia 20/4 (October 1996): 319-324.

9416. Hirsch, Milton. "Confidential Informants: When Crime Pays," University of Miami Law Review 39/1 (1986): 131-155.
    Reviews in substantial detail the issues and concerns raised by various federal court decisions involving police use of undercover informants, principally Williamson v. US.

9417. Hixson, Walter L. "What Was the Cold War and How Did We Win It?," Reviews in American History 22/3 (1994): 507-511.

A book review essay of two books concerned with US post-World War II foreign policy by H. W. Brands, The Devil We Knew: Americans and the Cold War; and Ernest R. May, American Cold War Strategy: Interpreting NSC-68.

9418. Hoerrner, Mark D. "Fire at Will: The CIA Director's Ability to Dismiss Homosexual Employees as National Security Risks," Boston College Law Review 31 (May 1990): 699-748.

Major sections discuss an overview of traditional judicial deference to executive or legislative authority; the Central Intelligence Agency director's potential defenses against claims by dismissed homosexual employees; a homosexual plaintiff's poor chances of successfully challenging his or her dismissal from CIA in court.

9419. Hoffman, Bruce. "Responding to Terrorism Across the Technological Spectrum," Terrorism and Political Violence 6/3 (1994): 366-390.

A detailed analysis of the implications of sophisticated American military ability to plan for terroristic attacks, many with increasing scales of loss and injury. Argues that deadly attacks by terrorists will continue and they will probably escalate in intensity, thus indicating a need for even more improved intelligence and planning.

9420. Hoffman, Christopher D. "Encrypted Digital Cash Transfers: Why Traditional Money Laundering Controls May Fail Without Uniform Cryptography Regulations," Fordham International Law Journal 21 (March 1998): 799-859.

9421. Hoffman, Jon T. "The Legacy and Lessons of Operation Overlord," Marine Corps Gazette 78/6 (1994): 68-72.

A useful background piece on the logistical preparations for the secret mission to invade Europe in June 1944.

9422. Hoffman, Tod. "The Mystery of Aldrich Ames," Queen's Quarterly 103 (Summer 1996): 385-397.

A book review essay concerning four books about CIA convicted spy and former employee Aldrich Ames: Sellout by James Adams; Killer Spy by Peter Maas; Betrayal by Tim Weiner, David Johnston, and Neil Lewis; and Nightmover by David Wise. Note: Not covered by this review, and published later, is another book on the Ames case by Peter Early, Confessions of a Spy.

9423. Hoffman, Tod. "Treason and Loyalties," Queen's Quarterly 104/1 (Spring 1997): 31-45.

Argues that the job of an intelligence officer can be reduced to two functions: detecting treason and inducing treason. Discusses various cases of modern treason to demonstrate the theory and principles involved.

1132 INTELLIGENCE, ESPIONAGE and RELATED TOPICS

9424. Hoffman, Tod. "LeCarre Weaves Through Greenland," Queen's Quarterly 104/3 (Fall 1997): 499-510.
    A book review essay in consideration of novelist John LeCarre's work, The Tailor of Panama (1996).

9425. Holland, Norman N. "Style As Character: The Secret Agent," Modern Fiction Studies 12/2 (Summer 1966): 221-231.
    A literary interpretation of Joseph Conrad's early spy novel, arguing that this novel is set off markedly from Conrad's other writings.

9426. Holstein, Linda L. and Karen E. Reilly. "Electronic Communications in the Workplace: New Limits on Employer Surveillance," Hennepin Lawyer 65 (January-February 1996): 4-12.

9427. Holt, Thaddeus. "The Deceivers," MHQ: The Quarterly Journal of Military History 7/1 (1994): 48-57.
    An account of the British special team in World War II assigned several secret tasks to deceive German and Japanese intelligence as to possible strategic and tactical intentions of Allied forces.

9428. Holzimmer, Kevin C. "Walter Kruger, Douglas MacArthur, and the Pacific War: The Wakde-Sarmi Campaign as a Case Study," Journal of Military History 59/4 (1995): 661-685.

9429. Horel, Ned C. "In Search of Migratory Isotopes," Studies in Intelligence 12/2 (Summer 1968).

9430. Horne, Alistair. "The Cuban Missile Crisis," Histoire, Economie et Socit 13/1 (1994): 171-184.
    In French, the author sets forth discussion of various events from 1958 to 1962 which escalated tensions between the US and the Soviet Union, culminating in the Missile Crisis.

9431. Houston, Lawrence R. "Executive Privilege in the Field of Intelligence," Studies in Intelligence 2 (Fall 1958).

9432. Houston, Lawrence R. "United States v. Harry A. Jarvinen," Studies in Intelligence 15/4 (Winter 1971).

9433. Houston, Lawrence R. "The John Richard Hawke Case," Studies in Intelligence 16/Special edition (1972).

9434. Howard, John. "The Library, the Park, and the Pervert: Public Space and Homosexual Encounter in Post-World War II Atlanta," Radical History Review

62 (1995): 166-187.

Historical analysis of the Atlanta Public Library perversion case and the efforts of the City of Atlanta to reduce homosexual activity in Piedmont Park, mainly backed by local religious groups who vigorously opposed gay demonstrations in search of wider social acceptance. Useful in studies of domestic or police intelligence targeting of gays or others who oppose conventional lifestyles.

9435. Howerton, Paul W. "Economic Intelligence," Studies in Intelligence 1 (Spring 1956).

9436. Howland, Richard C. "The Lessons of the September 30 Affair," Studies in Intelligence 14/3 (Fall 1970).

9437. Hubest, Alfred. "Audiosurveillance," Studies in Intelligence 4/2 (Summer 1960).

9438. Hudson, Gossie H. "Not for Entertainment Only," Negro History Bulletin 40/2 (1977): 682-683.

9439. Hugo, Grant. "The Political Influence of the Thriller," Contemporary Review 221 (1972): 274-285.

9440. Hugon, Alain. "L'Affaire l'Hoste ou la Tentation Expagnole (1604)," Revue d'Histoire Moderne et Contemporaine 42/3 (1995): 355-375.

9441. Hugon, Alain. "Les Rendez-vous Manques de Gerard de Raffis: Espionnage et Retournement Ideologique sous le Regne de Henri IV," Revue Historique 296/1 (1996): 59-82.

9442. Hull, James P. "'The Surest Augery for Ultimate Success': The Release of Propriety Technical Knowledge by U.S. Firms in the Early Century," Canadian Review of American History 24/2 (1994): 61-86.

A detailed account of strategies aimed at the competing values of open versus secret industrial production methods, as demonstrated during the early twentieth century. May be useful in studies of industrial espionage and technological secrecy.

9443. Hulnick, Arthur S. "Intelligence and Law Enforcement: The "Spies Are Not Cops" Problem," International Journal of Intelligence and Counterintelligence 10/3 (Fall 1997): 269-286.

Major sections discuss keeping intelligence out of law enforcement; CIA-FBI links; terrorism forces a change; effects of the Ames case; spies and cops; cultural and operational differences; what spies and cops want; the impact of the

Ames case; the Nicholson affair; capturing Fawaz Yunis; lessons learned; and the reality of tasking.

9444. Humphrey, David C. "NSC Meetings During the Johnson Presidency," Diplomatic History 18/1 (Winter 1994): 29-45.

An excellent overview of the Johnson administration's experience with National Security Council meetings, and LBJ's frequent use of the Council as a forum for briefings rather than advice and counsel from the membership.

9445. Hunter, Helen-Louise. "Zanzibar Revisited," Studies in Intelligence 11/1 (Spring 1967).

9446. Hunter, Jane. "ANC Activists: Inside the South African Government-- Interview with Sue and Peter Dobson," Covert Action Quarterly 34 (Summer 1990): 14-16.

9447. Huntington, Thomas. "The Berlin Spy Tunnel Affair," American Heritage of Invention and Technology 10/4 (Spring 1995): 44-52.

9448. Hurley, John A. "A Technique for Coastal Infiltration," Studies in Intelligence 6/2 (Summer 1962).

9449. "Hu's a Reformist, Hu's a Conservative," Studies in Intelligence 31/4 (Winter 1987).

This article is not listed by the Central Intelligence Agency among the collection of declassified items for public access.

9450. Ichikawa, Akira. "A Test of Religious Tolerance: Canadian Government and Jodo Shinshu Buddhism During the Pacific War, 1941-1945," Canadian Ethnic Studies 26/2 (1994): 46-69.

In a similar fashion to US policy with respect to the internment of Japanese-Americans during World War II, the Canadian government's forcible removal of Buddhist ministers from British Columbia challenged constitutionally granted civil liberties. Useful in studies of domestic security considerations in time of national security emergencies.

9451. Ilyashov, Anatoli and I. M. Lapitski. "Reconnaissance Flights in the Cold War Period," SShA: Ekonomika, Politika, Ideologiia 8-9 (1994): 121-132.

9452. Indinopulos, Thomas. "Shin Bet's Blind Side," International Journal of Intelligence and Counterintelligence 10/1 (Spring 1997): 91-96.

Major sections discuss features of the Israel internal intelligence function: the intelligence web; misreading the opposition; the blind side and the failure to protect Yitzhak Rabin; and ignoring the past.

9453. "Industrial Intelligence and Espionage," Studies in Intelligence 12/3 (Fall 1968).

This article is not listed among the collection of declassified items by the Central Intelligence Agency for public access.

9454. "In Memoriam," Intelligence and National Security 13/2 (Summer 1998): 213-214.

This is a brief tribute to Joan E. L. Murray (1917-1996), first and only woman to have served as a cryptanalyst at Hut 8 at Bletchley Park.

9455. Inquirer [pseud.]. "Porthole to the West," Studies in Intelligence 6/1 (Spring 1962).

9456. "Instructions for a Secret Mission to Russia," Studies in Intelligence 27/1 (Spring 1983).

9457. "The Intelligence Challenge in the 1980s," Studies in Intelligence 24/4 (Winter 1980).

This article is not listed among the collection of declassified items by the Central Intelligence Agency for public access.

9458. "The International Arena in the Year 2000," Studies in Intelligence 29/3 (Fall 1985).

This article is not listed among the declassified items by the Central Intelligence Agency for public access. Perhaps a researcher will reflect upon the predictions made in this article upon arrival of the millennium.

9459. "Interrogation of an Alleged CIA Agent," Studies in Intelligence 23/1 (Spring 1983).

This article is not listed among the declassified items by the Central Intelligence Agency for public access.

9460. "An Interview with Erna Flegel from the Fuerhrerbunker, November 1945," Studies in Intelligence 25/3 (Fall 1981).

This article is not listed among the declassified items by the Central Intelligence Agency for public access.

9461. Jackson, Susan M. "Cultural Lag and the International Law of Remote Sensing," Brooklyn Journal of International Law 23 (January 1998): 833-885.

Discusses the developing market for commercial remote sensing; commercialization of remote sensing; and the value of an international framework.

9462. Jacob, Abel. "Israel's Military Aid to Africa, 1960-66," Journal of Modern Africa 9/2 (1971): 165-187.

Major sections discuss the politics of military aid; the military and internal politics; international competition in military aid; and Nahal and Gadna paramilitary organizations.

9463. Jacobs, Bruce A. "Undercover Deception: Reconsidering Presentations of Self," Journal of Contemporary Ethnography 21/2 (July 1992): 200-225.

Discusses deception strategies used by undercover narcotics agents. Major sections discuss the study method; deception strategies; discussion of findings; and conclusions.

9464. Jacobs, Bruce A. "Undercover Drug-Use Evasion Tactics: Excuses and Neutralization," Symbolic Interaction 15 (1992): 435-453.

9465. Jacobs, Bruce A. "Getting Narced: Neutralization of Undercover Identity Discreditation," Deviant Behavior 14/3 (1993): 187-208.

9466. Jacobs, Bruce A. "Undercover Deception Clues: A Case of Restrictive Deterrence," Criminology 31/2 (May 1993): 281-299.

Discusses results of research on the perceptual shorthand used by drug dealers to detect under cover law enforcement personnel. Two major types of deception clues are associated with trend discontinuity: familiar customers introduce strangers to the buying process; and familiar customer increase the amount of their purchases by some significant amount.

9467. Jacobs, Bruce A. "Anticipatory Undercover Targeting in High Schools," Journal of Criminal Justice 22/5 (1994): 445-457.

Useful in domestic and police intelligence research.

9468. Jacobs, Bruce A. "Undercover Social-Distancing Techniques," Symbolic Interaction 17/4 (1994): 395-410.

9469. Jacobs, Bruce A. "Cognitive Bridges: The Case of High School Undercover Officers," Sociological Quarterly 37/3 (Summer 1996): 391-412.

Explores the methods used by undercover officers to bridge from a position of social isolation to a position of social integration in a high school drug enforcement setting. Sections discuss cognitive bridges; methods; bad kid identity performances; class clowning; retreatism; trouble making; and implications. Useful in studies of police intelligence research.

9470. Jacobs, Bruce A. "Crack Dealers and Restrictive Deterrence: Identifying Narcs," Criminology 34/3 (August 1996): 409-431.

Presents findings of a study of the "perceptual shorthand" that crack dealers use to determine whether buyers are narcotics enforcement officers. Considers the intersection of several variables in the crack dealing game.

9471. Jacobs, Bruce A. "Contingent Ties: Undercover Drug Officers' Use of Informants," British Journal of Sociology 48/1 (March 1997): 35-53.

9472. Jansen, Sabine. "L'Affaire Jean Moulin," Revue d'Histoire Moderne et Contemporaine 41/4 (1994): 710-715.
        In French, a brief account of the role Jean Moulin in World War II French Resistance efforts.

9473. Jardine, David. "Observations on the Historical Evidence Supporting the Implication of Lord Mounteagle as a Conspirator in the Gunpowder Treason," Archaeologia 29 (1844).
        Also contained in this old journal is another article by the same author, "Remarks Upon the Letters of Thomas Winter and Lord Mounteagle, Lately Discovered by John Bruce, Esq., F.S.A."

9474. Jeffreys-Jones, Rhodri. "Profit Over Class: A Study of American Industrial Espionage," Journal of American Studies 6/3 (December 1972): 233-248.
        This article is mainly aimed at the history of American labor spying, including the individuals and organizations that participated in undermining the labor movement.

9475. Jeffreys-Jones, Rhodri. "Why Was the CIA Established in 1947?," Intelligence and National Security 12/1 (January 1997): 21-40.
        Explores various historical arguments about the causative elements in the development of the Central Intelligence Agency in 1947.

9476. Jeffreys-Jones, Rhodri. "The Sins of the Founding Fathers," Intelligence and National Security 12/4 (October 1997): 211-214.
        This is a book review article and critique of Stephen F. Knott's book, Secret and Sanctioned: Covert Operations and the American Presidency.

9477. Jenkins, Philip. "The Assassination of Olof Palme: Evidence and Ideology," Contemporary Crises 13/1 (1989): 15-33.

9478. Jenkins, Philip. "'Spy Mad?' Investigating Subversion in Pennsylvania, 1917-1918," Pennsylvania History 63/2 (1996): 204-231.

9479. Jensen, Joan M. "The 'Hindu Conspiracy': A Reassessment," Pacific Historical Review 48 (February 1979): 65-83.

9480. Jeremy, David J. "Transatlantic Industrial Espionage in the Early Nineteenth Century: Barriers and Penetrations," Textile History 26/1 (1995): 95-122.

A detailed historical study of the collection of technological intelligence by American industrialists by means of travel to Britain in the early years of the nineteenth century. Useful in studies of trade secrets theft and commercial espionage.

9481. Jerez Mir, Miguel. "La Composicion de las Elites en los Etados Unidos," Revista de Estudios Polaticos 48 (1985): 77-104.

Appears in Spanish in this journal for political studies from Spain. Includes brief discussion of the intelligence services as part of the American elite establishment.

9482. Jessel, Walter. "A National Name Index Network," Studies in Intelligence 6/1 (Spring 1962).

9483. Johnson, Bruce D. and Mangai Natarajan. "Strategies to Avoid Arrest: Crack Sellers' Response to Intensified Policing," American Journal of Police 14/3-4 (1995): 49-69.

9484. Johnson, Donald O. "Wilson, Burleson and Censorship in the First World War," Journal of Southern History 28/1 (1962): 46-58.

9485. Johnson, Falk S. "The Battle of the Bulge Foreshadowed," Military Review 75/1 (1994-1995): 110-112.

Discusses the weaknesses in US intelligence with respect to the Battle of the Bulge attack by the German army in the winter of 1944, and the single point defenses of General George S. Patton.

9486. Johnson, Loch K. "Spymasters and the Cold War," Foreign Policy 105 (Winter 1996-1997): 179-192.

A book review essay concerning two intelligence books: From the Shadows: The Ultimate Insider's Story of Five Presidents and How They Won the Cold War by Robert M. Gates; and The First Directorate: My 32 Years in Intelligence and Espionage Against the West by Oleg Kalugin and Fen Montaigne.

9487. Johnson, Loch K. "The CIA and the Question of Accountability," Intelligence and National Security 12/1 (January 1997): 178-200.

The expert on CIA oversight discusses accountability issues in several major sections: the sharing of governmental power; the exceptional case of intelligence; on the merits of accountability; and adapting to the new era of accountability.

9488. Johnson, Loch K. "Balancing Security and Liberty," Freedom Review 28 (Summer 1997): 37-44.

A discussion of US intelligence oversight practices and the increasing pressures to make the intelligence community more accountable.

9489.   Johnson, Loch K.   "Intelligence and the Challenge of Collaborative Government," Intelligence and National Security 13/2 (Summer 1998): 177-182.

Responding to Stephen Knott's critique of his work on Executive-Legislative balance of power regarding the intelligence function, Johnson points out errors and misunderstandings in the Knott perspective. Affirmatively, Johnson argues that it is possible to have collaborative intelligence arrangements that produce beneficial results for national security policy. See also Johnson's book review of Knott's book which appears in American Political Science Review 91/1 (March 1997): 191-192.

9490.   Johnson, Loch K. and Annette Freyburg.   "Ambivalent Bedfellows: German-American Intelligence Relations, 1969-1991," International Journal of Intelligence and Counterintelligence 10/2 (Summer 1997): 165-179.

Major sections discuss incentives for intelligence cooperation; the scope of intelligence liaison; the risk of liaison; threat as a cohesive force for liaison relationships; and ambivalence and continuity.

9491. Johnson, L. Scott. "Toward a Functional Model of Information Warfare," Studies in Intelligence Unclassified edition (1997): 49-56.

Major sections discuss IW's ultimate target; a target model; three target layers; elements of IW; and IW orchestration.

9492. Johnson, Thomas M. "They Told All," American Legion Magazine 26 (February 1939): 14-17, 38-39.

9493. Johnson, William R.   "Recalling Snepp's Indecent Breach of Trust," International Journal of Intelligence and Counterintelligence 9/4 (Winter 1996-1997): 473-481.

A book review essay pertaining to former CIA case officer Frank Snepp's account of the last days of the Vietnam war, published in 1977. The reviewer had personal and professional involvement in the overall fact pattern of the situation.

9494. Johnston, Paul. "No Cloak and Dagger Required: Intelligence Support to UN Peacekeeping," Intelligence and National Security 12/4 (October 1997): 102-112.

Major sections discuss the UN aversion to intelligence; the essence of peacekeeping is intelligence; information/intelligence distinction; UN collection difficulties/sensitivities; new enthusiasms; levels of intelligence; the UNPROFOR example; possible solutions; and a permanent staff in New York.

9495. Jones, Archer. "The Vicksburg Campaign," Journal of Mississippi History 29/1 (1967): 12-27.

9496. Jones, David M. "Organization or Individual Corruption? An Examination of Operation Greylord," Justice Professional 7/1 (1992): 35-52.

9497. Jones, Reginald V. "Science, Intelligence and Policy," Royal United Services Institution Journal 124 (June 1979): 9-17.

9498. Jordan, Lloyd R. "The Case for Holistic Intelligence," Studies in Intelligence 19/2 (Summer 1975).

9499. Jorgensen, Jay A. "Scouting for Ulysses S. Grant: The 5th Ohio Cavalry in the Shiloh Campaign," Civil War Regiments 4/1 (1994): 44-77.
    A lengthy and detailed history of the missions of this unit during the early years of the American Civil War.

9500. Joubert, C. "Undercover Policing--A Comparative Study," European Journal of Crime, Criminal Law and Criminal Justice 2/1 (1994): 18-38.

9501. Kahn, David. "Toward a Theory of Intelligence," MHQ: The Quarterly Journal of Military History 7/2 (Winter 1995): 92-97.

9502. Kainen, Burton and Shel D. Myers. "Turning Off the Power on Employees: Using Surreptitious Tape-Recordings and E-Mail Intrusion by Employees in Pursuit of Employer Rights," Labor Law Journal 48 (April 1997): 199-213.
    Major sections discuss the employer as victim of surreptitious tape recordings or E-mail intrusions by employees; and various dimensions of federal and state laws invoked or challenged as to privacy rights of employers and employees.

9503. Kaiser, David. "Intelligence and the Assassination of John F. Kennedy," Intelligence and National Security 12/4 (October 1997): 165-195.
    A lengthy and detailed analysis of five books addressing the assassination of President John F. Kennedy: G. Robert Blakey and Richard Billings, Fatal Hour: The Assassination of President Kennedy and Organized Crime; Norman Mailer, Oswald's Tale: An American Mystery; John Newman, Oswald and the CIA; Ray and Mary La Fontaine, Oswald Talked: The New Evidence in the JFK Assassination; and James P. Hosty, Jr. and Thomas Hosty, Assignment: Oswald.

9504. Kalin, Berkley. "Young Abe Fortas," West Tennessee Historical Society Papers 34 (1980): 96-100+.

9505. Kalitka, Peter F. "The Equalizer Versus Competitive Intelligence," American Intelligence Journal 17/1&2 (1996): 43-45.

Discusses the counterintelligence struggle; the real operational environment; compromise of critical information; and three-phase neutralization plan of prevention, detection, and punishment.

9506. Kamenev, Viktor Y. "The Standardization of Foreign Personal Names," Studies in Intelligence 13/2 (Summer 1969).
Estimated to be 3 pages in length.

9507. Kaplan, Matthew N. "Who Will Guard the Guardians? Independent Counsel, State Secrets, and Judicial Review," Nova Law Review 18/3 (Spring 1994): 1787-1861.
Major sections discuss the background of the experience in the Iran-Contra case regarding independent counsel and availability of judicial recourse; statutes; the Constitution; and conclusions.

9508. Kaplan, Robert D. "Special Intelligence," Atlantic Monthly 281/2 (February 1998): 61-62.
Brief reflections and observations from the author's own experience regarding the relationship between the Central Intelligence Agency and military forces, especially US Special Forces. Speculates that the CIA may pass out of existence, but collaborative forms of intelligence organizations are only now entering a new golden era.

9509. Karabell, Zachary and Timothy Naftali. "History Declassified: The Perils and Promise of CIA Documents," Diplomatic History 18/4 (Fall 1994): 615-626.
This is a research note to offer guidelines to assist CIA records researchers in their quest for CIA materials, especially in light of the CIA's history branch declassification efforts in the 1990s.

9510. Kash, Douglas. "Abducting Terrorists Under PDD-39: Much Ado About Nothing New," American University International Law Review 13 (1997): 139-162.

9511. Kealey, Gregory S. "The RCMP, the Special Branch, and the Early Days of the Communist Party of Canada: A Documentary Article," Labour/Le Travail 30 (1992): 169-204.

9512. Kealey, Gregory S. "In the Canadian Archives on Security and Intelligence," Dalhousie Review 75/1 (Spring 1995): 26-38.

9513. Keatts, Dorothy J. "Footnote to Cicero (What Happened to Moyzisch's Secretary)," Studies in Intelligence 2 (Fall 1957).

9514. Keene, Jennifer D. "Uneasy Alliances: French Military Intelligence and the American Army during the First World War," <u>Intelligence and National Security</u> 13/1 (Spring 1998): 18-36.

This is a study of the French military intelligence aimed at US military intentions and operations in Europe in World War I. Useful in studies of secret intelligence liaison relationships.

9515. Kehm, Harold D. "Notes on Some Aspects of Intelligence Estimates," <u>Studies in Intelligence</u> 1 (Winter 1956).

9516. Keiger, J. F. V. "'Perfidious Albion?' French Perceptions of Britain as an Ally after the First World War," <u>Intelligence and National Security</u> 13/1 (Spring 1998): 37-52.

An analysis of the erosion of British and French relations after World War I, and the need to study perceptions between friends in the course of coping with liaison relationships in the area of intelligence analysis.

9517. Keithly, David M. "Leading Intelligence in the 21st Century: Past As Prologue?," <u>Defense Intelligence Journal</u> 7/1 (Spring 1998): 78-88.

Sections discuss today and the future; intelligence requirements; back to the future; and lessons learned.

9518. Kennan, George F. "The Sources of Soviet Conduct," <u>Foreign Affairs</u> 25 (July 1947): 566-582.

Not strictly a discussion of intelligence matters, authorship of this frequently cited piece was originally identified only as "X". See other citations by George Kennan in this bibliography. This piece addresses United States containment strategies aimed at Soviet Union expansionism in the early days of the Cold War.

9519. Kennedy, John F. "Valediction," <u>Studies in Intelligence</u> 6/4 (Winter 1962).

A reflection on the contributions of Allen Dulles, former director of the CIA, as delivered by President Kennedy.

9520. Kennett, Lee. "World War I Materials in the French Military Archives," <u>Military Affairs</u> 37/2 (April 1973): 60-61.

A brief overview of the papers and materials in the Chateau de Vincennes in Paris, where military records of the 19th and 20th centuries are kept. These files are useful resources for intelligence research.

9521. Kent, Sherman. "Notes on Capabilities in National Intelligence," <u>Studies in Intelligence</u> 1/1 (Fall 1955).

9522. Kent, Sherman. "The Summit Conference of 1960: An Intelligence Officer's View," <u>Studies in Intelligence</u> 16/Special edition (1972).

9523. Kerr, Sheila. "KGB Sources on the Cambridge Network of Soviet Agents: True or False?," Intelligence and National Security 11/3 (July 1996): 561-585.

A book review essay of four books pertaining to KGB efforts during the Cold War.

9524. Kevles, Daniel J. "Testing the Army's Intelligence: Psychologists and the Military in World War I," Journal of American History 55/3 (1968): 565-581.

May be useful in studies linking the role and practical applications of intelligence testing during World War I and operations of military intelligence organizations.

9525. Kielbowicz, Richard B. "The Telegraph, Censorship, and Politics at the Outset of the Civil War," Civil War History 40/2 (1994): 95-118.

Examines the practice of executive branch censorship, mainly aimed at the press, during the early stages of the American Civil War.

9526. Kimball, Walter B. "Singapore's People's Association," Studies in Intelligence 12/3 (Fall 1968).

Estimated to be 5 pages in length. Discusses insurgency activities of this group. See item 8682: Author's name located after first citation of this title.

9527. Kimble, Kerry L. "Corona: The First U.S. Photoreconnaissance Satellite," Military Intelligence 23/3 (July-September 1997): 46-49.

Discusses historical background; trial and error; cover story; security challenges; modifications; accomplishments; and the extended life of the program.

9528. Kimmel, David. "The Queer Career of Homosexual Security Vetting in Cold War Canada," Canadian Historical Review 75/3 (September 1994): 319-345.

9529. Kimsey, Herman E. "The Identi-Kit," Studies in Intelligence 4/4 (Winter 1960).

9530. King, David N. "Privacy Issues in the Private Sector Workplace: Protection from Electronic Surveillance and the Emerging 'Privacy' Gap," Southern California Law Review 67 (January 1994): 441-474.

9531. King, James T. "George Crook: Indian Fighter and Humanitarian," Arizona and the West 9/4 (1967): 333-348.

9532. Kirkpatrick, Lyman B., Jr. "The Quiet Canadian," Studies in Intelligence 7/2 (Summer 1963): 122-125.

A book review essay that discusses the circumstances under which the book, by the same title, was published. The Quiet Canadian by H. M. Hyde, also published in the United States under the title of Room 3603, provided theretofore unrevealed intelligence insights and the publication itself was substantially controversial.

9533. Kitchen, Martin. "SOE's Man in Moscow," Intelligence and National Security 12/3 (July 1997): 95-109.

A brief account of the career and intelligence liaison work of Major George "Pop" Hill, an SOE officer with World War I experience in Russia in association with luminaries such as Sydney Reilly, Somerset Maugham, R. H. Bruce Lockhart and others. Despite the apparent futility of many of his missions to Russia through the years, he should be considered a master of the Russian mind.

9534. Kitchens, James H., III. "The Bombing of Auschwitz Re-examined," Journal of Military History 58/2 (1994): 233-266.

Addresses the controversial issue of whether railroad lines and other methods of ingress to the Auschwitz camp could have been destroyed by bombing raids well before 1945. Among other variables, military intelligence complications are raised in defense of the position that such attacks appeared at the time to be less than useful in meeting military objectives.

9535. Kitcvh, Edmund W. "The Expansion of Trade Secrecy Protection and the Mobility of Management Employees: A New Problem for the Law," South Carolina Law Review 47 (Summer 1996): 659-672.

A detailed discussion of contracts of employment; unfair competition arising from employee mobility; and modern trade secrets protection.

9536. Kitts, Kenneth. "Commission Politics and National Security: Gerald Ford's Response to the CIA Controversy of 1975," Presidential Studies Quarterly 26/4 (Fall 1996): 1081-1098.

Major sections discuss the crisis and response in terms of the strategy taking place; "in certain other matters"; operating procedure; the final report; and conclusions.

9537. Knauft, Sage R. "Proposed Guidelines for Measuring the Propriety of Armed State Responses to Terrorist Attacks," Hastings International and Comparative Law Review 19 (Summer 1996): 763-788.

Major sections discuss transnational terrorism and the inadequacy of existing law; forcible state responses to transnational terrorism; and testing Israeli and US counterterror operations under the proposed guidelines.

9538. Knight, Amy. "The Future of the KGB," Problems of Communism 39/6 (November-December 1990): 20-33.

Major sections discuss Gorbachev's strategy toward the KGB; KGB initiatives; beyond Glasnost; dissension in the ranks; reform from within; legal controls over the KGB; and the end of the KGB.

9539. Knight, Amy. "The Coup That Never Was: Gorbachev and the Forces of Reaction," Problems of Communism 40/6 (November-December 1991): 36-46.
Sections consider history lessons; Gorbachev and the right wing; the post-coup security apparatus; and a law-governed state? Contains conclusions about the legacy of Feliks Dzerzhinsky.

9540. Knight, Amy. "Russian Security Services Under Yeltsin," Post-Soviet Affairs 9/1 (January-March 1993): 40-65.
Traces the development through March 1993 of confrontation between Boris Yeltsin and the Congress of People's Deputies, reflecting in part on the dissolution of the KGB. Discusses oversight of the Russian security service; the legal system and human rights; and the foreign intelligence service.

9541. Knight, Amy. "Internal Security and the Rule of Law in Russia," Current History 95 (October 1996): 311-315.
Major sections discuss the KGB as reorganized but not reformed; the question of whose protectors; the administration's long arm of the law; and securing the security services.

9542. Knobelspiesse, A. V. "Masterman Revisited," Studies in Intelligence 18/1 (Spring 1974).
A review and critique of issues raised in J. C. Masterman's book on British intelligence against Nazi Germany.

9543. Knott, James E. "Secrecy and Intelligence in a Free Society," Studies in Intelligence 19/2 (Summer 1975).
Estimated to be 8 pages in length.

9544. Knott, Stephen. "Executive Power and the Control of American Intelligence," Intelligence and National Security 13/2 (Summer 1998): 171-176.
A brief but strongly stated argument that the shift of power from the Executive to the Congress in the area of intelligence oversight has been a mistake, tied mainly to a misinterpretation of the Framers' behavior and intentions regarding the executive's need to carry out foreign policy sometimes in secrecy. This is a commentary on the writings of Loch Johnson. See Johnson citation in this "Late Entries" collection.

9545. Knowles, Owen. "Fishy Business in Conrad's The Secret Agent," Notes & Queries 37/4 (1990): 433-434.

9546. Kober, Stanley. "Spying and Security in the 90's," World & I 12 (August 1997): 52-57.

9547. Konovalov, A. A. and V. S. Sokolov. "Meetings with Agents," <u>Studies in Intelligence</u> 8/1 (Spring 1964).

9548. Kornweibel, Theodore, Jr. "Black on Black: The FBI's First Negro Informants and Agents and the Investigation of Black Radicalism During the Red Scare," <u>Criminal Justice History</u> 8 (1987): 121-136.

Discusses the need in the FBI for informant's who were black and working undercover; the first black special agent of the FBI; infiltrating Garvey's movement; black agent as professional; and racial and civil liberties dilemmas.

9549. Kornweibel, Theodore, Jr. "'The Most Dangerous of All Negro Journals': Federal Efforts to Suppress the Chicago Defender During World War I," <u>American Journalism</u> 11/2 (1994): 154-168.

The leading black newspaper, the <u>Chicago Defender</u>, was silenced in its efforts to expose lynching and other injustices by United States Post Office inspectors, Bureau of Investigation agents, and the United States Army's Military Intelligence Division. Useful in studies of domestic intelligence abuses, justified in wartime to be necessary national security measures.

9550. Kovacs, Amos. "Using Intelligence," <u>Intelligence and National Security</u> 12/4 (October 1997): 145-164.

This author's view is that users of intelligence are rarely discussed in the context of the intelligence process, and he wishes to change this outcome. Major sections discuss intelligence and its uses; usability characteristics of various kinds of intelligence; and conclusions.

9551. Kovacs, Amos. "The Nonuse of Intelligence," <u>International Journal of Intelligence and Counterintelligence</u> 10/4 (Winter 1997-1998): 383-417.

An analysis of the dynamics of the October 1973 war between Israeli and Egyptian armies, in particular the role of intelligence. Major sections discuss intelligence users; the extended producer-consumer intelligence cycle; the causes of not using intelligence; the information explosion; information flooding; failures of dissemination; politicization; the gap between the two communities; and analyzing the causes.

9552. Kovner, Milton. "Pricing Soviet Military Exports," <u>Studies in Intelligence</u> 12/1 (Spring 1968).

9553. Krepon, Michael and Jeffrey P. Tracey. "'Open Skies' and UN Peacekeeping," <u>Survival</u> 32/3 (May-June 1990): 251-263.

9554. Kress, Kenneth A. "Parapsychology in Intelligence: A Personal Review and Conclusions," <u>Studies in Intelligence</u> 21/4 (Winter 1977).

9555. Kronenbitter, Rita T. "Leon Trotsky, Dupe of the NKVD," Studies in Intelligence (1972).

Estimated to be 47 pages in length. Appears in a special edition in 1972, but appeared first in 1967.

9556. Kumaraswamy, P. R. "The Politics of Pardon: Israel and Jonathan Pollard," Arab Studies Quarterly 18/3 (1996): 17-35.

9557. Kuo, Warren. "CCP Wartime Secret Service and Underground Struggle, Part I," Issues and Studies (August 1970): 56-60.

9558. Kurkcu, Ertugrul. "Trapped in a Web of Covert Killers," Covert Action Quarterly (Summer 1997): 6-12.

9559. Kurland, Jordan E. "Keeping Tabs on Our Slavic Scholars: McCarthyism Endured," Slavic Review 52/1 (1993): 116-121.

9560. Kushner, Harvey W. "Suicide Bombers: Business As Usual," Studies in Conflict and Terrorism 19 (October-December 1996): 329-337.

9561. Kwasowski, Mark J. "Thermal Imaging Technology: Should Its Warrantless Use By Police Be Allowed in Residential Searches?," Texas Wesleyan Law Review 3/2 (Spring 1997): 393-420.

Major sections discuss the Fourth Amendment protection from unreasonable searches and seizures; warrantless Forward Looking Infrared (FLIR) imaging and recommended prohibition in residential settings; and conclusions.

9562. Lafferty, Brad, et al. "The Effects of Media Information on Enemy Capability: A Model for Conflict," Proteus 11/1 (1994): 3-10.

Analysis of the relationship between policies of government on media information in wartime and enemy capabilities to gather useful intelligence. Considers government-media relations in the Korean, Vietnam, and Gulf wars.

9563. Lagrone, James J. "The Hotel in Operations," Studies in Intelligence 9/3 (Fall 1965).

9564. Lambridge, Wayne. "A Note on KGB Style," Studies in Intelligence 15/4 (Winter 1971).

9565. LaMountain, Frank X. "Requirements and the American Scientist," Studies in Intelligence 7/1 (Spring 1963).

9566. Lanctt, Gustave. "The Scandalous Life of a Forger," Transactions of the Royal Society of Canada 50/1 (1956): 25-48.

This is an approximate translation of a title appearing in this English and French languages journal.

9567. Lang, Kurt. "Trends in Military Occupational Structure and Their Political Implications," Journal of Political and Military Sociology 1/1 (1973): 1-18.

9568. Langworthy, Robert H. "Do Stings Control Crime? An Evaluation of a Police Fencing Operation," Justice Quarterly 6/1 (March 1989): 27-45.
    Major sections discuss police organizational goals; the empirical literature on police stings and control of crime; data and methods; findings; and discussion of study results. Calls for changes in the way police conduct under cover sting operations.

9569. Langworthy, Robert H. and James L. LeBeau. "Spatial Evolution of a Sting Clientele," Journal of Criminal Justice 20/2 (1992): 135-145.

9570. Larres, Klaus. "Preserving Law and Order: Britain, the United States, and the East German Uprising of 1953," Twentieth Century British History 5/3 (1994): 320-350.
    Considers the dynamics of US and British diplomatic responses to the East German crackdown against internal disorder in 1953.

9571. Laskier, Michael M. "A Document on Anglo-Jewry's Intervention on Behalf of Egyptian Jews on Trial for Espionage and Sabotage, December 1954," Michael 10 (1986): 143-152.

9572. Laskowsky, Henry J. "Conrad's Under Western Eyes: A Marxian View," Minnesota Review 11 (Fall 1978): 90-104.
    Offers a contrasting perspective of Joseph Conrad's novel.

9573. Lavender, W. B. "The Old Winsockie Syndrome," Studies in Intelligence 13/4 (Winter 1969).

9574. Laville, Helen. "The Committee of Correspondence--CIA Funding of Women's Groups, 1952-1967," Intelligence and National Security 12/1 (January 1997): 104-121.
    A unique study of the Central Intelligence Agency's 15-year effort to learn more about the internal operations and funding of women's organizations which may have been influenced by Soviet propaganda. An attempt to set the record straight is the basis for this piece.

9575. Lawrence, R. E. and Harry W. Woo. "Infrared Imagery in Overhead Reconnaissance," Studies in Intelligence 11/2 (Summer 1967).

9576. Laycock, Keith. "Handwriting Analysis as an Assessment Aid," Studies in Intelligence 3 (Summer 1959).

9577. Laycock, Keith. "Intelligence Gathering in an Unlettered Land," Studies in Intelligence 3 (Summer 1959).

9578. Layton, B. E. "The Joint Debriefing of a Cuban," Studies in Intelligence 7/2 (Summer 1963).
    Useful in studies of defector information reliability.

9579. Leab, Daniel J. "The Red Menace and Justice in the Pacific Northwest: The 1946 Trial of the Soviet Naval Lieutenant Nikolai Gregorevitch Redin," Pacific Northwest Quarterly 87/2 (1996): 82-93.

9580. Leary, William M. "The CIA and the 'Secret War' in Laos: The Battle of Skyline Ridge, 1971-1972," Journal of Military History 59/3 (July 1995): 505-517.
    Aims to clarify the record of involvement of CIA in the decade-long secret war in Laos, which was not so secret after 1962, which lasted for twenty years between the early 1950s and the 1970s.

9581. Leary, William M. "Personality," Vietnam 10/4 (1997): 8-10.

9582. Leavitt, Robert W. "Developments in Air Targeting: The Military Resources Model," Studies in Intelligence 2 (Winter 1958).

9583. Le Calloc'h, Bernard. "Un Passage du Recit de Voyage de Joseph Wolff Relatif a Csoma de Kors," Acta Orientalia Academiae Scientiarum Hungaricae 45/1 (1991): 133-148.

9584. LeCarre, John. "The Spy to End Spies: On Richard Sorge," Encounter 27 (November 1966): 88-89.

9585. Lee, Chong K. "Secrecy Law in Korea," Dickinson Journal of International Law 14 (Spring 1996): 562-576.
    Major sections discuss confidentiality in the Presidential Order regarding financial institution secrecy; provisions of protected financial information with "Customer Request"; and various statutory protections to protect privacy within the realm of Korean financial institutions.

9586. Lee, M. "Across the Public-Private Divide? Private Policing, Grey Intelligence and Civil Actions in Local Drugs Control," European Journal of Crime, Criminal Law and Criminal Justice 3/4 (1995): 381-394.
    Discusses results of a study of police and security interaction in

communities in Britain. Major sections discuss methodology of the study; the local setting; community damage limitations; anti-drug strategies; routine activities and a security patrol function; grey (intelligence) information; the meshing of private policing and civil law; and conclusions.

9587. Leggett, Robert E. "Intelligence Monitoring of Reduction-of-Budget Arms Control Agreements," Studies in Intelligence 21/2 (Summer 1977).

9588. Leggett, Robert E. "The DCI's Center for the Study of Intelligence: Meeting the Challenges of a Changing World Environment," American Intelligence Journal 17/1&2 (1996): 47-51.
    Sections discuss background; organization; Historical Review Group; Academic Affairs Group; History Staff; Community Coordination Group; and looking ahead.

9589. Leib, Michael S. "E-Mail and the Wiretap Laws: Why Congress Should Add Electronic Communication to Title III's Statutory Exclusionary Rule and Expressly Reject a 'Good Faith' Exception," Harvard Journal on Legislation 34 (Summer 1997): 393-438.
    Discusses the background of wiretapping law; electronic communication and the statutory exclusionary rule; the question of a "good faith" exception to the exclusionary rule ofr Title III violations; and conclusions about the need for new statutory protections.

9590. Leidesdorf, Titus. "The Libyan as Agent," Studies in Intelligence 7/4 (Winter 1963).

9591. Leidesdorf, Titus. "The Vietnamese as Operational Target," Studies in Intelligence 12/3 (Fall 1968).

9592. Leigh, Ian. "Legal Access to Security Files: The Canadian Experience," Intelligence and National Security 12/2 (April 1997): 126-153.
    Major sections discuss document classification and ATIP regulations for protection of information in Canada; exemptions; access to intelligence information in practice; enforcement strategy; exempt databanks; and conclusions.

9593. Leonard, Robert G. "Covert Scientific Collection," Studies in Intelligence 3 (1959): 129-132.
    This is a letter to the journal editor which may be useful to researchers investigating issues regarding science policy and data collection.

9594. Lerner, Victoria. "Mexican Spies in North America (1914-1915)," New Mexico Historical Review 69/3 (1994): 230-247.
    Spies for Pancho Villa's raids into the US are discussed in the context

of border history of the period.

9595. Levchenko, Stanislav. "Is the KGB Dead?," World & I 8 (August 1992): 44-50.

9596. Levine, Michael. "I Volunteer to Kidnap Oliver North," Crime, Law and Social Change 20/1 (1993): 1-12.

9597. Levin, David. "Gaps in Narratives of the Hiss Case," Prospects 20 (1995): 257-283.

9598. Leviness, Robert M. "The Chinese as Agent," Studies in Intelligence 10/2 (Summer 1966).

9599. Lewis, Anthony M. "Re-examining Our Perceptions on Vietnam," Studies in Intelligence 17/4 (Winter 1973).
    This former Central Intelligence Agency insider examines how the internal analytical process regarding progress in Vietnam became increasingly attuned to the perceptions of bureaucratic and political superiors, thus leading to long term failure of the war effort from the US position. Estimated to be 32 pages in length.

9600. Lewis, Cliff. "John Steinbeck's Alternative to Internment Camps: A Policy for the President, December 15, 1941," Journal of the West 34/1 (1995): 55-61.
    Novelist and social critic John Steinbeck proposed to President Roosevelt that Japanese-Americans should be brought into the war effort as they were as loyal as any other Americans to the cause of victory. For his efforts, Steinbeck was investigated by the FBI on the allegation that he may have been disloyal by making the proposal. Useful in studies of the excesses of domestic security arising from national security imperatives.

9601. Lewis, Richard B. "JFACC: Problems Associated with Battlefield Preparation in Desert Storm," Airpower (Spring 1994): 4-15.

9602. Lexow, Wilton E. "The Science Attache Program," Studies in Intelligence 10/1 (Spring 1966).

9603. Lexow, Wilton E. and Julian Hoptman. "The Enigma of Soviet BW," Studies in Intelligence 9/1 (Spring 1965).

9604. Lhomme, Michel. "Autant en Emporte le Vent: La Pacification Inachevee ou Improbable du Perou," Defense Nationale 53 (November 1997): 123-132.

9605. Lieberman, Elli. "What Makes Deterrence Work? Lessons from the Egyptian-Israeli Enduring Rivalry," Security Studies 4/4 (Summer 1995): 880-885.

9606. Lippman, David H. "Bastogne Belatedly Besieged," Military History 11/5 (1994): 30-37.
         A recognition of the fiftieth anniversary of the Battle of the Bulge, a last effort by the German Army to break out in December 1944. The battle was largely the result of major intelligence blunders.

9607. Little, Douglas. "Gideon's Band: America and the Middle East Since 1945," Diplomatic History 18/4 (1994): 513-540.
         A detailed analysis of US foreign policy in the Middle East for the previous forty years, including the application of covert actions to change leadership in certain countries.

9608. Little, Douglas. "A Puppet in Search of a Puppeteer? The United States, King Hussein, and Jordan, 1953-1970," International History Review 17/3 (1995): 512-544.
         Amid discussion about of the foreign policy interests of the United States in links with King Hussein is argument that Jordan's stability and the long term survival of Hussein depended in part on US covert actions plans carried out by the Central Intelligence Agency at the direction of United States national security policy makers.

9609. Liubarskii, Kronid. "Pasportnaia Systema i Sistema Propiski v Rossii," Rossiiskii Biulleten' po Pravam Cheloveka 2 (1994): 14-24.
         Discusses the passport system and internal security controls on citizens and visitors to Russia.

9610. Livingston, Robert W. "Marine Corps Intelligence Activity: Excellence in Expeditionary Intelligence," American Intelligence Journal 17/1&2 (1996): 29-33.
         Major sections discuss organization; intelligence production; pre-deployment planning support; service specific exercise support; crisis support; support to combat development; support to acquisition; requirement process; and conclusions.

9611. Livingstone, Neil C. and David Halevy. "Phone Tag: Mossad Gives Terrorist Mastermind and Ear Full of Ordnance," Soldier of Fortune 23 (January 1998): 53-55+.
         Refers to Israeli Mossad activities to find and assassinate a Hamas bombing specialist.

9612. Livingstone, Neil C. "Myth & Conspiracy in International Affairs: Terrorism, Conspiracy, Myth and Reality," Fletcher Forum of World Affairs Journal 22 (Winter-Spring 1998): 1-19.

9613. Lohr, Michael F. "Legal Analysis of United States Military Responses to State-Sponsored International Terrorism," Naval Law Review 34 (1985): 1-48.
     Major sections discuss terrorism; military responses to state-sponsored international terrorism; War Powers Resolution and the effect on the use of military force against terrorism; and conclusions.

9614. Long, John W. "Searching for Sidney Reilly: The Lockhart Plot in Revolutionary Russia, 1918," Europe-East Asia Studies 47/7 (1995): 1225-1241.

9615. Long, Lewis R. "Concepts for a Philosophy of Air Intelligence," Studies in Intelligence 2 (Winter 1958).

9616. Lonner, Jonathan A. "Official Government Abductions in the Presence of Extradition Treaties," Journal of Criminal Law and Criminology 83/4 (Winter 1993): 998-1023.
     Considers issues involved in the Supreme Court decision in United States v. Alvarez-Machain. Majors sections discuss the facts and procedural history; Supreme Court opinions; cases analyses; and conclusions.

9617. Lopuzanski, A. "La Police Romaine et les Chretiens," Antiquite Classique 20 (1951): 5-46.

9618. Loving, Bill. "DMV Secrecy: Stalking and Suppression of Speech Rights," CommLaw Conspectus 4 (Summer 1996): 203-213.
     Concerns individual rights as to department of motor vehicle records. Suggests unique dimension for studies of domestic intelligence practices.

9619. Low, Morris. "Japan' Secret War?: 'Instant' Scientific Manpower and Japan's World War II Atomic Bomb Project," Annals of Science 47/4 (1990): 347-360.

9620. Lowell, Cym H. "Corporate Privacy: A Remedy for the Victim of Industrial Espionage," Patent Law Review 4 (1972): 407-449.
     The new title of this publication is Intellectual Property Law Review. Originally, this piece appeared in Duke Law Journal (1971): 391+. Sections consider common law response to the encroachments of technological surveillance; a right to privacy for the corporate victim of industrial espionage and surveillance; corporate privacy, its advocacy and existence; and preemption by federal patent policy.

9621. Lowenfish, Lee E. "The Odd Couple Revisited and Other Re-evaluations of American Communism and Anti-Communism," Minnesota Review 10 (Fall 1978): 117-125.

A book review essay considering three books on the Hiss-Chambers case: Alger Hiss by John C. Smith; Perjury by Allen Weinstein; and The Romance of American Communism by Vivian Gornick.

9622. Lowenhaupt, Henry S. "The Decryption of a Picture," Studies in Intelligence 11/2 (Summer 1967).

9623. Lowenhaupt, Henry S. "On the Soviet Nuclear Scent," Studies in Intelligence 11/3 (Fall 1967).

9624. Lowenhaupt, Henry S. "Somewhere in Siberia," Studies in Intelligence 15/4 (Winter 1971).

9625. Lowenhaupt, Henry S. "Chasing Bitterfeld Calcium, 1946-1950," Studies in Intelligence 17/1 (Spring 1973).

9626. Lowenhaupt, Henry S. "How We Identified the Technical Problems of Early Soviet Nuclear Submarines," Studies in Intelligence 18/3 (Fall 1974).

9627. Lpinasse, Pierre. "Toward a Transnational Economic Understanding? The Trilateral Commission," Revue Francaise d'Etudes Americaines 63 (1995): 107-116.

Refers in part to the Commission's use of insider information in its decision making activities toward its alleged intentions of world control of corporate organizations.

9628. Lucas, W. Scott. "Campaigns of Truth: The Psychological Strategy Board and American Ideology, 1951-1953," International History Review 18/2 (1996): 279-302.

9629. Lucas, W. Scott. "Escaping Suez: New Interpretations of Western Policy in the Middle East 1936-1961," Intelligence and National Security 12/2 (April 1997): 180-183.

A brief book review essay referring to three books: T. Shaw, Eden, Suez and the Mass Media; H. G. A. Nasser, Britain and the Egyptian Nationalist Movement, 1936-1952; and A. Rathmell, Secret War in the Middle East: The Covert Struggle for Syria, 1949-1961.

9630. Lucas, W. Scott. "Beyond the New Look: Policy and Operations in the Eisenhower Administration," Intelligence and National Security 12/3 (July 1997): 196-200.

A book review essay examining three related works: Saki Dockrill's Eisenhower's New-Look National Security Policy, 1953-61, 1996; Erika Alin's The United States and the 1958 Lebanon Crisis, 1994; and Audrey R. and George McT. Kahin's Subversion as Foreign Policy: The Secret Eisenhower and Dulles Debacle in Indonesia, 1995.

9631. Luckett, Thomas M. "Hunting for Spies and Whores: A Parisian Riot on the Eve of the French Revolution," Past & Present 156 (August 1997): 116-143.

A richly detailed discussion of the riots in Paris in 1787-1788 and more carefully evaluates the circumstances of the 1787 "Tonneau riot" which appears to have laid the groundwork for later popular violence. Considers also the search for spies and prostitutes.

9632. Lundin, John A. "Red Nautilus Under Way," Studies in Intelligence 11/1 (Spring 1967).

9633. Lyandres, S.; N. A. Sidorov; and E. S. Ul'ko. "Novye Dokumenty o Finansovykh Subsidiiakh Bol'shevikam v 1917 Godu," Otechestvennaia Istoriia 2 (1993): 128-143.

An edited collection of documents pertaining to secret finances supplied to the Bolsheviks in the Russian revolution.

9634. MacDonald, Callum A. "The Venlo Affair," European Studies Review 8 (1978): 443-464.

Recounts the story of two British intelligence officers who were kidnapped in November 1939 at Venlo, near the German-Dutch border. They were taken to Germany. The mysterious incident remains shrouded in secrecy as to what the British SIS knew about the incident. The author provides an analysis of the background circumstances to the incident.

9635. MacEachin, Douglas J. "CIA Assessments of the Soviet Union," Studies in Intelligence Unclassified edition (1997): 57-65.

A former high level CIA executive discusses what the CIA said; the failing Soviet system; Gorbachev; the showdown; failure to predict what did not happen; tyrannical numbers; and lessons.

9636. Mac Gregro, Felipe. "La Reconstrucion tras el Conflicto: El Peru Despues de Sendero Luminoso," Analysis Internacional: Revista del Centro Peruano de Estudos Internacionales (January-April 1995): 59-66.

9637. Mackie, J. D. "The Secret Diplomacy of King James VI in Italy Prior to His Accession to the English Throne," Scottish Historical Review 21 (1923-1924): 267-282.

An account of the covert actions of James VI prior to assuming the throne of England following Queen Elizabeth. Discusses the use of emissaries, ciphers and blanks, and false documents.

9638. Maclin, Tracey. "Informants and the Fourth Amendment: A Reconsideration," <u>Washington University Law Quarterly</u> 74 (Fall 1996): 573-635.
Considers circumstances involving use of private employees in a corporation to conduct surveillance and to serve as informants for police. Major sections discuss the history of the US Constitution's Fourth Amendment; the modern informant cases; the defective reasoning of the Supreme Court on privacy; and conclusions.

9639. Macleod, D. Peter. "Treason at Quebec: British Espionage in Canada During the Winter of 1759-1760," <u>Canadian Military History</u> 2/1 (1993): 49-62.

9640. Maddrell, Paul. "Fond 89 of the Archives of the Soviet Communist Party and Soviet State," <u>Intelligence and National Security</u> 12/2 (April 1997): 184-197.
A summation of the contents of this particular collection of microfilm reels, Fond 89, recently released by the State Archival Service of Russia and the Hoover Institution on War, Revolution and Peace. The set contains 25 reels and approximately 3000 documents.

9641. Maddrell, Paul. "Battlefield Germany," <u>Intelligence and National Security</u> 13/2 (Summer 1998): 190-212.
A lengthy book review essay pertaining to six books: <u>Headquarters Germany</u> by Klaus Eichner and Andreas Dobbert; <u>Bauernopfer der Deutschen Frage: Der Kommunist Kurt Vieweg im Dschungel der Geheimdienste</u> by Michael F. Scholz; <u>Spionage fuer den Frieden? Nachrichtendienste in Deutschland Wahrend des Kalten Krieges</u> by Wolfgang Krieger and Jurgen Weber (eds.); <u>Auftrag Winrose: Der Militarische Geheimdienst der DDR</u> by Andreas Kabus; <u>Battleground Berlin: CIA vs. KGB in the Cold War</u> by David E. Murphy, Sergei A Kondrashev, and George Bailey; and <u>Man without a Face</u> by Markus Wolf.

9642. Madsen, Wayne; David L. Sobel; Max Rotenberg, et al. "Cryptography and Liberty: An International Survey of Encryption Policy," <u>John Marshall Journal of Computer & Information Law</u> 16 (Spring 1998): 475-503.

9643. Maglio, Manuela. "Palestine, Israel and Egypt: New Scholarship on Middle Eastern Conflicts," <u>Intelligence and National Security</u> 12/2 (April 1997): 163-179.
A book review essay referring to six major new works: A. Ilan, <u>The Origins of the Arab-Israeli Arms Race</u>; E. Inbar and S. Sandler (eds.), <u>Middle Eastern Security: Prospects for an Arms Control Regime</u>; S. Zadka, <u>Blood in Zion: How the Jewish Guerillas Drove the British Out of Palestine</u>; J. Heller, <u>The</u>

Stern Gang: Ideology, Politics and Terror 1940-1949; W. S. Lucas, Britain and Gaza: The Lion's Last Roar; and R. Ginat, The Soviet Union and Egypt 1945-1955.

9644. Maguire, J. Robert. "Hand's Cove: Rendezvous of Ethan Allen and the Green Mountain Boys for the Capture of Fort Ticonderoga," Vermont History 33 (1965): 417-437.

9645. Maguire, J. Robert. "Dr. Robert Knox's Account of the Battle of Balcour, October 11-13, 1776," Vermont History 46 (1978): 141-150.

9646. Maguire, M. and T. John. "Covert and Deceptive Policing in England and Wales: Issues in Regulation and Practice," European Journal of Crime, Criminal Law and Criminal Justice 4/4 (1997): 316-334.
   Major sections discuss the shift to proactive investigation; the patchwork of regulation and coming changes; and concluding comments.

9647. Mahnken, Thomas G. "Gazing at the Sun: The Office of Naval Intelligence and Japanese Naval Innovation, 1918-1941," Intelligence and National Security 11/3 (July 1996): 424-441.
   Discussion of US Naval intelligence and the Japanese navy; incomplete and inaccurate data; inadequate analytical constructs; ingrained beliefs; and conclusions and insights.

9648. Malleson, W. "The British Military Mission to Turkestan, 1918-1920," Journal of the Central Asian Society 9 (1922): 96-110.

9649. Mallmann, Klaus-Michael. "Social Penetration and Police Action: Collaboration Structures in the Repertory of Gestapo Activities," International Review of Social History 42/1 (April 1997): 25-43.

9650. Malooly, Daniel J. "Physical Searches Under FISA: A Constitutional Analysis," American Criminal Law Review 35 (Winter 1998): 411-424.
   An analysis of search principles and rules under the Foreign Intelligence Surveillance Act.

9651. Managhan, Robert L. "Trends in African Forgeries," Studies in Intelligence 19/1 (Spring 1975).

9652. Mangano, Basil W. "The Communications Assistance for Law Enforcement Act and Protection of Cordless Telephone Communications: The Use of Technology As a Guide to Privacy," Cleveland State Law Review 44 (Winter 1996): 99-122.
   Major sections discuss the history of federal wiretap law; case law on

wiretapping; defining cordless telephone communication; and legislation and technology.

9653. Mangini, Publio and Anne Crudge. "Experience in War: Secret Mission to Tokyo," MHQ: The Quarterly Journal of Military History 5/4 (Summer 1993).

9654. Manrique, Nelson. "Lo Publico y lo Privado en al Ciberespacio," Que Hacer: Revista Bimestral (May-June 1996): 60-64.
     Includes discussion of encryption issues, legal aspects of encryption policies, and federal agencies that require encryption protection.

9655. Marcquenski, Thomas W. "A Name for Your Number," Studies in Intelligence 7/3 (Fall 1963).

9656. Marengo, Louis; Dean Moor; Richard Ober; and Dick Wood. "National Estimates: An Assessment of the Product and the Process," Studies in Intelligence 21/1 (Spring 1977).

9657. Marin Aranquren, Margarita. "El Gasto Militar Para Que? Los Gatos Militares en Colombia Son Desproporcionados Frente a la Efectividad de las Fuerzas Armadas," Economia Columbiana: Revista de la Contraloria General de la Republica (June 1996): 61-63.
     Concerns a variety of internal security issues facing the Colombian government.

9658. Mark, Eduard. "Venona's Source 19 and the 'Trident' Conference of May 1943: Diplomacy or Espionage?," Intelligence and National Security 13/2 (Summer 1998): 1-31.
     A lengthy accounting of the records of the Trident conference between the US ranking leadership and the Soviets on the prospective invasion of Western Europe in World War II. Apparently, the records strongly suggest that the source of the date for US invasion was Roosevelt's special assistant, Harry Hopkins.

9659. Marks, Tom. "Against All Odds: Columbia Army Battles Marx, Narcs and Politicos," Soldier of Fortune 23 (January 1998): 40-45+.

9660. Markvart, Fred A. "A Chinese Defects," Studies in Intelligence 11/2 (Summer 1967).

9661. Marl, David. "The Mayaguez Rescue Operation Revisited," Studies in Intelligence 23/2 (Summer 1979).

9662. Marquardt-Bigman, Petra. "American Intelligence Estimates of Nazi Germany," Tel Aviv Journal of German History 23 (1994): 325-344.

In German, this article describes some of the work of the Research and Analysis Branch of the wartime American Office of Strategic Services under the supervision of William Langer, with particular emphasis on the work of Franz Neumann.

9663. Marquart-Bigman, Petra. "The Research and Analysis Branch of the Office of Strategic Services in the Debate over US Policies towards Germany, 1943-46," Intelligence and National Security 12/2 (April 1997): 91-100.
A brief history of the subject, including the personal experiences of the author.

9664. Marquart-Bigman, Petra. "Project Communication: An Oral History of the Office of Strategic Services," Intelligence and National Security 12/2 (April 1997): 161-162.
A brief summary of available resources to continue this project sponsored by the Central Intelligence Agency.

9665. Marshall, Patrick. "Guarding the Wealth of Nations," Wilson Quarterly 21/1 (Winter 1997): 64-70.
Discussion of industrial espionage by theft of intellectual property and piracy as it affects foreign policy, trade policy, and international relations.

9666. Marsot, Alain-Gerard. "Background to the American Intervention in Cambodia: Sihanouk's Overthrow," Asian Profile 1/1 (1973): 75-90.

9667. Martenow, Daniel R. "Reentry Vehicle Analysis," Studies in Intelligence 12/2 (Summer 1968).

9668. Martin, Lawrence A. "The Battle of the Bulge in Retrospect," Military Review 75/1 (1994-1995): 116-118.
A brief analysis of the famous battle's characteristics in terms of surprise attack concepts.

9669. Marx, Gary T. "The New Police Undercover Work," Urban Life 8/4 (January 1980): 399-446.
Discusses types of undercover activity; intended and unintended consequences; inducing unwanted crimes; enforcing the law against each other; becoming what we pretend to be; expansion of proactive policing; and some implications for policy and theories of deviance.

9670. Marx, Gary T. "When the Guards Guard Themselves: Undercover Tactics Turned Inward," Policing and Society 2/3 (1992): 151-172.

9671. Mascolo, Edward G. "Controverting and Informant's Factual Basis for a

Search Warrant: <u>Franks v. Delaware</u> Revisited and Rejected Under Connecticut Law," <u>QLR</u> 15 (Spring 1995): 65-101.

This publication was originally <u>Bridgeport Law Review</u>. Major sections discuss veracity attacks upon affidavits for search warrants under the <u>Franks</u> rule; the "good faith" exception to the exclusionary rule; <u>Marsola</u> and the expanded scope of the exclusionary rule; and conclusions with respect to police use of informants who lie or who fabricate information for police use in search warrant affidavits.

9672. Mason, Geoffrey C. "Electronic Surveillance," <u>Georgetown Law Journal</u> 84 (April 1996): 821-842.

This is the annual review (95-96) of Supreme Court analyses of electronic surveillance pursuant to Title III of the Omnibus Crime Control and Safe Streets Act of 1968.

9673. Mastrofski, Stephen and Gary Potter. "Controlling Organized Crime: A Critique of Law Enforcement Policy," <u>Criminal Justice Policy Review</u> 2/3 (1987): 269-301.

9674. Mathes, W. Michael. "The Expedition of Juan Rodriguez Cabrillo, 1542-1543: An Historiographical Reexamination," <u>Southern California Quarterly</u> 76/3 (1994): 247-253.

Describes the cartographic work of Spanish explorers Sebastian Vizcaino and Juan Cabrillo, indicating that the latter's work has only reconnaissance value by comparison with Vizcaino's complex and far reaching explorations.

9675. Mathews, Charles W. "Technical Intelligence and Arms Inspection," <u>Studies in Intelligence</u> 2 (Fall 1957).

9676. Matsumara, Janice. "Internal Security in Wartime Japan (1937-45) and the Creation of Internal Insecurity," <u>Canadian Journal of History</u> 31/3 (December 1996): 395-411.

An excellent history of the internal dynamics of Japanese politics and civil society before and during World War II, with some references to spies and traitors in the context of domestic thought control.

9677. Matthias, Willard C. "How Three Estimates Went Wrong," <u>Studies in Intelligence</u> 12/4 (Winter 1968): 27-35.

Analysis of escalation of US actions in the Vietnam war. Author served as chairman of the intelligence community's Board of National Estimates.

9678. Mauch, Christof. "Dream of a Miracle War: The OSS and Germany, 1942-1945," <u>Prologue: Quarterly Journal of the National Archives</u> 27/2 (1995): 134-143.

Describes and interprets the work of the American Office of Strategic Services from 1942-1945, with particular emphasis on OSS's interpretation of the advancement of German internal resistance to the Nazi's and Adolph Hitler.

9679. Maxfield, Myles and Edward G. Greger. "VIP Health Watch," Studies in Intelligence 12/1 (Spring 1968).

9680. Maxfield, Myles; Robert Proper; and Sharol Case. "Remote Medical Diagnosis," Studies in Intelligence 23/1 (Spring 1979).

9681. Maximov, William J. and Edward Scrutchings. "The Metal Traces Test," Studies in Intelligence 11/3 (Fall 1967).

9682. Mayor, Adrienne. "Dirty Tricks in Ancient Warfare," MHQ: The Quarterly Journal of Military History 10/1 (Autumn 1997).

9683. McCadden, Harvey B. "Cover in Unconventional Operations," Studies in Intelligence 5/2 (Summer 1961).

9684. McCarrick, Earlean M. "American Anti-Nazism: A Cold War Casualty," Simon Wiesenthal Center Annual 6 (1989): 223-233.

9685. McConaghy, Jeanine P. "Criminal Law--Outrageous Misconduct--A Viable But Rarely Successful Defense," Suffolk University Law Review 28 (Fall 1994): 906-910.
Reviews the circumstances of the Santana case wherein government agents distributed a large quantity of heroin in a reverse sting operation, but they failed to re-acquire the drugs at the end of the investigation. The district court threw out the prosecution under the outrageous misconduct principle.

9686. McCracken, Michael C. "Computers in Economic Intelligence," Studies in Intelligence 13/1 (Spring 1969).

9687. McCrea, Brett A. "U.S. Counter-Terrorist Policy: A Proposed Strategy for a Non-traditional Threat," Low Intensity Conflict and Law Enforcement 3/3 (1994): 493-508.

9688. McCullough, James. "Commentary on 'Congress as a User of Intelligence,'" Studies in Intelligence Unclassified edition (Spring 1998): 71-74.
The author, a former CIA senior officer in the Directorate of Operations, remarks on the issues raised by L. Britt Snider in the article by the same title (see this section under Snider, L. Britt). This article is published in the unnumbered and unclassified issue of the CIA's internal journal. Sections discuss Congress, CIA, and aid to Cambodia; operations in the Gulf; and need for wider awareness.

9689.   McDonald, J. Kenneth.   "Commentary on "History Declassified,'" Diplomatic History 18/4 (Fall 1994): 627-634.

A commentary in further discussion and critique of the article by Z. Karabell and T. Naftali in the same issue (see above citation). Offers information the author believes was overlooked with respect to the CIA's intelligence declassification efforts.

9690. McDonald, Robert A.   "CORONA: Success for Space Reconnaissance, a Look into the Cold War, and a Revolution for Intelligence," Photogrammetric Engineering & Remote Sensing 61 (June 1995).

9691. McDonald, Walter. "African Numbers Game," Studies in Intelligence 8/3 (Fall 1964).

9692. McDowell, Jonathan. "US Reconnaissance Satellite Programs, Part I," Quest (Summer 1995): 28-31.

9693. McDowell, Jonathan. "US Reconnaissance Satellite Programs, Part II," Quest (Winter 1995): 41-42.

9694. McGee, Val L. "The Confederate Who Switched Sides: The Saga of Captain Joseph G. Sanders," Alabama Review 47/1 (1994): 20-28.

A brief history of a man who switched sides in the Civil War, from Confederate captain to Union lieutenant. Useful in studies of the meaning of treason in wartime.

9695.   McGuffy, Roger W.   "The Case Against Solzhenitsyn," Studies in Intelligence 13/2 (Summer 1969).

9696. McGuire, Andre. "CIA: Myth and Reality," Military Intelligence 20/4 (October-December 1994): 9-12.

From experience with the CIA, the author wishes to set the record straight to dispel myths, and to discuss the future relationships between CIA and Defense Intelligence Agency.

9697. McIninch, Thomas P. "The OXCART Story," Studies in Intelligence 15/4 (Winter 1971).

Estimated to be 22 pages in length. Also appeared in an issue of Air Force Magazine, and may have been reprinted in Studies in Intelligence in 1982. Observes the historic event of the first flight of the A-12 spy aircraft in 1962, flown by a test pilot named Louis Schalk. The plane was named OXCART, the code for the development program. The A-12 was the prototype of the SR-71 aircraft.

9698. McKay, C. G. "MI5 on OSTRO: A New Document from the Archives," Intelligence and National Security 12/3 (July 1997): 178-184.

Reports on the usefulness of an MI5 memoranda on OSTRO signal operations in World War II, particularly two reports in June 1944.

9699. McKeown, Margaret. "Trade Secret Enforcement in the United States," International Law Practicum 9 (Spring 1996): 22-28.

9700. McKnight, David. "Reassessing the Rosenberg and Petrov Affairs," Labour History 70 (May 1996): 182-190.

Discusses the debate over the authenticity of the Venona cables. This is an Australian journal.

9701. McKnight, David. "The Moscow-Canberra Cables: How Soviet Intelligence Obtained British Secrets through the Back Door," Intelligence and National Security 13/2 (Summer 1998): 159-170.

Drawing on decoded Soviet KGB cables, the author confirms the value of the 1954 Royal Commission on Espionage, particularly with respect to the domestic espionage activities of certain communists in the public service in Australia. Points out the value, also, of the Venona cables.

9702. McLaughlin, John E. "New Challenges and Priorities for Analysis," Defense Intelligence Journal 6/2 (Fall 1997): 11-21.

Discusses the analytical agenda, mainly of CIA; service of needs in the analytical and policy settings; and conclusions.

9703. McLean, David R. "Cranks, Nuts, and Screwballs," Studies in Intelligence 9/2 (Summer 1965).

9704. McMullan, John L. "The Arresting Eye: Discourse, Surveillance and Disciplinary Administration in Early English Police Thinking," Social and Legal Studies 7 (March 1998): 97-128.

9705. McNaughton, James C. "Desert Storm's Language Lessons: Can We Talk?," Army (June 1992): 20-25.

A useful warning regarding the shortfall in linguistic capabilities in the military intelligence ranks.

9706. McT. Kahin, Audrey and George. "The Debate Continues: The CIA in Indonesia: The Scholars vs. the Professionals, CIA Disingenuous," International Journal of Intelligence and Counterintelligence 10/2 (Summer 1997): 206-217.

This article is based on the author's book, Subversion as Foreign Policy: The Secret Eisenhower and Dulles Debacle in Indonesia, and it is a rebuttal to a book review essay appearing in volume 9, issue 3 of the Journal by J. Foster

Collins and B. Hugh Tovar. Major sections discuss the facts the authors offer; the author disagreements with Collins and Tovar; areas of the review which do not challenge the authors; taking Hugh to task; and dissing the killings in 1965-66.

9707. McWhiney, Grady. "Conservatism and the Military," Continuity 4&5 (1982): 93-126.

9708. Meares, Russell. "The Secret," Psychiatry 39 (1976): 258-265.
A psychiatric perspective on the implications of a secret.

9709. Meernik, James. "Presidential Decision Making and the Political Use of Military Force," International Studies Quarterly 38/1 (1994): 121-138.
A study of decision making criteria in international situations calling for presidential initiative, including the use of military force. Argues that national interest was more often than not the criterion for action than alternative political benefit.

9710. Melakopides, Constantine. "Libya Raids and the Western Alliance," International Perspectives (July-August 1986): 19-21.

9711. Melin, Marshall. "The 'Unknown' Satellite," Sky & Telescope (April 1960).

9712. Mendenhall, Lawrence K. "Misters Korematsu and Steffan: The Japanese Internment and the Military's Ban on Gays in the Armed Forces," New York University Law Review 70 (April 1995): 196-225.

9713. Meredith, Owen N. "The Sam Davis Home," Tennessee Historical Quarterly 24/4 (1965): 303-320.

9714. Merkle, Janet H. "Policy Bias," Studies in Intelligence 7/4 (Winter 1963).
Reflections on circumstances in Angola.

9715. Messer, Robert L. "Paths Not Taken: The United States Department of State and Alternatives to Containment, 1945-1946," Diplomatic History 1/4 (Fall 1977): 297-319.
Inquires into the making of foreign policy consensus, especially with respect to the role and limits of expert advice in the policy process. The focus is on US containment policy immediately following World War II.

9716. Metcalfe, N. P. and J. C. Smith. "Customs and Excise Management Act 1979, s.170(2)--Police and Criminal Evidence Act 1984, s.78--Use of Undercover Officer in Pakistan and Customs Officer as Courier--Enticement of Defendants to England--Admissibility of Evidence of Undercover Officer--No Abuse of Process,"

Criminal Law Review (June 1996): 414-416.

9717. Metcalfe, N. P. and J. C. Smith. "Police and Criminal Evidence Act 1984, s.78--Admissibility--Whether Evidence from Covert Electronic Device Properly Admitted," Criminal Law Review (October 1996): 733-735.

9718. Metz, Steven. "Deterring Conflict Short of War," Strategic Review 22/4 (Fall 1994): 48-58.

9719. Metzger, Laurent. "Joseph Ducroux, a French Agent of the Comintern in Singapore (1931-1932)," Journal of the Malaysian Branch of the Royal Asiatic Society 69/1 (1996): 1-20.
    Discusses Ducroux's early life; experience in Singapore; trial for subversion; sentence; Malay writings; and conclusions. Includes an extensive bibliography on Malaysian communism and politics.

9720. Meyerhoff, Hans. "Through the Liberal Looking Glass--Darkly," Partisan Review 22 (1955): 238-245.
    A viewpoint on the allegations against J. Robert Oppenheimer.

9721. Miester, Donald J., Jr. "Trade Secret Misappropriation under the Louisiana Trade Secrets Act," Louisiana Bar Journal 44 (December 1996): 326-330.

9722. Millar, James R., et al. "Survey Article: An Evaluation of the CIA's Analysis of Soviet Economic Performance, 1970-1990," Comparative Economic Studies 35/2 (Summer 1993): 33-57.

9723. Miller, Abraham H. "How the CIA Fell Victim to Myth Posing as Journalism," International Journal of Intelligence and Counterintelligence 10/3 (Fall 1997): 257-268.
    Discusses myths about CIA that have been reinforced in the media, such as the allegation that CIA had been a major drug dealer in Los Angeles. Sections discuss rapping the spooks; seeking a cause; the federal target; the role of Congresswoman Maxine Waters; the role of John Deutch; unraveling the Gary Webb; and backtracking on Webb.

9724. Miller, Abraham H. and Nicholas A. Damask. "The Dual Myths of Narco-Terrorism: How Myths Drive Policy," Terrorism and Political Violence 8/1 (Spring 1996): 114-131.

9725. Miller, J. Mitchell and Lance H. Selva. "Drug Enforcement's Double-Edged Sword: An Assessment of Asset Forfeiture Programs," Justice Quarterly 11/2 (June 1994): 313-335.
    A discussion of some ethnographic research by undercover operations

methods concerning asset forfeiture in the drug war. Major sections discuss the background of the study; the under cover research over a one year period; typical cases; the impact of forfeiture on police conduct; and an overall assessment of the program.

9726. Millican, E. Bowie; Robert M. Gelman; and Thomas A. Stanhope. "Lost Order, Lost Cause," Studies in Intelligence 2 (Winter 1958).

9727. Millikan, Max F. "The Nature and Methods of Economic Intelligence," Studies in Intelligence 1 (Spring 1956).

9728. Millis, Wade. "Spy Under the Common Law of War," American Bar Association Journal 11 (1925): 183-184.

9729. Millstein, Mark H. "Hez Hunters: Ringside as 'Grapes of Wrath,'" Soldier of Fortune 21 (September 1996): 31-34.
    A brief summary of Israeli actions to counter Hezbollah terrorists.

9730. Mineur, Michael L. "Defense Against Communist Interrogation Organizations," Studies in Intelligence 13/3 (Fall 1969).

9731. Minichello, Dennis. "Use and Abuse of Surveillance Videos," Illinois Bar Journal 85 (January 1997): 22-28.

9732. Minihan, Kenneth A. "Conflict in the Information Age: Threat and Response," American Intelligence Journal 17/1&2 (1996): 7-10.
    Discusses threats to industrial technology; the response; standards; technology; vulnerabilities; and the role of intelligence.

9733. Mirsky, Wendy L. "The Link Between Russian Organized Crime and Nuclear-Weapons Proliferation: Fighting Crime and Ensuring International Security," University of Pennsylvania Journal of International Business Law 16/4Winter 1996): 749-781.
    Major sections discuss fissile material's appearance in Europe on the black market; the growth of Russian organized crime since the fall of the Soviet Union; the link between Russian organized crime and nuclear-weapons proliferation in Europe; obstacles in combatting nuclear proliferation by organized crime and possible solutions; and conclusions.

9734. "The Missiles Leave Cuba," ONI Review 17/12 (1962): 511-512.
    A brief reflection on the missile crisis outcome.

9735. "Miss Menzies Wishes the Record to be Complete," New Jersey History 85/3-4 (1967): 217-224.

9736. Miyagi, Takemi. "Which Way Did They Go?," Studies in Intelligence 11/4 (Winter 1967).

Reflections on Japanese spies and espionage operations in World War II.

9737. "A Modest Suggestion for a Review of the Bidding," Studies in Intelligence 14/3 (Fall 1970).

9738. Moffat, Wendy. "Domestic Violence: The Simple Tale with The Secret Agent," English Literature in Transition 1880-1920 37/4 (1994): 465-489.

The author interprets Joseph Conrad's novel in terms of domestic violence and its impact on certain characters. Major sections discuss intention and irony; marriage, respectability, and agency; and the limits of irony.

9739. Molander, Roger C.; Andrew S. Riddle; and Peter A. Wilson. "Strategic Information Warfare: A New Face of War," Parameters: US Army War College Quarterly 26/3 (Autumn 1996): 81-92.

Discusses the definition of information warfare; strategic information warfare; basic features of strategic information warfare; and conclusions on the elusive bottom line on the threat.

9740. Monteiro, Alfred, Jr. "Cryptologic Support to Military Operations," American Intelligence Journal 17/3&4 (1997): 39-44.

Major sections discuss definitions of terms and roles; examining the military support process; USSS strengths and weaknesses; conducting military support, and conclusions.

9741. Moomaw, W. H. "The Denouement of General Howe's Campaign of 1777," English Historical Review 79/312 (1964): 498-512.

9742. Moore, Davis W., Jr. "Open Sources on Soviet Military Affairs," Studies in Intelligence 7/2 (Summer 1963).

9743. Moore, Jeffrey M. "Pacific Island Intelligence: The Assault on Tinian," American Intelligence Journal 18/1&2 (1998): 81-86.

A brief history of intelligence operations to estimate the conditions that would contribute to a successful attack on Tinian Island in July 1944. Sections discuss intelligence collection; how intelligence influenced the battle; the amphibious landings; geography; order of battle; mistakes; analysis of success; and conclusion.

9744. Moore, John H. "Measuring Soviet Economic Growth: Old Problems and New Complications," Journal of Institutional and Theoretical Economics 148/1 (1992): 72-92.

9745. Morfit, John C. "Who Has the Information I Want?," Studies in Intelligence 14/3 (Fall 1970).

9746. Morgan, Gerald. "A Glimpse at Russian Nineteenth Century Espionage," Contemporary Review 215/1246 (November 1969): 225-232.
    Argues that the Mongol conquerors of Russia had much to do with instilling intrigue and espionage into Russian society and thought. A brief account of intelligence gathering activities by and against Russia in the 19th century.

9747. Morris, Jack. "Disaster Over Armenia: A Personal Recollection," American Intelligence Journal 17/3&4 (1997): 5-6.
    Reflects the author's recollections of a Soviet shootdown of an American C-130 in Eastern Turkey in September 1958.

9748. Morris, John L. "MASINT," American Intelligence Journal 17/1&2 (1996): 24-27.
    Key sections discuss definition of Measurements and Signature Intelligence(MASINT); Central MASINT Office responsibilities; applications; and future directions.

9749. Morris, L. P. "British Secret Missions in Turkestan, 1918-19," Journal of Contemporary History 12/2 (April 1977): 363-379.
    Discusses British espionage work in various intrigues in the effort to secure India during World War I. Discusses the Military Intelligence Division of the War Office and its role in dispatching secret agents.

9750. Morris, Scott R. "America's Most Recent Prisoner of War: The Warrant Officer Bobby Hall Incident," Army Lawyer (September 1996): 3-30.

9751. Mossinghoff, Gerald J.; J. Derek Mason; and David A. Oblon. "The Economic Espionage Act: A New Federal Regime of Trade Secret Protection," Journal of the Patent and Trademark Office Society 79 (March 1997): 191-210.

9752. Moynihan, Daniel P. "The Culture of Secrecy," Public Interest 128 (Summer 1997): 55-72.
    Discusses the new world order; the Wright Commission; secrecy and inefficiency; a culture of openness; keeping secrets; and the right to know.

9753. Mozumbar, Chandana. "The Role of Mixed Bloods Among the Southeastern Indians During the Colonial Period," New England Journal of History 51/3 (1995): 2-9.
    A brief consideration of intermarriage and child rearing among traders and indians in Southeastern regions of America during the colonial era. Argues that this mixing of races produced benefits for colonial leaders, since new

generations filled roles as language interpreters and intelligence gatherers.

9754. Mulcahy, Kevin V. "Walt Rostow As National Security Adviser, 1966-69," Presidential Studies Quarterly 25/2 (1995): 223-236.

A revisitation of Walt Rostow's performance during the years he served as President Johnson's national security adviser. Considers his role in staffing and directing the National Security Council.

9755. Mulcahy, Kevin V. "Rethinking Groupthink: Walt Rostow and the National Security Advisory Process in the Johnson Administration," Presidential Studies Quarterly 25/2 (1995): 237-250.

Argues against the popular view that Walt Rostow, Lyndon Johnson's national security adviser, controlled information inputs on national security issues to the degree that a group think mindset was allegedly institutionalized. Author observes the active role of Rostow in providing Johnson with a wide range of information regarding the progress of the Vietnam war.

9756. Mulholland, Warren R. "Liaison Training," Studies in Intelligence 17/2 (Summer 1973).

9757. Mullaney, Steven. "Lying Like Truth: Riddle, Representation and Treason in Renaissance England," ELH 47 (1980): 32-47.

9758. Muller, Kurt E. "On the Military Significance of Language Competence," Modern Language Journal 65/4 (Winter 1981): 361-370.

Argues that the net decline in language competence carries significant negative implications for intelligence services and the military branches. Advances the view that a software should be developed to improve armed forces language capabilities.

9759. Mullins, Wayman C. "An Overview and Analysis of Nuclear, Biological, and Chemical Terrorism: The Weapons, Strategies, and Solutions to a Growing Problem," American Journal of Criminal Justice 16/2 (1992): 95-119.

9760. Munson, Harlow T. and W. P. Southard. "Two Witnesses for the Defense," Studies in Intelligence 8/3 (Fall 1964): 93-98.

9761. Murphy, Christopher K. "Electronic Surveillance," Georgetown Law Journal 85 (April 1997): 920-940.

This is the annual (1996-1997) review of electronic surveillance issues taken up by the Supreme Court.

9762. Murphy, David E. "They Called Him 'Misha,'" International Journal of Intelligence and Counterintelligence 11/1 (Spring 1998): 93-104.

A book review essay on <u>Man Without a Face: The Autobiography of Communism's Greatest Spymaster</u> by Marcus Wolf with Anne McElroy.

9763. Murphy, Frank B. "Ocean Surveillance: New Weapon of Naval Warfare," <u>U.S. Naval Institute Proceedings</u> 97/2 (1971): 38-41.

9764. Murphy, Mary L. "Tools for Trade Secret Litigation," <u>Practical Litigator</u> 7 (May 1996): 47-54.

9765. Murray, Williamson. "Overlord," <u>MHQ: The Quarterly Journal of Military History</u> 6/3 (Spring 1994): 6-21.
A detailed review of the plans for the allied invasion of Europe via Operation Overlord. Suggests that the plans did not entirely contemplate the losses suffered by the allies, but the main goals of the invasion were achieved.

9766. Nadel, Mark V. "Corporate Secrecy and Political Accountability," <u>Public Administration Review</u> 35 (1975): 14-23.
Major sections discuss sources of corporate secrecy; manifestation of corporate secrecy; the linkage between corporate and government secrecy; unilateral secrecy; and impact of corporate secrecy.

9767. Naffsinger, Peter A. "'Face' Among the Arabs," <u>Studies in Intelligence</u> 8/2 (Summer 1964).

9768. Nalivaiko, Boris Y. "'Konsol Bezhat' Otkasalsya," <u>Novoye Vremya</u> 37 (1993): 50-53.
The unclassified version of the author's description of Russian KGB's Gartenbau incident involving the author's investigation of the disappearance of Soviet defector Pyotr Deriabin. The author wrote a classified version of this investigation.

9769. Nance, William H. "Quality Elint," <u>Studies in Intelligence</u> 12/1 (Spring 1968).

9770. Nauck, A. "Friedrich der Grosse vor dem Ausbruch des Siebenjahrigen Krieges," <u>Historische Zeitschrift</u> 55 (1886): 425-462.
This article is continued in 56 (1887): 404-462. "Frederick the Great before the Outbreak of the Seven Years War."

9771. Naylor. R. T. "Loose Cannons: Covert Commerce and Underground Finance in the Modern Arms Black Market," <u>Crime, Law and Social Change</u> 22/1 (1995): 1-57.

9772. Needell, Allan A. "'Truth Is Our Weapon': Project TROY, Political

Warfare, and Government-Academic Relationships in the National Security State," <u>Diplomatic History</u> 17/3 (Summer 1993): 399-420.

Provides a history of the State Department's top secret project to bring twenty-one scientists, social scientists, and historians together to discuss the best insights into the internal circumstances of the post-war Soviet Union.

9773. Nekrasov, V. F. "Laventii Beriia," <u>Sovetskaia Militsiia</u> 3&4 (1990): 18-24; 40-46.

A two-part investigation into the life and intrigues of Stalinist head of the KGB.

9774. Nelson, Paul D. "Legacy of Controversy: Gates, Schuyler, and Arnold at Saratoga," <u>Military Affairs</u> 37 (1973): 41-47.

9775. Nelson, Paul D. "Guy Carleton versus Benedict Arnold: The Campaign of 1776 in Canada and on Lake Champlain," <u>New York History</u> 57 (1976): 339-366.

Discusses the campaign from British and American perspectives. Offers an explanation for British failure. Role of traitor Benedict Arnold is discussed.

9776. Neu, Charles E. "The Unfinished War," <u>Reviews in American History</u> 23/1 (1995): 144-152.

A book review essay.

9777. Neufeld, Robert T. "Mission Impossible: New York Cannot Face the Future without a Trade Secret Act," <u>Fordham Intellectual Property, Media & Entertainment Law Journal</u> 7 (Spring 1997): 883-926.

9778. Neuse, Steven M. "Bureaucratic Malaise in the Modern Spy Novel: Deighton, Greene, and LeCarre," <u>Public Administration</u> 60 (Autumn 1982): 293-306.

Discusses political themes in the modern spy novel; the bureaucratic malaise; the 'thriller'; the 'negative thriller'; the threat from within; the individual within the organization; and conclusions.

9779. "A New Analyst Replies," <u>Studies in Intelligence</u> 31/3 (Fall 1987).

This article is not listed among the collection of declassified items by the Central Intelligence Agency for public access.

9780. "A New Light on Old Spies," <u>Studies in Intelligence</u> 9/3 (Fall 1965).

A review of then-recent Soviet intelligence revelations. This article is not listed among the collection of declassified items by the Central Intelligence Agency for public access.

9781. Newton, William. "Rat-Race," Studies in Intelligence 21/3 (Fall 1977).

9782. Nguyen, Thinh. "Cryptography, Export Controls, and the First Amendment in Bernstein v. United States Department of State," Harvard Journal of Law and Technology 10 (Summer 1997): 667-684.

9783. Nicholls, Mark. "Treason's Reward: The Punishment of Conspirators in the Bye Plot of 1603," Historical Journal 38/4 (December 1995): 821-842.
    A reconsideration of a wide range of records pertaining to a celebrated but often forgotten treason plot in the early seventeenth century. Discusses the important elements in treason trials of the times, including the prisonerss conduct.

9784. Nicholls, William. "The Pollard Affair: Antisemitism in Government?," Midstream 42/5 (June-July 1996): 29-31.
    A review of the Jeffrey Pollard espionage case, and the authors opinions about what the case represents in terms of American government policy. Useful in studies of intelligence liaison.

9785. Nielsen, Nathan. "The National Intelligence Daily," Studies in Intelligence 20/1 (Spring 1976).

9786. Niu Xianming. "Kangzhan shiqi Zhongguo Qingbao zhan Suyi," Zhuanji Wenxue 27/6 (December 1975): 7-10.
    Roughly translated from the Chinese, this article concerns the author's reflections on Chinese intelligence warfare in the War of Resistance.

9787. Noonan, Robert W. "Split-Based Intelligence for Central Region Operations," American Intelligence Journal 17/3&4 (1997): 15-22.
    Discusses USCENTCOM theater strategy; the concept of intelligence operations; planning for split-based intelligence; how intelligence goes to war; the road ahead; and conclusions.

9788. Northrup, Doyle L. and Donald H. Rock. "The Detection of Joe 1," Studies in Intelligence 10/1 (Spring 1966).

9789. Norton, Robert; Charles Feldman; and Dennis Tafoya. "Risk Parameters Across Types of Secrets, Journal of Counseling Psychology 21 (1974): 450-454.
    Provides results of a content analysis of the frequency of themes for several hundred secrets obtained from an encounter group exercise. Seventeen categories of secrets were revealed in this individual-level study.

9790. Norwood, Stephen. "Ford's Brass Knuckles: Harry Bennett, the Cult of Muscularity, and Anti-Labor Terror - 1920-1945," Labor History 37/3 (1996): 365-391.

9791. "The NSA Journal," Studies in Intelligence 11/1 (Spring 1967).

9792. Nye, Joseph S. "Estimating the Future," American Intelligence Journal 17/1&2 (1996): 65-70.
    Originally published in the July-August issue of Foreign Affairs under a different title, sections discuss intelligence analysis in the Cold War era; after the Cold War; responses to uncertainty; and conclusions.

9793. Nystrm, Sune. "American Problems, V and VI," Kungliga Krigsvetenskaps Akademiens Handlingar och Tidskrift 172/4 & 8 (1968): 198-214; 466-480.

9794. Oberg, James. "Echoes of the Nedelin Catastrophe," Air & Space (December 1990): 76-77.
    A reflection on the Soviet rocket launch disaster in 1960 and the Soviet Union's rocket program headed by Marshal Mitrofan I. Nedelin. The disaster symbolized the stresses on both the American and Soviet secret satellite launch programs.

9795. Oberg, James. "The Moon Race (and Its Coverup) in Hindsight," Spaceflight (February 1993): 46-47.

9796. O'Connell, Robert L. "Arms and Men: The Wizards of German Weaponry," MHQ: The Quarterly Journal of Military History 1/3 (Spring 1989).

9797. O'Connell, Robert L. "Arms and Men: The Norden Bombsight," MHQ: The Quarterly Journal of Military History 2/4 (Summer 1990).

9798. Ogle, James V. "Intelligence of Literature," Studies in Intelligence 7/3 (Fall 1963).

9799. O'Halpin, Eunan. "'According to the Irish Minister in Rome...': British Decrypts and Irish Diplomacy in the Second World War," Irish Studies in International Affairs 6 (1995).

9800. Oldham, Max S. "A Value of Information," Studies in Intelligence 12/1 (Spring 1968).

9801. Olmsted, Kathryn. "Reclaiming Executive Power: The Ford Administration's Response to the Intelligence Investigations," Presidential Studies Quarterly 26/3 (Summer 1996): 725-737.
    Majors sections discuss early mistakes and lessons; monitoring, preempting, and discrediting Congress; media manipulation in the murder of Richard Welch; the Pike report leak; and conclusions.

9802. Olson, Gary D. "Thomas Brown, Loyalist Partisan, and the Revolutionary War in Georgia, 1777-1782," Georgia Historical Quarterly 54/1& 2 (1970): 1-19; 183-208.

9803. O'Malley, Edward. "Economic Espionage Act," American Intelligence Journal 18/1&2 (1998): 51-56.
      Summarizes the issues involved in developing the law; addressing the problem; statute provisions; arrests under EEA; and the 21st century.

9804. Omandere, Louise D. "The Covert Collection of Scientific Information," Studies in Intelligence 2 (Fall 1958).

9805. O'Mara, Michael D. "Thermal Surveillance and the Fourth Amendment: Heating Up the War on Drugs," Dickinson Law Review 100/2 (Winter 1996): 415-439.
      Major sections discuss thermal technology characteristics; sense-enhanced searches; judicial confirmation of the warrantless use of thermal surveillance; judicial scrutiny; Fourth Amendment analysis; and conclusions.

9806. O'Neal, William J. "Delation in the Early Empire," Classical Bulletin 55 (1978): 24-28.
      Discusses the role of information and informers in the early Roman empire.

9807. Orleans, Leo A. "The Problem of Chinese Statistics," Studies in Intelligence 17/1 (Spring 1973): 47-62.

9808. Orlov, Alexander S. "Operation Paperclip," Novaia i Noveishaia Istoriia 3 (1986): 206-211.
      This article appears in a Russian language journal.

9809. Orme, John. "Deterrence Failures: A Second Look," International Security 11/4 (Spring 1987): 96-124.
      Asks the question, when does deterrence fail to deter? Considers the Fashoda crisis of 1898; the Russo-Japanese war; Morocco 1911; July crisis 1914; the Korean war; the Cuban missile crisis; the Sino-Indian case; and the Arab-Israeli war.

9810. Orr, Kenneth G. "Training for Overseas Effectiveness: A Survey," Studies in Intelligence 4/3 (Fall 1960).

9811. Ostensoe, James G. "The Problem of Scientific Surprise," Studies in Intelligence 5/3 (Fall 1961).

9812. Ostermann, Christian R. "'Keeping the Pot Simmering': The United States and the East German Uprising of 1953," German Studies Review 19/1 (February 1996): 61-89.

Lengthy and detailed analysis of the work of the Eisenhower administration to support the grass roots uprising in East Germany in the summer and fall of 1953. Emphasis is placed on the role of Eisenhower's provision of food to embarrass the communist government while soliciting pro-US sentiment among the people. The strategy produced the desired short term positive effects for a favorable view of the US, but there were also negative implications with respect to reunification of Germany.

9813. Ostrovsky, Victor. "Bungled Amman Assassination Plot Exposes Rife with Israeli Government over Peace Negotiations," Washington Report on Middle East Affairs 16 (December 1997): 7-8+.

Includes discussion of Israeli intelligence operations and services.

9814. O'Toole, George J. A. "The Chesapeake Capes: American Intelligence Coup?," International Journal of Intelligence and Counterintelligence 10/2 (Summer 1997): 196-205.

Brief interpretation of aspects of the American Revolution's Battle of Yorktown as to intelligence dimensions. Majors sections discuss signalling ahead; knowing the moves; sailing by the book; mixed signals; and a grave loss.

9815. Ould, H. "Secret Agent: Criticism," English Review 35 (December 1922): 526-531.

A literary critique of Joseph Conrad's novel, Secret Agent.

9816. Owens, William A. "Intelligence in the 21st Century," Defense Intelligence Journal 7/1 (Spring 1998): 25-45.

Argues that changes are needed in the intelligence community in order for the community to fully accommodate the information revolution affecting DoD operations. Major sections discuss dominant battlespace knowledge; the shift from attrition to nodal warfare; larger implications; and role of intelligence.

9817. Paddock, Ira J. "Cipher Codes Simplified," Scientific American 113 (September 1915): 271.

A brief observation that the use of numeral values assigned to letters may simplify a cipher code for translation or detection. Note the year of publication of this article.

9818. Paine, Gary. "A Mine, the Military, and a Dry Lake: National Security and the Groom District, Lincoln County, Nevada," Nevada Historical Society Quarterly 39/1 (1996): 20-42.

9819. Palat, Madhaven K. "Police Socialism in Tsarist Russia, 1900-1905," Studies in History 2 (January-June 1986): 71-136.

9820. Pal'chikov, P. A. and A. A. Goncharov. "Chto Proizoshlo s Komanduiushchim Zapadnym Frontom Generalom D. G. Pavlovym v 1941 g.," Novaia i Noveishaia Istoriia 5 (1992): 114-135.
    Contemplates the disappearance of Russian General Pavlov who commanded Russian troops against the German advances in 1941.

9821. Palfrey, John G. "The AEC Security Program: Past and Present," Bulletin of the Atomic Scientists 11 (April 1955): 131-133.
    Discusses the Atomic Energy Commission; early security program; the later period; the effects of the interplay between two systems; and the meaning of AEC's personnel security system.

9822. Panjabi, Ranee K. L. "Terror at the Emperor's Birthday Party: An Analysis of the Hostage-Taking Incident at the Japanese Embassy in Lima, Peru," Dickinson Journal of International Law 16 (Fall 1997): 1-135.

9823. Panzarella, Robert and Joanna Funk. "Police Deception Tactics and Public Consent in the United States and Great Britain," Criminal Justice Policy Review 2/2 (1987): 133-149.

9824. Park, David M. "Re-examining the Attorney General's Guidelines for FBI Investigations of Domestic Groups," Arizona Law Review 39 (Summer 1997): 769-792.
    Provides discussion of the historical background of the FBI Guidelines; constitutional challenges and proposals for changing the Guidelines for use against domestic terrorism.

9825. Parker, Geoffrey. "Philip II, Knowledge and Power," MHQ: The Quarterly Journal of Military History 11/1 (Autumn 1998): 104-111.
    Discusses the seemingly perpetual problem of information overload as encountered in military planning and execution throughout modern history. Argues that Philip II faced this problem in the sixteenth century in connection with the amount of communication time and distance from critical points of potential and actual conflict.

9826. Parkerson, John E., Jr. "United States Compliance with Humanitarian Law Respecting Civilians during Operation Just Cause," Military Law Review 133 (Summer 1991): 31-148.

9827. Parkinson, Len. "Penkovskiy's Legacy and Strategic Research," Studies in Intelligence 16/1 (Spring 1972).

9828. Parks, W. Hays. "Memorandum of Law: Executive Order 12333 and Assassination," Army Lawyer (December 1989): 4-9.

Following issuance of various Presidential Orders precluding assassination by any government employee, the meaning of assassination in the military context remains unclear. This memorandum explains the term in the context of military operations.

9829. Parrish, Randolph. "The Lords of Diplomacy: The Dulles Brothers," Midstream 42/5 (June-July 1996): 11-13.

A brief summation of the lives and circumstances of John Foster Dulles and Allen Dulles, former CIA director.

9830. Parry-Giles, Shawn J. "The Eisenhower Administration's Conceptualization of the USIA: The Development of Overt and Covert Propaganda Strategies," Presidential Studies Quarterly 24/2 (1994): 263-276.

Detailed review of the propaganda policies and programs of the Eisenhower administration, particularly with respect to the central role of the US Information Agency.

9831. Parry, Helen and Susan S. Hunt. "Undercover Operations and White Collar Crime," Journal of Asset Protection and Financial Crime 2/2 (1994): 150-159.

9832. Pastor, Werner. "Der Besten Einer, Treu, Aufrecht, Fest! Willy Budich," Beitrage zur Geschichte der Arbeiterbewegung 32/2 (1990): 260-267.

Roughly translated from the German: "The Best One, True, Straight, Celebration! Willy Budich."

9833. Pate, James L. "We Have Met the Enemy--and He Is Us: America's New Internal Security Forces," Soldier of Fortune 21 (October 1996): 38-39+.

9834. Pattakos, Arion N. "Counterintelligence and the OPSEC Connection Past, Present, and Future," American Intelligence Journal 18/1&2 (1998): 43-50.

Major sections discuss the acronyms of the military intelligence CI programs; OPSEC and focus; CI in support of OPSEC; risk management; OPSEC and traditional security; new direction; the natural link between OPSEC and CI; and value added.

9835. Patterson, Bradley H., Jr. "Teams and Staff: Dwight D. Eisenhower's Innovations in the Structure and Operations of the Modern White House," Presidential Studies Quarterly 24/2 (1994): 277-298.

Argues that the Eisenhower administration established the model for the modern presidency, particularly with respect to the creation of new administrative functions, many of which have survived to recent presidencies.

9836. Patton, Thomas J. "The Monitoring of War Indicators," <u>Studies in Intelligence</u> 3/4 (Winter 1959).

9837. Pawa, J. M. "Black Radicals and White Spies: Harlem, 1919," <u>Negro History Bulletin</u> 35/6 (1972): 129-133.

9838. Payne, Randolph. "Production at an Aircraft Plant," <u>Studies in Intelligence</u> 6/1 (Spring 1962).

9839. Peake, Hayden B. "OSS and the Venona Decrypts," <u>Intelligence and National Security</u> 12/3 (July 1997): 14-34.
    This veteran CIA operations specialist analyzes recently declassified messages regarding Soviet espionage against the US atomic bomb project. Major sections discuss pre-1945 FBI counterintelligence; OSS and the mole problem; the Venona decrypts; Venona and the moles in OSS; Venona and validation of other OSS moles; and Venona and OSS surprises.

9840. Pearse, Ralph S. "What Size Is It?," <u>Studies in Intelligence</u> 15/4 (Winter 1971).

9841. Peebles, Curtis L. "The Guardians," <u>Spaceflight</u> (November 1978): 381-385.
    Discusses the Big Bird low altitude camera surveillance system of the Air Force for photographing Soviet missile silos. Photos were evaluated by the National Photographic Interpretation Center of the National Reconnaissance Office.

9842. Peebles, Curtis L. "A Traveller in the Night," <u>Journal of the British Interplanetary Society</u> 33 (August 1980): 282-286.
    Discusses the social and cultural backdrop to the American space effort in the Eisenhower years, and reflections upon how American society viewed the Soviet advancements in space.

9843. Pekary, T. "Seditio: Unruhen und Revolten im Romischen Reich von Augustus bis Commodus," <u>Ancient Society</u> 18 (1987): 133-150.

9844. Pekel, Kent. "Integrity, Ethics, and the CIA: The Need for Improvement," <u>Studies in Intelligence</u> Unclassified edition (Spring 1998): 85-94.
    This is a discussion of the author's views on ethical training at the CIA in the post-Aldrich Ames espionage case era. Major sections discuss the origins and overview of the new ethics policy and training; the elements of integrity; the challenges to integrity; cloudy moral purpose; encouraging dissent and accepting bad news; misdefining failure and the fear of taking risks; promotion and performance appraisal; and a program of ethics education. This article appears in

the unclassified and unnumbered issue of the CIA's internal journal.

9845.   Pennetier, Jean-Marc.   "The Springtime of French Intelligence," Intelligence and National Security 11/4 (October 1996):   780-798.

A book review essay concerning three books on the subject: Agent Secrete by Dominique Prieur; L'homme des Services Secrets by Paul Paillole; and Au Coeur du Secret, 1,500 Jours Aux Commandes de la DGS, 1989-1993 by Claude Siberzahn.

9846.   Perkins, David D.   "Counterintelligence and Human Intelligence Operations in Bosnia," Defense Intelligence Journal 6/1 (Spring 1997):   33-61.

A detailed outline of the subject.   Major topical sections are: past operations; the hard road to success in Bosnia; CI and Humint operations; CI and Humint collection management and single source analysis; automation and communication; lessons learned; and need for investment in the training base. A edited version of this article appears in American Intelligence Journal 18/1&2 (1998): 33-42.

9847. Perl, Raphael F. "United States Andean Drug Policy: Background Issues for Decisionmakers," Journal of Interamerican Studies and World Affairs 34/3 (1992): 13-35.

9848. Pesavento, Peter. "Secrets Revealed about the Early U.S. Navy Space Program," Spaceflight (July 1996): 239-245.

Also in this issue by the same author is "U.S. Navy's Untold Story of Space-Related Firsts."

9849. Petchell, Robert A. "Cash on Delivery," Studies in Intelligence 17/3 (Fall 1973).

9850. Peters, Ralph. "Comrades and Computers," Military Intelligence (July-September 1988): 22-27.

Discusses the extraordinary expansion of Soviet KGB's copying efforts of Western technologies, including advancements in automation of information resources.

9851. Petersen, John H. "Info Wars," U.S. Naval Institute Proceedings 119/5 (1993): 85-92.

9852. Peterson, Eric C. "Intelligence for Worldwide Transportation Command Operations," American Intelligence Journal 17/3&4 (1997): 29-32.

Discusses the mission and organization of the Air Force Joint Intelligence Center-Transportation.

9853. Petitat, Andre. "Secret et Morphogenese Sociale," Cahiers Internationaux de Sociologie 102 (January-July 1997): 139-160.

In French, this is a sociological analysis of the role of morphogenesis in secrecy relationships.

9854. Petrovski, L. P. "Tainyi Front Ernsta Genri," Kentavr 6 (1995): 114-125.

In Russian, this piece considers the espionage actions of Ernst Henry, an alias for Semyon N. Rostovsky, a Soviet intelligence operative in London who worked as a journalist to spread the alleged progress of anti-fascism in the early 1930s.

9855. Pfaff, William. "Confessions of a Green Beret," Commentary 49/1 (1970): 28-34.

9856. Pforzheimer, Walter. "Public Texts in Intelligence," Studies in Intelligence 5/1 (Spring 1961).

9857. Pforzheimer, Walter. "In Memoriam," Studies in Intelligence 5/3 (Fall 1961).

A recognition of the services of General Walter Bedell Smith.

9858. Pforzheimer, Walter. "Postwar Soviet Espionage," Studies in Intelligence 6/1 (Spring 1962).

This is a bibliographic collection.

9859. Pforzheimer, Walter. "Public Texts in Intelligence," Studies in Intelligence 8/4 (Winter 1964).

9860. Pforzheimer, Walter. "Passport to Death," Studies in Intelligence 11/3 (Fall 1967).

9861. Pforzheimer, Walter. "Philatelic KGB," Studies in Intelligence 12/1 (Spring 1968).

9862. Pierce, John G. "Some Mathematical Methods for Intelligence Analysis," Studies in Intelligence 21/2 (Summer 1977).

9863. Pierpaoli, Paul G., Jr. "Mobilizing for the Cold War: The Korean Conflict and the Birth of the National Security State," Essays in Economic and Business History 12 (1994): 106-117.

Discusses the role of mobilization for war in the Korean conflict, particularly with respect to the long range evolution of national security policy making during the cold war.

9864. Pike, Christopher A. "CANYON, RHYOLITE, and AQUACADE: US Signals Intelligence in the 1970s," Spaceflight 37/11 (November 1995): 381-383.

9865. Pincus, Walter. "No More Martinis," Washington Monthly 29/2 (January 1997): 44-46.
    Discusses the Central Intelligence Agency and recent works of nonfiction and autobiographies of insiders about Agency operations.

9866. Pizzicaro, John T. "The 30 September Movement in Indonesia," Studies in Intelligence 13/ 3 (Fall 1969).

9867. Plaster, Henry G. "Snooping on Space Pictures," Studies in Intelligence 8/3 (Fall 1964).

9868. Platig, E. Raymond. "Research and Analysis," Annals of the American Academy of Political and Social Science 380 (1968): 50-59.

9869. Poe, Larry L. "Naval Reserve Intelligence Command: Intelligence Support for the Fleet and Joint Warfighter," American Intelligence Journal 18/1&2 (1998): 5-14.
    Examines history and organization; how Naval Reserve Intelligence supports the active duty force; Naval Reserve Intelligence in a changing strategic environment; the future and personnel; and integrated solutions.

9870. Poirier, Robert G. "Rome East of the Jordan: The Archaeological Use of Satellite Photography," Studies in Intelligence 21/1 (Spring 1977).

9871. Poirier, Robert G. "Satellite View of a Historic Battlefield," Studies in Intelligence 22/1 (Spring 1978).

9872. Pogrebin, Mark R. and Eric D. Poole. "Vice Isn't Nice: A Look at the Effects of Working Undercover," Journal of Criminal Justice 21/4 (1993): 383-394.

9873. Polgar, Thomas. "Assignment: Skyjacker," Studies in Intelligence 16/3 (Fall 1972).

9874. Ponse, B. "Secrecy in the Lesbian World," Urban Life 5 (1976): 313-338.

9875. Poole, Eric D. and Mark R. Pogrebin. "Crime and Law Enforcement Policy in the Korean-American Community," Police Studies 13/2 (1990): 57-66.

9876. Pooley, James H. A. "Understanding the Economic Espionage Act of 1996," Texas Intellectual Property Law Journal 5 (1997): 177-229.

9877. Popplewell, Richard J. "The KGB and the Control of the Soviet Bloc: The Case of East Germany," Intelligence and National Security 13/1 (Spring 1998): 254-285.

Majors sections discuss Soviet intelligence and the communist parties of Eastern Europe; the KPD (the German Communist Party), the Comintern and Soviet intelligence, 1918-33; the creation of East German intelligence; the Berlin uprising and the fall of Zaisser; the purges and East Germany; Ernst Wollweber and the MFS; and Erich Mielke and the fall of Walter Ulbright.

9878. Porcaro, Anthony. "The Graphics Coordinator Program," Studies in Intelligence 8/2 (Summer 1964).

9879. Porteous, Samuel D. "Looking Out for Economic Interests: An Increased Role for Intelligence," Washington Quarterly 19 (Autumn 1996): 191-204.

Major sections discuss economic intelligence where government is the client; government support versus direct commercial impact; putting economic intelligence to work; and the future of economic intelligence.

9880. Posner, Richard A. "Trade Secret Misappropriation: A Cost-Benefit Response to the Fourth Amendment Analogy," Harvard Law Review 106 (December 1992): 461-478.

Argues that the Fourth Amendment protection for trade secrets is less persuasive than the cost-benefit view, wherein the expense of protecting a secret is balanced against the value of the secret. Major sections define a trade secret; point out the misguided Fourth Amendment analogy; explains an alternative framework; and offers brief conclusions.

9881. Post, Jerrold M. "On Aging Leaders," Studies in Intelligence 13/1 (Spring 1969).

9882. Post, Jerrold M. "The Anatomy of Treason," Studies in Intelligence 19/1 (Spring 1975).

9883. Post, Jerrold M. "Personality Profiles in Support of the Camp David Summit," Studies in Intelligence 23/2 (Summer 1979).

9884. Poulgrain, Greg. "The Loveday Exchange, Australia, 1942: The Japanese Naval Spies Return to Java," Indonesia 55 (1993): 140-149.

9885. Pounder, Chris N. M. "Data Protection and the Police," Journal of Law and Society 10/1 (Summer 1983): 109-118.

Commentary on the advancing capabilities of police and criminal information systems. Sections discuss criminal intelligence and computers; the problem of "use"; conclusions on collection and use of information in Britain.

9886. Powers, Robert D., Jr. "Treason by Domiciled Aliens," <u>Military Law Review</u> 17 (July 1962): 123-143.

Discusses the circumstances of treason conducted by aliens, and the legal principles involved in prosecution. Major sections discuss domiciled neutral aliens; domiciled enemy aliens; treasonable acts outside the jurisdiction of state of domicile; and conclusions regarding the role of a passport and allegiance to the country of origin.

9887. Prados, John. "No Reform Here," <u>Bulletin of the Atomic Scientists</u> 52 (September-October 1996): 55-59.

A discussion of the Aspin-Brown Commission to study the reform proposals applicable to the intelligence community, arguing that much more work is needed to carry out the intentions of reform. Suggests that little real reform has been accomplished to date.

9888. Pringle, Bruce D. "Present and Suggested Limitations on the Use of Secret Agents and Informers in Law Enforcement," <u>Colorado Law Review</u> 41/2 (1969): 261-284.

9889. Pringle, Robert W. "The Heritage and Future of Russian Intelligence," <u>International Journal of Intelligence and Counterintelligence</u> 11/2 (Summer 1998): 175-184.

Major sections discuss the evaluation of the past; the dead hand of ideology; the never-ending search for enemies; covert action, collection, and analysis; treason and corruption; implications; back to the future?; and a note for students of Russian intelligence. Includes an outline of the new Russian intelligence organizations.

9890. Proschan, Frank. "'Rumor, Innuendo, Propaganda, and Disinformation,'" <u>Bulletin of Concerned Asian Scholars</u> 28/1 (January-March 1996): 52-64.

A review essay of substantial length of <u>Tragic Mountains: The Hmong, the Americans, and the Secret Wars for Laos, 1942-1992</u> by Jane Hamilton-Merrit. Contains sections: the problem of the unverifiable; the unanimity of "the Hmong"; the singularity of the Hmong and their devotion to the Lao nation; genocide against the Hmong as a people?; betrayed and abandoned?; and "sensational tales [that] bear little resemblance to truth."

9891. "Prosecution Under the Espionage Act and the Lessons Therefrom," <u>Law Notes</u> 24 (1920): 165-166.

9892. Prunckun, Henry W., Jr. "Crime Analysis: Intelligence Techniques in Criminal Investigation," <u>Australian Police Journal</u> 42/4 (1988).

9893. Prunckun, Henry W., Jr. "The Intelligence Analyst as Social Scientist:

A Comparison of Research Methods," Police Studies 19/3 (1996): 67-80.
    Explores the relationship between police intelligence and social science research methods. Suggests that analysts working in the police field may benefit from the knowledge and skills of the social science community.

9894. Prunko, Donald H. "Recruitment in Moscow," Studies in Intelligence 13/1 (Spring 1969).
    Few articles exist on this subject.

9895. Puchalla, Edward F. "Communist Defense Against Aerial Surveillance in Southeast Asia," Studies in Intelligence 14/3 (Fall 1970).

9896. Purpura, G. "I Curiosi e la Schola Agentum in Rebus," ASGP 34 (1973): 165-275.

9897. Quigley, John. "Israel's Destruction of Iraq's Nuclear Reactor: A Reply," Temple International and Comparative Law Journal 9/2 (Fall 1995): 441-444.
    This is a brief critique of the piece on the same subject by authors Louis R. Beres and Yoash Tsiddon-Chatto (see citation above).

9898. Quintanilla, Hector, Jr. "The Investigation of UFOs," Studies in Intelligence 10/3 (Fall 1966): 95-110.
    A discussion of Project Grudge and the contributions on this matter by the Scientific Advisory Panel.

9899. Radlo, Edward J. "Legal Issues in Cryptography," Computer Lawyer 13 (May 1996): 1-11.

9900. Raminov. "The American Civil War (1861-1865)," Journal of the United Service Institution of India 89/375 & 376 (1959): 177-183; 261-276.

9901. Ramsey, Diane M. and Mark S. Boerner. "A Study in Indications Methodology," Studies in Intelligence 7/2 (Summer 1963).

9902. Randall, Willard S. "Benedict Arnold at Quebec," MHQ: The Quarterly Journal of Military History 2/4 (Summer 1990).

9903. Rathmell, Andrew. "Syria's Intelligence Services: Origins and Development," Journal of Conflict Studies 16/2 (Fall 1996): 75-96.

9904. Rathmell, Andrew. "Brotherly Enemies: The Rise and Fall of the Syrian-Egyptian Intelligence Axis, 1954-1967," Intelligence and National Security 13/1 (Spring 1998): 230-253.
    Discusses regional political developments; emergence of an alliance,

1954-57; consolidating the alliance, 1958-61; the Lebanese conflict of 1958; from allies to enemies, 1961-67; the Suez crisis; and the 1967 war.

9905. Rausch, G. Jay and Diane. "Developments in Espionage Fiction," Kansas Quarterly 10/4 (1978): 71-84.

9906. Raven-Hansen, Peter and William C. Banks. "From Vietnam to Desert Shield: The Commander in Chief's Spending Power," Iowa Law Review 81 (October 1995): 79-147.

Considers whether or not the President may constitutionally spend for national security without prior specific appropriation or in disregard of appropriation restrictions, write the authors. Major sections discuss case studies; the Contras and CIA involvement in Nicaragua; the President's discretionary spending power; spending despite appropriate restrictions; and conclusions.

9907. Ravid, Itzhak. "Military Decision, Game Theory and Intelligence: An Anecdote," Operations Research 38/2 (1990): 260-264.

9908. Rawnsley, Gary D. "Overt and Covert: The Voice of Britain and Black Radio Broadcasting in the Suez Crisis, 1956," Intelligence and National Security 11/3 (July 1996): 497-522.

Discusses British intelligence operations in the Middle East in the mid 1950s; the voice of Britain through the BBC; black broadcasting; and conclusions.

9909. Ray, Gerda W. "From Cossack to Trooper: Manliness, Police Reform, and the State," Journal of Social History 28/3 (1995): 565-586.

A unique interpretation of the rise and development of US state police organizations, particularly with respect to the New York State Police. Brief discussion of the author's association of state police agencies with the emergence of the FBI. May be useful in research of historical development of domestic intelligence organizations.

9910. Reagan, Ronald. "The President at Langley," Studies in Intelligence 26/3 (Fall 1982).

President Ronald Reagan's speech to Central Intelligence Agency employees and guests on the grounds of CIA headquarters building in Langley, Virginia.

9911. Redfearn, Mason and Richard J. Aldrich. "The Perfect Cover: British Intelligence, the Soviet Fleet and Distant Water Trawler Operations, 1963-1974," Intelligence and National Security 12/3 (July 1997): 166-177.

Major sections discuss British intelligence and photographic surveillance, 1945-64; and surveillance in the Barents Sea, 1963-74.

9912. Redlich, Shimon. "Rehabilitation of the Jewish Anti-Fascist Committee: Report No. 7," Soviet Jewish Affairs 20/2-3 (1990): 85-98.

9913. Redlich, Shimon. "Discovering Soviet Archives, the Papers of the Jewish Anti-Fascist Committee," Jewish Quarterly 39/4 (Winter 1992-1993): 15-19.

9914. Reese, John R. "A Case Study in Operational Intelligence," International Journal of Intelligence and Counterintelligence 11/1 (Spring 1998): 73-92.
    Addresses the important work accomplished by British and US intelligence to follow German development of the Messerschmitt Me 262 jet aircraft in the final stages of World War II. Major sections discuss the monitoring of German programs; bombing the heartland; looking at pictures; ULTRA's contribution; reappraising Nazi strength; sharing a fantasy; refining the "industrial web" model; challenging the forecasts; bombing strategy revisited; questionable results; a 'wicked airplane' in reference to the Me 262. This piece refers, also, to an article predicting the fall of the German Luftwaffe, appearing in the Army Air Corps classified magazine, Impact 3/1 (January 1945): 41.

9915. Rehnquist, William H. "The Milligan Decision, MHQ: The Quarterly Journal of Military History 11/2 (Winter 1999): 44-49.
    The chief justice of the US Supreme Court discusses legal history and issues of the Lambdin P. Milligan martial law case which unfolded during the American civil war. This is an excerpt of his book, All the Laws But One.

9916. Reiman, Phillip E. "Cryptography and the First Amendment: The Right to Be Unheard," John Marshall Journal of Computer & Information Law 14 (Winter 1996): 325-345.

9917. Reiser, Donald and Harry Wood. "Microtechnology," Studies in Intelligence 12/3 (Fall 1968).

9918. Reisman, W. Michael. "Covert Action," Yale Journal of International Law 20/2 (Summer 1995): 419-425.
    This is a brief explanation of selected points the author wished to make in response to a review of his book (co-authored with James E. Baker), Regulating Covert Action: Practices, Contexts, and Policies of Covert Coercion Abroad in International and American Law. See critique by Robert F. Turner in "Late Entries" below.

9919. Relyea, Harold C. "Opening Government to Public Scrutiny: A Decade of Federal Efforts," Public Administration Review 35/1 (January-February 1975): 3-10.

9920. Relyea, Harold C. "The Freedom of Information Act: Its Evolution and

Operational Status," Journalism Quarterly 54/3 (1977): 538-544.
    The author explains the evolution of the FOIA and argues that the law is reasonably successful in fulfilling needs of requesters for government-held information. He acknowledges agency resistance and recalcitrance in some cases.

9921. Renntauskas, Vincent. "The Estimation of Construction Jobs," Studies in Intelligence 7/3 (Fall 1963).

9922. Reynolds, Clark G. "Submarine Attacks on the Pacific Coast, 1942," Pacific Historical Review 33 (May 1964): 183-193.
    Discusses the psychological impact of attacks on the US population.

9923. Reynolds, David. "Lord Lothian and Anglo-American Relations, 1939-1940," Transactions of the American Philosophical Society 73/2 (1983): 1-65.
    A lengthy discussion of Lothian's role in a variety of diplomatic actions prior to World War II, including his participation in certain covert activities.

9924. Rhinehart, Marilyn D. "Spies in the Piney Woods: John Henry Kirby's Agents Provocateurs and the Brotherhood of Timber Workers in East Texas, 1910-1912," Locus 8/2 (1996): 169-182.

9925. Riccardelli, Richard F. "Warfighter Intelligence for Operations Other Than War," American Intelligence Journal 17/3&4 (1997): 49-54.
    Sections discuss Operation Uphold Democracy in Haiti; building an architecture and battlefield visualization in terms of setting the stage; planning considerations and intelligence preparation of the battlefield in OOTW; lessons learned and relearned: tactics, techniques and procedures; weather analysis and forecasting; open-source intelligence; command posts and intelligence; training; customer focus and menus; operational security; targeting and battlefield damage assessments; and intelligence XXI.

9926. Richard, Daniel. "Overseas Tasking of the CIA for Domestic Law Enforcement," National Security Studies Quarterly 2 (Summer 1996): 1-18.

9927. Richardson, Robert C., III. "Upgrading U.S. National Security for the 21st Century," Journal of Social, Political and Economic Studies 20 (Winter 1995): 387-404.

9928. Richelson, Jeffrey T. "Volume of Data Cripples Tactical Intelligence System," Armed Forces Journal International (June 1992): 35-37.
    Reference is to the Gulf War and the tactical intelligence problems encountered by the US military.

9929. Richelson, Jeffrey T. "High Flyin' Spies," Bulletin of the Atomic

Scientists 52 (September-October 1996): 48-54.

The author questions whether or not the US intelligence collection systems in the satellite realm are a match for the new sophistication in target secrecy methods. Says there is room for substantial improvement.

9930. Richelson, Jeffrey T. "The Wizards of Langley: The CIA's Directorate of Science and Technology," Intelligence and National Security 12/1 (January 1997): 82-103.

Major sections discuss origins; the Directorate of Research; the Directorate of Science and Technology; organizational evolution; collection systems development; collection operations; analysis and processing; research and development; and past impact and future roles.

9931. Richelson, Jeffrey T. "From MONARCH EAGLE to MODERN AGE: The Consolidation of U.S. Defense HUMINT," International Journal of Intelligence and Counterintelligence 10/2 (Summer 1997): 131-164.

The author, a senior fellow at the National Security Archives in Washington, D.C., discusses post world war US military human intelligence collection; Defense Department coordination and consolidation initiatives; the road to Defense Humint Service (DHS); creation of the DHS; DHS structure and operations; organizational options; and the search for better results.

9932. Richelson, Jeffrey T.   "Out of the Black: The Disclosure and Declassification of the National Reconnaissance Office," International Journal of Intelligence and Counterintelligence 11/1 (Spring 1998): 1-25.

Sections discuss undercover aspects of outer space; disclosure of National Reconnaissance Office's existence; going nowhere fast; a change of plans; one small step; navigating the slippery slope; FOIAs and flaps; final frontiers; and changing times.

9933. Richelson, Jeffrey T. "A Secret Journey: The Creation and Evolution of the National Reconnaissance Office," (1998 or 1999): forthcoming.

This article delves into the early secret correspondence (1961) between Secretary of Defense Robert McNamara and Allen Dulles with respect to the formation of this super secret space reconnaissance organization.

9934. Richman, Irwin. "Pauline Cushman: A Personality Profile," Civil War Times Illustrated 7/10 (October 1969): 38-44.

9935. Ridlon, David. "Shots in the Dark: British Tactical Intelligence in the Falklands War," Military Intelligence 15/2 (July-September 1989): 40-42, 49.

Discusses task force preparation; signals imagery, and human intelligence operations; and lessons learned.

9936. Riffice, Albert E. "Intelligence and Covert Action," <u>Studies in Intelligence</u> 6/4 (Winter 1962).

9937. Rigby, T. H. "Was Stalin a Disloyal Patron?," <u>Soviet Studies</u> 38/3 (July 1986): 311-324.

9938. Rimanelli, Marco. "East-West Arms Control and the Fall of the USSR, 1967-1994: Radical Change or Expedient Accommodation?," <u>East European Quarterly</u> 29/2 (1995): 237-273.
    An extensive and detailed review of arms negotiations between the US and the USSR during the period, including consideration of methods for verifying nuclear weapons arsenals over time.

9939. Rittenberg, E. S. "Your Man in Ohio," <u>Studies in Intelligence</u> 7/2 (Summer 1963).

9940. Roberts, Jerry. "Operation Overlord," <u>Sea History</u> 69 (1994): 10-16.
    A brief overview of the Overlord operation to surprise German defense forces at Normandy beach in June 1944.

9941. Robertson, K. G. "Recent Reform of Intelligence in the UK: Democratization or Risk Management?," <u>Intelligence and National Security</u> 13/2 (Summer 1998): 144-158.
    Evaluates the spate of recent UK legislation to democratize the British intelligence services. Major sections discuss Parliament and intelligence; the Intelligence Services Act 1994; the Intelligence and Security Committee; and conclusions about the total effort.

9942. Rocafort, W. W. "Colonel Abel's Assistant," <u>Studies in Intelligence</u> 3/3 (Fall 1959).

9943. Rodman, David. "Regime-Targeting: A Strategy for Israel," <u>Israeli Affairs</u> 2/1 (Autumn 1995): 153-167.

9944. Rodrigue, Aron. "Rearticulations of French Jewish Identities after the Dreyfus Affair," <u>Jewish Social Studies</u> 2/3 (Spring-Summer 1996): 1-24.

9945. Rogers, Lawrence E. "Project Ninos," <u>Studies in Intelligence</u> 7/4 (Winter 1963).

9946. Rogov, A. S. "Pitfalls of Civilian Cover," <u>Studies in Intelligence</u> 8/2 (Summer 1964).
    A discussion of certain tradecraft techniques and limitations.

9947. Rohde, William E. "What Is Info Warfare?," <u>U.S. Naval Institute Proceedings</u> 122 (Fall 1996): 34-38.

9948. Romano, George. "Coexistence and Covert Collection," <u>Studies in Intelligence</u> 2 (Summer 1958).

9949. Romich, Ron. "'Daddy, Why Do They Call It Collection Requirements Manglement?,'" <u>Defense Intelligence Journal</u> 6/1 (Spring 1997): 23-32.
     Major sections discuss the comparison of the business process and the collection requirements management process; a guide for the development of collections requirements; register requirements; validate requirements; prioritize requirements; levy requirements; monitor status and provide feedback to customers; and assess requirements satisfaction.

9950. Romig, Walter W. "Spy Mission to Montana," <u>Studies in Intelligence</u> 11/2 (Summer 1967).

9951. Ron, James. "Varying Methods of State Violence," <u>International Organizations</u> 51 (Spring 1997): 275-300.
     Includes brief discussion about interrogation techniques among international organizations.

9952. Roshchupkin, V. T. "'Razvedka Sysgrala Ochen' Bol'Shuiu Rol,'" <u>Voenno-Istoricheskii Zhurnal</u> 4-5 (1992): 35-37.
     In Russian.

9953. Roshchupkin, V. T. "Moskva Khotela Znat' Vse: Neizvestnye Stranitsy Karibskogo Krizisa," <u>Voenno-Istoricheskii Zhurnal</u> 9 (1992): 58-60.
     In Russian.

9954. Rossi, Luigi. "L'Etnia Italiana Nelle Americhe: La Strategia Statunitense Durante la Seconda Guerra Mondiale," <u>Nuova Revista Storica</u> 79/1 (1995): 115-142.
     In Italian, the title of this piece is roughly translated as follows: "The Ethnic Italians in the Americas and the Strategy of the United States in the Second World War."

9955. Rossi, Mario. "La Mission du Colonel Passy aux Etats-Unis: Inquietudes et Suspicions Americaines (Decembre 1944)," <u>Guerres Mondiales et Conflits Contemporains</u> 45/178 (1995): 115-118.

9956. Roth, Paul W. "Industriespionage im Zeitalter der Industriellen Revolution," <u>Blaetter fuer Technikgeschichte</u> 38 (1976): 40-54.
     Loosely translated, discusses industrial espionage in the era of the

industrial revolution.

9957. Rothenberg, Herbert C.   "Identifying the Future Threat," <u>Studies in Intelligence</u> 12/3 (Fall 1968).

9958. Rothstein, William G. "Professions in Process," <u>Bulletin of the History of Medicine</u> 70/4 (1996): 691-698.

9959. Rourke, Francis E. "Introduction" [Administrative secrecy articles], <u>Public Administration Review</u> 35/1 (January-February 1975): 1-4.
   This is a brief overview and introduction of a collection of articles by Harold C. Relyea; Robert L. Saloschin; James B. Christoph; and Itzhak Galnoor (see this bibliography).

9960. Rout, Leslie B., Jr. and John F. Bratzel. "Origins: US Intelligence in Latin America," <u>Studies in Intelligence</u> 29/4 (Winter 1985).

9961. Royden, Barry G. "CIA and National HUMINT Preparing for the 21st Century," <u>Defense Intelligence Journal</u> 6/1 (Spring 1997): 15-22.
   A discussion of the need for national Humint and issues facing CIA and national Humint.

9962. Rubel, Robert C. "Gettysburg and Midway: Historical Parallels in Operational Command," <u>Naval War College Review</u> 48/1 (Winter 1995): 96-100.
   Major sections discuss historical parallels and the study of war; the parallels between the Gettysburg and Midway battles; the inputs (including a discussion of the failures of scouting); and lessons.

9963. Rubin, F. "The Theory and Concept of National Security in the Warsaw Pact Countries," <u>International Affairs</u> (Great Britain) 58/4 (Autumn 1982): 648-657.
   Major sections discuss the fundamental tenet of communist national security; Soviet perception and interpretation of national security; and conclusions; KGB intelligence service is mentioned briefly.

9964. Rucker, Raymond B., Jr. "Criminal Intelligence: Enforcing Today, Managing Tomorrow," <u>Police Chief</u> 62/10 (October 1995): 34.
   A brief overview of one author's perspectives on the role of police intelligence, especially in connection with the trend toward community policing.

9965. Ruetten, Richard T. "Harry Elmer Barnes and the 'Historical Blackout,'" <u>Historian</u> 33 (February 1971): 202-214.
   A brief account of Barnes' role in the revisionist history of the Pearl Harbor attack and other aspects of post-World War II history.

9966. Ruffner, Kevin C. "CIA's Support to the Nazi War Criminal Investigation," Studies in Intelligence Unclassified edition (1997): 103-109.

Major sections discuss continuing suspicions; the Government Accounting Office's first investigation; formation of Office of Special Investigation; a surge of cases; GAO's findings; Mengele and Waldheim; more cases and more demands; the mixed record; and cooperation and controversy.

9967. Rumpelmayer, J. J. "The Missiles in Cuba," Studies in Intelligence 8/3 (Fall 1964): 87-92.

9968. Rush, Myron and James A. Byron. "The Impact of the USSR's Economic Predicament on Soviet Military Spending - A Speculative Debate," Studies in Intelligence 22/1 (Spring 1978).

9969. "Russian Spy System: The Azeff Scandals," English Review 1 (March 1909): 816-832.

A classic article on a topic of rare discussion.

9970. Rusu, Sharon. "The Role of Collector in Early Warning," International Journal of Refugee Law Special Issue (September 1990): 65-70.

9971. Rutledge, John W. "National Imagery and Mapping: Guaranteeing an Information Edge," American Intelligence Journal 17/3&4 (1997): 33-38.

Discusses the background of the National Imaging and Mapping Agency (originally the Army Map Service, then later the Defense Mapping Agency); support across the spectrum; and further improvements ahead.

9972. Ryan, Jill M. "Freedom to Speak Unintelligibly: The First Amendment Implications of Government-Controlled Encryption," William and Mary Bill of Rights Journal 4 (Summer 1996): 1165-1222.

9973. Rydell, Robert W. "'This Is America': The American Pavilion at the 1958 Brussels World's Fair," European Contributions to American Studies 26 (1995): 197-218.

9974. Sabatt, Randy. "International Harmonization on Electronic Commerce and Electronic Data Interchange: A Proposed First Step Toward Signing on the Digital Dotted Line," American University Law Review 46 (December 1996): 511-536.

9975. Safran, William. "The Dreyfus Affair, Political Consciousness and the Jews: A Centennial Retrospective," Contemporary French Civilization 19/1 (Winter-Spring 1995): 1-32.

9976. Salemme, Arthur J. "Beyond Webster and All That: Dictionaries of Unconventional Language," Studies in Intelligence 13/1 (Spring 1969): 63-69.

9977. Saloschin, Robert L. "The Freedom of Information Act: A Governmental Perspective," Public Administration Review 35/1 (January-February 1975): 10-14.

9978. Samii, Abbas W. "The Shah's Lebanon Policy: The Role of the SAVAK," Middle Eastern Studies 33 (January 1997): 66-91.
    Discusses the role of the Shah of Iran's secret police.

9979. Samuelson, Franz. "World War I Intelligence Testing and the Development of Psychology," Journal of the History of the Behavioral Sciences 13/3 (1977): 274-282.

9980. Sanders, M. L. "Wellington House and British Propaganda during the First World War," Historical Journal 18/1 (March 1975): 119-146.
    A history of the British efforts to counter German propaganda in 1914, centered in Wellington House. Discusses military propagand under the direction of the War Office MI-7. Includes organization charts of John Buchan's propaganda department.

9981. Sapp, Edwin G. "Decision Trees," Studies in Intelligence 18/4 (Winter 1974).

9982. Sarotte, M. E. "Under Cover of Boredom: Recent Publications on the 'Stasi', the East German Ministry for State Security," Intelligence and National Security 12/4 (October 1997): 196-210.
    A detailed book review article exploring the observations on the Stasi found in eight books, five of which have been published in Germany.

9983. Sarty, Roger. "The Limits of Ultra: The Schnorkel U-boat Offensive Against North America, November 1944-January 1945," Intelligence and National Security 12/2 (April 1997): 44-68.
    A detailed history of the subject, including maps. Concludes that even a relatively degraded application of the Ultra system, resulting from enemy counter strategies, "made possible an economical defence of Canadian waters."

9984. Savacool, James A. "Training Pays," Studies in Intelligence 9/2 (Summer 1965).

9985. Savage, Donald C. "Keeping Professors Out: The Immigration Department and the Idea of Academic Freedom, 1945-90," Dalhousie Review 69/4 (1989-1990): 499-524.

9986. Savage, Joseph F., Jr. "I Spy: The New Economic Espionage Act Can Be Risky Business," Criminal Justice 12 (Fall 1997): 12-18.

9987. Scheiber, Harry N. and Jane L. "Bayonets in Paradise: A Half-Century Retrospect on Martial Law in Hawaii, 1941-1946," University of Hawaii Law Review 19 (Fall 1997): 477+.

9988. Schiattareggia, M. H. "Counterintelligence in Counter-Guerilla Operations," Studies in Intelligence 6/2 (Summer 1962).

9989. Schleifman, Nurit. "The Internal Agency: Linchpin of the Political Police in Russia," Cahiers du Monde Russe et Sovietique 24 (1983): 151-177.

9990. Schneiderman, Jeremiah. "From the Files of the Moscow Gendarme Corps: A Lecture on Combatting Revolution," Canadian Slavic Studies 2 (Spring 1968): 86-99.

9991. Schnell, Jane. "Snapshots at Random," Studies in Intelligence 5/1 (Spring 1961).

9992. Schorreck, Henry F. "The Telegram that Changed History," Cryptologic Spectrum 1/3 (Summer 1970): 22-29.

9993. Schrecker, Ellen. "Immigration and Internal Security: Political Deportations During the McCarthy Era," Science and Society 60 (Winter 1996-1997): 393-426.
A detailed discussion of the history of repression visited upon immigrants, especially during the Cold War era. Sections discuss Cold War deportations; INS procedures and immigrants' rights; cases of Ellen Knauff, Kwong Hai Chew, Gerhart Eisler; the INS gets its law; and retrospective and conclusions. Discusses the role of the FBI.

9994. Schreckengost, R. C. "New Perspectives in ELINT," Studies in Intelligence 14/3 (Fall 1970).

9995. Schreckengost, R. C. "Some Limitations in Systems Analysis in Intelligence Activities," Studies in Intelligence 14/3 (Fall 1970).

9996. Schroeder, Gertrude. "Reflections on Economic Sovietology," Post-Soviet Affairs 11 (July-September 1995): 197-234.
Sections discuss the nature of the Soviet economic system; use and sources of evidence; the controversy over rates of economic growth (including Central Intelligence Agency studies); comparative size of the economy; depiction of Soviet economic problems and prospects; and accomplishments and shortcomings.

9997. Schumeyer, Gerard. "Medical Intelligence...Making a Difference," American Intelligence Journal 17/1&2 (1996): 11-15.

Sections discuss a brief history of medical intelligence; organization and mission; implications and impact of medical intelligence; and the future.

9998. Schwartz, David A. "The Digital Telephony Legislation of 1994: Law Enforcement Hitches a Ride on the Information Superhighway," Criminal Law Bulletin 31/3 (1995): 195-210.

Evaluates the impact of the 1994 statute on electronic surveillance by police. Major sections discuss the impact on criminal law; impact on Title III and the Electronic Communication Privacy Act of 1986; and impact on use of various interception devices.

9999. Schwartz, D. F. and E. Jacobson. "Organizational Communication Network Analysis: The Liaison Communication Role," Organizational Behavior and Human Performance 18 (1977): 158-174.

10000. Schwarzchild, Edward T. "The Assessment of Insurgency," Studies of Intelligence 7/3 (Fall 1963).

10001. Scidmore, R. R. "The Symptoms of Scientific Breakthrough," Studies in Intelligence 4/4 (Winter 1960).

Reflections on attempts at anticipation.

10002. Scott, E. J. "The Cheka," St. Antony's Papers 1 (1956): 1-23.

10003. Sears, Stephen W. "Raid on Richmond," MHQ: The Quarterly Journal of Military History 11/1 (Autumn 1998): 88-96.

A history, with maps and photographs, of the American civil war secret Kilpatrick-Dahlgren raid of 1864.

10004. Seifman, Donald H. and Craig W. Trepanier. "Evolution of the Paperless Office: Legal Issues Arising Out of Technology in the Workplace. Part I. E-Mail and Voicemail Systems," Employee Relations Law Journal 21/3 (Winter 1995-1996): 5-36.

Major sections discuss employee privacy rights; "On-Line" defamation, slander, and trade libel; harassment and discrimination via electronic communication; protecting trade secrets and confidential information; avoiding copyright infringement; union solicitation; discovery and admissibility of stored communications; and effective company policies.

10005. Seidel, Wallace E. "Great Frusina Revisited: The Problem of Priority Positive Intelligence," Studies in Intelligence 5/4 (Winter 1961).

10006. Seidel, Wallace E. "Intelligence for Defense Planning," <u>Studies in Intelligence</u> /1 (Spring 1964).

10007. "Senate Concurrent Resolution 133: Mr. Dole," <u>Studies in Intelligence</u> 30/3 (Fall 1986).

10008. Senn, Alfred E. "The Myth of German Money During the First World War," <u>Soviet Studies</u> 28 (January 1976): 83-90.
      Investigates the question of possible collusion between Lenin and the Germans between 1914 and 1917. The author insists that Lenin had no provable connection with German agents before March 1917, especially agents working secret missions in Bern.

10009. Sergeev, Feodosii M. "From the History of U.S. Intelligence Against the Soviet Union," <u>Voenno-Istoricheskii Zhurnal</u> 6 (1969): 119-127.
      This is an approximate translation of a title which appears in a Russian language history journal.

10010. Sergienko, Greg S. "Self Incrimination and Cryptographic Keys," <u>Richmond Journal of Law & Technology</u> 2 (1996): 1-23.
      Major sections discuss the Fifth Amendment and the compulsory production of cryptographic keys; the advantages of a traditional solution to the search and seizure issue; and conclusions.

10011. Serov, Ivan A. "Work with Walk-Ins," <u>Studies in Intelligence</u> 8/4 (Winter 1964).
      Discussion of the handling of walk-in defectors.

10012. "The Shah's Illness and the Fall of Iran," <u>Studies in Intelligence</u> 24/2 (Summer 1980): 61-63.
      This article is not listed among declassified items by the Central Intelligence Agency for public access.

10013. Shapiro, Howard M. "The FBI in the 21st Century," <u>Cornell International Law Journal</u> 28 (1995): 219-228.
      A speech given by the author, who served as General Counsel to the Federal Bureau of Investigation. Gives emphasis to the counterintelligence role of the FBI and discusses the Ames espionage case.

10014. Sharpe, Sybil. "Covert Policing: A Comparative View," <u>Anglo-American Law Review</u> 25 (April-June 1996): 163-187.
      Considers judicial attitudes towards evidence which is improperly obtained by means of covert police operations in England and the US. Major sections discuss the basis for excluding improperly obtained evidence in England

and Wales; the exercise of judicial discretion in section 78 of the Police and Criminal Evidence Act 1984; the basis of evidence exclusion in the US; the entrapment defense; the due process doctrine, and conclusions.

10015.   Shatz, Martin L.   "Psychological Problems in Singleton Cover Assignments," Studies in Intelligence 2 (Summer 1958).

10016. Shaw, Brackley. "Origins of the U-2: Interview with Richard M. Bissell, Jr.," Air Power History (Winter 1989).

10017. Shea, James R. "Winnowing Wheat from Chaff," Studies in Intelligence 13/3 (Fall 1969).

10018.   Shearing, Clifford D.; Phillip C. Stenning; and Susan M. Addario. "Public Perceptions of Private Security," Canadian Police College Journal 9/3 (1985): 225-253.

10019. Sheehan, Darrell C. "The Japanese Intelligence Community," National Security Studies Quarterly 2 (Winter 1996): 59-67.

10020.   Sheldon, Rose M.   "Clandestine Operations and Covert Action: The Ancient Imperative," Proceedings of the Military and Naval History Forum (March 1995): 1-14.

10021. Sheldon, Rose M. "The Ancient Imperative: Clandestine Operations and Covert Operations," International Journal of Intelligence and Counterintelligence 10/3 (Fall 1997): 299-315.
    An attempt to show evidence that in ancient societies covert action was a practical solution to the overt use of military force.   Sections discuss the obstacles to conducting research on the issue with respect to the Roman empire; Rome versus Parthia; the first contacts between Rome and Parthia; the battle over Syria; Antony's first campaign; the second try; Octavian; Augustus, the high point of covert action; covert operations under Tiberius; and masters of deceit.

10022. Sheldon, Rose M. "Intelligence and the Historians," International Journal of Intelligence and Counterintelligence 11/1 (Spring 1998): 104-115.
    A book review essay on Explorio: Military and Political Intelligence in the Roman World from the Second Punic War to the Battle of Adrianople by N. J. E. Austin and N. B. Rankov.

10023.   Shelton, David L.   "Intelligence Lessons Known and Revealed During Operation RESTORE HOPE Somalia," Marine Corps Gazette 79/2 (February 1995): 37-42.

10024. Shelton, H. Hugh and Timothy D. Vane. "Winning the War in Haiti," Military Review 75/6 (1995): 3-9.

10025. Shen, Yu. "SACO in History and Histories: Politics and Memory," Journal of American-East Asian Relations 5/1 (1996): 37-55.

10026. Sherrin, Christopher. "Problems with Their Use," Criminal Law Quarterly 40 (August 1997): 106-122.
Refers to the use of jailhouse informers in the Canadian justice system. This is Part I. Part II is found in the same journal (November 1997): 157-187.

10027. Shirley, Edward G. "Can't Anybody Here Play This Game?," Atlantic Monthly 281/2 (February 1998): 45-61.
The author, a former CIA case officer in the Agency's Directorate of Operations, reflects on his own experiences and argues that the DO has become increasingly dysfunctional. Sections are titled: A dysfunctional family; A Liars' Paradise; The numbers racket; Too many spooks--Too few spies; and Glasnost?

10028. Shlaim, Avi. "The Protocol of Sevres, 1956: Anatomy of a War Plot," International Affairs (Great Britain) 73/3 (1997): 509-530.
Major sections discuss secrecy and the sources on Sevres; invitation to a conspiracy; David Ben-Gurion's grand design; the reluctant conspirator (Selwyn Lloyd); the second day of Sevres; the third day of Sevres; the Protocol of Sevres; and conclusions.

10029. Shockley, Pat. "The Availability of 'Trade Secret' Protection for University Research," Journal of College and University Law 20 (Winter 1994): 309-332.
Relevant to the issue of protecting secrets resulting from the commercial or other activities of university academics, major sections discuss types of available protections; the Freedom of Information Act; policy considerations; and conclusions.

10030. Shoeman, Ferdinand. "Undercover Operations: Some Moral Questions About S. 804," Criminal Justice Ethics 5/2 (1986): 16-22.

10031. Shoen, Harriet H. "Pryce Lewis, Spy for the Union: Operations in Western Virginia, June-July 1861," Davis and Elkins Historical Magazine 2 (March-May 1949): 22-30.

10032. Shoham, J. "Does Nutritional Surveillance Have a Role to Play in Early Warning of Food Crisis and in the Management of Relief Operations?," Disasters 11/4 (1987): 282-285.

10033. Shreeve, Thomas W. and James J. Dowd, Jr. "Building a Learning Organization: Teaching with Cases at CIA," International Journal of Intelligence and Counterintelligence 10/1 (Spring 1997): 97-107.

Major sections discuss Central Intelligence Agency's case method approach; getting started in the training process; the case method teaching workshop; creating a library of cases; some rules for writing cases for internal use; results; taking the method on the road; problems encountered; and judgment and thinking.

10034. Shrivastava, B. K. "U.S. Military Assistance to Pakistan: A Reappraisal," India Quarterly: Journal of International Affairs 32/1 (1976): 26-41.

10035. Shryock, Richard W. "For an Eclectic Sovietology," Studies in Intelligence 8/4 (Winter 1964).

10036. Siddiqi, Asif. "Morning Star," Quest (Winter 1994): 39-48.

Discusses the Soviet rocket program and the associated secret space effort to launch spy satellites.

10037. Sigal, Leon V. "Antisatellite Accord Key to Summit," Bulletin of the Atomic Scientists 41/9 (1985): 16-18.

10038. Siklova, Jirina. "Lustration or the Czech Way of Screening," East European Constitutional Review 5 (Winter 1996): 57-75.

10039. Silver, Daniel B. "The CIA and the Law: The Evolving Role of CIA's General Counsel," Studies in Intelligence 25/2 (Summer 1981).

Estimated to be 6 pages in length. A discussion of the evolving role (as of 1981) of the CIA's General Counsel and the future of congressional oversight and internal regulation.

10040. Silverman, Debra L. "Freedom of Information: Will Blair Be Able to Break the Walls of Secrecy in Britain?," American University International Law Review 13 (1997): 471-532.

10041. Simmons, David A. "The Military and Administrative Abilities of James Wilkinson in the Old Northwest, 1792-1793," Old Northwest 3/3 (1977): 237-250.

10042. Simms, B. W. and E. R. Petersen. "The Economics of Criminal Investigation in a Municipal Police Force," Journal of Criminal Justice 17/3 (1989): 199-224.

Sections discuss an information processing model of criminal investigations; economic analysis; and conclusions. Mentions police intelligence contributions to the information data base.

10043. Simon, Jonathan. "Ghosts of the Disciplinary Machine: Lee Harvey Oswald, Life-History, and the Truth of Crime," Yale Journal of Law and Human Rights 10 (Winter 1998): 75+.

10044. Simpson, A. W. Brian. "Detention without Trial in the Second World War: Comparing the British and American Experiences," Florida State University Law Review 16 (Summer 1988): 225-259.

10045. Simpson, Christopher. "The Uses of Counter-Terrorism," Covert Action Quarterly (Fall 1996): 31-40.

10046. Sims, H. Blake. "Constitutional Law--The Sixth Amendment Right to Counsel--Admissibility of Testimony from a Voluntary Active Informant," Tennessee Law Review 63 (Winter 1996): 453-469.
        Considers the case of Hartmann v. State, 896 S.W.2d 94 (Tenn. 1995) in which the majority in the Tennessee Supreme Court held that "an informant's testimony containing incriminating statements obtained before law enforcement authorities became involved, is admissible and does not violate a defendant's Sixth Amendment right to counsel, even if the informant gathers the information with the intention of conveying the information to the Government."

10047. Smith, Abbot E. "Notes on 'Capabilities' in National Intelligence," Studies in Intelligence 1 (Winter 1956).

10048. Smith, Abbot E. "On the Accuracy of National Intelligence Estimates," Studies in Intelligence 13/3 (Fall 1969).

10049. Smith, Alan B. "Costing Nuclear Programs," Studies in Intelligence 10/4 (Winter 1966).

10050. Smith, Bruce. "The Great Chinese Mounds Puzzle," Studies in Intelligence 19/3 (Fall 1975).

10051. Smith, Joseph B. "Portrait of a Cold Warrior," Studies in Intelligence 20/4 (Winter 1976).

10052. Smith, R. J. "Coordination and Responsibility," Studies in Intelligence 2 (Fall 1957).

10053. Smith, Robert W. "The Analyst in a War Theater Role," Studies in Intelligence 8/4 (Winter 1964).

10054. Sinclair, William R. "Bombs Over Alberta," <u>Alberta History</u> 43/2 (1995): 2-8.

An account of the Japanese project to dispatch bombs carried by balloons over the Canadian Province of Alberta in 1945. According to published records, no damage or injuries were sustained in the course of nearly a dozen and one-half such balloon-bomb incidents.

10055. Singhal, Anjali. "The Piracy of Privacy?: A Fourth Amendment Analysis of Key Escrow Cryptography," <u>Stanford Law & Policy Review</u> 7 (Summer 1996): 189-210.

10056. Sinnigen, William G. "Tirones and Supernumeraii," <u>Classical Philology</u> 62 (1967): 108-112.

See numerous other citations by this scholar of ancient Roman intelligence services. This article discusses the steps by which a civilian became a soldier in the Late Empire Roman army.

10057. Slaby, David W.; James C. Chapman; and Gregory P. O'Hara. "Trade Secret Protection: An Analysis of the Concept 'Efforts Reasonable Under the Circumstances to Maintain Secrecy,'" <u>Santa Clara Computer and High Technology Law Journal</u> 5 (June 1989): 321-348.

10058. Smirnov, Iu. "Stalin i Atomnaia Bomba," <u>Voprosy Istorii Estestvoznaniia i Tekhniki</u> 2 (1994): 125-130.

10059. Smith, Bradley F. "The American Road to Central Intelligence," <u>Intelligence and National Security</u> 12/1 (January 1997): 1-20.

A summary history of the progress of events before and during World War II which ultimately yielded the 1947 creation of the CIA.

10060. Smith, Bradley F. "The Birth of SIS: A Newly Released Document," <u>Intelligence and National Security</u> 13/2 (Summer 1998): 183-189.

Contains a brief introduction to the typed transcript of the proceedings of the second meeting of the 1909 meeting of the Subcommittee on Intelligence, Committee of Imperial Defence. Document is relevant to the origins of MI-6.

10061. Smith, Dwight C., Jr. "Cooperative Action in Organized Crime Control," <u>Journal of Criminal Law, Criminology and Police Science</u> 59/4 (December 1968): 491-498.

Major sections consider a national organized crime intelligence board and the challenge of its creation; an inter-jurisdictional group to coordinate strategic planning; a channel for strategic estimates coordination and review; the means for sharing pertinent data; and some unanswered problems.

10062. Smith, Dwight C., Jr. and Ralph F. Salerno. "The Use of Strategies in Organized Crime Control," Journal of Criminal Law, Criminology and Police Science 61/1 (March 1970): 101-111.

Discusses strategies against organized crime, such as, attrition, exposure, harassment, and "Ostrich practice"; problems in defining strategies; the application of strategies; and conclusions regarding the intelligence process and the dependence of strategies on intelligence.

10063. Smith, Steven D. "Radically Subversive Speech and the Authority of Law," Michigan Law Review 94 (November 1995): 348-370.

Major sections in this essay discuss the special problem of radically subversive speech; the problem of legal authority; the nature of fictional authority; the free speech problem revisited; and a conclusion.

10064. Smyth, Denis. "'Les Chevaliers de Saint-George': La Grande-Bretagne et la Corruption des Generaux Espagnoles," Guerre Mondiales et Conflits Contemporains 162 (1991).

10065. Snider, L. Britt. "Sharing Secrets with Lawmakers: Congress as a User of Intelligence," Studies in Intelligence Unclassifed edition (Spring 1998): 47-69.

In this unnumbered unclassified issue of the CIA's internal journal, the author discusses the evolution of intelligence-sharing with the Congress; what distinguishes Congress as a user of intelligence; how intelligence-sharing works; the impact of intelligence-sharing; challenges and pitfalls; and recommendations.

10066. Snyder, Charles M. "With Benedict Arnold at Valcour Island: The Diary of Pascal De Angelis," Vermont History 42 (1974): 195-200.

10067. Snyder, Gregory H. "Alliances, Balances and Stability," International Organization 45/1 (Winter 1991): 121-142.

This piece is not specifically aimed at intelligence concerns, it may find application in studies of secret intelligence liaison relationships, especially where such relationships suggest spying on friendly nations and intelligence services.

10068. Snyder, John R. "The Spy Story as Modern Tragedy," Literature/Film Quarterly 5 (Summer 1977): 230-238.

10069. Sofaer, Abraham D. "Terrorism, the Law, and the National Defense," Military Law Review 126 (1989): 89-121.

Major sections of this 1989 lecture at the JAG School of the Army discuss the use of force; armed attack; necessity and proportionality; responsibility for aggression; territorial integrity; the War Powers Resolution; assassination; and conclusions about state-sponsored terrorism.

10070. Solin, Gail. "The Art of China-Watching," <u>Studies in Intelligence</u> 19/2 (Summer 1975).

10071. Soman, Appu K. "'Who's Daddy' in the Taiwan Strait?: The Offshore Islands Crisis of 1958," <u>Journal of American-East Asian Relations</u> 3/4 (1994): 373-398.

Discusses the dynamics of the Quemoy and Matsu crisis of 1958 in which nuclear weapons use was a clear option available to President Eisenhower and national security strategists. Useful in case studies of intelligence analysis in crisis situations.

10072. Soohoo, Edmund L. "An ELINT Vigil, Unmanned," <u>Studies in Intelligence</u> 12/1 (Spring 1968).

10073. Sopko, John F. "The Changing Proliferation Threat," <u>Foreign Policy</u> 105 (Winter 1996-1997): 3-20.

An overview of the new threats to international peace by terrorist groups and new weapons. Sections discuss new tools for terrorists (gas, bugs, and thugs); the Aum Shinrikyo; and the concern for American preparation for attack. Mentions the intelligence services.

10074. Sorge, Richard and A. A. Prokhozhev. "Tiuremnye Zapiski Rikharda Sorge," <u>Novaia i Noveishaia Istoriia</u> 4&5 (1994): 141-176.

In Russian, the former Russian spy against Japan relates his experiences. Discussion is continued in volume 6 (1994): 91-116.

10075. Sorge, Richard and A. A. Prokhozhev. "Tiuremnye Zapiski: Moi Issledovaniia v Iaponii," <u>Novaia i Noveishaia Istoriia</u> 2 (1995): 79-100.

In Russian, more accounts of the Russian spy against Japan.

10076. Soucy, Gilles. "A German Spy in New Carlisle," <u>Gaspsie</u> 30/1 (1992): 21-23.

In French, this article appears in a French Canadian journal. This title is approximate.

10077. "Soviet ELINT Capabilities," <u>ONI Review</u> 15/1 (1960): 13-15.

10078. "Soviet Intelligence and Security: Second Bibliography of Soviet Books and Articles," <u>Studies in Intelligence</u> 11/4 (Winter 1967).

This article is not listed by the Central Intelligence Agency in the collection of declassified items for public access.

10079. "The Soviets and Repetitive Formulae," <u>Studies in Intelligence</u> 14/3 (Fall 1970).

10080. "Soviet Space Reconnaissance Systems," ONI Review 16/12 (1961): 491-494.

10081. Spader, Dean J. "Conflicting Values and Laws: Understanding the Paradox of the Privacy Act and the Freedom of Information Act," Legal Studies Forum 19 (Winter 1995): 21-42.

10082. Sparrow, Malcolm K. "The Application of Network Analysis to Criminal Intelligence: An Assessment of the Prospects," Social Networks 13 (1991): 251-274.
    Useful in studies of domestic intelligence of criminal organizations, and police intelligence of organized crime.

10083. "Specialized Soviet Assassination Weapons," ONI Review 9/12 (1954): 510-512.

10084. Spence, Richard B. "Sidney Reilly's Lubianka "Diary" 30 October to 4 November 1925," Revolutionary Russia 8/2 (1995): 179-194.

10085. Spence, Richard B. "K. A. Jahnke and the German Sabotage Campaign in the United States and Mexico, 1914-1918," Historian 59/1 (1996): 89-112.

10086. Spencer, J. R. "Bugging and Burglary by Police," Cambridge Law Review 56 (March 1997): 6-8.
    Considers the holding in R. v. Khan (1996) wherein in the British Home Office had ordered police to burgle a house and to plant a listening device pursuant to Home Office Guidelines. Raises an objection to this form of home invasion and briefly considers the implications of the case.

10087. Speidel, M. P. "Exploratores: Mobile Elite Units of Roman Germany," Epigraphische Studien 13 (1983): 63-78.
    Contains insights into the Roman emperors intelligence gathering intentions in the farthest corners of the empire. Cited in the work of Rose Mary Sheldon, a frequent and rare modern contributor to the topic of intelligence in ancient times (see citations in this bibliography).

10088. Springer, Elisabeth. "Die Bruder Ridolfi in Rom: Habsburgische Agenten im Schatten des Bruderzwistes," Wiener Beitrage zur Geschichte der Neuzeit 20 (1993): 78-95.

10089. Squire, P. S. "Nicholas I and the Problem of Internal Security in Russia in 1826," Slavonic and East European Review 38/91 (June 1960).

10090. Stack, Kevin P. "A Negative View of Competitive Analysis,"

International Journal of Intelligence and Counterintelligence 10/4 (Winter 1997-1998): 456-464.

A brief reflection on the 1976 Team B concept and its potential for failure in the modern context of intelligence analysis.

10091. Stack, Kevin P. "The Cold War Intelligence Score," American Intelligence Journal 18/1&2 (1998): 69-72.

Discussion of covert action; analysis; collection; and counterintelligence.

10092. Starnes, Lucy. "Girl Spy of the Valley," Virginia Cavalcade (Spring 1961).

Discusses the espionage activities of Belle Boyd during the Civil War.

10093. Stashower, Daniel. "A Thin Man Who Made Memorable Use of His Spade," Smithsonian 25/2 (1994): 114-127.

The fictional works of former Pinkerton Detective Agency operative Dashiell Hammett are discussed in detail, mainly with reference to the detective characters created by the author.

10094. Stedman, John C. "Trade Secrets," Ohio State Law Journal 23 (1962): 4-34.

Major sections discuss the definition of trade secrets; the general law of trade secret protection; some special situations; underlying legal philosophy for trade secret protection; evaluation of existing legal approaches to trade secret protection; and a trade secret policy proposal.

10095. Steele, J. Michael. "Models for Managing Secrets," Management Science 35/2 (February 1989): 240-248.

Considers the goal of improving secrecy management by demonstrating mathematical probabilities applicable to different secrecy control strategies. In simple terms, the author points out that secrecy is a function of the number of people who know a secret, combined with the methods they use to secure it.

10096. Steele, Richard W. "Preparing the Public for War: Efforts to Establish a National Propaganda Agency, 1940-1941," American Historical Review 75/6 (October 1970): 1640-1653.

A brief history of Franklin Roosevelt's efforts to orchestrate a degree of popular support for US involvement in the impending world war. Emphasizes the care Roosevelt took to avoid the mistakes of the Wilson administration in World War I with respect to propaganda use to whip up popular support.

10097. Steele, Robert D. "Open Source Intelligence: What Is It? Why Is It Important to the Military?," American Intelligence Journal 17/1&2 (1996): 35-41.

Contains sections addressing introductory observations; open source intelligence and the military; the information continuum; commentary on representative national approaches; advantages and disadvantages; obstacles to military exploitation; opportunities for advantage; and role of the military reserve.

10098. Steely, Mel. "Col. A. L. Conger and America's Peacemaking Diplomacy in 1919," Journal of the Georgia Association of Historians 15 (1994): 64-82.

10099. Stefanac, Suzanne. "Dangerous Games," California Lawyer 14 (October 1994): 56-59+.
        Concerns espionage and computer crimes.

10100. Stein, Abe. "The Downfall of Beria," New International 19/3 (May-June 1953): 111-129.

10101. Steinbach, Peter. "Widerstandsorganisation Harnack/Schulze-Boysen die 'Rote Kapelle': Ein Vergleichsfall fuer die Widerstandsgeschichte," Geschichte in Wissenschaft und Unterricht 42/3 (1991): 133-152.

10102. Steinmeyer, Walter. "Installation Penetration," Studies in Intelligence 6/2 (Summer 1962).

10103. Steinmeyer, Walter. "The Intelligence Role in Counterinsurgency," Studies in Intelligence 9/3 (Fall 1965).

10104. Stekal, Oleg. "Ukraine: The New Secret Services," Transition 1/10 (June 1995): 1-4.

10105. Stender, J. Terrence. "Too Many Secrets: Challenges to Control of Strong Crypto and the National Security Perspective," Case Western Reserve Journal of International Law 30 (Winter 1998): 287-352.

10106. Stephenson, John L. "On Optimism," Studies in Intelligence 23/2 (Summer 1979): 41-42.

10107. Sterling, George E. "The U.S. Hunt for Axis Agent Radios," Studies in Intelligence 4/1 (Spring 1960).

10108. Stern, Guy. "The Jewish Exiles in the Service of US Intelligence: The Post-War Years," Yearbook of the Leo Baick Institute 40 (1995): 51-62
        Jewish exiles served with distinction in US intelligence activities during World War II from 1943-1945, then in various roles in the post-war era in connection with the Nuremberg trials and establishment of German newspaper and radio media.

10109. Stern, Suzanna W. "My Brush with History: My Doctor," <u>American Heritage</u> 47/2 (April 1996): 52-56.

A brief discussion of espionage and physicians.

10110. Stevens, Charles J. "The Use and Control of Executive Agreements: Recent Congressional Initiatives," <u>Orbis</u> 20/4 (1977): 905-931.

10111. Stevens, James W. and David W. MacKenna. "Assignment and Coordination of Tactical Units," <u>FBI Law Enforcement Bulletin</u> 58/3 (1989): 2-9.

A brief overview of tactical unit operations, including some statistics on tactical unit deployment, and the use of information and assessment by tactical units.

10112. Stevens, Linda K. "The Economic Espionage Act: New Criminal Penalties for Trade Secret Misappropriation," <u>Franchise Law Journal</u> 17 (Summer 1997): 3-8.

10113. Stevens, Sayre. "'Foretesting' ABM Systems: Some Hazards," <u>Studies in Intelligence</u> 12/2 (Summer 1968).

10114. Stewart, Averill T. and Joseph O. Matthews. "View from the Hot Shop," <u>Studies in Intelligence</u> 12/3 (Fall 1968).

10115. Stewart, Duncan. "Apples and Espionage," <u>New Zealand Law Journal</u> 1997 (June 1997): 213-214+.

Considers dimensions of the <u>Franklin v. Giddens</u> case reflecting on trade secrets law in New Zealand.

10116. Stewart, Walter J. "The Army's Reserve Component Intelligence Forces," <u>American Intelligence Journal</u> 18/1&2 (1998): 15-19.

Discusses the Army National Guard force and ARNG military intelligence linguist units; the Army Reserve force; AR MI units and linguists units; and training dimensions.

10117. Stoertz, Howard, Jr. "Intelligence Support to the US SALT Delegation," <u>Studies in Intelligence</u> 16/2 (Spring 1972).

10118. Stone, Barbara S. "The John Birch Society in California: A Profile," <u>Journal of Politics</u> 36/1 (February 1974): 184-197.

A study of the Society, a right wing political organization founded in 1958. Major sections discuss the research sample; the research findings; political conservatism and conclusions. May have application in assessments of internal political groups.

10119. Storm, Paul R. "Estimating the Soviet Gold Position," Studies in Intelligence 7/3 (Fall 1963).

10120. "Strategic Arms Limitations Talks: The Current Round," New World Review 38/4 (1970): 20-27.

10121. "Strategic Warning and Deception," Studies in Intelligence 17/1 (Spring 1973).
This article is not listed by the Central Intelligence Agency among declassified items for public access.

10122. Strayer, Joseph R. "The Role of the Consultant in Intelligence Estimates," Studies in Intelligence 2/3 (Fall 1958).

10123. Strotmann, Michael. "Die Last der Vergangenheit: Zum Umgang mit den Stasi-Aktenim Wierderverreinigten Deutschland," Deutschland Archiv: Zeitschrift fuer das Vereinigte Deutschland 28 (August 1995): 806-822.
In German, a discussion of the implications of secret police operations of the former East German Stasi.

10124. Strout, Cushing. "Telling the Oppenheimer Story: From the AEC to the BBC," Yale Review 73 (1983): 122-130.
A review of the American Playhouse Series seven-part dramatization of 'Oppenheimer,' a depiction of the life and circumstances involving the security clearance of atomic scientist J. Robert Oppenheimer.

10125. Studeman, William O. "Leading Intelligence Along the Byways of our Future: Acquiring C4ISR Architectures for the 21st Century," Defense Intelligence Journal 7/1 (Spring 1998): 47-65.
Discusses the interlocking nature of intelligence architectures in terms of the current challenges; leadership issues; and intelligence issues. Special emphasis is given to the intelligence issues.

10126. Stuteville, Joe. "Secret Casualties of the Gulf War," American Legion Magazine 142/3 (March 1997): 34-36.

10127. Sufrin, Mark. "The Story of Earl Ellis," Mankind 2/6 (1970): 70-76.

10128. Sullivan, Brian R. "From Little Brother to Senior Partner: Fascist Italian Perceptions of the Nazis and of Hitler's Regime, 1930-1936," Intelligence and National Security 13/1 (Spring 1998): 85-108.
A study of the intrigue in the relations between Mussolini and Hitler during the 1930s, including the role of intelligence in informing the shifts in the nature of the relationship. Major sections discuss attitudes of Italians toward

Germany and Hitler; statistics; envoys; soldiers; and leaders.

10129. Sulzberger, Carl F. "Why Is It Hard to Keep Secrets?," Psychoanalysis 2 (Fall 1953): 37-43.

10130. Sumida, Marshall M. and Paul M. Nagano. "Review, Resolve and Redress of the Internment of Japanese Americans During World War II," American Baptist Quarterly 13/1 (1994): 79-108.
An analysis of the impact of US national security policy of internment on Japanese-Americans. May be useful in discussions and debates about information collected and used by decision makers in the formation of the internment policy.

10131. Sunderland, Riley. "The Secret Embargo," Pacific Historical Review 29 (February 1960): 75-80.
Attempts to clarify the record with respect to the role of Chiang Kai-shek in the embargo of weapons to the Chinese to permit a defense of air fields against Japanese attack.

10132. Supperston, Michael. "The Intelligence Services Act 1994," Public Law (1994): 329-331.

10133. Suri, Jeremi. "America's Search for a Technological Solution to the Arms Race: The Surprise Attack Conference of 1958 and a Challenge for 'Eisenhower Revisionists,'" Diplomatic History 21/3 (Summer 1997): 417-451.

10134. Suss, Walter. "Entmachtung und Verfall der Staatssicherheit: Ein Kapital aus dem Spaetherbst 1989," Deutschland Archiv: Zeitschrift fuer das Vereinigte Deutschland 28 (February 1995): 122-151.

10135. Svent, Rozina. "Vladimir Vauhnik: Vojak in Obvescevalec," Zgodovinski Casopis 49/2 (1995): 281-288.
In Slovenian, this is a brief study of the espionage work of Vauhnik.

10136. Svetz, Holly E. "Japan's New Trade Secret Law: We Asked for It--Now What Have We Got?," George Washington Journal of International Law and Economics 26/2 (1992): 413-449.
Discusses the backgrounds of the US and Japan in trade secret protection and the pressure by the US on Japan to introduce formal protection; analysis of the new Japanese law; and conclusions.

10137. Sypher, Eileen. "Anarchism and Gender: James' The Princess Cassamassima and Conrad's The Secret Agent," Henry James Review 9/1 (1988): 1-16.

10138. Syrett, David. "Communications Intelligence and the Battle of the Atlantic, 1943-1945," Archives 22 (April 1995): 45-59.

10139. Szamuely, George. "Did the U.S. Recruit Nazi War Criminals?," Commentary 85/6 (June 1988): 50-53.
    A brief overview of some of the controversies surrounding the question of US support for former Nazis after World War II. Considers issues raised by several authors who have given book-length analysis to the matter.

10140. Szasz, Ferenc M. "Peppermint and Alsos," MHQ: The Quarterly Journal of Military History 6/3 (1994): 42-47.
    A brief overview of US covert actions against the Germans in 1944 aimed at discovery of German nuclear capabilities for the combat environment.

10141. Taft, H. W. "Freedom of Speech and the Espionage Act," American Law Review 55 (September 1921): 695-721.

10142. Talasco, Frederick J. "The Blockhouse in the Clove, 1782," North Jersey Highlander 9/3 (1973): 13-18.

10143. "The Tangled Web," Studies in Intelligence 31/1 (Spring 1987).
    This article is not listed by the Central Intelligence Agency among a collection of declassified items for public access.

10144. Taras, Ray. "The End of the Walesa Era in Poland," Current History 95/599 (March 1996): 124-128.
    Among numerous issues related to modern Poland, espionage is discussed.

10145. Tauss, Edward. "Foretesting a Soviet ABM System," Studies in Intelligence 12/4 (Winter 1968).

10146. Taylor, John M. "In Queen Victoria's Secret Service," Studies in Intelligence 29/4 (Winter 1985).

10147. Taylor, Philip M. "The Foreign Office and British Propaganda During the First World War," Historical Journal 23/4 (December 1980): 875-898.
    A detailed discussion of organizational politics associated with the Foreign Office role in propaganda administration during World War I.

10148. Taylor, Sandra C. "Long-Haired Women, Short-Haired Spies: Gender, Espionage, and America's War in Vietnam," Intelligence and National Security 13/2 (Summer 1998): 61-70.
    A brief exploration of the role of Vietnamese women in service as

military intelligence collection agents of the North Vietnamese cause. Based on secondary source accounts and some of the author's original research. She has recently published a book titled <u>Vietnamese Women At War: Fighting for Ho Chi Minh and the Revolution</u> (1998).

10149. Taylor, Stan A. and Daniel Snow. "Cold War Spies: Why They Spied and How They Got Caught," <u>Intelligence and National Security</u> 12/2 (April 1997): 101-125.

Sections discuss the authors' analyses of the subject: why they spied; how they got caught; and intelligence after the cold war.

10150. "Teaching Intelligence," <u>Studies in Intelligence</u> 26/4 (Winter 1982).

This article is not listed by the Central Intelligence Agency among a collection of declassified items for public access.

10151. Teagarden, Ernest M. "The Cambridge Five: The End of the Cold War Brings Forth Some Views from the Other Side," <u>American Intelligence Journal</u> 18/1&2 (1998): 63-68.

Summarizes the espionage actions of five British spies: Anthony Blunt; Guy Burgess; John Cairncross; Donald Maclean; and Kim Philby.

10152. Tebrich, Spencer. "Human Scent and its Detection," <u>Studies in Intelligence</u> 5/1 (Spring 1961).

10153. Teichholtz, Kermit B. "A Mirror for Agent Handlers," <u>Studies in Intelligence</u> 6/2 (Summer 1962).

10154. Temple, Wayne C. "A Signal Officer with Grant: The Letters of Captain Charles L. Davis," <u>Civil War History</u> 7/4 (December 1961): 428-437.

Contains some letters from Davis' military service from 1861 to 1865. In 1865, he was General Grant's Chief Signal Officer of the Army of the Potomac.

10155. Teplitz, Robert F. "Taking Assassination Attempts Seriously: Did the United States Violate International Law in Forcefully Responding to the Iraqi Plot to Kill George Bush?," <u>Cornell International Law Journal</u> 28 (Spring 1995): 569-617.

10156. Thacher, Thomas D., III. "Combatting Corruption and Racketeering: A New Strategy for Reforming Public Contracting in New York City's Construction Industry," <u>New York Law School Law Review</u> 40/1-2 (1995): 113-142.

Considers the operations of the New York Office of Inspector General, the work of the Office against organized crime, and the use of intelligence gathering and other strategies to effect prosecutions of organized crime members.

10157. "Theft of Trade Secrets: The Need for a Statutory Solution," University of Pennsylvania Law Review 120 (1972): 378-401.

Major issues under consideration are: internal confusions of trade secret law, the concepts of property and special relationship; Dupont v. Christopher and its implications; the federal preemption problem; and needed federal legislation.

10158. Thomas, Louis. "The Map in Field Reporting," Studies in Intelligence 6/1 (Spring 1962).

10159. Thomas, Louis. "Alexander Rado," Studies in Intelligence 12/2 (Summer 1968).

10160. Thomas, Martin. "The Discarded Leader: General Henri Giraud and the Foundation of the French Committee of National Liberation," French History 10/1 (1996): 100-131.

In addition to discussion of the political intrigues in French determination to lead French resistance to the Axis powers, this article discusses the US Office of Strategic Services' primacy in intelligence and covert operations in the Middle East.

10161. Thomas, Stafford T. "A Political Theory of the CIA," International Journal of Intelligence and Counterintelligence 11/1 (Spring 1998): 57-72.

Argues that a framework for analysis of the Central Intelligence Agency is useful in studies of the US intelligence effort. The framework considers the CIA's international policy context; the Washington political context; and the bureaucratic context. A final section addresses unrealistic expectations of CIA.

10162. Thomas, T. "Child Protection, Privacy and Covert Video Surveillance," Journal of Social Welfare and Family Law 17 (1995): 311-323.

10163. Thomas, Timothy L. "Deterring Information Warfare: A New Strategic Challenge," Parameters: US Army War College Quarterly 26/4 (Winter 1996-1997): 81-91.

Discusses the meaning of threat; threat subsets; deterrence reasoning; defining deterrence against information assault; means to deter information assaults; and conclusions.

10164. Thompkins, Peter. "The OSS and Italian Partisans in World War II: Intelligence and Operational Support for the Anti-Nazi Resistance," Studies in Intelligence Unclassified edition (Spring 1998): 95-103.

The author, a former OSS agent, discusses the assistance of the OSS to the Italian partisans, mainly in 1944. Major sections discuss the Gothic Line; partisan attacks; stalled offensive; liberating Ravenna; two key cities; uprising in Genoa; partisans prevail; retaking Turin; allied advances; a string of victories;

enter Mussolini; and the battle ends. The article appears in the unclassified and unnumbered issue of the CIA's internal journal.

10165. Thompson, Robert. "What Went Wrong? The Failure of American Strategy in Vietnam," Interplay 2/9 91969): 13-16.

10166. Thony, J. F. "Processing Financial Information in Money Laundering Matters: The Financial Intelligence Units," European Journal of Crime, Criminal Law and Criminal Justice 4/3 (1996): 257-282.
    A detailed consideration of financial investigative and information gathering units for combatting money laundering. Discusses the nature and type of financial intelligence units; and organization functions.

10167. Thurlow, Richard C. "'A Very Clever Capitalist Class': British Communism and State Surveillance, 1939-1945," Intelligence and National Security 12/2 (April 1997): 1-21.
    Major sections include: state management of political extremism, 1918-39; the 'imperialist war', 1939-41; the 'apostles of national unity,' 1941-45; and chicken feed triumph.

10168. Tidwell, William A. "Kim or Major North?," Studies in Intelligence 2/2 (Summer 1958).

10169. Tidwell, William A. "Charles County: Confederate Cauldron," Maryland Historical Magazine 91/1 (1996): 16-27.
    A brief history of the role of Charles County's leading citizens in supporting the Confederacy during the Civil War, in particular the underground actions in secret communications and transportation of equipment. Useful in Civil War intelligence studies.

10170. Tod, J. K. "The Malleson Mission to Transcaspia in 1918," Journal of the Central Asian Society 27/1 (January 1940): 45-67.

10171. Todd, Dana M. "In Defense of the Outrageous Government Conduct Defense in the Federal Courts," Kentucky Law Journal 84/2 (Winter 1995-1996): 415-445.
    The author reviews the federal entrapment defense; the due process defense of outrageous government conduct; and the future of the due process defense. Particularly useful in research on undercover police operations.

10172. Tollius, Paul. "Experience with Types of Agent Motivation," Studies in Intelligence 3/3 (Fall 1959).

10173. Tolzer, Warren W. "The Foreign Correspondents' Visit to Yenan in

1944: A Reassessment," Pacific Historical Review 41 (May 1972): 207-224.

An assessment of the nature and effect of the correspondents' visit, concluding that the visit had little effect on American policy toward China.

10174. Tomaselli, Keyan G. and P. Eric Louw. "Disinformation and the South African Defence Force's Theory of War," Social Justice 18/1&2 (Spring-Summer 1991): 124-140.

Major sections: the South African state's communication strategy in the 1980s; combating media terms; disinformation and dirty tricks; disinformation and misinformation (a case study); closing observations; postscript.

10175. Tomkins, Adam. "Government Information and Parliament: Misleading by Design or by Default?," Public Law (Autumn 1996): 472-489.

Discusses the background of the Iran-Iraq war, 1980-88; the ceasefire in 1988, and "Project Babylon (the Iraqi long-range gun project); intelligence services (MI-6 and SIS) interest in the Supergun affair; government disclosure to Parliament; constitutional implications; and publication of the Scott report in 1996.

10176. Tomkins, Adam. "Intelligence and Government," Parliamentary Affairs 50/1 (January 1997): 109-129.

Evaluates aspects of the Scott investigation regarding Britain's national security structure, including its intelligence activities.

10177. Tophol, L. "The Invisible Battle--Electronic Warfare," NATO's Sixteen Nations 42 (1996-1997): 21-22+.

10178. Toran, Janice. "Secrecy Orders and Government Litigants: 'A Northwest Passage Around the Freedom of Information Act,'" Georgia Law Review 27 (Fall 1992): 121-182.

Discusses the legislative history of the FOIA; illustrative cases; identifying problems; and conclusions.

10179. Toren, Peter J. G. "The Prosecution of Trade Secrets Thefts under Federal Law," Intellectual Property Law Review (1996): 511-550.

Major sections discuss the scope of the problem; specific federal statutes; and cases brought in federal courts; and recommendations. Originally published in Pepperdine Law Review 22 (1994): 59-98.

10180. Tovar, B. Hugh. "The Debate Continues: The CIA in Indonesia: The Scholars vs. the Professionals [The Professionals: The Kahins' CIA Fever]," International Journal of Intelligence and Counterintelligence 10/2 (Summer 1997): 218-221.

This is part of an on-going controversy surrounding a critique written about a book on the Indonesian revolt by Audrey and George McT. Kahin. Major sections discuss General Suharto's place; substantiation needed; and believing the worst.

10181.   Townshend, Charles.   "Bloody Sunday--Michael Collins Speaks," European Studies Review 9/3 (July 1979): 377-385.
Referring to the article by Tom Bowden (see citation 8915), this author critiques the Bowden perspective and some of the evidence used to explain the November 21, 1920 "Bloody Sunday" account involving Michael Collins and the IRA.

10182.   Townroe, B. S.   "Heroine of France: Helene Vagliano," Blackwood's Magazine 258 (October 1945): 281-284.
Briefly accounts for the spy work of Vagliano.

10183.   Toyne, S. M. "Guy Fawkes and the Powder Plot," History Today 1 (November 1951): 16-24.
An attempt to clarify the history of the plot to blow up Parliament in 1605, and the role of Guy Fawkes in the conspiracy.

10184.   Trahair, Richard C. S.   "A Psychohistorical Approach to Espionage: Klaus Fuchs (1911-1988)," Mentalities 9/2 (1994): 28-49.

10185.   Travers, Russ. "The Coming Intelligence Failure," Studies in Intelligence Unclassified edition (1997): 35-43.
A "back to the future" look at intelligence community problems and prospects associated with possible failures in the year 2001.   Major sections discuss the path to failure; and avoiding failure.

10186.   Trilling, Diana. "The Oppenheimer Case: A Reading of the Testimony," Partisan Review 21 (1954): 604-635.
A lengthy and detailed consideration of the contents of the Atomic Energy Commission investigation of J. Robert Oppenheimer, and the unexpected release of the findings published in In the Matter of J. Robert Oppenheimer: Transcript of Hearings Before the Personnel Security Board.

10187.   Trilling, Diana.   "A Rejoinder to M. Meyerhoff," Partisan Review 22 (1955): 248-251.
See the Meyerhoff citation in this bibliography. The exchange was over circumstances of the McCarthy era persecution of various people, including J. Robert Oppenheimer.

10188.   Trimble, Delmege.   "Defector Disposal," Studies in Intelligence 2 (Fall 1958).

10189. Trimble, Delmege. "The Defections of Dr. John," Studies in Intelligence 5/3 (Fall 1960).

10190. Troy, Thomas F. "The Coordinator of Information and British Intelligence," Studies in Intelligence 18/Supplement (Spring 1974).
An essay dealing with the origins of the COI, William Donovan's role, and the roles of Churchill and Kennedy. Estimated to be 116 pages in length.

10191. Trulock, Notra, III. "Intelligence and the Department of Energy: New Approaches for the 1990s," American Intelligence Journal 17/1&2 (1996): 17-22
Key sections discuss the evolving intelligence arena; DOE intelligence in a nutshell; Office of Energy Intelligence relationship to DOE; providing intelligence support to DOE; OEI and the intelligence community; challenges facing DOE intelligence.

10192. Tsaknis, Leo. "Commonwealth Secrecy Provisions: Time for Reform?," Criminal Law Journal 18 (October 1994): 254-270.
A detailed discussion of freedom of information issues and policy in Australian law.

10193. Tucker, Darren S. "The Federal Government's War on Economic Espionage," University of Pennsylvania Journal of International Law 18/3 (Fall 1997): 1109-1152.
Sections of this article discuss economic espionage against the US and the new role of intelligence agencies in its prevention; a definition of economic espionage; countries engaged in theft of corporate secrets of US corporations and types of information sought; losses from economic espionage; techniques of foreign intelligence services to acquire US trade secrets; prevention programs; civil and criminal remedies; and recommendations on further prevention efforts.

10194. Tucker, Robert C. "Svetlana Alliluyeva as Witness of Stalin," Slavic Review 27/2 (June 1968): 296-312.

10195. Tucker, Robert C. "The Rise of Stalin's Personality Cult," American Historical Review 84 (April 1979): 347-366.

10196. Turgeon, Charles F. "Windfall from Hong Kong," Studies in Intelligence 8/4 (Winter 1964).

10197. Turn, R.; N. Z. Shapiro; and M. L. Juncosa. "Privacy and Security in Centralized Versus Decentralized Databank Systems," Policy Sciences 7 (1976): 17-30.

10198. Turnbaugh, Roy. "Harry Elmer Barnes and World War I Revisionism:

An Absence of Dialogue," Peace and Change 5/2-3 (1978): 63-69.

A sharply critical view of the writings of Barnes, a 1920s social critic, who was known for propagandizing for Germany in the years after World War I.

10199. Twiddy, Andrew J. "The Recruitment of Soviet Officials," Studies in Intelligence 8/4 (Winter 1964).

10200. Ulsamer, Edgar. "The Military Decision-Makers' Top Tool," Air Force Magazine 54/7 (1971): 44-49.

10201. Unger, Jonathan. "The Making and Breaking of the Chinese Secret Societies," Journal of Contemporary Asia 5 (1975): 89-98.

10202. Unger, Stephen H. "The Growing Threat of Government Secrecy," Technology Review 85 (February-March 1982): 31-39, 84-85.

10203. Vandaveer, Robert. "Operation Lincoln," Studies in Intelligence 7/4 (Winter 1963).

10204. Vaneev, V. "From the History of the Radio War of the U.S.A. Against Japan," Voenno-Istoricheski Zhurnal 5 (1968): 46-54.

This is an approximate translation of the title of an article appearing in a Russian language journal.

10205. VanErt, Gibran. "Empty Air: Ezra Pound's World War Two Radio Broadcasts," Past Imperfect 3 (1994): 47-72.

A detailed analysis of poet Ezra Pound's work during World War II as a propagandist for the Italian government by means of radio broadcasts.

10206. Van Seters, Deborah. "The Munsinger Affair: Images of Espionage and Security in 1960s Canada," Intelligence and National Security 13/2 (Summer 1998): 71-84.

A discussion of an internal security scandal in Canada in the 1960s, including the role of the Royal Canadian Mounted Police investigation as compared with journalistic attention given to the case.

10207. Van Stappen, James. "Graphological Assessment in Action," Studies in Intelligence 3/3 (Fall 1959).

10208. Van Stappen, James. "Laboratory Analysis of Suspect Documents," Studies in Intelligence 4/2 (Summer 1960).

10209. Van Wagenen, James S. "A Review of Congressional Oversight," Studies in Intelligence Unclassified edition (1997): 97-102.

This article discusses the revolutionary war experience; early establishment of a secret fund; early attempts at oversight; period of benign neglect; getting tough; cooperation and legislation; renewed tension; reorganization; and the balance sheet.

10210. Vasse, Maurice. "France and the Cuban Crisis," <u>Histoire, Eonomie et Socit</u> 13/1 (1994): 185-194.

In French, this brief article discusses French support for the US actions during the 1962 Soviet missile crisis. Useful in studies of international security cooperation between countries with long histories of contentious relationships.

10211. Vaughn, Michael S. "The Parameters of Trickery as an Acceptable Police Practice," <u>American Journal of Police</u> 11/4 (1992): 71-95.

10212. Vermaat, J. A. Emerson. "The East German Secret Service Structure and Operational Focus," <u>Conflict Quarterly</u> 7/3 (Fall 1987): 44-57.

10213. Vermij, R. H. "Bedrijfsspionage in de Achttiende Eeuw: Een Agent van de Tsaar te Zijdebalen," <u>Maandblad Oud-Utrecht</u> 63 (1990): 107-110.

Concerns an incident in early modern european industrial espionage. Useful in studies of the theft of inventions and other industrial spying activities.

10214. Vetterling, Philip and Avis Waring. "Tonnage Through Tibet," <u>Studies in Intelligence</u> 7/1 (Spring 1963).

10215. Vick, James A., Jr. "Intelligence Support to Operation 'GIT'MO,'" <u>Military Intelligence</u> 19/2 (April-June 1993): 6-9, 50.

An in-depth look at the unique requirements for intelligence support in this politically volatile relief effort, particularly regarding the focus on the difficulties associated with nontactical operations.

10216. Villani, Pasquale. "Agenti e Diplomatici Francesi in Italia (1789-1795): Un Giacobino a Genova: Jean Tilly," <u>Societ e Storia</u> 17/65 (1994): 529-558.

In Italian, this is a lengthy discussion of Tilly's espionage work in Genoa thoroughout the French revolution.

10217. Viniar, Lester M. "With Rod & Reel in Afghanistan," <u>Studies in Intelligence</u> 11/1 (Spring 1967).

10218. Vita-Finzi, Paolo. "The Defender of Abel," <u>Nuova Antologia</u> 517/2066 (1973): 251-253.

10219. Vogel, Joseph L. "The Best Fighter I Ever Flew," <u>Aerospace Historian</u> 24/3 (1977): 146-148.

10220. Volpo, Dan and Sylvia Piggott. "Surfing for Corporate Intelligence," <u>Business Information Review</u> 13 (March 1996): 39-47.

10221. Volterra, Alessandro. "Verso La Colonia Eritrea: La Legislazione E L'Administrazione, 1887-1889," <u>Storea Contemporanea</u> 26/5 (1995): 817-850.

10222. von Mayrhauser, Richard T. "Making Intelligence Functional: Walter D. Scott and Applied Psychological Testing in World War I," <u>Journal of the History of the Behavioral Sciences</u> 25/1 (1989): 60-72.

10223. Waal, Carla. "The First Original Confederate Drama, 'The Guerillas,'" <u>Virginia Magazine of History and Biography</u> 70/4 (1962): 459-467.

10224. Waghelstein, John D. "Ruminations of a Pachyderm or What I Learned in the Counter-Insurgency Business," <u>Small Wars and Insurgencies</u> 5/3 (1994): 360-378.
    The author gives his detailed accounting of counter-insurgency and covert missions during his career, and evaluates the missions he believes were most productive of benefit to US interests.

10225. Walker, Clive. "Constitutional Governance and Special Powers Against Terrorism: Lessons from the United Kingdom's Prevention of Terrorism Acts," <u>Columbia Journal of Transnational Law</u> 35 (1997): 1-47.

10226. Walker, J. Samuel. "'No More Cold War': American Foreign Policy and the 1948 Soviet Peace Offensive," <u>Diplomatic History</u> 5/1 (Winter 1981): 75-91.
    Provides an overview of the circumstances leading to Soviet overtures of peace in 1948, particularly with respect to the Truman administration's apparent hostility toward improved relations.

10227. Wall, Irwin M. "The United States, Algeria, and the Fall of the Fourth Republic," <u>Diplomatic History</u> 18/4 (1994): 489-511.
    A detailed discussion of the strategy of the United States in maintaining friendly associations with the Algerians during the late 1950s insurgency conflict between Algeria and France. Useful in intelligence inquiries aimed at behind-the-scenes forces allegedly responsible for widening the divide between adversaries.

10228. Walsh, James H. "Strategic Thinking and Air Intelligence," <u>Studies in Intelligence</u> 2/1 (Winter 1958): 27-28.

10229. Wang, Jessica. "Science, Security, and the Cold War: The Case of E. U. Condon," <u>Isis</u> 83/2 (1992): 238-269.
    A detailed discussed of Condon's loyalty hearings.

10230. Ward, David. "Sisyphean Circles: The Communications Assistance for Law Enforcement Act," Rutgers Computer & Technology Law Journal 22 (Spring 1996): 267-299.

Discussion of the Act's background; an overview of the Act; analysis of the Act's components; the Act's impact on the future of the telecommunications industry; and conclusions.

10231. Ward, Stephen R. "Intelligence Surveillance of British Ex-Servicemen 1918-1920," Historical Journal 16/1 (March 1973): 179-188.

Summarizes the work of the Home Office Special Branch in its surveillance of British military veterans, mainly aimed at the search for enemy agents and espionage activities. Argues that the surveillance activities had a beneficial effect upon the relationship between government and the ex-servicemen.

10232. Wark, David L. "The Definition of Some Estimative Expressions," Studies in Intelligence 8/3 (Fall 1964).

10233. Warman, Roberta M. "The Erosion of Foreign Office Influence in the Making of Foreign Policy, 1916-1918," Historical Journal 15/1 (March 1972): 133-159.

The details of the demise of Foreign Office influence in the World War I years are discussed. Includes discussion of the role of the Military Intelligence Division and the Political Intelligence Bureau.

10234. Warner, Denis and Peggy. "The Doctrine of Surprise," MHQ: The Quarterly Journal of Military History 4/1 (Autumn 1991).

10235. Warner, Michael. "Sophisticated Spies: CIA's Links to Liberal Anti-Communists, 1949-1967," International Journal of Intelligence and Counter-intelligence 9/4 (Winter 1996-1997): 425-433.

This brief history explores the early years of covert action plans at CIA. Sections discuss a vanished world, and domestic intervention at issue.

10236. Warner, Michael. "The CIA's Office of Policy Coordination: From NSC 10/2 to NSC 68," International Journal of Intelligence and Counterintelligence 11/2 (Summer 1998): 211-220.

Major sections discuss peacetime covert action; OPC and the burst of activity in the early cold war era; shifting control; taking the offensive; and planned growth.

10237. Warner, Michael and Robert L. Benson. "Venona and Beyond: Thoughts on Work Undone," Intelligence and National Security 12/3 (July 1997): 1-13.

Reflections upon, and analysis of, the recently declassified messages pertaining to Soviet espionage against the US atomic bomb project in World War

II. Sections discuss Venona's limitations; solvable problems; eternal mysteries; and conclusions.

10238. Warner, Peggy. "Arms and Men: The Secret Weapon that Failed," MHQ: The Quarterly Journal of Military History 4/1 (Autumn 1991).

10239. Watanabe, Frank. "Fifteen Axioms for Intelligence Analysts," Studies in Intelligence Unclassified edition (1997): 45-47.
    Axioms consider professional judgments; aggressive posture; mistaken versus wrong; mirror imaging; dissemination; coordination; agreement among peers; consumer behavior; collection, and other fundamentals.

10240. Watanabe, Toru. "1991: American Perceptions of the Pearl Harbor Attack," Journal of American-East Asian Relations 3/3 (1994): 269-278.
    In the year of the fiftieth anniversary of the Pearl Harbor attack, it is useful to review American perceptions of the Japanese as to the lessons of the event and the implications for future relations.

10241. Watson, Alan. "Trade Secrets and Roman Law: The Myth Exploded," Tulane European and Civil Law Forum 11 (Winter 1996): 1151-1196.
    This is a response to an article by A. Arthur Schiller in Columbia Law Review 30 (1930): 837-851.

10242. Watson, David. "The Krasin-Savinkov Meeting of 1 December 1921," Cahiers du Monde Russe et Sovietique 27/3-4 (1986).

10243. Watson, George. "Were the Intellectuals Duped?," Encounter 36/12 (December 1973): 21-31.

10244. Waxman, Matthew C. "Emerging Intelligence Challenges," International Journal of Intelligence and Counterintelligence 10/3 (Fall 1997): 317-331.
    Major sections consider coercion and the assumption of control; an illustration of allied coercion and the former Yugoslavia; dislocation of authority: a counter coercive strategy?; emerging intelligence challenges regarding collection, coordination, and application; and identifying the adversary.

10245. Way, Roland A. "The BBC Monitoring Service and Its US Partner," Studies in Intelligence 2 (Summer 1958).
    Discusses cooperation between the US intelligence organizations and the British Broadcasting monitoring service.

10246. Weber, W. "Industriespionage als Technologischen Transfer in der Fruehindustrialisierung Deutschland," Technikgeschichte 42 (1975): 287-306.
    Loosely translated, discusses industrial espionage as technology transfer

in the early industrialization of Germany.

10247. Wecht, Cyril. "Why Is the Rockefeller Commission So Single-Minded About a Lone Assassin in the Kennedy Case?," Journal of Legal Medicine 3 (July-August 1975): 22-25.

10248. Wedgwood, Camilla H. "The Nature and Function of Secret Societies," Oceania 1 (1930): 129-141.

10249. Wege, Carl A. "Iranian Intelligence Organizations," International Journal of Intelligence and Counterintelligence 10/3 (Fall 1997): 287-298.
        Discusses Iran's security architecture; the Russian preference; killing dissidents; terrorism by the Revolutionary Guard; evaluating the Persian security establishment

10250. Weinrod, W. B. "U.S. Intelligence Priorities in the Post-Cold War Era," World Affairs 159 (Summer 1996): 3-11.

10251. Weinstein, Brian S. "In Defense of Jeffrey Wigand: A First Amendment Challenge to the Enforcement of Employee Confidentiality Agreements Against Whistleblowers," South Carolina Law Review 49 (Fall 1997): 129-178.

10252. Weis, W. Michael. "Government News Management, Bias and Distortion in American Press Coverage of the Brazilian Coup," Social Science Journal 34/1 (January 1997): 35-55.

10253. Weissman, James C.; Thomas A. Giacinti; and Francis W. Lanasa. "Undetected Opiate Use: A Comparison of Official Drug User Files and a Private Methadone Clinic's Patient Records," Journal of Criminal Justice 1/2 (Summer 1973): 135-144.
        A study comparing drug user population data from police intelligence files with data from walk-in patients at a private methadone treatment clinic. Study results showed that slightly more than half of the patients were unknown to police; more blacks were unknown to police than whites; and nearly three quarters of the population of addicts under thirty years old were unknown.

10254. Welch, David A. "The Organizational Politics and Bureaucratic Politics Paradigms," International Security 17/2 (Fall 1992): 112-146.
        Develops the theories relevant to the dynamics of the Cuban missile crisis of 1962.

10255. Weller, Geoffrey R. "Comparing Western Inspectors General of Intelligence and Security," International Journal of Intelligence and Counterintelligence 9/4 (Winter 1996-1997): 383-406.

Major sections discuss the demand for accountability; the mandates of the IGS; the IGS' work and methods; the ability to conduct the work; IG outputs and recommendations; relations with legislatures; relations with other oversight agencies; and improvements but no solutions.

10256. Weller, Jac. "Wellington Against Abrams: Were the Old Ways Better?," Army Quarterly and Defence Journal 100/1 (1970): 60-70.

10257. Wenger, William V. and Fredric W. Young. "The Los Angeles Riots and Tactical Intelligence," Military Intelligence 18/4 (October-December 1992): 30-34.
A brief summary of the information gathering work of the Army National Guard during the 1992 Los Angeles riots.

10258. Werbicki, Raymond J. "International Considerations in the Protection of Confidential Business Information," International Law Practicum 9 (Spring 1996): 37-43.

10259. Westad, Odd A. "Secrets of the Second World War: The Russian Archives and the Reinterpretation of Cold War History," Diplomatic History 21/2 (Spring 1997): 259-271.
Major sections discuss power and organization; ideologies and personalities; alliances; and establishing a historiography.

10260. Westerfield, H. Bradford. "America and the World of Intelligence Liaison," Intelligence and National Security 11/3 (July 1996): 523-560.
Major sections discuss America's addiction to liaison; keeping it secret; the forms and risks of liaison collaboration; and liaison and spying on friends.

10261. Westerfield, H. Bradford. "Inside Ivory Bunkers: CIA Analysts Resist Managers' 'Pandering'--Part I," International Journal of Intelligence and Counterintelligence 9/4 (Winter 1996-1997): 407-424.
Author discusses 'objective' versus 'actionable' analysis; the initial competition; acculturation in the analysis review process; analysts' suspicions of decisionmakers; decisisionmakers' suspicions of analysts; and a case study of evidence from the Robert Gates era.

10262. Westerfield, H. Bradford. "Inside Ivory Bunkers: CIA Analysts Resist Managers' 'Pandering'--Part II," International Journal of Intelligence and Counterintelligence 10/1 (July 1997): 19-55.
A continuation of the previous article in several sections: the 1991 Robert Gates confirmation hearings; making a principle of analysts' autonomy from managers; Gates' role-image; 'hard-liners' versus 'soft-liners' about the USSR; analysis manipulation by Gates at DI; self-compartmentation of analysts

of Soviet/Third World relations; 'objectivity'/'actionability' and the Soviet-economy analysts; skirting the Soviet-economy analysts' bunker; 'politicization,' 'actionability,' and management; and possible conclusions.

10263. Westerfield, H. Bradford. "American Exceptionalism and American Intelligence," Freedom Review 28 (Summer 1997): 27-36.

10264. Westley, William A. "Secrecy and the Police," Social Forces 34 (March 1956): 254-257.

A study of police secrecy was conducted by the author in a midwestern industrial town. Discusses the fundamental rule of secrecy among police; the strength of secrecy; sanctions supporting secrecy; the functions of secrecy; and indoctrination in the need for secrecy.

10265. Wetlaufer, Gerald B. "Justifying Secrecy: An Objection to the General Deliberative Privilege," Indiana Law Journal 65 (Fall 1990): 845-924.

A detailed discussion of issues related to privileges and immunities; separation of powers; executive authority; discovery and other civil procedures; and privileged communications.

10266. "What Sort of Improper Conduct Constitutes Misappropriation of a Trade Secret?," IDEA: The Journal of Law and Technology 30 (1990): 287-308.

10267. Wheaton, Kelly D. "Spycraft and Government Contracts: A Defense of Totten v. United States," Army Lawyer 1997 (August 1997): 9-18.

Discusses the case of Enoch Totten; the Totten progeny; OPLAN 34-A in North Vietnam and Laos, 1960-1966; the need to contract for secret services; the legal relationship between the parties when covert services are obtained; the viability of contracts for secret services; and conclusions.

10268. Wheelon, Albert D. and Sidney N. Graybeal. "Intelligence for the Space Race," Studies in Intelligence 5/3 (Fall 1961).

A useful article for studies in space intelligence gathering programs.

10269. Whitaker, Reginald. "Spies Who Might Have Been: Canada and the Myth of Cold War Counterintelligence," Intelligence and National Security 12/4 (October 1997):25-43.

Article is arranged in the following sections: the case of E. Herbert Norman; some lessons of the Norman case; the "Long Knife" betrayal; the "feather bed" concept; and when the war was over.

10270. White, Jeffrey B. "Irregular Warfare: A Different Kind of Threat," American Intelligence Journal 17/1&2 (1996): 57-63.

Major sections discuss implications for intelligence; operational environment; modern and irregular warfare; balance sheet; and intelligence considerations.

10271. Whitman, John.   "Better an Office of Sovietology," <u>Studies of Intelligence</u> 8/4 (Winter 1964).

10272. Whitmere, Frank A. and Edward G. Correll. "The Failure of Cosmos 57," <u>Studies in Intelligence</u> 10/2 (Summer 1966).

10273. Whitney, Kathleen M. "Sin, FRAPH, and the CIA: U.S. Covert Action in Haiti," <u>Southwestern Journal of Law and Trade in the Americas</u> 3 (Fall 1996): 303+.

10274. Wiehl, Lis. "Keeping Files on the File Keepers: When Prosecutors Are Forced to Turn Over the Personnel Files of Federal Agents to Defense Lawyers," <u>Washington Law Review</u> 72 (January 1997): 73-127.
        Considers the question of whether criminal defendants can compel federal prosecutors during pretrial discovery to review and turn over the personnel files of law enforcement officers who will testify. Includes discussion of several federal cases.

10275. Wiley, Bell I. "Women of the Lost Cause," <u>American History Illustrated</u> 8/8 (1973): 10-23.

10276. Wilhelm, Richard J. "The New NRO: A CMS Perspective," <u>American Intelligence Journal</u> 17/1&2 (1996): 53-55.
        Discusses the DCI's Community Management Staff; the Cold War National Reconnaissance Office; rethinking the NRO mission; imagery and the NRO; SIGINT and the NRO; and conclusions.

10277. Williams, Brian E. "Reserve Component Intelligence Integration: A Total Force Success Story," <u>American Intelligence Journal</u> 18/1&2 (1998): 27-31.
        Major sections discuss overview and background; peacetime use of reserve component intelligence elements; and manning and budget issues.

10278. Williams, J. R. and L. L. Guess.   "The Informant: A Narcotics Enforcement Dilemma," <u>Journal of Psychoactive Drugs</u> (July-September 1981): 235-245.

10279. Williams, Phil. "International Drug Trafficking: An Industry Analysis," <u>Low Intensity Conflict and Law Enforcement</u> 2/3 (1993): 397-420.

10280. Williams, Phil. "Transnational Criminal Organizations: Strategic Alliances," <u>Washington Quarterly</u> 18/1 (Winter 1995): 57-72.

Discusses the interconnections between criminal organizations in the larger context of transnational corporations and strategic alliances. Discusses implications for policy and mentions the role of intelligence agencies.

10281. Williams, Robert H. and Marcel Vigneras. "Ambush Detection," Military Review 44/11 (1964): 84-93.

10282. Williamson, James R. "The Quest for Mao Tse-tung," Studies in Intelligence 13/1 (Spring 1969).

10283. Williamson, John L. "Air Reserve Component Intelligence Forces: Integrating for Information Superiority," American Intelligence Journal 18/1&2 (1998): 21-26.
Discusses organization for a new culture; missions, roles, and organization of intelligence; and future concerns.

10284. Wilson, Richard B. "The Arrogance of Constitutional Power," Colorado Quarterly 16/3 (1968): 267-285.

10285. Windle, Kevin. "From Ogre to 'Uncle Lawrence': The Evolution of the Myth of Beria in Russian Fiction from 1953 to the Present," Australian Slavic & East European Studies 3/1 (1989): 1-16.

10286. Wingo, Harry. "Dumpster Diving and the Ethical Blindspot of Trade Secret Law," Yale Law & Policy Review 16/1 (1997): 195-219.
Major sections discuss the scope of dumpter diving and industrial espionage; the privacy analogy in the Winnie and Tennant decisions; Winne rationale's misplaced reliance on the Greenwood presumption; Christopher and the cost of absolute security; trade secrets law's ethical blindspot; the Connecticut solution and the Economic Espionage Act.

10287. Winton, Harold R. "The Battle of the Bulge," Military Review 75/1 (1994-1995): 107-115, 118-123.
An overview of the surprise attack by the German army in the winter of 1944 and the subsequent American counteroffensive.

10288. Wilson, Thomas R. "Joint Intelligence and Uphold Democracy," Joint Force Quarterly 7 (Spring 1995): 54-59.

10289. Wolf, John B. "Organization and Management Practices of Urban Terrorist Groups," Terrorism: An International Journal 1/2 (1978): 169-186.

10290. Wolfe, Bertram. "The Struggle for the Soviet Succession," Foreign Affairs 31/4 (July 1953): 548-565.

10291. Wolkomir, Richard and Joyce. "Where Staving Off Armageddon Is All in a Day's Work," <u>Smithsonian</u> 27/11 (November 1997): 114-128.

10292. Wood, John S., Jr. "Counterinsurgency Coordination as the National and Regional Level," <u>Military Review</u> 46/3 (1966): 80-85.

10293. Woodeman, Nathan X. "Yardley Revisited," <u>Studies in Intelligence</u> 27/2 (Summer 1983): 42-49.

10294. Woodruff, Joseph A. "Privileges Under the Military Rules of Evidence," <u>Military Law Review</u> 92 (Spring 1981): 5-76.
     Explores in detail the rules pertaining to general provisions; attorney-client privilege; communications to clergy; martial privilege; classified information and governmental information; informers; political vote and jury deliberations; involuntary disclosure of confidential communications; and comment upon or references from claim of privilege.

10295. Woodruff, Joseph A. "Practical Aspects of Trying Cases Involving Classified Information," <u>Army Lawyer</u> (June 1986): 50-54.
     Major sections discuss handling of classified information; handling the government's privilege; and conclusions. Provides practical guidance in the handling of classified materials while defending clients.

10296. Wooten, Clyde C. "Economic Intelligence in Defense Planning," <u>Studies in Intelligence</u> 10/4 (Winter 1966).

10297. Wormald, Jenny. "Gunpowder, Treason and Scots," <u>Journal of British Studies</u> 24/2 (April 1985): 141-168.
     A history of the treason plot of 1605, and attempts to anwer why there was a plot and what the plotters wanted to achieve.

10298. Worthy, Patricia M. "The Impact of New and Emerging Telecommunications Technologies: A Call to the Rescue of the Attorney-Client Privilege," <u>Howard Law Journal</u> 39 (Winter 1996): 437-475.
     Major sections discuss federal confidentiality laws, including Title III; historical background of the attorney-client privilege; a technology-neutral doctrine for the privilege; and conclusions regarding confidential communications.

10299. Wrege, Charles D. and Ronald G. Greenwood. "Frederick Taylor and Industrial Espionage: 1895-1897," <u>Business and Economic History</u> 15 (1990): 183-193.
     Provides details of circumstances involving the infamous management expert, Frederick W. Taylor, in spying on competitor ball bearing companies by the use of private detectives.

10300. Wright, Marshall N. "Battlespace 2000: Intelligence Communications for Deployed Naval Forces," American Intelligence Journal 17/3&4 (1997): 59-64.

Technical discussion of ISR products for battle group commanders; common high bandwidth data link-surface terminal; CHBDL-ST as part of network centric architecture; and battle group local area network interconnectivity demonstration.

10301. Wright, Patricia. "Loris-Melikov: Russia, 1880-1," History Today 24 (June 1974): 413-419.

A discussion of the grant of dictatorial powers to Russian general Loris-Melnikov to control the attacks upon the Tsar and to put down the brooding revolutionary movement. Mentions the role of the secret police.

10302. Wylie, Amos K. "Unfair Exchange," Studies in Intelligence 6/3 (Fall 1962).

10303. Wylie, Neville. "'Keeping the Swiss Sweet': Intelligence as a Factor in British Policy Towards Switzerland during the Second World War," Intelligence and National Security 11/3 (July 1996): 442-467.

A lengthy discussion of the topic in three main sections: the slow development of British espionage activities in Switzerland before the summer of 1940; complications and contradictions in British policy regarding espionage in Switzerland; and a net assessment of how useful was the intelligence from Switzerland, in terms of Britain's total output of intelligence.

10304. Yamashita, Kanshi S. "The Saga of the Japanese Americans: 1870-1942," American Baptist Quarterly 13/1 (1994): 4-47.

A detailed review of the experience of Japanese immigrants, mainly in the Southern California area up to the internment period from 1942-1945. Useful in historical analyses of hysteria in wartime and the origins of fears of Japanese espionage in America.

10305. Yates, Lawrence A. "Mounting an Intervention: The Dominican Republic, 1965," Military Review 69/3 (1989): 50-62.

10306. Yearns, W. Buck. "American Perceptions of Subhas Chandra Bose in World War II," Journal of Indian History 64/1-3 (1986): 247-261.

This journal is published in India.

10307. Yelin, Lev. "The Man Who Knows the Truth about Katyn," New Times 17 (1991): 28-31.

10308. Yorker, Beatrice C. "Court Video Surveillance of Munchausen Syndrome by Proxy: The Exigent Circumstances," Health Matrix 5 (Summer 1995): 325-346.

10309. Youngblood, Robert L. "Electronic Databases and Research on the Central Intelligence Agency in Asia," Bulletin of Concerned Asian Scholars 26/3 (July-September 1994): 61-65.

A review essay of the resources in two databases: CIABASE and NAMEBASE.

10310. Yung, Andrew W. "Regulating the Genie: Effective Wiretaps in the Information Age," Dickinson Law Review 101 (Fall 1996): 95-135.

Major sections discuss the importance of discussing technological advances in telecommunications and law enforcement; a primer on wiretaps and recent changes in the nature of telecommunications; current government initiatives to respond to wiretap difficulties; the unacceptable dangers of dumbing down technology; and conclusions on technical merits and procedural common sense.

10311. Zahn, Gordon C. "War and Its Conventions," Worldview 16/7 (1973): 46-49.

10312. Zeidel, Robin. "Closing the Courtroom for Undercover Police Witnesses: New York Must Adopt a Consistent Standard," Journal of Law and Policy 4 (Spring 1996): 659-717.

Discusses several cases involving undercover police operations against drug activity in New York; the buy-and-bust operation and undercover officers; the law before Waller v. Georgia; trial testimony of undercover officers after Waller; the four prong test in Waller; and conclusions.

10313. Zarate, Juan C. "The Emergence of a New Dog of War: Private International Security Companies, International Law, and the New World Disorder," Stanford Journal of International Law 34 (Winter 1998): 75-185.

Reflections on the legal issues associated with private organizations in security, intelligence, and related positions in the international arena.

10314. Zeira, Eli. "Israel's Intelligence Failure of 1973: New Evidence, a New Interpretation, and Theoretical Implications," Security Studies 4/3 (Spring 1995): 584-609.

The author, former Israeli military attache in Washington in 1973, focuses on new evidence of circumstances leading to the October war with Egypt.

10315. Zelikow, Philip. "American Economic Intelligence: Past Practice and Future Principles," Intelligence and National Security 12/1 (January 1997): 164-177.

Major sections discuss the organization of economic intelligence gathering; collection and analysis, and how it is produced; and four principles related to when to rely on government.

10316.   Zengel, Patricia.   "Assassination and the Law of Armed Conflict," Military Law Review 134 (1991): 123-135.

Examines the development of the customary prohibition of assassination during time of war and concludes that there is no longer any convincing justification for retaining a unique rule of international law that treats assassination apart from other uses of force.

10317.   Zervoudakis, Alexander.   "Nihil Mirare, Nihil Contemptare, Omnia Intelligere: Franco-Vietnamese Intelligence in Indochina, 1950-1954," Intelligence and National Security 13/1 (Spring 1998): 195-229.

Discusses French intelligence apparatus in Indochina in the early 1950s involvement in Vietnam; operational examples; the Route Coloniale 4 Disaster in 1950; Dien Bien Phu, 1953-54; Dong Trieu, 1951; the Day River battles, 1951; and conclusions.

10318.   Ziegler, Charles A.   "Intelligence Assessments of Soviet Atomic Capability, 1945-1949:   Myths, Monopolies and Maskirovka," Intelligence and National Security 12/4 (October 1997): 1-24.

Major sections discuss the background of the reigning explanatory schema; monopolies both imaginary and real; uranium's role in intelligence assessments; assumptions involved in projections; Sudoplatov's claims; and conclusions.

10319.   Zimbalist, Andrew.   "Why Did the U.S. Invade Panama?," Radical American 23/2-3 (1989): 7-13.

10320.   Zlotnick, Jack.   "A Theorem for Prediction," Studies in Intelligence 11/3 (Fall 1967).

10321.   Zopette, Glenn.   "The Edison of Secret Codes," American Heritage of Invention & Technology 10/1 (1994): 34-43.

A summation of the life and inventions of Edward Hebern, a man of criminal experience who invented the cipher machine later used by the military and diplomatic services.

10322.   Zubok, Vladislav.   "Soviet Intelligence and the Cold War: The 'Small' Committee of Information, 1952-53," Diplomatic History 19/3 (1995): 453-472.

Discusses the impact of the Soviet intelligence reports about US and other policies toward the Soviet Union before Josef Stalin's death.   Considers the balancing points between political leadership and character of intelligence reports.

10323. Zubok, Vladislav. "Stalin's Plans and Russian Archives," <u>Diplomatic History</u> 21/3 (Summer 1997): 383-415.

10324. Zweig, Ronald W. "British Plans for the Evacuation of Palestine in 1941-1942," <u>Studies in Zionism</u> 4 (Autumn 1983): 301+.

Section II, Late Entries:

10325. Amuchastegui, Domingo. "Cuban Intelligence and the October Crisis," <u>Intelligence and National Security</u> 13/3 (Autumn 1998): 88-119.

The author, a former member of Cuban intelligence, discusses the organization of Cuban intelligence; the crisis and Cuban intelligence; and the aftermath of the event.

10326. Anderson, Elizabeth E. "The Security Dilemma and Covert Action: The Truman Years," <u>International Journal of Intelligence and Counterintelligence</u> 11/4 (Winter 1998-1999): 403-427.

Major sections discuss covert action and international relations; the security issue; meeting security dilemmas in the Truman years; and success deemed immaterial.

10327. Bar-Joseph, Uri. "Israeli Intelligence Failure of 1973: New Evidence, a New Interpretation, and Theoretical Implications," <u>Security Studies</u> 4/3 (1995): 584-609.

Provides a description of Early Warning Systems of the Israeli defense system before the 1973 war.

10328. Bar-Joseph, Uri and Zachary Sheaffer. "Surprise and Its Causes in Business Administration and Strategic Studies," <u>International Journal of Intelligence and Counterintelligence</u> 11/3 (Fall 1998): 331-349.

Article contains the authors' further reflections on the Arab-Israeli war of October 1973, especially with respect to some lessons that can be learned from the common dimensions of surprise in both the strategic military and business realms. A link is offered between circumstances of the October war and failure of England's Barings Bank. Major sections discuss the main variables of surprise; the categories of explanations; the initial conclusions; and research agenda.

10329. Barrett, David M. "Glimpses of a Hidden History: Sen. Richard Russell, Congress, and Oversight of the CIA," <u>International Journal of Intelligence and Counterintelligence</u> 11/3 (Fall 1998): 271-298.

Major sections discuss the Truman era; the Eisenhower administration; the reign of the preeminent Senator Russell; the U-2 spy flights; the informal meetings; Senator Mansfield makes waves; alternate responses; and interim assessments.

10330. Blight, James G. and David A. Welch. "Risking 'The Destruction of Nations': Lessons of the Cuban Missile Crisis for New and Aspiring Nuclear States," Security Studies 4/4 (Summer 1994): 811-850.

10331. Blight, James G. and David A. Welch. "What Can Intelligence Tell Us About the Cuban Missile Crisis, and What Can the Cuban Missile Crisis Tell Us About Intelligence?," Intelligence and National Security 13/3 (Autumn 1998): 1-17.

   Major sections discuss a brief historiography of the missile crisis; the design and execution of the entire volume devoted to this question; and a little foreshadowing.

10332. Blight, James G. and David A. Welch. "The Cuban Missile Crisis and Intelligence Performance," Intelligence and National Security 13/3 (Autumn 1998): 173-217.

   This is an overview article reflecting the authors' interpretations of dimensions of the missile crisis as discussed by other authors in this issue. Major sections include: "What" questions; "Why" questions; evaluating intelligence performance; and conclusions on the theory and practice of intelligence assessment.

10333. Brenner, Philip. "Cuba and the Missile Crisis," Journal of Latin American Studies 22/1 (February 1990): 115-142.

10334. Burr, William and Jeffrey T. Richelson. "A Chinese Puzzle," Bulletin of the Atomic Scientists (July-August 1997).

   Attempts to compare Central Intelligence Agency estimates of Chinese nuclear capabilities with the actual historical experience of Chinese advanced weapons development.

10335. Champion, Brian. "Subreptitious Aircraft in Transnational Covert Operations," International Journal of Intelligence and Counterintelligence 11/4 (Winter 1998-1999): 453-478.

   Discusses a history of secret airplane uses in various covert actions since World War II. Defines subreptitious as a distinguishable concept from surreptitious. Major sections discuss the World War II legacy; flights to Palestine; airborne felines; winging out of China; meeting challenges; others flying for the red, white, and blue; downsizing the fleet; back in business; arming the enemy; ventures to faraway places; getting the facts; and business as usual.

10336. Charters, David A. "Eyes of the Underground: Jewish Insurgent Intelligence in Palestine, 1945-47," Intelligence and National Security 13/4 (Winter 1998): 163-177.

   Major sections consider insurgent strategy; insurgent intelligence organization; requirements; operations; internal security; operational effectiveness; and conclusions.

10337. Clemens, Peter. "Operation 'Cardinal': The OSS in Manchuria, August 1945," Intelligence and National Security 13/4 (Winter 1998): 71-106.

Considers a brief chapter in the history of the Office of Strategic Services. Major sections discuss prisoners and a mission for the OSS; 'Cardinal' relinquishes its POW mission; 'Cardinal' as an intelligence asset; and conclusions.

10338. Cohen, Sam. "Ted Hall: A Soldier from Venona," International Journal of Intelligence and Counterintelligence 11/3 (Fall 1998): 351-365.

This article contains the author's account of his associations with Ted Hall, bornTheodore Alvin Holtzberg, during their service on the Manhattan Project in Los Alamos in 1943-44. Also, it describes the Venona Papers.

10339. Croft, John. "Reminiscences of GCHQ and GCB 1942-45," Intelligence and National Security 13/4 (Winter 1998): 133-143.

Discusses the author's reflections on his experiences in cryptanalyis work at Bletchley Park in World War II. Sections discuss his first months at Bletchley park; and experiences at Berkeley Street and Aldford House.

10340. Davies, Philip H. J. "British Intelligence from Fenian Dynamite to the Docklands Bomb, By Way of Two World Wars, one Cold War, and a Jungle Full of Snakes," Intelligence and National Security 13/4 (Winter 1998): 237-244.

A book review essay regarding Michael Smith's book, New Cloak, Old Dagger: How Britain's Spies Came In From The Cold.

10341. Feer, Fredric S. "Intelligence Storytelling: Moshe Dayan and the 1970 Cease-Fire," International Journal of Intelligence and Counterintelligence 11/4 (Winter 1998-1999): 429-445.

In the context of the cease-fire action of 1970, the author discusses cognitive psychological factors; sources uneven; examining the situation; a matter of deciding; the big picture; alternative interpretations; why did no dog bark?; Washington's influence; and the bases of knowledge.

10342. Fischer, Beth A. "Perception, Intelligence Errors, and the Cuban Missile Crisis," Intelligence and National Security 13/3 (Autumn 1998): 150-172.

Article contains sections which discuss psychology and intelligence errors; critical perceptions in the Cuban missile crisis; and conclusions.

10343. Fursenko, Aleksandr and Timothy Naftali. "Using KGB Documents: The Scali-Feklisov Channel in the Cuban Missile Crisis," Cold War International History Project Bulletin 5 (Spring 1995): 58, 60-62.

10344. Fursenko, Aleksandr and Timothy Naftali. "Soviet Intelligence and the Cuban Missile Crisis," Intelligence and National Security 13/3 (Autumn 1998): 64-87.

These authors discuss the mechanics of the Soviet intelligence community; Soviet intelligence sources, 1962; the missile crisis in its several phases; the mystery of the Occidental meeting; and conclusions.

10345. Garthoff, Raymond L. "The Havana Conference on the Cuban Missile Crisis," Cold War International History Project Bulletin 1 (Spring 1992): 1, 3.

10346. Garthoff, Raymond L. "US Intelligence in the Cuban Missile Crisis," Intelligence and National Security 13/3 (Autumn 1998): 18-63.

Major sections discuss the US intelligence community; collection, analyses, and estimates; monitoring the Soviet buildup in Cuba; assessing Soviet motives; monitoring Soviet Union's forces in Cuba after 16 October 1962; assessing intelligence performance prior to and during the acute phase of the crisis; the settlement phase; post-crisis reviews; a retrospective evaluation; and conclusions.

10347. Gladman, Brad W. "Air Power and Intelligence in the Western Desert Campaign, 1940-43," Intelligence and National Security 13/4 (Winter 1998): 144-162.

Stresses the importance and limitations of intelligence operations to assist the Royal Air Force interdiction efforts against the Germans in the Western desert campaign mainly in 1942.

10348. Harris, John A. "Industrial Espionage in the Eighteenth Century," Industrial Archaeology 7 (1985): 127-138.

10349. Hastedt, Glenn. "Seeking Economic Security Through Intelligence," International Journal of Intelligence and Counterintelligence 11/4 (Winter 1998-1999): 385-401.

Addresses some of the realities associated with the failure of economic intelligence measures employed by the American intelligence community. Major sections discuss previous action requests; prior collection efforts; comparisons to other intelligence tasks; where tasks differ; private sector economic intelligence; how risk is defined; the uses of business intelligence; what are they looking at; doing the analysis; and intelligence's limited role.

10350. Higgins, E. Tory; William S. Rholes; and Carl R. Jones. "Category Accessibility and Impression Formation," Journal of Experimental Social Psychology 13/2 (March 1977): 141-157.

May be useful research in the study of strategic and other forms of surprise.

10351. Hindley, Meredith. "First Annual List of Dissertations on Intelligence," Intelligence and National Security 13/4 (Winter 1998): 208-230.

This journal begins an annual reporting of titles and authors of doctoral dissertations devoted to intelligence studies. It lists dissertations completed in 1996-1997 and projects underway in 1998.

10352. Imlay, Talbot. "Allied Economic Intelligence and Strategy during the 'Phoney War,'" Intelligence and National Security 13/4 (Winter 1998): 107-132.

Discusses the work of British and French intelligence organizations to discover and document the viability of the German economy during World War II. Analytical approaches and weaknesses of British and French intelligence organizations are considered along with implications of various assumptions about the enemy.

10353. Jeffreys-Jones, Rhodri. "The Myth of Recovered Innocence in US Intelligence History," Intelligence and National Security 13/4 (Winter 1998): 231-236.

A book review essay pertaining to two books: David E. Murphy et al., Battleground Berlin: CIA vs KGB in the Cold War; and James G. Blight and Peter Kornbluh, Politics of Illusion: The Bay of Pigs Reexamined.

10354. Marsden, Roy. "Operation 'Schooner/Nylon': RAF Flying in the Berlin Control Zone," Intelligence and National Security 13/4 (Winter 1998): 178-193.

Liaison activities between the British and other Allied intelligence services operated in various regions of formerly German-held territories in the years following World War II. The British Royal Air Force conducted highly valuable intelligence collection via its photographic missions using small aircraft and hand-held cameras to record conditions of Soviet military units and equipment. Selected photos are included.

10355. Miller, Davina and Mark Phythian. "Secrecy, Accountability and British Arms Exports: Issues for the Post-Scott Era," Contemporary Security Policy 19 (1998).

10356. Moran, Jonathan. "The Role of the Security Services in Democratization: An Analysis of South Korea's Agency for National Security Planning," Intelligence and National Security 13/4 (Winter 1998): 1-32.

Key sections of this article investigate national security and development in terms of South Korea as a comparative study; South Korea's security establishment; reform and democratisation; controlling the transition in two presidential administrations; historical legacies and political practice; national security, intelligence, and the 'problem' of civil society; external threat and security policy in terms of the North Korean threat; domestic dissent, national security and foreign policy; national security, democracy and oversight; recent developments; prospects for reform; and conclusions.

10357. Packard, Wyman H. "Notes on the Early History of Naval Intelligence in the United States," ONI Review 12 (April-May 1957): 169-175.

10358. Quiggin, Thomas. "Response to 'No Cloak and Dagger Required: Intelligence Support to UN Peacekeeping Missions,'" Intelligence and National Security 13/4 (Winter 1998): 203-207.
          A rebuttal to the article by Paul Johnston, item 9494. Sections discuss the operational level of intelligence; military intelligence; the compartmentalization of information; and conclusions.

10359. Riley, Patrick R. "CIA and Its Discontents," International Journal of Intelligence and Counterintelligence 11/3 (Fall 1998): 255-269.
          This is a discussion of organizational dynamics and problems within the Central Intelligence Agency. Major sections discuss four theses; bureaucratic problems; possible remedies; the question of inadequate intelligence; upgrading performance; promotions and the question of the numbers game; and a net assessment of the quality of work at CIA.

10360. Selth, Andrew. "Burma's Intelligence Apparatus," Intelligence and National Security 13/4 (Winter 1998): 33-70.
          Examines intelligence in Burma before 1988 and including several organizational charts; intelligence after 1988; military intelligence under the SLORC and SPDC political councils; and Burma and intelligence organizations.

10361. Stack, Kevin P. "Competitive Intelligence," Intelligence and National Security 13/4 (Winter 1998): 194-202.
          A brief essay on the question of whether or not the major analytical intelligence organizations of the US are capable of producing high quality analytical products in view of their current organizational structures. Major sections consider the background of A-Team and B-Team; reasons for failure; and conclusions.

10362. Stein, Janice G. "Political Learning by Doing: Gorbachev as Uncommitted Thinker and Motivated Learner," International Organization 48/2 (Spring 1994): 155-183.

10363. Swain, Geoffrey. "Bitten by the Russia Bug: Britons and Russia, 1894-1939," Intelligence and National Security 13/4 (Winter 1998): 245-250.
          Book review essay on three books: Keith Neilson's Britain and the Last Tsar: British Policy and Russia, 1894-1917; Michael Hughes' Inside the Enigma: British Officials in Russia, 1900-39; and G. W. Morrell's Britain Confronts the Stalin Revolution: Anglo-Soviet Relations and the Metro-Vickers Crisis.

10364. Thornton, Richard C. "The Unfulfilled Promise of Declassification," International Journal of Intelligence and Counterintelligence 11/4 (Winter 1998-1999): 447-451.

Overview of declassification of intelligence documents, particularly regarding failed implementation of E.O. 12958 signed by Bill Clinton in 1995.

10365. Waller, John H. "The Devil's Doctor: Felix Kersten," International Journal of Intelligence and Counterintelligence 11/3 (Fall 1998): 299-329.

Discussion of Heinrich Himmler's personal physical therapist and confidant, Felix Kersten, who saved the lives of some Jews from the horrors of Hitler's mass extermination program. Major sections discuss Kersten's skill as a therapist; the question of the defeat of the Vaterland; a partnership for treason; the darkest secret; delicate subjects; the American connection; new overtures; on a tightrope; northern strains; new faces on stage; stepping back; easing Jewish peril; sharing confidences; international assistance; and the failure of evil fantasies.

10366. Wirth, James J. "Organizing for Crisis Intelligence: Lessons from the Cuban Missile Crisis," Intelligence and National Security 13/3 (Autumn 1998): 120-149.

Cases of crises; intelligence failures and successes; and conclusions.

10367. Woodhouse, Christopher M. "Early Contacts with the Greek Resistance," Balkan Studies 12 (1971).

10368. Woolsey, R. James. "Intelligence Quotient: The Mission of the CIA in the New World," Harvard International Review (1994): 34-37, 80.

Former CIA director offers his views on the present and near-term roles of the CIA in the context of modern international dilemmas and challenges.

10369. Yesin, V. I. and Yu. V. Grekov. "Participation of the Strategic Rocket Forces in Operation 'Anadyr,'" Military Thought 5 (September-October 1997): 65-73.

This is a rough translation of an article in Russian in a Russian journal.

Appendix: Journals Cited

Note to user: This appendix lists journal and magazine titles appearing in this bibliography only. Some titles have changed through the years, and some titles have added, subtracted, or modified acronyms or word order. The appendix has been included mainly to demonstrate diversity of publications in which the topics investigated have been published, and to suggest to new authors in these subject areas possible outlets for scholarly work.

ABA Journal
Academe
Academy of Pacific Coast History
Acta
Acta Orientalia Academiae Scientiarum
  Hungaricae
Action Nationale
Adelaide Law Review
Administration and Society
Administrative Law Review
Administrative Science Quarterly
Advanced Management Journal
Advocate
Advocates' Society Journal
Aerospace Historian
Africa
Africa Insight
African Affairs
African Communist
African Studies Review
Africa Report
Africa Today
Afrika Segodnia
Agricultural History

AIPLA Quarterly Journal
Air & Space/Smithsonian
Air Classics
Air Defense Artillery
Air Defense Magazine
Air Force Comptroller
Air Force Law Review
Air Force Magazine
Air Force and Space Digest
Air International
Airlift Operations Review
Airman
Airpower
Airpower Historian
Air Power Journal
Air Progress Aviation Review
Air University Review
Akron Business and Economic Review
Akron Law Review
ALA Bulletin
Alabama Historical Quarterly
Alabama Review
Alaska Journal
Alaska Review

Albany Law Review
Alberta History
Albion
All Hands
Alternatives
Amerasia Journal
America
Americana
American Anthropologist
American Antiquarian Society Proceedings
American-Arab Affairs
American Archivist
American Aviation History Society Journal
American Baptist Quarterly
American Bar Association Journal
American Bar Foundation Research Journal
American Behavioral Scientist
American Business Law Journal
American Criminal Law Review
American Education
American Enterprise
American Heritage
American Heritage of Invention and
  Technology
American Historical Review
American History Illustrated
American Indian Culture and Research
  Journal
American Indian Quarterly
American Intelligence Journal
American Jewish Archives
American Jewish History
American Journalism Review
American Journal of Comparative Law
American Journal of Criminal Justice
American Journal of Criminal Law
American Journal of International Law
American Journal of Legal History
American Journal of Philology
American Journal of Police
American Journal of Political Science
American Journal of Physics
American Journal of Sociology
American Law Review
American Lawyer
American Legal News
American Legion Magazine
American Libraries
American Literature: Journal of Literary
  History
American Magazine
American Magazine of Aeronautics
American Mathematical Monthly

American Mercury
American Neptune
American Perspective
American Philosophical Society Proceedings
American Photography
American Political Science Review
American Politics Quarterly
American Prospect
American Psychologist
American Quarterly
American Review of Canadian Studies
American Review of Reviews
American Scholar
American Scientist
American Sociological Review
American Sociologist
American Spectator
American Studies
American University International Law
  Review
American University Law Review
American Visions
American West
Americas: Quarterly Review of Inter-
  American Cultural History
Analyse et Prevision (currently Futuribles)
Analysis Internacional: Revista del Centro
  Peruano de Estudos Internacionales
Analytical Chemistry
Analytical Methods Review
Ancient Macedonia
Ancient Society
Anglican and Episcopal History
Annales: Canadian Journal of History
Annali della Fondazione Giangiacomo
  Feltrinella
Annals of Iowa
Annals of Air and Space Law
Annals of Science
Annals of the American Academy of Political
  and Social Sciences
Annals of the History of Computing
Annals of the New York Academy of
  Sciences
Annee Politique et Economie
Annual Survey of American Law
Anthropological Quarterly
Antioch Review
Antiquite Classique
Anuario de Estudios Centroamericanos
Anuario Historia Derecho Espan
Applicationes Mathematicae
Arab Studies Quarterly

Archaeologia
Archaeology
Archivaria
Archives
Archives and Manuscripts
Archiv fuer Deutsche Postgeschichte
Arizona and the West
Arizona Journal of International and
  Comparative Law
Arizona Law Review
Arizona State Law Journal
Arkansas Historical Quarterly
Arlington Historical Magazine
ARMA Records Management Quarterly
Armed Forces and Society
Armed Forces Journal International
Armed Forces Management
Armement
Armor
Arms Control Today
Army (currently Field Artillery Journal)
Army Digest
Army Information Digest
Army Journal (currently Defence Force
  Journal)
Army Quarterly
Army Quarterly and Defence Journal
ASGP
Asian Affairs: An American Review
Asian Forum
Asian Profile
Asian Survey
Asia-Pacific Defence Reporter
Asia Quarterly
Assets Protection
Athenaeum
Atlanta History
Atlantic Advocate
Atlantic Community Quarterly
Atlantic Monthly
Atlas
ATQ
Auckland University Law Review
Aus Politik und Zeitgeschichte
Australian Defence Force Journal
Australian Foreign Affairs Record
Australian Historical Studies
Australian Journal of Politics and History
Australian Law Journal
Australian Outlook: Journal of the Australian
  Institute of International Affairs
Australian Quarterly
Australian Slavic & East European Studies

Aviation and Cosmonautics
Aziia i Afrika Segodnia
Background
Baconiana
Baker Street Journal: An Irregular Quarterly
  of Sherlockiana
Balkan Studies
Baokan Ziliao: Zhongguo Jindai Shi
BC Studies
Beadle's Monthly: A Magazine of To-day
Beaver
Behavioral Science
Behavioral Sciences and the Law
Beitrage zur Konfliktforschung
Beitrage zur Geschichte de Arbeiterbewegung
Bell System Technical Journal
Berlin Journal of Sociology
Bermudian Magazine
Bibliography Facsimiles
Bibliography Quarterly
Bill of Rights Journal
Biography
Biometrika
Black Scholar: Journal of Black Studies and
  Research
Black Studies Journal
Blackwood's Magazine
Blatter fuer Technikgeschichte
B'nai B'rith International Monthly
Boletin del Archivo General de la Nacion
Boletting Della Domus Mazziniana
Bookman
Boston College Law Review
Boston College Industrial and Commercial
  Law Review
Boston College International and
  Comparative Law Review
Boston University International Law Journal
Boston University Law Review
Boundary
British Army Review
British Heritage
British Journal of Criminology
British Journal of International Studies
British Journal of Law and Society
British Journal of Sociology
British Journal of the History of Science
British Legion Journal
British Society for Eighteenth-Century
  Studies
British Yearbook of International Law
Brooklyn Journal of International Law
Brooklyn Law Review

Buffalo Law Review
Bulletin (Institute for the Study of the Soviet
  USSR)
Bulletin of Concerned Asian Scholars
Bulletin of Peace Proposals
Bulletin of the American Association of
  University Professors
Bulletin of the Atomic Scientists
Bulletin of the Institute of Historical Research
Bulletin of the Institute of Modern History
Bulletin of the Institute of Mathematics and
  Its Applications
Bulletin of the Institue of Physics
Bulletin of the History of Medicine
Bulletin of the Jerusalem Institute for
  Western Defense
Bulletin of the London University Institute of
  Historical Research
Bulletin of the Missouri Historical Society
Bulletin of the New York Public Library
Bureaucrat
Business & Professional Ethics Journal
Business & Society Review
Business and Economic History
Business History Review
Business Horizons
Business Information Review
Business Lawyer
Byzantinische Zeitschrift
Cahiers/Bijdragen
Cahiers de l'Institut d'Histoire du Temps
  Present
Cahiers d'Histoire de la Seconde Guerre
  Mondiale
Cahiers du Monde Russe et Sovietique
Cahiers Internationaux de Sociologie
California Historical Society Quarterly
California History
California Law Review
California Lawyer
California Management Review
California Peace Officer
California State Bar Journal
California Western International Law Journal
California Western Law Review
Cambridge Historical Journal
Cambridge Law Journal
Cambridge Review of International Affairs
Canadian Army Journal
Candian Bankers Association Journal
Canadian Bar Review
Canadian Bulletin of Medical History
Canadian Business Law Journal

Canadian Business Review
Canadian Defence Quarterly
Canadian Dimension
Canadian Ethnic Studies
Canadian Forces Sentinel
Canadian Forum
Canadian Geographer
Canadian Geographical Journal
Canadian Historical Association Annual
  Report
Canadian Historical Review
Canadian Journal of Economics and Political
  Science
Canadian Journal of Electronics
Canadian Journal of Law & Society
Canadian Journal of Political Science
Canadian Journal of Sociology
Canadian Labour
Canadian Lawyer
Canadian Military History
Canadian Monthly
Canadian Police College Journal
Canadian Public Administration
Canadian Public Policy
Canadian Review of American History
Canadian Review of American Studies
Canadian Slavic Studies
Canadian-U.S. Law Journal
Capitol Studies
Cardoza Law Review
Caribbean Review
Carinthia
Casa de las Americas
Case and Comment
Case Western Reserve Journal of
  International Law
Case Western Reserve Law Review
Catalyst
Cathedra
Catholic Historical Review
Catholic University Law Review
Cavalry Journal
Center Magazine
Central European History
Century Illustrated Magazine
Century Magazine
Cesky Casopis Historicky
Challenge
Change
Chaucer Review
Chicago Bar Record
Chicago-Kent Law Review
China Law Register

China Law Reporter
China Quarterly
Chinese Studies in History
Chitty's Law Journal
Choice
Chronicles of St. Mary's
Cinerna
Cities
Civilization
Civil Justice Quarterly
Civil Liberties
Civil Liberties Law Review
Civil Liberties Review
Civil War History
Civil War Regiments
Civil War Times Illustrated
Civilta Cattolica
Classica et Medievalia
Classical Bulletin
Classical Journal
Classical Philology
Classical Quarterly
Classical Views
Cleveland-Marshall Law Review
Cleveland State Law Review
Coast Artillery Journal
Coevolution Quarterly
Cold War International History Project
  Bulletin
Collier's
Colorado Heritage
Colorado Law Review
Colorado Quarterly
Columbia Human Rights Law Review
Columbia Journalism Review
Columbia Journal of Law and Social
  Problems
Columbia Journal of Transnational Law
Columbia Law Review
Columbian Journalism Review
Columbia-VLA Journal of Law & the Arts
Combat Forces Journal
Commentary
CommLaw Conspectus
Communication
Communications and the Law
Communications Law
Communications of the ACM
Communita
Company Law
Comparative Economic Studies
Comparative Political Studies
Comparative Strategy

Computer
Computer Law Journal
Computer Lawyer
Computers and Automation
Computers and People
Conflict: An International Journal
Conflict Quarterly
Conflict Resolution (currently Journal of
  Conflict Resolution)
Conflict Studies
Congress & the Presidency
Congressional Digest
Congress Monthly
Connecticut History
Connecticut Law Review
Conquest
Conradiana
Constitutional Commentary
Contact
Contemporary Crises
Contemporary European History
Contemporary French Civilization
Contemporary Literature
Contemporary Record
Contemporary Review
Continuity
Cooperation and Conflict
Cooperation & Conflict: Nordic Journal of
  International Politics
Cornell International Law Journal
Cornell Law Quarterly
Cornell Law Review
Cornhill Magazine
Corrections Magazine
Corruption and Reform
Cosmos
Counterspy (currently National Reporter)
Covert Action Information Bulletin (currently
  Covert Action Quarterly)
CQ Researcher
Creighton Law Review
Crime and Delinquency
Crime and Social Justice
Crime, Law and Social Change (formerly
  Crime and Social Justice)
Crime Prevention Review
Criminal Justice
Criminal Justice Ethics
Criminal Justice History: An International
  Annual
Criminal Justice Journal
Criminal Justice Policy Review
Criminal Law Bulletin

Criminal Law Quarterly
Criminal Law Review
Criminologie
Criminology
Critical Inquiry
Critique
Crossroads: An International Socio-Political
  Journal
Cryptolog
Cryptologia
Cryptologic Spectrum
Current
Current History
Current Municipal Problems
Current World Leaders
Cybernetica
Cybernetics
Daedalus
Dalhousie Law Journal
Dalhousie Review
Damals
Data: Magazine of Military RDT&E
  Management
Daughters of the American Revolution
  Magazine
Davis and Elkins Historical Magazine
Decision Sciences
Defence
Defence and Foreign Affairs
Defense/85
Defense/86
Defense Analysis
Defense and Diplomacy
Defense and Foreign Affairs Digest
Defense Electronics (see Electronic Warfare)
Defense Intelligence Journal
Defense Science and Electronics
Defense Systems Review
Delaware History
Democracy
Democratic Review
Democrazia e Diritto
Demokratizatsiya: Journal of Post-Soviet
  Democratization
Denning Law Journal
Denver Journal of International Law and
  Politics
Department of State Bulletin
Depaul Law Review
Detective
Detroit College of Law Review
Detroit Journal of Urban Law
Deutsche Aussenpolitik

Deutschland Archiv: Zeitschrift fuer das
  Vereinigte Deutschland
Developmental Psychology
Deviant Behavior
Dialogue
Dickinson Journal of International Law
Dickinson Law Review
Dickman Law Review
Die Amerikanische Rundschau
Diplomatic History
Disarmament
Disarmament and Arms Control
Disasters
Discover
Dissent
Dokumentation der Zeit
Dossier: The Official Journal of the
  International Spy Society
Drake Law Review
Duke Law Journal
Dun's Review
Duquesne Law Review
Early American Life
East and West
East Asian History
East Europe
East European Constitutional Review
East European Quarterly
Eastern Horizon
Eastern Journal of International Law
East Tennessee Historical Society's
  Publications
East Texas Historical Journal
Ebony
Economia Columbiana: Revista de la
  Contraloria General de la Republica
Economic History Review
Educational Record
Eesti Teaduslihu Seltsi Noatsis Aastar Aamat
Eire-Ireland
Electronic Warfare/Defense Electronics
Electronics and Power
Electronics & Wireless World
ELH
Emory International Law Review
Emory Law Journal
Employee Relations Law Journal
Encore
Encounter
English Historical Journal
English Historical Review
English Historical Quarterly
English Literary History

Enforcement Journal
Environment
Epigraphische Studien
Escribano
Espionage
Esprit
Esquire
Essays in Economic and Business History
Est. et Quest
Estudios Sociales
ETC.: A Review of General Semantics
Ethics
Ethics and International Affairs
Europa-Archiv
European Affairs
European Contributions to American Studies
European History Quarterly
European Intellectual Property Review
European Journal of Crime, Criminal Law
    and Criminal Justice
European Journal of Sociology
European Journal on Criminal Policing and
    Research
European Law Review
European Studies Review
Europe-Asia Studies
Europe-East Asia Studies
Everybody's Magazine
Executive Intelligence
Extrapolation
Far Eastern Economic Review
FBI Law Enforcement Bulletin
Federal Bar Journal
Federal Communications Bar Journal
Federal Law Review
Federalist
Federal Probation
Federal Review of Documents
Field Artillery Journal
Film Library Quarterly
Filson Club History Quarterly
Fingerprints and Identification
Fletcher Forum of World Affairs
Florida Bar Journal
Florida Historical Quarterly
Florida State University Law Review
Flying
Flying Review International
Folklore & Mythology Studies
Fordham Intellectual Property, Media &
    Entertainment Law Journal
Fordham International Law Review
Fordham Law Review

Foreign Affairs
Foreign Policy
Foreign Service Journal
Forest History
Fortnightly
Fortnightly Review
Fortune
Forum
Franchise Law Journal
Franco-American Review
Frankfurter Hefte
Freedom At Issue
Freedom Review
Free Speech Yearbook
French Historical Studies
French History
Futures
Futurist
Fuyin Baokan Ziliao: Zhongguo Jindai Shi
Gaspsie
Gateway Heritage
Gazette
Geographical Review
George Mason University Law Review
Georgetown Law Journal
George Washington Journal of International
    Law and Economics
George Washington Law Review
Georgia Historical Quarterly
Georgia Journal of International and
    Comparative Law
Georgia Law Review
Georgia Review
German International
German Studies Review
Geschichte in Wissenschaft und Unterricht
Global Affairs
Golden Gate University Law Review
Government and Opposition
Government Executive
Government Information Quarterly
Government Publications Review
Grand Street
Great Plains Journal
Greece and Rome
Grotius Society Transactions
Gulf Coast Historical Review
Hadtrtnelmi Kzlemnyek
Hamdard Islamicus
Hamline Journal of Public Law and Policy
Harper's
Harriman Institute Forum
Harvard Business Review

Harvard Civil Rights and Civil Liberties Law
Review
Harvard International Law Journal
Harvard Journal of Law & Public Policy
Harvard Journal of Law and Technology
Harvard Journal on Legislation
Harvard Law Review
Harvard Political Review
Hastings Communications and Entertainment
Law Journal
Hastings Constitutional Law Quarterly
Hastings International and Comparative Law
Review
Hastings Law Review
Hawaii Law Review
Hawaiian Journal of History
Headline Series
Health Matrix
Hennepin Lawyer
Henry James Review
Hispanic American Historical Review
Histcrama
Histoire
Histoire, Economie et Socit
Histoire Magazina
Historama
Historia Mathematica
Historia Mexicana
Historia y Vida
Historian
Historical Journal
Historical Journal of Film, Radio and
Television
Historical Magazine
Historical New Hampshire
Historical Papers
Historical Records of Australian Science
Historical Research
Historical Review
Historical Society Proceedings
Historical Studies
Historical Studies in the Physical and
Biological Sciences
Historicky Casopis
Historie a Vojanstvl
Historisches Jahrbuch
Historische Zeitschrift
History
History and Social Science Teacher
History and Theory
History, Numbers, and War
History of Political Economy
History of Political Thought

History Today
Hofstra Law Review
Holocaust and Genocide Studies
Horizon
Houston Journal of International Law
Houston Law Review
Howard International Law Review
Howard Law Journal
Human Behavior
Human Events
Human Factors
Humanist
Humanites
Human Rights
Huntington Library Quarterly
IBM Journal of Research and Development
IDEA: The Journal of Law and Technology
IEEE Proceedings (Institute of Electrical and
Electronic Engineers)
IEEE Spectrum
IEEE Technology and Society
IEEE Transactions on Communications
IEEE Transactions on Pattern Analysis and
Machine Intelligence
IEEE Transactionns on Professional
Communication
Illinois Bar Journal
Illinois Historical Journal
Illinois Law Review
Imperial War Museum Review
Index on Censorship
India Quarterly: Journal of International
Affairs
Indian Defence Review
Indian Historical Quarterly
Indian Journal of International Law
Indian Journal of Political Science
Indian Journal of Politics
Indian Journal of Public Administration
Indian Political Science Review
Indiana Law Journal
Indiana Magazine of History
Indonesia
Industrial Archaeology Review
Infantry
Infantry Journal
Infantry School Quarterly
Information Society
Inland Seas
INSCOM Journal
Insight
Institute of Applied Psychology Review
Insurgent Sociologist

Issues in Science and Technology
Intellect
Intellectual Property Law: An International Analytical Journal
Intellectual Property Law Review
Intelligence and National Security
Intelligence Quarterly
Inter-American Economic Affairs
Interavia
Intercollegiate Review
Interdisciplinary Science Reviews
Internasjonal Politikk
International Affairs (Great Britain)
International Affairs (USSR)
International & Comparative Law Quarterly
International Combat Arms: The Journal of Defense Technology
International Commission of Jurists Review
International Criminal Police Review
International Defense Review
International Interactions
Internationale Wissenschaftliche Korrespondenz zur Geschichte der Deutschen Arbeiterbewegung
International Fiction Review
International Freedom Review
International History Review
International Interactions
International Journal
International Journal of African Historical Studies
International Journal of Imaging, Remote Sensing and Integrated Geographical Systems
International Journal of Intelligence and Counterintelligence
International Journal of Man-Machine Studies
International Journal of Middle East Studies
International Journal of Politics, Culture and Society
International Journal of Psychiatry
International Journal of Refugee Law
International Journal of Social Psychology
International Journal of Technology Management
International Journal of World Peace
International Journal of the Sociology of Law
International Law Practicum
International Lawyer
International Migration Review
International Organization
International Perspectives: A Canadian Journal of World Affairs

International Problems
International Relations
International Review
International Review of Administrative Science
International Review of History and Political Science
International Review of Social History
International Security
International Security Review
International Social Science Journal
International Studies Notes
International Studies Quarterly
International Symposium on Comparative Law
Internationella Studier
Interplay
Iowa Law Review
IQ: Intelligence Quarterly
Irish Historical Studies
Irish Studies
Irish Studies in International Affairs
Irish Sword
Isis
Islamic Defense
Israeli Affairs
Israel Law Review
Issues and Studies
Istoricheskii Arkhiv
Istorijski Casopis
Istorijski Glasnik
Jahrbuch des Instituts fuer Deutsche Geschichte
Jahrbucher fuer Geschichte Osteuropas
Jane's Intelligence Review
Jane's Soviet Intelligence Review
Japan Forum
Japan Quarterly
Jerusalem Journal of International Relations
Jerusalem Quarterly
Jewish History
Jewish Quarterly
Jewish Social Studies
John Marshall Journal of Computer & Information Law
John Marshall Law Review
Joint Forces Quarterly
Joint Perspectives
Journal of Air Law and Commerce
Journal of Algerian History
Journal of American-East Asian Relations
Journal of American History
Journal of American Studies

Journal of Anthropological Research
Journal of Applied Social Psychology
Journal of Arms Control
Journal of Asian Studies
Journal of Asiatique
Journal of Asset Protection and Financial
  Crime
Journal of Astronautical Sciences
Journal of Baltic Studies
Journal of Black Studies
Journal of British Studies
Journal of Broadcasting
Journal of Business Ethics
Journal of Business Strategy
Journal of California Law Enforcement
Journal of Canadian Studies
Journal of Central European Affairs
Journal of Church and State
Journal of College and University Law
Journal of Communication
Journal of Comparative Economics
Journal of Conflict Resolution
Journal of Conflict Studies
Journal of Contemporary Asia
Journal of Contemporary History
Journal of Contemporary Law
Journal of Contemporary Studies
Journal of Counseling Psychology
Journal of Criminal Justice
Journal of Criminal Law
Journal of Criminal Law and Criminology
Journal of Criminal Law, Criminology and
  Police Science (formerly Journal of the
  American Institute of Criminal Law and
  Criminology)
Journal of Defense and Diplomacy
Journal of East Asian Studies
Journal of Economic and Social Intelligence
Journal of Electronic Defense
Journal of Ethnic Studies
Journal of Ethno-Development
Journal of European Economic History
Journal of European Studies
Journal of Forensic Sciences
Journal of General Education
Journal of Hellenic Studies
Journal of Higher Education
Journal of Imperial and Commonwealth
  History
Journal of Indian History
Journal of Institutional and Theoretical
  Economics
Journal of Inter-American Studies and World

Affairs
Journal of Interdisciplinary History
Journal of International Affairs
Journal of International Business Studies
Journal of International Law and Economics
Journal of International Legal Studies
Journal of Italian History
Journal of Japanese Studies
Journal of Korean Affairs
Journal of Latin American Studies
Journal of Law and Policy
Journal of Law and Politics
Journal of Law and Society
Journal of Law and Society of Scotland
Journal of Legal Education
Journal of Legal History
Journal of Legal Medicine
Journal of Legislation
Journal of Libertarian Studies
Journal of Library History
Journal of Micrographics
Journal of Media Law and Practice
Journal of Medieval & Renaissance Studies
Journal of Memory and Language
Journal of Military History
Journal of Mississippi History
Journal of Modern Africa
Journal of Modern African Studies
Journal of Modern History
Journal of Modern South African Studies
Journal of Negro History
Journal of Nervous and Mental Disease
Journal of Northeast Asian Studies
Journal of Offender Rehabilitation
Journal of Pacific History
Journal of Palestine Studies
Journal of Peace Research
Journal of Peace Science
Journal of Personality and Social Psychology
Journal of Petroleum Technology
Journal of Police Science and Administration
Journal of Political and Military Sociology
Journal of Political Economy
Journal of Political Science
Journal of Politics
Journal of Policy Analysis and Management
Journal of Policy History
Journal of Popular Culture
Journal of Popular Film
Journal of Popular Film and Television
Journal of Public Law
Journal of Public Policy
Journal of Psychoactive Drugs

Journal of Psychohistory
Journal of Radio Law
Journal of Refugee Studies
Journal of Religion
Journal of Roman Studies
Journal of Security Administration
Journal of Semitic Studies
Journal of Social and Political Studies
Journal of Social History
Journal of Social Issues
Journal of Social, Political and Economic
  Studies
Journal of Social Psychology
Journal of Social Welfare and Family Law
Journal of South African Affairs
Journal of Southeast Asia and the Far East
Journal of Southeast Asian Studies
Journal of Southern History
Journal of Southwest Georgia History
Journal of Strategic Studies
Journal of Supreme Court History
Journal of Women's History
Journal of World Public Order
Journal of the Academy of War-Sciences
Journal of the Acoustical Society of America
Journal of the American Institute of Electric
  Engineers
Journal of the American Irish Historical
  Society
Journal of the American Medical Association
Journal of the American Oriental Society
Journal of the American Society of
  Information Science
Journal of the American Statistical
  Association
Journal of the Association for Global
  Strategic Information
Journal of the Audio Engineering Society
Journal of the Australian War Memorial
Journal of the British Interplanetary Society
Journal of the Central Asian Society
Journal of the Council of on America's
  Military Past
Journal of the Early Republic
Journal of the Georgia Association of
  Historians
Journal of the Hellenic Diaspora
Journal of the History of Behavioral Sciences
Journal of the History of Ideas
Journal of the Illinois Historical Society
Journal of the Institution of Electrical
  Engineers
Journal of the International Commission of

Jurists
Journal of the Interplanetary Society
Journal of the Kansas Bar Association
Journal of the Legal Profession
Journal of the Malaysian Branch of the Royal
  Asiatic Society
Journal of the Military Service Institution of
  the United States
Journal of the Minnesota Academy of Science
Journal of the Patent and Trademark Office
  Society
Journal of the Royal Artillery
Journal of the Royal Asiatic Society
Journal of the Royal United Services Institute
  (currently RUSI Defence Studies Journal)
Journal of the Society for Army Historical
  Research
Journal of the Society of Comparative
  Analysis
Journal of the Southwest
Journal of Soviet Military Studies
Journal of the United Service Institution of
  India
Journal of the United States Artillery
Journal of the University of Bombay
Journal of the U.S. Army Intelligence and
  Security Command
Journal of the U.S. Cavalry Association
Journal of the West
Journalism History
Journalism Quarterly
Judges Journal
Judicature
Juridical Review
Jurimetrics Journal
Justice Professional
Justice Quarterly
Kansas Historical Quarterly
Kansas History
Kansas Journal of Law and Public Policy
Kansas Quarterly
Kentavr
Kentucky Bench and Bar
Kentucky Law Journal
Kobe University Law Review
Kommunist
Kontinent
Korean Journal of Defense Analysis
Krasnaya Zvezda
Kriminalist
Kriminalistik
Kultura
Kungliga Krigsvetenskaps Akademiens

Handlingar och Tidskrift
Labor History
Labor Law Journal
Labor's Heritage
Labor Studies Journal
Labour/Le Travail: Journal of Canadian
  Labour Studies
Labour History
Labour Monthly
La Raza Law Journal
La Revolution Francaise
Latin American Art
Latin American Perspectives
Latin American Research Review
Law and Contemporary Problems
Law and History Review
Law and Order
Law and Policy in International Business
Law and Social Inquiry
Law and Social Order
Law and Society Review
Law Institute Journal
Law Library Journal
Law Notes
Law Quarterly Review
Law Times
Lawyer
Lawyers Guild Review
Le Debat
Legal Reference Services Quarterly
Legal Service Bulletin
Legal Studies
Legal Studies Forum
Legislative Studies Quarterly
L'Histoire
Liberation
Libraries and Culture
Library Trends
Lincoln Herald
Link
Listener
Literature and History
Literature/Film Quarterly
Lithopinion
Liverpool Law Review
Lockheed Horizons
Locus
London Magazine
Longman's Magazine
Louisiana Bar Journal
Louisiana History
Louisiana Law Review
Louisiana Studies

Low-Intensity Conflict and Law Enforcement
Loyala of Los Angeles International and
  Comparative Law Journal
Loyola of Los Angeles Law Review
Loyola University of Chicago Law Journal
Maandblad Oud-Utrecht
Maarachot IDF Journal
Maclean's
Macmillan's Magazine
Mademoiselle
Magazin Istoric
Magazine of American History
Man
Management Science
Manatoba Law Journal
Manchester Literary and Philosophical
  Society Memoirs and Proceedings
Mankind
Manuscripts
Marine Corps Gazette
Mariner's Mirror
Marine-Rundschau
Marquette Law Review
Maryland Historian
Maryland Historical Magazine
Maryland Law Review
Massachusetts Law Review
Massachusetts Review
Mathematical Intelligencer
Mathematical Monthly
McClure's Magazine
McGill Law Journal
Media, Culture and Society
Medical Historian
Medical Science and the Law
Medico-Legal Journal
Mediterranean Quarterly
Memoirs of the American Academy of Rome
Mennonite Life
Mennonite Quarterly Review
Menorah Journal
Mensaje
Mentalities
Mergers and Acquisitions
Merkur
Meteorological Magazine
Mezhdunarodnaia Zhizn'
MHQ: The Quarterly Journal of Military
  History
Michael
Michigan Academician
Michigan Alumnus Quarterly
Michigan History Magazine

Michigan Journal of International Law
Michigan Journal of Race & Law
Michigan Law Review
Mid-America
Mid-American Review of Sociology
Middle East
Middle East Affairs
Middle Eastern Studies
Middle East International
Middle East Journal
Middle East Review
Middle East Society Journal
Middle East Studies
Middle East Studies Association Bulletin
Midstream
Midwestern Archivist
Midwest Quarterly
Midwest Review of Public Administration
Militargeschichtliche Mitteilungen
Military Affairs
Military Collector and Historian
Military Electronics and Countermeasures
Military Engineer
Military History
Military Intelligence
Military Journal
Military Law Review
Military Logistics
Military Police Journal
Military Review
Military Science and Technology
Military Technology
Military Thought (English translation of title
    of Russian journal)
Millennium: Journal of International Studies
Miller Center Journal
Minerva: Quarterly Report on Women and
    the Military
Minnesota History
Minnesota Law Review
Minnesota Review
Miron de l'Histoire
Mirovaia Ekonomika i Mezhdunarodyne
    Otnasheniia
Mississippi College Law Review
Mississippi Quarterly
Mississippi Valley Historical Review
Missouri Historical Review
Missouri Law Review
Mitteilungen des Oberoestereichischen
Modern Age
Modern Asian Studies
Modern China

Modern Drama
Modern Fiction Studies
Modern Language Journal
Modern Language Review
Modern Law Review
Modern Maturity
Moirae
Monash University Law Review
Mongolian Studies
Montana
Montana Law Review
Month
More
Morskoi Skornik
Mosaic
Mother Jones
Musical Quarterly
Names
National Aeronautic Association Review
National Defense Magazine
National Geographic
National Guard
National Interest
National Journal of Criminal Defense
National Lawyers' Guild Practitioner
National Reporter
National Review
National Security Affairs Forum
National Security Studies Quarterly
Nation's Business
NATO Review
NATO's Fifteen Nations
NATO's Sixteen Nations
Naval Aviation Museum Foundation
Naval History
Naval Intelligence Professionals Quarterly
Naval Law Review
Naval Review
Naval War College Review
Navy
Navy International
Nebraska Law Review
Negro History Bulletin
Nevada Historical Society Quarterly
New Dominion
New England Galaxy
New England Historical and Geneological
    Register
New England Journal of History
New England Monthly
New England Quarterly
New Humanist
New International

New Jersey History
New Jersey Lawyer
New Law Journal
New Left Review
New Mexico Historical Review
New Outlook
New Politics
New Review
New Review of East European History
Newsletter of the American Committee of the
 History of the Second World War
Newsletter of the Society for Historians of
 American Foreign Relations
News Media and the Law
New Times
New York Historical Society Quarterly
New York History
New York Law Forum
New York Law School Journal of
 International and Comparative Law
New York Law School Law Review
New York Police Studies
New York Review
New York State Bar Journal
New York Times Biographical Service
New York University Environmental Law
 Journal
New York University Journal of International
 Law and Politics
New York University Law Review
New York University Law School Law
 Review
New York University Review of Law and
 Social Change
New World Review
New Zealand Universities Law Review
NICA Shield
Nineteenth Century
Nineteenth Century and After
Nineteenth Century Fiction
North America
North American Review
North Atlantic Regional Business Law
 Review
North British Review
North Carolina Journal of International Law
 and Commercial Regulation
North Carolina Law Review
North Dakota Quarterly
North Jersey Highlander
Northern Ireland Legal Quarterly
Northern Kentucky Law Review
North South Trader

Northwestern Journal of International Law &
 Business
Northwestern University Law Review
Notes & Queries
Notes and Records of the Royal Society of
 London
Notre Dame Law Review
Notre Dame Lawyer
Notre Dame Magazine
Nova Law Review
Novaia i Noveishaia Istoriia
Novel
Noviiy Mir
Noviy Zhurnal
Novoye Vremya
Novum Gabrauchsgraphik
Nowe Drogi
Nucleonics
Nuova Antologia
Nuova Revista Storica
Occasional Papers and Reprints in
 Contemporary Asian Studies
Occupational Outlook Quarterly
Ocean Development and International Law
Oceania
Officer
Ohio Northern University Law Review
Ohio State Law Journal
Oklahoma City University Law Review
Old Northwest
Old West
Omni
ONI Review
Ontario History
Open Court
Operations Research
Optimum, the Journal of Public Sector
 Management
Orbis
Oregon Law Review
Organizational Behavior and Human
 Performance
Orientations
Osgoode Hall Law Journal
Ottawa Law Review
Otechestvennaia Istoriia
Overland
Oxford Journal of Legal Studies
Oxford Slavonic Papers
Pacific Affairs
Pacific Defence Reporter
Pacific Historian
Pacific Historical Review

Pacific Law Journal
Pacific Northwest Quarterly
Pacific Quarterly
Pakistan Horizon
Pall Mall Magazine
Papers and Monographs of the American
  Academy of Rome
Papers of the Royal Engineer Corps
Papers on Language & Literature
Parameters: Journal of the U.S. Army War
  College
Parliamentary Affairs
Partisan Review
Partorteneti Kozlemenyek
Parttorteneti Kozlemenyek
Password
Past and Present
Past Imperfect
Patent Law Review
PC Computing
Peace and Change
Peacekeeping & International Relations
Peace Research Society International Papers
Peace Review
Pennsylvania Folklife
Pennsylvania History
Pennsylvania Magazine of History and
  Biography
Pepperdine Law Review
Periodical: Journal of America's Military
  Past
Perspective
Perspectives in American History
Pharmacy in History
Philadelphia History
Philippines Armed Forces Journal
Philogical Quarterly
Philologus
Phoenix
Photogrammetric Engineering
Photogrammetric Engineering and Remote
  Sensing (currently The Art of Photography:
  Photogrammetry and Remote Sensing)
Photographic Journal
Physics Today
Planning Review
PMLA (Publications of the Modern Language
  Association of America)
Police
Police Chief
Police College Magazine
Police Journal
Police Magazine

Police Research Bulletin
Police Studies
Policing and Society
Policy Review
Policy Sciences
Police Studies
Policy Studies Journal
Policy Studies Review
Policy Studies Review Annual
Polish American Studies
Polish Review
Politica Exterior
Politica Internazionale
Political Affairs
Political Communication and
  Persuasion Political Psychology
Political Quarterly
Political Science Quarterly
Political Studies
Political Theory
Political Warfare
Politiikka
Politique Internationale: Revue Trimestrille
Politics
Politics and Society
Politics Today
Politische Meinung
Politische Studien
Politischeskoe Samoobrazovanie
Polity
Popular Science
Posev
Post-Soviet Affairs
Post-Soviet Geography
Potomac Review
Practical Litigator
Present Tense
Presidential Studies Quarterly
Princeton University Library Chronicle
Privacy Journal
Problems of Communism
Problems of Post-Communism
Proceedings and Papers of the Georgia
  Association of History
Proceedings of the Academy of Political
  Science
Proceedings of the American Philosophical
  Society
Proceedings of the American Society of
  International Law
Proceedings of the Annual Meeting of the
  Western Society for French History
Proceedings of the Indian History Congress

Proceedings of the Institute of Electrical &
Electronic Engineers (IEEE)
Proceedings of the Massachusetts Historical
Society
Proceedings of the Military and Naval
History Forum
Proceedings of the New Jersey Historical
Society
Proceedings of the Royal Air Force Historical
Society
Profiles
Progressive
Progressive Labor
Prologue: Quarterly Journal of the National
Archives
Prospects
Proteus
Przeglad Historyczny
Przeglad Polonijny
PS
Psychiatry
Psychoanalysis
Psychology Today
Psychophysiology
Public Administration
Public Administration Review
Public Historian
Public Interest
Public Law
Public Opinion
Public Opinion Quarterly
Public Personnel Management
Public Policy
Public Policy and Administration
Public Relations Review
Publishing, Entertainment, Advertising and
Allied Fields Law Quarterly
Publius
Publizistik
QLR (formerly Bridgeport Law Review)
Quadrant
Quaker History
Quarterly Journal of Contemporary History
Quarterly Journal of Speech
Quarterly Review
Que Hacer: Revista Bimestral
Queen City Heritage
Queen's Quarterly
Quellen und Forschungen aus Italienishchen
Archiven und Bibliothehen
Quest
Quill
Race and Class

Radical American
Radical History Review
Radio-Electricite
R.A.F. Flying Review
Ramparts
Raritan
Rassegna Storica Toscana
RCAF Staff College Journal
RCMP Quarterly
Reason
Record of the Association of the Bar of the
City of New York
Records
Recruiter's Bulletin
Recusant History
Regardies
Register of the Kentucky Historical Society
Relations Internationales
Representations
Republican China
Research
Research-Technology Management
Reserve Officer
Retired Officer
Review of English Studies
Review of International Studies
Review of Litigation
Review of Military Literature
Review of Politics
Review of Public Personnel Administration
Review of Radical Political Economy
Review of Social Economy
Review of Socialist Law
Reviews in American History
Revista de Ciencians Sociales
Revista de Derecho Puertorriqueno
Revista de Estudios Polaticos
Revista de Hiseria Naval
Revista Istorica
Revista de Istorie
Revista de Louisiane
Revista de Marina
Revista di Storia della Chiesa in Italia
Revista di Studi Politici Internazionali
Revista General de Marina
Revista General de Mauvia
Revista Marittima
Revista Mexicana de Ciencias Politicas Y
Sociales
Revolutionary Russia
Revue Barreau Quebec
Revue Belge de Philologie et d'Histoire
Revue Belge d'Histoire Militaire

Revue d'Assyriologie et d'Archeologie
  Orientale
Revue de Defense Nationale
Revue d'Etudes Comparatives Est-Quest
Revue d'Histoire de la Deuxieme Guerre
  Mondiale
Revue d'Histoire de la Deuxieme Guerre
  Mondiale et des Conflits Contemporains
Revue d'Histoire Diplomatique
Revue d'Histoire Moderne et Contemporaine
Revue de l'Armee de l'Air
Revue Francaise d'Etudes Americaines
Revue Francaise de Sciencepolitique
Revue Histoire des Armees
Revue Historique
Revue International d'Histoire Militaire
Revue Internationale de Criminalistique
Revue Internationale de Criminologie et de
  Police Technique
Revista Juridica de la Universidad de Puerto
  Rico
Revue Militaire Francaise
Revue Militaire Generale
Rhode Island Historical Society Collections
Rhode Island History
Richmond Journal of Law & Technology
Ripon Forum
Rocky Mountain Social Science Journal
Roczniki Humanistyczne
Rose and the Laurel
Rossiiskii Biulleten' po Pravam Cheloveka
Roundel
Roundtable
Royal Society of Arts Journal
Round Table
Royal Australian Historical Society Journal
Royal United Services Journal
RUSI and Brassey's Annual
RUSI Journal of Defence Studies (formerly
  Royal United Services Institute Journal)
Russian History
Russian Review
Rutgers Computer & Technology Law
  Journal
Rutgers Law Journal
Saga
Saint Louis University Public Law Review
SAIS Review
SAM Advanced Management Journal
Samtiden
San Diego Law Review
San Fernando Valley Law Review
Santa Clara Computer and High-Technology

Law Journal
Santa Clara Law Review
Saskatchewan History
Saturday Review of Literature
Sbornik Archivnl ch Pracl
Scandinavian Economic History Review
Scandinavian Journal of Development
  Alternatives
Scandinavian Journal of History
Scandinavian Studies
Schweizerische Zeitschrift Geschichte
Science
Science and Society
Science Digest
Scientific American
Scottish Historical Review
Scribner's Magazine
Scripta Mathematica
Sea Classics
Sea History
Sea Power
Search and Seizure Law Reporter
Security Dialogue
Security Journal
Security Management
Security Studies
Sergeants
Seton Hall Law Review
Seton Hall Legislative Journal
Sewanee Review
Shakespeare Quarterly
Shakespeare Studies
Shigaku Zasshi
Show: The Magazine of the Arts
Shutterbug
Signal
Signal Corps Bulletin
Singapore Police Journal
Simon Wiesenthal Center Annual
Sixteenth Century Journal
Skeptic
Sky & Telescope
Skyways
Slaski Kwzrtalnik Historyozny Sob'tka
Slavic Review
Slavonic and East European Review
  (formerly Slavonic Review)
Sloan Management Review
Slovansky Prehled
Small Wars and Insurgencies
Smithsonian
Social and Legal Studies
Social Education

Social Forces
Social History
Social Justice
Social Networks
Social Policy
Social Problems
Social Research
Social Responsibility: Business, Journalism,
  Law, Medicine
Social Science
Social Science Journal
Social Studies
Socialist Register
Societ e Storia
Society
Society for Historians of American Foreign
  Relations Newsletter
Society of Archivists Journal
Society of Motion Picture Engineers
Sociological Quarterly
Sociological Symposium
Sociologisk Forskning
Sociometry
Software Law Journal
Soldier
Soldier of Fortune
South African Defence Review
South African Journal of South African
  Affairs
South Atlantic Quarterly
South Carolina Historical and Geneological
  Magazine
South Carolina Historical Magazine
South Carolina History Magazine
South Carolina Law Review
South Dakota History
Southeastern Political Review
Southern California Historical Society
  Quarterly
Southern California Law Review
Southern California Quarterly
Southern Exposure
Southern Historical Society Papers
Southern Illinois University Law Journal
Southern Quarterly
Southern Studies
Southern University Law Review
South Texas Law Review
Southwest Art
Southwest Folklore
Southwest Review
Southwestern Historical Quarterly
Southwestern Journal of Law and Trade in

  the Americas
Southwestern Law Journal
Southwestern Social Science Quarterly
Southwestern University Law Review
Sovetskaia Milisiia
Sovetskoe Gosudarstvo i Pravo
Soviet Armed Forces Review Annual
Soviet Economy
Soviet Jewish Affairs
Soviet Law and Government
Soviet Literature
Soviet Military Review
Soviet Studies
Soviet Union/Union Sovietique
Spaceflight
Special Libraries
Special Warfare
Speculum
Speech Monographs
Spiegel Historisch
SShA: Ekonomika, Politika, Ideologiia
Stanford Journal of International Law
Stanford Law & Policy Review
Stanford Law Review
St. Antony's Papers
Steirische Berichte
Stetson Law Review
St. John's Journal of Legal Commentary
St. John's University Law Review
St. Louis University Law Journal
St. Mary's Law Journal
Storea Contemporanea
Strategic Analysis
Strategic Management Journal
Strategic Review
Strategic Review for Southern Africa:
  Security and Intelligence in a Post-
  Apartheid South Africa
Strategy and Tactics
Student Law Journal
Studia Historyozne
Studies in Communications
Studies in Comparative Communism
Studies in Conflict and Terrorism
Studies in Eighteenth-Century Culture
Studies in History and Society
Studies in Intelligence
Studies in Law, Politics, and Society
Studies in Soviet Thought
Studies in Zionism
Stutthof Zaazyt y Muzaum
Suffolk Transnational Law Journal
Suffolk University Law Review

Supervision
Supreme Court Historical Society Yearbook
Supreme Court Review
Survey: A Journal of East and West Studies
Survival
Swiss American Historical Newsletter
Sydney Law Review
Symbolic Interaction
Syracuse Journal of International Law and
  Commerce
Syracuse Law Review
Tactical Air Reconnaissance Digest
TDR
Teaching Political Science
Technikgeschichte
Technology and Culture
Technology Review
Tel Aviv Journal of German History
Temple International and Comparative Law
  Journal
Temple Law Quarterly
Temple Law Review
Tennessee Historical Quarterly
Tennessee Law Review
Terrorism and Political Violence
Terrorism: An International Journal
Texana
Texas Bar Journal
Texas International Law Journal
Texas International Property Law Journal
Texas Law Review
Texas Police Journal
Texas Studies in Literature and Language: A
  Journal of the Humanities
Texas Wesleyan Law Review
Textile History
Theatre Survey
Third World Quarterly
Thought
Thurgood Marshall Law Review
Touro Journal of International Law
Towson State Journal of International Affairs
Traditio
Transaction
Transactions of the American Philosophical
  Society
Transactions of the Bibliographical Society
Transactions of the International Conference
  of Orientalists in Japan
Transactions of the Royal Historical Society
Transactions of the Royal Historical Society
  of Canada
Transactions of the Royal Society of Canada

Transactions of the Society of Biblical
  Archaelogy
Trans Africa Forum
Transition
Translations of U.S.S.R Military Affairs
Transnational Law and Contemporary
  Problems
Trial
Tulane European and Civil Law Forum
Tulane Law Review
Tulsa Journal of Comparative & International
  Law
Tulsa Law Journal
Turkish Studies Association Bulletin
Twentieth Century
Twentieth Century British History
U. C. Davis Law Review
UCLA History Journal
UCLA Law Review
Ufahamu
Ukrainian Quarterly
Ukrainian Review
Ukrains'kyi Istorychnyi Zhurnal
United Nations World
United Service Institution of India Journal
United Service Magazine
United States Air Force Judge Advocate
  General Law Review
United States Army Aviation Digest
University of Arkansas at Little Rock Law
  Journal
University of Baltimore Law Review
University of Bridgeport Law Review
University of Chicago Law Review
University of Chicago Legal Forum
University of Cincinnati Law Review
University of Dayton Law Review
University of Detroit Journal of Urban Law
University of Detroit Mercy Law Review
University of Florida Law Review
University of Illinois Law Forum
University of Illinois Law Review
University of Miami Inter-American Law
  Review
University of Miami Law Review
University of Michigan Journal of Law
  Reform
University of Michigan Law Review
University of Missouri-Kansas City Law
  Review
University of Nebraska Law Review
University of Pennsylvania Journal of
  Business Law

University of Pennsylvania Journal of
International Law
University of Pennsylvania Law Review
University of Pittsburg Law Review
University of Puget Sound Law Review
University of Queensland Law Journal
University of Queens Law Journal
University of Richmond Law Review
University of Tasmania Law Review
University of Toledo Law Review
University of Toronto Law Journal
University of Toronto Quarterly
University of Western Australia Law Review
University of Western Ontario Law Review
Urban Life
U.S. Air Services
U.S. Camera
U.S. Naval Institute Proceedings
Utah Historical Quarterly
Utah Law Review
Valley Forge Journal
Valparaiso University Law Review
Vanderbilt Journal of Transnational Law
Vanderbilt Law Review
Vermont History
Vestnik Leningradskogo Universiteta
Veyahasim Beinlevmi'im
Victoria University of Wellington Law
Review
Victorian Studies
Vierteljahrshefte fuer Zietgeschichte
Vietnam
Vietnam Generation
Vil Qtrtnet
Villanova Law Review
Virginia Cavalcade
Virginia Journal of International Law
Virginia Law Review
Virginia Magazine of History and Biography
Virginia Quarterly Review
Vital Issues
Voennaia Vestnik
Voennoistoricheskii Sbornik
Voenno-Istoricheskii Zhurnal
Voprosy Istorii
Voprosy Istorii Estestvoznaniia
Voprosy Istorii Estestvoznaniia i Tekhniki
Voyennaya Mysl
Voynaistoryski Glasnik
Vozrozhdenie
Wake Forest Law Review
Warship International
Washburn Law Journal

Washington Academy of Sciences Journal
Washington and Lee Law Review
Washingtonian
Washington Journalism Review
Washington Law Review
Washington Monthly
Washington Quarterly
Washington Report of Middle East Affairs
Washington State Bar News
Washington State University Law Review
Washington University Law Quarterly
Wayne Law Review
Weatherwise
West Indian Law Journal
Westminster
West's Federal Rules and Decisions
West Tennessee Historical Society Papers
West Virginia History
Western Historical Quarterly
Western Illinois Regional Studies
Western Monats
Western New England Law Review
Western Pennsylvania History Magazine
Western Political Quarterly
Western State University Law Review
Westways
Whole Earth Review
Wiener Beitrage zur Geschichte der Neuzeit
William and Mary Bill of Rights Journal
William and Mary Law Review
William and Mary Quarterly
William Mitchell Law Review
Wilson Library Bulletin
Wilson Quarterly
Wisconsin International Law Journal
Wisconsin Law Review
Wisconsin Magazine of History
WJR
Women's Rights Law Reporter
Working Papers for a New Society
World & I
World Affairs
World Air Power Journal
World Marxist Review
World Monitor
World Outlook
World Policy Journal
World Politics
World's Work
World Today
Worldview
World War II Investigator
Yad Vashem Bulletin

Yale Alumni Magazine and Journal
Yale Journal of International Law
Yale Journal of Law and Human Rights
Yale Journal of World Public Order
Yale Law & Policy Review
Yale Law Journal
Yale Review
Yale Review of Law and Social Action
Yale University Library Gazette
Yankee
Yearbook of Law, Computers & Technology
Yearbook of the Leo Baick Institute
Yonkers Historical Bulletin
Zeitgeschichte
Zeitschrift fuer Geschichtswissenschaft
Zeszyty Historyczne
Zgodovinski Casopis
Zhuanji Wenxue

Co-Author Index

Key Word or Term Index

Note to user: Following is a list of key words or terms appearing in the titles or annotations to articles in this book. Acronyms and proper names containing letters and numbers, e.g., A-12, appear at the beginning of the appropriate letter group. If a numeric representing a year, e.g. 1948, appears in the article title, the number can be found at the beginning of alphabetical group corresponding with number's spelling, e.g. 1578 in 'F'; 1600 or 1700 in 'S'; 1809 in 'E'; 1935 in 'N'; and 2000 in 'T'. When numeric parameters appear in a title, e.g. 1941-1945, the first number is used for index purposes: 1941 is listed to represent 1941-1945. Users can search for topics of interest within year parameters, e.g. 1941-1945, since most topics are cross-indexed at least two ways. For example, if the topics of interest included the war against Japan and the American homefront morale, 1941-1945, citations would appear under "war," "World War II," "Japan/Japanese," "homefront," "morale," and "1941." Most formal titles and ranks have been removed from personal names, such as Colonel, General, or Sir, etc.

A-12 9697, 9840
A-Team 10361
AAUP (American Association of University Professors) 4374, 8767
ABM (Advanced Ballistic Missile) 7854
AEWC (Airborne Early Warning Command) 4821
Aaronsohn house 8814
Abduction(s) 5312, 9616
Abel, Rudolph I. 2626, 9942, 10218, 10302
Abortion 940
Abrams, Jacob 1297, 6051, 7461, 8189
Abrams, Creighton 10256
Abramson 1681
Abscam 722, 8243, 9291
Abwehr 898, 6229, 7735, 8663, 9174, 9338
Academe/academia 214, 432, 963, 1108, 1921, 2012, 2014, 2106, 2329, 2349, 2414, 3670, 4323, 4374, 6216, 6912, 8003, 8722, 9588, 9772, 9985, 10029
Acheson, Dean 21
Accountability 709, 1576, 2506, 3466, 3877, 3886, 5123, 6255, 6530, 8096, 8159, 9487, 9488, 9766, 10355
Acrostics 2637
Active measures (see Soviet Union)
Adams, John 2411
Adams, Joseph Truslow 4274
Adams, Samuel 1713, 2980, 5891
Adenauer, Konrad 5062
Administrative process 1795, 6534, 6535, 7881
Adverse action 2695
Aerial 1090, 1142, 2575, 3187, 4463, 4747, 5059, 7245, 8250, 8398, 8458, 9263, 9895
Aeronautics 7205

Bolshevik(s) 3811, 4093, 4517, 4753, 5152, 6018, 6337, 6983, 7365, 7816, 9633
Bolyn, Anne 6705
Bombardment 4108
Bomb(ing) 3280, 5275, 5706, 8021, 9248, 9560
Bombe 248, 1886, 2005, 8094
Bona fide(s) 8928
Bond, James 771, 1231, 3024, 5732, 6149, 6745, 6746, 6785
Bonn, Germany 8478
Border(s) 1774, 3183, 3184, 6275, 6419, 8291
Book cipher 4640
Boolean 6639
Booth, John Wilkes 429, 1819, 2733
Bose, Subhas C. 10306
Bosnia 8756, 8787, 9269, 9846
Boston 2087
Boston Gazette 236
Botha, P. W. 6920
Bouck, William 6781, 6782
Bounds, Joseph M. 5929
Bourbon 4138
Bourke-White, Margaret 7147
Bourne, Robert 3310
Bourquin, George M. 3108, 3109
Bowen, William 3089
Bowler, Metcalf 1413
Boyd, Belle 1817, 1818, 7005, 7006, 10092
Brahmi 4040
Braille 4020
Brainwashing 1051
Brandenburg 7387
Brandt, Willie 1616
Brandywine 3380, 6638
Brase, Louis 2094
Brazil 715, 4376, 4578, 5951, 10252
Bregenzer, Karl 8737
Brett, Arthur 2450
Brezhnev, Leonid 168, 3277, 3282
Bridge(s) 9248
Bridge, game of 8260
Bright, Jesse 1602
Bright line 3884
Brissot, J. P. 1793
Bristow affair 8159
Britain/British 156, 446, 449, 483, 521, 533, 691, 937, 1137, 1149, 1289, 1326, 1333, 1413, 1472, 1593, 1619, 1648, 1759, 1815, 1905, 1915, 2006, 2057, 2059, 2148, 2149, 2203, 2263, 2452, 2453, 2456, 2457, 2469, 2589, 2614, 2617, 2621, 2668, 2771, 2823,

2849, 2910, 3042, 3063, 3079, 3087, 3119, 3147, 3195, 3199, 3231, 3267, 3269, 3298, 3308, 3375, 3408, 3411, 3452, 3456, 3457, 3458, 3459, 3460, 3461, 3462, 3471, 3486, 3501, 3502, 3508, 3538, 3558, 3589, 3636, 3683, 3702, 3773, 3805, 3834, 3841, 3912, 3923, 3926, 4004, 4074, 4210, 4212, 4261, 4347, 4358, 4499, 4504, 4505, 4587, 4631, 4632, 4678, 4706, 4872, 4882, 4890, 4909, 4911, 5175, 5231, 5263, 5361, 5372, 5373, 5429, 5430, 5474, 5511, 5561, 5562, 5585, 5687, 5694, 5715, 5747, 5768, 5881, 5883, 5889, 6031, 6132, 6072, 6073, 6075, 6085, 6150, 6158, 6313, 6361, 6394, 6417, 6479, 6627, 6643, 6644, 6645, 6646, 6794, 6841, 6914, 7000, 7089, 7104, 7119, 7142, 7210, 7211, 7212, 7213, 7332, 7368, 7369, 7382, 7428, 7518, 7552, 7568, 7599, 7635, 7661, 7687, 7810, 7899, 7957, 7966, 8012, 8019, 8021, 8076, 8118, 8131, 8142, 8220, 8226, 8347, 8381, 8384, 8396, 8426, 8429, 8482, 8521, 8550, 8556, 8705, 8713, 8717, 8750, 8826, 8877, 8878, 8896, 8956, 8970, 8991, 9019, 9027, 9040, 9057, 9069, 9163, 9182, 9190, 9194, 9249, 9287, 9289, 9304, 9325, 9376, 9384, 9516, 9570, 9586, 9634, 9639, 9646, 9648, 9716, 9749, 9757, 9885, 9908, 9911, 9935, 9941, 9980, 10040, 10044, 10060, 10064, 10147, 10176, 10225, 10231, 10324, 10340, 10352, 10355, 10363
British Foreign Office (see Foreign Office)
Broadcast(ing) 103, 1003, 1004, 3221, 3260 3640, 5299, 6158, 7157, 9908, 10205
Broadway House 2453
Brodsky, Joseph 1072
Brown Commission 8483
Brown, James G. 1846
Brown, John 5076
Brown, Thomas 9802
Brunei 9306
Brussels 4198, 9973
Buchan, John 5867, 6118, 7216
Buchanan, James 1845, 6834, 7440
Bucher, Lloyd M. 1046
Buckley, William F., Jr. 6660
Budapest 7473
Budget 2982, 7075, 8068, 8092, 9587
Budich, Willy 9832
Buendia, Manuel 6522
Buenos Aires 2693
Buddhism 9450
Bug(s)/bugging 3925 4334, 4662, 5575, 5708, 5745, 6284, 6569, 7910, 8242, 8970,

9511, 10206
Royal Commission on Espionage 2230
Royal North-West Mounted Police 3605
Rubik's Cube 5353
Rubles 3552, 9321
Rumford, Count (see also Thompson, Benjamin) 312, 999, 2191, 3141, 4835, 6117
Rumor 1052, 3710, 7222, 9890
Runic Inscriptions 4510
Ruse 594, 5920, 6407
Rushdie, Salman 5081, 5082
Russell, William 6801
Russia Committee 5231
Russia(n) 159, 175, 294, 454, 873, 1107, 1762, 1988, 2515, 2548, 2688, 2691, 2917, 2958, 3017, 3189, 3283, 3302, 3453, 3655, 3667, 3811, 3923, 3940, 4206, 4215, 4280, 4290, 4340, 4359, 4517, 4540, 4779, 4795, 4826, 4897, 4909, 5553, 5561, 5562, 5563, 5638, 5919, 6027, 6052, 6322, 6323, 6337, 6666, 6726, 6951, 6952, 6983, 7000, 7040, 7299, 7487, 7554, 7750, 7846, 7903, 7904, 7905, 7957, 8086, 8291, 8292, 8377, 8506, 8574, 8740, 8752, 8918, 9165, 9254, 9311, 9331, 9366, 9367, 9385, 9456, 9614, 9640, 9733, 9746, 9819, 9820, 9969, 9989, 10089, 10259, 10285, 10301, 10323, 10363
Russian intelligence service(s) 6027, 6052, 7902, 9540, 9541, 9889, 9969, 9989, 9990, 10089
Russia Section 9311
Russo, Anthony 2384
Russo-Czech alliance 8456
Russo-German campaign 7359
Russo-Japanese war 2402, 3490
Ruth, Samuel 1278, 7396
Rygor, operation 3401
1601 9271
1603 9783
1604 9440
1605 10183, 10297
1624 6793
1641 1372
1655 2488
1656 192
1661 7374
1683 6801
1696 6892
1710 9124
1715 2641
1755 6670
1759 4890, 9639
1762 3029

1766 1719, 2802
1772 8978
1773 7661
1775 6841
1776 481, 1116, 1527, 2554, 7303, 8672, 8902, 9645, 9775
1777 522, 6638, 8676, 9741, 9802
1778 872, 4163, 7812
1780 875, 5889
1781 5387, 6626, 6880
1782 4483, 4911, 10142
1783 3610
1784 1472
1787 689, 9631
1789 1473
1791 1735, 2293, 2813
1792 7173, 9280, 10041
1793 3712
1794 6344
1795 7174, 7346
1798 4076, 4344, 7109, 7626
S-2 934, 8009, 8196, 8440
SA (Nazi storm troops) 2490
SACO 10025
SALT I and II/SALT agreement (Strategic Arms Limitation Talks) 238, 1539, 2728, 2729, 2783, 2999, 3037, 3890, 4097, 4694, 4781, 5914, 6727, 7416, 7417, 7475, 9398, 10117, 10120
SAS 5584
SATBVC 3620, 5595
SAVAK 9978
SD (Sicherheitsdienst) 2211, 4349
SDI (see Strategic Defense Initiative)
SEP 1465
SIGABA 3899, 4430
SIOP 1392
SIRA 8101
SIS 1461, 1704, 2311, 6538, 6723, 7970, 8076, 10060, 10175
SLOC (Sino-American Cooperation Association) 6699
SPOT 6360, 8438
SOE (see Special Operations Executive)
SR-71 3855, 3864, 8560, 9697, 9841
SS (see Waffen SS)
SS-6 8319
SS-8 8923
SSO (Special Security Office) 2003
SSU 8750
STANO (Surveillance, Target Acquisition, and Night Observation) 4236
STASM 4736

About the Compiler

JAMES D. CALDER is Associate Professor of Criminal Justice at the University of Texas at San Antonio. His teaching and research specialties include intelligence, espionage, national security, organized and white collar crime, American criminal justice history, and private and government security practices. He recently published several topical articles on intelligence and espionage subjects in the *Encyclopedia of U.S. Foreign Policy* (1997), as well as an earlier book, *The Origins and Development of Federal Crime Control Policy: Herbert Hoover's Initiatives* (Praeger, 1993).

ISBN 0-313-29290-6

90000>

EAN

9 780313 292903

HARDCOVER BAR CODE